Econometric Exercises, Volume 1

Matrix Algebra

Matrix Algebra is the first volume of the *Econometric Exercises* series. It contains exercises relating to course material in matrix algebra that students are expected to know while enrolled in an (advanced) undergraduate or a postgraduate course in econometrics or statistics. The book contains a comprehensive collection of exercises, all with full answers. But the book is not just a collection of exercises; in fact, it is a textbook, though one that is organized in a completely different manner from the usual textbook. The volume can be used either as a self-contained course in matrix algebra or as a supplementary text.

Karim M. Abadir has held a joint Chair since 1996 in the Departments of Mathematics and Economics at the University of York, where he has been the founder and director of various degree programs. He has also taught at the American University in Cairo, the University of Oxford, and the University of Exeter. He became an Extramural Fellow at CentER (Tilburg University) in 2003. Professor Abadir is a holder of two Econometric Theory Awards and has authored many articles in top journals, including *The Annals of Statistics*, *Econometric Theory*, *Econometrica*, and *Journal of Physics A*. He is Coordinating Editor (and one of the founders) of *The Econometrics Journal* and Associate Editor of *Econometric Reviews*, *Econometric Theory*, *Journal of Financial Econometrics*, and *Portuguese Economic Journal*.

Jan R. Magnus is Professor of Econometrics at Tilburg University, The Netherlands. He has also taught at the University of Amsterdam, the University of British Columbia, the London School of Economics, the University of Montreal, and the European University Institute, among other places. His books include *Matrix Differential Calculus* (with H. Neudecker), *Linear Structures*, *Methodology and Tacit Knowledge* (with M. S. Morgan), and *Econometrics: A First Course* (in Russian with P. K. Katyshev and A. A. Peresetsky). Professor Magnus has written numerous articles in the leading journals, including *Econometrica*, *The Annals of Statistics*, *Journal of the American Statistical Association*, *Journal of Econometrics*, *Linear Algebra and Its Applications*, and *The Review of Income and Wealth*. He is a Fellow of the *Journal of Econometrics*, holder of the Econometric Theory Award, and Associate Editor of *The Journal of Economic Methodology*, *Computational Statistics and Data Analysis*, and *Journal of Multivariate Analysis*.

Econometric Exercises

Editors:

Karim M. Abadir, *Departments of Mathematics and Economics, University of York, UK*

Jan R. Magnus, *CentER and Department of Econometrics and Operations Research, Tilburg University, The Netherlands*

Peter C. B. Phillips, *Cowles Foundation for Research in Economics, Yale University, USA*

Titles in the Series (* = planned):

1 Matrix Algebra (K. M. Abadir and J. R. Magnus)
2 Statistics (K. M. Abadir, R. D. H. Heijmans, and J. R. Magnus)
3 Econometric Theory, I (P. Paruolo)
4 Empirical Applications, I (A. van Soest and M. Verbeek)
* Econometric Theory, II
* Empirical Applications, II
* Time Series Econometrics, I
* Time Series Econometrics, II
* Microeconometrics
* Panel Data
* Bayesian Econometrics
* Nonlinear Models
* Nonparametrics and Semiparametrics
* Simulation-Based Econometrics
* Computational Methods
* Financial Econometrics
* Robustness
* Econometric Methodology

Matrix Algebra

Karim M. Abadir
Departments of Mathematics and Economics, University of York, UK

Jan R. Magnus
CentER and Department of Econometrics and Operations Research, Tilburg University, The Netherlands

CAMBRIDGE
UNIVERSITY PRESS

CAMBRIDGE UNIVERSITY PRESS
Cambridge, New York, Melbourne, Madrid, Cape Town, Singapore, São Paulo

Cambridge University Press
40 West 20th Street, New York, NY 10011-4211, USA

www.cambridge.org
Information on this title: www.cambridge.org/9780521822893

First published 2005

Printed in the United States of America

A catalog record for this publication is available from the British Library.

Library of Congress Cataloging in Publication Data
Abadir, Karim M., 1964–
Matrix algebra / Karim M. Abadir, Jan R. Magnus.
p. cm. – (Econometric exercises ; 1)
Includes bibliographical references and index.
ISBN-13 978-0-521-82289-3
ISBN-10 0-521-82289-0
ISBN-13 978-0-521-53746-9 (pbk.)
ISBN-10 0-521-53746-0 (pbk.)
1. Matrices–Textbooks. I. Magnus, Jan R. II. Title. III. Series.
QA188.A195 2005
512.9′434 – dc22 2005002651

ISBN-13 978-0-521-82289-3 hardback
ISBN-10 0-521-82289-0 hardback

ISBN-13 978-0-521-53746-9 paperback
ISBN-10 0-521-53746-0 paperback

To my parents, and to Kouka, Ramez, Naguib, Névine
To Gideon and Hedda

Contents

List of exercises

Preface to the series

The past two decades have seen econometrics grow into a vast discipline. Many different branches of the subject now happily coexist with one another. These branches interweave econometric theory and empirical applications and bring econometric method to bear on a myriad of economic issues. Against this background, a guided treatment of the modern subject of econometrics in a series of volumes of worked econometric exercises seemed a natural and rather challenging idea.

The present series, *Econometric Exercises*, was conceived in 1995 with this challenge in mind. Now, one decade later, it has become an exciting reality with the publication of the first installment of a series of volumes of worked econometric exercises. How can these volumes work as a tool of learning that adds value to the many existing textbooks of econometrics? What readers do we have in mind as benefiting from this series? What format best suits the objective of helping these readers learn, practice, and teach econometrics? These questions we now address, starting with our overall goals for the series.

Econometric Exercises is published as an organized set of volumes. Each volume in the series provides a coherent sequence of exercises in a specific field or subfield of econometrics. Solved exercises are assembled in a structured and logical pedagogical framework that seeks to develop the subject matter of the field from its foundations through to its empirical applications and advanced reaches. As the Schaum series has done so successfully for mathematics, the overall goal of *Econometric Exercises* is to develop the subject matter of econometrics through solved exercises, providing a coverage of the subject that begins at an introductory level and moves through to more advanced undergraduate- and graduate-level material.

Problem solving and worked exercises play a major role in every scientific subject. They are particularly important in a subject like econometrics where there is a rapidly growing literature of statistical and mathematical technique and an ever-expanding core to the discipline. As students, instructors, and researchers, we all benefit by seeing carefully worked-out solutions to problems that develop the subject and illustrate its methods and workings. Regular exercises and problem sets consolidate learning and reveal applications of textbook material. Clearly laid out solutions, paradigm answers, and alternate routes to solutions all develop problem-solving skills. Exercises train students in clear analytical thinking and help them in preparing for tests and exams. Teachers, as well as students, find solved exercises useful in their classroom preparation and in designing problem sets, tests, and examinations. Worked problems and illustrative empirical applications appeal to researchers and professional economists wanting to learn about specific econometric techniques. Our intention for the *Econometric Exercises* series is to appeal to this wide range of potential users.

Each volume of the series follows the same general template. Chapters begin with a short outline that emphasizes the main ideas and overviews the most relevant theorems and results. The introductions are followed by a sequential development of the material by solved examples and applications, as well as computer exercises where these are appropriate. All problems are solved, and they are graduated in difficulty, with solution techniques evolving in a logical, sequential fashion. Problems are asterisked when they require more creative solutions or reach higher levels of technical difficulty. Each volume is self-contained. There is some commonality in material across volumes in the series in order to reinforce learning and to make each volume accessible to students and others who are working largely, or even completely, on their own.

Content is structured so that solutions follow immediately after the exercise is posed. This makes the text more readable and avoids repetition of the statement of the exercise when it is being solved. More importantly, posing the right question at the right moment in the development of a subject helps to anticipate and address future learning issues that students face. Furthermore, the methods developed in a solution and the precision and insights of the answers are often more important than the questions being posed. In effect, the inner workings of a good solution frequently provide benefit beyond what is relevant to the specific exercise.

Exercise titles are listed at the start of each volume, so that readers may see the overall structure of the book and its more detailed contents. This organization reveals the exercise progression, how the exercises relate to one another, and where the material is heading. It should also tantalize readers with the exciting prospect of advanced material and intriguing applications.

The series is intended for a readership that includes undergraduate students of econometrics with an introductory knowledge of statistics, first- and second-year graduate students of econometrics, as well as students and instructors from neighboring disciplines (like statistics, psychology, or political science) with interests in econometric methods. The volumes generally increase in difficulty as the topics become more specialized.

The early volumes in the series (particularly those covering matrix algebra, statistics, econometric theory, and empirical applications) provide a foundation to the study of econometrics. These volumes will be especially useful to students who are following the first-year econometrics course sequence in North American graduate schools and need to prepare for graduate comprehensive examinations in econometrics and to write an applied econometrics paper. The early volumes will equally be of value to advanced undergraduates studying econometrics in Europe, to advanced undergraduates and honors students in the Australasian system, and to masters and doctoral students in general. Subsequent volumes will be of interest to professional economists, applied workers, and econometricians who are working with techniques in those areas, as well as students who are taking an advanced course sequence in econometrics and statisticians with interests in those topics.

The *Econometric Exercises* series is intended to offer an independent learning-by-doing program in econometrics, and it provides a useful reference source for anyone wanting to learn more about econometric methods and applications. The individual volumes can be used in classroom teaching and examining in a variety of ways. For instance, instructors can work through some of the problems in class to demonstrate methods as they are introduced, they can illustrate theoretical material with some of the solved examples, and they can show real data applications of the methods by drawing on some of the empirical examples. For examining purposes, instructors may draw freely from the solved exercises in test preparation. The systematic development of the subject in individual volumes will make the material easily accessible both for students in revision and for instructors in test preparation.

In using the volumes, students and instructors may work through the material sequentially as part of a complete learning program, or they may dip directly into material where they are experiencing difficulty, in order to learn from solved exercises and illustrations. To promote intensive study, an instructor might announce to a class in advance of a test that some questions in the test will be selected from a certain chapter of one of the volumes. This approach encourages students to work through most of the exercises in a particular chapter by way of test preparation, thereby reinforcing classroom instruction.

Further details and updated information about individual volumes can be obtained from the *Econometric Exercises* website,

http://us.cambridge.org/economics/ee/econometricexercises.htm

The website also contains the basic notation for the series, which can be downloaded along with the LaTeX style files.

As series editors, we welcome comments, criticisms, suggestions, and, of course, corrections from all our readers on each of the volumes in the series as well as on the series itself. We bid you as much happy reading and problem solving as we have had in writing and preparing this series.

York, Tilburg, New Haven
June 2005

Karim M. Abadir
Jan R. Magnus
Peter C. B. Phillips

Preface

This volume on matrix algebra and its companion volume on statistics are the first two volumes of the *Econometric Exercises* series. The two books contain exercises in matrix algebra, probability, and statistics, relating to course material that students are expected to know while enrolled in an (advanced) undergraduate or a postgraduate course in econometrics.

When we started writing this volume, our aim was to provide a collection of interesting exercises with complete and rigorous solutions. In fact, we wrote the book that we — as students — would have liked to have had. Our intention was not to write a textbook, but to supply material that could be used together with a textbook. But when the volume developed we discovered that we did in fact write a textbook, be it one organized in a completely different manner. Thus, we do provide and prove theorems in this volume, because continually referring to other texts seemed undesirable. The volume can thus be used either as a self-contained course in matrix algebra or as a supplementary text.

We have attempted to develop new ideas slowly and carefully. The important ideas are introduced algebraically and sometimes geometrically, but also through examples. It is our experience that most students find it easier to assimilate the material through examples rather than by the theoretical development only.

In proving the more difficult theorems, we have always divided them up in smaller questions, so that the student is encouraged to understand the structure of the proof and will be able to answer at least some of the questions, even if he/she cannot prove the whole theorem. More difficult exercises are marked with an asterisk ($*$).

One approach to presenting the material is to prove a general result and then obtain a number of special cases. For the student, however, we believe it is more useful (and also closer to scientific development) to first prove a simple case, then a more difficult case, and finally the general result. This means that we sometimes prove the same result two or three times, in increasing complexity, but nevertheless essentially the same. This gives the student who could not solve the simple case a second chance in trying to solve the more general case, after having studied the solution of the simple case.

We have chosen to take real matrices as our unit of operation, although almost all results are equally valid for complex matrices. It was tempting — and possibly would have been more logical and aesthetic — to work with complex matrices throughout. We have resisted this temptation, solely for educational reasons. We emphasize from time to time that results are also valid for complex matrices. Of course, we explicitly need complex matrices in some important cases, most notably in decomposition theorems involving eigenvalues.

Occasionally we have illustrated matrix ideas in a statistical or econometric context, realizing that the student may not yet have studied these concepts. These exercises may be skipped at the first reading.

In contrast to statistics (in particular, probability theory), there only exist a few books of worked exercises in matrix algebra. First, there is Schaum's outline series with four volumes: *Matrices* by Ayres (1962), *Theory and Problems of Matrix Operations* by Bronson (1989), *3000 Solved Problems in Linear Algebra* by Lipschutz (1989), and *Theory and Problems of Linear Algebra* by Lipschutz and Lipson (2001). The only other examples of worked exercises in matrix algebra, as far as we are aware, are Proskuryakov (1978), Prasolov (1994), Zhang (1996, 1999), and Harville (2001).

Matrix algebra is by now an established field. Most of the results in this volume of exercises have been known for decades or longer. Readers wishing to go deeper into the material are advised to consult Mirsky (1955), Gantmacher (1959), Bellman (1970), Hadley (1961), Horn and Johnson (1985, 1991), Magnus (1988), or Magnus and Neudecker (1999), among many other excellent texts.

We are grateful to Josette Janssen at Tilburg University for expert and cheerful typing in LaTeX; to Jozef Pijnenburg for constant advice on difficult LaTeX questions; to Andrey Vasnev for help with the figures; to Sanne Zwart for editorial assistance; to Bertrand Melenberg, William Mikhail, Maxim Nazarov, Paolo Paruolo, Peter Phillips, Gabriel Talmain, undergraduates at Exeter University, PhD students at the NAKE program in Utrecht and at the European University Institute in Florence, and two anonymous referees, for their constructive comments; and to Scott Parris and his staff at Cambridge University Press for their patience and encouragement. The final version of this book was completed while Jan spent six months as a Jean Monnet Fellow at the European University Institute in Florence.

Updates and corrections of this volume can be obtained from the *Econometric Exercises* website,

http://us.cambridge.org/economics/ee/econometricexercises.htm

Of course, we welcome comments from our readers.

York, Tilburg
June 2005

Karim M. Abadir
Jan R. Magnus

1

Vectors

The set of (finite) real numbers (the *one-dimensional Euclidean space*) is denoted by $\mathbb{R}$. The *m-dimensional Euclidean space* $\mathbb{R}^m$ is the Cartesian product of m sets equal to $\mathbb{R}$:

$$\mathbb{R}^m := \mathbb{R} \times \mathbb{R} \times \cdots \times \mathbb{R} \quad (m \text{ times}).$$

A particular element in $\mathbb{R}^m$, say

$$\boldsymbol{x} := \begin{pmatrix} x_1 \\ x_2 \\ \vdots \\ x_m \end{pmatrix}$$

is called a (real) *vector* (or *column vector*). The quantities x_i are called the *components* (or *elements*) of $\boldsymbol{x}$, while m is called the *order* of $\boldsymbol{x}$. An m-component vector $\boldsymbol{x}$ is thus an ordered m-tuple of (real) numbers. Vectors will be denoted by lowercase bold-italic symbols such as $\boldsymbol{a}$, $\boldsymbol{x}$, $\boldsymbol{\omega}$ or $\boldsymbol{f}$. Vectors of order 1 are called *scalars*. These are the usual one-dimensional variables. The m-tuple of zeros is called the *null vector* (of order m), and is denoted by $\mathbf{0}$ or $\mathbf{0}_m$. The m-tuple of ones is called the *sum vector* (of order m), and is denoted by $\boldsymbol{\imath}$ or $\boldsymbol{\imath}_m$; the name "sum vector" is explained in Exercise 1.16.

Vector analysis can be treated algebraically or geometrically. Both viewpoints are important. If x_i denotes the income of the i-th family in a particular year in a particular country, then the vector $\boldsymbol{x}$ is best thought of as a *point* in $\mathbb{R}^m$. If, however, we think of quantities such as force and velocity, that is, quantities that possess both magnitude and direction, then these are best represented by *arrows*, emanating from some given reference point $\mathbf{0}$ (the origin). The first viewpoint is algebraic, the second is geometric.

Two vectors $\boldsymbol{x}$ and $\boldsymbol{y}$ of the same order are said to be equal, written $\boldsymbol{x} = \boldsymbol{y}$, if $x_i = y_i$ for $i = 1, \dots, m$. If $x_i > y_i$ for all i, we write $\boldsymbol{x} > \boldsymbol{y}$ or $\boldsymbol{y} < \boldsymbol{x}$. Similarly, if $x_i \geq y_i$ for all i, we write $\boldsymbol{x} \geq \boldsymbol{y}$ or $\boldsymbol{y} \leq \boldsymbol{x}$. The two basic operations associated with vectors are vector addition and scalar multiplication. The sum of two vectors $\boldsymbol{x}$ and $\boldsymbol{y}$ of the same order, written as $\boldsymbol{x}+\boldsymbol{y}$, is defined to be the vector

$$\boldsymbol{x}+\boldsymbol{y} := \begin{pmatrix} x_1+y_1 \\ x_2+y_2 \\ \vdots \\ x_m+y_m \end{pmatrix}.$$

Multiplication of a vector $\boldsymbol{x}$ by a scalar λ is defined by means of the relation

$$\lambda\boldsymbol{x} := \begin{pmatrix} \lambda x_1 \\ \lambda x_2 \\ \vdots \\ \lambda x_m \end{pmatrix},$$

which can also be written is $\boldsymbol{x}\lambda$. The geometric counterpart to these algebraic definitions is clarified in Figure 1.1. The sum $\boldsymbol{x}+\boldsymbol{y}$ is obtained as the diagonal of the parallelogram

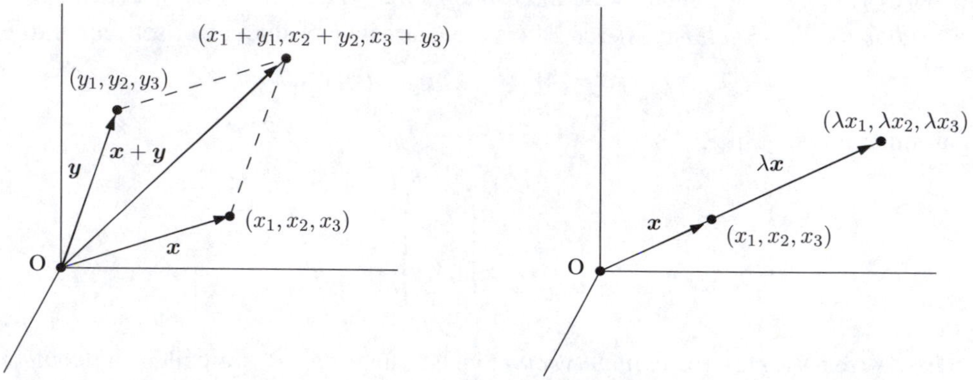

Figure 1.1 — Vector addition and scalar multiplication in $\mathbb{R}^3$.

formed by $\boldsymbol{x}$, $\boldsymbol{y}$ and the origin. The product $\lambda\boldsymbol{x}$ is obtained by multiplying the magnitude of $\boldsymbol{x}$ by λ and retaining the same direction if $\lambda > 0$ or the opposite direction if $\lambda < 0$. We say that two vectors $\boldsymbol{x}$ and $\boldsymbol{y}$ are *collinear* if either $\boldsymbol{x} = \mathbf{0}$ or $\boldsymbol{y} = \mathbf{0}$ or $\boldsymbol{y} = \lambda\boldsymbol{x}$ for some scalar λ. In Figure 1.1, $\boldsymbol{x}$ and $\boldsymbol{y}$ are not collinear, while $\boldsymbol{x}$ and $\lambda\boldsymbol{x}$ are collinear.

An important scalar function of two real vectors $\boldsymbol{x}$ and $\boldsymbol{y}$ of the same order is the *inner product* (also called *scalar* product),

$$\langle \boldsymbol{x}, \boldsymbol{y} \rangle := \sum_{i=1}^{m} x_i y_i,$$

which leads directly to the *norm*,

$$\|\boldsymbol{x}\| := \langle \boldsymbol{x}, \boldsymbol{x} \rangle^{1/2}.$$

The norm $\|\boldsymbol{x}\|$ represents the geometric idea of "length" of the vector $\boldsymbol{x}$. A vector $\boldsymbol{x}$ for which $\|\boldsymbol{x}\| = 1$ is said to be *normalized* (its norm equals 1). The famous Cauchy-Schwarz inequality (Exercise 1.9) asserts that

$$|\langle \boldsymbol{x}, \boldsymbol{y} \rangle|^{1/2} \leq \|\boldsymbol{x}\| \cdot \|\boldsymbol{y}\|.$$

Two vectors $\boldsymbol{x}$ and $\boldsymbol{y}$ for which $\langle \boldsymbol{x}, \boldsymbol{y} \rangle = 0$ are said to be *orthogonal*, and we write $\boldsymbol{x} \perp \boldsymbol{y}$. If, in addition, $\|\boldsymbol{x}\| = \|\boldsymbol{y}\| = 1$, the two vectors are said to be *orthonormal*. In m-dimensional Euclidean space, the *unit* vectors (or *elementary* vectors, hence the notation $\boldsymbol{e}_i$)

$$\boldsymbol{e}_1 := \begin{pmatrix} 1 \\ 0 \\ 0 \\ \vdots \\ 0 \end{pmatrix}, \quad \boldsymbol{e}_2 := \begin{pmatrix} 0 \\ 1 \\ 0 \\ \vdots \\ 0 \end{pmatrix}, \quad \ldots, \quad \boldsymbol{e}_m := \begin{pmatrix} 0 \\ 0 \\ 0 \\ \vdots \\ 1 \end{pmatrix}$$

are orthonormal. In the three-dimensional space of Figure 1.1, the vectors $\boldsymbol{e}_1$, $\boldsymbol{e}_2$, and $\boldsymbol{e}_3$ represent points at 1 on each of the three axes.

To define the *angle* between two nonzero vectors $\boldsymbol{x}$ and $\boldsymbol{y}$, consider the triangle OAB in Figure 1.2. The vectors $\boldsymbol{x}$ and $\boldsymbol{y}$ are indicated by arrows emanating from the origin. We

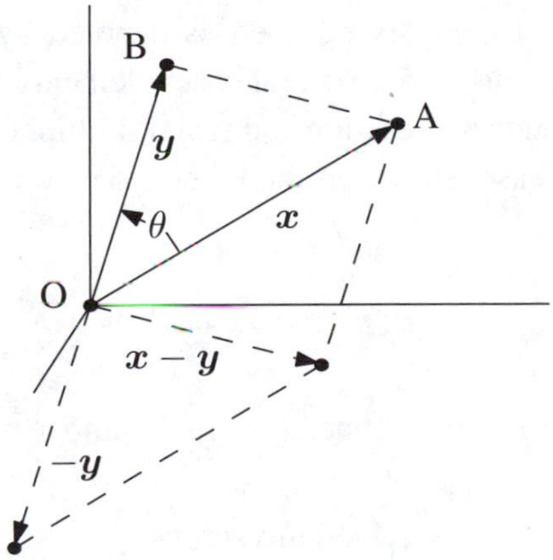

Figure 1.2 — Angle between $\boldsymbol{x}$ and $\boldsymbol{y}$.

construct the vector $-\boldsymbol{y}$ and the vector $\boldsymbol{x} - \boldsymbol{y} = \boldsymbol{x} + (-\boldsymbol{y})$. The length of $\boldsymbol{x} - \boldsymbol{y}$ is equal to the length of AB. Hence, by the cosine rule,

$$\|\boldsymbol{x} - \boldsymbol{y}\|^2 = \|\boldsymbol{x}\|^2 + \|\boldsymbol{y}\|^2 - 2\|\boldsymbol{x}\| \cdot \|\boldsymbol{y}\| \cos\theta.$$

After simplifying, this becomes

$$\langle \boldsymbol{x}, \boldsymbol{y} \rangle = \|\boldsymbol{x}\| \cdot \|\boldsymbol{y}\| \cos\theta,$$

and thus suggests the following definition of the angle θ between $\boldsymbol{x}$ and $\boldsymbol{y}$,

$$\cos\theta := \frac{\langle \boldsymbol{x}, \boldsymbol{y}\rangle}{\|\boldsymbol{x}\| \cdot \|\boldsymbol{y}\|} \quad (0 \leq \theta \leq \pi).$$

We briefly review complex numbers; these will play a small but important role in this book. Appendix A contains further details. A complex number, say u, is denoted by $u := a + \mathrm{i}b$, where a and b are real numbers and i is the imaginary unit defined by $\mathrm{i}^2 := -1$. We write $\mathrm{Re}(u) := a$ and $\mathrm{Im}(u) := b$. If $u := a + \mathrm{i}b$ and $v := c + \mathrm{i}d$ are two complex numbers, then they are said to be equal, written $u = v$, if $a = c$ and $b = d$. The sum is defined as

$$u + v := (a + c) + \mathrm{i}(b + d)$$

and the product by

$$uv := (ac - bd) + \mathrm{i}(ad + bc).$$

It follows from the definition that $uv = vu$ and $u + v = v + u$. The *complex conjugate* of u is defined by $u^* := a - \mathrm{i}b$. We then see that $u \cdot u^* = a^2 + b^2$, a nonnegative real number. We now define the *modulus* by $|u| := (u \cdot u^*)^{1/2}$, where we take the nonnegative value of the square root only. Thus, the modulus of a complex number is a nonnegative real number. Then, $u \cdot u^* = |u|^2$ and hence, when $u \neq 0$,

$$\frac{1}{u} = \frac{u^*}{|u|^2} = \frac{a}{a^2 + b^2} - \mathrm{i}\frac{b}{a^2 + b^2}.$$

The set of all m-tuples of complex numbers is denoted by $\mathbb{C}^m$ and is called the *m-dimensional complex space*. Just as in the real case, elements of $\mathbb{C}$ are called scalars and elements of $\mathbb{C}^m$ are called vectors. Addition and scalar multiplication are defined in exactly the same way as in the real case. However, the inner product of $\boldsymbol{u}$ and $\boldsymbol{v}$ is now defined as the complex number

$$\langle \boldsymbol{u}, \boldsymbol{v}\rangle := \sum_{i=1}^{m} u_i v_i^*.$$

The norm of a complex vector is the nonnegative real number $\|\boldsymbol{u}\| := \langle \boldsymbol{u}, \boldsymbol{u}\rangle^{1/2}$.

1.1 Real vectors

Exercise 1.1 (Vector equality)
(a) If $\boldsymbol{x} = \mathbf{0}$ and $\boldsymbol{y} = \mathbf{0}$, does it follow that $\boldsymbol{x} = \boldsymbol{y}$?
(b) Find x, y, z such that $(x + y, x + z, z - 1) = (2, 2, 0)$.

Solution
(a) Only if $\boldsymbol{x}$ and $\boldsymbol{y}$ are of the same order.
(b) We need to solve the three equations in three unknowns,

$$x + y = 2, \quad x + z = 2, \quad z - 1 = 0.$$

The solution is $x = y = z = 1$.

Exercise 1.2 (Vector addition, numbers) Let

$$\boldsymbol{x} = \begin{pmatrix} 1 \\ 2 \\ -3 \end{pmatrix} \quad \text{and} \quad \boldsymbol{y} = \begin{pmatrix} 7 \\ -1 \\ 2 \end{pmatrix}.$$

Compute $\boldsymbol{x} + \boldsymbol{y}$, $3\boldsymbol{x}$, $-\boldsymbol{y}$, and $5\boldsymbol{x} - 2\boldsymbol{y}$.

Solution

$$\boldsymbol{x} + \boldsymbol{y} = \begin{pmatrix} 8 \\ 1 \\ -1 \end{pmatrix}, \quad 3\boldsymbol{x} = \begin{pmatrix} 3 \\ 6 \\ -9 \end{pmatrix}, \quad -\boldsymbol{y} = \begin{pmatrix} -7 \\ 1 \\ -2 \end{pmatrix}, \quad 5\boldsymbol{x} - 2\boldsymbol{y} = \begin{pmatrix} -9 \\ 12 \\ -19 \end{pmatrix}.$$

Exercise 1.3 (Null vector) Show that the null vector $\mathbf{0}$ is similar to the scalar 0 in that, for any $\boldsymbol{x}$, we have $\boldsymbol{x} + \mathbf{0} = \boldsymbol{x}$.

Solution
We have

$$\boldsymbol{x} + \mathbf{0} = \begin{pmatrix} x_1 + 0 \\ x_2 + 0 \\ \vdots \\ x_m + 0 \end{pmatrix} = \begin{pmatrix} x_1 \\ x_2 \\ \vdots \\ x_m \end{pmatrix} = \boldsymbol{x}.$$

Exercise 1.4 (Vector addition) Let $\boldsymbol{x}$, $\boldsymbol{y}$, and $\boldsymbol{z}$ be vectors of the same order.
(a) Show that $\boldsymbol{x} + \boldsymbol{y} = \boldsymbol{y} + \boldsymbol{x}$ (*commutativity*).
(b) Show that $(\boldsymbol{x} + \boldsymbol{y}) + \boldsymbol{z} = \boldsymbol{x} + (\boldsymbol{y} + \boldsymbol{z})$ (*associativity*).
(c) Hence, show that $\boldsymbol{x} + \boldsymbol{y} + \boldsymbol{z}$ is an unambiguous vector.

Solution
Let x_i, y_i, z_i denote the i-th components of the vectors $\boldsymbol{x}, \boldsymbol{y}, \boldsymbol{z}$, respectively. It is sufficient to show that the corresponding components on each side of the vector equations are equal. The results follow since (a) $x_i + y_i = y_i + x_i$, (b) $= (x_i + y_i) + z_i = x_i + (y_i + z_i)$, and (c) $x_i + y_i + z_i$ is unambiguously defined.

Exercise 1.5 (Scalar multiplication)
(a) For vectors $\boldsymbol{x}$ and $\boldsymbol{y}$ of the same order, and scalars λ and μ, show that $(\lambda + \mu)(\boldsymbol{x} + \boldsymbol{y}) = \lambda\boldsymbol{x} + \lambda\boldsymbol{y} + \mu\boldsymbol{x} + \mu\boldsymbol{y}$.
(b) Show that the null vector is uniquely determined by the condition that $\lambda\mathbf{0} = \mathbf{0}$ for all finite scalars λ.

Solution
(a) The i-th component on the left side of the equation is $(\lambda + \mu)(x_i + y_i)$; the i-th component on the right side is $\lambda x_i + \lambda y_i + \mu x_i + \mu y_i$. The equality of these two expressions follows from scalar arithmetic.
(b) Consider the equation $\lambda \boldsymbol{x} = \boldsymbol{x}$. Since, for $i = 1, \ldots, m$, the i-th component on both sides must be equal, we obtain $\lambda x_i = x_i$, that is, $(\lambda - 1)x_i = 0$. Hence, $\lambda = 1$ or $x_i = 0$. Since the equation holds for all λ, it follows that $x_i = 0$ for all i. Hence, $\boldsymbol{x} = \boldsymbol{0}$.

Exercise 1.6 (Proportion of a line) Let $0 \le \lambda \le 1$. Prove that the point $\boldsymbol{z} := (1-\lambda)\boldsymbol{x} + \lambda \boldsymbol{y}$ divides the line segment joining $\boldsymbol{x}$ and $\boldsymbol{y}$ in the proportion $\lambda : (1-\lambda)$.

Solution
A *line* passing through the points $\boldsymbol{x}$ and $\boldsymbol{y}$ is the set of points $\{(1-\lambda)\boldsymbol{x} + \lambda\boldsymbol{y},\ \lambda \in \mathbb{R}\}$. The *line segment* joining $\boldsymbol{x}$ and $\boldsymbol{y}$ is defined as $L(\boldsymbol{x}, \boldsymbol{y}) := \{(1-\lambda)\boldsymbol{x} + \lambda\boldsymbol{y},\ 0 \le \lambda \le 1\}$. The point $\boldsymbol{z}$ lies on the line segment $L(\boldsymbol{x}, \boldsymbol{y})$, and

$$\|\boldsymbol{z} - \boldsymbol{x}\| = \|(1-\lambda)\boldsymbol{x} + \lambda\boldsymbol{y} - \boldsymbol{x}\| = \|\lambda(\boldsymbol{y} - \boldsymbol{x})\| = \lambda\|\boldsymbol{y} - \boldsymbol{x}\|,$$

$$\|\boldsymbol{y} - \boldsymbol{z}\| = \|\boldsymbol{y} - (1-\lambda)\boldsymbol{x} - \lambda\boldsymbol{y}\| = \|(1-\lambda)(\boldsymbol{y} - \boldsymbol{x})\| = (1-\lambda)\|\boldsymbol{y} - \boldsymbol{x}\|.$$

Hence, $\boldsymbol{z}$ divides $L(\boldsymbol{x}, \boldsymbol{y})$ in the proportion $\lambda : (1-\lambda)$. Notice that the proportion is the other way round than the coordinates.

Exercise 1.7 (Inner product) Recall that the inner product of two real vectors $\boldsymbol{x}$ and $\boldsymbol{y}$ in $\mathbb{R}^m$ is defined as $\langle \boldsymbol{x}, \boldsymbol{y} \rangle := \sum_{i=1}^m x_i y_i$. Prove that:
(a) $\langle \boldsymbol{x}, \boldsymbol{y} \rangle = \langle \boldsymbol{y}, \boldsymbol{x} \rangle$;
(b) $\langle \boldsymbol{x}, \boldsymbol{y} + \boldsymbol{z} \rangle = \langle \boldsymbol{x}, \boldsymbol{y} \rangle + \langle \boldsymbol{x}, \boldsymbol{z} \rangle$;
(c) $\langle \lambda\boldsymbol{x}, \boldsymbol{y} \rangle = \lambda\langle \boldsymbol{x}, \boldsymbol{y} \rangle$;
(d) $\langle \boldsymbol{x}, \boldsymbol{x} \rangle \ge 0$, with $\langle \boldsymbol{x}, \boldsymbol{x} \rangle = 0 \iff \boldsymbol{x} = \boldsymbol{0}$.

Solution
(a) $\langle \boldsymbol{x}, \boldsymbol{y} \rangle = \sum_i x_i y_i = \sum_i y_i x_i = \langle \boldsymbol{y}, \boldsymbol{x} \rangle$.
(b) $\langle \boldsymbol{x}, \boldsymbol{y} + \boldsymbol{z} \rangle = \sum_i x_i(y_i + z_i) = \sum_i x_i y_i + \sum_i x_i z_i = \langle \boldsymbol{x}, \boldsymbol{y} \rangle + \langle \boldsymbol{x}, \boldsymbol{z} \rangle$.
(c) $\langle \lambda\boldsymbol{x}, \boldsymbol{y} \rangle = \sum_i \lambda x_i y_i = \lambda \sum_i x_i y_i = \lambda\langle \boldsymbol{x}, \boldsymbol{y} \rangle$.
(d) $\langle \boldsymbol{x}, \boldsymbol{x} \rangle = \sum_i x_i^2 \ge 0$, and

$$\langle \boldsymbol{x}, \boldsymbol{x} \rangle = 0 \iff \sum_{i=1}^m x_i^2 = 0 \iff x_i = 0 \text{ for all } i \iff \boldsymbol{x} = \boldsymbol{0}.$$

Exercise 1.8 (Inner product, numbers) Let

$$\boldsymbol{x} = \begin{pmatrix} 1 \\ 2 \\ -3 \end{pmatrix}, \quad \boldsymbol{y} = \begin{pmatrix} 4 \\ -5 \\ 1 \end{pmatrix}, \quad \boldsymbol{z} = \begin{pmatrix} 1 \\ 1 \\ 1 \end{pmatrix}, \quad \boldsymbol{w} = \begin{pmatrix} 3 \\ \alpha \\ 1 \end{pmatrix}.$$

Compute $\langle \boldsymbol{x}, \boldsymbol{y} \rangle$, $\langle \boldsymbol{x}, \boldsymbol{z} \rangle$, and $\langle \boldsymbol{y}, \boldsymbol{z} \rangle$, and find α such that $\langle \boldsymbol{y}, \boldsymbol{w} \rangle = 0$.

Solution
Direct multiplication gives

$$\langle \boldsymbol{x}, \boldsymbol{y}\rangle = 1 \times 4 + 2 \times (-5) + (-3) \times 1 = -9,$$
$$\langle \boldsymbol{x}, \boldsymbol{z}\rangle = 1 \times 1 + 2 \times 1 + (-3) \times 1 = 0,$$
$$\langle \boldsymbol{y}, \boldsymbol{z}\rangle = 4 \times 1 + (-5) \times 1 + 1 \times 1 = 0,$$

and

$$\langle \boldsymbol{y}, \boldsymbol{w}\rangle = 4 \times 3 + (-5) \times \alpha + 1 \times 1 = 13 - 5\alpha.$$

Hence, $\langle \boldsymbol{y}, \boldsymbol{w}\rangle = 0$ when $\alpha = 13/5$.

Exercise 1.9 (Cauchy-Schwarz inequality)
(a) For any $\boldsymbol{x}, \boldsymbol{y}$ in $\mathbb{R}^m$ and any scalar λ, show that

$$0 \leq \langle \boldsymbol{x} - \lambda\boldsymbol{y}, \boldsymbol{x} - \lambda\boldsymbol{y}\rangle = \langle \boldsymbol{x}, \boldsymbol{x}\rangle - 2\lambda\langle \boldsymbol{x}, \boldsymbol{y}\rangle + \lambda^2\langle \boldsymbol{y}, \boldsymbol{y}\rangle.$$

(b) Hence, prove that

$$\langle \boldsymbol{x}, \boldsymbol{y}\rangle^2 \leq \langle \boldsymbol{x}, \boldsymbol{x}\rangle\langle \boldsymbol{y}, \boldsymbol{y}\rangle,$$

with equality if and only if $\boldsymbol{x}$ and $\boldsymbol{y}$ are collinear (*Cauchy-Schwarz*).

Solution
(a) This is obtained by direct multiplication, using the properties of the inner product.
(b) If $\boldsymbol{y} = \boldsymbol{0}$ then the result holds. Let $\boldsymbol{y} \neq \boldsymbol{0}$. Then, for any scalar λ, (a) holds. Setting $\lambda := \langle \boldsymbol{x}, \boldsymbol{y}\rangle / \langle \boldsymbol{y}, \boldsymbol{y}\rangle$, the inequality becomes

$$0 \leq \langle \boldsymbol{x}, \boldsymbol{x}\rangle - \frac{\langle \boldsymbol{x}, \boldsymbol{y}\rangle^2}{\langle \boldsymbol{y}, \boldsymbol{y}\rangle},$$

from which the Cauchy-Schwarz inequality follows. Next we consider when equality occurs. If $\boldsymbol{y} = \boldsymbol{0}$, then equality holds. If $\boldsymbol{y} \neq \boldsymbol{0}$, then equality occurs if and only if $\langle \boldsymbol{x} - \lambda\boldsymbol{y}, \boldsymbol{x} - \lambda\boldsymbol{y}\rangle = 0$, that is, if and only if $\boldsymbol{x} = \lambda\boldsymbol{y}$.

Exercise 1.10 (Triangle inequality) For any vector $\boldsymbol{x}$ in $\mathbb{R}^m$ the norm is defined as the scalar function $\|\boldsymbol{x}\| := \langle \boldsymbol{x}, \boldsymbol{x}\rangle^{1/2}$. Show that:
(a) $\|\lambda\boldsymbol{x}\| = |\lambda| \cdot \|\boldsymbol{x}\|$ for every scalar λ;
(b) $\|\boldsymbol{x}\| \geq 0$, with $\|\boldsymbol{x}\| = 0$ if and only if $\boldsymbol{x} = \boldsymbol{0}$;
(c) $\|\boldsymbol{x} + \boldsymbol{y}\| \leq \|\boldsymbol{x}\| + \|\boldsymbol{y}\|$ for every $\boldsymbol{x}, \boldsymbol{y} \in \mathbb{R}^m$, with equality if and only if $\boldsymbol{x}$ and $\boldsymbol{y}$ are collinear (*triangle inequality*).

Solution
(a) $\|\lambda\boldsymbol{x}\| = \langle \lambda\boldsymbol{x}, \lambda\boldsymbol{x}\rangle^{1/2} = |\lambda|\langle \boldsymbol{x}, \boldsymbol{x}\rangle^{1/2} = |\lambda| \cdot \|\boldsymbol{x}\|$.
(b) $\|\boldsymbol{x}\| = \langle \boldsymbol{x}, \boldsymbol{x}\rangle^{1/2} \geq 0$, with $\|\boldsymbol{x}\| = 0 \iff \langle \boldsymbol{x}, \boldsymbol{x}\rangle = 0 \iff \boldsymbol{x} = 0$.

(c) The Cauchy-Schwarz inequality (Exercise 1.9) gives $\langle \boldsymbol{x}, \boldsymbol{y}\rangle^2 \leq \|\boldsymbol{x}\|^2\|\boldsymbol{y}\|^2$. Hence,

$$\begin{aligned}\|\boldsymbol{x}+\boldsymbol{y}\|^2 &= \langle \boldsymbol{x}+\boldsymbol{y}, \boldsymbol{x}+\boldsymbol{y}\rangle = \langle \boldsymbol{x}, \boldsymbol{x}\rangle + 2\langle \boldsymbol{x}, \boldsymbol{y}\rangle + \langle \boldsymbol{y}, \boldsymbol{y}\rangle \\ &\leq \|\boldsymbol{x}\|^2 + 2\|\boldsymbol{x}\| \cdot \|\boldsymbol{y}\| + \|\boldsymbol{y}\|^2 = (\|\boldsymbol{x}\| + \|\boldsymbol{y}\|)^2.\end{aligned}$$

Taking the square root of both sides yields the triangle inequality. Equality occurs if and only if $\langle \boldsymbol{x}, \boldsymbol{y}\rangle = \|\boldsymbol{x}\| \cdot \|\boldsymbol{y}\|$, that is, if and only if $\boldsymbol{x}$ and $\boldsymbol{y}$ are collinear (Cauchy-Schwarz). The geometric interpretation of the inequality is that in any triangle, the sum of the lengths of two sides must exceed the length of the third side. In other words, that a straight line is the shortest distance between two points; see Figure 1.1.

Exercise 1.11 (Normalization) A vector $\boldsymbol{x}$ for which $\|\boldsymbol{x}\| = 1$ is said to be normalized (its norm equals 1). Any nonzero vector $\boldsymbol{x}$ can be normalized by

$$\boldsymbol{x}_\circ := \frac{1}{\|\boldsymbol{x}\|}\boldsymbol{x}.$$

(a) Show that $\|\boldsymbol{x}_\circ\| = 1$.
(b) Determine the norm of

$$\boldsymbol{a} = \begin{pmatrix}1\\2\end{pmatrix}, \quad \boldsymbol{b} = \begin{pmatrix}1\\0\end{pmatrix}, \quad \boldsymbol{c} = \begin{pmatrix}3\\4\end{pmatrix}.$$

(c) Normalize $\boldsymbol{a}$, $\boldsymbol{b}$, and $\boldsymbol{c}$.
(d) Show that $\boldsymbol{x}$ and $\lambda\boldsymbol{x}$ have the same normalized vector for any $\lambda > 0$.

Solution
(a) We have

$$\|\boldsymbol{x}_\circ\| = \|\frac{\boldsymbol{x}}{\|\boldsymbol{x}\|}\| = \frac{1}{\|\boldsymbol{x}\|}\|\boldsymbol{x}\| = 1.$$

(b) We have $\|\boldsymbol{a}\| = \sqrt{1^2+2^2} = \sqrt{5}$, $\|\boldsymbol{b}\| = 1$, and $\|\boldsymbol{c}\| = 5$.
(c) Normalizing gives

$$\boldsymbol{a}_\circ = \frac{\boldsymbol{a}}{\|\boldsymbol{a}\|} = \frac{1}{\sqrt{5}}\begin{pmatrix}1\\2\end{pmatrix}, \quad \boldsymbol{b}_\circ = \begin{pmatrix}1\\0\end{pmatrix}, \quad \boldsymbol{c}_\circ = \frac{1}{5}\begin{pmatrix}3\\4\end{pmatrix}.$$

(d) Let $\boldsymbol{w} := \lambda\boldsymbol{x}$. Then $\|\boldsymbol{w}\| = |\lambda| \cdot \|\boldsymbol{x}\|$, and

$$\boldsymbol{w}_\circ = \frac{\lambda}{|\lambda|} \cdot \frac{\boldsymbol{x}}{\|\boldsymbol{x}\|}.$$

Hence, $\boldsymbol{w}_\circ = \boldsymbol{x}_\circ$ if $\lambda > 0$, and $\boldsymbol{w}_\circ = -\boldsymbol{x}_\circ$ if $\lambda < 0$.

Exercise 1.12 (Orthogonal vectors) Two vectors $\boldsymbol{x}$ and $\boldsymbol{y}$ for which $\langle \boldsymbol{x}, \boldsymbol{y}\rangle = 0$ are said to be orthogonal, and we write $\boldsymbol{x} \perp \boldsymbol{y}$. Let

$$\boldsymbol{a} = \begin{pmatrix}1\\2\end{pmatrix} \quad \text{and} \quad \boldsymbol{b} = \begin{pmatrix}1\\0\end{pmatrix}.$$

(a) Determine all vectors that are orthogonal to $\boldsymbol{a}$.
(b) Determine all vectors that are orthogonal to $\boldsymbol{b}$.
(c) If $\boldsymbol{x} \perp \boldsymbol{y}$, prove that $\|\boldsymbol{x}+\boldsymbol{y}\|^2 = \|\boldsymbol{x}\|^2 + \|\boldsymbol{y}\|^2$ (*Pythagoras*).

Solution
(a) All vectors $\boldsymbol{x} := (x_1, x_2)'$ orthogonal to $\boldsymbol{a}$ satisfy $\langle \boldsymbol{x}, \boldsymbol{a} \rangle = 0$, that is, $x_1 + 2x_2 = 0$. Hence,

$$\boldsymbol{x} = \lambda \begin{pmatrix} 2 \\ -1 \end{pmatrix} \quad (\lambda \in \mathbb{R}) .$$

(b) Any vector $\boldsymbol{x} \perp \boldsymbol{b}$ must satisfy $\langle \boldsymbol{x}, \boldsymbol{b} \rangle = 0$, that is, $x_1 = 0$. Hence,

$$\boldsymbol{x} = \lambda \begin{pmatrix} 0 \\ 1 \end{pmatrix} \quad (\lambda \in \mathbb{R}) .$$

(c) If $\boldsymbol{x} \perp \boldsymbol{y}$, then $\langle \boldsymbol{x}, \boldsymbol{y} \rangle = 0$ and hence,

$$\begin{aligned} \|\boldsymbol{x}+\boldsymbol{y}\|^2 &= \langle \boldsymbol{x}+\boldsymbol{y}, \boldsymbol{x}+\boldsymbol{y} \rangle = \langle \boldsymbol{x}, \boldsymbol{x} \rangle + 2\langle \boldsymbol{x}, \boldsymbol{y} \rangle + \langle \boldsymbol{y}, \boldsymbol{y} \rangle \\ &= \langle \boldsymbol{x}, \boldsymbol{x} \rangle + \langle \boldsymbol{y}, \boldsymbol{y} \rangle = \|\boldsymbol{x}\|^2 + \|\boldsymbol{y}\|^2 . \end{aligned}$$

Exercise 1.13 (Orthonormal vectors) Two orthogonal vectors $\boldsymbol{x}$ and $\boldsymbol{y}$ that are normalized such that $\|\boldsymbol{x}\| = \|\boldsymbol{y}\| = 1$ are said to be orthonormal.
(a) Show that the unit vectors $\boldsymbol{e}_i$ are orthonormal.
(b) If $\boldsymbol{x} := \sum_{i=1}^m c_i \boldsymbol{e}_i$, determine the values of the c_i.
(c) Discuss the geometric meaning of this result.

Solution
(a) This follows from the fact that $\langle \boldsymbol{e}_i, \boldsymbol{e}_i \rangle = 1$ and $\langle \boldsymbol{e}_i, \boldsymbol{e}_j \rangle = 0$ $(i \neq j)$.
(b) We have

$$\boldsymbol{x} = c_1\boldsymbol{e}_1 + c_2\boldsymbol{e}_2 + \dots + c_m\boldsymbol{e}_m = \begin{pmatrix} c_1 \\ 0 \\ \vdots \\ 0 \end{pmatrix} + \begin{pmatrix} 0 \\ c_2 \\ \vdots \\ 0 \end{pmatrix} + \dots + \begin{pmatrix} 0 \\ 0 \\ \vdots \\ c_m \end{pmatrix} = \begin{pmatrix} c_1 \\ c_2 \\ \vdots \\ c_m \end{pmatrix} .$$

Hence, $c_i = x_i$. The c_i thus are the "rectangular coordinates" of $\boldsymbol{x}$.
(c) This simple result is of great importance, because it implies that every vector can be decomposed as a sum of orthogonal ("independent") vectors represented by perpendicular axes, as in Figure 1.1.

Exercise 1.14 (Orthogonality is not transitive) Demonstrate that $\boldsymbol{x} \perp \boldsymbol{y}$ and $\boldsymbol{y} \perp \boldsymbol{z}$ need not imply that $\boldsymbol{x} \perp \boldsymbol{z}$.

Solution

Take $\boldsymbol{z} := \boldsymbol{x}$. Then $\boldsymbol{x} \perp \boldsymbol{y}$ and $\boldsymbol{y} \perp \boldsymbol{x}$, but it is clearly not true that $\boldsymbol{x} \perp \boldsymbol{x}$ unless $\boldsymbol{x} = \mathbf{0}$. Another counterexample is provided by Exercise 1.8, where $\boldsymbol{x} \perp \boldsymbol{z}$ and $\boldsymbol{z} \perp \boldsymbol{y}$, but $\boldsymbol{x}$ is not orthogonal to $\boldsymbol{y}$.

Exercise 1.15 (Angle) The angle θ between two nonzero vectors $\boldsymbol{x}$ and $\boldsymbol{y}$ is defined by

$$\cos\theta := \frac{\langle \boldsymbol{x}, \boldsymbol{y} \rangle}{\|\boldsymbol{x}\| \cdot \|\boldsymbol{y}\|} \quad (0 \leq \theta \leq \pi).$$

(a) Show that

$$-1 \leq \frac{\langle \boldsymbol{x}, \boldsymbol{y} \rangle}{\|\boldsymbol{x}\| \cdot \|\boldsymbol{y}\|} \leq 1.$$

(b) Show that the angle between a vector and itself is zero.
(c) Show that the angle between $\boldsymbol{x}$ and $-\boldsymbol{x}$ is π.
(d) What is the angle between two orthogonal vectors?

Solution

(a) This follows from the Cauchy-Schwarz inequality (Exercise 1.9).
(b) Let θ $(0 \leq \theta \leq \pi)$ be the angle. Then,

$$\cos\theta = \frac{\langle \boldsymbol{x}, \boldsymbol{x} \rangle}{\|\boldsymbol{x}\| \cdot \|\boldsymbol{x}\|} = 1,$$

implying $\theta = 0$.
(c) Here,

$$\cos\theta = \frac{\langle \boldsymbol{x}, -\boldsymbol{x} \rangle}{\|\boldsymbol{x}\| \cdot \|-\boldsymbol{x}\|} = -1,$$

implying that $\theta = \pi$.
(d) Finally, if $\boldsymbol{x}$ and $\boldsymbol{y}$ are orthogonal, then

$$\cos\theta = \frac{\langle \boldsymbol{x}, \boldsymbol{y} \rangle}{\|\boldsymbol{x}\| \cdot \|\boldsymbol{y}\|} = 0,$$

and hence $\theta = \pi/2$.

Exercise 1.16 (Sum vector) The sum vector is defined as the vector consisting entirely of ones:

$$\boldsymbol{\imath} := \begin{pmatrix} 1 \\ 1 \\ \vdots \\ 1 \end{pmatrix}.$$

(a) Consider $\langle \imath, x \rangle$ and explain the name *sum vector*.
(b) What is $\|\imath\|$?

Solution
(a) The fact that $\langle \imath, x \rangle = \sum_i x_i$ explains the name.
(b) If $\imath$ is a vector of order m, then $\|\imath\| = \sqrt{m}$.

1.2 Complex vectors

Exercise 1.17 (Complex numbers) For complex numbers, $u := a + \mathrm{i}b$ and $v := c + \mathrm{i}d$, where a, b, c, d are real numbers, and i denotes the imaginary unit defined by $\mathrm{i}^2 := -1$, show that:
(a) $\lambda u = (\lambda a) + \mathrm{i}(\lambda b)$ for any real scalar λ;
(b) $uv = vu$ and $u + v = v + u$;
(c) the ratio of u and v is

$$\frac{u}{v} = \frac{ac + bd}{c^2 + d^2} - \mathrm{i}\frac{ad - bc}{c^2 + d^2},$$

when $v \neq 0$.

Solution
(a) This follows directly from the definition.
(b)

$$uv = (ac - bd) + \mathrm{i}(ad + bc) = (ca - db) + \mathrm{i}(cb + da) = vu$$

and

$$u + v = (a + c) + \mathrm{i}(b + d) = (c + a) + \mathrm{i}(d + b) = v + u.$$

(c)

$$\frac{u}{v} = \frac{a + \mathrm{i}b}{c + \mathrm{i}d} = \frac{(a + \mathrm{i}b)(c - \mathrm{i}d)}{(c + \mathrm{i}d)(c - \mathrm{i}d)} = \frac{(ac + bd) - \mathrm{i}(ad - bc)}{c^2 + d^2}.$$

Exercise 1.18 (Complex conjugates) If $u := a + \mathrm{i}b$ is a complex number, then the complex conjugate of u is defined as $u^* := a - \mathrm{i}b$. Show that:
(a) $(u^*)^* = u$;
(b) $(u + v)^* = u^* + v^*$;
(c) $(uv)^* = u^* v^*$;
(d) $uv^* \neq u^* v$ unless uv^* is a real number.

Solution

(a) Since $u^* = a - \mathrm{i}b$, we have $(u^*)^* = a - \mathrm{i}(-b) = a + \mathrm{i}b = u$.

(b) Let $v := c + \mathrm{i}d$. Then

$$\begin{aligned}(u+v)^* &= ((a+c) + \mathrm{i}(b+d))^* = (a+c) - \mathrm{i}(b+d) \\ &= (a - \mathrm{i}b) + (c - \mathrm{i}d) = u^* + v^*.\end{aligned}$$

(c) Since $uv = (ac - bd) + \mathrm{i}(ad + bc)$, we find

$$(uv)^* = (ac - bd) - \mathrm{i}(ad + bc) = (a - \mathrm{i}b)(c - \mathrm{i}d) = u^*v^*.$$

(d) Since

$$uv^* = (ac + bd) - \mathrm{i}(ad - bc) \quad \text{and} \quad u^*v = (ac + bd) + \mathrm{i}(ad - bc),$$

we see that uv^* and u^*v are each other's complex conjugate. Hence, they are equal if and only if $ad - bc = 0$, in which case both are real.

***Exercise 1.19 (Modulus)**

(a) Show that $|uv| = |u||v|$.

(b) Show that $|u + v| \leq |u| + |v|$ (*triangle inequality*).

Solution

(a) Let $u := a + \mathrm{i}b$ and $v := c + \mathrm{i}d$. Then,

$$|uv| = \sqrt{(ac - bd)^2 + (ad + bc)^2} = \sqrt{(a^2 + b^2)(c^2 + d^2)} = |u||v|.$$

(b) Write $\boldsymbol{x} := (\mathrm{Re}(u), \mathrm{Im}(u))'$ and $\boldsymbol{y} := (\mathrm{Re}(v), \mathrm{Im}(v))'$. The triangle inequality (Exercise 1.10(c)) then implies that

$$|u + v| = \|\boldsymbol{x} + \boldsymbol{y}\| \leq \|\boldsymbol{x}\| + \|\boldsymbol{y}\| = |u| + |v|.$$

Exercise 1.20 (Inner product in $\mathbb{C}^m$) The inner product between two complex vectors $\boldsymbol{u}$ and $\boldsymbol{v}$ is the complex number $\langle \boldsymbol{u}, \boldsymbol{v} \rangle := \sum_{i=1}^m u_i v_i^*$ and the norm is the real number $\|\boldsymbol{u}\| := \langle \boldsymbol{u}, \boldsymbol{u} \rangle^{1/2} = (\sum_{i=1}^m u_i u_i^*)^{1/2}$. Show that for any vectors $\boldsymbol{u}, \boldsymbol{v}, \boldsymbol{w}$ in $\mathbb{C}^m$ and any scalar λ in $\mathbb{C}$:

(a) $\langle \boldsymbol{u}, \boldsymbol{v} \rangle = \langle \boldsymbol{v}, \boldsymbol{u} \rangle^*$;

(b) $\langle \boldsymbol{u}, \boldsymbol{v} + \boldsymbol{w} \rangle = \langle \boldsymbol{u}, \boldsymbol{v} \rangle + \langle \boldsymbol{u}, \boldsymbol{w} \rangle$;

(c) $\langle \lambda \boldsymbol{u}, \boldsymbol{v} \rangle = \lambda \langle \boldsymbol{u}, \boldsymbol{v} \rangle$;

(d) $\langle \boldsymbol{u}, \boldsymbol{u} \rangle \geq 0$, with $\langle \boldsymbol{u}, \boldsymbol{u} \rangle = 0 \iff \boldsymbol{u} = \boldsymbol{0}$.

Solution

(a) $\langle \boldsymbol{u}, \boldsymbol{v} \rangle = \sum_i u_i v_i^* = \sum_i (v_i u_i^*)^* = \langle \boldsymbol{v}, \boldsymbol{u} \rangle^*$.

(b) We have

$$\begin{aligned}\langle \boldsymbol{u}, \boldsymbol{v} + \boldsymbol{w} \rangle &= \sum_i u_i (v_i + w_i)^* = \sum_i u_i (v_i^* + w_i^*) \\ &= \sum_i u_i v_i^* + \sum_i u_i w_i^* = \langle \boldsymbol{u}, \boldsymbol{v} \rangle + \langle \boldsymbol{u}, \boldsymbol{w} \rangle.\end{aligned}$$

(c) $\langle \lambda \boldsymbol{u}, \boldsymbol{v}\rangle = \sum_i \lambda u_i v_i^* = \lambda \sum_i u_i v_i^* = \lambda\langle \boldsymbol{u}, \boldsymbol{v}\rangle$.
(d) $\langle \boldsymbol{u}, \boldsymbol{u}\rangle = \sum_i u_i u_i^* = \|\boldsymbol{u}\|^2 \geq 0$, and $\|\boldsymbol{u}\| = 0$ if and only if $\boldsymbol{u} = \mathbf{0}$.

Exercise 1.21 (Complex inequalities) Show for any two vectors $\boldsymbol{u}$ and $\boldsymbol{v}$ in $\mathbb{C}^m$ that:
(a) $\langle \boldsymbol{u}, \lambda\boldsymbol{v}\rangle = \lambda^*\langle \boldsymbol{u}, \boldsymbol{v}\rangle$;
(b) $|\langle \boldsymbol{u}, \boldsymbol{v}\rangle| \leq \|\boldsymbol{u}\| \cdot \|\boldsymbol{v}\|$, with equality if and only if $\boldsymbol{u}$ and $\boldsymbol{v}$ are collinear (*Cauchy-Schwarz*);
(c) $\|\boldsymbol{u} + \boldsymbol{v}\| \leq \|\boldsymbol{u}\| + \|\boldsymbol{v}\|$, with equality if and only if $\boldsymbol{u}$ and $\boldsymbol{v}$ are collinear (*triangle inequality*).

Solution
(a) We have

$$\langle \boldsymbol{u}, \lambda\boldsymbol{v}\rangle = \sum_i u_i(\lambda v_i)^* = \sum_i u_i\lambda^* v_i^* = \lambda^* \sum_i u_i v_i^* = \lambda^*\langle \boldsymbol{u}, \boldsymbol{v}\rangle.$$

(b) The proof is almost identical to the proof in the real case (Exercise 1.9). We have

$$0 \leq \langle \boldsymbol{u} - \lambda\boldsymbol{v}, \boldsymbol{u} - \lambda\boldsymbol{v}\rangle = \langle \boldsymbol{u}, \boldsymbol{u}\rangle - \lambda\langle \boldsymbol{v}, \boldsymbol{u}\rangle - \lambda^*\langle \boldsymbol{u}, \boldsymbol{v}\rangle + |\lambda|^2\langle \boldsymbol{v}, \boldsymbol{v}\rangle.$$

Setting $\lambda := \langle \boldsymbol{u}, \boldsymbol{v}\rangle / \langle \boldsymbol{v}, \boldsymbol{v}\rangle$, the result follows as in the real case. Notice that $\lambda\langle \boldsymbol{v}, \boldsymbol{u}\rangle$ and $\lambda^*\langle \boldsymbol{u}, \boldsymbol{v}\rangle$ are complex conjugates.
(c) Again, the proof is almost identical to the proof of Exercise 1.10(c):

$$\begin{aligned}\|\boldsymbol{u} + \boldsymbol{v}\|^2 &= \langle \boldsymbol{u} + \boldsymbol{v}, \boldsymbol{u} + \boldsymbol{v}\rangle = \langle \boldsymbol{u}, \boldsymbol{u}\rangle + \langle \boldsymbol{u}, \boldsymbol{v}\rangle + \langle \boldsymbol{v}, \boldsymbol{u}\rangle + \langle \boldsymbol{v}, \boldsymbol{v}\rangle \\ &\leq \|\boldsymbol{u}\|^2 + 2\|\boldsymbol{u}\| \cdot \|\boldsymbol{v}\| + \|\boldsymbol{v}\|^2 = (\|\boldsymbol{u}\| + \|\boldsymbol{v}\|)^2,\end{aligned}$$

using the Cauchy-Schwarz inequality. Taking the positive square root of both sides yields the result.

Notes

There are many good introductory texts, see for example Hadley (1961), Bellman (1970), and Bretscher (1997). The reader interested in the origins of matrix theory should consult MacDuffee (1946) or Bretscher (1997).

The famous Cauchy-Schwarz inequality (Exercises 1.9 and 1.21) is named after the mathematicians Augustin-Louis Cauchy (1789–1857) from France and Hermann Amandus Schwarz (1843–1921) from Germany. It is sometimes called Schwarz's inequality, and in the Russian literature it is known as Bunyakovskii's inequality.

2

Matrices

An $m \times n$ matrix $\boldsymbol{A}$ is a rectangular array of scalar (real or complex) numbers,

$$\boldsymbol{A} := \begin{pmatrix} a_{11} & a_{12} & \dots & a_{1n} \\ a_{21} & a_{22} & \dots & a_{2n} \\ \vdots & \vdots & & \vdots \\ a_{m1} & a_{m2} & \dots & a_{mn} \end{pmatrix}.$$

The displayed matrix has m rows and n columns, and is called an m *by* n matrix or a matrix of *order* $m \times n$. Matrices will be denoted by uppercase symbols in bold-italic: $\boldsymbol{A}, \boldsymbol{B}, \dots, \boldsymbol{Z}$. They can also be denoted by Greek uppercase letters in bold-italic, such as $\boldsymbol{\Gamma}$ or $\boldsymbol{\Theta}$. We sometimes write $\boldsymbol{A} = (a_{ij})$. The quantities a_{ij} are called the *elements* of $\boldsymbol{A}$. Notice that a_{ij} is the element in row i and column j. When useful we may also write a_{ij} as $(\boldsymbol{A})_{ij}$. If we remove all but m_1 rows and all but n_1 columns of an $m \times n$ matrix $\boldsymbol{A}$, then the resulting $m_1 \times n_1$ matrix is called a *submatrix* of $\boldsymbol{A}$. For example, if

$$\boldsymbol{A} = \begin{pmatrix} 1 & 2 & 3 \\ 4 & 5 & 6 \end{pmatrix},$$

then both

$$\begin{pmatrix} 1 \\ 4 \end{pmatrix} \quad \text{and} \quad \begin{pmatrix} 1 & 3 \\ 4 & 6 \end{pmatrix}$$

are submatrices of $\boldsymbol{A}$.

The *transpose* of an $m \times n$ matrix $\boldsymbol{A} = (a_{ij})$ is the $n \times m$ matrix $\boldsymbol{A}' := (a_{ji})$. The rows of $\boldsymbol{A}'$ are the columns of $\boldsymbol{A}$ and the rows of $\boldsymbol{A}$ are the columns of $\boldsymbol{A}'$. We write the n

columns of $\boldsymbol{A}$ as $\boldsymbol{a}_{\bullet 1}, \boldsymbol{a}_{\bullet 2}, \dots, \boldsymbol{a}_{\bullet n}$, and the m rows as $\boldsymbol{a}'_{1\bullet}, \boldsymbol{a}'_{2\bullet}, \dots, \boldsymbol{a}'_{m\bullet}$. Hence,

$$\boldsymbol{A} = (\boldsymbol{a}_{\bullet 1}, \boldsymbol{a}_{\bullet 2}, \dots, \boldsymbol{a}_{\bullet n}) = \begin{pmatrix} \boldsymbol{a}'_{1\bullet} \\ \boldsymbol{a}'_{2\bullet} \\ \vdots \\ \boldsymbol{a}'_{m\bullet} \end{pmatrix}.$$

With this notation, $\boldsymbol{a}_{i\bullet}$ and $\boldsymbol{a}_{\bullet j}$ are both (column) vectors. Their transposes $\boldsymbol{a}'_{i\bullet}$ and $\boldsymbol{a}'_{\bullet j}$ are called *row vectors*. In practice, when there is no possibility of confusion, we often write $\boldsymbol{a}_j$ instead of $\boldsymbol{a}_{\bullet j}$, so that $\boldsymbol{A} = (\boldsymbol{a}_1, \boldsymbol{a}_2, \dots, \boldsymbol{a}_n)$, also written as $\boldsymbol{A} = (\boldsymbol{a}_1 : \boldsymbol{a}_2 : \dots : \boldsymbol{a}_n)$.

Two matrices $\boldsymbol{A}$ and $\boldsymbol{B}$ are called equal, written $\boldsymbol{A} = \boldsymbol{B}$, if and only if their corresponding elements are equal. The sum of two matrices $\boldsymbol{A}$ and $\boldsymbol{B}$ of the same order is defined as

$$\boldsymbol{A} + \boldsymbol{B} := (a_{ij}) + (b_{ij}) := (a_{ij} + b_{ij}),$$

and the product of a matrix by a scalar λ is

$$\lambda \boldsymbol{A} := \boldsymbol{A}\lambda := (\lambda a_{ij}).$$

For example, we have

$$\begin{pmatrix} 1 & 2 \\ 3 & 4 \end{pmatrix} + \begin{pmatrix} 5 & 6 \\ 7 & 8 \end{pmatrix} = \begin{pmatrix} 6 & 8 \\ 10 & 12 \end{pmatrix} = 2 \begin{pmatrix} 3 & 4 \\ 5 & 6 \end{pmatrix}.$$

Matrices whose elements are all real numbers are called *real matrices*, and we write $\boldsymbol{A} \in \mathbb{R}^{m \times n}$. Matrices (some of) whose elements are complex numbers are called *complex matrices*, and we write $\boldsymbol{A} \in \mathbb{C}^{m \times n}$ to indicate that $\boldsymbol{A}$ is a complex matrix of order $m \times n$.

A matrix whose elements are all zero is called a *null matrix*, and is denoted by $\mathbf{O}$. If we wish to stress the dimensions we write $\mathbf{O}_{mn}$ or $\mathbf{O}_{m,n}$, if the order is $m \times n$.

If $\boldsymbol{A}$ is an $m \times n$ matrix and $\boldsymbol{B}$ a $p \times q$ matrix, then we define the *product* of $\boldsymbol{A}$ and $\boldsymbol{B}$ as

$$\boldsymbol{AB} := \left(\sum_{j=1}^{n} a_{ij} b_{jk} \right),$$

provided $n = p$, so that $\boldsymbol{A}$ has the same number of columns as $\boldsymbol{B}$ has rows. Thus, $\boldsymbol{AB}$ is an $m \times q$ matrix and its ik-th element is $\sum_{j=1}^{n} a_{ij} b_{jk}$. Notice carefully the sequence of indices $ijjk$ in the sum defining the ik-th element. For example,

$$\begin{pmatrix} 1 & 2 \\ 3 & 4 \end{pmatrix} \begin{pmatrix} 5 & 6 \\ 7 & 8 \end{pmatrix} = \begin{pmatrix} 5 + 14 & 6 + 16 \\ 15 + 28 & 18 + 32 \end{pmatrix} = \begin{pmatrix} 19 & 22 \\ 43 & 50 \end{pmatrix}$$

and

$$\begin{pmatrix} 5 & 6 \\ 7 & 8 \end{pmatrix} \begin{pmatrix} 1 & 2 \\ 3 & 4 \end{pmatrix} = \begin{pmatrix} 5 + 18 & 10 + 24 \\ 7 + 24 & 14 + 32 \end{pmatrix} = \begin{pmatrix} 23 & 34 \\ 31 & 46 \end{pmatrix}.$$

When the orders of $\boldsymbol{A}$ and $\boldsymbol{B}$ are such that $\boldsymbol{AB}$ is defined, we say that $\boldsymbol{A}$ and $\boldsymbol{B}$ are *conformable*. More generally we shall say that matrices (and vectors) are conformable when their orders are such that the implied matrix operations (such as multiplication and addition) can be carried out. Notice that the product $\boldsymbol{BA}$ is given by

$$\boldsymbol{BA} = \left(\sum_{i=1}^{m} b_{ri}a_{ij}\right),$$

provided $q = m$. Thus, $\boldsymbol{BA}$ is a $p \times n$ matrix and its rj-th element is $\sum_{i=1}^{m} b_{ri}a_{ij}$. In the product $\boldsymbol{AB}$ we say that $\boldsymbol{B}$ is *premultiplied* by $\boldsymbol{A}$ and that $\boldsymbol{A}$ is *postmultiplied* by $\boldsymbol{B}$. The above example shows that, in general, $\boldsymbol{AB} \neq \boldsymbol{BA}$. Two matrices for which $\boldsymbol{AB} = \boldsymbol{BA}$ are said to *commute*.

The main property of the transpose is that $(\boldsymbol{AB})' = \boldsymbol{B}'\boldsymbol{A}'$ for any two matrices $\boldsymbol{A}$ and $\boldsymbol{B}$ for which $\boldsymbol{AB}$ is defined.

A matrix $\boldsymbol{A} = (a_{ij})$ is said to be *square* if it has as many rows as it has columns. An $n \times n$ square matrix is said to be of *order* n. A square matrix of particular importance is the *diagonal* matrix whose elements outside the diagonal are all zero, that is, $a_{ij} = 0$ for all $i \neq j$. For any square matrix $\boldsymbol{A}$, not necessarily diagonal, we define the matrix function $\operatorname{dg} \boldsymbol{A}$ or $\operatorname{dg}(\boldsymbol{A})$ as

$$\operatorname{dg}(\boldsymbol{A}) := \begin{pmatrix} a_{11} & 0 & \dots & 0 \\ 0 & a_{22} & \dots & 0 \\ \vdots & \vdots & & \vdots \\ 0 & 0 & \dots & a_{nn} \end{pmatrix}.$$

For any set of numbers $(a_1, a_2, \dots, a_n)$, we define $\operatorname{diag}(a_1, a_2, \dots, a_n)$ as the diagonal $n \times n$ matrix containing $a_1, a_2, \dots, a_n$ on the diagonal. Thus,

$$\operatorname{dg}(\boldsymbol{A}) = \operatorname{diag}(a_{11}, a_{22}, \dots, a_{nn}).$$

A diagonal matrix of special importance is the *identity matrix*,

$$\boldsymbol{I} := \begin{pmatrix} 1 & 0 & \dots & 0 \\ 0 & 1 & \dots & 0 \\ \vdots & \vdots & & \vdots \\ 0 & 0 & \dots & 1 \end{pmatrix}.$$

If the identity matrix is of order n, we often write $\boldsymbol{I}_n$ to emphasize this. Any matrix of the form $\lambda \boldsymbol{I}_n$ is called a *scalar matrix*. A square matrix $\boldsymbol{A}$ for which $a_{ij} = 0$ for $j > i$ is said to be *lower triangular*: all elements above the diagonal are zero. Similarly, when $a_{ij} = 0$ for $i > j$, the matrix is said to be *upper triangular*. A (lower, upper) triangular matrix is *strictly* (lower, upper) triangular if its diagonal elements are zero, and *unit* (lower, upper) triangular if its diagonal elements are one.

A square real matrix $\boldsymbol{A}$ is *symmetric* if $\boldsymbol{A} = \boldsymbol{A}'$. Symmetric matrices have attractive properties that are often not shared by nonsymmetric matrices. A square real matrix $\boldsymbol{A}$ is *skew-symmetric* if $\boldsymbol{A}' = -\boldsymbol{A}$. Every square matrix $\boldsymbol{A}$ can be written as

$$\boldsymbol{A} = \frac{\boldsymbol{A} + \boldsymbol{A}'}{2} + \frac{\boldsymbol{A} - \boldsymbol{A}'}{2},$$

that is, as the sum of a symmetric and a skew-symmetric matrix, if $\boldsymbol{A}$ is real.

If $\boldsymbol{a}$ and $\boldsymbol{x}$ are real vectors of the same order, then the scalar function $\boldsymbol{a}'\boldsymbol{x}$ is called a *linear form* in $\boldsymbol{x}$. If $\boldsymbol{A}$ is a real matrix and $\boldsymbol{x}$ a conformable real vector, then the scalar function $\boldsymbol{x}'\boldsymbol{A}\boldsymbol{x}$ is called a *quadratic form* in $\boldsymbol{x}$. In a quadratic form the matrix $\boldsymbol{A}$ can always be taken to be symmetric, because

$$\boldsymbol{x}'\boldsymbol{A}\boldsymbol{x} = \boldsymbol{x}'\left(\frac{\boldsymbol{A} + \boldsymbol{A}'}{2}\right)\boldsymbol{x}.$$

For example,

$$(x_1, x_2)\begin{pmatrix}1 & 2\\ 3 & 4\end{pmatrix}\begin{pmatrix}x_1\\ x_2\end{pmatrix} = (x_1, x_2)\begin{pmatrix}1 & 2.5\\ 2.5 & 4\end{pmatrix}\begin{pmatrix}x_1\\ x_2\end{pmatrix} = x_1^2 + 5x_1x_2 + 4x_2^2.$$

The *trace* of a square matrix $\boldsymbol{A}$ is the sum of its diagonal elements, and is written as $\operatorname{tr}\boldsymbol{A}$ or $\operatorname{tr}(\boldsymbol{A})$. The trace is a linear operator, $\operatorname{tr}(\boldsymbol{A}+\boldsymbol{B}) = \operatorname{tr}(\boldsymbol{A}) + \operatorname{tr}(\boldsymbol{B})$ and $\operatorname{tr}(\lambda\boldsymbol{A}) = \lambda\operatorname{tr}(\boldsymbol{A})$, and it has two principal properties:

$$\operatorname{tr}(\boldsymbol{A}') = \operatorname{tr}(\boldsymbol{A}) \quad \text{and} \quad \operatorname{tr}(\boldsymbol{A}\boldsymbol{B}) = \operatorname{tr}(\boldsymbol{B}\boldsymbol{A}),$$

where $\boldsymbol{A}$ must be square in the first equation (in which case $\boldsymbol{A}'$ is also square), and $\boldsymbol{A}\boldsymbol{B}$ must be square in the second equation (in which case $\boldsymbol{B}\boldsymbol{A}$ is also square, though not necessarily of the same order).

For any real square $\boldsymbol{A}$, we say that $\boldsymbol{A}$ is *orthogonal* if $\boldsymbol{A}'\boldsymbol{A} = \boldsymbol{A}\boldsymbol{A}' = \boldsymbol{I}$; that $\boldsymbol{A}$ is a *permutation matrix* if each row and each column of $\boldsymbol{A}$ contains a single element 1, and the remaining elements are zero; that $\boldsymbol{A}$ is *normal* if $\boldsymbol{A}'\boldsymbol{A} = \boldsymbol{A}\boldsymbol{A}'$. For any square matrix $\boldsymbol{A}$, real or complex, we say that $\boldsymbol{A}$ is *idempotent* if $\boldsymbol{A}\boldsymbol{A} = \boldsymbol{A}$. The *powers* of a square matrix $\boldsymbol{A}$ are defined as $\boldsymbol{A}^2 := \boldsymbol{A}\boldsymbol{A}$, $\boldsymbol{A}^3 := \boldsymbol{A}^2\boldsymbol{A}$, and so on. By convention, $\boldsymbol{A}^0 = \boldsymbol{I}$.

For two real matrices $\boldsymbol{A}$ and $\boldsymbol{B}$ of the same order we define the *inner product* as

$$\langle\boldsymbol{A}, \boldsymbol{B}\rangle := \sum_i\sum_j a_{ij}b_{ij} = \operatorname{tr}\boldsymbol{A}'\boldsymbol{B},$$

and the *norm* as

$$\|\boldsymbol{A}\| := \langle\boldsymbol{A}, \boldsymbol{A}\rangle^{1/2} = \sqrt{\sum_i\sum_j a_{ij}^2} = \sqrt{\operatorname{tr}\boldsymbol{A}'\boldsymbol{A}}.$$

Finally, a complex matrix $\boldsymbol{U}$ is a matrix whose elements are complex numbers. Recall that if $u := a + \mathrm{i}b$ is a complex number, then $u^* := a - \mathrm{i}b$ is its conjugate. Similarly, if $\boldsymbol{U} := \boldsymbol{A} + \mathrm{i}\boldsymbol{B}$ is a complex matrix ($\boldsymbol{A}$ and $\boldsymbol{B}$ are real matrices), then $\boldsymbol{U}^* := \boldsymbol{A}' - \mathrm{i}\boldsymbol{B}'$ is the *conjugate transpose* of $\boldsymbol{U}$. (Note carefully that the matrix generalization of $u^* = a - \mathrm{i}b$ is *not* $\boldsymbol{U}^* = \boldsymbol{A} - \mathrm{i}\boldsymbol{B}$.) A square matrix $\boldsymbol{U}$ is said to be *Hermitian* if $\boldsymbol{U}^* = \boldsymbol{U}$ (the complex analogue of a symmetric matrix); *skew-Hermitian* if $\boldsymbol{U}^* = -\boldsymbol{U}$ (the complex analogue of a skew-symmetric matrix); *unitary* if $\boldsymbol{U}^*\boldsymbol{U} = \boldsymbol{U}\boldsymbol{U}^* = \boldsymbol{I}$ (the complex analogue of an orthogonal matrix); and *normal* if $U^*U = UU^*$ (the complex analogue of a real normal matrix). For any complex-valued vector x, the function u^*x is called a *linear form*, as in the real case. However, the scalar function x^*Ux is called a *Hermitian form*, and not a quadratic form.

Remarks on the definitions: Many definitions, even of central concepts such as symmetry and orthogonality, are not standardized in the literature on matrix algebra. We believe that the most natural way is to take the definitions of the complex matrices (on which there is no controversy) as the starting point. Thus, the four concepts of a Hermitian matrix, a unitary matrix, a skew-Hermitian matrix, and a Hermitian form specialize in the real case to a symmetric matrix, an orthogonal matrix, a skew-symmetric matrix, and a quadratic form. For example, a symmetric matrix is simply a shorter name for a real Hermitian matrix, and all properties of Hermitian matrices apply to symmetric matrices. This is how we do it.

When reading other literature on matrix algebra, the reader should be aware that some authors define a symmetric matrix to be one that satisfies $A' = A$, where A may be real or complex, and similarly with the other three concepts. Only the properties of *real* symmetric matrices then follow from those of Hermitian matrices. *Complex-symmetric* matrices (that is, square complex matrices satisfying $A' = A$) and, similarly, *complex-orthogonal* matrices (that is, square complex matrices satisfying $A'A = I$) do not share the attractive properties of their real counterparts (see Exercises 7.23, 7.41, and 7.72) — they play a marginal role in matrix theory.

We also emphasize that an idempotent matrix is *not* necessarily symmetric, while a positive (semi)definite matrix (introduced in Chapter 8) *is* necessarily symmetric.

Finally, caution is required with the word "orthogonal". Of course, an orthogonal matrix should be named "orthonormal" instead, as many authors have already remarked, but the word seems too embedded in matrix language to change it now. Also, a sentence like "A and B are orthogonal" can mean that both matrices are orthogonal, but it can also mean that they are orthogonal *to each other*, that is, that $A'B = \mathrm{O}$. If the latter meaning is intended we write "A and B are orthogonal to each other" or "A is orthogonal to B" or "B is orthogonal to A" — the three statements are equivalent.

2.1 Real matrices

Exercise 2.1 (Matrix equality)
(a) For two matrices A and B, when is $A = B$?
(b) If $A = \mathrm{O}$ and $B = \mathrm{O}$, is $A = B$?
(c) When is it true that $ab' = ba'$?

Solution
(a) A and B must be of the same order, and have the same elements, $a_{ij} = b_{ij}$.
(b) Only if A and B are of the same order.
(c) First, a and b must be of the same order, say n. Then, $ab' = ba'$ holds if and only if $a_i b_j = a_j b_i$ for all $i, j = 1, \dots, n$. If $b = 0$ the relationship holds. If $b \neq 0$, then there

exists an integer j such that $b_j \neq 0$. For this value of j we have $b_j \boldsymbol{a} = a_j \boldsymbol{b}$ and hence $\boldsymbol{a} = \lambda \boldsymbol{b}$ for some λ. We conclude that $\boldsymbol{a}\boldsymbol{b}' = \boldsymbol{b}\boldsymbol{a}'$ if and only if $\boldsymbol{a}$ and $\boldsymbol{b}$ are collinear.

Exercise 2.2 (Matrix equality, numbers) Find a, b, c, d such that

$$\begin{pmatrix} a-b & 3c+d \\ a+b & c-d \end{pmatrix} = \begin{pmatrix} 2 & 6 \\ 4 & 2 \end{pmatrix}.$$

Solution
We solve four equations in four unknowns,

$$a-b=2, \quad 3c+d=6, \quad a+b=4, \quad c-d=2,$$

and find $a=3, b=1, c=2, d=0$.

Exercise 2.3 (Matrix addition)
(a) Show that there exists a unique matrix $\mathbf{O}$ such that $\boldsymbol{A}+\mathbf{O}=\boldsymbol{A}$.
(b) Show that $\boldsymbol{A}+\boldsymbol{B}=\boldsymbol{B}+\boldsymbol{A}$.
(c) Show that $(\boldsymbol{A}+\boldsymbol{B})+\boldsymbol{C}=\boldsymbol{A}+(\boldsymbol{B}+\boldsymbol{C})$.

Solution
(a) If $\boldsymbol{A}+\boldsymbol{X}=\boldsymbol{A}$, then $a_{ij}+x_{ij}=a_{ij}$ for all i,j. This implies $x_{ij}=0$ for all i,j, and hence $\boldsymbol{X}=\mathbf{O}$.
(b) $\boldsymbol{A}+\boldsymbol{B}=(a_{ij}+b_{ij})=(b_{ij}+a_{ij})=\boldsymbol{B}+\boldsymbol{A}$.
(c) $(\boldsymbol{A}+\boldsymbol{B})+\boldsymbol{C}=((a_{ij}+b_{ij})+c_{ij})=(a_{ij}+(b_{ij}+c_{ij}))=\boldsymbol{A}+(\boldsymbol{B}+\boldsymbol{C})$.

Exercise 2.4 (Transpose and inner product) Consider the matrices

$$\boldsymbol{A} = \begin{pmatrix} 1 & 2 \\ 2 & 1 \end{pmatrix} \quad \text{and} \quad \boldsymbol{B} = \begin{pmatrix} 1 & 2 & 3 \\ 2 & 1 & 5 \end{pmatrix}.$$

(a) Obtain $\boldsymbol{A}'$ and $\boldsymbol{B}'$.
(b) Prove that $(\boldsymbol{X}')' = \boldsymbol{X}$ for any matrix $\boldsymbol{X}$ and verify this on the matrices $\boldsymbol{A}$ and $\boldsymbol{B}$.
(c) What is the transpose of the row vector $\boldsymbol{b}' = (1,2,3)$?
(d) Show that $(\boldsymbol{A}+\boldsymbol{B})' = \boldsymbol{A}'+\boldsymbol{B}'$ for any two matrices $\boldsymbol{A}$ and $\boldsymbol{B}$ of the same order.
(e) For two real vectors $\boldsymbol{a}$ and $\boldsymbol{b}$, show that the inner product $\langle \boldsymbol{a}, \boldsymbol{b} \rangle = \boldsymbol{a}'\boldsymbol{b}$.

Solution
(a) Transposing gives

$$\boldsymbol{A}' = \begin{pmatrix} 1 & 2 \\ 2 & 1 \end{pmatrix} \quad \text{and} \quad \boldsymbol{B}' = \begin{pmatrix} 1 & 2 \\ 2 & 1 \\ 3 & 5 \end{pmatrix}.$$

Notice that $\boldsymbol{A} = \boldsymbol{A}'$, but that $\boldsymbol{B} \neq \boldsymbol{B}'$. Indeed, $\boldsymbol{B}$ and $\boldsymbol{B}'$ have different orders.

(b) We see that $(\boldsymbol{A}')' = \boldsymbol{A}$ and $(\boldsymbol{B}')' = \boldsymbol{B}$. In general, if $\boldsymbol{X} := (x_{ij})$ is an $m \times n$ matrix, then $\boldsymbol{X}' = (x_{ji})$ is an $n \times m$ matrix, and $(\boldsymbol{X}')' = (x_{ij})$ is an $m \times n$ matrix. Hence, $(\boldsymbol{X}')' = \boldsymbol{X}$.
(c) The transpose of the 1×3 matrix (row vector) $\boldsymbol{b}'$ is the 3×1 matrix (vector)

$$\boldsymbol{b} = \begin{pmatrix} 1 \\ 2 \\ 3 \end{pmatrix}.$$

(d) $(\boldsymbol{A} + \boldsymbol{B})' = (a_{ji} + b_{ji}) = (a_{ji}) + (b_{ji}) = \boldsymbol{A}' + \boldsymbol{B}'$.
(e) By definition, $\langle \boldsymbol{a}, \boldsymbol{b} \rangle = \sum_i a_i b_i$. Hence, $\langle \boldsymbol{a}, \boldsymbol{b} \rangle = \boldsymbol{a}'\boldsymbol{b}$.

Exercise 2.5 (Multiplication, 1) Let

$$\boldsymbol{A} = \begin{pmatrix} 1 & 2 & 3 \\ 4 & 5 & 6 \end{pmatrix} \quad \text{and} \quad \boldsymbol{B} = \begin{pmatrix} 4 & 5 & 6 \\ 1 & 2 & 3 \end{pmatrix}.$$

(a) Compute $\boldsymbol{A}\boldsymbol{B}'$, $\boldsymbol{B}\boldsymbol{A}'$, $\boldsymbol{A}'\boldsymbol{B}$, and $\boldsymbol{B}'\boldsymbol{A}$.
(b) Show that $\boldsymbol{I}_2\boldsymbol{A} = \boldsymbol{A}$ and $\boldsymbol{I}_2\boldsymbol{B} = \boldsymbol{B}$.

Solution
(a) We have

$$\boldsymbol{A}\boldsymbol{B}' = \begin{pmatrix} 1 & 2 & 3 \\ 4 & 5 & 6 \end{pmatrix} \begin{pmatrix} 4 & 1 \\ 5 & 2 \\ 6 & 3 \end{pmatrix} = \begin{pmatrix} 32 & 14 \\ 77 & 32 \end{pmatrix},$$

$$\boldsymbol{B}\boldsymbol{A}' = \begin{pmatrix} 4 & 5 & 6 \\ 1 & 2 & 3 \end{pmatrix} \begin{pmatrix} 1 & 4 \\ 2 & 5 \\ 3 & 6 \end{pmatrix} = \begin{pmatrix} 32 & 77 \\ 14 & 32 \end{pmatrix},$$

$$\boldsymbol{A}'\boldsymbol{B} = \begin{pmatrix} 1 & 4 \\ 2 & 5 \\ 3 & 6 \end{pmatrix} \begin{pmatrix} 4 & 5 & 6 \\ 1 & 2 & 3 \end{pmatrix} = \begin{pmatrix} 8 & 13 & 18 \\ 13 & 20 & 27 \\ 18 & 27 & 36 \end{pmatrix},$$

and

$$\boldsymbol{B}'\boldsymbol{A} = \begin{pmatrix} 4 & 1 \\ 5 & 2 \\ 6 & 3 \end{pmatrix} \begin{pmatrix} 1 & 2 & 3 \\ 4 & 5 & 6 \end{pmatrix} = \begin{pmatrix} 8 & 13 & 18 \\ 13 & 20 & 27 \\ 18 & 27 & 36 \end{pmatrix}.$$

Notice that $\boldsymbol{A}'\boldsymbol{B}$ is symmetric, but that $\boldsymbol{A}\boldsymbol{B}'$ is not symmetric. Of course, the matrix $\boldsymbol{A}'\boldsymbol{B}$ is only symmetric in this special case. However, the fact that the sum of the diagonal elements in each of the four products is the same (namely 64) is not a coincidence; see Exercise 2.26(a).
(b) This is shown by direct calculation. The identity matrix plays the role of the number 1.

Exercise 2.6 (Multiplication, 2) Let

$$A = \begin{pmatrix} 4 & 0 & 1 \\ 0 & 1 & 0 \\ 4 & 0 & 1 \end{pmatrix}, \quad B = \begin{pmatrix} 1 & 0 & 0 \\ 0 & 1 & 0 \\ 0 & 0 & 1 \end{pmatrix}, \quad a = \begin{pmatrix} 3 \\ -1 \\ 5 \end{pmatrix}, \quad b = \begin{pmatrix} 1 \\ 2 \\ 3 \end{pmatrix}.$$

(a) Compute $Aa, Bb, b5$.
(b) Find $a'a, a'b$, and ab'.

Solution
(a)

$$Aa = \begin{pmatrix} 17 \\ -1 \\ 17 \end{pmatrix}, \quad Bb = b, \quad b5 = \begin{pmatrix} 5 \\ 10 \\ 15 \end{pmatrix}.$$

(b)

$$a'a = (3, -1, 5) \begin{pmatrix} 3 \\ -1 \\ 5 \end{pmatrix} = 35, \quad a'b = (3, -1, 5) \begin{pmatrix} 1 \\ 2 \\ 3 \end{pmatrix} = 16,$$

and

$$ab' = \begin{pmatrix} 3 \\ -1 \\ 5 \end{pmatrix} (1, 2, 3) = \begin{pmatrix} 3 & 6 & 9 \\ -1 & -2 & -3 \\ 5 & 10 & 15 \end{pmatrix}.$$

Exercise 2.7 (True or false) Which of the following statements are true, and why?
(a) $(A + B)^2 = (B + A)^2$;
(b) $(A + B)^2 = A^2 + 2AB + B^2$;
(c) $(A + B)^2 = A(A + B) + B(A + B)$;
(d) $(A + B)^2 = (A + B)(B + A)$;
(e) $(A + B)^2 = A^2 + AB + BA + B^2$.

Solution
(a) True, because $A + B = B + A$.
(b) False, because $AB \neq BA$ in general.
(c) True, because $A(A + B) + B(A + B) = (A + B)(A + B)$.
(d) True, because $B + A = A + B$.
(e) True, by direct multiplication.

Exercise 2.8 (Matrix multiplication versus scalar multiplication) Give examples of real 2×2 matrices such that:
(a) $A^2 = -I$;
(b) $B^2 = O \quad (B \neq O)$;

(c) $\boldsymbol{CD} = -\boldsymbol{DC}$ $(\boldsymbol{CD} \neq \mathbf{O})$;
(d) $\boldsymbol{EF} = \mathbf{O}$ (no elements of $\boldsymbol{E}$ or $\boldsymbol{F}$ are zero).

Solution
These four statements show that matrix multiplication is essentially different from scalar multiplication.
(a) For example, there is no real scalar a such that $a^2 = -1$. However, the real matrix

$$\boldsymbol{A} = \begin{pmatrix} 0 & 1 \\ -1 & 0 \end{pmatrix}$$

satisfies $\boldsymbol{A}^2 = -\boldsymbol{I}$. This is an orthogonal matrix which, by premultiplying any point $(x, y)'$, rotates the point clockwise along a circle, centered at the origin, by an angle of 90°, to give $(y, -x)'$.
(b) The matrix

$$\boldsymbol{B} = \begin{pmatrix} 0 & 1 \\ 0 & 0 \end{pmatrix}$$

satisfies $\boldsymbol{B}^2 = \mathbf{O}$. Any matrix $\boldsymbol{B}$ satisfying $\boldsymbol{B}^{k-1} \neq \mathbf{O}$ and $\boldsymbol{B}^k = \mathbf{O}$ is said to be *nilpotent* of index k. Hence, the displayed matrix is nilpotent of index 2.
(c) The matrices

$$\boldsymbol{C} = \begin{pmatrix} 1 & 1 \\ 1 & -1 \end{pmatrix} \quad \text{and} \quad \boldsymbol{D} = \begin{pmatrix} 1 & -1 \\ -1 & -1 \end{pmatrix}$$

satisfy the requirement. Both are symmetric and $\boldsymbol{CD}$ is skew-symmetric.
(d) The matrices

$$\boldsymbol{E} = \begin{pmatrix} 1 & 1 \\ 1 & 1 \end{pmatrix} \quad \text{and} \quad \boldsymbol{F} = \begin{pmatrix} 1 & 1 \\ -1 & -1 \end{pmatrix}$$

satisfy $\boldsymbol{EF} = \mathbf{O}$.

Exercise 2.9 (Noncommutativity)
(a) Show that $\boldsymbol{BA}$ need not be defined, even if $\boldsymbol{AB}$ is.
(b) Show that, even if $\boldsymbol{AB}$ and $\boldsymbol{BA}$ are both defined, they are in general not equal.
(c) Find an example of two matrices $\boldsymbol{A}$ and $\boldsymbol{B}$ such that $\boldsymbol{AB} = \boldsymbol{BA}$. (Two matrices with this property are said to commute.)

Solution
(a) Let $\boldsymbol{A}$ be an $m \times n$ matrix and let $\boldsymbol{B}$ be a $p \times q$ matrix. Assuming that neither $\boldsymbol{A}$ nor $\boldsymbol{B}$ is a scalar (that is, it is not the case that $m = n = 1$ or $p = q = 1$), the product $\boldsymbol{AB}$ is defined only if $n = p$, whereas the product $\boldsymbol{BA}$ is defined only if $m = q$. For example, if $\boldsymbol{A}$ has order 2×3 and $\boldsymbol{B}$ has order 3×4, then $\boldsymbol{AB}$ is defined but $\boldsymbol{BA}$ is not.
(b) If $\boldsymbol{AB}$ and $\boldsymbol{BA}$ are both defined, that is, if $n = p$ and $m = q$, they may not be of the same order. For example, if $\boldsymbol{A}$ has order 2×3 and $\boldsymbol{B}$ has order 3×2 then $\boldsymbol{AB}$ has

order 2×2 and BA has order 3×3. If AB and BA are both defined and are of the same order, then both must be square. Even in that case $AB \neq BA$ is general. For example, the matrices

$$A = \begin{pmatrix} 0 & 1 \\ 1 & 0 \end{pmatrix} \quad \text{and} \quad B = \begin{pmatrix} 0 & 1 \\ -1 & 0 \end{pmatrix}$$

do not commute. The matrix A swaps the rows of B when it premultiplies it, while swapping the columns of B when it postmultiplies it.
(c) However, the matrices

$$A = \begin{pmatrix} 1 & 0 \\ 0 & 1 \end{pmatrix} \quad \text{and} \quad B = \begin{pmatrix} 1 & 0 \\ 0 & -1 \end{pmatrix}$$

do commute.

Exercise 2.10 (Noncommutativity and reshuffle) Consider two shuffling operations on an ordered sequence (a_1, a_2, a_3): $\mathcal{S}$ reverses the order and $\mathcal{T}$ wraps around the last element to the first position. Show that $\mathcal{S}\mathcal{T} \neq \mathcal{T}\mathcal{S}$, once with and once without matrices.

Solution
The operation $\mathcal{S}$ produces (a_3, a_2, a_1) and hence $\mathcal{T}\mathcal{S}$ produces (a_1, a_3, a_2). The operation $\mathcal{T}$ produces (a_3, a_1, a_2) and hence $\mathcal{S}\mathcal{T}$ produces (a_2, a_1, a_3). Using matrix algebra, we define the matrices

$$S = \begin{pmatrix} 0 & 0 & 1 \\ 0 & 1 & 0 \\ 1 & 0 & 0 \end{pmatrix} \quad \text{and} \quad T = \begin{pmatrix} 0 & 0 & 1 \\ 1 & 0 & 0 \\ 0 & 1 & 0 \end{pmatrix}.$$

Then S and T correspond to the operations $\mathcal{S}$ and $\mathcal{T}$, as can be verified by postmultiplying these matrices by the vector $(a_1, a_2, a_3)'$. Multiplying the two matrices shows that $ST \neq TS$.

Exercise 2.11 (Row scaling and column scaling) Consider the matrices

$$A := \begin{pmatrix} a_1 & 0 \\ 0 & a_2 \end{pmatrix} \quad \text{and} \quad B := \begin{pmatrix} b_{11} & b_{12} \\ b_{21} & b_{22} \end{pmatrix}.$$

(a) Calculate and interpret AB and BA.
(b) What does $AB = BA$ imply?

Solution
(a) We find

$$AB = \begin{pmatrix} a_1 b_{11} & a_1 b_{12} \\ a_2 b_{21} & a_2 b_{22} \end{pmatrix} \quad \text{and} \quad BA = \begin{pmatrix} a_1 b_{11} & a_2 b_{12} \\ a_1 b_{21} & a_2 b_{22} \end{pmatrix}.$$

Hence, AB scales the rows of B, while BA scales the columns of B.
(b) If $AB = BA$, then $b_{12}(a_1 - a_2) = 0$ and $b_{21}(a_1 - a_2) = 0$. Hence, $a_1 = a_2$ or $b_{12} = b_{21} = 0$, that is, either A is a scalar matrix or B is diagonal (or both).

Exercise 2.12 (Order of matrix) What are the orders of the matrices that guarantee that $\boldsymbol{ABC}$ is defined?

Solution

Let $\boldsymbol{A}$ $(m \times n)$, $\boldsymbol{B}$ $(p \times q)$, and $\boldsymbol{C}$ $(r \times s)$. Then $\boldsymbol{ABC}$ is defined when $n = p$ and $q = r$, but also when $m = n = 1$ and $q = r$, when $p = q = 1$ and $n = r$, or when $r = s = 1$ and $n = p$. It is also defined when any two of $\boldsymbol{A}$, $\boldsymbol{B}$, $\boldsymbol{C}$ are scalars.

***Exercise 2.13 (Generalization of $x^2 = 0 \iff x = 0$)** For real matrices $\boldsymbol{A}$, $\boldsymbol{B}$ and $\boldsymbol{C}$, show that:
(a) $\boldsymbol{A}'\boldsymbol{A} = \mathbf{O}$ if and only if $\boldsymbol{A} = \mathbf{O}$;
(b) $\boldsymbol{AB} = \mathbf{O}$ if and only if $\boldsymbol{A}'\boldsymbol{AB} = \mathbf{O}$;
(c) $\boldsymbol{AB} = \boldsymbol{AC}$ if and only if $\boldsymbol{A}'\boldsymbol{AB} = \boldsymbol{A}'\boldsymbol{AC}$.
(d) Why do we require the matrices to be real?

Solution

(a) Clearly, $\boldsymbol{A} = \mathbf{O}$ implies $\boldsymbol{A}'\boldsymbol{A} = \mathbf{O}$. Conversely, assume $\boldsymbol{A}'\boldsymbol{A} = \mathbf{O}$. Then, for all j, the j-th diagonal element of $\boldsymbol{A}'\boldsymbol{A}$ is zero, that is, $\sum_i a_{ij}^2 = 0$. This implies that $a_{ij} = 0$ for all i and j, and hence that $\boldsymbol{A} = \mathbf{O}$. Contrast this result with Exercise 2.8(b).
(b) Clearly, $\boldsymbol{AB} = \mathbf{O}$ implies $\boldsymbol{A}'\boldsymbol{AB} = \mathbf{O}$. Conversely, if $\boldsymbol{A}'\boldsymbol{AB} = \mathbf{O}$, then

$$(\boldsymbol{AB})'(\boldsymbol{AB}) = \boldsymbol{B}'\boldsymbol{A}'\boldsymbol{AB} = \mathbf{O}$$

and hence $\boldsymbol{AB} = \mathbf{O}$, by (a).
(c) This follows by replacing $\boldsymbol{B}$ by $\boldsymbol{B} - \boldsymbol{C}$ in (b).
(d) Consider $\boldsymbol{a} = (1 + \mathrm{i}, 1 - \mathrm{i})'$. Then $\boldsymbol{a}'\boldsymbol{a} = (1 + \mathrm{i})^2 + (1 - \mathrm{i})^2 = 0$, even though $\boldsymbol{a} \neq \mathbf{0}$. Hence, the above statements are, in general, not true for complex matrices. However, they are true if we replace $'$ by *.

Exercise 2.14 (Multiplication, 3)
(a) Show that $(\boldsymbol{AB})\boldsymbol{C} = \boldsymbol{A}(\boldsymbol{BC})$ for conformable $\boldsymbol{A}, \boldsymbol{B}, \boldsymbol{C}$.
(b) Show that $\boldsymbol{A}(\boldsymbol{B} + \boldsymbol{C}) = \boldsymbol{AB} + \boldsymbol{AC}$ for conformable $\boldsymbol{A}$, $\boldsymbol{B}$, $\boldsymbol{C}$.

Solution

(a) Let $\boldsymbol{D} := \boldsymbol{AB}$ and $\boldsymbol{E} := \boldsymbol{BC}$. Then,

$$\begin{aligned}(\boldsymbol{DC})_{ik} &= \sum_j d_{ij}c_{jk} = \sum_j \left(\sum_h a_{ih}b_{hj}\right) c_{jk} \\ &= \sum_h a_{ih} \left(\sum_j b_{hj}c_{jk}\right) = \sum_h a_{ih}e_{hk} = (\boldsymbol{AE})_{ik}.\end{aligned}$$

Hence, $\boldsymbol{DC} = \boldsymbol{AE}$.
(b) Let $\boldsymbol{D} := \boldsymbol{B} + \boldsymbol{C}$. Then,

$$\begin{aligned}(\boldsymbol{AD})_{ij} &= \sum_h a_{ih} d_{hj} = \sum_h a_{ih} (b_{hj} + c_{hj}) \\ &= \sum_h a_{ih} b_{hj} + \sum_h a_{ih} c_{hj} = (\boldsymbol{AB})_{ij} + (\boldsymbol{AC})_{ij}.\end{aligned}$$

Exercise 2.15 (Transpose and products)
(a) Show that $(\boldsymbol{AB})' = \boldsymbol{B}'\boldsymbol{A}'$.
(b) Show that $(\boldsymbol{ABC})' = \boldsymbol{C}'\boldsymbol{B}'\boldsymbol{A}'$.
(c) Under what condition is $(\boldsymbol{AB})' = \boldsymbol{A}'\boldsymbol{B}'$?

Solution
(a) We have

$$\begin{aligned}(\boldsymbol{B}'\boldsymbol{A}')_{ij} &= \sum_h (\boldsymbol{B}')_{ih} (\boldsymbol{A}')_{hj} = \sum_h (\boldsymbol{B})_{hi} (\boldsymbol{A})_{jh} \\ &= \sum_h (\boldsymbol{A})_{jh} (\boldsymbol{B})_{hi} = (\boldsymbol{AB})_{ji}.\end{aligned}$$

(b) Let $\boldsymbol{D} := \boldsymbol{BC}$. Then, using (a),

$$(\boldsymbol{ABC})' = (\boldsymbol{AD})' = \boldsymbol{D}'\boldsymbol{A}' = (\boldsymbol{BC})'\boldsymbol{A}' = \boldsymbol{C}'\boldsymbol{B}'\boldsymbol{A}'.$$

(c) This occurs if and only if $\boldsymbol{AB} = \boldsymbol{BA}$, that is, if and only if $\boldsymbol{A}$ and $\boldsymbol{B}$ commute.

Exercise 2.16 (Partitioned matrix) Let $\boldsymbol{A}$ and $\boldsymbol{B}$ be 3×5 matrices, partitioned as

$$\boldsymbol{A} = \left(\begin{array}{ccc|cc} 1 & 3 & -2 & 1 & 2 \\ 6 & 8 & 0 & -1 & 6 \\ \hline 0 & 0 & 1 & 4 & 1 \end{array}\right), \quad \boldsymbol{B} = \left(\begin{array}{ccc|cc} 1 & -3 & -2 & 4 & 1 \\ 6 & 2 & 6 & 2 & 0 \\ \hline 1 & 0 & 2 & 0 & 1 \end{array}\right),$$

and let $\boldsymbol{C}$ be a 5×4 matrix, partitioned as

$$\boldsymbol{C} = \left(\begin{array}{cc|cc} 1 & 0 & 5 & 1 \\ 0 & 2 & 0 & 0 \\ -1 & 0 & 3 & 1 \\ \hline 3 & 5 & 0 & 2 \\ 2 & -1 & 3 & 1 \end{array}\right).$$

Denoting the submatrices by

$$\boldsymbol{A} = \begin{pmatrix} \boldsymbol{A}_{11} & \boldsymbol{A}_{12} \\ \boldsymbol{A}_{21} & \boldsymbol{A}_{22} \end{pmatrix}, \quad \boldsymbol{B} = \begin{pmatrix} \boldsymbol{B}_{11} & \boldsymbol{B}_{12} \\ \boldsymbol{B}_{21} & \boldsymbol{B}_{22} \end{pmatrix}, \quad \boldsymbol{C} = \begin{pmatrix} \boldsymbol{C}_{11} & \boldsymbol{C}_{12} \\ \boldsymbol{C}_{21} & \boldsymbol{C}_{22} \end{pmatrix},$$

show that

$$\boldsymbol{A}+\boldsymbol{B}=\begin{pmatrix}\boldsymbol{A}_{11}+\boldsymbol{B}_{11} & \boldsymbol{A}_{12}+\boldsymbol{B}_{12}\\ \boldsymbol{A}_{21}+\boldsymbol{B}_{21} & \boldsymbol{A}_{22}+\boldsymbol{B}_{22}\end{pmatrix},$$

$$\boldsymbol{AC}=\begin{pmatrix}\boldsymbol{A}_{11}\boldsymbol{C}_{11}+\boldsymbol{A}_{12}\boldsymbol{C}_{21} & \boldsymbol{A}_{11}\boldsymbol{C}_{12}+\boldsymbol{A}_{12}\boldsymbol{C}_{22}\\ \boldsymbol{A}_{21}\boldsymbol{C}_{11}+\boldsymbol{A}_{22}\boldsymbol{C}_{21} & \boldsymbol{A}_{21}\boldsymbol{C}_{12}+\boldsymbol{A}_{22}\boldsymbol{C}_{22}\end{pmatrix},$$

and

$$\boldsymbol{A}'=\begin{pmatrix}\boldsymbol{A}'_{11} & \boldsymbol{A}'_{21}\\ \boldsymbol{A}'_{12} & \boldsymbol{A}'_{22}\end{pmatrix}.$$

Solution

$$\boldsymbol{A}+\boldsymbol{B}=\left(\begin{array}{ccc|cc}(1+1) & (3-3) & (-2-2) & (1+4) & (2+1)\\ (6+6) & (8+2) & (0+6) & (-1+2) & (6+0)\\ \hline (0+1) & (0+0) & (1+2) & (4+0) & (1+1)\end{array}\right)$$

$$=\left(\begin{array}{ccc|cc}2 & 0 & -4 & 5 & 3\\ 12 & 10 & 6 & 1 & 6\\ \hline 1 & 0 & 3 & 4 & 2\end{array}\right)=\begin{pmatrix}\boldsymbol{A}_{11}+\boldsymbol{B}_{11} & \boldsymbol{A}_{12}+\boldsymbol{B}_{12}\\ \boldsymbol{A}_{21}+\boldsymbol{B}_{21} & \boldsymbol{A}_{22}+\boldsymbol{B}_{22}\end{pmatrix},$$

$$\boldsymbol{AC}=\left(\begin{array}{ccc|cc}1 & 3 & -2 & 1 & 2\\ 6 & 8 & 0 & -1 & 6\\ \hline 0 & 0 & 1 & 4 & 1\end{array}\right)\left(\begin{array}{cc|cc}1 & 0 & 5 & 1\\ 0 & 2 & 0 & 0\\ -1 & 0 & 3 & 1\\ \hline 3 & 5 & 0 & 2\\ 2 & -1 & 3 & 1\end{array}\right)$$

$$=\left(\begin{array}{cc|cc}10 & 9 & 5 & 3\\ 15 & 5 & 48 & 10\\ \hline 13 & 19 & 6 & 10\end{array}\right)=\begin{pmatrix}\boldsymbol{A}_{11}\boldsymbol{C}_{11}+\boldsymbol{A}_{12}\boldsymbol{C}_{21} & \boldsymbol{A}_{11}\boldsymbol{C}_{12}+\boldsymbol{A}_{12}\boldsymbol{C}_{22}\\ \boldsymbol{A}_{21}\boldsymbol{C}_{11}+\boldsymbol{A}_{22}\boldsymbol{C}_{21} & \boldsymbol{A}_{21}\boldsymbol{C}_{12}+\boldsymbol{A}_{22}\boldsymbol{C}_{22}\end{pmatrix},$$

and

$$\boldsymbol{A}'=\left(\begin{array}{cc|c}1 & 6 & 0\\ 3 & 8 & 0\\ -2 & 0 & 1\\ \hline 1 & -1 & 4\\ 2 & 6 & 1\end{array}\right)=\begin{pmatrix}\boldsymbol{A}'_{11} & \boldsymbol{A}'_{21}\\ \boldsymbol{A}'_{12} & \boldsymbol{A}'_{22}\end{pmatrix}.$$

Exercise 2.17 (Sum of outer products) Let $\boldsymbol{A} := (\boldsymbol{a}_1, \boldsymbol{a}_2, \dots, \boldsymbol{a}_n)$ be an $m \times n$ matrix.
(a) Show that $\boldsymbol{AA}' = \sum_i \boldsymbol{a}_i\boldsymbol{a}_i'$.
(b) Show that $\boldsymbol{A}'\boldsymbol{A} = (\boldsymbol{a}_i'\boldsymbol{a}_j)$.

Solution
We write

$$AA' = (a_1, a_2, \dots, a_n)\begin{pmatrix} a_1' \\ a_2' \\ \vdots \\ a_n' \end{pmatrix}, \qquad A'A = \begin{pmatrix} a_1' \\ a_2' \\ \vdots \\ a_n' \end{pmatrix}(a_1, a_2, \dots, a_n),$$

and the results follow.

***Exercise 2.18 (Identity matrix)**
(a) Show that $Ix = x$ for all x, and that this relation uniquely determines I.
(b) Show that $IA = AI = A$ for any matrix A, and specify the orders of the identity matrices.

Solution
(a) If $A = I$, then $Ax = x$ holds for all x. Conversely, if $Ax = x$ holds for all x, then it holds in particular for the unit vectors $x = e_j$. This gives $Ae_j = e_j$, so that $a_{ij} = e_i'Ae_j = e_i'e_j$, which is zero when $i \neq j$ and one when $i = j$. Hence, $A = I$.
(b) Let A be an $m \times n$ matrix, and let $a_1, a_2, \dots, a_n$ denote its columns. Then,

$$I_m A = (I_m a_1, I_m a_2, \dots, I_m a_n) = (a_1, a_2, \dots, a_n) = A,$$

using (a). Since $I_m A = A$ for every A, it follows that $I_n A' = A'$ for every A, and hence that $AI_n = A$.

Exercise 2.19 (Diagonal matrix, permutation)
(a) Is the 3×3 matrix

$$A := \begin{pmatrix} 0 & 0 & a \\ 0 & b & 0 \\ c & 0 & 0 \end{pmatrix}$$

a diagonal matrix?
(b) With A defined in (a), show that AA' and $A'A$ are diagonal matrices.

Solution
(a) Although one might argue that a square matrix has two diagonals, only the diagonal $(a_{11}, a_{22}, \dots, a_{nn})$ is called *the* diagonal. So, the matrix A is *not* a diagonal matrix, unless $a = c = 0$.
(b) We have

$$AA' = \begin{pmatrix} 0 & 0 & a \\ 0 & b & 0 \\ c & 0 & 0 \end{pmatrix}\begin{pmatrix} 0 & 0 & c \\ 0 & b & 0 \\ a & 0 & 0 \end{pmatrix} = \begin{pmatrix} a^2 & 0 & 0 \\ 0 & b^2 & 0 \\ 0 & 0 & c^2 \end{pmatrix},$$

and, similarly,

$$A'A = \begin{pmatrix} c^2 & 0 & 0 \\ 0 & b^2 & 0 \\ 0 & 0 & a^2 \end{pmatrix}.$$

Exercise 2.20 (Diagonal matrices, commutation) Let A and B be diagonal matrices. Show that AB is also diagonal and that $AB = BA$.

Solution
Let $A := \operatorname{diag}(a_1, a_2, \dots, a_n)$ and $B := \operatorname{diag}(b_1, b_2, \dots, b_n)$. Then,

$$AB = \operatorname{diag}(a_1 b_1, \dots, a_n b_n) = \operatorname{diag}(b_1 a_1, \dots, b_n a_n) = BA.$$

A diagonal matrix is the simplest generalization of a scalar, and essentially all properties of scalars also hold for diagonal matrices.

Exercise 2.21 (Triangular matrix)
(a) Consider the lower triangular matrices

$$A = \begin{pmatrix} 1 & 0 & 0 \\ 1 & 1 & 0 \\ 0 & 0 & 1 \end{pmatrix} \quad \text{and} \quad B = \begin{pmatrix} 1 & 0 & 0 \\ 0 & 1 & 0 \\ 0 & -2 & 1 \end{pmatrix}.$$

Show that AB and BA are lower triangular, but that $AB \neq BA$.
(b) Show that the product of two lower triangular matrices is always lower triangular.

Solution
(a) We have

$$AB = \begin{pmatrix} 1 & 0 & 0 \\ 1 & 1 & 0 \\ 0 & -2 & 1 \end{pmatrix} \quad \text{and} \quad BA = \begin{pmatrix} 1 & 0 & 0 \\ 1 & 1 & 0 \\ -2 & -2 & 1 \end{pmatrix}.$$

(b) Let $A = (a_{ij})$ and $B = (b_{ij})$ be lower triangular $n \times n$ matrices. Consider the ij-th element of AB. We will show that $(AB)_{ij} = 0$ for $i < j$. Now,

$$(AB)_{ij} = \sum_{k=1}^{n} a_{ik} b_{kj} = \sum_{k=1}^{i} a_{ik} b_{kj} + \sum_{k=i+1}^{n} a_{ik} b_{kj}.$$

In the first sum, $b_{kj} = 0$ for all $k \leq i < j$; in the second sum, $a_{ik} = 0$ for all $k > i$. Hence, $(AB)_{ij} = 0$ for $i < j$, that is, AB is lower triangular.

Exercise 2.22 (Symmetry) Let A be a square real matrix.
(a) Show that $A + A'$ is symmetric, even if A is not symmetric.
(b) Show that AB is not necessarily symmetric if A and B are.
(c) Show that $A'BA$ is symmetric if B is symmetric, but that the converse need not be true.

Solution
(a) Since $(A + B)' = A' + B'$, we have $(A + A')' = A' + (A')' = A' + A = A + A'$. Hence, $A + A'$ is symmetric.
(b) For example,

$$A = \begin{pmatrix} 1 & 1 \\ 1 & 0 \end{pmatrix} \quad \text{and} \quad B = \begin{pmatrix} 0 & 1 \\ 1 & 1 \end{pmatrix}.$$

(c) We have $(A'BA)' = A'B'(A')' = A'BA$. To prove that the converse is not necessarily true, let e_i and e_j be unit vectors and define $A := e_i e_j'$. Then, for any matrix B, $A'BA = e_j e_i' B e_i e_j' = b_{ii} e_j e_j'$, which is symmetric.

Exercise 2.23 (Skew-symmetry) Let A be a square real matrix.
(a) Show that $A - A'$ is skew-symmetric.
(b) Hence, show that A can be decomposed as the sum of a symmetric and a skew-symmetric matrix.
(c) If A is skew-symmetric, show that its diagonal elements are all zero.

Solution
(a) We have $(A - A')' = A' - A = -(A - A')$.
(b) We write

$$A = \frac{A + A'}{2} + \frac{A - A'}{2}.$$

The first matrix on the right-hand side is symmetric; the second is skew-symmetric.
(c) Since the diagonal elements of A' are the diagonal elements of A, the defining equation $A' = -A$ implies that $a_{ii} = -a_{ii}$ for all i. Hence, $a_{ii} = 0$ for all i.

Exercise 2.24 (Trace as linear operator) The trace of a square matrix A is the sum of its diagonal elements, and is written as $\operatorname{tr}(A)$ or $\operatorname{tr} A$. Let A and B be square matrices of the same order, and let λ and μ be scalars. Show that:
(a) $\operatorname{tr}(A + B) = \operatorname{tr}(A) + \operatorname{tr}(B)$;
(b) $\operatorname{tr}(\lambda A + \mu B) = \lambda \operatorname{tr}(A) + \mu \operatorname{tr}(B)$;
(c) $\operatorname{tr}(A') = \operatorname{tr}(A)$;
(d) $\operatorname{tr}(AA') = \operatorname{tr}(A'A) = \sum_{ij} a_{ij}^2$;
(e) $\operatorname{tr}(aa') = a'a = \sum_i a_i^2$ for any vector a.

Solution
(a)–(b) This follows by direct verification or by noting that the trace is a linear operator.
(c) In the trace operation only *diagonal* elements are involved; what happens outside the diagonal is irrelevant.
(d) We have

$$\operatorname{tr} AA' = \sum_i (AA')_{ii} = \sum_i \sum_j a_{ij}^2 = \sum_j \sum_i a_{ij}^2 = \sum_j (A'A)_{jj} = \operatorname{tr} A'A.$$

(e) This follows from (d) because $\operatorname{tr} a'a = a'a$, since $a'a$ is a scalar.

Exercise 2.25 (Trace of $A'A$) For any real matrix $\boldsymbol{A}$, show that $\operatorname{tr} \boldsymbol{A}'\boldsymbol{A} \geq 0$, with $\operatorname{tr} \boldsymbol{A}'\boldsymbol{A} = 0$ if and only if $\boldsymbol{A} = \mathbf{O}$.

Solution
Since $\operatorname{tr} \boldsymbol{A}'\boldsymbol{A} = \sum_{ij} a_{ij}^2$ and $\boldsymbol{A}$ is real, the result follows.

Exercise 2.26 (Trace, cyclical property)
(a) Let $\boldsymbol{A}$ and $\boldsymbol{B}$ be $m \times n$ matrices. Prove that

$$\operatorname{tr}(\boldsymbol{A}'\boldsymbol{B}) = \operatorname{tr}(\boldsymbol{B}\boldsymbol{A}') = \operatorname{tr}(\boldsymbol{A}\boldsymbol{B}') = \operatorname{tr}(\boldsymbol{B}'\boldsymbol{A}).$$

(b) Show that $\operatorname{tr}(\boldsymbol{A}\boldsymbol{a}\boldsymbol{a}') = \boldsymbol{a}'\boldsymbol{A}\boldsymbol{a}$ for any square $\boldsymbol{A}$ and conformable $\boldsymbol{a}$.
(c) Show that $\operatorname{tr}(\boldsymbol{ABC}) = \operatorname{tr}(\boldsymbol{CAB}) = \operatorname{tr}(\boldsymbol{BCA})$ and specify the restrictions on the orders of $\boldsymbol{A}$, $\boldsymbol{B}$, and $\boldsymbol{C}$.
(d) Is it also true that $\operatorname{tr}(\boldsymbol{ABC}) = \operatorname{tr}(\boldsymbol{ACB})$?

Solution
(a) In view of Exercise 2.24(c) it is sufficient to prove $\operatorname{tr}(\boldsymbol{A}'\boldsymbol{B}) = \operatorname{tr}(\boldsymbol{B}\boldsymbol{A}')$. We have

$$\operatorname{tr}(\boldsymbol{A}'\boldsymbol{B}) = \sum_j (\boldsymbol{A}'\boldsymbol{B})_{jj} = \sum_j \sum_i a_{ij} b_{ij} = \sum_i \sum_j b_{ij} a_{ij} = \sum_i (\boldsymbol{B}\boldsymbol{A}')_{ii} = \operatorname{tr}(\boldsymbol{B}\boldsymbol{A}').$$

(b) This follows from (a).
(c) Let $\boldsymbol{A}$ $(m \times n)$, $\boldsymbol{B}$ $(n \times p)$, and $\boldsymbol{C}$ $(p \times m)$, so that $\boldsymbol{ABC}$ is defined and square. Then, using (a),

$$\operatorname{tr}(\boldsymbol{ABC}) = \operatorname{tr}((\boldsymbol{AB})\boldsymbol{C}) = \operatorname{tr}(\boldsymbol{C}(\boldsymbol{AB})) = \operatorname{tr}(\boldsymbol{CAB}),$$

and similarly for the second equality.
(d) No, this is not true. The expression $\boldsymbol{ACB}$ is not even defined in general.

Exercise 2.27 (Trace and sum vector) Show that

$$\boldsymbol{\imath}'\boldsymbol{A}\boldsymbol{\imath} = \boldsymbol{\imath}'(\operatorname{dg} \boldsymbol{A})\boldsymbol{\imath} + \operatorname{tr}\left((\boldsymbol{\imath}\boldsymbol{\imath}' - \boldsymbol{I}_n)\boldsymbol{A}\right)$$

for any $n \times n$ matrix $\boldsymbol{A}$.

Solution
We write

$$\operatorname{tr}\left((\boldsymbol{\imath}\boldsymbol{\imath}' - \boldsymbol{I}_n)\boldsymbol{A}\right) = \operatorname{tr}(\boldsymbol{\imath}\boldsymbol{\imath}'\boldsymbol{A}) - \operatorname{tr}(\boldsymbol{I}_n\boldsymbol{A}) = \operatorname{tr}(\boldsymbol{\imath}'\boldsymbol{A}\boldsymbol{\imath}) - \operatorname{tr}(\boldsymbol{A}) = \boldsymbol{\imath}'\boldsymbol{A}\boldsymbol{\imath} - \boldsymbol{\imath}'(\operatorname{dg} \boldsymbol{A})\boldsymbol{\imath}.$$

Exercise 2.28 (Orthogonal matrix, representation) A real square matrix $\boldsymbol{A}$ is orthogonal if $\boldsymbol{A}'\boldsymbol{A} = \boldsymbol{A}\boldsymbol{A}' = \boldsymbol{I}$.

(a) Show that every orthogonal 2×2 matrix takes one of the two forms

$$\boldsymbol{A}_1 := \begin{pmatrix} \cos\theta & -\sin\theta \\ \sin\theta & \cos\theta \end{pmatrix} \quad \text{or} \quad \boldsymbol{A}_2 := \begin{pmatrix} \cos\theta & -\sin\theta \\ -\sin\theta & -\cos\theta \end{pmatrix},$$

and describe its effect on a 2×1 vector $\boldsymbol{x}$.
(b) Show that, if a matrix $\boldsymbol{A}$ is orthogonal, its rows form an orthonormal set.
(c) Show that, if a matrix $\boldsymbol{A}$ is orthogonal, its columns also form an orthonormal set.

Solution
(a) This is essentially a generalization of the fact that any normalized real 2×1 vector $\boldsymbol{x}$ has a representation $\boldsymbol{x} = (\cos\theta, \sin\theta)'$. Let

$$\boldsymbol{A} := \begin{pmatrix} a & b \\ c & d \end{pmatrix}.$$

The equations $\boldsymbol{A}'\boldsymbol{A} = \boldsymbol{A}\boldsymbol{A}' = \boldsymbol{I}$ yield

$$a^2 + b^2 = 1, \quad a^2 + c^2 = 1, \quad b^2 + d^2 = 1, \quad c^2 + d^2 = 1,$$

and

$$ab + cd = 0, \quad ac + bd = 0,$$

implying

$$a^2 = d^2, \quad b^2 = c^2, \quad a^2 + b^2 = 1, \quad ab + cd = 0.$$

This gives

$$a = \cos\theta, \quad b = -\sin\theta, \quad c = \pm\sin\theta, \quad d = \pm\cos\theta.$$

The matrix $\boldsymbol{A}_1$ rotates any vector $\boldsymbol{x} := (x, y)'$ by an angle θ in the positive (counterclockwise) direction. For example, when $\theta = \pi/2$,

$$\boldsymbol{A}_1\boldsymbol{x} = \begin{pmatrix} \cos\pi/2 & -\sin\pi/2 \\ \sin\pi/2 & \cos\pi/2 \end{pmatrix} \begin{pmatrix} x \\ y \end{pmatrix} = \begin{pmatrix} 0 & -1 \\ 1 & 0 \end{pmatrix} \begin{pmatrix} x \\ y \end{pmatrix} = \begin{pmatrix} -y \\ x \end{pmatrix}.$$

The matrix $\boldsymbol{A}_2$ satisfies

$$\boldsymbol{A}_2\boldsymbol{x} = \begin{pmatrix} 1 & 0 \\ 0 & -1 \end{pmatrix} \boldsymbol{A}_1\boldsymbol{x},$$

so that $\boldsymbol{x}$ is rotated counterclockwise by an angle θ, and then reflected across the x-axis.
(b) Let $\boldsymbol{a}'_{1\bullet}, \dots, \boldsymbol{a}'_{n\bullet}$ denote the rows of $\boldsymbol{A}$. From $\boldsymbol{A}\boldsymbol{A}' = \boldsymbol{I}_n$ it follows that $\boldsymbol{a}'_{i\bullet}\boldsymbol{a}_{i\bullet} = 1$ and $\boldsymbol{a}'_{i\bullet}\boldsymbol{a}_{j\bullet} = 0$ $(i \neq j)$. Hence, the rows form an orthonormal set.
(c) Let $\boldsymbol{a}_{\bullet 1}, \dots, \boldsymbol{a}_{\bullet n}$ denote the columns of $\boldsymbol{A}$. Then, from $\boldsymbol{A}'\boldsymbol{A} = \boldsymbol{I}_n$ it follows that $\boldsymbol{a}'_{\bullet i}\boldsymbol{a}_{\bullet i} = 1$ and $\boldsymbol{a}'_{\bullet i}\boldsymbol{a}_{\bullet j} = 0$ $(i \neq j)$. Hence, the columns also form an orthonormal set.

Exercise 2.29 (Permutation matrix) A square matrix $\boldsymbol{A}$ is called a permutation matrix if each row and each column of $\boldsymbol{A}$ contains a single element 1, and the remaining elements are zero.

(a) Show that there exist 2 permutation matrices of order 2.
(b) Show that there exist 6 permutation matrices of order 3, and determine which of these transforms the matrix $\boldsymbol{A}$ of Exercise 2.19(a) into $\operatorname{diag}(a, b, c)$.
(c) Show that there exist $n!$ permutation matrices of order n.
(d) Show that every permutation matrix is orthogonal.

Solution
(a) The permutation matrices of order 2 are

$$\begin{pmatrix} 1 & 0 \\ 0 & 1 \end{pmatrix} \quad \text{and} \quad \begin{pmatrix} 0 & 1 \\ 1 & 0 \end{pmatrix}.$$

The latter matrix permutes (or swaps) the axes by premultiplication, since

$$\begin{pmatrix} 0 & 1 \\ 1 & 0 \end{pmatrix} \begin{pmatrix} x_1 \\ x_2 \end{pmatrix} = \begin{pmatrix} x_2 \\ x_1 \end{pmatrix}.$$

(b) The permutation matrices of order 3 are

$$\begin{pmatrix} 1 & 0 & 0 \\ 0 & 1 & 0 \\ 0 & 0 & 1 \end{pmatrix}, \quad \begin{pmatrix} 1 & 0 & 0 \\ 0 & 0 & 1 \\ 0 & 1 & 0 \end{pmatrix}, \quad \begin{pmatrix} 0 & 1 & 0 \\ 1 & 0 & 0 \\ 0 & 0 & 1 \end{pmatrix}, \quad \begin{pmatrix} 0 & 1 & 0 \\ 0 & 0 & 1 \\ 1 & 0 & 0 \end{pmatrix}, \quad \begin{pmatrix} 0 & 0 & 1 \\ 1 & 0 & 0 \\ 0 & 1 & 0 \end{pmatrix}, \quad \begin{pmatrix} 0 & 0 & 1 \\ 0 & 1 & 0 \\ 1 & 0 & 0 \end{pmatrix}.$$

To write the matrix $\boldsymbol{A}$ of Exercise 2.19 as $\operatorname{diag}(a, b, c)$, we need to swap the first and third columns. This is achieved by postmultiplying $\boldsymbol{A}$ by the last of the six displayed matrices; premultiplying would have swapped the rows instead.
(c) We proceed by induction. Suppose there are $(n-1)!$ permutation matrices of order $n-1$. For each $(n-1) \times (n-1)$ permutation matrix there are precisely n ways to form an $n \times n$ permutation matrix. Hence, there exist $n!$ permutation matrices of order n.
(d) Each row $\boldsymbol{p}'_{i\cdot}$ of the permutation matrix $\boldsymbol{P}$ contains one 1 and $(n-1)$ zeros. Hence, $\boldsymbol{p}'_{i\cdot}\boldsymbol{p}_{i\cdot} = 1$. Another row, say $\boldsymbol{p}'_{j\cdot}$, also contains only one 1, but in a different place. Hence, $\boldsymbol{p}'_{i\cdot}\boldsymbol{p}_{j\cdot} = 0$ $(i \neq j)$. Thus $\boldsymbol{P}$ is orthogonal.

Exercise 2.30 (Normal matrix) A real square matrix $\boldsymbol{A}$ is normal if $\boldsymbol{A}'\boldsymbol{A} = \boldsymbol{A}\boldsymbol{A}'$.
(a) Show that every symmetric matrix is normal.
(b) Show that every orthogonal matrix is normal.
(c) Let $\boldsymbol{A}$ be a normal 2×2 matrix. Show that $\boldsymbol{A}$ is either symmetric or has the form

$$\boldsymbol{A} = \lambda \begin{pmatrix} \alpha & 1 \\ -1 & \alpha \end{pmatrix} \quad (\lambda \neq 0).$$

Solution
(a) If $\boldsymbol{A} = \boldsymbol{A}'$ then $\boldsymbol{A}'\boldsymbol{A} = \boldsymbol{A}\boldsymbol{A} = \boldsymbol{A}\boldsymbol{A}'$.
(b) If $\boldsymbol{A}'\boldsymbol{A} = \boldsymbol{A}\boldsymbol{A}' = \boldsymbol{I}$, then clearly $\boldsymbol{A}'\boldsymbol{A} = \boldsymbol{A}\boldsymbol{A}'$.
(c) Let

$$\boldsymbol{A} := \begin{pmatrix} a & b \\ c & d \end{pmatrix}.$$

The definition $\boldsymbol{A}'\boldsymbol{A} = \boldsymbol{A}\boldsymbol{A}'$ implies that

$$\begin{pmatrix} a^2+c^2 & ab+cd \\ ab+cd & b^2+d^2 \end{pmatrix} = \begin{pmatrix} a^2+b^2 & ac+bd \\ ac+bd & c^2+d^2 \end{pmatrix}$$

and hence that $b^2 = c^2$ and $(a-d)(b-c) = 0$. This gives either $b = c$ (symmetry) or $b = -c \neq 0$ and $a = d$.

Exercise 2.31 (Commuting matrices) Consider the matrix

$$\boldsymbol{A} = \begin{pmatrix} 1 & 2 \\ 3 & 4 \end{pmatrix}.$$

Show that the class of matrices $\boldsymbol{B}$ satisfying $\boldsymbol{AB} = \boldsymbol{BA}$ is given by

$$\boldsymbol{B} = \alpha \begin{pmatrix} 1 & 0 \\ 0 & 1 \end{pmatrix} + \beta \begin{pmatrix} 0 & 2 \\ 3 & 3 \end{pmatrix}.$$

Solution
Let

$$\boldsymbol{B} := \begin{pmatrix} a & b \\ c & d \end{pmatrix}.$$

Then the equation $\boldsymbol{AB} = \boldsymbol{BA}$ gives

$$\begin{pmatrix} a+2c & b+2d \\ 3a+4c & 3b+4d \end{pmatrix} = \begin{pmatrix} a+3b & 2a+4b \\ c+3d & 2c+4d \end{pmatrix},$$

which leads to

$$3b - 2c = 0, \quad 2a + 3b - 2d = 0, \quad a + c - d = 0.$$

Hence,

$$c = (3/2)b \quad \text{and} \quad d = a + (3/2)b,$$

and the result follows.

Exercise 2.32 (Powers, quadratic's solution) Consider a real square matrix $\boldsymbol{A}$ of order 2.
(a) Show that $\boldsymbol{A}^2 = \mathbf{O}$ has a unique *symmetric* solution, namely $\boldsymbol{A} = \mathbf{O}$.
(b) Show that, in general, $\boldsymbol{A}^2 = \mathbf{O}$ has an infinite number of solutions, given by $\boldsymbol{A} = \boldsymbol{p}\boldsymbol{q}'$ with $\boldsymbol{p}'\boldsymbol{q} = 0$.

Solution
(a) Again, let

$$\boldsymbol{A} := \begin{pmatrix} a & b \\ c & d \end{pmatrix}.$$

The equation $\boldsymbol{A}^2 = \mathbf{O}$ can then be written as

$$\begin{pmatrix} a^2+bc & b(a+d) \\ c(a+d) & bc+d^2 \end{pmatrix} = \begin{pmatrix} 0 & 0 \\ 0 & 0 \end{pmatrix}$$

with general solution $a = -d, a^2 + bc = 0$. If $\boldsymbol{A}$ is symmetric, then $b = c$, and hence all elements are zero. (This also follows from Exercise 2.13.)
(b) If $\boldsymbol{A}$ is not symmetric, then the solution is given by $a = -d, a^2 + bc = 0, b \neq c$. If $a = 0$, the solutions are

$$\boldsymbol{A} = \begin{pmatrix} 0 & b \\ 0 & 0 \end{pmatrix} = \begin{pmatrix} 1 \\ 0 \end{pmatrix} \begin{pmatrix} 0 & b \end{pmatrix} \quad \text{and} \quad \boldsymbol{A} = \begin{pmatrix} 0 & 0 \\ c & 0 \end{pmatrix} = \begin{pmatrix} 0 \\ 1 \end{pmatrix} \begin{pmatrix} c & 0 \end{pmatrix}.$$

If $a \neq 0$, then all elements of $\boldsymbol{A}$ are nonzero and

$$\boldsymbol{A} = \begin{pmatrix} a & b \\ -a^2/b & -a \end{pmatrix} = \begin{pmatrix} 1 \\ -a/b \end{pmatrix} \begin{pmatrix} a & b \end{pmatrix}.$$

All three cases are of the form $\boldsymbol{A} = \boldsymbol{p}\boldsymbol{q}'$ with $\boldsymbol{p}'\boldsymbol{q} = 0$. Conversely, if $\boldsymbol{A} = \boldsymbol{p}\boldsymbol{q}'$ then $\boldsymbol{A}^2 = \boldsymbol{p}\boldsymbol{q}'\boldsymbol{p}\boldsymbol{q}' = \boldsymbol{p}(\boldsymbol{q}'\boldsymbol{p})\boldsymbol{q}' = \mathbf{O}$, whenever $\boldsymbol{p}'\boldsymbol{q} = 0$.

Exercise 2.33 (Powers of a symmetric matrix) Show that $\boldsymbol{A}^p$ is symmetric when $\boldsymbol{A}$ is symmetric.

Solution
We have

$$(\boldsymbol{A}^p)' = (\boldsymbol{A}\boldsymbol{A}\dots\boldsymbol{A})' = \boldsymbol{A}'\boldsymbol{A}'\dots\boldsymbol{A}' = \boldsymbol{A}\boldsymbol{A}\dots\boldsymbol{A} = \boldsymbol{A}^p.$$

Exercise 2.34 (Powers of the triangle) Consider an $n \times n$ triangular matrix $\boldsymbol{A}$. Show that the powers of $\boldsymbol{A}$ are also triangular and that the diagonal elements of $\boldsymbol{A}^p$ are given by a_{ii}^p for $i = 1, \dots, n$.

Solution
Assume that $\boldsymbol{A}$ is lower triangular. It suffices to prove the result for $p = 2$. Exercise 2.21(b) shows that the product of two lower triangular matrices is again lower triangular. Let $\boldsymbol{B} := \boldsymbol{A}^2$. Then its i-th diagonal element is given by $b_{ii} = \sum_k a_{ik}a_{ki} = a_{ii}^2$, since either $a_{ki} = 0$ or $a_{ik} = 0$ when $k \neq i$.

Exercise 2.35 (Fibonacci sequence) Consider the 2×2 matrix

$$\boldsymbol{A} = \begin{pmatrix} 1 & 1 \\ 1 & 0 \end{pmatrix}.$$

Show that

$$\boldsymbol{A}^n = \begin{pmatrix} x_n & x_{n-1} \\ x_{n-1} & x_{n-2} \end{pmatrix}$$

with $x_{-1} := 0$, $x_0 := 1$, and $x_n := x_{n-1} + x_{n-2}$ $(n \geq 1)$. (This is the *Fibonacci sequence*: $1, 2, 3, 5, 8, 13, \ldots$.)

Solution
Since $\boldsymbol{A}$ is symmetric, we know from Exercise 2.33 that $\boldsymbol{A}^n$ is symmetric. Let

$$\boldsymbol{A}^n := \begin{pmatrix} x_n & b_n \\ b_n & c_n \end{pmatrix}.$$

Then,

$$\boldsymbol{A}^{n+1} = \begin{pmatrix} 1 & 1 \\ 1 & 0 \end{pmatrix} \begin{pmatrix} x_n & b_n \\ b_n & c_n \end{pmatrix} = \begin{pmatrix} x_n + b_n & b_n + c_n \\ x_n & b_n \end{pmatrix} = \begin{pmatrix} x_{n+1} & b_{n+1} \\ b_{n+1} & c_{n+1} \end{pmatrix}.$$

Hence, $b_{n+1} = x_n$, $c_{n+1} = b_n = x_{n-1}$, and $x_{n+1} = x_n + b_n = x_n + x_{n-1}$. The condition $b_{n+1} = b_n + c_n$ is then automatically fulfilled. Thus,

$$\boldsymbol{A}^{n+1} = \begin{pmatrix} x_n + x_{n-1} & x_n \\ x_n & x_{n-1} \end{pmatrix}.$$

Exercise 2.36 (Difference equations) Consider the 2×2 matrices

$$\boldsymbol{A} = \begin{pmatrix} 1 & -1 \\ 1 & 0 \end{pmatrix} \quad \text{and} \quad \boldsymbol{B} = \begin{pmatrix} 0 & -1 \\ 1 & -1 \end{pmatrix}.$$

(a) Show that $\boldsymbol{B} = \boldsymbol{A}^2$ and $\boldsymbol{B}^2 = -\boldsymbol{A}$.
(b) Compute $\boldsymbol{A}^2, \boldsymbol{A}^3, \ldots, \boldsymbol{A}^6$.
(c) Conclude that $\boldsymbol{A}^6 = \boldsymbol{I}$ and $\boldsymbol{B}^3 = \boldsymbol{I}$.
(d) What is the relationship between the matrix $\boldsymbol{A}$ and the second-order difference equation $x_n = x_{n-1} - x_{n-2}$?

Solution
(a)–(c) We find

$$\boldsymbol{A}^2 = \begin{pmatrix} 1 & -1 \\ 1 & 0 \end{pmatrix} \begin{pmatrix} 1 & -1 \\ 1 & 0 \end{pmatrix} = \begin{pmatrix} 0 & -1 \\ 1 & -1 \end{pmatrix} = \boldsymbol{B},$$

and further $\boldsymbol{A}^3 = -\boldsymbol{I}$, $\boldsymbol{A}^4 = -\boldsymbol{A}$, $\boldsymbol{A}^5 = -\boldsymbol{B}$, and $\boldsymbol{A}^6 = \boldsymbol{I}$. Hence, $\boldsymbol{B}^2 = \boldsymbol{A}^4 = -\boldsymbol{A}$ and $\boldsymbol{B}^3 = \boldsymbol{A}^6 = \boldsymbol{I}$.
(d) Let $\boldsymbol{z}_n := (x_n, x_{n-1})'$ for $n = 0, 1, \ldots$. Then,

$$\boldsymbol{z}_n = \boldsymbol{A}\boldsymbol{z}_{n-1} \iff \begin{pmatrix} x_n \\ x_{n-1} \end{pmatrix} = \begin{pmatrix} 1 & -1 \\ 1 & 0 \end{pmatrix} \begin{pmatrix} x_{n-1} \\ x_{n-2} \end{pmatrix} = \begin{pmatrix} x_{n-1} - x_{n-2} \\ x_{n-1} \end{pmatrix},$$

so that the first-order vector equation $\boldsymbol{z}_n = \boldsymbol{A}\boldsymbol{z}_{n-1}$ is equivalent to the second-order difference equation $x_n = x_{n-1} - x_{n-2}$. Hence, the solution $\boldsymbol{z}_n = \boldsymbol{A}^n \boldsymbol{z}_0$ of the vector equation also solves the difference equation.

Exercise 2.37 (Idempotent) A square matrix $\boldsymbol{A}$ is idempotent if $\boldsymbol{A}^2 = \boldsymbol{A}$.
(a) Show that the only idempotent *symmetric* 2×2 matrices are

$$\boldsymbol{A} = \begin{pmatrix} 1 & 0 \\ 0 & 1 \end{pmatrix}, \quad \boldsymbol{A} = \begin{pmatrix} 0 & 0 \\ 0 & 0 \end{pmatrix}, \quad \boldsymbol{A} = \boldsymbol{a}\boldsymbol{a}' \quad (\boldsymbol{a}'\boldsymbol{a} = 1).$$

(b) Recall that $\boldsymbol{\imath} := (1, 1, \dots, 1)'$, denotes the $n \times 1$ vector of ones. Show that the matrix $\boldsymbol{I}_n - (1/n)\boldsymbol{\imath}\boldsymbol{\imath}'$ is idempotent and symmetric. What is the intuition behind this fact?
(c) Give an example of an $n \times n$ idempotent matrix that is *not* symmetric.

Solution
(a) The 2×2 matrix $\boldsymbol{A}$ is symmetric idempotent if and only if

$$\begin{pmatrix} a & b \\ b & d \end{pmatrix} \begin{pmatrix} a & b \\ b & d \end{pmatrix} = \begin{pmatrix} a & b \\ b & d \end{pmatrix},$$

that is, if and only if,

$$a^2 + b^2 = a, \quad b(a + d) = b, \quad d^2 + b^2 = d.$$

We distinguish between $a + d \neq 1$ and $a + d = 1$. If $a + d \neq 1$, then $b = 0$ and $a = d = 1$ or $a = d = 0$. If $a + d = 1$, then $b^2 = a(1 - a)$, so that $0 \leq a \leq 1$, $0 \leq d \leq 1$, and $b = \pm\sqrt{a(1 - a)}$. Then,

$$\begin{pmatrix} a & b \\ b & d \end{pmatrix} = \begin{pmatrix} a & \pm\sqrt{a(1-a)} \\ \pm\sqrt{a(1-a)} & 1 - a \end{pmatrix} = \begin{pmatrix} \sqrt{a} \\ \pm\sqrt{1-a} \end{pmatrix} \begin{pmatrix} \sqrt{a} \\ \pm\sqrt{1-a} \end{pmatrix}',$$

which is of the form $\boldsymbol{a}\boldsymbol{a}'$ ($\boldsymbol{a}'\boldsymbol{a} = 1$). Conversely, $(\boldsymbol{a}\boldsymbol{a}')(\boldsymbol{a}\boldsymbol{a}') = \boldsymbol{a}(\boldsymbol{a}'\boldsymbol{a})\boldsymbol{a}' = \boldsymbol{a}\boldsymbol{a}'$ if $\boldsymbol{a}'\boldsymbol{a} = 1$.
(b) Let $\boldsymbol{M} := \boldsymbol{I}_n - (1/n)\boldsymbol{\imath}\boldsymbol{\imath}'$. Then,

$$\begin{aligned} \boldsymbol{M}^2 &= (\boldsymbol{I}_n - \frac{1}{n}\boldsymbol{\imath}\boldsymbol{\imath}')(\boldsymbol{I}_n - \frac{1}{n}\boldsymbol{\imath}\boldsymbol{\imath}') = \boldsymbol{I}_n - \frac{1}{n}\boldsymbol{\imath}\boldsymbol{\imath}' - \frac{1}{n}\boldsymbol{\imath}\boldsymbol{\imath}' + \frac{1}{n^2}\boldsymbol{\imath}\boldsymbol{\imath}'\boldsymbol{\imath}\boldsymbol{\imath}' \\ &= \boldsymbol{I}_n - \frac{2}{n}\boldsymbol{\imath}\boldsymbol{\imath}' + \frac{1}{n^2}\boldsymbol{\imath}(\boldsymbol{\imath}'\boldsymbol{\imath})\boldsymbol{\imath}' = \boldsymbol{I}_n - \frac{2}{n}\boldsymbol{\imath}\boldsymbol{\imath}' + \frac{1}{n}\boldsymbol{\imath}\boldsymbol{\imath}' = \boldsymbol{M}. \end{aligned}$$

To understand the intuition, consider the vector equation $\boldsymbol{y} = \boldsymbol{M}\boldsymbol{x}$. We have

$$\boldsymbol{y} = \boldsymbol{M}\boldsymbol{x} = (\boldsymbol{I}_n - \frac{1}{n}\boldsymbol{\imath}\boldsymbol{\imath}')\boldsymbol{x} = \boldsymbol{x} - \frac{1}{n}\boldsymbol{\imath}(\boldsymbol{\imath}'\boldsymbol{x}) = \boldsymbol{x} - \overline{x}\boldsymbol{\imath},$$

where $\overline{x} := (1/n)\boldsymbol{\imath}'\boldsymbol{x}$ (the average). Hence, $y_i = x_i - \overline{x}$, and the transformation $\boldsymbol{M}$ thus puts $\boldsymbol{x}$ in deviations from its mean. Now consider $\boldsymbol{z} = \boldsymbol{M}\boldsymbol{y}$ and note that $\overline{y} = 0$. Hence, $\boldsymbol{z} = \boldsymbol{y}$, that is, $\boldsymbol{M}^2\boldsymbol{x} = \boldsymbol{M}\boldsymbol{x}$ for every $\boldsymbol{x}$. This gives $\boldsymbol{M}^2 = \boldsymbol{M}$. Associated with an idempotent matrix is an idempotent *operation* (in this case: "put the elements of a vector in deviation form"). Once the operation has been performed, repeating it has no further effect.
(c) In econometrics most idempotent matrices will be symmetric. But the matrix $\boldsymbol{A} = \boldsymbol{a}\boldsymbol{b}'$ with $\boldsymbol{b}'\boldsymbol{a} = 1$ is idempotent but not symmetric (unless $\boldsymbol{a} = \boldsymbol{b}$ or one of the vectors is the null vector).

Exercise 2.38 (Inner product, matrix) For two real matrices $\boldsymbol{A}$ and $\boldsymbol{B}$ of the same order, the inner product is defined as $\langle \boldsymbol{A}, \boldsymbol{B} \rangle := \sum_i \sum_j a_{ij} b_{ij} = \operatorname{tr} \boldsymbol{A}'\boldsymbol{B}$. Prove that:
(a) $\langle \boldsymbol{A}, \boldsymbol{B} \rangle = \langle \boldsymbol{B}, \boldsymbol{A} \rangle$;
(b) $\langle \boldsymbol{A}, \boldsymbol{B}+\boldsymbol{C} \rangle = \langle \boldsymbol{A}, \boldsymbol{B} \rangle + \langle \boldsymbol{A}, \boldsymbol{C} \rangle$;
(c) $\langle \lambda\boldsymbol{A}, \boldsymbol{B} \rangle = \lambda\langle \boldsymbol{A}, \boldsymbol{B} \rangle$;
(d) $\langle \boldsymbol{A}, \boldsymbol{A} \rangle \geq 0$, with $\langle \boldsymbol{A}, \boldsymbol{A} \rangle = 0 \iff \boldsymbol{A} = \mathbf{O}$.

Solution
We need to show that $\operatorname{tr} \boldsymbol{A}'\boldsymbol{B} = \operatorname{tr} \boldsymbol{B}'\boldsymbol{A}$, $\operatorname{tr} \boldsymbol{A}'(\boldsymbol{B}+\boldsymbol{C}) = \operatorname{tr} \boldsymbol{A}'\boldsymbol{B} + \operatorname{tr} \boldsymbol{A}'\boldsymbol{C}$, $\operatorname{tr}(\lambda\boldsymbol{A})'\boldsymbol{B} = \lambda \operatorname{tr} \boldsymbol{A}'\boldsymbol{B}$, $\operatorname{tr} \boldsymbol{A}'\boldsymbol{A} \geq 0$, and $\operatorname{tr} \boldsymbol{A}'\boldsymbol{A} = 0 \iff \boldsymbol{A} = \mathbf{O}$. All these properties have been proved before.

***Exercise 2.39 (Norm, matrix)** For a real matrix $\boldsymbol{A}$, we define the norm as

$$\|\boldsymbol{A}\| := \langle \boldsymbol{A}, \boldsymbol{A} \rangle^{1/2} = \sqrt{\sum_i \sum_j a_{ij}^2} = \sqrt{\operatorname{tr} \boldsymbol{A}'\boldsymbol{A}}.$$

Show that:
(a) $\|\lambda\boldsymbol{A}\| = |\lambda| \cdot \|\boldsymbol{A}\|$;
(b) $\|\boldsymbol{A}\| \geq 0$, with $\|\boldsymbol{A}\| = 0$ if and only if $\boldsymbol{A} = \mathbf{O}$;
(c) $\|\boldsymbol{A}+\boldsymbol{B}\| \leq \|\boldsymbol{A}\| + \|\boldsymbol{B}\|$ (*triangle inequality*).

Solution
(a) We have

$$\|\lambda\boldsymbol{A}\| = \sqrt{\operatorname{tr}(\lambda\boldsymbol{A})'(\lambda\boldsymbol{A})} = \sqrt{\lambda^2 \operatorname{tr} \boldsymbol{A}'\boldsymbol{A}} = |\lambda|\sqrt{\operatorname{tr} \boldsymbol{A}'\boldsymbol{A}} = |\lambda| \cdot \|\boldsymbol{A}\|.$$

(b) Further, $\|\boldsymbol{A}\| = \sqrt{\operatorname{tr} \boldsymbol{A}'\boldsymbol{A}} \geq 0$, with $\|\boldsymbol{A}\| = 0$ if and only if $\boldsymbol{A} = \mathbf{O}$, according to Exercise 2.25.
(c) Finally, let $\boldsymbol{A} := (a_{ij})$ and $\boldsymbol{B} := (b_{ij})$ be $m \times n$ matrices, and define $mn \times 1$ vectors $\boldsymbol{a}$ and $\boldsymbol{b}$ such that $\boldsymbol{a}$ contains the elements of $\boldsymbol{A}$ in a specific order and $\boldsymbol{b}$ contains the elements of $\boldsymbol{B}$ *in the same order*. For example,

$$\boldsymbol{a} := (a_{11}, a_{21}, \dots, a_{m1}, a_{12}, \dots, a_{m2}, \dots, a_{mn})',$$

which we shall later write as $\operatorname{vec} \boldsymbol{A}$; see Chapter 10. Then,

$$\operatorname{tr} \boldsymbol{A}'\boldsymbol{B} = \sum_{ij} a_{ij} b_{ij} = \boldsymbol{a}'\boldsymbol{b}$$

and similarly, $\operatorname{tr} \boldsymbol{A}'\boldsymbol{A} = \boldsymbol{a}'\boldsymbol{a}$ and $\operatorname{tr} \boldsymbol{B}'\boldsymbol{B} = \boldsymbol{b}'\boldsymbol{b}$. Hence,

$$\begin{aligned} \|\boldsymbol{A}+\boldsymbol{B}\| &= \sqrt{\operatorname{tr}(\boldsymbol{A}+\boldsymbol{B})'(\boldsymbol{A}+\boldsymbol{B})} = \sqrt{(\boldsymbol{a}+\boldsymbol{b})'(\boldsymbol{a}+\boldsymbol{b})} = \|\boldsymbol{a}+\boldsymbol{b}\| \\ &\leq \|\boldsymbol{a}\| + \|\boldsymbol{b}\| = \sqrt{\boldsymbol{a}'\boldsymbol{a}} + \sqrt{\boldsymbol{b}'\boldsymbol{b}} = \sqrt{\operatorname{tr} \boldsymbol{A}'\boldsymbol{A}} + \sqrt{\operatorname{tr} \boldsymbol{B}'\boldsymbol{B}} = \|\boldsymbol{A}\| + \|\boldsymbol{B}\|, \end{aligned}$$

using the triangle equality for vectors (Exercise 1.10(c)).

2.2 Complex matrices

Exercise 2.40 (Conjugate transpose) Recall that a complex matrix U can be written as $U := A + \mathrm{i}B$, where A and B are real matrices, and that the matrix $U^* := A' - \mathrm{i}B'$ is the conjugate transpose of U.
(a) If A is real, show that $A^* = A'$.
(b) Let

$$Z = \begin{pmatrix} 1+2\mathrm{i} & 3-5\mathrm{i} & 7 \\ 8+\mathrm{i} & 6\mathrm{i} & 2-\mathrm{i} \end{pmatrix}.$$

Compute Z', Z^*, and $(Z^*)^*$.
(c) For any matrix U, show that $(U^*)^* = U$, and verify with the matrix in (b).
(d) Show that $(UV)^* = V^*U^*$.
(e) Show that $\operatorname{tr} U^* \neq \operatorname{tr} U$, unless $\operatorname{tr} U$ is a real number.

Solution
(a) This follows from the definition.
(b) We have

$$Z' = \begin{pmatrix} 1+2\mathrm{i} & 8+\mathrm{i} \\ 3-5\mathrm{i} & 6\mathrm{i} \\ 7 & 2-\mathrm{i} \end{pmatrix}, \quad Z^* = \begin{pmatrix} 1-2\mathrm{i} & 8-\mathrm{i} \\ 3+5\mathrm{i} & -6\mathrm{i} \\ 7 & 2+\mathrm{i} \end{pmatrix},$$

and

$$(Z^*)^* = \begin{pmatrix} 1+2\mathrm{i} & 3-5\mathrm{i} & 7 \\ 8+\mathrm{i} & 6\mathrm{i} & 2-\mathrm{i} \end{pmatrix} = Z.$$

(c) Let $U := A + \mathrm{i}B$. Then $U^* = A' - \mathrm{i}B'$ and $(U^*)^* = (A')' + \mathrm{i}(B')' = A + \mathrm{i}B = U$. The verification is straightforward.
(d) Let $U := A + \mathrm{i}B$ and $V := C + \mathrm{i}D$. Then $UV = (AC - BD) + \mathrm{i}(AD + BC)$, so that

$$\begin{aligned}(UV)^* &= (AC - BD)' - \mathrm{i}(AD + BC)' = (C'A' - D'B') - \mathrm{i}(D'A' + C'B') \\ &= (C' - \mathrm{i}D')(A' - \mathrm{i}B') = (C + \mathrm{i}D)^*(A + \mathrm{i}B)^* = V^*U^*.\end{aligned}$$

(e) Let $U := A + \mathrm{i}B$. Then, $\operatorname{tr} U^* = \operatorname{tr} A - \mathrm{i} \operatorname{tr} B$ while $\operatorname{tr} U = \operatorname{tr} A + \mathrm{i} \operatorname{tr} B$. Hence, they are equal if and only if $\operatorname{tr} B = 0$, that is, if and only if $\operatorname{tr} U$ is real.

Exercise 2.41 (Hermitian matrix) A square matrix U is Hermitian if $U^* = U$. Show that:
(a) a real Hermitian matrix is symmetric;
(b) if $U := A + \mathrm{i}B$ is Hermitian (A, B real), then $A' = A$ and $B' = -B$;
(c) if $U := A + \mathrm{i}B$ is Hermitian, then U^*U is real if and only if $AB = -BA$;
(d) UU^* and U^*U are both Hermitian;
(e) the diagonal elements of a Hermitian matrix are real;
(f) if $U = U^*$, then the Hermitian form x^*Ux is real for every vector x.

Solution
(a) If $\boldsymbol{U}$ is real, then $\boldsymbol{U}^* = \boldsymbol{U}'$. If $\boldsymbol{U}$ is Hermitian, then $\boldsymbol{U}^* = \boldsymbol{U}$. Hence, $\boldsymbol{U} = \boldsymbol{U}'$ and $\boldsymbol{U}$ is symmetric.
(b) Let $\boldsymbol{U} = \boldsymbol{A} + \mathrm{i}\boldsymbol{B}$. If $\boldsymbol{U}$ is Hermitian, then $\boldsymbol{A}' - \mathrm{i}\boldsymbol{B}' = \boldsymbol{A} + \mathrm{i}\boldsymbol{B}$. Hence, $\boldsymbol{A}' = \boldsymbol{A}$ and $\boldsymbol{B}' = -\boldsymbol{B}$.
(c) In general we have

$$\boldsymbol{U}^*\boldsymbol{U} = (\boldsymbol{A}' - \mathrm{i}\boldsymbol{B}')(\boldsymbol{A} + \mathrm{i}\boldsymbol{B}) = (\boldsymbol{A}'\boldsymbol{A} + \boldsymbol{B}'\boldsymbol{B}) + \mathrm{i}(\boldsymbol{A}'\boldsymbol{B} - \boldsymbol{B}'\boldsymbol{A}).$$

If $\boldsymbol{U}$ is Hermitian, then (b) implies that $\boldsymbol{A}' = \boldsymbol{A}$ and $\boldsymbol{B}' = -\boldsymbol{B}$, so that $\boldsymbol{A}'\boldsymbol{B} = \boldsymbol{B}'\boldsymbol{A} \iff \boldsymbol{A}\boldsymbol{B} = -\boldsymbol{B}\boldsymbol{A}$.
(d) This follows because

$$(\boldsymbol{U}\boldsymbol{U}^*)^* = (\boldsymbol{U}^*)^*\boldsymbol{U}^* = \boldsymbol{U}\boldsymbol{U}^*, \quad (\boldsymbol{U}^*\boldsymbol{U})^* = \boldsymbol{U}^*(\boldsymbol{U}^*)^* = \boldsymbol{U}^*\boldsymbol{U}.$$

(e) Write $\boldsymbol{U} := \boldsymbol{A} + \mathrm{i}\boldsymbol{B}$. If $\boldsymbol{U}$ is Hermitian then we know from (b) that $\boldsymbol{A}$ is symmetric and $\boldsymbol{B}$ skew-symmetric. The diagonal elements of $\boldsymbol{B}$ are therefore zero (Exercise 2.23(c)), so that the diagonal elements of $\boldsymbol{U}$ are those of $\boldsymbol{A}$.
(f) Let $z := \boldsymbol{x}^*\boldsymbol{U}\boldsymbol{x}$. Then,

$$z^* = (\boldsymbol{x}^*\boldsymbol{U}\boldsymbol{x})^* = \boldsymbol{x}^*\boldsymbol{U}^*\boldsymbol{x} = \boldsymbol{x}^*\boldsymbol{U}\boldsymbol{x} = z.$$

Now, z is a scalar, equal to its complex conjugate. Hence, z is real.

Exercise 2.42 (Skew-Hermitian matrix) A square matrix $\boldsymbol{U}$ is skew-Hermitian if $\boldsymbol{U}^* = -\boldsymbol{U}$. If $\boldsymbol{U}$ is skew-Hermitian, show that:
(a) if $\boldsymbol{U}$ is real, then $\boldsymbol{U}$ is skew-symmetric;
(b) the matrix $\mathrm{i}\boldsymbol{U}$ is Hermitian;
(c) the diagonal elements of $\mathrm{Re}(\boldsymbol{U})$ are zero, but the diagonal elements of $\mathrm{Im}(\boldsymbol{U})$ are not necessarily zero.

Solution
(a) If $\boldsymbol{U}$ is real, then $\boldsymbol{U}' = \boldsymbol{U}^* = -\boldsymbol{U}$.
(b) Write $\boldsymbol{U} := \boldsymbol{A} + \mathrm{i}\boldsymbol{B}$. Then $\boldsymbol{U}^* = \boldsymbol{A}' - \mathrm{i}\boldsymbol{B}'$ and hence $(\mathrm{i}\boldsymbol{U})^* = \mathrm{i}^*\boldsymbol{U}^* = -\mathrm{i}\boldsymbol{U}^* = -\mathrm{i}\boldsymbol{A}' - \boldsymbol{B}'$. Since $\boldsymbol{U}$ is skew-Hermitian, we have $\boldsymbol{A}' = -\boldsymbol{A}$ and $\boldsymbol{B}' = \boldsymbol{B}$, so that $(\mathrm{i}\boldsymbol{U})^* = \mathrm{i}\boldsymbol{A} - \boldsymbol{B} = \mathrm{i}(\boldsymbol{A} + \mathrm{i}\boldsymbol{B}) = \mathrm{i}\boldsymbol{U}$.
(c) Write again $\boldsymbol{U} := \boldsymbol{A} + \mathrm{i}\boldsymbol{B}$. The equation $\boldsymbol{U}^* = -\boldsymbol{U}$ gives $\boldsymbol{A}' = -\boldsymbol{A}$ and $\boldsymbol{B}' = \boldsymbol{B}$. Hence, the diagonal elements of $\boldsymbol{A} = \mathrm{Re}(\boldsymbol{U})$ are zero, but the diagonal elements of $\boldsymbol{B} = \mathrm{Im}(\boldsymbol{U})$ need not be.

Exercise 2.43 (Unitary matrix) A square matrix $\boldsymbol{U}$ is unitary if $\boldsymbol{U}^*\boldsymbol{U} = \boldsymbol{U}\boldsymbol{U}^* = \boldsymbol{I}$. Show that:
(a) a real unitary matrix is orthogonal;
(b) $\boldsymbol{U}^*$ is unitary if and only if $\boldsymbol{U}$ is;
(c) $\boldsymbol{U}\boldsymbol{V}$ is unitary if $\boldsymbol{U}$ and $\boldsymbol{V}$ are unitary;
(d) the converse of (c) does not necessarily hold.

Solution
(a) If U is real then $U^* = U'$ and hence $U'U = UU' = I$.
(b) Let $V := U^*$. If U is unitary we have $U^*U = UU^* = I$, and hence

$$V^*V = UU^* = I \quad \text{and} \quad VV^* = U^*U = I.$$

This also proves the "only if" part.
(c) We have

$$(UV)^*(UV) = V^*U^*UV = V^*IV = V^*V = I$$

and, similarly, $(UV)(UV)^* = I$.
(d) The converse of (c) does not hold in general. The matrix UV is unitary if and only if $V^*U^*UV = I$. One counterexample is a matrix U such that $U^*U = \sigma^2 I$ and a matrix V such that $V^*V = \sigma^{-2}I$.

***Exercise 2.44 (Counting)** How many matrices are there that are simultaneously Hermitian, unitary, and diagonal?

Solution
Let $U := A + \mathrm{i}B$. Since U is diagonal, both A and B are diagonal, $A := \operatorname{diag}(a_1, \ldots, a_n)$ and $B := \operatorname{diag}(b_1, \ldots, b_n)$. Since U is Hermitian, $a_j + ib_j = a_j - ib_j$ for $j = 1, \ldots, n$. Hence, $B = O$, and $U = \operatorname{diag}(a_1, \ldots, a_n)$ is real. Since U is real unitary (that is, orthogonal), we have $a_j^2 = 1$. Hence, U is a diagonal matrix and its diagonal elements are ± 1. There are 2^n different matrices.

Exercise 2.45 (Normal matrix, complex) A square matrix U is called normal if $U^*U = UU^*$. Consider the matrices

$$A = \frac{1}{2}\begin{pmatrix} \mathrm{i} & -\sqrt{3} \\ \sqrt{3} & -\mathrm{i} \end{pmatrix}, \quad B = \frac{1}{2}\begin{pmatrix} 1+\mathrm{i} & 1-\mathrm{i} \\ 1-\mathrm{i} & 1+\mathrm{i} \end{pmatrix}, \quad C = \begin{pmatrix} 1 & 0 \\ 1-\mathrm{i} & \mathrm{i} \end{pmatrix}.$$

Which of the matrices A, B, C are normal? Which are unitary?

Solution
We find

$$\begin{aligned} A^*A &= \frac{1}{4}\begin{pmatrix} -\mathrm{i} & \sqrt{3} \\ -\sqrt{3} & \mathrm{i} \end{pmatrix}\begin{pmatrix} \mathrm{i} & -\sqrt{3} \\ \sqrt{3} & -\mathrm{i} \end{pmatrix} = \begin{pmatrix} 1 & 0 \\ 0 & 1 \end{pmatrix} \\ &= \frac{1}{4}\begin{pmatrix} \mathrm{i} & -\sqrt{3} \\ \sqrt{3} & -\mathrm{i} \end{pmatrix}\begin{pmatrix} -\mathrm{i} & \sqrt{3} \\ -\sqrt{3} & \mathrm{i} \end{pmatrix} = AA^* \end{aligned}$$

and

$$\begin{aligned} B^*B &= \frac{1}{4}\begin{pmatrix} 1-\mathrm{i} & 1+\mathrm{i} \\ 1+\mathrm{i} & 1-\mathrm{i} \end{pmatrix}\begin{pmatrix} 1+\mathrm{i} & 1-\mathrm{i} \\ 1-\mathrm{i} & 1+\mathrm{i} \end{pmatrix} = \begin{pmatrix} 1 & 0 \\ 0 & 1 \end{pmatrix} \\ &= \frac{1}{4}\begin{pmatrix} 1+\mathrm{i} & 1-\mathrm{i} \\ 1-\mathrm{i} & 1+\mathrm{i} \end{pmatrix}\begin{pmatrix} 1-\mathrm{i} & 1+\mathrm{i} \\ 1+\mathrm{i} & 1-\mathrm{i} \end{pmatrix} = BB^*. \end{aligned}$$

Hence, $\boldsymbol{A}$ and $\boldsymbol{B}$ are both unitary (and hence normal). In contrast,

$$\boldsymbol{C}^*\boldsymbol{C} = \begin{pmatrix} 1 & 1+\mathrm{i} \\ 0 & -\mathrm{i} \end{pmatrix} \begin{pmatrix} 1 & 0 \\ 1-\mathrm{i} & \mathrm{i} \end{pmatrix} = \begin{pmatrix} 3 & -1+\mathrm{i} \\ -1-\mathrm{i} & 1 \end{pmatrix},$$

while

$$\boldsymbol{C}\boldsymbol{C}^* = \begin{pmatrix} 1 & 0 \\ 1-\mathrm{i} & \mathrm{i} \end{pmatrix} \begin{pmatrix} 1 & 1+\mathrm{i} \\ 0 & -\mathrm{i} \end{pmatrix} = \begin{pmatrix} 1 & 1+\mathrm{i} \\ 1-\mathrm{i} & 3 \end{pmatrix}.$$

Hence, $\boldsymbol{C}$ is not normal (and hence not unitary).

Notes

Some excellent introductory texts are Hadley (1961), Bellman (1970), and Bretscher (1997). More advanced are Mirsky (1955), old but still very readable, and Horn and Johnson (1985, 1991).

If we take the Fibonacci numbers $1, 2, 3, 5, 8, 13, \ldots$ in Exercise 2.35, and consider the successive ratios $g_1 = 1/2$, $g_2 = 2/3$, $g_3 = 3/5$, and so on, then the sequence $\{g_i\}$ converges to $G := (\sqrt{5} - 1)/2 \approx 0.62$. Its reciprocal is the famous *golden ratio*. The number G divides a line such that the proportion of the smaller part to the larger part equals the proportion of the larger part to the whole.

3

Vector spaces

This chapter is the most abstract of the book. You may skip it at first reading, and jump directly to Chapter 4. But make sure you return to it later. Matrix theory can be viewed from an algebraic viewpoint or from a geometric viewpoint — both are equally important. The theory of vector spaces is essential in understanding the geometric viewpoint.

Associated with every vector space is a set of scalars, used to define scalar multiplication on the space. In the most abstract setting these scalars are required only to be elements of an algebraic field. We shall, however, always take the scalars to be the set of complex numbers (*complex vector space*) or, as an important special case, the set of real numbers (*real vector space*).

A *vector space* (or *linear space*) $\mathcal{V}$ is a nonempty set of elements (called *vectors*) together with two operations and a set of axioms. The first operation is *addition*, which associates with any two vectors $\boldsymbol{x}$, $\boldsymbol{y} \in \mathcal{V}$ a vector $\boldsymbol{x} + \boldsymbol{y} \in \mathcal{V}$ (the *sum* of $\boldsymbol{x}$ and $\boldsymbol{y}$). The second operation is *scalar multiplication*, which associates with any vector $\boldsymbol{x} \in \mathcal{V}$ and any real (or complex) scalar α, a vector $\alpha\boldsymbol{x} \in \mathcal{V}$. It is the scalar (rather than the vectors) that determines whether the space is real or complex.

The space $\mathcal{V}$ is called a real (complex) vector space if the following axioms hold for any vectors $\boldsymbol{x}$, $\boldsymbol{y}$, $\boldsymbol{z} \in \mathcal{V}$ and any real (complex) scalars α, β.

Axioms A: Addition

A1. $\boldsymbol{x} + \boldsymbol{y} = \boldsymbol{y} + \boldsymbol{x}$ (commutative law).
A2. $\boldsymbol{x} + (\boldsymbol{y} + \boldsymbol{z}) = (\boldsymbol{x} + \boldsymbol{y}) + \boldsymbol{z}$ (associative law).
A3. There exists a vector in $\mathcal{V}$ (denoted by $\mathbf{0}$) such that $\boldsymbol{x} + \mathbf{0} = \boldsymbol{x}$ for all $\boldsymbol{x}$ (null vector).
A4. For any $\boldsymbol{x} \in \mathcal{V}$ there exists a vector in $\mathcal{V}$ (denoted by $-\boldsymbol{x}$) such that $\boldsymbol{x} + (-\boldsymbol{x}) = \mathbf{0}$ (negative of $\boldsymbol{x}$).

Axioms B: Scalar multiplication
B1. $\alpha(\beta\boldsymbol{x}) = (\alpha\beta)\boldsymbol{x}$ (associative law).
B2. $1\boldsymbol{x} = \boldsymbol{x}$.

Axioms C: Distributive laws
C1. $\alpha(\boldsymbol{x}+\boldsymbol{y}) = \alpha\boldsymbol{x} + \alpha\boldsymbol{y}$ (distributive law for vectors).
C2. $(\alpha+\beta)\boldsymbol{x} = \alpha\boldsymbol{x} + \beta\boldsymbol{x}$ (distributive law for scalars).

Three types of vector spaces are discussed in this chapter, each being a special case of its predecessor. First, the complex vector space defined above. Concepts like subspace, linear independence, basis, and dimension can be discussed in this space. If we add one ingredient (the inner product) to this space, we obtain a subclass called the inner-product space. This allows us to discuss the important concept of orthogonality. If we add one more ingredient (completeness) then the inner-product space becomes a Hilbert space. This allows us to prove the famous projection theorem.

A nonempty subset $\mathcal{A}$ of a vector space $\mathcal{V}$ is called a *subspace* of $\mathcal{V}$ if, for all $\boldsymbol{x}, \boldsymbol{y} \in \mathcal{A}$, we have $\boldsymbol{x}+\boldsymbol{y} \in \mathcal{A}$ and $\alpha\boldsymbol{x} \in \mathcal{A}$ for any scalar α. The *intersection* of two subspaces $\mathcal{A}$ and $\mathcal{B}$ in a vector space $\mathcal{V}$, denoted by $\mathcal{A} \cap \mathcal{B}$, consists of all vectors that belong to both $\mathcal{A}$ and $\mathcal{B}$. The *union* of $\mathcal{A}$ and $\mathcal{B}$, denoted by $\mathcal{A} \cup \mathcal{B}$, consists of all vectors that belong to at least one of the sets $\mathcal{A}$ and $\mathcal{B}$. The *sum* of $\mathcal{A}$ and $\mathcal{B}$, denoted by $\mathcal{A} + \mathcal{B}$, consists of all vectors of the form $\boldsymbol{a} + \boldsymbol{b}$ where $\boldsymbol{a} \in \mathcal{A}$ and $\boldsymbol{b} \in \mathcal{B}$.

A *linear combination* of the vectors $\boldsymbol{x}_1, \boldsymbol{x}_2, \dots, \boldsymbol{x}_n$ in a vector space is a sum of the form $\alpha_1\boldsymbol{x}_1 + \alpha_2\boldsymbol{x}_2 + \cdots + \alpha_n\boldsymbol{x}_n$. A finite set of vectors $\boldsymbol{x}_1, \dots, \boldsymbol{x}_n$ $(n \geq 1)$ is said to be *linearly dependent* if there exist scalars $\alpha_1, \dots, \alpha_n$, not all zero, such that $\alpha_1\boldsymbol{x}_1 + \cdots + \alpha_n\boldsymbol{x}_n = \boldsymbol{0}$; otherwise it is linearly independent. An arbitrary set of elements A of $\mathcal{V}$ (containing possibly an infinite number of vectors) is linearly independent if every nonempty finite subset of A is linearly independent; otherwise it is linearly dependent. In Figure 1.1 of Chapter 1, suppose you wish to travel from the origin to the point $\boldsymbol{x} + \boldsymbol{y}$. If you are only allowed to travel along the line on which $\boldsymbol{x}$ and the origin lie, then it is not possible to reach $\boldsymbol{x} + \boldsymbol{y}$, unless $\boldsymbol{y}$ too is on the line $\alpha\boldsymbol{x}$. Hence, $\boldsymbol{x}$ and $\boldsymbol{y}$ are linearly independent.

Let A be a nonempty set of vectors from a vector space $\mathcal{V}$. The set $\mathcal{A}$ consisting of all linear combinations of vectors in A is called the subspace *spanned* (or *generated*) by A. Figure 3.1 shows two nonzero vectors $\boldsymbol{x}$ and $\boldsymbol{y}$ in $\mathbb{R}^2$, not proportional to each other. The horizontally shaded area is the span of $\boldsymbol{x}$ and $\boldsymbol{y}$ when only positive scalar multiples α and β are allowed in $\alpha\boldsymbol{x} + \beta\boldsymbol{y}$. For negative α and β we obtain the vertically shaded area. Any other point in $\mathbb{R}^2$ (such as $\boldsymbol{x} - \boldsymbol{y}$) can also be written as a linear combination of $\boldsymbol{x}$ and $\boldsymbol{y}$. Thus, all of $\mathbb{R}^2$ is spanned. Any pair of linearly independent vectors $\boldsymbol{x}$ and $\boldsymbol{y}$ spans $\mathbb{R}^2$, and, more generally, any set of linearly independent vectors $\boldsymbol{x}_1, \dots, \boldsymbol{x}_n$ spans $\mathbb{R}^n$. For example, in Figure 3.2, if we do the same as in Figure 3.1 with the points $\boldsymbol{x}$ and $\boldsymbol{y}$, they will span the whole plane linking them to the origin, but not all of $\mathbb{R}^3$. If a vector space $\mathcal{V}$ contains a finite set of n linearly independent vectors $\boldsymbol{x}_1, \dots, \boldsymbol{x}_n$, and moreover any

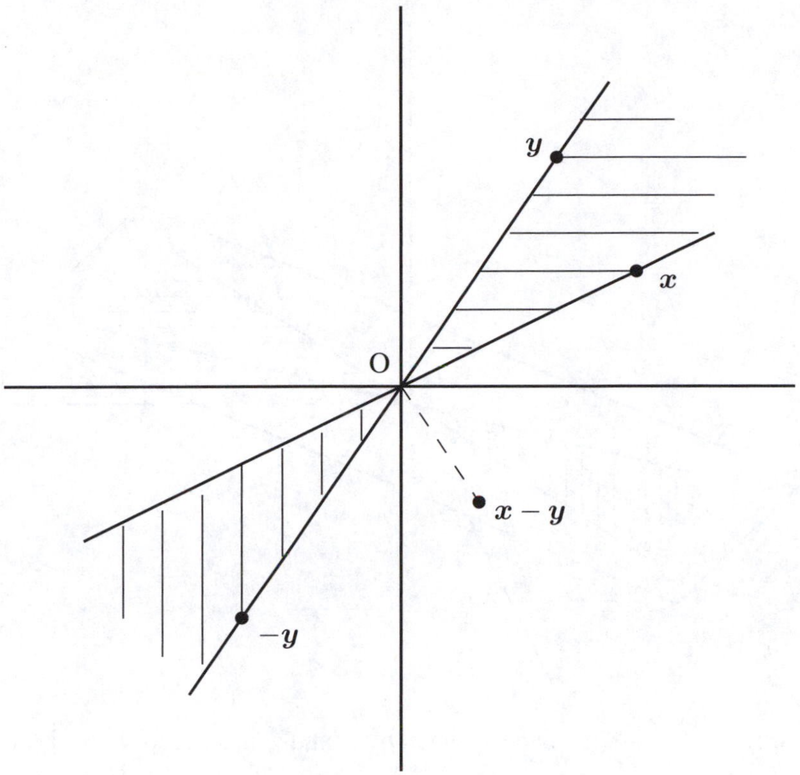

Figure 3.1 — $\boldsymbol{x}$ and $\boldsymbol{y}$ span $\mathbb{R}^2$.

set of $n + 1$ vectors is linearly dependent, we will say that the *dimension* of $\mathcal{V}$ is n, and write $\dim(\mathcal{V}) = n$. In this case $\mathcal{V}$ is said to be *finite dimensional.* (If $\mathcal{V} = \{\mathbf{0}\}$ we define $\dim(\mathcal{V}) = 0$.) If no such n exists, we say that $\mathcal{V}$ is *infinite dimensional.*

If $\mathcal{V}$ is a vector space, not necessarily finite dimensional, and A is a linearly independent set of vectors from $\mathcal{V}$, then A is a *basis* of $\mathcal{V}$ if $\mathcal{V}$ is spanned by A.

In accordance with the definitions in Chapters 1 and 2, the *inner product* of two vectors $\boldsymbol{x}$ and $\boldsymbol{y}$, denoted by $\langle \boldsymbol{x}, \boldsymbol{y} \rangle$, is defined as a complex-valued function, satisfying the following conditions:

(i) $\langle \boldsymbol{x}, \boldsymbol{y} \rangle = \langle \boldsymbol{y}, \boldsymbol{x} \rangle^*$, the complex conjugate of $\langle \boldsymbol{y}, \boldsymbol{x} \rangle$;
(ii) $\langle \boldsymbol{x} + \boldsymbol{y}, \boldsymbol{z} \rangle = \langle \boldsymbol{x}, \boldsymbol{z} \rangle + \langle \boldsymbol{y}, \boldsymbol{z} \rangle$;
(iii) $\langle \alpha\boldsymbol{x}, \boldsymbol{y} \rangle = \alpha\langle \boldsymbol{x}, \boldsymbol{y} \rangle$;
(iv) $\langle \boldsymbol{x}, \boldsymbol{x} \rangle \geq 0$, with $\langle \boldsymbol{x}, \boldsymbol{x} \rangle = 0$ if and only if $\boldsymbol{x} = \mathbf{0}$.

A complex vector space $\mathcal{V}$ together with an inner product is then said to be an *inner-product space.* A real vector space $\mathcal{V}$ is an inner-product space if for each $\boldsymbol{x}$, $\boldsymbol{y} \in \mathcal{V}$ there exists a *real* number $\langle \boldsymbol{x}, \boldsymbol{y} \rangle$ satisfying conditions (i)–(iv). Of course condition (i) reduces in this case to $\langle \boldsymbol{x}, \boldsymbol{y} \rangle = \langle \boldsymbol{y}, \boldsymbol{x} \rangle$.

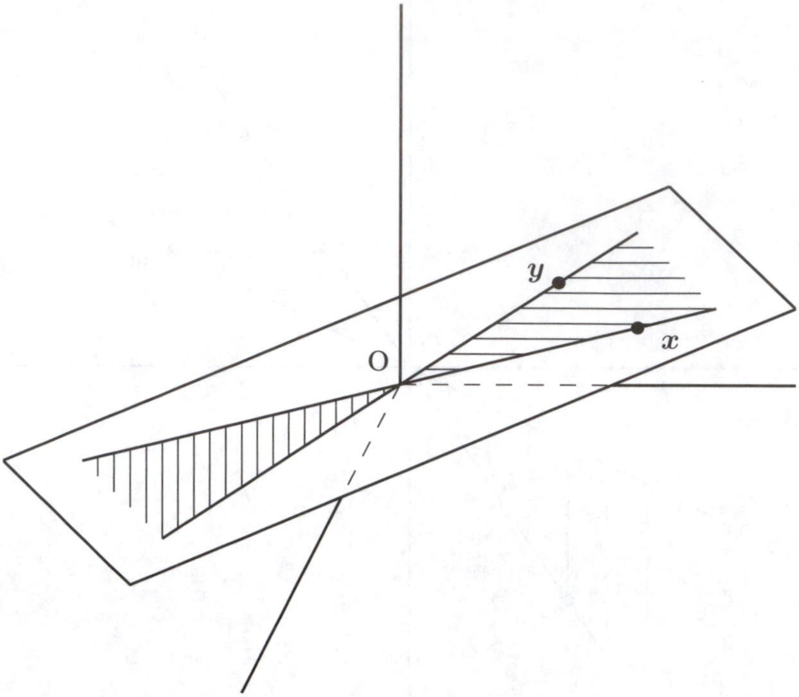

Figure 3.2 — The plane spanned by $\boldsymbol{x}$ and $\boldsymbol{y}$ is a subspace of $\mathbb{R}^3$.

The *norm* of a vector $\boldsymbol{x}$ in an inner-product space is defined to be the real number $\|\boldsymbol{x}\| := \sqrt{\langle \boldsymbol{x}, \boldsymbol{x} \rangle}$. The concept of an inner product not only induces the concept of "length" (the norm), but also of "distance". In an inner-product space the distance $d(\boldsymbol{x}, \boldsymbol{y})$ between two vectors $\boldsymbol{x}$ and $\boldsymbol{y}$ is defined as $d(\boldsymbol{x}, \boldsymbol{y}) := \|\boldsymbol{x} - \boldsymbol{y}\|$.

For two vectors $\boldsymbol{x}$, $\boldsymbol{y}$ in an inner-product space, we say that $\boldsymbol{x}$ and $\boldsymbol{y}$ are orthogonal if $\langle \boldsymbol{x}, \boldsymbol{y} \rangle = 0$, and we write $\boldsymbol{x} \perp \boldsymbol{y}$. Consider a set $A := \{\boldsymbol{x}_1, \dots, \boldsymbol{x}_r\}$ of nonzero vectors in an inner-product space $\mathcal{V}$. A is called an *orthogonal set* if each pair of vectors in A is orthogonal. If, in addition, each vector in A has unit length, then A is called an *orthonormal set*. For example, the unit $m \times 1$ vectors $\boldsymbol{e}_1, \dots, \boldsymbol{e}_r$ $(r \leq m)$ form an orthonormal set in $\mathbb{R}^m$. Two subspaces $\mathcal{A}$ and $\mathcal{B}$ of an inner-product space $\mathcal{V}$ are said to be *orthogonal* if every vector $\boldsymbol{a}$ in $\mathcal{A}$ is orthogonal to every vector $\boldsymbol{b}$ in $\mathcal{B}$. If $\mathcal{A}$ is a subspace of an inner-product space $\mathcal{V}$, then the space of all vectors orthogonal to $\mathcal{A}$ is called the *orthogonal complement* of $\mathcal{A}$ and is denoted by $\mathcal{A}^\perp$.

In finite-dimensional spaces (such as $\mathbb{R}^m$) an inner-product space is of sufficient generality. This is because all finite-dimensional inner-product spaces are "complete". But infinite-dimensional inner-product spaces are not necessarily complete. Hence, in order to develop the concept of orthogonality further and to prove the "projection theorem" we need a little more than the inner-product space. We need a complete inner-product space, that is, a Hilbert space. Now, what is completeness? Consider a sequence $\{\boldsymbol{x}_n\} := \{\boldsymbol{x}_1, \boldsymbol{x}_2, \dots\}$

in an inner-product space $\mathcal{V}$. If the sequence converges, say to $\boldsymbol{x}$, then its terms must ultimately become close to $\boldsymbol{x}$ and hence close to each other, more precisely: for every $\epsilon > 0$ there exists an $n_\epsilon > 0$ such that

$$\|\boldsymbol{x}_n - \boldsymbol{x}_m\| < \epsilon \quad \text{for all } m, n > n_\epsilon. \tag{3.1}$$

In some spaces (such as $\mathbb{R}^m$), the converse is also true; in other spaces it is not. A sequence $\{\boldsymbol{x}_n\}$ in an inner-product space $\mathcal{V}$ is called a *Cauchy sequence* if (3.1) holds. If every Cauchy sequence in $\mathcal{V}$ converges to a member of $\mathcal{V}$, then $\mathcal{V}$ is said to be *complete*, and we call $\mathcal{V}$ a *Hilbert space*. See Appendix A for more details on the notion of completeness.

3.1 Complex and real vector spaces

Exercise 3.1 (The null vector)
(a) Show that every vector space contains at least one vector, namely $\mathbf{0}$.
(b) Show that the set $\{\mathbf{0}\}$, containing only $\mathbf{0}$, is a vector space.

Solution
(a) This follows from axiom A3.
(b) This follows by verifying that all axioms are satisfied. For example, $\mathbf{0} + \mathbf{0} = \mathbf{0} + \mathbf{0}$, so A1 holds.

***Exercise 3.2 (Elementary properties of the sum)** Show that in any vector space:
(a) the sum $\boldsymbol{x}_1 + \boldsymbol{x}_2 + \cdots + \boldsymbol{x}_n$ is unambiguously defined;
(b) the null vector is unique;
(c) the negative $-\boldsymbol{x}$ of the vector $\boldsymbol{x}$ is unique;
(d) $\boldsymbol{x} + \boldsymbol{y} = \boldsymbol{x} + \boldsymbol{z}$ implies $\boldsymbol{y} = \boldsymbol{z}$.

Solution
(a) For $n = 3$ we have, using Axiom A2, $(\boldsymbol{x}_1 + \boldsymbol{x}_2) + \boldsymbol{x}_3 = \boldsymbol{x}_1 + (\boldsymbol{x}_2 + \boldsymbol{x}_3)$. The proof then follows by induction.
(b) Suppose two vectors $\boldsymbol{a}$ and $\boldsymbol{b}$ exist satisfying $\boldsymbol{x} + \boldsymbol{a} = \boldsymbol{x}$ for all $\boldsymbol{x}$ and $\boldsymbol{x} + \boldsymbol{b} = \boldsymbol{x}$ for all $\boldsymbol{x}$. Then, for $\boldsymbol{x} = \boldsymbol{b}$ and $\boldsymbol{x} = \boldsymbol{a}$, respectively, we find $\boldsymbol{b} + \boldsymbol{a} = \boldsymbol{b}$ and $\boldsymbol{a} + \boldsymbol{b} = \boldsymbol{a}$. Since $\boldsymbol{b} + \boldsymbol{a} = \boldsymbol{a} + \boldsymbol{b}$ (by A1), we conclude that $\boldsymbol{a} = \boldsymbol{b}$.
(c) Suppose two vectors $\boldsymbol{a}$ and $\boldsymbol{b}$ exist such that, for given $\boldsymbol{x}$, $\boldsymbol{x} + \boldsymbol{a} = \mathbf{0}$ and $\boldsymbol{x} + \boldsymbol{b} = \mathbf{0}$. Then, $\boldsymbol{a} = \mathbf{0} + \boldsymbol{a} = (\boldsymbol{x} + \boldsymbol{b}) + \boldsymbol{a} = (\boldsymbol{x} + \boldsymbol{a}) + \boldsymbol{b} = \mathbf{0} + \boldsymbol{b} = \boldsymbol{b}$.
(d) If $\boldsymbol{x}+\boldsymbol{y} = \boldsymbol{x}+\boldsymbol{z}$, then $\boldsymbol{y} = \mathbf{0}+\boldsymbol{y} = (-\boldsymbol{x}+\boldsymbol{x})+\boldsymbol{y} = -\boldsymbol{x}+(\boldsymbol{x}+\boldsymbol{y}) = -\boldsymbol{x}+(\boldsymbol{x}+\boldsymbol{z}) = (-\boldsymbol{x} + \boldsymbol{x}) + \boldsymbol{z} = \mathbf{0} + \boldsymbol{z} = \boldsymbol{z}$.

Exercise 3.3 (Elementary properties of scalar multiplication) Show that in any vector space:
(a) $\alpha\mathbf{0} = \mathbf{0}$;
(b) $0\boldsymbol{x} = \mathbf{0}$;

(c) $\alpha \boldsymbol{x} = \mathbf{0}$ implies $\alpha = 0$ or $\boldsymbol{x} = \mathbf{0}$ (or both);
(d) $(-\alpha)\boldsymbol{x} = \alpha(-\boldsymbol{x}) = -\alpha\boldsymbol{x}$;
(e) $\alpha\boldsymbol{x} = \alpha\boldsymbol{y}$ and $\alpha \neq 0$ implies $\boldsymbol{x} = \boldsymbol{y}$;
(f) $\alpha\boldsymbol{x} = \beta\boldsymbol{x}$ and $\boldsymbol{x} \neq \mathbf{0}$ implies $\alpha = \beta$;
(g) $(\alpha - \beta)\boldsymbol{x} = \alpha\boldsymbol{x} - \beta\boldsymbol{x}$;
(h) $\alpha(\boldsymbol{x} - \boldsymbol{y}) = \alpha\boldsymbol{x} - \alpha\boldsymbol{y}$.

Solution
(a) By Axiom A3, we have $\mathbf{0} + \mathbf{0} = \mathbf{0}$. Hence, by Axiom C1,

$$\alpha\mathbf{0} = \alpha(\mathbf{0} + \mathbf{0}) = \alpha\mathbf{0} + \alpha\mathbf{0}.$$

Now add $-\alpha\mathbf{0}$ to both sides.
(b) Axiom C2 gives $0\boldsymbol{x} = (0 + 0)\boldsymbol{x} = 0\boldsymbol{x} + 0\boldsymbol{x}$. Now add $-0\boldsymbol{x}$ to both sides.
(c) Suppose $\alpha\boldsymbol{x} = \mathbf{0}$ and $\alpha \neq 0$. Then there exists a scalar α^{-1} such that $\alpha^{-1}\alpha = 1$. Thus,

$$\boldsymbol{x} = 1\boldsymbol{x} = (\alpha^{-1}\alpha)\boldsymbol{x} = \alpha^{-1}(\alpha\boldsymbol{x}) = \alpha^{-1}\mathbf{0} = \mathbf{0}.$$

(This is not as trivial as it may seem. There are objects that have the property that $ab = 0$ without either a or b being zero. For example, the two matrices

$$\boldsymbol{A} = \begin{pmatrix} 0 & \alpha \\ 0 & 0 \end{pmatrix} \quad \text{and} \quad \boldsymbol{B} = \begin{pmatrix} 0 & \beta \\ 0 & 0 \end{pmatrix}$$

satisfy $\boldsymbol{AB} = \mathbf{O}$ without either being zero.)
(d) Using $\boldsymbol{x} + (-\boldsymbol{x}) = \mathbf{0}$ and $\alpha + (-\alpha) = 0$ gives

$$\mathbf{0} = \alpha\mathbf{0} = \alpha(\boldsymbol{x} + (-\boldsymbol{x})) = \alpha\boldsymbol{x} + \alpha(-\boldsymbol{x}), \quad \mathbf{0} = 0\boldsymbol{x} = (\alpha + (-\alpha))\boldsymbol{x} = \alpha\boldsymbol{x} + (-\alpha)\boldsymbol{x}.$$

Then, adding $-\alpha\boldsymbol{x}$ to both sides of both equations, we find $-\alpha\boldsymbol{x} = \alpha(-\boldsymbol{x})$ and $-\alpha\boldsymbol{x} = (-\alpha)\boldsymbol{x}$.
(e) Since $\alpha \neq 0$, α^{-1} exists. Hence,

$$\begin{aligned} \boldsymbol{x} = 1\boldsymbol{x} &= (\alpha^{-1}\alpha)\boldsymbol{x} = \alpha^{-1}(\alpha\boldsymbol{x}) = \alpha^{-1}(\alpha\boldsymbol{y}) \\ &= (\alpha^{-1}\alpha)\boldsymbol{y} = 1\boldsymbol{y} = \boldsymbol{y}. \end{aligned}$$

(f) Subtracting $\alpha\boldsymbol{x}$ from both sides of $\alpha\boldsymbol{x} = \beta\boldsymbol{x}$ gives $\mathbf{0} = \beta\boldsymbol{x} - \alpha\boldsymbol{x} = (\beta - \alpha)\boldsymbol{x}$. The result then follows from (c).
(g) We have $(\alpha - \beta)\boldsymbol{x} = (\alpha + (-\beta))\boldsymbol{x} = \alpha\boldsymbol{x} + (-\beta)\boldsymbol{x} = \alpha\boldsymbol{x} - \beta\boldsymbol{x}$.
(h) Property (d) gives $\alpha(-\boldsymbol{x}) = -\alpha\boldsymbol{x}$. Hence,

$$\alpha(\boldsymbol{x} - \boldsymbol{y}) = \alpha(\boldsymbol{x} + (-\boldsymbol{y})) = \alpha\boldsymbol{x} + \alpha(-\boldsymbol{y}) = \alpha\boldsymbol{x} + (-\alpha\boldsymbol{y}) = \alpha\boldsymbol{x} - \alpha\boldsymbol{y}.$$

Exercise 3.4 (Examples of real vector spaces) Show that the following sets are real vector spaces and indicate in each case what the "vectors" are and what the "null vector" is:
(a) $\mathbb{R}$, the set of real numbers;
(b) $\mathbb{R}^m$, the set of real $m \times 1$ vectors;
(c) $\mathbb{R}^{m \times n}$, the set of real $m \times n$ matrices.

Solution
(a) If we interpret $x + y$ and αx as the usual addition and multiplication of real numbers, then all parts of axioms A, B, and C hold. "Vectors" are simply real numbers, and the "null vector" is the number zero.
(b) If $\boldsymbol{x} := (x_1, \dots, x_m)'$ and $\boldsymbol{y} := (y_1, \dots, y_m)'$ are vectors in $\mathbb{R}^m$, we have, for $\alpha \in \mathbb{R}$,

$$\boldsymbol{x} + \boldsymbol{y} = (x_1 + y_1, \dots, x_m + y_m)' \quad \text{and} \quad \alpha\boldsymbol{x} = (\alpha x_1, \dots, \alpha x_m)'.$$

It is easy to verify that axioms A, B, and C are satisfied. For example the relation $x_i + 0 = x_i$ implies $\boldsymbol{x} + \boldsymbol{0} = \boldsymbol{x}$. A "vector" in $\mathbb{R}^m$ is an m-tuple of real numbers, and the "null" vector is $\boldsymbol{0} = (0, \dots, 0)'$.
(c) Defining the sum of two $m \times n$ matrices $\boldsymbol{A} = (a_{ij})$ and $\boldsymbol{B} = (b_{ij})$ as $\boldsymbol{A} + \boldsymbol{B} = (a_{ij} + b_{ij})$, and scalar multiplication as $\alpha\boldsymbol{A} = (\alpha a_{ij})$ (where $\alpha \in \mathbb{R}$), the three axioms are again satisfied. A "vector" is now a matrix and the "null vector" is the null matrix $\mathbf{O}$.

Exercise 3.5 (Space l_2) The set of real (or complex) sequences $(x_1, x_2, \dots)$ satisfying $\sum_{i=1}^{\infty} |x_i|^2 < \infty$ is called the real (or complex) l_2-space. Show that l_2 is a vector space.

Solution
Addition and scalar multiplication are defined as usual:

$$(x_1, x_2, \dots) + (y_1, y_2, \dots) = (x_1 + y_1, x_2 + y_2, \dots)$$

and

$$\alpha(x_1, x_2, \dots) = (\alpha x_1, \alpha x_2, \dots).$$

If $\boldsymbol{x} = (x_i) \in l_2$ and $\boldsymbol{y} = (y_i) \in l_2$, then $\boldsymbol{x} + \boldsymbol{y} \in l_2$, because

$$\sum_{i=1}^{\infty} |x_i + y_i|^2 \leq 2\sum_{i=1}^{\infty} |x_i|^2 + 2\sum_{i=1}^{\infty} |y_i|^2 < \infty.$$

Also, $\alpha\boldsymbol{x} \in l_2$, because $\sum_i |\alpha x_i|^2 = |\alpha|^2 \sum_i |x_i|^2 < \infty$. The other required properties are easily checked. The "null vector" is the sequence $(0, 0, \dots)$. (There is one very important difference between the spaces $\mathbb{R}^m$ and $\mathbb{C}^m$ on the one hand and the space l_2 on the other: the spaces $\mathbb{R}^m$ and $\mathbb{C}^m$ are finite dimensional, whereas the space l_2 is infinite dimensional. We don't know yet what this means, but this will become clear shortly.)

*__Exercise 3.6 (Space $L_2^{\dagger}$ of random variables, sample)__ Let $\{x_1, \dots, x_n\}$ be a finite collection of random variables with $\mathrm{E}(x_i^2) < \infty$ $(i = 1, \dots, n)$. Show that the set of all linear combinations $\sum_{i=1}^{n} \alpha_i x_i$ constitutes a vector space, which we denote by $L_2^{\dagger}$. (This is idiosyncratic notation, but is justified by the fact that $L_2^{\dagger}$ is a subspace of L_2, to be introduced in Exercise 3.7.)

Solution
If $y := \sum_i \alpha_i x_i \in L_2^{\dagger}$ and $z := \sum_i \beta_i x_i \in L_2^{\dagger}$, then $y + z = \sum_i (\alpha_i + \beta_i) x_i \in L_2^{\dagger}$, and $\lambda y = \sum_i (\lambda\alpha_i) x_i \in L_2^{\dagger}$. All properties of vector space are easily verified, except for one

difficulty. The difficulty is that a random variable $y = \sum_i \alpha_i x_i$ might also be expressible as $y = \sum_i \beta_i x_i$, where $(\alpha_1, \dots, \alpha_n) \neq (\beta_1, \dots, \beta_n)$. We resolve this difficulty by defining equivalence classes, as follows. The equality $\Pr(y = z) = 1$ defines an equivalence class for the coefficients of the representation. If y and z are in the same equivalence class, then they are equal with probability one; we say *almost surely* equal. Thus, instead of the random variables, we consider the induced equivalence classes. The "null vector" in $L_2^\dagger$ is then the equivalence class for which $\Pr(y = 0) = 1$, of which the vector $(\alpha_1, \dots, \alpha_n) = (0, \dots, 0)$ is obviously a member.

Exercise 3.7 (Space L_2 of random variables, population) Consider a collection $\mathcal{V}$ of all real random variables x satisfying the condition $\mathrm{E}(x^2) < \infty$. With the usual definition of multiplication by a real nonrandom scalar and addition of random variables, show that $\mathcal{V}$ is a real vector space.

Solution

We have, for all $x, y \in \mathcal{V}$ and $\alpha \in \mathbb{R}$,

$$\mathrm{E}\left((\alpha x)^2\right) = \alpha^2 \,\mathrm{E}(x^2) < \infty$$

and

$$\mathrm{E}\left((x + y)^2\right) \leq 2\,\mathrm{E}(x^2) + 2\,\mathrm{E}(y^2) < \infty.$$

The other required properties are easy to check. Notice that the "null vector" in L_2 is the class of random variables that are zero with probability 1 (almost surely).

Exercise 3.8 (Subspace) A nonempty subset $\mathcal{A}$ of a vector space $\mathcal{V}$ is a subspace of $\mathcal{V}$ if, for all $\boldsymbol{x}, \boldsymbol{y} \in \mathcal{A}$, we have $\boldsymbol{x} + \boldsymbol{y} \in \mathcal{A}$ and $\alpha\boldsymbol{x} \in \mathcal{A}$ for any scalar α.

(a) Show that $\mathcal{A}$ is a vector space.

(b) Show that every subspace contains the null vector.

(c) What is the smallest subspace of $\mathcal{V}$? What is the largest?

Solution

(a) By definition, a subspace is a subset that is "closed" under addition and scalar multiplication. These two operations follow the rules of the larger space $\mathcal{V}$, without taking us out of the subspace. Since the axioms of a vector space hold in $\mathcal{V}$, they will automatically hold in $\mathcal{A}$ as well.

(b) Choose $\alpha = 0$. Then $\alpha\boldsymbol{x} = 0\boldsymbol{x} = \boldsymbol{0}$ lies in $\mathcal{A}$.

(c) The smallest subspace is $\{\boldsymbol{0}\}$. The largest is $\mathcal{V}$.

Exercise 3.9 (Subspaces of $\mathbb{R}^2$)

(a) Show that the set of real 2×1 vectors whose first component is zero is a subspace of $\mathbb{R}^2$.

(b) Is the set of real 2×1 vectors whose first component is one also a subspace of $\mathbb{R}^2$?

(c) Is the set $\{(x,y), x \geq 0, y \geq 0\}$ a subspace of $\mathbb{R}^2$?
(d) Show that the only subspaces of $\mathbb{R}^2$ are $\mathbb{R}^2$ itself, the set $\{\mathbf{0}\}$, and any line through the origin.

Solution
(a) We take a linear combination of two arbitrary vectors in the subset,

$$\alpha \begin{pmatrix} 0 \\ x \end{pmatrix} + \beta \begin{pmatrix} 0 \\ y \end{pmatrix} = \begin{pmatrix} 0 \\ \alpha x + \beta y \end{pmatrix},$$

and see that the resulting vector also lies in the subset.
(b) No, because

$$2 \begin{pmatrix} 1 \\ x \end{pmatrix} = \begin{pmatrix} 2 \\ 2x \end{pmatrix} \neq \lambda \begin{pmatrix} 1 \\ 2x \end{pmatrix}.$$

(c) No, because $(1,1)'$ lies in the set, but $-(1,1)'$ does not.
(d) Let $\mathcal{A}$ be a subspace of $\mathbb{R}^2$, and assume that $\mathcal{A}$ is neither the set $\{\mathbf{0}\}$ nor a line through the origin. We need to show that $\mathcal{A} = \mathbb{R}^2$. Since $\mathcal{A} \neq \{\mathbf{0}\}$, $\mathcal{A}$ contains at least two (different) points (vectors), say $\boldsymbol{a}$ and $\boldsymbol{b}$. Since $\boldsymbol{a}$ and $\boldsymbol{b}$ are not on the same line through the origin, there are at least two lines in $\mathcal{A}$, intersecting at the origin. Any point in $\mathbb{R}^2$ can now be written as $\alpha\boldsymbol{a} + \beta\boldsymbol{b}$ for some α and β, and hence lies in $\mathcal{A}$.

Exercise 3.10 (Subspaces of $\mathbb{R}^3$) Which of the following subsets of $\mathbb{R}^3$ are subspaces?
(a) The plane of vectors $(x,y,z)'$ with $x = 0$ (the y-z plane).
(b) The plane of vectors $(x,y,z)'$ satisfying $xy = 0$ (the union of the y-z plane and the x-z plane).
(c) The null vector $(x,y,z)' = (0,0,0)'$.
(d) All linear combinations of two given vectors in $\mathbb{R}^3$.
(e) The vectors $(x,y,z)'$ satisfying $\alpha x + \beta y + \gamma z = 0$ (a plane through the origin).

Solution
Only the set in (b) is not a subspace, because the two vectors $(0,1,0)'$ and $(1,0,0)'$ are in the subset but their sum is not.

Exercise 3.11 (Subspaces of $\mathbb{R}^{3\times 3}$) In the vector space $\mathbb{R}^{3\times 3}$ (the set of real matrices of order 3×3), show that the set of lower triangular matrices is a subspace. Is the set of symmetric matrices also a subspace?

Solution
The set of lower triangular matrices is a subspace of $\mathbb{R}^{3\times 3}$, because if $\boldsymbol{A}$ and $\boldsymbol{B}$ are both lower triangular, then $\boldsymbol{A} + \boldsymbol{B}$ and $\alpha\boldsymbol{A}$ are also lower triangular. Similarly, if $\boldsymbol{A}$ and $\boldsymbol{B}$ are symmetric, then $\boldsymbol{A}+\boldsymbol{B}$ and $\alpha\boldsymbol{A}$ are also symmetric, implying that symmetric matrices also define a subspace.

Exercise 3.12 (Intersection, union, sum) The intersection $\mathcal{A} \cap \mathcal{B}$ of two subspaces $\mathcal{A}$ and $\mathcal{B}$ in a vector space $\mathcal{V}$ consists of all vectors that belong to both $\mathcal{A}$ and $\mathcal{B}$; the union $\mathcal{A} \cup \mathcal{B}$ consists of all vectors that belong to at least one of the sets $\mathcal{A}$ and $\mathcal{B}$; and the sum $\mathcal{A} + \mathcal{B}$ consists of all vectors of the form $\boldsymbol{a} + \boldsymbol{b}$ where $\boldsymbol{a} \in \mathcal{A}$ and $\boldsymbol{b} \in \mathcal{B}$.
(a) Show that the intersection of two subspaces of $\mathcal{V}$ is a subspace of $\mathcal{V}$.
(b) Show that the union of two subspaces of $\mathcal{V}$ is not necessarily a subspace of $\mathcal{V}$.
(c) Show that the sum of two subspaces of $\mathcal{V}$ is a subspace of $\mathcal{V}$.

Solution
(a) The intersection $\mathcal{A} \cap \mathcal{B}$ is not empty since the null vector lies in both $\mathcal{A}$ and $\mathcal{B}$. If $\boldsymbol{x}$ and $\boldsymbol{y}$ are in $\mathcal{A} \cap \mathcal{B}$, they are in both $\mathcal{A}$ and $\mathcal{B}$. Therefore $\alpha\boldsymbol{x} + \beta\boldsymbol{y}$ is in both $\mathcal{A}$ and $\mathcal{B}$ and hence in the intersection.
(b) Exercise 3.10(b) provides a counterexample.
(c) It is clear that $\mathcal{A} + \mathcal{B}$ contains the null vector. Let $\boldsymbol{x}$ and $\boldsymbol{y}$ be two vectors in $\mathcal{A} + \mathcal{B}$. Consider the vectors $\boldsymbol{a}_1, \boldsymbol{a}_2 \in \mathcal{A}$, and $\boldsymbol{b}_1, \boldsymbol{b}_2 \in \mathcal{B}$ such that $\boldsymbol{x} = \boldsymbol{a}_1 + \boldsymbol{b}_1$, $\boldsymbol{y} = \boldsymbol{a}_2 + \boldsymbol{b}_2$. We have $\boldsymbol{x} + \boldsymbol{y} = (\boldsymbol{a}_1 + \boldsymbol{a}_2) + (\boldsymbol{b}_1 + \boldsymbol{b}_2)$, and $\alpha\boldsymbol{x} = (\alpha\boldsymbol{a}_1) + (\alpha\boldsymbol{b}_1)$ for any scalar α. The result then follows, since $(\boldsymbol{a}_1 + \boldsymbol{a}_2)$ and $\alpha\boldsymbol{a}_1$ are in $\mathcal{A}$ and $(\boldsymbol{b}_1 + \boldsymbol{b}_2)$ and $\alpha\boldsymbol{b}_1$ are in $\mathcal{B}$.

Exercise 3.13 (Uniqueness of sum) If $\mathcal{A}$ and $\mathcal{B}$ are two subspaces of a vector space $\mathcal{V}$, then show that:
(a) if $\mathcal{A} \cap \mathcal{B} = \{\boldsymbol{0}\}$, then every vector in $\mathcal{A} + \mathcal{B}$ can be written uniquely as $\boldsymbol{a} + \boldsymbol{b}$, where $\boldsymbol{a} \in \mathcal{A}$ and $\boldsymbol{b} \in \mathcal{B}$;
(b) if $\mathcal{A} \cap \mathcal{B} \neq \{\boldsymbol{0}\}$, then there exist vectors in $\mathcal{A} + \mathcal{B}$ that *cannot* be written uniquely as $\boldsymbol{a} + \boldsymbol{b}$, $\boldsymbol{a} \in \mathcal{A}$, $\boldsymbol{b} \in \mathcal{B}$.

Solution
(a) Let $\mathcal{A} \cap \mathcal{B} = \{\boldsymbol{0}\}$, and assume that $\boldsymbol{x} \in \mathcal{A} + \mathcal{B}$ can be written as $\boldsymbol{x} = \boldsymbol{a}_1 + \boldsymbol{b}_1$ and also as $\boldsymbol{x} = \boldsymbol{a}_2 + \boldsymbol{b}_2$. This gives $\boldsymbol{a}_1 - \boldsymbol{a}_2 = \boldsymbol{b}_2 - \boldsymbol{b}_1$. But $\boldsymbol{a}_1 - \boldsymbol{a}_2 \in \mathcal{A}$ and $\boldsymbol{b}_2 - \boldsymbol{b}_1 \in \mathcal{B}$. Hence, $\boldsymbol{a}_1 - \boldsymbol{a}_2 = \boldsymbol{b}_2 - \boldsymbol{b}_1 = \boldsymbol{0}$, or $\boldsymbol{a}_1 = \boldsymbol{a}_2$, $\boldsymbol{b}_1 = \boldsymbol{b}_2$.
(b) Let $\boldsymbol{x} \neq \boldsymbol{0}$ and assume that $\boldsymbol{x} \in \mathcal{A} \cap \mathcal{B}$. Then $\boldsymbol{x}$ can be written as $\boldsymbol{x} + \boldsymbol{0}$ (with $\boldsymbol{x} \in \mathcal{A}$, $\boldsymbol{0} \in \mathcal{B}$), but also as $\boldsymbol{0} + \boldsymbol{x}$ ($\boldsymbol{0} \in \mathcal{A}$, $\boldsymbol{x} \in \mathcal{B}$).

Exercise 3.14 (Linear combination) A linear combination of the vectors $\boldsymbol{x}_1, \boldsymbol{x}_2, \dots, \boldsymbol{x}_n$ in a vector space is a sum of the form $\alpha_1\boldsymbol{x}_1 + \alpha_2\boldsymbol{x}_2 + \dots + \alpha_n\boldsymbol{x}_n$. Show that a linear combination of vectors from a subspace is also in the subspace.

Solution
Consider two linear combinations of $\boldsymbol{x}_1, \boldsymbol{x}_2, \dots, \boldsymbol{x}_n$,

$$\boldsymbol{y} := \alpha_1\boldsymbol{x}_1 + \alpha_2\boldsymbol{x}_2 + \dots + \alpha_n\boldsymbol{x}_n \quad \text{and} \quad \boldsymbol{z} := \beta_1\boldsymbol{x}_1 + \beta_2\boldsymbol{x}_2 + \dots + \beta_n\boldsymbol{x}_n.$$

Then,

$$\boldsymbol{x} + \boldsymbol{y} = (\alpha_1 + \beta_1)\boldsymbol{x}_1 + \dots + (\alpha_n + \beta_n)\boldsymbol{x}_n \quad \text{and} \quad \lambda\boldsymbol{y} = (\lambda\alpha_1)\boldsymbol{x}_1 + \dots + (\lambda\alpha_n)\boldsymbol{x}_n$$

are also linear combinations of $\boldsymbol{x}_1, \dots, \boldsymbol{x}_n$.

Exercise 3.15 (Linear dependence, theory) A finite set of vectors $\boldsymbol{x}_1, \ldots, \boldsymbol{x}_n$ ($n \geq 1$) is linearly dependent if there exist scalars $\alpha_1, \ldots, \alpha_n$, not all zero, such that $\alpha_1\boldsymbol{x}_1 + \cdots + \alpha_n\boldsymbol{x}_n = \mathbf{0}$; otherwise it is linearly independent. An arbitrary subset A of $\mathcal{V}$ (containing possibly an infinite number of vectors) is linearly independent if every nonempty finite subset of A is linearly independent; otherwise it is linearly dependent. Show that:
(a) the null vector by itself is a linearly dependent set;
(b) any set of vectors containing the null vector is a linearly dependent set;
(c) a set of nonzero vectors $\boldsymbol{x}_1, \ldots, \boldsymbol{x}_n$ is linearly dependent if and only if a member in the set is a linear combination of the others;
(d) a set of nonzero vectors $\boldsymbol{x}_1, \ldots, \boldsymbol{x}_n$ is linearly dependent if and only if some $\boldsymbol{x}_j$ ($2 \leq j \leq n$) is a linear combination of its predecessors.

Solution
(a) This is trivially true, because there exists a scalar $\alpha \neq 0$ such that $\alpha\mathbf{0} = \mathbf{0}$.
(b) Suppose $\boldsymbol{x}_1 = \mathbf{0}$. Then the set $(\alpha_1, \alpha_2, \ldots, \alpha_n) = (1, 0, \ldots, 0)$ is a nontrivial set that produces $\alpha_1\boldsymbol{x}_1 + \cdots + \alpha_n\boldsymbol{x}_n = \mathbf{0}$.
(c) Let a member be a linear combination of the others, say $\boldsymbol{x}_j = \sum_{i \neq j} \alpha_i\boldsymbol{x}_i$. Choosing $\alpha_j = -1$, gives $\sum_{i=1}^n \alpha_i\boldsymbol{x}_i = \mathbf{0}$. Conversely, linear dependence implies that $\sum_{i=1}^n \alpha_i\boldsymbol{x}_i = \mathbf{0}$ for some choice of $\alpha_1, \ldots, \alpha_n$, not all zero. Let $\alpha_j \neq 0$. Then $\boldsymbol{x}_j$ can be written as $\boldsymbol{x}_j = \sum_{i \neq j}(-\alpha_i/\alpha_j)\boldsymbol{x}_i$.
(d) If $\boldsymbol{x}_j$ is a linear combination of $\boldsymbol{x}_1, \ldots, \boldsymbol{x}_{j-1}$, say $\boldsymbol{x}_j = \sum_{i=1}^{j-1} \alpha_i\boldsymbol{x}_i$, then also $\boldsymbol{x}_j = \sum_{i \neq j} \alpha_i\boldsymbol{x}_i$ (by choosing $\alpha_i = 0$ for $i > j$). Hence, $\boldsymbol{x}_1, \ldots, \boldsymbol{x}_n$ are linearly dependent, by (c). Conversely, if $\sum_{i=1}^n \alpha_i\boldsymbol{x}_i = \mathbf{0}$, then $\boldsymbol{x}_n$ depends linearly on its predecessors or $\alpha_n = 0$. If $\alpha_n = 0$, then $\boldsymbol{x}_{n-1}$ depends on its predecessors or $\alpha_{n-1} = 0$. Continuing in this way, and using the fact that at least one of the α_i must be nonzero, we find that one of the $\boldsymbol{x}_i$ ($i \geq 2$) must depend on its predecessors (since $\boldsymbol{x}_1 \neq \mathbf{0}$).

Exercise 3.16 (Linear dependence and triangularity)
(a) Show that the columns of the $n \times n$ identity matrix $\boldsymbol{I}_n$ are linearly independent.
(b) Show that the columns of the matrix

$$\boldsymbol{A} = \begin{pmatrix} 1 & 3 & 2 & 0 \\ 1 & -5 & -3 & 1 \\ 5 & -1 & 0 & 2 \end{pmatrix}$$

are linearly dependent. How about the rows?
(c) Show that the columns of a triangular matrix are linearly independent if and only if all diagonal elements are nonzero.

Solution
(a) Let $\boldsymbol{e}_i$ ($i = 1, \ldots, n$) denote the columns of $\boldsymbol{I}_n$, and suppose $\sum_{i=1}^n \alpha_i\boldsymbol{e}_i = \mathbf{0}$. This implies $\alpha_1 = \alpha_2 = \cdots = \alpha_n = 0$.

(b) The columns $\boldsymbol{a}_{\bullet 1}, \ldots, \boldsymbol{a}_{\bullet 4}$ satisfy, for example, $3\boldsymbol{a}_{\bullet 1} - \boldsymbol{a}_{\bullet 2} - 8\boldsymbol{a}_{\bullet 4} = \mathbf{0}$. The rows $\boldsymbol{a}'_{1\bullet}$, $\boldsymbol{a}'_{2\bullet}$, $\boldsymbol{a}'_{3\bullet}$ satisfy $3\boldsymbol{a}_{1\bullet} + 2\boldsymbol{a}_{2\bullet} - \boldsymbol{a}_{3\bullet} = \mathbf{0}$. So, both the columns and the rows are linearly dependent.
(c) Suppose the matrix $\boldsymbol{X} = (x_{ij})$ is lower triangular. The linear combination $\alpha_1 \boldsymbol{x}_{\bullet 1} + \cdots + \alpha_n \boldsymbol{x}_{\bullet n}$ is equal to zero if and only if

$$\begin{aligned} \alpha_1 x_{11} &= 0 \\ \alpha_1 x_{21} + \alpha_2 x_{22} &= 0 \\ &\vdots \\ \alpha_1 x_{n1} + \alpha_2 x_{n2} + \cdots + \alpha_n x_{nn} &= 0. \end{aligned}$$

If $x_{ii} \neq 0$ for all i, then these equations imply successively that $\alpha_1 = 0$, $\alpha_2 = 0$, ..., $\alpha_n = 0$.

We prove the converse by contrapositive. Let $x_{ii} = 0$ for some i. If $x_{ii} = 0$ for more than one i, choose $i := \max\{j : x_{jj} = 0\}$, so that $x_{jj} \neq 0$ for $j > i$. Choose $\alpha_1 = \cdots = \alpha_{i-1} = 0$ and $\alpha_i = 1$. Then the first i equations are satisfied, and the last $n - i$ equations take the form

$$\begin{aligned} x_{i+1,i} + \alpha_{i+1} x_{i+1,i+1} &= 0, \\ &\vdots \\ x_{ni} + \alpha_{i+1} x_{n,i+1} + \cdots + \alpha_n x_{nn} &= 0. \end{aligned}$$

From these equations we successively solve $\alpha_{i+1}, \ldots, \alpha_n$. Hence, there exists a nontrivial set of α's (since $\alpha_i = 1$) such that $\sum_j \alpha_j \boldsymbol{x}_j = \mathbf{0}$.

Exercise 3.17 (Linear dependence, some examples)
(a) If $\boldsymbol{x}$, $\boldsymbol{y}$, and $\boldsymbol{z}$ are linearly independent vectors, are $\boldsymbol{x}+\boldsymbol{y}$, $\boldsymbol{x}+\boldsymbol{z}$, and $\boldsymbol{y}+\boldsymbol{z}$ also linearly independent?
(b) For which values of λ are the vectors $(\lambda, 1, 0)'$, $(1, \lambda, 1)'$, and $(0, 1, \lambda)'$ linearly dependent?

Solution
(a) Yes. We have

$$\alpha(\boldsymbol{x}+\boldsymbol{y}) + \beta(\boldsymbol{x}+\boldsymbol{z}) + \gamma(\boldsymbol{y}+\boldsymbol{z}) = (\alpha+\beta)\boldsymbol{x} + (\alpha+\gamma)\boldsymbol{y} + (\beta+\gamma)\boldsymbol{z}.$$

Since $\boldsymbol{x}$, $\boldsymbol{y}$, and $\boldsymbol{z}$ are linearly independent, the above expression vanishes if and only if $\alpha + \beta = 0$, $\alpha + \gamma = 0$, and $\beta + \gamma = 0$, that is, if and only if $\alpha = \beta = \gamma = 0$.
(b) We need to find $(\alpha, \beta, \gamma) \neq (0, 0, 0)$ such that

$$\alpha\lambda + \beta = 0, \quad \alpha + \beta\lambda + \gamma = 0, \quad \beta + \gamma\lambda = 0.$$

The solutions are $\lambda = 0$ associated with $(\alpha, \beta, \gamma) = \kappa(1, 0, -1)$ and $\lambda = \pm\sqrt{2}$ associated with $(\alpha, \beta, \gamma) = \kappa(1, \mp\sqrt{2}, 1)$.

Exercise 3.18 (Spanned subspace) Let A be a nonempty set of elements of a vector space $\mathcal{V}$. The set $\mathcal{A}$ consisting of all linear combinations of vectors in A is called the subspace spanned (or generated) by A.

(a) Show that $\mathcal{A}$ is in fact a subspace of $\mathcal{V}$.
(b) Show that $\mathcal{A}$ is the smallest subspace containing A.

Solution
(a) This follows from the fact that a linear combination of linear combinations is also a linear combination.
(b) Let $\mathcal{B}$ be a subspace of $\mathcal{V}$, such that A is contained in $\mathcal{B}$. Then $\mathcal{B}$ contains all linear combinations from A, and hence $\mathcal{A} \subseteq \mathcal{B}$.

Exercise 3.19 (Spanned subspace in $\mathbb{R}^3$)
(a) Let A be a circle in $\mathbb{R}^3$ centered at the origin. What is the space $\mathcal{A}$ spanned by A?
(b) Let A be a plane in $\mathbb{R}^3$ not passing through the origin. What is $\mathcal{A}$?
(c) Consider the vectors $\boldsymbol{e}_1 = (1, 0, 0)'$, $\boldsymbol{e}_2 = (0, 1, 0)'$, and $\boldsymbol{v} = (0, -2, 0)'$ in $\mathbb{R}^3$. Show that the three vectors span a plane (the x-y plane), that $\boldsymbol{e}_1$ and $\boldsymbol{e}_2$ alone span the same plane, and that $\boldsymbol{e}_2$ and $\boldsymbol{v}$ span only a line.

Solution
(a) The plane containing the circle.
(b) The whole of $\mathbb{R}^3$. Contrast this with the plane in Figure 3.2.
(c) Letting $\lambda := \alpha_2 - 2\alpha_3$, we have $\alpha_1\boldsymbol{e}_1 + \alpha_2\boldsymbol{e}_2 + \alpha_3\boldsymbol{v} = \alpha_1\boldsymbol{e}_1 + \lambda\boldsymbol{e}_2$, and $\alpha_2\boldsymbol{e}_2 + \alpha_3\boldsymbol{v} = \lambda\boldsymbol{e}_2$. Hence, $\{\boldsymbol{e}_1, \boldsymbol{e}_2, \boldsymbol{v}\}$ and $\{\boldsymbol{e}_1, \boldsymbol{e}_2\}$ alone span the x-y plane (the plane $z = 0$), and $\{\boldsymbol{e}_2, \boldsymbol{v}\}$ spans the y-axis (the line $x = z = 0$).

Exercise 3.20 (Dimension) If a vector space $\mathcal{V}$ contains a finite set of n linearly independent vectors $\boldsymbol{x}_1, \boldsymbol{x}_2, \dots, \boldsymbol{x}_n$, and moreover any set of $n+1$ vectors is linearly dependent, then the dimension of $\mathcal{V}$ is n, and we write $\dim(\mathcal{V}) = n$. In this case $\mathcal{V}$ is said to be finite dimensional. If no such n exists, we say that $\mathcal{V}$ is infinite dimensional. Show that in a finite-dimensional vector space $\mathcal{V}$ of dimension n:
(a) no set of more than n vectors can be linearly independent;
(b) no set of fewer than n vectors can span the space.

Solution
(a) If $\dim(\mathcal{V}) = n$, then any set of $n+1$ vectors is linearly dependent, by definition.
(b) Since $\dim(\mathcal{V}) = n$, $\mathcal{V}$ contains n linearly independent vectors $\boldsymbol{x}_1, \boldsymbol{x}_2, \dots, \boldsymbol{x}_n$. Suppose $n-1$ vectors, say $\boldsymbol{v}_1, \dots, \boldsymbol{v}_{n-1}$, span $\mathcal{V}$. Consider the set $\{\boldsymbol{x}_1, \boldsymbol{v}_1, \dots, \boldsymbol{v}_{n-1}\}$. The vector $\boldsymbol{x}_1$ is a linear combination of $\{\boldsymbol{v}_i\}$, since $\{\boldsymbol{v}_i\}$ spans $\mathcal{V}$. Accordingly, the set $\{\boldsymbol{x}_1, \boldsymbol{v}_1, \dots, \boldsymbol{v}_{n-1}\}$ is linearly dependent and also spans $\mathcal{V}$. By Exercise 3.15(d), one of the vectors is a linear combination of its predecessors, say $\boldsymbol{v}_i$. Thus, $\{\boldsymbol{x}_1, \boldsymbol{v}_1, \dots, \boldsymbol{v}_{i-1}, \boldsymbol{v}_{i+1}, \dots, \boldsymbol{v}_{n-1}\}$ spans $\mathcal{V}$. We next add $\boldsymbol{x}_2$ and consider the dependent set $\{\boldsymbol{x}_1, \boldsymbol{x}_2, \boldsymbol{v}_1, \dots, \boldsymbol{v}_{i-1}, \boldsymbol{v}_{i+1}, \dots, \boldsymbol{v}_{n-1}\}$. Another $\boldsymbol{v}$ is omitted. Continuing in this way, and observing that none of the $\boldsymbol{x}_i$ are to be omitted, we conclude that $\{\boldsymbol{x}_1, \boldsymbol{x}_2, \dots, \boldsymbol{x}_{n-1}\}$ spans $\mathcal{V}$. Hence, $\boldsymbol{x}_n$ must be a linear combination of $\boldsymbol{x}_1, \dots, \boldsymbol{x}_{n-1}$, which contradicts the fact that $\boldsymbol{x}_1, \dots, \boldsymbol{x}_n$ are linearly independent.

***Exercise 3.21 (Finite dimension of $L_2^\dagger$)** Show that the space $L_2^\dagger$ is finite dimensional.

Solution

The space $L_2^\dagger$ was introduced in Exercise 3.6. It consists of all random variables of the form $\boldsymbol{a}'\boldsymbol{x}$, where $\boldsymbol{x} := (x_1, \dots, x_n)'$ is a random vector whose components x_i have finite second moments, $\mathrm{E}(x_i^2) < \infty$, and the components a_i of $\boldsymbol{a}$ are finite constants. Since we can find at most n linearly independent vectors $\boldsymbol{a}_j$ of order $n \times 1$, the dimension of $L_2^\dagger$ is at most n, hence finite. Notice that, if the variance matrix $\mathrm{var}(\boldsymbol{x})$ is positive definite, then $\dim(L_2^\dagger) = n$. If, however, $\mathrm{var}(\boldsymbol{x})$ is singular and has rank $r < n$, then there will be $n - r$ nontrivial linear combinations $\boldsymbol{a}'\boldsymbol{x}$ such that $\Pr(\boldsymbol{a}'\boldsymbol{x} = 0) = 1$. Then, $\dim(L_2^\dagger) = r$. (We don't know yet what the words "positive definite", "singular", and "rank" mean, but we will get to this in later chapters.)

Not all spaces are finite dimensional. For example, L_2-space, introduced in Exercise 3.7, is infinite dimensional. As a second example, consider real l_2-space, introduced in Exercise 3.5. This is the real vector space of all infinite sequences $(x_1, x_2, \dots)$ satisfying $\sum_{i=1}^{\infty} x_i^2 < \infty$. Define an inner product $\langle \boldsymbol{x}, \boldsymbol{y} \rangle := \sum_{i=1}^{\infty} x_i y_i$. Then l_2 is an infinite-dimensional inner-product space; see Exercise 3.35(d). A third example is provided in Exercise 6.31: In the space of all polynomials $p(x) := a_0 + a_1 x + \dots + a_n x^n$ (of degree $\leq n$), the functions $1, x, \dots, x^n$ are linearly independent for every $n = 1, 2, \dots$. This space has finite dimension $n + 1$. But the space of *all* polynomials $p(x)$ (of *all* degrees) is infinite dimensional.

Exercise 3.22 (Basis) If $\mathcal{V}$ is a vector space, not necessarily finite dimensional, and A is a set of linearly independent vectors from $\mathcal{V}$, such that $\mathcal{V}$ is spanned by A, then A is a basis of $\mathcal{V}$.

(a) Find a basis of $\mathbb{R}^3$.

(b) Find another basis of $\mathbb{R}^3$.

(c) Show that there are infinitely many bases of $\mathbb{R}^3$.

Solution

(a) The unit vectors $\boldsymbol{e}_1$, $\boldsymbol{e}_2$, $\boldsymbol{e}_3$ are the simplest choice of basis. They are, in fact, a basis, because every $\boldsymbol{x} := (x_1, x_2, x_3)'$ in $\mathbb{R}^3$ can be written as $\boldsymbol{x} = x_1\boldsymbol{e}_1 + x_2\boldsymbol{e}_2 + x_3\boldsymbol{e}_3$.

(b) The columns of

$$\begin{pmatrix} 1 & 0 & 0 \\ 0 & 2 & 0 \\ 2 & 0 & \alpha \end{pmatrix}$$

are also a basis for $\mathbb{R}^3$, provided $\alpha \neq 0$, because every $\boldsymbol{x}$ can be written as

$$x_1 \begin{pmatrix} 1 \\ 0 \\ 2 \end{pmatrix} + \left(\frac{1}{2}x_2\right) \begin{pmatrix} 0 \\ 2 \\ 0 \end{pmatrix} + \left(\frac{x_3 - 2x_1}{\alpha}\right) \begin{pmatrix} 0 \\ 0 \\ \alpha \end{pmatrix}.$$

(c) The matrix in (b) is a basis for every $\alpha \neq 0$.

Exercise 3.23 (Basis, numbers) Consider the matrix

$$A = \begin{pmatrix} 1 & 1 & 1 & 1 & 1 & 1 & 2 & 2 & 5 \\ 0 & 1 & 1 & 2 & 2 & 3 & -1 & 3 & 3 \\ 1 & 1 & 2 & 3 & 5 & 5 & 1 & 0 & 4 \end{pmatrix}$$

and denote the nine columns by $\boldsymbol{a}_1, \dots, \boldsymbol{a}_9$. Which of the following form a basis of $\mathbb{R}^3$?
(a) $\boldsymbol{a}_1$ and $\boldsymbol{a}_2$;
(b) $\boldsymbol{a}_1, \boldsymbol{a}_4, \boldsymbol{a}_6, \boldsymbol{a}_8$;
(c) $\boldsymbol{a}_2, \boldsymbol{a}_4, \boldsymbol{a}_7$;
(d) $\boldsymbol{a}_3, \boldsymbol{a}_5, \boldsymbol{a}_9$.

Solution
(a)–(b) No, because a basis of $\mathbb{R}^3$ must contain three vectors.
(c) Yes. The three vectors are a basis if and only if they are linearly independent. This is the case, because the three linear equations

$$x_1 + x_2 + 2x_3 = 0, \quad x_1 + 2x_2 - x_3 = 0, \quad x_1 + 3x_2 + x_3 = 0$$

have only $x_1 = x_2 = x_3 = 0$ as solution.
(d) No, because the three vectors are linearly dependent: $7\boldsymbol{a}_3 - 2\boldsymbol{a}_5 - \boldsymbol{a}_9 = 0$.

Exercise 3.24 (Basis for matrices)
(a) In the space of 2×2 matrices find a basis for the subspace of matrices whose row sums and column sums are all equal.
(b) Also find a basis for the 3×3 matrices with this property.

Solution
(a) The 2×2 matrices all have the form

$$\begin{pmatrix} a & b \\ b & a \end{pmatrix} = a \begin{pmatrix} 1 & 0 \\ 0 & 1 \end{pmatrix} + b \begin{pmatrix} 0 & 1 \\ 1 & 0 \end{pmatrix}.$$

Notice that the two matrices on the right-hand side satisfy the restriction that row sums and column sums are equal, as of course they must.
(b) The 3×3 matrices have the form

$$\begin{pmatrix} a & b & c+d+e \\ c & d & a+b+e \\ b+d+e & a+c+e & -e \end{pmatrix} = a \begin{pmatrix} 1 & 0 & 0 \\ 0 & 0 & 1 \\ 0 & 1 & 0 \end{pmatrix} + b \begin{pmatrix} 0 & 1 & 0 \\ 0 & 0 & 1 \\ 1 & 0 & 0 \end{pmatrix}$$

$$+ c \begin{pmatrix} 0 & 0 & 1 \\ 1 & 0 & 0 \\ 0 & 1 & 0 \end{pmatrix} + d \begin{pmatrix} 0 & 0 & 1 \\ 0 & 1 & 0 \\ 1 & 0 & 0 \end{pmatrix} + e \begin{pmatrix} 0 & 0 & 1 \\ 0 & 0 & 1 \\ 1 & 1 & -1 \end{pmatrix}.$$

The last of the five matrices on the right-hand side contains two identical rows (and two identical columns); it is a "singular" matrix (a concept to be introduced later). Thus, elements of a basis for a space of square matrices, may be singular.

Exercise 3.25 (Existence of basis) Every vector space $\mathcal{V} \neq \{0\}$ has a basis. Prove this in the finite-dimensional case.

Solution
Choose sequentially nonzero vectors $\boldsymbol{x}_1, \boldsymbol{x}_2, \ldots$ in $\mathcal{V}$, such that none of the $\boldsymbol{x}_i$ is linearly dependent on its predecessors. If there is no limit to this process, then $\mathcal{V}$ is infinite dimensional. Since $\mathcal{V}$ is finite dimensional, there is a number n, such that $\boldsymbol{x}_1, \ldots, \boldsymbol{x}_n$ are linearly independent and no linearly independent vector is left in $\mathcal{V}$. Thus, $\{\boldsymbol{x}_1, \ldots, \boldsymbol{x}_n\}$ constitute a basis in $\mathcal{V}$.

Exercise 3.26 (Unique representation in terms of a basis) Show that every nonzero vector in a finite-dimensional vector space $\mathcal{V}$ has a unique representation in terms of a given basis.

Solution
Let A be the given basis and let $\boldsymbol{x} \in \mathcal{V}$, $\boldsymbol{x} \neq \mathbf{0}$. Then there exists a set of linearly independent $\{\boldsymbol{x}_1, \ldots, \boldsymbol{x}_n\} \subset A$ such that $\boldsymbol{x} = \sum_{i=1}^n \alpha_i \boldsymbol{x}_i$. Suppose that there also exists a set of linearly independent $\{\boldsymbol{y}_1, \ldots, \boldsymbol{y}_m\} \subset A$ such that $\boldsymbol{x} = \sum_{j=1}^m \beta_j \boldsymbol{y}_j$. Then,

$$\sum_{i=1}^n \alpha_i \boldsymbol{x}_i - \sum_{j=1}^m \beta_j \boldsymbol{y}_j = \mathbf{0}.$$

If the two sets $\{\boldsymbol{x}_1, \ldots, \boldsymbol{x}_n\}$ and $\{\boldsymbol{y}_1, \ldots, \boldsymbol{y}_m\}$ do not overlap, then all $m + n$ vectors are linearly independent, and we find $\alpha_i = 0$ and $\beta_j = 0$ for all i and j. This gives $\boldsymbol{x} = \mathbf{0}$, a contradiction. Hence, the two sets overlap. Let $\{\boldsymbol{x}_1, \ldots, \boldsymbol{x}_p\}$ be the overlap, such that $\boldsymbol{y}_j = \boldsymbol{x}_j$ for $j = 1, \ldots, p$. Then,

$$\sum_{i=1}^p (\alpha_i - \beta_i)\boldsymbol{x}_i + \sum_{i=p+1}^n \alpha_i \boldsymbol{x}_i - \sum_{j=p+1}^m \beta_j \boldsymbol{y}_j = \mathbf{0},$$

implying that $\alpha_i = \beta_i$ $(i = 1, \ldots, p)$, $\alpha_i = 0$ $(i = p + 1, \ldots, n)$, and $\beta_j = 0$ $(j = p + 1, \ldots, m)$, and hence that $\boldsymbol{x}$ has the unique representation $\boldsymbol{x} = \sum_{i=1}^p \alpha_i \boldsymbol{x}_i$.

Exercise 3.27 (Reduction and extension to basis) Show that in any finite-dimensional vector space $\mathcal{V}$:
(a) any spanning set can be reduced to a basis, by discarding vectors if necessary;
(b) any linearly independent set can be extended to a basis, by adding more vectors if necessary.

Solution
(a) Consider the set $A := \{\boldsymbol{x}_1, \ldots, \boldsymbol{x}_m\}$, which spans $\mathcal{V}$. We now construct a basis as follows. First, delete all null vectors from A. Next, for $i = 2, \ldots, m$, if $\boldsymbol{x}_i$ is linearly dependent on its predecessors, delete $\boldsymbol{x}_i$ from A. The resulting set B contains only linearly independent vectors and still spans $\mathcal{V}$. Hence, it is a basis.

(b) Let $\{\boldsymbol{x}_1, \dots, \boldsymbol{x}_n\}$ be a basis of $\mathcal{V}$, and let $\{\boldsymbol{y}_1, \dots, \boldsymbol{y}_m\}$ be a linearly independent set in $\mathcal{V}$. Now consider the set

$$A := \{\boldsymbol{y}_1, \dots, \boldsymbol{y}_m, \boldsymbol{x}_1, \dots, \boldsymbol{x}_n\}.$$

This set spans $\mathcal{V}$. Applying the reduction algorithm from (a), we obtain a set B containing $\boldsymbol{y}_1, \dots, \boldsymbol{y}_m$ and a selection of $n - m$ vectors from $\{\boldsymbol{x}_1, \dots, \boldsymbol{x}_n\}$. The set B is a basis of $\mathcal{V}$.

Exercise 3.28 (Span and linear independence) Let $\mathcal{V}$ be a finite-dimensional vector space. Assume that $\{\boldsymbol{x}_1, \dots, \boldsymbol{x}_n\}$ spans $\mathcal{V}$ (but that the vectors are not necessarily linearly independent), and that $\{\boldsymbol{y}_1, \dots, \boldsymbol{y}_m\}$ are linearly independent (but that the set does not necessarily span $\mathcal{V}$). Show that $n \geq m$.

Solution

Suppose that $n < m$. Consider the set $A_1 := \{\boldsymbol{y}_m, \boldsymbol{x}_1, \dots, \boldsymbol{x}_n\}$ containing $n + 1$ vectors. The set A_1 spans $\mathcal{V}$ (because the $\{\boldsymbol{x}_i\}$ span $\mathcal{V}$) and A_1 is linearly dependent (because it contains more than n vectors). Remove from A_1 the first $\boldsymbol{x}_i$ that is a linear combination of its predecessors. This produces a set B_1 containing n vectors. The set B_1 also spans $\mathcal{V}$. Now define the set A_2 as the set B_1 with $\boldsymbol{y}_{m-1}$ added as the first vector. Then A_2 spans $\mathcal{V}$ and is linearly dependent. Continuing in this way we obtain, after n steps, a set B_n containing the vectors $\boldsymbol{y}_{m-n+1}, \dots, \boldsymbol{y}_m$. By construction, B_n spans $\mathcal{V}$. Hence, the vectors $\boldsymbol{y}_1, \dots, \boldsymbol{y}_{m-n}$ are linear combinations of the vectors in B_n. This is a contradiction, because the $\{\boldsymbol{y}_i\}$ are linearly independent. Hence, $n \geq m$.

Exercise 3.29 (Dimension of basis) Let $\mathcal{V}$ be a finite-dimensional vector space. Use Exercise 3.28 to show that every basis contains the same number of vectors.

Solution

Let $\{\boldsymbol{x}_1, \dots, \boldsymbol{x}_n\}$ and $\{\boldsymbol{y}_1, \dots, \boldsymbol{y}_m\}$ be two bases of $\mathcal{V}$. Then, $\{\boldsymbol{x}_1, \dots, \boldsymbol{x}_n\}$ spans $\mathcal{V}$ and $\{\boldsymbol{y}_1, \dots, \boldsymbol{y}_m\}$ is linearly independent. Hence, by Exercise 3.28, $n \geq m$. Similarly, $\{\boldsymbol{y}_1, \dots, \boldsymbol{y}_m\}$ spans $\mathcal{V}$ and $\{\boldsymbol{x}_1, \dots, \boldsymbol{x}_n\}$ is linearly independent. Hence, $m \geq n$. The result follows.

Exercise 3.30 (Basis and dimension) Let $\mathcal{V}$ be a finite-dimensional vector space with $\dim(\mathcal{V}) = n$.

(a) Show that every set of n linearly independent vectors in $\mathcal{V}$ constitutes a basis of $\mathcal{V}$.

(b) Show that every basis of $\mathcal{V}$ contains n (linearly independent) vectors.

Solution

(a) Let $\boldsymbol{x}_1, \dots, \boldsymbol{x}_n$ be a set of linearly independent vectors in $\mathcal{V}$, and let $\boldsymbol{x} \in \mathcal{V}$ be arbitrary. Since the set $\{\boldsymbol{x}, \boldsymbol{x}_1, \dots, \boldsymbol{x}_n\}$ is linearly dependent (it contains $n + 1$ vectors), there exist scalars, not all zero, such that

$$\alpha \boldsymbol{x} + \alpha_1 \boldsymbol{x}_1 + \cdots + \alpha_n \boldsymbol{x}_n = \mathbf{0}.$$

If α were zero, this would imply that the $\{\boldsymbol{x}_i\}$ are linearly dependent, which they are not. Hence, $\alpha \neq 0$ and we can write $\boldsymbol{x}$ as a linear combination of $\boldsymbol{x}_1, \dots, \boldsymbol{x}_n$. Since $\boldsymbol{x}$ is an arbitrary vector in $\mathcal{V}$, this shows that the $\boldsymbol{x}_i$ span $\mathcal{V}$. Since they are also linearly independent, they constitute a basis.
(b) By (a) there exists a basis containing n vectors. By Exercise 3.29 every basis has the same number of vectors. Hence, every basis has n vectors.

Exercise 3.31 (Basis and dimension, numbers) Let $\mathcal{A}$ be the subspace of $\mathbb{R}^4$ spanned by the columns of the matrix

$$\boldsymbol{A} = \begin{pmatrix} 1 & 2 & 3 \\ -2 & 3 & 8 \\ 5 & 1 & -3 \\ -3 & -4 & -5 \end{pmatrix}.$$

(a) Find a basis of $\mathcal{A}$.
(b) What is the dimension of $\mathcal{A}$?
(c) Extend the basis of $\mathcal{A}$ to a basis of $\mathbb{R}^4$.

Solution
(a) Let $\boldsymbol{a}_1, \boldsymbol{a}_2, \boldsymbol{a}_3$ denote the columns of $\boldsymbol{A}$. It is clear that $\boldsymbol{a}_1$ and $\boldsymbol{a}_2$ are linearly independent (otherwise they would be proportional). But $\boldsymbol{a}_1 - 2\boldsymbol{a}_2 + \boldsymbol{a}_3 = 0$, so that $\{\boldsymbol{a}_1, \boldsymbol{a}_2, \boldsymbol{a}_3\}$ are linearly dependent. Hence, $\{\boldsymbol{a}_1, \boldsymbol{a}_2\}$ is a basis of $\mathcal{A}$.
(b) $\dim(\mathcal{A}) = 2$.
(c) There are infinitely many solutions. We need to find two vectors, say $\boldsymbol{v}_1$ and $\boldsymbol{v}_2$ such that $\{\boldsymbol{a}_1, \boldsymbol{a}_2, \boldsymbol{v}_1, \boldsymbol{v}_2\}$ is a basis of $\mathbb{R}^4$. A simple solution is $\boldsymbol{v}_1 = (0, 0, 1, 0)'$ and $\boldsymbol{v}_2 = (0, 0, 0, 1)'$.

Exercise 3.32 (Dimension of subspace) Let $\mathcal{A}$ be a subspace of a finite-dimensional vector space $\mathcal{V}$. Show that:
(a) $\dim(\mathcal{A}) \leq \dim(\mathcal{V})$;
(b) $\dim(\mathcal{A}) = \dim(\mathcal{V})$ if and only if $\mathcal{A} = \mathcal{V}$.

Solution
(a) Let $\dim(\mathcal{V}) = n$. Then any $n+1$ (or more) vectors in $\mathcal{V}$ are linearly dependent. Hence, any $n + 1$ (or more) vectors in $\mathcal{A}$ are linearly dependent. In particular, therefore, any basis of $\mathcal{A}$ cannot contain more than n vectors. Thus, $\dim(\mathcal{A}) \leq n$.
(b) If $A := \{\boldsymbol{x}_1, \dots, \boldsymbol{x}_n\}$ is a basis of $\mathcal{A}$, then A contains n linearly independent vectors in $\mathcal{V}$ and hence spans $\mathcal{V}$. Thus, $\mathcal{V} \subseteq \mathcal{A}$. Since obviously $\mathcal{A} \subseteq \mathcal{V}$, it follows that $\mathcal{A} = \mathcal{V}$.

Exercise 3.33 (Dimension of $\mathbb{C}^n$)
(a) What is the dimension of $\mathbb{C}^n$ when the field of scalars is $\mathbb{C}$?
(b) What is the dimension of $\mathbb{C}^n$ when the field of scalars is $\mathbb{R}$?

Solution
(a) A basis is $\{e_1, \dots, e_n\}$ and hence the dimension is n.
(b) A basis is $\{e_1, \dots, e_n, \mathrm{i}e_1, \dots, \mathrm{i}e_n\}$ and hence the dimension is $2n$.

Exercise 3.34 (Dimension of a sum) Let $\mathcal{A}$ and $\mathcal{B}$ be finite-dimensional subspaces of a vector space $\mathcal{V}$. Suppose that $A := \{\boldsymbol{a}_i\}$ spans $\mathcal{A}$ and that $B := \{\boldsymbol{b}_j\}$ spans $\mathcal{B}$.
(a) Show that $A \cup B$ spans $\mathcal{A} + \mathcal{B}$.
(b) If $\mathcal{A} \cap \mathcal{B} = \{\mathbf{0}\}$, show that $A \cup B$ is a basis of $\mathcal{A} + \mathcal{B}$.
(c) Hence, show that $\mathcal{A} \cap \mathcal{B} = \{\mathbf{0}\}$ implies that $\dim(\mathcal{A} + \mathcal{B}) = \dim(\mathcal{A}) + \dim(\mathcal{B})$.

Solution
(a) Let $\dim(\mathcal{A}) = m$, $\dim(\mathcal{B}) = n$, and let

$$C := \{\boldsymbol{a}_1, \dots, \boldsymbol{a}_m, \boldsymbol{b}_1, \dots, \boldsymbol{b}_n\}.$$

Then C spans $\mathcal{A}+\mathcal{B}$, because every vector in $\mathcal{A}+\mathcal{B}$ can be written as a linear combination of the $\{\boldsymbol{a}_i\}$ plus a linear combination of the $\{\boldsymbol{b}_j\}$, that is, as a linear combination of C. For example, two distinct planes through the origin span the whole of $\mathbb{R}^3$.
(b) Suppose that $\boldsymbol{a} + \boldsymbol{b} = \mathbf{0}$, where

$$\boldsymbol{a} := \sum_{i=1}^{m} \alpha_i \boldsymbol{a}_i \quad \text{and} \quad \boldsymbol{b} := \sum_{j=1}^{n} \beta_j \boldsymbol{b}_j$$

for some scalars $\alpha_1, \dots, \alpha_m$ and $\beta_1, \dots, \beta_n$. Then, $\boldsymbol{a} = -\boldsymbol{b} \in \mathcal{B}$. Since obviously $\boldsymbol{a} \in \mathcal{A}$, this gives $\boldsymbol{a} \in \mathcal{A} \cap \mathcal{B} = \{\mathbf{0}\}$, and hence $\boldsymbol{a} = \mathbf{0}$. Similarly, $\boldsymbol{b} = \mathbf{0}$. Since A and B are bases, we obtain $\alpha_i = 0$ for all i and $\beta_j = 0$ for all j. This shows that the $m + n$ vectors in C are linearly independent and, together with (a), that C is a basis of $\mathcal{A} + \mathcal{B}$.
(c) The dimension of $\mathcal{A} + \mathcal{B}$ is equal to the number of vectors in C (since C is a basis). Hence, $\dim(\mathcal{A} + \mathcal{B}) = m + n = \dim(\mathcal{A}) + \dim(\mathcal{B})$.

3.2 Inner-product space

Exercise 3.35 (Examples of inner-product spaces)
(a) Show that the space $\mathbb{R}^m$ with the usual inner product $\langle \boldsymbol{x}, \boldsymbol{y} \rangle := \sum_{i=1}^{m} x_i y_i$ is an inner-product space.
(b) Show that the space $\mathbb{C}^m$ with the inner product $\langle \boldsymbol{x}, \boldsymbol{y} \rangle := \sum_{i=1}^{m} x_i y_i^*$ is an inner-product space.
(c) Show that the space $\mathbb{R}^{m \times n}$ of real $m \times n$ matrices is an inner-product space when $\langle \boldsymbol{A}, \boldsymbol{B} \rangle := \operatorname{tr} \boldsymbol{A}'\boldsymbol{B}$.
(d) Let $\mathcal{V}$ be the real vector space of all infinite sequences $(x_1, x_2, \dots)$ satisfying $\sum_{i=1}^{\infty} x_i^2 < \infty$. Define an inner product $\langle \boldsymbol{x}, \boldsymbol{y} \rangle := \sum_{i=1}^{\infty} x_i y_i$. Show that $\mathcal{V}$ is an inner-product space (real l_2-space).

Solution
(a)–(c) This has been proved earlier, namely in Exercises 1.7, 1.20, and 2.38, respectively.
(d) In l_2-space, we know that $\langle \boldsymbol{x}, \boldsymbol{x} \rangle$ is finite. Hence, by the Cauchy-Schwarz inequality,

$\langle \boldsymbol{x}, \boldsymbol{y} \rangle^2 \leq \langle \boldsymbol{x}, \boldsymbol{x} \rangle \langle \boldsymbol{y}, \boldsymbol{y} \rangle < \infty$, so that $\langle \boldsymbol{x}, \boldsymbol{y} \rangle$ is finite. The four defining properties of the inner product are now easily verified. For example, $\langle \boldsymbol{x}, \boldsymbol{y} \rangle = \sum_i x_i y_i = \sum_i y_i x_i = \langle \boldsymbol{y}, \boldsymbol{x} \rangle$.

Exercise 3.36 (Norm and length) Recall that the norm of a vector $\boldsymbol{x}$ in an inner-product space is given by $\|\boldsymbol{x}\| := \sqrt{\langle \boldsymbol{x}, \boldsymbol{x} \rangle}$.
(a) Show that $\langle \boldsymbol{x}, \boldsymbol{x} \rangle$ is always a real number.
(b) What is the geometric interpretation of the norm in $\mathbb{R}^n$?

Solution
(a) Since $\langle \boldsymbol{x}, \boldsymbol{y} \rangle = \langle \boldsymbol{y}, \boldsymbol{x} \rangle^*$, we see that $\langle \boldsymbol{x}, \boldsymbol{x} \rangle = \langle \boldsymbol{x}, \boldsymbol{x} \rangle^*$.
(b) The norm is the idealization of "length" in Euclidean geometry, and its properties have been worked out in Exercises 1.10, 1.20(d), and 1.21(c).

Exercise 3.37 (Cauchy-Schwarz inequality, again) Show that in any inner-product space,

$$|\langle \boldsymbol{x}, \boldsymbol{y} \rangle| \leq \|\boldsymbol{x}\| \cdot \|\boldsymbol{y}\|$$

with equality if and only if $\boldsymbol{x}$ and $\boldsymbol{y}$ are collinear.

Solution
This follows in the same way as in the proof of Exercise 1.21(b).

***Exercise 3.38 (The parallelogram equality)**
(a) Show that in any inner-product space,

$$\|\boldsymbol{x} + \boldsymbol{y}\|^2 + \|\boldsymbol{x} - \boldsymbol{y}\|^2 = 2\|\boldsymbol{x}\|^2 + 2\|\boldsymbol{y}\|^2.$$

(b) Why is this equality called the "parallelogram equality"?

Solution
(a) We have

$$\begin{aligned}
\|\boldsymbol{x} + \boldsymbol{y}\|^2 + \|\boldsymbol{x} - \boldsymbol{y}\|^2 &= \langle \boldsymbol{x} + \boldsymbol{y}, \boldsymbol{x} + \boldsymbol{y} \rangle + \langle \boldsymbol{x} - \boldsymbol{y}, \boldsymbol{x} - \boldsymbol{y} \rangle \\
&= \langle \boldsymbol{x}, \boldsymbol{x} \rangle + \langle \boldsymbol{x}, \boldsymbol{y} \rangle + \langle \boldsymbol{y}, \boldsymbol{x} \rangle + \langle \boldsymbol{y}, \boldsymbol{y} \rangle + \langle \boldsymbol{x}, \boldsymbol{x} \rangle - \langle \boldsymbol{x}, \boldsymbol{y} \rangle - \langle \boldsymbol{y}, \boldsymbol{x} \rangle + \langle \boldsymbol{y}, \boldsymbol{y} \rangle \\
&= 2\langle \boldsymbol{x}, \boldsymbol{x} \rangle + 2\langle \boldsymbol{y}, \boldsymbol{y} \rangle = 2\|\boldsymbol{x}\|^2 + 2\|\boldsymbol{y}\|^2.
\end{aligned}$$

(b) Figure 3.3 explains the term in $\mathbb{R}^2$. If we think of A as the origin, B as the point $\boldsymbol{x}$, and D as the point $\boldsymbol{y}$, then we need to prove that $\mathrm{AC}^2 + \mathrm{BD}^2 = 2(\mathrm{AB}^2 + \mathrm{AD}^2)$, in other words that the sum of the squares of the two diagonals of the parallelogram is equal to the sum of the squares of the four sides. Now,

$$\begin{aligned}
\mathrm{AC}^2 + \mathrm{BD}^2 &= (a + b + a)^2 + h^2 + b^2 + h^2 \\
&= 2\left((a + b)^2 + (a^2 + h^2)\right) = 2(\mathrm{AB}^2 + \mathrm{AD}^2).
\end{aligned}$$

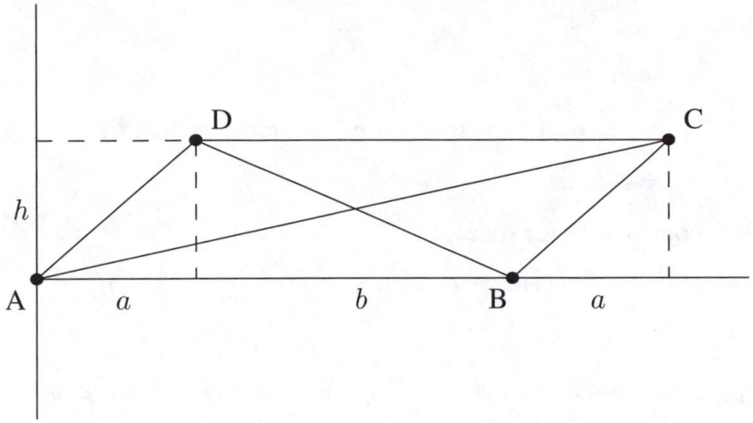

Figure 3.3 — The parallelogram equality.

Exercise 3.39 (Norm, general definition) Consider a real-valued function $\nu(\boldsymbol{x})$ defined on an inner-product space. Suppose $\nu(\boldsymbol{x})$ satisfies:

(i) $\nu(\alpha\boldsymbol{x}) = |\alpha|\nu(\boldsymbol{x})$;
(ii) $\nu(\boldsymbol{x}) \geq 0$, with $\nu(\boldsymbol{x}) = 0$ if and only if $\boldsymbol{x} = \mathbf{0}$;
(iii) $\nu(\boldsymbol{x}+\boldsymbol{y}) \leq \nu(\boldsymbol{x}) + \nu(\boldsymbol{y})$ (triangle inequality).

Show that the function $\nu(\boldsymbol{x}) := \|\boldsymbol{x}\|$ satisfies (i)–(iii). (Many authors call any real-valued function ν satisfying (i)–(iii) a norm. Our definition is more specialized; it is the norm induced by the inner product $\langle \boldsymbol{x}, \boldsymbol{y}\rangle$.)

Solution
This follows in exactly the same way as the solution to Exercise 1.10; see also Exercise 1.21(c).

Exercise 3.40 (Induced inner product) We know that an inner product induces a norm. But the converse is also true!
(a) In any real inner-product space, show that

$$\langle \boldsymbol{x}, \boldsymbol{y}\rangle = \frac{1}{4}\left(\|\boldsymbol{x}+\boldsymbol{y}\|^2 - \|\boldsymbol{x}-\boldsymbol{y}\|^2\right).$$

(b) In any complex inner-product space, show that

$$\operatorname{Re}\langle \boldsymbol{x}, \boldsymbol{y}\rangle = \frac{1}{4}\left(\|\boldsymbol{x}+\boldsymbol{y}\|^2 - \|\boldsymbol{x}-\boldsymbol{y}\|^2\right)$$

and

$$\operatorname{Im}\langle \boldsymbol{x}, \boldsymbol{y}\rangle = \frac{1}{4}\left(\|\boldsymbol{x}+\mathrm{i}\boldsymbol{y}\|^2 - \|\boldsymbol{x}-\mathrm{i}\boldsymbol{y}\|^2\right).$$

Solution

(a) In a real vector space,

$$\begin{aligned}\|\boldsymbol{x}+\boldsymbol{y}\|^2 - \|\boldsymbol{x}-\boldsymbol{y}\|^2 \\ &= \langle\boldsymbol{x},\boldsymbol{x}\rangle + 2\langle\boldsymbol{x},\boldsymbol{y}\rangle + \langle\boldsymbol{y},\boldsymbol{y}\rangle - \langle\boldsymbol{x},\boldsymbol{x}\rangle + 2\langle\boldsymbol{x},\boldsymbol{y}\rangle - \langle\boldsymbol{y},\boldsymbol{y}\rangle \\ &= 4\langle\boldsymbol{x},\boldsymbol{y}\rangle.\end{aligned}$$

(b) Similarly, in a complex vector space,

$$\|\boldsymbol{x}+\boldsymbol{y}\|^2 - \|\boldsymbol{x}-\boldsymbol{y}\|^2 = 2\left(\langle\boldsymbol{y},\boldsymbol{x}\rangle + \langle\boldsymbol{x},\boldsymbol{y}\rangle\right) = 2\left(\langle\boldsymbol{x},\boldsymbol{y}\rangle^* + \langle\boldsymbol{x},\boldsymbol{y}\rangle\right) = 4\,\mathrm{Re}\langle\boldsymbol{x},\boldsymbol{y}\rangle,$$

and

$$\|\boldsymbol{x}+\mathrm{i}\boldsymbol{y}\|^2 - \|\boldsymbol{x}-\mathrm{i}\boldsymbol{y}\|^2 = 2\mathrm{i}\left(\langle\boldsymbol{y},\boldsymbol{x}\rangle - \langle\boldsymbol{x},\boldsymbol{y}\rangle\right) = 4\,\mathrm{Im}\langle\boldsymbol{x},\boldsymbol{y}\rangle.$$

***Exercise 3.41 (Norm does not imply inner product)** Exercise 3.40 shows that the unique inner product can be induced from the norm, if we know that an inner product exists. It does not imply (and it is not true) that the existence of a norm implies the existence of an inner product. For example, in $\mathbb{R}^m$, consider the real-valued function $\nu(\boldsymbol{x}) := \sum_{i=1}^m |x_i|$.
(a) Show that ν is a norm, according to the definition of Exercise 3.39.
(b) Show that there is no inner-product space that induces this norm.

Solution

(a) We need to show that $\sum_i |x_i| \geq 0$, that $\sum_i |x_i| = 0$ if and only if $\boldsymbol{x} = \mathbf{0}$, that $\sum_i |\alpha x_i| = |\alpha| \sum_i |x_i|$, and that $\sum_i |x_i + y_i| \leq \sum_i |x_i| + \sum_i |y_i|$, all of which follow from Chapter 1.
(b) If an inner product existed, then the parallelogram equality would hold. Let $\boldsymbol{x} = (1,1)'$ and $\boldsymbol{y} = (1,-1)'$ in $\mathbb{R}^2$. Then, $\nu(\boldsymbol{x}+\boldsymbol{y}) = \nu(\boldsymbol{x}-\boldsymbol{y}) = \nu(\boldsymbol{x}) = \nu(\boldsymbol{y}) = 2$, and hence

$$(\nu(\boldsymbol{x}+\boldsymbol{y}))^2 + (\nu(\boldsymbol{x}-\boldsymbol{y}))^2 = 8 \neq 16 = 2(\nu(\boldsymbol{x}))^2 + 2(\nu(\boldsymbol{y}))^2.$$

This shows that the parallelogram equality does not hold, and hence that no inner product exists for this norm.

Exercise 3.42 (Distance) In an inner-product space, the distance $d(\boldsymbol{x},\boldsymbol{y})$ between two vectors $\boldsymbol{x}$ and $\boldsymbol{y}$ is defined as $d(\boldsymbol{x},\boldsymbol{y}) := \|\boldsymbol{x}-\boldsymbol{y}\|$. Show that:
(a) $d(\boldsymbol{x},\boldsymbol{x}) = 0$;
(b) $d(\boldsymbol{x},\boldsymbol{y}) > 0$ if $\boldsymbol{x} \neq \boldsymbol{y}$;
(c) $d(\boldsymbol{x},\boldsymbol{y}) = d(\boldsymbol{y},\boldsymbol{x})$;
(d) $d(\boldsymbol{x},\boldsymbol{y}) \leq d(\boldsymbol{x},\boldsymbol{z}) + d(\boldsymbol{z},\boldsymbol{y})$.
Discuss the geometric interpretation in $\mathbb{R}^2$.

Solution

Parts (a) and (b) follow from Exercise 3.39(ii), while part (c) follows from Exercise 3.39(i). To prove (d) we use the triangle inequality and obtain

$$\|\boldsymbol{x}-\boldsymbol{y}\| = \|(\boldsymbol{x}-\boldsymbol{z}) + (\boldsymbol{z}-\boldsymbol{y})\| \leq \|\boldsymbol{x}-\boldsymbol{z}\| + \|\boldsymbol{z}-\boldsymbol{y}\|.$$

The geometric interpretation in $\mathbb{R}^2$ is: (a), (b) the distance between two points is positive, unless the points coincide, in which case the distance is zero; (c) the distance between two points A and B is the same as the distance between B and A; (d) a straight line is the shortest distance between two points.

Exercise 3.43 (Continuity of the inner product) If $\{\boldsymbol{x}_n\}$ and $\{\boldsymbol{y}_n\}$ are sequences of vectors in an inner-product space, such that $\|\boldsymbol{x}_n - \boldsymbol{x}\| \to 0$ and $\|\boldsymbol{y}_n - \boldsymbol{y}\| \to 0$, then show that:
(a) $\|\boldsymbol{x}_n\| \to \|\boldsymbol{x}\|, \quad \|\boldsymbol{y}_n\| \to \|\boldsymbol{y}\|$;
(b) $\langle \boldsymbol{x}_n, \boldsymbol{y}_n \rangle \to \langle \boldsymbol{x}, \boldsymbol{y} \rangle$, if $\|\boldsymbol{x}\| < \infty$ and $\|\boldsymbol{y}\| < \infty$.

Solution
(a) The triangle inequality states that $\|\boldsymbol{x} + \boldsymbol{y}\| \leq \|\boldsymbol{x}\| + \|\boldsymbol{y}\|$ for any $\boldsymbol{x}, \boldsymbol{y}$. It follows that

$$\|\boldsymbol{x}_n\| \leq \|\boldsymbol{x}_n - \boldsymbol{x}\| + \|\boldsymbol{x}\|, \quad \|\boldsymbol{x}\| \leq \|\boldsymbol{x} - \boldsymbol{x}_n\| + \|\boldsymbol{x}_n\|,$$

and hence $|\|\boldsymbol{x}_n\| - \|\boldsymbol{x}\|| \leq \|\boldsymbol{x}_n - \boldsymbol{x}\|$, from which (a) follows.
(b) Next,

$$\begin{aligned}
|\langle \boldsymbol{x}_n, \boldsymbol{y}_n \rangle - \langle \boldsymbol{x}, \boldsymbol{y} \rangle| &= |\langle \boldsymbol{x}_n, \boldsymbol{y}_n - \boldsymbol{y} \rangle + \langle \boldsymbol{x}_n - \boldsymbol{x}, \boldsymbol{y} \rangle| \\
&\leq |\langle \boldsymbol{x}_n, \boldsymbol{y}_n - \boldsymbol{y} \rangle| + |\langle \boldsymbol{x}_n - \boldsymbol{x}, \boldsymbol{y} \rangle| \\
&\leq \|\boldsymbol{x}_n\| \cdot \|\boldsymbol{y}_n - \boldsymbol{y}\| + \|\boldsymbol{x}_n - \boldsymbol{x}\| \cdot \|\boldsymbol{y}\|,
\end{aligned}$$

where the last inequality follows from Cauchy-Schwarz. Since, from (a), $\|\boldsymbol{x}_n\| \to \|\boldsymbol{x}\|$, the result follows.

Exercise 3.44 (Orthogonal vectors in space) Recall that two vectors $\boldsymbol{x}$, $\boldsymbol{y}$ in an inner-product space are orthogonal if $\langle \boldsymbol{x}, \boldsymbol{y} \rangle = 0$, in which case we write $\boldsymbol{x} \perp \boldsymbol{y}$.
(a) Show that the null vector $\mathbf{0}$ is orthogonal to every vector in $\mathcal{V}$.
(b) Obtain all vectors in $\mathbb{R}^3$ orthogonal to $\boldsymbol{x} = (2, 2, -1)'$.

Solution
(a) For every $\boldsymbol{y} \in \mathcal{V}$ we have $\langle \mathbf{0}, \boldsymbol{y} \rangle = 0$.
(b) Any vector $\boldsymbol{y}$ orthogonal to $\boldsymbol{x}$ must satisfy the equation $\langle \boldsymbol{x}, \boldsymbol{y} \rangle = 0$, that is, $2y_1 + 2y_2 - y_3 = 0$. Hence,

$$\boldsymbol{y} = \begin{pmatrix} y_1 \\ y_2 \\ 2y_1 + 2y_2 \end{pmatrix} = y_1 \begin{pmatrix} 1 \\ 0 \\ 2 \end{pmatrix} + y_2 \begin{pmatrix} 0 \\ 1 \\ 2 \end{pmatrix}.$$

This is the equation of a plane through the origin; see also Exercise 3.10(e). All vectors in the plane are orthogonal to $\boldsymbol{x}$. We say that the vector $\boldsymbol{x}$ is *normal* to the plane.

Exercise 3.45 (Pythagoras)
(a) If $\boldsymbol{x} \perp \boldsymbol{y}$ in an inner-product space, show that $\|\boldsymbol{x} + \boldsymbol{y}\|^2 = \|\boldsymbol{x}\|^2 + \|\boldsymbol{y}\|^2$.
(b) Does the converse hold?

Solution
We have

$$\|\boldsymbol{x}+\boldsymbol{y}\|^2 = \langle \boldsymbol{x}+\boldsymbol{y}, \boldsymbol{x}+\boldsymbol{y}\rangle = \langle \boldsymbol{x},\boldsymbol{x}\rangle + \langle \boldsymbol{x},\boldsymbol{y}\rangle + \langle \boldsymbol{y},\boldsymbol{x}\rangle + \langle \boldsymbol{y},\boldsymbol{y}\rangle.$$

(a) If $\boldsymbol{x} \perp \boldsymbol{y}$, then $\langle \boldsymbol{x},\boldsymbol{y}\rangle = \langle \boldsymbol{y},\boldsymbol{x}\rangle = 0$ and hence $\|\boldsymbol{x}+\boldsymbol{y}\|^2 = \|\boldsymbol{x}\|^2 + \|\boldsymbol{y}\|^2$.
(b) Conversely, if $\|\boldsymbol{x}+\boldsymbol{y}\|^2 = \|\boldsymbol{x}\|^2+\|\boldsymbol{y}\|^2$, then $\langle \boldsymbol{x},\boldsymbol{y}\rangle+\langle \boldsymbol{y},\boldsymbol{x}\rangle = 0$, that is, $\operatorname{Re}\langle \boldsymbol{x},\boldsymbol{y}\rangle = 0$. So, the converse holds in $\mathbb{R}^n$, but not in $\mathbb{C}^n$. For example, in $\mathbb{C}^2$, if $\boldsymbol{x} = (1,\mathrm{i})'$ and $\boldsymbol{y} = (\mathrm{i},0)'$, then $\langle \boldsymbol{x},\boldsymbol{y}\rangle = -\mathrm{i}$ and $\langle \boldsymbol{y},\boldsymbol{x}\rangle = \mathrm{i}$, so that $\langle \boldsymbol{x},\boldsymbol{y}\rangle \neq 0$ despite the fact that $\|\boldsymbol{x}+\boldsymbol{y}\|^2 = \|\boldsymbol{x}\|^2 + \|\boldsymbol{y}\|^2$.

Exercise 3.46 (Orthogonality and linear independence) Let $A := \{\boldsymbol{x}_1,\dots,\boldsymbol{x}_r\}$ be a set of nonzero vectors in an inner-product space. A is an orthogonal set if each pair of vectors in A is orthogonal. If, in addition, each vector in A has unit length, then A is an orthonormal set.
(a) Show that the n columns of $\boldsymbol{I}_n$ are orthonormal and linearly independent.
(b) Prove that any orthonormal set is linearly independent.

Solution
(a) The columns of $\boldsymbol{I}_n$ are $\boldsymbol{e}_1,\dots,\boldsymbol{e}_n$. It is easy to see that $\boldsymbol{e}_i'\boldsymbol{e}_j = \delta_{ij}$, where δ_{ij} denotes the so-called *Kronecker delta*, taking the value one if $i=j$ and zero otherwise. Hence, the columns of $\boldsymbol{I}_n$ are orthonormal. They are also linearly independent, because $\alpha_1\boldsymbol{e}_1+\dots+\alpha_n\boldsymbol{e}_n = (\alpha_1,\dots,\alpha_n)'$ and this equals the null vector if and only if all α_i are zero.
(b) Let $B := \{\boldsymbol{b}_1,\dots,\boldsymbol{b}_n\}$ be an orthonormal set, and suppose that $\alpha_1\boldsymbol{b}_1+\dots+\alpha_n\boldsymbol{b}_n = \mathbf{0}$. For $i=1,\dots,n$ we have

$$0 = \langle \boldsymbol{b}_i, \alpha_1\boldsymbol{b}_1+\dots+\alpha_n\boldsymbol{b}_n\rangle = \sum_{j=1}^n \alpha_j\langle \boldsymbol{b}_i,\boldsymbol{b}_j\rangle = \alpha_i,$$

and hence $\alpha_i = 0$ for all i.

Exercise 3.47 (Orthogonal subspace) Recall that two subspaces $\mathcal{A}$ and $\mathcal{B}$ of an inner-product space are orthogonal if every vector $\boldsymbol{a}$ in $\mathcal{A}$ is orthogonal to every vector $\boldsymbol{b}$ in $\mathcal{B}$.
(a) Show the front wall and side wall of a room are *not* orthogonal.
(b) Show that the subspace $\{\mathbf{0}\}$ is orthogonal to all subspaces.

Solution
(a) This is somewhat counterintuitive, but only some of the lines in the two walls meet at right angles. Moreover, the line along the corner is in both walls, and it is not orthogonal to itself. In $\mathbb{R}^3$ no plane is orthogonal to another plane.
(b) This is true because $\langle \mathbf{0},\boldsymbol{x}\rangle = 0$ for all $\boldsymbol{x}$.

Exercise 3.48 (Orthogonal complement) Let $\mathcal{A}$ be a subspace of an inner-product space $\mathcal{V}$. The space $\mathcal{A}^\perp$ of all vectors orthogonal to $\mathcal{A}$ is the orthogonal complement of $\mathcal{A}$.

(a) What is the orthogonal complement of $\{\mathbf{0}\}$?
(b) Show that $\mathcal{A}^\perp$ is a subspace of $\mathcal{V}$.
(c) Show that $\mathcal{A} \cap \mathcal{A}^\perp = \{\mathbf{0}\}$.

Solution
(a) Every vector $\boldsymbol{x}$ in $\mathcal{V}$ satisfies $\langle \boldsymbol{x}, \mathbf{0} \rangle = 0$. Hence, the orthogonal complement of $\{\mathbf{0}\}$ is the whole space $\mathcal{V}$.
(b) Let $\boldsymbol{x} \in \mathcal{A}^\perp$, $\boldsymbol{y} \in \mathcal{A}^\perp$. Then, for any $\boldsymbol{z} \in \mathcal{A}$, we have $\langle \boldsymbol{x}, \boldsymbol{z} \rangle = \langle \boldsymbol{y}, \boldsymbol{z} \rangle = 0$ and hence also $\langle \boldsymbol{x} + \boldsymbol{y}, \boldsymbol{z} \rangle = 0$ and $\langle \alpha \boldsymbol{x}, \boldsymbol{z} \rangle = 0$. This shows that $\boldsymbol{x} + \boldsymbol{y} \in \mathcal{A}^\perp$ and $\alpha \boldsymbol{x} \in \mathcal{A}^\perp$, and hence that $\mathcal{A}^\perp$ is a subspace of $\mathcal{V}$.
(c) Let $\boldsymbol{x} \in \mathcal{A} \cap \mathcal{A}^\perp$. Since $\boldsymbol{x} \in \mathcal{A}^\perp$, we have that $\langle \boldsymbol{x}, \boldsymbol{y} \rangle = 0$ for all $\boldsymbol{y} \in \mathcal{A}$. But, since $\boldsymbol{x}$ is also in $\mathcal{A}$, this gives $\langle \boldsymbol{x}, \boldsymbol{x} \rangle = 0$, and hence $\boldsymbol{x} = \mathbf{0}$.

Exercise 3.49 (Gram-Schmidt orthogonalization) We already know that any vector space $\mathcal{V}$ has a basis. Now show that if $\mathcal{V}$ is a finite-dimensional inner-product space, $\mathcal{V}$ always has an orthonormal basis.

Solution
Let $\boldsymbol{x}_1, \boldsymbol{x}_2, \dots$ be a basis of $\mathcal{V}$. We define

$$\begin{aligned} \boldsymbol{y}_1 &:= \boldsymbol{x}_1 \\ \boldsymbol{y}_2 &:= \boldsymbol{x}_2 - a_{21}\boldsymbol{y}_1 \\ &\vdots \\ \boldsymbol{y}_n &:= \boldsymbol{x}_n - a_{n,n-1}\boldsymbol{y}_{n-1} - \dots - a_{n1}\boldsymbol{y}_1. \end{aligned}$$

The coefficients in the i-th equation are chosen in such a way that $\boldsymbol{y}_i$ is orthogonal to each of $\boldsymbol{y}_1, \dots, \boldsymbol{y}_{i-1}$. Thus, $\boldsymbol{y}_2 \perp \boldsymbol{y}_1$ yields $\langle \boldsymbol{x}_2, \boldsymbol{y}_1 \rangle = a_{21} \langle \boldsymbol{y}_1, \boldsymbol{y}_1 \rangle$ and $\boldsymbol{y}_3 \perp \boldsymbol{y}_1$, $\boldsymbol{y}_3 \perp \boldsymbol{y}_2$ yields $\langle \boldsymbol{x}_3, \boldsymbol{y}_1 \rangle = a_{31} \langle \boldsymbol{y}_1, \boldsymbol{y}_1 \rangle$ and $\langle \boldsymbol{x}_3, \boldsymbol{y}_2 \rangle = a_{32} \langle \boldsymbol{y}_2, \boldsymbol{y}_2 \rangle$. Continuing in this way we find all the coefficients from $\langle \boldsymbol{x}_i, \boldsymbol{y}_j \rangle = a_{ij} \langle \boldsymbol{y}_j, \boldsymbol{y}_j \rangle$, $j = 1, \dots, i-1$. (Note that $\langle \boldsymbol{y}_j, \boldsymbol{y}_j \rangle \neq 0$, because otherwise $\boldsymbol{y}_j = \mathbf{0}$ would imply linear dependence of the $\boldsymbol{x}_1, \dots, \boldsymbol{x}_j$.) The vectors $\boldsymbol{y}_1, \boldsymbol{y}_2, \dots$ constitute an orthogonal basis. The normalized set $\boldsymbol{y}_{\circ 1}, \boldsymbol{y}_{\circ 2}, \dots$, with $\boldsymbol{y}_{\circ i} := \boldsymbol{y}_i / \|\boldsymbol{y}_i\|$ constitutes an orthonormal basis.

3.3 Hilbert space

Exercise 3.50 ($\mathbb{R}^m$ is a Hilbert space) Show that $\mathbb{R}^m$ is a Hilbert space and hence, by the same argument, that $\mathbb{C}^m$, $\mathbb{R}^{m \times n}$, and $\mathbb{C}^{m \times n}$ are also Hilbert spaces. (You may use the fact that the set $\mathbb{R}$ of real numbers is complete.)

Solution
Suppose $\{\boldsymbol{x}^{(1)}, \boldsymbol{x}^{(2)}, \dots\}$ is a Cauchy sequence, where $\boldsymbol{x}^{(p)} := (x_1^{(p)}, x_2^{(p)}, \dots, x_m^{(p)})'$ denotes a real $m \times 1$ vector. Then,

$$\sum_{i=1}^m \left(x_i^{(p)} - x_i^{(q)} \right)^2 \to 0 \quad \text{as} \quad p, q \to \infty.$$

This implies that for each $i = 1, \dots, m$,

$$\left(x_i^{(p)} - x_i^{(q)}\right)^2 \to 0 \quad \text{as} \quad p, q \to \infty,$$

and hence, by the completeness of $\mathbb{R}$, that each sequence $x_i^{(p)}$ converges to, say, x_i. Letting $\boldsymbol{x}' := (x_1, \dots, x_m)$, it then follows that $\boldsymbol{x}^{(p)}$ converges to $\boldsymbol{x}$. Hence, every Cauchy sequence converges in $\mathbb{R}^m$, proving its completeness. We already know that $\mathbb{R}^m$ is an inner-product space. Hence, $\mathbb{R}^m$ is a complete inner-product space, that is, a Hilbert space. The complex case follows by applying the same argument to $\text{Re}(x_i^{(p)})$ and $\text{Im}(x_i^{(p)})$ separately.

Exercise 3.51 ($L_2^\dagger$ is a Hilbert space) Show that the space $L_2^\dagger$ of random variables, introduced in Exercises 3.6 and 3.21, is a Hilbert space.

Solution
This proceeds in essentially the same way as in Exercise 3.50. Both $\mathbb{R}^m$ and $L_2^\dagger$ are finite dimensional, and *any* finite-dimensional inner-product space is complete and therefore a Hilbert space.

Exercise 3.52 (Closed subspace) A subspace $\mathcal{A}$ of a vector space $\mathcal{V}$ is said to be a *closed subspace* of $\mathcal{V}$ if $\mathcal{A}$ contains all of its limit points, that is, if $\boldsymbol{x}_n \in \mathcal{A}$ and $\|\boldsymbol{x}_n - \boldsymbol{x}\| \to 0$ imply $\boldsymbol{x} \in \mathcal{A}$. If $\mathcal{V}$ is a Hilbert space and $\mathcal{A}$ is a closed subspace of $\mathcal{V}$, then show that:
(a) $\mathcal{A}$ is also a Hilbert space;
(b) $\mathcal{A}^\perp$ is a closed subspace of $\mathcal{V}$, and hence also a Hilbert space.

Solution
(a) Let $\{\boldsymbol{x}_n\}$ be a Cauchy sequence in $\mathcal{A}$. Since $\mathcal{V}$ is complete, $\boldsymbol{x}_n \to \boldsymbol{x} \in \mathcal{V}$. But, since $\mathcal{A}$ is closed, $\boldsymbol{x} \in \mathcal{A}$. Hence, the arbitrary Cauchy sequence $\{\boldsymbol{x}_n\}$ converges in $\mathcal{A}$, proving that $\mathcal{A}$ is complete.
(b) $\mathcal{A}^\perp$ is a subspace because a linear combination of vectors orthogonal to a set is also orthogonal to the set. $\mathcal{A}^\perp$ is closed because if $\{\boldsymbol{x}_n\}$ is a convergent sequence from $\mathcal{A}^\perp$, say $\boldsymbol{x}_n \to \boldsymbol{x}$, continuity of the inner product (Exercise 3.43) implies that $0 = \langle \boldsymbol{x}_n, \boldsymbol{y} \rangle \to \langle \boldsymbol{x}, \boldsymbol{y} \rangle$ for all $\boldsymbol{y} \in \mathcal{A}$. Hence, $\boldsymbol{x} \in \mathcal{A}^\perp$. Completeness then follows from (a).

***Exercise 3.53 (Projection theorem)** Let $\mathcal{V}$ be a Hilbert space and $\mathcal{A}$ a closed subspace of $\mathcal{V}$.
(a) Show that for any $\boldsymbol{y} \in \mathcal{V}$ there exists a vector $\hat{\boldsymbol{y}} \in \mathcal{A}$ such that $\|\boldsymbol{y} - \hat{\boldsymbol{y}}\| \le \|\boldsymbol{y} - \boldsymbol{x}\|$ for all $\boldsymbol{x} \in \mathcal{A}$, that is,

$$\|\boldsymbol{y} - \hat{\boldsymbol{y}}\| = \inf_{\boldsymbol{x} \in \mathcal{A}} \|\boldsymbol{y} - \boldsymbol{x}\|.$$

[Hint: Consider a sequence $\{\boldsymbol{x}_n\}$ achieving this infimum, then show that it is a Cauchy sequence.]
(b) Show that $\hat{\boldsymbol{y}}$, thus obtained, is unique. (The vector $\hat{\boldsymbol{y}}$ is called the *orthogonal projection* of $\boldsymbol{y}$ onto $\mathcal{A}$.)

Solution

(a) (existence). If $\boldsymbol{y} \in \mathcal{A}$, then the choice $\hat{\boldsymbol{y}} := \boldsymbol{y}$ solves the problem. Assume $\boldsymbol{y} \notin \mathcal{A}$, and let $d := \inf_{\boldsymbol{x} \in \mathcal{A}} \|\boldsymbol{y} - \boldsymbol{x}\|^2$. We will show that there exists a $\hat{\boldsymbol{y}} \in \mathcal{A}$ such that $\|\boldsymbol{y} - \hat{\boldsymbol{y}}\|^2 = d$, that is, that the infimum is in fact a minimum. Let $\{\boldsymbol{x}_n\}$ be a sequence of vectors in $\mathcal{A}$ such that $\|\boldsymbol{x}_n - \boldsymbol{x}\|^2 \to d$. Then, applying the parallelogram equality, we can write

$$\begin{aligned}\|(\boldsymbol{x}_n - \boldsymbol{x}) + (\boldsymbol{x} - \boldsymbol{x}_m)\|^2 &+ \|(\boldsymbol{x}_n - \boldsymbol{x}) - (\boldsymbol{x} - \boldsymbol{x}_m)\|^2 \\ &= 2\|\boldsymbol{x}_n - \boldsymbol{x}\|^2 + 2\|\boldsymbol{x}_m - \boldsymbol{x}\|^2.\end{aligned}$$

Rearranging yields

$$\|\boldsymbol{x}_n - \boldsymbol{x}_m\|^2 = 2\|\boldsymbol{x}_n - \boldsymbol{x}\|^2 + 2\|\boldsymbol{x}_m - \boldsymbol{x}\|^2 - 4\|\frac{\boldsymbol{x}_n + \boldsymbol{x}_m}{2} - \boldsymbol{x}\|^2.$$

Now, $(\boldsymbol{x}_n + \boldsymbol{x}_m)/2$ is in $\mathcal{A}$ because $\boldsymbol{x}_n$ and $\boldsymbol{x}_m$ are in $\mathcal{A}$. Hence, $\|(\boldsymbol{x}_n + \boldsymbol{x}_m)/2 - \boldsymbol{x}\|^2 \geq d$ and we obtain

$$0 \leq \|\boldsymbol{x}_n - \boldsymbol{x}_m\|^2 \leq 2\|\boldsymbol{x}_n - \boldsymbol{x}\|^2 + 2\|\boldsymbol{x}_m - \boldsymbol{x}\|^2 - 4d.$$

Since $\|\boldsymbol{x}_n - \boldsymbol{x}\|^2 \to d$ as $n \to \infty$, we find $\|\boldsymbol{x}_n - \boldsymbol{x}_m\| \to 0$ as $n, m \to \infty$, so that $\{\boldsymbol{x}_n\}$ is a Cauchy sequence. Since $\mathcal{V}$ is a Hilbert space, there now exists a vector $\hat{\boldsymbol{y}} \in \mathcal{V}$ such that $\|\boldsymbol{x}_n - \hat{\boldsymbol{y}}\| \to 0$. Furthermore, since $\mathcal{A}$ is closed, $\hat{\boldsymbol{y}} \in \mathcal{A}$. Finally, by the continuity of the inner product (Exercise 3.43),

$$\|\boldsymbol{y} - \hat{\boldsymbol{y}}\|^2 = \lim_{n \to \infty} \|\boldsymbol{y} - \boldsymbol{x}_n\|^2 = d.$$

(b) (uniqueness). Suppose $\widetilde{\boldsymbol{y}} \in \mathcal{A}$ exists such that $\|\boldsymbol{y} - \hat{\boldsymbol{y}}\|^2 = \|\boldsymbol{y} - \widetilde{\boldsymbol{y}}\|^2 = d$. Then, again using the parallelogram equality,

$$\begin{aligned}0 \leq \|\hat{\boldsymbol{y}} - \widetilde{\boldsymbol{y}}\|^2 &= 2\|\hat{\boldsymbol{y}} - \boldsymbol{y}\|^2 + 2\|\widetilde{\boldsymbol{y}} - \boldsymbol{y}\|^2 - 4\|\frac{\hat{\boldsymbol{y}} + \widetilde{\boldsymbol{y}}}{2} - \boldsymbol{y}\|^2 \\ &\leq 2d + 2d - 4d = 0,\end{aligned}$$

and hence $\widetilde{\boldsymbol{y}} = \hat{\boldsymbol{y}}$.

***Exercise 3.54 (Projection theorem, complement)** Let $\mathcal{V}$ be a Hilbert space, $\mathcal{A}$ a closed subspace of $\mathcal{V}$, and $\boldsymbol{y} \in \mathcal{V}$.
(a) If $\boldsymbol{y} - \hat{\boldsymbol{y}} \in \mathcal{A}^{\perp}$ for some $\hat{\boldsymbol{y}} \in \mathcal{A}$, show that $\|\boldsymbol{y} - \hat{\boldsymbol{y}}\| = \inf_{\boldsymbol{x} \in \mathcal{A}} \|\boldsymbol{y} - \boldsymbol{x}\|$.
(b) Conversely, if $\|\boldsymbol{y} - \hat{\boldsymbol{y}}\| = \inf_{\boldsymbol{x} \in \mathcal{A}} \|\boldsymbol{y} - \boldsymbol{x}\|$ for some $\hat{\boldsymbol{y}} \in \mathcal{A}$, show that $\boldsymbol{y} - \hat{\boldsymbol{y}} \in \mathcal{A}^{\perp}$.
[Hint: Use proof by contrapositive and the method in Exercise 1.9 (Cauchy-Schwarz).]

Solution

(a) If $\hat{\boldsymbol{y}} \in \mathcal{A}$ and $\boldsymbol{y} - \hat{\boldsymbol{y}} \in \mathcal{A}^{\perp}$, then, for any $\boldsymbol{x} \in \mathcal{A}$, we have $\hat{\boldsymbol{y}} - \boldsymbol{x} \in \mathcal{A}$ and hence $(\hat{\boldsymbol{y}} - \boldsymbol{x}) \perp (\boldsymbol{y} - \hat{\boldsymbol{y}})$. Application of Pythagoras's theorem (Exercise 3.45) gives

$$\begin{aligned}\|\boldsymbol{y} - \boldsymbol{x}\|^2 &= \|(\boldsymbol{y} - \hat{\boldsymbol{y}}) + (\hat{\boldsymbol{y}} - \boldsymbol{x})\|^2 \\ &= \|\boldsymbol{y} - \hat{\boldsymbol{y}}\|^2 + \|\hat{\boldsymbol{y}} - \boldsymbol{x}\|^2 \geq \|\boldsymbol{y} - \hat{\boldsymbol{y}}\|^2,\end{aligned}$$

with equality if and only if $\boldsymbol{x} = \hat{\boldsymbol{y}}$.

(b) Suppose $\boldsymbol{y} - \hat{\boldsymbol{y}} \notin \mathcal{A}^\perp$. If $\hat{\boldsymbol{y}} \in \mathcal{A}$, then $\beta := \langle \boldsymbol{y} - \hat{\boldsymbol{y}}, \boldsymbol{x} \rangle \neq 0$ for some $\boldsymbol{x} \in \mathcal{A}$. Clearly, $\boldsymbol{x} \neq \boldsymbol{0}$ since otherwise $\beta = 0$. For any scalar α,

$$\|\boldsymbol{y} - \hat{\boldsymbol{y}} - \alpha\boldsymbol{x}\|^2 = \|\boldsymbol{y} - \hat{\boldsymbol{y}}\|^2 - \alpha^*\beta - \alpha\beta^* + \alpha\alpha^*\|\boldsymbol{x}\|^2.$$

Choose $\alpha^* := \beta^*/\|\boldsymbol{x}\|^2$. This gives

$$\|\boldsymbol{y} - \hat{\boldsymbol{y}} - \frac{\beta\boldsymbol{x}}{\|\boldsymbol{x}\|^2}\| = \|\boldsymbol{y} - \hat{\boldsymbol{y}}\|^2 - \frac{|\beta|^2}{\|\boldsymbol{x}\|^2} < \|\boldsymbol{y} - \hat{\boldsymbol{y}}\|^2.$$

Hence, a vector $\widetilde{\boldsymbol{y}} := \hat{\boldsymbol{y}} + \beta\boldsymbol{x}/\|\boldsymbol{x}\|^2$ exists in $\mathcal{A}$ such that $\|\boldsymbol{y} - \widetilde{\boldsymbol{y}}\| < \|\boldsymbol{y} - \hat{\boldsymbol{y}}\|$. This implies that $\hat{\boldsymbol{y}}$ is not the minimizing vector. Since, in fact, $\hat{\boldsymbol{y}}$ *is* the minimizing vector, it follows that $\boldsymbol{y} - \hat{\boldsymbol{y}} \in \mathcal{A}^\perp$.

Exercise 3.55 (Unique representation, direct sum) Let $\mathcal{V}$ be a Hilbert space and let $\mathcal{A}$ be a closed subspace of $\mathcal{V}$. Show that each vector $\boldsymbol{y} \in \mathcal{V}$ has a unique representation $\boldsymbol{y} = \hat{\boldsymbol{y}} + \boldsymbol{e}$ where $\hat{\boldsymbol{y}} \in \mathcal{A}$ and $\boldsymbol{e} \in \mathcal{A}^\perp$. (This is sometimes written as $\mathcal{V} = \mathcal{A} \oplus \mathcal{A}^\perp$ where $\oplus$ denotes the *direct sum* operator.)

Solution

Let $\boldsymbol{y} \in \mathcal{V}$. By the projection theorem (Exercise 3.53), there is a unique vector $\hat{\boldsymbol{y}} \in \mathcal{A}$ such that $\|\boldsymbol{y} - \hat{\boldsymbol{y}}\| \leq \|\boldsymbol{y} - \boldsymbol{x}\|$ for all $\boldsymbol{x} \in \mathcal{A}$. Moreover, $\boldsymbol{e} := \boldsymbol{y} - \hat{\boldsymbol{y}} \in \mathcal{A}^\perp$ (Exercise 3.54(b)). Hence, $\boldsymbol{y} = \hat{\boldsymbol{y}} + \boldsymbol{e}$ with $\hat{\boldsymbol{y}} \in \mathcal{A}$ and $\boldsymbol{e} \in \mathcal{A}^\perp$.

To prove that the representation is unique, suppose that $\boldsymbol{y}$ can also be represented as $\boldsymbol{y} = \boldsymbol{a} + \boldsymbol{b}$, with $\boldsymbol{a} \in \mathcal{A}$, $\boldsymbol{b} \in \mathcal{A}^\perp$. Then, $(\boldsymbol{a} - \hat{\boldsymbol{y}}) + (\boldsymbol{b} - \boldsymbol{e}) = \boldsymbol{0}$ and $(\boldsymbol{a} - \hat{\boldsymbol{y}}) \perp (\boldsymbol{b} - \boldsymbol{e})$, since $\boldsymbol{a} - \hat{\boldsymbol{y}} \in \mathcal{A}$ and $\boldsymbol{b} - \boldsymbol{e} \in \mathcal{A}^\perp$. Pythagoras's theorem then gives

$$0 = \|(\boldsymbol{a} - \hat{\boldsymbol{y}}) + (\boldsymbol{b} + \boldsymbol{e})\|^2 = \|\boldsymbol{a} - \hat{\boldsymbol{y}}\|^2 + \|\boldsymbol{b} - \boldsymbol{e}\|^2,$$

implying that $\boldsymbol{a} = \hat{\boldsymbol{y}}$ and $\boldsymbol{b} = \boldsymbol{e}$.

Exercise 3.56 (Orthogonal complement, dimensions) Let $\mathcal{V}$ be a finite-dimensional inner-product space, and let $\mathcal{A}$ be a subspace of $\mathcal{V}$. Show that $\dim(\mathcal{A}) + \dim(\mathcal{A}^\perp) = \dim(\mathcal{V})$.

Solution

Exercises 3.34(c) and 3.48(c) together show that $\dim(\mathcal{A}) + \dim(\mathcal{A}^\perp) = \dim(\mathcal{A} + \mathcal{A}^\perp)$. Exercise 3.55 shows that $\mathcal{V} = \mathcal{A} \oplus \mathcal{A}^\perp$ and hence that $\dim(\mathcal{V}) = \dim(\mathcal{A} + \mathcal{A}^\perp)$. Hence, $\dim(\mathcal{A}) + \dim(\mathcal{A}^\perp) = \dim(\mathcal{V})$.

Exercise 3.57 (Orthogonal complement, iterated) Let $\mathcal{A}$ be a closed subspace of a Hilbert space $\mathcal{V}$. Show that $\mathcal{A}^{\perp\perp} = \mathcal{A}$.

Solution

Let $\boldsymbol{x} \in \mathcal{A}$. Then $\boldsymbol{x} \perp \boldsymbol{y}$ for all $\boldsymbol{y} \in \mathcal{A}^\perp$. Therefore, $\boldsymbol{x} \in \mathcal{A}^{\perp\perp}$. Conversely, let $\boldsymbol{x} \in \mathcal{A}^{\perp\perp}$. By Exercise 3.55 we can express $\boldsymbol{x}$ (uniquely) as $\boldsymbol{x} = \hat{\boldsymbol{x}} + \boldsymbol{e}$ with $\hat{\boldsymbol{x}} \in \mathcal{A}$, $\boldsymbol{e} \in \mathcal{A}^\perp$.

Since $\hat{x} \in \mathcal{A}$, it is also true that $\hat{x} \in \mathcal{A}^{\perp\perp}$. Hence, both x and $\hat{x}$ are in $\mathcal{A}^{\perp\perp}$. Therefore, $e = x - \hat{x} \in \mathcal{A}^{\perp\perp}$. But also $e \in \mathcal{A}^{\perp}$. Hence, $e = \mathbf{0}$ and $x = \hat{x} \in \mathcal{A}$.

Notes

Good intermediate texts on vector spaces are Shilov (1974) and Kreyszig (1978). More geared towards econometrics is Pollock (1979). In Exercise 3.25 we proved that every vector space $\mathcal{V} \neq \{\mathbf{0}\}$ has a basis in the finite-dimensional case. The result holds also in the infinite-dimensional case, but the proof is more difficult and requires Zorn's lemma; see Kreyszig (1978, Section 4.1). In Exercise 3.51 we showed that the space $L_2^\dagger$ of random variables is a Hilbert space. This is easy because *any* finite-dimensional inner-product space is complete (Kreyszig (1978, Theorem 2.4-2, pp. 73–74)) and therefore a Hilbert space. The difficulty only arises in infinite-dimensional spaces such as l_2. This space is, in fact, complete; for a proof see Kreyszig (1978, pp. 35–36).

4

Rank, inverse, and determinant

A real $m \times n$ matrix can be viewed as a collection of n columns in $\mathbb{R}^m$, but also as a collection of m rows in $\mathbb{R}^n$. Thus, associated with a matrix are *two* vector spaces: the collection of columns and the collection of rows. In each of the two spaces there are two subspaces of special importance. The *column space* of $\boldsymbol{A}$, denoted by $\operatorname{col} \boldsymbol{A}$, consists of all linear combinations of the columns of $\boldsymbol{A}$,

$$\operatorname{col} \boldsymbol{A} := \{\boldsymbol{x} \in \mathbb{R}^m : \boldsymbol{x} = \boldsymbol{A}\boldsymbol{y} \text{ for some } \boldsymbol{y} \in \mathbb{R}^n\}.$$

The *kernel* (or *null space*) of $\boldsymbol{A}$, denoted by $\ker \boldsymbol{A}$, is the set of all solutions to the equation $\boldsymbol{A}\boldsymbol{y} = \boldsymbol{0}$,

$$\ker \boldsymbol{A} := \{\boldsymbol{y} \in \mathbb{R}^n : \boldsymbol{A}\boldsymbol{y} = \boldsymbol{0}\}.$$

Notice that $\operatorname{col} \boldsymbol{A}$ is a subspace of the collection of columns, while $\ker \boldsymbol{A}$ is a subspace of the collection of rows. In the same way we can define the column space of $\boldsymbol{A}'$,

$$\operatorname{col} \boldsymbol{A}' := \{\boldsymbol{y} \in \mathbb{R}^n : \boldsymbol{y} = \boldsymbol{A}'\boldsymbol{x} \text{ for some } \boldsymbol{x} \in \mathbb{R}^m\},$$

and the kernel of $\boldsymbol{A}'$,

$$\ker \boldsymbol{A}' := \{\boldsymbol{x} \in \mathbb{R}^m : \boldsymbol{A}'\boldsymbol{x} = \boldsymbol{0}\}.$$

The kernels are more commonly known as *orthogonal complements*,

$$\operatorname{col}^{\perp}(\boldsymbol{A}) := \{\boldsymbol{x} \in \mathbb{R}^m : \boldsymbol{x} \perp \boldsymbol{A}\} = \ker \boldsymbol{A}'$$

and

$$\operatorname{col}^{\perp}(\boldsymbol{A}') := \{\boldsymbol{y} \in \mathbb{R}^n : \boldsymbol{y} \perp \boldsymbol{A}'\} = \ker \boldsymbol{A},$$

where $\operatorname{col}^{\perp}(\boldsymbol{A})$ denotes the orthogonal complement of $\boldsymbol{A}$ and $\operatorname{col}^{\perp}(\boldsymbol{A}')$ the orthogonal complement of $\boldsymbol{A}'$. The two subspaces $\operatorname{col} \boldsymbol{A}$ and $\operatorname{col}^{\perp}(\boldsymbol{A}) \equiv \ker \boldsymbol{A}'$ are orthogonal subspaces of $\mathbb{R}^m$, and their dimensions add up to m. Similarly, $\operatorname{col} \boldsymbol{A}'$ and $\operatorname{col}^{\perp}(\boldsymbol{A}') \equiv \ker \boldsymbol{A}$ are orthogonal subspaces of $\mathbb{R}^n$, and their dimensions add up to n. The two spaces are linked by the nontrivial fact that $\operatorname{col} \boldsymbol{A}$ and $\operatorname{col} \boldsymbol{A}'$ have the same dimension (proved in Exercise 4.5).

The *column rank* of $\boldsymbol{A}$ is the maximum number of linearly independent columns it contains. The *row rank* of $\boldsymbol{A}$ is the maximum number of linearly independent rows. The fact that $\operatorname{col} \boldsymbol{A}$ and $\operatorname{col} \boldsymbol{A}'$ have the same dimension implies that the column rank of $\boldsymbol{A}$ is equal to its row rank. Hence, the concept of *rank* is unambiguous. We denote the rank of $\boldsymbol{A}$ by $\operatorname{rk}(\boldsymbol{A})$. If an $m \times n$ matrix $\boldsymbol{A}$ has rank m we say that it has full row rank, if it has rank n we say it has full column rank. From the definitions of dimension and rank, it follows that

$$\operatorname{rk}(\boldsymbol{A}) = \dim(\operatorname{col} \boldsymbol{A})$$

for any matrix $\boldsymbol{A}$.

A square $n \times n$ matrix is said to be *nonsingular* (or *invertible*) if $\operatorname{rk}(\boldsymbol{A}) = n$; otherwise the matrix is *singular*. If there exists an $n \times n$ matrix $\boldsymbol{B}$ such that

$$\boldsymbol{AB} = \boldsymbol{BA} = \boldsymbol{I}_n,$$

then $\boldsymbol{B}$ is called the *inverse* of $\boldsymbol{A}$, denoted by $\boldsymbol{A}^{-1}$. For example, letting

$$\boldsymbol{A} = \begin{pmatrix} 2 & 1 \\ 1 & 1 \end{pmatrix} \quad \text{and} \quad \boldsymbol{B} = \begin{pmatrix} 1 & -1 \\ -1 & 2 \end{pmatrix},$$

we see that $\boldsymbol{AB} = \boldsymbol{I}_2$ and $\boldsymbol{BA} = \boldsymbol{I}_2$. Hence, $\boldsymbol{B}$ is the inverse of $\boldsymbol{A}$ and vice versa.

In order to define the determinant, consider first the set $(1, 2, \dots, n)$. Any rearrangement of the "natural order" $(1, 2, \dots, n)$ of n integers is called a *permutation* of these integers. The interchange of two integers (not necessarily adjacent) is called a *transposition*. For example, $(3, 2, 1)$ is a transposition of $(1, 2, 3)$. To obtain the permutation $(2, 3, 1)$ from $(1, 2, 3)$ requires two transpositions. But it can also be done in four (or any even number of) transpositions, for example,

$$(1, 2, 3) \mapsto (1, 3, 2) \mapsto (3, 1, 2) \mapsto (3, 2, 1) \mapsto (2, 3, 1).$$

The number of transpositions required to transform $(1, 2, \dots, n)$ to $(j_1, j_2, \dots, j_n)$ is always even or always odd (we shall not prove this). We define the function $\varphi(j_1, \dots, j_n)$ to equal 0 if the number of transpositions required to change $(1, \dots, n)$ into $(j_1, \dots, j_n)$ is even; it equals 1 otherwise.

Associated with any square matrix $\boldsymbol{A}$ of order n is the *determinant* $|\boldsymbol{A}|$ (or $\det \boldsymbol{A}$), defined by the *Laplace expansion*

$$|\boldsymbol{A}| := \sum (-1)^{\varphi(j_1, \dots, j_n)} \prod_{i=1}^{n} a_{ij_i}$$

where the summation is taken over all permutations $(j_1, \ldots, j_n)$ of the set of integers $(1, \ldots, n)$. For example, the determinant of a 2×2 matrix $\boldsymbol{A}$ is

$$|\boldsymbol{A}| = \begin{vmatrix} a_{11} & a_{12} \\ a_{21} & a_{22} \end{vmatrix} = (-1)^{\varphi(1,2)} a_{11}a_{22} + (-1)^{\varphi(2,1)} a_{12}a_{21}$$
$$= a_{11}a_{22} - a_{12}a_{21},$$

which is precisely the area of the parallelogram formed by the vectors $\boldsymbol{a}_1 := (a_{11}, a_{21})'$ and $\boldsymbol{a}_2 := (a_{12}, a_{22})'$. More generally, the determinant of an $n \times n$ matrix $\boldsymbol{A} := (\boldsymbol{a}_1, \ldots, \boldsymbol{a}_n)$ is the volume of the parallelotope of dimension n formed by the vectors $\boldsymbol{a}_1, \ldots, \boldsymbol{a}_n$.

Let $\boldsymbol{A}$ be a square matrix of order n and let $\boldsymbol{A}_{(ij)}$ be the $(n-1) \times (n-1)$ matrix obtained by deleting from $\boldsymbol{A}$ its i-th row and j-th column. The quantity

$$c_{ij} := (-1)^{i+j} |\boldsymbol{A}_{(ij)}|$$

is said to be the *cofactor* of the element a_{ij} of $\boldsymbol{A}$, and the matrix $\boldsymbol{C} = (c_{ij})$ is said to be the *cofactor matrix* of $\boldsymbol{A}$. The transpose of $\boldsymbol{C}$ is the *adjoint* of $\boldsymbol{A}$ and will be denoted by $\boldsymbol{A}^{\#}$.

All matrices in this chapter are real, unless specified otherwise.

4.1 Rank

Exercise 4.1 (Column space) Consider the 3×2 matrix

$$\boldsymbol{A} = \begin{pmatrix} 1 & 2 \\ 3 & 4 \\ 5 & 6 \end{pmatrix}.$$

(a) Show that

$$\operatorname{col} \boldsymbol{A} = \lambda_1 \begin{pmatrix} 1 \\ 0 \\ -1 \end{pmatrix} + \lambda_2 \begin{pmatrix} 0 \\ 1 \\ 2 \end{pmatrix}, \quad \ker \boldsymbol{A}' = \operatorname{col}^{\perp} \boldsymbol{A} = \lambda_3 \begin{pmatrix} 1 \\ -2 \\ 1 \end{pmatrix}.$$

(b) Show that

$$\operatorname{col} \boldsymbol{A}' = \mu_1 \begin{pmatrix} 1 \\ 0 \end{pmatrix} + \mu_2 \begin{pmatrix} 0 \\ 1 \end{pmatrix}, \quad \ker \boldsymbol{A} = \operatorname{col}^{\perp} \boldsymbol{A}' = \{\boldsymbol{0}\}.$$

(c) Show that $\operatorname{col} \boldsymbol{A} = \operatorname{col}(\boldsymbol{A}\boldsymbol{A}')$.

Solution

(a) The column space of $\boldsymbol{A}$ is given by

$$\operatorname{col} \boldsymbol{A} = y_1 \begin{pmatrix} 1 \\ 3 \\ 5 \end{pmatrix} + y_2 \begin{pmatrix} 2 \\ 4 \\ 6 \end{pmatrix}.$$

Let $\lambda_1 := y_1 + 2y_2$ and $\lambda_2 := 3y_1 + 4y_2$. Then $y_1 = -2\lambda_1 + \lambda_2$ and $2y_2 = 3\lambda_1 - \lambda_2$. Hence, $5y_1 + 6y_2 = -\lambda_1 + 2\lambda_2$. The orthogonal complement $\operatorname{col}^{\perp}(\boldsymbol{A})$ is given by the general solution to

$$\begin{pmatrix} 1 & 3 & 5 \\ 2 & 4 & 6 \end{pmatrix} \begin{pmatrix} x_1 \\ x_2 \\ x_3 \end{pmatrix} = \begin{pmatrix} 0 \\ 0 \end{pmatrix},$$

which yields $x_2 + 2x_3 = 0$ and $x_1 = x_3$.
(b) Similarly, the column space of $\boldsymbol{A}'$ is given by

$$\operatorname{col} \boldsymbol{A}' = x_1 \begin{pmatrix} 1 \\ 2 \end{pmatrix} + x_2 \begin{pmatrix} 3 \\ 4 \end{pmatrix} + x_3 \begin{pmatrix} 5 \\ 6 \end{pmatrix} = \mu_1 \begin{pmatrix} 1 \\ 0 \end{pmatrix} + \mu_2 \begin{pmatrix} 0 \\ 1 \end{pmatrix},$$

letting $\mu_1 := x_1 + 3x_2 + 5x_3$ and $\mu_2 := 2x_1 + 4x_2 + 6x_3$. The orthogonal complement $\operatorname{col}^{\perp}(\boldsymbol{A}')$ is the general solution to

$$\begin{pmatrix} 1 & 2 \\ 3 & 4 \\ 5 & 6 \end{pmatrix} \begin{pmatrix} y_1 \\ y_2 \end{pmatrix} = \begin{pmatrix} 0 \\ 0 \\ 0 \end{pmatrix},$$

yielding $y_1 = y_2 = 0$.
(c) We need to show that for each α, β, γ we can find λ_1, λ_2 such that

$$\alpha \begin{pmatrix} 5 \\ 11 \\ 17 \end{pmatrix} + \beta \begin{pmatrix} 11 \\ 25 \\ 39 \end{pmatrix} + \gamma \begin{pmatrix} 17 \\ 39 \\ 61 \end{pmatrix} = \lambda_1 \begin{pmatrix} 1 \\ 0 \\ -1 \end{pmatrix} + \lambda_2 \begin{pmatrix} 0 \\ 1 \\ 2 \end{pmatrix}.$$

Choosing $\lambda_1 := 5\alpha+11\beta+17\gamma$, $\lambda_2 := 11\alpha+25\beta+39\gamma$, shows that this is indeed possible.

Exercise 4.2 (Dimension of column space) Recall that the dimension of a vector space $\mathcal{V}$ (such as $\operatorname{col} \boldsymbol{A}$) is the minimum number of vectors required to span the space. For the matrix $\boldsymbol{A}$ of Exercise 4.1 show that:
(a) $\dim(\operatorname{col} \boldsymbol{A}) = \dim(\operatorname{col} \boldsymbol{A}') = 2$;
(b) $\dim(\operatorname{col} \boldsymbol{A}) + \dim(\operatorname{col}^{\perp} \boldsymbol{A}) = 3$;
(c) $\dim(\operatorname{col} \boldsymbol{A}') + \dim(\operatorname{col}^{\perp} \boldsymbol{A}') = 2$.

Solution
We see that $\dim(\operatorname{col} \boldsymbol{A}) = 2$, $\dim(\operatorname{col} \boldsymbol{A}') = 2$, $\dim(\operatorname{col}^{\perp} \boldsymbol{A}) = 1$, and $\dim(\operatorname{col}^{\perp} \boldsymbol{A}') = 0$. In the following three exercises we shall generalize these results to arbitrary $\boldsymbol{A}$.

Exercise 4.3 (Orthogonal complement) Let $\boldsymbol{A}$ be a real $m \times n$ matrix.
(a) Show that $\operatorname{col} \boldsymbol{A} \perp \ker \boldsymbol{A}'$.
(b) Show that $\ker \boldsymbol{A}' = \operatorname{col}^{\perp} \boldsymbol{A}$.
(c) Show that $\dim(\operatorname{col} \boldsymbol{A}) + \dim(\ker \boldsymbol{A}') = m$.

Solution
(a) Let $\boldsymbol{x}$ be an arbitrary vector in $\operatorname{col} \boldsymbol{A}$. Then $\boldsymbol{x} = \boldsymbol{A}\boldsymbol{v}$ for some vector $\boldsymbol{v}$. Let $\boldsymbol{y}$ be an arbitrary vector in $\ker \boldsymbol{A}'$. Then $\boldsymbol{A}'\boldsymbol{y} = \boldsymbol{0}$. Hence, $\boldsymbol{x}'\boldsymbol{y} = (\boldsymbol{A}\boldsymbol{v})'\boldsymbol{y} = \boldsymbol{v}'\boldsymbol{A}'\boldsymbol{y} = \boldsymbol{v}'\boldsymbol{0} = 0$.

(b) This is almost trivial. The space $\ker \boldsymbol{A}'$ contains all vectors orthogonal to the matrix $\boldsymbol{A}$, whereas the space $\operatorname{col}^{\perp} \boldsymbol{A}$ contains all vectors orthogonal to the space $\operatorname{col} \boldsymbol{A}$, that is, to the space spanned by the columns of $\boldsymbol{A}$. If $\boldsymbol{x} \in \operatorname{col}^{\perp} \boldsymbol{A}$, then $\boldsymbol{x}$ is orthogonal to every vector in $\operatorname{col} \boldsymbol{A}$ and, in particular, to the columns of $\boldsymbol{A}$. Hence, $\boldsymbol{x} \in \ker \boldsymbol{A}'$. Conversely, if $\boldsymbol{x} \in \ker \boldsymbol{A}'$, then $\boldsymbol{x} \in \operatorname{col}^{\perp} \boldsymbol{A}$, using (a). Hence, the two spaces are the same.
(c) The result now is an immediate consequence of Exercise 3.56.

***Exercise 4.4 (Fundamental link between rows and columns)** Let $\boldsymbol{A}$ be a real $m \times n$ matrix. Show that $\dim(\operatorname{col} \boldsymbol{A}) + \dim(\ker \boldsymbol{A}) = n$.

Solution
Recall that

$$\operatorname{col} \boldsymbol{A} := \{\boldsymbol{x} \in \mathbb{R}^m : \boldsymbol{x} = \boldsymbol{A}\boldsymbol{y} \text{ for some } \boldsymbol{y}\} \quad \text{and} \quad \ker \boldsymbol{A} := \{\boldsymbol{y} \in \mathbb{R}^n : \boldsymbol{A}\boldsymbol{y} = \boldsymbol{0}\}.$$

Consider a basis $(\boldsymbol{x}_1, \dots, \boldsymbol{x}_r)$ of $\operatorname{col} \boldsymbol{A}$ and a basis $(\boldsymbol{y}_1, \dots, \boldsymbol{y}_s)$ of $\ker \boldsymbol{A}$. For each $\boldsymbol{x}_j$ $(j = 1, \dots, r)$ there exists a $\boldsymbol{z}_j \neq \boldsymbol{0}$ such that $\boldsymbol{x}_j = \boldsymbol{A}\boldsymbol{z}_j$. Now consider the matrix

$$\boldsymbol{B} := (\boldsymbol{y}_1, \dots, \boldsymbol{y}_s, \boldsymbol{z}_1, \dots, \boldsymbol{z}_r).$$

The proof consists of two parts. In the first part we show that the columns of $\boldsymbol{B}$ span $\mathbb{R}^n$; in the second part we show that the columns in $\boldsymbol{B}$ are linearly independent. The two parts together imply that $\boldsymbol{B}$ is a basis of $\mathbb{R}^n$, and hence that $s + r = n$.

To prove that $\boldsymbol{B}$ spans $\mathbb{R}^n$, let $\boldsymbol{v} \in \mathbb{R}^n$ be arbitrary. Then $\boldsymbol{A}\boldsymbol{v} \in \operatorname{col} \boldsymbol{A}$, and hence $\boldsymbol{A}\boldsymbol{v} = \sum_j \alpha_j \boldsymbol{x}_j$ for some choice of $\alpha_1, \dots, \alpha_r$. Define $\tilde{\boldsymbol{y}} := \sum_j \alpha_j \boldsymbol{z}_j - \boldsymbol{v}$. Then,

$$\boldsymbol{A}\tilde{\boldsymbol{y}} = \sum_j \alpha_j \boldsymbol{A}\boldsymbol{z}_j - \boldsymbol{A}\boldsymbol{v} = \sum_j \alpha_j \boldsymbol{x}_j - \boldsymbol{A}\boldsymbol{v} = \boldsymbol{0},$$

and hence $\tilde{\boldsymbol{y}} \in \ker \boldsymbol{A}$. We can therefore write $\tilde{\boldsymbol{y}} = \sum_i \beta_i \boldsymbol{y}_i$ for some choice of $\beta_1, \dots, \beta_s$, so that $\boldsymbol{v} = -\sum_i \beta_i \boldsymbol{y}_i + \sum_j \alpha_j \boldsymbol{z}_j$. Hence, every vector $\boldsymbol{v} \in \mathbb{R}^n$ can be written as a linear combination of the columns of $\boldsymbol{B}$.

To prove the second part, assume that $\sum_j \alpha_j \boldsymbol{z}_j + \sum_i \beta_i \boldsymbol{y}_i = \boldsymbol{0}$. Then,

$$\boldsymbol{0} = \sum_j \alpha_j \boldsymbol{A}\boldsymbol{z}_j + \sum_i \beta_i \boldsymbol{A}\boldsymbol{y}_i = \sum_j \alpha_j \boldsymbol{x}_j,$$

because $\boldsymbol{A}\boldsymbol{y}_i = \boldsymbol{0}$ and $\boldsymbol{A}\boldsymbol{z}_j = \boldsymbol{x}_j$. This shows that $\sum_j \alpha_j \boldsymbol{x}_j = \boldsymbol{0}$ and, since $(\boldsymbol{x}_1, \dots, \boldsymbol{x}_r)$ is a basis, that $\alpha_j = 0$ for all j. This in turn implies that $\sum_i \beta_i \boldsymbol{y}_i = \boldsymbol{0}$ and, since $(\boldsymbol{y}_1, \dots, \boldsymbol{y}_s)$ is a basis, that $\beta_i = 0$ for all i. Hence, the columns of $\boldsymbol{B}$ are linearly independent, and the proof is complete.

Exercise 4.5 (The rank theorem)
(a) Show that, for any real matrix $\boldsymbol{A}$, $\dim(\operatorname{col} \boldsymbol{A}') = \dim(\operatorname{col} \boldsymbol{A})$, using Exercises 4.3 and 4.4.

(b) Conclude that the column rank of $\boldsymbol{A}$ is equal to its row rank, so that the concept of rank is unambiguous.
(c) Show that $\operatorname{rk}(\boldsymbol{A}) = \operatorname{rk}(\boldsymbol{A}')$.

Solution
(a) Applying Exercise 4.4 to $\boldsymbol{A}'$ instead of $\boldsymbol{A}$, gives $\dim(\operatorname{col} \boldsymbol{A}') + \dim(\ker \boldsymbol{A}') = m$. Combining this with the result of Exercise 4.3 immediately gives the required result.
(b) Since the column space of $\boldsymbol{A}'$ is the row space of $\boldsymbol{A}$, we conclude that the column space and the row space of $\boldsymbol{A}$ have the same dimension, and hence that the column rank and the row rank of $\boldsymbol{A}$ are the same.
(c) Since the column rank of $\boldsymbol{A}$ is the row rank of $\boldsymbol{A}'$, and, as we now know, column rank and row rank are the same, the result follows. (The rank theorem, although misleadingly simple in appearance, is in fact one of the most important theorems in matrix algebra.)

Exercise 4.6 (Rank, example) Consider the matrices

$$\boldsymbol{A} = \begin{pmatrix} 1 & 5 & 6 \\ 2 & 6 & 8 \\ 7 & 1 & 8 \end{pmatrix} \quad \text{and} \quad \boldsymbol{B} = \begin{pmatrix} 1 & 5 & 6 & 3 \\ 2 & 1 & 4 & 1 \\ 3 & 5 & 5 & 4 \end{pmatrix}.$$

(a) Find the rank of $\boldsymbol{A}$ and $\boldsymbol{B}$.
(b) Show that $\operatorname{rk}(\boldsymbol{A}) = \operatorname{rk}(\boldsymbol{A}') = \operatorname{rk}(\boldsymbol{A}\boldsymbol{A}') = \operatorname{rk}(\boldsymbol{A}'\boldsymbol{A})$.
(c) Is it possible to construct a 3×4 matrix of rank 4?

Solution
(a) The first two rows of both $\boldsymbol{A}$ and $\boldsymbol{B}$ are linearly independent. Hence, $\operatorname{rk}(\boldsymbol{A}) \geq 2$ and $\operatorname{rk}(\boldsymbol{B}) \geq 2$. Also, $\operatorname{rk}(\boldsymbol{A}) < 3$, because if we let $\boldsymbol{u} = (20, -17, 2)'$, then $\boldsymbol{A}'\boldsymbol{u} = \boldsymbol{0}$. Hence, $\operatorname{rk}(\boldsymbol{A}) = 2$. (Notice that the vector $\boldsymbol{v} = (1, 1, -1)'$ gives $\boldsymbol{A}\boldsymbol{v} = \boldsymbol{0}$. If the row rank of $\boldsymbol{A}$ is 2, then the column rank is 2 as well.) However, $\operatorname{rk}(\boldsymbol{B}) = 3$, since $\boldsymbol{B}'\boldsymbol{z} = \boldsymbol{0}$ implies $\boldsymbol{z} = \boldsymbol{0}$.
(b) We already know that $\operatorname{rk}(\boldsymbol{A}') = \operatorname{rk}(\boldsymbol{A}) = 2$. Writing out both $\boldsymbol{A}\boldsymbol{A}'$ and $\boldsymbol{A}'\boldsymbol{A}$ it becomes clear that their ranks must be 2 or 3. (If the rank is 0, then the matrix is the null matrix; if the rank is 1, then all columns are proportional to each other, and all rows are proportional to each other.) In fact, $\operatorname{rk}(\boldsymbol{A}\boldsymbol{A}') = \operatorname{rk}(\boldsymbol{A}'\boldsymbol{A}) = 2$, because $\boldsymbol{A}\boldsymbol{A}'\boldsymbol{u} = \boldsymbol{0}$ and $\boldsymbol{A}'\boldsymbol{A}\boldsymbol{v} = \boldsymbol{0}$, where $\boldsymbol{u}$ and $\boldsymbol{v}$ are given under (a).
(c) No, this is not possible. There are only three rows and these cannot generate a four-dimensional space.

Exercise 4.7 (Simple properties of rank) Let $\boldsymbol{A}$ be an $m \times n$ matrix.
(a) Show that $0 \leq \operatorname{rk}(\boldsymbol{A}) \leq \min(m, n)$.
(b) Show that $\operatorname{rk}(\boldsymbol{A}) = 0 \iff \boldsymbol{A} = \mathbf{O}$.
(c) Show that $\operatorname{rk}(\boldsymbol{I}_n) = n$.
(d) Show that $\operatorname{rk}(\lambda \boldsymbol{A}) = \operatorname{rk}(\boldsymbol{A})$ if $\lambda \neq 0$.

Solution

(a) It is clear that $\mathrm{rk}(\boldsymbol{A}) \geq 0$. The rank of $\boldsymbol{A}$ is equal to the number of linearly independent columns. Since there are only n columns, $\mathrm{rk}(\boldsymbol{A}) \leq n$. Also, $\mathrm{rk}(\boldsymbol{A})$ is equal to the number of linearly independent rows. Hence, $\mathrm{rk}(\boldsymbol{A}) \leq m$.
(b) If $\mathrm{rk}(\boldsymbol{A}) = 0$, then there are no linearly independent columns. Hence, $\boldsymbol{A} = \boldsymbol{O}$. Conversely, if $\boldsymbol{A} = \boldsymbol{O}$, then there are no linearly independent columns. Hence, $\mathrm{rk}(\boldsymbol{A}) = 0$.
(c) The identity matrix of order n has n linearly independent columns, since $\boldsymbol{I}_n\boldsymbol{x} = \boldsymbol{0}$ implies $\boldsymbol{x} = \boldsymbol{0}$.
(d) We have

$$\mathrm{rk}(\boldsymbol{A}) = \dim(\mathrm{col}(\boldsymbol{A})) = \dim(\mathrm{col}(\lambda\boldsymbol{A})) = \mathrm{rk}(\lambda\boldsymbol{A})$$

for any $\lambda \neq 0$.

Exercise 4.8 (Homogeneous vector equation) Let $\boldsymbol{A}$ be an $m \times n$ matrix and let $\boldsymbol{A}\boldsymbol{x} = \boldsymbol{0}$ for some $\boldsymbol{x} \neq \boldsymbol{0}$. Show that $\mathrm{rk}(\boldsymbol{A}) \leq n - 1$. Does the converse hold as well? (A generalization of this result is provided in Exercise 5.47(c).)

Solution

Let $\boldsymbol{A}\boldsymbol{x} = \boldsymbol{0}$ for some $\boldsymbol{x} := (x_1, \dots, x_n)' \neq \boldsymbol{0}$. If $\boldsymbol{a}_1, \dots, \boldsymbol{a}_n$ denote the columns of $\boldsymbol{A}$, then $x_1\boldsymbol{a}_1 + x_2\boldsymbol{a}_2 + \cdots + x_n\boldsymbol{a}_n = \boldsymbol{0}$. Hence, the columns of $\boldsymbol{A}$ are linearly dependent, and $\mathrm{rk}(\boldsymbol{A}) \leq n - 1$. The converse holds as well. If $\boldsymbol{A}\boldsymbol{x} \neq \boldsymbol{0}$ for all $\boldsymbol{x} \neq \boldsymbol{0}$, then the columns of $\boldsymbol{A}$ are linearly independent, and $\mathrm{rk}(\boldsymbol{A}) = n$.

Exercise 4.9 (Rank of diagonal matrix)

(a) Show that the rank of a diagonal matrix equals the number of nonzero diagonal elements it possesses.
(b) Is the same true for a triangular matrix?

Solution

(a) Let $\boldsymbol{A}$ be a diagonal matrix of order n. Suppose r of its diagonal elements are nonzero, say the first r. Then the diagonal matrix takes the form $\boldsymbol{A} = (a_{11}\boldsymbol{e}_1, \dots, a_{rr}\boldsymbol{e}_r, \boldsymbol{0}, \dots, \boldsymbol{0})$. The first r columns are then linearly independent, but the last $n - r$ columns depend (trivially) on the first r. Hence, $\mathrm{rk}(\boldsymbol{A}) = r$.
(b) The two examples

$$\boldsymbol{A} = \begin{pmatrix} 0 & 0 \\ 1 & 0 \end{pmatrix} \quad \text{and} \quad \boldsymbol{B} = \begin{pmatrix} 1 & 0 & 0 \\ 0 & 0 & 0 \\ 0 & 1 & 0 \end{pmatrix}$$

demonstrate that the same is not true for triangular matrices. The matrix $\boldsymbol{A}$ has rank 1, but no nonzero diagonal elements; the matrix $\boldsymbol{B}$ has rank 2 and has 1 nonzero diagonal element. However, the statement is true in the special case that $\boldsymbol{A}$ has full rank; see Exercise 3.16(c).

Exercise 4.10 (Matrix of rank one) Show that $\operatorname{rk}(\boldsymbol{A}) = 1$ if and only if there exist nonzero vectors $\boldsymbol{a}$ and $\boldsymbol{b}$ such that $\boldsymbol{A} = \boldsymbol{a}\boldsymbol{b}'$.

Solution

Let $\boldsymbol{A} := (\boldsymbol{a}_1, \dots, \boldsymbol{a}_n)$ be an $m \times n$ matrix. If $\boldsymbol{A} = \boldsymbol{a}\boldsymbol{b}'$ ($\boldsymbol{a} \neq \boldsymbol{0}, \boldsymbol{b} \neq \boldsymbol{0}$), then $\boldsymbol{A} = (b_1\boldsymbol{a}, \dots, b_n\boldsymbol{a})$ and hence all columns of $\boldsymbol{A}$ are linearly dependent on one $m \times 1$ vector $\boldsymbol{a}$, so that $\operatorname{rk}(\boldsymbol{A}) = 1$.

Conversely, let $\operatorname{rk}(\boldsymbol{A}) = 1$ and assume, without loss of generality, that $\boldsymbol{a}_1 \neq \boldsymbol{0}$. Then, for $2 \leq j \leq n$, $b_1\boldsymbol{a}_1 + b_j\boldsymbol{a}_j = \boldsymbol{0}$ for some b_1 and b_j, not both zero. If $b_j = 0$, then $b_1\boldsymbol{a}_1 = \boldsymbol{0}$ and hence $b_1 = 0$ (since $\boldsymbol{a}_1 \neq \boldsymbol{0}$). Since b_1 and b_j cannot both be zero, it follows that $b_j \neq 0$ and hence that $\boldsymbol{a}_j = -(b_1/b_j)\boldsymbol{a}_1$. Thus, each column of $\boldsymbol{A}$ is a multiple of $\boldsymbol{a}_1$, and we obtain $\boldsymbol{A} = (b_1\boldsymbol{a}, \dots, b_n\boldsymbol{a}) = \boldsymbol{a}\boldsymbol{b}'$.

Exercise 4.11 (Rank factorization theorem)
(a) Show that every $m \times n$ matrix $\boldsymbol{A}$ of rank r can be written as $\boldsymbol{A} = \boldsymbol{B}\boldsymbol{C}'$, where $\boldsymbol{B}$ ($m \times r$) and $\boldsymbol{C}$ ($n \times r$) both have rank r.
(b) Hence, show that $\boldsymbol{A}$ can be written as a sum of r matrices, each of rank one.

Solution

(a) Since $\boldsymbol{A}$ has rank r, it has r linearly independent columns, say $\boldsymbol{b}_1, \dots, \boldsymbol{b}_r$. Each column $\boldsymbol{a}_i$ of $\boldsymbol{A}$ is a linear combination of $\boldsymbol{b}_1, \dots, \boldsymbol{b}_r$. Hence there exist numbers c_{ij} ($i = 1, \dots, n; j = 1, \dots, r$) such that

$$\boldsymbol{a}_i = \sum_{j=1}^{r} c_{ij}\boldsymbol{b}_j.$$

Now let $\boldsymbol{B} := (\boldsymbol{b}_1, \dots, \boldsymbol{b}_r)$ and $\boldsymbol{C} := (c_{ij})$. Then, $\boldsymbol{A}\boldsymbol{e}_i = \boldsymbol{a}_i = \boldsymbol{B}(\boldsymbol{C}'\boldsymbol{e}_i) = (\boldsymbol{B}\boldsymbol{C}')\boldsymbol{e}_i$ for all i, and hence $\boldsymbol{A} = \boldsymbol{B}\boldsymbol{C}'$. (Of course, we could also have started with r linearly independent rows of $\boldsymbol{A}$, say $\boldsymbol{c}_1', \dots, \boldsymbol{c}_r'$.)
(b) Letting $\boldsymbol{B} := (\boldsymbol{b}_1, \dots, \boldsymbol{b}_r)$ and $\boldsymbol{C} := (\boldsymbol{c}_1, \dots, \boldsymbol{c}_r)$, we obtain $\boldsymbol{A} = \boldsymbol{B}\boldsymbol{C}' = \sum_{j=1}^{r} \boldsymbol{b}_j\boldsymbol{c}_j'$, a sum of r matrices, each of rank one.

Exercise 4.12 (Column rank and row rank) Given is an $m \times n$ matrix $\boldsymbol{A}$. You know that there exists an $m \times 1$ vector $\boldsymbol{a}$, such that, if $\boldsymbol{a}$ is added as an additional column to $\boldsymbol{A}$, the rank of $\boldsymbol{A}$ increases by 1. In other words, $\operatorname{rk}(\boldsymbol{A} : \boldsymbol{a}) = \operatorname{rk}(\boldsymbol{A}) + 1$. Show that this implies that the rows of $\boldsymbol{A}$ are linearly dependent.

Solution

This exercise is another example of the tight connection between row rank and column rank. Suppose that the m rows of $\boldsymbol{A}$ are linearly independent, so that $\operatorname{rk}(\boldsymbol{A}) = m$. After adding one column to $\boldsymbol{A}$, the matrix $(\boldsymbol{A} : \boldsymbol{a})$ still has m rows, and hence $\operatorname{rk}(\boldsymbol{A} : \boldsymbol{a}) \leq m$, by Exercise 4.7(a). We thus arrive at a contradiction. Hence, $\operatorname{rk}(\boldsymbol{A}) < m$ and the rows of $\boldsymbol{A}$ are linearly dependent.

Exercise 4.13 (A and AA' span same space) Show that:
(a) $\ker(A') = \ker(AA')$;
(b) $\mathrm{col}^{\perp}(A) = \mathrm{col}^{\perp}(AA')$;
(c) $\mathrm{col}(A) = \mathrm{col}(AA')$;
(d) $\mathrm{rk}(A) = \mathrm{rk}(AA') = \mathrm{rk}(A'A)$.

Solution
(a) If $x \in \ker A'$, then $A'x = 0$. This gives $AA'x = 0$, so that $x \in \ker(AA')$. Conversely, if $x \in \ker(AA')$, then $AA'x = 0$, and hence $(A'x)'(A'x) = x'AA'x = 0$. This gives $A'x = 0$, so that $x \in \ker A'$.
(b) Since $\ker A' = \mathrm{col}^{\perp}(A)$ and $\ker(AA') = \mathrm{col}^{\perp}(AA')$, using Exercise 4.3(b), the result follows immediately.
(c) Using Exercise 3.57, we find

$$\mathrm{col}\, A = (\mathrm{col}^{\perp} A)^{\perp} = (\mathrm{col}^{\perp}(AA'))^{\perp} = \mathrm{col}(AA').$$

(d) Clearly (c) implies that $\mathrm{rk}(A) = \mathrm{rk}(AA')$. By the same argument we also find $\mathrm{rk}(A') = \mathrm{rk}(A'A)$. Then, since $\mathrm{rk}(A) = \mathrm{rk}(A')$, the result follows.

Exercise 4.14 (Rank inequalities: sum)
(a) Show that $\mathrm{rk}(A + B) \leq \mathrm{rk}(A) + \mathrm{rk}(B)$.
(b) Show that $\mathrm{rk}(A - B) \geq |\,\mathrm{rk}(A) - \mathrm{rk}(B)|$.
(The same result will be proved in Exercise 5.51 using partitioned matrices.)

Solution
(a) Let $r := \mathrm{rk}(A)$ and $s := \mathrm{rk}(B)$. Denote by $x_1, \dots, x_r$ a set of r linearly independent columns of A, and by $y_1, \dots, y_s$ a set of s linearly independent columns of B. Then every column of $A + B$ can be expressed as a linear combination of the $r + s$ vectors of

$$C := (x_1, \dots, x_r, y_1, \dots, y_s).$$

The vector space $\mathcal{C}$ spanned by the columns of $A + B$ is also spanned by the $r + s$ vectors in C, and hence

$$\mathrm{rk}(A + B) = \dim(\mathcal{C}) \leq r + s = \mathrm{rk}(A) + \mathrm{rk}(B).$$

(b) Replace A by $A - B$ in (a), and use the fact that $\mathrm{rk}(A - B) = \mathrm{rk}(B - A)$.

Exercise 4.15 (Rank inequalities: product)
(a) Show that $\mathrm{col}(AB) \subseteq \mathrm{col}\, A$.
(b) Show that $\mathrm{rk}(AB) \leq \min(\mathrm{rk}(A), \mathrm{rk}(B))$.

Solution
(a) Let $x \in \mathrm{col}(AB)$. Then $x = ABz$ for some z. Hence, $x = Ay$ for $y := Bz$, so that $x \in \mathrm{col}\, A$.

(b) As a result,

$$\operatorname{rk}(\boldsymbol{AB}) = \dim(\operatorname{col}(\boldsymbol{AB})) \leq \dim(\operatorname{col} \boldsymbol{A}) = \operatorname{rk}(\boldsymbol{A}).$$

Since $\operatorname{rk}(\boldsymbol{AB}) \leq \operatorname{rk}(\boldsymbol{A})$ for any two matrices $\boldsymbol{A}$ and $\boldsymbol{B}$, it is also true that

$$\operatorname{rk}(\boldsymbol{AB}) = \operatorname{rk}(\boldsymbol{B}'\boldsymbol{A}') \leq \operatorname{rk}(\boldsymbol{B}') = \operatorname{rk}(\boldsymbol{B}).$$

This completes the proof.

Let us provide a second proof, based on the kernel. Let $\boldsymbol{A}$ be an $m \times n$ matrix and let $\boldsymbol{B}$ an $n \times p$ matrix. Then, $\boldsymbol{Bz} = \mathbf{0}$ implies $\boldsymbol{ABz} = \mathbf{0}$ for any $\boldsymbol{z}$, so that $\ker \boldsymbol{B} \subseteq \ker(\boldsymbol{AB})$. Hence, using Exercise 4.4,

$$p - \dim(\operatorname{col} \boldsymbol{B}) = \dim(\ker \boldsymbol{B}) \leq \dim(\ker \boldsymbol{AB}) = p - \dim(\operatorname{col} \boldsymbol{AB}),$$

from which it follows that $\dim(\operatorname{col} \boldsymbol{AB}) \leq \dim(\operatorname{col} \boldsymbol{B})$. From here the proof proceeds as before.

Exercise 4.16 (Rank of a product) Show that it is not true, in general, that $\operatorname{rk}(\boldsymbol{AB}) = \operatorname{rk}(\boldsymbol{BA})$ for two conformable matrices $\boldsymbol{A}$ and $\boldsymbol{B}$.

Solution
It suffices to consider

$$\boldsymbol{A} = \begin{pmatrix} 1 & 0 \\ 1 & 0 \end{pmatrix} \quad \text{and} \quad \boldsymbol{B} = \begin{pmatrix} 0 & 0 \\ 1 & 1 \end{pmatrix}.$$

Then, $\operatorname{rk}(\boldsymbol{AB}) = \operatorname{rk}(\mathbf{O}) = 0$ and $\operatorname{rk}(\boldsymbol{BA}) = 1$.

Exercise 4.17 (Rank of submatrix) Let $\boldsymbol{A}_1$ be a submatrix of $\boldsymbol{A}$. Show that $\operatorname{rk}(\boldsymbol{A}_1) \leq \operatorname{rk}(\boldsymbol{A})$.

Solution
We can write $\boldsymbol{A}_1 = \boldsymbol{EAF}$ for appropriate choices of selection matrices $\boldsymbol{E}$ and $\boldsymbol{F}$. Exercise 4.15(b) then shows that $\operatorname{rk}(\boldsymbol{A}_1) = \operatorname{rk}(\boldsymbol{EAF}) \leq \operatorname{rk}(\boldsymbol{AF}) \leq \operatorname{rk}(\boldsymbol{A})$.

***Exercise 4.18 (Rank equalities, 1)** Show that $\operatorname{rk}(\boldsymbol{A}'\boldsymbol{AB}) = \operatorname{rk}(\boldsymbol{AB}) = \operatorname{rk}(\boldsymbol{ABB}')$ for any conformable matrices $\boldsymbol{A}$ and $\boldsymbol{B}$.

Solution
Using Exercises 4.13(d) and 4.15(b) repeatedly, we obtain

$$\operatorname{rk}(\boldsymbol{AB}) = \operatorname{rk}(\boldsymbol{B}'\boldsymbol{A}'\boldsymbol{AB}) \leq \operatorname{rk}(\boldsymbol{A}'\boldsymbol{AB}) \leq \operatorname{rk}(\boldsymbol{AB})$$

and

$$\operatorname{rk}(\boldsymbol{AB}) = \operatorname{rk}(\boldsymbol{ABB}'\boldsymbol{A}') \leq \operatorname{rk}(\boldsymbol{ABB}') \leq \operatorname{rk}(\boldsymbol{AB}).$$

The results follow.

4.2 Inverse

Exercise 4.19 (Inverse of 2-by-2 matrix) Consider the matrices

$$A = \begin{pmatrix} 1 & 2 \\ 2 & 4 \end{pmatrix} \quad \text{and} \quad B = \begin{pmatrix} 1 & 3 \\ 2 & 4 \end{pmatrix}.$$

(a) Does A have an inverse? What is $\operatorname{rk}(A)$?
(b) Does B have an inverse? What is $\operatorname{rk}(B)$?

Solution
(a) Since the rows (and columns) of A are proportional, A has rank 1. If there exists a matrix C such that $AC = I$ then we must have

$$\begin{pmatrix} 1 & 2 \\ 2 & 4 \end{pmatrix} \begin{pmatrix} a & b \\ c & d \end{pmatrix} = \begin{pmatrix} 1 & 0 \\ 0 & 1 \end{pmatrix},$$

which leads to

$$a + 2c = 1, \quad b + 2d = 0, \quad 2a + 4c = 0, \quad 2b + 4d = 1.$$

Clearly there is no solution and hence there is no inverse.
(b) Now, $\operatorname{rk}(B) = 2$ because the rows are not proportional. We must solve

$$\begin{pmatrix} 1 & 3 \\ 2 & 4 \end{pmatrix} \begin{pmatrix} a & b \\ c & d \end{pmatrix} = \begin{pmatrix} 1 & 0 \\ 0 & 1 \end{pmatrix}, \quad \begin{pmatrix} a & b \\ c & d \end{pmatrix} \begin{pmatrix} 1 & 3 \\ 2 & 4 \end{pmatrix} = \begin{pmatrix} 1 & 0 \\ 0 & 1 \end{pmatrix}.$$

The first equation gives

$$a + 3c = 1, \quad b + 3d = 0, \quad 2a + 4c = 0, \quad 2b + 4d = 1,$$

and the second gives

$$a + 2b = 1, \quad 3a + 4b = 0, \quad c + 2d = 0, \quad 3c + 4d = 1.$$

Both sets of equations give the same solution (this is no coincidence), namely $(a, b, c, d) = (-2, 3/2, 1, -1/2)$.

Exercise 4.20 (Uniqueness of inverse)
(a) Show that an inverse, if it exists, is unique.
(b) If A has a left inverse ($BA = I$) and a right inverse ($AC = I$), then $B = C$.

Solution
(a) Suppose there are two matrices B and C such that $AB = BA = I$ and $AC = CA = I$. Then,

$$B = B(AC) = (BA)C = C.$$

(b) Noting that in (a) we have only used $BA = I$ and $AC = I$, the same argument applies.

Exercise 4.21 (Existence of inverse) Let A be a square matrix of order n. Show that the inverse exists if and only if A is nonsingular.

Solution

If $\boldsymbol{A}$ has an inverse, then a square matrix $\boldsymbol{B}$ of order n can be found such that $\boldsymbol{AB} = \boldsymbol{BA} = \boldsymbol{I}_n$. Then, using Exercise 4.15,

$$n = \text{rk}(\boldsymbol{AB}) \leq \min(\text{rk}(\boldsymbol{A}), \text{rk}(\boldsymbol{B})) \leq \text{rk}(\boldsymbol{A}) \leq n,$$

implying that $\text{rk}(\boldsymbol{A}) = n$. Conversely, suppose that $\text{rk}(\boldsymbol{A}) = n$. Then the columns of $\boldsymbol{A}$ span $\mathbb{R}^n$, and hence every vector in $\mathbb{R}^n$ can be expressed as a linear combination of the columns of $\boldsymbol{A}$. In particular, the i-th unit vector can be expressed as $\boldsymbol{e}_i = \boldsymbol{A}\boldsymbol{b}_i$ for some $\boldsymbol{b}_i$ ($i = 1, \dots, n$). The matrix $\boldsymbol{B} := (\boldsymbol{b}_1, \dots, \boldsymbol{b}_n)$ now satisfies $\boldsymbol{AB} = \boldsymbol{I}_n$. By an analogous argument, there exists a matrix $\boldsymbol{C}$ such that $\boldsymbol{CA} = \boldsymbol{I}_n$. Finally, by Exercise 4.20, $\boldsymbol{B} = \boldsymbol{C}$.

Exercise 4.22 (Properties of inverse) For any nonsingular matrix $\boldsymbol{A}$, show that:
(a) $(\lambda \boldsymbol{A})^{-1} = (1/\lambda)\boldsymbol{A}^{-1}$ $(\lambda \neq 0)$;
(b) $(\boldsymbol{A}^{-1})^{-1} = \boldsymbol{A}$;
(c) $(\boldsymbol{A}^{-1})' = (\boldsymbol{A}')^{-1}$;
(d) $(\boldsymbol{AB})^{-1} = \boldsymbol{B}^{-1}\boldsymbol{A}^{-1}$ if $\boldsymbol{B}$ is nonsingular and of the same order as $\boldsymbol{A}$;
(e) if $\boldsymbol{A}$ and $\boldsymbol{B}$ commute and $\boldsymbol{B}$ is nonsingular, then $\boldsymbol{A}$ and $\boldsymbol{B}^{-1}$ commute.

Solution

The results follow because:
(a) $\lambda \boldsymbol{A}(1/\lambda)\boldsymbol{A}^{-1} = \boldsymbol{A}\boldsymbol{A}^{-1} = \boldsymbol{I}$ and $(1/\lambda)\boldsymbol{A}^{-1}\lambda\boldsymbol{A} = \boldsymbol{A}^{-1}\boldsymbol{A} = \boldsymbol{I}$;
(b) $\boldsymbol{A}\boldsymbol{A}^{-1} = \boldsymbol{A}^{-1}\boldsymbol{A} = \boldsymbol{I}$;
(c) $\boldsymbol{A}'(\boldsymbol{A}^{-1})' = (\boldsymbol{A}^{-1}\boldsymbol{A})' = \boldsymbol{I}$ and $(\boldsymbol{A}^{-1})'\boldsymbol{A}' = (\boldsymbol{A}\boldsymbol{A}^{-1})' = \boldsymbol{I}$;
(d) $\boldsymbol{A}\boldsymbol{B}\boldsymbol{B}^{-1}\boldsymbol{A}^{-1} = \boldsymbol{A}\boldsymbol{A}^{-1} = \boldsymbol{I}$ and $\boldsymbol{B}^{-1}\boldsymbol{A}^{-1}\boldsymbol{A}\boldsymbol{B} = \boldsymbol{B}^{-1}\boldsymbol{B} = \boldsymbol{I}$;
(e) pre- and postmultiplying $\boldsymbol{AB} = \boldsymbol{BA}$ by $\boldsymbol{B}^{-1}$ gives $\boldsymbol{B}^{-1}\boldsymbol{A} = \boldsymbol{A}\boldsymbol{B}^{-1}$.

Exercise 4.23 (Semi-orthogonality)
(a) Let $\boldsymbol{A}$ and $\boldsymbol{B}$ be square matrices of the same order. Show that $\boldsymbol{AB} = \boldsymbol{I}$ if and only if $\boldsymbol{BA} = \boldsymbol{I}$.
(b) Now let $\boldsymbol{A}$ be a matrix of order $m \times n$. If $m < n$, show that no $m \times n$ matrix $\boldsymbol{B}$ exists such that $\boldsymbol{B}'\boldsymbol{A} = \boldsymbol{I}_n$.
(c) Give an example of an $m \times n$ matrix $\boldsymbol{A}$ $(m \neq n)$ such that $\boldsymbol{A}\boldsymbol{A}' = \boldsymbol{I}_m$ or $\boldsymbol{A}'\boldsymbol{A} = \boldsymbol{I}_n$. (A real $m \times n$ matrix $\boldsymbol{A}$ for which $\boldsymbol{A}\boldsymbol{A}' = \boldsymbol{I}_m$ or $\boldsymbol{A}'\boldsymbol{A} = \boldsymbol{I}_n$, but not necessarily both, is called *semi-orthogonal*.)

Solution

(a) Let $\boldsymbol{A}$ and $\boldsymbol{B}$ be matrices of order n. Since $\boldsymbol{AB} = \boldsymbol{I}_n$, we have

$$n = \text{rk}(\boldsymbol{AB}) \leq \min(\text{rk}(\boldsymbol{A}), \text{rk}(\boldsymbol{B})) \leq \text{rk}(\boldsymbol{A}) \leq n.$$

Hence, $\boldsymbol{A}$ (and $\boldsymbol{B}$) has full rank n, and is therefore nonsingular (Exercise 4.21). Since the inverse is unique, $\boldsymbol{BA} = \boldsymbol{I}$ holds also.
(b) If $\boldsymbol{B}'\boldsymbol{A} = \boldsymbol{I}_n$, then $n = \text{rk}(\boldsymbol{I}_n) = \text{rk}(\boldsymbol{B}'\boldsymbol{A}) \leq \text{rk}(\boldsymbol{A}) \leq m$, a contradiction.

(c) Let $\boldsymbol{x}$ be an $n \times 1$ vector ($n > 1$) such that $\boldsymbol{x}'\boldsymbol{x} = 1$, for example $\boldsymbol{x} := \boldsymbol{e}_i$. Letting $\boldsymbol{A} := \boldsymbol{x}'$ (and hence $m = 1$), we see that $\boldsymbol{A}\boldsymbol{A}' = \boldsymbol{x}'\boldsymbol{x} = 1$ (a scalar), but that $\boldsymbol{A}'\boldsymbol{A} = \boldsymbol{x}\boldsymbol{x}' \neq \boldsymbol{I}_n$.

Exercise 4.24 (Rank equalities, 2) Let $\boldsymbol{A}$ be an $m \times n$ matrix, and let $\boldsymbol{B}$ ($m \times m$) and $\boldsymbol{C}$ ($n \times n$) be nonsingular. Show that:
(a) $\operatorname{rk}(\boldsymbol{BA}) = \operatorname{rk}(\boldsymbol{A})$;
(b) $\operatorname{rk}(\boldsymbol{AC}) = \operatorname{rk}(\boldsymbol{A})$;
(c) $\operatorname{rk}(\boldsymbol{BAC}) = \operatorname{rk}(\boldsymbol{A})$.

Solution
We know from Exercise 4.15 that the rank of a matrix product can never exceed the ranks of the constituent matrices. Hence,

$$\operatorname{rk}(\boldsymbol{A}) = \operatorname{rk}(\boldsymbol{B}^{-1}\boldsymbol{BACC}^{-1}) \leq \operatorname{rk}(\boldsymbol{BAC}) \leq \operatorname{rk}(\boldsymbol{A}),$$

proving (c). Letting $\boldsymbol{C} := \boldsymbol{I}_n$ and $\boldsymbol{B} := \boldsymbol{I}_m$, respectively, yields (a) and (b) as special cases.

Exercise 4.25 (Rank equalities, 3) For conformable matrices $\boldsymbol{A}$, $\boldsymbol{B}$, $\boldsymbol{C}$ show that:
(a) $\operatorname{rk}(\boldsymbol{BA}) = \operatorname{rk}(\boldsymbol{B}'\boldsymbol{BA})$;
(b) $\operatorname{rk}(\boldsymbol{AC}) = \operatorname{rk}(\boldsymbol{ACC}')$;
(c) $\operatorname{rk}(\boldsymbol{BA}) = \operatorname{rk}(\boldsymbol{A})$ if $\boldsymbol{B}$ has full column rank;
(d) $\operatorname{rk}(\boldsymbol{AC}) = \operatorname{rk}(\boldsymbol{A})$ if $\boldsymbol{C}$ has full row rank.

Solution
(a)–(b) Since the matrices $\boldsymbol{A}$, $\boldsymbol{A}'$, $\boldsymbol{AA}'$, and $\boldsymbol{A}'\boldsymbol{A}$ all have the same rank (Exercise 4.13), we obtain

$$\operatorname{rk}(\boldsymbol{BA}) = \operatorname{rk}(\boldsymbol{A}'\boldsymbol{B}'\boldsymbol{BA}) \leq \operatorname{rk}(\boldsymbol{B}'\boldsymbol{BA}) \leq \operatorname{rk}(\boldsymbol{BA})$$

and

$$\operatorname{rk}(\boldsymbol{AC}) = \operatorname{rk}(\boldsymbol{ACC}'\boldsymbol{A}') \leq \operatorname{rk}(\boldsymbol{ACC}') \leq \operatorname{rk}(\boldsymbol{AC}).$$

(c) If $\boldsymbol{B}$ has full column rank, then $\boldsymbol{B}'\boldsymbol{B}$ is square and nonsingular. Hence, $\operatorname{rk}(\boldsymbol{BA}) = \operatorname{rk}(\boldsymbol{B}'\boldsymbol{BA}) = \operatorname{rk}(\boldsymbol{A})$, using Exercise 4.24.
(d) If $\boldsymbol{C}$ has full row rank, then $\boldsymbol{CC}'$ is square and nonsingular, and the proof follows as in (c).

Exercise 4.26 (Orthogonal matrix: real versus complex) Recall that a real square matrix $\boldsymbol{A}$ is orthogonal if $\boldsymbol{A}'\boldsymbol{A} = \boldsymbol{AA}' = \boldsymbol{I}$.
(a) Show that the matrix

$$\boldsymbol{A} = \frac{1}{\sqrt{2}}\begin{pmatrix} 1 & 0 & 1 \\ -1 & 0 & 1 \\ 0 & \sqrt{2} & 0 \end{pmatrix}$$

is orthogonal.

(b) Now consider the complex matrix

$$B = \begin{pmatrix} \beta & \mathrm{i} \\ -\mathrm{i} & \beta \end{pmatrix},$$

where β is a real number. For which value of β is B unitary?
(c) For which value of β is B complex-orthogonal, in the sense that $B'B = I_2$?
(d) For this value of β, are the two columns of B orthogonal to each other?

Solution
We have

$$A'A = \frac{1}{2}\begin{pmatrix} 1 & -1 & 0 \\ 0 & 0 & \sqrt{2} \\ 1 & 1 & 0 \end{pmatrix}\begin{pmatrix} 1 & 0 & 1 \\ -1 & 0 & 1 \\ 0 & \sqrt{2} & 0 \end{pmatrix} = \begin{pmatrix} 1 & 0 & 0 \\ 0 & 1 & 0 \\ 0 & 0 & 1 \end{pmatrix}$$

and similarly $AA' = I$.
(b) Here we have

$$B^*B = \begin{pmatrix} \beta & \mathrm{i} \\ -\mathrm{i} & \beta \end{pmatrix}\begin{pmatrix} \beta & \mathrm{i} \\ -\mathrm{i} & \beta \end{pmatrix} = \begin{pmatrix} 1+\beta^2 & 2\mathrm{i}\beta \\ -2\mathrm{i}\beta & 1+\beta^2 \end{pmatrix},$$

and this equals I_2 if and only if $\beta = 0$.
(c) Similarly,

$$B'B = \begin{pmatrix} \beta & -\mathrm{i} \\ \mathrm{i} & \beta \end{pmatrix}\begin{pmatrix} \beta & \mathrm{i} \\ -\mathrm{i} & \beta \end{pmatrix} = \begin{pmatrix} \beta^2 - 1 & 0 \\ 0 & \beta^2 - 1 \end{pmatrix},$$

so that we must choose $\beta = \pm\sqrt{2}$.
(d) No. The two columns are orthogonal to each other if and only if

$$0 = \begin{pmatrix} \beta \\ -\mathrm{i} \end{pmatrix}^* \begin{pmatrix} \mathrm{i} \\ \beta \end{pmatrix} = (\beta, \mathrm{i})\begin{pmatrix} \mathrm{i} \\ \beta \end{pmatrix} = 2\mathrm{i}\beta,$$

that is, if and only if $\beta = 0$. Hence, for $\beta = \pm\sqrt{2}$, the two columns are not orthogonal to each other. This is one of the reasons why we do not call a square complex matrix B satisfying $B'B = I$ orthogonal; Exercise 7.23 provides another reason. In our definition, an orthogonal matrix is always real.

Exercise 4.27 (Properties of orthogonal matrix) Let A be an orthogonal matrix of order n. Show that:
(a) A is nonsingular;
(b) $A' = A^{-1}$;
(c) A' is orthogonal;
(d) AB is orthogonal when B is orthogonal.

Solution
(a) The matrix A is nonsingular because $n = \mathrm{rk}(A'A) \leq \mathrm{rk}(A) \leq n$.
(b) Postmultiplying $A'A = I$ by A^{-1} (or premultiplying $AA' = I$ by A^{-1}) gives $A' = A^{-1}$.

(c) Let $\boldsymbol{B} := \boldsymbol{A}'$. Then $\boldsymbol{B}'\boldsymbol{B} = \boldsymbol{A}\boldsymbol{A}' = \boldsymbol{I}$ and $\boldsymbol{B}\boldsymbol{B}' = \boldsymbol{A}'\boldsymbol{A} = \boldsymbol{I}$.
(d) We have $(\boldsymbol{AB})'\boldsymbol{AB} = \boldsymbol{B}'\boldsymbol{A}'\boldsymbol{AB} = \boldsymbol{B}'\boldsymbol{B} = \boldsymbol{I}$ and $\boldsymbol{AB}(\boldsymbol{AB})' = \boldsymbol{ABB}'\boldsymbol{A}' = \boldsymbol{AA}' = \boldsymbol{I}$.

Exercise 4.28 (Inverse of $\boldsymbol{A} + \boldsymbol{ab}'$) Let $\boldsymbol{A}$ be a nonsingular $n \times n$ matrix, and let $\boldsymbol{a}$ and $\boldsymbol{b}$ be $n \times 1$ vectors.
(a) If $\boldsymbol{a}'\boldsymbol{A}^{-1}\boldsymbol{a} \neq -1$, show that

$$(\boldsymbol{A} + \boldsymbol{aa}')^{-1} = \boldsymbol{A}^{-1} - \frac{1}{1 + \boldsymbol{a}'\boldsymbol{A}^{-1}\boldsymbol{a}}\boldsymbol{A}^{-1}\boldsymbol{aa}'\boldsymbol{A}^{-1}.$$

(b) If $\boldsymbol{a}'\boldsymbol{A}^{-1}\boldsymbol{a} \neq 1$, show that

$$(\boldsymbol{A} - \boldsymbol{aa}')^{-1} = \boldsymbol{A}^{-1} + \frac{1}{1 - \boldsymbol{a}'\boldsymbol{A}^{-1}\boldsymbol{a}}\boldsymbol{A}^{-1}\boldsymbol{aa}'\boldsymbol{A}^{-1}.$$

(c) If $\boldsymbol{b}'\boldsymbol{A}^{-1}\boldsymbol{a} \neq -1$, show that

$$(\boldsymbol{A} + \boldsymbol{ab}')^{-1} = \boldsymbol{A}^{-1} - \frac{1}{1 + \boldsymbol{b}'\boldsymbol{A}^{-1}\boldsymbol{a}}\boldsymbol{A}^{-1}\boldsymbol{ab}'\boldsymbol{A}^{-1}.$$

Solution
We prove only (c), since (a) and (b) are special cases. Let $\lambda := (1 + \boldsymbol{b}'\boldsymbol{A}^{-1}\boldsymbol{a})^{-1}$. Then,

$$\begin{aligned}
&(\boldsymbol{A} + \boldsymbol{ab}')(\boldsymbol{A}^{-1} - \lambda\boldsymbol{A}^{-1}\boldsymbol{ab}'\boldsymbol{A}^{-1}) \\
&\quad = \boldsymbol{AA}^{-1} - \lambda\boldsymbol{AA}^{-1}\boldsymbol{ab}'\boldsymbol{A}^{-1} + \boldsymbol{ab}'\boldsymbol{A}^{-1} - \lambda\boldsymbol{a}(\boldsymbol{b}'\boldsymbol{A}^{-1}\boldsymbol{a})\boldsymbol{b}'\boldsymbol{A}^{-1} \\
&\quad = \boldsymbol{I} - (\lambda - 1 + \lambda\boldsymbol{b}'\boldsymbol{A}^{-1}\boldsymbol{a})\boldsymbol{ab}'\boldsymbol{A}^{-1} = \boldsymbol{I},
\end{aligned}$$

because $\lambda(1 + \boldsymbol{b}'\boldsymbol{A}^{-1}\boldsymbol{a}) = 1$.

4.3 Determinant

Exercise 4.29 (Determinant of order 3) Show that the determinant of a 3×3 matrix $\boldsymbol{A} = (a_{ij})$ is

$$|\boldsymbol{A}| = \begin{vmatrix} a_{11} & a_{12} & a_{13} \\ a_{21} & a_{22} & a_{23} \\ a_{31} & a_{32} & a_{33} \end{vmatrix} = a_{11}a_{22}a_{33} - a_{11}a_{23}a_{32}$$
$$- a_{12}a_{21}a_{33} + a_{12}a_{23}a_{31} + a_{13}a_{21}a_{32} - a_{13}a_{22}a_{31}.$$

Solution
There are six permutations (in general, for an $n \times n$ matrix, there are $n!$ permutations):

(1,2,3), (1,3,2), (2,1,3), (2,3,1), (3,1,2), (3,2,1). Hence,

$$\begin{aligned}|\boldsymbol{A}| &= (-1)^{\varphi(1,2,3)}a_{11}a_{22}a_{33} + (-1)^{\varphi(1,3,2)}a_{11}a_{23}a_{32} \\ &\quad + (-1)^{\varphi(2,1,3)}a_{12}a_{21}a_{33} + (-1)^{\varphi(2,3,1)}a_{12}a_{23}a_{31} \\ &\quad + (-1)^{\varphi(3,1,2)}a_{13}a_{21}a_{32} + (-1)^{\varphi(3,2,1)}a_{13}a_{22}a_{31} \\ &= a_{11}a_{22}a_{33} - a_{11}a_{23}a_{32} - a_{12}a_{21}a_{33} \\ &\quad + a_{12}a_{23}a_{31} + a_{13}a_{21}a_{32} - a_{13}a_{22}a_{31}.\end{aligned}$$

Exercise 4.30 (Determinant of the transpose) For any square matrix $\boldsymbol{A}$, show that $|\boldsymbol{A}'| = |\boldsymbol{A}|$.

Solution

Let the same permutation that changes $(j_1, \dots, j_n)$ into $(1, \dots, n)$, change $(1, \dots, n)$ into $(i_1, \dots, i_n)$. Then, noting that $\varphi(1, \dots, n) = 0$, we obtain

$$\begin{aligned}|\boldsymbol{A}| &= \sum_{(j_1,\dots,j_n)} (-1)^{\varphi(j_1,\dots,j_n)} a_{1j_1}a_{2j_2}\dots a_{nj_n} \\ &= \sum_{(j_1,\dots,j_n)} (-1)^{\varphi(1,\dots,n)}(-1)^{\varphi(j_1,\dots,j_n)} a_{1j_1}a_{2j_2}\dots a_{nj_n} \\ &= \sum_{(i_1,\dots,i_n)} (-1)^{\varphi(i_1,\dots,i_n)}(-1)^{\varphi(1,\dots,n)} a_{i_11}a_{i_22}\dots a_{i_nn} = |\boldsymbol{A}'|.\end{aligned}$$

We remark that, if $\boldsymbol{A}$ is complex, the determinant of its conjugate transpose is given by $|\boldsymbol{A}^*| = |\boldsymbol{A}|^*$, and that it is therefore not true that $|\boldsymbol{A}^*| = |\boldsymbol{A}|$, unless $|\boldsymbol{A}|$ is real.

Exercise 4.31 (Find the determinant) Let

$$\boldsymbol{A} = \begin{pmatrix} 1 & \alpha & 0 \\ 4 & 5 & 3 \\ 1 & 0 & 2 \end{pmatrix}.$$

(a) For which α is $|\boldsymbol{A}| = 0$? Show that the columns of $\boldsymbol{A}$ are linearly dependent in that case.
(b) If we interchange the second and third row, show that $|\boldsymbol{A}|$ changes sign.
(c) If we multiply the first column by 2, show that $|\boldsymbol{A}|$ is also multiplied by 2.
(d) If we subtract 4 times the first row from the second row, show that $|\boldsymbol{A}|$ does not change.

Solution

In addition to the matrix $\boldsymbol{A}$ we define the matrices

$$\boldsymbol{B} = \begin{pmatrix} 1 & \alpha & 0 \\ 1 & 0 & 2 \\ 4 & 5 & 3 \end{pmatrix}, \quad \boldsymbol{C} = \begin{pmatrix} 2 & \alpha & 0 \\ 8 & 5 & 3 \\ 2 & 0 & 2 \end{pmatrix}, \quad \boldsymbol{D} = \begin{pmatrix} 1 & \alpha & 0 \\ 0 & 5-4\alpha & 3 \\ 1 & 0 & 2 \end{pmatrix}.$$

(a) We find $|\boldsymbol{A}| = 10 - 5\alpha$ and hence $|\boldsymbol{A}| = 0$ when $\alpha = 2$. The vector $\boldsymbol{x} = (2, -1, -1)'$ satisfies $\boldsymbol{A}\boldsymbol{x} = \boldsymbol{0}$, showing that the columns of $\boldsymbol{A}$ are linearly dependent in that case.
(b)–(d) The matrices $\boldsymbol{B}$, $\boldsymbol{C}$, and $\boldsymbol{D}$ correspond to the operations described in (b)–(d), respectively. We find $|\boldsymbol{B}| = -10 + 5\alpha$, $|\boldsymbol{C}| = 20 - 10\alpha$, and $|\boldsymbol{D}| = 10 - 5\alpha$.

Exercise 4.32 (Elementary operations of determinant, 1) Show that, if we interchange rows (columns) i and j of the matrix $\boldsymbol{A}$, then $|\boldsymbol{A}|$ changes sign. (This is called an *elementary operation* on the matrix $\boldsymbol{A}$.)

Solution
We first show that a single transposition of two elements in a permutation will change an odd permutation to an even one, and vice versa. Let $(k_1, \dots, k_n)$ be a permutation of $(1, \dots, n)$. Suppose that k_i and k_j are interchanged ($j > i$). It involves $j - i$ transpositions to move k_j to pass k_i, and another $j - i - 1$ transpositions to move k_i to pass k_{j-1}. So, $2(j - i) - 1$ transpositions are required, which is always an odd number. Hence, if the original permutation was even, the new permutation is odd, and vice versa.

Now suppose that rows i and j are interchanged. This involves interchanging two first subscripts in each term of

$$|\boldsymbol{A}| := \sum_{(j_1,\dots,j_n)} (-1)^{\varphi(j_1,\dots,j_n)} a_{1j_1} a_{2j_2} \dots a_{nj_n}.$$

Hence, each term changes sign, and hence the determinant changes sign.

Exercise 4.33 (Zero determinant) Let $\boldsymbol{A}$ be a square matrix of order n. Show that:
(a) if $\boldsymbol{A}$ has two identical rows (columns), then $|\boldsymbol{A}| = 0$;
(b) if $\boldsymbol{A}$ has a row (column) of zeros, then $|\boldsymbol{A}| = 0$.

Solution
(a) Let $d_1 := |\boldsymbol{A}|$ and let d_2 be the determinant obtained after interchanging the two identical rows. Then obviously $d_1 = d_2$. But, by Exercise 4.32, $d_2 = -d_1$. Hence, $d_1 = 0$.
(b) By definition, the determinant of $\boldsymbol{A}$ is the sum of $n!$ terms, each of which is a product of n elements of the matrix $\boldsymbol{A}$. In each product there will be exactly one element from the i-th row. If the i-th row is zero then all products vanish, and $|\boldsymbol{A}| = 0$.

Exercise 4.34 (Elementary operations of determinant, 2) Prove the remaining two so-called elementary operations on a square matrix $\boldsymbol{A}$:
(a) if we multiply row (column) i by a scalar λ, then $|\boldsymbol{A}|$ is multiplied by λ;
(b) if we add a scalar multiple of one row (column) to another row (column), $|\boldsymbol{A}|$ does not change.

Solution
(a) This follows from the fact that an element from each row and column appears precisely once in each of the $n!$ terms of the definition of the determinant. Multiplying each element in row i by λ will multiply each term by λ, and hence will multiply the whole determinant by λ.

(b) Let B denote the matrix obtained from A by adding c times the k-th row to the i-th row. Then a typical term in $|B|$ takes the form

$$\begin{aligned} &a_{1j_1}a_{2j_2}\dots(a_{ij_i}+ca_{kj_k})\dots a_{nj_n} \\ &\qquad = (a_{1j_1}a_{2j_2}\dots a_{ij_i}\dots a_{nj_n}) + c(a_{1j_1}a_{2j_2}\dots a_{kj_k}\dots a_{nj_n}). \end{aligned}$$

Summing over all permutations gives $|B| = |A| + c|\widetilde{A}|$, where $\widetilde{A}$ is obtained from A by replacing the i-th row by the k-th row. Thus, $\widetilde{A}$ has two identical rows and hence, by Exercise 4.33(a), determinant zero. This gives $|B| = |A|$, which we wanted to prove.

Exercise 4.35 (Some simple properties of the determinant) Show that:
(a) $|\lambda A| = \lambda^n |A|$ where n is the order of A;
(b) $|I_n| = 1$;
(c) the determinant of a diagonal matrix is the product of its diagonal elements.

Solution
(a) This is a direct consequence of Exercise 4.34(a).
(b) Consider a term t of the determinant of A,

$$t := (-1)^{\varphi(j_1,\dots,j_n)} a_{1j_1}a_{2j_2}\dots a_{nj_n}.$$

If $A = I_n$, then this term is always zero, unless $(j_1,\dots,j_n) = (1,\dots,n)$, in which case it equals 1.
(c) As in (b), the term t is always zero, unless $(j_1,\dots,j_n) = (1,\dots,n)$, in which case

$$|A| = (-1)^{\varphi(1,\dots,n)} a_{11}a_{22}\dots a_{nn},$$

which is the product of the diagonal elements.

***Exercise 4.36 (Expansions by rows or columns)** Let $A = (a_{ij})$ be a square matrix of order n, and let c_{ij} be the cofactor of a_{ij}. Show that:
(a) $|A| = \sum_{j=1}^n a_{ij}c_{ij} \quad (i = 1,\dots,n)$;
(b) $|A| = \sum_{i=1}^n a_{ij}c_{ij} \quad (j = 1,\dots,n)$.

Solution
Consider first a 3×3 matrix $A = (a_{ij})$. Then, by Exercise 4.29,

$$\begin{aligned} |A| &= a_{11}a_{22}a_{33} - a_{11}a_{23}a_{32} - a_{12}a_{21}a_{33} \\ &\quad + a_{12}a_{23}a_{31} + a_{13}a_{21}a_{32} - a_{13}a_{22}a_{31} \\ &= a_{11}(a_{22}a_{33} - a_{23}a_{32}) + a_{12}(-a_{21}a_{33} + a_{23}a_{31}) \\ &\quad + a_{13}(a_{21}a_{32} - a_{22}a_{31}) \\ &= a_{11}c_{11} + a_{12}c_{12} + a_{13}c_{13}. \end{aligned}$$

Let us now prove result (a) for $i = 1$. The other results then follow in the same way. Since each term in $\boldsymbol{A}$ contains precisely one element from the first row, we can write the determinant as

$$|\boldsymbol{A}| = \sum_{(j_1,\dots,j_n)} (-1)^{\varphi(j_1,\dots,j_n)} a_{1j_1} a_{2j_2} \dots a_{nj_n}$$
$$= a_{11}d_{11} + a_{12}d_{12} + \dots + a_{1n}d_{1n}.$$

Notice that d_{1j} is a sum of terms involving no element of the first row of $\boldsymbol{A}$. We must show that $d_{1j} = c_{1j}$ for all j.

For $j = 1$ we have

$$a_{11}d_{11} = \sum (-1)^{\varphi(j_1,\dots,j_n)} a_{1j_1} a_{2j_2} \dots a_{nj_n},$$

where the summation is over all permutations $(j_1, \dots, j_n)$ for which $j_1 = 1$. This implies that

$$d_{11} = \sum (-1)^{\varphi(j_2,\dots,j_n)} a_{2j_2} \dots a_{nj_n},$$

where the summation is now over all permutations $(j_2, \dots, j_n)$. This is precisely $|\boldsymbol{A}_{(11)}|$, where $\boldsymbol{A}_{(1j)}$ denotes the $(n-1) \times (n-1)$ matrix obtained from $\boldsymbol{A}$ by deleting the first row and the j-th column. Thus,

$$d_{11} = |\boldsymbol{A}_{(11)}| = (-1)^{1+1}|\boldsymbol{A}_{(11)}| = c_{11}.$$

Next we consider an arbitrary $j > 1$. Interchange the j-th column with each preceding column until it becomes the first column. This involves $j - 1$ transpositions. The determinant $|\boldsymbol{A}_{(1j)}|$ is not affected by these transpositions. Hence,

$$d_{1j} = (-1)^{j-1}|\boldsymbol{A}_{(1j)}| = (-1)^{j+1}|\boldsymbol{A}_{(1j)}| = c_{1j}.$$

Exercise 4.37 (Cofactors) Show that:
(a) $\sum_{j=1}^{n} a_{ij}c_{kj} = 0$ if $i \neq k$;
(b) $\sum_{i=1}^{n} a_{ij}c_{ik} = 0$ if $j \neq k$;
(c) $\boldsymbol{AC}' = \boldsymbol{C}'\boldsymbol{A} = |\boldsymbol{A}|\boldsymbol{I}_n$.

Solution
(a)–(b) Again we only prove (a) for the case $k = 1$. Thus we wish to show that, for all $i \neq 1$,

$$a_{i1}c_{11} + a_{i2}c_{12} + \dots + a_{in}c_{1n} = 0.$$

Let $\boldsymbol{B}$ be the matrix obtained from $\boldsymbol{A}$ by replacing the first row of $\boldsymbol{A}$ by the i-th row. Then, $|\boldsymbol{B}| = 0$, because $\boldsymbol{B}$ has two identical rows. Also, expanding $|\boldsymbol{B}|$ by the first row,

$$|\boldsymbol{B}| = a_{i1}c_{11} + a_{i2}c_{12} + \dots + a_{in}c_{1n}.$$

The result follows.

(c) From (a) and (b) and Exercise 4.36, we obtain

$$\sum_{j=1}^{n} a_{ij}c_{kj} = \delta_{ik}|\boldsymbol{A}| \quad \text{and} \quad \sum_{i=1}^{n} c_{ik}a_{ij} = \delta_{kj}|\boldsymbol{A}|,$$

where δ_{ik} denotes the Kronecker delta. Hence, $\boldsymbol{AC}' = \boldsymbol{C}'\boldsymbol{A} = |\boldsymbol{A}|\boldsymbol{I}_n$.

Exercise 4.38 (Determinant of triangular matrix)
Show that the determinant of a triangular matrix is the product of its diagonal elements.

Solution
Suppose $\boldsymbol{A}$ is lower triangular, so that $a_{ij} = 0$ for $i < j$. Now consider a term t of the determinant of $\boldsymbol{A}$,

$$t := (-1)^{\varphi(j_1,\dots,j_n)} a_{1j_1}a_{2j_2}\dots a_{nj_n}.$$

If $j_1 \neq 1$ then $j_1 > 1$ so that $a_{1j_1} = 0$. Hence, $t = 0$ whenever $j_1 \neq 1$. Next suppose $j_1 = 1$ but $j_2 \neq 2$. Then $j_2 > 2$ so that $a_{2j_2} = 0$, and hence $t = 0$. Continuing in this way, we find that the only nonzero term is the one where $j_1 = 1$, $j_2 = 2$, …, $j_n = n$. Thus, $|\boldsymbol{A}| = a_{11}a_{22}\dots a_{nn}$, the product of the diagonal elements.

Exercise 4.39 (Weierstrass's axiomatic definition) Let $\boldsymbol{A}$ be a square matrix of order n, and define a scalar function p that assigns to $\boldsymbol{A}$ a number $p(\boldsymbol{A})$ such that:

(i) $p(\boldsymbol{A})$ is a linear function of each of the columns of $\boldsymbol{A}$, if the others are held fixed;
(ii) if $\boldsymbol{B}$ is obtained from $\boldsymbol{A}$ by interchanging two columns, then $p(\boldsymbol{B}) = -p(\boldsymbol{A})$;
(iii) $p(\boldsymbol{I}_n) = 1$.

Show that the determinant $|\boldsymbol{A}|$ satisfies properties (i)–(iii). (In fact, the determinant is the *only* function that satisfies (i)–(iii). The determinant can thus be *defined* in terms of these properties.)

Solution
To prove that $|\boldsymbol{A}|$ is a linear function of its columns, it suffices to note that each of the $n!$ products in the definition of the determinant contains exactly one factor from each column. This proves (i). Part (ii) follows from Exercise 4.32, and part (iii) from Exercise 4.35(b).

Exercise 4.40 (A tridiagonal matrix) Consider the $n \times n$ "tridiagonal" matrix

$$\boldsymbol{A}_n = \begin{pmatrix} 2 & -1 & 0 & \dots & 0 & 0 \\ -1 & 2 & -1 & \dots & 0 & 0 \\ \vdots & \vdots & \vdots & & \vdots & \vdots \\ 0 & 0 & 0 & \dots & 2 & -1 \\ 0 & 0 & 0 & \dots & -1 & 2 \end{pmatrix}.$$

Show that $|\boldsymbol{A}_n| = n + 1$.

Solution
Expand the determinant of $\boldsymbol{A}_n$ by the first row. This gives

$$|\boldsymbol{A}_n| = 2|\boldsymbol{A}_{n-1}| - (-1) \begin{vmatrix} -1 & -1 & 0 & \dots & 0 \\ 0 & 2 & -1 & \dots & 0 \\ 0 & -1 & 2 & \dots & 0 \\ \vdots & \vdots & \vdots & & \vdots \\ 0 & 0 & 0 & \dots & 2 \end{vmatrix} = 2|\boldsymbol{A}_{n-1}| - |\boldsymbol{A}_{n-2}|,$$

where the second equality follows by expanding the displayed reduced determinant by its first row. Hence, $|\boldsymbol{A}_n| - |\boldsymbol{A}_{n-1}| = |\boldsymbol{A}_{n-1}| - |\boldsymbol{A}_{n-2}|$. Since $|\boldsymbol{A}_1| = 2$ and $|\boldsymbol{A}_2| = 3$, we thus find that $|\boldsymbol{A}_n| - |\boldsymbol{A}_{n-1}| = 1$, so that $|\boldsymbol{A}_n| = 2 + 1 + \cdots + 1 = n + 1$.

***Exercise 4.41 (Vandermonde determinant)** Consider the $(n+1) \times (n+1)$ matrix

$$\boldsymbol{V} := \begin{pmatrix} 1 & 1 & \dots & 1 \\ a_0 & a_1 & \dots & a_n \\ a_0^2 & a_1^2 & \dots & a_n^2 \\ \vdots & \vdots & & \vdots \\ a_0^n & a_1^n & \dots & a_n^n \end{pmatrix},$$

where $a_0, a_1, \dots, a_n$ are all distinct. This matrix is called a *Vandermonde* matrix. Show that

$$|\boldsymbol{V}| = \prod_{j<i} (a_i - a_j),$$

Solution
We proceed by induction. For $n = 1$ (that is, for a 2×2 matrix) we find $|\boldsymbol{V}| = a_1 - a_0$, so that the result holds for $n = 1$. Now consider

$$\varphi(t) := \begin{vmatrix} 1 & 1 & \dots & 1 \\ a_0 & a_1 & \dots & t \\ a_0^2 & a_1^2 & \dots & t^2 \\ \vdots & \vdots & & \vdots \\ a_0^n & a_1^n & \dots & t^n \end{vmatrix}.$$

The determinant is linear in the last column (Exercise 4.39), and hence $\varphi(t)$ is a polynomial of the n-th degree. Suppose now that Vandermonde's formula holds for $n-1$ (that is, for an $n \times n$ matrix). The coefficient, say k, of t^n in the polynomial is the determinant of the $n \times n$ submatrix obtained by deleting the last row and the last column. Thus, by the induction hypothesis,

$$k = \prod_{0 \le j < i \le n-1} (a_i - a_j).$$

Clearly, $\varphi(a_0) = \varphi(a_1) = \cdots = \varphi(a_{n-1}) = 0$, because two identical columns yield a zero determinant. Hence,

$$\varphi(t) = k(t - a_0)(t - a_1) \dots (t - a_{n-1})$$

Substituting $t = a_n$ completes the proof.

*__Exercise 4.42 (Determinant of a product)__ Show that for any two square matrices of the same order, $|\boldsymbol{AB}| = |\boldsymbol{A}||\boldsymbol{B}|$.

Solution

Let $\boldsymbol{B} = (b_{ij})$ have columns $\boldsymbol{b}_1, \dots, \boldsymbol{b}_n$. The columns of $\boldsymbol{AB}$ are then $\boldsymbol{Ab}_1, \dots, \boldsymbol{Ab}_n$. Expressing $\boldsymbol{b}_1$ as $\sum_{i=1}^n b_{i1}\boldsymbol{e}_i$, where the $\boldsymbol{e}_i$ are unit vectors, we obtain

$$|\boldsymbol{AB}| = \left|\sum_{i=1}^n b_{i1}\boldsymbol{Ae}_i, \boldsymbol{Ab}_2, \dots, \boldsymbol{Ab}_n\right| = \sum_{i=1}^n \left[b_{i1}\left|\boldsymbol{Ae}_i, \boldsymbol{Ab}_2, \dots, \boldsymbol{Ab}_n\right|\right],$$

using the fact that the determinant is a linear function of the first column, if the others are held fixed (Exercise 4.39(i)). Repeating this process with $\boldsymbol{b}_2, \dots, \boldsymbol{b}_n$ gives

$$|\boldsymbol{AB}| = \sum_{i_1=1}^n \cdots \sum_{i_n=1}^n \left[b_{i_1,1}b_{i_2,2}\dots b_{i_n,n}\left|\boldsymbol{Ae}_{i_1}, \boldsymbol{Ae}_{i_2}, \dots, \boldsymbol{Ae}_{i_n}\right|\right].$$

Now consider the matrix $\boldsymbol{C} := (\boldsymbol{Ae}_{i_1}, \dots, \boldsymbol{Ae}_{i_n})$. If $i_j = i_k$ for some pair (j, k), then $|\boldsymbol{C}| = 0$ (two equal columns, Exercise 4.33(a)). We may therefore assume that $(i_1, \dots, i_n)$ is a permutation of $(1, \dots, n)$, so that $\boldsymbol{C}$ contains all n columns of $\boldsymbol{A}$, be it in a different order. By Exercise 4.39(ii) we then have $|\boldsymbol{C}| = t(i_1, \dots, i_n)|\boldsymbol{A}|$, where $t(i_1, \dots, i_n)$ is either $+1$ or -1. Hence,

$$|\boldsymbol{AB}| = \left[\sum t(i_1, \dots, i_n)b_{i_1,1}\dots b_{i_n,n}\right]|\boldsymbol{A}|,$$

where the sum is taken over all ordered n-tuples $(i_1, \dots, i_n)$ with $1 \leq i_j \leq n$. Taking $\boldsymbol{A} = \boldsymbol{I}_n$, and using Exercise 4.39(iii), we see that the sum in square brackets is in fact $|\boldsymbol{B}|$. This completes the proof. (An alternative proof, requiring partitioned matrices, is provided in Exercise 5.27.)

Exercise 4.43 (Rank and zero determinant) Let $\boldsymbol{A}$ be a square matrix of order n. Show that $|\boldsymbol{A}| = 0$ if and only if $\operatorname{rk}(\boldsymbol{A}) < n$.

Solution

Suppose that $\operatorname{rk}(\boldsymbol{A}) < n$. Then the columns of $\boldsymbol{A}$ are linearly dependent. If $\boldsymbol{A}$ has a zero column, then its determinant is zero (Exercise 4.33(b)). If $\boldsymbol{A}$ has no zero column, we can transform $\boldsymbol{A}$ into a matrix having a zero column by performing elementary column-operations. Hence, $|\boldsymbol{A}| = 0$. Next, suppose that $\operatorname{rk}(\boldsymbol{A}) = n$. Then $\boldsymbol{A}$ has an inverse (Exercise 4.21), and hence $1 = |\boldsymbol{A}^{-1}\boldsymbol{A}| = |\boldsymbol{A}^{-1}| \cdot |\boldsymbol{A}|$, implying that $|\boldsymbol{A}| \neq 0$.

Exercise 4.44 (Determinant of the inverse)
(a) If $\boldsymbol{A}$ is nonsingular, show that $|\boldsymbol{A}^{-1}| = |\boldsymbol{A}|^{-1}$.
(b) If $\boldsymbol{A}$ is orthogonal, show that $|\boldsymbol{A}| = \pm 1$.

Solution
(a) Taking determinants of $\boldsymbol{A}\boldsymbol{A}^{-1} = \boldsymbol{I}$ gives $|\boldsymbol{A}\boldsymbol{A}^{-1}| = |\boldsymbol{A}||\boldsymbol{A}^{-1}| = 1$.
(b) Taking determinants of $\boldsymbol{A}'\boldsymbol{A} = \boldsymbol{I}$ gives $|\boldsymbol{A}|^2 = 1$.

Exercise 4.45 (Orthogonal matrix: rotation and reflection) Consider the matrices introduced in Exercise 2.28,

$$\boldsymbol{A}_1 := \begin{pmatrix} \cos\theta & -\sin\theta \\ \sin\theta & \cos\theta \end{pmatrix} \quad \text{and} \quad \boldsymbol{A}_2 := \begin{pmatrix} \cos\theta & -\sin\theta \\ -\sin\theta & -\cos\theta \end{pmatrix}.$$

Show that $|\boldsymbol{A}_1| = 1$ while $|\boldsymbol{A}_2| = -1$, and comment on this result.

Solution
We find $|\boldsymbol{A}_1| = (\cos\theta)^2 + (\sin\theta)^2 = 1$ and $|\boldsymbol{A}_2| = -(\cos\theta)^2 - (\sin\theta)^2 = -1$. An orthogonal matrix $\boldsymbol{A}$ with $|\boldsymbol{A}| = 1$ (like $\boldsymbol{A}_1$) is called a *rotation matrix*. Writing $\boldsymbol{A}_2 = \operatorname{diag}(1, -1)\boldsymbol{A}_1$, we see that the additional operation of reflecting one of the axes changes the sign of the determinant. Two reflections, if applied to different axes, are equivalent to a rotation by π. If applied to the same axis, they are equivalent to a rotation by 2π, that is, back to the original position. This follows from

$$\begin{pmatrix} 1 & 0 \\ 0 & -1 \end{pmatrix}\begin{pmatrix} -1 & 0 \\ 0 & 1 \end{pmatrix} = -\boldsymbol{I}_2 \quad \text{and} \quad \begin{pmatrix} 1 & 0 \\ 0 & -1 \end{pmatrix}^2 = \boldsymbol{I}_2,$$

both rotations having positive determinant (as rotations should have).

***Exercise 4.46 (Adjoint)**
(a) Show that $\boldsymbol{A}\boldsymbol{A}^{\#} = \boldsymbol{A}^{\#}\boldsymbol{A} = |\boldsymbol{A}|\boldsymbol{I}$.
(b) Hence, show that $\boldsymbol{A}^{-1} = (1/|\boldsymbol{A}|)\boldsymbol{A}^{\#}$, if $\boldsymbol{A}$ is nonsingular.
(c) Show that $|\boldsymbol{A}^{\#}| = |\boldsymbol{A}|^{n-1}$.
(d) Show that $(\boldsymbol{A}\boldsymbol{B})^{\#} = \boldsymbol{B}^{\#}\boldsymbol{A}^{\#}$.

Solution
(a) Since $\boldsymbol{A}^{\#} = \boldsymbol{C}'$, the first result follows from Exercise 4.37(c).
(b) If $\boldsymbol{A}$ is nonsingular, then premultiply both sides of $\boldsymbol{A}\boldsymbol{A}^{\#} = |\boldsymbol{A}|\boldsymbol{I}$ by $\boldsymbol{A}^{-1}$. This gives $\boldsymbol{A}^{\#} = |\boldsymbol{A}|\boldsymbol{A}^{-1}$ and the result follows.
(c) Taking determinants on both sides of $\boldsymbol{A}\boldsymbol{A}^{\#} = |\boldsymbol{A}|\boldsymbol{I}$ gives $|\boldsymbol{A}||\boldsymbol{A}^{\#}| = |\boldsymbol{A}|^n$. If $\boldsymbol{A}$ is nonsingular the result follows. If $\boldsymbol{A}$ is singular then $\boldsymbol{A}^{\#}$ is also singular, and the result follows too.
(d) We write

$$\begin{aligned} |\boldsymbol{A}||\boldsymbol{B}|\boldsymbol{B}^{\#}\boldsymbol{A}^{\#} &= |\boldsymbol{A}\boldsymbol{B}|\boldsymbol{I}\boldsymbol{B}^{\#}\boldsymbol{A}^{\#} = (\boldsymbol{A}\boldsymbol{B})^{\#}(\boldsymbol{A}\boldsymbol{B})\boldsymbol{B}^{\#}\boldsymbol{A}^{\#} \\ &= (\boldsymbol{A}\boldsymbol{B})^{\#}\boldsymbol{A}|\boldsymbol{B}|\boldsymbol{I}\boldsymbol{A}^{\#} = |\boldsymbol{A}||\boldsymbol{B}|(\boldsymbol{A}\boldsymbol{B})^{\#}. \end{aligned}$$

If $|A| \neq 0$ and $|B| \neq 0$, the result follows. If either A or B (or both) is singular, then the proof requires an additional step. All three expressions $\varphi := |A||B|$, $F := B^{\#}A^{\#}$, and $G := (AB)^{\#}$ are polynomials in the $2n^2$ elements of A and B. Since $\varphi F = \varphi G$ and φ does not vanish identically, it follows that $F = G$.

A different proof of the case where either A or B (or both) is singular, is based on a continuity argument that is often useful. Consider the matrices $A(\epsilon) := A + \epsilon I$ and $B(\epsilon) := B + \epsilon I$. We can always choose $\delta > 0$ such that $A(\epsilon)$ and $B(\epsilon)$ are nonsingular for every $0 < \epsilon < \delta$. Hence, $(A(\epsilon)B(\epsilon))^{\#} = (B(\epsilon))^{\#}(A(\epsilon))^{\#}$ for every $0 < \epsilon < \delta$. Letting $\epsilon \to 0$ gives the result.

Exercise 4.47 (Find the inverse) Obtain the inverse of the matrix A in Exercise 4.31 for $\alpha = 1$, using the formula in Exercise 4.46(b).

Solution

We need the determinant and the cofactor matrix C. We have

$$A = \begin{pmatrix} 1 & 1 & 0 \\ 4 & 5 & 3 \\ 1 & 0 & 2 \end{pmatrix} \quad \text{and hence} \quad C = \begin{pmatrix} 10 & -5 & -5 \\ -2 & 2 & 1 \\ 3 & -3 & 1 \end{pmatrix}.$$

The determinant of A is 5, and hence

$$A^{\#} = C' = \begin{pmatrix} 10 & -2 & 3 \\ -5 & 2 & -3 \\ -5 & 1 & 1 \end{pmatrix}, \quad A^{-1} = \frac{1}{|A|}A^{\#} = \begin{pmatrix} 2 & -0.4 & 0.6 \\ -1 & 0.4 & -0.6 \\ -1 & 0.2 & 0.2 \end{pmatrix}.$$

After finding an inverse it is usually a good idea to check that it satisfies $AA^{-1} = I$.

Notes

In defining the determinant we needed the concept of a transposition, and in particular the fact that the number of transpositions required to transform $(1, 2, \dots, n)$ to $(j_1, j_2, \dots, j_n)$ is always even or always odd; see Mirsky (1955, p. 3). The fact that the determinant can be characterized by the three properties in Exercise 4.39 was first recognized by Weierstrass in the 1880s. In advanced courses it is often taken as the definition, because it allows for a more elegant presentation. A proof that these three properties indeed define the determinant can be found, for example, in Mirsky (1955, Section 6.6). For a long time, the theory of determinants was considered to be the cornerstone of linear algebra, and it owes a great debt to Vandermonde (1735–1796). The matrix named after him (Exercise 4.41) has many applications, see, for example, Exercises 6.30 and 6.31. There are two proofs of the important fact that $|AB| = |A||B|$. The one in Exercise 4.42 is based on Rudin (1976, Chapter 9). An alternative proof, using results of partitioned matrices, is provided in Exercise 5.27. The adjoint matrix also has a long history. Exercise 4.46(c) was already known to Cauchy in 1812.

5

Partitioned matrices

A partitioned matrix is a matrix of the form

$$Z := \begin{pmatrix} A & B \\ C & D \end{pmatrix}.$$

None of the matrices needs to be square, but A and B must have the same number of rows (say m), A and C must have the same number of columns (say p), and so on. Throughout the chapter, unless specified otherwise, we shall adopt the following convention as to the orders of the submatrices: A $(m \times p)$, B $(m \times q)$, C $(n \times p)$, and D $(n \times q)$. If the matrix A is square, it is of order $m \times m$. If the matrix D is square, it is of order $n \times n$.

The chapter is almost entirely concerned with partitioned matrices with two row blocks and two column blocks, like the matrix Z above. Extensions to m row blocks and n column blocks, such as

$$\begin{pmatrix} Z_{11} & Z_{12} & \dots & Z_{1n} \\ Z_{21} & Z_{22} & \dots & Z_{2n} \\ \vdots & \vdots & & \vdots \\ Z_{m1} & Z_{m2} & \dots & Z_{mn} \end{pmatrix},$$

are conceptually and mathematically straightforward, but notationally cumbersome. As a special case, we say that a square matrix is *block-diagonal* if it takes the form

$$\begin{pmatrix} Z_{11} & \mathrm{O} & \dots & \mathrm{O} \\ \mathrm{O} & Z_{22} & \dots & \mathrm{O} \\ \vdots & \vdots & & \vdots \\ \mathrm{O} & \mathrm{O} & \dots & Z_{rr} \end{pmatrix},$$

where all diagonal blocks are square, not necessarily of the same order. A block-diagonal matrix is thus the direct sum (in the sense of Exercise 3.55) of its blocks $Z_{11}, \dots, Z_{rr}$. If a square matrix is diagonal, then it is block-diagonal, but not vice versa.

The main tool in obtaining the inverse, determinant, and rank of a partitioned matrix is to write the matrix as a product of simpler matrices, that is, matrices of which one (or two) of the four blocks is the null matrix. Many examples of this general principle will be provided.

We first provide some basic results, and then apply and extend these to find inverses (Section 5.2), determinants (Section 5.3), and ranks (Section 5.3) of partitioned matrices. A final section is devoted to the *sweep operator*, closely related to the Gram-Schmidt orthogonalization (see Exercise 3.49). The sweep operator has become popular in computer packages as a matrix inversion routine. If $\boldsymbol{A} := (a_{ij})$ is an $n \times n$ matrix, then we define the $n \times n$ matrix $\boldsymbol{B} := (b_{ij})$ as

$$b_{kk} := -1/a_{kk}, \quad b_{ik} := a_{ik}/a_{kk}, \quad b_{kj} := a_{kj}/a_{kk}, \quad b_{ij} := a_{ij} - a_{ik}a_{kj}/a_{kk},$$

where $k \neq i$, $k \neq j$, and it is assumed that a_{kk} (the *pivot*) is not zero. We write $\boldsymbol{B} := \mathrm{SWP}(\boldsymbol{A}, k)$ to indicate that the k-th row and column of $\boldsymbol{A}$ are being swept.

5.1 Basic results and multiplication relations

Exercise 5.1 (Partitioned sum) Let

$$\boldsymbol{Z}_1 := \begin{pmatrix} \boldsymbol{A}_1 & \boldsymbol{B}_1 \\ \boldsymbol{C}_1 & \boldsymbol{D}_1 \end{pmatrix} \quad \text{and} \quad \boldsymbol{Z}_2 := \begin{pmatrix} \boldsymbol{A}_2 & \boldsymbol{B}_2 \\ \boldsymbol{C}_2 & \boldsymbol{D}_2 \end{pmatrix}.$$

Show that

$$\boldsymbol{Z} := \boldsymbol{Z}_1 + \boldsymbol{Z}_2 = \begin{pmatrix} \boldsymbol{A}_1 + \boldsymbol{A}_2 & \boldsymbol{B}_1 + \boldsymbol{B}_2 \\ \boldsymbol{C}_1 + \boldsymbol{C}_2 & \boldsymbol{D}_1 + \boldsymbol{D}_2 \end{pmatrix}.$$

Which are the order conditions that need to be satisfied?

Solution
The rule for addition of partitioned matrices is the same as the rule for addition or ordinary matrices: we just add the corresponding elements in the two matrices. Hence, $\boldsymbol{Z}_1$ and $\boldsymbol{Z}_2$ can be added "by blocks" if they are partitioned in the same way, that is to say, if the corresponding submatrices are of the same order.

Exercise 5.2 (Partitioned product) Let

$$\boldsymbol{Z}_1 := \begin{pmatrix} \boldsymbol{A}_1 & \boldsymbol{B}_1 \\ \boldsymbol{C}_1 & \boldsymbol{D}_1 \end{pmatrix} \quad \text{and} \quad \boldsymbol{Z}_2 := \begin{pmatrix} \boldsymbol{A}_2 & \boldsymbol{B}_2 \\ \boldsymbol{C}_2 & \boldsymbol{D}_2 \end{pmatrix}.$$

Show that

$$\boldsymbol{Z} := \boldsymbol{Z}_1\boldsymbol{Z}_2 = \begin{pmatrix} \boldsymbol{A}_1\boldsymbol{A}_2 + \boldsymbol{B}_1\boldsymbol{C}_2 & \boldsymbol{A}_1\boldsymbol{B}_2 + \boldsymbol{B}_1\boldsymbol{D}_2 \\ \boldsymbol{C}_1\boldsymbol{A}_2 + \boldsymbol{D}_1\boldsymbol{C}_2 & \boldsymbol{C}_1\boldsymbol{B}_2 + \boldsymbol{D}_1\boldsymbol{D}_2 \end{pmatrix}.$$

What are the conditions on the orders of the submatrices?

Solution
Let $\boldsymbol{Z}_1$ be an $(m+n) \times (p+q)$ matrix and $\boldsymbol{Z}_2$ a $(p+q) \times (r+s)$ matrix, such that $\boldsymbol{A}_1$ is of order $m \times p$ and $\boldsymbol{A}_2$ is of order $p \times r$. Then all submatrices are well-defined. By the

rules of ordinary matrix multiplication we have

$$
\begin{aligned}
\boldsymbol{Z}_{ij} &= (\boldsymbol{Z}_1\boldsymbol{Z}_2)_{ij} = \sum_{k=1}^{p+q}(\boldsymbol{Z}_1)_{ik}(\boldsymbol{Z}_2)_{kj} \\
&= \sum_{k=1}^{p}\begin{pmatrix}\boldsymbol{A}_1\\ \boldsymbol{C}_1\end{pmatrix}_{ik}(\boldsymbol{A}_2:\boldsymbol{B}_2)_{kj} + \sum_{k=1}^{q}\begin{pmatrix}\boldsymbol{B}_1\\ \boldsymbol{D}_1\end{pmatrix}_{ik}(\boldsymbol{C}_2:\boldsymbol{D}_2)_{kj} \\
&= \left(\sum_{k=1}^{p}\begin{pmatrix}\boldsymbol{A}_1\\ \boldsymbol{C}_1\end{pmatrix}_{\bullet k}(\boldsymbol{A}_2:\boldsymbol{B}_2)_{k\bullet}\right)_{ij} + \left(\sum_{k=1}^{q}\begin{pmatrix}\boldsymbol{B}_1\\ \boldsymbol{D}_1\end{pmatrix}_{\bullet k}(\boldsymbol{C}_2:\boldsymbol{D}_2)_{k\bullet}\right)_{ij} \\
&= \begin{pmatrix}\boldsymbol{A}_1\boldsymbol{A}_2 & \boldsymbol{A}_1\boldsymbol{B}_2\\ \boldsymbol{C}_1\boldsymbol{A}_2 & \boldsymbol{C}_1\boldsymbol{B}_2\end{pmatrix}_{ij} + \begin{pmatrix}\boldsymbol{B}_1\boldsymbol{C}_2 & \boldsymbol{B}_1\boldsymbol{D}_2\\ \boldsymbol{D}_1\boldsymbol{C}_2 & \boldsymbol{D}_1\boldsymbol{D}_2\end{pmatrix}_{ij} \\
&= \begin{pmatrix}\boldsymbol{A}_1\boldsymbol{A}_2+\boldsymbol{B}_1\boldsymbol{C}_2 & \boldsymbol{A}_1\boldsymbol{B}_2+\boldsymbol{B}_1\boldsymbol{D}_2\\ \boldsymbol{C}_1\boldsymbol{A}_2+\boldsymbol{D}_1\boldsymbol{C}_2 & \boldsymbol{C}_1\boldsymbol{B}_2+\boldsymbol{D}_1\boldsymbol{D}_2\end{pmatrix}_{ij}.
\end{aligned}
$$

Exercise 5.3 (Partitioned transpose) Show that

$$\begin{pmatrix}\boldsymbol{A} & \boldsymbol{B}\\ \boldsymbol{C} & \boldsymbol{D}\end{pmatrix}' = \begin{pmatrix}\boldsymbol{A}' & \boldsymbol{C}'\\ \boldsymbol{B}' & \boldsymbol{D}'\end{pmatrix},$$

with $\boldsymbol{A}$ $(m \times p)$, $\boldsymbol{B}$ $(m \times q)$, $\boldsymbol{C}$ $(n \times p)$, and $\boldsymbol{D}$ $(n \times q)$.

Solution

This is almost trivial. A formal proof proceeds as follows. Let

$$\boldsymbol{Z} := \begin{pmatrix}\boldsymbol{A} & \boldsymbol{B}\\ \boldsymbol{C} & \boldsymbol{D}\end{pmatrix} \quad \text{and} \quad \boldsymbol{X} := \begin{pmatrix}\boldsymbol{A}' & \boldsymbol{C}'\\ \boldsymbol{B}' & \boldsymbol{D}'\end{pmatrix}.$$

Then,

$$
\begin{aligned}
\boldsymbol{Z}_{ij} &= \begin{cases}\boldsymbol{A}_{ij} & (1 \le i \le m,\ 1 \le j \le p),\\ \boldsymbol{B}_{i,j-p} & (1 \le i \le m,\ p+1 \le j \le p+q),\\ \boldsymbol{C}_{i-m,j} & (m+1 \le i \le m+n,\ 1 \le j \le p),\\ \boldsymbol{D}_{i-m,j-p} & (m+1 \le i \le m+n,\ p+1 \le j \le p+q)\end{cases} \\
&= \begin{cases}(\boldsymbol{A}')_{ji} & (1 \le j \le p,\ 1 \le i \le m),\\ (\boldsymbol{C}')_{j,i-m} & (1 \le j \le p,\ m+1 \le i \le m+n),\\ (\boldsymbol{B}')_{j-p,i} & (p+1 \le j \le p+q,\ 1 \le i \le m),\\ (\boldsymbol{D}')_{j-p,i-m} & (p+1 \le j \le p+q,\ m+1 \le i \le m+n)\end{cases} \\
&= \boldsymbol{X}_{ji}.
\end{aligned}
$$

Exercise 5.4 (Trace of partitioned matrix) If A and D are square, not necessarily of the same order, show that

$$\operatorname{tr}\begin{pmatrix} A & B \\ C & D \end{pmatrix} = \operatorname{tr} A + \operatorname{tr} D.$$

Solution

Since A and D are both square, the diagonal elements of Z are precisely those of A and D. The result follows.

Exercise 5.5 (Preservation of form) Let

$$Z := \begin{pmatrix} A & B \\ C & D \end{pmatrix},$$

where A and D are square matrices, not necessarily of the same order.
(a) If Z is symmetric, show that A and D are symmetric.
(b) If Z is diagonal, show that A and D are diagonal.
(c) If Z is upper triangular, show that A and D are upper triangular.
(d) What additional requirements are needed for the reverse implications?

Solution

(a) It follows from Exercise 5.3 that $Z = Z'$ if and only if $A = A'$, $B = C'$, and $D = D'$. Hence the symmetry of A and D is necessary but not sufficient for the symmetry of Z.
(b) We see by direct inspection that Z is diagonal if and only if A and D are diagonal and $B = \mathrm{O}$, $C = \mathrm{O}$. Diagonality of A and D is therefore a necessary but not a sufficient condition for the diagonality of Z.
(c) Z is upper triangular if and only if A and D are upper triangular and $C = \mathrm{O}$.
(d) All three statements are necessary but not sufficient. The additional requirements are: (a) $B = C'$, (b) $B = \mathrm{O}$ and $C = \mathrm{O}$, and (c) $C = \mathrm{O}$.

Exercise 5.6 (Elementary row-block operations) Prove the following elementary row-block operations:

$$\begin{pmatrix} \mathrm{O} & I_n \\ I_m & \mathrm{O} \end{pmatrix}\begin{pmatrix} A & B \\ C & D \end{pmatrix} = \begin{pmatrix} C & D \\ A & B \end{pmatrix},$$

$$\begin{pmatrix} E & \mathrm{O} \\ \mathrm{O} & I_n \end{pmatrix}\begin{pmatrix} A & B \\ C & D \end{pmatrix} = \begin{pmatrix} EA & EB \\ C & D \end{pmatrix},$$

and

$$\begin{pmatrix} I_m & E \\ \mathrm{O} & I_n \end{pmatrix}\begin{pmatrix} A & B \\ C & D \end{pmatrix} = \begin{pmatrix} A+EC & B+ED \\ C & D \end{pmatrix}.$$

Solution
The results follow directly from the rules of partitioned matrix multiplication (Exercise 5.2).

Exercise 5.7 (Elementary column-block operations) Prove the following elementary column-block operations:

$$\begin{pmatrix} A & B \\ C & D \end{pmatrix} \begin{pmatrix} O & I_p \\ I_q & O \end{pmatrix} = \begin{pmatrix} B & A \\ D & C \end{pmatrix},$$

$$\begin{pmatrix} A & B \\ C & D \end{pmatrix} \begin{pmatrix} F & O \\ O & I_q \end{pmatrix} = \begin{pmatrix} AF & B \\ CF & D \end{pmatrix},$$

and

$$\begin{pmatrix} A & B \\ C & D \end{pmatrix} \begin{pmatrix} I_p & F \\ O & I_q \end{pmatrix} = \begin{pmatrix} A & B+AF \\ C & D+CF \end{pmatrix}.$$

Solution
These results also follow directly from the rules of partitioned matrix multiplication (Exercise 5.2).

Exercise 5.8 (Unipotence) Show that the matrix

$$Z := \begin{pmatrix} -I_m & B \\ C & I_n \end{pmatrix}$$

satisfies $Z^2 = I_{m+n}$, if $B = O$ or $C = O$. Is this condition necessary?

Solution
We have

$$Z^2 = \begin{pmatrix} -I_m & B \\ C & I_n \end{pmatrix} \begin{pmatrix} -I_m & B \\ C & I_n \end{pmatrix} = \begin{pmatrix} I_m + BC & O \\ O & I_n + CB \end{pmatrix},$$

and hence $Z^2 = I_{m+n}$ if and only if $BC = O$ and $CB = O$. This shows the result, and also shows that the condition, while sufficient, is not necessary.

Exercise 5.9 (Commuting partitioned matrices) Show that the matrices

$$Z_1 := \begin{pmatrix} I_m & B_1 \\ O & I_n \end{pmatrix} \quad \text{and} \quad Z_2 := \begin{pmatrix} I_m & B_2 \\ O & I_n \end{pmatrix}$$

commute, that is, $Z_1 Z_2 = Z_2 Z_1$.

Solution
We write $Z_1 = I_{m+n} + X_1$ and $Z_2 = I_{m+n} + X_2$ with

$$X_1 := \begin{pmatrix} O & B_1 \\ O & O \end{pmatrix} \quad \text{and} \quad X_2 := \begin{pmatrix} O & B_2 \\ O & O \end{pmatrix}.$$

Then, $X_1X_2 = X_2X_1 = O$, and hence

$$
\begin{aligned}
Z_1Z_2 &= (I_{m+n} + X_1)(I_{m+n} + X_2) = I_{m+n} + X_1 + X_2 \\
&= I_{m+n} + X_2 + X_1 = (I_{m+n} + X_2)(I_{m+n} + X_1) = Z_2Z_1.
\end{aligned}
$$

Exercise 5.10 (Schur complement of diagonal block, 1) If A is nonsingular, show that

$$
\begin{pmatrix} I_m & O \\ -CA^{-1} & I_n \end{pmatrix} \begin{pmatrix} A & B \\ C & D \end{pmatrix} = \begin{pmatrix} A & B \\ O & D - CA^{-1}B \end{pmatrix},
$$

$$
\begin{pmatrix} A & B \\ C & D \end{pmatrix} \begin{pmatrix} I_m & -A^{-1}B \\ O & I_q \end{pmatrix} = \begin{pmatrix} A & O \\ C & D - CA^{-1}B \end{pmatrix},
$$

and hence

$$
\begin{pmatrix} I_m & O \\ -CA^{-1} & I_n \end{pmatrix} \begin{pmatrix} A & B \\ C & D \end{pmatrix} \begin{pmatrix} I_m & -A^{-1}B \\ O & I_q \end{pmatrix} = \begin{pmatrix} A & O \\ O & D - CA^{-1}B \end{pmatrix}.
$$

The matrix $D - CA^{-1}B$ is called the *Schur complement* of A. The result is somewhat easier to remember if we write

$$
Z := \begin{pmatrix} Z_{11} & Z_{12} \\ Z_{21} & Z_{22} \end{pmatrix}.
$$

The Schur complement of Z_{11} is then $Z_{22|1} := Z_{22} - Z_{21}Z_{11}^{-1}Z_{12}$.

Solution

Consider the equation

$$
\begin{pmatrix} I_m & O \\ R & I_n \end{pmatrix} \begin{pmatrix} A & B \\ C & D \end{pmatrix} = \begin{pmatrix} A & B \\ C + RA & D + RB \end{pmatrix}.
$$

We can create a zero in the off-diagonal block if $C + RA = O$. Hence, we choose $R := -CA^{-1}$, in which case $D + RB = D - CA^{-1}B$. Next consider the equation

$$
\begin{pmatrix} A & B \\ C & D \end{pmatrix} \begin{pmatrix} I_m & Q \\ O & I_q \end{pmatrix} = \begin{pmatrix} A & B + AQ \\ C & D + CQ \end{pmatrix}.
$$

Here we choose Q such that $B + AQ = O$, that is, $Q := -A^{-1}B$, in which case $D + CQ = D - CA^{-1}B$. The final result is an immediate consequence of the first two.

Exercise 5.11 (Schur complement of diagonal block, 2) If D is nonsingular, show that

$$
\begin{pmatrix} I_m & -BD^{-1} \\ O & I_n \end{pmatrix} \begin{pmatrix} A & B \\ C & D \end{pmatrix} = \begin{pmatrix} A - BD^{-1}C & O \\ C & D \end{pmatrix},
$$

$$
\begin{pmatrix} A & B \\ C & D \end{pmatrix} \begin{pmatrix} I_p & O \\ -D^{-1}C & I_n \end{pmatrix} = \begin{pmatrix} A - BD^{-1}C & B \\ O & D \end{pmatrix},
$$

and hence

$$\begin{pmatrix} I_m & -BD^{-1} \\ O & I_n \end{pmatrix} \begin{pmatrix} A & B \\ C & D \end{pmatrix} \begin{pmatrix} I_p & O \\ -D^{-1}C & I_n \end{pmatrix} = \begin{pmatrix} A - BD^{-1}C & O \\ O & D \end{pmatrix}.$$

The matrix $A - BD^{-1}C$ is the Schur complement of D.

Solution

The proof is analogous to the proof in Exercise 5.10, or can be obtained directly by performing the required block multiplications.

5.2 Inverses

Exercise 5.12 (Two zero blocks, inverse)

(a) If A and D are nonsingular, show that

$$\begin{pmatrix} A & O \\ O & D \end{pmatrix}^{-1} = \begin{pmatrix} A^{-1} & O \\ O & D^{-1} \end{pmatrix}.$$

(b) If B and C are nonsingular, show that

$$\begin{pmatrix} O & B \\ C & O \end{pmatrix}^{-1} = \begin{pmatrix} O & C^{-1} \\ B^{-1} & O \end{pmatrix} \quad \text{and} \quad \begin{pmatrix} O & B \\ B^{-1} & O \end{pmatrix}^{-1} = \begin{pmatrix} O & B \\ B^{-1} & O \end{pmatrix}.$$

(c) When are the matrices in (b) orthogonal?

Solution

(a) In general, if we know (or suspect), for a given matrix A, that $A^{-1} = B$, then all we need to do in order to prove this result is check that $AB = I$ (or that $BA = I$, one of the two suffices). This method is not "constructive", so it does not help us if we do *not* know the inverse. Result (a) is immediate by direct verification. In a constructive proof we would solve

$$\begin{pmatrix} A & O \\ O & D \end{pmatrix} \begin{pmatrix} P & Q \\ R & S \end{pmatrix} = \begin{pmatrix} I_m & O \\ O & I_n \end{pmatrix},$$

which gives the four equations

$$AP = I_m, \quad AQ = O, \quad DR = O, \quad DS = I_n.$$

Since A and D are nonsingular, we find $P = A^{-1}$, $Q = O$, $R = O$, and $S = D^{-1}$.

(b) Of course, direct verification works here too. But suppose we conjecture that the inverse is of the same type. Then we may try and solve

$$\begin{pmatrix} O & B \\ C & O \end{pmatrix} \begin{pmatrix} O & Q \\ R & O \end{pmatrix} = \begin{pmatrix} I_m & O \\ O & I_n \end{pmatrix}.$$

This gives $BR = I_m$ and $CQ = I_n$, and hence $R = B^{-1}$, $Q = C^{-1}$. The second result of (b) is obtained by setting $C = B^{-1}$.

(c) Given (b), the first matrix,

$$\begin{pmatrix} \mathbf{O} & \boldsymbol{B} \\ \boldsymbol{C} & \mathbf{O} \end{pmatrix},$$

is orthogonal if and only if both $\boldsymbol{B}$ and $\boldsymbol{C}$ are orthogonal. Replacing $\boldsymbol{C}$ by $\boldsymbol{B}^{-1}$ shows that the second matrix is orthogonal if and only $\boldsymbol{B}$ is orthogonal.

Exercise 5.13 (One off-diagonal zero block, inverse)
(a) Show that

$$\begin{pmatrix} \boldsymbol{I}_m & \boldsymbol{B} \\ \mathbf{O} & \boldsymbol{I}_n \end{pmatrix}^{-1} = \begin{pmatrix} \boldsymbol{I}_m & -\boldsymbol{B} \\ \mathbf{O} & \boldsymbol{I}_n \end{pmatrix} \quad \text{and} \quad \begin{pmatrix} \boldsymbol{I}_m & \mathbf{O} \\ \boldsymbol{C} & \boldsymbol{I}_n \end{pmatrix}^{-1} = \begin{pmatrix} \boldsymbol{I}_m & \mathbf{O} \\ -\boldsymbol{C} & \boldsymbol{I}_n \end{pmatrix}.$$

(b) More generally, if $\boldsymbol{A}$ and $\boldsymbol{D}$ are nonsingular, show that

$$\begin{pmatrix} \boldsymbol{A} & \boldsymbol{B} \\ \mathbf{O} & \boldsymbol{D} \end{pmatrix}^{-1} = \begin{pmatrix} \boldsymbol{A}^{-1} & -\boldsymbol{A}^{-1}\boldsymbol{B}\boldsymbol{D}^{-1} \\ \mathbf{O} & \boldsymbol{D}^{-1} \end{pmatrix}$$

and

$$\begin{pmatrix} \boldsymbol{A} & \mathbf{O} \\ \boldsymbol{C} & \boldsymbol{D} \end{pmatrix}^{-1} = \begin{pmatrix} \boldsymbol{A}^{-1} & \mathbf{O} \\ -\boldsymbol{D}^{-1}\boldsymbol{C}\boldsymbol{A}^{-1} & \boldsymbol{D}^{-1} \end{pmatrix}.$$

Solution
(a) We verify that

$$\begin{pmatrix} \boldsymbol{I}_m & \boldsymbol{B} \\ \mathbf{O} & \boldsymbol{I}_n \end{pmatrix} \begin{pmatrix} \boldsymbol{I}_m & -\boldsymbol{B} \\ \mathbf{O} & \boldsymbol{I}_n \end{pmatrix} = \begin{pmatrix} \boldsymbol{I}_m & \mathbf{O} \\ \mathbf{O} & \boldsymbol{I}_n \end{pmatrix}$$

and similarly for the second result.
(b) Direct verification works of course. Instead, let us conjecture that

$$\begin{pmatrix} \boldsymbol{A} & \boldsymbol{B} \\ \mathbf{O} & \boldsymbol{D} \end{pmatrix} \begin{pmatrix} \boldsymbol{A}^{-1} & \boldsymbol{Q} \\ \mathbf{O} & \boldsymbol{D}^{-1} \end{pmatrix} = \begin{pmatrix} \boldsymbol{I}_m & \mathbf{O} \\ \mathbf{O} & \boldsymbol{I}_n \end{pmatrix}.$$

for some matrix $\boldsymbol{Q}$. The equation is satisfied if and only if $\boldsymbol{A}\boldsymbol{Q} + \boldsymbol{B}\boldsymbol{D}^{-1} = \mathbf{O}$, that is, if and only if $\boldsymbol{Q} = -\boldsymbol{A}^{-1}\boldsymbol{B}\boldsymbol{D}^{-1}$. The second result follows in the same way, or by direct verification, or by considering the transpose and using the first result.

Exercise 5.14 (One diagonal zero block, inverse)
(a) Show that

$$\begin{pmatrix} \boldsymbol{A} & \boldsymbol{I}_m \\ \boldsymbol{I}_n & \mathbf{O} \end{pmatrix}^{-1} = \begin{pmatrix} \mathbf{O} & \boldsymbol{I}_n \\ \boldsymbol{I}_m & -\boldsymbol{A} \end{pmatrix} \quad \text{and} \quad \begin{pmatrix} \mathbf{O} & \boldsymbol{I}_m \\ \boldsymbol{I}_n & \boldsymbol{D} \end{pmatrix}^{-1} = \begin{pmatrix} -\boldsymbol{D} & \boldsymbol{I}_n \\ \boldsymbol{I}_m & \mathbf{O} \end{pmatrix}.$$

(b) More generally, if $\boldsymbol{B}$ and $\boldsymbol{C}$ are nonsingular, show that

$$\begin{pmatrix} \boldsymbol{A} & \boldsymbol{B} \\ \boldsymbol{C} & \mathbf{O} \end{pmatrix}^{-1} = \begin{pmatrix} \mathbf{O} & \boldsymbol{C}^{-1} \\ \boldsymbol{B}^{-1} & -\boldsymbol{B}^{-1}\boldsymbol{A}\boldsymbol{C}^{-1} \end{pmatrix}$$

and

$$\begin{pmatrix} \mathbf{O} & \boldsymbol{B} \\ \boldsymbol{C} & \boldsymbol{D} \end{pmatrix}^{-1} = \begin{pmatrix} -\boldsymbol{C}^{-1}\boldsymbol{D}\boldsymbol{B}^{-1} & \boldsymbol{C}^{-1} \\ \boldsymbol{B}^{-1} & \mathbf{O} \end{pmatrix}.$$

Solution

All four results follow by direct verification. Let us prove one of them constructively. From the equation

$$\begin{pmatrix} \boldsymbol{A} & \boldsymbol{B} \\ \boldsymbol{C} & \mathbf{O} \end{pmatrix} \begin{pmatrix} \boldsymbol{P} & \boldsymbol{Q} \\ \boldsymbol{R} & \boldsymbol{S} \end{pmatrix} = \begin{pmatrix} \boldsymbol{I}_m & \mathbf{O} \\ \mathbf{O} & \boldsymbol{I}_n \end{pmatrix},$$

we find

$$\boldsymbol{AP} + \boldsymbol{BR} = \boldsymbol{I}_m, \quad \boldsymbol{AQ} + \boldsymbol{BS} = \mathbf{O}, \quad \boldsymbol{CP} = \mathbf{O}, \quad \boldsymbol{CQ} = \boldsymbol{I}_n.$$

The last two equations give $\boldsymbol{P} = \mathbf{O}$ and $\boldsymbol{Q} = \boldsymbol{C}^{-1}$. Inserting these in the first two equations gives $\boldsymbol{BR} = \boldsymbol{I}_m$ and $\boldsymbol{AC}^{-1} + \boldsymbol{BS} = \mathbf{O}$, implying $\boldsymbol{R} = \boldsymbol{B}^{-1}$ and $\boldsymbol{S} = -\boldsymbol{B}^{-1}\boldsymbol{AC}^{-1}$.

Exercise 5.15 (Scalar diagonal block, inverse)

(a) If $\boldsymbol{A}$ is nonsingular and $\varepsilon := \delta - \boldsymbol{c}'\boldsymbol{A}^{-1}\boldsymbol{b} \neq 0$, show that

$$\begin{pmatrix} \boldsymbol{A} & \boldsymbol{b} \\ \boldsymbol{c}' & \delta \end{pmatrix}^{-1} = \begin{pmatrix} \boldsymbol{A}^{-1} & \mathbf{0} \\ \mathbf{0}' & 0 \end{pmatrix} + \frac{1}{\varepsilon} \begin{pmatrix} \boldsymbol{A}^{-1}\boldsymbol{b} \\ -1 \end{pmatrix} (\boldsymbol{c}'\boldsymbol{A}^{-1} : -1).$$

(b) Similarly, if $\boldsymbol{D}$ is nonsingular and $\phi := \alpha - \boldsymbol{b}'\boldsymbol{D}^{-1}\boldsymbol{c} \neq 0$, show that

$$\begin{pmatrix} \alpha & \boldsymbol{b}' \\ \boldsymbol{c} & \boldsymbol{D} \end{pmatrix}^{-1} = \begin{pmatrix} 0 & \mathbf{0}' \\ \mathbf{0} & \boldsymbol{D}^{-1} \end{pmatrix} + \frac{1}{\phi} \begin{pmatrix} -1 \\ \boldsymbol{D}^{-1}\boldsymbol{c} \end{pmatrix} (-1 : \boldsymbol{b}'\boldsymbol{D}^{-1}).$$

Solution

We only prove (a), since (b) is proved in the same way. Thus, we try and find the solution to

$$\begin{pmatrix} \boldsymbol{A} & \boldsymbol{b} \\ \boldsymbol{c}' & \delta \end{pmatrix} \begin{pmatrix} \boldsymbol{P} & \boldsymbol{q} \\ \boldsymbol{r}' & \sigma \end{pmatrix} = \begin{pmatrix} \boldsymbol{I}_m & \mathbf{0} \\ \mathbf{0}' & 1 \end{pmatrix}.$$

This gives four equations:

$$\boldsymbol{AP} + \boldsymbol{br}' = \boldsymbol{I}_m, \quad \boldsymbol{Aq} + \sigma\boldsymbol{b} = \mathbf{0}, \quad \boldsymbol{c}'\boldsymbol{P} + \delta\boldsymbol{r}' = \mathbf{0}', \quad \boldsymbol{c}'\boldsymbol{q} + \delta\sigma = 1.$$

We "solve" $\boldsymbol{P}$ (in terms of $\boldsymbol{r}$) from the first equation as $\boldsymbol{P} = \boldsymbol{A}^{-1} - \boldsymbol{A}^{-1}\boldsymbol{br}'$, and insert this in the third equation, $\boldsymbol{c}'\boldsymbol{A}^{-1} - (\boldsymbol{c}'\boldsymbol{A}^{-1}\boldsymbol{b})\boldsymbol{r}' + \delta\boldsymbol{r}' = \mathbf{0}'$, giving $\varepsilon\boldsymbol{r}' = -\boldsymbol{c}'\boldsymbol{A}^{-1}$, and hence $\boldsymbol{r}' = -(1/\varepsilon)\boldsymbol{c}'\boldsymbol{A}^{-1}$ and $\boldsymbol{P} = \boldsymbol{A}^{-1} + (1/\varepsilon)\boldsymbol{A}^{-1}\boldsymbol{bc}'\boldsymbol{A}^{-1}$. Similarly, "solving" $\boldsymbol{q}$ from the second equation as $\boldsymbol{q} = -\sigma\boldsymbol{A}^{-1}\boldsymbol{b}$, and inserting in the fourth equation, gives $(\delta - \boldsymbol{c}'\boldsymbol{A}^{-1}\boldsymbol{b})\sigma = 1$, and hence $\sigma = 1/\varepsilon$ and $\boldsymbol{q} = -(1/\varepsilon)\boldsymbol{A}^{-1}\boldsymbol{b}$.

Exercise 5.16 (Inverse of a partitioned matrix: main result)
(a) If A and $E := D - CA^{-1}B$ are nonsingular, show that

$$\begin{pmatrix} A & B \\ C & D \end{pmatrix}^{-1} = \begin{pmatrix} A^{-1} + A^{-1}BE^{-1}CA^{-1} & -A^{-1}BE^{-1} \\ -E^{-1}CA^{-1} & E^{-1} \end{pmatrix}.$$

(b) If D and $F := A - BD^{-1}C$ are nonsingular, show that

$$\begin{pmatrix} A & B \\ C & D \end{pmatrix}^{-1} = \begin{pmatrix} F^{-1} & -F^{-1}BD^{-1} \\ -D^{-1}CF^{-1} & D^{-1} + D^{-1}CF^{-1}BD^{-1} \end{pmatrix}.$$

Solution
(a) We use the Schur complement of Exercise 5.10,

$$\begin{pmatrix} I_m & O \\ -CA^{-1} & I_n \end{pmatrix} \begin{pmatrix} A & B \\ C & D \end{pmatrix} = \begin{pmatrix} A & B \\ O & E \end{pmatrix},$$

where $E := D - CA^{-1}B$. Then, using Exercise 5.13(b), we obtain

$$\begin{aligned} \begin{pmatrix} A & B \\ C & D \end{pmatrix}^{-1} &= \begin{pmatrix} A & B \\ O & E \end{pmatrix}^{-1} \begin{pmatrix} I_m & O \\ -CA^{-1} & I_n \end{pmatrix} \\ &= \begin{pmatrix} A^{-1} & -A^{-1}BE^{-1} \\ O & E^{-1} \end{pmatrix} \begin{pmatrix} I_m & O \\ -CA^{-1} & I_n \end{pmatrix} \\ &= \begin{pmatrix} A^{-1} + A^{-1}BE^{-1}CA^{-1} & -A^{-1}BE^{-1} \\ -E^{-1}CA^{-1} & E^{-1} \end{pmatrix}. \end{aligned}$$

(b) This result may be proved analogously. So, let us provide a different, more direct, proof. We consider the equation

$$\begin{pmatrix} A & B \\ C & D \end{pmatrix} \begin{pmatrix} P & Q \\ R & S \end{pmatrix} = \begin{pmatrix} I_m & O \\ O & I_n \end{pmatrix},$$

leading to two equations in P and R:

$$AP + BR = I_m, \quad CP + DR = O,$$

and two equations in Q and S:

$$AQ + BS = O, \quad CQ + DS = I_n.$$

The first set of equations gives $R = -D^{-1}CP$ and hence

$$I_m = AP + BR = AP - BD^{-1}CP = (A - BD^{-1}C)P = FP,$$

so that $P = F^{-1}$ and $R = -D^{-1}CF^{-1}$. The second set of equations gives $S = D^{-1} - D^{-1}CQ$ and hence

$$O = AQ + BS = AQ + BD^{-1} - BD^{-1}CQ = FQ + BD^{-1},$$

so that $Q = -F^{-1}BD^{-1}$ and $S = D^{-1} + D^{-1}CF^{-1}BD^{-1}$.

Exercise 5.17 (Inverse of $A - BD^{-1}C$) If the inverses exist, show that

$$(A - BD^{-1}C)^{-1} = A^{-1} + A^{-1}B(D - CA^{-1}B)^{-1}CA^{-1}$$

and

$$(D - CA^{-1}B)^{-1} = D^{-1} + D^{-1}C(A - BD^{-1}C)^{-1}BD^{-1}.$$

(These results provide a generalization of Exercise 4.28.)

Solution
In Exercise 5.16 we obtained two expressions for the inverse of a partitioned matrix. Since the inverse is unique, they must be equal to each other.

Exercise 5.18 (Positive definite counterpart of the main inversion result) Let $(A : B)$ be an $n \times (k + m)$ matrix of full column rank, and define

$$Z := (A : B)'(A : B) = \begin{pmatrix} A'A & A'B \\ B'A & B'B \end{pmatrix}.$$

Let

$$M_A := I_n - A(A'A)^{-1}A', \quad M_B := I_n - B(B'B)^{-1}B',$$

and

$$E := B'M_AB, \quad F := A'M_BA.$$

(a) Show that Z^{-1} can be expressed as

$$Z^{-1} = \begin{pmatrix} (A'A)^{-1} + (A'A)^{-1}A'BE^{-1}B'A(A'A)^{-1} & -(A'A)^{-1}A'BE^{-1} \\ -E^{-1}B'A(A'A)^{-1} & E^{-1} \end{pmatrix}.$$

(b) Alternatively, show that Z^{-1} can also be expressed as

$$Z^{-1} = \begin{pmatrix} F^{-1} & -F^{-1}A'B(B'B)^{-1} \\ -(B'B)^{-1}B'AF^{-1} & (B'B)^{-1} + (B'B)^{-1}B'AF^{-1}A'B(B'B)^{-1} \end{pmatrix}.$$

Solution
This is a direct consequence of Exercise 5.16.

Exercise 5.19 (A 3-by-3 block matrix inverse) Consider the symmetric matrix

$$Z := \begin{pmatrix} A & B & C \\ B' & D & O \\ C' & O & E \end{pmatrix}.$$

If $\boldsymbol{D}$, $\boldsymbol{E}$, and $\boldsymbol{Q} := \boldsymbol{A}-\boldsymbol{B}\boldsymbol{D}^{-1}\boldsymbol{B}'-\boldsymbol{C}\boldsymbol{E}^{-1}\boldsymbol{C}'$ are nonsingular, show that $\boldsymbol{Z}$ is nonsingular with inverse

$$\begin{pmatrix} \boldsymbol{Q}^{-1} & -\boldsymbol{Q}^{-1}\boldsymbol{B}\boldsymbol{D}^{-1} & -\boldsymbol{Q}^{-1}\boldsymbol{C}\boldsymbol{E}^{-1} \\ -\boldsymbol{D}^{-1}\boldsymbol{B}'\boldsymbol{Q}^{-1} & \boldsymbol{D}^{-1}+\boldsymbol{D}^{-1}\boldsymbol{B}'\boldsymbol{Q}^{-1}\boldsymbol{B}\boldsymbol{D}^{-1} & \boldsymbol{D}^{-1}\boldsymbol{B}'\boldsymbol{Q}^{-1}\boldsymbol{C}\boldsymbol{E}^{-1} \\ -\boldsymbol{E}^{-1}\boldsymbol{C}'\boldsymbol{Q}^{-1} & \boldsymbol{E}^{-1}\boldsymbol{C}'\boldsymbol{Q}^{-1}\boldsymbol{B}\boldsymbol{D}^{-1} & \boldsymbol{E}^{-1}+\boldsymbol{E}^{-1}\boldsymbol{C}'\boldsymbol{Q}^{-1}\boldsymbol{C}\boldsymbol{E}^{-1} \end{pmatrix}.$$

Solution

By postmultiplying $\boldsymbol{Z}$ by the supposed matrix $\boldsymbol{Z}^{-1}$, we obtain nine (matrix) equations in the five unknown matrices, which all have to be satisfied. For example,

$$\boldsymbol{A}\boldsymbol{Q}^{-1}-\boldsymbol{B}\boldsymbol{D}^{-1}\boldsymbol{B}'\boldsymbol{Q}^{-1}-\boldsymbol{C}\boldsymbol{E}^{-1}\boldsymbol{C}'\boldsymbol{Q}^{-1}=\boldsymbol{Q}\boldsymbol{Q}^{-1}=\boldsymbol{I}$$

and

$$\begin{aligned} -\boldsymbol{A}\boldsymbol{Q}^{-1}\boldsymbol{B}\boldsymbol{D}^{-1}+\boldsymbol{B}\boldsymbol{D}^{-1}+\boldsymbol{B}\boldsymbol{D}^{-1}\boldsymbol{B}'\boldsymbol{Q}^{-1}\boldsymbol{B}\boldsymbol{D}^{-1}+\boldsymbol{C}\boldsymbol{E}^{-1}\boldsymbol{C}'\boldsymbol{Q}^{-1}\boldsymbol{B}\boldsymbol{D}^{-1} \\ =(-\boldsymbol{A}+\boldsymbol{Q}+\boldsymbol{B}\boldsymbol{D}^{-1}\boldsymbol{B}'+\boldsymbol{C}\boldsymbol{E}^{-1}\boldsymbol{C}')\boldsymbol{Q}^{-1}\boldsymbol{B}\boldsymbol{D}^{-1}=\mathbf{O}. \end{aligned}$$

Continuing in this way, one verifies that all nine equations hold. Having thus established the existence of a square matrix $\boldsymbol{X}$ satisfying $\boldsymbol{Z}\boldsymbol{X}=\boldsymbol{I}$, the nonsingularity of $\boldsymbol{Z}$ is established as well.

Exercise 5.20 (Inverse of a bordered matrix) Let $\boldsymbol{A}$ be a nonsingular $m \times m$ matrix, and let $\alpha \neq 0$. Show that

$$\begin{pmatrix} \mathbf{0} & \boldsymbol{A} \\ \alpha & \boldsymbol{a}' \end{pmatrix}^{-1} = \frac{1}{\alpha}\begin{pmatrix} -\boldsymbol{a}'\boldsymbol{A}^{-1} & 1 \\ \alpha\boldsymbol{A}^{-1} & \mathbf{0} \end{pmatrix}.$$

Solution

If we know the answer, it is easy. We just check that multiplication results in the identity matrix. If we do not know the answer, we write

$$\begin{pmatrix} \mathbf{0} & \boldsymbol{A} \\ \alpha & \boldsymbol{a}' \end{pmatrix}\begin{pmatrix} \boldsymbol{p}' & q \\ \boldsymbol{R} & \boldsymbol{s} \end{pmatrix} = \begin{pmatrix} \boldsymbol{I}_m & \mathbf{0} \\ \mathbf{0}' & 1 \end{pmatrix},$$

which leads to the equations

$$\boldsymbol{A}\boldsymbol{R}=\boldsymbol{I}_m, \quad \boldsymbol{A}\boldsymbol{s}=\mathbf{0}, \quad \alpha\boldsymbol{p}'+\boldsymbol{a}'\boldsymbol{R}=\mathbf{0}', \quad \alpha q+\boldsymbol{a}'\boldsymbol{s}=1,$$

from which we obtain $\boldsymbol{R}=\boldsymbol{A}^{-1}$, $\boldsymbol{s}=\mathbf{0}$, $\boldsymbol{p}'=-(1/\alpha)\boldsymbol{a}'\boldsymbol{A}^{-1}$, and $q=1/\alpha$.

Exercise 5.21 (Powers of partitioned matrix)

(a) If $\boldsymbol{A}$ and $\boldsymbol{D}$ are square, show that

$$\begin{pmatrix} \boldsymbol{A} & \boldsymbol{B} \\ \mathbf{O} & \boldsymbol{D} \end{pmatrix}^k = \begin{pmatrix} \boldsymbol{A}^k & \boldsymbol{Q}_k \\ \mathbf{O} & \boldsymbol{D}^k \end{pmatrix} \quad (k=1,2,\dots),$$

where $\boldsymbol{Q}_k := \sum_{j=1}^{k} \boldsymbol{A}^{k-j}\boldsymbol{B}\boldsymbol{D}^{j-1}$.

(b) What is $\boldsymbol{Q}_k$ if $\boldsymbol{D} = \boldsymbol{I}_n$ and $\boldsymbol{I}_m - \boldsymbol{A}$ is nonsingular?
(c) Does the result in (a) also hold for negative integers?

Solution

(a) This follows by induction, because

$$\begin{pmatrix} \boldsymbol{A} & \boldsymbol{B} \\ \mathbf{O} & \boldsymbol{D} \end{pmatrix} \begin{pmatrix} \boldsymbol{A}^k & \boldsymbol{Q}_k \\ \mathbf{O} & \boldsymbol{D}^k \end{pmatrix} = \begin{pmatrix} \boldsymbol{A}^{k+1} & \boldsymbol{A}\boldsymbol{Q}_k + \boldsymbol{B}\boldsymbol{D}^k \\ \mathbf{O} & \boldsymbol{D}^{k+1} \end{pmatrix} = \begin{pmatrix} \boldsymbol{A}^{k+1} & \boldsymbol{Q}_{k+1} \\ \mathbf{O} & \boldsymbol{D}^{k+1} \end{pmatrix},$$

using the fact that

$$\boldsymbol{Q}_{k+1} = \sum_{j=1}^{k+1} \boldsymbol{A}^{k+1-j}\boldsymbol{B}\boldsymbol{D}^{j-1}$$

$$= \boldsymbol{A}\sum_{j=1}^{k} \boldsymbol{A}^{k-j}\boldsymbol{B}\boldsymbol{D}^{j-1} + \boldsymbol{B}\boldsymbol{D}^k = \boldsymbol{A}\boldsymbol{Q}_k + \boldsymbol{B}\boldsymbol{D}^k.$$

(b) If $\boldsymbol{D} = \boldsymbol{I}_n$, then $\boldsymbol{Q}_k = (\boldsymbol{I}_m + \boldsymbol{A} + \cdots + \boldsymbol{A}^{k-1})\boldsymbol{B}$. Since

$$(\boldsymbol{I}_m - \boldsymbol{A})(\boldsymbol{I}_m + \boldsymbol{A} + \cdots + \boldsymbol{A}^{k-1}) = \boldsymbol{I}_m - \boldsymbol{A}^k,$$

this gives $\boldsymbol{Q}_k = (\boldsymbol{I}_m - \boldsymbol{A})^{-1}(\boldsymbol{I}_m - \boldsymbol{A}^k)\boldsymbol{B}$.
(c) If $\boldsymbol{A}$ and $\boldsymbol{D}$ are nonsingular, then

$$\begin{pmatrix} \boldsymbol{A} & \boldsymbol{B} \\ \mathbf{O} & \boldsymbol{D} \end{pmatrix} \begin{pmatrix} \boldsymbol{A}^{-1} & -\boldsymbol{A}^{-1}\boldsymbol{B}\boldsymbol{D}^{-1} \\ \mathbf{O} & \boldsymbol{D}^{-1} \end{pmatrix} = \boldsymbol{I}_{m+n}$$

(by Exercise 5.13(b)), and hence

$$\begin{pmatrix} \boldsymbol{A} & \boldsymbol{B} \\ \mathbf{O} & \boldsymbol{D} \end{pmatrix}^{-k} = \begin{pmatrix} \boldsymbol{A}^{-1} & -\boldsymbol{A}^{-1}\boldsymbol{B}\boldsymbol{D}^{-1} \\ \mathbf{O} & \boldsymbol{D}^{-1} \end{pmatrix}^{k} = \begin{pmatrix} \boldsymbol{A}^{-k} & \boldsymbol{R}_k \\ \mathbf{O} & \boldsymbol{D}^{-k} \end{pmatrix}$$

with

$$\boldsymbol{R}_k := \sum_{j=1}^{k} (\boldsymbol{A}^{-1})^{k-j}(-\boldsymbol{A}^{-1}\boldsymbol{B}\boldsymbol{D}^{-1})(\boldsymbol{D}^{-1})^{j-1} = -\sum_{j=1}^{k} \boldsymbol{A}^{-(k-j+1)}\boldsymbol{B}\boldsymbol{D}^{-j}.$$

5.3 Determinants

Exercise 5.22 (Two off-diagonal zero blocks, determinant) If $\boldsymbol{A}$ and $\boldsymbol{D}$ are square matrices, show that

$$\begin{vmatrix} \boldsymbol{A} & \mathbf{O} \\ \mathbf{O} & \boldsymbol{D} \end{vmatrix} = |\boldsymbol{A}||\boldsymbol{D}|.$$

Solution

Let $\boldsymbol{A}$ be an $m \times m$ matrix and $\boldsymbol{D}$ an $n \times n$ matrix. Consider the matrices

$$\boldsymbol{\Delta}_m := \begin{pmatrix} \boldsymbol{I}_m & \mathbf{O} \\ \mathbf{O} & \boldsymbol{D} \end{pmatrix} \quad \text{and} \quad \boldsymbol{\Lambda}_n := \begin{pmatrix} \boldsymbol{A} & \mathbf{O} \\ \mathbf{O} & \boldsymbol{I}_n \end{pmatrix}.$$

Since

$$\boldsymbol{\Delta}_m = \begin{pmatrix} 1 & \mathbf{0}' \\ 0 & \boldsymbol{\Delta}_{m-1} \end{pmatrix} \quad \text{and} \quad \boldsymbol{\Lambda}_n = \begin{pmatrix} \boldsymbol{\Lambda}_{n-1} & \mathbf{0} \\ \mathbf{0}' & 1 \end{pmatrix},$$

we obtain $|\boldsymbol{\Delta}_m| = |\boldsymbol{\Delta}_{m-1}|$ (expansion by the first row, Exercise 4.36) and $|\boldsymbol{\Lambda}_n| = |\boldsymbol{\Lambda}_{n-1}|$ (expansion by the last row). A simple recursion then gives $|\boldsymbol{\Delta}_m| = |\boldsymbol{D}|$ and $|\boldsymbol{\Lambda}_n| = |\boldsymbol{A}|$. Hence,

$$\begin{vmatrix} \boldsymbol{A} & \mathrm{O} \\ \mathrm{O} & \boldsymbol{D} \end{vmatrix} = \left| \begin{pmatrix} \boldsymbol{A} & \mathrm{O} \\ \mathrm{O} & \boldsymbol{I}_n \end{pmatrix} \begin{pmatrix} \boldsymbol{I}_m & \mathrm{O} \\ \mathrm{O} & \boldsymbol{D} \end{pmatrix} \right| = \begin{vmatrix} \boldsymbol{A} & \mathrm{O} \\ \mathrm{O} & \boldsymbol{I}_n \end{vmatrix} \begin{vmatrix} \boldsymbol{I}_m & \mathrm{O} \\ \mathrm{O} & \boldsymbol{D} \end{vmatrix} = |\boldsymbol{A}||\boldsymbol{D}|.$$

***Exercise 5.23 (Two diagonal zero blocks, determinant)**
(a) Show that

$$\begin{vmatrix} \mathrm{O} & \boldsymbol{I}_m \\ \boldsymbol{I}_n & \mathrm{O} \end{vmatrix} = (-1)^{mn}.$$

(b) Use (a) to show that

$$\begin{vmatrix} \mathrm{O} & \boldsymbol{B} \\ \boldsymbol{C} & \mathrm{O} \end{vmatrix} = (-1)^{mn}|\boldsymbol{B}||\boldsymbol{C}|$$

when $\boldsymbol{B}$ and $\boldsymbol{C}$ are square matrices of orders m and n, respectively.
(c) If $m = n$, the result in (b) specializes to $(-1)^m|\boldsymbol{B}||\boldsymbol{C}|$. Why?
(d) What happens when $\boldsymbol{B}$ and $\boldsymbol{C}$ are not square?

Solution
(a) This is an exercise in counting. Move column $n+1$ back repeatedly by one position until it becomes the first column (n permutations), then move column $n+2$ back until it becomes the second column (again n permutations), and so on until column $n+m$. In total we require nm permutations to transform the matrix of part (a) to the identity matrix $\boldsymbol{I}_{mn}$. We now invoke Exercise 4.32 and the fact that $|\boldsymbol{I}| = 1$ (Exercise 4.35).
(b) Observe that

$$\begin{pmatrix} \mathrm{O} & \boldsymbol{B} \\ \boldsymbol{C} & \mathrm{O} \end{pmatrix} = \begin{pmatrix} \boldsymbol{B} & \mathrm{O} \\ \mathrm{O} & \boldsymbol{C} \end{pmatrix} \begin{pmatrix} \mathrm{O} & \boldsymbol{I}_m \\ \boldsymbol{I}_n & \mathrm{O} \end{pmatrix}.$$

Taking determinants, the result follows from Exercise 5.22 and part (a).
(c) This is true because m^2 is even if and only if m is even.
(d) We will show that $\boldsymbol{Z}$ is singular. Let $\boldsymbol{B}$ be a matrix of order $m_1 \times n_2$ and let $\boldsymbol{C}$ be of order $m_2 \times n_1$, such that $m_1 + m_2 = n_1 + n_2$. Denote the partitioned matrix by $\boldsymbol{Z}$. Then,

$$\boldsymbol{Z}'\boldsymbol{Z} = \begin{pmatrix} \mathrm{O} & \boldsymbol{B} \\ \boldsymbol{C} & \mathrm{O} \end{pmatrix}' \begin{pmatrix} \mathrm{O} & \boldsymbol{B} \\ \boldsymbol{C} & \mathrm{O} \end{pmatrix} = \begin{pmatrix} \boldsymbol{C}'\boldsymbol{C} & \mathrm{O} \\ \mathrm{O} & \boldsymbol{B}'\boldsymbol{B} \end{pmatrix},$$

so that $|\boldsymbol{Z}|^2 = |\boldsymbol{Z}'\boldsymbol{Z}| = |\boldsymbol{B}'\boldsymbol{B}||\boldsymbol{C}'\boldsymbol{C}|$. Suppose $\boldsymbol{Z}$ is nonsingular. Then, $|\boldsymbol{B}'\boldsymbol{B}| \neq 0$ and $|\boldsymbol{C}'\boldsymbol{C}| \neq 0$. Hence, $\mathrm{rk}(\boldsymbol{B}) = n_2 \leq m_1$ and $\mathrm{rk}(\boldsymbol{C}) = n_1 \leq m_2$. But $n_1 + n_2 = m_1 + m_2$, implying that $m_1 = n_2$ and $m_2 = n_1$. This contradicts the fact that $\boldsymbol{B}$ and $\boldsymbol{C}$ are not square. We conclude that $\boldsymbol{Z}$ must be singular if $\boldsymbol{B}$ and $\boldsymbol{C}$ are not square.

Exercise 5.24 (Two diagonal zero blocks, special case) Find the determinant of

$$\begin{pmatrix} \mathrm{O} & \boldsymbol{B} \\ \boldsymbol{B}' & \mathrm{O} \end{pmatrix} \quad \text{and} \quad \begin{pmatrix} \mathrm{O} & \boldsymbol{B} \\ \boldsymbol{B}^{-1} & \mathrm{O} \end{pmatrix}.$$

Solution
Exercise 5.23 immediately implies

$$\begin{vmatrix} \mathrm{O} & \boldsymbol{B} \\ \boldsymbol{B}' & \mathrm{O} \end{vmatrix} = \begin{cases} (-1)^m |\boldsymbol{B}|^2 & (\boldsymbol{B} \text{ square}), \\ 0 & (\boldsymbol{B} \text{ not square}), \end{cases}$$

and

$$\begin{vmatrix} \mathrm{O} & \boldsymbol{B} \\ \boldsymbol{B}^{-1} & \mathrm{O} \end{vmatrix} = (-1)^m |\boldsymbol{B}||\boldsymbol{B}^{-1}| = (-1)^m.$$

Exercise 5.25 (One off-diagonal zero block, determinant)
(a) Show that

$$\begin{vmatrix} \boldsymbol{I}_m & \boldsymbol{B} \\ \mathrm{O} & \boldsymbol{I}_n \end{vmatrix} = 1.$$

(b) Hence, show for square matrices $\boldsymbol{A}$ and $\boldsymbol{D}$ that

$$\begin{vmatrix} \boldsymbol{A} & \boldsymbol{B} \\ \mathrm{O} & \boldsymbol{D} \end{vmatrix} = \begin{vmatrix} \boldsymbol{A} & \mathrm{O} \\ \boldsymbol{C} & \boldsymbol{D} \end{vmatrix} = |\boldsymbol{A}||\boldsymbol{D}|.$$

Solution
(a) Denoting the matrix by $\boldsymbol{\Delta}_m$, expansion by the first column gives $|\boldsymbol{\Delta}_m| = |\boldsymbol{\Delta}_{m-1}|$, and hence

$$|\boldsymbol{\Delta}_m| = |\boldsymbol{\Delta}_{m-1}| = \cdots = |\boldsymbol{\Delta}_0| = |\boldsymbol{I}_n| = 1.$$

(b) This follows from the equalities

$$\begin{pmatrix} \boldsymbol{I}_m & \mathrm{O} \\ \mathrm{O} & \boldsymbol{D} \end{pmatrix} \begin{pmatrix} \boldsymbol{I}_m & \boldsymbol{B} \\ \mathrm{O} & \boldsymbol{I}_n \end{pmatrix} \begin{pmatrix} \boldsymbol{A} & \mathrm{O} \\ \mathrm{O} & \boldsymbol{I}_n \end{pmatrix} = \begin{pmatrix} \boldsymbol{A} & \boldsymbol{B} \\ \mathrm{O} & \boldsymbol{D} \end{pmatrix}$$

and

$$\begin{pmatrix} \boldsymbol{A} & \mathrm{O} \\ \mathrm{O} & \boldsymbol{I}_n \end{pmatrix} \begin{pmatrix} \boldsymbol{I}_m & \mathrm{O} \\ \boldsymbol{C} & \boldsymbol{I}_n \end{pmatrix} \begin{pmatrix} \boldsymbol{I}_m & \mathrm{O} \\ \mathrm{O} & \boldsymbol{D} \end{pmatrix} = \begin{pmatrix} \boldsymbol{A} & \mathrm{O} \\ \boldsymbol{C} & \boldsymbol{D} \end{pmatrix}.$$

Exercise 5.26 (More column-block operations) Show that

$$\begin{vmatrix} I_m & B \\ B' & B'B + D \end{vmatrix} = |D|.$$

Solution
This follows from the elementary column-block operation

$$\begin{pmatrix} I_m & B \\ B' & B'B + D \end{pmatrix} \begin{pmatrix} I_m & -B \\ O & I_n \end{pmatrix} = \begin{pmatrix} I_m & O \\ B' & D \end{pmatrix}.$$

Exercise 5.27 (Determinant of a product, alternative proof) Use Exercise 5.25 to provide an alternative proof of the fundamental fact that $|AB| = |A||B|$ for any two square matrices of the same order. (Compare Exercise 4.42.)

Solution
Consider the $2n \times 2n$ matrices

$$P := \begin{pmatrix} I_n & A \\ O & I_n \end{pmatrix}, \quad Q := \begin{pmatrix} A & O \\ -I_n & B \end{pmatrix}, \quad R := \begin{pmatrix} O & AB \\ -I_n & B \end{pmatrix}.$$

One verifies easily that $PQ = R$. We shall show that $|PQ| = |A||B|$ and that $|R| = |AB|$. The multiplication PQ amounts to premultiplying the last n rows of Q by A (that is, taking n linear combinations of such rows) and adding them to the first n rows. By Exercise 4.34(b) this leaves the determinant unchanged: $|PQ| = |Q|$. But, by Exercise 5.25(b), $|Q| = |A||B|$. Hence, $|PQ| = |A||B|$. Further,

$$\begin{aligned} |R| &= \begin{vmatrix} O & AB \\ -I_n & B \end{vmatrix} = (-1)^n \begin{vmatrix} AB & O \\ B & -I_n \end{vmatrix} \\ &= (-1)^n |AB||-I_n| = (-1)^{2n}|AB| = |AB|, \end{aligned}$$

where the second equality follows from Exercise 4.32, the third from Exercise 5.25(b), and the fourth from the fact that $|-I_n| = (-1)^n$. We now know that $|PQ| = |A||B|$ and that $|R| = |AB|$. We also know that $PQ = R$. The result follows.

Exercise 5.28 (One diagonal zero block, determinant)
(a) For nonsingular A, show that

$$\begin{vmatrix} A & b \\ c' & 0 \end{vmatrix} = -|A|(c'A^{-1}b).$$

(b) Generalize (a) by showing that

$$\begin{vmatrix} A & B \\ C & O \end{vmatrix} = (-1)^n |A||CA^{-1}B|,$$

when A is nonsingular and n denotes the order of the square null matrix.
(c) Similarly, show that

$$\begin{vmatrix} O & B \\ C & D \end{vmatrix} = (-1)^m |D||BD^{-1}C|,$$

when D is nonsingular and m denotes the order of the square null matrix.

Solution
All three determinants follow from matrix equalities in Exercise 5.10. We have, respectively,

$$\begin{pmatrix} I_m & 0 \\ -c'A^{-1} & 1 \end{pmatrix} \begin{pmatrix} A & b \\ c' & 0 \end{pmatrix} = \begin{pmatrix} A & b \\ 0' & -c'A^{-1}b \end{pmatrix},$$

$$\begin{pmatrix} I_m & O \\ -CA^{-1} & I_n \end{pmatrix} \begin{pmatrix} A & B \\ C & O \end{pmatrix} = \begin{pmatrix} A & B \\ O & -CA^{-1}B \end{pmatrix},$$

and

$$\begin{pmatrix} I_m & -BD^{-1} \\ O & I_n \end{pmatrix} \begin{pmatrix} O & B \\ C & D \end{pmatrix} = \begin{pmatrix} -BD^{-1}C & O \\ C & D \end{pmatrix}.$$

Exercise 5.29 (Scalar diagonal block, determinant) Consider the matrices

$$Z_1 := \begin{pmatrix} A & b \\ c' & \delta \end{pmatrix} \quad \text{and} \quad Z_2 := \begin{pmatrix} \alpha & b' \\ c & D \end{pmatrix}.$$

Show that:
(a) if A is nonsingular, then $|Z_1| = |A|(\delta - c'A^{-1}b)$;
(b) if $\delta \neq 0$, then $|Z_1| = \delta|A - \delta^{-1}bc'|$;
(c) if D is nonsingular, then $|Z_2| = |D|(\alpha - b'D^{-1}c)$;
(d) if $\alpha \neq 0$, then $|Z_2| = \alpha|D - \alpha^{-1}cb'|$.

Solution
The results follow by taking determinants in the following four equalities:

$$\begin{pmatrix} I_m & 0 \\ -c'A^{-1} & 1 \end{pmatrix} \begin{pmatrix} A & b \\ c' & \delta \end{pmatrix} = \begin{pmatrix} A & b \\ 0' & (\delta - c'A^{-1}b) \end{pmatrix},$$

$$\begin{pmatrix} I_m & -\delta^{-1}b \\ 0' & 1 \end{pmatrix} \begin{pmatrix} A & b \\ c' & \delta \end{pmatrix} = \begin{pmatrix} A - \delta^{-1}bc' & 0 \\ c' & \delta \end{pmatrix},$$

$$\begin{pmatrix} 1 & -b'D^{-1} \\ 0 & I_n \end{pmatrix} \begin{pmatrix} \alpha & b' \\ c & D \end{pmatrix} = \begin{pmatrix} (\alpha - b'D^{-1}c) & 0' \\ c & D \end{pmatrix},$$

and

$$\begin{pmatrix} 1 & \mathbf{0}' \\ -\alpha^{-1}\mathbf{c} & \mathbf{I}_n \end{pmatrix} \begin{pmatrix} \alpha & \mathbf{b}' \\ \mathbf{c} & \mathbf{D} \end{pmatrix} = \begin{pmatrix} \alpha & \mathbf{b}' \\ \mathbf{0} & \mathbf{D} - \alpha^{-1}\mathbf{c}\mathbf{b}' \end{pmatrix}.$$

Exercise 5.30 (Determinant of a partitioned matrix: main result) Consider the matrix

$$\mathbf{Z} := \begin{pmatrix} \mathbf{A} & \mathbf{B} \\ \mathbf{C} & \mathbf{D} \end{pmatrix}.$$

(a) If $\mathbf{A}$ is nonsingular, show that

$$|\mathbf{Z}| = |\mathbf{A}||\mathbf{D} - \mathbf{C}\mathbf{A}^{-1}\mathbf{B}|,$$

and notice how this generalizes the familiar formula for the determinant of a 2-by-2 matrix.
(b) If $\mathbf{D}$ is nonsingular, show that

$$|\mathbf{Z}| = |\mathbf{D}||\mathbf{A} - \mathbf{B}\mathbf{D}^{-1}\mathbf{C}|.$$

(c) Is it possible that $\mathbf{A}$ and $\mathbf{D}$ are both singular, but $\mathbf{Z}$ is nonsingular?

Solution
(a)–(b) This is a very important result, so let us give a constructive proof. Consider the equalities

$$\begin{pmatrix} \mathbf{I}_m & \mathbf{Q} \\ \mathbf{O} & \mathbf{I}_n \end{pmatrix} \begin{pmatrix} \mathbf{A} & \mathbf{B} \\ \mathbf{C} & \mathbf{D} \end{pmatrix} = \begin{pmatrix} \mathbf{A} + \mathbf{Q}\mathbf{C} & \mathbf{B} + \mathbf{Q}\mathbf{D} \\ \mathbf{C} & \mathbf{D} \end{pmatrix}$$

and

$$\begin{pmatrix} \mathbf{I}_m & \mathbf{O} \\ \mathbf{R} & \mathbf{I}_n \end{pmatrix} \begin{pmatrix} \mathbf{A} & \mathbf{B} \\ \mathbf{C} & \mathbf{D} \end{pmatrix} = \begin{pmatrix} \mathbf{A} & \mathbf{B} \\ \mathbf{R}\mathbf{A} + \mathbf{C} & \mathbf{R}\mathbf{B} + \mathbf{D} \end{pmatrix}.$$

We wish to choose $\mathbf{Q}$ and $\mathbf{R}$ such that $\mathbf{B} + \mathbf{Q}\mathbf{D} = \mathbf{O}$ and $\mathbf{R}\mathbf{A} + \mathbf{C} = \mathbf{O}$. If $|\mathbf{A}| \neq 0$, we can choose $\mathbf{R} := -\mathbf{C}\mathbf{A}^{-1}$ and (a) follows. If $|\mathbf{D}| \neq 0$, we can choose $\mathbf{Q} := -\mathbf{B}\mathbf{D}^{-1}$ and (b) follows.
(c) This is certainly possible. For example, see the matrix of Exercise 5.23(a).

Exercise 5.31 (Positive definite counterpart of the main determinantal result) Let $(\mathbf{A} : \mathbf{B})$ be an $n \times (k + m)$ matrix.
(a) If $\mathbf{A}$ has full column rank, show that

$$\begin{vmatrix} \mathbf{A}'\mathbf{A} & \mathbf{A}'\mathbf{B} \\ \mathbf{B}'\mathbf{A} & \mathbf{B}'\mathbf{B} \end{vmatrix} = |\mathbf{A}'\mathbf{A}||\mathbf{B}'(\mathbf{I}_n - \mathbf{A}(\mathbf{A}'\mathbf{A})^{-1}\mathbf{A}')\mathbf{B}|.$$

(b) If $\mathbf{B}$ has full column rank, show that

$$\begin{vmatrix} \mathbf{A}'\mathbf{A} & \mathbf{A}'\mathbf{B} \\ \mathbf{B}'\mathbf{A} & \mathbf{B}'\mathbf{B} \end{vmatrix} = |\mathbf{B}'\mathbf{B}||\mathbf{A}'(\mathbf{I}_n - \mathbf{B}(\mathbf{B}'\mathbf{B})^{-1}\mathbf{B}')\mathbf{A}|.$$

Solution
This follows directly from Exercise 5.30.

Exercise 5.32 (Row-block operations and determinants) Let $\boldsymbol{A}$ and $\boldsymbol{D}$ be square matrices, of orders m and n, respectively.
(a) For any $m \times m$ matrix $\boldsymbol{E}$, show that

$$\begin{vmatrix} \boldsymbol{EA} & \boldsymbol{EB} \\ \boldsymbol{C} & \boldsymbol{D} \end{vmatrix} = |\boldsymbol{E}| \begin{vmatrix} \boldsymbol{A} & \boldsymbol{B} \\ \boldsymbol{C} & \boldsymbol{D} \end{vmatrix}.$$

(b) For any $n \times m$ matrix $\boldsymbol{E}$, show that

$$\begin{vmatrix} \boldsymbol{A} & \boldsymbol{B} \\ \boldsymbol{C}+\boldsymbol{EA} & \boldsymbol{D}+\boldsymbol{EB} \end{vmatrix} = \begin{vmatrix} \boldsymbol{A} & \boldsymbol{B} \\ \boldsymbol{C} & \boldsymbol{D} \end{vmatrix}.$$

Solution
(a) This follows from

$$\begin{pmatrix} \boldsymbol{E} & \mathrm{O} \\ \mathrm{O} & \boldsymbol{I}_n \end{pmatrix} \begin{pmatrix} \boldsymbol{A} & \boldsymbol{B} \\ \boldsymbol{C} & \boldsymbol{D} \end{pmatrix} = \begin{pmatrix} \boldsymbol{EA} & \boldsymbol{EB} \\ \boldsymbol{C} & \boldsymbol{D} \end{pmatrix}.$$

(b) And this follows from

$$\begin{pmatrix} \boldsymbol{I}_m & \mathrm{O} \\ \boldsymbol{E} & \boldsymbol{I}_n \end{pmatrix} \begin{pmatrix} \boldsymbol{A} & \boldsymbol{B} \\ \boldsymbol{C} & \boldsymbol{D} \end{pmatrix} = \begin{pmatrix} \boldsymbol{A} & \boldsymbol{B} \\ \boldsymbol{C}+\boldsymbol{EA} & \boldsymbol{D}+\boldsymbol{EB} \end{pmatrix}.$$

Exercise 5.33 (Determinant of one block in the inverse) Let

$$\boldsymbol{Z} := \begin{pmatrix} \boldsymbol{A} & \boldsymbol{B} \\ \boldsymbol{C} & \boldsymbol{D} \end{pmatrix} \quad \text{and} \quad \boldsymbol{Z}^{-1} := \begin{pmatrix} \boldsymbol{P} & \boldsymbol{Q} \\ \boldsymbol{R} & \boldsymbol{S} \end{pmatrix},$$

where $\boldsymbol{A}$ and $\boldsymbol{D}$ are square matrices and $\boldsymbol{Z}$ is nonsingular (although $\boldsymbol{A}$ and $\boldsymbol{D}$ may be singular). Show that

$$|\boldsymbol{S}| = \frac{|\boldsymbol{A}|}{|\boldsymbol{Z}|} \quad \text{and} \quad |\boldsymbol{P}| = \frac{|\boldsymbol{D}|}{|\boldsymbol{Z}|}.$$

Solution
Multiplying out $\boldsymbol{Z}\boldsymbol{Z}^{-1} = \boldsymbol{I}_{m+n}$, we obtain

$$\boldsymbol{AP}+\boldsymbol{BR} = \boldsymbol{I}_m, \quad \boldsymbol{AQ}+\boldsymbol{BS} = \mathrm{O}, \quad \boldsymbol{CP}+\boldsymbol{DR} = \mathrm{O}, \quad \boldsymbol{CQ}+\boldsymbol{DS} = \boldsymbol{I}_n.$$

Hence,

$$\begin{pmatrix} \boldsymbol{A} & \boldsymbol{B} \\ \boldsymbol{C} & \boldsymbol{D} \end{pmatrix} \begin{pmatrix} \boldsymbol{I}_m & \boldsymbol{Q} \\ \mathrm{O} & \boldsymbol{S} \end{pmatrix} = \begin{pmatrix} \boldsymbol{A} & \mathrm{O} \\ \boldsymbol{C} & \boldsymbol{I}_n \end{pmatrix}, \quad \begin{pmatrix} \boldsymbol{A} & \boldsymbol{B} \\ \boldsymbol{C} & \boldsymbol{D} \end{pmatrix} \begin{pmatrix} \boldsymbol{P} & \mathrm{O} \\ \boldsymbol{R} & \boldsymbol{I}_n \end{pmatrix} = \begin{pmatrix} \boldsymbol{I}_m & \boldsymbol{B} \\ \mathrm{O} & \boldsymbol{D} \end{pmatrix},$$

and the results follow.

Exercise 5.34 (Relationship between $|I_m - BB'|$ and $|I_n - B'B|$) Show that

$$\begin{vmatrix} I_m & B \\ B' & I_n \end{vmatrix} = |I_n - B'B| = |I_m - BB'|.$$

Solution
Consider the equation

$$\begin{pmatrix} I_m & O \\ R & I_n \end{pmatrix} \begin{pmatrix} I_m & B \\ B' & I_n \end{pmatrix} = \begin{pmatrix} I_m & B \\ R + B' & RB + I_n \end{pmatrix}.$$

Choosing $R := -B'$, the first result follows. The second result follows from

$$\begin{pmatrix} I_m & B \\ B' & I_n \end{pmatrix} \begin{pmatrix} I_m & O \\ -B' & I_n \end{pmatrix} = \begin{pmatrix} I_m - BB' & B \\ O & I_n \end{pmatrix}.$$

*__Exercise 5.35 (Determinant when two blocks commute)__ If A and C commute ($AC = CA$), show that

$$\begin{vmatrix} A & B \\ C & D \end{vmatrix} = |AD - CB|.$$

Solution
We use a continuity argument. Assume first that $|A| \neq 0$. Then, by Exercise 5.30,

$$\begin{aligned} \begin{vmatrix} A & B \\ C & D \end{vmatrix} &= |A||D - CA^{-1}B| = |AD - ACA^{-1}B| \\ &= |AD - CAA^{-1}B| = |AD - CB|. \end{aligned}$$

Now assume that $|A| = 0$. Then there exists a $\delta > 0$ such that $|A + \epsilon I_m| \neq 0$ for all ϵ satisfying $0 < \epsilon < \delta$. Then,

$$\begin{vmatrix} A + \epsilon I_m & B \\ C & D \end{vmatrix} = |(A + \epsilon I_m)D - CB| = |AD - CB + \epsilon D| \quad (0 < \epsilon < \delta).$$

Since both sides are continuous in ϵ, we let $\epsilon \to 0$ and find the required result.

Exercise 5.36 (One identity block, determinant) Show that

$$\begin{vmatrix} I_m & B \\ C & D \end{vmatrix} = |D - CB|.$$

Solution
If C is a square matrix, then I_m and C commute, and the result follows from Exercise 5.35.

In general, if C is not square, then Exercise 5.30(a) implies that

$$\begin{vmatrix} I_m & B \\ C & D \end{vmatrix} = |I_m||D - CB| = |D - CB|.$$

Exercise 5.37 (Relationship between $|I_m - BC|$ and $|I_n - CB|$)
(a) Show that

$$\begin{vmatrix} I_m & B \\ C & I_n \end{vmatrix} = \begin{vmatrix} I_n & C \\ B & I_m \end{vmatrix}.$$

(b) Hence, show that

$$|I_m - BC| = |I_n - CB|.$$

(c) Let A and D be nonsingular matrices of orders m and n, respectively. Use (b) to show that

$$|A + BDC| = |A||D||D^{-1} + CA^{-1}B|.$$

Solution
(a)–(b) The result follows directly from Exercises 5.30(a) and (b). Here we provide a different solution. Denote the two matrices in (a) by Z_1 and Z_2. Then

$$\begin{pmatrix} I_m & O \\ C & I_n \end{pmatrix} \begin{pmatrix} I_m & B \\ O & I_n - CB \end{pmatrix} = Z_1 = \begin{pmatrix} I_m & B \\ O & I_n \end{pmatrix} \begin{pmatrix} I_m - BC & O \\ C & I_n \end{pmatrix}$$

and

$$\begin{pmatrix} I_n - CB & C \\ O & I_m \end{pmatrix} \begin{pmatrix} I_n & O \\ B & I_m \end{pmatrix} = Z_2 = \begin{pmatrix} I_n & O \\ B & I_m - BC \end{pmatrix} \begin{pmatrix} I_n & C \\ O & I_m \end{pmatrix}.$$

Taking determinants we find

$$|Z_1| = |I_n - CB| = |I_m - BC|, \quad |Z_2| = |I_n - CB| = |I_m - BC|$$

implying both (a) and (b).
(c) It follows from (b) that

$$|I_m + (A^{-1}B)(DC)| = |I_n + (DC)(A^{-1}B)|.$$

A little manipulation then yields

$$|A(I_m + A^{-1}BDC)| = |A||D||D^{-1}(I_n + DCA^{-1}B)|,$$

and the result follows.

Exercise 5.38 (Matrix generalization of $a^2 - b^2 = (a+b)(a-b)$) If A and B are square matrices of the same order, show that

$$\begin{vmatrix} A & B \\ B & A \end{vmatrix} = |A + B||A - B|.$$

Solution
We write

$$\begin{pmatrix} I_m & I_m \\ O & I_m \end{pmatrix}\begin{pmatrix} A & B \\ B & A \end{pmatrix} = \begin{pmatrix} A+B & B+A \\ B & A \end{pmatrix} = \begin{pmatrix} A+B & O \\ O & I_m \end{pmatrix}\begin{pmatrix} I_m & I_m \\ B & A \end{pmatrix}$$

$$= \begin{pmatrix} A+B & O \\ O & I_m \end{pmatrix}\begin{pmatrix} I_m & O \\ B & I_m \end{pmatrix}\begin{pmatrix} I_m & I_m \\ O & A-B \end{pmatrix}.$$

Taking determinants, the result follows.

Exercise 5.39 (A 3-by-3 block matrix determinant) Consider the symmetric matrix of Exercise 5.19,

$$Z := \begin{pmatrix} A & B & C \\ B' & D & O \\ C' & O & E \end{pmatrix}.$$

Show that

$$|Z| = |D||E||A - BD^{-1}B' - CE^{-1}C'|$$

if the matrices D and E are nonsingular.

Solution
Let

$$\widetilde{A} := A, \quad \widetilde{B} := (B : C), \quad \widetilde{C} := (B : C)', \quad \widetilde{D} := \begin{pmatrix} D & O \\ O & E \end{pmatrix}.$$

Then,

$$|Z| = \begin{vmatrix} \widetilde{A} & \widetilde{B} \\ \widetilde{C} & \widetilde{D} \end{vmatrix} = |\widetilde{D}||\widetilde{A} - \widetilde{B}\widetilde{D}^{-1}\widetilde{C}|$$

$$= |D||E||A - BD^{-1}B' - CE^{-1}C'| = |D||E||Q|,$$

using Exercise 5.30(b).

Exercise 5.40 (Determinant of a bordered matrix) Let A be a nonsingular $m \times m$ matrix, and let $\alpha \neq 0$. Show that

$$\begin{vmatrix} 0 & A \\ \alpha & a' \end{vmatrix} = (-1)^m \alpha |A|.$$

Solution
We expand the determinant by the first column. This gives

$$\begin{vmatrix} 0 & A \\ \alpha & a' \end{vmatrix} = (-1)^{m+1}(-\alpha)|A| = (-1)^m \alpha |A|.$$

5.4 Rank (in)equalities

Exercise 5.41 (Two zero blocks, rank)
(a) For any two matrices $\boldsymbol{A}$ and $\boldsymbol{D}$ (not necessarily square), show that

$$\operatorname{rk}\begin{pmatrix} \boldsymbol{A} & \mathrm{O} \\ \mathrm{O} & \boldsymbol{D} \end{pmatrix} = \operatorname{rk}(\boldsymbol{A}) + \operatorname{rk}(\boldsymbol{D}).$$

(b) For any two matrices $\boldsymbol{B}$ and $\boldsymbol{C}$ (not necessarily square), show that

$$\operatorname{rk}\begin{pmatrix} \mathrm{O} & \boldsymbol{B} \\ \boldsymbol{C} & \mathrm{O} \end{pmatrix} = \operatorname{rk}(\boldsymbol{B}) + \operatorname{rk}(\boldsymbol{C}).$$

Solution
(a) The rank of a matrix is equal to the number of its linearly independent columns. Let

$$\boldsymbol{Z} := \begin{pmatrix} \boldsymbol{A} & \mathrm{O} \\ \mathrm{O} & \boldsymbol{D} \end{pmatrix}, \quad \widetilde{\boldsymbol{A}} := \begin{pmatrix} \boldsymbol{A} \\ \mathrm{O} \end{pmatrix}, \quad \widetilde{\boldsymbol{D}} := \begin{pmatrix} \mathrm{O} \\ \boldsymbol{D} \end{pmatrix}.$$

Let $\widetilde{\boldsymbol{a}} := (\boldsymbol{a}', \boldsymbol{0}')'$ and $\widetilde{\boldsymbol{d}} := (\boldsymbol{0}', \boldsymbol{d}')'$ be two nonzero columns of $\widetilde{\boldsymbol{A}}$ and $\widetilde{\boldsymbol{D}}$, respectively. Then $\widetilde{\boldsymbol{a}}$ and $\widetilde{\boldsymbol{d}}$ are linearly independent, because if

$$\lambda_1\widetilde{\boldsymbol{a}} + \lambda_2\widetilde{\boldsymbol{d}} = \lambda_1\begin{pmatrix} \boldsymbol{a} \\ \boldsymbol{0} \end{pmatrix} + \lambda_2\begin{pmatrix} \boldsymbol{0} \\ \boldsymbol{d} \end{pmatrix} = \begin{pmatrix} \lambda_1\boldsymbol{a} \\ \lambda_2\boldsymbol{d} \end{pmatrix} = \boldsymbol{0},$$

then $\lambda_1 = \lambda_2 = 0$ (since $\widetilde{\boldsymbol{a}}$ and $\widetilde{\boldsymbol{d}}$ are nonzero). This implies that $\operatorname{rk}(\widetilde{\boldsymbol{A}} : \widetilde{\boldsymbol{D}}) = \operatorname{rk}(\widetilde{\boldsymbol{A}}) + \operatorname{rk}(\widetilde{\boldsymbol{D}})$ and hence that $\operatorname{rk}(\boldsymbol{Z}) = \operatorname{rk}(\boldsymbol{A}) + \operatorname{rk}(\boldsymbol{D})$.
(b) The rank does not change if we interchange columns. Hence,

$$\operatorname{rk}\begin{pmatrix} \mathrm{O} & \boldsymbol{B} \\ \boldsymbol{C} & \mathrm{O} \end{pmatrix} = \operatorname{rk}\begin{pmatrix} \boldsymbol{B} & \mathrm{O} \\ \mathrm{O} & \boldsymbol{C} \end{pmatrix} = \operatorname{rk}(\boldsymbol{B}) + \operatorname{rk}(\boldsymbol{C}),$$

using (a).

Exercise 5.42 (One off-diagonal zero block, rank) Consider the matrices

$$\boldsymbol{Z}_1 := \begin{pmatrix} \boldsymbol{A} & \boldsymbol{B} \\ \mathrm{O} & \boldsymbol{D} \end{pmatrix} \quad \text{and} \quad \boldsymbol{Z}_2 := \begin{pmatrix} \boldsymbol{A} & \mathrm{O} \\ \boldsymbol{C} & \boldsymbol{D} \end{pmatrix}.$$

Show that it is *not* true, in general, that $\operatorname{rk}(\boldsymbol{Z}_1) = \operatorname{rk}(\boldsymbol{A}) + \operatorname{rk}(\boldsymbol{D})$ or that $\operatorname{rk}(\boldsymbol{Z}_2) = \operatorname{rk}(\boldsymbol{A}) + \operatorname{rk}(\boldsymbol{D})$.

Solution
Take $\boldsymbol{A} = \mathbf{O}$ and $\boldsymbol{D} = \mathbf{O}$. Then $\operatorname{rk}(\boldsymbol{A}) = \operatorname{rk}(\boldsymbol{D}) = 0$, but $\operatorname{rk}(\boldsymbol{Z}_1) = \operatorname{rk}(\boldsymbol{B})$ and $\operatorname{rk}(\boldsymbol{Z}_2) = \operatorname{rk}(\boldsymbol{C})$, which are not zero, unless $\boldsymbol{B} = \mathbf{O}$ and $\boldsymbol{C} = \mathbf{O}$.

Exercise 5.43 (Nonsingular diagonal block, rank) Consider the matrices $\boldsymbol{Z}_1$ and $\boldsymbol{Z}_2$ of Exercise 5.42. If either $\boldsymbol{A}$ or $\boldsymbol{D}$ (or both) is nonsingular, show that

$$\operatorname{rk}(\boldsymbol{Z}_1) = \operatorname{rk}(\boldsymbol{Z}_2) = \operatorname{rk}(\boldsymbol{A}) + \operatorname{rk}(\boldsymbol{D}).$$

Is this condition necessary?

Solution

First, if $A = I_m$ and $D = I_n$, then both Z_1 and Z_2 are nonsingular (their determinant is 1 by Exercise 5.25). Now assume that $|A| \neq 0$. Then,

$$\begin{pmatrix} A & B \\ O & D \end{pmatrix} \begin{pmatrix} I_m & -A^{-1}B \\ O & I_q \end{pmatrix} = \begin{pmatrix} A & O \\ O & D \end{pmatrix} = \begin{pmatrix} I_m & O \\ -CA^{-1} & I_n \end{pmatrix} \begin{pmatrix} A & O \\ C & D \end{pmatrix}$$

and the result follows from Exercise 4.24. Similarly, if $|D| \neq 0$, we have

$$\begin{pmatrix} I_m & -BD^{-1} \\ O & I_n \end{pmatrix} \begin{pmatrix} A & B \\ O & D \end{pmatrix} = \begin{pmatrix} A & O \\ O & D \end{pmatrix} = \begin{pmatrix} A & O \\ C & D \end{pmatrix} \begin{pmatrix} I_p & O \\ -D^{-1}C & I_n \end{pmatrix}.$$

The condition is not necessary. For example, if $B = O$ and $C = O$, then $\operatorname{rk}(Z_1)$ and $\operatorname{rk}(Z_2)$ are both equal to $\operatorname{rk}(A) + \operatorname{rk}(D)$ whatever the ranks of A and D.

Exercise 5.44 (Nonsingular off-diagonal block, rank) Consider again the matrices Z_1 and Z_2 of Exercise 5.42. Show that

$$\operatorname{rk}(Z_1) = \operatorname{rk}(B) + \operatorname{rk}(DB^{-1}A)$$

if B is square and nonsingular, and

$$\operatorname{rk}(Z_2) = \operatorname{rk}(C) + \operatorname{rk}(AC^{-1}D)$$

if C is square and nonsingular.

Solution

The results follow from the equalities

$$\begin{pmatrix} I_m & O \\ -DB^{-1} & I_n \end{pmatrix} \begin{pmatrix} A & B \\ O & D \end{pmatrix} \begin{pmatrix} O & I_p \\ I_m & -B^{-1}A \end{pmatrix} = \begin{pmatrix} B & O \\ O & -DB^{-1}A \end{pmatrix}$$

and

$$\begin{pmatrix} O & I_n \\ I_m & -AC^{-1} \end{pmatrix} \begin{pmatrix} A & O \\ C & D \end{pmatrix} \begin{pmatrix} I_n & -C^{-1}D \\ O & I_q \end{pmatrix} = \begin{pmatrix} C & O \\ O & -AC^{-1}D \end{pmatrix}.$$

Exercise 5.45 (Rank inequalities, 1)

(a) Prove that

$$\operatorname{rk}\begin{pmatrix} A & B \\ O & D \end{pmatrix} \geq \operatorname{rk}(A) + \operatorname{rk}(D), \quad \operatorname{rk}\begin{pmatrix} A & O \\ C & D \end{pmatrix} \geq \operatorname{rk}(A) + \operatorname{rk}(D).$$

(b) Show that it is not true, in general, that

$$\operatorname{rk}\begin{pmatrix} A & B \\ C & D \end{pmatrix} \geq \operatorname{rk}(A) + \operatorname{rk}(D).$$

Solution

(a) Let

$$Z := \begin{pmatrix} A & B \\ O & D \end{pmatrix},$$

where the orders of the matrices are: A $(m \times p)$, B $(m \times q)$, and D $(n \times q)$. Suppose that $r := \operatorname{rk}(A) \leq p$ and that $s := \operatorname{rk}(D) \leq q$. Then A has r linearly independent columns, say $a_1, \dots, a_r$, and D has s linearly independent columns, say $d_1, \dots, d_s$. Let b_j denote the column of B directly above d_j in the matrix Z. Now consider the set of $r + s$ columns of Z,

$$\begin{pmatrix} a_1 \\ 0 \end{pmatrix}, \begin{pmatrix} a_2 \\ 0 \end{pmatrix}, \begin{pmatrix} a_r \\ 0 \end{pmatrix}, \dots, \begin{pmatrix} b_1 \\ d_1 \end{pmatrix}, \begin{pmatrix} b_2 \\ d_2 \end{pmatrix}, \begin{pmatrix} b_s \\ d_s \end{pmatrix}.$$

We shall show that these $r + s$ columns are linearly independent. Suppose they are linearly dependent. Then there exist numbers $\alpha_1, \dots, \alpha_r$ and $\beta_1, \dots, \beta_s$, not all zero, such that

$$\sum_{i=1}^{r} \alpha_i \begin{pmatrix} a_i \\ 0 \end{pmatrix} + \sum_{j=1}^{s} \beta_j \begin{pmatrix} b_j \\ d_j \end{pmatrix} = 0.$$

This gives the two equations

$$\sum_{i=1}^{r} \alpha_i a_i + \sum_{j=1}^{s} \beta_j b_j = 0, \quad \sum_{j=1}^{s} \beta_j d_j = 0.$$

Since the $\{d_j\}$ are linearly independent, the second equation implies that $\beta_j = 0$ for all j. The first equation then reduces to $\sum_{i=1}^{r} \alpha_i a_i = 0$. Since the $\{a_i\}$ are linearly independent as well, all α_i are zero. We now have a contradiction. The matrix Z thus possesses (at least) $r + s$ linearly independent columns, so that $\operatorname{rk}(Z) \geq r + s = \operatorname{rk}(A) + \operatorname{rk}(D)$.

The second result can be proved analogously. Alternatively, it can be proved from the first result by considering the transpose:

$$\begin{aligned} \operatorname{rk} \begin{pmatrix} A & O \\ C & D \end{pmatrix} &= \operatorname{rk} \begin{pmatrix} A & O \\ C & D \end{pmatrix}' = \operatorname{rk} \begin{pmatrix} A' & C' \\ O & D' \end{pmatrix} \\ &\geq \operatorname{rk}(A') + \operatorname{rk}(D') = \operatorname{rk}(A) + \operatorname{rk}(D). \end{aligned}$$

(b) Consider

$$Z := \begin{pmatrix} A & B \\ C & D \end{pmatrix} = \begin{pmatrix} I_m & I_m \\ I_m & I_m \end{pmatrix}.$$

Then $\operatorname{rk}(A) = \operatorname{rk}(D) = \operatorname{rk}(Z) = m$, so that the inequality does not hold.

Exercise 5.46 (Rank inequalities, 2) Consider the matrices

$$Z_1 := \begin{pmatrix} A & B \\ C & O \end{pmatrix} \quad \text{and} \quad Z_2 := \begin{pmatrix} O & B \\ C & D \end{pmatrix}.$$

(a) If either $\boldsymbol{B}$ or $\boldsymbol{C}$ (or both) is nonsingular, then show that

$$\operatorname{rk}(\boldsymbol{Z}_1) = \operatorname{rk}(\boldsymbol{Z}_2) = \operatorname{rk}(\boldsymbol{B}) + \operatorname{rk}(\boldsymbol{C}).$$

(b) Show that

$$\operatorname{rk}(\boldsymbol{Z}_1) = \operatorname{rk}(\boldsymbol{A}) + \operatorname{rk}(\boldsymbol{C}\boldsymbol{A}^{-1}\boldsymbol{B})$$

if $\boldsymbol{A}$ is square and nonsingular, and

$$\operatorname{rk}(\boldsymbol{Z}_2) = \operatorname{rk}(\boldsymbol{D}) + \operatorname{rk}(\boldsymbol{B}\boldsymbol{D}^{-1}\boldsymbol{C})$$

if $\boldsymbol{D}$ is square and nonsingular.
(c) Show that

$$\operatorname{rk}(\boldsymbol{Z}_1) \geq \operatorname{rk}(\boldsymbol{B}) + \operatorname{rk}(\boldsymbol{C}), \quad \operatorname{rk}(\boldsymbol{Z}_2) \geq \operatorname{rk}(\boldsymbol{B}) + \operatorname{rk}(\boldsymbol{C}).$$

Solution
Since the rank does not change if we interchange columns, we have

$$\operatorname{rk}(\boldsymbol{Z}_1) = \operatorname{rk}\begin{pmatrix} \boldsymbol{B} & \boldsymbol{A} \\ \mathbf{O} & \boldsymbol{C} \end{pmatrix}, \quad \operatorname{rk}(\boldsymbol{Z}_2) = \operatorname{rk}\begin{pmatrix} \boldsymbol{B} & \mathbf{O} \\ \boldsymbol{D} & \boldsymbol{C} \end{pmatrix}.$$

Results (a)–(c) now follow from Exercises 5.43–5.45.

Exercise 5.47 (The inequalities of Frobenius and Sylvester)
(a) Use Exercise 5.46 to obtain the following famous inequality:

$$\operatorname{rk}(\boldsymbol{AB}) + \operatorname{rk}(\boldsymbol{BC}) \leq \operatorname{rk}(\boldsymbol{B}) + \operatorname{rk}(\boldsymbol{ABC}),$$

if the product $\boldsymbol{ABC}$ exists (*Frobenius*).
(b) From (a) obtain another famous inequality:

$$\operatorname{rk}(\boldsymbol{AB}) \geq \operatorname{rk}(\boldsymbol{A}) + \operatorname{rk}(\boldsymbol{B}) - p$$

for any $m \times p$ matrix $\boldsymbol{A}$ and $p \times n$ matrix $\boldsymbol{B}$ (*Sylvester's law of nullity*).
(c) Show that $\boldsymbol{AB} = \mathbf{O}$ implies that $\operatorname{rk}(\boldsymbol{A}) \leq p - \operatorname{rk}(\boldsymbol{B})$ for any $m \times p$ matrix $\boldsymbol{A}$ and $p \times n$ matrix $\boldsymbol{B}$. (This generalizes Exercise 4.8.)

Solution
(a) Consider the identity

$$\begin{pmatrix} \boldsymbol{I}_m & -\boldsymbol{A} \\ \mathbf{O} & \boldsymbol{I}_n \end{pmatrix} \begin{pmatrix} \mathbf{O} & \boldsymbol{AB} \\ \boldsymbol{BC} & \boldsymbol{B} \end{pmatrix} \begin{pmatrix} \boldsymbol{I}_q & \mathbf{O} \\ -\boldsymbol{C} & \boldsymbol{I}_p \end{pmatrix} = \begin{pmatrix} -\boldsymbol{ABC} & \mathbf{O} \\ \mathbf{O} & \boldsymbol{B} \end{pmatrix}.$$

Of the four matrices, the first and third are nonsingular. Hence,

$$\operatorname{rk}\begin{pmatrix} \mathbf{O} & \boldsymbol{AB} \\ \boldsymbol{BC} & \boldsymbol{B} \end{pmatrix} = \operatorname{rk}(\boldsymbol{ABC}) + \operatorname{rk}(\boldsymbol{B}).$$

Also, by Exercise 5.46(c),

$$\operatorname{rk}\begin{pmatrix} \mathbf{O} & \boldsymbol{AB} \\ \boldsymbol{BC} & \boldsymbol{B} \end{pmatrix} \geq \operatorname{rk}(\boldsymbol{AB}) + \operatorname{rk}(\boldsymbol{BC}),$$

and the result follows.
(b) From Frobenius's inequality we obtain

$$\operatorname{rk}(\boldsymbol{AX}) + \operatorname{rk}(\boldsymbol{XB}) \leq \operatorname{rk}(\boldsymbol{X}) + \operatorname{rk}(\boldsymbol{AXB})$$

for any square matrix $\boldsymbol{X}$ of order p. Setting $\boldsymbol{X} = \boldsymbol{I}_p$ gives the result.
(c) Since $\boldsymbol{AB} = \mathbf{O}$, Sylvester's inequality gives $0 = \operatorname{rk}(\boldsymbol{AB}) \geq \operatorname{rk}(\boldsymbol{A}) + \operatorname{rk}(\boldsymbol{B}) - p$.

Exercise 5.48 (Rank of a partitioned matrix: main result) Let

$$\boldsymbol{Z} := \begin{pmatrix} \boldsymbol{A} & \boldsymbol{B} \\ \boldsymbol{C} & \boldsymbol{D} \end{pmatrix}.$$

Show that

$$\operatorname{rk}(\boldsymbol{Z}) = \operatorname{rk}(\boldsymbol{A}) + \operatorname{rk}(\boldsymbol{D} - \boldsymbol{CA}^{-1}\boldsymbol{B}) \quad (\text{if } |\boldsymbol{A}| \neq 0)$$

and

$$\operatorname{rk}(\boldsymbol{Z}) = \operatorname{rk}(\boldsymbol{D}) + \operatorname{rk}(\boldsymbol{A} - \boldsymbol{BD}^{-1}\boldsymbol{C}) \quad (\text{if } |\boldsymbol{D}| \neq 0).$$

Solution
If $\boldsymbol{A}$ is nonsingular we can write

$$\begin{pmatrix} \boldsymbol{I}_m & \mathbf{O} \\ -\boldsymbol{CA}^{-1} & \boldsymbol{I}_n \end{pmatrix} \begin{pmatrix} \boldsymbol{A} & \boldsymbol{B} \\ \boldsymbol{C} & \boldsymbol{D} \end{pmatrix} \begin{pmatrix} \boldsymbol{I}_m & -\boldsymbol{A}^{-1}\boldsymbol{B} \\ \mathbf{O} & \boldsymbol{I}_q \end{pmatrix} = \begin{pmatrix} \boldsymbol{A} & \mathbf{O} \\ \mathbf{O} & \boldsymbol{D} - \boldsymbol{CA}^{-1}\boldsymbol{B} \end{pmatrix}.$$

Similarly, if $\boldsymbol{D}$ is nonsingular, we can write

$$\begin{pmatrix} \boldsymbol{I}_m & -\boldsymbol{BD}^{-1} \\ \mathbf{O} & \boldsymbol{I}_n \end{pmatrix} \begin{pmatrix} \boldsymbol{A} & \boldsymbol{B} \\ \boldsymbol{C} & \boldsymbol{D} \end{pmatrix} \begin{pmatrix} \boldsymbol{I}_p & \mathbf{O} \\ -\boldsymbol{D}^{-1}\boldsymbol{C} & \boldsymbol{I}_n \end{pmatrix} = \begin{pmatrix} \boldsymbol{A} - \boldsymbol{BD}^{-1}\boldsymbol{C} & \mathbf{O} \\ \mathbf{O} & \boldsymbol{D} \end{pmatrix}.$$

Since for any matrix $\boldsymbol{Z}$, $\operatorname{rk}(\boldsymbol{Z}) = \operatorname{rk}(\boldsymbol{EZF})$ whenever $\boldsymbol{E}$ and $\boldsymbol{F}$ are nonsingular, the results follow.

Exercise 5.49 (Relationship between the ranks of $\boldsymbol{I}_m - \boldsymbol{BB}'$ and $\boldsymbol{I}_n - \boldsymbol{B}'\boldsymbol{B}$) Show that

$$\operatorname{rk}\begin{pmatrix} \boldsymbol{I}_m & \boldsymbol{B} \\ \boldsymbol{B}' & \boldsymbol{I}_n \end{pmatrix} = m + \operatorname{rk}(\boldsymbol{I}_n - \boldsymbol{B}'\boldsymbol{B}) = n + \operatorname{rk}(\boldsymbol{I}_m - \boldsymbol{BB}').$$

Solution
From Exercise 5.48 we obtain

$$\operatorname{rk}\begin{pmatrix} \boldsymbol{I}_m & \boldsymbol{B} \\ \boldsymbol{B}' & \boldsymbol{I}_n \end{pmatrix} = \operatorname{rk}(\boldsymbol{I}_m) + \operatorname{rk}(\boldsymbol{I}_n - \boldsymbol{B}'\boldsymbol{B}) = m + \operatorname{rk}(\boldsymbol{I}_n - \boldsymbol{B}'\boldsymbol{B})$$

and also

$$\operatorname{rk}\begin{pmatrix} \boldsymbol{I}_m & \boldsymbol{B} \\ \boldsymbol{B}' & \boldsymbol{I}_n \end{pmatrix} = \operatorname{rk}(\boldsymbol{I}_n) + \operatorname{rk}(\boldsymbol{I}_m - \boldsymbol{B}\boldsymbol{B}') = n + \operatorname{rk}(\boldsymbol{I}_m - \boldsymbol{B}\boldsymbol{B}').$$

Exercise 5.50 (Relationship between the ranks of $\boldsymbol{I}_m - \boldsymbol{B}\boldsymbol{C}$ and $\boldsymbol{I}_n - \boldsymbol{C}\boldsymbol{B}$)
(a) Let $\boldsymbol{B}$ and $\boldsymbol{C}$ be square $n \times n$ matrices. Show that

$$\operatorname{rk}(\boldsymbol{I}_n - \boldsymbol{B}\boldsymbol{C}) = \operatorname{rk}(\boldsymbol{I}_n - \boldsymbol{C}\boldsymbol{B}).$$

(b) Now let $\boldsymbol{B}$ be an $m \times n$ matrix and $\boldsymbol{C}$ an $n \times m$ matrix. Extend the result under (a) by showing that

$$\operatorname{rk}(\boldsymbol{I}_m - \boldsymbol{B}\boldsymbol{C}) = \operatorname{rk}(\boldsymbol{I}_n - \boldsymbol{C}\boldsymbol{B}) + m - n.$$

Solution
(a) We have

$$\begin{pmatrix} \boldsymbol{I}_n & -\boldsymbol{B} \\ \mathrm{O} & \boldsymbol{I}_n \end{pmatrix}\begin{pmatrix} \boldsymbol{I}_n & \boldsymbol{B} \\ \boldsymbol{C} & \boldsymbol{I}_n \end{pmatrix}\begin{pmatrix} \boldsymbol{I}_n & \mathrm{O} \\ -\boldsymbol{C} & \boldsymbol{I}_n \end{pmatrix} = \begin{pmatrix} \boldsymbol{I}_n - \boldsymbol{B}\boldsymbol{C} & \mathrm{O} \\ \mathrm{O} & \boldsymbol{I}_n \end{pmatrix}$$

and

$$\begin{pmatrix} \boldsymbol{I}_n & \mathrm{O} \\ -\boldsymbol{C} & \boldsymbol{I}_n \end{pmatrix}\begin{pmatrix} \boldsymbol{I}_n & \boldsymbol{B} \\ \boldsymbol{C} & \boldsymbol{I}_n \end{pmatrix}\begin{pmatrix} \boldsymbol{I}_n & -\boldsymbol{B} \\ \mathrm{O} & \boldsymbol{I}_n \end{pmatrix} = \begin{pmatrix} \boldsymbol{I}_n & \mathrm{O} \\ \mathrm{O} & \boldsymbol{I}_n - \boldsymbol{C}\boldsymbol{B} \end{pmatrix}.$$

This proves (a) and shows in addition that

$$\operatorname{rk}(\boldsymbol{I}_n - \boldsymbol{B}\boldsymbol{C}) = \operatorname{rk}(\boldsymbol{I}_n - \boldsymbol{C}\boldsymbol{B}) = \operatorname{rk}\begin{pmatrix} \boldsymbol{I}_n & \boldsymbol{B} \\ \boldsymbol{C} & \boldsymbol{I}_n \end{pmatrix}.$$

(b) The argument is identical to the argument under (a), except for the order of the identity matrices. Thus, we conclude that

$$\operatorname{rk}\begin{pmatrix} \boldsymbol{I}_m - \boldsymbol{B}\boldsymbol{C} & \mathrm{O} \\ \mathrm{O} & \boldsymbol{I}_n \end{pmatrix} = \operatorname{rk}\begin{pmatrix} \boldsymbol{I}_m & \mathrm{O} \\ \mathrm{O} & \boldsymbol{I}_n - \boldsymbol{C}\boldsymbol{B} \end{pmatrix}$$

and the result follows.

Exercise 5.51 (Upper bound for the rank of a sum) Let $\boldsymbol{A}$ and $\boldsymbol{B}$ be matrices of the same order. We know from Exercise 4.14 that

$$\operatorname{rk}(\boldsymbol{A} + \boldsymbol{B}) \leq \operatorname{rk}(\boldsymbol{A}) + \operatorname{rk}(\boldsymbol{B}).$$

Provide an alternative proof, using partitioned matrices.

Solution
The argument builds on the two matrices

$$\boldsymbol{Z}_1 := \begin{pmatrix} \boldsymbol{A} & \mathrm{O} \\ \mathrm{O} & \boldsymbol{B} \end{pmatrix} \quad \text{and} \quad \boldsymbol{Z}_2 := \begin{pmatrix} \boldsymbol{A} + \boldsymbol{B} & \boldsymbol{B} \\ \boldsymbol{B} & \boldsymbol{B} \end{pmatrix}.$$

The matrices $\boldsymbol{Z}_1$ and $\boldsymbol{Z}_2$ have the same rank, because

$$\begin{pmatrix} \boldsymbol{I}_m & \boldsymbol{I}_m \\ \mathbf{O} & \boldsymbol{I}_m \end{pmatrix} \begin{pmatrix} \boldsymbol{A} & \mathbf{O} \\ \mathbf{O} & \boldsymbol{B} \end{pmatrix} \begin{pmatrix} \boldsymbol{I}_n & \mathbf{O} \\ \boldsymbol{I}_n & \boldsymbol{I}_n \end{pmatrix} = \begin{pmatrix} \boldsymbol{A}+\boldsymbol{B} & \boldsymbol{B} \\ \boldsymbol{B} & \boldsymbol{B} \end{pmatrix}.$$

Clearly, $\operatorname{rk}(\boldsymbol{Z}_1) = \operatorname{rk}(\boldsymbol{A}) + \operatorname{rk}(\boldsymbol{B})$. Also, since $\boldsymbol{A}+\boldsymbol{B}$ is a submatrix of $\boldsymbol{Z}_2$ we must have $\operatorname{rk}(\boldsymbol{Z}_2) \geq \operatorname{rk}(\boldsymbol{A}+\boldsymbol{B})$ (Exercise 4.17). Hence,

$$\operatorname{rk}(\boldsymbol{A}+\boldsymbol{B}) \leq \operatorname{rk}(\boldsymbol{Z}_2) = \operatorname{rk}(\boldsymbol{Z}_1) = \operatorname{rk}(\boldsymbol{A}) + \operatorname{rk}(\boldsymbol{B}).$$

Exercise 5.52 (Rank of a 3-by-3 block matrix) Consider the symmetric matrix $\boldsymbol{Z}$ of Exercise 5.19. Show that

$$\operatorname{rk}(\boldsymbol{Z}) = \operatorname{rk}(\boldsymbol{D}) + \operatorname{rk}(\boldsymbol{E}) + \operatorname{rk}(\boldsymbol{A} - \boldsymbol{B}\boldsymbol{D}^{-1}\boldsymbol{B}' - \boldsymbol{C}\boldsymbol{E}^{-1}\boldsymbol{C}')$$

if $\boldsymbol{D}$ and $\boldsymbol{E}$ are nonsingular.

Solution
Let

$$\widetilde{\boldsymbol{A}} := \boldsymbol{A}, \quad \widetilde{\boldsymbol{B}} := (\boldsymbol{B} : \boldsymbol{C}), \quad \widetilde{\boldsymbol{C}} := (\boldsymbol{B} : \boldsymbol{C})', \quad \widetilde{\boldsymbol{D}} := \begin{pmatrix} \boldsymbol{D} & \mathbf{O} \\ \mathbf{O} & \boldsymbol{E} \end{pmatrix}.$$

Then, using Exercise 5.48,

$$\begin{aligned} \operatorname{rk}(\boldsymbol{Z}) &= \operatorname{rk}(\widetilde{\boldsymbol{D}}) + \operatorname{rk}(\widetilde{\boldsymbol{A}} - \widetilde{\boldsymbol{B}}\widetilde{\boldsymbol{D}}^{-1}\widetilde{\boldsymbol{C}}) \\ &= \operatorname{rk}(\boldsymbol{D}) + \operatorname{rk}(\boldsymbol{E}) + \operatorname{rk}(\boldsymbol{A} - \boldsymbol{B}\boldsymbol{D}^{-1}\boldsymbol{B}' - \boldsymbol{C}\boldsymbol{E}^{-1}\boldsymbol{C}'). \end{aligned}$$

Exercise 5.53 (Rank of a bordered matrix) Let

$$\boldsymbol{Z} := \begin{pmatrix} \mathbf{0} & \boldsymbol{A} \\ \alpha & \boldsymbol{a}' \end{pmatrix}.$$

Show that

$$\operatorname{rk}(\boldsymbol{Z}) = \begin{cases} \operatorname{rk}(\boldsymbol{A}) & (\alpha = 0 \text{ and } \boldsymbol{a} \in \operatorname{col}(\boldsymbol{A}')), \\ \operatorname{rk}(\boldsymbol{A}) + 1 & (\text{otherwise}). \end{cases}$$

Solution
If $\alpha \neq 0$ then $\operatorname{rk}(\boldsymbol{Z}) = \operatorname{rk}(\boldsymbol{A}) + 1$ by Exercise 5.46(a). If $\alpha = 0$ then $\operatorname{rk}(\boldsymbol{Z}) = \operatorname{rk}(\boldsymbol{A}' : \boldsymbol{a})$. If $\boldsymbol{a} \in \operatorname{col}(\boldsymbol{A}')$ then

$$\operatorname{rk}(\boldsymbol{A}' : \boldsymbol{a}) = \operatorname{rk}(\boldsymbol{A}') = \operatorname{rk}(\boldsymbol{A}).$$

If $\boldsymbol{a} \notin \operatorname{col}(\boldsymbol{A}')$ then

$$\operatorname{rk}(\boldsymbol{A}' : \boldsymbol{a}) = \operatorname{rk}(\boldsymbol{A}') + 1 = \operatorname{rk}(\boldsymbol{A}) + 1.$$

5.5 The sweep operator

Exercise 5.54 (Simple sweep) Consider the 2×2 matrix

$$A := \begin{pmatrix} a & b \\ c & d \end{pmatrix}.$$

(a) Compute $A^{(1)} := \mathrm{SWP}(A, 1)$ and state the condition(s) under which it is defined.
(b) Compute $A^{(2)} := \mathrm{SWP}(A^{(1)}, 2)$ and state the condition(s) under which it is defined.
(c) Show that $A^{(2)} = -A^{-1}$.

Solution
(a) By definition, we have

$$A^{(1)} = \mathrm{SWP}(A, 1) = \begin{pmatrix} -1/a & b/a \\ c/a & d - bc/a \end{pmatrix},$$

provided $a \neq 0$.
(b) Applying the definition to $A^{(1)}$ gives

$$A^{(2)} = \mathrm{SWP}(A^{(1)}, 2) = \frac{a}{ad-bc} \begin{pmatrix} -\frac{ad-bc}{a^2} - \frac{cb}{a^2} & \frac{b}{a} \\ \frac{c}{a} & -1 \end{pmatrix} = \frac{-1}{ad-bc} \begin{pmatrix} d & -b \\ -c & a \end{pmatrix},$$

provided $a \neq 0$ and $ad - bc \neq 0$.
(c) We recognize $-A^{(2)}$ as the inverse of A or, if we don't, we can verify that $AA^{(2)} = -I_2$.

Exercise 5.55 (General sweep)
(a) Let A be a 3×3 matrix. Compute $\mathrm{SWP}(A, 2)$ and state the condition(s) under which it is defined.
(b) Let A be an $n \times n$ matrix. For $1 \leq p \leq n$, compute $\mathrm{SWP}(A, p)$ and state the condition(s) under which it is defined.

Solution
(a) Let

$$A := \begin{pmatrix} a_{11} & a_{12} & a_{13} \\ a_{21} & a_{22} & a_{23} \\ a_{31} & a_{32} & a_{33} \end{pmatrix}.$$

Then, applying the definition,

$$\mathrm{SWP}(A, 2) = \begin{pmatrix} a_{11} - a_{12}a_{21}/a_{22} & a_{12}/a_{22} & a_{13} - a_{12}a_{23}/a_{22} \\ a_{21}/a_{22} & -1/a_{22} & a_{23}/a_{22} \\ a_{31} - a_{32}a_{21}/a_{22} & a_{32}/a_{22} & a_{33} - a_{32}a_{23}/a_{22} \end{pmatrix},$$

provided $a_{22} \neq 0$.

(b) More generally, if

$$A := \begin{pmatrix} A_{11} & a_{12} & A_{13} \\ a'_{21} & a_{22} & a'_{23} \\ A_{31} & a_{32} & A_{33} \end{pmatrix},$$

where A_{11} has order $p-1$, a_{22} is a scalar, and A_{33} has order $n-p$, then we obtain in the same way

$$\mathrm{SWP}(A, p) = \begin{pmatrix} A_{11} - a_{12}a'_{21}/a_{22} & a_{12}/a_{22} & A_{13} - a_{12}a'_{23}/a_{22} \\ a'_{21}/a_{22} & -1/a_{22} & a'_{23}/a_{22} \\ A_{31} - a_{32}a'_{21}/a_{22} & a_{32}/a_{22} & A_{33} - a_{32}a'_{23}/a_{22} \end{pmatrix},$$

provided a_{22} is nonzero.

*__Exercise 5.56 (The sweeping theorem)__ Let A be an $n \times n$ matrix and let $1 \le p \le n$. Define $A^{(k)}$ recursively by $A^{(k)} := \mathrm{SWP}(A^{(k-1)}, k)$ for $k = 1, \dots, p$ with starting value $A^{(0)} := A$.

(a) If A is partitioned as

$$A := \begin{pmatrix} P & Q \\ R & S \end{pmatrix},$$

where P is a $p \times p$ matrix, show that

$$A^{(p)} = \begin{pmatrix} -P^{-1} & P^{-1}Q \\ RP^{-1} & S - RP^{-1}Q \end{pmatrix}.$$

(b) Hence show that $A^{(n)} = -A^{-1}$.

Solution

(a) We prove this by induction on p. The result is true for $p = 1$, because $A^{(1)} = \mathrm{SWP}(A, 1)$ and the definition of the sweep operator or Exercise 5.54(a). Next, assume that the result holds for $p-1$, and let A be partitioned as

$$A = \begin{pmatrix} A_{11} & a_{12} & A_{13} \\ a'_{21} & a_{22} & a'_{23} \\ A_{31} & a_{32} & A_{33} \end{pmatrix},$$

where A_{11} has order $p-1$, a_{22} is a scalar, and A_{33} has order $n-p$. Then, by the induction hypothesis, we have

$$A^{(p-1)} = \begin{pmatrix} -A_{11}^{-1} & A_{11}^{-1}a_{12} & A_{11}^{-1}A_{13} \\ a'_{21}A_{11}^{-1} & a_{22} - a'_{21}A_{11}^{-1}a_{12} & a'_{23} - a'_{21}A_{11}^{-1}A_{13} \\ A_{31}A_{11}^{-1} & a_{32} - A_{31}A_{11}^{-1}a_{12} & A_{33} - A_{31}A_{11}^{-1}A_{13} \end{pmatrix}.$$

We now use Exercise 5.55(b); this shows that $\mathrm{SWP}(A^{(p-1)}, p)$ is equal to

$$\begin{pmatrix} -B_{11} & -b_{12} & B_{11}A_{13} + b_{12}a'_{23} \\ -b'_{21} & -b_{22} & b'_{21}A_{13} + b_{22}a'_{23} \\ A_{31}B_{11} + a_{32}b'_{21} & A_{31}b_{12} + a_{32}b_{22} & A_{33} - D \end{pmatrix},$$

where

$$\begin{aligned}
B_{11} &:= A_{11}^{-1} + A_{11}^{-1}a_{12}a_{21}'A_{11}^{-1}/\beta, \\
b_{12} &:= -A_{11}^{-1}a_{12}/\beta, \quad b_{21}' := -a_{21}'A_{11}^{-1}/\beta, \\
b_{22} &:= 1/\beta, \quad \beta := a_{22} - a_{21}'A_{11}^{-1}a_{12}, \\
D &:= A_{31}A_{11}^{-1}A_{13} + (a_{32} - A_{31}A_{11}^{-1}a_{12})(a_{23}' - a_{21}'A_{11}^{-1}A_{13})/\beta.
\end{aligned}$$

Noticing that

$$\begin{pmatrix} A_{11} & a_{12} \\ a_{21}' & a_{22} \end{pmatrix}^{-1} = \begin{pmatrix} B_{11} & b_{12} \\ b_{21}' & b_{22} \end{pmatrix},$$

using Exercise 5.16(a), and that

$$D = (A_{31} : a_{32}) \begin{pmatrix} B_{11} & b_{12} \\ b_{21}' & b_{22} \end{pmatrix} \begin{pmatrix} A_{13} \\ a_{23}' \end{pmatrix},$$

the result follows.
(b) This follows directly from (a). The inverse of A can thus be computed by n sequential sweep operations, a very useful fact in numerical inversion routines.

Exercise 5.57 (Sweeping and linear equations)
(a) Show how the sweep operator can be used to solve the linear system $PX = Q$ for nonsingular P.
(b) In particular, solve the system $2x_1 + 3x_2 = 8$ and $4x_1 + 5x_2 = 14$ using the sweep operator.

Solution
(a) We know from Exercise 5.56 that

$$A := \begin{pmatrix} P & Q \\ R & S \end{pmatrix} \implies A^{(p)} = \begin{pmatrix} -P^{-1} & P^{-1}Q \\ RP^{-1} & S - RP^{-1}Q \end{pmatrix}.$$

Hence, the solution $P^{-1}Q$ appears as the $(1,2)$-block of $A^{(p)}$, where p denotes the order of the square matrix P.
(b) Denoting irrelevant elements by $*$s, we define

$$A^{(0)} := \begin{pmatrix} 2 & 3 & 8 \\ 4 & 5 & 14 \\ * & * & * \end{pmatrix}.$$

This gives

$$A^{(1)} := \mathrm{SWP}(A^{(0)}, 1) = \begin{pmatrix} -1/2 & 3/2 & 4 \\ 2 & -1 & -2 \\ * & * & * \end{pmatrix}$$

and

$$A^{(2)} := \mathrm{SWP}(A^{(1)}, 2) = \begin{pmatrix} 5/2 & -3/2 & 1 \\ -2 & 1 & 2 \\ * & * & * \end{pmatrix},$$

so that the solution is $x_1 = 1$, $x_2 = 2$.

Notes

A good survey of results with partitioned matrices can be found in Chapter 2 of Zhang (1999). The inequalities in Exercise 5.47 were first obtained by Sylvester in 1884 and Frobenius in 1911. Sylvester's inequality is called the "law of nullity", because it implies that

$$\dim(\ker(AB)) \leq \dim(\ker(A)) + \dim(\ker(B)),$$

and the dimension of the kernel of a matrix is known as its "nullity". The sweep operator (Exercises 5.54–5.57) plays a role in inversion routines. It was introduced by Beaton (1964); see also Dempster (1969).

6

Systems of equations

Sets of simultaneous linear equations appear frequently in linear econometric models and elsewhere. We shall be concerned with deriving criteria for the existence and uniqueness of solutions, and with the properties of solutions. We begin by considering some simple operations on the rows (columns) of a matrix without changing its rank. Three types of operations on the rows of a matrix (called *elementary row operations*) are of importance; they are:

(i) interchange of two rows;
(ii) multiplication of a row by any scalar $\lambda \neq 0$;
(iii) addition to the i-th row of λ times the j-th row ($i \neq j$).

Let us perform these three row operations, one at a time, on the identity matrix $\boldsymbol{I}_m$. We denote by $\boldsymbol{E}_{ij}$ the identity matrix with rows i and j interchanged, by $\boldsymbol{E}_i(\lambda)$ the identity matrix whose i-th row is multiplied by $\lambda \neq 0$, and by $\boldsymbol{E}_i(\lambda|j)$ the identity matrix where λ times row j is added to a row i ($i \neq j$). For example, when $m = 3$,

$$\boldsymbol{E}_{13} = \begin{pmatrix} 0 & 0 & 1 \\ 0 & 1 & 0 \\ 1 & 0 & 0 \end{pmatrix}, \quad \boldsymbol{E}_2(7) = \begin{pmatrix} 1 & 0 & 0 \\ 0 & 7 & 0 \\ 0 & 0 & 1 \end{pmatrix}, \quad \boldsymbol{E}_3(5|2) = \begin{pmatrix} 1 & 0 & 0 \\ 0 & 1 & 0 \\ 0 & 5 & 1 \end{pmatrix}.$$

Elementary *column* operations are defined in the same way; they are:

(i) interchange of two columns;
(ii) multiplication of a column by any scalar $\lambda \neq 0$;
(iii) addition to the i-th column of λ times the j-th column ($i \neq j$).

We now perform these three column operations on the identity matrix $\boldsymbol{I}_n$. Let $\boldsymbol{F}_{ij}$ denote $\boldsymbol{I}_n$ with columns i and j interchanged, $\boldsymbol{F}_i(\lambda)$ when the i-th column is multiplied by $\lambda \neq 0$, and $\boldsymbol{F}_i(\lambda|j)$ when λ times column j is added to column i ($i \neq j$). When $n = 3$, we have

$$\boldsymbol{F}_{13} = \begin{pmatrix} 0 & 0 & 1 \\ 0 & 1 & 0 \\ 1 & 0 & 0 \end{pmatrix}, \quad \boldsymbol{F}_2(7) = \begin{pmatrix} 1 & 0 & 0 \\ 0 & 7 & 0 \\ 0 & 0 & 1 \end{pmatrix}, \quad \boldsymbol{F}_3(5|2) = \begin{pmatrix} 1 & 0 & 0 \\ 0 & 1 & 5 \\ 0 & 0 & 1 \end{pmatrix}.$$

Notice that, when $m = n$, we have $\boldsymbol{F}_{ij} = \boldsymbol{E}_{ij}$, $\boldsymbol{F}_i(\lambda) = \boldsymbol{E}_i(\lambda)$, but $\boldsymbol{F}_i(\lambda|j) = \boldsymbol{E}_j(\lambda|i) = \boldsymbol{E}'_i(\lambda|j)$.

We shall see (Exercise 6.13) that by means of a series of elementary row operations, any $m \times n$ matrix $\boldsymbol{A}$ can be reduced to a so-called *echelon* matrix, which has the following structure:

(i) if a row has nonzero elements, then the first nonzero element (called the *leading* element or *pivot*) is 1;
(ii) if a column contains a leading 1, then all elements in that column below the leading 1 are zero;
(iii) if a row has a leading 1, then each row above contains a leading 1 further to the left.

A typical example of an echelon matrix is

$$\boldsymbol{H} = \begin{pmatrix} 0 & \textcircled{1} & h_{13} & h_{14} & h_{15} & h_{16} \\ 0 & 0 & 0 & \textcircled{1} & h_{25} & h_{26} \\ 0 & 0 & 0 & 0 & \textcircled{1} & h_{36} \\ 0 & 0 & 0 & 0 & 0 & 0 \end{pmatrix},$$

where the three leading ones have been circled. One of the useful properties of $\boldsymbol{H}$ is that its rank is very easy to determine. It is simply the number of nonzero rows (here 3), see Exercise 6.12.

If $\boldsymbol{A}$ is a nonsingular matrix, then not only can we reduce $\boldsymbol{A}$ to echelon form by a sequence of elementary operations, say $\boldsymbol{E}_1\boldsymbol{A} = \boldsymbol{H}$ (*forward elimination*), but we can further reduce $\boldsymbol{H}$ to the identity matrix, $\boldsymbol{E}_2\boldsymbol{H} = \boldsymbol{I}_n$ (*backward elimination*). Hence, $\boldsymbol{E}_2\boldsymbol{E}_1\boldsymbol{A} = \boldsymbol{I}_n$ and $\boldsymbol{A}^{-1} = \boldsymbol{E}_2\boldsymbol{E}_1$. This is the idea behind Gaussian elimination, discussed in Section 6.3.

In Sections 6.4 and 6.5 we discuss the homogeneous equation $\boldsymbol{Ax} = \boldsymbol{0}$ and the nonhomogeneous equation $\boldsymbol{Ax} = \boldsymbol{b}$, respectively.

6.1 Elementary matrices

Exercise 6.1 (Elementary example) Consider the matrix

$$\boldsymbol{A} = \begin{pmatrix} 1 & 2 \\ 3 & 4 \\ 5 & 6 \end{pmatrix}.$$

Show that $\boldsymbol{B} = \boldsymbol{EA}$ for some elementary matrix $\boldsymbol{E}$, when:
(a) $\boldsymbol{B}$ is obtained from $\boldsymbol{A}$ by interchanging the first and third rows in $\boldsymbol{A}$;
(b) $\boldsymbol{B}$ is obtained from $\boldsymbol{A}$ by multiplying the second row by 7;
(c) $\boldsymbol{B}$ is obtained from $\boldsymbol{A}$ by adding five times the second row to the third row.

Solution

Denote the solutions to (a)–(c) by $\boldsymbol{E}_{13}$, $\boldsymbol{E}_2(7)$, and $\boldsymbol{E}_3(5|2)$, respectively. Then,

$$\boldsymbol{E}_{13} = \begin{pmatrix} 0 & 0 & 1 \\ 0 & 1 & 0 \\ 1 & 0 & 0 \end{pmatrix}, \quad \boldsymbol{E}_2(7) = \begin{pmatrix} 1 & 0 & 0 \\ 0 & 7 & 0 \\ 0 & 0 & 1 \end{pmatrix}, \quad \boldsymbol{E}_3(5|2) = \begin{pmatrix} 1 & 0 & 0 \\ 0 & 1 & 0 \\ 0 & 5 & 1 \end{pmatrix}$$

satisfy the requirements. Apparently, if $\boldsymbol{B}$ is obtained from $\boldsymbol{A}$ by an elementary row operation, then $\boldsymbol{B} = \boldsymbol{E}\boldsymbol{A}$ for some elementary matrix $\boldsymbol{E}$. We next prove that this holds generally.

Exercise 6.2 (Elementary row operations) Let $\boldsymbol{B}$ be obtained from $\boldsymbol{A}$ by an elementary row operation. Show that $\boldsymbol{B} = \boldsymbol{E}\boldsymbol{A}$ for some elementary matrix $\boldsymbol{E}$.

Solution

Let $\boldsymbol{A}$ be a matrix of order $m \times n$. Then so is $\boldsymbol{B}$ and hence $\boldsymbol{E}$ must be square of order $m \times m$. There are three elementary row operations. Without loss of generality we set $m = 3$ and $n = 1$, so that $\boldsymbol{A}$ is a 3×1 matrix, that is, a vector $\boldsymbol{a} := (a_1, a_2, a_3)'$. It suffices to show that

$$\boldsymbol{E}_{12}\boldsymbol{a} = \begin{pmatrix} a_2 \\ a_1 \\ a_3 \end{pmatrix}, \quad \boldsymbol{E}_1(\lambda)\boldsymbol{a} = \begin{pmatrix} \lambda a_1 \\ a_2 \\ a_3 \end{pmatrix}, \quad \boldsymbol{E}_1(\lambda|2)\boldsymbol{a} = \begin{pmatrix} a_1 + \lambda a_2 \\ a_2 \\ a_3 \end{pmatrix}.$$

But this follows from the fact that

$$\boldsymbol{E}_{12} = \begin{pmatrix} 0 & 1 & 0 \\ 1 & 0 & 0 \\ 0 & 0 & 1 \end{pmatrix}, \quad \boldsymbol{E}_1(\lambda) = \begin{pmatrix} \lambda & 0 & 0 \\ 0 & 1 & 0 \\ 0 & 0 & 1 \end{pmatrix}, \quad \boldsymbol{E}_1(\lambda|2) = \begin{pmatrix} 1 & \lambda & 0 \\ 0 & 1 & 0 \\ 0 & 0 & 1 \end{pmatrix}.$$

*__Exercise 6.3 (Explicit expression of elementary matrices)__ Show that the elementary matrices can be expressed in terms of the unit vectors $\boldsymbol{e}_i$ and $\boldsymbol{e}_j$. In particular,

$$\boldsymbol{E}_{ij} = \boldsymbol{I}_m - (\boldsymbol{e}_i - \boldsymbol{e}_j)(\boldsymbol{e}_i - \boldsymbol{e}_j)',$$

$$\boldsymbol{E}_i(\lambda) = \boldsymbol{I}_m + (\lambda - 1)\boldsymbol{e}_i\boldsymbol{e}_i', \quad \boldsymbol{E}_i(\lambda|j) = \boldsymbol{I}_m + \lambda\boldsymbol{e}_i\boldsymbol{e}_j'.$$

Solution

We have

$$\begin{aligned} \boldsymbol{E}_{ij} &= \left(\sum_{k \notin \{i,j\}} \boldsymbol{e}_k\boldsymbol{e}_k' \right) + \boldsymbol{e}_i\boldsymbol{e}_j' + \boldsymbol{e}_j\boldsymbol{e}_i' \\ &= \left(\sum_{k=1}^{m} \boldsymbol{e}_k\boldsymbol{e}_k' \right) - (\boldsymbol{e}_i\boldsymbol{e}_i' + \boldsymbol{e}_j\boldsymbol{e}_j' - \boldsymbol{e}_i\boldsymbol{e}_j' - \boldsymbol{e}_j\boldsymbol{e}_i') \\ &= \boldsymbol{I}_m - (\boldsymbol{e}_i - \boldsymbol{e}_j)(\boldsymbol{e}_i - \boldsymbol{e}_j)'. \end{aligned}$$

Also,

$$E_i(\lambda) = \left(\sum_{k\neq i} e_k e_k'\right) + \lambda e_i e_i' = \left(\sum_{k=1}^{m} e_k e_k'\right) - e_i e_i' + \lambda e_i e_i' = I_m + (\lambda - 1) e_i e_i'.$$

Finally,

$$\begin{aligned} E_i(\lambda|j) &= \left(\sum_{k\neq i} e_k e_k'\right) + e_i(e_i + \lambda e_j)' \\ &= \left(\sum_{k=1}^{m} e_k e_k'\right) - e_i e_i' + e_i e_i' + \lambda e_i e_j' = I_m + \lambda e_i e_j'. \end{aligned}$$

Exercise 6.4 (Transpose of an elementary matrix)
(a) Show that

$$E_{ij}' = E_{ij}, \quad E_i'(\lambda) = E_i(\lambda), \quad E_i'(\lambda|j) = E_j(\lambda|i).$$

(b) Conclude that the transpose of an elementary matrix is itself elementary.

Solution
(a) Using Exercise 6.3 (or by direct inspection) we see that E_{ij} and $E_i(\lambda)$ are symmetric and that

$$E_i'(\lambda|j) = (I_m + \lambda e_i e_j')' = I_m + \lambda e_j e_i' = E_j(\lambda|i).$$

(b) The conclusion is evident from (a).

Exercise 6.5 (Inverse of an elementary matrix)
(a) Show that

$$E_{ij}^{-1} = E_{ij}, \quad E_i^{-1}(\lambda) = E_i(\lambda^{-1}), \quad E_i^{-1}(\lambda|j) = E_i(-\lambda|j).$$

(b) Conclude that the inverse of an elementary matrix is itself elementary.

Solution
(a) First, letting $d := e_i - e_j$, we find, using Exercise 6.3,

$$\begin{aligned} E_{ij} E_{ij} &= (I_m - dd')^2 = I_m - dd' - dd' + (d'd)dd' \\ &= I_m + (d'd - 2)dd' = I_m, \end{aligned}$$

because if $i \neq j$ then $d'd = (e_i - e_j)'(e_i - e_j) = 2$, and if $i = j$ then $d = 0$. Second,

$$\begin{aligned} E_i(\lambda) E_i(\lambda^{-1}) &= \left(I_m + (\lambda - 1) e_i e_i'\right)\left(I_m + (\lambda^{-1} - 1) e_i e_i'\right) \\ &= I_m + \left(\lambda^{-1} - 1 + \lambda - 1 + (\lambda - 1)(\lambda^{-1} - 1)\right) e_i e_i' = I_m. \end{aligned}$$

Third,

$$\begin{aligned}\boldsymbol{E}_i(\lambda|j)\boldsymbol{E}_i(-\lambda|j) &= (\boldsymbol{I}_m + \lambda \boldsymbol{e}_i\boldsymbol{e}_j')(\boldsymbol{I}_m - \lambda \boldsymbol{e}_i\boldsymbol{e}_j') \\ &= \boldsymbol{I}_m - \lambda \boldsymbol{e}_i\boldsymbol{e}_j' + \lambda \boldsymbol{e}_i\boldsymbol{e}_j' - \lambda^2 \boldsymbol{e}_i\boldsymbol{e}_j'\boldsymbol{e}_i\boldsymbol{e}_j' = \boldsymbol{I}_m,\end{aligned}$$

because $\boldsymbol{e}_j'\boldsymbol{e}_i = 0$, since $i \neq j$.
(b) The conclusion follows.

Exercise 6.6 (Product of elementary matrices) Show that the product of two elementary matrices is, in general, not elementary.

Solution
For example,

$$\boldsymbol{E}_{13}\boldsymbol{E}_2(7) = \begin{pmatrix} 0 & 0 & 1 \\ 0 & 1 & 0 \\ 1 & 0 & 0 \end{pmatrix} \begin{pmatrix} 1 & 0 & 0 \\ 0 & 7 & 0 \\ 0 & 0 & 1 \end{pmatrix} = \begin{pmatrix} 0 & 0 & 1 \\ 0 & 7 & 0 \\ 1 & 0 & 0 \end{pmatrix},$$

which is not elementary.

Exercise 6.7 (Elementary checks) Check the theoretical results of Exercises 6.4 and 6.5 by considering the 3×3 identity matrix and the elementary matrices $\boldsymbol{E}_{23}$, $\boldsymbol{E}_1(5)$, $\boldsymbol{E}_2(4|1)$, $\boldsymbol{E}_1(4|2)$, and $\boldsymbol{E}_2(0|1)$.

Solution
First we consider

$$\boldsymbol{E}_{23} = \begin{pmatrix} 1 & 0 & 0 \\ 0 & 0 & 1 \\ 0 & 1 & 0 \end{pmatrix} \quad \text{and} \quad \boldsymbol{E}_1(5) = \begin{pmatrix} 5 & 0 & 0 \\ 0 & 1 & 0 \\ 0 & 0 & 1 \end{pmatrix}.$$

Both matrices are symmetric. It is easy to show that $\boldsymbol{E}_{23}^2 = \boldsymbol{I}_3$. The matrix $\boldsymbol{E}_1(5)$ is diagonal and hence its inverse is $\boldsymbol{E}_1(1/5)$. Now consider

$$\boldsymbol{E}_2(4|1) = \begin{pmatrix} 1 & 0 & 0 \\ 4 & 1 & 0 \\ 0 & 0 & 1 \end{pmatrix}, \quad \boldsymbol{E}_1(4|2) = \begin{pmatrix} 1 & 4 & 0 \\ 0 & 1 & 0 \\ 0 & 0 & 1 \end{pmatrix},$$

and

$$\boldsymbol{E}_2(0|1) = \begin{pmatrix} 1 & 0 & 0 \\ 0 & 1 & 0 \\ 0 & 0 & 1 \end{pmatrix}.$$

We see that $\boldsymbol{E}_2'(4|1) = \boldsymbol{E}_1(4|2)$ and $\boldsymbol{E}_2'(0|1) = \boldsymbol{E}_1(0|2) = \boldsymbol{I}_3$. The inverses follow by direct computation.

Exercise 6.8 (Do elementary matrices commute?)
(a) Find the matrix E which, when postmultiplied by

$$A = \begin{pmatrix} 1 & 2 & 3 \\ 4 & 5 & 6 \end{pmatrix},$$

interchanges rows 1 and 2, then multiplies row 2 by 5. Does the order of the two operations matter?
(b) Find the matrix E which, when postmultiplied by A, interchanges rows 1 and 2, then adds 3 times row 1 to row 2. Does the order of the operations matter?
(c) Do elementary matrices commute?

Solution
(a) We have

$$E_2(5)E_{12}A = \begin{pmatrix} 1 & 0 \\ 0 & 5 \end{pmatrix}\begin{pmatrix} 0 & 1 \\ 1 & 0 \end{pmatrix}\begin{pmatrix} 1 & 2 & 3 \\ 4 & 5 & 6 \end{pmatrix} = \begin{pmatrix} 4 & 5 & 6 \\ 5 & 10 & 15 \end{pmatrix}$$
$$\neq \begin{pmatrix} 20 & 25 & 30 \\ 1 & 2 & 3 \end{pmatrix} = E_{12}E_2(5)A.$$

This is because

$$E_2(5)E_{12} = \begin{pmatrix} 0 & 1 \\ 5 & 0 \end{pmatrix} \quad \text{and} \quad E_{12}E_2(5) = \begin{pmatrix} 0 & 5 \\ 1 & 0 \end{pmatrix}.$$

(b) Here,

$$E = E_2(3|1)E_{12} = \begin{pmatrix} 0 & 1 \\ 1 & 3 \end{pmatrix} \quad \text{and} \quad E_{12}E_2(3|1) = \begin{pmatrix} 3 & 1 \\ 1 & 0 \end{pmatrix}.$$

(c) No, they do not commute.

Exercise 6.9 (Determinant of an elementary matrix) Show that

$$|E_{ij}| = -1, \quad |E_i(\lambda)| = \lambda, \quad |E_i(\lambda|j)| = 1,$$

and hence that the determinant is nonzero and does not depend on the order of the matrix.

Solution
This follows from Exercises 4.32 and 4.34.

Exercise 6.10 (Elementary column operations) Let B be obtained from A by an elementary column operation. Show that $B = AF$ for some elementary matrix F.

Solution
If B is obtained from A by an elementary column operation, then B' is obtained from A' by an elementary row operation. Then, by Exercise 6.2, $B' = EA'$ for some elementary matrix E. Hence, $B = AE'$. Letting $F := E'$ and noting that F is an elementary matrix (Exercise 6.4), the result follows.

Exercise 6.11 (More elementary checks) For the 3×2 matrix of Exercise 6.1 find the 2×2 elementary column matrices $\boldsymbol{F}_{12}$, $\boldsymbol{F}_1(3)$, and $\boldsymbol{F}_2(5|1)$, and check that they perform the operations they are supposed to perform.

Solution
We have

$$\boldsymbol{AF}_{12} = \begin{pmatrix} 1 & 2 \\ 3 & 4 \\ 5 & 6 \end{pmatrix} \begin{pmatrix} 0 & 1 \\ 1 & 0 \end{pmatrix} = \begin{pmatrix} 2 & 1 \\ 4 & 3 \\ 6 & 5 \end{pmatrix},$$

$$\boldsymbol{AF}_1(3) = \begin{pmatrix} 1 & 2 \\ 3 & 4 \\ 5 & 6 \end{pmatrix} \begin{pmatrix} 3 & 0 \\ 0 & 1 \end{pmatrix} = \begin{pmatrix} 3 & 2 \\ 9 & 4 \\ 15 & 6 \end{pmatrix},$$

and

$$\boldsymbol{AF}_2(5|1) = \begin{pmatrix} 1 & 2 \\ 3 & 4 \\ 5 & 6 \end{pmatrix} \begin{pmatrix} 1 & 5 \\ 0 & 1 \end{pmatrix} = \begin{pmatrix} 1 & 7 \\ 3 & 19 \\ 5 & 31 \end{pmatrix}.$$

6.2 Echelon matrices

Exercise 6.12 (Rank of an echelon matrix) Let $\boldsymbol{H}$ be an echelon matrix. Show that $\operatorname{rk}(\boldsymbol{H})$ is equal to the number of nonzero rows in $\boldsymbol{H}$.

Solution
Let $\boldsymbol{H}$ be an $m \times n$ matrix and suppose there are r nonzero rows (a nonzero row is one that contains at least one nonzero element). We want to show that precisely r of the m rows of $\boldsymbol{H}$ are linearly independent. Now, $\operatorname{rk}(\boldsymbol{H})$ cannot be greater than r, because there are $m - r$ zero rows. Let $\boldsymbol{h}'_1, \dots, \boldsymbol{h}'_r$ denote the first r rows of $\boldsymbol{H}$ (the nonzero rows). We need to show that the equation $\sum_i \lambda_i \boldsymbol{h}_i = \boldsymbol{0}$ implies that $\lambda_1 = \lambda_2 = \dots = \lambda_r = 0$. If row $\boldsymbol{h}'_1$ has its leading 1 in column $\boldsymbol{c}_1$, then all other rows have zeros in this column. Hence, $\lambda_1 = 0$. In the same way, $\lambda_2 = \dots = \lambda_r = 0$. Therefore, the first r rows are linearly independent and $\operatorname{rk}(\boldsymbol{H}) = r$.

***Exercise 6.13 (Reduction to echelon form)** Show that every $m \times n$ matrix $\boldsymbol{A}$ can be reduced to echelon form by elementary row operations. In other words, show that for every $m \times n$ matrix $\boldsymbol{A}$, there exist a finite number of elementary $m \times m$ matrices $\boldsymbol{E}_1, \dots, \boldsymbol{E}_k$ such that

$$\boldsymbol{E}_k \boldsymbol{E}_{k-1} \dots \boldsymbol{E}_1 \boldsymbol{A} = \boldsymbol{H}$$

where the $m \times n$ matrix $\boldsymbol{H}$ is in echelon form.

Solution

The following solution is "constructive", that is, we do not only show that it is possible to find elementary matrices $\boldsymbol{E}_1, \ldots, \boldsymbol{E}_k$, but we also show how. The algorithm entails an iteration consisting of three steps.

For $i = 1, 2, \ldots, m$ do:
Step 1: Define j_i to be the first column that has at least one nonzero element below row $i-1$ ($j_i > j_{i-1}$, $j_0 := 0$). If there is no such column, then STOP.
Step 2: If $a_{i,j_i} = 0$, interchange row i with any row (with row index $> i$) having a nonzero element in column j_i.
Step 3: Reduce any other nonzero elements in column j_i (with row index $> i$) to zero by subtracting suitable multiples of row i from the other rows.

The resulting matrix is in echelon form except that the leading element (that is, the first nonzero element) in each row is not yet 1. So, for $i = 1, 2, \ldots, m$, we divide each nonzero row by its leading element. The matrix is now in echelon form.

Exercise 6.14 (Echelon example, 1) Reduce the 3×5 matrix

$$\boldsymbol{A} = \begin{pmatrix} 0 & 0 & 1 & 2 & 3 \\ 2 & 4 & -2 & 0 & 4 \\ 2 & 4 & -1 & 2 & 7 \end{pmatrix}$$

to echelon forms through a series of elementary row operations.

Solution

We follow precisely the algorithm described in the solution of Exercise 6.13.

$i = 1$, step 1: $j_1 = 1$
$i = 1$, step 2: Since $a_{11} = 0$, we interchange rows 1 and 2:

$$\boldsymbol{A}_2 := \boldsymbol{E}_{12}\boldsymbol{A} = \begin{pmatrix} \textcircled{2} & 4 & -2 & 0 & 4 \\ 0 & 0 & 1 & 2 & 3 \\ 2 & 4 & -1 & 2 & 7 \end{pmatrix}.$$

$i = 1$, step 3: Subtract row 1 from row 3:

$$\boldsymbol{A}_3 := \boldsymbol{E}_3(-1|1)\boldsymbol{A}_2 = \begin{pmatrix} \textcircled{2} & 4 & -2 & 0 & 4 \\ 0 & 0 & \textcircled{1} & 2 & 3 \\ 0 & 0 & 1 & 2 & 3 \end{pmatrix}.$$

$i = 2$, step 1: $j_2 = 3$.
$i = 2$, step 2: $a_{23} \neq 0$, so no action required.

$\underline{i = 2, \text{ step 3:}}$ Subtract row 2 from row 3:

$$A_4 := E_3(-1|2)A_3 = \begin{pmatrix} ② & 4 & -2 & 0 & 4 \\ 0 & 0 & ① & 2 & 3 \\ 0 & 0 & 0 & 0 & 0 \end{pmatrix}.$$

$\underline{i = 3, \text{ step 1:}}$ STOP.

Finally, divide row 1 by 2:

$$A_5 := E_1(1/2)A_4 = \begin{pmatrix} ① & 2 & -1 & 0 & 2 \\ 0 & 0 & ① & 2 & 3 \\ 0 & 0 & 0 & 0 & 0 \end{pmatrix}.$$

Hence,

$$H := A_5 := E_1(1/2)E_3(-1|2)E_3(-1|1)E_{12}A.$$

Exercise 6.15 (Echelon example, 2) Let H be the 3×5 echelon matrix of Exercise 6.14. Show, through a series of elementary column operations, that we can reduce H to the form

$$\begin{pmatrix} 1 & 0 & 0 & 0 & 0 \\ 0 & 1 & 0 & 0 & 0 \\ 0 & 0 & 0 & 0 & 0 \end{pmatrix}.$$

Solution

First interchange columns 2 and 3:

$$H_2 := HF_{23} = \begin{pmatrix} 1 & -1 & 2 & 0 & 2 \\ 0 & 1 & 0 & 2 & 3 \\ 0 & 0 & 0 & 0 & 0 \end{pmatrix}.$$

Then, use column 1 to produce zeros in the first row of columns 2, 3, and 5:

$$H_3 := H_2F_2(1|1)F_3(-2|1)F_5(-2|1) = \begin{pmatrix} 1 & 0 & 0 & 0 & 0 \\ 0 & 1 & 0 & 2 & 3 \\ 0 & 0 & 0 & 0 & 0 \end{pmatrix}.$$

Finally, use column 2 to produce zeros in the second row of columns 4 and 5:

$$H_4 := H_3F_4(-2|2)F_5(-3|2) = \begin{pmatrix} 1 & 0 & 0 & 0 & 0 \\ 0 & 1 & 0 & 0 & 0 \\ 0 & 0 & 0 & 0 & 0 \end{pmatrix}.$$

Exercise 6.16 (Reduction from echelon to diagonal form) Show that every $m \times n$ echelon matrix H of rank r can be reduced to the $m \times n$ matrix

$$\begin{pmatrix} I_r & O \\ O & O \end{pmatrix}$$

by elementary column operations. That is, show that elementary $n \times n$ matrices $\boldsymbol{F}_1, \dots, \boldsymbol{F}_l$ exist such that

$$\boldsymbol{H}\boldsymbol{F}_1\boldsymbol{F}_2 \dots \boldsymbol{F}_l = \begin{pmatrix} \boldsymbol{I}_r & \mathrm{O} \\ \mathrm{O} & \mathrm{O} \end{pmatrix}.$$

Solution

The solution follows exactly the example of Exercise 6.15. First use elementary matrices $\boldsymbol{F}_i$ to transform $\boldsymbol{H}$ to the form

$$\boldsymbol{H}_2 := \begin{pmatrix} \boldsymbol{I}_r + \boldsymbol{U} & \boldsymbol{Q} \\ \mathrm{O} & \mathrm{O} \end{pmatrix},$$

where $\boldsymbol{U}$ is an upper triangular $r \times r$ matrix, and $\boldsymbol{Q}$ is an $r \times (m - r)$ matrix. Then, use column j ($j = 1, 2, \dots, r$) to produce zeros in the j-th row of $\boldsymbol{H}_2$.

Exercise 6.17 (Factorization using echelon matrices) Use Exercises 6.13 and 6.16 to show that every $m \times n$ matrix $\boldsymbol{A}$ of rank r can be represented as

$$\boldsymbol{E}\boldsymbol{A}\boldsymbol{F} = \begin{pmatrix} \boldsymbol{I}_r & \mathrm{O} \\ \mathrm{O} & \mathrm{O} \end{pmatrix}$$

where $\boldsymbol{E}$ and $\boldsymbol{F}$ are nonsingular matrices.

Solution

We know from Exercises 6.13 and 6.16, that

$$\boldsymbol{E}\boldsymbol{A} = \boldsymbol{H} \quad \text{and} \quad \boldsymbol{H}\boldsymbol{F} = \begin{pmatrix} \boldsymbol{I}_r & \mathrm{O} \\ \mathrm{O} & \mathrm{O} \end{pmatrix},$$

where $\boldsymbol{E}$ ($m \times m$) and $\boldsymbol{F}$ ($n \times n$) are products of elementary matrices, and $\boldsymbol{H}$ is an $m \times n$ echelon matrix. Hence,

$$\boldsymbol{E}\boldsymbol{A}\boldsymbol{F} = \boldsymbol{H}\boldsymbol{F} = \begin{pmatrix} \boldsymbol{I}_r & \mathrm{O} \\ \mathrm{O} & \mathrm{O} \end{pmatrix}.$$

The matrices $\boldsymbol{E}$ and $\boldsymbol{F}$ are nonsingular, because every elementary matrix is nonsingular and hence products of elementary matrices are nonsingular too.

Exercise 6.18 (A property of nonsingular matrices)

(a) If $\boldsymbol{A}$ is a nonsingular $n \times n$ matrix, show that nonsingular matrices $\boldsymbol{E}$ and $\boldsymbol{F}$ exist such that $\boldsymbol{E}\boldsymbol{A}\boldsymbol{F} = \boldsymbol{I}_n$.

(b) Hence, show that every nonsingular matrix can be written as the product of elementary matrices.

Solution

Part (a) is an immediate consequence of Exercise 6.17, since $r = n$ in the nonsingular case. Further, since $\boldsymbol{E}\boldsymbol{A}\boldsymbol{F} = \boldsymbol{I}_n$, we obtain

$$\boldsymbol{A} = \boldsymbol{E}^{-1}\boldsymbol{F}^{-1} = (\boldsymbol{E}_k\boldsymbol{E}_{k-1} \dots \boldsymbol{E}_1)^{-1} (\boldsymbol{F}_1\boldsymbol{F}_2 \dots \boldsymbol{F}_l)^{-1} = \boldsymbol{E}_1^{-1} \dots \boldsymbol{E}_k^{-1}\boldsymbol{F}_l^{-1} \dots \boldsymbol{F}_1^{-1},$$

which is a product of elementary matrices. (Remember from Exercise 6.5 that the inverse of an elementary matrix is elementary as well.)

Exercise 6.19 (Equivalence) Let $\boldsymbol{A}$ and $\boldsymbol{B}$ be matrices of order $m \times n$. Show that nonsingular matrices $\boldsymbol{E}$ and $\boldsymbol{F}$ exist such that $\boldsymbol{B} = \boldsymbol{EAF}$ if and only if $\operatorname{rk}(\boldsymbol{A}) = \operatorname{rk}(\boldsymbol{B})$. (Two matrices of the same order and the same rank are said to be *equivalent*.)

Solution
If $\boldsymbol{E}$ and $\boldsymbol{F}$ are nonsingular, then $\operatorname{rk}(\boldsymbol{EAF}) = \operatorname{rk}(\boldsymbol{A})$. Conversely, if $\operatorname{rk}(\boldsymbol{A}) = \operatorname{rk}(\boldsymbol{B}) = r$, then

$$\boldsymbol{E}_1\boldsymbol{A}\boldsymbol{F}_1 = \begin{pmatrix} \boldsymbol{I}_r & \mathbf{O} \\ \mathbf{O} & \mathbf{O} \end{pmatrix} = \boldsymbol{E}_2\boldsymbol{B}\boldsymbol{F}_2$$

for some nonsingular matrices $\boldsymbol{E}_1$, $\boldsymbol{E}_2$, $\boldsymbol{F}_1$, $\boldsymbol{F}_2$ (Exercise 6.17). Hence, $\boldsymbol{B} = \boldsymbol{E}_2^{-1}\boldsymbol{E}_1\boldsymbol{A}\boldsymbol{F}_1\boldsymbol{F}_2^{-1}$. Letting $\boldsymbol{E} := \boldsymbol{E}_2^{-1}\boldsymbol{E}_1$, $\boldsymbol{F} := \boldsymbol{F}_1\boldsymbol{F}_2^{-1}$, it follows that $\boldsymbol{B} = \boldsymbol{EAF}$ and that $\boldsymbol{E}$ and $\boldsymbol{F}$ are nonsingular.

Exercise 6.20 (Rank through echelon) Find the rank of the matrix

$$\boldsymbol{A} = \begin{pmatrix} 2 & 1 & 4 & 0 & 6 & 7 & 10 \\ 3 & 5 & 9 & 1 & 0 & 4 & 3 \\ 7 & 7 & 3 & 2 & 8 & 1 & 1 \\ -9 & -8 & 7 & -3 & -10 & 9 & 11 \\ 4 & 2 & -20 & 2 & 4 & -20 & -24 \end{pmatrix}$$

by reducing it to echelon form.

Solution
By successive reduction we first obtain

$$\boldsymbol{A}_2 = \begin{pmatrix} \circled{2} & 1 & 4 & 0 & 6 & 7 & 10 \\ 0 & \circled{3.5} & 3 & 1 & -9 & -6.5 & -12 \\ 0 & 3.5 & -11 & 2 & -13 & -23.5 & -34 \\ 0 & -3.5 & 25 & -3 & 17 & 40.5 & 56 \\ 0 & 0 & -28 & 2 & -8 & -34 & -44 \end{pmatrix}$$

and then, annihilating the second column,

$$\boldsymbol{A}_3 = \begin{pmatrix} \circled{2} & 1 & 4 & 0 & 6 & 7 & 10 \\ 0 & \circled{3.5} & 3 & 1 & -9 & -6.5 & -12 \\ 0 & 0 & \circled{-14} & 1 & -4 & -17 & -22 \\ 0 & 0 & 28 & -2 & 8 & 34 & 44 \\ 0 & 0 & -28 & 2 & -8 & -34 & -44 \end{pmatrix}.$$

We can reduce this further (the last two rows can be made zero), but it is already apparent that $\operatorname{rk}(\boldsymbol{A}_3) = 3$, and hence $\operatorname{rk}(\boldsymbol{A}) = 3$.

Exercise 6.21 (Extending the echelon) Suppose we wish to reduce $\boldsymbol{A}$ to echelon form and, at the same time, find the matrix $\boldsymbol{E}$ which carries out the reduction. How can this be achieved?

Solution
Suppose that $\boldsymbol{EA} = \boldsymbol{H}$. Then, $\boldsymbol{E}(\boldsymbol{A} : \boldsymbol{I}) = (\boldsymbol{H} : \boldsymbol{E})$. So, instead of reducing the $m \times n$ matrix $\boldsymbol{A}$ to echelon form, we reduce the $m \times (n+m)$ matrix $(\boldsymbol{A} : \boldsymbol{I}_m)$ to echelon form.

Exercise 6.22 (Inverse by echelon: theory)
(a) If $\boldsymbol{A}$ is a nonsingular $n \times n$ matrix, show that there exists a matrix $\boldsymbol{E}$ such that $\boldsymbol{EA} = \boldsymbol{I}_n$, where $\boldsymbol{E}$ is the product of elementary matrices.
(b) Use (a) and Exercise 6.21 to develop a procedure for finding the inverse of a nonsingular matrix.

Solution
(a) From Exercise 6.18 we can write $\boldsymbol{EAF} = \boldsymbol{I}_n$. Now premultiply by $\boldsymbol{F}$ and postmultiply by $\boldsymbol{F}^{-1}$. This gives $\boldsymbol{FEA} = \boldsymbol{I}_n$. The matrix $\boldsymbol{FE}$ is a product of elementary matrices.
(b) It follows from (a) that we can reduce $\boldsymbol{A}$ to $\boldsymbol{I}_n$, say through $\boldsymbol{EA} = \boldsymbol{I}_n$ (where this $\boldsymbol{E}$ is not the same as the one in (a)). Hence,

$$\boldsymbol{E}(\boldsymbol{A} : \boldsymbol{I}_n) = (\boldsymbol{EA} : \boldsymbol{E}) = (\boldsymbol{I} : \boldsymbol{A}^{-1}).$$

So, if we reduce $(\boldsymbol{A} : \boldsymbol{I}_n)$ to echelon form, such that the first block is the identity matrix, then the second block will be the inverse.

Exercise 6.23 (Inverse by echelon: practice) Use the method of Exercise 6.22 to find the inverse of

$$\boldsymbol{A} = \begin{pmatrix} 0 & 1 & 1 \\ 1 & 1 & 1 \\ 3 & 4 & 3 \end{pmatrix}.$$

Solution
We form the extended matrix

$$\widetilde{\boldsymbol{A}}_1 = \left(\begin{array}{ccc|ccc} 0 & 1 & 1 & 1 & 0 & 0 \\ 1 & 1 & 1 & 0 & 1 & 0 \\ 3 & 4 & 3 & 0 & 0 & 1 \end{array}\right).$$

Interchange rows 1 and 2:

$$\widetilde{\boldsymbol{A}}_2 = \left(\begin{array}{ccc|ccc} \textcircled{1} & 1 & 1 & 0 & 1 & 0 \\ 0 & 1 & 1 & 1 & 0 & 0 \\ 3 & 4 & 3 & 0 & 0 & 1 \end{array}\right).$$

Subtract 3 times row 1 from row 3:

$$\widetilde{\boldsymbol{A}}_3 = \left(\begin{array}{ccc|ccc} \textcircled{1} & 1 & 1 & 0 & 1 & 0 \\ 0 & \textcircled{1} & 1 & 1 & 0 & 0 \\ 0 & 1 & 0 & 0 & -3 & 1 \end{array}\right).$$

Subtract row 2 from row 3, and multiply row 3 by -1:

$$\widetilde{\boldsymbol{A}}_4 = \left(\begin{array}{ccc|ccc} \textcircled{1} & 1 & 1 & 0 & 1 & 0 \\ 0 & \textcircled{1} & 1 & 1 & 0 & 0 \\ 0 & 0 & \textcircled{1} & 1 & 3 & -1 \end{array}\right).$$

The matrix $\boldsymbol{A}$ is now in echelon form. To reduce further we subtract row 3 from rows 1 and 2:

$$\widetilde{\boldsymbol{A}}_5 = \left(\begin{array}{ccc|ccc} 1 & 1 & 0 & -1 & -2 & 1 \\ 0 & 1 & 0 & 0 & -3 & 1 \\ 0 & 0 & 1 & 1 & 3 & -1 \end{array}\right).$$

And, finally, we subtract row 2 from row 1:

$$\widetilde{\boldsymbol{A}}_6 = \left(\begin{array}{ccc|ccc} 1 & 0 & 0 & -1 & 1 & 0 \\ 0 & 1 & 0 & 0 & -3 & 1 \\ 0 & 0 & 1 & 1 & 3 & -1 \end{array}\right).$$

Hence,

$$\boldsymbol{A}^{-1} = \begin{pmatrix} -1 & 1 & 0 \\ 0 & -3 & 1 \\ 1 & 3 & -1 \end{pmatrix}.$$

6.3 Gaussian elimination

Exercise 6.24 (A problem posed by Euler) A Swiss farmer buys sheep, goats, and hogs, totalling 100 in number, for 100 crowns. The sheep cost him $\frac{1}{2}$ a crown apiece; the goats $1\frac{1}{3}$ crowns; and the hogs $3\frac{1}{2}$ crowns. How many had he of each?

Solution

Denote the number of sheep, goats, and hogs by x_1, x_2, and x_3. We need to solve the equation

$$\begin{pmatrix} 1 & 1 & 1 \\ 1/2 & 4/3 & 7/2 \end{pmatrix} \begin{pmatrix} x_1 \\ x_2 \\ x_3 \end{pmatrix} = \begin{pmatrix} 100 \\ 100 \end{pmatrix}.$$

We have three unknowns and only two equations. By subtracting $1/2$ times the first equation from the second equation, and then multiplying the second equation by $6/5$, we obtain

$$\begin{pmatrix} 1 & 1 & 1 \\ 0 & 1 & 3.6 \end{pmatrix} \begin{pmatrix} x_1 \\ x_2 \\ x_3 \end{pmatrix} = \begin{pmatrix} 100 \\ 60 \end{pmatrix}.$$

The matrix is now in echelon form. We cannot solve x_1, x_2, and x_3, but if we think of x_3 as a "free" parameter, say $x_3 = \lambda$, then we can express x_2 and x_1 in terms of λ:

$$x_2 = 60 - 3.6\lambda, \quad x_1 = 100 - \lambda - x_2 = 40 + 2.6\lambda.$$

Hence,

$$(x_1, x_2, x_3) = (40, 60, 0) + \lambda(2.6, -3.6, 1).$$

However, since we are dealing with animals, we do in fact have additional information on x_1, x_2, and x_3. First, we know that $x_1 \geq 0$, $x_2 \geq 0$, $x_3 \geq 0$. This implies $0 \leq \lambda \leq 16\frac{2}{3}$. Second, all three x_i must be integers. This gives four solutions, for $\lambda = 0, 5, 10$, and 15, namely: (40, 60, 0), (53, 42, 5), (66, 24, 10), and (79, 6, 15).

Exercise 6.25 (Euler's problem, continued) Suppose Euler had forgotten to provide the information: "He had eleven more sheep than goats." Now solve this problem again.

Solution

Of the previous four solutions, only the second qualifies. Hence, the solution is (53, 42, 5). Let us now proceed to solve the problem without this previous knowledge. We write the three equations as

$$\begin{pmatrix} 1 & 1 & 1 \\ 1/2 & 4/3 & 7/2 \\ 1 & -1 & 0 \end{pmatrix} \begin{pmatrix} x_1 \\ x_2 \\ x_3 \end{pmatrix} = \begin{pmatrix} 100 \\ 100 \\ 11 \end{pmatrix}.$$

Subtract (a multiple of) row 1 from rows 2 and 3, thus putting zeros below the first leading element:

$$\begin{pmatrix} 1 & 1 & 1 \\ 0 & 5/6 & 3 \\ 0 & -2 & -1 \end{pmatrix} \begin{pmatrix} x_1 \\ x_2 \\ x_3 \end{pmatrix} = \begin{pmatrix} 100 \\ 50 \\ -89 \end{pmatrix}.$$

Next add $12/5$ times row 2 to row 3:

$$\begin{pmatrix} 1 & 1 & 1 \\ 0 & 5/6 & 3 \\ 0 & 0 & 31/5 \end{pmatrix} \begin{pmatrix} x_1 \\ x_2 \\ x_3 \end{pmatrix} = \begin{pmatrix} 100 \\ 50 \\ 31 \end{pmatrix}.$$

Multiply row 2 by $6/5$ and row 3 by $5/31$. This produces the echelon form:

$$\begin{pmatrix} 1 & 1 & 1 \\ 0 & 1 & 3.6 \\ 0 & 0 & 1 \end{pmatrix} \begin{pmatrix} x_1 \\ x_2 \\ x_3 \end{pmatrix} = \begin{pmatrix} 100 \\ 60 \\ 5 \end{pmatrix}.$$

This is the end of stage A, called forward elimination. Now comes stage B, backward elimination. Subtract appropriate multiples of row 3 from rows 1 and 2:

$$\begin{pmatrix} 1 & 1 & 0 \\ 0 & 1 & 0 \\ 0 & 0 & 1 \end{pmatrix} \begin{pmatrix} x_1 \\ x_2 \\ x_3 \end{pmatrix} = \begin{pmatrix} 95 \\ 42 \\ 5 \end{pmatrix}.$$

Finally, subtract row 2 from row 1:

$$\begin{pmatrix} 1 & 0 & 0 \\ 0 & 1 & 0 \\ 0 & 0 & 1 \end{pmatrix} \begin{pmatrix} x_1 \\ x_2 \\ x_3 \end{pmatrix} = \begin{pmatrix} 53 \\ 42 \\ 5 \end{pmatrix}.$$

The procedure spelled out above is called *Gaussian elimination*.

Exercise 6.26 (The Gaussian elimination algorithm) Use the example of Exercise 6.25 and the theoretical result of Exercise 6.22 to describe a formal solution algorithm, the so-called *Gaussian elimination method*.

Solution

Let $\boldsymbol{A}$ be a nonsingular matrix and consider the equation $\boldsymbol{Ax} = \boldsymbol{b}$. We want to solve $\boldsymbol{x}$. We use the fact, established in Exercise 6.22, that there exists a nonsingular matrix $\boldsymbol{E}$ (a product of elementary matrices) such that $\boldsymbol{EA} = \boldsymbol{I}$. In fact, we think of $\boldsymbol{E}$ as the product of two matrices, $\boldsymbol{E} = \boldsymbol{E}_2\boldsymbol{E}_1$, such that $\boldsymbol{E}_1\boldsymbol{A} = \boldsymbol{H}$ (echelon form) and $\boldsymbol{E}_2\boldsymbol{H} = \boldsymbol{I}$.

Consider the *augmented matrix* $(\boldsymbol{A} : \boldsymbol{b})$. In stage A (forward elimination) we perform a series of elementary row operations such that $\boldsymbol{E}_1(\boldsymbol{A} : \boldsymbol{b}) = (\boldsymbol{H} : \boldsymbol{E}_1\boldsymbol{b})$. This is achieved by putting zeros *below* each pivot, working from the top row down. In stage B (backward elimination) we perform further elementary row operations such that $\boldsymbol{E}_2(\boldsymbol{H} : \boldsymbol{E}_1\boldsymbol{b}) = (\boldsymbol{I} : \boldsymbol{E}_2\boldsymbol{E}_1\boldsymbol{b})$. This is achieved by putting zeros *above* each pivot, working from the bottom row up. The vector $\boldsymbol{x} = \boldsymbol{E}_2\boldsymbol{E}_1\boldsymbol{b}$ is the required solution. This follows immediately from the fact that $\boldsymbol{E}_2\boldsymbol{E}_1\boldsymbol{A} = \boldsymbol{E}_2\boldsymbol{H} = \boldsymbol{I}$, so that $\boldsymbol{A}^{-1} = \boldsymbol{E}_2\boldsymbol{E}_1$ and hence $\boldsymbol{A}^{-1}\boldsymbol{b} = \boldsymbol{E}_2\boldsymbol{E}_1\boldsymbol{b}$.

Exercise 6.27 (Examples of Gauss's algorithm) Solve the equations

$$\begin{pmatrix} 2 & 1 & -3 \\ 5 & 2 & -6 \\ 3 & -1 & -4 \end{pmatrix} \begin{pmatrix} x_1 \\ x_2 \\ x_3 \end{pmatrix} = \begin{pmatrix} 1 \\ 5 \\ 7 \end{pmatrix} \quad \text{and} \quad \begin{pmatrix} 2 & 1 & -2 \\ 3 & 2 & 2 \\ 5 & 4 & 3 \end{pmatrix} \begin{pmatrix} x_1 \\ x_2 \\ x_3 \end{pmatrix} = \begin{pmatrix} 10 \\ 1 \\ 4 \end{pmatrix}$$

by Gaussian elimination.

Solution

We perform row operations on the augmented matrices

$$\begin{pmatrix} 2 & 1 & -3 & 1 \\ 5 & 2 & -6 & 5 \\ 3 & -1 & -4 & 7 \end{pmatrix} \quad \text{and} \quad \begin{pmatrix} 2 & 1 & -2 & 10 \\ 3 & 2 & 2 & 1 \\ 5 & 4 & 3 & 4 \end{pmatrix}.$$

This produces, by forward elimination, the matrix $\boldsymbol{A}$ in echelon form:

$$\begin{pmatrix} 1 & 0.5 & -1.5 & 0.5 \\ 0 & 1 & -3 & -5 \\ 0 & 0 & 1 & 1 \end{pmatrix} \quad \text{and} \quad \begin{pmatrix} 1 & 0.5 & -1 & 5 \\ 0 & 1 & 10 & -28 \\ 0 & 0 & 1 & -3 \end{pmatrix}.$$

Then, by backward elimination,

$$\begin{pmatrix} 1 & 0 & 0 & 3 \\ 0 & 1 & 0 & -2 \\ 0 & 0 & 1 & 1 \end{pmatrix} \quad \text{and} \quad \begin{pmatrix} 1 & 0 & 0 & 1 \\ 0 & 1 & 0 & 2 \\ 0 & 0 & 1 & -3 \end{pmatrix}.$$

Hence, the solutions are $(x_1, x_2, x_3) = (3, -2, 1)$ and $(1, 2, -3)$, respectively.

Exercise 6.28 (Cramer's rule) Let $\boldsymbol{A} = (a_{ij})$ be a square matrix of order n, and let $\boldsymbol{A}_{(ij)}$ be the $(n-1) \times (n-1)$ matrix obtained from $\boldsymbol{A}$ by deleting row i and column j. Recall from Chapter 4 that the cofactor of a_{ij} is given by $c_{ij} := (-1)^{i+j}|\boldsymbol{A}_{(ij)}|$. Let $\boldsymbol{C} = (c_{ij})$ be the $n \times n$ matrix of cofactors. If $\boldsymbol{A}$ is nonsingular, then Exercise 4.37(c) tells us that $\boldsymbol{A}^{-1} = |\boldsymbol{A}|^{-1}\boldsymbol{C}'$. Now consider the equation $\boldsymbol{A}\boldsymbol{x} = \boldsymbol{b}$.
(a) If $\boldsymbol{A}$ is nonsingular, show that

$$x_j = \frac{\sum_{i=1}^{n} b_i c_{ij}}{|\boldsymbol{A}|} \quad (j = 1, \dots, n).$$

(b) Let $\boldsymbol{A}^{(j)}$ denote the matrix obtained from $\boldsymbol{A}$ when the j-th column is replaced by $\boldsymbol{b}$. Show that $x_j = |\boldsymbol{A}^{(j)}|/|\boldsymbol{A}|$ for $j = 1, \dots, n$ (*Cramer*).

Solution
(a) Since $\boldsymbol{x} = \boldsymbol{A}^{-1}\boldsymbol{b} = |\boldsymbol{A}|^{-1}\boldsymbol{C}'\boldsymbol{b}$, we obtain

$$x_j = \frac{\boldsymbol{e}_j'\boldsymbol{C}'\boldsymbol{b}}{|\boldsymbol{A}|} = \frac{\sum_{i=1}^{n} b_i c_{ij}}{|\boldsymbol{A}|}.$$

(b) Since $\boldsymbol{C}'\boldsymbol{A} = |\boldsymbol{A}|\boldsymbol{I}_n$, all diagonal elements of $\boldsymbol{C}'\boldsymbol{A}$ are equal to $|\boldsymbol{A}|$, that is, $|\boldsymbol{A}| = \sum_i a_{ij}c_{ij}$ $(j = 1, \dots, n)$. This is called the expansion of $|\boldsymbol{A}|$ by the j-th column (Exercise 4.36). Now consider the expansion of $|\boldsymbol{A}^{(j)}|$ by the j-th column (that is, $\boldsymbol{b}$). The cofactor of the ij-th element of $\boldsymbol{A}^{(j)}$ is obtained by deleting the j-th column of $\boldsymbol{A}^{(j)}$ and the i-th row. Hence, it is equal to c_{ij}, the cofactor of the ij-th element of $\boldsymbol{A}$. As a consequence, $|\boldsymbol{A}^{(j)}| = \sum_i b_i c_{ij}$, and the result follows from (a). (Cramer's rule is of great theoretical importance; it is *not*, however, an efficient way to solve linear equations.)

Exercise 6.29 (Cramer's rule in practice) Solve the two equations of Exercise 6.27 by Cramer's rule.

Solution
For the first equation we have

$$|\boldsymbol{A}^{(1)}| = \begin{vmatrix} 1 & 1 & -3 \\ 5 & 2 & -6 \\ 7 & -1 & -4 \end{vmatrix} = 21, \quad |\boldsymbol{A}^{(2)}| = \begin{vmatrix} 2 & 1 & -3 \\ 5 & 5 & -6 \\ 3 & 7 & -4 \end{vmatrix} = -14,$$

$$|\boldsymbol{A}^{(3)}| = \begin{vmatrix} 2 & 1 & 1 \\ 5 & 2 & 5 \\ 3 & -1 & 7 \end{vmatrix} = 7, \quad |\boldsymbol{A}| = \begin{vmatrix} 2 & 1 & -3 \\ 5 & 2 & -6 \\ 3 & -1 & -4 \end{vmatrix} = 7.$$

Hence, $x_1 = 3$, $x_2 = -2$, $x_3 = 1$. Similarly, for the second equation, $|\boldsymbol{A}^{(1)}| = -7$, $|\boldsymbol{A}^{(2)}| = -14$, $|\boldsymbol{A}^{(3)}| = 21$, and $|\boldsymbol{A}| = -7$, implying that $x_1 = 1$, $x_2 = 2$, $x_3 = -3$.

***Exercise 6.30 (Fitting a polynomial)** Suppose we wish to fit an n-th degree polynomial $p(x) := \sum_{j=0}^{n} a_j x^j$ to $n+1$ (possibly unevenly spaced) data points. Our data consist of $x_1, \dots, x_{n+1}$ and $y_1, \dots, y_{n+1}$, where $y_i := p(x_i)$ for $i = 1, \dots, n+1$, and the x_i are all distinct. Determine the coefficients $a_0, a_1, \dots, a_n$.

Solution
We write

$$\begin{aligned} a_0 + a_1 x_1 + \dots + a_n x_1^n &= y_1 \\ a_0 + a_1 x_2 + \dots + a_n x_2^n &= y_2 \\ &\vdots \\ a_0 + a_1 x_{n+1} + \dots + a_n x_{n+1}^n &= y_{n+1}. \end{aligned}$$

Now consider

$$\boldsymbol{V} := \begin{pmatrix} 1 & 1 & \dots & 1 \\ x_1 & x_2 & \dots & x_{n+1} \\ x_1^2 & x_2^2 & \dots & x_{n+1}^2 \\ \vdots & \vdots & & \vdots \\ x_1^n & x_2^n & \dots & x_{n+1}^n \end{pmatrix}, \quad \boldsymbol{y} := \begin{pmatrix} y_1 \\ y_2 \\ \vdots \\ y_{n+1} \end{pmatrix}, \quad \boldsymbol{a} := \begin{pmatrix} a_0 \\ a_1 \\ \vdots \\ a_n \end{pmatrix},$$

where $\boldsymbol{V}$ is the $(n+1) \times (n+1)$ Vandermonde matrix. We know from Exercise 4.41 that $\boldsymbol{V}$ is nonsingular, because $x_1, x_2, \dots, x_{n+1}$ are all distinct, and that its determinant is given by $|\boldsymbol{V}| = \prod_{j<i}(x_i - x_j)$. Hence, the system of $n+1$ equations can be written as $\boldsymbol{V}'\boldsymbol{a} = \boldsymbol{y}$ with solution $\boldsymbol{a} = \boldsymbol{V}'^{-1}\boldsymbol{y}$.

Now let η_j be the determinant of the $(n+1) \times (n+1)$ matrix obtained from $\boldsymbol{V}$ by replacing the $(j+1)$-th *row* of $\boldsymbol{V}$ by $\boldsymbol{y}'$. Then Cramer's rule gives $a_j = \eta_j / |\boldsymbol{V}|$ for $j = 0, 1, \dots, n$ (Exercise 6.28).

Exercise 6.31 (Linear independence of powers) Consider the Hilbert space of all polynomials $p(x) := a_0 + a_1 x + \dots + a_n x^n$ (of all degrees).
(a) Show that the functions $1, x, \dots, x^n$ are linearly independent for every $n = 1, 2, \dots$
(b) Show that this space is infinite dimensional.

Solution
(a) Suppose a relation $a_0 + a_1x + \cdots + a_nx^n = 0$ holds. Successively setting x equal to distinct values $x_1, x_2, \dots, x_{n+1}$, we obtain the system

$$a_0 + a_1x_1 + \cdots + a_nx_1^n = 0$$
$$a_0 + a_1x_2 + \cdots + a_nx_2^n = 0$$
$$\vdots$$
$$a_0 + a_1x_{n+1} + \cdots + a_nx_{n+1}^n = 0,$$

that is, $\boldsymbol{V}'\boldsymbol{a} = \boldsymbol{0}$, using the notation of Exercise 6.30. Since $\boldsymbol{V}$ is nonsingular, this implies that $\boldsymbol{a} = \boldsymbol{0}$. Hence, the only numbers that solve $a_0 + a_1x + \cdots + a_nx^n = 0$ are $a_0 = a_1 = \cdots = a_n = 0$, thus establishing the linear independence.
(b) There is no finite n for which the Vandermonde determinant is zero. Hence, the space is infinite dimensional.

6.4 Homogeneous equations

Exercise 6.32 (One or infinitely many solutions) Consider the homogeneous equation $\boldsymbol{Ax} = \boldsymbol{0}$.
(a) Show that there always exists a solution for $\boldsymbol{x}$.
(b) If there exist two solutions, then show there are infinitely many.

Solution
(a) Clearly $\boldsymbol{x} = \boldsymbol{0}$ is always a solution, called the *trivial* solution.
(b) Suppose $\boldsymbol{x}_1$ and $\boldsymbol{x}_2$ are two solutions. Then $\boldsymbol{Ax}_1 = \boldsymbol{Ax}_2 = \boldsymbol{0}$, and, for any λ and μ, the vector $\boldsymbol{x} := \lambda\boldsymbol{x}_1 + \mu\boldsymbol{x}_2$ is also a solution.

Exercise 6.33 (Existence of nontrivial solutions) Naturally the question arises under what conditions the homogeneous equation $\boldsymbol{Ax} = \boldsymbol{0}$ possesses nontrivial solutions.
(a) Show that nontrivial solutions exist if and only if $\text{rk}(\boldsymbol{A}) < n$, where n denotes the number of columns of $\boldsymbol{A}$.
(b) Hence, show that, if $\text{rk}(\boldsymbol{A}) < n$, infinitely many solutions exist.

Solution
(a) If $\text{rk}(\boldsymbol{A}) = n$, then $\boldsymbol{Ax} = \boldsymbol{0}$ implies that $\boldsymbol{A}'\boldsymbol{Ax} = \boldsymbol{0}$, and hence that $\boldsymbol{x} = \boldsymbol{0}$, since $\boldsymbol{A}'\boldsymbol{A}$ is nonsingular. Thus, if a nontrivial solution exists, then $\text{rk}(\boldsymbol{A}) < n$. Conversely, if $\text{rk}(\boldsymbol{A}) < n$, then the n columns $\boldsymbol{a}_1, \boldsymbol{a}_2, \dots, \boldsymbol{a}_n$ of $\boldsymbol{A}$ are linearly dependent, and hence there exist numbers $x_1, x_2, \dots, x_n$ (not all zero) such that $x_1\boldsymbol{a}_1 + x_2\boldsymbol{a}_2 + \cdots + x_n\boldsymbol{a}_n = \boldsymbol{0}$, that is, such that $\boldsymbol{Ax} = \boldsymbol{0}$. Hence, a nontrivial solution exists.
(b) If $\boldsymbol{x} \neq \boldsymbol{0}$ is a solution, then $\lambda\boldsymbol{x}$ is also a solution for any scalar λ.

Exercise 6.34 (As many equations as unknowns) In the homogeneous equation $\boldsymbol{Ax} = \mathbf{0}$, suppose $\boldsymbol{A}$ is a square matrix. Show that nontrivial solutions exist if and only if $\boldsymbol{A}$ is singular.

Solution
This follows directly from Exercise 6.33.

Exercise 6.35 (Few equations, many unknowns) If there are fewer equations than unknowns in a homogeneous equation, show that a nontrivial solution always exists.

Solution
Let $\boldsymbol{Ax} = \mathbf{0}$, where $\boldsymbol{A}$ is an $m \times n$ matrix. If $m < n$, then $\text{rk}(\boldsymbol{A}) \leq m < n$. Hence, by Exercise 6.33, nontrivial solutions exist.

Exercise 6.36 (Kernel dimension) Let $\boldsymbol{A}$ be an $m \times n$ matrix.
(a) Show that there exists $n - \text{rk}(\boldsymbol{A})$ linearly independent vectors $\boldsymbol{y}$ satisfying $\boldsymbol{Ay} = \mathbf{0}$. [Hint: Use the concepts of column space and kernel.]
(b) In particular, when $\text{rk}(\boldsymbol{A}) = n$, show that the equation $\boldsymbol{Ay} = \mathbf{0}$ only has the trivial solution $\boldsymbol{y} = \mathbf{0}$. (Compare Exercise 6.33.)

Solution
(a) Exercise 4.4 proves that $\dim(\ker \boldsymbol{A}) = n - \dim(\text{col}\, \boldsymbol{A})$. Since $\dim(\text{col}\, \boldsymbol{A}) = \text{rk}(\boldsymbol{A})$, this means that the dimension of $\ker(\boldsymbol{A})$ is equal to $n - \text{rk}(\boldsymbol{A})$ and hence that there are $n - \text{rk}(\boldsymbol{A})$ linearly independent vectors $\boldsymbol{y}$ satisfying $\boldsymbol{Ay} = \mathbf{0}$.
(b) If $\text{rk}(\boldsymbol{A}) = n$ then (a) implies that there are no linearly independent vectors $\boldsymbol{y}$ satisfying $\boldsymbol{Ay} = \mathbf{0}$. In other words, that $\boldsymbol{y} = \mathbf{0}$ is the only solution.

Exercise 6.37 (Homogeneous example, 1) Find the solution(s) of the equations

$$x_1 + 3x_2 + 2x_3 = 0, \quad 2x_1 + 7x_2 + 3x_3 = 0.$$

Solution
Since there are fewer equations than unknowns, there exists a nontrivial solution. Transforming the matrix $\boldsymbol{A}$ to echelon form, we obtain

$$\begin{pmatrix} 1 & 3 & 2 \\ 2 & 7 & 3 \end{pmatrix} \mapsto \begin{pmatrix} 1 & 3 & 2 \\ 0 & 1 & -1 \end{pmatrix}.$$

Hence, the general solution is given by $(x_1, x_2, x_3) = \lambda(-5, 1, 1)$.

Exercise 6.38 (Homogeneous example, 2) Find the solution(s) of the equations

$$x_1 + 3x_2 = 0, \quad 2x_1 + kx_2 = 0.$$

Solution
Since $m = n$, there may only be the trivial solution $\boldsymbol{x} = \mathbf{0}$ (if $|\boldsymbol{A}| \neq 0$) or there may be nontrivial solutions (if $|\boldsymbol{A}| = 0$). Transform $\boldsymbol{A}$ to echelon form:

$$\begin{pmatrix} 1 & 3 \\ 2 & k \end{pmatrix} \mapsto \begin{pmatrix} 1 & 3 \\ 0 & k-6 \end{pmatrix}.$$

If $k \neq 6$, then $|\boldsymbol{A}| = k - 6 \neq 0$, and the only solution is $(x_1, x_2) = (0, 0)$. If $k = 6$, then the solution is given by $x_1 + 3x_2 = 0$, that is, $(x_1, x_2) = \lambda(-3, 1)$.

Exercise 6.39 (Homogeneous example, 3) Find the solution(s) of the equations

$$x_1 + 2x_2 = 0, \quad 3x_1 + 6x_2 = 0, \quad 2x_1 + kx_2 = 0.$$

Solution
Again, we transform $\boldsymbol{A}$ to echelon form:

$$\begin{pmatrix} 1 & 2 \\ 3 & 6 \\ 2 & k \end{pmatrix} \mapsto \begin{pmatrix} 1 & 2 \\ 0 & 0 \\ 0 & k-4 \end{pmatrix}.$$

If $k \neq 4$, then $\text{rk}(\boldsymbol{A}) = 2$, and the only solution is $(x_1, x_2) = (0, 0)$. If $k = 4$, then $\text{rk}(\boldsymbol{A}) = 1$, and the solution is given by $x_1 + 2x_2 = 0$, that is, $(x_1, x_2) = \lambda(-2, 1)$.

Exercise 6.40 (Homogeneous example, 4) Solve the homogeneous system of linear equations

$$\begin{aligned} x_1 - x_2 + 5x_3 - x_4 &= 0, \\ x_1 + x_2 - 2x_3 + 3x_4 &= 0, \\ 3x_1 - x_2 + 8x_3 + x_4 &= 0, \\ x_1 + 3x_2 - 9x_3 + 7x_4 &= 0. \end{aligned}$$

Solution
We transform the system to echelon form:

$$\begin{pmatrix} 1 & -1 & 5 & -1 \\ 1 & 1 & -2 & 3 \\ 3 & -1 & 8 & 1 \\ 1 & 3 & -9 & 7 \end{pmatrix} \mapsto \begin{pmatrix} 1 & -1 & 5 & -1 \\ 0 & 1 & -7/2 & 2 \\ 0 & 0 & 0 & 0 \\ 0 & 0 & 0 & 0 \end{pmatrix}.$$

Hence, $\text{rk}(\boldsymbol{A}) = 2$. Let $x_3 := 2\lambda$ and $x_4 := \mu$. Then,

$$x_2 = 7\lambda - 2\mu, \quad x_1 = x_2 - 10\lambda + \mu = -3\lambda - \mu.$$

Hence, we obtain $(x_1, x_2, x_3, x_4) = \lambda(-3, 7, 2, 0) + \mu(-1, -2, 0, 1)$.

6.5 Nonhomogeneous equations

Exercise 6.41 (A simple nonhomogeneous example) Consider the two equations

$$x_1 + x_2 = 1, \quad 2x_1 + 2x_2 = k.$$

For which values of k does a solution exist? If a solution exists, is it unique? (If the equation has at least one solution, we say that it is a *consistent* equation.)

Solution

If $k = 2$, then every (x_1, x_2) satisfying $x_1 + x_2 = 1$ is a solution, but if $k \neq 2$, then there is no solution. Hence, a nonhomogeneous equation $\boldsymbol{A}\boldsymbol{x} = \boldsymbol{b}$ does not necessarily have a solution. Let us consider the matrix $\boldsymbol{A}$ and the augmented matrix $(\boldsymbol{A} : \boldsymbol{b})$,

$$\boldsymbol{A} = \begin{pmatrix} 1 & 1 \\ 2 & 2 \end{pmatrix} \quad \text{and} \quad (\boldsymbol{A} : \boldsymbol{b}) = \begin{pmatrix} 1 & 1 & 1 \\ 2 & 2 & k \end{pmatrix}.$$

We see that $\operatorname{rk}(\boldsymbol{A}) = 1$, and that $\operatorname{rk}(\boldsymbol{A} : \boldsymbol{b})$ equals 1 for $k = 2$ and equals 2 for $k \neq 2$. Hence, $\operatorname{rk}(\boldsymbol{A} : \boldsymbol{b}) = \operatorname{rk}(\boldsymbol{A})$ if and only if $k = 2$, that is, if and only if the system is consistent. The next exercise shows that this is a general result.

Exercise 6.42 (Necessary and sufficient condition for consistency) Consider a system of equations $\boldsymbol{A}\boldsymbol{x} = \boldsymbol{b}$ to be solved for $\boldsymbol{x}$. Show that the system is consistent (has a solution) if and only if $\operatorname{rk}(\boldsymbol{A} : \boldsymbol{b}) = \operatorname{rk}(\boldsymbol{A})$.

Solution

We notice first that the rank of $(\boldsymbol{A} : \boldsymbol{b})$ is either equal to the rank of $\boldsymbol{A}$ or exceeds it by one. Let $\boldsymbol{a}_1, \dots, \boldsymbol{a}_n$ be the columns of $\boldsymbol{A}$. We write the system as

$$x_1\boldsymbol{a}_1 + x_2\boldsymbol{a}_2 + \dots + x_n\boldsymbol{a}_n = \boldsymbol{b}.$$

The system thus has a solution if and only if we can write $\boldsymbol{b}$ as a linear combination of the columns of $\boldsymbol{A}$. This is possible if and only if $\boldsymbol{b}$ lies in $\operatorname{col}(\boldsymbol{A})$. This, in turn, happens if and only if $\operatorname{rk}(\boldsymbol{A} : \boldsymbol{b}) = \operatorname{rk}(\boldsymbol{A})$. (Notice that $\operatorname{rk}(\boldsymbol{A} : \boldsymbol{0}) = \operatorname{rk}(\boldsymbol{A})$, so that $\boldsymbol{A}\boldsymbol{x} = \boldsymbol{0}$ is always consistent; see Exercise 6.32.)

Exercise 6.43 (Solution with full row rank)

(a) Is it possible to construct a matrix $\boldsymbol{A}$ such that $\boldsymbol{A}\boldsymbol{x} = \boldsymbol{b}$ is inconsistent for every $\boldsymbol{b}$?
(b) Is it possible to construct a matrix $\boldsymbol{A}$ such that $\boldsymbol{A}\boldsymbol{x} = \boldsymbol{b}$ is consistent for every $\boldsymbol{b}$?

Solution

(a) No, this is not possible. Whatever the rank of $\boldsymbol{A}$, we can always find a $\boldsymbol{b}$, such that $\operatorname{rk}(\boldsymbol{A} : \boldsymbol{b}) = \operatorname{rk}(\boldsymbol{A})$, for example the first column of $\boldsymbol{A}$.
(b) Yes, if $\boldsymbol{A}$ has full row rank. Suppose $\boldsymbol{A}$ is an $m \times n$ matrix with $\operatorname{rk}(\boldsymbol{A}) = m$. Then the augmented matrix $(\boldsymbol{A} : \boldsymbol{b})$ has m rows and $n + 1$ columns. Hence, $\operatorname{rk}(\boldsymbol{A} : \boldsymbol{b}) \leq m$. But also, for any matrix $\boldsymbol{A}$ and vector $\boldsymbol{b}$, $\operatorname{rk}(\boldsymbol{A} : \boldsymbol{b}) \geq \operatorname{rk}(\boldsymbol{A})$. It follows that $\operatorname{rk}(\boldsymbol{A} : \boldsymbol{b}) = m$ and hence that $\operatorname{rk}(\boldsymbol{A} : \boldsymbol{b}) = \operatorname{rk}(\boldsymbol{A})$.

Exercise 6.44 (Solution with full column rank)
(a) Is $\boldsymbol{Ax} = \boldsymbol{b}$ always consistent if $\boldsymbol{A}$ has full column rank?
(b) Assume that $\boldsymbol{Ax} = \boldsymbol{b}$ is consistent. Show that the solution is unique if and only if $\boldsymbol{A}$ has full column rank.
(c) In that case, what is the unique solution?

Solution
(a) The equation can be consistent (when $\boldsymbol{A}$ is square), but in general it is not. For example, for $m = 2$ and $n = 1$, let $\boldsymbol{A} := (1, 0)'$ and $\boldsymbol{b} := (0, 1)'$. Then no vector (in this case, scalar) $\boldsymbol{x}$ exists such that $\boldsymbol{Ax} = \boldsymbol{b}$.
(b) We prove the "if" part by contradiction and the "only if" part by contrapositive. Let $\boldsymbol{A}$ be a matrix of order $m \times n$. Suppose $\text{rk}(\boldsymbol{A}) = n$ and let $\boldsymbol{x}_1$ and $\boldsymbol{x}_2$ be two distinct solutions. Then $\boldsymbol{Ax}_1 = \boldsymbol{b}$ and $\boldsymbol{Ax}_2 = \boldsymbol{b}$, and hence $\boldsymbol{A}(\boldsymbol{x}_1 - \boldsymbol{x}_2) = \boldsymbol{0}$. We know from Exercise 6.33 that the homogeneous equation $\boldsymbol{Ax} = \boldsymbol{0}$ has a unique solution (namely $\boldsymbol{x} = \boldsymbol{0}$) if (and only if) $\text{rk}(\boldsymbol{A}) = n$. This implies that $\boldsymbol{x}_1 - \boldsymbol{x}_2 = \boldsymbol{0}$, a contradiction.

Now suppose that $\text{rk}(\boldsymbol{A}) < n$. Then the equation $\boldsymbol{Ax} = \boldsymbol{0}$ has infinitely many solutions (Exercise 6.33). Let $\boldsymbol{x}_1$ and $\boldsymbol{x}_2$ be two solutions. If $\boldsymbol{x}_0$ is a solution of $\boldsymbol{Ax} = \boldsymbol{b}$, then both $\boldsymbol{x}_0 - \boldsymbol{x}_1$ and $\boldsymbol{x}_0 - \boldsymbol{x}_2$ are also solutions, so that the solution is not unique.
(c) Premultiply both sides of $\boldsymbol{Ax} = \boldsymbol{b}$ by $\boldsymbol{A}'$. This gives $\boldsymbol{A}'\boldsymbol{Ax} = \boldsymbol{A}'\boldsymbol{b}$. Since $\text{rk}(\boldsymbol{A}) = n$, the matrix $\boldsymbol{A}'\boldsymbol{A}$ is nonsingular. Hence, $\boldsymbol{x} = (\boldsymbol{A}'\boldsymbol{A})^{-1}\boldsymbol{A}'\boldsymbol{b}$ is the unique solution.

Exercise 6.45 (Complete characterization of solution) Give a complete characterization of the existence and uniqueness of solutions of a system $\boldsymbol{Ax} = \boldsymbol{b}$.

Solution
This is the characterization, assuming that $\boldsymbol{A}$ is an $m \times n$ matrix:

$$\begin{aligned} \text{rk}(\boldsymbol{A} : \boldsymbol{b}) = \text{rk}(\boldsymbol{A}) = n &\implies \text{unique solution;} \\ \text{rk}(\boldsymbol{A} : \boldsymbol{b}) = \text{rk}(\boldsymbol{A}) < n &\implies \text{multiple solution;} \\ \text{rk}(\boldsymbol{A} : \boldsymbol{b}) = \text{rk}(\boldsymbol{A}) + 1 &\implies \text{no solution.} \end{aligned}$$

Exercise 6.42 shows that the system is consistent if and only if $\text{rk}(\boldsymbol{A} : \boldsymbol{b}) = \text{rk}(\boldsymbol{A})$. Now assume that the system is consistent, so that there exists an $\widetilde{\boldsymbol{x}}$ such that $\boldsymbol{A}\widetilde{\boldsymbol{x}} = \boldsymbol{b}$. Then $\boldsymbol{Ax} = \boldsymbol{b}$ has a unique solution if and only if $\boldsymbol{A}(\boldsymbol{x} - \widetilde{\boldsymbol{x}}) = \boldsymbol{0}$ has a unique (namely the trivial) solution. By Exercise 6.33 this is the case if and only if $\text{rk}(\boldsymbol{A}) = n$.

Exercise 6.46 (Is this consistent?) Is there a solution to

$$\begin{aligned} 2x_1 + 3x_2 + x_3 &= 7, \\ x_1 + 2x_2 - 2x_3 &= 8, \\ 3x_1 + 4x_2 + 4x_3 &= 20? \end{aligned}$$

Solution
We have

$$(\boldsymbol{A}:\boldsymbol{b}) = \begin{pmatrix} 2 & 3 & 1 & 7 \\ 1 & 2 & -2 & 8 \\ 3 & 4 & 4 & 20 \end{pmatrix}.$$

After reduction to echelon form, this becomes

$$\begin{pmatrix} 1 & 1.5 & 0.5 & 3.5 \\ 0 & 1 & -5 & 9 \\ 0 & 0 & 0 & 14 \end{pmatrix}$$

from which we see that $\mathrm{rk}(\boldsymbol{A}:\boldsymbol{b}) = 3$ and $\mathrm{rk}(\boldsymbol{A}) = 2$. Hence, the system is inconsistent.

Exercise 6.47 (A more difficult nonhomogeneous example) Consider the three-equation system

$$\begin{aligned} \alpha x_1 + \beta x_2 + 2x_3 &= 1, \\ \alpha x_1 + (2\beta - 1)x_2 + 3x_3 &= 1, \\ \alpha x_1 + \beta x_2 + (\beta + 3)x_3 &= 2\beta - 1. \end{aligned}$$

When is there a solution? When is the solution unique?

Solution
The augmented matrix is

$$(\boldsymbol{A}:\boldsymbol{b}) = \begin{pmatrix} \alpha & \beta & 2 & 1 \\ \alpha & 2\beta - 1 & 3 & 1 \\ \alpha & \beta & \beta + 3 & 2\beta - 1 \end{pmatrix}.$$

In echelon form:

$$\widetilde{\boldsymbol{A}} = \begin{pmatrix} \alpha & 1 & 1 & 1 \\ 0 & \beta - 1 & 1 & 0 \\ 0 & 0 & \beta + 1 & 2(\beta - 1) \end{pmatrix}.$$

Let $\widetilde{\boldsymbol{A}}^{(j)}$ denote the 3×3 submatrix of $\widetilde{\boldsymbol{A}}$ obtained by deleting column j. Then, $|\widetilde{\boldsymbol{A}}^{(1)}| = -(\beta-1)(\beta-5)$, $|\widetilde{\boldsymbol{A}}^{(2)}| = 2\alpha(\beta-1)$, $|\widetilde{\boldsymbol{A}}^{(3)}| = 2\alpha(\beta-1)^2$, and $|\widetilde{\boldsymbol{A}}^{(4)}| = |\boldsymbol{A}| = \alpha(\beta^2-1)$. Hence, we need to distinguish six cases:

$$\begin{aligned} \beta \notin \{-1, 1, 5\},\ \alpha \neq 0 : \mathrm{rk}(\boldsymbol{A}) = 3, \mathrm{rk}(\boldsymbol{A}:\boldsymbol{b}) = 3 &\implies \text{unique solution} \\ \beta \notin \{-1, 1, 5\},\ \alpha = 0 : \mathrm{rk}(\boldsymbol{A}) = 2, \mathrm{rk}(\boldsymbol{A}:\boldsymbol{b}) = 3 &\implies \text{no solution} \\ \beta = 5,\ \alpha \neq 0 : \mathrm{rk}(\boldsymbol{A}) = 3, \mathrm{rk}(\boldsymbol{A}:\boldsymbol{b}) = 3 &\implies \text{unique solution} \\ \beta = 5,\ \alpha = 0 : \mathrm{rk}(\boldsymbol{A}) = 2, \mathrm{rk}(\boldsymbol{A}:\boldsymbol{b}) = 2 &\implies \text{multiple solutions} \\ \beta = 1 : \mathrm{rk}(\boldsymbol{A}) = 2, \mathrm{rk}(\boldsymbol{A}:\boldsymbol{b}) = 2 &\implies \text{multiple solutions} \\ \beta = -1 : \mathrm{rk}(\boldsymbol{A}) = 2, \mathrm{rk}(\boldsymbol{A}:\boldsymbol{b}) = 3 &\implies \text{no solution.} \end{aligned}$$

Notes

The problem in Exercise 6.24 was posed by Euler in 1770; see Bretscher (1997). The algorithm in Exercise 6.26 is the so-called Gaussian elimination method, published by Gauss in 1809, but already used by him in 1801 in order to solve 17 linear equations. Cramer's rule in Exercise 6.28 was obtained by Cramer in 1750, although Leibniz knew essentially the same result around 1700.

7

Eigenvalues, eigenvectors, and factorizations

Although we considered complex numbers and complex matrices in the previous chapters, it is only in this chapter that we really start to need them. This is because eigenvalues (to be defined shortly) are, in general, complex numbers.

We recall briefly that if $\boldsymbol{A}$ and $\boldsymbol{B}$ are real matrices of the same order, a complex matrix $\boldsymbol{U}$ can be written as $\boldsymbol{U} := \boldsymbol{A} + \mathrm{i}\boldsymbol{B}$, where i denotes the imaginary unit with the property $\mathrm{i}^2 = -1$. The conjugate transpose of $\boldsymbol{U}$, denoted by $\boldsymbol{U}^*$, is defined as $\boldsymbol{U}^* := \boldsymbol{A}' - \mathrm{i}\boldsymbol{B}'$. If $\boldsymbol{U}$ is real, then $\boldsymbol{U}^* = \boldsymbol{U}'$. If $\boldsymbol{U}$ is a scalar, say u, then the conjugate transpose u^* is also a scalar, called the complex conjugate. A square matrix $\boldsymbol{U}$ is said to be Hermitian if $\boldsymbol{U}^* = \boldsymbol{U}$ (the complex equivalent to a symmetric matrix) and unitary if $\boldsymbol{U}^*\boldsymbol{U} = \boldsymbol{I}$ (the complex equivalent to an orthogonal matrix).

Let $\boldsymbol{A}$ be a square matrix, real or complex, say of order n. The *eigenvalues* (or *characteristic roots*) of $\boldsymbol{A}$ are defined as the roots of the *characteristic equation*

$$p_{\boldsymbol{A}}(\lambda) := |\lambda \boldsymbol{I}_n - \boldsymbol{A}| = 0.$$

The function $p_{\boldsymbol{A}}(\lambda)$ is called the *characteristic polynomial* of $\boldsymbol{A}$. From the "fundamental theorem of algebra" we know that the n-th degree equation $p_{\boldsymbol{A}}(\lambda) = 0$ has n roots. Not all these roots need to be different, but if a root is counted a number of times equal to its multiplicity, there are n roots, which may be either real or complex.

The characteristic polynomial can be represented as

$$p_{\boldsymbol{A}}(\lambda) = p_0 + p_1\lambda + \cdots + p_{n-1}\lambda^{n-1} + \lambda^n = (\lambda - \lambda_1)(\lambda - \lambda_2)\ldots(\lambda - \lambda_n).$$

If $\boldsymbol{A}$ is a real matrix, then $p_0, \ldots, p_{n-1}$ are also real, and therefore complex eigenvalues of a real matrix can only occur in conjugate pairs (Exercise 7.17).

The numbers $\lambda_1, \ldots, \lambda_n$ thus denote the eigenvalues of the matrix $\boldsymbol{A}$. We sometimes write $\lambda_i(\boldsymbol{A})$ to emphasize this. If λ_i appears $n_i > 1$ times then it is called a *multiple* eigenvalue and the number n_i is the *multiplicity* of λ_i; if λ_i appears only once it is called a *simple* eigenvalue.

Given a set of numbers $\lambda_1, \dots, \lambda_n$, we now define the *elementary symmetric functions* of $\{\lambda_1, \dots, \lambda_n\}$ as

$$s_1 := \sum_{i=1}^{n} \lambda_i = \lambda_1 + \lambda_2 + \cdots + \lambda_n,$$

$$s_2 := \sum_{i<j} \lambda_i \lambda_j = \lambda_1\lambda_2 + \cdots + \lambda_1\lambda_n + \lambda_2\lambda_3 + \cdots + \lambda_2\lambda_n + \cdots + \lambda_{n-1}\lambda_n,$$

$$\vdots$$

$$s_r := \sum_{i_1<i_2<\cdots<i_r} \lambda_{i_1}\lambda_{i_2}\dots\lambda_{i_r},$$

$$\vdots$$

$$s_n := \lambda_1\lambda_2\dots\lambda_n.$$

One can show that the coefficients in the characteristic polynomial are related to the elementary symmetric functions by

$$p_{n-1} = -s_1, \quad p_{n-2} = (-1)^2 s_2, \quad \dots, \quad p_1 = (-1)^{n-1} s_{n-1}, \quad p_0 = (-1)^n s_n.$$

Moreover, if we define the *power sums*,

$$\sigma_k := \sum_{i=1}^{n} \lambda_i^k \quad (k = 1, 2, \dots, n),$$

then there is a one-to-one relationship between the two sets $\{s_i\}$ and $\{\sigma_i\}$.

Recall that a $k \times k$ submatrix of an $n \times n$ matrix $\boldsymbol{A}$ is obtained by deleting $n - k$ rows and $n - k$ columns of $\boldsymbol{A}$. If the deleted row indices and the deleted column indices are the same we obtain a *principal* submatrix of $\boldsymbol{A}$. For example, the 3×3 matrix consisting of the first, third, and seventh row, and the first, third, and seventh column of $\boldsymbol{A}$ is a principal submatrix. If the selected principal submatrix is in fact a north-west corner of the matrix $\boldsymbol{A}$, then it is a *leading* principal submatrix. So, the above 3×3 principal submatrix is not leading; the leading principal 3×3 submatrix consists of the first, second, and third row, and the first, second, and third column of $\boldsymbol{A}$. The determinant of a (leading) principal submatrix is called a *(leading) principal minor*. There are $\binom{n}{k}$ different $k \times k$ principal minors of $\boldsymbol{A}$, and we denote the sum of these by E_k or by $E_k(\boldsymbol{A})$. In particular, $E_1(\boldsymbol{A}) = \operatorname{tr}(\boldsymbol{A})$ and $E_n(\boldsymbol{A}) = |\boldsymbol{A}|$. One can show that the coefficients in the characteristic polynomial are related to the functions E_k by

$$p_{n-1} = -E_1, \quad p_{n-2} = (-1)^2 E_2, \quad \dots, \quad p_1 = (-1)^{n-1} E_{n-1}, \quad p_0 = (-1)^n E_n.$$

Hence, if $\lambda_1, \dots, \lambda_n$ are the eigenvalues of $\boldsymbol{A}$, then

$$s_k(\lambda_1, \dots, \lambda_n) = E_k(\boldsymbol{A}) \quad (k = 1, \dots, n).$$

If λ is an eigenvalue of $\boldsymbol{A}$, then there is at least one $\boldsymbol{x} \neq \boldsymbol{0}$ that satisfies $\boldsymbol{Ax} = \lambda\boldsymbol{x}$. Any such $\boldsymbol{x}$ is called a (right) *eigenvector* of $\boldsymbol{A}$ associated with the eigenvalue λ. Eigenvectors are usually normalized in some way to make them unique (apart from sign), typically by $\boldsymbol{x}^*\boldsymbol{x} = 1$ ($\boldsymbol{x}'\boldsymbol{x} = 1$ when $\boldsymbol{x}$ is real). It is remarkable that we can find a vector $\boldsymbol{x}$ such that $\boldsymbol{Ax}$ becomes just a multiple of $\boldsymbol{x}$ (see Figure 1.1). We know from Chapter 6 that, if $(\lambda\boldsymbol{I}_n - \boldsymbol{A})\boldsymbol{x} = \boldsymbol{0}$ for some $\boldsymbol{x} \neq \boldsymbol{0}$, then $\lambda\boldsymbol{I}_n - \boldsymbol{A}$ is singular. This corresponds with the characteristic equation $|\lambda\boldsymbol{I}_n - \boldsymbol{A}| = 0$ defining the eigenvalues above.

Let i be some positive integer. If a vector $\boldsymbol{x}_i$ satisfies

$$(\boldsymbol{A} - \lambda\boldsymbol{I}_n)^i \boldsymbol{x}_i = \boldsymbol{0} \quad \text{but} \quad (\boldsymbol{A} - \lambda\boldsymbol{I}_n)^{i-1} \boldsymbol{x}_i \neq \boldsymbol{0},$$

then it is called a *generalized eigenvector of degree* i associated with λ. When $i = 1$, using the convention $\boldsymbol{C}^0 = \boldsymbol{I}$ for any square matrix $\boldsymbol{C}$, the definition of $\boldsymbol{x}_1$ boils down to that of the usual eigenvector; hence the term *generalized*. Suppose that there exists a vector $\boldsymbol{x}_p$ satisfying this definition, but no $\boldsymbol{x}_{p+1}$. The sequence $\{\boldsymbol{x}_p, \boldsymbol{x}_{p-1}, \dots, \boldsymbol{x}_1\}$ generated by $\boldsymbol{x}_p$ through

$$\boldsymbol{x}_{p-i} = (\boldsymbol{A} - \lambda\boldsymbol{I}_n)^i \boldsymbol{x}_p \quad (i = 1, \dots, p-1),$$

or recursively by

$$\boldsymbol{x}_i = (\boldsymbol{A} - \lambda\boldsymbol{I}_n) \boldsymbol{x}_{i+1} \quad (i = p-1, \dots, 1),$$

is called a *Jordan chain of length* p associated with λ. Clearly, $\boldsymbol{x}_1 = (\boldsymbol{A} - \lambda\boldsymbol{I}_n)^{p-1} \boldsymbol{x}_p$.

When two matrices $\boldsymbol{A}$ and $\boldsymbol{B}$, of the same order, also have the same rank, they are said to be *equivalent*, a concept first encountered in Exercise 6.19. When, in addition, $\boldsymbol{A}$ and $\boldsymbol{B}$ are square and there exists a nonsingular matrix $\boldsymbol{T}$ such that $\boldsymbol{T}^{-1}\boldsymbol{AT} = \boldsymbol{B}$, then they are said to be *similar*. Similar matrices will play an important role in this chapter.

The chapter is divided into six sections. The first section gives some general results on eigenvalues and eigenvectors and presents the diagonalization theorem when the eigenvalues are all distinct (Exercise 7.32). The QR decomposition is also presented. In Section 7.2 we consider the special case of symmetric matrices. These matrices have five important properties that are not shared, in general, by other matrices, real or complex:

(i) the eigenvalues are all real;
(ii) eigenvectors associated with distinct eigenvalues are orthogonal;
(iii) the eigenvectors span $\mathbb{R}^n$;
(iv) the rank is equal to the number of nonzero eigenvalues;
(v) the matrix can be diagonalized (by means of an orthogonal transformation).

Each of these properties is proved and examples are provided. Section 7.3 is an interlude on triangular matrices and presents some results that are used later. Section 7.4 presents Schur's triangularization theorem (Exercise 7.62) and some of its consequences. Sections 7.5 and 7.6 are devoted to the Jordan decomposition. The Jordan theorem states that, for any square matrix $\boldsymbol{A}$, there exists a nonsingular $\boldsymbol{T}$ and a "Jordan matrix" $\boldsymbol{J}$ such that $\boldsymbol{T}^{-1}\boldsymbol{AT} = \boldsymbol{J}$. The theorem itself is presented in Exercise 7.79. The question on how to construct the matrix $\boldsymbol{T}$ is discussed in Section 7.6.

A major question in this chapter is when a matrix can be diagonalized (is similar to a diagonal matrix). A full characterization of such matrices is provided. When a matrix cannot be diagonalized, we ask how close to a diagonal representation we can get. The answer is given by Jordan's theorem, a full proof of which is provided.

Because of the central role of factorization theorems, let us list the ones we prove in this chapter, together with two results obtained before.

If $\boldsymbol{A}$ is an $m \times n$ matrix of rank r, then:

- $\boldsymbol{A} = \boldsymbol{B}\boldsymbol{C}'$ with $\boldsymbol{B}$ $(m \times r)$ and $\boldsymbol{C}$ $(n \times r)$ both of rank r (Exercise 4.11).
- $\boldsymbol{E}\boldsymbol{A}\boldsymbol{F} = \operatorname{diag}(\boldsymbol{I}_r, \mathrm{O})$ with $\boldsymbol{E}$ and $\boldsymbol{F}$ nonsingular (Exercise 6.17).
- $\boldsymbol{A} = \boldsymbol{Q}\boldsymbol{R}$ (when $r = n$) with $\boldsymbol{Q}^*\boldsymbol{Q} = \boldsymbol{I}_n$ and $\boldsymbol{R}$ upper triangular matrix with positive diagonal elements; if $\boldsymbol{A}$ is real, then $\boldsymbol{Q}$ and $\boldsymbol{R}$ are real as well (Exercises 7.34 and 7.35).

If $\boldsymbol{A}$ is a square matrix of order n, then:

- $\boldsymbol{S}^*\boldsymbol{A}\boldsymbol{S} = \boldsymbol{M}$ with $\boldsymbol{S}$ unitary and $\boldsymbol{M}$ upper triangular (Schur, Exercise 7.62).
- $\boldsymbol{S}^*\boldsymbol{A}\boldsymbol{S} = \boldsymbol{\Lambda}$ (diagonal) with $\boldsymbol{S}$ unitary, if and only if $\boldsymbol{A}$ is normal (Exercise 7.71).
- $\boldsymbol{S}'\boldsymbol{A}\boldsymbol{S} = \boldsymbol{\Lambda}$ (diagonal) with $\boldsymbol{S}$ orthogonal, if $\boldsymbol{A}$ is symmetric (Exercise 7.46).
- $\boldsymbol{S}'\boldsymbol{A}\boldsymbol{S} = \boldsymbol{\Lambda}$ (diagonal) and $\boldsymbol{S}'\boldsymbol{B}\boldsymbol{S} = \boldsymbol{M}$ (diagonal) with $\boldsymbol{A}$ and $\boldsymbol{B}$ symmetric and $\boldsymbol{S}$ orthogonal, if and only if $\boldsymbol{A}$ and $\boldsymbol{B}$ commute (Exercise 7.51).

If $\boldsymbol{A}$ is a square matrix of order n, then also:

- $\boldsymbol{T}^{-1}\boldsymbol{A}\boldsymbol{T} = \boldsymbol{J}$ (Jordan matrix) with $\boldsymbol{T}$ nonsingular (Jordan, Exercise 7.79).
- $\boldsymbol{T}^{-1}\boldsymbol{A}\boldsymbol{T} = \boldsymbol{\Lambda}$ (diagonal) with $\boldsymbol{T}$ nonsingular, if $\boldsymbol{A}$ has distinct eigenvalues (Exercise 7.32).
- $\boldsymbol{T}^{-1}\boldsymbol{A}\boldsymbol{T} = \operatorname{dg}(\boldsymbol{A})$ with $\boldsymbol{T}$ unit upper triangular, if $\boldsymbol{A}$ upper triangular with distinct diagonal elements (Exercise 7.59).
- $\boldsymbol{T}^{-1}\boldsymbol{A}\boldsymbol{T} = \boldsymbol{\Lambda}$ (diagonal) and $\boldsymbol{T}^{-1}\boldsymbol{B}\boldsymbol{T} = \boldsymbol{M}$ (diagonal) with $\boldsymbol{T}$ nonsingular, if $\boldsymbol{A}$ has only simple eigenvalues and commutes with $\boldsymbol{B}$ (Exercise 7.39).

7.1 Eigenvalues and eigenvectors

Exercise 7.1 (Find two eigenvalues) Find the eigenvalues of the 2×2 matrices

$$\boldsymbol{A} = \begin{pmatrix} 3 & 5 \\ -2 & -4 \end{pmatrix}, \quad \boldsymbol{B} = \begin{pmatrix} 3 & 4 \\ -5 & -5 \end{pmatrix}, \quad \boldsymbol{C} = \begin{pmatrix} 3 & 5 \\ 5 & 7 \end{pmatrix}.$$

Solution
We have

$$|\lambda \boldsymbol{I}_2 - \boldsymbol{A}| = \begin{vmatrix} \lambda - 3 & -5 \\ 2 & \lambda + 4 \end{vmatrix} = (\lambda - 3)(\lambda + 4) + 10 = (\lambda - 1)(\lambda + 2)$$

and hence the eigenvalues are 1 and -2. Similarly,

$$|\lambda \boldsymbol{I}_2 - \boldsymbol{B}| = \begin{vmatrix} \lambda - 3 & -4 \\ 5 & \lambda + 5 \end{vmatrix} = (\lambda - 3)(\lambda + 5) + 20 = (\lambda + 1)^2 + 4.$$

Hence, the (complex) eigenvalues of $\boldsymbol{B}$ are given by the equation $(\lambda + 1)^2 = -4$, so that $\lambda_{1,2} = -1 \pm 2\mathrm{i}$. Finally,

$$|\lambda \boldsymbol{I}_2 - \boldsymbol{C}| = \begin{vmatrix} \lambda - 3 & -5 \\ -5 & \lambda - 7 \end{vmatrix} = (\lambda - 3)(\lambda - 7) - 25 = (\lambda - 5)^2 - 29.$$

The eigenvalues of $\boldsymbol{C}$ are therefore $\lambda_{1,2} = 5 \pm \sqrt{29}$. We see from this exercise that a nonsymmetric matrix (like $\boldsymbol{A}$ and $\boldsymbol{B}$) may or may not have real eigenvalues. We shall see later (Exercise 7.40) that a symmetric matrix (like $\boldsymbol{C}$) always has real eigenvalues.

Exercise 7.2 (Find three eigenvalues) Find the eigenvalues of the 3×3 matrices

$$\boldsymbol{A} = \begin{pmatrix} 7 & 0 & 0 \\ 0 & 3 & 0 \\ 0 & 0 & 3 \end{pmatrix}, \quad \boldsymbol{B} = \begin{pmatrix} 7 & 0 & 0 \\ 0 & 3 & 5 \\ 0 & 5 & 4 \end{pmatrix}, \quad \boldsymbol{C} = \begin{pmatrix} 7 & 0 & 0 \\ 0 & 3 & 1 \\ 0 & 0 & 3 \end{pmatrix}.$$

Solution

Since

$$|\lambda \boldsymbol{I}_3 - \boldsymbol{A}| = \begin{vmatrix} \lambda - 7 & 0 & 0 \\ 0 & \lambda - 3 & 0 \\ 0 & 0 & \lambda - 3 \end{vmatrix} = (\lambda - 7)(\lambda - 3)^2,$$

the eigenvalues of $\boldsymbol{A}$ are 7 and 3 (twice). To find the eigenvalues of $\boldsymbol{B}$ we write

$$|\lambda \boldsymbol{I}_3 - \boldsymbol{B}| = (\lambda - 7) \begin{vmatrix} \lambda - 3 & -5 \\ -5 & \lambda - 4 \end{vmatrix} = (\lambda - 7)\left((\lambda - 7/2)^2 - 101/4\right),$$

and the eigenvalues are 7 and $\frac{1}{2}(7 \pm \sqrt{101})$. To find the eigenvalues of $\boldsymbol{C}$ we write

$$|\lambda \boldsymbol{I}_3 - \boldsymbol{C}| = \begin{vmatrix} \lambda - 7 & 0 & 0 \\ 0 & \lambda - 3 & -1 \\ 0 & 0 & \lambda - 3 \end{vmatrix} = (\lambda - 7)(\lambda - 3)^2,$$

and the eigenvalues are therefore 7 and 3 (twice).

Exercise 7.3 (Characteristic equation)

(a) Find the characteristic equation and the eigenvalues of

$$\boldsymbol{A} = \begin{pmatrix} 1 & 3 & 0 \\ 0 & 1 & 0 \\ 2 & 1 & 5 \end{pmatrix}.$$

(b) What is the rank of $\boldsymbol{A}$?

Solution

(a) The characteristic polynomial is

$$p_{\boldsymbol{A}}(\lambda) = |\lambda \boldsymbol{I}_3 - \boldsymbol{A}| = \begin{vmatrix} \lambda - 1 & -3 & 0 \\ 0 & \lambda - 1 & 0 \\ -2 & -1 & \lambda - 5 \end{vmatrix} = (\lambda - 1)^2(\lambda - 5).$$

Hence, the characteristic equation is $(\lambda - 1)^2(\lambda - 5) = 0$, and the eigenvalues are 5 and 1 (twice).

(b) Setting $\lambda = 0$ in $p_{\boldsymbol{A}}(\lambda)$ we find

$$p_{\boldsymbol{A}}(0) = |-\boldsymbol{A}| = (-1)^3|\boldsymbol{A}| = (-1)^2(-5) = -5,$$

so that $|\boldsymbol{A}| = 5$. Hence, $\boldsymbol{A}$ is nonsingular and $\operatorname{rk}(\boldsymbol{A}) = 3$.

Exercise 7.4 (Characteristic polynomial)

(a) Find the characteristic polynomial and the eigenvalues λ_1 and λ_2 of the 2×2 matrix

$$\boldsymbol{A} := \begin{pmatrix} a & b \\ c & d \end{pmatrix}.$$

(b) Show that

$$\lambda_1\lambda_2 = |\boldsymbol{A}| \quad \text{and} \quad \lambda_1 + \lambda_2 = \operatorname{tr} \boldsymbol{A}.$$

Solution

(a) The characteristic polynomial is given by

$$p_{\boldsymbol{A}}(\lambda) = \begin{vmatrix} \lambda - a & -b \\ -c & \lambda - d \end{vmatrix} = (\lambda - a)(\lambda - d) - bc = \lambda^2 - (a + d)\lambda + (ad - bc).$$

The eigenvalues follow from the equation $p_{\boldsymbol{A}}(\lambda) = 0$. We find

$$\lambda_{1,2} = \frac{a + d}{2} \pm \frac{1}{2}\sqrt{(a - d)^2 + 4bc}.$$

(b) Since $\operatorname{tr} \boldsymbol{A} = a + d$ and $|\boldsymbol{A}| = ad - bc$, we find

$$(\lambda - \lambda_1)(\lambda - \lambda_2) = \lambda^2 - (\operatorname{tr} \boldsymbol{A})\lambda + |\boldsymbol{A}|,$$

and the result follows.

Exercise 7.5 (Complex eigenvalues of a real matrix, 1) Consider the same 2×2 matrix $\boldsymbol{A}$ of Exercise 7.4, now assuming that $\boldsymbol{A}$ is real.

(a) Show that, if one eigenvalue is complex, both are.

(b) If the eigenvalues are complex, show that one is the complex conjugate of the other.

(c) If $\boldsymbol{A} = \boldsymbol{A}'$ (that is, if $b = c$), show that the eigenvalues must be real.

Solution

(a) Let $\mu := (a - d)^2 + 4bc$. If $\mu \geq 0$, then both eigenvalues are real, but if $\mu < 0$, then both are complex.

(b) If $\mu < 0$, the eigenvalues are

$$\lambda_{1,2} = \frac{a+d}{2} \pm \frac{1}{2}\mathrm{i}\sqrt{|\mu|}.$$

(c) If $b = c$, then $\mu = (a-d)^2 + 4b^2 \geq 0$.

Exercise 7.6 ($\boldsymbol{A} \neq \boldsymbol{B}$ may have the same eigenvalues) Suppose that two matrices $\boldsymbol{A}$ and $\boldsymbol{B}$ (of the same order) have the same characteristic polynomial. Is it necessarily true that $\boldsymbol{A} = \boldsymbol{B}$?

Solution
No. Take

$$\boldsymbol{A} = \begin{pmatrix} 1 & \alpha \\ 0 & 2 \end{pmatrix}.$$

Then $p_{\boldsymbol{A}}(\lambda) = (\lambda - 1)(\lambda - 2)$ for every α. So, although the eigenvalues are an excellent way to characterize a matrix, they do not characterize a matrix completely.

Exercise 7.7 (The eigenvector) If λ is an eigenvalue of $\boldsymbol{A}$, show that $\boldsymbol{A}\boldsymbol{x} = \lambda\boldsymbol{x}$ for some $\boldsymbol{x} \neq \boldsymbol{0}$.

Solution
Let $\boldsymbol{A}$ be a matrix of order $n \times n$. If λ is an eigenvalue of $\boldsymbol{A}$, then $|\lambda\boldsymbol{I}_n - \boldsymbol{A}| = 0$. The n columns of $\lambda\boldsymbol{I}_n - \boldsymbol{A}$ must therefore be linearly dependent, and hence $(\lambda\boldsymbol{I}_n - \boldsymbol{A})\boldsymbol{x} = \boldsymbol{0}$ for some $\boldsymbol{x} \neq \boldsymbol{0}$. This gives $\boldsymbol{A}\boldsymbol{x} = \lambda\boldsymbol{x}$.

Exercise 7.8 (Eigenvectors are not unique)
(a) Show that an eigenvector cannot be associated with two distinct eigenvalues.
(b) But can two distinct vectors be associated with the same eigenvalue?

Solution
(a) Suppose $\lambda_1 \neq \lambda_2$ are eigenvalues of a matrix $\boldsymbol{A}$ and that $\boldsymbol{x} \neq \boldsymbol{0}$ satisfies $\boldsymbol{A}\boldsymbol{x} = \lambda_1\boldsymbol{x}$ and $\boldsymbol{A}\boldsymbol{x} = \lambda_2\boldsymbol{x}$. Then $\lambda_1\boldsymbol{x} = \lambda_2\boldsymbol{x}$, and, since $\lambda_1 \neq \lambda_2$, $\boldsymbol{x} = \boldsymbol{0}$. But $\boldsymbol{x} = \boldsymbol{0}$ is not permitted as an eigenvector, so we arrive at a contradiction.
(b) Yes. The identity matrix $\boldsymbol{I}_n$, for example, possesses only eigenvalues one and *every* $n \times 1$ vector $\boldsymbol{x} \neq \boldsymbol{0}$ is an eigenvector.

Exercise 7.9 (Linear combination of eigenvectors with same eigenvalue) If $\boldsymbol{x}_1, \dots, \boldsymbol{x}_m$ are all eigenvectors of $\boldsymbol{A}$ associated with the same λ, show that $\sum_{i=1}^m \mu_i\boldsymbol{x}_i$ is also an eigenvector of $\boldsymbol{A}$.

Solution
If $\boldsymbol{A}\boldsymbol{x}_i = \lambda\boldsymbol{x}_i$ $(i = 1, \dots, m)$, then

$$\boldsymbol{A}\sum_{i=1}^m \mu_i\boldsymbol{x}_i = \sum_{i=1}^m \mu_i(\boldsymbol{A}\boldsymbol{x}_i) = \sum_{i=1}^m \mu_i(\lambda\boldsymbol{x}_i) = \lambda\sum_{i=1}^m \mu_i\boldsymbol{x}_i.$$

Exercise 7.10 (Find the eigenvectors, 1) Consider the matrices

$$\boldsymbol{A} = \begin{pmatrix} 1 & 1 \\ 0 & 1 \end{pmatrix} \quad \text{and} \quad \boldsymbol{B} = \begin{pmatrix} 2 & 0 \\ 0 & 2 \end{pmatrix}.$$

(a) What are the eigenvalues and eigenvectors of $\boldsymbol{A}$?
(b) What are the eigenvalues and eigenvectors of $\boldsymbol{B}$?

Solution
(a) The eigenvalues of $\boldsymbol{A}$ are 1 (twice). The eigenvectors are found from the equation

$$\begin{pmatrix} 1 & 1 \\ 0 & 1 \end{pmatrix} \begin{pmatrix} x_1 \\ x_2 \end{pmatrix} = \begin{pmatrix} x_1 \\ x_2 \end{pmatrix}$$

which gives

$$x_1 + x_2 = x_1, \quad x_2 = x_2,$$

and hence $x_2 = 0$. The normalized eigenvector is thus $(x_1, x_2) := (1, 0)$. Notice that there is only one eigenvector. Hence, the number of linearly independent eigenvectors associated with a multiple eigenvalue is not necessarily equal to the multiplicity. See also the next exercise.
(b) The eigenvalues of $\boldsymbol{B}$ are 2 (twice). *Every* vector $\boldsymbol{x} \neq \boldsymbol{0}$ satisfies

$$\begin{pmatrix} 2 & 0 \\ 0 & 2 \end{pmatrix} \begin{pmatrix} x_1 \\ x_2 \end{pmatrix} = \begin{pmatrix} 2x_1 \\ 2x_2 \end{pmatrix},$$

and the complete set of eigenvectors can be written as

$$\boldsymbol{x} := \mu_1 \begin{pmatrix} 1 \\ 0 \end{pmatrix} + \mu_2 \begin{pmatrix} 0 \\ 1 \end{pmatrix}$$

with $(\mu_1, \mu_2) \neq (0, 0)$. In contrast to (a), here there are two eigenvectors associated with the multiple eigenvalue.

Exercise 7.11 (Geometric multiplicity, 1) What are the eigenvectors of the matrix $\boldsymbol{A}$ in Exercise 7.3? Are they linearly independent? Are they orthogonal?

Solution
The eigenvalues are 1 (twice) and 5. The eigenvectors associated with $\lambda = 1$ are determined by $\boldsymbol{A}\boldsymbol{x} = \lambda \boldsymbol{x}$, that is,

$$\begin{pmatrix} 1 & 3 & 0 \\ 0 & 1 & 0 \\ 2 & 1 & 5 \end{pmatrix} \begin{pmatrix} x_1 \\ x_2 \\ x_3 \end{pmatrix} = \begin{pmatrix} x_1 \\ x_2 \\ x_3 \end{pmatrix}.$$

This gives

$$x_1 + 3x_2 = x_1, \quad x_2 = x_2, \quad 2x_1 + x_2 + 5x_3 = x_3,$$

and hence $x_2 = 0$ and $x_1 + 2x_3 = 0$, so that $(x_1, x_2, x_3) = (2, 0, -1)$ or a multiple thereof. Notice that in this example (and also the previous exercise) there is only one eigenvector (rather than two) associated with the multiple eigenvalue 1. We say that the (algebraic) multiplicity of this eigenvalue is 2, and that its *geometric multiplicity* is 1. The geometric multiplicity of an eigenvalue is thus the dimension of the space spanned by the associated eigenvectors. This dimension cannot exceed the (algebraic) multiplicity. Hence,

$$\text{geometric multiplicity} \leq \text{(algebraic) multiplicity.}$$

The eigenvector associated with $\lambda = 5$ is found analogously; it is $(x_1, x_2, x_3) = (0, 0, 1)$ or a multiple thereof. The two eigenvectors are linearly independent, but they are not orthogonal.

Exercise 7.12 (Multiples of eigenvalues and eigenvectors)
(a) If λ is an eigenvalue of $\boldsymbol{A}$, show that $t\lambda$ is an eigenvalue of $t\boldsymbol{A}$, with the same eigenvector(s).
(b) If $\boldsymbol{x}$ is an eigenvector of $\boldsymbol{A}$, show that $t\boldsymbol{x}$ $(t \neq 0)$ is also an eigenvector of $\boldsymbol{A}$, associated with the same eigenvalue.

Solution
(a) If $\boldsymbol{Ax} = \lambda\boldsymbol{x}$, then $(t\boldsymbol{A})\boldsymbol{x} = t(\boldsymbol{Ax}) = t(\lambda\boldsymbol{x}) = (t\lambda)\boldsymbol{x}$.
(b) If $\boldsymbol{Ax} = \lambda\boldsymbol{x}$, then $\boldsymbol{A}(t\boldsymbol{x}) = t(\boldsymbol{Ax}) = t(\lambda\boldsymbol{x}) = \lambda(t\boldsymbol{x})$.

Exercise 7.13 (Do $\boldsymbol{A}$ and $\boldsymbol{A}'$ have the same eigenvalues?)
(a) Show that $\boldsymbol{A}$ and $\boldsymbol{A}'$ have the same eigenvalues.
(b) Do they also have the same eigenvectors?
(c) Do $\boldsymbol{A}$ and $\boldsymbol{A}^*$ have the same eigenvalues?

Solution
(a) Since $|\boldsymbol{B}'| = |\boldsymbol{B}|$ for every square matrix $\boldsymbol{B}$, we have $|\lambda\boldsymbol{I} - \boldsymbol{A}'| = |(\lambda\boldsymbol{I} - \boldsymbol{A})'| = |\lambda\boldsymbol{I} - \boldsymbol{A}|$. The characteristic polynomials of $\boldsymbol{A}$ and $\boldsymbol{A}'$ are therefore the same and hence their eigenvalues too.
(b) No, they do not, in general. If

$$\boldsymbol{A} := \begin{pmatrix} 2 & 1 \\ 0 & 1 \end{pmatrix},$$

then the eigenvalues of $\boldsymbol{A}$ (and $\boldsymbol{A}'$) are 2 and 1. The eigenvectors of $\boldsymbol{A}$ are $(1, 0)'$ and $(1, -1)'$, but the eigenvectors of $\boldsymbol{A}'$ are $(1, 1)'$ and $(0, 1)'$.
(c) No, unless all eigenvalues of $\boldsymbol{A}$ are real. The eigenvalues of $\boldsymbol{A}^*$ are λ^*, because

$$|\lambda^*\boldsymbol{I} - \boldsymbol{A}^*| = |(\lambda\boldsymbol{I} - \boldsymbol{A})^*| = |\lambda\boldsymbol{I} - \boldsymbol{A}|^* = 0.$$

Exercise 7.14 (Eigenvalues of a power) Let λ be an eigenvalue of $\boldsymbol{A}$ associated with an eigenvector $\boldsymbol{x}$. Show that:
(a) $\boldsymbol{x}$ is an eigenvector of $s\boldsymbol{I} - t\boldsymbol{A}$, for any scalars s and t, associated with the eigenvalue $s - t\lambda$;

(b) $\boldsymbol{x}$ is an eigenvector of $\boldsymbol{A}^k$ ($k = 2, 3, \dots$), associated with the eigenvalue λ^k;
(c) $\boldsymbol{x}$ is an eigenvector of $\boldsymbol{A}^{-1}$ (if $\boldsymbol{A}$ is nonsingular), associated with the eigenvalue λ^{-1}.

Solution
(a) This follows from

$$(s\boldsymbol{I} - t\boldsymbol{A})\boldsymbol{x} = s\boldsymbol{x} - t\lambda\boldsymbol{x} = (s - t\lambda)\boldsymbol{x}.$$

(b) And this follows from

$$\boldsymbol{A}^k\boldsymbol{x} = \boldsymbol{A}^{k-1}(\boldsymbol{A}\boldsymbol{x}) = \lambda\boldsymbol{A}^{k-1}\boldsymbol{x} = \cdots = \lambda^k\boldsymbol{x}.$$

(c) If $\boldsymbol{A}\boldsymbol{x} = \lambda\boldsymbol{x}$, then $\boldsymbol{A}^{-1}\boldsymbol{A}\boldsymbol{x} = \lambda\boldsymbol{A}^{-1}\boldsymbol{x}$ and hence, $\lambda\boldsymbol{A}^{-1}\boldsymbol{x} = \boldsymbol{x}$. If $\lambda = 0$, then this implies $\boldsymbol{x} = \boldsymbol{0}$, a contradiction. Hence, $\lambda \neq 0$ and $\boldsymbol{A}^{-1}\boldsymbol{x} = \lambda^{-1}\boldsymbol{x}$.

Exercise 7.15 (Eigenvalues of a triangular matrix)
(a) What are the eigenvalues of a diagonal matrix?
(b) What are the eigenvalues of a triangular matrix?

Solution
(a) The eigenvalues are the diagonal elements. This follows directly from the fact that the determinant of a diagonal matrix is equal to the product of the diagonal elements.
(b) Here too, the eigenvalues are the diagonal elements, because the determinant of a triangular matrix is equal to the product of its diagonal elements.

Exercise 7.16 (Singularity and zero eigenvalue) Show that $\boldsymbol{A}$ is nonsingular if and only if all its eigenvalues are nonzero. (Equivalently, show that a matrix is singular if and only if at least one of its eigenvalues is zero.)

Solution
If $\lambda = 0$ is an eigenvalue of the $n \times n$ matrix $\boldsymbol{A}$, then $|\lambda\boldsymbol{I}_n - \boldsymbol{A}| = |-\boldsymbol{A}| = (-1)^n|\boldsymbol{A}| = 0$ and hence, $|\boldsymbol{A}| = 0$. Conversely, if $|\boldsymbol{A}| = 0$ then $|\lambda\boldsymbol{I}_n - \boldsymbol{A}| = 0$ for $\lambda = 0$.

Exercise 7.17 (Complex eigenvalues of a real matrix, 2)
(a) Show that complex eigenvalues of a real matrix can only occur in conjugate pairs.
(b) Hence, show that a real matrix of odd order has at least one real eigenvalue.

Solution
(a) If $\boldsymbol{A}\boldsymbol{x} = \lambda\boldsymbol{x}$, then $\boldsymbol{x}^*\boldsymbol{A}^* = (\boldsymbol{A}\boldsymbol{x})^* = (\lambda\boldsymbol{x})^* = \lambda^*\boldsymbol{x}^*$. If $\boldsymbol{A}$ is real, then $(\boldsymbol{A}^*)' = \boldsymbol{A}$ and hence, for $\boldsymbol{y} := (\boldsymbol{x}^*)'$, we obtain $\boldsymbol{A}\boldsymbol{y} = \lambda^*\boldsymbol{y}$.
(b) This is a consequence of (a).

***Exercise 7.18 (Eigenvalues of a skew-symmetric matrix)**
(a) Let $\boldsymbol{A}$ be a skew-symmetric matrix, so that $\boldsymbol{A}$ is real and $\boldsymbol{A}' = -\boldsymbol{A}$. Show that the eigenvalues are either zero or pure imaginary.
(b) What if n is odd?

Solution
(a) Since $\boldsymbol{Ax} = \lambda\boldsymbol{x}$, we have $\boldsymbol{A}^2\boldsymbol{x} = \lambda\boldsymbol{Ax} = \lambda^2\boldsymbol{x}$. Now,

$$(\boldsymbol{Ax})^*\boldsymbol{Ax} = \boldsymbol{x}^*\boldsymbol{A}^*\boldsymbol{Ax} = \boldsymbol{x}^*\boldsymbol{A}'\boldsymbol{Ax} = -\boldsymbol{x}^*\boldsymbol{A}^2\boldsymbol{x} = -\lambda^2\boldsymbol{x}^*\boldsymbol{x},$$

and hence $\lambda^2 \leq 0$.
(b) Since $\boldsymbol{A}$ is real, its complex roots (if any) occur in conjugate pairs (Exercise 7.17). Since n is odd, there exists at least one real eigenvalue, and this eigenvalue is zero by (a). Hence, by Exercise 7.16, the matrix $\boldsymbol{A}$ is singular.

Exercise 7.19 (Rank and number of nonzero eigenvalues, 1) Find the eigenvalues and the rank of the matrix

$$\boldsymbol{J} = \begin{pmatrix} 0 & 1 & 0 & \dots & 0 \\ 0 & 0 & 1 & \dots & 0 \\ \vdots & \vdots & \vdots & & \vdots \\ 0 & 0 & 0 & \dots & 1 \\ 0 & 0 & 0 & \dots & 0 \end{pmatrix}.$$

Solution
If $\boldsymbol{J}$ ($\boldsymbol{J}$ for "Jordan") is an $n \times n$ matrix, then all its n eigenvalues are zero, but it possesses $n-1$ linearly independent columns, so that $\text{rk}(\boldsymbol{J}) = n - 1$.

Exercise 7.20 (Nonsingularity of $\boldsymbol{A} - \mu\boldsymbol{I}$) If μ is *not* an eigenvalue of $\boldsymbol{A}$, show that $\boldsymbol{A} - \mu\boldsymbol{I}$ is nonsingular.

Solution
Let $\lambda_1, \dots, \lambda_n$ be the eigenvalues of $\boldsymbol{A}$. Then the eigenvalues of $\boldsymbol{B} := \boldsymbol{A} - \mu\boldsymbol{I}$ are $\lambda_i - \mu$ ($i = 1, \dots, n$). Since $\lambda_i \neq \mu$, all eigenvalues of $\boldsymbol{B}$ are nonzero. Hence, by Exercise 7.16, $\boldsymbol{B}$ is nonsingular.

Exercise 7.21 (A continuity argument) If $\boldsymbol{A}$ is singular, show that we can always find a scalar $\epsilon \neq 0$ such that $\boldsymbol{A} + \epsilon\boldsymbol{I}$ is nonsingular.

Solution
Let $\lambda_1, \dots, \lambda_n$ be the eigenvalues of $\boldsymbol{A}$. Then the eigenvalues of $\boldsymbol{A} + \epsilon\boldsymbol{I}$ are $\lambda_i + \epsilon$ ($i = 1, \dots, n$). Hence, any $\epsilon \neq -\lambda_i$ will make $\boldsymbol{A} + \epsilon\boldsymbol{I}$ nonsingular. In particular, if we let $\delta := \min_i\{|\lambda_i|, \lambda_i \neq 0\}$, then $\boldsymbol{A} + \epsilon\boldsymbol{I}$ is nonsingular for any ϵ in the interval $(0, \delta)$.

***Exercise 7.22 (Eigenvalues of an orthogonal or a unitary matrix)**
(a) Show, through a 2×2 example, that an orthogonal matrix will, in general, have complex eigenvalues.

(b) Show that the complex eigenvalues, if any, of an orthogonal matrix occur in conjugate pairs.
(c) Show that all eigenvalues of a unitary (and hence, in particular, of an orthogonal) matrix have unit modulus.

Solution
(a) Consider the example of Exercise 2.28:

$$\boldsymbol{A} := \begin{pmatrix} \cos\theta & -\sin\theta \\ \sin\theta & \cos\theta \end{pmatrix}.$$

The eigenvalues of $\boldsymbol{A}$ are found by solving $0 = |\boldsymbol{A} - \lambda \boldsymbol{I}_2| = (\cos\theta - \lambda)^2 + (\sin\theta)^2 = 0$, giving eigenvalues $\lambda = \cos\theta + \mathrm{i}\sin\theta = \mathrm{e}^{\mathrm{i}\theta}$ and $\lambda^* = \cos\theta - \mathrm{i}\sin\theta = \mathrm{e}^{-\mathrm{i}\theta}$. Notice that the modulus of λ (and of λ^*) is one.
(b) Since an orthogonal matrix is real (by definition), its complex roots (if any) occur in conjugate pairs (Exercise 7.17).
(c) If $\boldsymbol{A}$ is unitary, then $\boldsymbol{A}^*\boldsymbol{A} = \boldsymbol{I}$. Thus, if $\boldsymbol{A}\boldsymbol{x} = \lambda\boldsymbol{x}$, then $\boldsymbol{x}^*\boldsymbol{A}^* = \lambda^*\boldsymbol{x}^*$. Hence

$$\boldsymbol{x}^*\boldsymbol{x} = \boldsymbol{x}^*\boldsymbol{A}^*\boldsymbol{A}\boldsymbol{x} = \lambda^*\lambda\boldsymbol{x}^*\boldsymbol{x}.$$

Since $\boldsymbol{x}^*\boldsymbol{x} \neq 0$, we obtain $\lambda^*\lambda = 1$ and hence $|\lambda| = 1$.

Exercise 7.23 (Eigenvalues of a complex-orthogonal matrix) Let us reconsider the matrix introduced in Exercise 4.26(b). In particular, let

$$\boldsymbol{B}_1 = \begin{pmatrix} \sqrt{2} & \mathrm{i} \\ -\mathrm{i} & \sqrt{2} \end{pmatrix} \quad \text{and} \quad \boldsymbol{B}_2 = \begin{pmatrix} 0 & \mathrm{i} \\ -\mathrm{i} & 0 \end{pmatrix}.$$

(a) Show that $|\boldsymbol{B}_1| = 1$ and $|\boldsymbol{B}_2| = -1$.
(b) Find the eigenvalues of $\boldsymbol{B}_1$ and $\boldsymbol{B}_2$.

Solution
The matrix $\boldsymbol{B}_1$ satisfies $\boldsymbol{B}_1'\boldsymbol{B}_1 = \boldsymbol{I}_2$, but it is a complex matrix. Hence, $\boldsymbol{B}_1$ is not orthogonal; we call it complex-orthogonal. The matrix $\boldsymbol{B}_2$ satisfies $\boldsymbol{B}_2^*\boldsymbol{B}_2 = \boldsymbol{I}_2$ and is therefore unitary. Both matrices are Hermitian.
(a) We have $|\boldsymbol{B}_1| = (\sqrt{2})^2 + \mathrm{i}^2 = 2 - 1 = 1$ and $|\boldsymbol{B}_2| = \mathrm{i}^2 = -1$. This suggests (and this is indeed the case) that the determinant of a complex-orthogonal matrix equals ± 1.
(b) The eigenvalues of $\boldsymbol{B}_1$ are $\sqrt{2} \pm 1$, and the eigenvalues of $\boldsymbol{B}_2$ (in agreement with Exercise 7.22) are ± 1. Hence, the eigenvalues of a complex-orthogonal matrix do *not* in general have modulus one. This is one important reason for restricting the word "orthogonal" to real matrices.

Exercise 7.24 (Similarity) If there exists a nonsingular matrix $\boldsymbol{T}$ such that $\boldsymbol{B} = \boldsymbol{T}^{-1}\boldsymbol{A}\boldsymbol{T}$, the square matrices $\boldsymbol{A}$ and $\boldsymbol{B}$ are said to be similar.
(a) Show that similar matrices have the same set of eigenvalues (with the same multiplicities).
(b) Do they have the same set of eigenvectors as well?

Solution

(a) From

$$\lambda \boldsymbol{I}_n - \boldsymbol{T}^{-1}\boldsymbol{A}\boldsymbol{T} = \boldsymbol{T}^{-1}(\lambda \boldsymbol{I}_n - \boldsymbol{A})\boldsymbol{T},$$

we obtain

$$|\lambda \boldsymbol{I}_n - \boldsymbol{T}^{-1}\boldsymbol{A}\boldsymbol{T}| = |\boldsymbol{T}^{-1}||\lambda \boldsymbol{I}_n - \boldsymbol{A}||\boldsymbol{T}| = |\lambda \boldsymbol{I}_n - \boldsymbol{A}|.$$

(b) No. If $\boldsymbol{A}\boldsymbol{x} = \lambda \boldsymbol{x}$, then $\boldsymbol{B}(\boldsymbol{T}^{-1}\boldsymbol{x}) = \lambda(\boldsymbol{T}^{-1}\boldsymbol{x})$.

Exercise 7.25 (Eigenvalues of AB and BA compared) Let $\boldsymbol{A}$ be an $m \times n$ matrix and $\boldsymbol{B}$ an $n \times m$ matrix.
(a) Show that $|\boldsymbol{I}_m - \boldsymbol{A}\boldsymbol{B}| = |\boldsymbol{I}_n - \boldsymbol{B}\boldsymbol{A}|$.
(b) Hence, show that the nonzero eigenvalues of $\boldsymbol{B}\boldsymbol{A}$ and $\boldsymbol{A}\boldsymbol{B}$ are identical.
(c) If $n > m$, show that the $n \times n$ matrix $\boldsymbol{B}\boldsymbol{A}$ contains at least $n - m$ zero eigenvalues. Why *at least*?

Solution

(a) Taking determinants on both sides of the equality

$$\begin{pmatrix} \boldsymbol{I}_m - \boldsymbol{A}\boldsymbol{B} & \boldsymbol{A} \\ \mathrm{O} & \boldsymbol{I}_n \end{pmatrix} \begin{pmatrix} \boldsymbol{I}_m & \mathrm{O} \\ \boldsymbol{B} & \boldsymbol{I}_n \end{pmatrix} = \begin{pmatrix} \boldsymbol{I}_m & \mathrm{O} \\ \boldsymbol{B} & \boldsymbol{I}_n \end{pmatrix} \begin{pmatrix} \boldsymbol{I}_m & \boldsymbol{A} \\ \mathrm{O} & \boldsymbol{I}_n - \boldsymbol{B}\boldsymbol{A} \end{pmatrix},$$

we obtain $|\boldsymbol{I}_m - \boldsymbol{A}\boldsymbol{B}| = |\boldsymbol{I}_n - \boldsymbol{B}\boldsymbol{A}|$.
(b) Let $\lambda \neq 0$. Then,

$$\begin{aligned} |\lambda \boldsymbol{I}_n - \boldsymbol{B}\boldsymbol{A}| &= \lambda^n |\boldsymbol{I}_n - \boldsymbol{B}(\lambda^{-1}\boldsymbol{A})| \\ &= \lambda^n |\boldsymbol{I}_m - (\lambda^{-1}\boldsymbol{A})\boldsymbol{B}| = \lambda^{n-m}|\lambda \boldsymbol{I}_m - \boldsymbol{A}\boldsymbol{B}|. \end{aligned}$$

Hence, the nonzero eigenvalues of $\boldsymbol{B}\boldsymbol{A}$ are the same as the nonzero eigenvalues of $\boldsymbol{A}\boldsymbol{B}$.
(c) By the proof of (b), $|\lambda \boldsymbol{I}_n - \boldsymbol{B}\boldsymbol{A}| = 0$ if and only if $\lambda^{n-m}|\lambda \boldsymbol{I}_m - \boldsymbol{A}\boldsymbol{B}| = 0$. The latter equation has (at least) $n - m$ zero roots. If the equation $|\lambda \boldsymbol{I}_m - \boldsymbol{A}\boldsymbol{B}| = 0$ has no zero roots, then there are precisely $n - m$ zero eigenvalues; if the equation does have one or more zero roots, then there are more than $n - m$ zero eigenvalues.

Exercise 7.26 (Determinant and eigenvalues) Show that the determinant of a square matrix equals the product of its eigenvalues, $|\boldsymbol{A}| = \prod_{i=1}^n \lambda_i$.

Solution

If the eigenvalues of $\boldsymbol{A}$ are denoted by $\lambda_1, \lambda_2, \dots, \lambda_n$, then

$$|\lambda \boldsymbol{I}_n - \boldsymbol{A}| = (\lambda - \lambda_1)(\lambda - \lambda_2)\dots(\lambda - \lambda_n).$$

Now, set $\lambda = 0$. This gives $|-\boldsymbol{A}| = (-1)^n \prod_i \lambda_i$ and hence $|\boldsymbol{A}| = \prod_i \lambda_i$.

Exercise 7.27 (Trace and eigenvalues)
(a) If $\boldsymbol{A}$ is a square matrix of order n, show that

$$|\lambda \boldsymbol{I}_n - \boldsymbol{A}| = \lambda^n - (\operatorname{tr} \boldsymbol{A})\lambda^{n-1} + P_{n-2}(\lambda),$$

where $P_{n-2}(\lambda)$ denotes a polynomial in λ of degree $n-2$ or less.
(b) If the eigenvalues of $\boldsymbol{A}$ are $\lambda_1, \dots, \lambda_n$, show that

$$|\lambda \boldsymbol{I}_n - \boldsymbol{A}| = \lambda^n - \left(\sum_{i=1}^n \lambda_i\right)\lambda^{n-1} + P_{n-2}(\lambda).$$

(c) Conclude that

$$\operatorname{tr} \boldsymbol{A} = \sum_{i=1}^n \lambda_i.$$

Solution
(a) Let $\boldsymbol{A}_{(k)}$ ($k = 1, \dots, n$) denote the $k \times k$ leading principal submatrix of $\boldsymbol{A}$, so that $\boldsymbol{A}_{(1)} = a_{11}$ and $\boldsymbol{A}_{(n)} = \boldsymbol{A}$. Denoting irrelevant elements by a $*$, we may write

$$|\lambda \boldsymbol{I}_n - \boldsymbol{A}| = \begin{vmatrix} \lambda \boldsymbol{I}_{n-1} - \boldsymbol{A}_{(n-1)} & * \\ * & \lambda - a_{nn} \end{vmatrix} = (\lambda - a_{nn})|\lambda \boldsymbol{I}_{n-1} - \boldsymbol{A}_{(n-1)}| + P_{n-2}(\lambda),$$

because in each term of the remainder two of the diagonal elements are missing. Hence,

$$\begin{aligned} |\lambda \boldsymbol{I}_n - \boldsymbol{A}| &= (\lambda - a_{nn})(\lambda - a_{n-1,n-1})|\lambda \boldsymbol{I}_{n-2} - \boldsymbol{A}_{(n-2)}| + P_{n-2}(\lambda) \\ &= (\lambda - a_{nn})(\lambda - a_{n-1,n-1}) \dots (\lambda - a_{11}) + P_{n-2}(\lambda) \\ &= \lambda^n - (a_{nn} + a_{n-1,n-1} + \dots + a_{11})\lambda^{n-1} + P_{n-2}(\lambda) \\ &= \lambda^n - (\operatorname{tr} \boldsymbol{A})\lambda^{n-1} + P_{n-2}(\lambda). \end{aligned}$$

(b) We also have

$$\begin{aligned} |\lambda \boldsymbol{I}_n - \boldsymbol{A}| &= (\lambda - \lambda_1)(\lambda - \lambda_2) \dots (\lambda - \lambda_n) \\ &= \lambda^n - (\lambda_1 + \lambda_2 + \dots + \lambda_n)\lambda^{n-1} + P_{n-2}(\lambda). \end{aligned}$$

(c) Equating the coefficients of λ^{n-1} in the two expressions gives $\operatorname{tr} \boldsymbol{A} = \sum_i \lambda_i$.

Exercise 7.28 (Trace, powers, and eigenvalues, 1) For any $n \times n$ matrix $\boldsymbol{A}$ with eigenvalues $\lambda_1, \dots, \lambda_n$, show that

$$\operatorname{tr} \boldsymbol{A}^k = \sum_{i=1}^n \lambda_i^k \quad (k = 1, 2, \dots).$$

Solution
This is an immediate consequence of Exercise 7.27(c) because the eigenvalues of $\boldsymbol{A}^k$ are $\lambda_1^k, \lambda_2^k, \dots, \lambda_n^k$ by Exercise 7.14(b).

Exercise 7.29 (Elementary symmetric functions) Consider the polynomial

$$p(\lambda) := (\lambda - \lambda_1)(\lambda - \lambda_2)(\lambda - \lambda_3) = p_0 + p_1\lambda + p_2\lambda^2 + \lambda^3.$$

Define the elementary symmetric functions

$$s_1 := \lambda_1 + \lambda_2 + \lambda_3, \quad s_2 := \lambda_1\lambda_2 + \lambda_1\lambda_3 + \lambda_2\lambda_3, \quad s_3 := \lambda_1\lambda_2\lambda_3,$$

and the power sums

$$\sigma_1 := \lambda_1 + \lambda_2 + \lambda_3, \quad \sigma_2 := \lambda_1^2 + \lambda_2^2 + \lambda_3^2, \quad \sigma_3 := \lambda_1^3 + \lambda_2^3 + \lambda_3^3.$$

(a) Show that

$$p_0 = -s_3, \quad p_1 = s_2, \quad p_2 = -s_1.$$

(b) Show that between the sets $\{s_1, s_2, s_3\}$ and $\{\sigma_1, \sigma_2, \sigma_3\}$ there exists a one-to-one relationship. (This result generalizes to polynomials of arbitrary degree.)

Solution

(a) We have

$$\begin{aligned}
p(\lambda) &= (\lambda - \lambda_1)(\lambda - \lambda_2)(\lambda - \lambda_3) \\
&= (\lambda - \lambda_1)(\lambda^2 - (\lambda_2 + \lambda_3)\lambda + \lambda_2\lambda_3) \\
&= \lambda^3 - (\lambda_1 + \lambda_2 + \lambda_3)\lambda^2 + (\lambda_1\lambda_2 + \lambda_1\lambda_3 + \lambda_2\lambda_3)\lambda - \lambda_1\lambda_2\lambda_3 \\
&= -s_3 + s_2\lambda - s_1\lambda^2 + \lambda^3.
\end{aligned}$$

(b) One verifies that

$$\begin{aligned}
\sigma_1 &= s_1 \\
\sigma_2 &= s_1^2 - 2s_2 \\
\sigma_3 &= s_1^3 - 3s_1s_2 + 3s_3
\end{aligned}$$

and

$$\begin{aligned}
s_1 &= \sigma_1 \\
s_2 &= \frac{1}{2}(\sigma_1^2 - \sigma_2) \\
s_3 &= \frac{1}{6}(\sigma_1^3 - 3\sigma_1\sigma_2 + 2\sigma_3).
\end{aligned}$$

Exercise 7.30 (When do A and B have the same eigenvalues?) Use the one-to-one correspondence between the sets $\{s_i\}$ and $\{\sigma_i\}$ to show that two $n \times n$ matrices $\boldsymbol{A}$ and $\boldsymbol{B}$ have the same set of eigenvalues if and only if $\operatorname{tr} \boldsymbol{A}^k = \operatorname{tr} \boldsymbol{B}^k$ $(k = 1, 2, \dots, n)$.

Solution

If $\boldsymbol{A}$ and $\boldsymbol{B}$ have the same set of eigenvalues, say $\lambda_1, \dots, \lambda_n$, then, by Exercise 7.28,

$$\operatorname{tr} \boldsymbol{A}^k = \sum_{i=1}^{n} \lambda_i^k = \operatorname{tr} \boldsymbol{B}^k.$$

To prove the converse, it is sufficient to show that $\boldsymbol{A}$ and $\boldsymbol{B}$ have the same characteristic polynomial or, equivalently, that the elementary symmetric functions $s_k(\boldsymbol{A})$ and $s_k(\boldsymbol{B})$ of the eigenvalues of $\boldsymbol{A}$ and $\boldsymbol{B}$, respectively, are identical for $k = 1, 2, \dots, n$. Let

$$\sigma_k(\boldsymbol{A}) := \sum_{i=1}^{n} \lambda_i^k(\boldsymbol{A}), \quad \sigma_k(\boldsymbol{B}) := \sum_{i=1}^{n} \lambda_i^k(\boldsymbol{B}) \quad (k = 1, \dots, n).$$

We need to demonstrate that if $\sigma_k(\boldsymbol{A}) = \sigma_k(\boldsymbol{B})$ for $k = 1, \dots, n$, then also $s_k(\boldsymbol{A}) = s_k(\boldsymbol{B})$ for $k = 1, \dots, n$. But this follows from the fact that the sets $\{s_k\}$ and $\{\sigma_k\}$ are in one-to-one correspondence, a fact stated (without proof) in the introduction and proved for $n = 3$ in Exercise 7.29.

Exercise 7.31 (Linear independence of eigenvectors)

(a) Show that eigenvectors associated with distinct eigenvalues are linearly independent.
(b) Are these eigenvectors orthogonal to each other?

Solution

(a) Our proof is by contradiction. Consider a set $\boldsymbol{x}_1, \dots, \boldsymbol{x}_s$ of eigenvectors of $\boldsymbol{A}$ such that $\boldsymbol{x}_j$ is associated with the eigenvalue λ_j and no two λ_j are equal. Suppose this set is linearly dependent. Rearrange the eigenvectors (if necessary) such that $\boldsymbol{x}_1, \dots, \boldsymbol{x}_r$ $(r \leq s)$ are linearly independent. Then, for $j = r+1, \dots, s$, $\boldsymbol{x}_j = \sum_{i=1}^{r} \alpha_{ij} \boldsymbol{x}_i$. Hence,

$$\lambda_j \boldsymbol{x}_j = \lambda_j \sum_{i=1}^{r} \alpha_{ij} \boldsymbol{x}_i,$$

and also

$$\lambda_j \boldsymbol{x}_j = \boldsymbol{A} \boldsymbol{x}_j = \sum_{i=1}^{r} \alpha_{ij} \boldsymbol{A} \boldsymbol{x}_i = \sum_{i=1}^{r} \alpha_{ij} \lambda_i \boldsymbol{x}_i.$$

Thus we obtain $\sum_{i=1}^{r} \alpha_{ij}(\lambda_i - \lambda_j)\boldsymbol{x}_i = \mathbf{0}$. Since $\boldsymbol{x}_1, \dots, \boldsymbol{x}_r$ are linearly independent, this implies that $\alpha_{ij}(\lambda_i - \lambda_j) = 0$ for all $i = 1, \dots, r$ and $j = r+1, \dots, s$. But $\lambda_i \neq \lambda_j$ by assumption. Hence, $\alpha_{ij} = 0$ for all $i = 1, \dots, r$ and $j = r+1, \dots, s$, and hence $\boldsymbol{x}_{r+1} = \dots = \boldsymbol{x}_s = 0$. This contradicts the fact that $\boldsymbol{x}_{r+1}, \dots, \boldsymbol{x}_s$ are eigenvectors and therefore nonzero.

(b) If the matrix $\boldsymbol{A}$ is symmetric, then these eigenvectors are indeed orthogonal to each other (Exercise 7.44), but if $\boldsymbol{A}$ is not symmetric then they may or may not be orthogonal. For example, let

$$\boldsymbol{A} = \begin{pmatrix} 4 & 1 \\ 1 & 2 \end{pmatrix} \quad \text{and} \quad \boldsymbol{B} = \begin{pmatrix} 4 & 1 \\ 2 & 2 \end{pmatrix}.$$

The eigenvalues of $\boldsymbol{A}$ are $\lambda_1 = 3 + \sqrt{2}$ and $\lambda_2 = 3 - \sqrt{2}$. The associated eigenvectors are

$$\boldsymbol{x}_1 = \begin{pmatrix} 1 \\ -1 + \sqrt{2} \end{pmatrix} \quad \text{and} \quad \boldsymbol{x}_2 = \begin{pmatrix} 1 \\ -1 - \sqrt{2} \end{pmatrix},$$

and we see that $\boldsymbol{x}_1'\boldsymbol{x}_2 = 1 - 1 = 0$. On the other hand, the eigenvalues of $\boldsymbol{B}$ are $\lambda_1 = 3 + \sqrt{3}$ and $\lambda_2 = 3 - \sqrt{3}$, and the associated eigenvectors are

$$\boldsymbol{x}_1 = \begin{pmatrix} 1 \\ -1 + \sqrt{3} \end{pmatrix} \quad \text{and} \quad \boldsymbol{x}_2 = \begin{pmatrix} 1 \\ -1 - \sqrt{3} \end{pmatrix},$$

so that $\boldsymbol{x}_1'\boldsymbol{x}_2 = -1 \neq 0$.

In this example, the eigenvectors are orthogonal to each other when the matrix is symmetric, but not orthogonal when the matrix is not symmetric. One may wonder whether symmetry is necessary and sufficient for the eigenvectors to be orthogonal. This is *not* the case. Symmetry, though sufficient, is not necessary. Necessity is provided by the class of *normal* matrices (Exercise 7.73).

Exercise 7.32 (Diagonalization of matrices with distinct eigenvalues) Let $\boldsymbol{A}$ be an $n \times n$ matrix with distinct eigenvalues. Then there exist a nonsingular $n \times n$ matrix $\boldsymbol{T}$ and a diagonal $n \times n$ matrix $\boldsymbol{\Lambda}$ whose diagonal elements are the eigenvalues of $\boldsymbol{A}$, such that $\boldsymbol{T}^{-1}\boldsymbol{A}\boldsymbol{T} = \boldsymbol{\Lambda}$.

Solution

Let $\lambda_1, \dots, \lambda_n$ be the eigenvalues of $\boldsymbol{A}$, and let $\boldsymbol{A}\boldsymbol{x}_i = \lambda_i \boldsymbol{x}_i$ for $i = 1, \dots, n$. Let $\boldsymbol{T} := (\boldsymbol{x}_1, \boldsymbol{x}_2, \dots, \boldsymbol{x}_n)$. Then,

$$\boldsymbol{A}\boldsymbol{T} = (\boldsymbol{A}\boldsymbol{x}_1, \dots, \boldsymbol{A}\boldsymbol{x}_n) = (\lambda_1\boldsymbol{x}_1, \dots, \lambda_n\boldsymbol{x}_n) = \boldsymbol{T}\boldsymbol{\Lambda},$$

where $\boldsymbol{\Lambda} := \operatorname{diag}(\lambda_1, \dots, \lambda_n)$. The eigenvectors $\boldsymbol{x}_1, \dots, \boldsymbol{x}_n$ are linearly independent, because the eigenvalues are distinct (Exercise 7.31). Hence, the matrix $\boldsymbol{T}$ is nonsingular, and we obtain $\boldsymbol{T}^{-1}\boldsymbol{A}\boldsymbol{T} = \boldsymbol{\Lambda}$.

Exercise 7.33 (Can all matrices be diagonalized?) Show that the matrix

$$\boldsymbol{A} = \begin{pmatrix} 1 & 1 & 0 \\ 0 & 1 & 1 \\ 0 & 0 & 1 \end{pmatrix}$$

cannot be diagonalized. That is, no matrix $\boldsymbol{T}$ exists such that $\boldsymbol{T}^{-1}\boldsymbol{A}\boldsymbol{T} = \boldsymbol{\Lambda}$, where $\boldsymbol{\Lambda}$ is a diagonal matrix containing the eigenvalues of $\boldsymbol{A}$.

Solution

The eigenvalues of $\boldsymbol{A}$ are 1 (3 times). Consider the equation $\boldsymbol{A}\boldsymbol{x} = \boldsymbol{x}$. The only solution is $\boldsymbol{x} = (1, 0, 0)'$ (or multiples thereof), and hence there exists no nonsingular $\boldsymbol{T}$ such that $\boldsymbol{A}\boldsymbol{T} = \boldsymbol{T}$. The problem lies in the fact that the eigenvectors do not span $\mathbb{R}^3$; in fact, they only span $\mathbb{R}$. This is sometimes expressed by saying that the (algebraic) multiplicity of the eigenvalue is three and the geometric multiplicity is one.

Exercise 7.34 (QR factorization) Let $\boldsymbol{A}$ be an $m \times n$ matrix of rank n (so that $m \geq n$). Use the Gram-Schmidt process of Exercise 3.49 to show that there exist an $m \times n$ matrix $\boldsymbol{Q}$ satisfying $\boldsymbol{Q}^*\boldsymbol{Q} = \boldsymbol{I}_n$ and an $n \times n$ upper triangular matrix $\boldsymbol{R}$ with positive diagonal elements, such that $\boldsymbol{A} = \boldsymbol{QR}$.

Solution

This proceeds in the same way as the Gram-Schmidt process described in Exercise 3.49. Let $\boldsymbol{a}_1, \boldsymbol{a}_2, \dots, \boldsymbol{a}_n$ be the columns of $\boldsymbol{A}$, and define

$$\begin{aligned}
\boldsymbol{q}_1 &:= \boldsymbol{a}_1 \\
\boldsymbol{q}_2 &:= \boldsymbol{a}_2 - r_{12}\boldsymbol{q}_1 \\
&\ \vdots \\
\boldsymbol{q}_n &:= \boldsymbol{a}_n - r_{n-1,n}\boldsymbol{q}_{n-1} - \dots - r_{1n}\boldsymbol{q}_1.
\end{aligned}$$

The coefficients in the i-th equation are chosen in such a way that $\boldsymbol{q}_i$ is orthogonal to each of $\boldsymbol{q}_1, \dots, \boldsymbol{q}_{i-1}$. Thus, $\boldsymbol{q}_2 \perp \boldsymbol{q}_1$ yields $\boldsymbol{a}_2^*\boldsymbol{q}_1 = r_{12}\boldsymbol{q}_1^*\boldsymbol{q}_1$ and $\boldsymbol{q}_3 \perp \boldsymbol{q}_1$, $\boldsymbol{q}_3 \perp \boldsymbol{q}_2$ yields $\boldsymbol{a}_3^*\boldsymbol{q}_1 = r_{13}\boldsymbol{q}_1^*\boldsymbol{q}_1$ and $\boldsymbol{a}_3^*\boldsymbol{q}_2 = r_{23}\boldsymbol{q}_2^*\boldsymbol{q}_2$. Continuing in this way we find all the coefficients from $\boldsymbol{a}_j^*\boldsymbol{q}_i = r_{ij}\boldsymbol{q}_i^*\boldsymbol{q}_i$, $i = 1, \dots, j-1$. Now let $\boldsymbol{Q}_1 := (\boldsymbol{q}_1, \dots, \boldsymbol{q}_n)$ and

$$\boldsymbol{R}_1 := \begin{pmatrix} 1 & r_{12} & \dots & r_{1n} \\ 0 & 1 & \dots & r_{2n} \\ \vdots & \vdots & \dots & \vdots \\ 0 & 0 & \dots & 1 \end{pmatrix}.$$

Then $\boldsymbol{A} = \boldsymbol{Q}_1\boldsymbol{R}_1$. By construction, the columns of $\boldsymbol{Q}_1$ are orthogonal, but not yet orthonormal. Let $\lambda_i := \boldsymbol{q}_i^*\boldsymbol{q}_i$ and $\boldsymbol{\Lambda} := \operatorname{diag}(\lambda_1, \dots, \lambda_n)$. Define $\boldsymbol{Q} := \boldsymbol{Q}_1\boldsymbol{\Lambda}^{-1/2}$ and $\boldsymbol{R} := \boldsymbol{\Lambda}^{1/2}\boldsymbol{R}_1$. Then $\boldsymbol{Q}$ and $\boldsymbol{R}$ satisfy the required properties.

Exercise 7.35 (QR factorization, real) If $\boldsymbol{A}$ is a real $m \times n$ matrix of rank n, then show that there exist an $m \times n$ semi-orthogonal matrix $\boldsymbol{Q}$ (that is, a real matrix satisfying $\boldsymbol{Q}'\boldsymbol{Q} = \boldsymbol{I}_n$) and an $n \times n$ real upper triangular matrix $\boldsymbol{R}$ with positive diagonal elements, such that $\boldsymbol{A} = \boldsymbol{QR}$.

Solution

If we assume that $\boldsymbol{A}$ is real in the solution to Exercise 7.34, then it follows that $\boldsymbol{q}_1$ is real, hence that r_{12} is real, hence that $\boldsymbol{q}_2$ is real, and so on.

Exercise 7.36 (A matrix of rank one) Let $\boldsymbol{x}$ and $\boldsymbol{y}$ be $n \times 1$ vectors.

(a) Prove that $\boldsymbol{xy}'$ has $n-1$ zero eigenvalues and one eigenvalue $\boldsymbol{y}'\boldsymbol{x}$.

(b) Show that $|\boldsymbol{I}_n + \boldsymbol{x}\boldsymbol{y}'| = 1 + \boldsymbol{y}'\boldsymbol{x}$.
(c) Let $\mu := 1 + \boldsymbol{y}'\boldsymbol{x}$. If $\mu \neq 0$, show that $(\boldsymbol{I}_n + \boldsymbol{x}\boldsymbol{y}')^{-1} = \boldsymbol{I}_n - \mu^{-1}\boldsymbol{x}\boldsymbol{y}'$.

Solution
(a) Since there are $n-1$ linearly independent vectors $\boldsymbol{u}_i$ satisfying $\boldsymbol{y}'\boldsymbol{u}_i = 0$, each of these satisfy the equation $\boldsymbol{x}\boldsymbol{y}'\boldsymbol{u}_i = \boldsymbol{0}$. Hence, the $\boldsymbol{u}_i$ form a set of linearly independent eigenvectors associated with the eigenvalue 0, which has multiplicity $n-1$. Since $\operatorname{tr}(\boldsymbol{x}\boldsymbol{y}') = \boldsymbol{y}'\boldsymbol{x}$ equals the sum of the n eigenvalues, the only possibly nonzero eigenvalue is $\boldsymbol{y}'\boldsymbol{x}$.
(b) The eigenvalues of $\boldsymbol{I}_n + \boldsymbol{x}\boldsymbol{y}'$ are 1 ($n-1$ times) and $1 + \boldsymbol{y}'\boldsymbol{x}$. Since the determinant is the product of the eigenvalues, we have $|\boldsymbol{I}_n + \boldsymbol{x}\boldsymbol{y}'| = 1 + \boldsymbol{y}'\boldsymbol{x}$. (The result also follows directly from Exercise 7.25.)
(c) We just check that

$$\begin{aligned}(\boldsymbol{I}_n + \boldsymbol{x}\boldsymbol{y}')(\boldsymbol{I}_n - \mu^{-1}\boldsymbol{x}\boldsymbol{y}') &= \boldsymbol{I}_n - \mu^{-1}\boldsymbol{x}\boldsymbol{y}' + \boldsymbol{x}\boldsymbol{y}' - \mu^{-1}\boldsymbol{x}\boldsymbol{y}'\boldsymbol{x}\boldsymbol{y}' \\ &= \boldsymbol{I}_n - \mu^{-1}\left(1 - \mu + \boldsymbol{y}'\boldsymbol{x}\right)\boldsymbol{x}\boldsymbol{y}' = \boldsymbol{I}_n,\end{aligned}$$

or we apply the result of Exercise 4.28(c).

Exercise 7.37 (Left eigenvector) A left eigenvector of $\boldsymbol{A}$ associated with the eigenvalue λ is a nonzero vector $\boldsymbol{y}$ such that $\boldsymbol{y}^*\boldsymbol{A} = \lambda\boldsymbol{y}^*$.
(a) Show that a left eigenvector $\boldsymbol{y}$ associated with an eigenvalue λ of $\boldsymbol{A}$ is a right eigenvector of $\boldsymbol{A}^*$ associated with λ^*.
(b) If $\lambda \neq \mu$ are two eigenvalues of $\boldsymbol{A}$, show that any left eigenvector associated with μ is orthogonal to any right eigenvector associated with λ.

Solution
(a) We have

$$\boldsymbol{A}^*\boldsymbol{y} = (\boldsymbol{y}^*\boldsymbol{A})^* = (\lambda\boldsymbol{y}^*)^* = \lambda^*\boldsymbol{y}.$$

(b) Let $\boldsymbol{A}\boldsymbol{x} = \lambda\boldsymbol{x}$ and $\boldsymbol{y}^*\boldsymbol{A} = \mu\boldsymbol{y}^*$. Then,

$$\boldsymbol{y}^*\boldsymbol{A}\boldsymbol{x} = \boldsymbol{y}^*(\lambda\boldsymbol{x}) = \lambda(\boldsymbol{y}^*\boldsymbol{x})$$

and also

$$\boldsymbol{y}^*\boldsymbol{A}\boldsymbol{x} = (\mu\boldsymbol{y}^*)\boldsymbol{x} = \mu(\boldsymbol{y}^*\boldsymbol{x}).$$

Since $\lambda \neq \mu$, we must have $\boldsymbol{y}^*\boldsymbol{x} = 0$. Hence, $\boldsymbol{x}$ and $\boldsymbol{y}$ are orthogonal to each other.

Exercise 7.38 (Companion matrix) Show that the matrix

$$\boldsymbol{C} := \begin{pmatrix} 0 & 1 & 0 & \dots & 0 & 0 \\ 0 & 0 & 1 & \dots & 0 & 0 \\ 0 & 0 & 0 & \dots & 0 & 0 \\ \vdots & \vdots & \vdots & & \vdots & \vdots \\ 0 & 0 & 0 & \dots & 0 & 1 \\ -a_0 & -a_1 & -a_2 & \dots & -a_{n-2} & -a_{n-1} \end{pmatrix}$$

has as its characteristic equation

$$p_C(\lambda) = |\lambda \boldsymbol{I}_n - \boldsymbol{C}| = \lambda^n + a_{n-1}\lambda^{n-1} + a_{n-2}\lambda^{n-2} + \cdots + a_1\lambda + a_0.$$

The matrix $\boldsymbol{C}$ is called the *companion matrix* for this characteristic equation.

Solution

Define the $j \times j$ matrix

$$\boldsymbol{A}_{(j)}[x] := \begin{pmatrix} \lambda & -1 & 0 & \dots & 0 & 0 \\ 0 & \lambda & -1 & \dots & 0 & 0 \\ 0 & 0 & \lambda & \dots & 0 & 0 \\ \vdots & \vdots & \vdots & & \vdots & \vdots \\ 0 & 0 & 0 & \dots & \lambda & -1 \\ a_0 & a_1 & a_2 & \dots & a_{j-2} & x \end{pmatrix}.$$

Then,

$$\begin{aligned} |\lambda \boldsymbol{I}_n - \boldsymbol{C}| &= |\boldsymbol{A}_{(n)}[\lambda + a_{n-1}]| = (\lambda + a_{n-1})\lambda^{n-1} + |\boldsymbol{A}_{(n-1)}[a_{n-2}]| \\ &= \lambda^n + a_{n-1}\lambda^{n-1} + a_{n-2}\lambda^{n-2} + |\boldsymbol{A}_{(n-2)}[a_{n-3}]| = \dots \\ &= \lambda^n + a_{n-1}\lambda^{n-1} + a_{n-2}\lambda^{n-2} + \cdots + a_2\lambda^2 + \begin{vmatrix} \lambda & -1 \\ a_0 & a_1 \end{vmatrix} \\ &= \lambda^n + a_{n-1}\lambda^{n-1} + a_{n-2}\lambda^{n-2} + \cdots + a_2\lambda^2 + a_1\lambda + a_0. \end{aligned}$$

Exercise 7.39 (Simultaneous reduction to diagonal form, 1)
(a) Let λ be a simple eigenvalue of a square matrix $\boldsymbol{A}$, so that $\boldsymbol{Ax} = \lambda \boldsymbol{x}$ for some eigenvector $\boldsymbol{x}$. If $\boldsymbol{A}$ and $\boldsymbol{B}$ commute, show that $\boldsymbol{x}$ is an eigenvector of $\boldsymbol{B}$ too.
(b) Hence, show that, if $\boldsymbol{A}$ has only simple eigenvalues and commutes with $\boldsymbol{B}$, then a nonsingular matrix $\boldsymbol{T}$ exists such that $\boldsymbol{T}^{-1}\boldsymbol{AT} = \boldsymbol{\Lambda}$ (diagonal) and $\boldsymbol{T}^{-1}\boldsymbol{BT} = \boldsymbol{M}$ (diagonal). (Compare Exercise 7.51 for the case where $\boldsymbol{A}$ and $\boldsymbol{B}$ are symmetric.)

Solution

(a) We have $\boldsymbol{Ax} = \lambda \boldsymbol{x}$ and also

$$\boldsymbol{A}(\boldsymbol{Bx}) = \boldsymbol{ABx} = \boldsymbol{BAx} = \boldsymbol{B}(\lambda \boldsymbol{x}) = \lambda(\boldsymbol{Bx}).$$

Hence, both $\boldsymbol{Bx}$ and $\boldsymbol{x}$ are eigenvectors associated with λ. Now, since λ is a simple eigenvalue, it follows that $\boldsymbol{Bx}$ and $\boldsymbol{x}$ are collinear, that is, $\boldsymbol{Bx} = \mu \boldsymbol{x}$ for some scalar μ, so that $\boldsymbol{x}$ is an eigenvector of $\boldsymbol{B}$ too.
(b) We know from Exercise 7.32 that there exist a nonsingular $n \times n$ matrix $\boldsymbol{T}$ and a diagonal $n \times n$ matrix $\boldsymbol{\Lambda}$ whose diagonal elements are the eigenvalues of $\boldsymbol{A}$, such that $\boldsymbol{T}^{-1}\boldsymbol{AT} = \boldsymbol{\Lambda}$. In addition, we know from (a) that $\boldsymbol{A}$ and $\boldsymbol{B}$ have the same set of eigenvectors. Hence, $\boldsymbol{BT} = \boldsymbol{TM}$ for some diagonal matrix $\boldsymbol{M}$ and the result follows.

7.2 Symmetric matrices

Exercise 7.40 (Real eigenvalues) Show that the eigenvalues of a symmetric matrix are real. How about the eigenvalues of a Hermitian matrix?

Solution

Let $\boldsymbol{A}\boldsymbol{x} = \lambda \boldsymbol{x}$. Then, $\boldsymbol{x}^*\boldsymbol{A}\boldsymbol{x} = \lambda \boldsymbol{x}^*\boldsymbol{x}$. Taking conjugate transposes gives $\boldsymbol{x}^*\boldsymbol{A}^*\boldsymbol{x} = \lambda^*\boldsymbol{x}^*\boldsymbol{x}$. But $\boldsymbol{A}^* = \boldsymbol{A}$, implying that $\lambda^*\boldsymbol{x}^*\boldsymbol{x} = \lambda\boldsymbol{x}^*\boldsymbol{x}$, and hence that $\lambda^* = \lambda$. We conclude that λ is real. Since this holds for Hermitian matrices, it holds for real Hermitian (that is, symmetric) matrices in particular.

Exercise 7.41 (Eigenvalues of a complex-symmetric matrix) Show that the eigenvalues of a complex matrix $\boldsymbol{A}$ satisfying $\boldsymbol{A}' = \boldsymbol{A}$ are not necessarily real.

Solution

Consider the matrix

$$\boldsymbol{A} = \begin{pmatrix} 1 & \mathrm{i} \\ \mathrm{i} & 1 \end{pmatrix}.$$

Its eigenvalues are found from the equation $(1-\lambda)^2 = -1$ and hence they are $1 \pm \mathrm{i}$.

Exercise 7.42 (A symmetric orthogonal matrix) Show that a symmetric orthogonal matrix has only eigenvalues 1 and -1.

Solution

We know from Exercise 7.22 that all eigenvalues of an orthogonal matrix have unit modulus, that is, if $\lambda = a + ib$ is an eigenvalue, then $a^2 + b^2 = 1$. However, if $\boldsymbol{A}$ is symmetric, then all eigenvalues must be real, so that $b = 0$ and $\lambda = \pm 1$.

Exercise 7.43 (Real eigenvectors) Show that the eigenvectors of a symmetric matrix can always be chosen to be real.

Solution

Let λ (real) be an eigenvalue of the symmetric matrix $\boldsymbol{A}$, and let $\boldsymbol{x}$ be an associated eigenvector. Write $\boldsymbol{x} = \operatorname{Re}(\boldsymbol{x}) + \mathrm{i}\operatorname{Im}(\boldsymbol{x})$. Then, $\boldsymbol{A}(\operatorname{Re}(\boldsymbol{x}) + \mathrm{i}\operatorname{Im}(\boldsymbol{x})) = \lambda(\operatorname{Re}(\boldsymbol{x}) + \mathrm{i}\operatorname{Im}(\boldsymbol{x}))$, giving $\boldsymbol{A}\operatorname{Re}(\boldsymbol{x}) = \lambda\operatorname{Re}(\boldsymbol{x})$ and also $\boldsymbol{A}\operatorname{Im}(\boldsymbol{x}) = \lambda\operatorname{Im}(\boldsymbol{x})$. If $\operatorname{Re}(\boldsymbol{x}) \neq \boldsymbol{0}$, then $\operatorname{Re}(\boldsymbol{x})$ is a real eigenvector of $\boldsymbol{A}$. If $\operatorname{Re}(\boldsymbol{x}) = \boldsymbol{0}$, then $\operatorname{Im}(\boldsymbol{x})$ is a real eigenvector.

Exercise 7.44 (Orthogonal eigenvectors with distinct eigenvalues) When $\boldsymbol{A}$ is a symmetric matrix, show that eigenvectors associated with distinct eigenvalues are orthogonal to each other (not just linearly independent as in Exercise 7.31).

Solution

Let λ_i and λ_j be two eigenvalues of $\boldsymbol{A}$ and assume that $\lambda_i \neq \lambda_j$. Then eigenvectors $\boldsymbol{x}_i$ and $\boldsymbol{x}_j$ exist such that

$$\boldsymbol{A}\boldsymbol{x}_i = \lambda_i \boldsymbol{x}_i \quad \text{and} \quad \boldsymbol{A}\boldsymbol{x}_j = \lambda_j \boldsymbol{x}_j.$$

As a result,

$$\lambda_i \boldsymbol{x}_j' \boldsymbol{x}_i = \boldsymbol{x}_j' \boldsymbol{A} \boldsymbol{x}_i = \boldsymbol{x}_i' \boldsymbol{A}' \boldsymbol{x}_j = \boldsymbol{x}_i' \boldsymbol{A} \boldsymbol{x}_j = \lambda_j \boldsymbol{x}_i' \boldsymbol{x}_j,$$

because of the symmetry of $\boldsymbol{A}$. Since $\lambda_i \neq \lambda_j$, we obtain $\boldsymbol{x}_i' \boldsymbol{x}_j = 0$.

Exercise 7.45 (Eigenvectors: independence and orthogonality) Consider the 2×2 matrix

$$\boldsymbol{A} = \begin{pmatrix} a & 1 \\ ab & b \end{pmatrix} \qquad (a \neq 0, b \neq 0).$$

(a) Obtain the eigenvalues and normalized eigenvectors of $\boldsymbol{A}$.
(b) Show that the two eigenvectors are linearly independent, unless $a + b = 0$. Why?
(c) Show that the two eigenvectors are not orthogonal, unless $ab = 1$. Why?

Solution

(a) The eigenvalues can be found from the characteristic equation

$$|\lambda \boldsymbol{I}_2 - \boldsymbol{A}| = \begin{vmatrix} \lambda - a & -1 \\ -ab & \lambda - b \end{vmatrix} = \lambda^2 - (a+b)\lambda = 0,$$

so that the eigenvalues are $\lambda_1 = 0$ and $\lambda_2 = a + b$. Alternatively, they can be found from the equations

$$\lambda_1 + \lambda_2 = \operatorname{tr} \boldsymbol{A} = a + b, \qquad \lambda_1 \lambda_2 = |\boldsymbol{A}| = 0.$$

To find the eigenvectors we must solve the equations $(\lambda_i \boldsymbol{I}_2 - \boldsymbol{A})\boldsymbol{x}_i = \boldsymbol{0}$. Let us take $\lambda_1 = 0$ first. The set of equations becomes

$$\begin{pmatrix} -a & -1 \\ -ab & -b \end{pmatrix} \begin{pmatrix} x_1 \\ x_2 \end{pmatrix} = \begin{pmatrix} 0 \\ 0 \end{pmatrix}$$

and hence $ax_1 + x_2 = 0$. The first eigenvector is therefore $\boldsymbol{x}_1 := \mu_1(1, -a)'$. Similarly, the second eigenvector (associated with λ_2) is $\boldsymbol{x}_2 := \mu_2(1, b)'$. After normalization, the eigenvectors become

$$\boldsymbol{x}_1 = \frac{1}{\sqrt{1+a^2}} \begin{pmatrix} 1 \\ -a \end{pmatrix} \quad \text{and} \quad \boldsymbol{x}_2 = \frac{1}{\sqrt{1+b^2}} \begin{pmatrix} 1 \\ b \end{pmatrix}.$$

Even then, the eigenvectors are not unique; the vector $-\boldsymbol{x}_1$ is also an eigenvector of length 1. To achieve uniqueness one sometimes requires that the first nonzero component of the eigenvector is positive, like here.

(b) The two eigenvectors are linearly dependent if and only if

$$\begin{vmatrix} 1 & 1 \\ -a & b \end{vmatrix} = a + b = 0,$$

in which case $\lambda_1 = \lambda_2$. So, in accordance with Exercise 7.31, the eigenvectors are linearly independent if the associated eigenvalues are distinct.
(c) The vectors $\boldsymbol{x}_1$ and $\boldsymbol{x}_2$ are orthogonal if and only if $\boldsymbol{x}_1'\boldsymbol{x}_2 = 0$, which occurs if and only if $ab = 1$. In that case, $\boldsymbol{A}$ is symmetric, thus agreeing with Exercise 7.44.

*__Exercise 7.46 (Diagonalization of symmetric matrices, 1)__ Let $\boldsymbol{A}$ be a symmetric $n \times n$ matrix. Then there exist an orthogonal $n \times n$ matrix $\boldsymbol{S}$ (satisfying $\boldsymbol{S}'\boldsymbol{S} = \boldsymbol{I}_n$) and a diagonal matrix $\boldsymbol{\Lambda}$ whose diagonal elements are the eigenvalues of $\boldsymbol{A}$, such that $\boldsymbol{S}'\boldsymbol{A}\boldsymbol{S} = \boldsymbol{\Lambda}$.
(a) Prove this result for $n = 2$.
(b) Use induction to prove the general result.

Solution
(a) Let λ_1 and λ_2 be the eigenvalues of $\boldsymbol{A}$, and let $\boldsymbol{x}_1$ be an eigenvector, normalized by $\boldsymbol{x}_1'\boldsymbol{x}_1 = 1$, associated with λ_1. Now choose $\boldsymbol{x}_2$ such that $\boldsymbol{x}_2'\boldsymbol{x}_1 = 0$, and normalize so that $\boldsymbol{x}_2'\boldsymbol{x}_2 = 1$. Let $\boldsymbol{X} := (\boldsymbol{x}_1 : \boldsymbol{x}_2)$. Then, $\boldsymbol{X}'\boldsymbol{X} = \boldsymbol{I}_2$ and

$$\boldsymbol{X}'\boldsymbol{A}\boldsymbol{X} = \begin{pmatrix} \boldsymbol{x}_1'\boldsymbol{A}\boldsymbol{x}_1 & \boldsymbol{x}_1'\boldsymbol{A}\boldsymbol{x}_2 \\ \boldsymbol{x}_2'\boldsymbol{A}\boldsymbol{x}_1 & \boldsymbol{x}_2'\boldsymbol{A}\boldsymbol{x}_2 \end{pmatrix} = \begin{pmatrix} \lambda_1\boldsymbol{x}_1'\boldsymbol{x}_1 & \lambda_1\boldsymbol{x}_1'\boldsymbol{x}_2 \\ \lambda_1\boldsymbol{x}_2'\boldsymbol{x}_1 & \boldsymbol{x}_2'\boldsymbol{A}\boldsymbol{x}_2 \end{pmatrix} = \begin{pmatrix} \lambda_1 & 0 \\ 0 & \boldsymbol{x}_2'\boldsymbol{A}\boldsymbol{x}_2 \end{pmatrix},$$

where we have used the symmetry of $\boldsymbol{A}$ to show that

$$\boldsymbol{x}_1'\boldsymbol{A} = \boldsymbol{x}_1'\boldsymbol{A}' = (\boldsymbol{A}\boldsymbol{x}_1)' = \lambda\boldsymbol{x}_1'.$$

The eigenvalues of $\boldsymbol{X}'\boldsymbol{A}\boldsymbol{X}$ are therefore λ_1 and $\boldsymbol{x}_2'\boldsymbol{A}\boldsymbol{x}_2$. But, since $\boldsymbol{X}$ is orthogonal, we have $|\boldsymbol{X}|^2 = |\boldsymbol{X}'\boldsymbol{X}| = |\boldsymbol{I}| = 1$ and hence

$$|\lambda\boldsymbol{I} - \boldsymbol{X}'\boldsymbol{A}\boldsymbol{X}| = |\boldsymbol{X}'(\lambda\boldsymbol{I} - \boldsymbol{A})\boldsymbol{X}| = |\boldsymbol{X}||\lambda\boldsymbol{I} - \boldsymbol{A}||\boldsymbol{X}| = |\lambda\boldsymbol{I} - \boldsymbol{A}|.$$

The eigenvalues of $\boldsymbol{X}'\boldsymbol{A}\boldsymbol{X}$ are therefore the eigenvalues of $\boldsymbol{A}$, and hence $\boldsymbol{x}_2'\boldsymbol{A}\boldsymbol{x}_2 = \lambda_2$.
(b) Let $\lambda_1, \lambda_2, \dots, \lambda_n$ be the eigenvalues of $\boldsymbol{A}$, and let $\boldsymbol{x}_1$ be a normalized eigenvector associated with λ_1. Choose $\boldsymbol{x}_2, \dots, \boldsymbol{x}_n$ such that the matrix

$$\boldsymbol{X}_n := (\boldsymbol{x}_1, \boldsymbol{x}_2, \dots, \boldsymbol{x}_n) = (\boldsymbol{x}_1 : \boldsymbol{X}_{n-1})$$

satisfies $\boldsymbol{X}_n'\boldsymbol{X}_n = \boldsymbol{I}_n$. Then,

$$\boldsymbol{X}_n'\boldsymbol{A}\boldsymbol{X}_n = \begin{pmatrix} \boldsymbol{x}_1'\boldsymbol{A}\boldsymbol{x}_1 & \boldsymbol{x}_1'\boldsymbol{A}\boldsymbol{X}_{n-1} \\ \boldsymbol{X}_{n-1}'\boldsymbol{A}\boldsymbol{x}_1 & \boldsymbol{X}_{n-1}'\boldsymbol{A}\boldsymbol{X}_{n-1} \end{pmatrix} = \begin{pmatrix} \lambda_1 & \boldsymbol{0}' \\ \boldsymbol{0} & \boldsymbol{X}_{n-1}'\boldsymbol{A}\boldsymbol{X}_{n-1} \end{pmatrix}.$$

Since $\boldsymbol{X}_n'\boldsymbol{A}\boldsymbol{X}_n$ and $\boldsymbol{A}$ have the same eigenvalues, it follows that $\boldsymbol{X}_{n-1}'\boldsymbol{A}\boldsymbol{X}_{n-1}$ has eigenvalues $\lambda_2, \lambda_3, \dots, \lambda_n$. Now assume (induction hypothesis) that symmetric matrices of order $n-1$ can be diagonalized by means of an orthogonal matrix. Then there exists an orthogonal matrix $\boldsymbol{T}_{n-1}$ of order $n-1$ such that

$$\boldsymbol{T}_{n-1}'\boldsymbol{X}_{n-1}'\boldsymbol{A}\boldsymbol{X}_{n-1}\boldsymbol{T}_{n-1} = \begin{pmatrix} \lambda_2 & 0 & \dots & 0 \\ 0 & \lambda_3 & \dots & 0 \\ \vdots & \vdots & & \vdots \\ 0 & 0 & \dots & \lambda_n \end{pmatrix}.$$

Defining the $n \times n$ matrix

$$\boldsymbol{S}_n := (\boldsymbol{x}_1 : \boldsymbol{X}_{n-1}\boldsymbol{T}_{n-1}),$$

we then have

$$\boldsymbol{S}_n'\boldsymbol{S}_n = \begin{pmatrix} \boldsymbol{x}_1'\boldsymbol{x}_1 & \boldsymbol{x}_1'\boldsymbol{X}_{n-1}\boldsymbol{T}_{n-1} \\ \boldsymbol{T}_{n-1}'\boldsymbol{X}_{n-1}'\boldsymbol{x}_1 & \boldsymbol{T}_{n-1}'\boldsymbol{X}_{n-1}'\boldsymbol{X}_{n-1}\boldsymbol{T}_{n-1} \end{pmatrix} = \begin{pmatrix} 1 & \boldsymbol{0}' \\ \boldsymbol{0} & \boldsymbol{I}_{n-1} \end{pmatrix} = \boldsymbol{I}_n,$$

and also

$$\boldsymbol{S}_n'\boldsymbol{A}\boldsymbol{S}_n = \begin{pmatrix} \boldsymbol{x}_1'\boldsymbol{A}\boldsymbol{x}_1 & \boldsymbol{x}_1'\boldsymbol{A}\boldsymbol{X}_{n-1}\boldsymbol{T}_{n-1} \\ \boldsymbol{T}_{n-1}'\boldsymbol{X}_{n-1}'\boldsymbol{A}\boldsymbol{x}_1 & \boldsymbol{T}_{n-1}'\boldsymbol{X}_{n-1}'\boldsymbol{A}\boldsymbol{X}_{n-1}\boldsymbol{T}_{n-1} \end{pmatrix} = \begin{pmatrix} \lambda_1 & 0 & \dots & 0 \\ 0 & \lambda_2 & \dots & 0 \\ \vdots & \vdots & & \vdots \\ 0 & 0 & \dots & \lambda_n \end{pmatrix}.$$

Hence, if the result holds for matrices of order $n-1$, it holds for matrices of order n. This, combined with the fact, proved in (a), that the result holds for $n = 2$, concludes the proof.

Exercise 7.47 (Multiple eigenvalues) Let λ be an eigenvalue of a symmetric $n \times n$ matrix $\boldsymbol{A}$, and assume that λ has multiplicity $k \geq 2$.
(a) Show that there exist k orthonormal (and linearly independent) eigenvectors associated with λ.
(b) Show that, in fact, there exist not one but an infinite number of sets of k orthonormal eigenvectors associated with λ.
(c) Show that there cannot be more than k linearly independent eigenvectors associated with λ.
(d) Conclude that the eigenvectors associated with λ span a subspace of $\mathbb{R}^n$ of dimension k.

Solution
From the diagonalization theorem for symmetric matrices (Exercise 7.46), we know that an orthogonal matrix $\boldsymbol{S}$ exists such that $\boldsymbol{A}\boldsymbol{S} = \boldsymbol{S}\boldsymbol{\Lambda}$. Let λ_1 be the multiple eigenvalue of multiplicity $k \geq 2$, and partition $\boldsymbol{\Lambda} := \operatorname{diag}(\lambda_1 \boldsymbol{I}_k, \boldsymbol{\Lambda}_2)$, where the diagonal matrix $\boldsymbol{\Lambda}_2$ contains the $n-k$ eigenvalues of $\boldsymbol{A}$, distinct from λ_1. Partition $\boldsymbol{S} = (\boldsymbol{S}_1 : \boldsymbol{S}_2)$ accordingly. Then,

$$\boldsymbol{A}\boldsymbol{S}_1 = \lambda_1 \boldsymbol{S}_1 \quad \text{and} \quad \boldsymbol{A}\boldsymbol{S}_2 = \boldsymbol{S}_2\boldsymbol{\Lambda}_2,$$

with

$$\boldsymbol{S}_1'\boldsymbol{S}_1 = \boldsymbol{I}_k, \quad \boldsymbol{S}_2'\boldsymbol{S}_2 = \boldsymbol{I}_{n-k}, \quad \boldsymbol{S}_1'\boldsymbol{S}_2 = \mathbf{O}.$$

(a) The matrix $\boldsymbol{S}_1$ has k columns. Since $\boldsymbol{S}_1'\boldsymbol{S}_1 = \boldsymbol{I}_k$, we see that the k columns of $\boldsymbol{S}_1$ are linearly independent and orthonormal. Since $\boldsymbol{A}\boldsymbol{S}_1 = \lambda_1\boldsymbol{S}_1$, each column is an eigenvector associated with λ_1.
(b) Let $\boldsymbol{Q}$ be an arbitrary orthogonal $k \times k$ matrix. Then the matrix $\boldsymbol{T}_1 := \boldsymbol{S}_1\boldsymbol{Q}$ also satisfies $\boldsymbol{T}_1'\boldsymbol{T}_1 = \boldsymbol{I}_k$ and $\boldsymbol{A}\boldsymbol{T}_1 = \lambda_1\boldsymbol{T}_1$.
(c) Each eigenvector associated with λ_1 is orthogonal to every other eigenvector associated with an eigenvalue distinct from λ_1. Let $\boldsymbol{x}_1$ be an eigenvector associated with λ_1 and write $\boldsymbol{x}_1 = \boldsymbol{S}_1\boldsymbol{p}_1 + \boldsymbol{S}_2\boldsymbol{p}_2$. (There is no loss of generality here, because $(\boldsymbol{S}_1 : \boldsymbol{S}_2)$ is nonsingular.) Now, $\boldsymbol{S}_2'\boldsymbol{x}_1 = \boldsymbol{0}$. Hence, $\boldsymbol{S}_2'\boldsymbol{S}_1\boldsymbol{p}_1 + \boldsymbol{S}_2'\boldsymbol{S}_2\boldsymbol{p}_2 = \boldsymbol{0}$, implying that $\boldsymbol{p}_2 = \boldsymbol{0}$ and $\boldsymbol{x}_1 = \boldsymbol{S}_1\boldsymbol{p}_1$. So every eigenvector associated with λ_1 must be a linear combination of the k columns of $\boldsymbol{S}_1$.
(d) The foregoing implies that any set of n orthonormal eigenvectors of $\boldsymbol{A}$ will contain exactly k eigenvectors associated with λ_1.

Exercise 7.48 (Eigenvectors span) Show that the eigenvectors of an $n \times n$ symmetric matrix $\boldsymbol{A}$ span $\mathbb{R}^n$.

Solution
Since $\boldsymbol{S}'\boldsymbol{A}\boldsymbol{S} = \boldsymbol{\Lambda}$ for some orthogonal $n \times n$ matrix $\boldsymbol{S}$, the n columns of $\boldsymbol{S}$ are linearly independent eigenvectors of $\boldsymbol{A}$. Hence, the orthonormal set of eigenvectors contains at least n vectors. However, there cannot be more than n orthonormal vectors in $\mathbb{R}^n$, and hence the eigenvectors span $\mathbb{R}^n$.

Exercise 7.49 (Rank and number of nonzero eigenvalues, 2) If $\boldsymbol{A}$ is a symmetric matrix with r nonzero eigenvalues, show that $\operatorname{rk}(\boldsymbol{A}) = r$.

Solution
Using Exercise 7.46, we have $\boldsymbol{S}'\boldsymbol{A}\boldsymbol{S} = \boldsymbol{\Lambda}$. Since $\boldsymbol{S}$ is nonsingular, we see that $\operatorname{rk}(\boldsymbol{A}) = \operatorname{rk}(\boldsymbol{\Lambda})$. But $\boldsymbol{\Lambda}$ is a diagonal matrix, and hence its rank is equal to the number (in this case r) of its nonzero diagonal elements. Hence, $\operatorname{rk}(\boldsymbol{A}) = \operatorname{rk}(\boldsymbol{\Lambda}) = r$.

Exercise 7.50 (Sylvester's law of nullity, again) Let $\boldsymbol{A}$ be an $m \times n$ matrix of rank r.
(a) Use Exercise 7.47 to show that there exists an $n \times (n-r)$ matrix $\boldsymbol{S}$ such that $\boldsymbol{A}\boldsymbol{S} = \boldsymbol{O}$ and $\boldsymbol{S}'\boldsymbol{S} = \boldsymbol{I}_{n-r}$.
(b) Let $\boldsymbol{S}$ be a matrix such that $\boldsymbol{A}\boldsymbol{S} = \boldsymbol{O}$. Show that $\operatorname{rk}(\boldsymbol{S}) \leq n - r$.

Solution
In essence, both results follow from the fact that $\boldsymbol{A}\boldsymbol{S} = \boldsymbol{O}$ if and only if $\boldsymbol{A}'\boldsymbol{A}\boldsymbol{S} = \boldsymbol{O}$.
(a) The matrix $\boldsymbol{A}'\boldsymbol{A}$ is a symmetric $n \times n$ matrix and has rank r. Hence, there exists a set of $n - r$ orthonormal eigenvectors associated with the eigenvalue 0 (multiplicity $n - r$).

Let S be the $n \times (n-r)$ matrix containing these eigenvectors. Then,

$$A'AS = O \quad \text{and} \quad S'S = I_{n-r}.$$

Since $A'AS = O$, we have $S'A'AS = O$ and hence $AS = O$ by Exercise 2.13(a).
(b) If $AS = O$, then $A'AS = O$, so that the columns of S can be taken as the eigenvectors associated with the eigenvalue $\lambda = 0$ of $A'A$. Since there are precisely $n-r$ linearly independent eigenvectors associated with $\lambda = 0$, there cannot be more than $n-r$ linearly independent columns in S. Hence $\text{rk}(S) \leq n-r$. In fact, this is Sylvester's law of nullity again, because Exercise 5.47(b) implies directly that $0 = \text{rk}(AS) \geq \text{rk}(A) + \text{rk}(S) - n$. Also compare Exercise 6.36(a).

*__Exercise 7.51 (Simultaneous reduction to diagonal form, 2)__ Let A and B be symmetric matrices. Show that an orthogonal matrix S exists such that $S'AS = \Lambda$ (diagonal) and $S'BS = M$ (diagonal) if and only if A and B commute.

Solution
If $S'AS = \Lambda$ and $S'BS = M$, then

$$AB = S\Lambda S'SMS' = S\Lambda MS' = SM\Lambda S' = SMS'S\Lambda S' = BA,$$

since Λ and M are diagonal and diagonal matrices commute.

The converse is more difficult. Suppose λ is an eigenvalue of A with multiplicity k. Let $X := (x_1, \dots, x_k)$ be a set of orthonormal eigenvectors associated with λ, so that $X'X = I_k$ and $AX = \lambda X$. Now consider

$$A(BX) = BAX = B\lambda X = \lambda(BX),$$

from which we see that each column of BX is an eigenvector of A associated with λ. Since X contains a full set of eigenvectors associated with λ, each column of BX must be a linear combination of the columns of X. There exists therefore a $k \times k$ matrix C such that $BX = XC$. Premultiplying by X' we see that $C = X'BX$, hence symmetric. Let S be an orthogonal matrix such that $S'CS = R$ (diagonal), $S'S = I_k$. Then,

$$S'X'AXS = \lambda I_k \quad \text{and} \quad S'X'BXS = R,$$

so that the semi-orthogonal $n \times k$ matrix XS (with $S'X'XS = I_k$) simultaneously diagonalizes A and B.

But the process is not yet complete. Let $\lambda_1, \dots, \lambda_s$ be the *distinct* eigenvalues of A with multiplicities $n_1, \dots, n_s$ $(n_1 + n_2 + \dots + n_s = n)$, and let $X := (X_1 : X_2 : \dots : X_s)$ be the orthogonal $n \times n$ matrix of eigenvectors of A, such that $AX_j = \lambda_j X_j$. (Note that X_j is an $n \times n_j$ matrix.) For $j = 1, \dots, s$, define S_j as the orthogonal $n_j \times n_j$ matrix that diagonalizes $X_j'BX_j$, so that $S_j'X_j'BX_jS_j = R_j$ (diagonal). Then the $n \times n$ matrix

$$T := (X_1S_1 : X_2S_2 : \dots : X_sS_s)$$

is orthogonal, because $S_j'X_j'X_jS_j = I_{n_j}$ and $X_i'X_j = \mathrm{O}$ $(i \neq j)$, and

$$T'AT = \begin{pmatrix} \lambda_1 I_{n_1} & \mathrm{O} & \dots & \mathrm{O} \\ \mathrm{O} & \lambda_2 I_{n_2} & \dots & \mathrm{O} \\ \vdots & \vdots & & \vdots \\ \mathrm{O} & \mathrm{O} & \dots & \lambda_s I_{n_s} \end{pmatrix}, \quad T'BT = \begin{pmatrix} R_1 & \mathrm{O} & \dots & \mathrm{O} \\ \mathrm{O} & R_2 & \dots & \mathrm{O} \\ \vdots & \vdots & & \vdots \\ \mathrm{O} & \mathrm{O} & \dots & R_s \end{pmatrix}.$$

***Exercise 7.52 (Craig-Sakamoto lemma)** Let A and B be symmetric matrices of the same order. Show that

$$AB = \mathrm{O} \iff |I - sA||I - tB| = |I - sA - tB|$$

for all real scalars s and t.

Solution

Clearly, if $AB = \mathrm{O}$, then

$$|I - sA||I - tB| = |I - sA - tB + stAB| = |I - sA - tB|.$$

The converse is more difficult. Assume that $|I - sA||I - tB| = |I - sA - tB|$ for all s and t. Then this holds in particular for all s satisfying $s^{-1} > |\lambda_{\max}(A)|$. For such s, two things happen, both of which will be used. First, the eigenvalues of sA are all smaller than one in absolute value; second, the eigenvalues of $I - sA$ are all nonzero.

Now define $C := (I - sA)^{-1}$. Then

$$|I - tB| = |C||C^{-1} - tB| = |I - tCB|$$

for all t. This implies that the matrices B and CB have the same characteristic polynomial and hence the same eigenvalues. In particular,

$$\begin{aligned} \operatorname{tr} B^2 &= \operatorname{tr}(CB)^2 = \operatorname{tr}((I - sA)^{-1}B)^2 = \operatorname{tr}((I + sA + s^2A^2 + \dots)B)^2 \\ &= \operatorname{tr} B^2 + s \operatorname{tr}(BAB + AB^2) + s^2 \operatorname{tr}(BA^2B + ABAB + A^2B^2) + O(s^3) \end{aligned}$$

for all s sufficiently small. Hence,

$$\operatorname{tr} AB^2 = 0 \quad \text{and} \quad \operatorname{tr}(AB)^2 + 2 \operatorname{tr} A^2B^2 = 0.$$

Now,

$$\begin{aligned} \operatorname{tr}(AB)^2 + 2 \operatorname{tr} A^2B^2 &\geq 2 \operatorname{tr} A^2B^2 \\ &= 2 \operatorname{tr}(AB)(AB)' \geq 0 \end{aligned}$$

with equality if and only if $AB = \mathrm{O}$.

Exercise 7.53 (Bounds of Rayleigh quotient) Let A be a symmetric $n \times n$ matrix with eigenvalues $\lambda_1 \geq \lambda_2 \geq \dots \geq \lambda_n$.

(a) Show that

$$\lambda_n \leq \frac{\boldsymbol{x}'\boldsymbol{A}\boldsymbol{x}}{\boldsymbol{x}'\boldsymbol{x}} \leq \lambda_1.$$

(b) Hence, show that, for any $m \times n$ matrix $\boldsymbol{A}$,

$$\|\boldsymbol{A}\boldsymbol{x}\| \leq \sqrt{\mu}\|\boldsymbol{x}\|,$$

where μ denotes the largest eigenvalue of $\boldsymbol{A}'\boldsymbol{A}$.

Solution

(a) Let $\boldsymbol{S}'\boldsymbol{A}\boldsymbol{S} = \boldsymbol{\Lambda}$, $\boldsymbol{S}'\boldsymbol{S} = \boldsymbol{I}_n$, and define $\boldsymbol{y} := \boldsymbol{S}'\boldsymbol{x}$. Then,

$$\begin{aligned}\boldsymbol{x}'\boldsymbol{A}\boldsymbol{x} = \boldsymbol{x}'\boldsymbol{S}\boldsymbol{\Lambda}\boldsymbol{S}'\boldsymbol{x} = \boldsymbol{y}'\boldsymbol{\Lambda}\boldsymbol{y} &= \sum_{i=1}^{n} \lambda_i y_i^2 \leq \lambda_1 \sum_{i=1}^{n} y_i^2 \\ &= \lambda_1 \boldsymbol{y}'\boldsymbol{y} = \lambda_1 \boldsymbol{x}'\boldsymbol{S}\boldsymbol{S}'\boldsymbol{x} = \lambda_1 \boldsymbol{x}'\boldsymbol{x}.\end{aligned}$$

The other inequality is proved in analogous fashion. The ratio $\boldsymbol{x}'\boldsymbol{A}\boldsymbol{x}/\boldsymbol{x}'\boldsymbol{x}$ is called the *Rayleigh quotient*.

(b) Recall that the norm $\|\boldsymbol{x}\|$ of a vector $\boldsymbol{x}$ is given by $\sqrt{\boldsymbol{x}'\boldsymbol{x}}$. We need to show that $\boldsymbol{x}'\boldsymbol{A}'\boldsymbol{A}\boldsymbol{x} \leq \mu \boldsymbol{x}'\boldsymbol{x}$, and this follows from (a).

7.3 Some results for triangular matrices

Exercise 7.54 (Normal matrices and triangularity) A square matrix $\boldsymbol{A}$ is normal if and only if $\boldsymbol{A}^*\boldsymbol{A} = \boldsymbol{A}\boldsymbol{A}^*$ ($\boldsymbol{A}'\boldsymbol{A} = \boldsymbol{A}\boldsymbol{A}'$ in the real case). Show that a triangular matrix is normal if and only if it is diagonal.

Solution

Assume that $\boldsymbol{A}$ is a real upper triangular matrix. If $\boldsymbol{A}$ is diagonal, then clearly $\boldsymbol{A}'\boldsymbol{A} = \boldsymbol{A}\boldsymbol{A}'$. To prove the converse, assume that $\boldsymbol{A}'\boldsymbol{A} = \boldsymbol{A}\boldsymbol{A}'$. Equating $(\boldsymbol{A}\boldsymbol{A}')_{ii}$ and $(\boldsymbol{A}'\boldsymbol{A})_{ii}$ for $i = 1, \dots, n$ gives the n equations:

$$\begin{aligned}a_{11}^2 + a_{12}^2 + a_{13}^2 + \cdots + a_{1n}^2 &= a_{11}^2 \\ a_{22}^2 + a_{23}^2 + \cdots + a_{2n}^2 &= a_{12}^2 + a_{22}^2 \\ a_{33}^2 + \cdots + a_{3n}^2 &= a_{13}^2 + a_{23}^2 + a_{33}^2 \\ &\vdots \\ a_{nn}^2 &= a_{1n}^2 + a_{2n}^2 + \cdots + a_{nn}^2.\end{aligned}$$

The first equation yields $a_{1j} = 0$ for $j = 2, \dots, n$. The second equation then yields $a_{2j} = 0$ for $j = 3, \dots, n$. Continuing in this way yields $a_{ij} = 0$ for all $j > i$. Hence, $\boldsymbol{A}$ is diagonal.

If $\boldsymbol{A}$ is complex, the proof is similar. If $\boldsymbol{A}$ is lower triangular, we work back from the last equation to the first.

***Exercise 7.55 (A strictly triangular matrix is nilpotent)** Let $\boldsymbol{A}$ be a strictly upper triangular $n \times n$ matrix.
(a) Show that $\boldsymbol{A}$ is nilpotent of index $\leq n$ (that is, $\boldsymbol{A}^n = \mathbf{O}$).
(b) If $r_j := \operatorname{rk}(\boldsymbol{A}^j)$, show that $r_{j+1} < r_j$ if $r_j > 0$.

Solution
(a) The statement is trivially true for $n = 1$. Assume that it is true for all strictly upper triangular matrices of order $n-1$. Let

$$\boldsymbol{A} := \begin{pmatrix} \boldsymbol{B} & \boldsymbol{b} \\ \mathbf{0}' & 0 \end{pmatrix}$$

be a strictly upper triangular matrix of order $n \times n$, where $\boldsymbol{B}$ is of order $(n-1) \times (n-1)$. By successive multiplication we see that

$$\boldsymbol{A}^2 = \begin{pmatrix} \boldsymbol{B}^2 & \boldsymbol{B}\boldsymbol{b} \\ \mathbf{0}' & 0 \end{pmatrix}, \quad \ldots, \quad \boldsymbol{A}^n = \begin{pmatrix} \boldsymbol{B}^n & \boldsymbol{B}^{n-1}\boldsymbol{b} \\ \mathbf{0}' & 0 \end{pmatrix}.$$

By the induction hypothesis, $\boldsymbol{B}^{n-1} = \mathbf{O}$. Hence, $\boldsymbol{A}^n = \mathbf{O}$. By the definition of nilpotency (Exercise 2.8(b)), $\boldsymbol{A}$ is nilpotent of index m if $\boldsymbol{A}^{m-1} \neq \mathbf{O}$ and $\boldsymbol{A}^m = \mathbf{O}$. We have proved that $\boldsymbol{A}^n = \mathbf{O}$, but we don't know whether $\boldsymbol{A}^{n-1} \neq \mathbf{O}$. Hence, the index could be smaller than n.
(b) The statement is true for $n = 1$ and $n = 2$. Assume that it is true for all strictly upper triangular matrices of order $n-1$. Let $\boldsymbol{A}$ be defined as under (a). Then,

$$\boldsymbol{A}^j = \begin{pmatrix} \boldsymbol{B}^j & \boldsymbol{B}^{j-1}\boldsymbol{b} \\ \mathbf{0}' & 0 \end{pmatrix},$$

and hence

$$r_j = \operatorname{rk}(\boldsymbol{A}^j) = \operatorname{rk}(\boldsymbol{B}^j : \boldsymbol{B}^{j-1}\boldsymbol{b}),$$

so that

$$\operatorname{rk}(\boldsymbol{B}^j) \leq r_j \leq \operatorname{rk}(\boldsymbol{B}^j) + 1.$$

We distinguish between three cases.
(i) If $\boldsymbol{B}^j = \mathbf{O}$, then $r_j = 1$ if $\boldsymbol{B}^{j-1}\boldsymbol{b} \neq \mathbf{0}$, and $r_j = 0$ if $\boldsymbol{B}^{j-1}\boldsymbol{b} = \mathbf{0}$. Also, $r_{j+1} = 0$. Hence, $r_{j+1} < r_j$ if $r_j > 0$.
(ii) If $\boldsymbol{B}^j \neq \mathbf{O}$ and $r_j = \operatorname{rk}(\boldsymbol{B}^j) + 1$, then $r_j > 0$ and $r_{j+1} \leq \operatorname{rk}(\boldsymbol{B}^{j+1}) + 1$. Hence, using the fact that $\operatorname{rk}(\boldsymbol{B}^{j+1}) < \operatorname{rk}(\boldsymbol{B}^j)$ (induction hypothesis), it follows that

$$r_{j+1} \leq \operatorname{rk}(\boldsymbol{B}^{j+1}) + 1 < \operatorname{rk}(\boldsymbol{B}^j) + 1 = r_j.$$

(iii) If $\boldsymbol{B}^j \neq \mathbf{O}$ and $r_j = \operatorname{rk}(\boldsymbol{B}^j)$, then $r_j > 0$ and there exists an $\boldsymbol{x}$ such that $\boldsymbol{B}^j\boldsymbol{x} = \boldsymbol{B}^{j-1}\boldsymbol{b}$. Then, premultiplying by $\boldsymbol{B}$, we obtain $\boldsymbol{B}^{j+1}\boldsymbol{x} = \boldsymbol{B}^j\boldsymbol{b}$, implying that $r_{j+1} =$

$\text{rk}(\boldsymbol{B}^{j+1})$. Then, using the fact that $\text{rk}(\boldsymbol{B}^{j+1}) < \text{rk}(\boldsymbol{B}^{j})$ (induction hypothesis), it follows that

$$r_{j+1} = \text{rk}(\boldsymbol{B}^{j+1}) < \text{rk}(\boldsymbol{B}^{j}) = r_j.$$

We conclude that $r_{j+1} < r_j$ when $r_j > 0$ in all three cases. Notice that (a) is an immediate consequence of (b).

Exercise 7.56 (Product of triangular matrices) Let $\boldsymbol{A} := (a_{ij})$ and $\boldsymbol{B} := (b_{ij})$ be two upper triangular $n \times n$ matrices such that $a_{ij} = 0$ for $1 \leq i \leq k$ and $1 \leq j \leq k$, and $b_{k+1,k+1} = 0$. Show that the matrix $\boldsymbol{C} := \boldsymbol{AB}$ is upper triangular with $c_{ij} = 0$ for $1 \leq i \leq k+1$ and $1 \leq j \leq k+1$.

Solution
Let us partition

$$\boldsymbol{A} = \begin{pmatrix} \mathrm{O} & \boldsymbol{A}_{12} \\ \mathrm{O} & \boldsymbol{A}_{22} \end{pmatrix}, \quad \boldsymbol{B} = \begin{pmatrix} \boldsymbol{B}_{11} & \boldsymbol{B}_{12} \\ \mathrm{O} & \boldsymbol{B}_{22} \end{pmatrix}, \quad \boldsymbol{C} = \boldsymbol{AB} = \begin{pmatrix} \mathrm{O} & \boldsymbol{A}_{12}\boldsymbol{B}_{22} \\ \mathrm{O} & \boldsymbol{A}_{22}\boldsymbol{B}_{22} \end{pmatrix},$$

where the first block in the partition is of order $k \times k$ and the other blocks are conformable. All we need to prove is that the first column of $\boldsymbol{A}_{12}\boldsymbol{B}_{22}$ is zero, and that the first diagonal element of the upper triangular matrix $\boldsymbol{A}_{22}\boldsymbol{B}_{22}$ is zero too. Since, by assumption, the first diagonal element of $\boldsymbol{B}_{22}$ is zero, and $\boldsymbol{B}_{22}$ is upper triangular, it follows that the first column of $\boldsymbol{B}_{22}$ is zero. Hence, for any matrix $\boldsymbol{E}$, the first column of $\boldsymbol{E}\boldsymbol{B}_{22}$ is zero, in particular the first column of $\boldsymbol{A}_{12}\boldsymbol{B}_{22}$ and the first column of $\boldsymbol{A}_{22}\boldsymbol{B}_{22}$.

Exercise 7.57 (Perturbed identity) Let $\boldsymbol{e}_i$ and $\boldsymbol{e}_j$ be unit vectors of order $n \times 1$, and define the $n \times n$ matrix $\boldsymbol{T}(\theta) := \boldsymbol{I}_n - \theta \boldsymbol{e}_i \boldsymbol{e}_j'$ where θ is some real scalar.
(a) Show that $\boldsymbol{T}(\theta)$ is nonsingular for every $i \neq j$ and for every θ, and that $\boldsymbol{T}^{-1}(\theta) = \boldsymbol{T}(-\theta)$.
(b) Let $\boldsymbol{A}$ be an upper triangular $n \times n$ matrix. For $i < j$, show that

$$\boldsymbol{T}^{-1}(\theta)\boldsymbol{A}\boldsymbol{T}(\theta) = \boldsymbol{A} + \theta(\boldsymbol{e}_i\boldsymbol{e}_j'\boldsymbol{A} - \boldsymbol{A}\boldsymbol{e}_i\boldsymbol{e}_j') = \boldsymbol{A} + \theta\boldsymbol{P}$$

where

$$\boldsymbol{P} := \begin{pmatrix} \mathrm{O} & \boldsymbol{Q} \\ \mathrm{O} & \mathrm{O} \end{pmatrix}, \quad \boldsymbol{Q} := \begin{pmatrix} -a_{1i} & 0 & \dots & 0 \\ -a_{2i} & 0 & \dots & 0 \\ \vdots & \vdots & & \vdots \\ -a_{i-1,i} & 0 & \dots & 0 \\ a_{jj} - a_{ii} & a_{j,j+1} & \dots & a_{jn} \end{pmatrix},$$

and the submatrices in $\boldsymbol{P}$ have i and $n-i$ rows, and $j-1$ and $n-j+1$ columns, respectively.
(c) If $a_{ii} \neq a_{jj}$, choose $\theta := a_{ij}/(a_{ii} - a_{jj})$. With this choice of θ, what is the effect of the transformation $\boldsymbol{T}^{-1}(\theta)\boldsymbol{A}\boldsymbol{T}(\theta)$ on the elements of $\boldsymbol{A}$?

Solution
(a) We verify that

$$(\boldsymbol{I}_n + \theta \boldsymbol{e}_i \boldsymbol{e}_j')(\boldsymbol{I}_n - \theta \boldsymbol{e}_i \boldsymbol{e}_j') = \boldsymbol{I}_n - \theta \boldsymbol{e}_i \boldsymbol{e}_j' + \theta \boldsymbol{e}_i \boldsymbol{e}_j' - \theta^2 \boldsymbol{e}_i (\boldsymbol{e}_j' \boldsymbol{e}_i) \boldsymbol{e}_j' = \boldsymbol{I}_n,$$

because $\boldsymbol{e}_j' \boldsymbol{e}_i = 0$ for $i \neq j$. (For $i = j$, $\boldsymbol{T}(\theta)$ is singular when $\theta = 1$.)
(b) We have

$$\begin{aligned}(\boldsymbol{I}_n + \theta \boldsymbol{e}_i \boldsymbol{e}_j')\boldsymbol{A}(\boldsymbol{I}_n - \theta \boldsymbol{e}_i \boldsymbol{e}_j') &= \boldsymbol{A} - \theta \boldsymbol{A} \boldsymbol{e}_i \boldsymbol{e}_j' + \theta \boldsymbol{e}_i \boldsymbol{e}_j' \boldsymbol{A} - \theta^2 \boldsymbol{e}_i (\boldsymbol{e}_j' \boldsymbol{A} \boldsymbol{e}_i) \boldsymbol{e}_j' \\ &= \boldsymbol{A} + \theta \boldsymbol{P},\end{aligned}$$

because $\boldsymbol{e}_j' \boldsymbol{A} \boldsymbol{e}_i = a_{ji} = 0$ if $i < j$. Since $\boldsymbol{A}$ is upper triangular, we find

$$\boldsymbol{A}\boldsymbol{e}_i = (a_{1i}, a_{2i}, \ldots, a_{ii}, 0, \ldots, 0)', \quad \boldsymbol{e}_j' \boldsymbol{A} = (0, \ldots, 0, a_{jj}, a_{j,j+1}, \ldots, a_{jn}).$$

Hence, $\boldsymbol{P} = \boldsymbol{e}_i \boldsymbol{e}_j' \boldsymbol{A} - \boldsymbol{A} \boldsymbol{e}_i \boldsymbol{e}_j'$ has zeros everywhere, except that it has $\boldsymbol{e}_j' \boldsymbol{A}$ as its i-th row, and $-\boldsymbol{A}\boldsymbol{e}_i$ as its j-th column (so that $a_{jj} - a_{ii}$ appears at the intersection).
(c) The effect of the transformation $\boldsymbol{T}^{-1}\boldsymbol{A}\boldsymbol{T}$ is that it makes the ij-th element of $\boldsymbol{A}$ zero, and disturbs *only* the elements of $\boldsymbol{A}$ in row i to the *right* of a_{ij} and in column j *above* a_{ij}.

Exercise 7.58 (Ingredient for Jordan's proof) Let $\boldsymbol{A}$ be an $n \times n$ upper triangular matrix, and assume that $\boldsymbol{A}$ has k distinct diagonal elements $\lambda_1, \ldots, \lambda_k$, arranged contiguously so that the diagonal elements are λ_1 (n_1 times), λ_2 (n_2 times), ..., λ_k (n_k times), with $n_1 + n_2 + \cdots + n_k = n$. Let

$$\boldsymbol{A} := \begin{pmatrix} \boldsymbol{A}_1 & * & \ldots & * \\ \mathbf{O} & \boldsymbol{A}_2 & \ldots & * \\ \vdots & \vdots & & \vdots \\ \mathbf{O} & \mathbf{O} & \ldots & \boldsymbol{A}_k \end{pmatrix} \quad \text{and} \quad \boldsymbol{B} := \begin{pmatrix} \boldsymbol{A}_1 & \mathbf{O} & \ldots & \mathbf{O} \\ \mathbf{O} & \boldsymbol{A}_2 & \ldots & \mathbf{O} \\ \vdots & \vdots & & \vdots \\ \mathbf{O} & \mathbf{O} & \ldots & \boldsymbol{A}_k \end{pmatrix},$$

where each $\boldsymbol{A}_j$ is an upper triangular $n_j \times n_j$ matrix, all whose diagonal elements are equal to λ_j, and the blocks indicated by a $*$ are unspecified. Use Exercise 7.57 to show that there exists a nonsingular $n \times n$ matrix $\boldsymbol{T}$ such that $\boldsymbol{T}^{-1}\boldsymbol{A}\boldsymbol{T} = \boldsymbol{B}$; in other words, show that $\boldsymbol{A}$ and $\boldsymbol{B}$ are similar. (We need this result in the proof of Jordan's theorem, Exercise 7.79.)

Solution
For $i < j$, let $\boldsymbol{T}_{ij} := \boldsymbol{I}_n - \theta_{ij} \boldsymbol{e}_i \boldsymbol{e}_j'$, so that $\boldsymbol{T}_{ij}^{-1} = \boldsymbol{I}_n + \theta_{ij} \boldsymbol{e}_i \boldsymbol{e}_j'$. Inspired by Exercise 7.57 we choose

$$\theta_{ij} := \begin{cases} \frac{a_{ij}}{\lambda_i - \lambda_j} & (\text{if } \lambda_i \neq \lambda_j), \\ 0 & (\text{if } \lambda_i = \lambda_j). \end{cases}$$

If $\lambda_i = \lambda_j$, the transformation $\boldsymbol{T}_{ij}^{-1}\boldsymbol{A}\boldsymbol{T}_{ij}$ leaves $\boldsymbol{A}$ unchanged. But if $\lambda_i \neq \lambda_j$ then the matrix $\boldsymbol{T}_{ij}^{-1}\boldsymbol{A}\boldsymbol{T}_{ij}$ differs from $\boldsymbol{A}$ in that it makes the ij-th element 0 and disturbs *only* the elements of $\boldsymbol{A}$ in row i to the right of a_{ij} and in column j above a_{ij}.

We now perform a sequence of transformations $T_{ij}^{-1}AT_{ij}$ for all values of $i < j$, but in a carefully chosen order, namely: $(i,j) = (n-1,n)$, $(n-2,n-1)$, $(n-2,n)$, $(n-3,n-2)$, $(n-3,n-1)$, $(n-3,n)$, ..., $(1,2)$, ..., $(1,n)$. Each transformation will create a 0 in the ij-th position if $\lambda_i \neq \lambda_j$, and no previously created 0 will be disturbed. Thus, $\boldsymbol{A}$ is transformed into $\boldsymbol{B}$.

Exercise 7.59 (Diagonalization of triangular matrices) Let $\boldsymbol{A}$ be an upper triangular matrix with distinct diagonal elements. Show that there exists a *unit* upper triangular matrix $\boldsymbol{T}$ (that is, an upper triangular matrix with ones on the diagonal) such that

$$\boldsymbol{T}^{-1}\boldsymbol{A}\boldsymbol{T} = \operatorname{dg}(\boldsymbol{A}).$$

Solution
Consider the $\frac{1}{2}n(n-1)$ equations in $\frac{1}{2}n(n-1)$ unknowns t_{ij} $(i < j)$ given by $\boldsymbol{A}\boldsymbol{T} = \boldsymbol{T}\operatorname{dg}(\boldsymbol{A})$. Equating the ij-th element of $\boldsymbol{A}\boldsymbol{T}$ with the ij-th element of $\boldsymbol{T}\operatorname{dg}(\boldsymbol{A})$ gives

$$a_{ii}t_{ij} + \dots + a_{ij}t_{jj} = a_{jj}t_{ij} \quad (i < j)$$

where $t_{jj} = 1$. We write these equations for $j = i+1, i+2, \dots, n$ as

$$\begin{aligned} a_{ii}t_{i,i+1} + a_{i,i+1} &= a_{i+1,i+1}t_{i,i+1} \\ a_{ii}t_{i,i+2} + a_{i,i+1}t_{i+1,i+2} + a_{i,i+2} &= a_{i+2,i+2}t_{i,i+2} \\ &\vdots \\ a_{ii}t_{in} + a_{i,i+1}t_{i+1,n} + \dots + a_{in} &= a_{nn}t_{in}. \end{aligned}$$

Now solve $t_{i,i+1}$ from the first equation, then $t_{i,i+2}$ from the second equation, and so on.

Exercise 7.60 (Inverse of triangular matrix)
(a) Let $\boldsymbol{A}$ be an upper triangular matrix with nonzero diagonal elements. Show that $\boldsymbol{A}^{-1}$ is of the same type.
(b) Let $\boldsymbol{A}$ be a unit upper triangular matrix with integers above the diagonal. Show that $\boldsymbol{A}^{-1}$ is of the same type.

Solution
(a) If $\boldsymbol{A}$ and $\boldsymbol{B}$ are two upper triangular matrices of the same order, then $(\boldsymbol{A}\boldsymbol{B})_{ij} = 0$ for $j < i$, and, for $j \geq i$,

$$(\boldsymbol{A}\boldsymbol{B})_{ij} = \sum_{k=i}^{j} a_{ik}b_{kj}.$$

(Compare Exercise 2.21.) Hence, the equation $\boldsymbol{AB} = \boldsymbol{I}$ generates the equations $b_{ii} = 1/a_{ii}$ for all i, and, for $j > i$,

$$\sum_{k=i}^{j} a_{ik} b_{kj} = 0,$$

which we can solve sequentially as in Exercise 7.59.
(b) Since all diagonal elements of $\boldsymbol{A}$ are one, we have $|\boldsymbol{A}| = 1$. Hence, by Exercise 4.37(c), $\boldsymbol{A}^{-1} = \boldsymbol{C}'$, where $\boldsymbol{C}$ denotes the matrix of cofactors. But each cofactor is an integer and the result follows.

7.4 Schur's decomposition theorem and its consequences

Exercise 7.61 (A necessary and sufficient condition for diagonal reduction)
(a) Show that a nonsingular matrix $\boldsymbol{T}$ exists such that $\boldsymbol{T}^{-1}\boldsymbol{AT} = \boldsymbol{\Lambda}$ (diagonal) if and only if there is a set of n linearly independent vectors, each of which is an eigenvector of $\boldsymbol{A}$.
(b) Show that a unitary matrix $\boldsymbol{S}$ exists such that $\boldsymbol{S}^*\boldsymbol{AS} = \boldsymbol{\Lambda}$ (diagonal) if and only if there is a set of orthonormal vectors, each of which is an eigenvector of $\boldsymbol{A}$.

Solution
(a) If $\boldsymbol{A}$ has n linearly independent eigenvectors $\boldsymbol{x}_1, \dots, \boldsymbol{x}_n$, then $\boldsymbol{T} := (\boldsymbol{x}_1, \dots, \boldsymbol{x}_n)$ is nonsingular and satisfies

$$\begin{aligned}\boldsymbol{AT} &= \boldsymbol{A}(\boldsymbol{x}_1, \dots, \boldsymbol{x}_n) = (\boldsymbol{Ax}_1, \dots, \boldsymbol{Ax}_n) = (\lambda_1 \boldsymbol{x}_1, \dots, \lambda_n \boldsymbol{x}_n) \\ &= (\boldsymbol{x}_1, \dots, \boldsymbol{x}_n)\boldsymbol{\Lambda} = \boldsymbol{T\Lambda},\end{aligned}$$

where $\boldsymbol{\Lambda} := \text{diag}(\lambda_1, \dots, \lambda_n)$ and $\lambda_1, \dots, \lambda_n$ are eigenvalues of $\boldsymbol{A}$. Hence, $\boldsymbol{T}^{-1}\boldsymbol{AT} = \boldsymbol{\Lambda}$.
Conversely, if $\boldsymbol{AT} = \boldsymbol{T\Lambda}$ for some diagonal matrix $\boldsymbol{\Lambda}$, then

$$\boldsymbol{A}(\boldsymbol{Te}_i) = (\boldsymbol{AT})\boldsymbol{e}_i = (\boldsymbol{T\Lambda})\boldsymbol{e}_i = \boldsymbol{T}(\boldsymbol{\Lambda e}_i) = \boldsymbol{T}(\lambda_i \boldsymbol{e}_i) = \lambda_i(\boldsymbol{Te}_i),$$

where $\boldsymbol{e}_i$ denotes the i-th unit vector. Hence, each column of $\boldsymbol{T}$ is an eigenvector of $\boldsymbol{A}$, and, since $\boldsymbol{T}$ is nonsingular, these eigenvectors are linearly independent.
(b) The proof is identical except that the columns of $\boldsymbol{S}$ are now not only independent but also orthonormal, so that $\boldsymbol{S}$ is unitary and $\boldsymbol{S}^{-1} = \boldsymbol{S}^*$.

Exercise 7.62 (Schur's decomposition theorem) Let $\boldsymbol{A}$ be an $n \times n$ matrix. Then there exist a unitary $n \times n$ matrix $\boldsymbol{S}$ (that is, $\boldsymbol{S}^*\boldsymbol{S} = \boldsymbol{I}_n$) and an upper triangular matrix $\boldsymbol{M}$ whose diagonal elements are the eigenvalues of $\boldsymbol{A}$, such that $\boldsymbol{S}^*\boldsymbol{AS} = \boldsymbol{M}$.
(a) Follow the steps of the solution to Exercise 7.46 to prove this result for $n = 2$.
(b) Then use induction to prove the general result.

Solution
(a) Let λ_1 and λ_2 be the eigenvalues of $\boldsymbol{A}$, and let $\boldsymbol{x}_1$ be an eigenvector, normalized by $\boldsymbol{x}_1^*\boldsymbol{x}_1 = 1$, associated with λ_1. Choose $\boldsymbol{x}_2$ such that $\boldsymbol{x}_2^*\boldsymbol{x}_1 = 0$, and normalize so that

$\boldsymbol{x}_2^*\boldsymbol{x}_2 = 1$. Let $\boldsymbol{X} := (\boldsymbol{x}_1 : \boldsymbol{x}_2)$. Then, $\boldsymbol{X}^*\boldsymbol{X} = \boldsymbol{I}_2$ and

$$\boldsymbol{X}^*\boldsymbol{A}\boldsymbol{X} = \begin{pmatrix} \boldsymbol{x}_1^*\boldsymbol{A}\boldsymbol{x}_1 & \boldsymbol{x}_1^*\boldsymbol{A}\boldsymbol{x}_2 \\ \boldsymbol{x}_2^*\boldsymbol{A}\boldsymbol{x}_1 & \boldsymbol{x}_2^*\boldsymbol{A}\boldsymbol{x}_2 \end{pmatrix} = \begin{pmatrix} \lambda_1\boldsymbol{x}_1^*\boldsymbol{x}_1 & \boldsymbol{x}_1^*\boldsymbol{A}\boldsymbol{x}_2 \\ \lambda_1\boldsymbol{x}_2^*\boldsymbol{x}_1 & \boldsymbol{x}_2^*\boldsymbol{A}\boldsymbol{x}_2 \end{pmatrix} = \begin{pmatrix} \lambda_1 & \boldsymbol{x}_1^*\boldsymbol{A}\boldsymbol{x}_2 \\ 0 & \boldsymbol{x}_2^*\boldsymbol{A}\boldsymbol{x}_2 \end{pmatrix}.$$

The eigenvalues of $\boldsymbol{X}^*\boldsymbol{A}\boldsymbol{X}$ are therefore λ_1 and $\boldsymbol{x}_2^*\boldsymbol{A}\boldsymbol{x}_2$. But, since $\boldsymbol{X}$ is unitary, we have

$$|\lambda\boldsymbol{I}_2 - \boldsymbol{X}^*\boldsymbol{A}\boldsymbol{X}| = |\boldsymbol{X}^*(\lambda\boldsymbol{I}_2 - \boldsymbol{A})\boldsymbol{X}| = |\lambda\boldsymbol{I}_2 - \boldsymbol{A}|.$$

The eigenvalues of $\boldsymbol{X}^*\boldsymbol{A}\boldsymbol{X}$ are therefore the eigenvalues of $\boldsymbol{A}$, and hence $\boldsymbol{x}_2^*\boldsymbol{A}\boldsymbol{x}_2 = \lambda_2$.
(b) Let $\lambda_1, \lambda_2, \dots, \lambda_n$ be the eigenvalues of $\boldsymbol{A}$, and let $\boldsymbol{x}_1$ be a normalized eigenvector associated with λ_1. Choose $\boldsymbol{x}_2, \dots, \boldsymbol{x}_n$ such that the matrix

$$\boldsymbol{X}_n := (\boldsymbol{x}_1, \boldsymbol{x}_2, \dots, \boldsymbol{x}_n) = (\boldsymbol{x}_1 : \boldsymbol{X}_{n-1})$$

satisfies $\boldsymbol{X}_n^*\boldsymbol{X}_n = \boldsymbol{I}_n$. Then

$$\boldsymbol{X}_n^*\boldsymbol{A}\boldsymbol{X}_n = \begin{pmatrix} \boldsymbol{x}_1^*\boldsymbol{A}\boldsymbol{x}_1 & \boldsymbol{x}_1^*\boldsymbol{A}\boldsymbol{X}_{n-1} \\ \boldsymbol{X}_{n-1}^*\boldsymbol{A}\boldsymbol{x}_1 & \boldsymbol{X}_{n-1}^*\boldsymbol{A}\boldsymbol{X}_{n-1} \end{pmatrix} = \begin{pmatrix} \lambda_1 & \boldsymbol{x}_1^*\boldsymbol{A}\boldsymbol{X}_{n-1} \\ \boldsymbol{0} & \boldsymbol{X}_{n-1}^*\boldsymbol{A}\boldsymbol{X}_{n-1} \end{pmatrix}.$$

Since $\boldsymbol{X}_n^*\boldsymbol{A}\boldsymbol{X}_n$ and $\boldsymbol{A}$ have the same eigenvalues, it follows that $\boldsymbol{X}_{n-1}^*\boldsymbol{A}\boldsymbol{X}_{n-1}$ has eigenvalues $\lambda_2, \lambda_3, \dots, \lambda_n$. Now assume (induction hypothesis) that all matrices of order $n-1$ can be triangularized by means of a unitary matrix. Then there exists a unitary matrix $\boldsymbol{T}_{n-1}$ of order $n-1$ such that

$$\boldsymbol{T}_{n-1}^*\boldsymbol{X}_{n-1}^*\boldsymbol{A}\boldsymbol{X}_{n-1}\boldsymbol{T}_{n-1} = \begin{pmatrix} \lambda_2 & * & \dots & * \\ 0 & \lambda_3 & \dots & * \\ \vdots & \vdots & & \vdots \\ 0 & 0 & \dots & \lambda_n \end{pmatrix},$$

where a $*$ denotes a possibly nonzero element. Now define the $n \times n$ matrix

$$\boldsymbol{S}_n := (\boldsymbol{x}_1 : \boldsymbol{X}_{n-1}\boldsymbol{T}_{n-1}).$$

We have

$$\boldsymbol{S}_n^*\boldsymbol{S}_n = \begin{pmatrix} \boldsymbol{x}_1^*\boldsymbol{x}_1 & \boldsymbol{x}_1^*\boldsymbol{X}_{n-1}\boldsymbol{T}_{n-1} \\ \boldsymbol{T}_{n-1}^*\boldsymbol{X}_{n-1}^*\boldsymbol{x}_1 & \boldsymbol{T}_{n-1}^*\boldsymbol{X}_{n-1}^*\boldsymbol{X}_{n-1}\boldsymbol{T}_{n-1} \end{pmatrix} = \begin{pmatrix} 1 & \boldsymbol{0}' \\ \boldsymbol{0} & \boldsymbol{I}_{n-1} \end{pmatrix} = \boldsymbol{I}_n$$

and also

$$\boldsymbol{S}_n^*\boldsymbol{A}\boldsymbol{S}_n = \begin{pmatrix} \boldsymbol{x}_1^*\boldsymbol{A}\boldsymbol{x}_1 & \boldsymbol{x}_1^*\boldsymbol{A}\boldsymbol{X}_{n-1}\boldsymbol{T}_{n-1} \\ \boldsymbol{T}_{n-1}^*\boldsymbol{X}_{n-1}^*\boldsymbol{A}\boldsymbol{x}_1 & \boldsymbol{T}_{n-1}^*\boldsymbol{X}_{n-1}^*\boldsymbol{A}\boldsymbol{X}_{n-1}\boldsymbol{T}_{n-1} \end{pmatrix}$$
$$= \begin{pmatrix} \lambda_1 & * & * & \dots & * \\ 0 & \lambda_2 & * & \dots & * \\ 0 & 0 & \lambda_3 & \dots & * \\ \vdots & \vdots & \vdots & & \vdots \\ 0 & 0 & 0 & \dots & \lambda_n \end{pmatrix}.$$

Hence, if the result holds for matrices of order $n-1$, it holds for matrices of order n. This, combined with the fact, proved in (a), that the result holds for $n = 2$, concludes the proof.

Exercise 7.63 (Diagonalization of symmetric matrices, 2) Use Schur's theorem to provide a shorter proof of the diagonalization theorem for symmetric matrices (Exercise 7.46).

Solution

Using Exercise 7.62, there exists a unitary matrix $\boldsymbol{S}$ and an upper triangular matrix $\boldsymbol{M}$ such that $\boldsymbol{S}^*\boldsymbol{A}\boldsymbol{S} = \boldsymbol{M}$. Then,

$$\boldsymbol{M}^* = (\boldsymbol{S}^*\boldsymbol{A}\boldsymbol{S})^* = \boldsymbol{S}^*\boldsymbol{A}^*\boldsymbol{S} = \boldsymbol{S}^*\boldsymbol{A}\boldsymbol{S} = \boldsymbol{M}.$$

Hence, $\boldsymbol{M}$ is Hermitian. But, since $\boldsymbol{M}$ is also triangular, $\boldsymbol{M}$ must be diagonal. By Schur's theorem, its diagonal elements are its eigenvalues. By Exercise 7.40 its eigenvalues are real. Finally, by Exercise 7.43, the eigenvector matrix $\boldsymbol{S}$ can be chosen real as well.

Exercise 7.64 (Determinant, trace, and eigenvalues) Use Schur's theorem to provide a short proof of

$$\operatorname{tr} \boldsymbol{A} = \sum_{i=1}^{n} \lambda_i, \quad |\boldsymbol{A}| = \prod_{i=1}^{n} \lambda_i,$$

where $\lambda_1, \dots, \lambda_n$ are the eigenvalues of the $n \times n$ matrix $\boldsymbol{A}$. (See Exercises 7.26 and 7.27.)

Solution

Writing $\boldsymbol{S}^*\boldsymbol{A}\boldsymbol{S} = \boldsymbol{M}$ (upper triangular), where $\boldsymbol{S}$ is unitary, we obtain

$$\operatorname{tr} \boldsymbol{A} = \operatorname{tr} \boldsymbol{S}\boldsymbol{M}\boldsymbol{S}^* = \operatorname{tr} \boldsymbol{M}\boldsymbol{S}^*\boldsymbol{S} = \operatorname{tr} \boldsymbol{M} = \sum_{i=1}^{n} \lambda_i$$

and

$$|\boldsymbol{A}| = |\boldsymbol{S}\boldsymbol{M}\boldsymbol{S}^*| = |\boldsymbol{M}||\boldsymbol{S}^*\boldsymbol{S}| = |\boldsymbol{M}| = \prod_{i=1}^{n} \lambda_i.$$

Exercise 7.65 (Trace, powers, and eigenvalues, 2) Use Schur's theorem to provide an alternative proof of the fact that

$$\operatorname{tr} \boldsymbol{A}^k = \sum_{i=1}^{n} \lambda_i^k \quad (k = 1, 2, \dots)$$

where $\lambda_1, \dots, \lambda_n$ are the eigenvalues of the $n \times n$ matrix $\boldsymbol{A}$ (Exercise 7.28.)

Solution

Writing again $\boldsymbol{S}^*\boldsymbol{A}\boldsymbol{S} = \boldsymbol{M}$ (upper triangular), we have $\boldsymbol{A} = \boldsymbol{S}\boldsymbol{M}\boldsymbol{S}^*$ and hence $\boldsymbol{A}^k = \boldsymbol{S}\boldsymbol{M}^k\boldsymbol{S}^*$. This gives

$$\operatorname{tr} \boldsymbol{A}^k = \operatorname{tr} \boldsymbol{S}\boldsymbol{M}^k\boldsymbol{S}^* = \operatorname{tr} \boldsymbol{M}^k = \sum_{i=1}^{n} \lambda_i^k,$$

because $\boldsymbol{M}^k$ is an upper triangular matrix with $\lambda_1^k, \dots, \lambda_n^k$ on the diagonal.

Exercise 7.66 (Number of nonzero eigenvalues does not exceed rank) If A has r nonzero eigenvalues, then show that $\operatorname{rk}(A) \geq r$.

Solution
We write again, using Schur's decomposition theorem, $S^* AS = M$. Partition

$$M = \begin{pmatrix} M_1 & M_2 \\ O & M_3 \end{pmatrix},$$

where M_1 is a nonsingular upper triangular $r \times r$ matrix and M_3 is *strictly* upper triangular. Since $\operatorname{rk}(A) = \operatorname{rk}(M) \geq \operatorname{rk}(M_1) = r$, the result follows.

Exercise 7.67 (A simple eigenvalue) Let A be an $n \times n$ matrix. If λ is a simple eigenvalue of A, show that $\operatorname{rk}(\lambda I_n - A) = n - 1$. Conversely, if $\operatorname{rk}(\lambda I_n - A) = n - 1$, show that λ is an eigenvalue of A, but not necessarily a simple eigenvalue.

Solution
Let $\lambda_1, \dots, \lambda_n$ be the eigenvalues of A. Then $B := \lambda I_n - A$ has eigenvalues $\lambda - \lambda_i$ $(i = 1, \dots, n)$. Since λ is an eigenvalue of A, B has at least one eigenvalue zero and hence $\operatorname{rk}(B) \leq n - 1$. In fact, λ is a simple eigenvalue of A, so that B has one eigenvalue 0 and $n - 1$ nonzero eigenvalues. Hence, $\operatorname{rk}(B) \geq n - 1$ (Exercise 7.66), and we conclude that $\operatorname{rk}(B) = n - 1$.

Conversely, if $\operatorname{rk}(B) = n - 1$, then B has at least one zero eigenvalue and hence $\lambda = \lambda_i$ for at least one i. The eigenvalue need not be simple as Exercise 7.19 shows.

Exercise 7.68 (A simple zero eigenvalue)
(a) If an $n \times n$ matrix A has a simple eigenvalue 0, show that $\operatorname{rk}(A) = n - 1$.
(b) If A has $k \geq 2$ eigenvalues 0, show that $\operatorname{rk}(A)$ is not necessarily equal to $n - k$.

Solution
(a) Setting $\lambda = 0$ in Exercise 7.67, shows that if 0 is a simple eigenvalue of A, then $\operatorname{rk}(A) = n - 1$, and conversely that if $\operatorname{rk}(A) = n - 1$, there is at least one 0 eigenvalue.
(b) Consider the matrix

$$A = \begin{pmatrix} 1 & -1 \\ 1 & -1 \end{pmatrix}.$$

Then $\operatorname{rk}(A) = 1$ and both eigenvalues of A are zero. In general, if A has p zero eigenvalues then its rank can be larger than or equal to $n - p$, but not smaller (Exercise 7.66). However, if A is symmetric then $\operatorname{rk}(A) = n - p$ (Exercise 7.49).

****Exercise 7.69 (Cayley-Hamilton, 1)** Let A be an $n \times n$ matrix with eigenvalues $\lambda_1, \dots, \lambda_n$. Show that A *satisfies its own characteristic equation*. That is,

$$(\lambda_1 I_n - A)(\lambda_2 I_n - A) \dots (\lambda_n I_n - A) = O.$$

Solution
By Schur's theorem there exists a unitary matrix $\boldsymbol{S}$ such that $\boldsymbol{S}^*\boldsymbol{A}\boldsymbol{S} = \boldsymbol{M}$ (upper triangular). Let $\boldsymbol{B}_i := \lambda_i \boldsymbol{I}_n - \boldsymbol{M}$. Then,

$$\prod_{i=1}^{n}(\lambda_i \boldsymbol{I}_n - \boldsymbol{A}) = \boldsymbol{S}\boldsymbol{B}_1\boldsymbol{S}^*\boldsymbol{S}\boldsymbol{B}_2\boldsymbol{S}^* \dots \boldsymbol{S}\boldsymbol{B}_n\boldsymbol{S}^* = \boldsymbol{S}\left(\prod_{i=1}^{n}\boldsymbol{B}_i\right)\boldsymbol{S}^*.$$

We wish to show that $\prod_i \boldsymbol{B}_i = \mathbf{O}$. This follows by repeated application of Exercise 7.56, using the fact that $\boldsymbol{B}_i$ is upper triangular and has 0 in the i-th diagonal position. The upper left 1-by-1 block of $\boldsymbol{B}_1$ is 0 and the second diagonal element of $\boldsymbol{B}_2$ is 0. Hence, the upper left 2-by-2 block of $\boldsymbol{B}_1\boldsymbol{B}_2$ is $\mathbf{O}$. The third diagonal element of $\boldsymbol{B}_3$ is 0. Hence, the upper left 3-by-3 block of $\boldsymbol{B}_1\boldsymbol{B}_2\boldsymbol{B}_3$ is $\mathbf{O}$. Continuing in this way we find that $\boldsymbol{B}_1\boldsymbol{B}_2 \dots \boldsymbol{B}_n = \mathbf{O}$.

Exercise 7.70 (Normal matrices)
(a) Show that unitary ($\boldsymbol{A}^*\boldsymbol{A} = \boldsymbol{I}$), Hermitian ($\boldsymbol{A}^* = \boldsymbol{A}$), and skew-Hermitian ($\boldsymbol{A}^* = -\boldsymbol{A}$) matrices are all normal.
(b) Give an example of a normal 2×2 matrix that is neither unitary, Hermitian, or skew-Hermitian.

Solution
(a) If $\boldsymbol{A}$ is unitary then $\boldsymbol{A}\boldsymbol{A}^* = \boldsymbol{I} = \boldsymbol{A}^*\boldsymbol{A}$; if $\boldsymbol{A}$ is Hermitian then $\boldsymbol{A}\boldsymbol{A}^* = \boldsymbol{A}^2 = \boldsymbol{A}^*\boldsymbol{A}$; and if $\boldsymbol{A}$ is skew-Hermitian then $\boldsymbol{A}\boldsymbol{A}^* = -\boldsymbol{A}^2 = \boldsymbol{A}^*\boldsymbol{A}$.
(b) Any matrix of the form

$$\boldsymbol{A} = \begin{pmatrix} a & b \\ -b & a \end{pmatrix},$$

with $a \neq 0$, $b \neq 0$, and $a^2 + b^2 \neq 1$ provides an example. In fact, it is the only example.

Exercise 7.71 (Spectral theorem for normal matrices) Given an $n \times n$ matrix $\boldsymbol{A}$, show that there exists a unitary $n \times n$ matrix $\boldsymbol{S}$ such that $\boldsymbol{S}^*\boldsymbol{A}\boldsymbol{S} = \boldsymbol{\Lambda}$ (diagonal) if and only if $\boldsymbol{A}$ is normal.

Solution
If $\boldsymbol{S}^*\boldsymbol{A}\boldsymbol{S} = \boldsymbol{\Lambda}$, then $\boldsymbol{A} = \boldsymbol{S}\boldsymbol{\Lambda}\boldsymbol{S}^*$ and $\boldsymbol{A}^* = \boldsymbol{S}\boldsymbol{\Lambda}^*\boldsymbol{S}^*$, so that $\boldsymbol{A}\boldsymbol{A}^* = \boldsymbol{S}\boldsymbol{\Lambda}\boldsymbol{\Lambda}^*\boldsymbol{S}^*$ and $\boldsymbol{A}^*\boldsymbol{A} = \boldsymbol{S}\boldsymbol{\Lambda}^*\boldsymbol{\Lambda}\boldsymbol{S}^*$. Since $\boldsymbol{\Lambda}\boldsymbol{\Lambda}^* = \boldsymbol{\Lambda}^*\boldsymbol{\Lambda}$, it follows that $\boldsymbol{A}\boldsymbol{A}^* = \boldsymbol{A}^*\boldsymbol{A}$.

Conversely, let $\boldsymbol{S}^*\boldsymbol{A}\boldsymbol{S} = \boldsymbol{M}$ (upper triangular). Then $\boldsymbol{A} = \boldsymbol{S}\boldsymbol{M}\boldsymbol{S}^*$ and $\boldsymbol{A}^* = \boldsymbol{S}\boldsymbol{M}^*\boldsymbol{S}^*$, so that $\boldsymbol{A}\boldsymbol{A}^* = \boldsymbol{S}\boldsymbol{M}\boldsymbol{M}^*\boldsymbol{S}^*$ and $\boldsymbol{A}^*\boldsymbol{A} = \boldsymbol{S}\boldsymbol{M}^*\boldsymbol{M}\boldsymbol{S}^*$. Since $\boldsymbol{A}$ is normal, we have $\boldsymbol{A}\boldsymbol{A}^* = \boldsymbol{A}^*\boldsymbol{A}$ and hence $\boldsymbol{M}\boldsymbol{M}^* = \boldsymbol{M}^*\boldsymbol{M}$. This shows that $\boldsymbol{M}$ is normal. But then, by Exercise 7.54, $\boldsymbol{M}$ must be diagonal.

Exercise 7.72 (Further properties of a complex-symmetric matrix) We have seen in Exercise 7.41 that the eigenvalues of a complex matrix $\boldsymbol{A}$ satisfying $\boldsymbol{A}' = \boldsymbol{A}$ (a complex-symmetric matrix) are not necessarily real. Now consider the complex-symmetric matrix

$$A = \begin{pmatrix} 1 & \mathrm{i} \\ \mathrm{i} & -1 \end{pmatrix}.$$

(a) Show that its eigenvalues are both 0 and that $\mathrm{rk}(A) = 1$. Conclude that the rank of A is not equal to the number of nonzero eigenvalues.
(b) Use Exercise 7.71 to show that A cannot be diagonalized.

Solution
(a) The eigenvalues of A are found from the equation $\lambda^2 = 0$ and hence they are both zero. Hence, the matrix is singular and $\mathrm{rk}(A) \leq 1$. Also, $\mathrm{rk}(A) \geq 1$ because A is not the null matrix. Hence, $\mathrm{rk}(A) = 1$.
(b) We write

$$A^*A = \begin{pmatrix} 1 & -\mathrm{i} \\ -\mathrm{i} & -1 \end{pmatrix} \begin{pmatrix} 1 & \mathrm{i} \\ \mathrm{i} & -1 \end{pmatrix} = 2 \begin{pmatrix} 1 & \mathrm{i} \\ -\mathrm{i} & 1 \end{pmatrix}$$

and

$$AA^* = \begin{pmatrix} 1 & \mathrm{i} \\ \mathrm{i} & -1 \end{pmatrix} \begin{pmatrix} 1 & -\mathrm{i} \\ -\mathrm{i} & -1 \end{pmatrix} = 2 \begin{pmatrix} 1 & -\mathrm{i} \\ \mathrm{i} & 1 \end{pmatrix}.$$

We see that A is not normal and hence, by Exercise 7.71, it cannot be diagonalized.

Exercise 7.73 (Normal matrix and orthonormal eigenvectors) Show that an orthonormal set of n eigenvectors of an $n \times n$ matrix A exists if and only if A is normal.

Solution
Exercise 7.71 says that A can be diagonalized through a unitary matrix if and only if A is normal. Exercise 7.61(b) says that A has n orthonormal eigenvectors if and only if A can be diagonalized through a unitary matrix. The statement in the exercise is a combination of these two statements.

7.5 Jordan's decomposition theorem

Exercise 7.74 (The basic Jordan block) Consider the $k \times k$ upper triangular matrix

$$J_k := \begin{pmatrix} 0 & 1 & 0 & \dots & 0 \\ 0 & 0 & 1 & \dots & 0 \\ \vdots & \vdots & \vdots & & \vdots \\ 0 & 0 & 0 & \dots & 1 \\ 0 & 0 & 0 & \dots & 0 \end{pmatrix}.$$

(a) Show that J_k cannot be diagonalized.
(b) Show that

$$J_k'J_k = \begin{pmatrix} 0 & \mathbf{0}' \\ \mathbf{0} & I_{k-1} \end{pmatrix}, \quad J_kJ_k' = \begin{pmatrix} I_{k-1} & \mathbf{0} \\ \mathbf{0}' & 0 \end{pmatrix}.$$

(c) Also show that J_k is nilpotent of index k, that is, $J_k^k = \mathbf{O}$ and $J_k^{k-1} \neq \mathbf{O}$.

Solution
(a) According to Exercise 7.61(a), an $n \times n$ matrix can be diagonalized if and only if there are n linearly independent eigenvectors. The matrix $\boldsymbol{J}$ has only *one* eigenvector, because $\boldsymbol{J}_k \boldsymbol{x} = \boldsymbol{0}$ implies that $x_2 = x_3 = \cdots = x_n = 0$, so that $\boldsymbol{x} = (1, 0, \dots, 0)'$ or a multiple thereof.
(b) One verifies easily that

$$\boldsymbol{J}_k' \boldsymbol{J}_k = \begin{pmatrix} 0 & 0 & \dots & 0 & 0 \\ 1 & 0 & \dots & 0 & 0 \\ \vdots & \vdots & & \vdots & \vdots \\ 0 & 0 & \dots & 0 & 0 \\ 0 & 0 & \dots & 1 & 0 \end{pmatrix} \begin{pmatrix} 0 & 1 & 0 & \dots & 0 \\ 0 & 0 & 1 & \dots & 0 \\ \vdots & \vdots & \vdots & & \vdots \\ 0 & 0 & 0 & \dots & 1 \\ 0 & 0 & 0 & \dots & 0 \end{pmatrix} = \begin{pmatrix} 0 & 0 & \dots & 0 & 0 \\ 0 & 1 & \dots & 0 & 0 \\ \vdots & \vdots & & \vdots & \vdots \\ 0 & 0 & \dots & 1 & 0 \\ 0 & 0 & \dots & 0 & 1 \end{pmatrix}$$

and similarly the second result.
(c) Let $\boldsymbol{e}_i$ be the i-th unit vector of order k. Then,

$$\boldsymbol{J}_k \boldsymbol{e}_i = \begin{cases} \boldsymbol{0} & (\text{if } i = 1), \\ \boldsymbol{e}_{i-1} & (\text{if } 2 \le i \le k). \end{cases}$$

Hence, by successive multiplication,

$$\boldsymbol{J}_k^2 \boldsymbol{e}_i = \begin{cases} \boldsymbol{0} & (\text{if } i = 1, 2), \\ \boldsymbol{e}_{i-2} & (\text{if } 3 \le i \le k), \end{cases} \quad \dots, \quad \boldsymbol{J}_k^{k-1} \boldsymbol{e}_i = \begin{cases} \boldsymbol{0} & (\text{if } 1 \le i \le k-1), \\ \boldsymbol{e}_1 & (\text{if } i = k), \end{cases}$$

and finally, $\boldsymbol{J}_k^k \boldsymbol{e}_i = \boldsymbol{0}$ for all i. Hence, $\boldsymbol{J}_k^k = \mathbf{O}$ and $\boldsymbol{J}_k^{k-1} \neq \mathbf{O}$. (The result also follows from Exercise 7.55(a).)

Exercise 7.75 (Forward and backward shift) Consider a basic Jordan block $\boldsymbol{J}_k$ of order $k \times k$ and an arbitrary vector $\boldsymbol{x} := (x_1, \dots, x_k)'$. Obtain the transformations:
(a) $\boldsymbol{J}_k \boldsymbol{x}$ (*forward shift*);
(b) $\boldsymbol{J}_k' \boldsymbol{x}$ (*backward shift*);
(c) $(\boldsymbol{I} - \boldsymbol{J}_k')\boldsymbol{x}$ (*difference*);
(d) $(\boldsymbol{I} - \boldsymbol{J}_k')^{-1}\boldsymbol{x}$ (*partial sum*).

Solution
(a)–(b) We have

$$\boldsymbol{J}_k \begin{pmatrix} x_1 \\ x_2 \\ \vdots \\ x_{k-1} \\ x_k \end{pmatrix} = \begin{pmatrix} x_2 \\ x_3 \\ \vdots \\ x_k \\ 0 \end{pmatrix} \quad \text{and} \quad \boldsymbol{J}_k' \begin{pmatrix} x_1 \\ x_2 \\ \vdots \\ x_{k-1} \\ x_k \end{pmatrix} = \begin{pmatrix} 0 \\ x_1 \\ \vdots \\ x_{k-2} \\ x_{k-1} \end{pmatrix},$$

thus defining a *forward shift* and a *backward shift* (or *lag*) operator, respectively.

(c) Here,

$$(\boldsymbol{I}_k - \boldsymbol{J}_k')\boldsymbol{x} = \begin{pmatrix} 1 & 0 & 0 & \dots & 0 & 0 \\ -1 & 1 & 0 & \dots & 0 & 0 \\ 0 & -1 & 1 & \dots & 0 & 0 \\ \vdots & \vdots & \vdots & & \vdots & \vdots \\ 0 & 0 & 0 & \dots & -1 & 1 \end{pmatrix} \begin{pmatrix} x_1 \\ x_2 \\ x_3 \\ \vdots \\ x_k \end{pmatrix} = \begin{pmatrix} x_1 \\ x_2 - x_1 \\ x_3 - x_2 \\ \vdots \\ x_k - x_{k-1} \end{pmatrix}.$$

(d) And finally,

$$(\boldsymbol{I}_k - \boldsymbol{J}_k')^{-1}\boldsymbol{x} = \begin{pmatrix} 1 & 0 & 0 & \dots & 0 & 0 \\ 1 & 1 & 0 & \dots & 0 & 0 \\ 1 & 1 & 1 & \dots & 0 & 0 \\ \vdots & \vdots & \vdots & & \vdots & \vdots \\ 1 & 1 & 1 & \dots & 1 & 1 \end{pmatrix} \begin{pmatrix} x_1 \\ x_2 \\ x_3 \\ \vdots \\ x_k \end{pmatrix} = \begin{pmatrix} x_1 \\ x_1 + x_2 \\ x_1 + x_2 + x_3 \\ \vdots \\ x_1 + \dots + x_k \end{pmatrix}.$$

Exercise 7.76 (Symmetric version of Jordan's block) Let $\boldsymbol{A} := \boldsymbol{J}_k + \boldsymbol{J}_k'$, so that $\boldsymbol{A}$ is a symmetric $k \times k$ matrix given by

$$\boldsymbol{A} = \begin{pmatrix} 0 & 1 & 0 & \dots & 0 & 0 & 0 \\ 1 & 0 & 1 & \dots & 0 & 0 & 0 \\ 0 & 1 & 0 & \dots & 0 & 0 & 0 \\ \vdots & \vdots & \vdots & & \vdots & \vdots & \vdots \\ 0 & 0 & 0 & \dots & 1 & 0 & 1 \\ 0 & 0 & 0 & \dots & 0 & 1 & 0 \end{pmatrix}.$$

(a) Show that

$$|\boldsymbol{A}| = \begin{cases} 0 & \text{(if } k \text{ is odd)}, \\ (-1)^{k/2} & \text{(if } k \text{ is even)}. \end{cases}$$

(b) Show that

$$\operatorname{tr} \boldsymbol{A} = 0, \quad \operatorname{tr} \boldsymbol{A}^2 = 2(k-1), \quad \operatorname{tr} \boldsymbol{A}^3 = 0, \quad \operatorname{tr} \boldsymbol{A}^4 = 2(3k-5).$$

Solution

(a) If we denote the $k \times k$ matrix by $\boldsymbol{A}_k$ to emphasize the order, we expand the determinant by the first row and obtain $|\boldsymbol{A}_k| = -|\boldsymbol{A}_{k-2}|$. Since $|\boldsymbol{A}_1| = 0$ and $|\boldsymbol{A}_2| = -1$, the result follows.

(b) Since $A = J_k + J_k'$ we obtain:

$$\begin{aligned}
\operatorname{tr} A &= 2 \operatorname{tr} J_k, \\
\operatorname{tr} A^2 &= 2 \operatorname{tr} J_k^2 + 2 \operatorname{tr} J_k J_k', \\
\operatorname{tr} A^3 &= 2 \operatorname{tr} J_k^3 + 6 \operatorname{tr} J_k (J_k J_k'), \\
\operatorname{tr} A^4 &= 2 \operatorname{tr} J_k^4 + 8 \operatorname{tr} J_k^2 (J_k J_k') + 4 \operatorname{tr}(J_k J_k')(J_k' J_k) + 2 \operatorname{tr}(J_k J_k')^2.
\end{aligned}$$

From the structure of J_k we see that $\operatorname{tr} J_k^p = 0$ and also $\operatorname{tr} J_k^p (J_k J_k') = 0$ for $p = 1, 2, \ldots$. The nonzero components are

$$\operatorname{tr} J_k J_k' = k - 1, \quad \operatorname{tr}(J_k J_k')(J_k' J_k) = k - 2, \quad \operatorname{tr}(J_k J_k')^2 = k - 1.$$

The result follows.

Exercise 7.77 (A lemma for Jordan, 1) Consider the following lemma: Let A be a *strictly* upper triangular $n \times n$ matrix, that is, an upper triangular matrix with zeros on the diagonal. Then, a nonsingular $n \times n$ matrix T exists and integers $n_1, \ldots, n_k$ with $n_1 \geq n_2 \geq \cdots \geq n_k \geq 1$ and $n_1 + n_2 + \cdots + n_k = n$, such that

$$T^{-1} A T = \begin{pmatrix} J_{n_1} & O & \ldots & O \\ O & J_{n_2} & \ldots & O \\ \vdots & \vdots & & \vdots \\ O & O & \ldots & J_{n_k} \end{pmatrix}, \quad J_{n_i} = \begin{pmatrix} 0 & 1 & 0 & \ldots & 0 \\ 0 & 0 & 1 & \ldots & 0 \\ \vdots & \vdots & \vdots & & \vdots \\ 0 & 0 & 0 & \ldots & 1 \\ 0 & 0 & 0 & \ldots & 0 \end{pmatrix},$$

where J_{n_i} is of order $n_i \times n_i$.

(a) Show that the lemma holds for $n = 2$.
(b) Show that the lemma holds for $n = 3$.

Solution
(a) For $n = 2$, we write

$$A := \begin{pmatrix} 0 & a \\ 0 & 0 \end{pmatrix}, \quad T_1 := \begin{pmatrix} 1 & 0 \\ 0 & 1 \end{pmatrix}, \quad T_2 := \begin{pmatrix} a & 0 \\ 0 & 1 \end{pmatrix}.$$

If $a = 0$, then $A = O$ and we choose $T := T_1$ giving $T_1^{-1} A T_1 = O$. This is the case $n_1 = n_2 = 1$. If $a \neq 0$, we choose $T := T_2$ giving

$$A T_2 = \begin{pmatrix} 0 & a \\ 0 & 0 \end{pmatrix} = T_2 \begin{pmatrix} 0 & 1 \\ 0 & 0 \end{pmatrix}.$$

This is the case $n_1 = 2$. Hence, for every value of a there exists a nonsingular matrix T such that $T^{-1} A T$ has the required form.

(b) For $n = 3$, we write

$$\boldsymbol{A} := \begin{pmatrix} 0 & a & b \\ 0 & 0 & c \\ 0 & 0 & 0 \end{pmatrix}.$$

Five cases need to be distinguished: (1) $a = b = c = 0$, (2) $a = 0, c = 0, b \neq 0$, (3) $a = 0, c \neq 0$, (4) $a \neq 0, c = 0$, and (5) $a \neq 0, c \neq 0$.

Case (1) corresponds to $n_1 = n_2 = n_3 = 1$. Then $\boldsymbol{A} = \mathbf{O}$ and we chose $\boldsymbol{T} := \boldsymbol{T}_1 := \boldsymbol{I}_3$. Cases (2)–(4) correspond to $n_1 = 2$, $n_2 = 1$, and case (5) corresponds to $n_1 = 3$. For cases (2)–(4) we define

$$\boldsymbol{T}_2 := \begin{pmatrix} b & 0 & 0 \\ 0 & 0 & 1 \\ 0 & 1 & 0 \end{pmatrix}, \quad \boldsymbol{T}_3 := \begin{pmatrix} b & 0 & 1 \\ c & 0 & 0 \\ 0 & 1 & 0 \end{pmatrix}, \quad \boldsymbol{T}_4 := \begin{pmatrix} a & 0 & 0 \\ 0 & 1 & -b \\ 0 & 0 & a \end{pmatrix},$$

and one verifies that

$$\boldsymbol{A}\boldsymbol{T}_i = \boldsymbol{T}_i \begin{pmatrix} 0 & 1 & 0 \\ 0 & 0 & 0 \\ 0 & 0 & 0 \end{pmatrix} \qquad (i = 2, 3, 4)$$

in each of these three cases. Finally, in case (5),

$$\boldsymbol{A}\boldsymbol{T}_5 = \boldsymbol{T}_5 \begin{pmatrix} 0 & 1 & 0 \\ 0 & 0 & 1 \\ 0 & 0 & 0 \end{pmatrix}, \quad \boldsymbol{T}_5 := \begin{pmatrix} ac & b & 0 \\ 0 & c & 0 \\ 0 & 0 & 1 \end{pmatrix}.$$

Hence, for every value of (a, b, c) there exists a nonsingular matrix $\boldsymbol{T}$ such that $\boldsymbol{T}^{-1}\boldsymbol{A}\boldsymbol{T}$ has the required form.

*__Exercise 7.78 (A lemma for Jordan, 2)__ Let $\boldsymbol{A}$ be a strictly upper triangular $n \times n$ matrix. We wish to prove the lemma of Exercise 7.77 by induction. The result holds for $n = 1$ (trivially), and, by Exercise 7.77, also for $n = 2$ and $n = 3$. Now assume it holds for $n - 1$. Partition $\boldsymbol{A}$ as

$$\boldsymbol{A} := \begin{pmatrix} 0 & \boldsymbol{a}' \\ \mathbf{0} & \boldsymbol{A}_1 \end{pmatrix},$$

where $\boldsymbol{a}$ is an $(n-1) \times 1$ vector and $\boldsymbol{A}_1$ is a strictly upper triangular matrix of order $n-1$. By the induction hypothesis there exists a nonsingular matrix $\boldsymbol{S}_1$ of order $n - 1$ such that $\boldsymbol{S}_1^{-1}\boldsymbol{A}_1\boldsymbol{S}_1 = \boldsymbol{J}_{(1)}$, where

$$\boldsymbol{J}_{(1)} := \begin{pmatrix} \boldsymbol{J}_{k_1} & \mathbf{O} & \dots & \mathbf{O} \\ \mathbf{O} & \boldsymbol{J}_{k_2} & \dots & \mathbf{O} \\ \vdots & \vdots & & \vdots \\ \mathbf{O} & \mathbf{O} & \dots & \boldsymbol{J}_{k_s} \end{pmatrix}$$

with $k_1 \geq k_2 \geq \cdots \geq k_s \geq 1$ and $k_1 + k_2 + \cdots + k_s = n - 1$.

(a) Show that $\boldsymbol{A}$ is similar to the matrix

$$\boldsymbol{A}_{(1)} := \begin{pmatrix} 0 & \boldsymbol{a}'\boldsymbol{S}_1 - \boldsymbol{q}'\boldsymbol{J}_{(1)} \\ \boldsymbol{0} & \boldsymbol{J}_{(1)} \end{pmatrix}$$

for any $(n-1) \times 1$ vector $\boldsymbol{q}$.
(b) Choose $\boldsymbol{q}$ such that $\boldsymbol{A}_{(1)}$ (and hence $\boldsymbol{A}$ itself) is similar to

$$\boldsymbol{A}_{(2)} := \begin{pmatrix} 0 & \beta\boldsymbol{e}_1' & \boldsymbol{b}' \\ \boldsymbol{0} & \boldsymbol{J}_{k_1} & \mathbf{O} \\ \boldsymbol{0} & \mathbf{O} & \boldsymbol{J}_{(2)} \end{pmatrix},$$

where $\beta := \boldsymbol{e}_1'\boldsymbol{S}_{11}'\boldsymbol{a}$, $\boldsymbol{b} := \boldsymbol{S}_{12}'\boldsymbol{a}$ (of order $(n-k_1-1) \times 1$), $\boldsymbol{S}_1 := (\boldsymbol{S}_{11} : \boldsymbol{S}_{12})$, $\boldsymbol{e}_1 := (1, 0, \dots, 0)'$ (of order $k_1 \times 1$), and

$$\boldsymbol{J}_{(2)} := \begin{pmatrix} \boldsymbol{J}_{k_2} & \mathbf{O} & \dots & \mathbf{O} \\ \mathbf{O} & \boldsymbol{J}_{k_3} & \dots & \mathbf{O} \\ \vdots & \vdots & & \vdots \\ \mathbf{O} & \mathbf{O} & \dots & \boldsymbol{J}_{k_s} \end{pmatrix}.$$

(c) Assume that $\beta \neq 0$. Then show that $\boldsymbol{A}_{(2)}$ is similar to

$$\boldsymbol{A}_{(3)} := \begin{pmatrix} \boldsymbol{J}_{k_1+1} & \tilde{\boldsymbol{e}}_1\boldsymbol{b}' \\ \mathbf{O} & \boldsymbol{J}_{(2)} \end{pmatrix},$$

where $\tilde{\boldsymbol{e}}_i$ denotes a unit vector of order $(k_1+1) \times 1$, which in turn is similar to

$$\begin{pmatrix} \boldsymbol{J}_{k_1+1} & \mathbf{O} \\ \mathbf{O} & \boldsymbol{J}_{(2)} \end{pmatrix},$$

a Jordan matrix of the required form.
(d) Finally, assume that $\beta = 0$. Then show that

$$\boldsymbol{A}_{(2)} := \begin{pmatrix} 0 & \boldsymbol{0}' & \boldsymbol{b}' \\ \boldsymbol{0} & \boldsymbol{J}_{k_1} & \mathbf{O} \\ \boldsymbol{0} & \mathbf{O} & \boldsymbol{J}_{(2)} \end{pmatrix} \quad \text{and} \quad \boldsymbol{A}_{(4)} := \begin{pmatrix} \boldsymbol{J}_{k_1} & \boldsymbol{0} & \mathbf{O} \\ \boldsymbol{0}' & 0 & \boldsymbol{b}' \\ \mathbf{O} & \boldsymbol{0} & \boldsymbol{J}_{(2)} \end{pmatrix}$$

are similar, and that $\boldsymbol{A}_{(4)}$, in turn, is similar to a Jordan matrix of the required form.
(e) Conclude that the validity of the lemma is thus established.

Solution
(a) Define the $n \times n$ matrix

$$\boldsymbol{T} := \begin{pmatrix} 1 & \boldsymbol{q}' \\ 0 & \boldsymbol{S}_1 \end{pmatrix} \quad \text{with} \quad \boldsymbol{T}^{-1} = \begin{pmatrix} 1 & -\boldsymbol{q}'\boldsymbol{S}_1^{-1} \\ 0 & \boldsymbol{S}_1^{-1} \end{pmatrix}.$$

Then we verify that $\boldsymbol{T}^{-1}\boldsymbol{A}\boldsymbol{T} = \boldsymbol{A}_{(1)}$.
(b) Choose

$$\boldsymbol{q} := \begin{pmatrix} \boldsymbol{J}_{k_1}\boldsymbol{S}_{11}'\boldsymbol{a} \\ \boldsymbol{0} \end{pmatrix}.$$

Then,

$$q'J_{(1)} = (a'S_{11}J'_{k_1} : 0')\begin{pmatrix} J_{k_1} & O \\ O & J_{(2)} \end{pmatrix} = (a'S_{11}J'_{k_1}J_{k_1} : 0'),$$

and hence

$$a'S_1 - q'J_{(1)} = \left(a'S_{11}(I_{k_1} - J'_{k_1}J_{k_1}) : a'S_{12}\right) = (\beta e'_1 : b'),$$

because $J'_{k_1}J_{k_1} = I_{k_1} - e_1e'_1$ by Exercise 7.74(b).
(c) If $\beta \neq 0$, then

$$\begin{pmatrix} 1/\beta & 0' & 0' \\ 0 & I_{k_1} & O \\ 0 & O & (1/\beta)I_{n-k_1-1} \end{pmatrix}\begin{pmatrix} 0 & \beta e'_1 & b' \\ 0 & J_{k_1} & O \\ 0 & O & J_{(2)} \end{pmatrix}\begin{pmatrix} \beta & 0' & 0' \\ 0 & I_{k_1} & O \\ 0 & O & \beta I_{n-k_1-1} \end{pmatrix}$$

$$= \begin{pmatrix} 0 & e'_1 & b' \\ 0 & J_{k_1} & O \\ 0 & O & J_{(2)} \end{pmatrix} = \begin{pmatrix} J_{k_1+1} & \tilde{e}_1 b' \\ O & J_{(2)} \end{pmatrix} = A_{(3)},$$

as required. Now, observe that for any vector c of order $(n - k_1 - 1) \times 1$,

$$\begin{pmatrix} I_{k_1+1} & \tilde{e}_{i+1}c' \\ O & I_{n-k_1-1} \end{pmatrix}\begin{pmatrix} J_{k_1+1} & \tilde{e}_i c' \\ O & J_{(2)} \end{pmatrix}\begin{pmatrix} I_{k_1+1} & -\tilde{e}_{i+1}c' \\ O & I_{n-k_1-1} \end{pmatrix} = \begin{pmatrix} J_{k_1+1} & \tilde{e}_{i+1}c'J_{(2)} \\ O & J_{(2)} \end{pmatrix},$$

because $J_{k_1+1}\tilde{e}_{i+1} = \tilde{e}_i$ for $i = 1, \dots, k_1$ by Exercise 7.74(c). Hence, choosing $c' := b'J_{(2)}^{i-1}$ for $i = 1, \dots, k_1$, and noting that $J_{(2)}^{k_1} = O$, we arrive at the requested Jordan form.
(d) If $\beta = 0$, then the matrices

$$A_{(2)} := \begin{pmatrix} 0 & 0' & b' \\ 0 & J_{k_1} & O \\ 0 & O & J_{(2)} \end{pmatrix} \quad \text{and} \quad \begin{pmatrix} J_{k_1} & 0 & O \\ 0' & 0 & b' \\ O & 0 & J_{(2)} \end{pmatrix},$$

are similar, because the second matrix, $A_{(4)}$, is obtained from the first by row- and column-block permutations. Now consider $A_{(4)}$, and, in particular, its $(n-k_1)\times(n-k_1)$ submatrix

$$\begin{pmatrix} 0 & b' \\ 0 & J_{(2)} \end{pmatrix}.$$

By the induction hypothesis, this submatrix is similar to a Jordan matrix with zero diagonal elements, say $J_{(3)}$. Then $\operatorname{diag}(J_{k_1}, J_{(3)})$ is similar to $A_{(4)}$ and hence to A. This is a Jordan matrix with zero diagonal elements. Finally we put its Jordan blocks in nonincreasing order by applying block permutations.
(e) We have thus proved that if the lemma holds for matrices of order $n - 1$, it also holds for matrices of order n. This, together with the fact that the result holds for $n = 1$ (and $n = 2$ and 3), completes the proof.

Exercise 7.79 (Jordan's decomposition theorem) Let $\boldsymbol{A}$ be an $n \times n$ matrix and denote by $\boldsymbol{J}_k(\lambda)$ a Jordan block, that is, a $k \times k$ matrix of the form

$$\boldsymbol{J}_k(\lambda) := \begin{pmatrix} \lambda & 1 & 0 & \dots & 0 \\ 0 & \lambda & 1 & \dots & 0 \\ \vdots & \vdots & \vdots & & \vdots \\ 0 & 0 & 0 & \dots & 1 \\ 0 & 0 & 0 & \dots & \lambda \end{pmatrix}.$$

For $k = 1$ we let $\boldsymbol{J}_1(\lambda) := \lambda$. Show that there exists a nonsingular $n \times n$ matrix $\boldsymbol{T}$ such that $\boldsymbol{T}^{-1}\boldsymbol{A}\boldsymbol{T} = \boldsymbol{J}$, where

$$\boldsymbol{J} := \begin{pmatrix} \boldsymbol{J}_{n_1}(\lambda_1) & \mathbf{O} & \dots & \mathbf{O} \\ \mathbf{O} & \boldsymbol{J}_{n_2}(\lambda_2) & \dots & \mathbf{O} \\ \vdots & \vdots & & \vdots \\ \mathbf{O} & \mathbf{O} & \dots & \boldsymbol{J}_{n_k}(\lambda_k) \end{pmatrix}$$

with $n_1 + n_2 + \dots + n_k = n$. The λ_i are the eigenvalues of $\boldsymbol{A}$, not necessarily distinct.

Solution

The proof consists of three steps, each of which has already been demonstrated. Schur's decomposition theorem (Exercise 7.62) guarantees the existence of a nonsingular (in fact, unitary) matrix $\boldsymbol{S}_1$ such that $\boldsymbol{S}_1^{-1}\boldsymbol{A}\boldsymbol{S}_1 = \boldsymbol{M}$, where $\boldsymbol{M}$ is upper triangular and has the eigenvalues of $\boldsymbol{A}$ on its diagonal. If necessary, we re-order the columns of $\boldsymbol{S}_1$ in such a way that multiple eigenvalues take contiguous positions on the diagonal of $\boldsymbol{M}$. Assume that $\boldsymbol{A}$ has s distinct eigenvalues $\lambda_1, \dots, \lambda_s$ with multiplicities $n_1, \dots, n_s$. Then,

$$\boldsymbol{S}_1^{-1}\boldsymbol{A}\boldsymbol{S}_1 = \begin{pmatrix} \boldsymbol{M}_1 & * & \dots & * \\ \mathbf{O} & \boldsymbol{M}_2 & \dots & * \\ \vdots & \vdots & & \vdots \\ \mathbf{O} & \mathbf{O} & \dots & \boldsymbol{M}_s \end{pmatrix}$$

where each $\boldsymbol{M}_i$ is an upper triangular $n_i \times n_i$ matrix, all whose diagonal elements are equal to λ_i and a $*$ indicates an unspecified matrix, not necessarily the null matrix.

In the second step, we use Exercise 7.58. This guarantees the existence of a nonsingular (but not necessarily unitary) matrix $\boldsymbol{S}_2$ such that

$$\boldsymbol{S}_2^{-1}\boldsymbol{S}_1^{-1}\boldsymbol{A}\boldsymbol{S}_1\boldsymbol{S}_2 = \begin{pmatrix} \boldsymbol{M}_1 & \mathbf{O} & \dots & \mathbf{O} \\ \mathbf{O} & \boldsymbol{M}_2 & \dots & \mathbf{O} \\ \vdots & \vdots & & \vdots \\ \mathbf{O} & \mathbf{O} & \dots & \boldsymbol{M}_s \end{pmatrix}.$$

We write $\boldsymbol{M}_i := \lambda_i \boldsymbol{I}_{n_i} + \boldsymbol{U}_i$, where $\boldsymbol{U}_i$ is a *strictly* upper triangular $n_i \times n_i$ matrix. In the third and final step we use Exercise 7.77. This guarantees the existence, for each $i = 1, \dots, s$ of a nonsingular matrix $\boldsymbol{T}_i$ such that $\boldsymbol{T}_i^{-1}\boldsymbol{U}_i\boldsymbol{T}_i$ has a block-diagonal "Jordan structure" (with all diagonal elements equal to 0), say $\boldsymbol{J}^{(i)}(0)$. Then,

$$\boldsymbol{T}_i^{-1}\boldsymbol{M}_i\boldsymbol{T}_i = \boldsymbol{T}_i^{-1}(\lambda_i\boldsymbol{I}_{n_i} + \boldsymbol{U}_i)\boldsymbol{T}_i = \lambda_i\boldsymbol{I}_{n_i} + \boldsymbol{J}^{(i)}(0) = \boldsymbol{J}^{(i)}(\lambda_i),$$

and hence, letting $\boldsymbol{S}_3 := \operatorname{diag}(\boldsymbol{T}_1, \boldsymbol{T}_2, \dots, \boldsymbol{T}_s)$,

$$\boldsymbol{S}_3^{-1}\boldsymbol{S}_2^{-1}\boldsymbol{S}_1^{-1}\boldsymbol{A}\boldsymbol{S}_1\boldsymbol{S}_2\boldsymbol{S}_3 = \begin{pmatrix} \boldsymbol{J}^{(1)}(\lambda_1) & \mathbf{O} & \dots & \mathbf{O} \\ \mathbf{O} & \boldsymbol{J}^{(2)}(\lambda_2) & \dots & \mathbf{O} \\ \vdots & \vdots & & \vdots \\ \mathbf{O} & \mathbf{O} & \dots & \boldsymbol{J}^{(s)}(\lambda_s) \end{pmatrix}.$$

If we now define $\boldsymbol{T} := \boldsymbol{S}_1\boldsymbol{S}_2\boldsymbol{S}_3$, then $\boldsymbol{T}$ is nonsingular and $\boldsymbol{T}^{-1}\boldsymbol{A}\boldsymbol{T}$ transforms $\boldsymbol{A}$ to Jordan form. Notice that $\lambda_1, \dots, \lambda_s$ are all distinct, but that within each block $\boldsymbol{J}^{(i)}(\lambda_i)$ several Jordan blocks may occur with the same λ_i. The total number of Jordan blocks is $k \geq s$.

Exercise 7.80 (Example of a Jordan matrix) Let $\boldsymbol{A}$ be a 5×5 matrix with eigenvalues λ_1 (3 times) and λ_2 (twice) such that $\lambda_1 \neq \lambda_2$. Write down the general form of the Jordan matrix $\boldsymbol{J}$.

Solution

The general form is

$$\boldsymbol{J} := \begin{pmatrix} \lambda_1 & \beta_1 & 0 & 0 & 0 \\ 0 & \lambda_1 & \beta_2 & 0 & 0 \\ 0 & 0 & \lambda_1 & 0 & 0 \\ 0 & 0 & 0 & \lambda_2 & \beta_3 \\ 0 & 0 & 0 & 0 & \lambda_2 \end{pmatrix},$$

where the value of β_1, β_2, β_3 is either 0 or 1. There are therefore eight possible forms in this case.

Exercise 7.81 (How many Jordan blocks?) Show that:
(a) The number k of Jordan blocks is the number of linearly independent eigenvectors of $\boldsymbol{J}$;
(b) The matrix $\boldsymbol{J}$ can be diagonalized if and only if $k = n$.

Solution

(a) It is easy to see that a $k \times k$ Jordan block $\boldsymbol{J}_k(\lambda)$ has rank $k - 1$ and possesses only one eigenvector associated with the eigenvalue λ, namely $(1, 0, \dots, 0)'$. Because of the block-diagonal structure of $\boldsymbol{J}$, eigenvectors associated with different blocks are linearly independent. Hence, each block contributes precisely one eigenvector.
(b) According to Exercise 7.61(a), the $n \times n$ matrix $\boldsymbol{J}$ can be diagonalized if and only if there exist n linearly independent vectors, each of which is an eigenvector of $\boldsymbol{A}$. This occurs if and only if $k = n$.

Exercise 7.82 (Cayley-Hamilton, 2) Use Exercise 7.74(c) to provide an alternative proof of the Cayley-Hamilton theorem (Exercise 7.69).

Solution
Because of the Jordan decomposition theorem, it suffices to prove that

$$(\lambda_1 \boldsymbol{I}_n - \boldsymbol{J})^{n_1}(\lambda_2 \boldsymbol{I}_n - \boldsymbol{J})^{n_2} \dots (\lambda_k \boldsymbol{I}_n - \boldsymbol{J})^{n_k} = \mathbf{O}.$$

Since $\boldsymbol{J}$ is block-diagonal, this happens if and only if, for $i = 1, \dots, k$,

$$(\lambda_1 \boldsymbol{I}_{n_i} - \boldsymbol{J}_{n_i}(\lambda_i))^{n_1} (\lambda_2 \boldsymbol{I}_{n_i} - \boldsymbol{J}_{n_i}(\lambda_i))^{n_2} \dots (\lambda_k \boldsymbol{I}_{n_i} - \boldsymbol{J}_{n_i}(\lambda_i))^{n_k} = \mathbf{O}.$$

But this is true because, for each i, the i-th term in the product vanishes:

$$(\lambda_i \boldsymbol{I}_{n_i} - \boldsymbol{J}_{n_i}(\lambda_i))^{n_i} = (-\boldsymbol{J}_{n_i}(0))^{n_i} = \mathbf{O},$$

by Exercise 7.74(c).

7.6 Jordan chains and generalized eigenvectors

Exercise 7.83 (Recursion within a Jordan chain) Let λ be a multiple eigenvalue of the $n \times n$ matrix $\boldsymbol{A}$, and let $\{\boldsymbol{x}_p, \boldsymbol{x}_{p-1}, \dots, \boldsymbol{x}_1\}$ be a Jordan chain associated with λ and generated recursively from the generalized eigenvector $\boldsymbol{x}_p$ by

$$\boldsymbol{x}_i = (\boldsymbol{A} - \lambda \boldsymbol{I}_n)\, \boldsymbol{x}_{i+1} \quad (i = p-1, \dots, 1).$$

Show that $\boldsymbol{x}_{p-1}, \dots, \boldsymbol{x}_1$ obtained in this way are generalized eigenvectors of degrees $p - 1, \dots, 1$.

Solution
Let $\boldsymbol{C} := \boldsymbol{A} - \lambda \boldsymbol{I}_n$. The definition of the generalized eigenvector $\boldsymbol{x}_p$ is

$$\boldsymbol{C}^p \boldsymbol{x}_p = \mathbf{0} \quad \text{but} \quad \boldsymbol{C}^{p-1} \boldsymbol{x}_p \neq \mathbf{0}.$$

We need to show that the next vector in the Jordan chain, generated by $\boldsymbol{x}_{p-1} = \boldsymbol{C}\boldsymbol{x}_p$, is a generalized eigenvector of degree $p - 1$. This follows from

$$\boldsymbol{C}^{p-1} \boldsymbol{x}_{p-1} = \boldsymbol{C}^{p-1}(\boldsymbol{C}\boldsymbol{x}_p) = \mathbf{0} \quad \text{but} \quad \boldsymbol{C}^{p-2} \boldsymbol{x}_{p-1} = \boldsymbol{C}^{p-2}(\boldsymbol{C}\boldsymbol{x}_p) \neq \mathbf{0},$$

by the definition of $\boldsymbol{x}_p$. Repeating this procedure for $\boldsymbol{x}_i = \boldsymbol{C}\boldsymbol{x}_{i+1}$, where $i = p-2, \dots, 1$, completes the solution.

Exercise 7.84 (One Jordan chain and one Jordan block) Let $\boldsymbol{A}$ be an $n \times n$ matrix, and suppose there exists a nonsingular matrix $\boldsymbol{T}$ such that $\boldsymbol{T}^{-1}\boldsymbol{A}\boldsymbol{T} = \boldsymbol{J}$, where

$$\boldsymbol{J} := \begin{pmatrix} \lambda & 1 & 0 & \dots & 0 & 0 \\ 0 & \lambda & 1 & \dots & 0 & 0 \\ \vdots & \vdots & \vdots & & \vdots & \vdots \\ 0 & 0 & 0 & \dots & \lambda & 1 \\ 0 & 0 & 0 & \dots & 0 & \lambda \end{pmatrix}.$$

What can you say about the columns of the matrix $\boldsymbol{T}$?

Solution

Let us write $\boldsymbol{T} := (\boldsymbol{x}_1, \boldsymbol{x}_2, \dots, \boldsymbol{x}_n)$. The equation $\boldsymbol{AT} = \boldsymbol{TJ}$ gives

$$\boldsymbol{A}\boldsymbol{x}_1 = \lambda \boldsymbol{x}_1 \quad \text{and} \quad \boldsymbol{A}\boldsymbol{x}_{i+1} = \boldsymbol{x}_i + \lambda \boldsymbol{x}_{i+1} \quad (i = 1, \dots, n-1),$$

which can be rewritten as

$$(\boldsymbol{A} - \lambda \boldsymbol{I}_n)\boldsymbol{x}_1 = \boldsymbol{0} \quad \text{and} \quad (\boldsymbol{A} - \lambda \boldsymbol{I}_n)\boldsymbol{x}_{i+1} = \boldsymbol{x}_i \quad (i = 1, \dots, n-1).$$

Hence, the n columns of $\boldsymbol{T}$ are generalized eigenvectors associated with the eigenvalue λ, and form a Jordan chain of length n associated with λ.

Exercise 7.85 (Independence within a Jordan chain) Let λ be a multiple eigenvalue of the $n \times n$ matrix $\boldsymbol{A}$. Show that the vectors in a Jordan chain $\{\boldsymbol{x}_p, \dots, \boldsymbol{x}_1\}$ associated with λ are linearly independent.

Solution

Suppose that $\boldsymbol{y} := \sum_{j=1}^{p} \alpha_j \boldsymbol{x}_j = \boldsymbol{0}$. We will show that this implies that $\alpha_j = 0$ for all j. Since $\boldsymbol{x}_j$ is a generalized eigenvector, we have

$$(\boldsymbol{A} - \lambda \boldsymbol{I}_n)^j \boldsymbol{x}_j = \boldsymbol{0}, \quad \text{but} \quad (\boldsymbol{A} - \lambda \boldsymbol{I}_n)^{j-1} \boldsymbol{x}_j \neq \boldsymbol{0}.$$

Hence, $(\boldsymbol{A} - \lambda \boldsymbol{I}_n)^{j+i} \boldsymbol{x}_j = \boldsymbol{0}$ for $i = 0, 1, \dots$. Premultiplying $\boldsymbol{y}$ by $(\boldsymbol{A} - \lambda \boldsymbol{I}_n)^{p-1}$ gives

$$\boldsymbol{0} = (\boldsymbol{A} - \lambda \boldsymbol{I}_n)^{p-1} \sum_{j=1}^{p} \alpha_j \boldsymbol{x}_j = \alpha_p (\boldsymbol{A} - \lambda \boldsymbol{I}_n)^{p-1} \boldsymbol{x}_p,$$

which holds if and only if $\alpha_p = 0$. If we premultiply $\boldsymbol{y}$ by $(\boldsymbol{A} - \lambda \boldsymbol{I}_n)^{p-2}$, then it follows that $\alpha_{p-1} = 0$. Continuing this procedure, we obtain $\alpha_j = 0$ for all j.

Exercise 7.86 (Independence of Jordan chains belonging to different eigenvalues) Let $\lambda_1 \neq \lambda_2$ be two eigenvalues of the $n \times n$ matrix $\boldsymbol{A}$. Let $\{\boldsymbol{x}_p, \dots, \boldsymbol{x}_1\}$ be a Jordan chain associated with λ_1, and $\{\boldsymbol{y}_q, \dots, \boldsymbol{y}_1\}$ be a Jordan chain associated with λ_2. Show that the vectors $\boldsymbol{x}_p, \dots, \boldsymbol{x}_1$ are linearly independent of the vectors $\boldsymbol{y}_q, \dots, \boldsymbol{y}_1$.

Solution

We need to show that the two vectors $\sum_{i=1}^{p} \alpha_i \boldsymbol{x}_i$ and $\sum_{j=1}^{q} \beta_j \boldsymbol{y}_j$ are linearly independent for any choice of the coefficients α_i (not all zero) and β_j (not all zero). Suppose that $\sum_{i=1}^{p} \alpha_i \boldsymbol{x}_i = \sum_{j=1}^{q} \beta_j \boldsymbol{y}_j$. If we can show that this implies that $\alpha_i = 0$ $(i = 1, \dots, p)$ and $\beta_j = 0$ $(j = 1, \dots, q)$, then we have demonstrated the required linear independence.

By definition, $(\boldsymbol{A} - \lambda_1 \boldsymbol{I}_n)^p \boldsymbol{x}_i = \boldsymbol{0}$ for all $i \leq p$, so that

$$\boldsymbol{0} = (\boldsymbol{A} - \lambda_1 \boldsymbol{I}_n)^p \sum_{i=1}^{p} \alpha_i \boldsymbol{x}_i = (\boldsymbol{A} - \lambda_1 \boldsymbol{I}_n)^p \sum_{j=1}^{q} \beta_j \boldsymbol{y}_j.$$

Now premultiply by $(\boldsymbol{A} - \lambda_2 \boldsymbol{I}_n)^{q-1}$. Since $(\boldsymbol{A} - \lambda_1 \boldsymbol{I}_n)^p$ and $(\boldsymbol{A} - \lambda_2 \boldsymbol{I}_n)^{q-1}$ commute (because $\boldsymbol{A}$ commutes with scalar matrices; see Exercise 2.11), we obtain

$$\mathbf{0} = (\boldsymbol{A} - \lambda_1 \boldsymbol{I}_n)^p \sum_{j=1}^{q} \beta_j \, (\boldsymbol{A} - \lambda_2 \boldsymbol{I}_n)^{q-1} \boldsymbol{y}_j.$$

Since $(\boldsymbol{A} - \lambda_2 \boldsymbol{I}_n)^{q-1} \boldsymbol{y}_j = \mathbf{0}$ for all $j \leq q-1$, the only nonzero term in the sum is the one where $j = q$, and we get

$$\mathbf{0} = \beta_q \, (\boldsymbol{A} - \lambda_1 \boldsymbol{I}_n)^p \, (\boldsymbol{A} - \lambda_2 \boldsymbol{I}_n)^{q-1} \, \boldsymbol{y}_q = \beta_q \, (\boldsymbol{A} - \lambda_1 \boldsymbol{I}_n)^p \, \boldsymbol{y}_1.$$

Recall that $\boldsymbol{y}_1$ is an eigenvector of $\boldsymbol{A}$ associated with λ_2. Hence, $(\boldsymbol{A} - \lambda_1 \boldsymbol{I}_n)\boldsymbol{y}_1 = (\lambda_2 - \lambda_1)\boldsymbol{y}_1$, and we obtain $\mathbf{0} = \beta_q(\lambda_2 - \lambda_1)^p \boldsymbol{y}_1$. Since $\lambda_2 \neq \lambda_1$, we find that $\beta_q = 0$.

Repeating the process by premultiplying both sides of $\mathbf{0} = (\boldsymbol{A} - \lambda_1 \boldsymbol{I}_n)^p \sum_{j=1}^{q} \beta_j \boldsymbol{y}_j$ by $(\boldsymbol{A} - \lambda_2 \boldsymbol{I}_n)^{q-2}$, we find that $\beta_{q-1} = 0$, and continuing in this way shows that $\beta_j = 0$ for all j. Finally, $\sum_{i=1}^{p} \alpha_i \boldsymbol{x}_i = \mathbf{0}$ implies that $\alpha_i = 0$ for all i by Exercise 7.85.

Exercise 7.87 (Independence of Jordan chains starting with independent eigenvectors) Let λ_1 and λ_2 be two eigenvalues (not necessarily distinct) of the $n \times n$ matrix $\boldsymbol{A}$. Let $\{\boldsymbol{x}_p, \dots, \boldsymbol{x}_1\}$ be a Jordan chain associated with λ_1, and let $\{\boldsymbol{y}_q, \dots, \boldsymbol{y}_1\}$ be a Jordan chain associated with λ_2, where $\boldsymbol{x}_1$ and $\boldsymbol{y}_1$ are linearly independent eigenvectors of $\boldsymbol{A}$.
(a) Show that the vectors $\boldsymbol{x}_p, \dots, \boldsymbol{x}_1$ are linearly independent of the vectors $\boldsymbol{y}_q, \dots, \boldsymbol{y}_1$.
(b) Does this result apply to more than two Jordan chains?

Solution
(a) When $\lambda_1 \neq \lambda_2$, the result follows from Exercise 7.86. When $\lambda_1 = \lambda_2 = \lambda$, say, let $q \geq p$ without loss of generality. Suppose that $\sum_{i=1}^{p} \alpha_i \boldsymbol{x}_i = \sum_{j=1}^{q} \beta_j \boldsymbol{y}_j$. Premultiplying both sides by $(\boldsymbol{A} - \lambda \boldsymbol{I}_n)^{q-1}$ gives

$$\begin{aligned} \alpha_p (\boldsymbol{A} - \lambda \boldsymbol{I}_n)^{q-1} \boldsymbol{x}_p &= \sum_{i=1}^{p} \alpha_i (\boldsymbol{A} - \lambda \boldsymbol{I}_n)^{q-1} \boldsymbol{x}_i = \sum_{j=1}^{q} \beta_j (\boldsymbol{A} - \lambda \boldsymbol{I}_n)^{q-1} \boldsymbol{y}_j \\ &= \beta_q (\boldsymbol{A} - \lambda \boldsymbol{I}_n)^{q-1} \boldsymbol{y}_q = \beta_q \boldsymbol{y}_1. \end{aligned}$$

If $q = p$, then the above equality implies that $\alpha_p \boldsymbol{x}_1 = \beta_q \boldsymbol{y}_1$, and hence — since $\boldsymbol{x}_1$ and $\boldsymbol{y}_1$ are linearly independent — that $\beta_q = 0$ (and also that $\alpha_p = 0$). If $q > p$, then the above equality implies that $0 = \beta_q \boldsymbol{y}_1$, and hence also that $\beta_q = 0$.

Premultiplying both sides by $(\boldsymbol{A} - \lambda \boldsymbol{I}_n)^{q-2}$ gives $\beta_{q-1} = 0$, and continuing in this way shows that $\beta_j = 0$ for all j. Finally, $\sum_{i=1}^{p} \alpha_i \boldsymbol{x}_i = \mathbf{0}$ implies that $\alpha_i = 0$ for all i by Exercise 7.85.
(b) The same proof applies to any number of Jordan chains, by writing

$$\sum_{i=1}^{p} \alpha_i \boldsymbol{x}_i + \sum_{j=1}^{q} \beta_j \boldsymbol{y}_j + \sum_{k=1}^{r} \gamma_k \boldsymbol{z}_k + \cdots = \mathbf{0},$$

and showing that $\alpha_i, \beta_j, \gamma_k, \dots$ are all zero.

***Exercise 7.88 (As many independent generalized eigenvectors as the multiplicity)** Let λ be an eigenvalue of multiplicity m of the $n \times n$ matrix $\boldsymbol{A}$. Show that the Jordan chains associated with λ have lengths adding up to m exactly:
(a) when $m = n$;
(b) when $m < n$.

Solution
(a) By Schur's decomposition, $\boldsymbol{A} - \lambda \boldsymbol{I}_m = \boldsymbol{S}\boldsymbol{M}\boldsymbol{S}^*$ where $\boldsymbol{S}\boldsymbol{S}^* = \boldsymbol{I}_m$ and $\boldsymbol{M}$ is strictly upper triangular. The definition of generalized eigenvectors can be rewritten as

$$\boldsymbol{M}^j \boldsymbol{y}_j = \boldsymbol{0} \quad \text{but} \quad \boldsymbol{M}^{j-1}\boldsymbol{y}_j \neq \boldsymbol{0},$$

where $\boldsymbol{y}_j := \boldsymbol{S}^*\boldsymbol{x}_j$. Let $r_1 := \operatorname{rk}(\boldsymbol{M}) < m$. Then, Exercise 6.36(a) shows that there are $\dim(\ker \boldsymbol{M}) = m - r_1$ linearly independent solutions to $\boldsymbol{M}\boldsymbol{y}_1 = \boldsymbol{0}$. If $r_1 = 0$, we have m linearly independent solutions to $\boldsymbol{y}_1$, hence m linearly independent eigenvectors $\boldsymbol{x}_1$ since $\boldsymbol{S}$ is unitary. If $r_1 > 0$, then $r_2 := \operatorname{rk}(\boldsymbol{M}^2) < r_1$ by Exercise 7.55(b). The rewritten definition of generalized eigenvectors then yields $r_1 - r_2 > 0$ additional generalized eigenvectors. Each one of these goes to a different Jordan chain for λ, because, whenever $\boldsymbol{y}_{i+1}$ exists, there is a corresponding $\boldsymbol{y}_i$ obtained by the definition of the Jordan chain $\boldsymbol{M}\boldsymbol{y}_{i+1} = \boldsymbol{y}_i$. This also implies that $m - r_1 \geq r_1 - r_2$.

Now, since $\boldsymbol{M}$ is strictly upper triangular, there exists an integer p such that $\boldsymbol{M}^p = \boldsymbol{O}$ while $\boldsymbol{M}^{p-1} \neq \boldsymbol{O}$. Hence, $r_p := \operatorname{rk}(\boldsymbol{M}^p) = 0$, and the total number of generalized eigenvectors is

$$(m - r_1) + (r_1 - r_2) + \cdots + (r_{p-2} - r_{p-1}) + (r_{p-1} - 0) = m,$$

as required. Note that this generalizes the earlier inequality to

$$m - r_1 \geq r_1 - r_2 \geq \cdots \geq r_{p-2} - r_{p-1} \geq r_{p-1} > 0,$$

by the definition of the Jordan chain. The number $p \leq m$ is the length of the longest Jordan chain, and the geometric multiplicity $m - r_1$ is equal to the number of Jordan chains for any particular eigenvalue.
(b) When $m < n$, Schur's decomposition gives $\boldsymbol{A} - \lambda \boldsymbol{I}_n = \boldsymbol{S}\boldsymbol{U}\boldsymbol{S}^*$, where $\boldsymbol{S}\boldsymbol{S}^* = \boldsymbol{I}_n$ and

$$\boldsymbol{U} = \begin{pmatrix} \boldsymbol{M} & * \\ \boldsymbol{O} & \boldsymbol{P} \end{pmatrix},$$

where the $m \times m$ submatrix $\boldsymbol{M}$ is strictly upper triangular as in (a), but $\boldsymbol{P}$ is upper triangular with nonzero diagonal elements since the multiplicity of λ is $m < n$. We have

$$\boldsymbol{U}^i = \begin{pmatrix} \boldsymbol{M}^i & * \\ \boldsymbol{O} & \boldsymbol{P}^i \end{pmatrix} \quad (i = 1, 2, \dots).$$

The diagonal elements of $\boldsymbol{P}^i$ being nonzero, Exercise 5.43 yields

$$r_i := \operatorname{rk}(\boldsymbol{U}^i) = \operatorname{rk}(\boldsymbol{M}^i) + \operatorname{rk}(\boldsymbol{P}^i) = \operatorname{rk}(\boldsymbol{M}^i) + n - m.$$

Therefore, as in (a), there exists an integer p such that $\boldsymbol{M}^p = \mathbf{O}$ while $\boldsymbol{M}^{p-1} \neq \mathbf{O}$. Then solving

$$\boldsymbol{U}^j \boldsymbol{y}_j = \mathbf{0} \quad \text{but} \quad \boldsymbol{U}^{j-1} \boldsymbol{y}_j \neq \mathbf{0},$$

where $\boldsymbol{y}_j := \boldsymbol{S}^* \boldsymbol{x}_j$ and $j = 1, \dots, p$, gives rise to the total number of generalized eigenvectors

$$\begin{aligned}
&(n - r_1) + \cdots + (r_{p-1} - r_p) \\
&\quad = (n - (\operatorname{rk}(\boldsymbol{M}) + n - m)) + \cdots + \left((\operatorname{rk}(\boldsymbol{M}^{p-1}) + n - m) - (n - m)\right) \\
&\quad = m.
\end{aligned}$$

There can be no further generalized eigenvectors for λ obtainable from $\boldsymbol{U}^{p+1}$,$\boldsymbol{U}^{p+2}$,..., since these are all of the same rank $n - m$ as $\boldsymbol{P}^i$ for all i.

Exercise 7.89 (Jordan in chains) By using generalized eigenvectors, prove that any $n \times n$ matrix $\boldsymbol{A}$ possesses a Jordan decomposition.

Solution

Recall, from Exercise 5.7, that

$$(\boldsymbol{T}_1, \dots, \boldsymbol{T}_k) \operatorname{diag}\left(\boldsymbol{J}_{n_1}(\lambda_1), \dots, \boldsymbol{J}_{n_k}(\lambda_k)\right) = \left(\boldsymbol{T}_1 \boldsymbol{J}_{n_1}(\lambda_1), \dots, \boldsymbol{T}_k \boldsymbol{J}_{n_k}(\lambda_k)\right),$$

for $\boldsymbol{T}_i$ and $\boldsymbol{J}_{n_i}(\lambda_i)$ conformable for multiplication, $i = 1, \dots, k$. Exercise 7.88 demonstrates that there are as many generalized eigenvectors as the order n of the matrix $\boldsymbol{A}$, so that $\sum_{i=1}^k n_i = n$. This, together with the linear independence established in Exercises 7.87 and 7.88, implies that the generalized eigenvectors are linearly independent, and hence that $\boldsymbol{T} := (\boldsymbol{T}_1, \dots, \boldsymbol{T}_k)$ is a nonsingular $n \times n$ matrix. Within each of the $n \times n_i$ blocks $\boldsymbol{T}_i$, the columns are generalized eigenvectors satisfying the same recursion as in Exercise 7.84, so that

$$\left(\boldsymbol{T}_1 \boldsymbol{J}_{n_1}(\lambda_1), \dots, \boldsymbol{T}_k \boldsymbol{J}_{n_k}(\lambda_k)\right) = \left(\boldsymbol{A}\boldsymbol{T}_1, \dots, \boldsymbol{A}\boldsymbol{T}_k\right).$$

Hence, $\boldsymbol{A}\boldsymbol{T} = \boldsymbol{T}\boldsymbol{J}$, where $\boldsymbol{J} := \operatorname{diag}(\boldsymbol{J}_{n_1}(\lambda_1), \dots, \boldsymbol{J}_{n_k}(\lambda_k))$.

Exercise 7.90 (Find the eigenvectors, 2) Consider

$$\boldsymbol{A} = \begin{pmatrix} 1 & 1 \\ 0 & 1 \end{pmatrix}.$$

Find the generalized eigenvectors of $\boldsymbol{A}$ and hence its Jordan decomposition $\boldsymbol{A} = \boldsymbol{T}\boldsymbol{J}\boldsymbol{T}^{-1}$. Compare the result to Exercise 7.10(a).

Solution

We notice that the matrix is already in its Jordan form, with one multiple eigenvalue of 1 and a single Jordan chain of length 2. Define

$$\boldsymbol{C} := \boldsymbol{A} - \lambda \boldsymbol{I}_2 = \begin{pmatrix} 0 & 1 \\ 0 & 0 \end{pmatrix}.$$

We need to solve $\boldsymbol{C}^2\boldsymbol{x}_2 = \mathbf{0}$ such that $\boldsymbol{C}\boldsymbol{x}_2 \neq \mathbf{0}$. The first equation places no restriction on $\boldsymbol{x}_2$ since $\boldsymbol{C}^2 = \mathbf{O}$. Letting $\boldsymbol{x}_2 := (x, y)'$, the inequality $\boldsymbol{C}\boldsymbol{x}_2 \neq \mathbf{0}$ implies $y \neq 0$, so that $\boldsymbol{x}_1 = \boldsymbol{C}\boldsymbol{x}_2 = (y, 0)'$. Hence,

$$\boldsymbol{T} := (\boldsymbol{x}_1, \boldsymbol{x}_2) = \begin{pmatrix} y & x \\ 0 & y \end{pmatrix},$$

giving

$$\begin{pmatrix} y & x \\ 0 & y \end{pmatrix}\begin{pmatrix} 1 & 1 \\ 0 & 1 \end{pmatrix}\begin{pmatrix} 1/y & -x/y^2 \\ 0 & 1/y \end{pmatrix} = \begin{pmatrix} 1 & 1 \\ 0 & 1 \end{pmatrix},$$

as expected.

Since $\boldsymbol{A}$ was already in its Jordan form, one possible choice of $\boldsymbol{T}$ is a scalar multiple of $\boldsymbol{I}_2$, which is obtained by setting $x = 0$. In Exercise 7.10(a) we obtained the eigenvector $(1, 0)'$, and we have now shown that $(0, 1)'$ is a suitable corresponding generalized eigenvector.

Note carefully the order of obtaining generalized eigenvectors in a Jordan chain. We started with $\boldsymbol{x}_2$ and then obtained $\boldsymbol{x}_1$. Had we selected $\boldsymbol{x}_1 = (1, 0)'$ first and $\boldsymbol{x}_2 = (x, y)'$ next, then the solution would have been incorrect:

$$\begin{pmatrix} 1 & x \\ 0 & y \end{pmatrix}\begin{pmatrix} 1 & 1 \\ 0 & 1 \end{pmatrix}\begin{pmatrix} 1 & x \\ 0 & y \end{pmatrix}^{-1} = \begin{pmatrix} 1 & 1/y \\ 0 & 1 \end{pmatrix} \neq \boldsymbol{A} \quad \text{if } y \neq 1.$$

This is why we prefer to keep the subscript of the eigenvector $\boldsymbol{x}_1$, to stress that it is in a Jordan chain, rather than drop it as we usually write $\boldsymbol{x}$ for an eigenvector.

Exercise 7.91 (Geometric multiplicity, 2) The matrix

$$\boldsymbol{A} = \begin{pmatrix} 1 & 3 & 0 \\ 0 & 1 & 0 \\ 2 & 1 & 5 \end{pmatrix}.$$

was already considered in Exercises 7.3 and 7.11. Now derive the generalized eigenvectors of $\boldsymbol{A}$ and its Jordan decomposition $\boldsymbol{A} = \boldsymbol{T}\boldsymbol{J}\boldsymbol{T}^{-1}$.

Solution

We know from Exercise 7.11 that the eigenvalues of $\boldsymbol{A}$ are 1 (twice) and 5, and that the multiple eigenvalue 1 has geometric multiplicity 1, so that we cannot find two linearly independent eigenvectors associated with the eigenvalue 1. Associated with the eigenvalue 1 is an eigenvector $(2, 0, -1)'$ (or a multiple thereof) and associated with the eigenvalue 5 is an eigenvector $(0, 0, 1)'$ (or a multiple thereof).

To find the Jordan chain associated with the eigenvalue 1, we define $\boldsymbol{C} := \boldsymbol{A} - \boldsymbol{I}_3$ and try to solve $\boldsymbol{x}_2 := (x, y, z)'$ from $\boldsymbol{C}^2\boldsymbol{x}_2 = \mathbf{0}$, while $\boldsymbol{C}\boldsymbol{x}_2 \neq \mathbf{0}$. This gives

$$\begin{pmatrix} 0 & 3 & 0 \\ 0 & 0 & 0 \\ 2 & 1 & 4 \end{pmatrix}^2 \begin{pmatrix} x \\ y \\ z \end{pmatrix} = \begin{pmatrix} 0 & 0 & 0 \\ 0 & 0 & 0 \\ 8 & 10 & 16 \end{pmatrix}\begin{pmatrix} x \\ y \\ z \end{pmatrix} = \begin{pmatrix} 0 \\ 0 \\ 8x + 10y + 16z \end{pmatrix} = \begin{pmatrix} 0 \\ 0 \\ 0 \end{pmatrix}$$

and

$$\begin{pmatrix} 0 & 3 & 0 \\ 0 & 0 & 0 \\ 2 & 1 & 4 \end{pmatrix} \begin{pmatrix} x \\ y \\ z \end{pmatrix} = \begin{pmatrix} 3y \\ 0 \\ 2x+y+4z \end{pmatrix} \neq \begin{pmatrix} 0 \\ 0 \\ 0 \end{pmatrix}.$$

The solution $(x, y, z)'$ must satisfy $y \neq 0$ and $4x + 5y + 8z = 0$, and we may take, for example, $\boldsymbol{x}_2 = (-1/2, 1, -3/8)'$. This implies

$$\boldsymbol{x}_1 = \begin{pmatrix} 0 & 3 & 0 \\ 0 & 0 & 0 \\ 2 & 1 & 4 \end{pmatrix} \begin{pmatrix} -1/2 \\ 1 \\ -3/8 \end{pmatrix} = \begin{pmatrix} 3 \\ 0 \\ -3/2 \end{pmatrix},$$

which is 1.5 times the eigenvector found in Exercise 7.11. As in Exercise 7.90, the scale is crucial for the construction of a correct Jordan chain in $\boldsymbol{T}$. Note that, as expected from Exercise 7.88, there is no generalized eigenvector of order 3 (that is, satisfying $\boldsymbol{C}^3\boldsymbol{x}_3 = \boldsymbol{0}$ and $\boldsymbol{C}^2\boldsymbol{x}_3 \neq \boldsymbol{0}$) associated with $\lambda = 1$, since $\boldsymbol{C}^3 = 4\boldsymbol{C}^2$.

Putting the generalized eigenvectors together and recalling that $(0, 0, t)'$ is an eigenvector associated with $\lambda = 5$ for any $t \neq 0$, for example $t = 3/8$, we obtain the decomposition

$$\begin{aligned} &\begin{pmatrix} 0 & 3 & -1/2 \\ 0 & 0 & 1 \\ 3/8 & -3/2 & -3/8 \end{pmatrix}^{-1} \begin{pmatrix} 1 & 3 & 0 \\ 0 & 1 & 0 \\ 2 & 1 & 5 \end{pmatrix} \begin{pmatrix} 0 & 3 & -1/2 \\ 0 & 0 & 1 \\ 3/8 & -3/2 & -3/8 \end{pmatrix} \\ &= \begin{pmatrix} 0 & 3 & -1/2 \\ 0 & 0 & 1 \\ 3/8 & -3/2 & -3/8 \end{pmatrix}^{-1} \begin{pmatrix} 0 & 3 & 5/2 \\ 0 & 0 & 1 \\ 15/8 & -3/2 & -15/8 \end{pmatrix} \\ &= \begin{pmatrix} 4/3 & 5/3 & 8/3 \\ 1/3 & 1/6 & 0 \\ 0 & 1 & 0 \end{pmatrix} \begin{pmatrix} 0 & 3 & 5/2 \\ 0 & 0 & 1 \\ 15/8 & -3/2 & -15/8 \end{pmatrix} \\ &= \begin{pmatrix} 5 & 0 & 0 \\ 0 & 1 & 1 \\ 0 & 0 & 1 \end{pmatrix} \end{aligned}$$

as expected. Again, careful that an incorrect scale for $\boldsymbol{x}_1$ could lead to

$$\begin{pmatrix} 0 & 2 & -1/2 \\ 0 & 0 & 1 \\ 3/8 & -1 & -3/8 \end{pmatrix} \begin{pmatrix} 5 & 0 & 0 \\ 0 & 1 & 1 \\ 0 & 0 & 1 \end{pmatrix} \begin{pmatrix} 0 & 2 & -1/2 \\ 0 & 0 & 1 \\ 3/8 & -1 & -3/8 \end{pmatrix}^{-1} = \begin{pmatrix} 1 & 2 & 0 \\ 0 & 1 & 0 \\ 2 & 3/2 & 5 \end{pmatrix},$$

which is not equal to $\boldsymbol{A}$.

Notes

The fact that there is a one-to-one relationship between the elementary symmetric functions and the power sums, and between the power sums and the functions E_k of the introduction, can be found in Hadley (1961, p. 273) or Horn and Johnson (1985, p. 42). The Craig-Sakamoto lemma (Exercise 7.52) is closely associated with the problem of the independence of quadratic forms in normal variables; see the *Econometric Exercises* volume by Abadir, Heijmans, and Magnus (2006, Chapter 8). The history of this problem is discussed in Driscoll and Gundberg (1986). If the algebraic multiplicities are known, but the geometric ones are not, then see Bronson (1989, pp. 82–83) for a numerical algorithm implied by Exercise 7.88. Jordan chains and generalized eigenvectors are discussed in Gantmacher (1959, Volume 1, Chapters 6 and 7), both from the analytic and the geometric point of view. See also Kostrikin and Manin (1981, Chapter 1, Section 9), Halmos (1974, Chapter II, Section 58), and Ortega (1987, Chapter 3, Section 3.2).

8

Positive (semi)definite and idempotent matrices

In this chapter we generalize the notion of a positive (nonnegative) number to a positive (semi)definite matrix, and the notion of zero and one to an idempotent matrix.

A symmetric (hence real) $n \times n$ matrix $\boldsymbol{A}$ is said to be *positive definite* (and we write $\boldsymbol{A} > \mathbf{O}$) if $\boldsymbol{x}'\boldsymbol{A}\boldsymbol{x} > 0$ for all real $\boldsymbol{x} \neq \mathbf{0}$; it is *positive semidefinite* (written $\boldsymbol{A} \geq \mathbf{O}$) if $\boldsymbol{x}'\boldsymbol{A}\boldsymbol{x} \geq 0$ for all $\boldsymbol{x}$. Similarly, $\boldsymbol{A}$ is *negative definite* ($\boldsymbol{A} < \mathbf{O}$) if $\boldsymbol{x}'\boldsymbol{A}\boldsymbol{x} < 0$ for all $\boldsymbol{x} \neq \mathbf{0}$ and *negative semidefinite* ($\boldsymbol{A} \leq \mathbf{O}$) if $\boldsymbol{x}'\boldsymbol{A}\boldsymbol{x} \leq 0$ for all $\boldsymbol{x}$. Most symmetric matrices are neither $\geq \mathbf{O}$ nor $\leq \mathbf{O}$; these are called *indefinite*. We write $\boldsymbol{A} > \boldsymbol{B}$ to indicate that $\boldsymbol{A} - \boldsymbol{B} > \mathbf{O}$, and similarly for $\boldsymbol{A} < \boldsymbol{B}$, $\boldsymbol{A} \geq \boldsymbol{B}$, and $\boldsymbol{A} \leq \boldsymbol{B}$.

We notice the following points:

(a) Symmetry is implicit in the definition. Of course, the quadratic form

$$\boldsymbol{x}'\boldsymbol{A}\boldsymbol{x} = (x_1, x_2)\begin{pmatrix} 4 & 4 \\ 0 & 4 \end{pmatrix}\begin{pmatrix} x_1 \\ x_2 \end{pmatrix} = (x_1 + 2x_2)^2 + 3x_1^2$$

is positive for all $(x_1, x_2) \neq (0, 0)$, but we do *not* call $\boldsymbol{A}$ positive definite. There is no need to do so, because

$$(x_1, x_2)\begin{pmatrix} 4 & 4 \\ 0 & 4 \end{pmatrix}\begin{pmatrix} x_1 \\ x_2 \end{pmatrix} = (x_1, x_2)\begin{pmatrix} 4 & 2 \\ 2 & 4 \end{pmatrix}\begin{pmatrix} x_1 \\ x_2 \end{pmatrix}.$$

In general, the transformation $\boldsymbol{B} := (\boldsymbol{A} + \boldsymbol{A}')/2$ makes $\boldsymbol{A}$ symmetric and leaves the quadratic form unchanged.

(b) All properties of negative (semi)definite matrices follow immediately from those of positive (semi)definite matrices, because $\boldsymbol{A}$ is positive (semi)definite if and only if $-\boldsymbol{A}$ is negative (semi)definite. The results for negative (semi)definite matrices are often more cumbersome, however. For example, if an $n \times n$ matrix $\boldsymbol{A}$ is positive definite, then $|\boldsymbol{A}| > 0$, but if it is negative definite then $(-1)^n|\boldsymbol{A}| > 0$ and hence the sign of $|\boldsymbol{A}|$ depends on the

order of the matrix. For these reasons we confine our attention to positive (semi)definite matrices.
(c) Most properties of positive semidefinite matrices follow from those of positive definite matrices by replacing $>$ by $\geq$. Thus, the statement "$\boldsymbol{A} > \mathbf{O}$ implies $|\boldsymbol{A}| > 0$" suggests that it is also true that "$\boldsymbol{A} \geq \mathbf{O}$ implies $|\boldsymbol{A}| \geq 0$", and this is indeed the case. But this does not always work! For example, if the n leading principal minors of $\boldsymbol{A}$ are positive then $\boldsymbol{A}$ is positive definite. But if the leading principal minors of $\boldsymbol{A}$ are nonnegative then $\boldsymbol{A}$ is not necessarily positive semidefinite; for this, *all* principal minors must be nonnegative.
(d) We restrict our attention to real matrices. If $\boldsymbol{A}$ is complex and Hermitian ($\boldsymbol{A}^* = \boldsymbol{A}$), then $\boldsymbol{A} > \mathbf{O}$ if the Hermitian form $\boldsymbol{x}^*\boldsymbol{A}\boldsymbol{x} > 0$ for all $\boldsymbol{x} \neq \mathbf{0}$, and $\boldsymbol{A} \geq \mathbf{O}$, $\boldsymbol{A} < \mathbf{O}$, and $\boldsymbol{A} \leq \mathbf{O}$ are defined analogously. The properties of complex (semi)definite matrices are similar to the properties of real (semi)definite matrices.

While a positive definite matrix generalizes the notion of positivity to matrices, an idempotent matrix generalizes the notion of both zero and one. As defined in Chapter 2, a square matrix $\boldsymbol{A}$ is idempotent if $\boldsymbol{A}^2 = \boldsymbol{A}$. Although most idempotent matrices used in statistics and econometrics are symmetric, symmetry is *not* part of the definition. We only consider real idempotent matrices. An idempotent matrix corresponds to an idempotent operation. As an example consider the matrix

$$\boldsymbol{A} := \boldsymbol{I}_n - \frac{1}{n}\boldsymbol{\imath}\boldsymbol{\imath}'.$$

This is an idempotent matrix. The transformation $\boldsymbol{y} := \boldsymbol{A}\boldsymbol{x}$ puts the variables $x_1, \ldots, x_n$ in deviation from their mean. The operation is idempotent because, once in deviation form, repeating the process does not lead to further changes. An idempotent matrix $\boldsymbol{A}(\boldsymbol{A}'\boldsymbol{A})^{-1}\boldsymbol{A}'$ is a projection (because its eigenvalues are 0 and 1 only) onto a space spanned by the columns of $\boldsymbol{A}$, namely the space $\operatorname{col} \boldsymbol{A}$ introduced in Chapter 3. This particular idempotent matrix is symmetric, so the projection is orthogonal; for a nonsymmetric idempotent matrix the projection is oblique.

Results for positive (semi)definite and idempotent matrices can be checked quite easily by proving or disproving the result for a diagonal matrix, one with positive (nonnegative) elements in the case of a positive (semi)definite matrix and one with only zeros and ones in the case of an idempotent matrix. If a statement does not hold for the diagonal matrix, it is false; if it does hold it is very likely (but not guaranteed) true.

When $\boldsymbol{A}$ is a positive semidefinite $n \times n$ matrix of rank r, we obtain in this chapter some additional decomposition theorems, among which:

- $\boldsymbol{A} = \boldsymbol{T}\boldsymbol{T}'$, $\boldsymbol{T}'\boldsymbol{T} = \boldsymbol{\Lambda}$ (diagonal) with $\boldsymbol{T}$ of order $n \times r$ and $\boldsymbol{\Lambda}$ containing the positive eigenvalues of $\boldsymbol{A}$ (Exercise 8.21).
- $\boldsymbol{A} = \boldsymbol{L}\boldsymbol{L}'$ with $\boldsymbol{L}$ lower triangular matrix with r positive and $n - r$ zero diagonal elements (Cholesky, Exercise 8.23).

- $\boldsymbol{A} = \boldsymbol{T}\boldsymbol{T}'$, $\boldsymbol{B} = \boldsymbol{T}\boldsymbol{\Lambda}\boldsymbol{T}'$ with $\boldsymbol{T}$ nonsingular and $\boldsymbol{\Lambda}$ diagonal, if $\boldsymbol{A}$ is positive definite and $\boldsymbol{B}$ symmetric (Exercise 8.37).

Also, if $\boldsymbol{A}$ is a real $m \times n$ matrix of rank $r > 0$, then:

- $\boldsymbol{A} = \boldsymbol{S}\boldsymbol{\Lambda}^{1/2}\boldsymbol{T}'$ with $\boldsymbol{S}'\boldsymbol{S} = \boldsymbol{T}'\boldsymbol{T} = \boldsymbol{I}_r$ and $\boldsymbol{\Lambda}$ $(r \times r)$ diagonal with positive diagonal elements (singular-value decomposition, Exercise 8.38).
- $\boldsymbol{A} = \boldsymbol{P}\boldsymbol{V}$, if $\operatorname{rk}(\boldsymbol{A}) = n$, with $\boldsymbol{P}$ semi-orthogonal and $\boldsymbol{V}$ positive definite (polar decomposition, Exercise 8.40).

8.1 Positive (semi)definite matrices

Exercise 8.1 (Symmetry and quadratic forms)
(a) For every square matrix $\boldsymbol{A}$, show that

$$\boldsymbol{x}'\boldsymbol{A}\boldsymbol{x} = \boldsymbol{x}'\left(\frac{\boldsymbol{A} + \boldsymbol{A}'}{2}\right)\boldsymbol{x}.$$

(b) Conclude that there is no loss in generality in confining the study of quadratic forms to symmetric matrices.

Solution
(a) We have

$$\boldsymbol{x}'\left(\frac{\boldsymbol{A} + \boldsymbol{A}'}{2}\right)\boldsymbol{x} = \frac{1}{2}(\boldsymbol{x}'\boldsymbol{A}\boldsymbol{x} + \boldsymbol{x}'\boldsymbol{A}'\boldsymbol{x}) = \frac{1}{2}(\boldsymbol{x}'\boldsymbol{A}\boldsymbol{x} + \boldsymbol{x}'\boldsymbol{A}\boldsymbol{x}) = \boldsymbol{x}'\boldsymbol{A}\boldsymbol{x}$$

because $\boldsymbol{x}'\boldsymbol{A}\boldsymbol{x}$ is a scalar and hence equal to its transpose:

$$\boldsymbol{x}'\boldsymbol{A}'\boldsymbol{x} = (\boldsymbol{x}'\boldsymbol{A}\boldsymbol{x})' = \boldsymbol{x}'\boldsymbol{A}\boldsymbol{x}.$$

(b) We see from (a) that the matrix in a quadratic form can always be made symmetric.

Exercise 8.2 (Matrix representation of quadratic forms) Write the following quadratic forms in matrix notation with a symmetric matrix: (a) $x^2 + y^2 - xy$, (b) $4x^2 + 5y^2 + z^2 + 2xy + 2yz$, (c) $-x^2 + 2y^2 + xy$. Verify whether these forms are positive (or negative) definite, semidefinite, or indefinite.

Solution
(a)

$$(x, y)\begin{pmatrix} 1 & -\frac{1}{2} \\ -\frac{1}{2} & 1 \end{pmatrix}\begin{pmatrix} x \\ y \end{pmatrix} = x^2 + y^2 - xy = \left(x - \frac{1}{2}y\right)^2 + \frac{3}{4}y^2 > 0$$

for all $(x, y) \neq (0, 0)$. Hence, the quadratic form is positive and the matrix is positive definite.

(b)

$$(x, y, z) \begin{pmatrix} 4 & 1 & 0 \\ 1 & 5 & 1 \\ 0 & 1 & 1 \end{pmatrix} \begin{pmatrix} x \\ y \\ z \end{pmatrix} = 4x^2 + 5y^2 + z^2 + 2xy + 2yz$$

$$= (x + y)^2 + (y + z)^2 + 3x^2 + 3y^2 > 0$$

for all $(x, y, z) \neq (0, 0, 0)$. Hence, the matrix is positive definite.

(c)

$$(x, y) \begin{pmatrix} -1 & \frac{1}{2} \\ \frac{1}{2} & 2 \end{pmatrix} \begin{pmatrix} x \\ y \end{pmatrix} = -x^2 + 2y^2 + xy = \left(\frac{3}{2}y\right)^2 - \left(x - \frac{1}{2}y\right)^2.$$

This can take positive values ($x = 1$, $y = 2$) or negative ones ($x = 1$, $y = 0$). Hence, the matrix is indefinite.

Exercise 8.3 (Symmetry and skew-symmetry)
(a) For any real matrix $\boldsymbol{A}$, show that $\boldsymbol{x}'\boldsymbol{A}\boldsymbol{x} = 0$ for all real $\boldsymbol{x}$ if and only if $\boldsymbol{A}$ is skew-symmetric.
(b) For any symmetric matrix $\boldsymbol{A}$, show that $\boldsymbol{x}'\boldsymbol{A}\boldsymbol{x} = 0$ for all real $\boldsymbol{x}$ if and only if $\boldsymbol{A} = \mathbf{O}$.
(c) Hence, show, if $\boldsymbol{A}$ and $\boldsymbol{B}$ are symmetric, that $\boldsymbol{x}'\boldsymbol{A}\boldsymbol{x} = \boldsymbol{x}'\boldsymbol{B}\boldsymbol{x}$ for all real $\boldsymbol{x}$ if and only if $\boldsymbol{A} = \boldsymbol{B}$.

Solution
(a) If $\boldsymbol{x}'\boldsymbol{A}\boldsymbol{x} = 0$ for all $\boldsymbol{x}$, then choose $\boldsymbol{x} := \boldsymbol{e}_i$ and $\boldsymbol{x} := \boldsymbol{e}_i + \boldsymbol{e}_j$, respectively. This gives

$$\boldsymbol{e}_i'\boldsymbol{A}\boldsymbol{e}_i = a_{ii} = 0, \quad (\boldsymbol{e}_i + \boldsymbol{e}_j)'\boldsymbol{A}(\boldsymbol{e}_i + \boldsymbol{e}_j) = a_{ii} + a_{ij} + a_{ji} + a_{jj} = 0.$$

This implies $a_{ii} = 0$ for all i and $a_{ij} = -a_{ji}$ for all i, j. Since $\boldsymbol{A}$ is real, it follows that $\boldsymbol{A}$ is skew-symmetric. Conversely, if $\boldsymbol{A}' = -\boldsymbol{A}$, then $\boldsymbol{x}'\boldsymbol{A}\boldsymbol{x} = \boldsymbol{x}'\boldsymbol{A}'\boldsymbol{x} = -\boldsymbol{x}'\boldsymbol{A}\boldsymbol{x}$, and hence $\boldsymbol{x}'\boldsymbol{A}\boldsymbol{x} = 0$.
(b) The only matrix that is both symmetric *and* skew-symmetric is the null matrix.
(c) Replace $\boldsymbol{A}$ by $\boldsymbol{A} - \boldsymbol{B}$ in (b) and the result follows.

Exercise 8.4 (Orthogonal transformation preserves length)
(a) Prove that a linear transformation $\boldsymbol{Q}\boldsymbol{x}$ of $\boldsymbol{x}$ preserves length, if $\boldsymbol{Q}$ is orthogonal.
(b) Does the converse hold?
(c) If $\|\boldsymbol{Q}\boldsymbol{x}\| = \|\boldsymbol{x}\|$ for every $\boldsymbol{x}$, and $\boldsymbol{Q}$ is a square matrix whose elements do not depend on $\boldsymbol{x}$, then show that $\boldsymbol{Q}$ is orthogonal.

Solution
(a) If $\boldsymbol{Q}$ is orthogonal, then $\boldsymbol{Q}'\boldsymbol{Q} = \boldsymbol{I}$ and hence

$$\|\boldsymbol{Q}\boldsymbol{x}\| = \sqrt{\boldsymbol{x}'\boldsymbol{Q}'\boldsymbol{Q}\boldsymbol{x}} = \sqrt{\boldsymbol{x}'\boldsymbol{x}} = \|\boldsymbol{x}\|.$$

(b) No. Let $\boldsymbol{x}$ be an arbitrary nonzero vector, and define $\boldsymbol{Q}$ to be any matrix such that $\boldsymbol{Q}\boldsymbol{x} = \boldsymbol{x}$, for example the idempotent matrix $\boldsymbol{Q} := (1/\boldsymbol{x}'\boldsymbol{x})\boldsymbol{x}\boldsymbol{x}'$. This $\boldsymbol{Q}$ is not orthogonal, but $\boldsymbol{x}'\boldsymbol{Q}'\boldsymbol{Q}\boldsymbol{x} = \boldsymbol{x}'\boldsymbol{x}$, so that $\|\boldsymbol{Q}\boldsymbol{x}\| = \|\boldsymbol{x}\|$.
(c) From $\|\boldsymbol{Q}\boldsymbol{x}\| = \|\boldsymbol{x}\|$, we see that $\boldsymbol{x}'(\boldsymbol{I} - \boldsymbol{Q}'\boldsymbol{Q})\boldsymbol{x} = 0$ for every $\boldsymbol{x}$. Since the matrix $\boldsymbol{I} - \boldsymbol{Q}'\boldsymbol{Q}$ is symmetric, and $\boldsymbol{Q}$ is constant (does not depend on $\boldsymbol{x}$), it must be the null matrix, by Exercise 8.3(b). Hence, $\boldsymbol{Q}'\boldsymbol{Q} = \boldsymbol{I}$.

Exercise 8.5 (Positive versus negative)
(a) Show that $\boldsymbol{A} > \mathbf{O}$ if and only if $-\boldsymbol{A} < \mathbf{O}$.
(b) Show that $\boldsymbol{A} \geq \mathbf{O}$ if and only if $-\boldsymbol{A} \leq \mathbf{O}$.
(c) Can a matrix be both positive definite and negative definite?
(d) Can a matrix be both positive semidefinite and negative semidefinite?

Solution
(a) $\boldsymbol{A}$ is positive definite if and only if $\boldsymbol{x}'\boldsymbol{A}\boldsymbol{x} > 0$ for all $\boldsymbol{x} \neq \mathbf{0}$, that is, if and only if $\boldsymbol{x}'(-\boldsymbol{A})\boldsymbol{x} < 0$ for all $\boldsymbol{x} \neq \mathbf{0}$, which occurs, by definition, if and only if $-\boldsymbol{A}$ is negative definite.
(b) Similarly, $\boldsymbol{x}'\boldsymbol{A}\boldsymbol{x} \geq 0$ for all $\boldsymbol{x}$ if and only if $\boldsymbol{x}'(-\boldsymbol{A})\boldsymbol{x} \leq 0$ for all $\boldsymbol{x}$.
(c) No. It is not possible that, for all $\boldsymbol{x} \neq \mathbf{0}$, $\boldsymbol{x}'\boldsymbol{A}\boldsymbol{x}$ is both positive and negative.
(d) Yes. This is only possible if $\boldsymbol{x}'\boldsymbol{A}\boldsymbol{x} = 0$ for every $\boldsymbol{x}$. We know from Exercise 8.3 that the only symmetric solution is the null matrix.

Exercise 8.6 (Positivity of diagonal matrix) If $\boldsymbol{A} := \operatorname{diag}(a_{11}, \dots, a_{nn})$ is a diagonal matrix, show that $\boldsymbol{A} > \mathbf{O}$ ($\boldsymbol{A} \geq \mathbf{O}$) if and only if $a_{ii} > 0$ ($a_{ii} \geq 0$) for all $i = 1, \dots, n$.

Solution
In this case, $\boldsymbol{x}'\boldsymbol{A}\boldsymbol{x} = a_{11}x_1^2 + \cdots + a_{nn}x_n^2$. If $a_{ii} > 0$ for all i, then $\boldsymbol{x}'\boldsymbol{A}\boldsymbol{x} > 0$ unless $\boldsymbol{x} = \mathbf{0}$. If $a_{ii} \geq 0$, then $\boldsymbol{x}'\boldsymbol{A}\boldsymbol{x} \geq 0$ for all $\boldsymbol{x}$. Conversely, if $\boldsymbol{x}'\boldsymbol{A}\boldsymbol{x} > 0$ for all $\boldsymbol{x} \neq \mathbf{0}$, then in particular $a_{ii} = \boldsymbol{e}_i'\boldsymbol{A}\boldsymbol{e}_i > 0$ for all i. And, if $\boldsymbol{x}'\boldsymbol{A}\boldsymbol{x} \geq 0$ for all $\boldsymbol{x}$, then $a_{ii} = \boldsymbol{e}_i'\boldsymbol{A}\boldsymbol{e}_i \geq 0$ for all i.

***Exercise 8.7 (Positive diagonal elements)** Let $\boldsymbol{A} = (a_{ij})$ be a positive definite $n \times n$ matrix.
(a) Show that the diagonal elements of $\boldsymbol{A}$ are positive.
(b) Show that $a_{ij}^2 < a_{ii}a_{jj}$ for all $i \neq j$.
(c) Use (b) to show that $\max_{i,j} |a_{ij}|$ must be one of the diagonal elements of $\boldsymbol{A}$.
(d) How do these results change for a positive semidefinite matrix $\boldsymbol{A}$?

Solution
(a) If $\boldsymbol{A} > \mathbf{O}$, then $\boldsymbol{x}'\boldsymbol{A}\boldsymbol{x} > 0$ for all $\boldsymbol{x} \neq \mathbf{0}$. Take $\boldsymbol{x} := \boldsymbol{e}_i$, the i-th unit vector. Then $a_{ii} = \boldsymbol{e}_i'\boldsymbol{A}\boldsymbol{e}_i > 0$.

(b) Take $\boldsymbol{x} := \alpha \boldsymbol{e}_i + \beta \boldsymbol{e}_j$ $(i \neq j)$. Then,

$$(\alpha \boldsymbol{e}_i + \beta \boldsymbol{e}_j)' \boldsymbol{A} (\alpha \boldsymbol{e}_i + \beta \boldsymbol{e}_j) = \alpha^2 a_{ii} + \beta^2 a_{jj} + 2\alpha\beta a_{ij} > 0$$

for all α and β, not both zero. For $\alpha := a_{ij}$ and $\beta := -a_{ii}$ we find in particular that $a_{ii}(a_{ii}a_{jj} - a_{ij}^2) > 0$, and hence $a_{ii}a_{jj} - a_{ij}^2 > 0$.
(c) Suppose that the largest element of $\boldsymbol{A}$ (in absolute value) does not lie on the diagonal. Let a_{ij} $(i \neq j)$ be the largest element. Then, $|a_{ij}| \geq a_{ii}$ and $|a_{ij}| \geq a_{jj}$ and hence $a_{ij}^2 \geq a_{ii}a_{jj}$. This is in contradiction with (b).
(d) If $\boldsymbol{A}$ is positive semidefinite rather than positive definite, then $a_{ii} \geq 0$ for all i and $a_{ij}^2 \leq a_{ii}a_{jj}$ for all $i \neq j$. The largest element of $\boldsymbol{A}$ (in absolute value) is still on the diagonal of $\boldsymbol{A}$, but now there may be off-diagonal elements that are equal (but not larger) to this diagonal element. The matrix $\boldsymbol{A} := \boldsymbol{\imath}\boldsymbol{\imath}'$ provides an example.

Exercise 8.8 (Positivity of $\boldsymbol{A} + \boldsymbol{B}$) Let $\boldsymbol{A}$ be a positive semidefinite $n \times n$ matrix. Show that:
(a) $\boldsymbol{A} = \mathbf{O} \iff \operatorname{tr} \boldsymbol{A} = 0$;
(b) if $\boldsymbol{B}$ is positive (semi)definite, then $\boldsymbol{A} + \boldsymbol{B}$ is positive (semi)definite.

Solution
(a) If $\boldsymbol{A} \geq \mathbf{O}$ then Exercise 8.7 tells us that $a_{ii} \geq 0$ for all i and $a_{ij}^2 \leq a_{ii}a_{jj}$ for all $i \neq j$. If $\operatorname{tr} \boldsymbol{A} = 0$ then all diagonal elements must be zero, and $a_{ij}^2 \leq 0$. Hence, $\boldsymbol{A} = \mathbf{O}$. The converse is trivial.
(b) If $\boldsymbol{A} \geq \mathbf{O}$ then

$$\boldsymbol{x}'(\boldsymbol{A} + \boldsymbol{B})\boldsymbol{x} = \boldsymbol{x}'\boldsymbol{A}\boldsymbol{x} + \boldsymbol{x}'\boldsymbol{B}\boldsymbol{x} \geq \boldsymbol{x}'\boldsymbol{B}\boldsymbol{x}.$$

If $\boldsymbol{B} > \mathbf{O}$, then $\boldsymbol{x}'\boldsymbol{B}\boldsymbol{x} > 0$ for all $\boldsymbol{x} \neq \mathbf{0}$ and hence $\boldsymbol{x}'(\boldsymbol{A} + \boldsymbol{B})\boldsymbol{x} > 0$. If $\boldsymbol{B} \geq \mathbf{O}$, then $\boldsymbol{x}'\boldsymbol{B}\boldsymbol{x} \geq 0$ for all $\boldsymbol{x}$ and hence $\boldsymbol{x}'(\boldsymbol{A} + \boldsymbol{B})\boldsymbol{x} \geq 0$.

Exercise 8.9 (Positivity of $\boldsymbol{A}\boldsymbol{A}'$) For any $m \times n$ matrix $\boldsymbol{A}$, show that:
(a) $\boldsymbol{A}'\boldsymbol{A}$ and $\boldsymbol{A}\boldsymbol{A}'$ are positive semidefinite;
(b) $\boldsymbol{A} = \mathbf{O} \iff \boldsymbol{A}'\boldsymbol{A} = \mathbf{O} \iff \operatorname{tr} \boldsymbol{A}'\boldsymbol{A} = 0$.

Solution
(a) We have $\boldsymbol{x}'\boldsymbol{A}'\boldsymbol{A}\boldsymbol{x} = (\boldsymbol{A}\boldsymbol{x})'(\boldsymbol{A}\boldsymbol{x}) \geq 0$ and $\boldsymbol{y}'\boldsymbol{A}\boldsymbol{A}'\boldsymbol{y} = (\boldsymbol{A}'\boldsymbol{y})'(\boldsymbol{A}'\boldsymbol{y}) \geq 0$.
(b) This follows from

$$\boldsymbol{A} = \mathbf{O} \implies \boldsymbol{A}'\boldsymbol{A} = \mathbf{O} \implies \operatorname{tr} \boldsymbol{A}'\boldsymbol{A} = \sum_{ij} a_{ij}^2 = 0$$

$$\implies a_{ij} = 0 \text{ for all } i, j \implies \boldsymbol{A} = \mathbf{O}.$$

(Part (b) was earlier proved in Exercise 2.25.)

Exercise 8.10 (Diagonalization of positive definite matrices) If $\boldsymbol{A}$ is positive definite (positive semidefinite), show that there exists an orthogonal matrix $\boldsymbol{S}$ and a diagonal matrix $\boldsymbol{\Lambda}$ with positive (nonnegative) diagonal elements such that $\boldsymbol{S}'\boldsymbol{A}\boldsymbol{S} = \boldsymbol{\Lambda}$.

Solution

This follows directly from the diagonalization theorem for symmetric matrices (Exercise 7.46).

Exercise 8.11 (Positive eigenvalues)

(a) Show that a symmetric matrix $\boldsymbol{A}$ is positive definite if and only if all its eigenvalues are positive.

(b) Show that a symmetric matrix $\boldsymbol{A}$ is positive semidefinite if and only if all its eigenvalues are nonnegative.

Solution

(a) If λ is an eigenvalue of $\boldsymbol{A}$ with associated eigenvector $\boldsymbol{x}$, then $\boldsymbol{x}'\boldsymbol{A}\boldsymbol{x} = \boldsymbol{x}'(\lambda\boldsymbol{x}) = \lambda\boldsymbol{x}'\boldsymbol{x}$. Since $\boldsymbol{A} > \mathbf{O}$ we have $\boldsymbol{x}'\boldsymbol{A}\boldsymbol{x} > 0$. Notice that $\boldsymbol{x} \neq \mathbf{0}$, because $\boldsymbol{x}$ is an eigenvector. Hence, $\boldsymbol{x}'\boldsymbol{x}$ is positive and we obtain $\lambda > 0$. Conversely, assume that all eigenvalues $\lambda_1, \dots, \lambda_n$ are positive. We diagonalize the symmetric matrix $\boldsymbol{A}$ by means of an orthogonal matrix $\boldsymbol{S}$, such that

$$\boldsymbol{S}'\boldsymbol{A}\boldsymbol{S} = \boldsymbol{\Lambda} := \operatorname{diag}(\lambda_1, \dots, \lambda_n), \quad \boldsymbol{S}'\boldsymbol{S} = \boldsymbol{I}_n.$$

Let $\boldsymbol{x} \neq \mathbf{0}$ and define $\boldsymbol{y} := \boldsymbol{S}'\boldsymbol{x}$. Then $\boldsymbol{y} \neq \mathbf{0}$ and

$$\boldsymbol{x}'\boldsymbol{A}\boldsymbol{x} = \boldsymbol{x}'\boldsymbol{S}\boldsymbol{S}'\boldsymbol{A}\boldsymbol{S}\boldsymbol{S}'\boldsymbol{x} = \boldsymbol{y}'\boldsymbol{\Lambda}\boldsymbol{y} = \sum_{i=1}^{n} \lambda_i y_i^2 > 0$$

because $\lambda_i > 0$ and $\boldsymbol{y} \neq \mathbf{0}$. Hence, $\boldsymbol{A} > \mathbf{O}$.

(b) This works the same way. We just replace every $>$ sign with a $\geq$ sign.

Exercise 8.12 (Positive determinant and trace) Suppose that $\boldsymbol{A} > \mathbf{O}$.

(a) Show that $|\boldsymbol{A}| > 0$.

(b) Show that $\operatorname{tr} \boldsymbol{A} > 0$.

(c) Show that $|\boldsymbol{A}| > 0$ and $\operatorname{tr} \boldsymbol{A} > 0$ together do not guarantee that $\boldsymbol{A} > \mathbf{O}$.

Solution

(a) The determinant is equal to the product of the eigenvalues. If all eigenvalues are > 0, then their product is also > 0.

(b) The trace is equal to the sum of the eigenvalues. If all eigenvalues are > 0, then their sum is also > 0.

(c) The example $\boldsymbol{A} = \operatorname{diag}(3, -1, -1)$ shows that the converse is not true, in general. We have $\operatorname{tr} \boldsymbol{A} > 0$ and $|\boldsymbol{A}| > 0$, but $\boldsymbol{A}$ is not positive definite.

Exercise 8.13 (Nonnegative determinant and trace) Suppose that $\boldsymbol{A} \geq \mathbf{O}$.
(a) Show that $|\boldsymbol{A}| \geq 0$, with equality if and only if $\boldsymbol{A}$ is singular.
(b) Show that $\operatorname{tr} \boldsymbol{A} \geq 0$, with equality if and only if $\boldsymbol{A} = \mathbf{O}$.

Solution
(a) The determinant is equal to the product of the eigenvalues. If all eigenvalues are ≥ 0, then their product is also ≥ 0. One of the eigenvalues is zero if and only if $\boldsymbol{A}$ is singular.
(b) The trace is equal to the sum of the eigenvalues. If all eigenvalues are ≥ 0, then their sum is also ≥ 0. Equality was demonstrated in Exercise 8.8(a).

Exercise 8.14 (Nonsingularity and positive definiteness)
(a) Show that a positive definite matrix is nonsingular.
(b) Show that a positive semidefinite matrix is positive definite if and only if it is nonsingular.
(c) Show that $\boldsymbol{A} > \mathbf{O}$ if and only if $\boldsymbol{A}^{-1} > \mathbf{O}$.

Solution
(a) Since $|\boldsymbol{A}| > 0$, the determinant is nonzero and hence $\boldsymbol{A}$ is nonsingular.
(b) If $\boldsymbol{A} \geq \mathbf{O}$ and nonsingular, then all eigenvalues must be nonzero, hence positive. Hence, $\boldsymbol{A} > \mathbf{O}$. The converse was proved under (a).
(c) Let $\boldsymbol{A} > \mathbf{O}$ and $\boldsymbol{x} \neq \mathbf{0}$. Then,

$$\boldsymbol{x}\boldsymbol{A}^{-1}\boldsymbol{x} = \boldsymbol{x}'\boldsymbol{A}^{-1}\boldsymbol{A}\boldsymbol{A}^{-1}\boldsymbol{x} = (\boldsymbol{A}^{-1}\boldsymbol{x})'\boldsymbol{A}(\boldsymbol{A}^{-1}\boldsymbol{x}) > 0,$$

since $\boldsymbol{A}^{-1}\boldsymbol{x} \neq \mathbf{0}$ if $\boldsymbol{x} \neq \mathbf{0}$. So, if $\boldsymbol{A} > \mathbf{O}$ then $\boldsymbol{A}^{-1} > \mathbf{O}$. The converse is then trivial.

Exercise 8.15 (Completion of square) Let $\boldsymbol{A}$ and $\boldsymbol{B}$ be positive definite $n \times n$ matrices, and define

$$\boldsymbol{C}^{-1} := \boldsymbol{A}^{-1} + \boldsymbol{B}^{-1} \quad \text{and} \quad \boldsymbol{D} := \boldsymbol{A} + \boldsymbol{B}.$$

(a) Show that

$$\boldsymbol{D}^{-1} = \boldsymbol{A}^{-1} - \boldsymbol{A}^{-1}\boldsymbol{C}\boldsymbol{A}^{-1} = \boldsymbol{B}^{-1} - \boldsymbol{B}^{-1}\boldsymbol{C}\boldsymbol{B}^{-1} = \boldsymbol{A}^{-1}\boldsymbol{C}\boldsymbol{B}^{-1} = \boldsymbol{B}^{-1}\boldsymbol{C}\boldsymbol{A}^{-1}.$$

(b) Let $\boldsymbol{x}$, $\boldsymbol{a}$, and $\boldsymbol{b}$ be $n \times 1$ vectors. Show that a vector $\boldsymbol{\mu}$ exists such that

$$(\boldsymbol{x} - \boldsymbol{a})'\boldsymbol{A}^{-1}(\boldsymbol{x} - \boldsymbol{a}) + (\boldsymbol{x} - \boldsymbol{b})'\boldsymbol{B}^{-1}(\boldsymbol{x} - \boldsymbol{b}) = (\boldsymbol{x} - \boldsymbol{\mu})'\boldsymbol{C}^{-1}(\boldsymbol{x} - \boldsymbol{\mu}) + Q(\boldsymbol{a}, \boldsymbol{b}),$$

where $Q(\boldsymbol{a}, \boldsymbol{b})$ does not depend on $\boldsymbol{x}$.
(c) Show that

$$Q(\boldsymbol{a}, \boldsymbol{b}) = (\boldsymbol{a} - \boldsymbol{b})'\boldsymbol{D}^{-1}(\boldsymbol{a} - \boldsymbol{b}).$$

Solution

(a) We need to prove four equalities. First,

$$\begin{aligned}(A+B)\left(A^{-1}-A^{-1}CA^{-1}\right)&\\ &=I-CA^{-1}+BA^{-1}-BA^{-1}CA^{-1}\\ &=I-B\left(B^{-1}-C^{-1}+A^{-1}\right)CA^{-1}=I.\end{aligned}$$

Interchanging A and B then gives $(A+B)(B^{-1}-B^{-1}CB^{-1})=I$. Next,

$$\begin{aligned}A^{-1}CB^{-1}&=A^{-1}(A^{-1}+B^{-1})^{-1}B^{-1}\\ &=\left(B(A^{-1}+B^{-1})A\right)^{-1}=(B+A)^{-1}=D^{-1}.\end{aligned}$$

The previous reasoning shows that $A^{-1}CB^{-1}$ is symmetric. Hence, also $B^{-1}CA^{-1}=D^{-1}$.

(b) We write

$$\begin{aligned}(x-a)'A^{-1}(x-a)+(x-b)'B^{-1}(x-b)&\\ &=x'A^{-1}x-2a'A^{-1}x+a'A^{-1}a+x'B^{-1}x-2b'B^{-1}x+b'B^{-1}b\\ &=x'(A^{-1}+B^{-1})x-2(a'A^{-1}+b'B^{-1})x+(a'A^{-1}a+b'B^{-1}b).\end{aligned}$$

Note that $x'A^{-1}a=a'A^{-1}x$, because A^{-1} is symmetric and a scalar is equal to its transpose. Also,

$$\begin{aligned}(x-\mu)'C^{-1}(x-\mu)+Q(a,b)&\\ &=x'C^{-1}x-2\mu'C^{-1}x+\mu'C^{-1}\mu+Q(a,b).\end{aligned}$$

Hence, equality occurs if we choose

$$C^{-1}=A^{-1}+B^{-1}\quad\text{and}\quad\mu=C(A^{-1}a+B^{-1}b).$$

(c) We note from (a) and (b) that

$$\begin{aligned}Q(a,b)&=a'A^{-1}a+b'B^{-1}b-\mu'C^{-1}\mu\\ &=a'A^{-1}a+b'B^{-1}b-(A^{-1}a+B^{-1}b)'C(A^{-1}a+B^{-1}b)\\ &=a'(A^{-1}-A^{-1}CA^{-1})a+b'(B^{-1}-B^{-1}CB^{-1})b-2a'A^{-1}CB^{-1}b\\ &=a'D^{-1}a+b'D^{-1}b-2a'D^{-1}b=(a-b)'D^{-1}(a-b).\end{aligned}$$

Exercise 8.16 (Powers are positive too) If $A>O$ ($A\geq O$), show that $A^k>O$ ($A^k\geq O$) for $k=1,2\ldots$.

Solution

If the eigenvalues of A are $\lambda_1,\ldots,\lambda_n$, then the eigenvalues of A^k are $\lambda_1^k,\ldots,\lambda_n^k$ (Exercise 7.14). If $\lambda_i>0$ (≥ 0) then $\lambda_i^k>0$ (≥ 0). Hence, all eigenvalues of A^k are positive (nonnegative), so that $A>O$ ($A\geq O$).

Exercise 8.17 (From symmetry to positivity) For every symmetric $n \times n$ matrix $\boldsymbol{A}$, show that a real number k exists such that $k\boldsymbol{I}_n + \boldsymbol{A}$ is positive definite.

Solution
If $\lambda_1, \dots, \lambda_n$ are the eigenvalues of $\boldsymbol{A}$, then $k + \lambda_1, \dots, k + \lambda_n$ are the eigenvalues of $k\boldsymbol{I}_n + \boldsymbol{A}$. Hence, any $k > -\min_i \lambda_i$ makes $k + \lambda_i > 0$ for all i.

***Exercise 8.18 (Kato's lemma)** If $\boldsymbol{A}$ is a symmetric matrix with no eigenvalue in the interval $[a, b]$, show that $(\boldsymbol{A} - a\boldsymbol{I})(\boldsymbol{A} - b\boldsymbol{I})$ is positive definite.

Solution
Let $\boldsymbol{B} := (\boldsymbol{A} - a\boldsymbol{I}_n)(\boldsymbol{A} - b\boldsymbol{I}_n)$. Then

$$\boldsymbol{B} = \boldsymbol{A}^2 - (a + b)\boldsymbol{A} + ab\boldsymbol{I}_n.$$

If $\boldsymbol{S}'\boldsymbol{A}\boldsymbol{S} = \boldsymbol{\Lambda}$, where $\boldsymbol{S}$ is orthogonal and $\boldsymbol{\Lambda}$ diagonal, then $\boldsymbol{A} = \boldsymbol{S}\boldsymbol{\Lambda}\boldsymbol{S}'$, $\boldsymbol{A}^2 = \boldsymbol{S}\boldsymbol{\Lambda}^2\boldsymbol{S}'$, and $\boldsymbol{I}_n = \boldsymbol{S}\boldsymbol{S}'$, so that $\boldsymbol{B} = \boldsymbol{S}(\boldsymbol{\Lambda}^2 - (a + b)\boldsymbol{\Lambda} + ab\boldsymbol{I}_n)\boldsymbol{S}'$. Hence, if λ is an eigenvalue of $\boldsymbol{A}$, then $\lambda^2 - (a + b)\lambda + ab$ is an eigenvalue of $\boldsymbol{B}$. So, all we need to show is that the quadratic form $\lambda^2 - (a+b)\lambda + ab$ is positive outside the interval $[a, b]$. This in turn follows from the fact that $\lambda^2 - (a + b)\lambda + ab = (\lambda - a)(\lambda - b)$.

Exercise 8.19 (The matrix $\boldsymbol{aa}' + \boldsymbol{bb}'$) Let $\boldsymbol{a}$ and $\boldsymbol{b}$ be two linearly independent $n \times 1$ vectors, and consider the $n \times n$ matrix $\boldsymbol{A} := \boldsymbol{aa}' + \boldsymbol{bb}'$.
(a) Show that $\boldsymbol{A} \geq \mathbf{O}$ with $\operatorname{rk}(\boldsymbol{A}) = 2$.
(b) Show that the two nonzero (positive) eigenvalues of $\boldsymbol{A}$ are obtained from the equation

$$\begin{pmatrix} \lambda - \boldsymbol{a}'\boldsymbol{a} & -\boldsymbol{a}'\boldsymbol{b} \\ -\boldsymbol{a}'\boldsymbol{b} & \lambda - \boldsymbol{b}'\boldsymbol{b} \end{pmatrix} \begin{pmatrix} \theta_1 \\ \theta_2 \end{pmatrix} = \begin{pmatrix} 0 \\ 0 \end{pmatrix}.$$

(c) Show that the corresponding eigenvectors are given by $\boldsymbol{x} = \theta_1\boldsymbol{a} + \theta_2\boldsymbol{b}$.

Solution
(a) We see that $\boldsymbol{x}'\boldsymbol{A}\boldsymbol{x} = \boldsymbol{x}'\boldsymbol{aa}'\boldsymbol{x} + \boldsymbol{x}'\boldsymbol{bb}'\boldsymbol{x} = (\boldsymbol{a}'\boldsymbol{x})^2 + (\boldsymbol{b}'\boldsymbol{x})^2 \geq 0$. Let $\boldsymbol{B} := (\boldsymbol{a}, \boldsymbol{b})$, so that $\boldsymbol{A} = \boldsymbol{B}\boldsymbol{B}'$. Since $\boldsymbol{a}$ and $\boldsymbol{b}$ are linearly independent, $\operatorname{rk}(\boldsymbol{B}) = 2$. Hence, $\operatorname{rk}(\boldsymbol{A}) = \operatorname{rk}(\boldsymbol{B}\boldsymbol{B}') = \operatorname{rk}(\boldsymbol{B}) = 2$.
(b) The nonzero eigenvalues of the $n \times n$ matrix $\boldsymbol{A} = \boldsymbol{B}\boldsymbol{B}'$ are the same as those of the 2×2 matrix $\boldsymbol{B}'\boldsymbol{B}$ (Exercise 7.25).
(c) Since $(\lambda\boldsymbol{I}_2 - \boldsymbol{B}'\boldsymbol{B})\boldsymbol{\theta} = \mathbf{0}$, where $\boldsymbol{\theta} := (\theta_1, \theta_2)'$, we obtain

$$\boldsymbol{A}(\boldsymbol{B}\boldsymbol{\theta}) = \boldsymbol{B}\boldsymbol{B}'(\boldsymbol{B}\boldsymbol{\theta}) = \boldsymbol{B}(\boldsymbol{B}'\boldsymbol{B}\boldsymbol{\theta}) = \boldsymbol{B}(\lambda\boldsymbol{\theta}) = \lambda(\boldsymbol{B}\boldsymbol{\theta}).$$

Hence, $\boldsymbol{B}\boldsymbol{\theta} = \theta_1\boldsymbol{a} + \theta_2\boldsymbol{b}$ is an eigenvector of $\boldsymbol{A}$ associated with λ.

Exercise 8.20 (The matrix $\boldsymbol{aa}' - \boldsymbol{bb}'$) Let $\boldsymbol{a}$ and $\boldsymbol{b}$ be two linearly independent $n \times 1$ vectors, and consider $\boldsymbol{A} := \boldsymbol{aa}' - \boldsymbol{bb}'$.

(a) Show that $\operatorname{rk}(\boldsymbol{A}) = 2$.
(b) Show that the two eigenvalues of $\boldsymbol{A}$ have opposite signs, so that $\boldsymbol{A}$ is indefinite.
(c) Show that the two nonzero eigenvalues of $\boldsymbol{A}$ are obtained from the equation

$$\begin{pmatrix} \lambda - a'a & a'b \\ -a'b & \lambda + b'b \end{pmatrix} \begin{pmatrix} \theta_1 \\ \theta_2 \end{pmatrix} = \begin{pmatrix} 0 \\ 0 \end{pmatrix}.$$

(d) Show that the corresponding eigenvectors are given by $\boldsymbol{x} = \theta_1 \boldsymbol{a} - \theta_2 \boldsymbol{b}$.

Solution
(a) Let $\boldsymbol{B} := (\boldsymbol{a}, -\boldsymbol{b})$ and $\boldsymbol{C} := (\boldsymbol{a}, \boldsymbol{b})$. Then $\boldsymbol{A} = \boldsymbol{B}\boldsymbol{C}'$. The rank of $\boldsymbol{B}\boldsymbol{C}'$ is equal to the rank of $\boldsymbol{C}'\boldsymbol{B}$. Since $|\boldsymbol{C}'\boldsymbol{B}| = -(\boldsymbol{a}'\boldsymbol{a})(\boldsymbol{b}'\boldsymbol{b}) + (\boldsymbol{a}'\boldsymbol{b})^2 < 0$ by the Cauchy-Schwarz inequality (remember that $\boldsymbol{a}$ and $\boldsymbol{b}$ are linearly independent, so that $(\boldsymbol{a}'\boldsymbol{a})(\boldsymbol{b}'\boldsymbol{b}) \neq (\boldsymbol{a}'\boldsymbol{b})^2$), it follows that $\operatorname{rk}(\boldsymbol{B}\boldsymbol{C}') = \operatorname{rk}(\boldsymbol{C}'\boldsymbol{B}) = 2$.
(b) We see from (a) that $|\boldsymbol{C}'\boldsymbol{B}| < 0$. Hence, the product of the two nonzero eigenvalues is negative, say $\lambda_1 > 0$ and $\lambda_2 < 0$. The matrix $\boldsymbol{A}$ is therefore neither positive semidefinite nor negative semidefinite, hence indefinite.
(c) The eigenvalues are found from the equation $(\lambda \boldsymbol{I}_2 - \boldsymbol{C}'\boldsymbol{B})\boldsymbol{\theta} = \boldsymbol{0}$.
(d) Since $\boldsymbol{C}'\boldsymbol{B}\boldsymbol{\theta} = \lambda\boldsymbol{\theta}$, we have $\boldsymbol{A}(\boldsymbol{B}\boldsymbol{\theta}) = \boldsymbol{B}\boldsymbol{C}'\boldsymbol{B}\boldsymbol{\theta} = \lambda(\boldsymbol{B}\boldsymbol{\theta})$.

Exercise 8.21 (Decomposition of a positive semidefinite matrix, 1) If $\boldsymbol{A}$ is a positive semidefinite $n \times n$ matrix of rank r, show that an $n \times r$ matrix $\boldsymbol{T}$ and a diagonal $r \times r$ matrix $\boldsymbol{\Lambda}$ exist such that

$$\boldsymbol{A} = \boldsymbol{T}\boldsymbol{T}' \quad \text{and} \quad \boldsymbol{T}'\boldsymbol{T} = \boldsymbol{\Lambda},$$

where $\boldsymbol{\Lambda}$ contains the nonzero (that is, positive) eigenvalues of $\boldsymbol{A}$. If $\boldsymbol{A}$ is positive definite, then $\boldsymbol{T}$ is square and nonsingular.

Solution
We write $\boldsymbol{S}'\boldsymbol{A}\boldsymbol{S} = \boldsymbol{\Lambda}_0$ (diagonal) with $\boldsymbol{S}'\boldsymbol{S} = \boldsymbol{I}_n$. Since $\operatorname{rk}(\boldsymbol{A}) = r$, there are $n - r$ zero eigenvalues. Let $\boldsymbol{\Lambda}$ be the diagonal $r \times r$ submatrix of $\boldsymbol{\Lambda}_0$ containing the nonzero (hence positive) eigenvalues of $\boldsymbol{A}$. Partitioning $\boldsymbol{S} = (\boldsymbol{S}_1 : \boldsymbol{S}_2)$ we obtain from $\boldsymbol{A}\boldsymbol{S} = \boldsymbol{S}\boldsymbol{\Lambda}_0$,

$$\boldsymbol{A}\boldsymbol{S}_1 = \boldsymbol{S}_1\boldsymbol{\Lambda} \quad \text{and} \quad \boldsymbol{A}\boldsymbol{S}_2 = \boldsymbol{O},$$

with

$$\boldsymbol{S}_1'\boldsymbol{S}_1 = \boldsymbol{I}_r, \quad \boldsymbol{S}_2'\boldsymbol{S}_2 = \boldsymbol{I}_{n-r}, \quad \boldsymbol{S}_1'\boldsymbol{S}_2 = \boldsymbol{O}.$$

Notice that $\boldsymbol{A} = \boldsymbol{S}\boldsymbol{\Lambda}_0\boldsymbol{S}' = \boldsymbol{S}_1\boldsymbol{\Lambda}\boldsymbol{S}_1'$. Now let $\boldsymbol{T} := \boldsymbol{S}_1\boldsymbol{\Lambda}^{1/2}$, where $\boldsymbol{\Lambda}^{1/2}$ is the diagonal $r \times r$ matrix containing the positive square roots of the positive eigenvalues of $\boldsymbol{A}$. Then, $\boldsymbol{T}\boldsymbol{T}' = \boldsymbol{S}_1\boldsymbol{\Lambda}\boldsymbol{S}_1' = \boldsymbol{A}$ and $\boldsymbol{T}'\boldsymbol{T} = \boldsymbol{\Lambda}^{1/2}\boldsymbol{S}_1'\boldsymbol{S}_1\boldsymbol{\Lambda}^{1/2} = \boldsymbol{\Lambda}$.

Exercise 8.22 (Decomposition of a positive semidefinite matrix, 2) If $\boldsymbol{A}$ is a positive semidefinite $n \times n$ matrix of rank r, show that there exists an $n \times m$ matrix $\boldsymbol{B}$ with $r \leq m \leq n$ such that $\boldsymbol{A} = \boldsymbol{B}\boldsymbol{B}'$.

Solution
Let $\boldsymbol{T}$ be an $n \times r$ matrix, such that $\boldsymbol{A} = \boldsymbol{T}\boldsymbol{T}'$ and $\boldsymbol{T}'\boldsymbol{T} = \boldsymbol{\Lambda}$ (diagonal). Such a matrix exists by Exercise 8.21. Now define $\boldsymbol{B} := (\boldsymbol{T} : \mathbf{O})$, where the null matrix is of order $n \times (m - r)$. Then $\boldsymbol{B}\boldsymbol{B}' = (\boldsymbol{T} : \mathbf{O})(\boldsymbol{T} : \mathbf{O})' = \boldsymbol{T}\boldsymbol{T}' = \boldsymbol{A}$. This exercise shows that there are many matrices $\boldsymbol{B}$ such that $\boldsymbol{A} = \boldsymbol{B}\boldsymbol{B}'$.

Exercise 8.23 (Cholesky decomposition) If an $n \times n$ matrix $\boldsymbol{A}$ is positive semidefinite of rank $r \leq n$, then it can be written as $\boldsymbol{A} = \boldsymbol{L}\boldsymbol{L}'$, where $\boldsymbol{L}$ is a lower triangular matrix with r positive and $n - r$ zero diagonal elements. Prove this statement for the special case $r = n$.

Solution
For any nonsingular $n \times n$ matrix $\boldsymbol{A}$, the QR decomposition (Exercise 7.35) implies that there exist an orthogonal $n \times n$ matrix $\boldsymbol{Q}$ and a lower triangular $n \times n$ matrix $\boldsymbol{L}$ with positive diagonal elements, such that $\boldsymbol{A} = \boldsymbol{L}\boldsymbol{Q}$. Hence, $\boldsymbol{A}\boldsymbol{A}' = \boldsymbol{L}\boldsymbol{Q}\boldsymbol{Q}'\boldsymbol{L}' = \boldsymbol{L}\boldsymbol{L}'$.

***Exercise 8.24 (Square root)** Let $\boldsymbol{A}$ be a positive semidefinite $n \times n$ matrix.
(a) Show that there exists a positive semidefinite matrix $\boldsymbol{B}$ such that $\boldsymbol{B}^2 = \boldsymbol{A}$. This matrix is called the *square root* of $\boldsymbol{A}$ and is denoted by $\boldsymbol{A}^{1/2}$.
(b) There are many matrices $\boldsymbol{B}$ satisfying $\boldsymbol{B}^2 = \boldsymbol{A}$. Show that there is only one positive semidefinite $\boldsymbol{B}$, so that the square root $\boldsymbol{A}^{1/2}$ is unique.
(c) How can $\boldsymbol{A}^{1/2}$ be calculated?

Solution
(a) Decompose $\boldsymbol{A} = \boldsymbol{S}\boldsymbol{\Lambda}\boldsymbol{S}'$, where $\boldsymbol{S}'\boldsymbol{S} = \boldsymbol{I}_n$ and $\boldsymbol{\Lambda} := \operatorname{diag}(\lambda_1, \dots, \lambda_n)$ contains the eigenvalues of $\boldsymbol{A}$ on its diagonal. Let $\boldsymbol{\Lambda}^{1/2} := \operatorname{diag}(\lambda_1^{1/2}, \dots, \lambda_n^{1/2})$, where the unique positive (nonnegative) square root is taken in each case, and define $\boldsymbol{B} := \boldsymbol{S}\boldsymbol{\Lambda}^{1/2}\boldsymbol{S}'$. Then $\boldsymbol{B}$ is a symmetric matrix satisfying $\boldsymbol{B}^2 = \boldsymbol{A}$ and $\boldsymbol{B}$ is positive (semi)definite.
(b) Suppose the opposite, and let $\boldsymbol{C}$ be another positive (semi)definite matrix satisfying $\boldsymbol{C}^2 = \boldsymbol{A}$. The eigenvalues $\mu_1, \dots, \mu_n$ of $\boldsymbol{C}$ satisfy $\mu_i^2 = \lambda_i$. Since $\boldsymbol{C}$ is positive semidefinite, $\mu_i = \lambda_i^{1/2}$ (and not $-\lambda_i^{1/2}$).

We now show that $\boldsymbol{B}$ and $\boldsymbol{C}$ commute. Write $\boldsymbol{B} = \boldsymbol{S}\boldsymbol{\Lambda}^{1/2}\boldsymbol{S}'$ and $\boldsymbol{C} = \boldsymbol{T}\boldsymbol{\Lambda}^{1/2}\boldsymbol{T}'$ where $\boldsymbol{S}$ and $\boldsymbol{T}$ are both orthogonal. Since $\boldsymbol{B}^2 = \boldsymbol{C}^2$ we obtain $\boldsymbol{S}\boldsymbol{\Lambda}\boldsymbol{S}' = \boldsymbol{T}\boldsymbol{\Lambda}\boldsymbol{T}'$. Now let $\boldsymbol{P} := \boldsymbol{S}'\boldsymbol{T}$. This is an orthogonal matrix satisfying $\boldsymbol{\Lambda}\boldsymbol{P} = \boldsymbol{P}\boldsymbol{\Lambda}$. Let $\boldsymbol{p}_j$ be the j-th column of $\boldsymbol{P}$. Then $\boldsymbol{\Lambda}\boldsymbol{p}_j = \lambda_j\boldsymbol{p}_j$ $(j = 1, \dots, n)$ and hence $\boldsymbol{\Lambda}^{1/2}\boldsymbol{p}_j = \lambda_j^{1/2}\boldsymbol{p}_j$ (because $\lambda_i = \lambda_j$ if and only if $\lambda_i^{1/2} = \lambda_j^{1/2}$). Hence, $\boldsymbol{\Lambda}^{1/2}\boldsymbol{P} = \boldsymbol{P}\boldsymbol{\Lambda}^{1/2}$. Now,

$$\boldsymbol{B}\boldsymbol{C} = \boldsymbol{S}\boldsymbol{\Lambda}^{1/2}\boldsymbol{S}'\boldsymbol{T}\boldsymbol{\Lambda}^{1/2}\boldsymbol{T}' = \boldsymbol{T}\boldsymbol{P}'\boldsymbol{\Lambda}^{1/2}\boldsymbol{P}\boldsymbol{\Lambda}^{1/2}\boldsymbol{P}'\boldsymbol{S}' = \boldsymbol{T}\boldsymbol{\Lambda}^{1/2}\boldsymbol{P}'\boldsymbol{\Lambda}^{1/2}\boldsymbol{S}' = \boldsymbol{C}\boldsymbol{B}.$$

Since $\boldsymbol{B}$ and $\boldsymbol{C}$ commute, they can be simultaneously diagonalized (Exercise 7.51). Thus, there exists an orthogonal matrix $\boldsymbol{Q}$ such that $\boldsymbol{Q}'\boldsymbol{B}\boldsymbol{Q} = \boldsymbol{M}_1$ (diagonal) and $\boldsymbol{Q}'\boldsymbol{C}\boldsymbol{Q} = \boldsymbol{M}_2$ (diagonal). Since $\boldsymbol{B}^2 = \boldsymbol{C}^2$ we obtain $\boldsymbol{M}_1^2 = \boldsymbol{M}_2^2$ and hence, since the nonnegative square root of a nonnegative number is unique, $\boldsymbol{M}_1 = \boldsymbol{M}_2$ and so $\boldsymbol{B} = \boldsymbol{C}$.

(c) Find $\boldsymbol{S}$ (orthogonal) and $\boldsymbol{\Lambda} := \operatorname{diag}(\lambda_1, \dots, \lambda_n)$ such that $\boldsymbol{A} = \boldsymbol{S\Lambda S}'$. Then construct $\boldsymbol{\Lambda}^{1/2} := \operatorname{diag}(\lambda_1^{1/2}, \dots, \lambda_n^{1/2})$, where the unique positive (nonnegative) square root is taken in each case. Finally set $\boldsymbol{A}^{1/2} := \boldsymbol{S\Lambda}^{1/2}\boldsymbol{S}'$.

Exercise 8.25 (Inverse of square root) Let $\boldsymbol{A} > \mathbf{O}$. Show that $(\boldsymbol{A}^{-1})^{1/2} = (\boldsymbol{A}^{1/2})^{-1}$. This matrix is denoted by $\boldsymbol{A}^{-1/2}$.

Solution
Let $\boldsymbol{A} = \boldsymbol{S\Lambda S}'$, $\boldsymbol{S}'\boldsymbol{S} = \boldsymbol{I}_n$. Then $\boldsymbol{A}^{-1} = \boldsymbol{S\Lambda}^{-1}\boldsymbol{S}'$ and hence, by Exercise 8.24,

$$(\boldsymbol{A}^{-1})^{1/2} = \boldsymbol{S\Lambda}^{-1/2}\boldsymbol{S}',$$

where $\boldsymbol{\Lambda}^{-1/2}$ denotes the diagonal matrix with elements $\lambda_i^{-1/2}$ on the diagonal. Also,

$$(\boldsymbol{A}^{1/2})^{-1} = (\boldsymbol{S\Lambda}^{1/2}\boldsymbol{S}')^{-1} = \boldsymbol{S}(\boldsymbol{\Lambda}^{1/2})^{-1}\boldsymbol{S}' = \boldsymbol{S\Lambda}^{-1/2}\boldsymbol{S}'.$$

Exercise 8.26 (The matrix $\boldsymbol{B}'\boldsymbol{AB}$ when $\boldsymbol{A} > \mathbf{O}$) Let $\boldsymbol{A}$ be a positive definite $n \times n$ matrix and let $\boldsymbol{B}$ be an $n \times m$ matrix. Consider the "matrix quadratic form" $\boldsymbol{B}'\boldsymbol{AB}$ and show that:
(a) $\operatorname{rk}(\boldsymbol{B}'\boldsymbol{AB}) = \operatorname{rk}(\boldsymbol{B})$;
(b) $\boldsymbol{B}'\boldsymbol{AB} > \mathbf{O} \iff \operatorname{rk}(\boldsymbol{B}) = m$;
(c) $\boldsymbol{B}'\boldsymbol{AB} = \mathbf{O} \iff \boldsymbol{B} = \mathbf{O}$.

Solution
(a) We use the fact that $\operatorname{rk}(\boldsymbol{C}'\boldsymbol{C}) = \operatorname{rk}(\boldsymbol{C})$ for any matrix $\boldsymbol{C}$. To this end we write $\boldsymbol{A} = \boldsymbol{TT}'$, where $\boldsymbol{T}$ is a nonsingular $n \times n$ matrix (Exercise 8.21). Then, $\boldsymbol{B}'\boldsymbol{AB} = \boldsymbol{B}'\boldsymbol{TT}'\boldsymbol{B} = (\boldsymbol{T}'\boldsymbol{B})'(\boldsymbol{T}'\boldsymbol{B})$ and hence $\operatorname{rk}(\boldsymbol{B}'\boldsymbol{AB}) = \operatorname{rk}(\boldsymbol{T}'\boldsymbol{B}) = \operatorname{rk}(\boldsymbol{B})$, since $\boldsymbol{T}$ is nonsingular.
(b) We have $\boldsymbol{B}'\boldsymbol{AB} > \mathbf{O}$ if and only if $\boldsymbol{B}'\boldsymbol{AB}$ is nonsingular (Exercise 8.14(b)), which is the case if and only if $\operatorname{rk}(\boldsymbol{B}'\boldsymbol{AB}) = m$, that is, if and only if $\operatorname{rk}(\boldsymbol{B}) = m$.
(c) If $\boldsymbol{B}'\boldsymbol{AB} = \mathbf{O}$, then $\operatorname{rk}(\boldsymbol{B}'\boldsymbol{AB}) = 0$. Hence, $\operatorname{rk}(\boldsymbol{B}) = 0$, and so $\boldsymbol{B} = \mathbf{O}$. The converse is trivial.

Exercise 8.27 (The matrix $\boldsymbol{B}'\boldsymbol{AB}$ when $\boldsymbol{A} \geq \mathbf{O}$) Let $\boldsymbol{A}$ be a positive semidefinite $n \times n$ matrix and let $\boldsymbol{B}$ be an $n \times m$ matrix. Show that:
(a) $\operatorname{rk}(\boldsymbol{B}'\boldsymbol{AB}) = \operatorname{rk}(\boldsymbol{AB})$;
(b) $\boldsymbol{B}'\boldsymbol{AB} \geq \mathbf{O}$;
(c) $\boldsymbol{B}'\boldsymbol{AB} = \mathbf{O} \iff \boldsymbol{AB} = \mathbf{O}$;
(d) if $\operatorname{rk}(\boldsymbol{B}) = m < n$, then $\boldsymbol{B}'\boldsymbol{AB} > \mathbf{O}$ does not necessarily imply that $\boldsymbol{A} > \mathbf{O}$.

Solution
(a) If $\operatorname{rk}(\boldsymbol{A}) = r$, we have $\boldsymbol{A} = \boldsymbol{TT}'$ for some $n \times r$ matrix $\boldsymbol{T}$. Then, $\boldsymbol{B}'\boldsymbol{AB} = \boldsymbol{B}'\boldsymbol{TT}'\boldsymbol{B} = (\boldsymbol{T}'\boldsymbol{B})'(\boldsymbol{T}'\boldsymbol{B})$, and

$$\operatorname{rk}(\boldsymbol{T}'\boldsymbol{B}) = \operatorname{rk}((\boldsymbol{T}'\boldsymbol{B})'(\boldsymbol{T}'\boldsymbol{B})) = \operatorname{rk}(\boldsymbol{B}'\boldsymbol{TT}'\boldsymbol{B}) \leq \operatorname{rk}(\boldsymbol{TT}'\boldsymbol{B}) \leq \operatorname{rk}(\boldsymbol{T}'\boldsymbol{B}),$$

so that $\operatorname{rk}(\boldsymbol{B}'\boldsymbol{AB}) = \operatorname{rk}(\boldsymbol{AB})$.

(b) For any $m \times 1$ vector $\boldsymbol{x}$ we have $\boldsymbol{x}'\boldsymbol{B}'\boldsymbol{A}\boldsymbol{B}\boldsymbol{x} = (\boldsymbol{B}\boldsymbol{x})'\boldsymbol{A}(\boldsymbol{B}\boldsymbol{x}) \geq 0$ since $\boldsymbol{A} \geq \mathbf{O}$. Hence, $\boldsymbol{B}'\boldsymbol{A}\boldsymbol{B} \geq \mathbf{O}$.
(c) We have

$$\begin{aligned} \boldsymbol{B}'\boldsymbol{A}\boldsymbol{B} = \mathbf{O} &\iff \boldsymbol{B}'\boldsymbol{T}\boldsymbol{T}'\boldsymbol{B} = \mathbf{O} \iff \boldsymbol{T}'\boldsymbol{B} = \mathbf{O} \\ &\iff \boldsymbol{T}\boldsymbol{T}'\boldsymbol{B} = \mathbf{O} \iff \boldsymbol{A}\boldsymbol{B} = \mathbf{O}. \end{aligned}$$

(d) For example, let

$$\boldsymbol{A} = \begin{pmatrix} 1 & 1 \\ 1 & 1 \end{pmatrix} \quad \text{and} \quad \boldsymbol{b} = \begin{pmatrix} 1 \\ 0 \end{pmatrix}.$$

Then, $\boldsymbol{b}'\boldsymbol{A}\boldsymbol{b} = 1 > 0$, but $\boldsymbol{A}$ is positive semidefinite and not positive definite.

Exercise 8.28 (Positivity of $\boldsymbol{B}'\boldsymbol{A}\boldsymbol{B}$) If $\boldsymbol{A}$ is symmetric and $\boldsymbol{B}$ nonsingular, both of the same order, then show:
(a) $\boldsymbol{B}'\boldsymbol{A}\boldsymbol{B} > \mathbf{O} \iff \boldsymbol{A} > \mathbf{O}$;
(b) $\boldsymbol{B}'\boldsymbol{A}\boldsymbol{B} \geq \mathbf{O} \iff \boldsymbol{A} \geq \mathbf{O}$.

Solution
(a) If $\boldsymbol{A} > \mathbf{O}$ then $\boldsymbol{B}'\boldsymbol{A}\boldsymbol{B} > \mathbf{O}$ by Exercise 8.26(b). Conversely, if $\boldsymbol{B}'\boldsymbol{A}\boldsymbol{B} > \mathbf{O}$, then $\boldsymbol{A} = \boldsymbol{B}^{-1\prime}(\boldsymbol{B}'\boldsymbol{A}\boldsymbol{B})\boldsymbol{B}^{-1} > \mathbf{O}$.
(b) This works the same, now using Exercise 8.27(b).

Exercise 8.29 (Eigenvalue bounds for $(\boldsymbol{A}+\boldsymbol{B})^{-1}\boldsymbol{A}$) Prove that the eigenvalues λ_i of $(\boldsymbol{A}+\boldsymbol{B})^{-1}\boldsymbol{A}$, where $\boldsymbol{A}$ is positive semidefinite and $\boldsymbol{B}$ positive definite, satisfy $0 \leq \lambda_i < 1$.

Solution
Let $\boldsymbol{C} := \boldsymbol{B}^{-1/2}\boldsymbol{A}\boldsymbol{B}^{-1/2}$ with eigenvalues $\mu_1, \dots, \mu_n$. These are nonnegative by Exercises 8.27 and 8.11(b). Then,

$$\boldsymbol{A} = \boldsymbol{B}^{1/2}\boldsymbol{C}\boldsymbol{B}^{1/2} \quad \text{and} \quad \boldsymbol{A}+\boldsymbol{B} = \boldsymbol{B}^{1/2}(\boldsymbol{I}+\boldsymbol{C})\boldsymbol{B}^{1/2},$$

so that

$$(\boldsymbol{A}+\boldsymbol{B})^{-1}\boldsymbol{A} = \boldsymbol{B}^{-1/2}(\boldsymbol{I}+\boldsymbol{C})^{-1}\boldsymbol{B}^{-1/2}\boldsymbol{B}^{1/2}\boldsymbol{C}\boldsymbol{B}^{1/2} = \boldsymbol{B}^{-1/2}(\boldsymbol{I}+\boldsymbol{C})^{-1}\boldsymbol{C}\boldsymbol{B}^{1/2},$$

and the eigenvalues of $(\boldsymbol{A}+\boldsymbol{B})^{-1}\boldsymbol{A}$ are the eigenvalues of $(\boldsymbol{I}+\boldsymbol{C})^{-1}\boldsymbol{C}$, where $\boldsymbol{C}$ is a positive semidefinite matrix. Let $\boldsymbol{S}'\boldsymbol{C}\boldsymbol{S} = \boldsymbol{M}$ (diagonal). Then, $(\boldsymbol{I}+\boldsymbol{C})^{-1}\boldsymbol{C} = \boldsymbol{S}(\boldsymbol{I}+\boldsymbol{M})^{-1}\boldsymbol{S}'\boldsymbol{S}\boldsymbol{M}\boldsymbol{S}'$, and the eigenvalues of $(\boldsymbol{I}+\boldsymbol{C})^{-1}\boldsymbol{C}$ are therefore the diagonal elements of $(\boldsymbol{I}+\boldsymbol{M})^{-1}\boldsymbol{M}$. Since $\mu_i \geq 0$, we obtain $0 \leq \mu_i/(1+\mu_i) < 1$.

Exercise 8.30 (Positivity of principal submatrices)
(a) If $\boldsymbol{A}$ is positive semidefinite, show that every principal submatrix of $\boldsymbol{A}$ is positive semidefinite as well.
(b) If $\boldsymbol{A}$ is positive definite, show that every principal submatrix of $\boldsymbol{A}$ is positive definite as well.

Solution
Let $\boldsymbol{S}_k := (\boldsymbol{I}_k : \mathbf{O})'$ or a row permutation thereof. Then every principal submatrix of $\boldsymbol{A}$ (of order k) can be represented as $\boldsymbol{S}_k'\boldsymbol{A}\boldsymbol{S}_k$. Both (a) and (b) then follow from Exercise 8.28.

***Exercise 8.31 (The principal minors criterion for $\boldsymbol{A} > \mathbf{O}$)** Show that $\boldsymbol{A}$ is positive definite if and only if all *leading* principal minors are positive. That is, if we denote by $\boldsymbol{A}_{(k)}$ the $k \times k$ north-west submatrix of $\boldsymbol{A}$ defined by

$$\boldsymbol{A}_{(k)} := \begin{pmatrix} a_{11} & \dots & a_{1k} \\ \vdots & & \vdots \\ a_{k1} & \dots & a_{kk} \end{pmatrix} \qquad (k = 1, \dots, n),$$

then $\boldsymbol{A} > \mathbf{O}$ if and only if $|\boldsymbol{A}_{(k)}| > 0$ for $k = 1, \dots, n$.

Solution
By Exercise 8.30, $\boldsymbol{A}_{(k)} > \mathbf{O}$ for all k, and hence, in particular, $|\boldsymbol{A}_{(k)}| > 0$. The converse is proved by induction. Assume that $|\boldsymbol{A}_{(k)}| > 0$ for $k = 1, \dots, n$, and partition $\boldsymbol{A}_{(k+1)}$ as

$$\boldsymbol{A}_{(k+1)} = \begin{pmatrix} \boldsymbol{A}_{(k)} & \boldsymbol{a}_{k+1} \\ \boldsymbol{a}'_{k+1} & a_{k+1,k+1} \end{pmatrix}.$$

Now assume (induction hypothesis) that $\boldsymbol{A}_{(k)} > \mathbf{O}$ and consider the equality

$$\begin{pmatrix} \boldsymbol{I}_k & \mathbf{0} \\ -\boldsymbol{a}'_{k+1}\boldsymbol{A}_{(k)}^{-1} & 1 \end{pmatrix} \begin{pmatrix} \boldsymbol{A}_{(k)} & \boldsymbol{a}_{k+1} \\ \boldsymbol{a}'_{k+1} & a_{k+1,k+1} \end{pmatrix} \begin{pmatrix} \boldsymbol{I}_k & -\boldsymbol{A}_{(k)}^{-1}\boldsymbol{a}_{k+1} \\ \mathbf{0}' & 1 \end{pmatrix} = \begin{pmatrix} \boldsymbol{A}_{(k)} & \mathbf{0} \\ \mathbf{0}' & \beta_{k+1} \end{pmatrix},$$

where $\beta_{k+1} := a_{k+1,k+1} - \boldsymbol{a}'_{k+1}\boldsymbol{A}_{(k)}^{-1}\boldsymbol{a}_{k+1}$ The equality shows that $\boldsymbol{A}_{(k+1)} > \mathbf{O}$ if and only if $\boldsymbol{A}_{(k)} > \mathbf{O}$ and $\beta_{k+1} > 0$; and also that $|\boldsymbol{A}_{(k+1)}| = \beta_{k+1}|\boldsymbol{A}_{(k)}|$. Since $|\boldsymbol{A}_{(k)}| > 0$ and $|\boldsymbol{A}_{(k+1)}| > 0$, it follows that $\beta_{k+1} > 0$. Also, $\boldsymbol{A}_{(k)} > \mathbf{O}$ by the induction hypothesis. Hence, $\boldsymbol{A}_{(k+1)} > \mathbf{O}$.

***Exercise 8.32 (The principal minors criterion for $\boldsymbol{A} \geq \mathbf{O}$)** Show that $\boldsymbol{A}$ is positive semidefinite if and only if *all* principal minors (not only the leading ones) are nonnegative.

Solution
By Exercise 8.30, $\boldsymbol{A}_{(k)} \geq \mathbf{O}$ for all k, and hence, in particular, $|\boldsymbol{A}_{(k)}| \geq 0$. Suppose, conversely, that all principal minors of $\boldsymbol{A}$ are nonnegative. Recall that there are $\binom{n}{k}$ different $k \times k$ principal minors of $\boldsymbol{A}$, and that the sum of these is denoted by E_k or $E_k(\boldsymbol{A})$. We know from the introduction to Chapter 7 that we can write the characteristic polynomial in terms of the functions E_k:

$$|\lambda\boldsymbol{I}_n - \boldsymbol{A}| = \lambda^n - E_1\lambda^{n-1} + E_2\lambda^{n-2} + \dots + (-1)^{n-1}E_{n-1}\lambda + (-1)^n E_n.$$

In particular, we obtain for $\epsilon > 0$,

$$|\boldsymbol{A}_{(k)} + \epsilon\boldsymbol{I}_k| = \epsilon^k + E_1(\boldsymbol{A}_{(k)})\epsilon^{k-1} + E_2(\boldsymbol{A}_{(k)})\epsilon^{k-2} + \dots + E_{k-1}(\boldsymbol{A}_{(k)})\epsilon + E_k(\boldsymbol{A}_{(k)}).$$

If all principal minors of $\boldsymbol{A}$ are nonnegative, then all $E_j \geq 0$ and hence $|\boldsymbol{A}_{(k)} + \epsilon \boldsymbol{I}_k| \geq \epsilon^k > 0$. This implies that all leading principal minors of $\boldsymbol{A} + \epsilon \boldsymbol{I}_n$ are positive. Then, by Exercise 8.31, $\boldsymbol{A} + \epsilon \boldsymbol{I}_n > \mathbf{O}$ and hence $\boldsymbol{x}'\boldsymbol{A}\boldsymbol{x} + \epsilon \boldsymbol{x}'\boldsymbol{x} > 0$ for all $\boldsymbol{x} \neq \mathbf{0}$. Letting $\epsilon \to 0$ gives $\boldsymbol{x}'\boldsymbol{A}\boldsymbol{x} \geq 0$ for all $\boldsymbol{x}$.

Exercise 8.33 (Small minors) Consider the matrices

$$\boldsymbol{A} = \begin{pmatrix} 0 & 0 \\ 0 & p \end{pmatrix} \quad \text{and} \quad \boldsymbol{B} = \begin{pmatrix} 1 & a & b \\ a & a^2 & ab \\ b & ab & p \end{pmatrix}.$$

(a) For which values of p are $\boldsymbol{A}$ and $\boldsymbol{B}$ positive (semi)definite?
(b) Obtain the principal minors of $\boldsymbol{A}$ and $\boldsymbol{B}$.
(c) For both $\boldsymbol{A}$ and $\boldsymbol{B}$, confirm that the leading principal minors are ≥ 0 for all values of p, but that $\boldsymbol{A}$ and $\boldsymbol{B}$ are only positive semidefinite when *all* principal minors are ≥ 0.

Solution
(a) Both $\boldsymbol{A}$ and $\boldsymbol{B}$ are singular, so they cannot be positive definite. We have, writing $\boldsymbol{B} = (1, a, b)'(1, a, b) + \operatorname{diag}(0, 0, p - b^2)$,

$$\boldsymbol{x}'\boldsymbol{A}\boldsymbol{x} = px_2^2 \quad \text{and} \quad \boldsymbol{x}'\boldsymbol{B}\boldsymbol{x} = (x_1 + ax_2 + bx_3)^2 + (p - b^2)x_3^2.$$

Hence, $\boldsymbol{A} \geq \mathbf{O}$ when $p \geq 0$ and $\boldsymbol{B} \geq 0$ when $p \geq b^2$.
(b) For $\boldsymbol{A}$, the principal minors of order 1 are 0 (leading) and p; and of order 2, 0 (leading). For $\boldsymbol{B}$, the principal minors of order 1 are 1 (leading), a^2 and p; of order 2, 0 (leading), $p - b^2$ and $a^2(p - b^2)$; and of order 3, 0 (leading).
(c) This follows immediately from the calculations in (b).

Exercise 8.34 (Bigger minors) The examples in Exercise 8.33 show that it is *not* true that $\boldsymbol{A} \geq \mathbf{O}$ if and only if the leading principal minors $|\boldsymbol{A}_{(k)}| \geq 0$ for $k = 1, \dots, n$. However, if $|\boldsymbol{A}_{(k)}| > 0$ for $k = 1, \dots, n-1$ and $|\boldsymbol{A}| = 0$, then $\boldsymbol{A} \geq \mathbf{O}$. Prove this.

Solution
Assume that $|\boldsymbol{A}_{(1)}| > 0, \dots, |\boldsymbol{A}_{(n-1)}| > 0$, and that $|\boldsymbol{A}| = 0$. Suppose that $\boldsymbol{A}$ is not positive semidefinite. Then an $\boldsymbol{x} := (x_1, \dots, x_n)'$ exists such that $\boldsymbol{x}'\boldsymbol{A}\boldsymbol{x} = -c$ for some $c > 0$. We note that $x_n \neq 0$, because if $x_n = 0$, then $(x_1, \dots, x_{n-1}, 0)'\boldsymbol{A}(x_1, \dots, x_{n-1}, 0) = (x_1, \dots, x_{n-1})'\boldsymbol{A}_{(n-1)}(x_1, \dots, x_{n-1}) > 0$ since $\boldsymbol{A}_{(n-1)} > \mathbf{O}$ (Exercise 8.31). Let $t := c/x_n^2 > 0$, and define $\boldsymbol{B} := \boldsymbol{A} + t\boldsymbol{e}_n\boldsymbol{e}_n'$. Then,

$$\boldsymbol{x}'\boldsymbol{B}\boldsymbol{x} = \boldsymbol{x}'\boldsymbol{A}\boldsymbol{x} + tx_n^2 = -c + tx_n^2 = 0$$

and

$$|\boldsymbol{B}| = |\boldsymbol{A} + t\boldsymbol{e}_n\boldsymbol{e}_n'| = |\boldsymbol{A}| + t|\boldsymbol{A}_{(n-1)}| = t|\boldsymbol{A}_{(n-1)}| > 0.$$

All leading principal minors of $\boldsymbol{B}$ are positive and hence $\boldsymbol{B} > \mathbf{O}$. The equality $\boldsymbol{x}'\boldsymbol{B}\boldsymbol{x} = 0$ then implies $\boldsymbol{x} = \mathbf{0}$, which contradicts the fact that $x_n \neq 0$. It follows that $\boldsymbol{x}'\boldsymbol{A}\boldsymbol{x} \geq 0$.

Exercise 8.35 (Determinantal inequality) Let $A > O$ and $B \geq O$. Show that $|A + B| \geq |A|$ with equality if and only if $B = O$. (This is a special case of a more general result to be proved in Exercise 12.7.)

Solution
Since $A > O$, the matrix $C := A^{-1/2}BA^{-1/2}$ exists. We write

$$A + B = A^{1/2}(I + C)A^{1/2},$$

so that

$$|A + B| = |A||I + C|.$$

The matrix C is positive semidefinite. Hence, $|I + C| \geq 1$ and $|A + B| \geq |A|$. If $B = O$ then $C = O$ and $|A + B| = |A|$. If $B \neq O$, then the eigenvalues of C will be nonnegative and at least one eigenvalue will be positive. Hence, $|I + C| > 1$ and $|A + B| > |A|$.

Exercise 8.36 (Real eigenvalues for AB) If A and B are symmetric and $A \geq O$ (or $B \geq O$), show that the eigenvalues of AB are real.

Solution
Assume that $A \geq O$ and write $A = TT'$. The nonzero eigenvalues of $TT'B$ are those of $T'BT$ (Exercise 7.25). But $T'BT$ is symmetric and therefore has only real eigenvalues (Exercise 7.40).

Exercise 8.37 (Simultaneous reduction to diagonal form, again) Let $A > O$ and let B be symmetric of the same order. Show that there exist a nonsingular matrix T and a diagonal matrix Λ such that

$$A = TT' \quad \text{and} \quad B = T\Lambda T',$$

where Λ contains the eigenvalues of $A^{-1}B$.

Solution
Let $C := A^{-1/2}BA^{-1/2}$. Since C is symmetric, there exist an orthogonal matrix S and a diagonal matrix Λ such that $S'CS = \Lambda$, $S'S = I$. Now define $T := A^{1/2}S$. Then,

$$TT' = A^{1/2}SS'A^{1/2} = A^{1/2}A^{1/2} = A$$

and

$$T\Lambda T' = A^{1/2}S\Lambda S'A^{1/2} = A^{1/2}CA^{1/2} = A^{1/2}A^{-1/2}BA^{-1/2}A^{1/2} = B.$$

Exercise 8.38 (Singular-value decomposition) Let A be a real $m \times n$ matrix with $\text{rk}(A) = r > 0$. Show that there exist an $m \times r$ matrix S such that $S'S = I_r$, an $n \times r$ matrix T such that $T'T = I_r$, and an $r \times r$ diagonal matrix Λ with positive diagonal elements, such that $A = S\Lambda^{1/2}T'$.

Solution
Since $\boldsymbol{AA}'$ is an $m \times m$ symmetric (in fact, positive semidefinite) matrix of rank r, its nonzero eigenvalues are all positive. From the diagonalization theorem for symmetric matrices we know that there exists an orthogonal $m \times m$ matrix $(\boldsymbol{S}_1 : \boldsymbol{S}_2)$ such that

$$\boldsymbol{AA}'\boldsymbol{S}_1 = \boldsymbol{S}_1\boldsymbol{\Lambda}, \quad \boldsymbol{AA}'\boldsymbol{S}_2 = \mathbf{O}, \quad \boldsymbol{S}_1\boldsymbol{S}_1' + \boldsymbol{S}_2\boldsymbol{S}_2' = \boldsymbol{I}_m,$$

where $\boldsymbol{\Lambda}$ is an $r \times r$ diagonal matrix having these r positive eigenvalues as diagonal elements. Define $\boldsymbol{T} := \boldsymbol{A}'\boldsymbol{S}_1\boldsymbol{\Lambda}^{-1/2}$. Then we see that

$$\boldsymbol{A}'\boldsymbol{AT} = \boldsymbol{T\Lambda}, \quad \boldsymbol{T}'\boldsymbol{T} = \boldsymbol{I}_r.$$

Since $\boldsymbol{A}'\boldsymbol{S}_2 = \mathbf{O}$, we obtain

$$\boldsymbol{A} = (\boldsymbol{S}_1\boldsymbol{S}_1' + \boldsymbol{S}_2\boldsymbol{S}_2')\boldsymbol{A} = \boldsymbol{S}_1\boldsymbol{S}_1'\boldsymbol{A} = \boldsymbol{S}_1\boldsymbol{\Lambda}^{1/2}\boldsymbol{\Lambda}^{-1/2}\boldsymbol{S}_1'\boldsymbol{A} = \boldsymbol{S}_1\boldsymbol{\Lambda}^{1/2}\boldsymbol{T}'.$$

The r diagonal elements of $\boldsymbol{\Lambda}^{1/2}$ are the *singular values* of the matrix $\boldsymbol{A}$. Their squares (the diagonal elements of $\boldsymbol{\Lambda}$) are the nonzero (hence positive) eigenvalues of $\boldsymbol{A}'\boldsymbol{A}$ or, equivalently, the r nonzero (hence positive) eigenvalues of $\boldsymbol{AA}'$. These are *not* the same as the eigenvalues of $\boldsymbol{A}^2$.

Exercise 8.39 (SVD warning) In the singular-value decomposition, the semi-orthogonal matrices $\boldsymbol{S}$ and $\boldsymbol{T}$ satisfy $\boldsymbol{AA}'\boldsymbol{S} = \boldsymbol{S\Lambda}$ and $\boldsymbol{A}'\boldsymbol{AT} = \boldsymbol{T\Lambda}$. Hence, $\boldsymbol{\Lambda}$ contains the r nonzero eigenvalues of $\boldsymbol{AA}'$ (which are equal to the nonzero eigenvalues of $\boldsymbol{A}'\boldsymbol{A}$), and $\boldsymbol{S}$ (by construction) and $\boldsymbol{T}$ contain corresponding eigenvectors. A common mistake in applying the singular-value decomposition is to find $\boldsymbol{S}$, $\boldsymbol{T}$, and $\boldsymbol{\Lambda}$ from the equations $\boldsymbol{AA}'\boldsymbol{S} = \boldsymbol{S\Lambda}$, $\boldsymbol{A}'\boldsymbol{AT} = \boldsymbol{T\Lambda}$.
(a) What is wrong with this?
(b) What would be right?

Solution
(a) This is incorrect because, given $\boldsymbol{S}$, $\boldsymbol{T}$ obtained in that way would not be unique.
(b) The correct procedure is to find $\boldsymbol{S}$ and $\boldsymbol{\Lambda}$ from $\boldsymbol{AA}'\boldsymbol{S} = \boldsymbol{S\Lambda}$ and then define $\boldsymbol{T} := \boldsymbol{A}'\boldsymbol{S\Lambda}^{-1/2}$. Alternatively, we can find $\boldsymbol{T}$ and $\boldsymbol{\Lambda}$ from $\boldsymbol{A}'\boldsymbol{AT} = \boldsymbol{T\Lambda}$ and define $\boldsymbol{S} := \boldsymbol{AT\Lambda}^{-1/2}$.

Exercise 8.40 (Polar decomposition) Let $\boldsymbol{A}$ be a real $m \times n$ matrix.
(a) If $\boldsymbol{A}$ has full column rank n, show that $\boldsymbol{A}$ can be written as $\boldsymbol{A} = \boldsymbol{PV}$, where $\boldsymbol{P}$ is a semi-orthogonal $m \times n$ matrix ($\boldsymbol{P}'\boldsymbol{P} = \boldsymbol{I}_n$) and $\boldsymbol{V}$ is a positive definite $n \times n$ matrix.
(b) If $\boldsymbol{A}$ has full row rank m, show that $\boldsymbol{A}$ can be written as $\boldsymbol{A} = \boldsymbol{VP}'$, where $\boldsymbol{P}$ is a semi-orthogonal $n \times m$ matrix ($\boldsymbol{P}'\boldsymbol{P} = \boldsymbol{I}_m$) and $\boldsymbol{V}$ is a positive definite $m \times m$ matrix.

Solution
(a) From the singular-value decomposition (Exercise 8.38) there exist an $m \times n$ semi-orthogonal matrix $\boldsymbol{S}$ such that $\boldsymbol{S}'\boldsymbol{S} = \boldsymbol{I}_n$, an $n \times n$ orthogonal matrix $\boldsymbol{T}$, and an $n \times n$

diagonal matrix $\boldsymbol{\Lambda}$ with positive diagonal elements, such that $\boldsymbol{A} = \boldsymbol{S}\boldsymbol{\Lambda}^{1/2}\boldsymbol{T}'$. Hence,

$$\boldsymbol{A} = \boldsymbol{S}\boldsymbol{\Lambda}^{1/2}\boldsymbol{T}' = \boldsymbol{S}(\boldsymbol{T}'\boldsymbol{T})\boldsymbol{\Lambda}^{1/2}\boldsymbol{T}' = (\boldsymbol{S}\boldsymbol{T}')(\boldsymbol{T}\boldsymbol{\Lambda}^{1/2}\boldsymbol{T}') = \boldsymbol{P}\boldsymbol{V},$$

where $\boldsymbol{P} := \boldsymbol{S}\boldsymbol{T}'$ is semi-orthogonal and $\boldsymbol{V} := \boldsymbol{T}\boldsymbol{\Lambda}^{1/2}\boldsymbol{T}'$ is positive definite.
(b) If $\boldsymbol{A}$ has full row rank m, then $\boldsymbol{B} := \boldsymbol{A}'$ is a real $n \times m$ matrix with full column rank m. Hence, by (a), we can write $\boldsymbol{B} = \boldsymbol{P}\boldsymbol{V}$. This gives $\boldsymbol{A} = \boldsymbol{B}' = (\boldsymbol{P}\boldsymbol{V})' = \boldsymbol{V}\boldsymbol{P}'$.

Exercise 8.41 (Singular relatives) If $\boldsymbol{A} \geq \boldsymbol{B} \geq \mathbf{O}$ and $|\boldsymbol{A}| = 0$, show that $|\boldsymbol{B}| = 0$ and $|\boldsymbol{A} - \boldsymbol{B}| = 0$.

Solution
Since $\boldsymbol{A} \geq \mathbf{O}$ but not $\boldsymbol{A} > \mathbf{O}$, there is an $\boldsymbol{x} \neq \mathbf{0}$ such that $\boldsymbol{x}'\boldsymbol{A}\boldsymbol{x} = 0$. Now, $\boldsymbol{B}$ and $\boldsymbol{A} - \boldsymbol{B}$ are both positive semidefinite. For this $\boldsymbol{x}$,

$$0 \leq \boldsymbol{x}'(\boldsymbol{A} - \boldsymbol{B})\boldsymbol{x} = -\boldsymbol{x}'\boldsymbol{B}\boldsymbol{x} \leq 0,$$

implying that both $\boldsymbol{x}'\boldsymbol{B}\boldsymbol{x} = 0$ and $\boldsymbol{x}'(\boldsymbol{A} - \boldsymbol{B})\boldsymbol{x} = 0$. Hence, both matrices are singular.

Exercise 8.42 (Linear independence) For all $\boldsymbol{A} \geq \mathbf{O}$, show that two vectors $\boldsymbol{A}^{1/2}\boldsymbol{x}$ and $\boldsymbol{A}^{1/2}\boldsymbol{y}$ are linearly dependent if and only if $\boldsymbol{A}\boldsymbol{x}$ and $\boldsymbol{A}\boldsymbol{y}$ are linearly dependent.

Solution
The essence of the proof is the simple observation that for any diagonal matrix $\boldsymbol{\Lambda}$ with nonnegative diagonal elements, we have $\boldsymbol{\Lambda}\boldsymbol{q} = \mathbf{0}$ if and only if $\boldsymbol{\Lambda}^{1/2}\boldsymbol{q} = \mathbf{0}$ for any vector $\boldsymbol{q}$. Let $\boldsymbol{S}'\boldsymbol{A}\boldsymbol{S} = \boldsymbol{\Lambda}$ with $\boldsymbol{S}'\boldsymbol{S} = \boldsymbol{I}_n$. Then,

$$\begin{aligned} \boldsymbol{A}\boldsymbol{q} = \mathbf{0} &\iff \boldsymbol{S}\boldsymbol{\Lambda}\boldsymbol{S}'\boldsymbol{q} = \mathbf{0} \iff \boldsymbol{\Lambda}\boldsymbol{S}'\boldsymbol{q} = \mathbf{0} \iff \boldsymbol{\Lambda}^{1/2}\boldsymbol{S}'\boldsymbol{q} = \mathbf{0} \\ &\iff \boldsymbol{S}\boldsymbol{\Lambda}^{1/2}\boldsymbol{S}'\boldsymbol{q} = \mathbf{0} \iff \boldsymbol{A}^{1/2}\boldsymbol{q} = \mathbf{0}. \end{aligned}$$

Now let $\boldsymbol{q} := \alpha_1\boldsymbol{x} + \alpha_2\boldsymbol{y}$. Then, $\alpha_1\boldsymbol{A}\boldsymbol{x} + \alpha_2\boldsymbol{A}\boldsymbol{y} = \mathbf{0}$ if and only if $\alpha_1\boldsymbol{A}^{1/2}\boldsymbol{x} + \alpha_2\boldsymbol{A}^{1/2}\boldsymbol{y} = \mathbf{0}$.

Exercise 8.43 (The matrix $\boldsymbol{A} - \boldsymbol{a}\boldsymbol{a}'$) If $\boldsymbol{A} > \mathbf{O}$, show that $\boldsymbol{A} - \boldsymbol{a}\boldsymbol{a}' > \mathbf{O}$ if and only if $\boldsymbol{a}'\boldsymbol{A}^{-1}\boldsymbol{a} < 1$.

Solution
Let $\boldsymbol{A} > \mathbf{O}$ and write $\boldsymbol{A} = \boldsymbol{S}\boldsymbol{\Lambda}\boldsymbol{S}'$, $\boldsymbol{S}'\boldsymbol{S} = \boldsymbol{I}$. Then $\boldsymbol{A}^{1/2} = \boldsymbol{S}\boldsymbol{\Lambda}^{1/2}\boldsymbol{S}'$, $\boldsymbol{A}^{-1} = \boldsymbol{S}\boldsymbol{\Lambda}^{-1}\boldsymbol{S}'$, and $\boldsymbol{A}^{-1/2} = \boldsymbol{S}\boldsymbol{\Lambda}^{-1/2}\boldsymbol{S}'$. Hence,

$$\boldsymbol{A} - \boldsymbol{a}\boldsymbol{a}' = \boldsymbol{A}^{1/2}(\boldsymbol{I}_n - \boldsymbol{A}^{-1/2}\boldsymbol{a}\boldsymbol{a}'\boldsymbol{A}^{-1/2})\boldsymbol{A}^{1/2}.$$

Since $\boldsymbol{A}^{1/2}$ is symmetric and nonsingular, it follows that $\boldsymbol{A} - \boldsymbol{a}\boldsymbol{a}' > \mathbf{O}$ if and only if $\boldsymbol{I}_n - \boldsymbol{A}^{-1/2}\boldsymbol{a}\boldsymbol{a}'\boldsymbol{A}^{-1/2} > \mathbf{O}$. The eigenvalues of $\boldsymbol{A}^{-1/2}\boldsymbol{a}\boldsymbol{a}'\boldsymbol{A}^{-1/2}$ are 0 ($n - 1$ times) and $\boldsymbol{a}'\boldsymbol{A}^{-1}\boldsymbol{a}$ (once). Hence, the eigenvalues of $\boldsymbol{I}_n - \boldsymbol{A}^{-1/2}\boldsymbol{a}\boldsymbol{a}'\boldsymbol{A}^{-1/2}$ are 1 ($n - 1$ times) and $1 - \boldsymbol{a}'\boldsymbol{A}^{-1}\boldsymbol{a}$. Positivity thus requires $\boldsymbol{a}\boldsymbol{A}^{-1}\boldsymbol{a} < 1$.

8.2 Partitioning and positive (semi)definite matrices

Exercise 8.44 (Block diagonality) Show that

$$Z := \begin{pmatrix} A & O \\ O & D \end{pmatrix}$$

is positive (semi)definite if and only if A and D are both positive (semi)definite.

Solution
The matrix Z is positive definite if and only if $x'Ax + y'Dy > 0$ for all x and y, not both zero. This occurs if and only if $x'Ax > 0$ for all nonzero x, and $y'Dy > 0$ for all nonzero y, that is, if and only if A and D are positive definite. The same argument proves the positive semidefinite case. Notice that $A \geq O$ and $D > O$ implies $Z \geq O$ but not $Z > O$.

Exercise 8.45 (Jumbled blocks) Show that

$$\begin{pmatrix} A & B \\ B' & D \end{pmatrix} > O \iff \begin{pmatrix} D & B' \\ B & A \end{pmatrix} > O.$$

Solution
Let x and y be arbitrary conformable vectors. Then,

$$(x', y') \begin{pmatrix} A & B \\ B' & D \end{pmatrix} \begin{pmatrix} x \\ y \end{pmatrix} = (y', x') \begin{pmatrix} D & B' \\ B & A \end{pmatrix} \begin{pmatrix} y \\ x \end{pmatrix}.$$

Hence, one quadratic form is positive for all x and y, not both zero, if and only if the other is.

Exercise 8.46 (Fischer's inequality) Show that

$$Z := \begin{pmatrix} A & B \\ B' & D \end{pmatrix} \geq O \implies |Z| \leq |A||D|.$$

Solution
Since $Z \geq O$, it follows that $A \geq O$ and $D \geq O$. Suppose that $|A| = 0$. Then $|Z| = 0$ (Exercise 8.31) and the result holds. Thus, suppose $A > O$. Then it follows from Exercise 5.30 that $|Z| = |A||D - B'A^{-1}B|$. Also, $|D - B'A^{-1}B| \leq |D|$ by Exercise 8.35. Hence, $|Z| \leq |A||D|$. (See also Exercise 12.34.)

Exercise 8.47 (Positivity of Schur complement) Show that

$$Z := \begin{pmatrix} A & B \\ B' & D \end{pmatrix}$$

is positive definite if and only if $\boldsymbol{A}$ and $\boldsymbol{D} - \boldsymbol{B}'\boldsymbol{A}^{-1}\boldsymbol{B}$ are both positive definite (or, equivalently, if and only if $\boldsymbol{D}$ and $\boldsymbol{A} - \boldsymbol{B}\boldsymbol{D}^{-1}\boldsymbol{B}'$ are both positive definite).

Solution

If $\boldsymbol{Z} > \mathrm{O}$, then all its principal submatrices are positive definite, in particular $\boldsymbol{A}$. Hence, we may write

$$\begin{pmatrix} \boldsymbol{I}_m & \mathrm{O} \\ -\boldsymbol{B}'\boldsymbol{A}^{-1} & \boldsymbol{I}_n \end{pmatrix} \begin{pmatrix} \boldsymbol{A} & \boldsymbol{B} \\ \boldsymbol{B}' & \boldsymbol{D} \end{pmatrix} \begin{pmatrix} \boldsymbol{I}_m & -\boldsymbol{A}^{-1}\boldsymbol{B} \\ \mathrm{O} & \boldsymbol{I}_n \end{pmatrix} = \begin{pmatrix} \boldsymbol{A} & \mathrm{O} \\ \mathrm{O} & \boldsymbol{D} - \boldsymbol{B}'\boldsymbol{A}^{-1}\boldsymbol{B} \end{pmatrix}.$$

This shows that the block-diagonal matrix on the right is positive definite and hence that $\boldsymbol{D} - \boldsymbol{B}'\boldsymbol{A}^{-1}\boldsymbol{B} > \mathrm{O}$. Conversely, if $\boldsymbol{A}$ and $\boldsymbol{D} - \boldsymbol{B}'\boldsymbol{A}^{-1}\boldsymbol{B}$ are both positive definite, then the above equality shows that $\boldsymbol{Z}$ is positive definite. (If $\boldsymbol{P}'\boldsymbol{Z}\boldsymbol{P} > 0$ and $|\boldsymbol{P}| \neq 0$, then $\boldsymbol{Z} > \mathrm{O}$ by Exercise 8.26(b).)

***Exercise 8.48 (Contractions)** Show that the matrix $\boldsymbol{Z}$ of Exercise 8.47 is positive semidefinite if and only if $\boldsymbol{A}$ and $\boldsymbol{D}$ are positive semidefinite and there exists a matrix $\boldsymbol{C}$ such that $\boldsymbol{A}^{1/2}\boldsymbol{C}\boldsymbol{D}^{1/2} = \boldsymbol{B}$, $\boldsymbol{C}'\boldsymbol{C} \leq \boldsymbol{I}_n$. A matrix $\boldsymbol{C}$ satisfying $\boldsymbol{C}'\boldsymbol{C} \leq \boldsymbol{I}_n$ is called a *contraction*.

Solution

If $\boldsymbol{A} \geq \mathrm{O}$, $\boldsymbol{D} \geq \mathrm{O}$, and a contraction $\boldsymbol{C}$ exists such that $\boldsymbol{B} = \boldsymbol{A}^{1/2}\boldsymbol{C}\boldsymbol{D}^{1/2}$, then we may write

$$\begin{aligned} \boldsymbol{Z} &= \begin{pmatrix} \boldsymbol{A}^{1/2}\boldsymbol{A}^{1/2} & \boldsymbol{A}^{1/2}\boldsymbol{C}\boldsymbol{D}^{1/2} \\ \boldsymbol{D}^{1/2}\boldsymbol{C}'\boldsymbol{A}^{1/2} & \boldsymbol{D}^{1/2}\boldsymbol{D}^{1/2} \end{pmatrix} \geq \begin{pmatrix} \boldsymbol{A}^{1/2}\boldsymbol{A}^{1/2} & \boldsymbol{A}^{1/2}\boldsymbol{C}\boldsymbol{D}^{1/2} \\ \boldsymbol{D}^{1/2}\boldsymbol{C}'\boldsymbol{A}^{1/2} & \boldsymbol{D}^{1/2}\boldsymbol{C}'\boldsymbol{C}\boldsymbol{D}^{1/2} \end{pmatrix} \\ &= \begin{pmatrix} \boldsymbol{A}^{1/2} \\ \boldsymbol{D}^{1/2}\boldsymbol{C}' \end{pmatrix} (\boldsymbol{A}^{1/2} : \boldsymbol{C}\boldsymbol{D}^{1/2}) \geq \mathrm{O}. \end{aligned}$$

Conversely, suppose that $\boldsymbol{Z} \geq \mathrm{O}$. First consider the case when $\boldsymbol{A} > \mathrm{O}$ and $\boldsymbol{D} > \mathrm{O}$. Letting $\boldsymbol{C} := \boldsymbol{A}^{-1/2}\boldsymbol{B}\boldsymbol{D}^{-1/2}$, we decompose

$$\begin{pmatrix} \boldsymbol{A} & \boldsymbol{B} \\ \boldsymbol{B}' & \boldsymbol{D} \end{pmatrix} = \begin{pmatrix} \boldsymbol{A}^{1/2} & \mathrm{O} \\ \boldsymbol{D}^{1/2}\boldsymbol{C}' & \boldsymbol{D}^{1/2} \end{pmatrix} \begin{pmatrix} \boldsymbol{I}_m & \mathrm{O} \\ \mathrm{O} & \boldsymbol{I}_n - \boldsymbol{C}'\boldsymbol{C} \end{pmatrix} \begin{pmatrix} \boldsymbol{A}^{1/2} & \boldsymbol{C}\boldsymbol{D}^{1/2} \\ \mathrm{O} & \boldsymbol{D}^{1/2} \end{pmatrix}.$$

Hence, if $\boldsymbol{Z} \geq \mathrm{O}$ and $\boldsymbol{A} > \mathrm{O}$, $\boldsymbol{D} > \mathrm{O}$, then $\boldsymbol{C}$ is a contraction and $\boldsymbol{B} = \boldsymbol{A}^{1/2}\boldsymbol{C}\boldsymbol{D}^{1/2}$.

Next consider the general case when $\boldsymbol{A} \geq \mathrm{O}$ and $\boldsymbol{D} \geq \mathrm{O}$. Then, for any positive integer k, the matrices $\boldsymbol{A} + k^{-1}\boldsymbol{I}_m$ and $\boldsymbol{D} + k^{-1}\boldsymbol{I}_n$ are both positive definite. Hence, replacing $\boldsymbol{A}$ by $\boldsymbol{A} + k^{-1}\boldsymbol{I}_m$, $\boldsymbol{D}$ by $\boldsymbol{D} + k^{-1}\boldsymbol{I}_n$, and hence $\boldsymbol{Z}$ by $\boldsymbol{Z} + k^{-1}\boldsymbol{I}_{m+n}$, the previous argument shows that there exists a contraction $\boldsymbol{C}_k$ such that $\boldsymbol{B} = (\boldsymbol{A}+k^{-1}\boldsymbol{I}_m)^{1/2}\boldsymbol{C}_k(\boldsymbol{D}+k^{-1}\boldsymbol{I}_n)^{1/2}$. Now, $\boldsymbol{C}_k'\boldsymbol{C}_k \leq \boldsymbol{I}_n$. Hence, for finite n, the sequence $\{\boldsymbol{C}_k\}_{k=1}^{\infty}$ is bounded. We know from the theory of sequences and subsequences that every bounded sequence in $\mathbb{R}^{mn}$ contains a convergent subsequence (Bolzano-Weierstrass theorem, Appendix A, Section A.3). Let $\boldsymbol{C}$ be the limit of this subsequence. Then $\boldsymbol{C}$ is a contraction and, letting $k \to \infty$, $\boldsymbol{B} = \boldsymbol{A}^{1/2}\boldsymbol{C}\boldsymbol{D}^{1/2}$.

***Exercise 8.49 (Nonsingularity of the bordered Gramian)** Let $\boldsymbol{A}$ be a positive semidefinite $m \times m$ matrix and $\boldsymbol{B}$ an $m \times n$ matrix. The symmetric $(m+n) \times (m+n)$ matrix

$$\boldsymbol{Z} := \begin{pmatrix} \boldsymbol{A} & \boldsymbol{B} \\ \boldsymbol{B}' & \mathbf{O} \end{pmatrix},$$

is called the *bordered Gramian* matrix.
(a) Give an example where $\boldsymbol{A}$ is singular, but where nevertheless $\boldsymbol{Z}$ is nonsingular. In that case, is the matrix $\boldsymbol{A} + \boldsymbol{B}\boldsymbol{B}'$ also singular?
(b) Show that $\boldsymbol{Z}$ is nonsingular if and only if $\operatorname{rk}(\boldsymbol{B}) = n$ and $\boldsymbol{A} + \boldsymbol{B}\boldsymbol{B}' > \mathbf{O}$. (In fact, it is even true that $\operatorname{rk}(\boldsymbol{Z}) = \operatorname{rk}(\boldsymbol{A} + \boldsymbol{B}\boldsymbol{B}') + \operatorname{rk}(\boldsymbol{B})$.)

Solution
(a) Taking an example similar to the one in the solution to Exercise 8.27, let

$$\boldsymbol{A} = \begin{pmatrix} 1 & 1 \\ 1 & 1 \end{pmatrix} \quad \text{and} \quad \boldsymbol{b} = \begin{pmatrix} 1 \\ \beta \end{pmatrix}.$$

The determinant of $\boldsymbol{Z}$ is then $|\boldsymbol{Z}| = -(\beta - 1)^2$, which is nonzero unless $\beta = 1$. The determinant of $\boldsymbol{A} + \boldsymbol{b}\boldsymbol{b}'$ is $(\beta - 1)^2$. We conclude (in this example) that $\boldsymbol{Z}$ is nonsingular if and only $\boldsymbol{A} + \boldsymbol{b}\boldsymbol{b}'$ is nonsingular. This is *not* a coincidence.
(b) We prove this is three steps. First, if $\operatorname{rk}(\boldsymbol{B}) < n$, then $\boldsymbol{Z}$ must be singular, because the last n columns of $\boldsymbol{Z}$ are linearly dependent. Second, if $\operatorname{rk}(\boldsymbol{B}) = n$ and $\boldsymbol{A} + \boldsymbol{B}\boldsymbol{B}'$ is singular, then there exists an $\boldsymbol{x} \neq \mathbf{0}$ such that

$$0 = \boldsymbol{x}'(\boldsymbol{A} + \boldsymbol{B}\boldsymbol{B}')\boldsymbol{x} = \boldsymbol{x}'\boldsymbol{A}\boldsymbol{x} + \boldsymbol{x}'\boldsymbol{B}\boldsymbol{B}'\boldsymbol{x},$$

implying that both $\boldsymbol{x}'\boldsymbol{A}\boldsymbol{x} = 0$ and $\boldsymbol{x}'\boldsymbol{B}\boldsymbol{B}'\boldsymbol{x} = 0$, and hence that $\boldsymbol{A}\boldsymbol{x} = \mathbf{0}$ and $\boldsymbol{B}'\boldsymbol{x} = \mathbf{0}$. This gives

$$\begin{pmatrix} \boldsymbol{A} & \boldsymbol{B} \\ \boldsymbol{B}' & \mathbf{O} \end{pmatrix} \begin{pmatrix} \boldsymbol{x} \\ \mathbf{0} \end{pmatrix} = \begin{pmatrix} \mathbf{0} \\ \mathbf{0} \end{pmatrix},$$

implying that $\boldsymbol{Z}$ is singular. Finally, if $\operatorname{rk}(\boldsymbol{B}) = n$ and $\boldsymbol{A} + \boldsymbol{B}\boldsymbol{B}' > \mathbf{O}$, we show that $\boldsymbol{Z}$ is nonsingular. Suppose $\boldsymbol{Z}$ is singular. Then there exist vectors $\boldsymbol{x}$ and $\boldsymbol{y}$, not both zero, such that

$$\begin{pmatrix} \boldsymbol{A} & \boldsymbol{B} \\ \boldsymbol{B}' & \mathbf{O} \end{pmatrix} \begin{pmatrix} \boldsymbol{x} \\ \boldsymbol{y} \end{pmatrix} = \begin{pmatrix} \mathbf{0} \\ \mathbf{0} \end{pmatrix}.$$

This gives $\boldsymbol{A}\boldsymbol{x} + \boldsymbol{B}\boldsymbol{y} = \mathbf{0}$ and $\boldsymbol{B}'\boldsymbol{x} = \mathbf{0}$, and hence $(\boldsymbol{A} + \boldsymbol{B}\boldsymbol{B}')\boldsymbol{x} + \boldsymbol{B}\boldsymbol{y} = \mathbf{0}$ and $\boldsymbol{B}'\boldsymbol{x} = \mathbf{0}$. Solving produces $\boldsymbol{x} = -(\boldsymbol{A} + \boldsymbol{B}\boldsymbol{B}')^{-1}\boldsymbol{B}\boldsymbol{y}$ and hence $\boldsymbol{B}'(\boldsymbol{A} + \boldsymbol{B}\boldsymbol{B}')^{-1}\boldsymbol{B}\boldsymbol{y} = \mathbf{0}$. Given our assumptions, the matrix $\boldsymbol{B}'(\boldsymbol{A} + \boldsymbol{B}\boldsymbol{B}')^{-1}\boldsymbol{B}$ is nonsingular; hence $\boldsymbol{y} = \mathbf{0}$. But then $(\boldsymbol{A} + \boldsymbol{B}\boldsymbol{B}')\boldsymbol{x} = \mathbf{0}$ too, so that both $\boldsymbol{x}$ and $\boldsymbol{y}$ are zero, and we arrive at a contradiction.

Exercise 8.50 (Inverse of the bordered Gramian) Suppose that $\boldsymbol{Z}$ is nonsingular and let $\boldsymbol{G} := \boldsymbol{A} + \boldsymbol{B}\boldsymbol{B}'$ and $\boldsymbol{H} := \boldsymbol{B}'\boldsymbol{G}^{-1}\boldsymbol{B}$. Show that the inverse of $\boldsymbol{Z}$ is given by

$$\boldsymbol{Z}^{-1} = \begin{pmatrix} \boldsymbol{G}^{-1} - \boldsymbol{G}^{-1}\boldsymbol{B}\boldsymbol{H}^{-1}\boldsymbol{B}'\boldsymbol{G}^{-1} & \boldsymbol{G}^{-1}\boldsymbol{B}\boldsymbol{H}^{-1} \\ \boldsymbol{H}^{-1}\boldsymbol{B}'\boldsymbol{G}^{-1} & \boldsymbol{I}_n - \boldsymbol{H}^{-1} \end{pmatrix}.$$

Solution
We simply check that $ZZ^{-1} = I_{m+n}$. We need to show that

$$AG^{-1} - AG^{-1}BH^{-1}B'G^{-1} + BH^{-1}B'G^{-1} = I_m,$$
$$AG^{-1}BH^{-1} - BH^{-1} + BHH^{-1} = O,$$
$$B'G^{-1} - B'G^{-1}BH^{-1}B'G^{-1} = O,$$
$$B'G^{-1}BH^{-1} = I_n.$$

We obtain this by replacing A by $G - BB'$ and using the definition of H.

Exercise 8.51 (Determinant of the bordered Gramian)
(a) If $A + BB'$ is nonsingular, show that $|Z| = (-1)^n|A + BB'||B'(A + BB')^{-1}B|$.
(b) If we impose the stronger condition that A is nonsingular, then show that $|Z| = (-1)^n|A||B'A^{-1}B|$.
(c) Conclude that for positive definite A we have

$$|A + BB'||B'(A + BB')^{-1}B| = |A||B'A^{-1}B|.$$

Solution
We notice that

$$\begin{pmatrix} I_m & B \\ O & I_n \end{pmatrix} \begin{pmatrix} A & B \\ B' & O \end{pmatrix} = \begin{pmatrix} A + BB' & B \\ B' & O \end{pmatrix}.$$

The results then follow from Exercise 5.28.

8.3 Idempotent matrices

Exercise 8.52 (A diagonal idempotent) If A is idempotent and diagonal, what are its diagonal elements?

Solution
The equation $\lambda^2 = \lambda$ has roots 0 and 1 only. Consequently, for $\Lambda := \operatorname{diag}(\lambda_1, \dots \lambda_n)$, the equation $\Lambda^2 = \Lambda$ implies $\lambda_i^2 = \lambda_i$ for all i. Hence, an idempotent diagonal matrix has diagonal elements 0 and 1 only.

Exercise 8.53 (Transpose, powers, and complements) If A is idempotent, show that A', A^k $(k = 1, 2, \dots)$, and $I - A$ are also idempotent. Is $-A$ idempotent?

Solution
We have

$$(A')^2 = A'A' = (AA)' = A',$$

$$(A^k)^2 = (A^2)^k = A^k,$$

and

$$(\boldsymbol{I}-\boldsymbol{A})^2=\boldsymbol{I}-\boldsymbol{A}-\boldsymbol{A}+\boldsymbol{A}^2=\boldsymbol{I}-\boldsymbol{A}-\boldsymbol{A}+\boldsymbol{A}=\boldsymbol{I}-\boldsymbol{A}.$$

However, $(-\boldsymbol{A})^2=\boldsymbol{A}\neq-\boldsymbol{A}$, so that $-\boldsymbol{A}$ is not idempotent.

Exercise 8.54 (Block diagonality) Show that $\boldsymbol{A}$ and $\boldsymbol{B}$ are idempotent if and only if

$$\boldsymbol{Z}:=\begin{pmatrix}\boldsymbol{A} & \mathbf{O}\\ \mathbf{O} & \boldsymbol{B}\end{pmatrix}$$

is idempotent.

Solution
We have

$$\boldsymbol{Z}^2=\begin{pmatrix}\boldsymbol{A} & \mathbf{O}\\ \mathbf{O} & \boldsymbol{B}\end{pmatrix}\begin{pmatrix}\boldsymbol{A} & \mathbf{O}\\ \mathbf{O} & \boldsymbol{B}\end{pmatrix}=\begin{pmatrix}\boldsymbol{A}^2 & \mathbf{O}\\ \mathbf{O} & \boldsymbol{B}^2\end{pmatrix}.$$

Hence, $\boldsymbol{Z}^2=\boldsymbol{Z}$ if and only if $\boldsymbol{A}^2=\boldsymbol{A}$ and $\boldsymbol{B}^2=\boldsymbol{B}$.

Exercise 8.55 (A nonsymmetric idempotent) Give an example of an idempotent matrix of rank >1 that is not symmetric.

Solution
There are many nonsymmetric idempotent matrices, see Exercise 2.37(c) for an example with $\operatorname{rk}(\boldsymbol{A})=1$. A more general example is provided by the matrix $\boldsymbol{A}(\boldsymbol{B}'\boldsymbol{A})^{-1}\boldsymbol{B}'$, because

$$\boldsymbol{A}(\boldsymbol{B}'\boldsymbol{A})^{-1}\boldsymbol{B}'\boldsymbol{A}(\boldsymbol{B}'\boldsymbol{A})^{-1}\boldsymbol{B}'=\boldsymbol{A}(\boldsymbol{B}'\boldsymbol{A})^{-1}\boldsymbol{B}',$$

if $\boldsymbol{A}$ and $\boldsymbol{B}$ are matrices of the same order, and $\boldsymbol{B}'\boldsymbol{A}$ has full rank.

Exercise 8.56 (Eigenvalues of idempotent)
(a) Show that the eigenvalues of an idempotent matrix are 0 and 1.
(b) Does the converse hold?

Solution
(a) Let $\boldsymbol{A}$ be idempotent. Then $\boldsymbol{A}^2=\boldsymbol{A}$. Thus, if $\boldsymbol{A}\boldsymbol{x}=\lambda\boldsymbol{x}$, we have

$$\lambda\boldsymbol{x}=\boldsymbol{A}\boldsymbol{x}=\boldsymbol{A}^2\boldsymbol{x}=\lambda\boldsymbol{A}\boldsymbol{x}=\lambda^2\boldsymbol{x}$$

and hence $\lambda=\lambda^2$. This implies that $\lambda=0$ or $\lambda=1$.
(b) No. For example

$$\begin{pmatrix}1&1&1\\0&1&1\\0&0&0\end{pmatrix}\begin{pmatrix}1&1&1\\0&1&1\\0&0&0\end{pmatrix}=\begin{pmatrix}1&2&2\\0&1&1\\0&0&0\end{pmatrix},$$

despite the fact that the eigenvalues are 0 and 1.

Exercise 8.57 (A symmetric matrix with $0, 1$ eigenvalues is idempotent) We know from Exercise 8.56 that a matrix may have only eigenvalues 0 and 1 and not be idempotent. Now show that if $\boldsymbol{A}$ is symmetric and has only eigenvalues 0 and 1, it is idempotent.

Solution

If $\boldsymbol{A}$ is symmetric, it can be diagonalized: $\boldsymbol{S}'\boldsymbol{A}\boldsymbol{S} = \boldsymbol{\Lambda}$ (diagonal), $\boldsymbol{S}'\boldsymbol{S} = \boldsymbol{I}$. If the eigenvalues are only 0 and 1, then $\boldsymbol{\Lambda}^2 = \boldsymbol{\Lambda}$, so that

$$\boldsymbol{A}^2 = \boldsymbol{S}\boldsymbol{\Lambda}\boldsymbol{S}'\boldsymbol{S}\boldsymbol{\Lambda}\boldsymbol{S}' = \boldsymbol{S}\boldsymbol{\Lambda}^2\boldsymbol{S}' = \boldsymbol{S}\boldsymbol{\Lambda}\boldsymbol{S}' = \boldsymbol{A}.$$

Exercise 8.58 (Ordering of idempotent matrices) Let $\boldsymbol{A}$ and $\boldsymbol{B}$ be symmetric idempotent matrices of the same order. Show that $\boldsymbol{A} \geq \boldsymbol{B}$ if and only if $\boldsymbol{A}\boldsymbol{B} = \boldsymbol{B}$.

Solution

If $\boldsymbol{A}\boldsymbol{B} = \boldsymbol{B}$, then

$$(\boldsymbol{A} - \boldsymbol{B})^2 = \boldsymbol{A}^2 - \boldsymbol{A}\boldsymbol{B} - \boldsymbol{B}\boldsymbol{A} + \boldsymbol{B}^2 = \boldsymbol{A} - \boldsymbol{B},$$

because $\boldsymbol{A}\boldsymbol{B} = \boldsymbol{B} = \boldsymbol{B}' = \boldsymbol{B}\boldsymbol{A}$. Since $\boldsymbol{A} - \boldsymbol{B}$ is symmetric, it is symmetric idempotent, hence positive semidefinite (because its eigenvalues are nonnegative, namely 0 and 1).

To prove the converse, let $\boldsymbol{A} \geq \boldsymbol{B}$ and define $\boldsymbol{C} := (\boldsymbol{I} - \boldsymbol{A})\boldsymbol{B}$. Clearly, $\boldsymbol{C}'\boldsymbol{C} \geq \mathbf{O}$. But also

$$\boldsymbol{C}'\boldsymbol{C} = \boldsymbol{B}(\boldsymbol{I} - \boldsymbol{A})\boldsymbol{B} = -\boldsymbol{B}(\boldsymbol{A} - \boldsymbol{B})\boldsymbol{B} \leq \mathbf{O}.$$

This implies that $\boldsymbol{C}'\boldsymbol{C} = \mathbf{O}$, and hence that $\boldsymbol{C} = \mathbf{O}$, that is, $\boldsymbol{A}\boldsymbol{B} = \boldsymbol{B}$.

Exercise 8.59 (Extreme cases: $\boldsymbol{A} = \mathbf{O}$ and $\boldsymbol{A} = \boldsymbol{I}$) Let $\boldsymbol{A}$ be an idempotent $n \times n$ matrix.

(a) Show that $\operatorname{rk}(\boldsymbol{A}) = n$ if and only if $\boldsymbol{A} = \boldsymbol{I}_n$.

(b) Show that all eigenvalues of $\boldsymbol{A}$ are zero if and only if $\boldsymbol{A} = \mathbf{O}$.

Solution

(a) If $\boldsymbol{A}$ is the identity matrix, then obviously $\operatorname{rk}(\boldsymbol{A}) = n$. Conversely, if $\boldsymbol{A}$ is nonsingular, then

$$\boldsymbol{A} = \boldsymbol{A}^{-1}\boldsymbol{A}\boldsymbol{A} = \boldsymbol{A}^{-1}\boldsymbol{A} = \boldsymbol{I}_n.$$

(b) If $\boldsymbol{A}$ is the null matrix, then all its eigenvalues are 0. Conversely, assume that all eigenvalues of $\boldsymbol{A}$ are 0. By Schur's decomposition theorem (Exercise 7.62) there exists a unitary matrix $\boldsymbol{S}$ and a *strictly* upper triangular matrix $\boldsymbol{M}$ such that $\boldsymbol{S}^*\boldsymbol{A}\boldsymbol{S} = \boldsymbol{M}$. Since $\boldsymbol{M}$ is strictly upper triangular, we know from Exercise 7.55(a) that $\boldsymbol{M}^n = \mathbf{O}$. Hence, $\boldsymbol{A}^n = \boldsymbol{S}\boldsymbol{M}^n\boldsymbol{S}^* = \mathbf{O}$. But $\boldsymbol{A}$ is idempotent. So, $\boldsymbol{A}^n = \boldsymbol{A}\boldsymbol{A}\ldots\boldsymbol{A} = \boldsymbol{A}$. We conclude that $\boldsymbol{A} = \mathbf{O}$.

Exercise 8.60 (Similarity of idempotent) If $\boldsymbol{A}$ is an idempotent $n \times n$ matrix with r eigenvalues equal to 1 (and $n-r$ eigenvalues equal to 0), show that there exists a nonsingular matrix $\boldsymbol{T}$ and a unitary matrix $\boldsymbol{S}$ such that

$$\boldsymbol{T}^{-1}\boldsymbol{A}\boldsymbol{T} = \begin{pmatrix} \boldsymbol{I}_r & \mathbf{O} \\ \mathbf{O} & \mathbf{O} \end{pmatrix} \quad \text{and} \quad \boldsymbol{S}^*\boldsymbol{A}\boldsymbol{S} = \begin{pmatrix} \boldsymbol{I}_r & \boldsymbol{Q} \\ \mathbf{O} & \mathbf{O} \end{pmatrix}$$

for some matrix $\boldsymbol{Q}$.

Solution

To prove the first result, we use Jordan's theorem (Exercise 7.79) by which there exists a nonsingular matrix $\boldsymbol{T}$ such that $\boldsymbol{T}^{-1}\boldsymbol{A}\boldsymbol{T} = \boldsymbol{J}$ (Jordan form). Since the eigenvalues of $\boldsymbol{A}$ are 1 and 0 only, we partition

$$\boldsymbol{J} := \begin{pmatrix} \boldsymbol{J}_1 & \mathbf{O} \\ \mathbf{O} & \boldsymbol{J}_0 \end{pmatrix}$$

with

$$\boldsymbol{J}_1 := \begin{pmatrix} 1 & \beta_1 & 0 & \dots & 0 \\ 0 & 1 & \beta_2 & \dots & 0 \\ \vdots & \vdots & \vdots & & \vdots \\ 0 & 0 & 0 & \dots & \beta_{r-1} \\ 0 & 0 & 0 & \dots & 1 \end{pmatrix}, \quad \boldsymbol{J}_0 := \begin{pmatrix} 0 & \gamma_1 & 0 & \dots & 0 \\ 0 & 0 & \gamma_2 & \dots & 0 \\ \vdots & \vdots & \vdots & & \vdots \\ 0 & 0 & 0 & \dots & \gamma_{n-r-1} \\ 0 & 0 & 0 & \dots & 0 \end{pmatrix},$$

where the β_i and γ_j are either 0 or 1. Since $\boldsymbol{A}$ is idempotent, so is $\boldsymbol{J}$ and so are $\boldsymbol{J}_1$ and $\boldsymbol{J}_0$. But $\boldsymbol{J}_1^2 = \boldsymbol{J}_1$ implies that $\boldsymbol{J}_1$ is diagonal and $\boldsymbol{J}_0^2 = \boldsymbol{J}_0$ implies that $\boldsymbol{J}_0$ is diagonal; see also Exercise 9.17. Hence, all β_i and γ_j are zero and the first result follows.

To prove the second result, we use Schur's theorem (Exercise 7.62) by which there exists a unitary matrix $\boldsymbol{S}$ such that $\boldsymbol{S}^*\boldsymbol{A}\boldsymbol{S} = \boldsymbol{M}$ (upper triangular). Since the eigenvalues of $\boldsymbol{A}$ are 1 and 0 only, we partition

$$\boldsymbol{M} := \begin{pmatrix} \boldsymbol{P} & \boldsymbol{Q} \\ \mathbf{O} & \boldsymbol{R} \end{pmatrix},$$

where $\boldsymbol{P}$ is a unit upper triangular $r \times r$ matrix (that is, it has only ones on the diagonal), and $\boldsymbol{R}$ a *strictly* upper triangular matrix. Since $\boldsymbol{A}$ is idempotent, so is $\boldsymbol{M}$ and hence

$$\begin{pmatrix} \boldsymbol{P}^2 & \boldsymbol{P}\boldsymbol{Q} + \boldsymbol{Q}\boldsymbol{R} \\ \mathbf{O} & \boldsymbol{R}^2 \end{pmatrix} = \begin{pmatrix} \boldsymbol{P} & \boldsymbol{Q} \\ \mathbf{O} & \boldsymbol{R} \end{pmatrix}.$$

This implies that $\boldsymbol{P}$ is idempotent; it is nonsingular, hence, $\boldsymbol{P} = \boldsymbol{I}_r$ (Exercise 8.59(a)). Also, $\boldsymbol{R}$ is idempotent and all its eigenvalues are zero; hence, $\boldsymbol{R} = \mathbf{O}$ (Exercise 8.59(b)). Thus,

$$\boldsymbol{M} = \begin{pmatrix} \boldsymbol{I}_r & \boldsymbol{Q} \\ \mathbf{O} & \mathbf{O} \end{pmatrix}.$$

Exercise 8.61 (Rank equals trace) For any idempotent matrix $\boldsymbol{A}$, show that $\operatorname{rk}(\boldsymbol{A}) = \operatorname{tr}(\boldsymbol{A})$.

Solution

We know from Exercise 8.60 that $\boldsymbol{S}^*\boldsymbol{A}\boldsymbol{S} = \boldsymbol{M}$, where $\boldsymbol{S}$ is unitary and

$$\boldsymbol{M} := \begin{pmatrix} \boldsymbol{I}_r & \boldsymbol{Q} \\ \mathrm{O} & \mathrm{O} \end{pmatrix}.$$

Hence, $\operatorname{rk}(\boldsymbol{A}) = \operatorname{rk}(\boldsymbol{M}) = r$ and $\operatorname{tr}(\boldsymbol{A}) = \operatorname{tr}(\boldsymbol{M}) = r$.

Exercise 8.62 (A necessary and sufficient condition for idempotency, 1) Show that a symmetric $n \times n$ matrix $\boldsymbol{A}$ is idempotent if and only if

$$\operatorname{rk}(\boldsymbol{A}) + \operatorname{rk}(\boldsymbol{I}_n - \boldsymbol{A}) = n.$$

Solution

Let n_0 denote the number of zero eigenvalues of $\boldsymbol{A}$, and n_1 the number of unit eigenvalues. Then, $\operatorname{rk}(\boldsymbol{A}) = n - n_0$ and $\operatorname{rk}(\boldsymbol{I}_n - \boldsymbol{A}) = n - n_1$. Hence,

$$\operatorname{rk}(\boldsymbol{A}) + \operatorname{rk}(\boldsymbol{I}_n - \boldsymbol{A}) = n + (n - n_0 - n_1),$$

and this equals n if and only if $n_0 + n_1 = n$, that is, if and only if $\boldsymbol{A}$ only has eigenvalues 0 and 1. By Exercise 8.57, this happens (because of the symmetry) if and only if $\boldsymbol{A}$ is idempotent.

Exercise 8.63 (A necessary and sufficient condition for idempotency, 2) In fact, the result of Exercise 8.62 holds generally. Thus, show that an $n \times n$ matrix $\boldsymbol{A}$ is idempotent if and only if

$$\operatorname{rk}(\boldsymbol{A}) + \operatorname{rk}(\boldsymbol{I}_n - \boldsymbol{A}) = n.$$

Solution

If $\boldsymbol{A}$ is idempotent, then $\boldsymbol{I}_n - \boldsymbol{A}$ is also idempotent. Hence,

$$\operatorname{rk}(\boldsymbol{A}) + \operatorname{rk}(\boldsymbol{I}_n - \boldsymbol{A}) = \operatorname{tr}(\boldsymbol{A}) + \operatorname{tr}(\boldsymbol{I}_n - \boldsymbol{A}) = \operatorname{tr}(\boldsymbol{A} + \boldsymbol{I}_n - \boldsymbol{A}) = \operatorname{tr}(\boldsymbol{I}_n) = n.$$

To prove the converse, let $\boldsymbol{A}$ possess r nonzero eigenvalues. We establish first that $\operatorname{rk}(\boldsymbol{A}) = r$. By Exercise 7.66, $\operatorname{rk}(\boldsymbol{A}) \geq r$. The matrix $\boldsymbol{I}_n - \boldsymbol{A}$ has $n - r$ eigenvalues 1 and r other eigenvalues. Hence, $\boldsymbol{I}_n - \boldsymbol{A}$ has *at least* $n - r$ nonzero eigenvalues, so that $\operatorname{rk}(\boldsymbol{I}_n - \boldsymbol{A}) \geq n - r$. But $\operatorname{rk}(\boldsymbol{A}) + \operatorname{rk}(\boldsymbol{I}_n - \boldsymbol{A}) = n$. Hence, $\operatorname{rk}(\boldsymbol{A}) = r$ and $\operatorname{rk}(\boldsymbol{I}_n - \boldsymbol{A}) = n - r$.

Now consider the Jordan decomposition of $\boldsymbol{A}$,

$$\boldsymbol{T}^{-1}\boldsymbol{A}\boldsymbol{T} = \begin{pmatrix} \boldsymbol{J}_1 & \mathrm{O} \\ \mathrm{O} & \boldsymbol{J}_0 \end{pmatrix},$$

where $\boldsymbol{J}_1$ has the r nonzero eigenvalues of $\boldsymbol{A}$ on the diagonal and $\boldsymbol{J}_0$ the $n - r$ zero eigenvalues. Since $\operatorname{rk}(\boldsymbol{J}_1) = r$ and $\operatorname{rk}(\boldsymbol{J}_1) + \operatorname{rk}(\boldsymbol{J}_0) = \operatorname{rk}(\boldsymbol{A}) = r$, it follows that $\operatorname{rk}(\boldsymbol{J}_0) = 0$;

hence, $\boldsymbol{J}_0 = \mathbf{O}$. Similarly we write the Jordan decomposition of $\boldsymbol{I}_n - \boldsymbol{A}$ as

$$\boldsymbol{T}^{-1}(\boldsymbol{I}_n - \boldsymbol{A})\boldsymbol{T} = \begin{pmatrix} \boldsymbol{I}_r - \boldsymbol{J}_1 & \mathbf{O} \\ \mathbf{O} & \boldsymbol{I}_{n-r} - \boldsymbol{J}_0 \end{pmatrix} = \begin{pmatrix} \boldsymbol{I}_r - \boldsymbol{J}_1 & \mathbf{O} \\ \mathbf{O} & \boldsymbol{I}_{n-r} \end{pmatrix}.$$

Since $\operatorname{rk}(\boldsymbol{I}_n - \boldsymbol{A}) = n - r$, it follows that $\operatorname{rk}(\boldsymbol{I}_r - \boldsymbol{J}_1) = 0$; hence, $\boldsymbol{J}_1 = \boldsymbol{I}_r$. We conclude that

$$\boldsymbol{A}(\boldsymbol{I}_n - \boldsymbol{A}) = \boldsymbol{T}\begin{pmatrix} \boldsymbol{I}_r & \mathbf{O} \\ \mathbf{O} & \mathbf{O} \end{pmatrix}\boldsymbol{T}^{-1}\boldsymbol{T}\begin{pmatrix} \mathbf{O} & \mathbf{O} \\ \mathbf{O} & \boldsymbol{I}_{n-r} \end{pmatrix}\boldsymbol{T}^{-1} = \mathbf{O},$$

and hence $\boldsymbol{A}^2 = \boldsymbol{A}$.

Exercise 8.64 (Idempotency of $\boldsymbol{A} + \boldsymbol{B}$) Let $\boldsymbol{A}$ and $\boldsymbol{B}$ be idempotent matrices of the same order.
(a) Show that $\boldsymbol{A} + \boldsymbol{B}$ is idempotent if and only if $\boldsymbol{AB} = \boldsymbol{BA} = \mathbf{O}$.
(b) If $\boldsymbol{A} + \boldsymbol{B}$ is idempotent, show that $\operatorname{rk}(\boldsymbol{A} + \boldsymbol{B}) = \operatorname{rk}(\boldsymbol{A}) + \operatorname{rk}(\boldsymbol{B})$.

Solution
(a) If $\boldsymbol{AB} = \boldsymbol{BA} = \mathbf{O}$, then

$$(\boldsymbol{A}+\boldsymbol{B})(\boldsymbol{A}+\boldsymbol{B}) = \boldsymbol{A}^2 + \boldsymbol{AB} + \boldsymbol{BA} + \boldsymbol{B}^2 = \boldsymbol{A}^2 + \boldsymbol{B}^2 = \boldsymbol{A} + \boldsymbol{B}.$$

Conversely, if $\boldsymbol{A} + \boldsymbol{B}$ is idempotent, then $\boldsymbol{AB} + \boldsymbol{BA} = \mathbf{O}$. Premultiplying by $\boldsymbol{A}$ gives $\boldsymbol{AB} + \boldsymbol{ABA} = \mathbf{O}$. Postmultiplying by $\boldsymbol{A}$ gives $\boldsymbol{ABA} + \boldsymbol{BA} = \mathbf{O}$. Hence, $\boldsymbol{AB} = \boldsymbol{BA} = \mathbf{O}$.
(b) If $\boldsymbol{A} + \boldsymbol{B}$ is idempotent, then

$$\operatorname{rk}(\boldsymbol{A} + \boldsymbol{B}) = \operatorname{tr}(\boldsymbol{A} + \boldsymbol{B}) = \operatorname{tr}(\boldsymbol{A}) + \operatorname{tr}(\boldsymbol{B}) = \operatorname{rk}(\boldsymbol{A}) + \operatorname{rk}(\boldsymbol{B}).$$

Exercise 8.65 (Condition for A and B to both be idempotent) If $\boldsymbol{AB} = \boldsymbol{A}$ and $\boldsymbol{BA} = \boldsymbol{B}$, show that both $\boldsymbol{A}$ and $\boldsymbol{B}$ are idempotent.

Solution
We have

$$\boldsymbol{A}^2 = (\boldsymbol{AB})^2 = \boldsymbol{ABAB} = \boldsymbol{ABA} = \boldsymbol{AB} = \boldsymbol{A}$$

and

$$\boldsymbol{B}^2 = (\boldsymbol{BA})^2 = \boldsymbol{BABA} = \boldsymbol{BAB} = \boldsymbol{BA} = \boldsymbol{B}.$$

Exercise 8.66 (Decomposition of symmetric idempotent matrices) Let $\boldsymbol{A}$ be a *symmetric* idempotent $n \times n$ matrix of rank r.
(a) Show that $\boldsymbol{A}$ is positivesemidefinite.

(b) Show that a semi-orthogonal $n \times r$ matrix $\boldsymbol{S}$ exists such that

$$\boldsymbol{A} = \boldsymbol{S}\boldsymbol{S}', \quad \boldsymbol{S}'\boldsymbol{S} = \boldsymbol{I}_r.$$

Solution

(a) If $\boldsymbol{A}$ is idempotent *and* symmetric, then it is positive semidefinite, because all its eigenvalues are nonnegative.

(b) This follows directly from Exercise 8.21, using the fact the eigenvalues are only 0 and 1. Let us present a more direct proof. It follows from the diagonalization theorem for symmetric matrices (Exercise 7.46) that an orthogonal matrix $\tilde{\boldsymbol{S}}$ exists such that

$$\tilde{\boldsymbol{S}}'\boldsymbol{A}\tilde{\boldsymbol{S}} = \boldsymbol{\Lambda} = \begin{pmatrix} \boldsymbol{I}_r & \mathbf{O} \\ \mathbf{O} & \mathbf{O} \end{pmatrix}.$$

Let us partition $\tilde{\boldsymbol{S}} := (\boldsymbol{S} : \boldsymbol{T})$. Then, $\boldsymbol{S}'\boldsymbol{S} = \boldsymbol{I}_r$ and

$$\boldsymbol{A} = \tilde{\boldsymbol{S}}\boldsymbol{\Lambda}\tilde{\boldsymbol{S}}' = \boldsymbol{S}\boldsymbol{I}_r\boldsymbol{S}' + \boldsymbol{T}\mathbf{O}\boldsymbol{T}' = \boldsymbol{S}\boldsymbol{S}'.$$

Exercise 8.67 (Orthogonal complements and idempotency) Let $\boldsymbol{A} := (\boldsymbol{A}_1 : \boldsymbol{A}_2)$ be a square matrix of order n. If $\operatorname{rk}(\boldsymbol{A}_1) + \operatorname{rk}(\boldsymbol{A}_2) = n$ and $\boldsymbol{A}_1'\boldsymbol{A}_2 = \mathbf{O}$, show that

$$\boldsymbol{A}_1(\boldsymbol{A}_1'\boldsymbol{A}_1)^{-1}\boldsymbol{A}_1' + \boldsymbol{A}_2(\boldsymbol{A}_2'\boldsymbol{A}_2)^{-1}\boldsymbol{A}_2' = \boldsymbol{I}_n.$$

Solution

Consider the matrix

$$\boldsymbol{A}'\boldsymbol{A} = \begin{pmatrix} \boldsymbol{A}_1'\boldsymbol{A}_1 & \boldsymbol{A}_1'\boldsymbol{A}_2 \\ \boldsymbol{A}_2'\boldsymbol{A}_1 & \boldsymbol{A}_2'\boldsymbol{A}_2 \end{pmatrix} = \begin{pmatrix} \boldsymbol{A}_1'\boldsymbol{A}_1 & \mathbf{O} \\ \mathbf{O} & \boldsymbol{A}_2'\boldsymbol{A}_2 \end{pmatrix}.$$

Since $\boldsymbol{A}$ is nonsingular, $\boldsymbol{A}'\boldsymbol{A}$ is nonsingular too (because $\boldsymbol{A}$ is square), and so are $\boldsymbol{A}_1'\boldsymbol{A}_1$ and $\boldsymbol{A}_2'\boldsymbol{A}_2$. Let $\boldsymbol{A}_1$ have n_1 columns and let $\boldsymbol{A}_2$ have $n_2 = n - n_1$ columns. Then $\operatorname{rk}(\boldsymbol{A}_1) = n_1$ and $\operatorname{rk}(\boldsymbol{A}_2) = n_2$. We now present two proofs. The first proof is based on the fact that $\boldsymbol{A}(\boldsymbol{A}'\boldsymbol{A})^{-1}\boldsymbol{A}' = \boldsymbol{I}_n$. This gives

$$\begin{aligned} \boldsymbol{I}_n = \boldsymbol{A}(\boldsymbol{A}'\boldsymbol{A})^{-1}\boldsymbol{A}' &= (\boldsymbol{A}_1 : \boldsymbol{A}_2) \begin{pmatrix} \boldsymbol{A}_1'\boldsymbol{A}_1 & \mathbf{O} \\ \mathbf{O} & \boldsymbol{A}_2'\boldsymbol{A}_2 \end{pmatrix}^{-1} \begin{pmatrix} \boldsymbol{A}_1' \\ \boldsymbol{A}_2' \end{pmatrix} \\ &= \boldsymbol{A}_1(\boldsymbol{A}_1'\boldsymbol{A}_1)^{-1}\boldsymbol{A}_1' + \boldsymbol{A}_2(\boldsymbol{A}_2'\boldsymbol{A}_2)^{-1}\boldsymbol{A}_2'. \end{aligned}$$

In the second proof we define $\boldsymbol{C}_1 := \boldsymbol{A}_1(\boldsymbol{A}_1'\boldsymbol{A}_1)^{-1}\boldsymbol{A}_1'$ and $\boldsymbol{C}_2 := \boldsymbol{A}_2(\boldsymbol{A}_2'\boldsymbol{A}_2)^{-1}\boldsymbol{A}_2'$. Then $\boldsymbol{C}_1$ and $\boldsymbol{C}_2$ are idempotent, and $\boldsymbol{C}_1\boldsymbol{C}_2 = \boldsymbol{C}_2\boldsymbol{C}_1 = \mathbf{O}$. Hence, by Exercise 8.64, $\boldsymbol{C}_1 + \boldsymbol{C}_2$ is idempotent, and

$$\operatorname{rk}(\boldsymbol{C}_1 + \boldsymbol{C}_2) = \operatorname{rk}(\boldsymbol{C}_1) + \operatorname{rk}(\boldsymbol{C}_2) = \operatorname{rk}(\boldsymbol{A}_1) + \operatorname{rk}(\boldsymbol{A}_2) = n,$$

because $\operatorname{rk}(\boldsymbol{A}_1(\boldsymbol{A}_1'\boldsymbol{A}_1)^{-1}\boldsymbol{A}_1') = \operatorname{rk}((\boldsymbol{A}_1'\boldsymbol{A}_1)^{-1}\boldsymbol{A}_1'\boldsymbol{A}_1) = \operatorname{rk}(\boldsymbol{I}_{n_1}) = \operatorname{rk}(\boldsymbol{A}_1)$, and similarly with $\boldsymbol{A}_2$. It follows that $\boldsymbol{C}_1 + \boldsymbol{C}_2$ is idempotent and nonsingular; hence, $\boldsymbol{C}_1 + \boldsymbol{C}_2 = \boldsymbol{I}_n$ (Exercise 8.59(a)).

Exercise 8.68 (A fundamental matrix in econometrics, 1) Let $\boldsymbol{X}$ be a matrix of order $n \times k$ and rank k. The matrix $\boldsymbol{M} := \boldsymbol{I}_n - \boldsymbol{X}(\boldsymbol{X}'\boldsymbol{X})^{-1}\boldsymbol{X}'$ is a very important one in econometrics.
(a) Show that $\boldsymbol{M}$ is symmetric idempotent.
(b) Show that $\boldsymbol{M}\boldsymbol{X} = \mathbf{O}$.
(c) Show that $\operatorname{rk}(\boldsymbol{M}) = n - k$.

Solution
(a) This follows from

$$
\begin{aligned}
(\boldsymbol{I}_n - &\boldsymbol{X}(\boldsymbol{X}'\boldsymbol{X})^{-1}\boldsymbol{X}')(\boldsymbol{I}_n - \boldsymbol{X}(\boldsymbol{X}'\boldsymbol{X})^{-1}\boldsymbol{X}') \\
&= \boldsymbol{I}_n - \boldsymbol{X}(\boldsymbol{X}'\boldsymbol{X})^{-1}\boldsymbol{X}' - \boldsymbol{X}(\boldsymbol{X}'\boldsymbol{X})^{-1}\boldsymbol{X}' + \boldsymbol{X}(\boldsymbol{X}'\boldsymbol{X})^{-1}\boldsymbol{X}'\boldsymbol{X}(\boldsymbol{X}'\boldsymbol{X})^{-1}\boldsymbol{X}' \\
&= \boldsymbol{I}_n - \boldsymbol{X}(\boldsymbol{X}'\boldsymbol{X})^{-1}\boldsymbol{X}' - \boldsymbol{X}(\boldsymbol{X}'\boldsymbol{X})^{-1}\boldsymbol{X}' + \boldsymbol{X}(\boldsymbol{X}'\boldsymbol{X})^{-1}\boldsymbol{X}' \\
&= \boldsymbol{I}_n - \boldsymbol{X}(\boldsymbol{X}'\boldsymbol{X})^{-1}\boldsymbol{X}'.
\end{aligned}
$$

(b) We verify that

$$
\boldsymbol{M}\boldsymbol{X} = (\boldsymbol{I}_n - \boldsymbol{X}(\boldsymbol{X}'\boldsymbol{X})^{-1}\boldsymbol{X}')\boldsymbol{X} = \boldsymbol{X} - \boldsymbol{X}(\boldsymbol{X}'\boldsymbol{X})^{-1}\boldsymbol{X}'\boldsymbol{X} = \boldsymbol{X} - \boldsymbol{X} = \mathbf{O}.
$$

(c) Finally,

$$
\begin{aligned}
\operatorname{rk}(\boldsymbol{M}) = \operatorname{tr}(\boldsymbol{M}) &= \operatorname{tr}(\boldsymbol{I}_n - \boldsymbol{X}(\boldsymbol{X}'\boldsymbol{X})^{-1}\boldsymbol{X}') = \operatorname{tr}(\boldsymbol{I}_n) - \operatorname{tr}(\boldsymbol{X}(\boldsymbol{X}'\boldsymbol{X})^{-1}\boldsymbol{X}') \\
&= n - \operatorname{tr}(\boldsymbol{X}'\boldsymbol{X}(\boldsymbol{X}'\boldsymbol{X})^{-1}) = n - \operatorname{tr}(\boldsymbol{I}_k) = n - k.
\end{aligned}
$$

***Exercise 8.69 (A fundamental matrix in econometrics, 2)** Let $\boldsymbol{X}$ be a matrix of order $n \times k$ and rank k, let $\boldsymbol{M} := \boldsymbol{I}_n - \boldsymbol{X}(\boldsymbol{X}'\boldsymbol{X})^{-1}\boldsymbol{X}'$, and let $\boldsymbol{V}$ be positive definite of order n. Show that the following three statements are equivalent:
(a) $\boldsymbol{X}'\boldsymbol{V}^{-1}\boldsymbol{M} = \mathbf{O}$;
(b) $\left(\boldsymbol{X}'\boldsymbol{V}^{-1}\boldsymbol{X}\right)^{-1}\boldsymbol{X}'\boldsymbol{V}^{-1} = (\boldsymbol{X}'\boldsymbol{X})^{-1}\boldsymbol{X}'$;
(c) $\left(\boldsymbol{X}'\boldsymbol{V}^{-1}\boldsymbol{X}\right)^{-1} = (\boldsymbol{X}'\boldsymbol{X})^{-1}\boldsymbol{X}'\boldsymbol{V}\boldsymbol{X}(\boldsymbol{X}'\boldsymbol{X})^{-1}$.

Solution
We show this in three steps.
(a) $\iff$ (b): This follows from

$$
\begin{aligned}
\boldsymbol{X}'\boldsymbol{V}^{-1}\boldsymbol{M} = \mathbf{O} &\iff \boldsymbol{X}'\boldsymbol{V}^{-1} = \boldsymbol{X}'\boldsymbol{V}^{-1}\boldsymbol{X}(\boldsymbol{X}'\boldsymbol{X})^{-1}\boldsymbol{X}' \\
&\iff \left(\boldsymbol{X}'\boldsymbol{V}^{-1}\boldsymbol{X}\right)^{-1}\boldsymbol{X}'\boldsymbol{V}^{-1} = (\boldsymbol{X}'\boldsymbol{X})^{-1}\boldsymbol{X}'.
\end{aligned}
$$

(b) $\Longrightarrow$ (c): It suffices to postmultiply both sides of the equality

$$
\left(\boldsymbol{X}'\boldsymbol{V}^{-1}\boldsymbol{X}\right)^{-1}\boldsymbol{X}'\boldsymbol{V}^{-1} = (\boldsymbol{X}'\boldsymbol{X})^{-1}\boldsymbol{X}'
$$

by $\boldsymbol{V}\boldsymbol{X}(\boldsymbol{X}'\boldsymbol{X})^{-1}$.

(c) $\Longrightarrow$ (b): This is a little trickier. We have

$$\begin{aligned}
\left(X'V^{-1}X\right)^{-1} &= \left(X'X\right)^{-1} X'VX \left(X'X\right)^{-1} \\
&\Longrightarrow X'X\left(X'V^{-1}X\right)^{-1} X'X = X'VX \\
&\Longrightarrow X'V^{1/2}V^{-1/2}X\left(X'V^{-1}X\right)^{-1} X'V^{-1/2}V^{1/2}X = X'V^{1/2}V^{1/2}X \\
&\Longrightarrow X'V^{1/2}\left(I - V^{-1/2}X\left(X'V^{-1}X\right)^{-1} X'V^{-1/2}\right)V^{1/2}X = O.
\end{aligned}$$

Now we observe that the matrix $Q := I - V^{-1/2}X\left(X'V^{-1}X\right)^{-1}X'V^{-1/2}$ is symmetric idempotent. Therefore, the fact that

$$O = X'V^{1/2}QV^{1/2}X = X'V^{1/2}Q'QV^{1/2}X$$

implies that $QV^{1/2}X = O$, that is,

$$\left(I - V^{-1/2}X\left(X'V^{-1}X\right)^{-1} X'V^{-1/2}\right)V^{1/2}X = O.$$

Now premultiply both sides by $(X'X)^{-1}X'V^{1/2}$ and postmultiply both sides by $(X'X)^{-1}$, and we obtain the required equality. (Compare Exercise 12.29.)

Exercise 8.70 (Two projection results) Let A be a symmetric idempotent $n \times n$ matrix and let B be an $n \times m$ matrix of rank m.
(a) If $AB = B$ and $\operatorname{rk}(A) = \operatorname{rk}(B)$, show that $A = B(B'B)^{-1}B'$.
(b) If $AB = O$ and $\operatorname{rk}(A) + \operatorname{rk}(B) = n$, show that $A = I_n - B(B'B)^{-1}B'$.

Solution
(a) Let $C := A - B(B'B)^{-1}B'$. Then,

$$\begin{aligned}
C^2 &= (A - B(B'B)^{-1}B')(A - B(B'B)^{-1}B') \\
&= A^2 - AB(B'B)^{-1}B' - B(B'B)^{-1}B'A + B(B'B)^{-1}B'B(B'B)^{-1}B' \\
&= A - B(B'B)^{-1}B' - B(B'B)^{-1}B' + B(B'B)^{-1}B' = C.
\end{aligned}$$

Hence, C is idempotent and

$$\operatorname{rk}(C) = \operatorname{tr} C = \operatorname{tr} A - \operatorname{tr} B(B'B)^{-1}B' = \operatorname{rk}(A) - \operatorname{rk}(B) = 0,$$

so that $C = O$ and $A = B(B'B)^{-1}B'$.
(b) Let $C := I_n - A$. Then C is symmetric idempotent and $CB = B$. Also, $\operatorname{rk}(C) = n - \operatorname{rk}(A) = \operatorname{rk}(B)$. Hence, by (a), $C = B(B'B)^{-1}B'$ and hence $A = I_n - C = I_n - B(B'B)^{-1}B'$.

Exercise 8.71 (Deviations from the mean, 1)
(a) Show that the matrix $M := I_n - (1/n)\imath\imath'$ is symmetric idempotent.
(b) Show that the j-th component of the vector Mx is $x_j - \bar{x}$, where $\bar{x} := (1/n)\sum_{k=1}^{n} x_k$.
(c) Show that $M\imath = 0$.

(d) Prove that, for any $\boldsymbol{A} \geq \mathbf{O}$,

$$\operatorname{tr} \boldsymbol{A}^2 - \frac{1}{n}(\operatorname{tr} \boldsymbol{A})^2 \geq 0.$$

Solution

(a) This can be verified directly. Alternatively, it follows from Exercise 8.68(a) by taking $\boldsymbol{X} := \boldsymbol{\imath}$, and noting that $\boldsymbol{\imath}'\boldsymbol{\imath} = n$.

(b) Since $\bar{x} = \boldsymbol{\imath}'\boldsymbol{x}/n$, we have $\boldsymbol{M}\boldsymbol{x} = \boldsymbol{x} - (1/n)\boldsymbol{\imath}\boldsymbol{\imath}'\boldsymbol{x} = \boldsymbol{x} - \bar{x}\boldsymbol{\imath}$, and the j-th component of this vector is $x_j - \bar{x}$.

(c) If $\boldsymbol{x} := \boldsymbol{\imath}$ in (b), then $x_j - \bar{x} = 0$ for all j.

(d) Let $\boldsymbol{S}'\boldsymbol{A}\boldsymbol{S} = \boldsymbol{\Lambda}$ (diagonal) with $\boldsymbol{S}'\boldsymbol{S} = \boldsymbol{I}_n$, and let $\boldsymbol{\lambda}$ be the $n \times 1$ vector containing the eigenvalues, $\boldsymbol{\lambda} := (\lambda_1, \dots, \lambda_n)'$. Then,

$$\begin{aligned}
\operatorname{tr} \boldsymbol{A}^2 - \frac{1}{n}(\operatorname{tr} \boldsymbol{A})^2 &= \operatorname{tr}(\boldsymbol{S}\boldsymbol{\Lambda}\boldsymbol{S}')^2 - \frac{1}{n}(\operatorname{tr} \boldsymbol{S}\boldsymbol{\Lambda}\boldsymbol{S}')^2 \\
&= \operatorname{tr} \boldsymbol{\Lambda}^2 - \frac{1}{n}(\operatorname{tr} \boldsymbol{\Lambda})^2 = \boldsymbol{\lambda}'\boldsymbol{\lambda} - \frac{1}{n}(\boldsymbol{\imath}'\boldsymbol{\lambda})^2 \\
&= \boldsymbol{\lambda}'\left(\boldsymbol{I}_n - \frac{1}{n}\boldsymbol{\imath}\boldsymbol{\imath}'\right)\boldsymbol{\lambda} \geq 0,
\end{aligned}$$

because the matrix $\boldsymbol{I}_n - (1/n)\boldsymbol{\imath}\boldsymbol{\imath}'$ is symmetric idempotent, hence positive semidefinite.

Exercise 8.72 (Many idempotent matrices) Let $\boldsymbol{A}_1, \boldsymbol{A}_2, \dots, \boldsymbol{A}_m$ be symmetric idempotent $n \times n$ matrices with $\operatorname{rk}(\boldsymbol{A}_i) = r_i$, such that $\boldsymbol{A}_1 + \boldsymbol{A}_2 + \dots + \boldsymbol{A}_m = \boldsymbol{I}_n$.

(a) Show that $r_1 + r_2 + \dots + r_m = n$.

(b) Show that $\boldsymbol{A}_i + \boldsymbol{A}_j$ is symmetric idempotent $(i \neq j)$.

(c) Show that $\boldsymbol{A}_i\boldsymbol{A}_j = \mathbf{O}$ $(i \neq j)$.

Solution

(a) This follows from

$$\sum_{i=1}^m r_i = \sum_{i=1}^m \operatorname{tr}(\boldsymbol{A}_i) = \operatorname{tr} \sum_{i=1}^m \boldsymbol{A}_i = \operatorname{tr}(\boldsymbol{I}_n) = n.$$

(b) Let $\boldsymbol{B} := \boldsymbol{A}_i + \boldsymbol{A}_j$ and $\boldsymbol{C} := \boldsymbol{I}_n - \boldsymbol{B}$. For any two matrices $\boldsymbol{P}$ and $\boldsymbol{Q}$ (of the same order) we have $\operatorname{rk}(\boldsymbol{P} + \boldsymbol{Q}) \leq \operatorname{rk}(\boldsymbol{P}) + \operatorname{rk}(\boldsymbol{Q})$; see Exercise 4.14 or Exercise 5.51. Thus,

$$\begin{aligned}
n = \operatorname{rk}(\boldsymbol{I}_n) &= \operatorname{rk}(\boldsymbol{B} + \boldsymbol{C}) \leq \operatorname{rk}(\boldsymbol{B}) + \operatorname{rk}(\boldsymbol{C}) \\
&= \operatorname{rk}(\boldsymbol{A}_i + \boldsymbol{A}_j) + \operatorname{rk}\left(\sum_{k \notin \{i,j\}} \boldsymbol{A}_k\right) \leq \sum_{i=1}^m \operatorname{rk}(\boldsymbol{A}_i) = n.
\end{aligned}$$

Hence, $\operatorname{rk}(\boldsymbol{B}) + \operatorname{rk}(\boldsymbol{I} - \boldsymbol{B}) = n$. Exercise 8.63(b) then implies that $\boldsymbol{B}$ is idempotent.

(c) Since $\boldsymbol{A}_i$, $\boldsymbol{A}_j$, and $\boldsymbol{A}_i + \boldsymbol{A}_j$ are all idempotent, Exercise 8.64(a) implies that $\boldsymbol{A}_i\boldsymbol{A}_j = \mathbf{O}$.

Exercise 8.73 (A weighted sum of idempotent matrices) Let $\boldsymbol{A}_1, \boldsymbol{A}_2, \dots, \boldsymbol{A}_m$ be symmetric idempotent $n \times n$ matrices with $\operatorname{rk}(\boldsymbol{A}_i) = r_i$ such that $\boldsymbol{A}_1 + \boldsymbol{A}_2 + \cdots + \boldsymbol{A}_m = \boldsymbol{I}_n$. Define

$$\boldsymbol{A} := \alpha_1 \boldsymbol{A}_1 + \alpha_2 \boldsymbol{A}_2 + \cdots + \alpha_m \boldsymbol{A}_m.$$

(a) Show that the eigenvalues of $\boldsymbol{A}$ are given by α_i (with multiplicity r_i), $i = 1, \dots, m$.
(b) Hence, show that $|\boldsymbol{A}| = \alpha_1^{r_1} \alpha_2^{r_2} \dots \alpha_m^{r_m}$.
(c) If $\alpha_i \neq 0$ for all i, show that $\boldsymbol{A}^{-1} = \alpha_1^{-1} \boldsymbol{A}_1 + \alpha_2^{-1} \boldsymbol{A}_2 + \cdots + \alpha_m^{-1} \boldsymbol{A}_m$.

Solution
(a) Since $\boldsymbol{A}_i \boldsymbol{A}_j = \mathbf{O}$ $(i \neq j)$ by Exercise 8.72, we obtain $\boldsymbol{A}(\boldsymbol{A}_i \boldsymbol{x}) = \alpha_i(\boldsymbol{A}_i \boldsymbol{x})$ for any $\boldsymbol{x}$. Hence, α_i is an eigenvalue with multiplicity r_i, because we can choose r_i linearly independent combinations of the columns of $\boldsymbol{A}_i$.
(b) The determinant is the product of the eigenvalues.
(c) We verify by direct multiplication, using the fact that $\boldsymbol{A}_i \boldsymbol{A}_j = \mathbf{O}$ for all $i \neq j$.

Exercise 8.74 (Equicorrelation matrix)
(a) Obtain the eigenvalues of the $n \times n$ *equicorrelation* matrix

$$\boldsymbol{A} := \begin{pmatrix} 1 & t & \dots & t \\ t & 1 & \dots & t \\ \vdots & \vdots & & \vdots \\ t & t & \dots & 1 \end{pmatrix}.$$

(b) What is the determinant? And the inverse?
(c) For which values of t is $\boldsymbol{A}$ positive definite?
(d) Obtain the eigenvectors of $\boldsymbol{A}$.

Solution
(a) Let $\boldsymbol{B} := \boldsymbol{\imath}\boldsymbol{\imath}'/n$. Notice that $\boldsymbol{B}$ is symmetric idempotent with $\operatorname{rk}(\boldsymbol{B}) = 1$. Now,

$$\begin{aligned} \boldsymbol{A} &= \boldsymbol{I}_n + t(\boldsymbol{\imath}\boldsymbol{\imath}' - \boldsymbol{I}_n) = (1-t)\boldsymbol{I}_n + (nt)\boldsymbol{B} \\ &= ((n-1)t + 1)\boldsymbol{B} + (1-t)(\boldsymbol{I}_n - \boldsymbol{B}) = \alpha_1 \boldsymbol{B} + \alpha_2(\boldsymbol{I}_n - \boldsymbol{B}), \end{aligned}$$

with $\alpha_1 := (n-1)t + 1$ and $\alpha_2 := 1 - t$. Since $\boldsymbol{B}$ and $\boldsymbol{I}_n - \boldsymbol{B}$ are idempotent and sum to $\boldsymbol{I}_n$, the eigenvalues of $\boldsymbol{A}$ are α_1 (once) and α_2 ($n-1$ times).
(b) The determinant is

$$|\boldsymbol{A}| = \alpha_1 \alpha_2^{n-1} = ((n-1)t + 1)(1-t)^{n-1}.$$

For $t \neq 1$ and $t \neq -1/(n-1)$, the matrix $\boldsymbol{A}$ is nonsingular, and

$$\boldsymbol{A}^{-1} = \alpha_1^{-1} \boldsymbol{B} + \alpha_2^{-1}(\boldsymbol{I}_n - \boldsymbol{B}).$$

(c) $\boldsymbol{A}$ is positive definite if (and only if) $\alpha_1 > 0$ and $\alpha_2 > 0$. This happens for $-1/(n-1) < t < 1$.

(d) Since $\boldsymbol{A} = \alpha_1 \boldsymbol{B} + \alpha_2(\boldsymbol{I}_n - \boldsymbol{B})$, the eigenvectors of $\boldsymbol{A}$ are those of $\boldsymbol{B}$, namely $\boldsymbol{\imath}/\sqrt{n}$, together with any set of $n-1$ linearly independent vectors orthogonal to $\boldsymbol{\imath}$.

Exercise 8.75 (Deviations from the mean, 2) Find the eigenvalues and eigenvectors associated with the quadratic form $\sum_{i,j=1}^{n}(x_i - x_j)^2$.

Solution

We write, letting $\boldsymbol{x} := (x_1, \dots, x_n)'$,

$$\begin{aligned}\sum_{ij}(x_i - x_j)^2 &= \sum_{ij}(x_i^2 + x_j^2 - 2x_i x_j) \\ &= 2n\sum_i x_i^2 - 2\left(\sum_i x_i\right)^2 = (2n)\boldsymbol{x}'\boldsymbol{x} - 2(\boldsymbol{\imath}'\boldsymbol{x})^2 \\ &= (2n)\,\boldsymbol{x}'\left(\boldsymbol{I}_n - \frac{1}{n}\boldsymbol{\imath}\boldsymbol{\imath}'\right)\boldsymbol{x} = (2n)\boldsymbol{x}'\boldsymbol{M}\boldsymbol{x},\end{aligned}$$

where the matrix $\boldsymbol{M} := \boldsymbol{I}_n - (1/n)\boldsymbol{\imath}\boldsymbol{\imath}'$ is symmetric idempotent of rank $n-1$. Hence, $\boldsymbol{M}$ has eigenvalues 1 ($n-1$ times) and 0 (once). As a result, $2n\boldsymbol{M}$ has eigenvalues $2n$ ($n-1$ times) and 0 (once). The eigenvectors are $\boldsymbol{\imath}$ (associated with the zero eigenvalue) and any linearly independent set of $n-1$ vectors orthogonal to $\boldsymbol{\imath}$ (associated with the eigenvalue $2n$).

Notes

The important Cholesky decomposition (Exercise 8.23) was only proved for the case where $\boldsymbol{A}$ is positive definite (hence nonsingular). In fact, it holds also for positive semidefinite matrices; see Horn and Johnson (1985). The concept of contractions, needed in Exercise 8.48, is discussed in Zhan (2002). The bordered Gramian matrix (Exercise 8.49) is treated more fully in Magnus (1990). Exercise 8.58 comes from Liu and Polasek (1995). More results of the kind discussed in Exercise 8.72 can be found in Graybill and Marsaglia (1957). Ayres (1962, pp. 170–171) extends Exercise 8.73 to the representation of any diagonalizable matrix $\boldsymbol{A}$, the so-called *spectral decomposition of a matrix.* The idempotents form a matrix basis and the coefficients of the representation are the distinct eigenvalues of $\boldsymbol{A}$.

9

Matrix functions

This chapter is concerned with using powers of an $n \times n$ matrix $\boldsymbol{A}$ to represent an $n \times n$ matrix function $\boldsymbol{F}(\boldsymbol{A})$. Simple examples of matrix functions are the powers $\boldsymbol{A}^p$ themselves, first encountered in Chapter 2, and the inverse $\boldsymbol{A}^{-1}$, defined in Chapter 4. In order to understand how matrix functions should be defined, let us reconsider the notion of a positive definite matrix. This is a matrix that is supposed to generalize the idea of a positive number to matrices. We did *not* define a positive definite matrix to be a matrix all of whose elements are positive. (Such matrices play a role in some areas of statistics and mathematical economics; they are called *positive matrices*.) Our definition was equivalent to requiring that all *eigenvalues* of $\boldsymbol{A}$ are positive. In the same way, we shall see that a matrix function is closely related to the same function defined on the eigenvalues of $\boldsymbol{A}$.

The eigenvalues of $\boldsymbol{A}$ are denoted by $\lambda_1, \dots, \lambda_n$, and we define the *spectral radius* of $\boldsymbol{A}$ as

$$\varrho(\boldsymbol{A}) := \max_i |\lambda_i|.$$

Suppose that there exists a *series expansion* (or *series representation*)

$$\boldsymbol{F}(\boldsymbol{A}) = \sum_{j=0}^{\infty} c_j \boldsymbol{A}^j,$$

where, by convention, we take $\boldsymbol{A}^0 = \boldsymbol{I}_n$. Series expansions are not unique, as we shall see in (a) below. The matrix series *converges absolutely* (or is *absolutely convergent*) if and only if each of the n^2 elements of the matrix $\sum_j c_j \boldsymbol{A}^j$ converges absolutely. This occurs if $\sum_{j=0}^{\infty} |c_j(\varrho(\boldsymbol{A}))^j| < \infty$ (see Exercise 9.19). The special case where the series terminates after m terms (that is, $c_j = 0$ or $\boldsymbol{A}^j = \mathbf{O}$ for $j \geq m$) is called a *matrix polynomial of order* $m-1$ or a *finite series*. The three functions most commonly encountered are the following:

(a) Let $\nu \in \mathbb{R}$ and $j = 0, 1, \dots$, and denote the binomial coefficients by

$$\binom{\nu}{j} := \frac{(\nu)(\nu-1)\cdots(\nu-j+1)}{j!},$$

sometimes also written by means of the combinations symbol C_j^ν (a generalization of this symbol will be introduced in Exercise 9.9). The *binomial expansion* of the power function, represented by

$$(\boldsymbol{I}_n + \boldsymbol{A})^\nu = \sum_{j=0}^{\infty} \binom{\nu}{j} \boldsymbol{A}^j,$$

converges absolutely for $\varrho(\boldsymbol{A}) < 1$ (Exercise 9.19(c)). There are alternative expansions for values of $\varrho(\boldsymbol{A})$ other than $\varrho(\boldsymbol{A}) < 1$; see Exercises 9.1 and 9.20. Absolute convergence occurs here when all eigenvalues of $\boldsymbol{A}$ lie within the unit circle. (In general, if a series converges absolutely for $\varrho(\boldsymbol{A}) < r$, then the largest such r is called the *radius of convergence* of the series.) Note the terminology: a unit circle is a circle in the complex plane of radius 1 with center at some point b, that is, the collection of points λ satisfying $|\lambda - b| < 1$. However, *the* unit circle refers to the unit circle with center 0.

(b) The *exponential function*

$$\exp(\boldsymbol{A}) := \sum_{j=0}^{\infty} \frac{1}{j!} \boldsymbol{A}^j,$$

also written as $e^{\boldsymbol{A}}$, converges absolutely for $\varrho(\boldsymbol{A}) < \infty$ (Exercise 9.19(b)). The resulting matrix $\boldsymbol{B} := \exp(\boldsymbol{A})$ is nonsingular, whatever the argument $\boldsymbol{A}$ (Exercise 9.21).

(c) The *logarithmic function* is defined implicitly as the inverse of the exponential function by $\log(\exp(\boldsymbol{A})) := \boldsymbol{A}$, or by $\exp(\log(\boldsymbol{B})) := \boldsymbol{B}$, where $\boldsymbol{B}$ is nonsingular. The function has the explicit representation

$$\log(\boldsymbol{I}_n + \boldsymbol{A}) = \sum_{j=0}^{\infty} \frac{(-1)^j}{j+1} \boldsymbol{A}^{j+1} = -\sum_{i=1}^{\infty} \frac{(-1)^i}{i} \boldsymbol{A}^i,$$

which converges absolutely for $\varrho(\boldsymbol{A}) < 1$, as implied by (a) and (b); see Exercises 9.8 and 9.19(c).

A series may or may not converge when the condition on $\varrho(\boldsymbol{A})$ is violated. For example, the expansion of $(\boldsymbol{I}_n + \boldsymbol{A})^2$ is $\boldsymbol{I}_n + 2\boldsymbol{A} + \boldsymbol{A}^2$, which terminates after the third term ($j = 2$) and is therefore convergent for any $\boldsymbol{A}$. Another example is given by the fact that the series expansion of $\log(1 + \lambda)$ converges to $\log 2$ for $\lambda = 1$, but not absolutely so:

$$\lim_{\lambda \to 1^-} \sum_{j=0}^{\infty} \frac{|-1|^j}{j+1} |\lambda^{j+1}| = \lim_{\lambda \to 1^-} \lambda \sum_{j=0}^{\infty} \frac{\lambda^j}{j+1} = \lim_{\lambda \to 1^-} -\log(1-\lambda) = \infty,$$

where the notation $\lambda \to 1^-$ indicates that the limit is taken from below. A series that converges, but not absolutely, is called *conditionally convergent*. For more on these issues, see Appendix A, where we also discuss the concept of principal value when a function is multiple-valued. Such is the case for the square root, the binomial, and the logarithmic functions.

We shall use Jordan's decomposition theorem to represent $\boldsymbol{F}(\boldsymbol{A}) := \sum_{j=0}^{\infty} c_j \boldsymbol{A}^j$ in terms of the scalar function $f(\lambda) := \sum_{j=0}^{\infty} c_j \lambda^j$. We recall from Chapter 7 that the Jordan decomposition of $\boldsymbol{A}$ is given by $\boldsymbol{A} = \boldsymbol{T}\boldsymbol{J}\boldsymbol{T}^{-1}$, where $\boldsymbol{J} := \operatorname{diag}(\boldsymbol{J}_{n_1}(\lambda_1), \dots, \boldsymbol{J}_{n_k}(\lambda_k))$, with $n_1 + \dots + n_k = n$ and the λ's need not be distinct. This implies (Exercise 9.18) that

$$\boldsymbol{F}(\boldsymbol{A}) = \boldsymbol{T}\boldsymbol{F}(\boldsymbol{J})\boldsymbol{T}^{-1},$$

where $\boldsymbol{F}(\boldsymbol{J}) := \operatorname{diag}(\boldsymbol{F}(\boldsymbol{J}_{n_1}(\lambda_1)), \dots, \boldsymbol{F}(\boldsymbol{J}_{n_k}(\lambda_k)))$ and

$$\boldsymbol{F}(\boldsymbol{J}_{n_i}(\lambda_i)) := \begin{pmatrix} f(\lambda_i) & f'(\lambda_i) & \dots & \frac{f^{(n_i-1)}(\lambda_i)}{(n_i-1)!} \\ 0 & f(\lambda_i) & \dots & \frac{f^{(n_i-2)}(\lambda_i)}{(n_i-2)!} \\ \vdots & \vdots & & \vdots \\ 0 & 0 & \dots & f(\lambda_i) \end{pmatrix}$$

for $i = 1, \dots, k$.

The Jordan representation of $\boldsymbol{F}(\boldsymbol{A})$ shows that of the scalar function $f(\lambda)$ only the derivatives up to order $n_i - 1$, evaluated at λ_i, are needed. So, any polynomial fitting these values will suffice. Let there be $l \le k$ distinct eigenvalues denoted by λ_s ($s = 1, \dots, l$) and let the maximal dimension of $\boldsymbol{J}_{n_i}(\lambda_s)$ for any given λ_s be denoted by m_s. For example, the matrix

$$\begin{pmatrix} 3 & 0 & 0 & 0 \\ 0 & 3 & 1 & 0 \\ 0 & 0 & 3 & 0 \\ 0 & 0 & 0 & 7 \end{pmatrix}$$

has $\boldsymbol{J} = \operatorname{diag}(\boldsymbol{J}_1(3), \boldsymbol{J}_2(3), \boldsymbol{J}_1(7))$ and the maximal dimension associated with $\lambda = 3$ is 2. Then, defining $m := \sum_{s=1}^{l} m_s$ and $p(\lambda) := \sum_{j=0}^{m-1} p_j \lambda^j$, we get (Exercise 9.29) the representation

$$\boldsymbol{F}(\boldsymbol{A}) := \sum_{j=0}^{\infty} c_j \boldsymbol{A}^j = p_0 \boldsymbol{I}_n + p_1 \boldsymbol{A} + \dots + p_{m-1} \boldsymbol{A}^{m-1},$$

where the polynomial's coefficients $p_0, \dots, p_{m-1}$ are obtained from equating

$$f^{(t)}(\lambda)\Big|_{\lambda_s} = p^{(t)}(\lambda)\Big|_{\lambda_s}$$

for $s = 1, \dots, l$ and $t = 0, 1, \dots, m_s - 1$. This representation has the advantage that we need not work out $\boldsymbol{T}$; it only requires us to solve a system of equations. Note that the scalar coefficients in the polynomial are in general *not* polynomial functions of theeigenvalues.

In fitting the polynomial of order $m-1$, we did not require $\boldsymbol{T}$ but we assumed $\boldsymbol{J}$ was known. Suppose instead that we only know $\operatorname{dg}(\boldsymbol{J})$, that is, the l distinct eigenvalues and their multiplicities. We can still use the approach of fitting a polynomial, albeit of order $n-1$ (hence larger than before), that reproduces the required derivatives of $f(\lambda_s)$. We obtain $q(\lambda) := \sum_{j=0}^{n-1} q_j \lambda^j$ from equating

$$f^{(t)}(\lambda)\Big|_{\lambda_s} = q^{(t)}(\lambda)\Big|_{\lambda_s}$$

for $s = 1, \dots, l$ and $t = 0, 1, \dots, r_s - 1$, where r_s denotes the multiplicity of λ_s. The coefficients of the polynomials $p(\lambda)$ and $q(\lambda)$ are not the same, in general; see Exercise 9.30.

9.1 Simple functions

Exercise 9.1 (Functions of diagonal matrices, numbers) Let

$$\boldsymbol{A} = \begin{pmatrix} a & 0 \\ 0 & b \end{pmatrix}.$$

(a) Obtain $\exp(\boldsymbol{A})$ in terms of a and b.
(b) For $|a| < 1$ and $|b| < 1$, obtain $(\boldsymbol{I}_n + \boldsymbol{A})^\nu$ and $\log(\boldsymbol{I}_n + \boldsymbol{A})$.
(c) For $|a| > 1$ and $|b| > 1$, obtain $(\boldsymbol{I}_n + \boldsymbol{A})^\nu$ assuming ν is an integer.

Solution
(a) By definition,

$$\exp(\boldsymbol{A}) = \sum_{j=0}^{\infty} \frac{1}{j!} \begin{pmatrix} a & 0 \\ 0 & b \end{pmatrix}^j = \sum_{j=0}^{\infty} \frac{1}{j!} \begin{pmatrix} a^j & 0 \\ 0 & b^j \end{pmatrix} = \begin{pmatrix} \sum_{j=0}^{\infty} \frac{a^j}{j!} & 0 \\ 0 & \sum_{j=0}^{\infty} \frac{b^j}{j!} \end{pmatrix}$$
$$= \begin{pmatrix} \exp(a) & 0 \\ 0 & \exp(b) \end{pmatrix}.$$

(b) Since the eigenvalues of $\boldsymbol{A}$, namely a and b, have moduli smaller than 1, we have $\varrho(\boldsymbol{A}) < 1$ and hence

$$(\boldsymbol{I}_n + \boldsymbol{A})^\nu = \sum_{j=0}^{\infty} \binom{\nu}{j} \begin{pmatrix} a^j & 0 \\ 0 & b^j \end{pmatrix} = \begin{pmatrix} (1+a)^\nu & 0 \\ 0 & (1+b)^\nu \end{pmatrix}$$

and

$$\log(\boldsymbol{I}_n + \boldsymbol{A}) = \sum_{j=0}^{\infty} \frac{(-1)^j}{j+1} \begin{pmatrix} a^{j+1} & 0 \\ 0 & b^{j+1} \end{pmatrix} = \begin{pmatrix} \log(1+a) & 0 \\ 0 & \log(1+b) \end{pmatrix}.$$

(c) If $|a| > 1$, $|b| > 1$, and ν is an integer (possibly negative), then we write

$$(\boldsymbol{I}_n + \boldsymbol{A})^\nu = \boldsymbol{A}^\nu (\boldsymbol{I}_n + \boldsymbol{A}^{-1})^\nu,$$

which can be proved by induction, using the fact that a matrix commutes with its own powers. The matrix $(\boldsymbol{I}_n + \boldsymbol{A}^{-1})^\nu$ has a convergent binomial expansion, because $\varrho(\boldsymbol{A}^{-1}) < 1$.

Thus,

$$(\boldsymbol{I}_n + \boldsymbol{A})^\nu = \boldsymbol{A}^\nu \left(\boldsymbol{I}_n + \boldsymbol{A}^{-1}\right)^\nu = \begin{pmatrix} a^\nu & 0 \\ 0 & b^\nu \end{pmatrix} \sum_{j=0}^{\infty} \binom{\nu}{j} \begin{pmatrix} a^{-j} & 0 \\ 0 & b^{-j} \end{pmatrix}$$

$$= \begin{pmatrix} a^\nu & 0 \\ 0 & b^\nu \end{pmatrix} \begin{pmatrix} \left(1+a^{-1}\right)^\nu & 0 \\ 0 & \left(1+b^{-1}\right)^\nu \end{pmatrix} = \begin{pmatrix} (1+a)^\nu & 0 \\ 0 & (1+b)^\nu \end{pmatrix}.$$

This shows that if the condition $\varrho(\boldsymbol{A}) < 1$ is *not* satisfied, it is sometimes still possible to express the function in terms of another series expansion.

Exercise 9.2 (Functions of diagonal matrices)
(a) Let $\boldsymbol{A} := \operatorname{diag}(a_1, \dots, a_n)$. If the series

$$\boldsymbol{F}(\boldsymbol{A}) := \sum_{j=0}^{\infty} c_j \boldsymbol{A}^j$$

is convergent, show that

$$\boldsymbol{F}(\boldsymbol{A}) = \operatorname{diag}(f(a_1), \dots, f(a_n)),$$

where $f(x) := \sum_{j=0}^{\infty} c_j x^j$.
(b) In particular, show that $\exp(\boldsymbol{I}_n) = (\mathrm{e})\boldsymbol{I}_n$.

Solution
(a) We have

$$\boldsymbol{F}(\boldsymbol{A}) = \sum_{j=0}^{\infty} c_j \boldsymbol{A}^j = \sum_{j=0}^{\infty} c_j (\operatorname{diag}(a_1, \dots, a_n))^j$$

$$= \operatorname{diag}\left(\sum_{j=0}^{\infty} c_j a_1^j, \dots, \sum_{j=0}^{\infty} c_j a_n^j\right) = \operatorname{diag}\left(f(a_1), \dots, f(a_n)\right).$$

(b) This follows by setting $c_j = 1/j!$, $\boldsymbol{A} = \boldsymbol{I}_n$, and $f(x) = \mathrm{e}^x$ in (a).

Exercise 9.3 (Nilpotent terminator) Let $\boldsymbol{A}$ be an $n \times n$ nilpotent matrix of index k. Show that

$$\boldsymbol{F}(\boldsymbol{A}) := \sum_{j=0}^{\infty} c_j \boldsymbol{A}^j$$

is a polynomial of finite order.

Solution
By definition, $\boldsymbol{A}^k = \mathbf{O}$, so that $\boldsymbol{A}^j = \mathbf{O}$ for all $j \geq k$. This implies that the series terminates after k terms.

Exercise 9.4 (Idempotent replicator) Let $\boldsymbol{A}$ be an $n \times n$ idempotent matrix. Show that:
(a) $(\boldsymbol{I}_n + \boldsymbol{A})^{-1} = \boldsymbol{I}_n - \frac{1}{2}\boldsymbol{A}$;
(b) $\exp(\boldsymbol{A}) = \boldsymbol{I}_n + (\mathrm{e}-1)\boldsymbol{A}$;
(c) $\log(\boldsymbol{I}_n + \boldsymbol{A}) = (\log 2)\boldsymbol{A}$.

Solution
(a) Direct verification gives

$$(\boldsymbol{I}_n + \boldsymbol{A})\left(\boldsymbol{I}_n - \frac{1}{2}\boldsymbol{A}\right) = \boldsymbol{I}_n + \boldsymbol{A} - \frac{1}{2}\boldsymbol{A} - \frac{1}{2}\boldsymbol{A}^2 = \boldsymbol{I}_n.$$

For a constructive proof, we use $\boldsymbol{A}^j = \boldsymbol{A}$ for $j \geq 1$, and the fact that $\varrho(\boldsymbol{A}) = 1$ but none of the eigenvalues is -1. Then,

$$(\boldsymbol{I}_n + \boldsymbol{A})^{-1} = \sum_{j=0}^{\infty} \binom{-1}{j} \boldsymbol{A}^j = \boldsymbol{I}_n + \sum_{j=1}^{\infty} \binom{-1}{j} \boldsymbol{A}.$$

Using $\sum_{j=1}^{\infty} \binom{-1}{j} = (1+1)^{-1} - 1 = -\frac{1}{2}$ gives the required result. Notice that this series is summable (see Appendix A), but not convergent.
(b) Similarly,

$$\exp(\boldsymbol{A}) = \boldsymbol{I}_n + \sum_{j=1}^{\infty} \frac{1}{j!}\boldsymbol{A} = \boldsymbol{I}_n + (\mathrm{e}-1)\boldsymbol{A}.$$

(c) Finally,

$$\log(\boldsymbol{I}_n + \boldsymbol{A}) = \sum_{j=0}^{\infty} \frac{(-1)^j}{j+1}\boldsymbol{A}^{j+1} = \sum_{j=0}^{\infty} \frac{(-1)^j}{j+1}\boldsymbol{A} = (\log 2)\boldsymbol{A}.$$

Exercise 9.5 (Inverse of $\boldsymbol{A} + \boldsymbol{a}\boldsymbol{b}'$, revisited) Let $\boldsymbol{A}$ be a nonsingular $n \times n$ matrix, and let $\boldsymbol{a}$ and $\boldsymbol{b}$ be $n \times 1$ vectors.
(a) If $\boldsymbol{b}'\boldsymbol{A}^{-1}\boldsymbol{a}$ is real and lies in the interval $(-1, 1]$, show that

$$(\boldsymbol{A} + \boldsymbol{a}\boldsymbol{b}')^{-1} = \boldsymbol{A}^{-1} - \frac{1}{1 + \boldsymbol{b}'\boldsymbol{A}^{-1}\boldsymbol{a}}\boldsymbol{A}^{-1}\boldsymbol{a}\boldsymbol{b}'\boldsymbol{A}^{-1}.$$

(b) What if $\boldsymbol{b}'\boldsymbol{A}^{-1}\boldsymbol{a} \neq -1$, but is unrestricted otherwise, and is possibly complex?

Solution
(a) We have $(\boldsymbol{A} + \boldsymbol{a}\boldsymbol{b}')^{-1} = \boldsymbol{A}^{-1}\left(\boldsymbol{I}_n + \boldsymbol{a}\boldsymbol{b}'\boldsymbol{A}^{-1}\right)^{-1}$. The matrix $\boldsymbol{a}\boldsymbol{b}'\boldsymbol{A}^{-1}$ has only one nonzero eigenvalue given by $\boldsymbol{b}'\boldsymbol{A}^{-1}\boldsymbol{a}$. Since $-1 < \boldsymbol{b}'\boldsymbol{A}^{-1}\boldsymbol{a} \leq 1$, we may expand the

binomial as

$$\left(\boldsymbol{I}_n+\boldsymbol{a}\boldsymbol{b}'\boldsymbol{A}^{-1}\right)^{-1}=\boldsymbol{I}_n+\sum_{j=1}^{\infty}\binom{-1}{j}\left(\boldsymbol{a}\boldsymbol{b}'\boldsymbol{A}^{-1}\right)^j$$
$$=\boldsymbol{I}_n+\boldsymbol{a}\sum_{j=1}^{\infty}\binom{-1}{j}\left(\boldsymbol{b}'\boldsymbol{A}^{-1}\boldsymbol{a}\right)^{j-1}\boldsymbol{b}'\boldsymbol{A}^{-1}$$
$$=\boldsymbol{I}_n-\boldsymbol{a}\frac{1}{1+\boldsymbol{b}'\boldsymbol{A}^{-1}\boldsymbol{a}}\boldsymbol{b}'\boldsymbol{A}^{-1},$$

because $\sum_{j=1}^{\infty}\binom{-1}{j}x^{j-1}=-1/(1+x)$. Premultiplying both sides of the equation by $\boldsymbol{A}^{-1}$ gives

$$\left(\boldsymbol{A}+\boldsymbol{a}\boldsymbol{b}'\right)^{-1}=\boldsymbol{A}^{-1}-\frac{1}{1+\boldsymbol{b}'\boldsymbol{A}^{-1}\boldsymbol{a}}\boldsymbol{A}^{-1}\boldsymbol{a}\boldsymbol{b}'\boldsymbol{A}^{-1}.$$

(b) Since the inverse of $\boldsymbol{A}+\boldsymbol{a}\boldsymbol{b}'$ is unique and the right-hand side does not contain a series expansion, it is also the inverse for any $\boldsymbol{b}'\boldsymbol{A}^{-1}\boldsymbol{a}\neq -1$. This can be verified by multiplying both sides by $\boldsymbol{A}+\boldsymbol{a}\boldsymbol{b}'$; see Exercise 4.28.

Exercise 9.6 (Geometric progression) Let $\boldsymbol{I}_n-\boldsymbol{A}$ be nonsingular.
(a) Show that

$$(\boldsymbol{I}_n-\boldsymbol{A})^{-1}=(\boldsymbol{I}_n-\boldsymbol{A})^{-1}\boldsymbol{A}^k+\sum_{j=0}^{k-1}\boldsymbol{A}^j$$

for any finite integer $k\geq 0$.
(b) Also show that

$$(\boldsymbol{I}_n-\boldsymbol{A})^{-1}=\sum_{j=0}^{\infty}\boldsymbol{A}^j$$

for any matrix $\boldsymbol{A}$ satisfying $\varrho(\boldsymbol{A})<1$.

Solution
(a) This follows by multiplying both sides by $\boldsymbol{I}_n-\boldsymbol{A}$ and then collecting terms. Alternatively, a constructive proof follows along the lines of Exercise 9.5 by taking the first k terms (instead of just one term) from the binomial expansion, then collecting the remainder.
(b) Since $\varrho(\boldsymbol{A})<1$ we may write

$$(\boldsymbol{I}_n-\boldsymbol{A})^{-1}=\sum_{j=0}^{\infty}\binom{-1}{j}(-\boldsymbol{A})^j=\sum_{j=0}^{\infty}\frac{(-1)(-2)\dots(-j)}{j!}(-1)^j\boldsymbol{A}^j=\sum_{j=0}^{\infty}\boldsymbol{A}^j.$$

Exercise 9.7 (Exponential as limit of the binomial) Let $\boldsymbol{A}$ be an $n\times n$ matrix with finite elements.

(a) Show that

$$\lim_{\nu \to 0} (\boldsymbol{I}_n + \nu \boldsymbol{A})^{\mu/\nu} = \exp(\mu \boldsymbol{A})$$

for any finite $\mu \in \mathbb{R}$.
(b) Hence, show that $(\exp(\boldsymbol{A}))^{\mu} = \exp(\mu \boldsymbol{A})$.

Solution
(a) Because $\varrho(\nu \boldsymbol{A}) \to 0$ as $\nu \to 0$, we have

$$(\boldsymbol{I}_n + \nu \boldsymbol{A})^{\mu/\nu} = \sum_{j=0}^{\infty} \binom{\mu/\nu}{j} \nu^j \boldsymbol{A}^j = \sum_{j=0}^{\infty} \frac{\prod_{i=0}^{j-1} \left(\frac{\mu}{\nu} - i\right)}{j!} \nu^j \boldsymbol{A}^j = \sum_{j=0}^{\infty} \frac{\prod_{i=0}^{j-1} (\mu - i\nu)}{j!} \boldsymbol{A}^j.$$

Letting $\nu \to 0$ gives the required limit.
(b) This follows from $\left((\boldsymbol{I}_n + \nu \boldsymbol{A})^{1/\nu}\right)^{\mu} \to (\exp(\boldsymbol{A}))^{\mu}$.

Exercise 9.8 (Logarithmic expansion) Let $\boldsymbol{A}$ be an $n \times n$ matrix whose eigenvalues are all different from -1. Using the definition $\exp(\log(\boldsymbol{I}_n + \boldsymbol{A})) := \boldsymbol{I}_n + \boldsymbol{A}$,
(a) show that $\log(\boldsymbol{I}_n + \boldsymbol{A})^{\nu} = \nu \log(\boldsymbol{I}_n + \boldsymbol{A})$; and
(b) derive the explicit representation

$$\log(\boldsymbol{I}_n + \boldsymbol{A}) = -\sum_{j=1}^{\infty} \frac{(-1)^j}{j} \boldsymbol{A}^j$$

for $\varrho(\boldsymbol{A}) < 1$. What does this representation imply for the definition of the function?

Solution
(a) Raising both sides of the definition to the power ν gives

$$(\boldsymbol{I}_n + \boldsymbol{A})^{\nu} = (\exp(\log(\boldsymbol{I}_n + \boldsymbol{A})))^{\nu} = \exp(\nu \log(\boldsymbol{I}_n + \boldsymbol{A})),$$

by Exercise 9.7. The result follows because the definition can also be written as

$$(\boldsymbol{I}_n + \boldsymbol{A})^{\nu} = \exp\left(\log(\boldsymbol{I}_n + \boldsymbol{A})^{\nu}\right).$$

(b) Expanding both sides of

$$\frac{1}{\nu}\left(\exp\left(\nu \log(\boldsymbol{I}_n + \boldsymbol{A})\right) - \boldsymbol{I}_n\right) = \frac{1}{\nu}\left((\boldsymbol{I}_n + \boldsymbol{A})^{\nu} - \boldsymbol{I}_n\right)$$

by the exponential and binomial series, respectively, gives

$$\log(\boldsymbol{I}_n + \boldsymbol{A}) + O(\nu) = \frac{1}{\nu} \sum_{j=1}^{\infty} \frac{\prod_{i=0}^{j-1}(\nu - i)}{j!} \boldsymbol{A}^j = \sum_{j=1}^{\infty} \frac{\prod_{i=1}^{j-1}(\nu - i)}{j!} \boldsymbol{A}^j.$$

Letting $\nu \to 0$ and noting that $\prod_{i=1}^{j-1}(-i) = (-1)^{j-1}(j-1)!$ gives the required result. This explicit representation shows that the inverse of the exponential function does indeed exist, at least for some values of $\varrho(\boldsymbol{A})$, and that the definition of logarithms is not vacuous. This is not yet a proof of absolute convergence. What we have done here is to work out a representation of the logarithmic function, *assuming* the binomial expansion stated in the introduction. Exercise 9.19(c) will establish that the binomial expansion is absolutely convergent when $\varrho(\boldsymbol{A}) < 1$. This then implies that the series expansion of $\log(\boldsymbol{I}_n + \boldsymbol{A})$ is also absolutely convergent when $\varrho(\boldsymbol{A}) < 1$.

***Exercise 9.9 (Binomial with two matrices)** Let $\boldsymbol{A}$ and $\boldsymbol{B}$ be two $n \times n$ matrices, and let p be a positive integer.
(a) Show that, in general, $(\boldsymbol{A}+\boldsymbol{B})^p \neq \boldsymbol{A}^p\left(\boldsymbol{I}_n + \boldsymbol{A}^{-1}\boldsymbol{B}\right)^p$.
(b) Introduce the new symbol $\boldsymbol{C}\{\boldsymbol{A}^{p-j}, \boldsymbol{B}^j\}$ to denote the sum of the $\binom{p}{j}$ combinations of $p-j$ matrices $\boldsymbol{A}$ with j matrices $\boldsymbol{B}$, for example,

$$\boldsymbol{C}\{\boldsymbol{A}^2, \boldsymbol{B}\} = \boldsymbol{A}^2\boldsymbol{B} + \boldsymbol{ABA} + \boldsymbol{BA}^2$$

and

$$\boldsymbol{C}\{\boldsymbol{A}^2, \boldsymbol{B}^2\} = \boldsymbol{A}^2\boldsymbol{B}^2 + \boldsymbol{ABAB} + \boldsymbol{AB}^2\boldsymbol{A} + \boldsymbol{BA}^2\boldsymbol{B} + \boldsymbol{BABA} + \boldsymbol{B}^2\boldsymbol{A}^2.$$

Show that

$$(\boldsymbol{A}+\boldsymbol{B})^p = \sum_{j=0}^{p} \boldsymbol{C}\{\boldsymbol{A}^{p-j}, \boldsymbol{B}^j\}.$$

(c) For $p \in \mathbb{N}$ show that $(\boldsymbol{A}+\boldsymbol{B})^p = \sum_{j=0}^{p} \binom{p}{j} \boldsymbol{A}^{p-j}\boldsymbol{B}^j$ if $\boldsymbol{A}$ and $\boldsymbol{B}$ commute.
(d) Show that the reverse implication holds for $p = 2$, but not generally.

Solution
(a) The inverse of $\boldsymbol{A}$ may not even exist. Even if it did exist, then

$$(\boldsymbol{A}+\boldsymbol{B})^2 = \boldsymbol{A}^2 + \boldsymbol{AB} + \boldsymbol{BA} + \boldsymbol{B}^2,$$

whereas

$$\begin{aligned}\boldsymbol{A}^2\left(\boldsymbol{I}_n + \boldsymbol{A}^{-1}\boldsymbol{B}\right)^2 &= \boldsymbol{A}^2\left(\boldsymbol{I}_n + 2\boldsymbol{A}^{-1}\boldsymbol{B} + \boldsymbol{A}^{-1}\boldsymbol{BA}^{-1}\boldsymbol{B}\right)\\ &= \boldsymbol{A}^2 + 2\boldsymbol{AB} + \boldsymbol{ABA}^{-1}\boldsymbol{B}.\end{aligned}$$

The two expressions are equal if $\boldsymbol{A}$ and $\boldsymbol{B}$ commute, but they will differ in general.
(b) We proceed by induction. For $p = 1$ the result holds trivially. As seen in (a) for $p = 2$, the $\binom{2}{1}$ combinations $\boldsymbol{C}\{\boldsymbol{A}, \boldsymbol{B}\}$ are $\boldsymbol{AB}$ and $\boldsymbol{BA}$, and there is only one combination $\boldsymbol{C}\{\boldsymbol{A}^2, \boldsymbol{I}_n\} = \boldsymbol{A}^2$. Now suppose that the formula holds for some p. Then it will also hold for $p+1$, because

$$\begin{aligned}(\boldsymbol{A}+\boldsymbol{B})^{p+1} &= (\boldsymbol{A}+\boldsymbol{B})\sum_{j=0}^{p} \boldsymbol{C}\{\boldsymbol{A}^{p-j}, \boldsymbol{B}^j\}\\ &= \sum_{j=0}^{p}\left(\boldsymbol{AC}\{\boldsymbol{A}^{p-j}, \boldsymbol{B}^j\} + \boldsymbol{BC}\{\boldsymbol{A}^{p-j}, \boldsymbol{B}^j\}\right)\\ &= \sum_{j=0}^{p+1} \boldsymbol{C}\{\boldsymbol{A}^{p+1-j}, \boldsymbol{B}^j\},\end{aligned}$$

using the fact that $\binom{p+1}{j+1} = \binom{p}{j} + \binom{p}{j+1}$ from Pascal's triangle.

(c) If $\boldsymbol{A}$ and $\boldsymbol{B}$ commute, then $\boldsymbol{C}\{\boldsymbol{A}^{p-j}, \boldsymbol{B}^j\} = \binom{p}{j} \boldsymbol{A}^{p-j}\boldsymbol{B}^j$ and the result follows.
(d) For $p = 2$, suppose that the formula

$$(\boldsymbol{A}+\boldsymbol{B})^2 = \boldsymbol{A}^2 + 2\boldsymbol{A}\boldsymbol{B} + \boldsymbol{B}^2$$

holds. Then, since also

$$(\boldsymbol{A}+\boldsymbol{B})^2 = \boldsymbol{A}^2 + \boldsymbol{A}\boldsymbol{B} + \boldsymbol{B}\boldsymbol{A} + \boldsymbol{B}^2,$$

we find $\boldsymbol{A}\boldsymbol{B} = \boldsymbol{B}\boldsymbol{A}$. However, for $p = 3$,

$$\begin{aligned}(\boldsymbol{A}+\boldsymbol{B})^3 &= \boldsymbol{A}^3 + \boldsymbol{A}\boldsymbol{B}\boldsymbol{A} + \boldsymbol{A}^2\boldsymbol{B} + \boldsymbol{B}\boldsymbol{A}^2 \\ &\quad + \boldsymbol{B}\boldsymbol{A}\boldsymbol{B} + \boldsymbol{B}^2\boldsymbol{A} + \boldsymbol{A}\boldsymbol{B}^2 + \boldsymbol{B}^3\end{aligned}$$

may equal

$$\sum_{j=0}^{3} \binom{3}{j} \boldsymbol{A}^{3-j}\boldsymbol{B}^j = \boldsymbol{A}^3 + 3\boldsymbol{A}^2\boldsymbol{B} + 3\boldsymbol{A}\boldsymbol{B}^2 + \boldsymbol{B}^3$$

even if $\boldsymbol{A}$ and $\boldsymbol{B}$ do not commute. To show this, we need two matrices $\boldsymbol{A}$ and $\boldsymbol{B}$ satisfying

$$\boldsymbol{A}\boldsymbol{B}\boldsymbol{A} + \boldsymbol{B}\boldsymbol{A}^2 + \boldsymbol{B}\boldsymbol{A}\boldsymbol{B} + \boldsymbol{B}^2\boldsymbol{A} = 2\boldsymbol{A}^2\boldsymbol{B} + 2\boldsymbol{A}\boldsymbol{B}^2.$$

For example, the matrices

$$\boldsymbol{A} = \begin{pmatrix} 0 & 0 & 1 \\ 0 & 0 & 1 \\ 0 & 0 & 0 \end{pmatrix} \quad \text{and} \quad \boldsymbol{B} = \begin{pmatrix} 0 & 1 & 0 \\ 0 & 0 & 1 \\ 0 & 0 & 0 \end{pmatrix},$$

which are nilpotent of indices 2 and 3, respectively, satisfy this relationship, but $\boldsymbol{A}\boldsymbol{B} = \mathbf{O}$ while $\boldsymbol{B}\boldsymbol{A} = \boldsymbol{B}^2 \neq \mathbf{O}$, so that they do not commute.

***Exercise 9.10 (Multiplicative exponential?)** Let $\boldsymbol{A}$ and $\boldsymbol{B}$ be two $n \times n$ matrices. Show that $\exp(x\boldsymbol{A} + x\boldsymbol{B}) = \exp(x\boldsymbol{A})\exp(x\boldsymbol{B})$ for all finite $x \in \mathbb{R}$ if and only if $\boldsymbol{A}$ and $\boldsymbol{B}$ commute. [Hint: Appendix A gives a formula to rewrite an infinite double series as an infinite sum of a finite series: $\sum_{j=0}^{\infty}\sum_{k=0}^{\infty} g_{j,k}(x) = \sum_{j=0}^{\infty}\sum_{k=0}^{j} g_{j-k,k}(x)$.]

Solution

Compare the powers of x in

$$\exp(x\boldsymbol{A} + x\boldsymbol{B}) = \sum_{j=0}^{\infty} \frac{x^j}{j!} (\boldsymbol{A}+\boldsymbol{B})^j$$

and

$$\begin{aligned}\exp(x\boldsymbol{A})\exp(x\boldsymbol{B}) &= \sum_{j=0}^{\infty}\sum_{k=0}^{\infty} \frac{x^{j+k}}{j!k!} \boldsymbol{A}^j\boldsymbol{B}^k = \sum_{j=0}^{\infty} x^j \sum_{k=0}^{j} \frac{1}{(j-k)!k!} \boldsymbol{A}^{j-k}\boldsymbol{B}^k \\ &= \sum_{j=0}^{\infty} \frac{x^j}{j!} \sum_{k=0}^{j} \binom{j}{k} \boldsymbol{A}^{j-k}\boldsymbol{B}^k,\end{aligned}$$

the rearrangement of the sum in k being allowed because the double series is absolutely convergent. Since the two formulas hold for all x (and, in particular, for $x \to 0$), we see that $\exp(x\boldsymbol{A} + x\boldsymbol{B}) = \exp(x\boldsymbol{A})\exp(x\boldsymbol{B})$ for all x if and only if $(\boldsymbol{A}+\boldsymbol{B})^j = \sum_{k=0}^{j}\binom{j}{k}\boldsymbol{A}^{j-k}\boldsymbol{B}^k$ for all j. If $\boldsymbol{A}$ and $\boldsymbol{B}$ commute, then Exercise 9.9(c) implies that $(\boldsymbol{A}+\boldsymbol{B})^j = \sum_{k=0}^{j}\binom{j}{k}\boldsymbol{A}^{j-k}\boldsymbol{B}^k$ for all j. Conversely, if $(\boldsymbol{A}+\boldsymbol{B})^j = \sum_{k=0}^{j}\binom{j}{k}\boldsymbol{A}^{j-k}\boldsymbol{B}^k$ for all j, then it holds in particular for $j = 2$, and hence $\boldsymbol{A}$ and $\boldsymbol{B}$ commute, using Exercise 9.9(d). The result follows.

To understand the subtle role of x (and j) in this proof, take $x \to 0$ in

$$\begin{aligned}&\frac{2}{x^2}\left(\exp(x\boldsymbol{A}+x\boldsymbol{B}) - \exp(x\boldsymbol{A})\exp(x\boldsymbol{B})\right)\\ &\quad = (\boldsymbol{A}+\boldsymbol{B})^2 - \sum_{k=0}^{2}\binom{2}{k}\boldsymbol{A}^{2-k}\boldsymbol{B}^k + O(x)\\ &\quad = \boldsymbol{B}\boldsymbol{A} - \boldsymbol{A}\boldsymbol{B} + O(x).\end{aligned}$$

Notice that we may have $\boldsymbol{A}$ and $\boldsymbol{B}$ *not* commuting while, for $x = 1$, the equalities $\exp(\boldsymbol{A}+\boldsymbol{B}) = \exp(\boldsymbol{A})\exp(\boldsymbol{B})$ or $\exp(\boldsymbol{A})\exp(\boldsymbol{B}) = \exp(\boldsymbol{B})\exp(\boldsymbol{A})$ hold. This can happen if

$$\exp(x\boldsymbol{A}+x\boldsymbol{B}) \neq \exp(x\boldsymbol{A})\exp(x\boldsymbol{B})$$

for some x in the neighborhood of zero; see Exercise 9.15 below.

Exercise 9.11 (Additive logarithmic?) Let $\boldsymbol{C}$ and $\boldsymbol{D}$ be two $n \times n$ matrices, and define $\boldsymbol{A} := \exp(\boldsymbol{C})$ and $\boldsymbol{B} := \exp(\boldsymbol{D})$.
(a) Show that $\log(\boldsymbol{A})$ and $\log(\boldsymbol{B})$ commute if and only if $\log(\boldsymbol{A}^x\boldsymbol{B}^x) = \log(\boldsymbol{A}^x) + \log(\boldsymbol{B}^x)$ for all finite $x \in \mathbb{R}$.
(b) Show that, when $\boldsymbol{A}$ is nonsingular,

$$\log(\boldsymbol{I}_n + \boldsymbol{A}) = \log(\boldsymbol{I}_n + \boldsymbol{A}^{-1}) - \log(\boldsymbol{A}^{-1}).$$

(c) Obtain $\log(\boldsymbol{I}_n + \boldsymbol{A})$ for

$$\boldsymbol{A} = \begin{pmatrix} a & 0\\ 0 & b\end{pmatrix}$$

in terms of a and b, when $a > 1$ and $b > 1$.

Solution
(a) From Exercise 9.10, $\log(\boldsymbol{A}) = \boldsymbol{C}$ and $\log(\boldsymbol{B}) = \boldsymbol{D}$ commute if and only if

$$\exp(x\boldsymbol{C})\exp(x\boldsymbol{D}) = \exp(x\boldsymbol{C} + x\boldsymbol{D})$$

for all x. Taking logarithms on both sides, then using the definitions of $\boldsymbol{A}$ and $\boldsymbol{B}$, gives the required result.
(b) Any $\boldsymbol{A}$ commutes with its own powers, hence also with power series in $\boldsymbol{A}$. (But be careful: $\boldsymbol{A}$ commutes with $\boldsymbol{A}'$ if and only if $\boldsymbol{A}$ is normal.) Hence,

$$\log(\boldsymbol{I} + \boldsymbol{A}^{-1}) = \log\left((\boldsymbol{I}+\boldsymbol{A})\boldsymbol{A}^{-1}\right) = \log(\boldsymbol{I}+\boldsymbol{A}) + \log(\boldsymbol{A}^{-1}),$$

using (a).

(c) Since the two eigenvalues of $\boldsymbol{A}^{-1}$ lie in the interval $(0,1)$, using (b) and the expansion derived in Exercise 9.8(b) gives

$$\begin{aligned}\log(\boldsymbol{I}_n+\boldsymbol{A}) &= \log(\boldsymbol{I}_n+\boldsymbol{A}^{-1}) - \log\left(\boldsymbol{I}_n-(\boldsymbol{I}_n-\boldsymbol{A}^{-1})\right)\\ &= \begin{pmatrix} a^{-1} & 0\\ 0 & b^{-1}\end{pmatrix}\sum_{j=0}^{\infty}\frac{(-1)^j}{j+1}\begin{pmatrix} a^{-j} & 0\\ 0 & b^{-j}\end{pmatrix}\\ &\quad + \begin{pmatrix} 1-a^{-1} & 0\\ 0 & 1-b^{-1}\end{pmatrix}\sum_{j=0}^{\infty}\frac{1}{j+1}\begin{pmatrix} (1-a^{-1})^j & 0\\ 0 & (1-b^{-1})^j\end{pmatrix}\\ &= \begin{pmatrix} \log(1+a^{-1}) & 0\\ 0 & \log(1+b^{-1})\end{pmatrix} - \begin{pmatrix} \log(a^{-1}) & 0\\ 0 & \log(b^{-1})\end{pmatrix}\\ &= \begin{pmatrix} \log(1+a) & 0\\ 0 & \log(1+b)\end{pmatrix},\end{aligned}$$

as in Exercise 9.1(b), where a and b were inside the unit circle.

Exercise 9.12 (Orthogonal representation, 1)
(a) Generalize Exercise 2.28 in the following way. Let $\boldsymbol{\Lambda} := \operatorname{diag}(\boldsymbol{\Lambda}_1,\dots,\boldsymbol{\Lambda}_n)$ be an $2n\times 2n$ block-diagonal matrix, where

$$\boldsymbol{\Lambda}_i := \begin{pmatrix} \cos\theta_i & -\sin\theta_i\\ \sin\theta_i & \cos\theta_i\end{pmatrix} \quad (i=1,\dots,n).$$

Show that $\boldsymbol{A} := \boldsymbol{S}\boldsymbol{\Lambda}\boldsymbol{S}'$ is orthogonal when $\boldsymbol{S}$ is orthogonal, and that $|\boldsymbol{A}|=1$.
(b) Now let $\boldsymbol{\Lambda} := \operatorname{diag}(\boldsymbol{\Lambda}_1,\dots,\boldsymbol{\Lambda}_n,1)$. Show that $\boldsymbol{A} := \boldsymbol{S}\boldsymbol{\Lambda}\boldsymbol{S}'$ is orthogonal when $\boldsymbol{S}$ is orthogonal, and that $|\boldsymbol{A}|=1$.
(c) Why do (a)–(b) provide a representation for all orthogonal matrices $\boldsymbol{A}$ having $|\boldsymbol{A}|=1$ (that is, rotation matrices) when all θ_i are real?

Solution
(a) We have $\boldsymbol{A}'\boldsymbol{A} = \boldsymbol{S}\boldsymbol{\Lambda}'\boldsymbol{S}'\boldsymbol{S}\boldsymbol{\Lambda}\boldsymbol{S}' = \boldsymbol{S}\boldsymbol{\Lambda}'\boldsymbol{\Lambda}\boldsymbol{S}'$. The matrix $\boldsymbol{\Lambda}'\boldsymbol{\Lambda}$ is block-diagonal, and its i-th diagonal block is given by

$$\begin{pmatrix} \cos\theta_i & \sin\theta_i\\ -\sin\theta_i & \cos\theta_i\end{pmatrix}\begin{pmatrix} \cos\theta_i & -\sin\theta_i\\ \sin\theta_i & \cos\theta_i\end{pmatrix} = \boldsymbol{I}_2$$

because $(\cos\theta_i)^2+(\sin\theta_i)^2=1$, so that $\boldsymbol{A}'\boldsymbol{A}=\boldsymbol{I}_n$. The determinant of $\boldsymbol{A}$ is

$$|\boldsymbol{A}| = \prod_{i=1}^{n}\begin{vmatrix} \cos\theta_i & -\sin\theta_i\\ \sin\theta_i & \cos\theta_i\end{vmatrix} = 1.$$

(b) This follows as in (a).
(c) By the definition of the cosine and sine functions in terms of the exponential, the eigenvalues implied by each $\boldsymbol{\Lambda}_i$ are the conjugate pairs $\mathrm{e}^{\pm\mathrm{i}\theta_i}$ having unit modulus, as expected from Exercise 7.22. Orthogonal matrices are normal, because they commute with

their transposes, that is, $A'A = AA' = I_n$. The spectral theorem for normal matrices (Exercise 7.71) proves that orthogonal matrices are diagonalizable by a unitary matrix, hence block-diagonalizable into Λ by a unitary matrix T (alternatively, the product of two unitary matrices is unitary). Since $AT = T\Lambda$,

$$\operatorname{Re}(AT) = \operatorname{Re}(T\Lambda) \iff A\operatorname{Re}(T) = \operatorname{Re}(T)\Lambda,$$

so that T can be taken to be real, that is, $\operatorname{Re}(T) = S$ is orthogonal; see Exercise 7.43.

Exercise 9.13 (Skew-symmetric representation) Let A be an $n \times n$ skew-Hermitian matrix.
(a) If A is real (hence skew-symmetric), show that its eigenvalues take one of two forms: they come in pairs $-\lambda, \lambda$ or they are zero.
(b) In general, show that the eigenvalues of A are pure imaginary, so that $-\lambda, \lambda$ are a conjugate pair.
(c) Show that $|A| = 0$ for n odd, and $|A| \geq 0$ for n even.
(d) If A is real, show that $A = S\Lambda S'$ for some orthogonal S and $\Lambda := \operatorname{diag}(\Lambda_1, \dots, \Lambda_m, \mathbf{O})$ for some integer $m \leq n/2$, where

$$\Lambda_i := \begin{pmatrix} 0 & -\theta_i \\ \theta_i & 0 \end{pmatrix} \quad (i = 1, \dots, m),$$

and the θ_i are real.

Solution
(a) Since the eigenvalues of A and A' are the same, we have

$$|\lambda I_n - A| = |\lambda I_n - A'| = |\lambda I_n + A| = (-1)^n |-\lambda I_n - A| .$$

Equating the first and the last determinant to zero gives the result.
(b) Let B be Hermitian. Then $A := \mathrm{i}B$ is skew-Hermitian since $A^* = -\mathrm{i}B^* = -\mathrm{i}B = -A$. The eigenvalues of B are all real (Exercise 7.40), and the eigenvalues of A are i times these. The result follows, and is a generalization of Exercise 7.18. We have here an example where a more general result can be proved more easily than the special case.
(c) For n odd, one of the eigenvalues of A must be zero, so that A is singular. For n even, the product of the conjugate pairs $-\lambda, \lambda$ is $|\lambda|^2 \geq 0$.
(d) The eigenvalues of Λ are obtained from $\lambda_i^2 = -\theta_i^2$ and possibly zeros. The representation follows as in Exercise 9.12(c) since skew-symmetric matrices are normal.

9.2 Jordan representation

Exercise 9.14 (Jordan representation, diagonalizable) Let A be an $n \times n$ symmetric matrix, and write $A = S\Lambda S'$, where Λ is the diagonal matrix of eigenvalues of A, and S is an orthogonal matrix of eigenvectors. Define the matrix function

$$F(A) := \sum_{j=0}^{\infty} c_j A^j$$

and the corresponding scalar function $f(\lambda) := \sum_{j=0}^{\infty} c_j \lambda^j$. Show that

$$F(A) = S \operatorname{diag}(f(\lambda_1), \dots, f(\lambda_n)) S'.$$

Solution

Substituting $A = S\Lambda S'$ in the matrix function $F(A)$, we obtain

$$F(A) = \sum_{j=0}^{\infty} c_j \left(S\Lambda S'\right)^j = S \sum_{j=0}^{\infty} c_j \Lambda^j S' = SF(\Lambda)S'$$

since $S'S = I_n$. The result then follows from Exercise 9.2.

Exercise 9.15 (Multiplicative exponential, by Jordan) Let

$$A = \begin{pmatrix} 0 & \pi \\ -\pi & 0 \end{pmatrix} \quad \text{and} \quad B = \begin{pmatrix} 0 & -\pi \\ 0 & 0 \end{pmatrix}.$$

(a) Show that A and B do not commute, but that $\exp(A)$ and $\exp(B)$ do commute.
(b) Also show that

$$\exp(A)\exp(B) \neq \exp(A + B).$$

Solution

(a) Direct multiplication shows that

$$AB = \begin{pmatrix} 0 & \pi \\ -\pi & 0 \end{pmatrix} \begin{pmatrix} 0 & -\pi \\ 0 & 0 \end{pmatrix} = \begin{pmatrix} 0 & 0 \\ 0 & \pi^2 \end{pmatrix}$$

and

$$BA = \begin{pmatrix} 0 & -\pi \\ 0 & 0 \end{pmatrix} \begin{pmatrix} 0 & \pi \\ -\pi & 0 \end{pmatrix} = \begin{pmatrix} \pi^2 & 0 \\ 0 & 0 \end{pmatrix} \neq AB.$$

The matrix A is skew-symmetric and its eigenvalues are $\pm i\pi$. Hence, there exists a nonsingular matrix T such that $A = T\Lambda T^{-1}$, with $\Lambda := \operatorname{diag}(i\pi, -i\pi)$. Then,

$$\exp(A) = T \exp(\Lambda) T^{-1} = T(-I_2)T^{-1} = -I_2,$$

since $\exp(\pm i\pi) = -1$. Hence, $\exp(B)$ commutes with $\exp(A)$.

We notice three things. First, it was not necessary to work out the eigenvectors explicitly in this case. One may verify, however, that

$$T = \frac{1}{\sqrt{2}} \begin{pmatrix} 1 & 1 \\ i & -i \end{pmatrix} \quad \text{and} \quad T^{-1} = \frac{1}{\sqrt{2}} \begin{pmatrix} 1 & -i \\ 1 & i \end{pmatrix}.$$

Second, T is unitary, as expected from the spectral theorem for normal matrices (Exercise 7.71). Third, A is skew-symmetric and $\exp(A)$ is orthogonal, a relation that is no coincidence and will be studied further in Exercise 9.22. The eigenvalues of Exercises 9.12 and 9.13 already suggested the relation.

(b) The matrix $\boldsymbol{B}$ is nilpotent, hence its series expansion terminates and $\exp(\boldsymbol{B}) = \boldsymbol{I}_2 + \boldsymbol{B}$. Therefore,

$$\exp(\boldsymbol{A})\exp(\boldsymbol{B}) = \exp(\boldsymbol{B})\exp(\boldsymbol{A}) = -\boldsymbol{I}_2 - \boldsymbol{B},$$

but

$$\exp(\boldsymbol{A}+\boldsymbol{B}) = \exp\begin{pmatrix} 0 & 0 \\ -\pi & 0 \end{pmatrix} = \boldsymbol{I}_2 + \boldsymbol{B}' \neq -\boldsymbol{I}_2 - \boldsymbol{B}.$$

Exercise 9.16 (Exponential, by Jordan) Let

$$\boldsymbol{A} = \begin{pmatrix} 1 & 3 & 0 \\ 0 & 1 & 0 \\ 2 & 1 & 5 \end{pmatrix}.$$

We have seen in Exercise 7.91 that

$$\boldsymbol{A} = \begin{pmatrix} 0 & 3 & -1/2 \\ 0 & 0 & 1 \\ 3/8 & -3/2 & -3/8 \end{pmatrix} \begin{pmatrix} 5 & 0 & 0 \\ 0 & 1 & 1 \\ 0 & 0 & 1 \end{pmatrix} \begin{pmatrix} 4/3 & 5/3 & 8/3 \\ 1/3 & 1/6 & 0 \\ 0 & 1 & 0 \end{pmatrix}.$$

Use this decomposition to work out $\exp(\boldsymbol{A})$ explicitly.

Solution

We have

$$\exp(\boldsymbol{A}) = \begin{pmatrix} 0 & 3 & -1/2 \\ 0 & 0 & 1 \\ 3/8 & -3/2 & -3/8 \end{pmatrix} \begin{pmatrix} \exp(5) & \boldsymbol{0}' \\ \boldsymbol{0} & \exp(\boldsymbol{J}_2(1)) \end{pmatrix} \begin{pmatrix} 4/3 & 5/3 & 8/3 \\ 1/3 & 1/6 & 0 \\ 0 & 1 & 0 \end{pmatrix}.$$

Since $\boldsymbol{J}_2(1) = \boldsymbol{I}_2 + \boldsymbol{J}_2(0)$, where $\boldsymbol{J}_2(0)$ is nilpotent of index 2, we can expand its powers by the binomial, yielding

$$\begin{aligned} \exp(\boldsymbol{J}_2(1)) &= \sum_{j=0}^{\infty} \frac{1}{j!} (\boldsymbol{I}_2 + \boldsymbol{J}_2(0))^j = \sum_{j=0}^{\infty} \frac{1}{j!} (\boldsymbol{I}_2 + j\boldsymbol{J}_2(0) + \mathbf{O}) \\ &= \left(\sum_{j=0}^{\infty} \frac{1}{j!}\right) \boldsymbol{I}_2 + \left(\sum_{j=0}^{\infty} \frac{1}{j!} j\right) \boldsymbol{J}_2(0) = \begin{pmatrix} \mathrm{e} & \mathrm{e} \\ 0 & \mathrm{e} \end{pmatrix}. \end{aligned}$$

Hence, $\exp(\boldsymbol{J}_2(1))$ can be written as $\mathrm{e}\boldsymbol{I}_2 + \mathrm{e}\boldsymbol{J}_2(0)$, a linear polynomial in $\boldsymbol{J}_2(0)$, where the first coefficient is e and the second coefficient, also e, equals $\mathrm{d}\mathrm{e}^{\lambda}/\,\mathrm{d}\lambda$ evaluated at $\lambda = 1$. Direct multiplication gives

$$\begin{aligned} \exp(\boldsymbol{A}) &= \begin{pmatrix} 0 & 3 & -1/2 \\ 0 & 0 & 1 \\ 3/8 & -3/2 & -3/8 \end{pmatrix} \begin{pmatrix} \mathrm{e}^5 & 0 & 0 \\ 0 & \mathrm{e} & \mathrm{e} \\ 0 & 0 & \mathrm{e} \end{pmatrix} \begin{pmatrix} 4/3 & 5/3 & 8/3 \\ 1/3 & 1/6 & 0 \\ 0 & 1 & 0 \end{pmatrix} \\ &= \begin{pmatrix} \mathrm{e} & 3\mathrm{e} & 0 \\ 0 & \mathrm{e} & 0 \\ \frac{1}{2}\mathrm{e}^5 - \frac{1}{2}\mathrm{e} & \frac{5}{8}\mathrm{e}^5 - \frac{17}{8}\mathrm{e} & \mathrm{e}^5 \end{pmatrix}. \end{aligned}$$

Exercise 9.17 (Powers of Jordan) Let $\boldsymbol{J}_n := \boldsymbol{J}_n(\lambda)$ be a Jordan block of size n corresponding to an eigenvalue λ.
(a) Obtain $\boldsymbol{J}_2^2, \boldsymbol{J}_2^3$ and deduce $\boldsymbol{J}_2^j$ when j is a natural number. Then use this result to calculate $\exp(\boldsymbol{J}_2)$, thus generalizing the expression obtained in Exercise 9.16 for $\lambda = 1$, to arbitrary λ.
(b) Obtain $\boldsymbol{J}_3^2, \boldsymbol{J}_3^3, \boldsymbol{J}_3^4$ and deduce $\boldsymbol{J}_3^j$.
(c) Now obtain $\boldsymbol{J}_n^j$.

Solution
(a) We find

$$\begin{pmatrix} \lambda & 1 \\ 0 & \lambda \end{pmatrix}^2 = \begin{pmatrix} \lambda^2 & 2\lambda \\ 0 & \lambda^2 \end{pmatrix} \quad \text{and} \quad \begin{pmatrix} \lambda & 1 \\ 0 & \lambda \end{pmatrix}^3 = \begin{pmatrix} \lambda^3 & 3\lambda^2 \\ 0 & \lambda^3 \end{pmatrix}.$$

This suggests that

$$\boldsymbol{J}_2^j = \begin{pmatrix} \lambda^j & j\lambda^{j-1} \\ 0 & \lambda^j \end{pmatrix}.$$

Assume that this is in fact correct for j. Then,

$$\begin{pmatrix} \lambda & 1 \\ 0 & \lambda \end{pmatrix}^{j+1} = \begin{pmatrix} \lambda & 1 \\ 0 & \lambda \end{pmatrix} \begin{pmatrix} \lambda^j & j\lambda^{j-1} \\ 0 & \lambda^j \end{pmatrix} = \begin{pmatrix} \lambda^{j+1} & (j+1)\lambda^j \\ 0 & \lambda^{j+1} \end{pmatrix},$$

which shows that the formula holds, by induction. Hence,

$$\begin{aligned} \exp(\boldsymbol{J}_2) &= \sum_{j=0}^{\infty} \frac{1}{j!} \boldsymbol{J}_2^j = \sum_{j=0}^{\infty} \frac{1}{j!} \begin{pmatrix} \lambda^j & j\lambda^{j-1} \\ 0 & \lambda^j \end{pmatrix} = \sum_{j=0}^{\infty} \frac{1}{j!} \begin{pmatrix} \lambda^j & \frac{\mathrm{d}}{\mathrm{d}\lambda}\lambda^j \\ 0 & \lambda^j \end{pmatrix} \\ &= \begin{pmatrix} \exp(\lambda) & \frac{\mathrm{d}\exp(\lambda)}{\mathrm{d}\lambda} \\ 0 & \exp(\lambda) \end{pmatrix} = \mathrm{e}^{\lambda} \begin{pmatrix} 1 & 1 \\ 0 & 1 \end{pmatrix} = \mathrm{e}^{\lambda} \left(\boldsymbol{I}_2 + \boldsymbol{J}_2(0) \right), \end{aligned}$$

a linear polynomial in $\boldsymbol{J}_2(0)$.
(b) For $n = 3$, we have

$$\begin{pmatrix} \lambda & 1 & 0 \\ 0 & \lambda & 1 \\ 0 & 0 & \lambda \end{pmatrix}^2 = \begin{pmatrix} \lambda^2 & 2\lambda & 1 \\ 0 & \lambda^2 & 2\lambda \\ 0 & 0 & \lambda^2 \end{pmatrix},$$

$$\begin{pmatrix} \lambda & 1 & 0 \\ 0 & \lambda & 1 \\ 0 & 0 & \lambda \end{pmatrix}^3 = \begin{pmatrix} \lambda^3 & 3\lambda^2 & 3\lambda \\ 0 & \lambda^3 & 3\lambda^2 \\ 0 & 0 & \lambda^3 \end{pmatrix},$$

and

$$\begin{pmatrix} \lambda & 1 & 0 \\ 0 & \lambda & 1 \\ 0 & 0 & \lambda \end{pmatrix}^4 = \begin{pmatrix} \lambda^4 & 4\lambda^3 & 6\lambda^2 \\ 0 & \lambda^4 & 4\lambda^3 \\ 0 & 0 & \lambda^4 \end{pmatrix}.$$

This suggests that

$$\boldsymbol{J}_3^j = \begin{pmatrix} \lambda^j & j\lambda^{j-1} & \frac{j(j-1)}{2}\lambda^{j-2} \\ 0 & \lambda^j & j\lambda^{j-1} \\ 0 & 0 & \lambda^j \end{pmatrix}$$

for $j \geq 2$ or, more generally for any j,

$$\boldsymbol{J}_3^j = \begin{pmatrix} f(\lambda) & f'(\lambda) & \frac{1}{2}f''(\lambda) \\ 0 & f(\lambda) & f'(\lambda) \\ 0 & 0 & f(\lambda) \end{pmatrix},$$

where $f(\lambda) := \lambda^j$. If the formula holds for j, then

$$\boldsymbol{J}_3^{j+1} = \begin{pmatrix} \lambda & 1 & 0 \\ 0 & \lambda & 1 \\ 0 & 0 & \lambda \end{pmatrix} \begin{pmatrix} \lambda^j & j\lambda^{j-1} & \frac{j(j-1)\lambda^{j-2}}{2} \\ 0 & \lambda^j & j\lambda^{j-1} \\ 0 & 0 & \lambda^j \end{pmatrix}$$

$$= \begin{pmatrix} \lambda^{j+1} & (j+1)\lambda^j & \frac{(j+1)j}{2}\lambda^{j-1} \\ 0 & \lambda^{j+1} & (j+1)\lambda^j \\ 0 & 0 & \lambda^{j+1} \end{pmatrix},$$

so that the formula holds also for $j+1$, hence for all j, by induction.
(c) We now repeat the induction argument for general n. Assume that

$$\boldsymbol{J}_n^j = \begin{pmatrix} f(\lambda) & f'(\lambda) & \dots & \frac{f^{(n-1)}(\lambda)}{(n-1)!} \\ 0 & f(\lambda) & \dots & \frac{f^{(n-2)}(\lambda)}{(n-2)!} \\ \vdots & \vdots & & \vdots \\ 0 & 0 & \dots & f(\lambda) \end{pmatrix},$$

where $f(\lambda) := \lambda^j$. Then,

$$\boldsymbol{J}_n^{j+1} = \begin{pmatrix} \lambda & 1 & 0 & \dots & 0 \\ 0 & \lambda & 1 & \dots & 0 \\ \vdots & \vdots & \vdots & & \vdots \\ 0 & 0 & 0 & \dots & \lambda \end{pmatrix} \begin{pmatrix} f(\lambda) & f'(\lambda) & \dots & \frac{f^{(n-1)}(\lambda)}{(n-1)!} \\ 0 & f(\lambda) & \dots & \frac{f^{(n-2)}(\lambda)}{(n-2)!} \\ \vdots & \vdots & & \vdots \\ 0 & 0 & \dots & f(\lambda) \end{pmatrix}$$

$$= \begin{pmatrix} \lambda f(\lambda) & \lambda f'(\lambda) + f(\lambda) & \dots & \lambda\frac{f^{(n-1)}(\lambda)}{(n-1)!} + \frac{f^{(n-2)}(\lambda)}{(n-2)!} \\ 0 & \lambda f(\lambda) & \dots & \lambda\frac{f^{(n-2)}(\lambda)}{(n-2)!} + \frac{f^{(n-3)}(\lambda)}{(n-3)!} \\ \vdots & \vdots & & \vdots \\ 0 & 0 & \dots & \lambda f(\lambda) \end{pmatrix}$$

$$= \begin{pmatrix} g(\lambda) & g'(\lambda) & \dots & \frac{g^{(n-1)}(\lambda)}{(n-1)!} \\ 0 & g(\lambda) & \dots & \frac{g^{(n-2)}(\lambda)}{(n-2)!} \\ \vdots & \vdots & & \vdots \\ 0 & 0 & \dots & g(\lambda) \end{pmatrix},$$

where $g(\lambda) := \lambda f(\lambda) = \lambda^{j+1}$. This confirms that the formula holds for $j + 1$ and hence, by induction, generally.

Exercise 9.18 (Jordan representation, general) Let $\boldsymbol{A}$ be an $n \times n$ matrix having the Jordan decomposition $\boldsymbol{A} = \boldsymbol{T}\boldsymbol{J}\boldsymbol{T}^{-1}$, where $\boldsymbol{J} := \operatorname{diag}(\boldsymbol{J}_{n_1}(\lambda_1), \dots, \boldsymbol{J}_{n_k}(\lambda_k))$, with $n_1 + \cdots + n_k = n$ and the λ's need not be distinct. Show that

$$\boldsymbol{F}(\boldsymbol{A}) := \sum_{j=0}^{\infty} c_j \boldsymbol{A}^j = \boldsymbol{T}\boldsymbol{F}(\boldsymbol{J})\boldsymbol{T}^{-1},$$

where $\boldsymbol{F}(\boldsymbol{J}) := \operatorname{diag}(\boldsymbol{F}(\boldsymbol{J}_{n_1}(\lambda_1)), \dots, \boldsymbol{F}(\boldsymbol{J}_{n_k}(\lambda_k)))$, $f(\lambda) := \sum_{j=0}^{\infty} c_j \lambda^j$, and

$$\boldsymbol{F}(\boldsymbol{J}_{n_i}(\lambda_i)) := \begin{pmatrix} f(\lambda_i) & f'(\lambda_i) & \dots & \frac{f^{(n_i-1)}(\lambda_i)}{(n_i-1)!} \\ 0 & f(\lambda_i) & \dots & \frac{f^{(n_i-2)}(\lambda_i)}{(n_i-2)!} \\ \vdots & \vdots & & \vdots \\ 0 & 0 & \dots & f(\lambda_i) \end{pmatrix}$$

for $i = 1, \dots, k$. What does this imply for the eigenvalues and eigenvectors of $\boldsymbol{F}(\boldsymbol{A})$?

Solution

Substituting $\boldsymbol{A} = \boldsymbol{T}\boldsymbol{J}\boldsymbol{T}^{-1}$ in $\boldsymbol{F}(\boldsymbol{A})$, we obtain

$$\boldsymbol{F}(\boldsymbol{A}) = \sum_{j=0}^{\infty} c_j \left(\boldsymbol{T}\boldsymbol{J}\boldsymbol{T}^{-1}\right)^j = \boldsymbol{T}\left(\sum_{j=0}^{\infty} c_j \boldsymbol{J}^j\right)\boldsymbol{T}^{-1} = \boldsymbol{T}\boldsymbol{F}(\boldsymbol{J})\boldsymbol{T}^{-1}.$$

The representation then follows from Exercise 9.17(c) and the property that powers of block-diagonal matrices are block-diagonal. Since $\boldsymbol{F}(\boldsymbol{J})$ is upper triangular, its eigenvalues are on the diagonal and are given by $f(\lambda_i)$. The eigenvectors (but not the other generalized eigenvectors) of $\boldsymbol{A}$ and $\boldsymbol{F}(\boldsymbol{A})$ are the same. These eigenvectors are the columns of $\boldsymbol{T}$ corresponding to the very first element of each $\boldsymbol{F}(\boldsymbol{J}_{n_i}(\lambda_i))$ for $i = 1, \dots, k$, namely the vector $\boldsymbol{x}_1$ of any given Jordan chain of generalized eigenvectors. Notice that $\boldsymbol{F}(\boldsymbol{J}_{n_i}(\lambda_i))$ is *not* in general a matrix in Jordan form.

Exercise 9.19 (Absolute convergence of series)

(a) Let $\boldsymbol{A}$ be an $n \times n$ matrix. Show that the series $\boldsymbol{F}(\boldsymbol{A}) := \sum_{j=0}^{\infty} c_j \boldsymbol{A}^j$ converges absolutely if $\sum_{j=0}^{\infty} |c_j(\varrho(\boldsymbol{A}))^j| < \infty$. [Hint: Use the property that if a power series converges absolutely, then its term-by-term derivative converges absolutely as well; see Appendix A.]

(b) Hence, show that the series expansion of $\exp(\boldsymbol{A})$ converges absolutely for all finite $\boldsymbol{A}$, and thus defines the function.

(c) Also show that the binomial expansion

$$(\boldsymbol{I}_n + \boldsymbol{A})^{\nu} = \sum_{j=0}^{\infty} \binom{\nu}{j} \boldsymbol{A}^j,$$

converges absolutely for $\varrho(\boldsymbol{A}) < 1$.

Solution

(a) Let $\rho := \varrho(\boldsymbol{A})$. Exercise 9.18 implies that we only need to show that $\boldsymbol{F}(\boldsymbol{J})$ converges absolutely when $\sum_{j=0}^{\infty} |c_j \rho^j| < \infty$; that is, that, for $f(\lambda) := \sum_{j=0}^{\infty} c_j \lambda^j$, the series

$$\boldsymbol{F}(\boldsymbol{J}_{n_i}(\lambda_i)) = \begin{pmatrix} f(\lambda_i) & f'(\lambda_i) & \dots & \frac{f^{(n_i-1)}(\lambda_i)}{(n_i-1)!} \\ 0 & f(\lambda_i) & \dots & \frac{f^{(n_i-2)}(\lambda_i)}{(n_i-2)!} \\ \vdots & \vdots & & \vdots \\ 0 & 0 & \dots & f(\lambda_i) \end{pmatrix}$$

all converge absolutely. The condition $\sum_{j=0}^{\infty} |c_j \rho^j| < \infty$ implies that ρ is within the radius of convergence of the power series, and hence that

$$f(\rho) = \sum_{j=0}^{\infty} c_j \rho^j, \quad f'(\rho) = \sum_{j=0}^{\infty} j c_j \rho^{j-1}, \quad \dots$$

all converge absolutely. The result follows.

(b) We have

$$\sum_{j=0}^{\infty} \left| \frac{1}{j!} \rho^j \right| = \exp(\rho) < \infty,$$

and the absolute convergence follows from (a).

(c) Since the scalar binomial series

$$f(\rho) = \sum_{j=0}^{\infty} \binom{\nu}{j} \rho^j$$

converges absolutely for $\rho < 1$ (recall that ρ is nonnegative), the result follows. The same is also valid for $f(\rho) = -\sum_{j=1}^{\infty} (-\rho)^j / j$, so the series expansion of the logarithmic function derived in Exercise 9.8(b) converges absolutely when $\rho < 1$.

***Exercise 9.20 (Noninteger powers)** Let $\boldsymbol{A}$ and $\boldsymbol{B}$ be $n \times n$ matrices related by $\boldsymbol{B} = \boldsymbol{A}^{\nu}$, and let λ_i $(i = 1, \dots, n)$ be the eigenvalues of $\boldsymbol{A}$. Rewrite this relationship:

(a) in terms of the Jordan decompositions

$$\boldsymbol{A} = \boldsymbol{T}_1 \boldsymbol{J}_1 \boldsymbol{T}_1^{-1} \quad \text{and} \quad \boldsymbol{B} = \boldsymbol{T}_2 \boldsymbol{J}_2 \boldsymbol{T}_2^{-1}$$

for $\nu \in \mathbb{N}$ and $\nu \in \mathbb{Q}$;

(b) for $\nu \in \mathbb{R}$ and $|\lambda_i - 1| < 1$ for all i;

(c) for $\nu \in \mathbb{R}$ and $\left|\lambda_i^{-1} - 1\right| < 1$ for all i;

(d) for $\nu \in \mathbb{R}$ and $|\lambda_i / \mu - 1| < 1$ for all i $(\mu \neq 0)$.

Solution

(a) We already know that if ν a natural number, then

$$\boldsymbol{B} = \boldsymbol{A}^{\nu} = \prod_{i=1}^{\nu} (\boldsymbol{T}_1 \boldsymbol{J}_1 \boldsymbol{T}_1^{-1}) = \boldsymbol{T}_1 \left(\prod_{i=1}^{\nu} \boldsymbol{J}_1 \right) \boldsymbol{T}_1^{-1} = \boldsymbol{T}_1 \boldsymbol{J}_1^{\nu} \boldsymbol{T}_1^{-1}.$$

If ν is a rational number, then we can write $\nu = p/q$ for some integers p and q such that $q > 0$, and

$$\boldsymbol{B}^q = \boldsymbol{A}^p \iff \boldsymbol{T}_2\boldsymbol{J}_2^q\boldsymbol{T}_2^{-1} = \boldsymbol{T}_1\boldsymbol{J}_1^p\boldsymbol{T}_1^{-1}.$$

The powers of all the matrices are integers, which we know how to compute, but note that the last equality is generally not one-to-one. Also note that the rationals are dense in the reals (that is, any real number is the limit of a rational sequence), so that one can take $\nu \in \mathbb{R}$ as a limiting case of $\nu \in \mathbb{Q}$.
(b) The eigenvalues of $\boldsymbol{A}$ lie within a unit circle centered at 1, so that $\varrho(\boldsymbol{A} - \boldsymbol{I}_n) < 1$. Therefore, we can use the binomial expansion

$$\boldsymbol{A}^\nu = (\boldsymbol{I}_n + (\boldsymbol{A} - \boldsymbol{I}_n))^\nu = \sum_{j=0}^{\infty} \binom{\nu}{j} (\boldsymbol{A} - \boldsymbol{I}_n)^j .$$

(c) Similarly,

$$\boldsymbol{A}^\nu = \left(\boldsymbol{A}^{-1}\right)^{-\nu} = \left(\boldsymbol{I}_n + \left(\boldsymbol{A}^{-1} - \boldsymbol{I}_n\right)\right)^{-\nu} = \sum_{j=0}^{\infty} \binom{-\nu}{j} \left(\boldsymbol{A}^{-1} - \boldsymbol{I}_n\right)^j .$$

(d) Finally,

$$\boldsymbol{A}^\nu = \mu^\nu \left(\frac{1}{\mu}\boldsymbol{A}\right)^\nu = \mu^\nu \left(\boldsymbol{I}_n + \left(\frac{1}{\mu}\boldsymbol{A} - \boldsymbol{I}_n\right)\right)^\nu = \mu^\nu \sum_{j=0}^{\infty} \binom{\nu}{j} \left(\frac{1}{\mu}\boldsymbol{A} - \boldsymbol{I}_n\right)^j .$$

This latter solution may be multiple-valued depending on μ^ν; see Appendix A for some examples.

Exercise 9.21 (Determinant and trace of matrix functions) Let $\boldsymbol{A}$ be an $n \times n$ matrix with eigenvalues $\lambda_1, \dots, \lambda_n$. Define $\boldsymbol{F}(\boldsymbol{A}) := \sum_{j=0}^{\infty} c_j \boldsymbol{A}^j$ and $f(\lambda) := \sum_{j=0}^{\infty} c_j \lambda^j$. Show that:
(a) $|\boldsymbol{F}(\boldsymbol{A})| = \prod_{i=1}^{n} f(\lambda_i)$ and $\operatorname{tr} \boldsymbol{F}(\boldsymbol{A}) = \sum_{i=1}^{n} f(\lambda_i)$;
(b) $|\exp(\boldsymbol{A})| = \operatorname{etr}(\boldsymbol{A})$, where $\operatorname{etr}(\boldsymbol{A}) := \exp(\operatorname{tr} \boldsymbol{A})$;
(c) $\exp(\boldsymbol{A})$ is nonsingular for any finite $\boldsymbol{A}$;
(d) $\log |\boldsymbol{I}_n - \boldsymbol{A}| = -\sum_{j=1}^{\infty} \frac{1}{j} \operatorname{tr}(\boldsymbol{A}^j)$ for $\varrho(\boldsymbol{A}) < 1$.

Solution
(a) This follows from the Jordan representation $\boldsymbol{F}(\boldsymbol{A}) = \boldsymbol{T}\boldsymbol{F}(\boldsymbol{J})\boldsymbol{T}^{-1}$ in Exercise 9.18, because

$$|\boldsymbol{F}(\boldsymbol{A})| = |\boldsymbol{T}\boldsymbol{F}(\boldsymbol{J})\boldsymbol{T}^{-1}| = |\boldsymbol{F}(\boldsymbol{J})| \quad \text{and} \quad \operatorname{tr}(\boldsymbol{F}(\boldsymbol{A})) = \operatorname{tr}(\boldsymbol{T}\boldsymbol{F}(\boldsymbol{J})\boldsymbol{T}^{-1}) = \operatorname{tr}(\boldsymbol{F}(\boldsymbol{J})).$$

(b) As a special case, we obtain from (a),

$$|\exp(\boldsymbol{A})| = \prod_{i=1}^{n} \exp(\lambda_i) = \exp\left(\sum_{i=1}^{n} \lambda_i\right) = \exp(\operatorname{tr} \boldsymbol{A}).$$

(c) We show that $\exp(\boldsymbol{A})$ is nonsingular by demonstrating that its determinant is nonzero. From (b), $|\exp(\boldsymbol{A})| = 0$ if and only if $\exp(\operatorname{tr} \boldsymbol{A}) = 0$, that is, if and only if $\operatorname{tr} \boldsymbol{A} = -\infty$.

Since A is finite, its trace is also finite. Hence $\exp(\operatorname{tr} A) \neq 0$ and $\exp(A)$ is nonsingular.
(d) Also from (b),

$$\exp\left(-\sum_{j=1}^{\infty}\frac{1}{j}\operatorname{tr}(A^j)\right) = \operatorname{etr}\left(-\sum_{j=1}^{\infty}\frac{1}{j}A^j\right) = \left|\exp\left(-\sum_{j=1}^{\infty}\frac{1}{j}A^j\right)\right|$$
$$= \left|\exp\left(\log(I_n - A)\right)\right| = |I_n - A|.$$

The result follows by taking logarithms.

Exercise 9.22 (Orthogonal representation, 2) The representation of Exercise 9.12 is not constructive (because one needs to have an orthogonal S to begin with). Let B be a real nonsingular matrix and C a skew-symmetric matrix, both of order $n \times n$. Show that:
(a) $A := B(B'B)^{-1/2}$ is orthogonal, with $|A| = \pm 1$;
(b) $A := (I_n - C)(I_n + C)^{-1}$ is orthogonal, with $|A| = 1$;
(c) $A := \exp(C)$ is orthogonal, with $|A| = 1$.

Solution
(a) We have

$$A'A = (B'B)^{-1/2}B'B(B'B)^{-1/2} = I_n$$

and

$$AA' = B(B'B)^{-1}B' = I_n$$

by the nonsingularity of B. Since $B'B$ is positive definite, A is real and

$$|A| = \frac{|B|}{\sqrt{|B^2|}} = \operatorname{sgn}(|B|).$$

This proves (a) and also shows that we can always choose B such that either $|A| = 1$ or $|A| = -1$.
(b) The eigenvalues of $I_n + C$ have positive moduli (by Exercise 9.13), so that $I_n + C$ is nonsingular. Then,

$$\begin{aligned} AA' &= (I_n - C)(I_n + C)^{-1}(I_n + C')^{-1}(I_n - C') \\ &= (I_n - C)(I_n + C)^{-1}(I_n - C)^{-1}(I_n + C) \\ &= (I_n - C)(I_n - C)^{-1}(I_n + C)^{-1}(I_n + C) = I_n \end{aligned}$$

and, similarly, $A'A = I_n$. Alternatively, one may prove this by inverting A directly, as

$$\begin{aligned} A^{-1} &= (I_n + C)\left(I_n - C\right)^{-1} = \left(I_n - C'\right)\left(I_n + C'\right)^{-1} \\ &= \left(I_n + C'\right)^{-1}\left(I_n - C'\right) = A'. \end{aligned}$$

The determinant follows from

$$|A| = \frac{|I_n - C|}{|I_n + C|} = \frac{|I_n - C|}{|I_n + C'|} = \frac{|I_n - C|}{|I_n - C|} = 1.$$

(c) We have

$$A^{-1} = \exp(-C) = \exp(C') = \sum_{j=0}^{\infty} \frac{1}{j!}(C')^j = \left(\sum_{j=0}^{\infty} \frac{1}{j!} C^j \right)' = A'$$

and

$$|A| = |\exp(C)| = \exp(\operatorname{tr} C) = \exp(0) = 1.$$

Exercise 9.23 (Unitary representation) Let C be an $n \times n$ skew-Hermitian matrix. Show that:
(a) $A := (I_n - C)(I_n + C)^{-1}$ is unitary, with $|\det A| = 1$ (*Cayley's transform*);
(b) $A := \exp(C)$ is unitary, with $|\det A| = 1$. (We use the notation $\det A$ rather than $|A|$ for determinant in this exercise, so that we can write $|\det A|$ to denote the modulus of the determinant.)

Solution
(a) The proof of $A^*A = AA^* = I_n$ is analogous to the solution of Exercise 9.22(b), using conjugate transposes. For the determinant, denoting by λ_i $(i = 1, \dots, n)$ the eigenvalues of C, we obtain

$$\det A = \frac{\det(I_n - C)}{\det(I_n + C)} = \frac{\det(I_n + C^*)}{\det(I_n + C)} = \prod_{i=1}^{n} \frac{1 + \lambda_i^*}{1 + \lambda_i}.$$

Taking the modulus gives the required result. Notice that, by the same steps used in the solution of Exercise 9.13(a), the paired eigenvalues of C are $-\lambda^*, \lambda$. Exercise 9.13(b) implies that $\lambda^* = -\lambda$, so that the pairs in C are multiple eigenvalues λ, λ, hence not conjugates. This explains why, unlike in Exercise 9.22(b), $\det A$ is not restricted to $+1$ only.
(b) Here we have

$$A^{-1} = \exp(-C) = \exp(C^*) = (\exp(C))^* = A^*$$

and

$$\det A = \det(\exp(C)) = \exp(\operatorname{tr} C).$$

Exercise 9.13(b) shows that the eigenvalues of C are pure imaginary, so that $\operatorname{tr} C$ is pure imaginary and $\exp(\operatorname{tr} C)$ is on the unit circle (has unit modulus).

9.3 Matrix-polynomial representation

Exercise 9.24 (Exponential of Jordan) Let $\boldsymbol{J}_2(\mu)$ be a Jordan block of size 2. Obtain the polynomial representation of $\exp(a\boldsymbol{J}_2(\mu))$.

Solution
Let

$$\boldsymbol{A} = \begin{pmatrix} a\mu & a \\ 0 & a\mu \end{pmatrix},$$

where there is only one Jordan block (of size 2), corresponding to the multiple eigenvalue $\lambda = a\mu$. We need to find

$$\exp(\boldsymbol{A}) = p_0 \boldsymbol{I}_2 + p_1 \boldsymbol{A},$$

where the coefficients in $p(x) := p_0 + p_1 x$ are obtained by equating

$$\exp(\lambda) = p(\lambda) \quad \text{and} \quad \frac{\mathrm{d}\exp(\lambda)}{\mathrm{d}\lambda} = \frac{\mathrm{d}p(\lambda)}{\mathrm{d}\lambda},$$

that is, by solving

$$\exp(\lambda) = p_0 + p_1\lambda \quad \text{and} \quad \exp(\lambda) = p_1.$$

We find

$$p_1 = \mathrm{e}^{\lambda} = \mathrm{e}^{a\mu} \quad \text{and} \quad p_0 = (1-\lambda)\mathrm{e}^{\lambda} = (1-a\mu)\mathrm{e}^{a\mu},$$

so that

$$\exp(\boldsymbol{A}) = (1-a\mu)\mathrm{e}^{a\mu}\boldsymbol{I}_2 + \mathrm{e}^{a\mu}\boldsymbol{A} = \mathrm{e}^{a\mu}\begin{pmatrix} 1 & a \\ 0 & 1 \end{pmatrix}.$$

When $a = 1$, this reduces to the exponential obtained in Exercise 9.17(a).

Exercise 9.25 (Skew's exponential, by polynomial) Let

$$\boldsymbol{A} = \begin{pmatrix} 0 & -\theta \\ \theta & 0 \end{pmatrix},$$

where $\theta \neq 0$ and possibly complex. Obtain the corresponding Jordan matrix and the polynomial representation of $\exp(\boldsymbol{A})$. What happens when $\theta \to 0$?

Solution
This is a generalization of the 2×2 matrix encountered in Exercise 9.15, where we considered the special case $\theta = -\pi$. The eigenvalues of $\boldsymbol{A}$ are $\pm\mathrm{i}\theta$, which are obviously distinct, so the Jordan matrix is $\operatorname{diag}(-\mathrm{i}\theta, \mathrm{i}\theta)$. The coefficients of $p(\lambda) := p_0 + p_1\lambda$ are obtained by solving

$$\begin{pmatrix} \exp(-\mathrm{i}\theta) \\ \exp(\mathrm{i}\theta) \end{pmatrix} = \begin{pmatrix} p_0 - \mathrm{i}\theta p_1 \\ p_0 + \mathrm{i}\theta p_1 \end{pmatrix} = \begin{pmatrix} 1 & -\mathrm{i}\theta \\ 1 & \mathrm{i}\theta \end{pmatrix}\begin{pmatrix} p_0 \\ p_1 \end{pmatrix},$$

which yields

$$\begin{pmatrix} p_0 \\ p_1 \end{pmatrix} = \begin{pmatrix} 1 & -\mathrm{i}\theta \\ 1 & \mathrm{i}\theta \end{pmatrix}^{-1} \begin{pmatrix} \exp(-\mathrm{i}\theta) \\ \exp(\mathrm{i}\theta) \end{pmatrix}$$

$$= \frac{1}{2} \begin{pmatrix} 1 & 1 \\ \mathrm{i}\theta^{-1} & -\mathrm{i}\theta^{-1} \end{pmatrix} \begin{pmatrix} \exp(-\mathrm{i}\theta) \\ \exp(\mathrm{i}\theta) \end{pmatrix} = \begin{pmatrix} \cos\theta \\ \theta^{-1}\sin\theta \end{pmatrix},$$

using the definitions of the cosine and sine functions. Hence,

$$\exp(\boldsymbol{A}) = \begin{pmatrix} \cos\theta & 0 \\ 0 & \cos\theta \end{pmatrix} + \begin{pmatrix} 0 & -\sin\theta \\ \sin\theta & 0 \end{pmatrix} = \begin{pmatrix} \cos\theta & -\sin\theta \\ \sin\theta & \cos\theta \end{pmatrix}$$

as expected from Exercises 9.12, 9.13, and 9.22. When $\theta \to 0$, using l'Hôpital's rule,

$$\lim_{\theta \to 0} \begin{pmatrix} p_0 \\ p_1 \end{pmatrix} = \lim_{\theta \to 0} \begin{pmatrix} \cos\theta \\ \theta^{-1}\sin\theta \end{pmatrix} = \begin{pmatrix} \cos(0) \\ (\mathrm{d}\sin\theta / \mathrm{d}\theta)|_{\theta=0} \end{pmatrix} = \begin{pmatrix} 1 \\ 1 \end{pmatrix},$$

which should be compared to Exercise 9.24 where there was one equation from $p(\lambda)$ and one from $p'(\lambda)$. Therefore, when $\theta = 0$, $\exp(\boldsymbol{A}) = \boldsymbol{I}_2 + \boldsymbol{A} = \boldsymbol{I}_2$, and the formula for $\exp(\boldsymbol{A})$ in terms of $\cos\theta$ and $\sin\theta$ is valid for all θ.

Exercise 9.26 (Exponential for two blocks with distinct eigenvalues) Obtain the polynomial representation of $\exp(\boldsymbol{A})$ for

$$\boldsymbol{A} = \begin{pmatrix} 1 & 3 & 0 \\ 0 & 1 & 0 \\ 2 & 1 & 5 \end{pmatrix},$$

which has the Jordan matrix

$$\boldsymbol{J} = \begin{pmatrix} 5 & 0 & 0 \\ 0 & 1 & 1 \\ 0 & 0 & 1 \end{pmatrix}.$$

Solution

The matrix $\boldsymbol{J} = \operatorname{diag}(\boldsymbol{J}_1(5), \boldsymbol{J}_2(1))$ indicates that $\lambda_1 = 5$ and $\lambda_2 = 1$, with $m_1 = 1$ and $m_2 = 2$. Then, defining $p(\lambda) := \sum_{j=0}^{2} p_j \lambda^j$, we solve

$$\mathrm{e}^5 = p_0 + 5p_1 + 25p_2, \quad \mathrm{e} = p_0 + p_1 + p_2, \quad \mathrm{e} = p_1 + 2p_2,$$

by writing

$$\begin{pmatrix} p_0 \\ p_1 \\ p_2 \end{pmatrix} = \begin{pmatrix} 1 & 5 & 25 \\ 1 & 1 & 1 \\ 0 & 1 & 2 \end{pmatrix}^{-1} \begin{pmatrix} \mathrm{e}^5 \\ \mathrm{e} \\ \mathrm{e} \end{pmatrix} = \begin{pmatrix} \frac{1}{16} & \frac{15}{16} & -\frac{5}{4} \\ -\frac{1}{8} & \frac{1}{8} & \frac{3}{2} \\ \frac{1}{16} & -\frac{1}{16} & -\frac{1}{4} \end{pmatrix} \begin{pmatrix} \mathrm{e}^5 \\ \mathrm{e} \\ \mathrm{e} \end{pmatrix} = \frac{\mathrm{e}}{16} \begin{pmatrix} \mathrm{e}^4 - 5 \\ -2\mathrm{e}^4 + 26 \\ \mathrm{e}^4 - 5 \end{pmatrix},$$

where we note that $p_0 = p_2$. Therefore,

$$\begin{aligned}\exp(\boldsymbol{A}) &= \frac{\mathrm{e}}{16}\left(\mathrm{e}^4 - 5\right)\left(\boldsymbol{I}_3 + \boldsymbol{A}^2\right) - \frac{\mathrm{e}}{16}\left(2\mathrm{e}^4 - 26\right)\boldsymbol{A} \\ &= \frac{\mathrm{e}}{16}\left(\mathrm{e}^4 - 5\right)\left(\begin{pmatrix} 1 & 0 & 0 \\ 0 & 1 & 0 \\ 0 & 0 & 1 \end{pmatrix} + \begin{pmatrix} 1 & 6 & 0 \\ 0 & 1 & 0 \\ 12 & 12 & 25 \end{pmatrix}\right) \\ &\quad - \frac{\mathrm{e}}{16}\left(2\mathrm{e}^4 - 26\right)\begin{pmatrix} 1 & 3 & 0 \\ 0 & 1 & 0 \\ 2 & 1 & 5 \end{pmatrix} \\ &= \begin{pmatrix} \mathrm{e} & 3\mathrm{e} & 0 \\ 0 & \mathrm{e} & 0 \\ \frac{1}{2}\mathrm{e}^5 - \frac{1}{2}\mathrm{e} & \frac{5}{8}\mathrm{e}^5 - \frac{17}{8}\mathrm{e} & \mathrm{e}^5 \end{pmatrix},\end{aligned}$$

which is not surprising in view of Exercise 9.16.

Exercise 9.27 (Matrix of order three, linear polynomial, 1) Obtain the polynomial representation of $\exp(\boldsymbol{A})$ for

$$\boldsymbol{A} = \begin{pmatrix} 3 & 0 & 0 \\ 0 & 3 & 1 \\ 0 & 0 & 3 \end{pmatrix}.$$

Solution

The matrix $\boldsymbol{A} = \boldsymbol{J} = \operatorname{diag}(\boldsymbol{J}_1(3), \boldsymbol{J}_2(3))$ indicates that there is a single eigenvalue $\lambda = 3$, with maximal Jordan-block size of $m = 2$. Thus, defining $p(\lambda) := p_0 + p_1\lambda$, we solve

$$\mathrm{e}^3 = p_0 + 3p_1 \quad \text{and} \quad \mathrm{e}^3 = p_1$$

as

$$\begin{pmatrix} p_0 \\ p_1 \end{pmatrix} = \begin{pmatrix} 1 & 3 \\ 0 & 1 \end{pmatrix}^{-1}\begin{pmatrix} \mathrm{e}^3 \\ \mathrm{e}^3 \end{pmatrix} = \begin{pmatrix} 1 & -3 \\ 0 & 1 \end{pmatrix}\begin{pmatrix} \mathrm{e}^3 \\ \mathrm{e}^3 \end{pmatrix} = \begin{pmatrix} -2\mathrm{e}^3 \\ \mathrm{e}^3 \end{pmatrix},$$

so that

$$\exp(\boldsymbol{A}) = -2\mathrm{e}^3\boldsymbol{I}_3 + \mathrm{e}^3\boldsymbol{A} = \mathrm{e}^3\begin{pmatrix} 1 & 0 & 0 \\ 0 & 1 & 1 \\ 0 & 0 & 1 \end{pmatrix}.$$

In this instance, since $\boldsymbol{A} = \boldsymbol{J}$ and $\boldsymbol{T} = \boldsymbol{I}_3$, it would have been equally easy to use the method of the previous section and calculate $\exp(\boldsymbol{A})$ directly, rather than indirectly through its polynomial representation. It is nonetheless useful to see how the polynomial can be of order one, despite the fact that the matrix is of order three and is not nilpotent. Another advantage follows in Exercise 9.28.

Exercise 9.28 (Matrix of order three, linear polynomial, 2) Let

$$B = \begin{pmatrix} 6 & -9 & -3 \\ 1 & 0 & -1 \\ 0 & 0 & 3 \end{pmatrix},$$

which has the same Jordan matrix as A of Exercise 9.27. Calculate $\exp(B)$.

Solution
Since the Jordan matrix is the same as before, we obtain

$$\exp(B) = -2e^3 I_3 + e^3 B = e^3 \begin{pmatrix} 4 & -9 & -3 \\ 1 & -2 & -1 \\ 0 & 0 & 1 \end{pmatrix}.$$

Note that we did not need to work out the matrix T in $B = TAT^{-1}$, and that the polynomial representation is valid for *any* matrix B similar to A, that is, for $B = CAC^{-1}$, where C is *any* nonsingular matrix.

Exercise 9.29 (Matrix-polynomial representation) Write a typical Jordan block as $J_m(\lambda) = \lambda I_m + E$, where

$$E := J_m(0) = \begin{pmatrix} 0 & 1 & 0 & \dots & 0 \\ 0 & 0 & 1 & \dots & 0 \\ \vdots & \vdots & \vdots & & \vdots \\ 0 & 0 & 0 & \dots & 1 \\ 0 & 0 & 0 & \dots & 0 \end{pmatrix}.$$

Define $F(J_m(\lambda)) := \sum_{j=0}^{\infty} c_j J_m^j(\lambda)$ and $f(\lambda) := \sum_{j=0}^{\infty} c_j \lambda^j$.
(a) Show that $J_m^j(\lambda) = \sum_{t=0}^{j} \binom{j}{t} \lambda^{j-t} E^t$.
(b) Show that $F(J_m(\lambda)) = \sum_{t=0}^{m-1} \frac{1}{t!} f^{(t)}(\lambda) E^t$.
(c) Deduce that $\exp(x J_m(\lambda)) = \exp(x\lambda) \sum_{t=0}^{m-1} \frac{x^t}{t!} E^t$.
(d) Now let $A := T J_m(\lambda) T^{-1}$, where T is nonsingular, and define $P(A) := \sum_{t=0}^{m-1} p_t A^t$ and $p(\lambda) := \sum_{t=0}^{m-1} p_t \lambda^t$. Show that $F(A)$ and $P(A)$ have the same polynomial representation in terms of E if and only if $f^{(t)}(\lambda) = p^{(t)}(\lambda)$ for $t = 0, 1, \dots, m-1$. Would this result be valid if $p(\lambda)$ were a polynomial of order m or larger?

Solution
(a) This follows from Exercise 9.9(c), since λI_m is a scalar matrix and thus commutes with any conformable matrix. Note that if $j > m$, the series terminates after $t = m-1$ because E is nilpotentof index m.

(b) We will require the same manipulation of double series employed in Exercise 9.10, namely

$$\sum_{j=0}^{\infty}\sum_{t=0}^{j} g_{j-t,t}(x) = \sum_{j=0}^{\infty}\sum_{t=0}^{\infty} g_{j,t}(x)$$

for any function $g(\cdot)$. Substituting from (a),

$$\begin{aligned}\boldsymbol{F}(\boldsymbol{J}_m(\lambda)) &= \sum_{j=0}^{\infty} c_j \sum_{t=0}^{j} \binom{j}{t} \lambda^{j-t}\boldsymbol{E}^t = \sum_{j=0}^{\infty}\sum_{t=0}^{\infty} c_{j+t}\binom{j+t}{t}\lambda^j \boldsymbol{E}^t \\ &= \sum_{t=0}^{\infty} \boldsymbol{E}^t \sum_{j=0}^{\infty} c_{j+t}\binom{j+t}{t}\lambda^j = \sum_{t=0}^{m-1}\boldsymbol{E}^t \sum_{j=0}^{\infty}\binom{j+t}{t} c_{j+t}\lambda^j,\end{aligned}$$

because $\boldsymbol{E}^m = \mathbf{O}$. The result then follows from

$$f^{(t)}(\lambda) = \sum_{j=t}^{\infty} \frac{j!}{(j-t)!} c_j \lambda^{j-t} = \sum_{j=0}^{\infty} \frac{(j+t)!}{j!} c_{j+t}\lambda^j.$$

This is effectively an alternative proof to Exercise 9.17, without the detailed analysis of the elements of the matrices.
(c) This follows directly from (b) by writing $f(\lambda) = \exp(x\lambda)$, and generalizes Exercise 9.24.
(d) The polynomial representation of $\boldsymbol{F}(\boldsymbol{A})$ in terms of $\boldsymbol{E}$ follows from (b), and

$$\boldsymbol{T}^{-1}\boldsymbol{F}(\boldsymbol{A})\boldsymbol{T} = \sum_{t=0}^{m-1} \frac{1}{t!} f^{(t)}(\lambda)\boldsymbol{E}^t.$$

The same procedure leads to

$$\boldsymbol{T}^{-1}\boldsymbol{P}(\boldsymbol{A})\boldsymbol{T} = \sum_{t=0}^{m-1} \frac{1}{t!} p^{(t)}(\lambda)\boldsymbol{E}^t.$$

The result now follows by comparing the two equations, and using the fact that the nonzero elements of the nilpotents $\boldsymbol{E}^{t_1}$ and $\boldsymbol{E}^{t_2}$ are in different positions when $t_1 \neq t_2$. This implies that one can use the polynomial $\boldsymbol{P}(\boldsymbol{J}_m(\lambda))$ instead of the infinite series $\boldsymbol{F}(\boldsymbol{J}_m(\lambda))$ when calculating the function $\boldsymbol{F}$ of any matrix similar to $\boldsymbol{J}_m(\lambda)$. The result is valid even if the polynomial $p(\lambda)$ were of order m or larger.

Exercise 9.30 (Matrix of order three, overfitting) Suppose you are given the matrix $\boldsymbol{B}$ of Exercise 9.28, but you are only told that $\boldsymbol{B}$ has an eigenvalue 3 with multiplicity 3. Calculate $\exp(\boldsymbol{B})$.

Solution
Defining $q(\lambda) := \sum_{j=0}^{2} q_j\lambda^j$, we solve

$$\mathrm{e}^3 = q_0 + 3q_1 + 9q_2, \quad \mathrm{e}^3 = q_1 + 6q_2, \quad \mathrm{e}^3 = 2q_2$$

as

$$\begin{pmatrix} q_0 \\ q_1 \\ q_2 \end{pmatrix} = \begin{pmatrix} 1 & 3 & 9 \\ 0 & 1 & 6 \\ 0 & 0 & 2 \end{pmatrix}^{-1} \begin{pmatrix} \mathrm{e}^3 \\ \mathrm{e}^3 \\ \mathrm{e}^3 \end{pmatrix} = \begin{pmatrix} 1 & -3 & \frac{9}{2} \\ 0 & 1 & -3 \\ 0 & 0 & \frac{1}{2} \end{pmatrix} \begin{pmatrix} \mathrm{e}^3 \\ \mathrm{e}^3 \\ \mathrm{e}^3 \end{pmatrix} = \mathrm{e}^3 \begin{pmatrix} \frac{5}{2} \\ -2 \\ \frac{1}{2} \end{pmatrix}.$$

Hence,

$$\begin{aligned} \exp(\boldsymbol{B}) &= \frac{5}{2}\mathrm{e}^3 \boldsymbol{I}_3 - 2\mathrm{e}^3 \boldsymbol{B} + \frac{1}{2}\mathrm{e}^3 \boldsymbol{B}^2 \\ &= \frac{5}{2}\mathrm{e}^3 \begin{pmatrix} 1 & 0 & 0 \\ 0 & 1 & 0 \\ 0 & 0 & 1 \end{pmatrix} - 2\mathrm{e}^3 \begin{pmatrix} 6 & -9 & -3 \\ 1 & 0 & -1 \\ 0 & 0 & 3 \end{pmatrix} + \frac{1}{2}\mathrm{e}^3 \begin{pmatrix} 27 & -54 & -18 \\ 6 & -9 & -6 \\ 0 & 0 & 9 \end{pmatrix} \\ &= \mathrm{e}^3 \begin{pmatrix} 4 & -9 & -3 \\ 1 & -2 & -1 \\ 0 & 0 & 1 \end{pmatrix}, \end{aligned}$$

in accordance with Exercise 9.28.

Notes

The implicit definition of logarithms, $\exp(\log(\boldsymbol{B})) := \boldsymbol{B}$, hides some complications when one requires $\log(\boldsymbol{B})$ to be real-valued. For example, the function $\log x$ is defined for x negative, by using the polar form $x = |x| \exp(-\mathrm{i}\pi)$, in which case $\log x = \log|x| - \mathrm{i}\pi$. This has been avoided in Exercise 9.11(c). Also, noninteger powers of complex numbers introduce complications, such as having to deal with multiple-valued functions (see Appendix A) and having to define the principal values. We have avoided this as much as possible here. Details are in Horn and Johnson (1991).

The process of extending a given series expansion of a function beyond the original radius of convergence, is called *analytic continuation*, which is quite common in the analysis of complex variables. For example, in Exercise 9.5, if $\boldsymbol{b}'\boldsymbol{A}^{-1}\boldsymbol{a}$ is within a unit circle centered at 1, a binomial expansion of the denominator of

$$\frac{1/2}{1 + (\boldsymbol{b}'\boldsymbol{A}^{-1}\boldsymbol{a} - 1)/2}$$

gives again the same result. This reasoning holds for all points in $\mathbb{C}$ except $\boldsymbol{b}'\boldsymbol{A}^{-1}\boldsymbol{a} = -1$, so that the whole of $\mathbb{C}$ (except the point -1) can be covered by the formula we have obtained for the inverse. More details can be found in Whittaker and Watson (1996).

For the representation of some types of orthogonal matrices useful in statistics, see Hedayat and Wallis (1978).

In the development of this chapter, we have shown how to represent the infinite series $\boldsymbol{F}(\boldsymbol{A})$ in terms of a polynomial by using the Jordan decomposition theorem. See, for example, Horn and Johnson (1991) who also study the Lagrange-Hermite interpolation formula for fitting polynomials.

There is, however, a second approach. Recall the Cayley-Hamilton theorem, which states that every matrix satisfies its own characteristic equation. The matrix function $\boldsymbol{B} :=$ $\boldsymbol{F}(\boldsymbol{A})$ is itself a matrix of order n, hence satisfying its *own* characteristic equation. This is a matrix polynomial of order n that is equivalent to the null matrix. Thus there exists a representation of $\boldsymbol{F}(\boldsymbol{A})$ as a matrix polynomial of maximal order $n-1$.

10

Kronecker product, vec-operator, and Moore-Penrose inverse

The Kronecker product transforms two matrices $\boldsymbol{A} := (a_{ij})$ and $\boldsymbol{B} := (b_{st})$ into a matrix containing all products $a_{ij}b_{st}$. More precisely, let $\boldsymbol{A}$ be a matrix of order $m \times n$ and $\boldsymbol{B}$ a matrix of order $p \times q$. Then the $mp \times nq$ matrix defined by

$$\begin{pmatrix} a_{11}\boldsymbol{B} & \dots & a_{1n}\boldsymbol{B} \\ \vdots & & \vdots \\ a_{m1}\boldsymbol{B} & \dots & a_{mn}\boldsymbol{B} \end{pmatrix}$$

is called the *Kronecker product* of $\boldsymbol{A}$ and $\boldsymbol{B}$ and is written $\boldsymbol{A} \otimes \boldsymbol{B}$. We notice that the Kronecker product $\boldsymbol{A} \otimes \boldsymbol{B}$ is defined for any pair of matrices $\boldsymbol{A}$ and $\boldsymbol{B}$, irrespective of their orders.

The *vec-operator* transforms a matrix into a vector by stacking its columns one underneath the other. Let $\boldsymbol{A}$ be an $m \times n$ matrix and $\boldsymbol{a}_i$ its i-th column. Then $\operatorname{vec} \boldsymbol{A}$ is the $mn \times 1$ vector

$$\operatorname{vec} \boldsymbol{A} := \begin{pmatrix} \boldsymbol{a}_1 \\ \boldsymbol{a}_2 \\ \vdots \\ \boldsymbol{a}_n \end{pmatrix}.$$

Notice that $\operatorname{vec} \boldsymbol{A}$ is defined for any matrix $\boldsymbol{A}$, not just for square matrices. We shall see that the Kronecker product and the vec-operator are intimately connected. Also notice the notation. The expression $\operatorname{vec} \boldsymbol{A}'$ denotes $\operatorname{vec}(\boldsymbol{A}')$ and not $(\operatorname{vec} \boldsymbol{A})'$. Occasionally we shall use parentheses and write, for example, $\operatorname{vec}(\boldsymbol{AB})$ instead of $\operatorname{vec} \boldsymbol{AB}$, but only if there is a possibility of confusion.

The inverse of a matrix is defined when the matrix is square and nonsingular. For many purposes it is useful to generalize the concept of invertibility to singular matrices and, indeed, to nonsquare matrices. One such generalization that is particularly useful because of its uniqueness is the *Moore-Penrose* (MP) inverse. Let $\boldsymbol{A}$ be a given real matrix of order $m \times n$. Then an $n \times m$ matrix $\boldsymbol{X}$ is said to be the MP-inverse of $\boldsymbol{A}$ if the following four conditions are satisfied:

$$\boldsymbol{AXA} = \boldsymbol{A}, \quad \boldsymbol{XAX} = \boldsymbol{X}, \quad (\boldsymbol{AX})' = \boldsymbol{AX}, \quad (\boldsymbol{XA})' = \boldsymbol{XA}.$$

We shall denote the MP-inverse of $\boldsymbol{A}$ by $\boldsymbol{A}^+$. Occasionally a more general inverse, the so-called *generalized inverse* $\boldsymbol{A}^-$, suffices. This matrix only satisfies one of the four equations, $\boldsymbol{AXA} = \boldsymbol{A}$, and it is not unique.

All matrices in this chapter are real, unless specified otherwise. However, most statements, for example the definition of the Moore-Penrose inverse above, generalize straightforwardly to complex matrices by replacing the transpose (′) by the conjugate transpose (*).

10.1 The Kronecker product

Exercise 10.1 (Kronecker examples) Let

$$\boldsymbol{A} = \begin{pmatrix} 2 & 5 & 2 \\ 0 & 6 & 3 \end{pmatrix}, \quad \boldsymbol{B} = \begin{pmatrix} 2 & 4 & 1 \\ 3 & 5 & 0 \end{pmatrix}, \quad \boldsymbol{e}' = (0, 0, 1).$$

(a) Compute $\boldsymbol{I}_2 \otimes \boldsymbol{A}$ and $\boldsymbol{A} \otimes \boldsymbol{I}_2$.
(b) Compute $\boldsymbol{A}' \otimes \boldsymbol{B}$.
(c) Compute $\boldsymbol{A} \otimes \boldsymbol{e}$ and $\boldsymbol{A} \otimes \boldsymbol{e}'$.

Solution
(a) We have

$$\boldsymbol{I}_2 \otimes \boldsymbol{A} = \begin{pmatrix} \boldsymbol{A} & \mathbf{O} \\ \mathbf{O} & \boldsymbol{A} \end{pmatrix} = \begin{pmatrix} 2 & 5 & 2 & 0 & 0 & 0 \\ 0 & 6 & 3 & 0 & 0 & 0 \\ 0 & 0 & 0 & 2 & 5 & 2 \\ 0 & 0 & 0 & 0 & 6 & 3 \end{pmatrix}$$

and

$$\boldsymbol{A} \otimes \boldsymbol{I}_2 = \begin{pmatrix} 2\boldsymbol{I}_2 & 5\boldsymbol{I}_2 & 2\boldsymbol{I}_2 \\ \mathbf{O} & 6\boldsymbol{I}_2 & 3\boldsymbol{I}_2 \end{pmatrix} = \begin{pmatrix} 2 & 0 & 5 & 0 & 2 & 0 \\ 0 & 2 & 0 & 5 & 0 & 2 \\ 0 & 0 & 6 & 0 & 3 & 0 \\ 0 & 0 & 0 & 6 & 0 & 3 \end{pmatrix}.$$

(b) Similarly,

$$\boldsymbol{A}' \otimes \boldsymbol{B} = \begin{pmatrix} 2\boldsymbol{B} & \mathbf{O} \\ 5\boldsymbol{B} & 6\boldsymbol{B} \\ 2\boldsymbol{B} & 3\boldsymbol{B} \end{pmatrix} = \begin{pmatrix} 4 & 8 & 2 & 0 & 0 & 0 \\ 6 & 10 & 0 & 0 & 0 & 0 \\ 10 & 20 & 5 & 12 & 24 & 6 \\ 15 & 25 & 0 & 18 & 30 & 0 \\ 4 & 8 & 2 & 6 & 12 & 3 \\ 6 & 10 & 0 & 9 & 15 & 0 \end{pmatrix}.$$

(c) Finally,

$$A \otimes e = \begin{pmatrix} 0 & 0 & 0 \\ 0 & 0 & 0 \\ 2 & 5 & 2 \\ 0 & 0 & 0 \\ 0 & 0 & 0 \\ 0 & 6 & 3 \end{pmatrix}, \quad A \otimes e' = \begin{pmatrix} 0 & 0 & 2 & 0 & 0 & 5 & 0 & 0 & 2 \\ 0 & 0 & 0 & 0 & 0 & 6 & 0 & 0 & 3 \end{pmatrix}.$$

Exercise 10.2 (Noncommutativity of Kronecker product) Show that:
(a) $\mathbf{O} \otimes \boldsymbol{A} = \boldsymbol{A} \otimes \mathbf{O} = \mathbf{O}$;
(b) $\mathrm{dg}(\boldsymbol{A} \otimes \boldsymbol{B}) = \mathrm{dg}(\boldsymbol{A}) \otimes \mathrm{dg}(\boldsymbol{B})$ ($\boldsymbol{A}$ and $\boldsymbol{B}$ square);
(c) $\boldsymbol{A} \otimes \boldsymbol{B} \neq \boldsymbol{B} \otimes \boldsymbol{A}$, in general.

Solution
(a) The matrix $\boldsymbol{A} \otimes \boldsymbol{B}$ contains elements $a_{ij}b_{st}$. If either $a_{ij} = 0$ for all i, j or if $b_{st} = 0$ for all s, t, then $\boldsymbol{A} \otimes \boldsymbol{B} = \mathbf{O}$.
(b) Let $\boldsymbol{A}$ be a matrix of order $n \times n$. Then,

$$\mathrm{dg}(\boldsymbol{A} \otimes \boldsymbol{B}) = \mathrm{dg}\begin{pmatrix} a_{11}\boldsymbol{B} & \mathbf{O} & \dots & \mathbf{O} \\ \mathbf{O} & a_{22}\boldsymbol{B} & \dots & \mathbf{O} \\ \vdots & \vdots & & \vdots \\ \mathbf{O} & \mathbf{O} & \dots & a_{nn}\boldsymbol{B} \end{pmatrix}$$

$$= \begin{pmatrix} a_{11}\,\mathrm{dg}(\boldsymbol{B}) & \mathbf{O} & \dots & \mathbf{O} \\ \mathbf{O} & a_{22}\,\mathrm{dg}(\boldsymbol{B}) & \dots & \mathbf{O} \\ \vdots & \vdots & & \vdots \\ \mathbf{O} & \mathbf{O} & \dots & a_{nn}\,\mathrm{dg}(\boldsymbol{B}) \end{pmatrix} = \mathrm{dg}(\boldsymbol{A}) \otimes \mathrm{dg}(\boldsymbol{B}).$$

(c) If $\boldsymbol{A}$ is of order $m \times n$ and $\boldsymbol{B}$ of order $p \times q$, then $\boldsymbol{A} \otimes \boldsymbol{B}$ and $\boldsymbol{B} \otimes \boldsymbol{A}$ have the same order $mp \times nq$ (in contrast to $\boldsymbol{AB}$ and $\boldsymbol{BA}$, which may be of different orders). Exercise 10.1(a) contains an example of noncommutativity. Another example is

$$\begin{pmatrix} 1 & 0 \end{pmatrix} \otimes \begin{pmatrix} 0 & 1 \end{pmatrix} = \begin{pmatrix} 0 & 1 & 0 & 0 \end{pmatrix}$$

and

$$\begin{pmatrix} 0 & 1 \end{pmatrix} \otimes \begin{pmatrix} 1 & 0 \end{pmatrix} = \begin{pmatrix} 0 & 0 & 1 & 0 \end{pmatrix}.$$

Exercise 10.3 (Kronecker rules) Show that the Kronecker product satisfies the following rules:
(a) $(\boldsymbol{A}_1 + \boldsymbol{A}_2) \otimes \boldsymbol{B} = \boldsymbol{A}_1 \otimes \boldsymbol{B} + \boldsymbol{A}_2 \otimes \boldsymbol{B}$ ($\boldsymbol{A}_1$ and $\boldsymbol{A}_2$ of the same order);
(b) $\boldsymbol{A} \otimes (\boldsymbol{B}_1 + \boldsymbol{B}_2) = \boldsymbol{A} \otimes \boldsymbol{B}_1 + \boldsymbol{A} \otimes \boldsymbol{B}_2$ ($\boldsymbol{B}_1$ and $\boldsymbol{B}_2$ of the same order);
(c) $\alpha\boldsymbol{A} \otimes \beta\boldsymbol{B} = \alpha\beta(\boldsymbol{A} \otimes \boldsymbol{B})$;
(d) $(\boldsymbol{A} \otimes \boldsymbol{B})(\boldsymbol{C} \otimes \boldsymbol{D}) = \boldsymbol{AC} \otimes \boldsymbol{BD}$.

Solution

(a) The typical block in the matrix $\boldsymbol{A} \otimes \boldsymbol{B}$ is the submatrix $a_{ij}\boldsymbol{B}$. Hence, the typical block in $(\boldsymbol{A}_1 + \boldsymbol{A}_2) \otimes \boldsymbol{B}$ is

$$(\boldsymbol{A}_1 + \boldsymbol{A}_2)_{ij}\boldsymbol{B} = ((\boldsymbol{A}_1)_{ij} + (\boldsymbol{A}_2)_{ij})\boldsymbol{B} = (\boldsymbol{A}_1)_{ij}\boldsymbol{B} + (\boldsymbol{A}_2)_{ij}\boldsymbol{B}.$$

(b) Let $\boldsymbol{B} := \boldsymbol{B}_1 + \boldsymbol{B}_2$. Then for each submatrix $a_{ij}\boldsymbol{B}$ of $\boldsymbol{A} \otimes \boldsymbol{B}$, we have $a_{ij}\boldsymbol{B} = a_{ij}\boldsymbol{B}_1 + a_{ij}\boldsymbol{B}_2$.

(c) In each typical submatrix we have $(\alpha\boldsymbol{A})_{ij}(\beta\boldsymbol{B}) = (\alpha\beta)a_{ij}\boldsymbol{B}$.

(d) Let $\boldsymbol{A}$ $(m \times n)$, $\boldsymbol{B}$ $(q \times r)$, $\boldsymbol{C}$ $(n \times p)$, and $\boldsymbol{D}$ $(r \times s)$ be given matrices. Then both products $\boldsymbol{AC}$ and $\boldsymbol{BD}$ are defined. Since $\boldsymbol{A} \otimes \boldsymbol{B}$ has nr columns and $\boldsymbol{C} \otimes \boldsymbol{D}$ has nr rows, the product $(\boldsymbol{A} \otimes \boldsymbol{B})(\boldsymbol{C} \otimes \boldsymbol{D})$ is defined as well. Let $\boldsymbol{A} = (a_{ij})$ and $\boldsymbol{C} = (c_{st})$. Then,

$$\begin{aligned}(\boldsymbol{A} \otimes \boldsymbol{B})(\boldsymbol{C} \otimes \boldsymbol{D}) &= \begin{pmatrix} a_{11}\boldsymbol{B} & \dots & a_{1n}\boldsymbol{B} \\ \vdots & & \vdots \\ a_{m1}\boldsymbol{B} & \dots & a_{mn}\boldsymbol{B} \end{pmatrix} \begin{pmatrix} c_{11}\boldsymbol{D} & \dots & c_{1p}\boldsymbol{D} \\ \vdots & & \vdots \\ c_{n1}\boldsymbol{D} & \dots & c_{np}\boldsymbol{D} \end{pmatrix} \\ &= \begin{pmatrix} (\sum_i a_{1i}c_{i1})\boldsymbol{BD} & \dots & (\sum_i a_{1i}c_{ip})\boldsymbol{BD} \\ \vdots & & \vdots \\ (\sum_i a_{mi}c_{i1})\boldsymbol{BD} & \dots & (\sum_i a_{mi}c_{ip})\boldsymbol{BD} \end{pmatrix} \\ &= \begin{pmatrix} (\boldsymbol{AC})_{11}\boldsymbol{BD} & \dots & (\boldsymbol{AC})_{1p}\boldsymbol{BD} \\ \vdots & & \vdots \\ (\boldsymbol{AC})_{m1}\boldsymbol{BD} & \dots & (\boldsymbol{AC})_{mp}\boldsymbol{BD} \end{pmatrix} = \boldsymbol{AC} \otimes \boldsymbol{BD}.\end{aligned}$$

Exercise 10.4 (Kronecker twice) Show that

$$\boldsymbol{A} \otimes (\boldsymbol{B} \otimes \boldsymbol{C}) = (\boldsymbol{A} \otimes \boldsymbol{B}) \otimes \boldsymbol{C},$$

and hence that $\boldsymbol{A} \otimes \boldsymbol{B} \otimes \boldsymbol{C}$ is unambiguous.

Solution

Let $\boldsymbol{A}$ be a matrix of order $m \times n$. Then,

$$\begin{aligned}(\boldsymbol{A} \otimes \boldsymbol{B}) \otimes \boldsymbol{C} &= \begin{pmatrix} a_{11}\boldsymbol{B} & \dots & a_{1n}\boldsymbol{B} \\ \vdots & & \vdots \\ a_{m1}\boldsymbol{B} & \dots & a_{mn}\boldsymbol{B} \end{pmatrix} \otimes \boldsymbol{C} \\ &= \begin{pmatrix} (a_{11}\boldsymbol{B}) \otimes \boldsymbol{C} & \dots & (a_{1n}\boldsymbol{B}) \otimes \boldsymbol{C} \\ \vdots & & \vdots \\ (a_{m1}\boldsymbol{B}) \otimes \boldsymbol{C} & \dots & (a_{mn}\boldsymbol{B}) \otimes \boldsymbol{C} \end{pmatrix} \\ &= \begin{pmatrix} a_{11}(\boldsymbol{B} \otimes \boldsymbol{C}) & \dots & a_{1n}(\boldsymbol{B} \otimes \boldsymbol{C}) \\ \vdots & & \vdots \\ a_{m1}(\boldsymbol{B} \otimes \boldsymbol{C}) & \dots & a_{mn}(\boldsymbol{B} \otimes \boldsymbol{C}) \end{pmatrix} = \boldsymbol{A} \otimes (\boldsymbol{B} \otimes \boldsymbol{C}).\end{aligned}$$

Exercise 10.5 (Kroneckered by a scalar)
(a) Show, for any scalar α, that $\alpha \otimes \boldsymbol{A} = \alpha\boldsymbol{A} = \boldsymbol{A}\alpha = \boldsymbol{A} \otimes \alpha$.
(b) Hence, show that $(\boldsymbol{A} \otimes \boldsymbol{b})\boldsymbol{B} = (\boldsymbol{AB}) \otimes \boldsymbol{b}$ for any vector $\boldsymbol{b}$ (if $\boldsymbol{AB}$ is defined).

Solution
(a) This follows directly from the definition.
(b) In proofs, if at all possible, we wish to work with matrices and vectors, and not with the individual elements. So, we write

$$(\boldsymbol{A} \otimes \boldsymbol{b})\boldsymbol{B} = (\boldsymbol{A} \otimes \boldsymbol{b})(\boldsymbol{B} \otimes 1) = (\boldsymbol{AB}) \otimes \boldsymbol{b}.$$

(Check that all multiplications are allowed!)

Exercise 10.6 (Kronecker product of vectors) For any two vectors $\boldsymbol{a}$ and $\boldsymbol{b}$, not necessarily of the same order, show that $\boldsymbol{a} \otimes \boldsymbol{b}' = \boldsymbol{ab}' = \boldsymbol{b}' \otimes \boldsymbol{a}$.

Solution
Let $\boldsymbol{a} := (a_1, \dots, a_m)'$ and $\boldsymbol{b} := (b_1, \dots, b_n)'$. Then,

$$\boldsymbol{a} \otimes \boldsymbol{b}' = \begin{pmatrix} a_1\boldsymbol{b}' \\ \vdots \\ a_m\boldsymbol{b}' \end{pmatrix} = \boldsymbol{ab}' = (b_1\boldsymbol{a}, \dots, b_n\boldsymbol{a}) = \boldsymbol{b}' \otimes \boldsymbol{a}.$$

Exercise 10.7 (Transpose and trace of a Kronecker product) Show that:
(a) $(\boldsymbol{A} \otimes \boldsymbol{B})' = \boldsymbol{A}' \otimes \boldsymbol{B}'$;
(b) $\operatorname{tr}(\boldsymbol{A} \otimes \boldsymbol{B}) = (\operatorname{tr} \boldsymbol{A})(\operatorname{tr} \boldsymbol{B})$;
(c) $\boldsymbol{A} \otimes \boldsymbol{B}$ is idempotent if $\boldsymbol{A}$ and $\boldsymbol{B}$ are idempotent;
and specify the order conditions where appropriate.

Solution
(a) We have

$$(\boldsymbol{A} \otimes \boldsymbol{B})' = \begin{pmatrix} a_{11}\boldsymbol{B} & \dots & a_{1n}\boldsymbol{B} \\ \vdots & & \vdots \\ a_{m1}\boldsymbol{B} & \dots & a_{mn}\boldsymbol{B} \end{pmatrix}' = \begin{pmatrix} a_{11}\boldsymbol{B}' & \dots & a_{m1}\boldsymbol{B}' \\ \vdots & & \vdots \\ a_{1n}\boldsymbol{B}' & \dots & a_{mn}\boldsymbol{B}' \end{pmatrix} = \boldsymbol{A}' \otimes \boldsymbol{B}'.$$

This holds for matrices $\boldsymbol{A}$ and $\boldsymbol{B}$ of any order.
(b) Here, $\boldsymbol{A}$ and $\boldsymbol{B}$ must be square, but not necessarily of the same order. Then,

$$\begin{aligned} \operatorname{tr}(\boldsymbol{A} \otimes \boldsymbol{B}) &= \operatorname{tr} \begin{pmatrix} a_{11}\boldsymbol{B} & \dots & a_{1m}\boldsymbol{B} \\ \vdots & & \vdots \\ a_{m1}\boldsymbol{B} & \dots & a_{mm}\boldsymbol{B} \end{pmatrix} = \operatorname{tr}(a_{11}\boldsymbol{B}) + \dots + \operatorname{tr}(a_{mm}\boldsymbol{B}) \\ &= (a_{11} + \dots + a_{mm}) \operatorname{tr} \boldsymbol{B} = (\operatorname{tr} \boldsymbol{A})(\operatorname{tr} \boldsymbol{B}). \end{aligned}$$

(c) Again, $\boldsymbol{A}$ and $\boldsymbol{B}$ must be square, but not necessarily of the same order. Then,

$$(\boldsymbol{A} \otimes \boldsymbol{B})(\boldsymbol{A} \otimes \boldsymbol{B}) = (\boldsymbol{A}\boldsymbol{A}) \otimes (\boldsymbol{B}\boldsymbol{B}) = \boldsymbol{A} \otimes \boldsymbol{B}.$$

Exercise 10.8 (Inverse of a Kronecker product) Show that

$$(\boldsymbol{A} \otimes \boldsymbol{B})^{-1} = \boldsymbol{A}^{-1} \otimes \boldsymbol{B}^{-1}$$

when $\boldsymbol{A}$ and $\boldsymbol{B}$ are both nonsingular, not necessarily of the same order.

Solution

Let $\boldsymbol{A}$ and $\boldsymbol{B}$ be nonsingular matrices of orders m and n, respectively. Then,

$$(\boldsymbol{A} \otimes \boldsymbol{B})(\boldsymbol{A}^{-1} \otimes \boldsymbol{B}^{-1}) = (\boldsymbol{A}\boldsymbol{A}^{-1}) \otimes (\boldsymbol{B}\boldsymbol{B}^{-1}) = \boldsymbol{I}_m \otimes \boldsymbol{I}_n = \boldsymbol{I}_{mn},$$

and hence one is the inverse of the other.

Exercise 10.9 (Kronecker product of a partitioned matrix) If $\boldsymbol{A}$ is a partitioned matrix,

$$\boldsymbol{A} = \begin{pmatrix} \boldsymbol{A}_{11} & \boldsymbol{A}_{12} \\ \boldsymbol{A}_{21} & \boldsymbol{A}_{22} \end{pmatrix},$$

then show that

$$\boldsymbol{A} \otimes \boldsymbol{B} = \begin{pmatrix} \boldsymbol{A}_{11} \otimes \boldsymbol{B} & \boldsymbol{A}_{12} \otimes \boldsymbol{B} \\ \boldsymbol{A}_{21} \otimes \boldsymbol{B} & \boldsymbol{A}_{22} \otimes \boldsymbol{B} \end{pmatrix}.$$

Solution

Suppose $\boldsymbol{A}_{ij}$ has order $m_i \times n_j$, with $m_1 + m_2 = m$, $n_1 + n_2 = n$, so that the order of $\boldsymbol{A}$ is $m \times n$. Then,

$$\boldsymbol{A} \otimes \boldsymbol{B} = \begin{pmatrix} a_{1,1}\boldsymbol{B} & \dots & a_{1,n_1}\boldsymbol{B} & a_{1,n_1+1}\boldsymbol{B} & \dots & a_{1,n}\boldsymbol{B} \\ \vdots & & \vdots & \vdots & & \vdots \\ a_{m_1,1}\boldsymbol{B} & \dots & a_{m_1,n_1}\boldsymbol{B} & a_{m_1,n_1+1}\boldsymbol{B} & \dots & a_{m_1,n}\boldsymbol{B} \\ a_{m_1+1,1}\boldsymbol{B} & \dots & a_{m_1+1,n_1} & a_{m_1+1,n_1+1}\boldsymbol{B} & \dots & a_{m_1+1,n}\boldsymbol{B} \\ \vdots & & \vdots & \vdots & & \vdots \\ a_{m,1}\boldsymbol{B} & \dots & a_{m,n_1}\boldsymbol{B} & a_{m,n_1+1}\boldsymbol{B} & \dots & a_{m,n}\boldsymbol{B} \end{pmatrix}$$

$$= \begin{pmatrix} \boldsymbol{A}_{11} \otimes \boldsymbol{B} & \boldsymbol{A}_{12} \otimes \boldsymbol{B} \\ \boldsymbol{A}_{21} \otimes \boldsymbol{B} & \boldsymbol{A}_{22} \otimes \boldsymbol{B} \end{pmatrix}.$$

Exercise 10.10 (Eigenvalues of a Kronecker product) Let $\boldsymbol{A}$ be an $m \times m$ matrix with eigenvalues $\lambda_1, \dots, \lambda_m$, and let $\boldsymbol{B}$ be an $n \times n$ matrix with eigenvalues $\mu_1, \dots, \mu_n$. Show that the mn eigenvalues of $\boldsymbol{A} \otimes \boldsymbol{B}$ are $\lambda_i\mu_j (i = 1, \dots, m; j = 1, \dots, n)$.

Solution

By Schur's theorem (Exercise 7.62) there exist unitary matrices $\boldsymbol{S}$ and $\boldsymbol{T}$ such that

$$\boldsymbol{S}^*\boldsymbol{A}\boldsymbol{S} = \boldsymbol{L}, \quad \boldsymbol{T}^*\boldsymbol{B}\boldsymbol{T} = \boldsymbol{M},$$

where L and M are upper triangular matrices whose diagonal elements are the eigenvalues of A and B, respectively. This gives

$$(S^* \otimes T^*)(A \otimes B)(S \otimes T) = L \otimes M.$$

Since $S^{-1} = S^*$ and $T^{-1} = T^*$, it follows that $(S \otimes T)^{-1} = S^* \otimes T^*$, and hence, using Exercise 7.24, that $(S^* \otimes T^*)(A \otimes B)(S \otimes T)$ and $A \otimes B$ have the same set of eigenvalues. This implies that $A \otimes B$ and $L \otimes M$ have the same set of eigenvalues. But $L \otimes M$ is an upper triangular matrix and hence (Exercise 7.15(b)) its eigenvalues are equal to its diagonal elements $\lambda_i \mu_j$.

Exercise 10.11 (Eigenvectors of a Kronecker product)
(a) Show that, if x is an eigenvector of A and y is an eigenvector of B, then $x \otimes y$ is an eigenvector of $A \otimes B$.
(b) Is it true that each eigenvector of $A \otimes B$ is of the form $x \otimes y$, where x is an eigenvector of A and y is an eigenvector of B?

Solution
(a) If $Ax = \lambda x$ and $By = \mu y$, then

$$(A \otimes B)(x \otimes y) = Ax \otimes By = \lambda x \otimes \mu y = \lambda\mu(x \otimes y).$$

(b) No. For example, let

$$A = B = \begin{pmatrix} 0 & 1 \\ 0 & 0 \end{pmatrix}, \quad e_1 = \begin{pmatrix} 1 \\ 0 \end{pmatrix}, \quad e_2 = \begin{pmatrix} 0 \\ 1 \end{pmatrix}.$$

Both eigenvalues of A (and both eigenvalues of B) are zero. The only eigenvector is e_1. The four eigenvalues of $A \otimes B$ are all zero, but $A \otimes B$ has three eigenvectors: $e_1 \otimes e_1$, $e_1 \otimes e_2$, and $e_2 \otimes e_1$.

Exercise 10.12 (Determinant and rank of a Kronecker product)
(a) If A and B are positive (semi)definite, show that $A \otimes B$ is positive (semi)definite.
(b) Show that

$$|A \otimes B| = |A|^n |B|^m,$$

when A and B are square matrices of orders m and n, respectively.
(c) Show that

$$\operatorname{rk}(A \otimes B) = \operatorname{rk}(A) \operatorname{rk}(B).$$

Solution
(a) If A and B are positive (semi)definite, then the eigenvalues λ_i of A and the eigenvalues μ_j of B are all positive (nonnegative), and hence all eigenvalues $\lambda_i \mu_j$ of $A \otimes B$ are also positive (nonnegative), so that $A \otimes B$ is positive (semi)definite (Exercise 8.11).

(b) The determinant is the product of the eigenvalues, so

$$|\boldsymbol{A} \otimes \boldsymbol{B}| = \prod_{i=1}^{m} \prod_{j=1}^{n} (\lambda_i \mu_j) = \prod_{i=1}^{m} (\lambda_i^n |\boldsymbol{B}|) = |\boldsymbol{B}|^m \left(\prod_{i=1}^{m} \lambda_i \right)^n = |\boldsymbol{A}|^n |\boldsymbol{B}|^m.$$

(c) Our starting point is

$$\text{rk}(\boldsymbol{A} \otimes \boldsymbol{B}) = \text{rk}(\boldsymbol{A} \otimes \boldsymbol{B})(\boldsymbol{A} \otimes \boldsymbol{B})' = \text{rk}(\boldsymbol{A}\boldsymbol{A}' \otimes \boldsymbol{B}\boldsymbol{B}').$$

The matrix $\boldsymbol{A}\boldsymbol{A}' \otimes \boldsymbol{B}\boldsymbol{B}'$ is symmetric (in fact, positive semidefinite) and hence its rank equals the number of nonzero eigenvalues (Exercise 7.49). Now, the eigenvalues of $\boldsymbol{A}\boldsymbol{A}' \otimes \boldsymbol{B}\boldsymbol{B}'$ are $\{\lambda_i \mu_j\}$, where $\{\lambda_i\}$ are the eigenvalues of $\boldsymbol{A}\boldsymbol{A}'$ and $\{\mu_j\}$ are the eigenvalues of $\boldsymbol{B}\boldsymbol{B}'$. The eigenvalue $\lambda_i \mu_j$ is nonzero if and only if both λ_i and μ_j are nonzero. Hence, the number of nonzero eigenvalues of $\boldsymbol{A}\boldsymbol{A}' \otimes \boldsymbol{B}\boldsymbol{B}'$ equals the product of the number of nonzero eigenvalues of $\boldsymbol{A}\boldsymbol{A}'$ and the number of nonzero eigenvalues of $\boldsymbol{B}\boldsymbol{B}'$. This implies $\text{rk}(\boldsymbol{A} \otimes \boldsymbol{B}) = \text{rk}(\boldsymbol{A})\,\text{rk}(\boldsymbol{B})$.

Exercise 10.13 (Nonsingularity of a Kronecker product)
If $\boldsymbol{A}$ and $\boldsymbol{B}$ are not square, then it is still possible that $\boldsymbol{A} \otimes \boldsymbol{B}$ is a square matrix. Show that $\boldsymbol{A} \otimes \boldsymbol{B}$ is singular, unless both $\boldsymbol{A}$ and $\boldsymbol{B}$ are square and nonsingular.

Solution
If the order of $\boldsymbol{A}$ is $m \times p$ and the order of $\boldsymbol{B}$ is $n \times q$, then $\boldsymbol{A} \otimes \boldsymbol{B}$ is square if and only if $mn = pq$. Now, by Exercises 10.12 and 4.7(a),

$$\text{rk}(\boldsymbol{A} \otimes \boldsymbol{B}) = \text{rk}(\boldsymbol{A})\,\text{rk}(\boldsymbol{B}) \leq \min(m, p) \min(n, q).$$

If $\boldsymbol{A} \otimes \boldsymbol{B}$ is nonsingular, we conclude from $\text{rk}(\boldsymbol{A} \otimes \boldsymbol{B}) = mn$ that $m \leq p$, $n \leq q$, and from $\text{rk}(\boldsymbol{A} \otimes \boldsymbol{B}) = pq$ that $p \leq m$ and $q \leq n$. Hence, $p = m$ and $q = n$, and $\boldsymbol{A}$ and $\boldsymbol{B}$ are both square. Since $\text{rk}(\boldsymbol{A})\,\text{rk}(\boldsymbol{B}) = mn$, it follows that $\text{rk}(\boldsymbol{A}) = m$ and $\text{rk}(\boldsymbol{B}) = n$.

Exercise 10.14 (When is $\boldsymbol{A} \otimes \boldsymbol{A} \geq \boldsymbol{B} \otimes \boldsymbol{B}$?) If $\boldsymbol{A}$ and $\boldsymbol{B}$ are positive semidefinite, show that $\boldsymbol{A} \otimes \boldsymbol{A} \geq \boldsymbol{B} \otimes \boldsymbol{B}$ if and only if $\boldsymbol{A} \geq \boldsymbol{B}$.

Solution
If $\boldsymbol{A} \geq \boldsymbol{B}$, then

$$\begin{aligned}\boldsymbol{A} \otimes \boldsymbol{A} - \boldsymbol{B} \otimes \boldsymbol{B} &= \boldsymbol{A} \otimes \boldsymbol{A} - \boldsymbol{A} \otimes \boldsymbol{B} + \boldsymbol{A} \otimes \boldsymbol{B} - \boldsymbol{B} \otimes \boldsymbol{B} \\ &= \boldsymbol{A} \otimes (\boldsymbol{A} - \boldsymbol{B}) + (\boldsymbol{A} - \boldsymbol{B}) \otimes \boldsymbol{B} \geq \mathbf{O},\end{aligned}$$

since $\boldsymbol{A}$, $\boldsymbol{B}$, and $\boldsymbol{A} - \boldsymbol{B}$ are all positive semidefinite. Conversely, if $\boldsymbol{A} \otimes \boldsymbol{A} \geq \boldsymbol{B} \otimes \boldsymbol{B}$, then for any conformable $\boldsymbol{x}$,

$$\begin{aligned}0 &\leq (\boldsymbol{x} \otimes \boldsymbol{x})'(\boldsymbol{A} \otimes \boldsymbol{A} - \boldsymbol{B} \otimes \boldsymbol{B})(\boldsymbol{x} \otimes \boldsymbol{x}) = (\boldsymbol{x}'\boldsymbol{A}\boldsymbol{x})^2 - (\boldsymbol{x}'\boldsymbol{B}\boldsymbol{x})^2 \\ &= \boldsymbol{x}'(\boldsymbol{A} + \boldsymbol{B})\boldsymbol{x} \cdot \boldsymbol{x}'(\boldsymbol{A} - \boldsymbol{B})\boldsymbol{x}.\end{aligned}$$

Since $A \geq O$ and $B \geq O$, we have $x'(A+B)x \geq 0$. If $x'(A+B)x > 0$, then the above inequality implies that $x'(A-B)x \geq 0$. If $x'(A+B)x = 0$, then $x'Ax = x'Bx = 0$, so that $x'(A-B)x = 0$. It follows that $x'(A-B)x \geq 0$ for all x. Hence, $A \geq B$.

10.2 The vec-operator

Exercise 10.15 (Examples of vec) Compute vec A, vec A', vec B, vec B', vec e, vec e' of the matrices A and B, and the vector e in Exercise 10.1.

Solution

We have

$$\operatorname{vec} A = \begin{pmatrix} 2 \\ 0 \\ 5 \\ 6 \\ 2 \\ 3 \end{pmatrix}, \quad \operatorname{vec} A' = \begin{pmatrix} 2 \\ 5 \\ 2 \\ 0 \\ 6 \\ 3 \end{pmatrix}, \quad \operatorname{vec} B = \begin{pmatrix} 2 \\ 3 \\ 4 \\ 5 \\ 1 \\ 0 \end{pmatrix}, \quad \operatorname{vec} B' = \begin{pmatrix} 2 \\ 4 \\ 1 \\ 3 \\ 5 \\ 0 \end{pmatrix},$$

and $\operatorname{vec} e = \operatorname{vec} e' = e = (0, 0, 1)'$.

Exercise 10.16 (Linearity of vec) If A and B have the same order, show that:
(a) $\operatorname{vec}(A + B) = \operatorname{vec}(A) + \operatorname{vec}(B)$;
(b) $\operatorname{vec}(\alpha A) = \alpha \operatorname{vec} A$.

Solution

(a) Let $A := (a_1, \dots, a_n)$, $B := (b_1, \dots, b_n)$, and $C := A + B$. Denoting the columns of C by $c_1, \dots, c_n$, we obtain

$$\operatorname{vec} C = \begin{pmatrix} c_1 \\ \vdots \\ c_n \end{pmatrix} = \begin{pmatrix} a_1 + b_1 \\ \vdots \\ a_n + b_n \end{pmatrix} = \begin{pmatrix} a_1 \\ \vdots \\ a_n \end{pmatrix} + \begin{pmatrix} b_1 \\ \vdots \\ b_n \end{pmatrix} = \operatorname{vec} A + \operatorname{vec} B.$$

(b) Here,

$$\operatorname{vec}(\alpha A) = \begin{pmatrix} \alpha a_1 \\ \vdots \\ \alpha a_n \end{pmatrix} = \alpha \begin{pmatrix} a_1 \\ \vdots \\ a_n \end{pmatrix} = \alpha \operatorname{vec} A.$$

Exercise 10.17 (Equality?)
(a) Does $\operatorname{vec} A = \operatorname{vec} B$ imply that $A = B$?
(b) Show that $\operatorname{vec} a' = \operatorname{vec} a = a$ for any vector a.

Solution

(a) If and only if $\boldsymbol{A}$ and $\boldsymbol{B}$ have the same order.

(b) Let $\boldsymbol{a} := (a_1, \ldots, a_n)'$. Then,

$$\operatorname{vec} \boldsymbol{a}' = \operatorname{vec}(a_1, \ldots, a_n) = \boldsymbol{a} = \operatorname{vec} \boldsymbol{a}.$$

This provides a counterexample for (a), because $\operatorname{vec} \boldsymbol{a}' = \operatorname{vec} \boldsymbol{a}$ does not imply that $\boldsymbol{a}' = \boldsymbol{a}$, unless $\boldsymbol{a}$ is a scalar.

***Exercise 10.18 (Relationship of vec-operator and Kronecker product)**

(a) Show that, for any two vectors $\boldsymbol{a}$ and $\boldsymbol{b}$, $\operatorname{vec} \boldsymbol{a}\boldsymbol{b}' = \boldsymbol{b} \otimes \boldsymbol{a}$.

(b) Use this fact to establish

$$\operatorname{vec} \boldsymbol{ABC} = (\boldsymbol{C}' \otimes \boldsymbol{A}) \operatorname{vec} \boldsymbol{B},$$

whenever the product $\boldsymbol{ABC}$ is defined (*Roth*).

Solution

(a) Let $\boldsymbol{b} := (b_1, \ldots, b_n)'$. Then,

$$\operatorname{vec} \boldsymbol{a}\boldsymbol{b}' = \operatorname{vec}(b_1\boldsymbol{a}, \ldots, b_n\boldsymbol{a}) = \begin{pmatrix} b_1\boldsymbol{a} \\ \vdots \\ b_n\boldsymbol{a} \end{pmatrix} = \boldsymbol{b} \otimes \boldsymbol{a}.$$

(b) Let $\boldsymbol{B} := (\boldsymbol{b}_1, \ldots, \boldsymbol{b}_n)$ be an $m \times n$ matrix and let the n columns of $\boldsymbol{I}_n$ be denoted by $\boldsymbol{e}_1, \ldots, \boldsymbol{e}_n$. Then $\boldsymbol{B}$ can be written as $\boldsymbol{B} = \sum_{i=1}^n \boldsymbol{b}_i\boldsymbol{e}_i'$. Hence, using (a),

$$\begin{aligned}\operatorname{vec} \boldsymbol{ABC} &= \operatorname{vec} \sum_{i=1}^n \boldsymbol{A}\boldsymbol{b}_i\boldsymbol{e}_i'\boldsymbol{C} = \sum_{i=1}^n \operatorname{vec}\left((\boldsymbol{A}\boldsymbol{b}_i)(\boldsymbol{C}'\boldsymbol{e}_i)'\right) \\ &= \sum_{i=1}^n (\boldsymbol{C}'\boldsymbol{e}_i) \otimes (\boldsymbol{A}\boldsymbol{b}_i) = (\boldsymbol{C}' \otimes \boldsymbol{A}) \sum_{i=1}^n (\boldsymbol{e}_i \otimes \boldsymbol{b}_i) \\ &= (\boldsymbol{C}' \otimes \boldsymbol{A}) \sum_{i=1}^n \operatorname{vec} \boldsymbol{b}_i\boldsymbol{e}_i' = (\boldsymbol{C}' \otimes \boldsymbol{A}) \operatorname{vec} \boldsymbol{B}.\end{aligned}$$

Exercise 10.19 (Special relationships) Let $\boldsymbol{A}$ be an $m \times n$ matrix, $\boldsymbol{B}$ an $n \times p$ matrix, and $\boldsymbol{d}$ a $p \times 1$ vector. Show that:

(a) $\operatorname{vec} \boldsymbol{AB} = (\boldsymbol{B}' \otimes \boldsymbol{I}_m) \operatorname{vec} \boldsymbol{A} = (\boldsymbol{B}' \otimes \boldsymbol{A}) \operatorname{vec} \boldsymbol{I}_n = (\boldsymbol{I}_p \otimes \boldsymbol{A}) \operatorname{vec} \boldsymbol{B}$;

(b) $\boldsymbol{ABd} = (\boldsymbol{d}' \otimes \boldsymbol{A}) \operatorname{vec} \boldsymbol{B} = (\boldsymbol{A} \otimes \boldsymbol{d}') \operatorname{vec} \boldsymbol{B}'$;

(c) $\operatorname{vec} \boldsymbol{A} = (\boldsymbol{I}_n \otimes \boldsymbol{A}) \operatorname{vec} \boldsymbol{I}_n = (\boldsymbol{A}' \otimes \boldsymbol{I}_m) \operatorname{vec} \boldsymbol{I}_m$.

Solution

(a) We have $\operatorname{vec} \boldsymbol{AB} = \operatorname{vec} \boldsymbol{I}_m\boldsymbol{AB} = (\boldsymbol{B}' \otimes \boldsymbol{I}_m) \operatorname{vec} \boldsymbol{A}$, and similarly, $\operatorname{vec} \boldsymbol{AB} = \operatorname{vec} \boldsymbol{A}\boldsymbol{I}_n\boldsymbol{B} = (\boldsymbol{B}' \otimes \boldsymbol{A}) \operatorname{vec} \boldsymbol{I}_n$, and $\operatorname{vec} \boldsymbol{AB} = \operatorname{vec} \boldsymbol{AB}\boldsymbol{I}_p = (\boldsymbol{I}_p \otimes \boldsymbol{A}) \operatorname{vec} \boldsymbol{B}$.

(b) This follows because

$$\boldsymbol{ABd} = \operatorname{vec} \boldsymbol{ABd} = (\boldsymbol{d}' \otimes \boldsymbol{A}) \operatorname{vec} \boldsymbol{B},$$

and also

$$\boldsymbol{ABd} = \operatorname{vec}(\boldsymbol{ABd})' = \operatorname{vec} \boldsymbol{d}'\boldsymbol{B}'\boldsymbol{A}' = (\boldsymbol{A} \otimes \boldsymbol{d}') \operatorname{vec} \boldsymbol{B}'.$$

(c) Finally,

$$\operatorname{vec} \boldsymbol{A} = \operatorname{vec} \boldsymbol{A}\boldsymbol{I}_n\boldsymbol{I}_n = (\boldsymbol{I}_n \otimes \boldsymbol{A}) \operatorname{vec} \boldsymbol{I}_n, \quad \operatorname{vec} \boldsymbol{A} = \operatorname{vec} \boldsymbol{I}_m\boldsymbol{I}_m\boldsymbol{A} = (\boldsymbol{A}' \otimes \boldsymbol{I}_m) \operatorname{vec} \boldsymbol{I}_m.$$

Exercise 10.20 (Relationship of vec-operator and trace)
(a) For any two matrices of the same order, show that

$$(\operatorname{vec} \boldsymbol{A})' \operatorname{vec} \boldsymbol{B} = \operatorname{tr} \boldsymbol{A}'\boldsymbol{B}.$$

(b) Use this fact to show that

$$\operatorname{tr} \boldsymbol{ABCD} = (\operatorname{vec} \boldsymbol{D}')'(\boldsymbol{C}' \otimes \boldsymbol{A}) \operatorname{vec} \boldsymbol{B} = (\operatorname{vec} \boldsymbol{D})'(\boldsymbol{A} \otimes \boldsymbol{C}') \operatorname{vec} \boldsymbol{B}',$$

when the product $\boldsymbol{ABCD}$ is defined and square.
(c) In particular, show that

$$\begin{aligned}(\operatorname{vec} \boldsymbol{V})'(\boldsymbol{A} \otimes \boldsymbol{B}) \operatorname{vec} \boldsymbol{V} &= (\operatorname{vec} \boldsymbol{V})'(\boldsymbol{B} \otimes \boldsymbol{A}) \operatorname{vec} \boldsymbol{V}, \\ &= (\operatorname{vec} \boldsymbol{V})'(\boldsymbol{A}' \otimes \boldsymbol{B}') \operatorname{vec} \boldsymbol{V} = (\operatorname{vec} \boldsymbol{V})'(\boldsymbol{B}' \otimes \boldsymbol{A}') \operatorname{vec} \boldsymbol{V},\end{aligned}$$

when $\boldsymbol{A}$, $\boldsymbol{B}$, and $\boldsymbol{V}$ are square of the same order, and $\boldsymbol{V}$ is symmetric.

Solution
(a) Let $\boldsymbol{A} = (a_{ij})$ and $\boldsymbol{B} = (b_{ij})$. Then,

$$(\operatorname{vec} \boldsymbol{A})' \operatorname{vec} \boldsymbol{B} = \sum_{ij} a_{ij}b_{ij} = \sum_j (\boldsymbol{A}'\boldsymbol{B})_{jj} = \operatorname{tr} \boldsymbol{A}'\boldsymbol{B}.$$

(b) This follows because

$$\operatorname{tr} \boldsymbol{ABCD} = \operatorname{tr} \boldsymbol{D}(\boldsymbol{ABC}) = (\operatorname{vec} \boldsymbol{D}')' \operatorname{vec} \boldsymbol{ABC} = (\operatorname{vec} \boldsymbol{D}')'(\boldsymbol{C}' \otimes \boldsymbol{A}) \operatorname{vec} \boldsymbol{B}$$

and also

$$\begin{aligned}\operatorname{tr} \boldsymbol{ABCD} &= \operatorname{tr}(\boldsymbol{ABCD})' = \operatorname{tr} \boldsymbol{D}'(\boldsymbol{C}'\boldsymbol{B}'\boldsymbol{A}') \\ &= (\operatorname{vec} \boldsymbol{D})' \operatorname{vec} \boldsymbol{C}'\boldsymbol{B}'\boldsymbol{A}' = (\operatorname{vec} \boldsymbol{D})'(\boldsymbol{A} \otimes \boldsymbol{C}') \operatorname{vec} \boldsymbol{B}'.\end{aligned}$$

We note that other equalities can be obtained by rearranging the order in $\operatorname{tr} \boldsymbol{ABCD}$ cyclically. There are four ways to do this. In addition we can take the transpose. Hence, there are eight equivalent expressions for $\operatorname{tr} \boldsymbol{ABCD}$ of the type $(\operatorname{vec} \boldsymbol{P})'(\boldsymbol{Q} \otimes \boldsymbol{R}) \operatorname{vec} \boldsymbol{S}$.
(c) Putting $\boldsymbol{B} := \boldsymbol{D} := \boldsymbol{V}$ in (b) proves the first equality. Taking transposes then proves the remaining equalities, because a quadratic form is a scalar and thus equals its transpose.

Exercise 10.21 (The matrix $\boldsymbol{A} \otimes \boldsymbol{A} - \alpha(\operatorname{vec} \boldsymbol{A})(\operatorname{vec} \boldsymbol{A})'$) Consider the $n^2 \times n^2$ matrices

$$\boldsymbol{B} := \boldsymbol{I}_n \otimes \boldsymbol{I}_n - \alpha(\operatorname{vec} \boldsymbol{I}_n)(\operatorname{vec} \boldsymbol{I}_n)' \quad \text{and} \quad \boldsymbol{C} := \boldsymbol{A} \otimes \boldsymbol{A} - \alpha(\operatorname{vec} \boldsymbol{A})(\operatorname{vec} \boldsymbol{A})',$$

with $\boldsymbol{A} > \mathbf{O}$ of order $n \times n$. Show that:
(a) the eigenvalues of $\boldsymbol{B}$ are $1 - n\alpha$ (once) and 1 ($n^2 - 1$ times);
(b) $|\boldsymbol{B}| = 1 - n\alpha$;
(c) $\boldsymbol{B} > \mathbf{O} \iff \alpha < 1/n$, and $\boldsymbol{B} \geq \mathbf{O} \iff \alpha \leq 1/n$;
(d) $\boldsymbol{C} > \mathbf{O} \iff \alpha < 1/n$, and $\boldsymbol{C} \geq \mathbf{O} \iff \alpha \leq 1/n$.

Solution
(a) The matrix $(\operatorname{vec} \boldsymbol{I}_n)(\operatorname{vec} \boldsymbol{I}_n)'$ is symmetric of rank one, and hence all its eigenvalues are zero except one, which equals $(\operatorname{vec} \boldsymbol{I}_n)'(\operatorname{vec} \boldsymbol{I}_n) = n$. Hence, the matrix $\alpha(\operatorname{vec} \boldsymbol{I}_n)(\operatorname{vec} \boldsymbol{I}_n)'$ has eigenvalues $n\alpha$ (once) and zero ($n^2 - 1$ times), and $\boldsymbol{B}$ has eigenvalues $1 - n\alpha$ (once) and 1 ($n^2 - 1$ times).
(b)–(c) This follows directly from (a).
(d) Since $(\boldsymbol{A}^{1/2} \otimes \boldsymbol{A}^{1/2})(\boldsymbol{A}^{1/2} \otimes \boldsymbol{A}^{1/2}) = \boldsymbol{A} \otimes \boldsymbol{A}$ and $(\boldsymbol{A}^{1/2} \otimes \boldsymbol{A}^{1/2}) \operatorname{vec} \boldsymbol{I}_n = \operatorname{vec} \boldsymbol{A}$, we obtain $\boldsymbol{C} = (\boldsymbol{A}^{1/2} \otimes \boldsymbol{A}^{1/2})\boldsymbol{B}(\boldsymbol{A}^{1/2} \otimes \boldsymbol{A}^{1/2})$ and the result follows.

10.3 The Moore-Penrose inverse

Exercise 10.22 (MP examples)
(a) What is the MP-inverse of a nonsingular matrix?
(b) What is the MP-inverse of a scalar?
(c) What is the MP-inverse of a diagonal matrix?
(d) What is the MP-inverse of a null matrix?

Solution
All four statements are proved by verifying that the four defining conditions hold.
(a) If $\boldsymbol{A}$ is nonsingular, then $\boldsymbol{A}^+ = \boldsymbol{A}^{-1}$.
(b) Let λ be a scalar. Then $\lambda^+ = 1/\lambda$ if $\lambda \neq 0$, and $\lambda^+ = 0$ if $\lambda = 0$.
(c) Let $\boldsymbol{\Lambda} := \operatorname{diag}(\lambda_1, \dots, \lambda_n)$ be a diagonal matrix. Then, $\boldsymbol{\Lambda}^+ = \operatorname{diag}(\lambda_1^+, \dots, \lambda_n^+)$.
(d) If $\boldsymbol{A} = \mathbf{O}$, then $\boldsymbol{A}^+ = \mathbf{O}$ (but if $\boldsymbol{A}$ has order $m \times n$, then $\boldsymbol{A}^+$ has order $n \times m$, so the two null matrices are not equal).

***Exercise 10.23 (Existence of MP)** Show the existence of the MP-inverse.

Solution
Let $\boldsymbol{A}$ be an $m \times n$ matrix with $\operatorname{rk}(\boldsymbol{A}) = r$. If $r = 0$, then $\boldsymbol{A} = \mathbf{O}$. In that case $\boldsymbol{A}^+ = \mathbf{O}$ satisfies the four definition equations. Assume next that $r > 0$. By the singular-value decomposition (Exercise 8.38), there exist an $m \times r$ matrix $\boldsymbol{S}$ satisfying $\boldsymbol{S}'\boldsymbol{S} = \boldsymbol{I}_r$, an $n \times r$ matrix $\boldsymbol{T}$ satisfying $\boldsymbol{T}'\boldsymbol{T} = \boldsymbol{I}_r$, and an $r \times r$ diagonal matrix $\boldsymbol{\Lambda}$ with positive diagonal

elements, such that $\boldsymbol{A} = \boldsymbol{S}\boldsymbol{\Lambda}^{1/2}\boldsymbol{T}'$. Now let $\boldsymbol{B} = \boldsymbol{T}\boldsymbol{\Lambda}^{-1/2}\boldsymbol{S}'$. Then,

$$\begin{aligned}
\boldsymbol{ABA} &= \boldsymbol{S}\boldsymbol{\Lambda}^{1/2}\boldsymbol{T}'\boldsymbol{T}\boldsymbol{\Lambda}^{-1/2}\boldsymbol{S}'\boldsymbol{S}\boldsymbol{\Lambda}^{1/2}\boldsymbol{T}' = \boldsymbol{S}\boldsymbol{\Lambda}^{1/2}\boldsymbol{T}' = \boldsymbol{A},\\
\boldsymbol{BAB} &= \boldsymbol{T}\boldsymbol{\Lambda}^{-1/2}\boldsymbol{S}'\boldsymbol{S}\boldsymbol{\Lambda}^{1/2}\boldsymbol{T}'\boldsymbol{T}\boldsymbol{\Lambda}^{-1/2}\boldsymbol{S}' = \boldsymbol{T}\boldsymbol{\Lambda}^{-1/2}\boldsymbol{S}' = \boldsymbol{B},\\
(\boldsymbol{AB})' &= \boldsymbol{S}\boldsymbol{\Lambda}^{1/2}\boldsymbol{T}'\boldsymbol{T}\boldsymbol{\Lambda}^{-1/2}\boldsymbol{S}' = \boldsymbol{SS}',\\
(\boldsymbol{BA})' &= \boldsymbol{T}\boldsymbol{\Lambda}^{-1/2}\boldsymbol{S}'\boldsymbol{S}\boldsymbol{\Lambda}^{1/2}\boldsymbol{T}' = \boldsymbol{TT}',
\end{aligned}$$

and hence $\boldsymbol{B}$ is an MP-inverse of $\boldsymbol{A}$.

***Exercise 10.24 (Uniqueness of MP)** Show that the MP-inverse is unique.

Solution

We provide two solutions. Suppose that $\boldsymbol{B}$ and $\boldsymbol{C}$ both satisfy the four defining conditions: (i) $\boldsymbol{AXA} = \boldsymbol{A}$, (ii) $\boldsymbol{XAX} = \boldsymbol{X}$, (iii) $(\boldsymbol{AX})' = \boldsymbol{AX}$, and (iv) $(\boldsymbol{XA})' = \boldsymbol{XA}$. We shall show that $\boldsymbol{B} = \boldsymbol{C}$.

In the first solution we note that

$$\boldsymbol{AB} = (\boldsymbol{AB})' = \boldsymbol{B}'\boldsymbol{A}' = \boldsymbol{B}'(\boldsymbol{ACA})' = \boldsymbol{B}'\boldsymbol{A}'\boldsymbol{C}'\boldsymbol{A}' = (\boldsymbol{AB})'(\boldsymbol{AC})' = \boldsymbol{ABAC} = \boldsymbol{AC},$$

using conditions (i) and (iii) only. Similarly, using (i) and (iv),

$$\boldsymbol{BA} = (\boldsymbol{BA})' = \boldsymbol{A}'\boldsymbol{B}' = (\boldsymbol{ACA})'\boldsymbol{B}' = \boldsymbol{A}'\boldsymbol{C}'\boldsymbol{A}'\boldsymbol{B}' = (\boldsymbol{CA})'(\boldsymbol{BA})' = \boldsymbol{CABA} = \boldsymbol{CA}.$$

Finally, using (ii),

$$\boldsymbol{B} = \boldsymbol{BAB} = \boldsymbol{BAC} = \boldsymbol{CAC} = \boldsymbol{C}.$$

This proves uniqueness.

In the second solution we let $\boldsymbol{Z} = \boldsymbol{B} - \boldsymbol{C}$ and show that $\boldsymbol{Z} = \mathbf{O}$. From the defining conditions we obtain (i) $\boldsymbol{AZA} = \mathbf{O}$, (ii) $\boldsymbol{Z} = \boldsymbol{ZAZ} + \boldsymbol{ZAC} + \boldsymbol{CAZ}$, (iii) $(\boldsymbol{AZ})' = \boldsymbol{AZ}$, (iv) $(\boldsymbol{ZA})' = \boldsymbol{ZA}$. From (i) and (iii) we see that $(\boldsymbol{AZ})'(\boldsymbol{AZ}) = \boldsymbol{AZAZ} = \mathbf{O}$, and hence $\boldsymbol{AZ} = \mathbf{O}$. Similarly, from (i) and (iv) we find $\boldsymbol{ZA} = \mathbf{O}$. Then, from (ii), $\boldsymbol{Z} = \mathbf{O}$.

Exercise 10.25 (MP-inverse of transpose) Show that:
(a) $(\boldsymbol{A}^+)^+ = \boldsymbol{A}$;
(b) $(\boldsymbol{A}')^+ = (\boldsymbol{A}^+)'$;
(c) $(\boldsymbol{A} \otimes \boldsymbol{B})^+ = \boldsymbol{A}^+ \otimes \boldsymbol{B}^+$.

Solution

(a) To check the four defining equations, we need to show that if (i) $\boldsymbol{A}^+\boldsymbol{X}\boldsymbol{A}^+ = \boldsymbol{A}^+$, (ii) $\boldsymbol{X}\boldsymbol{A}^+\boldsymbol{X} = \boldsymbol{X}$, (iii) $(\boldsymbol{A}^+\boldsymbol{X})' = \boldsymbol{A}^+\boldsymbol{X}$, and (iv) $(\boldsymbol{X}\boldsymbol{A}^+)' = \boldsymbol{X}\boldsymbol{A}^+$, then $\boldsymbol{X} = \boldsymbol{A}$. We can easily verify that $\boldsymbol{X} = \boldsymbol{A}$ satisfies these four equations. Since the solution is known to be unique, $\boldsymbol{X} = \boldsymbol{A}$ is the only solution.

(b) Here we need to prove that $X = (A^+)'$ satisfies the equations (i) $A'XA' = A'$, (ii) $XA'X = X$, (iii) $(A'X)' = A'X$, (iv) $(XA')' = XA'$. This follows immediately from the defining equations of A^+.
(c) Again, this follows from checking the four defining equations.

Exercise 10.26 (Idempotent matrices involving the MP-inverse) Let A be an $m \times n$ matrix of rank r. Show that the following matrices are symmetric idempotent:
(a) AA^+ and A^+A;
(b) $I_m - AA^+$ and $I_n - A^+A$;
(c) $A(A'A)^+A'$ and $A'(AA')^+A$.

Solution
(a) Symmetry holds by definition. Also, we have $AA^+AA^+ = (AA^+A)A^+ = AA^+$ and $A^+AA^+A = A^+(AA^+A) = A^+A$.
(b) This follows directly from (a).
(c) Symmetry is obvious. Idempotency follows by direct multiplication.

Exercise 10.27 (Condition for $A^+ = A$)
(a) If A is symmetric and idempotent, show that $A^+ = A$.
(b) Does the converse hold?
(c) For any A, show that $(AA^+)^+ = AA^+$ and $(A^+A)^+ = A^+A$.

Solution
(a) If $A = A' = A^2$, then $A^3 = A$ and $(A^2)' = A^2$. Hence the four defining equations are satisfied, and since the MP-inverse is unique, it follows that $A^+ = A$.
(b) No. For example, if $A = -I$, then $A^+ = A$, but A is not idempotent.
(c) This follows from (a), because AA^+ and A^+A are symmetric idempotent (Exercise 10.26(a)).

Exercise 10.28 (Rank of MP) Show that the matrices A, A^+, AA^+, and A^+A all have the same rank.

Solution
The results follow by pre- and postmultiplication:

$$\operatorname{rk}(A) = \operatorname{rk}(AA^+A) \leq \operatorname{rk}(A^+) = \operatorname{rk}(A^+AA^+) \leq \operatorname{rk}(A),$$
$$\operatorname{rk}(A) = \operatorname{rk}(AA^+A) \leq \operatorname{rk}(AA^+) \leq \operatorname{rk}(A),$$

and

$$\operatorname{rk}(A) = \operatorname{rk}(AA^+A) \leq \operatorname{rk}(A^+A) \leq \operatorname{rk}(A).$$

Exercise 10.29 (MP equalities, 1) Show that:
(a) $A'AA^+ = A' = A^+AA'$;
(b) $A'A^{+\prime}A^+ = A^+ = A^+A^{+\prime}A'$;
(c) $(A'A)^+ = A^+A^{+\prime}$;
(d) $(AA')^+ = A^{+\prime}A^+$;
(e) $A^+ = (A'A)^+A' = A'(AA')^+$.

Solution
(a) Since A^+A and AA^+ are both symmetric (by definition), we find

$$A'AA^+ = A'(AA^+)' = A'A^{+\prime}A' = (A^+A)'A' = A^+AA'.$$

This, together with the fact that $A'A^{+\prime}A' = (AA^+A)' = A'$ proves (a).
(b) Similarly,

$$A'A^{+\prime}A^+ = (A^+A)'A^+ = A^+AA^+ = A^+$$

and

$$A^+A^{+\prime}A' = A^+(AA^+)' = A^+AA^+ = A^+.$$

(c) We check the four defining equations, using (a) and (b):

$$A'AA^+A^{+\prime}A'A = A'A^{+\prime}A'A = (AA^+A)'A = A'A,$$

$$A^+A^{+\prime}A'AA^+A^{+\prime} = A^+A^{+\prime}A'A^{+\prime} = A^+(A^+AA^+)' = A^+A^{+\prime},$$

$$A'AA^+A^{+\prime} = A'A^{+\prime} = A^+A \quad \text{is symmetric},$$

$$A^+A^{+\prime}A'A = A^+A \quad \text{is symmetric}.$$

(d) This is proved exactly as (c).
(e) Using (b) and (c) we find $A^+ = A^+A^{+\prime}A' = (A'A)^+A'$. Similarly, using (b) and (c), $A^+ = A'A^{+\prime}A^+ = A'(AA')^+$.

Exercise 10.30 (MP equalities, 2)
(a) Show that $A(A'A)^+A'A = A = AA'(AA')^+A$.
(b) Hence, show that for positive definite V,

$$(X'V^{-1}X)(X'V^{-1}X)^+X' = X'.$$

(c) Also show, using (a), that

$$AB(B'B)^+B'A'(AB(B'B)^+B'A')^+AB = AB.$$

Solution
(a) We use Exercise 10.29(e). Then, $A(A'A)^+A'A = AA^+A = A$, and, similarly, $AA'(AA')^+A = AA^+A = A$.

(b) Let $A := V^{-1/2}X$. Then, inserting in (a), we obtain

$$V^{-1/2}X(X'V^{-1}X)^{+}X'V^{-1}X = V^{-1/2}X.$$

Premultiplying with $V^{1/2}$ and transposing gives the result.
(c) Let $C := (B'B)^{+}$ and $Q := ABC^{1/2}$. Then, since $QQ'(QQ')^{+}Q = Q$, we have

$$ABCB'A'(ABCB'A')^{+}ABC^{1/2} = ABC^{1/2}.$$

Now postmultiply by $C^{1/2}B'B$ and use (a).

Exercise 10.31 (Explicit expressions for A^{+})
(a) Show that $A^{+} = (A'A)^{-1}A'$ if A has full column rank.
(b) Show also that $A^{+} = A'(AA')^{-1}$ if A has full row rank.
(c) Show that $AA^{+} = I$ if A has full row rank and $A^{+}A = I$ if A has full column rank.

Solution
(a) If A has full column rank, then $A'A$ is nonsingular, and hence, using Exercise 10.29(e),

$$A^{+} = (A'A)^{+}A' = (A'A)^{-1}A'.$$

(b) Similarly, if A has full row rank, then AA' is nonsingular, and, again using Exercise 10.29(e),

$$A^{+} = A'(AA')^{+} = A'(AA')^{-1}.$$

(c) This follows directly from (a) and (b).

Exercise 10.32 (Condition for $AB = O$) Show that:
(a) $A = O \iff A^{+} = O$;
(b) $AB = O \iff B^{+}A^{+} = O$;
(c) $A^{+}B = O \iff A'B = O$.

Solution
(a) We already know (Exercise 10.22(d)) that if $A = O$, then $A^{+} = O$. The converse follows since $(A^{+})^{+} = A$ (Exercise 10.25(a)).
(b) If $AB = O$, then $B^{+}A^{+} = (B'B)^{+}B'A'(AA')^{+} = O$. To prove the converse, let $C := A^{+}$ and $D := B^{+}$. We just established that $DC = O$ implies $C^{+}D^{+} = O$. Hence, $B^{+}A^{+} = O$ implies $AB = O$.
(c) If $A'B = O$, then $A^{+}B = (A'A)^{+}A'B = O$. Conversely, if $A^{+}B = O$, then, by Exercise 10.30(a),

$$A'B = A'A(A'A)^{+}A'B = A'AA^{+}B = O.$$

Exercise 10.33 (MP-inverse of a vector)
(a) If $\operatorname{rk}(A) = 1$, then show that $A^{+} = (\operatorname{tr} AA')^{-1}A'$.
(b) In particular, what is the MP-inverse of a vector a?

Solution

(a) If $\operatorname{rk}(\boldsymbol{A}) = 1$, then $\boldsymbol{A} = \boldsymbol{a}\boldsymbol{b}'$ for some $\boldsymbol{a} \neq \boldsymbol{0}$, $\boldsymbol{b} \neq \boldsymbol{0}$. Then, letting $\lambda := (\boldsymbol{a}'\boldsymbol{a})(\boldsymbol{b}'\boldsymbol{b})$, we obtain from the defining equations, $\boldsymbol{A}^+ = \lambda^{-1}\boldsymbol{b}\boldsymbol{a}' = (\operatorname{tr} \boldsymbol{A}\boldsymbol{A}')^{-1}\boldsymbol{A}'$.
(b) In the special case where $b = 1$, we have $\boldsymbol{a}^+ = (1/\boldsymbol{a}'\boldsymbol{a})\boldsymbol{a}'$ if $\boldsymbol{a} \neq \boldsymbol{0}$. If $\boldsymbol{a} = \boldsymbol{0}$, then $\boldsymbol{a}^+ = \boldsymbol{0}'$.

Exercise 10.34 (MP-inverse of a block-diagonal matrix) Consider the partitioned matrices

$$\boldsymbol{A} := \begin{pmatrix} \boldsymbol{A}_1 & \mathrm{O} \\ \mathrm{O} & \boldsymbol{A}_2 \end{pmatrix} \quad \text{and} \quad \boldsymbol{B} := \begin{pmatrix} \boldsymbol{A}_1^+ & \mathrm{O} \\ \mathrm{O} & \boldsymbol{A}_2^+ \end{pmatrix}.$$

Show that $\boldsymbol{B} = \boldsymbol{A}^+$.

Solution

This follows from the properties of $\boldsymbol{A}^+$ and $\boldsymbol{B}^+$ and the four defining equations.

Exercise 10.35 (MP-inverse of a symmetric matrix) Let $\boldsymbol{A} = \boldsymbol{S}\boldsymbol{\Lambda}\boldsymbol{S}'$ be a symmetric $n \times n$ matrix of rank r, where $\boldsymbol{\Lambda}$ is a diagonal $r \times r$ matrix with nonzero diagonal elements, and $\boldsymbol{S}$ is a semi-orthogonal $n \times r$ matrix ($\boldsymbol{S}'\boldsymbol{S} = \boldsymbol{I}_r$). Show that $\boldsymbol{A}^+ = \boldsymbol{S}\boldsymbol{\Lambda}^{-1}\boldsymbol{S}'$.

Solution

This, again, follows from the four defining equations. For example,

$$\boldsymbol{A}\boldsymbol{A}^+\boldsymbol{A} = \boldsymbol{S}\boldsymbol{\Lambda}\boldsymbol{S}'\boldsymbol{S}\boldsymbol{\Lambda}^{-1}\boldsymbol{S}'\boldsymbol{S}\boldsymbol{\Lambda}\boldsymbol{S}' = \boldsymbol{S}\boldsymbol{\Lambda}\boldsymbol{S}' = \boldsymbol{A}.$$

Exercise 10.36 (Condition for $(\boldsymbol{A}\boldsymbol{B})^+ = \boldsymbol{B}^+\boldsymbol{A}^+$)

(a) Show that $(\boldsymbol{A}\boldsymbol{B})^+ = \boldsymbol{B}'\boldsymbol{A}^+$ if $\boldsymbol{B}\boldsymbol{B}' = \boldsymbol{I}$.
(b) Show that $(\boldsymbol{A}\boldsymbol{B})^+ = \boldsymbol{B}^+\boldsymbol{A}^+$ if $\boldsymbol{A}$ has full column rank and $\boldsymbol{B}$ has full row rank.
(c) We know from the rank factorization theorem (Exercise 4.11) that every $m \times n$ matrix $\boldsymbol{A}$ of rank r can be written as $\boldsymbol{A} = \boldsymbol{B}\boldsymbol{C}'$, where $\boldsymbol{B}$ $(m \times r)$ and $\boldsymbol{C}$ $(n \times r)$ both have full column rank r. Use this result to show that $\boldsymbol{A}^+ = \boldsymbol{C}(\boldsymbol{B}'\boldsymbol{B}\boldsymbol{C}'\boldsymbol{C})^{-1}\boldsymbol{B}'$.

Solution

(a) We check the four defining equations:

$$\begin{aligned} \boldsymbol{A}\boldsymbol{B}\boldsymbol{B}'\boldsymbol{A}^+\boldsymbol{A}\boldsymbol{B} &= \boldsymbol{A}\boldsymbol{A}^+\boldsymbol{A}\boldsymbol{B} = \boldsymbol{A}\boldsymbol{B}, \\ \boldsymbol{B}'\boldsymbol{A}^+\boldsymbol{A}\boldsymbol{B}\boldsymbol{B}'\boldsymbol{A}^+ &= \boldsymbol{B}'\boldsymbol{A}^+\boldsymbol{A}\boldsymbol{A}^+ = \boldsymbol{B}'\boldsymbol{A}^+, \\ \boldsymbol{A}\boldsymbol{B}\boldsymbol{B}'\boldsymbol{A}^+ &= \boldsymbol{A}\boldsymbol{A}^+ \quad \text{is symmetric}, \\ \boldsymbol{B}'\boldsymbol{A}^+\boldsymbol{A}\boldsymbol{B} & \quad \text{is symmetric}. \end{aligned}$$

(b) Again we check the defining equations, using $BB^+ = I$ and $A^+A = I$:

$$\begin{aligned} ABB^+A^+AB &= AB, \\ B^+A^+ABB^+A^+ &= B^+A^+, \\ ABB^+A^+ &= AA^+ \quad \text{is symmetric}, \\ B^+A^+AB &= B^+B \quad \text{is symmetric}. \end{aligned}$$

(c) This follows from (b), because

$$A^+ = (BC')^+ = (C')^+B^+ = C(C'C)^{-1}(B'B)^{-1}B' = C(B'BC'C)^{-1}B'.$$

*__Exercise 10.37 (When is $AA^+ = A^+A$?)__ Let A be a square matrix of order n and rank r.
(a) If $A = A'$, show that $AA^+ = A^+A$.
(b) Does the converse hold?
(c) Show that $AA^+ = A^+A$ if and only if $\text{col}(A) = \text{col}(A')$.

Solution
(a) This follows from $AA^+ = (AA^+)' = A^{+\prime}A' = (A')^+A' = A^+A$.
(b) No. Any nonsingular matrix A satisfies $AA^+ = A^+A = I$, whether symmetric or not. Less trivially, any matrix A of the form $A = SQS'$ with $S'S = I_r$ $(r \geq 2)$ and nonsingular Q has MP-inverse $A^+ = SQ^{-1}S'$ and hence $AA^+ = A^+A = SS'$. But A is not symmetric unless Q is symmetric.
(c) Write $A = BC'$, where B and C are $n \times r$ matrices of full column rank r (see Exercise 4.11(a)). Then, by Exercise 10.36,

$$A^+ = (BC')^+ = C'^+B^+ = C(C'C)^{-1}(B'B)^{-1}B',$$

and hence $AA^+ = B(B'B)^{-1}B'$ and $A^+A = C(C'C)^{-1}C'$. If $AA^+ = A^+A$, then $B(B'B)^{-1}B' = C(C'C)^{-1}C'$. Postmultiplying by B and C, respectively, shows that $B = CQ$ and $C = BQ^{-1}$ for some nonsingular matrix Q. Hence, $\text{col}(B) = \text{col}(C)$. Since A and B have the same rank and $A = BC'$, we have $\text{col}(B) = \text{col}(A)$. Similarly, since A' and C have the same rank and $A' = CB'$, we have $\text{col}(A') = \text{col}(C)$. Hence, $\text{col}(A) = \text{col}(A')$.

Conversely, if $\text{col}(A) = \text{col}(A')$, then $\text{col}(B) = \text{col}(C)$ and hence $B = CQ$ for some nonsingular matrix Q. Then, by Exercise 10.36(b), $B^+ = Q^{-1}C^+$ and hence

$$AA^+ = BB^+ = CQQ^{-1}C^+ = CC^+ = A^+A.$$

Exercise 10.38 (MP-inverse of a positive semidefinite matrix) Let A be a positive semidefinite $n \times n$ matrix of rank r. Recall from Exercise 8.22 that there exists an $n \times r$ matrix B of rank r such that $A = BB'$. Show that $A^+ = B(B'B)^{-2}B'$.

Solution
We can check the four defining equations. Alternatively, we know from Exercise 10.36(c) that $A^+ = B(B'BB'B)^{-1}B'$ and the result follows immediately.

Exercise 10.39 (An important MP equivalence) Show that

$$A'AB = A'C \iff AB = AA^+C.$$

Solution
We provide two proofs of the equivalence. If $A'AB = A'C$, then, using Exercises 10.30(a) and 10.29(e),

$$AB = A(A'A)^+A'AB = A(A'A)^+A'C = AA^+C.$$

Conversely, if $AB = AA^+C$, then, using Exercise 10.29(a),

$$A'AB = A'AA^+C = A'C.$$

The second proof uses the singular-value decomposition. We write $A = S\Lambda^{1/2}T'$ and $A^+ = T\Lambda^{-1/2}S'$, where $S'S = T'T = I_r$ and r is the rank of A. Then,

$$A'AB = A'C \iff T\Lambda^{1/2}S'S\Lambda^{1/2}T'B = T\Lambda^{1/2}S'C \iff \Lambda^{1/2}T'B = S'C$$
$$\iff S\Lambda^{1/2}T'B = SS'C \iff AB = AA^+C.$$

Exercise 10.40 (When is $(AB)(AB)^+ = AA^+$?)
(a) If B has full row rank, show that $AB(AB)^+ = AA^+$.
(b) Is the converse true?

Solution
(a) Since $A' = A'AA^+$ (Exercise 10.29(a)) and $BB^+ = I$ (Exercise 10.31(c)), we find

$$\begin{aligned} AB(AB)^+ &= (AB)^{+\prime}(AB)' = (AB)^{+\prime}B'A' = (AB)^{+\prime}B'A'AA^+ \\ &= (AB)^{+\prime}(AB)'AA^+ = AB(AB)^+AA^+ \\ &= AB(AB)^+ABB^+A^+ = ABB^+A^+ = AA^+. \end{aligned}$$

(b) No. If $B = A^+$, then $AB(AB)^+ = AA^+(AA^+)^+ = AA^+AA^+ = AA^+$, irrespective of the rank.

Exercise 10.41 (Is the difference of two idempotent matrices idempotent?) Let A be a symmetric idempotent matrix.
(a) If $AB = B$, show that $A - BB^+$ is symmetric idempotent with rank $\text{rk}(A) - \text{rk}(B)$.
(b) Does the converse hold?

Solution
(a) Let $\boldsymbol{C} := \boldsymbol{A} - \boldsymbol{B}\boldsymbol{B}^+$. Then $\boldsymbol{C} = \boldsymbol{C}'$, $\boldsymbol{C}\boldsymbol{B} = \mathbf{O}$, and

$$\begin{aligned}\boldsymbol{C}^2 &= (\boldsymbol{A} - \boldsymbol{B}\boldsymbol{B}^+)(\boldsymbol{A} - \boldsymbol{B}\boldsymbol{B}^+) = \boldsymbol{A}^2 - \boldsymbol{A}\boldsymbol{B}\boldsymbol{B}^+ - \boldsymbol{B}\boldsymbol{B}^+\boldsymbol{A} + \boldsymbol{B}\boldsymbol{B}^+\boldsymbol{B}\boldsymbol{B}^+ \\ &= \boldsymbol{A} - \boldsymbol{B}\boldsymbol{B}^+\boldsymbol{A} = \boldsymbol{A} - \boldsymbol{B}\boldsymbol{B}^+,\end{aligned}$$

because

$$\boldsymbol{B}\boldsymbol{B}^+\boldsymbol{A} = (\boldsymbol{B}\boldsymbol{B}^+)'\boldsymbol{A}' = (\boldsymbol{A}\boldsymbol{B}\boldsymbol{B}^+)' = (\boldsymbol{B}\boldsymbol{B}^+)' = \boldsymbol{B}\boldsymbol{B}^+.$$

Hence, $\boldsymbol{C}$ is idempotent. Its rank is

$$\operatorname{rk}(\boldsymbol{C}) = \operatorname{tr}(\boldsymbol{C}) = \operatorname{tr}\boldsymbol{A} - \operatorname{tr}\boldsymbol{B}\boldsymbol{B}^+ = \operatorname{rk}(\boldsymbol{A}) - \operatorname{rk}(\boldsymbol{B}).$$

(b) Yes. If $\boldsymbol{C}$ is idempotent, then $(\boldsymbol{A} - \boldsymbol{B}\boldsymbol{B}^+)(\boldsymbol{A} - \boldsymbol{B}\boldsymbol{B}^+) = \boldsymbol{A} - \boldsymbol{B}\boldsymbol{B}^+$, and hence $\boldsymbol{A}\boldsymbol{B}\boldsymbol{B}^+ + \boldsymbol{B}\boldsymbol{B}^+\boldsymbol{A} = 2\boldsymbol{B}\boldsymbol{B}^+$. Premultiplying with $\boldsymbol{A}$ gives $\boldsymbol{A}\boldsymbol{B}\boldsymbol{B}^+\boldsymbol{A} = \boldsymbol{A}\boldsymbol{B}\boldsymbol{B}^+$ and thus shows that $\boldsymbol{A}\boldsymbol{B}\boldsymbol{B}^+$ is symmetric. Hence, $\boldsymbol{A}\boldsymbol{B}\boldsymbol{B}^+ = \boldsymbol{B}\boldsymbol{B}^+\boldsymbol{A} = \boldsymbol{B}\boldsymbol{B}^+$, implying that $\boldsymbol{A}\boldsymbol{B} = \boldsymbol{B}$.

Exercise 10.42 (A necessary and sufficient condition for $\boldsymbol{A} = \boldsymbol{B}\boldsymbol{B}^+$) Let $\boldsymbol{A}$ be a symmetric idempotent $n \times n$ matrix. Use Exercise 10.41 to show:
(a) if $\boldsymbol{A}\boldsymbol{B} = \boldsymbol{B}$ and $\operatorname{rk}(\boldsymbol{A}) = \operatorname{rk}(\boldsymbol{B})$, then $\boldsymbol{A} = \boldsymbol{B}\boldsymbol{B}^+$;
(b) if $\boldsymbol{A}\boldsymbol{B} = \mathbf{O}$ and $\operatorname{rk}(\boldsymbol{A}) + \operatorname{rk}(\boldsymbol{B}) = n$, then $\boldsymbol{A} = \boldsymbol{I}_n - \boldsymbol{B}\boldsymbol{B}^+$.

Solution
(a) Exercise 10.41(a) shows that $\boldsymbol{A} - \boldsymbol{B}\boldsymbol{B}^+$ has rank 0. Hence, $\boldsymbol{A} = \boldsymbol{B}\boldsymbol{B}^+$.
(b) Let $\boldsymbol{C} := \boldsymbol{I}_n - \boldsymbol{A}$. Then $\boldsymbol{C}$ is symmetric idempotent and $\boldsymbol{C}\boldsymbol{B} = \boldsymbol{B}$. Also, $\operatorname{rk}(\boldsymbol{C}) = n - \operatorname{rk}(\boldsymbol{A}) = \operatorname{rk}(\boldsymbol{B})$. Hence, by (a), $\boldsymbol{C} = \boldsymbol{B}\boldsymbol{B}^+$, that is, $\boldsymbol{A} = \boldsymbol{I}_n - \boldsymbol{B}\boldsymbol{B}^+$. (Compare Exercise 8.64(b).)

10.4 Linear vector and matrix equations

Exercise 10.43 (The homogeneous equation $\boldsymbol{A}\boldsymbol{x} = \mathbf{0}$) Consider the homogeneous vector equation $\boldsymbol{A}\boldsymbol{x} = \mathbf{0}$.
(a) Show that the general solution of $\boldsymbol{A}\boldsymbol{x} = \mathbf{0}$ is given by $\boldsymbol{x} = (\boldsymbol{I} - \boldsymbol{A}^+\boldsymbol{A})\boldsymbol{q}$, where $\boldsymbol{q}$ is an arbitrary (conformable) vector.
(b) Show that the solution of $\boldsymbol{A}\boldsymbol{x} = \mathbf{0}$ is unique if and only if $\boldsymbol{A}$ has full column rank. What is the unique solution in that case?
(c) If the solution of $\boldsymbol{A}\boldsymbol{x} = \mathbf{0}$ is not unique, show that there are infinitely many solutions.

Solution
(a) Premultiplying $\boldsymbol{x} = (\boldsymbol{I} - \boldsymbol{A}^+\boldsymbol{A})\boldsymbol{q}$ by $\boldsymbol{A}$ shows that $\boldsymbol{x}$ is a solution of $\boldsymbol{A}\boldsymbol{x} = \mathbf{0}$ for any $\boldsymbol{q}$. Conversely, if $\boldsymbol{x}$ is a solution of $\boldsymbol{A}\boldsymbol{x} = \mathbf{0}$, then $\boldsymbol{x} = (\boldsymbol{I} - \boldsymbol{A}^+\boldsymbol{A})\boldsymbol{x}$. Hence, there exists a vector $\boldsymbol{q}$ (namely $\boldsymbol{x}$) such that $\boldsymbol{x} = (\boldsymbol{I} - \boldsymbol{A}^+\boldsymbol{A})\boldsymbol{q}$. (Experience shows that many students are not convinced by this simple proof, so look carefully at what happens.)

(b) $\boldsymbol{A}$ has full column rank if and only if $\boldsymbol{A}^+\boldsymbol{A} = \boldsymbol{I}$, in which case the general solution is $\boldsymbol{x} = \boldsymbol{0}$.
(c) If the solution is not unique, then $\boldsymbol{A}^+\boldsymbol{A} \neq \boldsymbol{I}$ and there are infinitely many solutions given by $\boldsymbol{x} = (\boldsymbol{I} - \boldsymbol{A}^+\boldsymbol{A})\boldsymbol{q}$.

Exercise 10.44 ($\boldsymbol{Ax} = \boldsymbol{b}$ may not have a solution) Show that the nonhomogeneous vector equation $\boldsymbol{Ax} = \boldsymbol{b}$ does not necessarily have a solution when $\boldsymbol{b} \neq \boldsymbol{0}$. In other words, show that a nonhomogeneous vector equation is not necessarily consistent.

Solution
For example, let

$$\boldsymbol{A} = \begin{pmatrix} 1 & 2 \\ 1 & 2 \end{pmatrix} \quad \text{and} \quad \boldsymbol{b} = \begin{pmatrix} 1 \\ 2 \end{pmatrix}.$$

Then $\boldsymbol{Ax} = \boldsymbol{b}$ has no solution.

Exercise 10.45 (Consistency of $\boldsymbol{Ax} = \boldsymbol{b}$) Let $\boldsymbol{A}$ be a given $m \times n$ matrix and $\boldsymbol{b}$ a given $m \times 1$ vector. Show that the following four statements are equivalent:
(a) the vector equation $\boldsymbol{Ax} = \boldsymbol{b}$ has a solution for $\boldsymbol{x}$,
(b) $\boldsymbol{b} \in \operatorname{col}(\boldsymbol{A})$,
(c) $\operatorname{rk}(\boldsymbol{A} : \boldsymbol{b}) = \operatorname{rk}(\boldsymbol{A})$,
(d) $\boldsymbol{AA}^+\boldsymbol{b} = \boldsymbol{b}$.

Solution
It is easy to show that (a), (b), and (c) are equivalent. Let us show that (a) and (d) are equivalent. Suppose $\boldsymbol{Ax} = \boldsymbol{b}$ is consistent. Then there exists an $\tilde{\boldsymbol{x}}$ such that $\boldsymbol{A}\tilde{\boldsymbol{x}} = \boldsymbol{b}$. Hence, $\boldsymbol{b} = \boldsymbol{A}\tilde{\boldsymbol{x}} = \boldsymbol{AA}^+\boldsymbol{A}\tilde{\boldsymbol{x}} = \boldsymbol{AA}^+\boldsymbol{b}$. Conversely, suppose that $\boldsymbol{AA}^+\boldsymbol{b} = \boldsymbol{b}$ and let $\tilde{\boldsymbol{x}} = \boldsymbol{A}^+\boldsymbol{b}$. Then $\boldsymbol{A}\tilde{\boldsymbol{x}} = \boldsymbol{AA}^+\boldsymbol{b} = \boldsymbol{b}$.

Exercise 10.46 (Solution of $\boldsymbol{Ax} = \boldsymbol{b}$) If the vector equation $\boldsymbol{Ax} = \boldsymbol{b}$ is consistent, show that the general solution is given by $\boldsymbol{x} = \boldsymbol{A}^+\boldsymbol{b} + (\boldsymbol{I} - \boldsymbol{A}^+\boldsymbol{A})\boldsymbol{q}$, where $\boldsymbol{q}$ is an arbitrary (conformable) vector.

Solution
Consistency implies that $\boldsymbol{AA}^+\boldsymbol{b} = \boldsymbol{b}$. Define $\tilde{\boldsymbol{x}} := \boldsymbol{x} - \boldsymbol{A}^+\boldsymbol{b}$. Then, using Exercise 10.43,

$$\begin{aligned} \boldsymbol{Ax} = \boldsymbol{b} &\iff \boldsymbol{Ax} = \boldsymbol{AA}^+\boldsymbol{b} \iff \boldsymbol{A}\tilde{\boldsymbol{x}} = \boldsymbol{0} \\ &\iff \tilde{\boldsymbol{x}} = (\boldsymbol{I} - \boldsymbol{A}^+\boldsymbol{A})\boldsymbol{q} \iff \boldsymbol{x} = \boldsymbol{A}^+\boldsymbol{b} + (\boldsymbol{I} - \boldsymbol{A}^+\boldsymbol{A})\boldsymbol{q}. \end{aligned}$$

Exercise 10.47 (Least squares)
(a) Whether the equation $\boldsymbol{Ax} = \boldsymbol{b}$ is consistent or not, show that

$$(\boldsymbol{Ax} - \boldsymbol{b})'(\boldsymbol{Ax} - \boldsymbol{b}) = (\boldsymbol{x} - \boldsymbol{A}^+\boldsymbol{b})'\boldsymbol{A}'\boldsymbol{A}(\boldsymbol{x} - \boldsymbol{A}^+\boldsymbol{b}) + \boldsymbol{b}'(\boldsymbol{I} - \boldsymbol{AA}^+)\boldsymbol{b}.$$

(b) Conclude that $\hat{\boldsymbol{x}} := \boldsymbol{A}^+\boldsymbol{b}$ minimizes $\|\boldsymbol{Ax} - \boldsymbol{b}\|$ (*least squares*).

Solution
(a) Let $\hat{x} := A^+b$. Then,

$$Ax - b = A(x - \hat{x}) - (I - AA^+)b.$$

Since A and $I - AA^+$ are orthogonal to each other, we obtain (a) by taking the inner product on both sides.
(b) Since $(x - A^+b)'A'A(x - A^+b) \geq 0$, the minimum of $(Ax - b)'(Ax - b)$ is obtained when $Ax = AA^+b$, in particular for $x = \hat{x}$.

Exercise 10.48 (Uniqueness of solution, 1)
(a) Show that the equation $Ax = b$ is consistent for every b if and only if A has full row rank.
(b) If $Ax = b$ is consistent, show that its solution is unique if and only if A has full column rank.

Solution
(a) This follows from Exercise 10.46, because $AA^+ = I$ in that case.
(b) This follows because $A^+A = I$ in that case. Note in particular that a unique solution may exist without A being square or nonsingular.

Exercise 10.49 (The matrix equation $AXB = C$) Consider the matrix equation $AXB = C$.
(a) Show that the equation is consistent if and only if $AA^+CB^+B = C$.
(b) If the equation is consistent, show that the general solution is given by

$$X = A^+CB^+ + Q - A^+AQBB^+,$$

where Q is an arbitrary (conformable) matrix.

Solution
We write the matrix equation $AXB = C$ as a vector equation $(B' \otimes A) \operatorname{vec} X = \operatorname{vec} C$.
(a) Using Exercise 10.45(d) consistency requires that

$$(B' \otimes A)(B' \otimes A)^+ \operatorname{vec} C = \operatorname{vec} C.$$

Noticing that $(B' \otimes A)(B' \otimes A)^+ = B^+B \otimes AA^+$, we obtain (a).
(b) Using Exercise 10.46, the general solution is

$$\begin{aligned}
\operatorname{vec} X &= (B' \otimes A)^+ \operatorname{vec} C + (I - (B' \otimes A)^+(B' \otimes A)) \operatorname{vec} Q \\
&= \operatorname{vec} A^+CB^+ + \operatorname{vec} Q - (BB^+ \otimes A^+A) \operatorname{vec} Q \\
&= \operatorname{vec}(A^+CB^+ + Q - A^+AQBB^+)
\end{aligned}$$

and the result follows.

Exercise 10.50 (Uniqueness of solution, 2)
(a) Show that the matrix equation $AXB = C$ is consistent for every C if and only if A has full row rank and B has full column rank.

(b) Show that the matrix equation $\boldsymbol{AXB} = \boldsymbol{C}$, if consistent, has a unique solution if and only if $\boldsymbol{A}$ has full column rank and $\boldsymbol{B}$ has full row rank.

Solution

(a) The equation $\boldsymbol{AXB} = \boldsymbol{C}$ is consistent for every $\boldsymbol{C}$ if and only if $(\boldsymbol{B}' \otimes \boldsymbol{A})(\boldsymbol{B}' \otimes \boldsymbol{A})^{+} = \boldsymbol{I}$. This is the case if and only if $\boldsymbol{B}^{+}\boldsymbol{B} = \boldsymbol{I}$ and $\boldsymbol{AA}^{+} = \boldsymbol{I}$, that is, if and only if $\boldsymbol{A}$ has full row rank and $\boldsymbol{B}$ has full column rank.
(b) The solution is unique if and only if $\boldsymbol{A}^{+}\boldsymbol{A} = \boldsymbol{I}$ and $\boldsymbol{BB}^{+} = \boldsymbol{I}$, that is, if and only if $\boldsymbol{A}$ has full column rank and $\boldsymbol{B}$ has full row rank.

Exercise 10.51 (Solution of $\boldsymbol{AX} = \mathbf{O}$ and $\boldsymbol{XA} = \mathbf{O}$)
(a) Show that the general solution of $\boldsymbol{AX} = \mathbf{O}$ is given by $\boldsymbol{X} = (\boldsymbol{I} - \boldsymbol{A}^{+}\boldsymbol{A})\boldsymbol{Q}$.
(b) Show that the general solution of $\boldsymbol{XA} = \mathbf{O}$ is given by $\boldsymbol{X} = \boldsymbol{Q}(\boldsymbol{I} - \boldsymbol{AA}^{+})$.

Solution

(a) Set $\boldsymbol{B} := \boldsymbol{I}$ and $\boldsymbol{C} := \mathbf{O}$ in the equation $\boldsymbol{AXB} = \boldsymbol{C}$. Since $\boldsymbol{C} = \mathbf{O}$, the equation is homogeneous and thus always has a solution given by Exercise 10.49(b).
(b) Similarly, we see that the general solution of the homogeneous equation $\boldsymbol{IXA} = \mathbf{O}$ is given by $\boldsymbol{X} = \mathbf{O} + \boldsymbol{Q} - \boldsymbol{IQAA}^{+} = \boldsymbol{Q}(\boldsymbol{I} - \boldsymbol{AA}^{+})$.

10.5 The generalized inverse

Exercise 10.52 (Generalized inverse) Any matrix $\boldsymbol{X}$ satisfying $\boldsymbol{AXA} = \boldsymbol{A}$ is called a generalized inverse of $\boldsymbol{A}$ and is denoted by $\boldsymbol{A}^{-}$.
(a) Show that $\boldsymbol{A}^{-}$ exists.
(b) Show that $\boldsymbol{A}^{-} = \boldsymbol{A}^{+} + \boldsymbol{Q} - \boldsymbol{A}^{+}\boldsymbol{AQAA}^{+}$ ($\boldsymbol{Q}$ arbitrary).

Solution

(a) Clearly, $\boldsymbol{X} := \boldsymbol{A}^{+}$ satisfies $\boldsymbol{AXA} = \boldsymbol{A}$, so that there exists at least one solution.
(b) From Exercise 10.49(b) we have

$$\boldsymbol{X} = \boldsymbol{A}^{+}\boldsymbol{AA}^{+} + \boldsymbol{Q} - \boldsymbol{A}^{+}\boldsymbol{AQAA}^{+}$$

and the result follows.

Exercise 10.53 (Idempotency of $\boldsymbol{A}^{-}\boldsymbol{A}$)
(a) Show that $\boldsymbol{A}^{-}\boldsymbol{A}$ is idempotent.
(b) Show that $\boldsymbol{A}^{-}\boldsymbol{A}$ is, in general, not symmetric.
(c) If $\boldsymbol{A}^{-}\boldsymbol{A}$ is symmetric, then show that $\boldsymbol{A}^{-}\boldsymbol{A} = \boldsymbol{A}^{+}\boldsymbol{A}$ and hence that $\boldsymbol{A}^{-}\boldsymbol{A}$ is unique. (Similar results hold, of course, for $\boldsymbol{AA}^{-}$.)

Solution

(a) We have

$$(\boldsymbol{A}^{-}\boldsymbol{A})(\boldsymbol{A}^{-}\boldsymbol{A}) = \boldsymbol{A}^{-}(\boldsymbol{AA}^{-}\boldsymbol{A}) = \boldsymbol{A}^{-}\boldsymbol{A}.$$

(b) Using the explicit expression for A^- (Exercise 10.52(b)), we obtain

$$A^-A = (A^+ + Q - A^+AQAA^+)A = A^+A + (I - A^+A)QA$$

which is, in general, not symmetric.
(c) If A^-A is symmetric, then $(I - A^+A)QA = A'Q'(I - A^+A)$. Postmultiplying both sides by $A'Q'(I - A^+A)$ yields

$$(I - A^+A)QAA'Q'(I - A^+A) = O,$$

and hence $(I - A^+A)QA = O$. The result then follows from (b).

Exercise 10.54 (Uniqueness of $A(A'A)^-A'$) Show that $A(A'A)^-A' = A(A'A)^+A'$ and hence that this matrix is symmetric, idempotent, and unique.

Solution
From the general expression for a generalized inverse (Exercise 10.52(b)) we obtain

$$(A'A)^- = (A'A)^+ + Q - (A'A)^+A'AQA'A(A'A)^+.$$

Premultiplying by A and postmultiplying by A' then gives the result, by Exercise 10.30(a).

Exercise 10.55 (Rank of A^-) Let A be a symmetric idempotent matrix.
(a) Show that the general solution of A^- is given by

$$A^- = A + Q - AQA \quad (Q \text{ arbitrary}).$$

(b) Show that $B := A + \alpha(I - A)$ is a generalized inverse of A for any α.
(c) Show that B is nonsingular for every $\alpha \neq 0$.
(d) Conclude that, in general, $\text{rk}(A^-) \neq \text{rk}(A)$.

Solution
(a) This follows from Exercise 10.52(b).
(b) Choose $Q = \alpha I$.
(c) Since the eigenvalues of A are 0 and 1, and writing $B = \alpha I + (1 - \alpha)A$, we see that the eigenvalues of B are α and 1. If $\alpha \neq 0$, then all eigenvalues of B are nonzero, so that B is nonsingular.
(d) The matrix B is a generalized inverse of A and has full rank when $\alpha \neq 0$, whatever the rank of A. Hence, $\text{rk}(A^-) \neq \text{rk}(A)$, in general.

Exercise 10.56 (The vector equation again)
(a) Show that a necessary and sufficient condition for the vector equation $Ax = b$ to be consistent is that $AA^-b = b$.
(b) Show that the vector equation $Ax = b$, if consistent, has the general solution $x = A^-b + (I - A^-A)q$, where q is an arbitrary (conformable) vector.

Solution

This is easiest proved by repeating the steps in the proofs of Exercises 10.45, 10.43(a), and 10.46, respectively, replacing $\boldsymbol{A}^+$ by $\boldsymbol{A}^-$ throughout.

Notes

The Kronecker product has a long history, especially the determinant result, $|\boldsymbol{A} \otimes \boldsymbol{B}| = |\boldsymbol{A}|^n |\boldsymbol{B}|^m$, for any two square matrices $\boldsymbol{A}$ and $\boldsymbol{B}$ of orders m and n, respectively (Exercise 10.12); see MacDuffee (1946, pp. 81–84) for references. For the use of tensors as an alternative to Kronecker products, see Kay (1988) and, for applications in statistics, see McCullagh (1987). The vec-operator was introduced by Koopmans, Rubin, and Leipnik (1950). The fundamental result $\operatorname{vec} \boldsymbol{ABC} = (\boldsymbol{C}' \otimes \boldsymbol{A}) \operatorname{vec} \boldsymbol{B}$ (Exercise 10.18) is due to Roth (1934). The Moore-Penrose inverse was introduced by Moore (1920, 1935) and rediscovered by Penrose (1955). There is a great volume of literature on the MP-inverse. The reader may wish to consult Rao and Mitra (1971) or Magnus and Neudecker (1999). The consistency and solution of the matrix equation $\boldsymbol{AXB} = \boldsymbol{C}$ (Exercise 10.49) is taken from Penrose (1956).

11

Patterned matrices: commutation- and duplication matrix

Let $\boldsymbol{A}$ be a real $m \times n$ matrix. The two vectors $\operatorname{vec} \boldsymbol{A}$ and $\operatorname{vec} \boldsymbol{A}'$ contain the same mn components, but in a different order. Hence, there exists a unique permutation matrix that transforms $\operatorname{vec} \boldsymbol{A}$ into $\operatorname{vec} \boldsymbol{A}'$. This $mn \times mn$ matrix is called the *commutation matrix*, denoted by $\boldsymbol{K}_{mn}$, and defined implicitly by the operation

$$\boldsymbol{K}_{mn} \operatorname{vec} \boldsymbol{A} = \operatorname{vec} \boldsymbol{A}'.$$

The order of the indices matters: $\boldsymbol{K}_{mn}$ and $\boldsymbol{K}_{nm}$ are two different matrices when $m \neq n$, except when either $m = 1$ or $n = 1$. The reason for the name "commutation" matrix will become apparent in Exercise 11.3. If $m = n$ we write $\boldsymbol{K}_n$ instead of $\boldsymbol{K}_{nn}$.

Closely related to the commutation matrix is the $n^2 \times n^2$ matrix $\boldsymbol{N}_n$ with the property

$$\boldsymbol{N}_n \operatorname{vec} \boldsymbol{A} = \operatorname{vec} \frac{1}{2}(\boldsymbol{A} + \boldsymbol{A}'),$$

for every square $n \times n$ matrix $\boldsymbol{A}$. Thus, $\boldsymbol{N}_n$ transforms an arbitrary square matrix $\boldsymbol{A}$ into the *symmetric* matrix $\frac{1}{2}(\boldsymbol{A} + \boldsymbol{A}')$. For this reason we call $\boldsymbol{N}_n$ the *symmetrizer* (matrix). It is easy to see that $\boldsymbol{N}_n = \frac{1}{2}(\boldsymbol{I}_{n^2} + \boldsymbol{K}_n)$.

Next we introduce the half-vec operator $\operatorname{vech}(\cdot)$. Again, let $\boldsymbol{A}$ be a square $n \times n$ matrix. Then $\operatorname{vech}(\boldsymbol{A})$ denotes the $\frac{1}{2}n(n+1) \times 1$ vector that is obtained from $\operatorname{vec} \boldsymbol{A}$ by eliminating all supradiagonal elements of $\boldsymbol{A}$. For example, for $n = 2$,

$$\operatorname{vec} \boldsymbol{A} = (a_{11}, a_{21}, a_{12}, a_{22})' \quad \text{and} \quad \operatorname{vech}(\boldsymbol{A}) = (a_{11}, a_{21}, a_{22})',$$

where the supradiagonal element a_{12} has been removed. Thus, for symmetric $\boldsymbol{A}$, $\operatorname{vech}(\boldsymbol{A})$ only contains the distinct elements of $\boldsymbol{A}$. Now, if $\boldsymbol{A}$ is symmetric, the elements of $\operatorname{vec} \boldsymbol{A}$ are those of $\operatorname{vech}(\boldsymbol{A})$ with some repetitions. Hence, there exists a unique $n^2 \times \frac{1}{2}n(n+1)$ matrix $\boldsymbol{D}_n$, called the *duplication matrix*, that transforms, for symmetric $\boldsymbol{A}$, $\operatorname{vech}(\boldsymbol{A})$ into $\operatorname{vec} \boldsymbol{A}$, that is,

$$\boldsymbol{D}_n \operatorname{vech}(\boldsymbol{A}) = \operatorname{vec} \boldsymbol{A} \quad (\boldsymbol{A} = \boldsymbol{A}').$$

We will see in Exercise 11.28 that $\boldsymbol{D}_n$ and $\boldsymbol{N}_n$ are connected through $\boldsymbol{D}_n\boldsymbol{D}_n^+ = \boldsymbol{N}_n$. Particular attention will be given to the matrices $\boldsymbol{D}^+(\boldsymbol{A}\otimes\boldsymbol{A})\boldsymbol{D}$ and $\boldsymbol{D}'(\boldsymbol{A}\otimes\boldsymbol{A})\boldsymbol{D}$, and their inverse and determinant, which play an important role in many statistical applications, for example in determining the variance of the Wishart distribution (Exercise 11.35) and evaluating Jacobians in Chapter 13 (Exercises 13.37 and 13.38).

Finally, we consider a generalization of the duplication matrix, called a linear structure. Let $\boldsymbol{X} = (x_{ij})$ be an $m \times n$ matrix and suppose that there exist $mn - s$ linear relationships among the mn elements of $\boldsymbol{X}$. If these restrictions are linearly independent, then $\boldsymbol{X}$ has only s "free" variables. A linear structure is then the collection of all real $m\times n$ matrices that satisfy a given set of linear restrictions. One example of a linear structure is the class of symmetric $n\times n$ matrices, where there are $\frac{1}{2}n(n-1)$ restrictions $x_{ij} = x_{ji}$, so that $s = \frac{1}{2}n(n+1)$.

More formally, let $\mathcal{D}$ be an s-dimensional ($s \geq 1$) subspace of the real vector space $\mathbb{R}^{mn}$ and let $\{\boldsymbol{d}_1, \boldsymbol{d}_2, \dots, \boldsymbol{d}_s\}$ be a basis of $\mathcal{D}$. Let $\boldsymbol{\Delta} := (\boldsymbol{d}_1, \boldsymbol{d}_2, \dots, \boldsymbol{d}_s)$. Then the collection of real $m \times n$ matrices

$$\mathrm{L}(\boldsymbol{\Delta}) = \{\boldsymbol{X} : \boldsymbol{X} \in \mathbb{R}^{m\times n}, \operatorname{vec}\boldsymbol{X} \in \mathcal{D}\}$$

is called a *linear structure*, s is called the *dimension*, and $m \times n$ the *order* of the linear structure. Of course, a basis matrix $\boldsymbol{\Delta}$ is not unique. For example, interchanging two columns of $\boldsymbol{\Delta}$ produces another basis matrix. However, as we shall see, the matrix $\boldsymbol{\Delta}\boldsymbol{\Delta}^+$ *is* unique.

11.1 The commutation matrix

Exercise 11.1 (Orthogonality of $\boldsymbol{K}_{mn}$)
(a) Show that $\boldsymbol{K}_{mn}$ is a permutation matrix.
(b) Hence, show that $\boldsymbol{K}_{mn}$ is orthogonal.
(c) Show that $\boldsymbol{K}_{nm}\boldsymbol{K}_{mn} = \boldsymbol{I}_{mn}$.
(d) Conclude that $\boldsymbol{K}'_{mn} = \boldsymbol{K}^{-1}_{mn} = \boldsymbol{K}_{nm}$.

Solution
(a) Let $\boldsymbol{A}$ be a matrix of order $m \times n$. Since $\operatorname{vec}\boldsymbol{A}$ and $\operatorname{vec}\boldsymbol{A}'$ contain the same mn elements, but in a different order, the matrix $\boldsymbol{K}_{mn}$, defined by the relation $\boldsymbol{K}_{mn}\operatorname{vec}\boldsymbol{A} = \operatorname{vec}\boldsymbol{A}'$, is a column permutation of the identity matrix $\boldsymbol{I}_{mn}$, and hence a permutation matrix.
(b) *Every* permutation matrix is orthogonal (Exercise 2.29(d)).
(c) Premultiply $\boldsymbol{K}_{mn}\operatorname{vec}\boldsymbol{A} = \operatorname{vec}\boldsymbol{A}'$ by $\boldsymbol{K}_{nm}$. This yields

$$\boldsymbol{K}_{nm}\boldsymbol{K}_{mn}\operatorname{vec}\boldsymbol{A} = \boldsymbol{K}_{nm}\operatorname{vec}\boldsymbol{A}' = \operatorname{vec}\boldsymbol{A}.$$

Since this holds for every vector $\operatorname{vec}\boldsymbol{A}$, we obtain $\boldsymbol{K}_{nm}\boldsymbol{K}_{mn} = \boldsymbol{I}_{mn}$.
(d) This follows from (b) and (c). Notice that $\boldsymbol{K}_{mn}$ is symmetric when $m = n$, but not when $m \neq n$, unless $m = 1$ or $n = 1$; see Exercise 11.2.

Exercise 11.2 (What is $\boldsymbol{K}_{n1}$?) Show that $\boldsymbol{K}_{n1} = \boldsymbol{K}_{1n} = \boldsymbol{I}_n$.

Solution

Let $\boldsymbol{a}$ be an $n \times 1$ vector. Then, by the definition of the commutation matrix, $\boldsymbol{K}_{n1} \operatorname{vec} \boldsymbol{a} = \operatorname{vec} \boldsymbol{a}'$ and $\boldsymbol{K}_{1n} \operatorname{vec} \boldsymbol{a}' = \operatorname{vec} \boldsymbol{a}$. But, $\operatorname{vec} \boldsymbol{a} = \operatorname{vec} \boldsymbol{a}'$. Hence, $\boldsymbol{K}_{n1} = \boldsymbol{K}_{1n} = \boldsymbol{I}_n$.

Exercise 11.3 (The commutation property, 1) Let $\boldsymbol{A}$ be an $m \times n$ matrix and $\boldsymbol{B}$ a $p \times q$ matrix. Show that

$$(\boldsymbol{A} \otimes \boldsymbol{B})\boldsymbol{K}_{nq} = \boldsymbol{K}_{mp}(\boldsymbol{B} \otimes \boldsymbol{A}).$$

Solution

Let $\boldsymbol{X}$ be an arbitrary $n \times q$ matrix. Then,

$$\begin{aligned}(\boldsymbol{A} \otimes \boldsymbol{B})\boldsymbol{K}_{nq} \operatorname{vec} \boldsymbol{X} &= (\boldsymbol{A} \otimes \boldsymbol{B}) \operatorname{vec} \boldsymbol{X}' = \operatorname{vec} \boldsymbol{B}\boldsymbol{X}'\boldsymbol{A}' \\ &= \boldsymbol{K}_{mp} \operatorname{vec} \boldsymbol{A}\boldsymbol{X}\boldsymbol{B}' = \boldsymbol{K}_{mp}(\boldsymbol{B} \otimes \boldsymbol{A}) \operatorname{vec} \boldsymbol{X}.\end{aligned}$$

Since $\boldsymbol{X}$ is arbitrary, the result follows. Note carefully the order of the indices of the various commutation matrices.

Exercise 11.4 (The commutation property, 2) For any matrix $\boldsymbol{A}$ $(m \times n)$ and $\boldsymbol{B}$ $(p \times q)$, show that

$$\boldsymbol{K}_{pm}(\boldsymbol{A} \otimes \boldsymbol{B})\boldsymbol{K}_{nq} = \boldsymbol{B} \otimes \boldsymbol{A}.$$

Solution

This follows from Exercise 11.3 by premultiplying both sides by $\boldsymbol{K}_{pm}$, using the fact that $\boldsymbol{K}_{pm}\boldsymbol{K}_{mp} = \boldsymbol{I}_{mp}$.

Exercise 11.5 (Commuting with vectors) For any $m \times 1$ vector $\boldsymbol{a}$ and $p \times 1$ vector $\boldsymbol{b}$, show that

$$\boldsymbol{K}_{pm}(\boldsymbol{a} \otimes \boldsymbol{b}) = \boldsymbol{b} \otimes \boldsymbol{a}.$$

Solution

Using the fact that $\boldsymbol{a} \otimes \boldsymbol{b} = \operatorname{vec} \boldsymbol{b}\boldsymbol{a}'$, we have $\boldsymbol{K}_{pm}(\boldsymbol{a} \otimes \boldsymbol{b}) = \boldsymbol{K}_{pm} \operatorname{vec} \boldsymbol{b}\boldsymbol{a}' = \operatorname{vec} \boldsymbol{a}\boldsymbol{b}' = \boldsymbol{b} \otimes \boldsymbol{a}$.

Exercise 11.6 (Commuting back and forth) For any $m \times n$ matrix $\boldsymbol{A}$ and $p \times 1$ vector $\boldsymbol{b}$, show that:

(a) $\boldsymbol{K}_{pm}(\boldsymbol{A} \otimes \boldsymbol{b}) = \boldsymbol{b} \otimes \boldsymbol{A}$;
(b) $\boldsymbol{K}_{mp}(\boldsymbol{b} \otimes \boldsymbol{A}) = \boldsymbol{A} \otimes \boldsymbol{b}$;
(c) $(\boldsymbol{A} \otimes \boldsymbol{b}')\boldsymbol{K}_{np} = \boldsymbol{b}' \otimes \boldsymbol{A}$;
(d) $(\boldsymbol{b}' \otimes \boldsymbol{A})\boldsymbol{K}_{pn} = \boldsymbol{A} \otimes \boldsymbol{b}'$.

Solution

(a) We have $\boldsymbol{K}_{pm}(\boldsymbol{A} \otimes \boldsymbol{b}) = (\boldsymbol{b} \otimes \boldsymbol{A})\boldsymbol{K}_{1n} = \boldsymbol{b} \otimes \boldsymbol{A}$.
(b) Similarly, $\boldsymbol{K}_{mp}(\boldsymbol{b} \otimes \boldsymbol{A}) = (\boldsymbol{A} \otimes \boldsymbol{b})\boldsymbol{K}_{n1} = \boldsymbol{A} \otimes \boldsymbol{b}$.

(c) Also, $(\boldsymbol{A} \otimes \boldsymbol{b}')\boldsymbol{K}_{np} = \boldsymbol{K}_{m1}(\boldsymbol{b}' \otimes \boldsymbol{A}) = \boldsymbol{b}' \otimes \boldsymbol{A}$.
(d) And finally, $(\boldsymbol{b}' \otimes \boldsymbol{A})\boldsymbol{K}_{pn} = \boldsymbol{K}_{1m}(\boldsymbol{A} \otimes \boldsymbol{b}') = \boldsymbol{A} \otimes \boldsymbol{b}'$.

Exercise 11.7 (The commutation property: a generalization) For $\boldsymbol{A}$ $(m \times n)$, $\boldsymbol{B}$ $(p \times q)$, $\boldsymbol{C}$ $(q \times s)$, and $\boldsymbol{D}$ $(n \times t)$, show that

$$\begin{aligned}\boldsymbol{K}_{mp}(\boldsymbol{BC} \otimes \boldsymbol{AD}) &= (\boldsymbol{A} \otimes \boldsymbol{B})\boldsymbol{K}_{nq}(\boldsymbol{C} \otimes \boldsymbol{D}) = (\boldsymbol{AD} \otimes \boldsymbol{BC})\boldsymbol{K}_{ts} \\ &= (\boldsymbol{I}_m \otimes \boldsymbol{BC})\boldsymbol{K}_{ms}(\boldsymbol{I}_s \otimes \boldsymbol{AD}) = (\boldsymbol{AD} \otimes \boldsymbol{I}_p)\boldsymbol{K}_{tp}(\boldsymbol{BC} \otimes \boldsymbol{I}_t).\end{aligned}$$

Solution
We have

$$\begin{aligned}\boldsymbol{K}_{mp}(\boldsymbol{BC} \otimes \boldsymbol{AD}) &= \boldsymbol{K}_{mp}(\boldsymbol{B} \otimes \boldsymbol{A})(\boldsymbol{C} \otimes \boldsymbol{D}) = (\boldsymbol{A} \otimes \boldsymbol{B})\boldsymbol{K}_{nq}(\boldsymbol{C} \otimes \boldsymbol{D}) \\ &= (\boldsymbol{A} \otimes \boldsymbol{B})(\boldsymbol{D} \otimes \boldsymbol{C})\boldsymbol{K}_{ts} = (\boldsymbol{AD} \otimes \boldsymbol{BC})\boldsymbol{K}_{ts} \\ &= (\boldsymbol{I}_m \otimes \boldsymbol{BC})(\boldsymbol{AD} \otimes \boldsymbol{I}_s)\boldsymbol{K}_{ts} = (\boldsymbol{I}_m \otimes \boldsymbol{BC})\boldsymbol{K}_{ms}(\boldsymbol{I}_s \otimes \boldsymbol{AD}),\end{aligned}$$

and also

$$\begin{aligned}(\boldsymbol{AD} \otimes \boldsymbol{BC})\boldsymbol{K}_{ts} &= (\boldsymbol{AD} \otimes \boldsymbol{I}_p)(\boldsymbol{I}_t \otimes \boldsymbol{BC})\boldsymbol{K}_{ts} \\ &= (\boldsymbol{AD} \otimes \boldsymbol{I}_p)\boldsymbol{K}_{tp}(\boldsymbol{BC} \otimes \boldsymbol{I}_t).\end{aligned}$$

Exercise 11.8 (Explicit form of $\boldsymbol{K}_{mn}$) Let $\boldsymbol{E}_{ij}$ denote the $m \times n$ matrix with 1 in its ij-th position and zeros elsewhere. Show that

$$\boldsymbol{K}_{mn} = \sum_{i=1}^{m}\sum_{j=1}^{n}(\boldsymbol{E}_{ij} \otimes \boldsymbol{E}'_{ij}).$$

Solution
We show again that the two matrices are equal by showing that their effect on an arbitrary vector is the same. Thus, let $\boldsymbol{X}$ be an arbitrary $m \times n$ matrix. Let $\boldsymbol{e}_i$ denote the i-th column of $\boldsymbol{I}_m$ and $\boldsymbol{u}_j$ the j-th column of $\boldsymbol{I}_n$, so that $\boldsymbol{E}_{ij} = \boldsymbol{e}_i\boldsymbol{u}'_j$. Then,

$$\begin{aligned}\boldsymbol{X}' = \boldsymbol{I}_n\boldsymbol{X}'\boldsymbol{I}_m &= \left(\sum_{j=1}^{n}\boldsymbol{u}_j\boldsymbol{u}'_j\right)\boldsymbol{X}'\left(\sum_{i=1}^{m}\boldsymbol{e}_i\boldsymbol{e}'_i\right) \\ &= \sum_{ij}\boldsymbol{u}_j(\boldsymbol{u}'_j\boldsymbol{X}'\boldsymbol{e}_i)\boldsymbol{e}'_i = \sum_{ij}\boldsymbol{u}_j(\boldsymbol{e}'_i\boldsymbol{X}\boldsymbol{u}_j)\boldsymbol{e}'_i \\ &= \sum_{ij}(\boldsymbol{u}_j\boldsymbol{e}'_i)\boldsymbol{X}(\boldsymbol{u}_j\boldsymbol{e}'_i) = \sum_{ij}\boldsymbol{E}'_{ij}\boldsymbol{X}\boldsymbol{E}'_{ij}.\end{aligned}$$

Taking vecs we obtain

$$\operatorname{vec}\boldsymbol{X}' = \sum_{ij}\operatorname{vec}\boldsymbol{E}'_{ij}\boldsymbol{X}\boldsymbol{E}'_{ij} = \sum_{ij}(\boldsymbol{E}_{ij} \otimes \boldsymbol{E}'_{ij})\operatorname{vec}\boldsymbol{X}.$$

Exercise 11.9 (Two examples of K_{mn})
(a) Display the matrix K_{23} and verify that $K_{23} \operatorname{vec} A = \operatorname{vec} A'$ for any 2×3 matrix A.
(b) And also for K_{42}.

Solution
(a) Let $A = (a_{ij})$ be a 2×3 matrix. Then,

$$K_{23} \operatorname{vec} A = \left(\begin{array}{cc|cc|cc} 1 & 0 & 0 & 0 & 0 & 0 \\ 0 & 0 & 1 & 0 & 0 & 0 \\ 0 & 0 & 0 & 0 & 1 & 0 \\ \hline 0 & 1 & 0 & 0 & 0 & 0 \\ 0 & 0 & 0 & 1 & 0 & 0 \\ 0 & 0 & 0 & 0 & 0 & 1 \end{array}\right) \begin{pmatrix} a_{11} \\ a_{21} \\ a_{12} \\ a_{22} \\ a_{13} \\ a_{23} \end{pmatrix} = \begin{pmatrix} a_{11} \\ a_{12} \\ a_{13} \\ a_{21} \\ a_{22} \\ a_{23} \end{pmatrix} = \operatorname{vec} A'.$$

(b) Similarly, let $A = (a_{ij})$ be a 4×2 matrix. Then,

$$K_{42} \operatorname{vec} A = \left(\begin{array}{cccc|cccc} 1 & 0 & 0 & 0 & 0 & 0 & 0 & 0 \\ 0 & 0 & 0 & 0 & 1 & 0 & 0 & 0 \\ \hline 0 & 1 & 0 & 0 & 0 & 0 & 0 & 0 \\ 0 & 0 & 0 & 0 & 0 & 1 & 0 & 0 \\ \hline 0 & 0 & 1 & 0 & 0 & 0 & 0 & 0 \\ 0 & 0 & 0 & 0 & 0 & 0 & 1 & 0 \\ \hline 0 & 0 & 0 & 1 & 0 & 0 & 0 & 0 \\ 0 & 0 & 0 & 0 & 0 & 0 & 0 & 1 \end{array}\right) \begin{pmatrix} a_{11} \\ a_{21} \\ a_{31} \\ a_{41} \\ a_{12} \\ a_{22} \\ a_{32} \\ a_{42} \end{pmatrix} = \begin{pmatrix} a_{11} \\ a_{12} \\ a_{21} \\ a_{22} \\ a_{31} \\ a_{32} \\ a_{41} \\ a_{42} \end{pmatrix} = \operatorname{vec} A'.$$

Exercise 11.10 (Alternative expressions for K_{mn})
(a) Let u_j denote the j-th column of I_n. Show that

$$K_{mn} = \sum_{j=1}^{n} (u_j' \otimes I_m \otimes u_j).$$

(b) Let e_i denote the i-th column of I_m. Show that

$$K_{mn} = \sum_{i=1}^{m} (e_i \otimes I_n \otimes e_i').$$

Solution
(a) We use the explicit expression obtained in Exercise 11.8 and the fact that $a \otimes b' = ab' = b' \otimes a$ for any two vectors a and b. Then,

$$\begin{aligned} K_{mn} &= \sum_{i=1}^{m} \sum_{j=1}^{n} (e_i u_j' \otimes u_j e_i') = \sum_{ij} (u_j' \otimes e_i \otimes e_i' \otimes u_j) \\ &= \sum_j \left(u_j' \otimes (\sum_i e_i \otimes e_i') \otimes u_j \right) = \sum_j (u_j' \otimes \sum_i e_i e_i' \otimes u_j) \\ &= \sum_j (u_j' \otimes I_m \otimes u_j). \end{aligned}$$

(b) Similarly,

$$\begin{aligned} \boldsymbol{K}_{mn} &= \sum_{ij}(\boldsymbol{e}_i \otimes \boldsymbol{u}_j' \otimes \boldsymbol{u}_j \otimes \boldsymbol{e}_i') = \sum_i \left(\boldsymbol{e}_i \otimes (\sum_j \boldsymbol{u}_j' \otimes \boldsymbol{u}_j) \otimes \boldsymbol{e}_i' \right) \\ &= \sum_i (\boldsymbol{e}_i \otimes \sum_j \boldsymbol{u}_j \boldsymbol{u}_j' \otimes \boldsymbol{e}_i) = \sum_i (\boldsymbol{e}_i \otimes \boldsymbol{I}_n \otimes \boldsymbol{e}_i'). \end{aligned}$$

Exercise 11.11 (Application of $\boldsymbol{K}_{mn}$ to outer product) Hence, show that, for any $\boldsymbol{A}$ $(m \times p)$, $\boldsymbol{b}$ $(n \times 1)$, and $\boldsymbol{c}$ $(q \times 1)$:
(a) $\boldsymbol{K}_{nm}(\boldsymbol{A} \otimes \boldsymbol{b}\boldsymbol{c}') = \boldsymbol{b} \otimes \boldsymbol{A} \otimes \boldsymbol{c}'$;
(b) $\boldsymbol{K}_{mn}(\boldsymbol{b}\boldsymbol{c}' \otimes \boldsymbol{A}) = \boldsymbol{c}' \otimes \boldsymbol{A} \otimes \boldsymbol{b}$.

Solution
(a) Using Exercise 11.10, and letting $\boldsymbol{b} := (b_1, \dots, b_n)'$, we have

$$\begin{aligned} \boldsymbol{K}_{mn}(\boldsymbol{b} \otimes \boldsymbol{A} \otimes \boldsymbol{c}') &= \sum_{j=1}^{n} (\boldsymbol{u}_j' \otimes \boldsymbol{I}_m \otimes \boldsymbol{u}_j)(\boldsymbol{b} \otimes \boldsymbol{A} \otimes \boldsymbol{c}') \\ &= \sum_j (\boldsymbol{u}_j'\boldsymbol{b}) \otimes \boldsymbol{A} \otimes (\boldsymbol{u}_j \boldsymbol{c}') = \boldsymbol{A} \otimes (\sum_j b_j \boldsymbol{u}_j)\boldsymbol{c}' = \boldsymbol{A} \otimes \boldsymbol{b}\boldsymbol{c}'. \end{aligned}$$

Premultiplying by $\boldsymbol{K}_{nm}$ gives the result.
(b) Similarly,

$$\begin{aligned} \boldsymbol{K}_{nm}(\boldsymbol{c}' \otimes \boldsymbol{A} \otimes \boldsymbol{b}) &= \sum_{j=1}^{n} (\boldsymbol{u}_j \otimes \boldsymbol{I}_m \otimes \boldsymbol{u}_j')(\boldsymbol{c}' \otimes \boldsymbol{A} \otimes \boldsymbol{b}) \\ &= \sum_j (\boldsymbol{u}_j \boldsymbol{c}') \otimes \boldsymbol{A} \otimes (\boldsymbol{u}_j'\boldsymbol{b}) = (\sum_j b_j \boldsymbol{u}_j)\boldsymbol{c}' \otimes \boldsymbol{A} = \boldsymbol{b}\boldsymbol{c}' \otimes \boldsymbol{A}. \end{aligned}$$

Exercise 11.12 (Trace and commutation) Let $\boldsymbol{A}$ and $\boldsymbol{B}$ be $m \times n$ matrices. Show that

$$\operatorname{tr}(\boldsymbol{K}_{mn}(\boldsymbol{A}' \otimes \boldsymbol{B})) = \operatorname{tr}(\boldsymbol{A}'\boldsymbol{B}).$$

Solution
Employing the explicit expression (Exercise 11.8), we find

$$\begin{aligned} \operatorname{tr} \boldsymbol{K}_{mn}(\boldsymbol{A}' \otimes \boldsymbol{B}) &= \operatorname{tr} \sum_{ij} (\boldsymbol{E}_{ij} \otimes \boldsymbol{E}_{ij}')(\boldsymbol{A}' \otimes \boldsymbol{B}) \\ &= \sum_{ij} \operatorname{tr}(\boldsymbol{E}_{ij} \otimes \boldsymbol{E}_{ij}')(\boldsymbol{A}' \otimes \boldsymbol{B}) = \sum_{ij} \operatorname{tr}(\boldsymbol{E}_{ij}\boldsymbol{A}' \otimes \boldsymbol{E}_{ij}'\boldsymbol{B}) \\ &= \sum_{ij} (\operatorname{tr} \boldsymbol{E}_{ij}\boldsymbol{A}')(\operatorname{tr} \boldsymbol{E}_{ij}'\boldsymbol{B}) = \sum_{ij} (\operatorname{tr} \boldsymbol{e}_i \boldsymbol{u}_j' \boldsymbol{A}')(\operatorname{tr} \boldsymbol{u}_j \boldsymbol{e}_i' \boldsymbol{B}) \\ &= \sum_{ij} (\boldsymbol{u}_j' \boldsymbol{A}' \boldsymbol{e}_i)(\boldsymbol{e}_i' \boldsymbol{B} \boldsymbol{u}_j) = \sum_{ij} a_{ij} b_{ij} = \operatorname{tr}(\boldsymbol{A}'\boldsymbol{B}). \end{aligned}$$

Exercise 11.13 (Trace and determinant of K_n)
(a) Show that $\operatorname{tr} K_n = n$.
(b) Show that the eigenvalues of K_n are $+1$ and -1 with multiplicities $\frac{1}{2}n(n+1)$ and $\frac{1}{2}n(n-1)$, respectively.
(c) Show that $|K_n| = (-1)^{\frac{1}{2}n(n-1)}$.

Solution
(a) This follows from Exercise 11.12 by letting $A = B = I_n$. Alternatively, let u_j be the j-th column of I_n. Then,

$$\operatorname{tr} K_n = \operatorname{tr} \sum_{i=1}^{n} \sum_{j=1}^{n} (u_i u_j' \otimes u_j u_i') = \sum_{ij} \operatorname{tr}(u_i u_j' \otimes u_j u_i')$$
$$= \sum_{ij} (\operatorname{tr} u_i u_j')(\operatorname{tr} u_j u_i') = \sum_{ij} \delta_{ij}^2 = n,$$

where δ_{ij} denotes the Kronecker delta.
(b) Since K_n is symmetric and orthogonal, it has eigenvalues $+1$ and -1 only (Exercise 7.42). Let p be the multiplicity of the eigenvalue -1. Then the multiplicity $+1$ is $(n^2 - p)$, and

$$n = \operatorname{tr} K_n = \text{ sum of eigenvalues of } K_n = n^2 - 2p.$$

This gives $p = \frac{1}{2}n(n-1)$.
(c) Finally,

$$|K_n| = (-1)^p = (-1)^{\frac{1}{2}n(n-1)}.$$

(The trace and determinant of K_{mn} ($m \neq n$) are more difficult to find, because K_{mn} is not symmetric when $m \neq n$ unless $m = 1$ or $n = 1$.)

Exercise 11.14 (The matrix $\frac{1}{2}(I_{n^2} - K_n)$)
(a) Show that the matrix $\frac{1}{2}(I_{n^2} - K_n)$ is symmetric idempotent.
(b) Show that, for any square matrix A, $\operatorname{tr} A^2 \leq \operatorname{tr} A'A$, with equality if and only if A is symmetric (*Schur's inequality*). (A different proof, not relying on the commutation matrix, will be provided in Exercise 12.6.)

Solution
(a) Symmetry follows from the fact that K_n is symmetric, and idempotency follows from

$$\left(\frac{1}{2}(I_{n^2} - K_n)\right)^2 = \frac{1}{4}\left(I_{n^2} - K_n - K_n + K_n^2\right) = \frac{1}{2}\left(I_{n^2} - K_n\right),$$

since $K_n^2 = I_{n^2}$. The role of this matrix is to transform $\operatorname{vec} A$ into its skew-symmetric counterpart $\frac{1}{2}\operatorname{vec}(A - A')$. It is thus called the *skew-symmetrizer*.

(b) We have, using the relationship between the trace- and vec-operator obtained in Exercise 10.20,

$$\begin{aligned}\operatorname{tr} \boldsymbol{A}'\boldsymbol{A} - \operatorname{tr} \boldsymbol{A}^2 &= (\operatorname{vec} \boldsymbol{A})'(\operatorname{vec} \boldsymbol{A}) - (\operatorname{vec} \boldsymbol{A}')'(\operatorname{vec} \boldsymbol{A}) \\ &= (\operatorname{vec} \boldsymbol{A})'(\operatorname{vec} \boldsymbol{A}) - (\operatorname{vec} \boldsymbol{A})'\boldsymbol{K}_n(\operatorname{vec} \boldsymbol{A}) \\ &= (\operatorname{vec} \boldsymbol{A})'(\boldsymbol{I}_{n^2} - \boldsymbol{K}_n)(\operatorname{vec} \boldsymbol{A}) \geq 0,\end{aligned}$$

because $\frac{1}{2}(\boldsymbol{I}_{n^2} - \boldsymbol{K}_n)$ is symmetric idempotent, hence positive semidefinite.

***Exercise 11.15 (Three indices in the commutation matrix)**

(a) Show that $\boldsymbol{K}_{s,tn}\boldsymbol{K}_{t,ns} = \boldsymbol{K}_{t,ns}\boldsymbol{K}_{s,tn} = \boldsymbol{K}_{st,n}$.
(b) Show that $\boldsymbol{K}_{ts,n}\boldsymbol{K}_{sn,t}\boldsymbol{K}_{nt,s} = \boldsymbol{I}_{tsn}$.
(c) Show that each pair of the matrices $\boldsymbol{K}_{n,st}$, $\boldsymbol{K}_{s,tn}$, and $\boldsymbol{K}_{t,ns}$ commutes.

Solution

(a) Let $\boldsymbol{a}$ $(n \times 1)$, $\boldsymbol{b}$ $(s \times 1)$, and $\boldsymbol{c}$ $(t \times 1)$ be arbitrary vectors. Then,

$$\boldsymbol{K}_{st,n}(\boldsymbol{a} \otimes \boldsymbol{b} \otimes \boldsymbol{c}) = \boldsymbol{b} \otimes \boldsymbol{c} \otimes \boldsymbol{a} = \boldsymbol{K}_{s,tn}\boldsymbol{K}_{t,ns}(\boldsymbol{a} \otimes \boldsymbol{b} \otimes \boldsymbol{c}).$$

Hence,

$$\boldsymbol{K}_{st,n} = \boldsymbol{K}_{s,tn}\boldsymbol{K}_{t,ns}.$$

Since $\boldsymbol{K}_{st,n} = \boldsymbol{K}_{ts,n}$, we may interchange s and t. This gives

$$\boldsymbol{K}_{st,n} = \boldsymbol{K}_{ts,n} = \boldsymbol{K}_{t,sn}\boldsymbol{K}_{s,nt} = \boldsymbol{K}_{t,ns}\boldsymbol{K}_{s,tn}.$$

(b) Postmultiply both sides of $\boldsymbol{K}_{st,n} = \boldsymbol{K}_{s,tn}\boldsymbol{K}_{t,ns}$ by $\boldsymbol{K}_{n,st}$ and transpose.
(c) Let $\boldsymbol{A} := \boldsymbol{K}_{n,st}$, $\boldsymbol{B} := \boldsymbol{K}_{s,tn}$, and $\boldsymbol{C} := \boldsymbol{K}_{t,ns}$. Given vectors $\boldsymbol{a}$, $\boldsymbol{b}$, and $\boldsymbol{c}$, we obtain

$$\begin{aligned}\boldsymbol{A}(\boldsymbol{b} \otimes \boldsymbol{c} \otimes \boldsymbol{a}) &= \boldsymbol{a} \otimes \boldsymbol{b} \otimes \boldsymbol{c}, \quad & \boldsymbol{A}(\boldsymbol{c} \otimes \boldsymbol{b} \otimes \boldsymbol{a}) &= \boldsymbol{a} \otimes \boldsymbol{c} \otimes \boldsymbol{b}, \\ \boldsymbol{B}(\boldsymbol{a} \otimes \boldsymbol{c} \otimes \boldsymbol{b}) &= \boldsymbol{b} \otimes \boldsymbol{a} \otimes \boldsymbol{c}, \quad & \boldsymbol{B}(\boldsymbol{c} \otimes \boldsymbol{a} \otimes \boldsymbol{b}) &= \boldsymbol{b} \otimes \boldsymbol{c} \otimes \boldsymbol{a}, \\ \boldsymbol{C}(\boldsymbol{a} \otimes \boldsymbol{b} \otimes \boldsymbol{c}) &= \boldsymbol{c} \otimes \boldsymbol{a} \otimes \boldsymbol{b}, \quad & \boldsymbol{C}(\boldsymbol{b} \otimes \boldsymbol{a} \otimes \boldsymbol{c}) &= \boldsymbol{c} \otimes \boldsymbol{b} \otimes \boldsymbol{a}.\end{aligned}$$

This implies

$$\begin{aligned}\boldsymbol{BA}(\boldsymbol{c} \otimes \boldsymbol{b} \otimes \boldsymbol{a}) &= \boldsymbol{b} \otimes \boldsymbol{a} \otimes \boldsymbol{c} = \boldsymbol{C}'(\boldsymbol{c} \otimes \boldsymbol{b} \otimes \boldsymbol{a}), \\ \boldsymbol{CA}(\boldsymbol{b} \otimes \boldsymbol{c} \otimes \boldsymbol{a}) &= \boldsymbol{c} \otimes \boldsymbol{a} \otimes \boldsymbol{b} = \boldsymbol{B}'(\boldsymbol{b} \otimes \boldsymbol{c} \otimes \boldsymbol{a}), \\ \boldsymbol{BC}(\boldsymbol{a} \otimes \boldsymbol{b} \otimes \boldsymbol{c}) &= \boldsymbol{b} \otimes \boldsymbol{c} \otimes \boldsymbol{a} = \boldsymbol{A}'(\boldsymbol{a} \otimes \boldsymbol{b} \otimes \boldsymbol{c}),\end{aligned}$$

and hence,

$$\boldsymbol{BA} = \boldsymbol{C}', \quad \boldsymbol{CA} = \boldsymbol{B}', \quad \boldsymbol{BC} = \boldsymbol{A}'.$$

Since $\boldsymbol{A}$, $\boldsymbol{B}$, and $\boldsymbol{C}$ are orthogonal, this gives

$$\boldsymbol{ABC} = \boldsymbol{ACB} = \boldsymbol{BAC} = \boldsymbol{BCA} = \boldsymbol{CAB} = \boldsymbol{CBA} = \boldsymbol{I},$$

and shows that $BC = CB$, $BA = AB$, $CA = AC$, and also, by suitable pre- and postmultiplication, that $BC' = C'B$, $BA' = A'B$, and $CA' = A'C$. The remaining six identities are found by transposition.

11.2 The symmetrizer matrix

Exercise 11.16 (Idempotency of N_n) Show that the symmetrizer satisfies:
(a) $N_n = \frac{1}{2}(I_{n^2} + K_n)$;
(b) $N_n = N_n' = N_n^2$;
(c) $\operatorname{rk}(N_n) = \operatorname{tr}(N_n) = \frac{1}{2}n(n+1)$.

Solution
(a) From the definition of N_n we know that $N_n \operatorname{vec} A = \operatorname{vec} \frac{1}{2}(A + A')$ for every $n \times n$ matrix A. Hence, $N_n \operatorname{vec} A = \frac{1}{2}(I_{n^2} + K_n) \operatorname{vec} A$ for every $n \times n$ matrix A, and hence $N_n = \frac{1}{2}(I_{n^2} + K_n)$.
(b) Since K_n is symmetric, so is N_n. Further,

$$N_n^2 = \frac{1}{4}(I_{n^2} + K_n)(I_{n^2} + K_n) = \frac{1}{4}(I_{n^2} + K_n + K_n + K_n^2) = \frac{1}{2}(I_{n^2} + K_n),$$

since $K_n^2 = I_{n^2}$.
(c) Since N_n is idempotent, its rank equals its trace. Further,

$$\operatorname{tr}(N_n) = \frac{1}{2}(n^2 + \operatorname{tr} K_n) = \frac{1}{2}(n^2 + n) = \frac{1}{2}n(n+1),$$

using the fact that $\operatorname{tr} K_n = n$ (Exercise 11.13).

Exercise 11.17 (Symmetrizer and skew-symmetrizer are orthogonal to each other)
(a) Show that $N_n K_n = N_n = K_n N_n$.
(b) Hence, show that symmetrizer matrix and the skew-symmetrizer matrix are orthogonal to each other.

Solution
(a) Since $N_n = \frac{1}{2}(I_{n^2} + K_n)$ and $K_n^2 = I_{n^2}$, we obtain

$$N_n K_n = \frac{1}{2}(I_{n^2} + K_n)K_n = \frac{1}{2}(K_n + K_n^2) = \frac{1}{2}(K_n + I_{n^2}) = N_n.$$

The second equality is proved similarly or by noting that $N_n K_n = K_n N_n$ because both N_n and K_n are symmetric.
(b) The symmetrizer is N_n, and the skew-symmetrizer is $\frac{1}{2}(I_{n^2} - K_n)$. We have

$$(N_n)'\left(\frac{1}{2}(I_{n^2} - K_n)\right) = \frac{1}{2}(N_n - N_n K_n) = \mathbf{O},$$

because of (a).

Exercise 11.18 (Kronecker properties of N_n) For any two $n \times n$ matrices A and B, show that:

(a) $\boldsymbol{N}_n(\boldsymbol{A}\otimes\boldsymbol{B})\boldsymbol{N}_n = \boldsymbol{N}_n(\boldsymbol{B}\otimes\boldsymbol{A})\boldsymbol{N}_n$;
(b)

$$\begin{aligned}\boldsymbol{N}_n(\boldsymbol{A}\otimes\boldsymbol{B}+\boldsymbol{B}\otimes\boldsymbol{A})\boldsymbol{N}_n &= \boldsymbol{N}_n(\boldsymbol{A}\otimes\boldsymbol{B}+\boldsymbol{B}\otimes\boldsymbol{A})\\ &= (\boldsymbol{A}\otimes\boldsymbol{B}+\boldsymbol{B}\otimes\boldsymbol{A})\boldsymbol{N}_n = 2\boldsymbol{N}_n(\boldsymbol{A}\otimes\boldsymbol{B})\boldsymbol{N}_n;\end{aligned}$$

(c) $\boldsymbol{N}_n(\boldsymbol{A}\otimes\boldsymbol{A})\boldsymbol{N}_n = \boldsymbol{N}_n(\boldsymbol{A}\otimes\boldsymbol{A}) = (\boldsymbol{A}\otimes\boldsymbol{A})\boldsymbol{N}_n$.

Solution
(a) We have $\boldsymbol{N}_n(\boldsymbol{A}\otimes\boldsymbol{B})\boldsymbol{N}_n = \boldsymbol{N}_n\boldsymbol{K}_n(\boldsymbol{B}\otimes\boldsymbol{A})\boldsymbol{K}_n\boldsymbol{N}_n = \boldsymbol{N}_n(\boldsymbol{B}\otimes\boldsymbol{A})\boldsymbol{N}_n$.
(b) Here we have

$$\begin{aligned}\boldsymbol{N}_n(\boldsymbol{A}\otimes\boldsymbol{B}+\boldsymbol{B}\otimes\boldsymbol{A})\boldsymbol{N}_n &= \frac{1}{2}\boldsymbol{N}_n(\boldsymbol{A}\otimes\boldsymbol{B}+\boldsymbol{B}\otimes\boldsymbol{A})(\boldsymbol{I}_{n^2}+\boldsymbol{K}_n)\\ &= \frac{1}{2}\boldsymbol{N}_n\left(\boldsymbol{A}\otimes\boldsymbol{B}+\boldsymbol{B}\otimes\boldsymbol{A}+\boldsymbol{K}_n(\boldsymbol{B}\otimes\boldsymbol{A}+\boldsymbol{A}\otimes\boldsymbol{B})\right)\\ &= \boldsymbol{N}_n^2(\boldsymbol{A}\otimes\boldsymbol{B}+\boldsymbol{B}\otimes\boldsymbol{A}) = \boldsymbol{N}_n(\boldsymbol{A}\otimes\boldsymbol{B}+\boldsymbol{B}\otimes\boldsymbol{A}).\end{aligned}$$

The second relationship is proved similarly. The third relationship follows from (a).
(c) This follows from (b) by letting $\boldsymbol{B} = \boldsymbol{A}$.

Exercise 11.19 (Symmetrizing with a vector) For any $n \times n$ matrix $\boldsymbol{A}$ and $n \times 1$ vector $\boldsymbol{b}$, show that

$$\boldsymbol{N}_n(\boldsymbol{A}\otimes\boldsymbol{b}) = \boldsymbol{N}_n(\boldsymbol{b}\otimes\boldsymbol{A}) = \frac{1}{2}(\boldsymbol{A}\otimes\boldsymbol{b}+\boldsymbol{b}\otimes\boldsymbol{A}).$$

Solution
Since $\boldsymbol{K}_n(\boldsymbol{A}\otimes\boldsymbol{b}) = \boldsymbol{b}\otimes\boldsymbol{A}$ and $\boldsymbol{K}_n(\boldsymbol{b}\otimes\boldsymbol{A}) = \boldsymbol{A}\otimes\boldsymbol{b}$ (Exercise 11.6), we obtain

$$\begin{aligned}\boldsymbol{N}_n(\boldsymbol{A}\otimes\boldsymbol{b}) &= \frac{1}{2}(\boldsymbol{I}_{n^2}+\boldsymbol{K}_n)(\boldsymbol{A}\otimes\boldsymbol{b}) = \frac{1}{2}(\boldsymbol{A}\otimes\boldsymbol{b}+\boldsymbol{b}\otimes\boldsymbol{A})\\ &= \frac{1}{2}(\boldsymbol{b}\otimes\boldsymbol{A}+\boldsymbol{A}\otimes\boldsymbol{b}) = \frac{1}{2}(\boldsymbol{I}_{n^2}+\boldsymbol{K}_n)(\boldsymbol{b}\otimes\boldsymbol{A}) = \boldsymbol{N}_n(\boldsymbol{b}\otimes\boldsymbol{A}).\end{aligned}$$

Exercise 11.20 (Two examples of $\boldsymbol{N}_n$) Display the matrix $\boldsymbol{N}_n$ for $n = 2$ and $n = 3$ and verify that the defining property holds.

Solution
Let $\boldsymbol{A} := (a_{ij})$ be a 2×2 matrix. Then,

$$\boldsymbol{N}_n \operatorname{vec}\boldsymbol{A} = \left(\begin{array}{cc|cc} 1 & 0 & 0 & 0\\ 0 & \frac{1}{2} & \frac{1}{2} & 0\\ \hline 0 & \frac{1}{2} & \frac{1}{2} & 0\\ 0 & 0 & 0 & 1\end{array}\right)\begin{pmatrix}a_{11}\\ a_{21}\\ a_{12}\\ a_{22}\end{pmatrix} = \begin{pmatrix}a_{11}\\ \frac{1}{2}(a_{21}+a_{12})\\ \frac{1}{2}(a_{21}+a_{12})\\ a_{22}\end{pmatrix} = \frac{1}{2}\operatorname{vec}(\boldsymbol{A}+\boldsymbol{A}').$$

Similarly, let $A = (a_{ij})$ be a 3×3 matrix. Then

$$N_n \operatorname{vec} A = \left(\begin{array}{ccc|ccc|ccc} 1 & 0 & 0 & 0 & 0 & 0 & 0 & 0 & 0 \\ 0 & \frac{1}{2} & 0 & \frac{1}{2} & 0 & 0 & 0 & 0 & 0 \\ 0 & 0 & \frac{1}{2} & 0 & 0 & 0 & \frac{1}{2} & 0 & 0 \\ \hline 0 & \frac{1}{2} & 0 & \frac{1}{2} & 0 & 0 & 0 & 0 & 0 \\ 0 & 0 & 0 & 0 & 1 & 0 & 0 & 0 & 0 \\ 0 & 0 & 0 & 0 & 0 & \frac{1}{2} & 0 & \frac{1}{2} & 0 \\ \hline 0 & 0 & \frac{1}{2} & 0 & 0 & 0 & \frac{1}{2} & 0 & 0 \\ 0 & 0 & 0 & 0 & 0 & \frac{1}{2} & 0 & \frac{1}{2} & 0 \\ 0 & 0 & 0 & 0 & 0 & 0 & 0 & 0 & 1 \end{array}\right) \begin{pmatrix} a_{11} \\ a_{21} \\ a_{31} \\ a_{12} \\ a_{22} \\ a_{32} \\ a_{13} \\ a_{23} \\ a_{33} \end{pmatrix} = \frac{1}{2} \operatorname{vec}(A+A').$$

***Exercise 11.21 (N_n and the normal distribution, 1)** Let $x \sim \mathrm{N}(0, I_n)$. Show that $\operatorname{var}(x \otimes x) = 2N_n$, and verify the result for $n = 1$.

Solution

In the scalar case ($n = 1$), $x \otimes x = x^2$, where $x \sim \mathrm{N}(0, 1)$, so that $x \otimes x \sim \chi^2(1)$ and hence $\operatorname{var}(x \otimes x) = 2$. We seek a generalization of this result.

Let A be an arbitrary real $n \times n$ matrix. The strategy of the proof is to find two expressions for $\operatorname{var}(x'Ax)$, both of which are quadratic forms in $\operatorname{vec} A$. If the matrices in the quadratic forms are symmetric, the matrices must be equal. Notice that the matrix A is *not* assumed to be symmetric.

First let $B := (A+A')/2$ and let S be an orthogonal $n \times n$ matrix such that $S'BS = \Lambda$, where Λ is the diagonal matrix whose diagonal elements $\lambda_1, \dots, \lambda_n$ are the eigenvalues of B. Let $y := S'x$ with components $y_1, \dots, y_n$. Then,

$$x'Ax = x'Bx = x'S\Lambda S'x = y'\Lambda y = \sum_{i=1}^{n} \lambda_i y_i^2.$$

Since $y \sim \mathrm{N}(0, I_n)$, it follows that $y_1^2, \dots, y_n^2$ are independently distributed with $\operatorname{var}(y_i^2) = 2$, so that

$$\begin{aligned} \operatorname{var}(x'Ax) &= \operatorname{var}\left(\sum_{i=1}^{n} \lambda_i y_i^2\right) = \sum_{i=1}^{n} \lambda_i^2 \operatorname{var}(y_i^2) = 2 \operatorname{tr} \Lambda^2 = 2 \operatorname{tr} B^2 \\ &= \operatorname{tr} A'A + \operatorname{tr} A^2 = (\operatorname{vec} A)'(I_{n^2} + K_n) \operatorname{vec} A, \end{aligned}$$

by Exercise 10.20.

Second, since $x'Ax = \operatorname{vec} x'Ax = (x \otimes x)' \operatorname{vec} A$, we find

$$\operatorname{var}(x'Ax) = \operatorname{var}\left((x \otimes x)' \operatorname{vec} A\right) = (\operatorname{vec} A)' \left(\operatorname{var}(x \otimes x)\right) \operatorname{vec} A.$$

We now have two expressions for $\operatorname{var}(x'Ax)$. Hence,

$$(\operatorname{vec} A)' \left(\operatorname{var}(x \otimes x)\right) \operatorname{vec} A = (\operatorname{vec} A)'(I_{n^2} + K_n) \operatorname{vec} A$$

for every $n \times n$ matrix $\boldsymbol{A}$. Since the two matrices in the quadratic forms are symmetric, the result follows from Exercise 8.3(c).

***Exercise 11.22 ($\boldsymbol{N}_n$ and the normal distribution, 2)** Let $\boldsymbol{x} \sim \mathrm{N}(\boldsymbol{\mu}, \boldsymbol{V})$, where $\boldsymbol{V}$ is a positive semidefinite $n \times n$ matrix. Show that

$$\operatorname{var}(\boldsymbol{x} \otimes \boldsymbol{x}) = 2\boldsymbol{N}_n(\boldsymbol{V} \otimes \boldsymbol{V} + \boldsymbol{V} \otimes \boldsymbol{\mu}\boldsymbol{\mu}' + \boldsymbol{\mu}\boldsymbol{\mu}' \otimes \boldsymbol{V}).$$

Solution

We write $\boldsymbol{x} = \boldsymbol{V}^{1/2}\boldsymbol{y} + \boldsymbol{\mu}$ with $\boldsymbol{y} \sim \mathrm{N}(\boldsymbol{0}, \boldsymbol{I}_n)$, so that

$$\begin{aligned}
\boldsymbol{x} \otimes \boldsymbol{x} &= \boldsymbol{V}^{1/2}\boldsymbol{y} \otimes \boldsymbol{V}^{1/2}\boldsymbol{y} + \boldsymbol{V}^{1/2}\boldsymbol{y} \otimes \boldsymbol{\mu} + \boldsymbol{\mu} \otimes \boldsymbol{V}^{1/2}\boldsymbol{y} + \boldsymbol{\mu} \otimes \boldsymbol{\mu} \\
&= (\boldsymbol{V}^{1/2} \otimes \boldsymbol{V}^{1/2})(\boldsymbol{y} \otimes \boldsymbol{y}) + (\boldsymbol{I}_{n^2} + \boldsymbol{K}_n)(\boldsymbol{V}^{1/2}\boldsymbol{y} \otimes \boldsymbol{\mu}) + \boldsymbol{\mu} \otimes \boldsymbol{\mu} \\
&= (\boldsymbol{V}^{1/2} \otimes \boldsymbol{V}^{1/2})(\boldsymbol{y} \otimes \boldsymbol{y}) + 2\boldsymbol{N}_n(\boldsymbol{V}^{1/2} \otimes \boldsymbol{\mu})\boldsymbol{y} + \boldsymbol{\mu} \otimes \boldsymbol{\mu},
\end{aligned}$$

because $\boldsymbol{y} \otimes 1 = \boldsymbol{y}$. Since the two vectors $\boldsymbol{y} \otimes \boldsymbol{y}$ and $\boldsymbol{y}$ are uncorrelated with $\operatorname{var}(\boldsymbol{y} \otimes \boldsymbol{y}) = 2\boldsymbol{N}_n$ and $\operatorname{var}(\boldsymbol{y}) = \boldsymbol{I}_n$, we obtain

$$\begin{aligned}
\operatorname{var}(\boldsymbol{x} \otimes \boldsymbol{x}) &= \operatorname{var}\left((\boldsymbol{V}^{1/2} \otimes \boldsymbol{V}^{1/2})(\boldsymbol{y} \otimes \boldsymbol{y})\right) + \operatorname{var}\left(2\boldsymbol{N}_n(\boldsymbol{V}^{1/2} \otimes \boldsymbol{\mu})\boldsymbol{y}\right) \\
&= 2(\boldsymbol{V}^{1/2} \otimes \boldsymbol{V}^{1/2})\boldsymbol{N}_n(\boldsymbol{V}^{1/2} \otimes \boldsymbol{V}^{1/2}) + 4\boldsymbol{N}_n(\boldsymbol{V}^{1/2} \otimes \boldsymbol{\mu})(\boldsymbol{V}^{1/2} \otimes \boldsymbol{\mu})'\boldsymbol{N}_n \\
&= 2\boldsymbol{N}_n(\boldsymbol{V} \otimes \boldsymbol{V}) + 4\boldsymbol{N}_n(\boldsymbol{V} \otimes \boldsymbol{\mu}\boldsymbol{\mu}')\boldsymbol{N}_n \\
&= 2\boldsymbol{N}_n(\boldsymbol{V} \otimes \boldsymbol{V} + \boldsymbol{V} \otimes \boldsymbol{\mu}\boldsymbol{\mu}' + \boldsymbol{\mu}\boldsymbol{\mu}' \otimes \boldsymbol{V}),
\end{aligned}$$

since $(\boldsymbol{V}^{1/2} \otimes \boldsymbol{V}^{1/2})\boldsymbol{N}_n = \boldsymbol{N}_n(\boldsymbol{V}^{1/2} \otimes \boldsymbol{V}^{1/2})$ and $2\boldsymbol{N}_n(\boldsymbol{V} \otimes \boldsymbol{\mu}\boldsymbol{\mu}')\boldsymbol{N}_n = \boldsymbol{N}_n(\boldsymbol{V} \otimes \boldsymbol{\mu}\boldsymbol{\mu}' + \boldsymbol{\mu}\boldsymbol{\mu}' \otimes \boldsymbol{V})$; see Exercise 11.18.

***Exercise 11.23 ($\boldsymbol{N}_n$ and the Wishart distribution)** Let $\boldsymbol{Z}$ follow a Wishart distribution, $\mathrm{W}_m(n, \boldsymbol{V}, \boldsymbol{M}'\boldsymbol{M})$, where $\boldsymbol{V}$ is a positive semidefinite $m \times m$ matrix.
(a) Show that $\mathrm{E}(\boldsymbol{Z}) = n\boldsymbol{V} + \boldsymbol{M}'\boldsymbol{M}$.
(b) Show that

$$\operatorname{var}(\operatorname{vec} \boldsymbol{Z}) = 2\boldsymbol{N}_m(n(\boldsymbol{V} \otimes \boldsymbol{V}) + \boldsymbol{V} \otimes \boldsymbol{M}'\boldsymbol{M} + \boldsymbol{M}'\boldsymbol{M} \otimes \boldsymbol{V}).$$

(c) Show that $\operatorname{var}(\operatorname{vec} \boldsymbol{Z})$ is symmetric and that its rank is $\leq \frac{1}{2}m(m+1)$.

Solution

Recall that if we have n random $m \times 1$ vectors $\boldsymbol{x}_1, \dots, \boldsymbol{x}_n$, distributed independently as $\boldsymbol{x}_i \sim \mathrm{N}(\boldsymbol{\mu}_i, \boldsymbol{V})$ $(i = 1, \dots, n)$, then the joint distribution of the elements of the matrix $\boldsymbol{Z} = \sum_{i=1}^n \boldsymbol{x}_i\boldsymbol{x}_i'$ is said to be Wishart with n degrees of freedom. This is often written as $\boldsymbol{Z} \sim \mathrm{W}_m(n, \boldsymbol{V}, \boldsymbol{M}'\boldsymbol{M})$, where $\boldsymbol{M}$ denotes the $n \times m$ matrix $\boldsymbol{M} := (\boldsymbol{\mu}_1, \dots, \boldsymbol{\mu}_n)'$. The matrix $\boldsymbol{M}'\boldsymbol{M}$ is the $m \times m$ unscaled *noncentrality matrix*. If $\boldsymbol{M} = \mathbf{O}$ then the distribution is said to be central, and we write $\boldsymbol{Z} \sim \mathrm{W}_m(n, \boldsymbol{V})$.

(a) Noting that $\sum_{i=1}^{n} \boldsymbol{\mu}_i \boldsymbol{\mu}_i' = \boldsymbol{M}'\boldsymbol{M}$, we obtain

$$\mathrm{E}(\boldsymbol{Z}) = \mathrm{E}\left(\sum_i \boldsymbol{x}_i \boldsymbol{x}_i'\right) = \sum_i \mathrm{E}(\boldsymbol{x}_i \boldsymbol{x}_i') = \sum_i (\boldsymbol{V} + \boldsymbol{\mu}_i \boldsymbol{\mu}_i') = n\boldsymbol{V} + \boldsymbol{M}'\boldsymbol{M}.$$

(b) Also, using Exercise 11.22,

$$\begin{aligned} \mathrm{var}(\mathrm{vec}\, \boldsymbol{Z}) &= \mathrm{var}\left(\mathrm{vec} \sum_i \boldsymbol{x}_i \boldsymbol{x}_i'\right) = \mathrm{var}\left(\sum_i \boldsymbol{x}_i \otimes \boldsymbol{x}_i\right) = \sum_i \mathrm{var}(\boldsymbol{x}_i \otimes \boldsymbol{x}_i) \\ &= \sum_i 2\boldsymbol{N}_m (\boldsymbol{V} \otimes \boldsymbol{V} + \boldsymbol{V} \otimes \boldsymbol{\mu}_i \boldsymbol{\mu}_i' + \boldsymbol{\mu}_i \boldsymbol{\mu}_i' \otimes \boldsymbol{V}) \\ &= 2\boldsymbol{N}_m \left(n(\boldsymbol{V} \otimes \boldsymbol{V}) + \boldsymbol{V} \otimes \boldsymbol{M}'\boldsymbol{M} + \boldsymbol{M}'\boldsymbol{M} \otimes \boldsymbol{V}\right). \end{aligned}$$

(c) Using Exercise 11.18(b) and (c), we see that

$$\begin{aligned} \mathrm{var}(\mathrm{vec}\, \boldsymbol{Z}) &= 2\boldsymbol{N}_m \left(n(\boldsymbol{V} \otimes \boldsymbol{V}) + \boldsymbol{V} \otimes \boldsymbol{M}'\boldsymbol{M} + \boldsymbol{M}'\boldsymbol{M} \otimes \boldsymbol{V}\right) \\ &= 2\boldsymbol{N}_m \left(n(\boldsymbol{V} \otimes \boldsymbol{V}) + \boldsymbol{V} \otimes \boldsymbol{M}'\boldsymbol{M} + \boldsymbol{M}'\boldsymbol{M} \otimes \boldsymbol{V}\right) \boldsymbol{N}_m, \end{aligned}$$

implying symmetry. The rank of the $m^2 \times m^2$ matrix is $\leq \frac{1}{2}m(m+1)$, because this is the rank of $\boldsymbol{N}_m$, by Exercise 11.16(c).

11.3 The vech-operator and the duplication matrix

Exercise 11.24 (Examples of vech) Let

$$\boldsymbol{A} = \begin{pmatrix} 1 & 2 & 3 \\ 0 & 4 & 5 \\ 0 & 0 & 6 \end{pmatrix}.$$

Show that

$$\mathrm{vech}(\boldsymbol{A}) = \mathrm{vech}(\mathrm{dg}\, \boldsymbol{A}) = \begin{pmatrix} 1 \\ 0 \\ 0 \\ 4 \\ 0 \\ 6 \end{pmatrix} \quad \text{and} \quad \mathrm{vech}(\boldsymbol{A}') = \begin{pmatrix} 1 \\ 2 \\ 3 \\ 4 \\ 5 \\ 6 \end{pmatrix}.$$

Solution

The vech-operator eliminates all supradiagonal elements of $\boldsymbol{A}$ from vec $\boldsymbol{A}$. Thus,

$$\mathrm{vech}(\boldsymbol{A}) = \begin{pmatrix} 1 \\ 0 \\ 0 \\ 4 \\ 0 \\ 6 \end{pmatrix} \quad \text{and} \quad \mathrm{vech}(\boldsymbol{A}') = \begin{pmatrix} 1 \\ 2 \\ 3 \\ 4 \\ 5 \\ 6 \end{pmatrix}.$$

The matrix $\operatorname{dg} \boldsymbol{A}$ is obtained from $\boldsymbol{A}$ by setting the nonzero off-diagonal elements (2,3,5) equal to zero. But since all these elements are above the diagonal of $\boldsymbol{A}$, this does not affect $\operatorname{vech}(\boldsymbol{A})$.

Exercise 11.25 (Basic properties of vech) Let $\boldsymbol{E}_{ij}$ be the $n \times n$ matrix with 1 in its ij-th position and zeros elsewhere, and let $\boldsymbol{u}_{ij} := \operatorname{vech}(\boldsymbol{E}_{ij})$ for $i \geq j$.
(a) Show that

$$(\boldsymbol{u}_{11}, \boldsymbol{u}_{21}, \dots, \boldsymbol{u}_{n1}, \boldsymbol{u}_{22}, \dots, \boldsymbol{u}_{n2}, \boldsymbol{u}_{33}, \dots, \boldsymbol{u}_{nn}) = \boldsymbol{I}_{\frac{1}{2}n(n+1)}.$$

(b) Show that $\sum_{i \geq j} \boldsymbol{u}_{ij} \boldsymbol{u}'_{ij} = \boldsymbol{I}_{\frac{1}{2}n(n+1)}$.

Solution
(a) We note that $\boldsymbol{u}'_{ij} \operatorname{vech}(\boldsymbol{A}) = \boldsymbol{a}_{ij}$ for $i \geq j$. Hence,

$$\begin{pmatrix} \boldsymbol{u}'_{11} \\ \boldsymbol{u}'_{21} \\ \vdots \\ \boldsymbol{u}'_{nn} \end{pmatrix} \operatorname{vech}(\boldsymbol{A}) = \begin{pmatrix} a_{11} \\ a_{21} \\ \vdots \\ a_{nn} \end{pmatrix} = \operatorname{vech}(\boldsymbol{A}).$$

Since this holds for every vector $\operatorname{vech}(\boldsymbol{A})$, the result follows.
(b) The matrix $\boldsymbol{u}_{ij} \boldsymbol{u}'_{ij}$ $(i \geq j)$ is of order $\frac{1}{2}n(n+1)$ and has 1 in one of the diagonal positions and zeros everywhere else. Summing over all $\frac{1}{2}n(n+1)$ different matrices thus produces the identity matrix.

Exercise 11.26 (Basic properties of $\boldsymbol{D}_n$) Show that:
(a) $\boldsymbol{D}_n$ has full column rank $\frac{1}{2}n(n+1)$;
(b) $\boldsymbol{D}_n^+ = (\boldsymbol{D}'_n \boldsymbol{D}_n)^{-1} \boldsymbol{D}'_n$;
(c) $\boldsymbol{D}_n^+ \boldsymbol{D}_n = \boldsymbol{I}_{\frac{1}{2}n(n+1)}$.

Solution
(a) Since symmetry implies $\frac{1}{2}n(n-1)$ restrictions, namely $a_{ij} = a_{ji}$ $(i < j)$, there are $\frac{1}{2}n(n+1)$ "free" elements. These are contained in the "half-vector" $\operatorname{vech}(\boldsymbol{A})$. Given symmetry of $\boldsymbol{A}$, the vectors $\operatorname{vech}(\boldsymbol{A})$ and $\operatorname{vec} \boldsymbol{A}$ contain precisely the same information. Hence, the equation $\boldsymbol{D}_n \operatorname{vech}(\boldsymbol{A}) = \operatorname{vec} \boldsymbol{A}$ has a *unique* solution, that is, $\boldsymbol{D}_n$ has full column rank (Exercise 6.44(b)).
(b) If $\boldsymbol{D}_n$ has full column rank, then $\boldsymbol{D}'_n \boldsymbol{D}_n$ is nonsingular. Hence $\boldsymbol{D}_n^+ = (\boldsymbol{D}'_n \boldsymbol{D}_n)^+ \boldsymbol{D}'_n = (\boldsymbol{D}'_n \boldsymbol{D}_n)^{-1} \boldsymbol{D}'_n$.
(c) This follows from (b).

Exercise 11.27 (From vec to vech) Let $\boldsymbol{A}$ be a symmetric $n \times n$ matrix.
(a) We already know that $\boldsymbol{D}_n \operatorname{vech}(\boldsymbol{A}) = \operatorname{vec} \boldsymbol{A}$. Now show the inverse relationship $\boldsymbol{D}_n^+ \operatorname{vec} \boldsymbol{A} = \operatorname{vech}(\boldsymbol{A})$,
(b) Show that $\boldsymbol{D}_n \boldsymbol{D}_n^+ \operatorname{vec} \boldsymbol{A} = \operatorname{vec} \boldsymbol{A}$.

Solution

(a) Since $\boldsymbol{A}$ is symmetric, we have $\boldsymbol{D}_n \operatorname{vech}(\boldsymbol{A}) = \operatorname{vec} \boldsymbol{A}$, and hence

$$\boldsymbol{D}_n^+ \operatorname{vec} \boldsymbol{A} = \boldsymbol{D}_n^+ \boldsymbol{D}_n \operatorname{vech}(\boldsymbol{A}) = \operatorname{vech}(\boldsymbol{A}),$$

since $\boldsymbol{D}_n^+ \boldsymbol{D}_n = \boldsymbol{I}$.

(b) Also, $\boldsymbol{D}_n \boldsymbol{D}_n^+ \operatorname{vec} \boldsymbol{A} = \boldsymbol{D}_n \operatorname{vech}(\boldsymbol{A}) = \operatorname{vec} \boldsymbol{A}$, despite the fact that $\boldsymbol{D}_n \boldsymbol{D}_n^+ \neq \boldsymbol{I}_{n^2}$ (unless $n = 1$).

Exercise 11.28 (Relationship between $\boldsymbol{D}_n$ and $\boldsymbol{K}_n$) Show that:

(a) $\boldsymbol{K}_n \boldsymbol{D}_n = \boldsymbol{D}_n = \boldsymbol{N}_n \boldsymbol{D}_n$;

(b) $\boldsymbol{D}_n^+ \boldsymbol{K}_n = \boldsymbol{D}_n^+ = \boldsymbol{D}_n^+ \boldsymbol{N}_n$;

(c) $\boldsymbol{D}_n \boldsymbol{D}_n^+ = \boldsymbol{N}_n$. [Hint: Use Exercise 10.42.]

Solution

(a) For symmetric $\boldsymbol{X}$ we have

$$\boldsymbol{K}_n \boldsymbol{D}_n \operatorname{vech}(\boldsymbol{X}) = \boldsymbol{K}_n \operatorname{vec} \boldsymbol{X} = \operatorname{vec} \boldsymbol{X} = \boldsymbol{D}_n \operatorname{vech}(\boldsymbol{X})$$

and

$$\boldsymbol{N}_n \boldsymbol{D}_n \operatorname{vech}(\boldsymbol{X}) = \boldsymbol{N}_n \operatorname{vec} \boldsymbol{X} = \operatorname{vec} \boldsymbol{X} = \boldsymbol{D}_n \operatorname{vech}(\boldsymbol{X}).$$

Since the symmetry of $\boldsymbol{X}$ does not restrict $\operatorname{vech}(\boldsymbol{X})$ (although it obviously does restrict $\operatorname{vec} \boldsymbol{X}$), we obtain (a).

(b) Since $\boldsymbol{D}_n^+ = (\boldsymbol{D}_n' \boldsymbol{D}_n)^{-1} \boldsymbol{D}_n'$, the result follows from (a) by postmultiplying with $(\boldsymbol{D}_n' \boldsymbol{D}_n)^{-1}$ and then transposing.

(c) We know from (a) that $\boldsymbol{N}_n \boldsymbol{D}_n = \boldsymbol{D}_n$. We know from Exercise 11.16 that $\boldsymbol{N}_n$ is symmetric idempotent and that $\operatorname{rk}(\boldsymbol{N}_n) = \operatorname{rk}(\boldsymbol{D}_n) = \frac{1}{2}n(n+1)$. The result now follows from Exercise 10.42.

Exercise 11.29 (Examples of the duplication matrix) Display the matrix $\boldsymbol{D}_n$ for $n = 2$ and $n = 3$ and verify that the defining property holds.

Solution

Let $\boldsymbol{A} = (a_{ij})$ be a square matrix of order 2. Then,

$$\boldsymbol{D}_2 \operatorname{vech}(\boldsymbol{A}) = \left(\begin{array}{cc|c} 1 & 0 & 0 \\ 0 & 1 & 0 \\ \hline 0 & 1 & 0 \\ 0 & 0 & 1 \end{array}\right) \begin{pmatrix} a_{11} \\ a_{21} \\ a_{22} \end{pmatrix} = \begin{pmatrix} a_{11} \\ a_{21} \\ a_{21} \\ a_{22} \end{pmatrix} = \operatorname{vec} \boldsymbol{A},$$

if $\boldsymbol{A}$ is symmetric. Also, for $n = 3$,

$$\boldsymbol{D}_3 \operatorname{vech}(\boldsymbol{A}) = \left(\begin{array}{ccc|cc|c} 1 & 0 & 0 & 0 & 0 & 0 \\ 0 & 1 & 0 & 0 & 0 & 0 \\ 0 & 0 & 1 & 0 & 0 & 0 \\ \hline 0 & 1 & 0 & 0 & 0 & 0 \\ 0 & 0 & 0 & 1 & 0 & 0 \\ 0 & 0 & 0 & 0 & 1 & 0 \\ \hline 0 & 0 & 1 & 0 & 0 & 0 \\ 0 & 0 & 0 & 0 & 1 & 0 \\ 0 & 0 & 0 & 0 & 0 & 1 \end{array}\right) \begin{pmatrix} a_{11} \\ a_{21} \\ a_{31} \\ a_{22} \\ a_{32} \\ a_{33} \end{pmatrix} = \begin{pmatrix} a_{11} \\ a_{21} \\ a_{31} \\ a_{21} \\ a_{22} \\ a_{32} \\ a_{31} \\ a_{32} \\ a_{33} \end{pmatrix} = \operatorname{vec} \boldsymbol{A},$$

if $\boldsymbol{A}$ is symmetric.

Exercise 11.30 (Properties of $\boldsymbol{D}_n'\boldsymbol{D}_n$)
(a) Show that the matrix $\boldsymbol{D}_n'\boldsymbol{D}_n$ is a diagonal $\frac{1}{2}n(n+1) \times \frac{1}{2}n(n+1)$ matrix with diagonal elements 1 (n times) and 2 ($\frac{1}{2}n(n-1)$ times).
(b) Hence, show that

$$\operatorname{tr} \boldsymbol{D}_n'\boldsymbol{D}_n = n^2, \quad |\boldsymbol{D}_n'\boldsymbol{D}_n| = 2^{\frac{1}{2}n(n-1)}.$$

Solution
(a) Let $\boldsymbol{X} = (x_{ij})$ be a symmetric, but otherwise arbitrary, $n \times n$ matrix. Then,

$$\begin{aligned} \operatorname{vech}(\boldsymbol{X})'\boldsymbol{D}_n'\boldsymbol{D}_n \operatorname{vech}(\boldsymbol{X}) &= (\operatorname{vec} \boldsymbol{X})' \operatorname{vec} \boldsymbol{X} = \sum_{ij} x_{ij}^2 \\ &= 2\sum_{i \geq j} x_{ij}^2 - \sum_i x_{ii}^2 \\ &= 2 \operatorname{vech}(\boldsymbol{X})' \operatorname{vech}(\boldsymbol{X}) - \sum_i \operatorname{vech}(\boldsymbol{X})'\boldsymbol{u}_{ii}\boldsymbol{u}_{ii}' \operatorname{vech}(\boldsymbol{X}) \\ &= \operatorname{vech}(\boldsymbol{X})'(2\boldsymbol{I}_{\frac{1}{2}n(n+1)} - \sum_{i=1}^n \boldsymbol{u}_{ii}\boldsymbol{u}_{ii}') \operatorname{vech}(\boldsymbol{X}), \end{aligned}$$

where $\boldsymbol{u}_{ii}$ is defined in Exercise 11.25. Since the matrices in both quadratic forms are *symmetric* (this is essential, why?), and $\operatorname{vech}(\boldsymbol{X})$ is unrestricted, it follows that

$$\boldsymbol{D}_n'\boldsymbol{D}_n = 2\boldsymbol{I}_{\frac{1}{2}n(n+1)} - \sum_{i=1}^n \boldsymbol{u}_{ii}\boldsymbol{u}_{ii}'.$$

This is a diagonal matrix with diagonal elements 1 (n times) and 2 ($\frac{1}{2}n(n-1)$ times).
(b) The trace of $\boldsymbol{D}_n'\boldsymbol{D}_n$ equals $n + n(n-1) = n^2$ and the determinant is $|\boldsymbol{D}_n'\boldsymbol{D}_n| = 1^n 2^{\frac{1}{2}n(n-1)} = 2^{\frac{1}{2}n(n-1)}$.

Exercise 11.31 (Kronecker property of the duplication matrix) Let $\boldsymbol{A}$ be an arbitrary $n \times n$ matrix. Show that:
(a) $\boldsymbol{D}_n\boldsymbol{D}_n^+(\boldsymbol{A}\otimes\boldsymbol{A})\boldsymbol{D}_n = (\boldsymbol{A}\otimes\boldsymbol{A})\boldsymbol{D}_n$;
(b) $(\boldsymbol{D}_n^+(\boldsymbol{A}\otimes\boldsymbol{A})\boldsymbol{D}_n)^{-1} = \boldsymbol{D}_n^+(\boldsymbol{A}^{-1}\otimes\boldsymbol{A}^{-1})\boldsymbol{D}_n \quad$ ($\boldsymbol{A}$ nonsingular).

Solution
(a) We have

$$\begin{aligned}\boldsymbol{D}_n\boldsymbol{D}_n^+(\boldsymbol{A}\otimes\boldsymbol{A})\boldsymbol{D}_n &= \boldsymbol{N}_n(\boldsymbol{A}\otimes\boldsymbol{A})\boldsymbol{D}_n\\ &= (\boldsymbol{A}\otimes\boldsymbol{A})\boldsymbol{N}_n\boldsymbol{D}_n = (\boldsymbol{A}\otimes\boldsymbol{A})\boldsymbol{D}_n,\end{aligned}$$

using the facts $\boldsymbol{D}_n\boldsymbol{D}_n^+ = \boldsymbol{N}_n$, $\boldsymbol{N}_n(\boldsymbol{A}\otimes\boldsymbol{A}) = (\boldsymbol{A}\otimes\boldsymbol{A})\boldsymbol{N}_n$, and $\boldsymbol{N}_n\boldsymbol{D}_n = \boldsymbol{D}_n$. Alternatively, we can prove (a) from the fact that $\boldsymbol{D}_n\boldsymbol{D}_n^+ \operatorname{vec}\boldsymbol{X} = \operatorname{vec}\boldsymbol{X}$ for *symmetric* $\boldsymbol{X}$, so that

$$\begin{aligned}\boldsymbol{D}_n\boldsymbol{D}_n^+(\boldsymbol{A}\otimes\boldsymbol{A})\boldsymbol{D}_n \operatorname{vech}(\boldsymbol{X}) &= \boldsymbol{D}_n\boldsymbol{D}_n^+(\boldsymbol{A}\otimes\boldsymbol{A})\operatorname{vec}\boldsymbol{X} = \boldsymbol{D}_n\boldsymbol{D}_n^+\operatorname{vec}\boldsymbol{A}\boldsymbol{X}\boldsymbol{A}'\\ &= \operatorname{vec}\boldsymbol{A}\boldsymbol{X}\boldsymbol{A}' = (\boldsymbol{A}\otimes\boldsymbol{A})\operatorname{vec}\boldsymbol{X} = (\boldsymbol{A}\otimes\boldsymbol{A})\boldsymbol{D}_n\operatorname{vech}(\boldsymbol{X}).\end{aligned}$$

The essence of this proof is that $\boldsymbol{A}\boldsymbol{X}\boldsymbol{A}'$ is symmetric for every $\boldsymbol{A}$, whenever $\boldsymbol{X}$ is symmetric. We call property (a) the "Kronecker" property of the duplication matrix.
(b) Letting $\boldsymbol{A}$ be nonsingular and using (a), we see that

$$\begin{aligned}\boldsymbol{D}_n^+(\boldsymbol{A}\otimes\boldsymbol{A})\boldsymbol{D}_n\boldsymbol{D}_n^+(\boldsymbol{A}^{-1}\otimes\boldsymbol{A}^{-1})\boldsymbol{D}_n &= \boldsymbol{D}_n^+(\boldsymbol{A}\otimes\boldsymbol{A})(\boldsymbol{A}^{-1}\otimes\boldsymbol{A}^{-1})\boldsymbol{D}_n\\ &= \boldsymbol{D}_n^+(\boldsymbol{I}_n\otimes\boldsymbol{I}_n)\boldsymbol{D}_n = \boldsymbol{D}_n^+\boldsymbol{D}_n = \boldsymbol{I}_{\frac{1}{2}n(n+1)}.\end{aligned}$$

***Exercise 11.32 (The matrix $\boldsymbol{D}_n^+(\boldsymbol{A}\otimes\boldsymbol{A})\boldsymbol{D}_n$, triangular case)** If $\boldsymbol{A} := (a_{ij})$ is an upper triangular $n \times n$ matrix, show that $\boldsymbol{D}_n^+(\boldsymbol{A}\otimes\boldsymbol{A})\boldsymbol{D}_n$ is also upper triangular, and that its diagonal elements are $a_{ii}a_{jj}$ $(1 \le j \le i \le n)$.

Solution
Let $\boldsymbol{E}_{ij}$ be the $n \times n$ matrix with one in the ij-th position and zeros elsewhere, and define the symmetric matrix $\boldsymbol{T}_{ij} := \boldsymbol{E}_{ij} + \boldsymbol{E}_{ji} - \delta_{ij}\boldsymbol{E}_{ii}$, where δ_{ij} is the Kronecker delta. Then, for $i \ge j$,

$$\begin{aligned}\boldsymbol{D}_n^+(\boldsymbol{A}\otimes\boldsymbol{A})\boldsymbol{D}_n\operatorname{vech}(\boldsymbol{E}_{ij}) &= \boldsymbol{D}_n^+(\boldsymbol{A}\otimes\boldsymbol{A})\boldsymbol{D}_n\operatorname{vech}(\boldsymbol{T}_{ij}) = \boldsymbol{D}_n^+(\boldsymbol{A}\otimes\boldsymbol{A})\operatorname{vec}\boldsymbol{T}_{ij}\\ &= \boldsymbol{D}_n^+\operatorname{vec}\boldsymbol{A}\boldsymbol{T}_{ij}\boldsymbol{A}' = \operatorname{vech}(\boldsymbol{A}\boldsymbol{T}_{ij}\boldsymbol{A}'),\end{aligned}$$

and therefore, for $i \ge j$ and $s \ge t$,

$$\begin{aligned}(\operatorname{vech}(\boldsymbol{E}_{st}))'\boldsymbol{D}_n^+(\boldsymbol{A}\otimes\boldsymbol{A})\boldsymbol{D}_n\operatorname{vech}(\boldsymbol{E}_{ij}) &= (\operatorname{vech}(\boldsymbol{E}_{st}))'\operatorname{vech}(\boldsymbol{A}\boldsymbol{T}_{ij}\boldsymbol{A}')\\ &= (\boldsymbol{A}\boldsymbol{T}_{ij}\boldsymbol{A}')_{st} = a_{si}a_{tj} + a_{sj}a_{ti} - \delta_{ij}a_{si}a_{ti}.\end{aligned}$$

Since $i \geq j$ and $s \geq t$, there are six cases to consider:

$$t \leq s \leq j \leq i, \quad t \leq j \leq s \leq i, \quad t \leq j \leq i \leq s,$$
$$j \leq t \leq s \leq i, \quad j \leq t \leq i \leq s, \quad j \leq i \leq t \leq s.$$

Now, $\boldsymbol{A}$ is upper triangular, so the last four of these yield zero or become special cases of the first two. The only cases not yielding zero are therefore $t \leq s \leq j \leq i$ and $t \leq j \leq s \leq i$, or equivalently

$$t \leq s \leq j = i, \quad t \leq s \leq j < i, \quad t \leq j < s \leq i.$$

Hence,

$$(\operatorname{vech}(\boldsymbol{E}_{st}))' \boldsymbol{D}_n^+ (\boldsymbol{A} \otimes \boldsymbol{A}) \boldsymbol{D}_n \operatorname{vech}(\boldsymbol{E}_{ij})$$
$$= \begin{cases} a_{si} a_{tj} & (t \leq s \leq j = i \quad \text{or} \quad t \leq j < s \leq i), \\ a_{si} a_{tj} + a_{sj} a_{ti} & (t \leq s \leq j < i), \\ 0 & (\text{otherwise}). \end{cases}$$

so that $\boldsymbol{D}_n^+ (\boldsymbol{A} \otimes \boldsymbol{A}) \boldsymbol{D}_n$ is upper triangular if $\boldsymbol{A}$ is, and

$$(\operatorname{vech}(\boldsymbol{E}_{ij}))' \boldsymbol{D}_n^+ (\boldsymbol{A} \otimes \boldsymbol{A}) \boldsymbol{D}_n \operatorname{vech}(\boldsymbol{E}_{ij}) = a_{ii} a_{jj} \quad (j \leq i)$$

are its diagonal elements.

Exercise 11.33 (The matrix $\boldsymbol{D}_n^+ (\boldsymbol{A} \otimes \boldsymbol{A}) \boldsymbol{D}_n$, eigenvalues) Let $\boldsymbol{A}$ be an $n \times n$ matrix with eigenvalues $\lambda_1, \lambda_2, \dots, \lambda_n$. Show that:
(a) the eigenvalues of $\boldsymbol{D}_n^+ (\boldsymbol{A} \otimes \boldsymbol{A}) \boldsymbol{D}_n$ are $\lambda_i \lambda_j$ $(1 \leq j \leq i \leq n)$;
(b) $\operatorname{tr}(\boldsymbol{D}_n^+ (\boldsymbol{A} \otimes \boldsymbol{A}) \boldsymbol{D}_n) = \frac{1}{2} (\operatorname{tr} \boldsymbol{A})^2 + \frac{1}{2} \operatorname{tr}(\boldsymbol{A}^2)$;
(c) $|\boldsymbol{D}_n^+ (\boldsymbol{A} \otimes \boldsymbol{A}) \boldsymbol{D}_n| = |\boldsymbol{A}|^{n+1}$.

Solution
By Schur's Theorem (Exercise 7.62) there exists a nonsingular matrix $\boldsymbol{S}$ such that $\boldsymbol{S}^{-1} \boldsymbol{A} \boldsymbol{S} = \boldsymbol{M}$, where $\boldsymbol{M}$ is an upper triangular matrix with the eigenvalues $\lambda_1, \dots, \lambda_n$ of $\boldsymbol{A}$ on its diagonal. Thus, by Exercise 11.31,

$$\boldsymbol{D}_n^+ (\boldsymbol{S}^{-1} \otimes \boldsymbol{S}^{-1}) \boldsymbol{D}_n \boldsymbol{D}_n^+ (\boldsymbol{A} \otimes \boldsymbol{A}) \boldsymbol{D}_n \boldsymbol{D}_n^+ (\boldsymbol{S} \otimes \boldsymbol{S}) \boldsymbol{D}_n = \boldsymbol{D}_n^+ (\boldsymbol{M} \otimes \boldsymbol{M}) \boldsymbol{D}_n.$$

Since $\boldsymbol{D}_n^+ (\boldsymbol{S}^{-1} \otimes \boldsymbol{S}^{-1}) \boldsymbol{D}_n$ is the inverse of $\boldsymbol{D}_n^+ (\boldsymbol{S} \otimes \boldsymbol{S}) \boldsymbol{D}_n$, it follows that $\boldsymbol{D}_n^+ (\boldsymbol{A} \otimes \boldsymbol{A}) \boldsymbol{D}_n$ and $\boldsymbol{D}_n^+ (\boldsymbol{M} \otimes \boldsymbol{M}) \boldsymbol{D}_n$ have the same set of eigenvalues. Exercise 11.32 shows that the latter matrix is upper triangular with eigenvalues (diagonal elements) $\lambda_i \lambda_j$ $(1 \leq j \leq i \leq n)$. These are therefore the eigenvalues of $\boldsymbol{D}_n^+ (\boldsymbol{A} \otimes \boldsymbol{A}) \boldsymbol{D}_n$ too.

The trace and determinant, being the sum and the product of the eigenvalues, respectively, are

$$\operatorname{tr} \boldsymbol{D}_n^+ (\boldsymbol{A} \otimes \boldsymbol{A}) \boldsymbol{D}_n = \sum_{i \geq j} \lambda_i \lambda_j = \frac{1}{2} \sum_i \lambda_i^2 + \frac{1}{2} \sum_{ij} \lambda_i \lambda_j$$
$$= \frac{1}{2} \operatorname{tr} \boldsymbol{A}^2 + \frac{1}{2} (\operatorname{tr} \boldsymbol{A})^2,$$

and

$$|D_n^+(A \otimes A)D_n| = \prod_{i \geq j} \lambda_i \lambda_j = \prod_i \lambda_i^{n+1} = |A|^{n+1}.$$

Exercise 11.34 (The matrix $D_n'(A \otimes A)D_n$) Let A be an $n \times n$ matrix. Show that:
(a) $|D_n'(A \otimes A)D_n| = 2^{\frac{1}{2}n(n-1)}|A|^{n+1}$;
(b) $(D_n'(A \otimes A)D_n)^{-1} = D_n^+(A^{-1} \otimes A^{-1})D_n^{+\prime}$ (A nonsingular).

Solution
(a) Since $D_n^+ = (D_n'D_n)^{-1}D_n'$, we have

$$D_n'(A \otimes A)D_n = (D_n'D_n)D_n^+(A \otimes A)D_n$$

and hence

$$|D_n'(A \otimes A)D_n| = |D_n'D_n||D_n^+(A \otimes A)D_n| = 2^{\frac{1}{2}n(n-1)}|A|^{n+1},$$

using Exercises 11.30 and 11.33.
(b) Similarly,

$$\begin{aligned}(D_n'(A \otimes A)D_n)^{-1} &= (D_n^+(A \otimes A)D_n)^{-1}(D_n'D_n)^{-1} \\ &= D_n^+(A^{-1} \otimes A^{-1})D_n(D_n'D_n)^{-1} = D_n^+(A^{-1} \otimes A^{-1})D_n^{+\prime},\end{aligned}$$

using Exercise 11.31.

Exercise 11.35 (Variance of the Wishart distribution) Let Z follow a central Wishart distribution, $\mathrm{W}_m(n, V)$, where V is a positive definite $m \times m$ matrix. We have seen in Exercise 11.23 that the variance of vec Z is given by $\mathrm{var}(\mathrm{vec}\, Z) = 2nN_m(V \otimes V)$.
(a) Obtain $\mathrm{var}(\mathrm{vech}(Z))$ and show that it is nonsingular.
(b) Find its inverse.
(c) Find its determinant.

Solution
(a) Since $\mathrm{vech}(Z) = D_m^+ \mathrm{vec}\, Z$, we find

$$\begin{aligned}\mathrm{var}(\mathrm{vech}(Z)) &= \mathrm{var}(D_m^+ \mathrm{vec}\, Z) = D_m^+ \mathrm{var}(\mathrm{vec}\, Z)D_m^{+\prime} \\ &= 2nD_m^+N_m(V \otimes V)D_m^{+\prime} = 2nD_m^+(V \otimes V)D_m^{+\prime},\end{aligned}$$

using Exercise 11.28(b). Its nonsingularity follows from Exercise 11.34.
(b) Again by Exercise 11.34(b), the inverse is given by

$$\left(\mathrm{var}(\mathrm{vech}(Z))\right)^{-1} = \frac{1}{2n}\left(D_m^+(V \otimes V)D_m^{+\prime}\right)^{-1} = \frac{1}{2n}D_m'(V^{-1} \otimes V^{-1})D_m.$$

(c) By Exercise 11.34(a), the determinant is given by

$$\begin{aligned}\left|\mathrm{var}(\mathrm{vech}(Z))\right| &= (2n)^{\frac{1}{2}m(m+1)}\left|D_m'(V^{-1} \otimes V^{-1})D_m\right|^{-1} \\ &= (2n)^{\frac{1}{2}m(m+1)}2^{\frac{1}{2}m(m-1)}|V^{-1}|^{m+1} = n^{\frac{1}{2}m(m+1)}2^{m^2}|V|^{-(m+1)}.\end{aligned}$$

11.4 Linear structures

Exercise 11.36 (Examples of linear structures) Show that the collection of $n \times n$ lower triangular matrices, strictly lower triangular matrices, and diagonal matrices are all linear structures.

Solution

All these classes have in common that a typical matrix $\boldsymbol{X}$ obeys linear restrictions (of the form $x_{ij} = x_{kl}$ or $x_{ij} = 0$). Hence for each class, there exists a vector function $\boldsymbol{\psi}(\boldsymbol{X})$ (like $\operatorname{vech}(\boldsymbol{X})$ for symmetry) containing the s "free" elements of $\boldsymbol{X}$, and a matrix $\boldsymbol{\Delta}$ (like $\boldsymbol{D}$ for symmetry), such that

$$\boldsymbol{\Delta}\boldsymbol{\psi}(\boldsymbol{X}) = \operatorname{vec} \boldsymbol{X} \quad \text{for all} \quad \boldsymbol{X} \in \mathrm{L}(\boldsymbol{\Delta}).$$

The dimension s of the linear structure is $\frac{1}{2}n(n+1)$ in the case of symmetry. For the other linear structures we have $\frac{1}{2}n(n+1)$ (lower triangular), $\frac{1}{2}n(n-1)$ (strictly lower triangular), and n (diagonal).

Exercise 11.37 (Basic properties of a linear structure) Let $\mathrm{L}(\boldsymbol{\Delta})$ be a linear structure of dimension s. Show that the following three statements are equivalent:
(i) $\boldsymbol{A} \in \mathrm{L}(\boldsymbol{\Delta})$;
(ii) $(\boldsymbol{I} - \boldsymbol{\Delta}\boldsymbol{\Delta}^+) \operatorname{vec} \boldsymbol{A} = \boldsymbol{0}$;
(iii) $\operatorname{vec} \boldsymbol{A} = \boldsymbol{\Delta}\boldsymbol{\psi}(\boldsymbol{A})$ for some $s \times 1$ vector $\boldsymbol{\psi}(\boldsymbol{A})$.

Solution

(i) $\Longleftrightarrow$ (iii): $\boldsymbol{A} \in \mathrm{L}(\boldsymbol{\Delta}) \Longleftrightarrow \operatorname{vec} \boldsymbol{A}$ lies in the space generated by the columns of $\boldsymbol{\Delta} \Longleftrightarrow$ a vector $\boldsymbol{\psi}(\boldsymbol{A})$ exists such that $\operatorname{vec} \boldsymbol{A} = \boldsymbol{\Delta}\boldsymbol{\psi}(\boldsymbol{A})$.
(ii) $\Longrightarrow$ (iii): $\operatorname{vec} \boldsymbol{A} = \boldsymbol{\Delta}\boldsymbol{\Delta}^+ \operatorname{vec} \boldsymbol{A}$ implies that there exists a vector $\boldsymbol{\psi}(\boldsymbol{A})$, namely $\boldsymbol{\psi}(\boldsymbol{A}) = \boldsymbol{\Delta}^+ \operatorname{vec} \boldsymbol{A}$, such that $\operatorname{vec} \boldsymbol{A} = \boldsymbol{\Delta}\boldsymbol{\psi}(\boldsymbol{A})$.
(iii) $\Longrightarrow$ (ii): $\operatorname{vec} \boldsymbol{A} = \boldsymbol{\Delta}\boldsymbol{\psi}(\boldsymbol{A})$ implies that $\boldsymbol{\Delta}\boldsymbol{\Delta}^+ \operatorname{vec} \boldsymbol{A} = \boldsymbol{\Delta}\boldsymbol{\Delta}^+\boldsymbol{\Delta}\boldsymbol{\psi}(\boldsymbol{A}) = \boldsymbol{\Delta}\boldsymbol{\psi}(\boldsymbol{A}) = \operatorname{vec} \boldsymbol{A}$.

Exercise 11.38 (Invariance of $\boldsymbol{N}_{\boldsymbol{\Delta}}$) Let $\mathrm{L}(\boldsymbol{\Delta})$ be a linear structure of dimension s, and define $\boldsymbol{N}_{\boldsymbol{\Delta}} := \boldsymbol{\Delta}\boldsymbol{\Delta}^+$. Show that:
(a) $\boldsymbol{N}_{\boldsymbol{\Delta}}$ is symmetric idempotent of rank s;
(b) $\boldsymbol{N}_{\boldsymbol{\Delta}} \operatorname{vec} \boldsymbol{A} = \operatorname{vec} \boldsymbol{A}$ for every $\boldsymbol{A} \in \mathrm{L}(\boldsymbol{\Delta})$;
(c) $\boldsymbol{N}_{\boldsymbol{\Delta}}$ is invariant to the choice of $\boldsymbol{\Delta}$.

Solution

(a) From the properties of the Moore-Penrose inverse we know that $\boldsymbol{\Delta}\boldsymbol{\Delta}^+$ is symmetric idempotent and that $\operatorname{rk}(\boldsymbol{\Delta}\boldsymbol{\Delta}^+) = \operatorname{rk}(\boldsymbol{\Delta}) = s$.
(b) This follows from Exercise 11.37((i) $\Longrightarrow$ (ii)).
(c) Let $\boldsymbol{\Delta}_1$ and $\boldsymbol{\Delta}_2$ be two basis matrices of an s-dimensional subspace $\mathcal{D}$ of $\mathbb{R}^{mn}$. Then $\boldsymbol{\Delta}_1 = \boldsymbol{\Delta}_2\boldsymbol{E}$ for some nonsingular matrix $\boldsymbol{E}$. Now, since $\boldsymbol{\Delta}_2' = (\boldsymbol{\Delta}_2\boldsymbol{\Delta}_2^+\boldsymbol{\Delta}_2)' = \boldsymbol{\Delta}_2'\boldsymbol{\Delta}_2\boldsymbol{\Delta}_2^+$,

we have $\Delta_1' = E'\Delta_2' = E'\Delta_2'\Delta_2\Delta_2^+ = \Delta_1'\Delta_2\Delta_2^+$. Hence,

$$\begin{aligned}\Delta_2\Delta_2^+ &= \Delta_2 E E^{-1}\Delta_2^+ = \Delta_1 E^{-1}\Delta_2^+ = \Delta_1\Delta_1^+\Delta_1 E^{-1}\Delta_2^+ \\ &= \Delta_1\Delta_1^+\Delta_2\Delta_2^+ = \Delta_1^{+\prime}\Delta_1'\Delta_2\Delta_2^+ = \Delta_1^{+\prime}\Delta_1' = \Delta_1\Delta_1^+.\end{aligned}$$

Exercise 11.39 (From vec to ψ) Let $\mathrm{L}(\Delta)$ be a linear structure of dimension s. We already know (Exercise 11.37) that $A \in \mathrm{L}(\Delta)$ if and only if there exists an $s \times 1$ vector, say $\psi(A)$, such that $\Delta\psi(A) = \operatorname{vec} A$. Show that $\psi(A)$ can be solved uniquely, the unique solution being

$$\psi(A) = \Delta^+ \operatorname{vec} A \quad (A \in \mathrm{L}(\Delta)).$$

Solution
This follows directly from the fact that Δ has full column rank.

Exercise 11.40 (Kronecker property of a linear structure) Let $\mathrm{L}(\Delta_1)$ and $\mathrm{L}(\Delta_2)$ be two given linear structures, let A and B be given matrices, and assume that $BXA' \in \mathrm{L}(\Delta_2)$ for all $X \in \mathrm{L}(\Delta_1)$. Show that:
(a) $\Delta_2\Delta_2^+(A \otimes B)\Delta_1 = (A \otimes B)\Delta_1$;
(b) $(\Delta_2^+(A \otimes B)\Delta_1)^{-1} = \Delta_1^+(A^{-1} \otimes B^{-1})\Delta_2$ (A and B nonsingular);
(c) $(\Delta_2'(A \otimes B)\Delta_1)^{-1} = \Delta_1^+(A^{-1} \otimes B^{-1})\Delta_2^{+\prime}$ (A and B nonsingular).

Solution
(a) Let $\psi_1(X)$ be such that $\Delta_1\psi_1(X) = \operatorname{vec} X$ for all $X \in \mathrm{L}(\Delta_1)$. Then,

$$\begin{aligned}\Delta_2\Delta_2^+(A \otimes B)\Delta_1\psi_1(X) &= \Delta_2\Delta_2^+(A \otimes B)\operatorname{vec} X \\ &= \Delta_2\Delta_2^+ \operatorname{vec} BXA' = \operatorname{vec} BXA' \\ &= (A \otimes B)\operatorname{vec} X = (A \otimes B)\Delta_1\psi_1(X).\end{aligned}$$

Since the restriction $X \in \mathrm{L}(\Delta_1)$ does not restrict $\psi_1(X)$ the result follows.
(b) We use (a) and write

$$\begin{aligned}\Delta_1^+(A^{-1} \otimes B^{-1})\Delta_2\Delta_2^+(A \otimes B)\Delta_1 &= \Delta_1^+(A^{-1} \otimes B^{-1})(A \otimes B)\Delta_1 \\ &= \Delta_1^+\Delta_1 = I_s.\end{aligned}$$

(c) Since $\Delta_2^{+\prime}\Delta_2' = \Delta_2\Delta_2^+$, the result follows from

$$\Delta_1^+(A^{-1} \otimes B^{-1})\Delta_2^{+\prime}\Delta_2'(A \otimes B)\Delta_1 = I_s.$$

Exercise 11.41 (Same linear structure for X and BXA'?) Give some examples of a linear structure such that $X \in \mathrm{L}(\Delta)$ implies $BXA' \in \mathrm{L}(\Delta)$ for a suitable choice of A and B.

Solution

We give four examples. If $\boldsymbol{X}$ is symmetric then $\boldsymbol{AXA}'$ is also symmetric, if $\boldsymbol{X}$ is skew-symmetric than so is $\boldsymbol{AXA}'$. If $\boldsymbol{A}'$ and $\boldsymbol{B}$ are both lower triangular, then $\boldsymbol{BXA}'$ is lower triangular if $\boldsymbol{X}$ is lower triangular, and $\boldsymbol{BXA}'$ is strictly lower triangular if $\boldsymbol{X}$ is strictly lower triangular.

Notes

The commutation matrix $\boldsymbol{K}_{mn}$ was rigorously studied by Magnus and Neudecker (1979), the symmetrizer matrix $\boldsymbol{N}_n$ was introduced by Browne (1974), and the duplication matrix $\boldsymbol{D}_n$ by Browne (1974) and Magnus and Neudecker (1980). In Exercise 11.13 we present the trace and determinant of $\boldsymbol{K}_n$. The trace and determinant of $\boldsymbol{K}_{mn}$ $(m \neq n)$ was obtained by Magnus and Neudecker (1979). An overview of results on linear structures (including further results on the commutation matrix, symmetrizer matrix, and duplication matrix) can be found in Magnus (1988).

12

Matrix inequalities

Matrix inequalities play an important role in matrix algebra and its applications. This chapter has two purposes. First, we will provide a number of important matrix inequalities, centered around four themes: (a) matrix generalizations of the Cauchy-Schwarz type, (b) inequalities for positive (semi)definite matrices, (c) inequalities based on the Schur complement, and (d) eigenvalue-related inequalities, especially the theorems of Fischer and Poincaré.

The second purpose is to demonstrate some of the most important principles by which inequalities can be derived. The principles discussed in this chapter can be listed as follows:

(a) Squares are nonnegative. For example, $\operatorname{tr} \boldsymbol{A}'\boldsymbol{A} \geq 0$ for any $\boldsymbol{A}$. Letting $\boldsymbol{A} := \boldsymbol{a}\boldsymbol{b}' - \boldsymbol{b}\boldsymbol{a}'$, Cauchy-Schwarz follows directly (Exercise 12.1(a)).

(b) Sums of nonnegative quantities are nonnegative. See Exercise 12.1(c) for an example.

(c) The product of nonnegative quantities is nonnegative. This is obviously true for a product of scalars, but for the matrix product we have to be careful. The Hadamard product (Exercise 12.32) is a more natural tool in this respect than the usual matrix product. Nevertheless, if $\boldsymbol{A} \geq \mathbf{O}$ then $\boldsymbol{B}'\boldsymbol{A}\boldsymbol{B} \geq \mathbf{O}$ for every $\boldsymbol{B}$. As an example, let $\boldsymbol{A}$ be idempotent symmetric. Then, $\boldsymbol{A} \geq \mathbf{O}$ and hence $\boldsymbol{B}'(\boldsymbol{I} - \boldsymbol{A})\boldsymbol{B} \geq \mathbf{O}$, so that we obtain the inequality $\boldsymbol{B}'\boldsymbol{A}\boldsymbol{B} \leq \boldsymbol{B}'\boldsymbol{B}$; see Exercise 12.15.

(d) Calculus. If we wish to demonstrate that $\phi_1(\boldsymbol{X}) \geq \phi_2(\boldsymbol{X})$ for all matrices $\boldsymbol{X}$, then we can also try and minimize the function $\phi(\boldsymbol{X}) := \phi_1(\boldsymbol{X}) - \phi_2(\boldsymbol{X})$ with respect to $\boldsymbol{X}$. If $\widetilde{\boldsymbol{X}}$ minimizes ϕ and $\phi(\widetilde{\boldsymbol{X}}) = 0$ then the inequality has been established. Chapter 13 contains a number of examples of this type.

(e) Quasilinearization. Consider a symmetric matrix $\boldsymbol{A}$ and let λ_1 denote its largest eigenvalue. We shall see that we can express λ_1 as $\max_{x} \boldsymbol{x}'\boldsymbol{A}\boldsymbol{x}/\boldsymbol{x}'\boldsymbol{x}$ (Exercise 12.39). Thus we can express a *nonlinear* function $\lambda_1(\boldsymbol{A})$ as an envelope of *linear* functions of $\boldsymbol{A}$. Because of the (quasi)linearity it is now easy to prove that $\lambda_1(\boldsymbol{A}+\boldsymbol{B}) \leq \lambda_1(\boldsymbol{A}) + \lambda_1(\boldsymbol{B})$ (Exercise 12.40).

(f) Continuity arguments. Suppose we have proved an inequality for a positive definite matrix $\boldsymbol{A}$. Does the same result also hold for positive semidefinite $\boldsymbol{A}$? We can introduce the matrix $\boldsymbol{B} := \boldsymbol{A} + \epsilon\boldsymbol{I}$ for $\epsilon > 0$. If $\boldsymbol{A} \geq \mathbf{O}$ then $\boldsymbol{B} > \mathbf{O}$ for every $\epsilon > 0$. We now apply the result to $\boldsymbol{B}$ and let $\epsilon \to 0$. Some care needs to be taken with this technique, because the functions need to be continuous in order for the limit to be valid. See Exercise 12.19 for an example of this technique.

(g) Schur complements. This technique — to which we devote a whole section — is based on partitioned matrices. Sometimes a problem becomes easier when we embed it into a higher-dimensional problem. The Schur-complement technique is an example of this idea.

All matrices in this chapter are real. When we investigate eigenvalues of symmetric matrices, we adopt the convention to arrange the eigenvalues $\lambda_1, \lambda_2, \ldots, \lambda_n$ in decreasing order, so that

$$\lambda_1 \geq \lambda_2 \geq \cdots \geq \lambda_n.$$

12.1 Cauchy-Schwarz type inequalities

Exercise 12.1 (Cauchy-Schwarz inequality, once more) Let $\boldsymbol{a}$ and $\boldsymbol{b}$ be two $n \times 1$ vectors. Then,

$$(\boldsymbol{a}'\boldsymbol{b})^2 \leq (\boldsymbol{a}'\boldsymbol{a})(\boldsymbol{b}'\boldsymbol{b}),$$

with equality if and only if $\boldsymbol{a}$ and $\boldsymbol{b}$ are linearly dependent. Prove this result by considering:
(a) the matrix $\boldsymbol{A} = \boldsymbol{a}\boldsymbol{b}' - \boldsymbol{b}\boldsymbol{a}'$;
(b) the matrix $\boldsymbol{A} = \boldsymbol{I}_n - (1/\boldsymbol{b}'\boldsymbol{b})\boldsymbol{b}\boldsymbol{b}'$ for $\boldsymbol{b} \neq \mathbf{0}$;
(c) the 2×2 matrices $\boldsymbol{A}_i := \boldsymbol{c}_i\boldsymbol{c}_i'$, where $\boldsymbol{c}_i' := (a_i : b_i)$ denotes the i-th row of $\boldsymbol{C} := (\boldsymbol{a} : \boldsymbol{b})$.

Solution
(a) We know from Exercise 2.25 that for any real matrix $\boldsymbol{A}$, $\operatorname{tr} \boldsymbol{A}'\boldsymbol{A} \geq 0$ with equality if and only if $\boldsymbol{A} = \mathbf{O}$. Now define $\boldsymbol{A} := \boldsymbol{a}\boldsymbol{b}' - \boldsymbol{b}\boldsymbol{a}'$. Then,

$$\operatorname{tr} \boldsymbol{A}'\boldsymbol{A} = 2(\boldsymbol{a}'\boldsymbol{a})(\boldsymbol{b}'\boldsymbol{b}) - 2(\boldsymbol{a}'\boldsymbol{b})^2 \geq 0$$

with equality if and only if $\boldsymbol{a}\boldsymbol{b}' = \boldsymbol{b}\boldsymbol{a}'$, that is, if and only if $\boldsymbol{a}$ and $\boldsymbol{b}$ are collinear.
(b) If $\boldsymbol{b} = \mathbf{0}$ the result is trivial. Assume that $\boldsymbol{b} \neq \mathbf{0}$, and consider the matrix $\boldsymbol{A} = \boldsymbol{I}_n - (1/\boldsymbol{b}\boldsymbol{b}')\boldsymbol{b}\boldsymbol{b}'$. The matrix $\boldsymbol{A}$ is symmetric idempotent, and therefore positive semidefinite

(Exercise 8.66(a)). Hence,

$$(\boldsymbol{a}'\boldsymbol{a})(\boldsymbol{b}'\boldsymbol{b}) - (\boldsymbol{a}'\boldsymbol{b})^2 = (\boldsymbol{b}'\boldsymbol{b})\left(\boldsymbol{a}'\boldsymbol{a} - \frac{\boldsymbol{a}'\boldsymbol{b}\boldsymbol{b}'\boldsymbol{a}}{\boldsymbol{b}'\boldsymbol{b}}\right) = (\boldsymbol{b}'\boldsymbol{b})\boldsymbol{a}'\boldsymbol{A}\boldsymbol{a} \geq 0.$$

Equality implies that $\boldsymbol{a}'\boldsymbol{A}\boldsymbol{a} = 0$, and hence $\boldsymbol{A}\boldsymbol{a} = \boldsymbol{0}$, that is, $\boldsymbol{a} = \alpha\boldsymbol{b}$ with $\alpha := \boldsymbol{a}'\boldsymbol{b}/\boldsymbol{b}'\boldsymbol{b}$.
(c) Since the matrices $\boldsymbol{A}_i$ are positive semidefinite (Exercise 8.9(a)), their sum $\boldsymbol{A} := \sum_i \boldsymbol{A}_i$ is also positive semidefinite (Exercise 8.8(b)). Now,

$$\boldsymbol{A} = \sum_{i=1}^{n} \boldsymbol{A}_i = \begin{pmatrix} \sum_i a_i^2 & \sum_i a_i b_i \\ \sum_i b_i a_i & \sum_i b_i^2 \end{pmatrix} = \begin{pmatrix} \boldsymbol{a}'\boldsymbol{a} & \boldsymbol{a}'\boldsymbol{b} \\ \boldsymbol{b}'\boldsymbol{a} & \boldsymbol{b}'\boldsymbol{b} \end{pmatrix},$$

and since $|\boldsymbol{A}| \geq 0$ (Exercise 8.13(a)), the result follows. Equality occurs if and only $\boldsymbol{A}$ is singular. Since $\boldsymbol{A} = \boldsymbol{C}'\boldsymbol{C}$, this occurs if and only if $\boldsymbol{C} = \mathbf{O}$ or $\operatorname{rk}(\boldsymbol{C}) = 1$, that is, if and only if $\boldsymbol{a}$ and $\boldsymbol{b}$ are collinear.

Exercise 12.2 (Bound for a_{ij}) Let $\boldsymbol{A} := (a_{ij})$ be a positive semidefinite $n \times n$ matrix.
(a) Show that $(\boldsymbol{x}'\boldsymbol{A}\boldsymbol{y})^2 \leq (\boldsymbol{x}'\boldsymbol{A}\boldsymbol{x})(\boldsymbol{y}'\boldsymbol{A}\boldsymbol{y})$, with equality if and only if $\boldsymbol{A}\boldsymbol{x}$ and $\boldsymbol{A}\boldsymbol{y}$ are collinear.
(b) Hence, show that $|a_{ij}| \leq \max\{a_{11}, \dots, a_{nn}\}$ for all i and j. (Compare Exercise 8.7.)

Solution
(a) Let $\boldsymbol{a} := \boldsymbol{A}^{1/2}\boldsymbol{x}$ and $\boldsymbol{b} := \boldsymbol{A}^{1/2}\boldsymbol{y}$. Application of Exercise 12.1 then gives the inequality. Equality occurs if and only if $\boldsymbol{A}^{1/2}\boldsymbol{x}$ and $\boldsymbol{A}^{1/2}\boldsymbol{y}$ are collinear, that is, if and only if $\boldsymbol{A}\boldsymbol{x}$ and $\boldsymbol{A}\boldsymbol{y}$ are collinear.
(b) Let $\boldsymbol{x} := \boldsymbol{e}_i$ and $\boldsymbol{y} := \boldsymbol{e}_j$, where $\boldsymbol{e}_i$ and $\boldsymbol{e}_j$ denote unit vectors. Then (a) shows that $a_{ij}^2 \leq a_{ii}a_{jj} \leq \max\{a_{ii}^2, a_{jj}^2\}$, and the result follows.

Exercise 12.3 (Bergstrom's inequality) Let $\boldsymbol{A}$ be positive definite.
(a) Show that $(\boldsymbol{x}'\boldsymbol{y})^2 \leq (\boldsymbol{x}'\boldsymbol{A}^{-1}\boldsymbol{x})(\boldsymbol{y}'\boldsymbol{A}\boldsymbol{y})$, with equality if and only if $\boldsymbol{A}^{-1}\boldsymbol{x}$ and $\boldsymbol{y}$ are collinear.
(b) For given $\boldsymbol{x} \neq \boldsymbol{0}$, define $\psi(\boldsymbol{A}) := (\boldsymbol{x}'\boldsymbol{A}^{-1}\boldsymbol{x})^{-1}$. Show that

$$\psi(\boldsymbol{A}) = \min_{\boldsymbol{y}} \frac{\boldsymbol{y}'\boldsymbol{A}\boldsymbol{y}}{(\boldsymbol{y}'\boldsymbol{x})^2}.$$

(c) Use (b) to prove that

$$\boldsymbol{x}'(\boldsymbol{A}+\boldsymbol{B})^{-1}\boldsymbol{x} \leq \frac{(\boldsymbol{x}'\boldsymbol{A}^{-1}\boldsymbol{x})(\boldsymbol{x}'\boldsymbol{B}^{-1}\boldsymbol{x})}{\boldsymbol{x}'(\boldsymbol{A}^{-1}+\boldsymbol{B}^{-1})\boldsymbol{x}}$$

for any two positive definite matrices $\boldsymbol{A}$ and $\boldsymbol{B}$ and $\boldsymbol{x} \neq \boldsymbol{0}$ (*Bergstrom*).

Solution
(a) Let $\boldsymbol{a} := \boldsymbol{A}^{-1/2}\boldsymbol{x}$ and $\boldsymbol{b} := \boldsymbol{A}^{1/2}\boldsymbol{y}$. Application of Exercise 12.1 then gives the inequality. Equality occurs if and only if $\boldsymbol{A}^{-1/2}\boldsymbol{x}$ and $\boldsymbol{A}^{1/2}\boldsymbol{y}$ are collinear, that is, if and

only if $\boldsymbol{x}$ and $\boldsymbol{Ay}$ are collinear. (Or, equivalently, if $\boldsymbol{A}^{-1}\boldsymbol{x}$ and $\boldsymbol{y}$ are collinear.)
(b) We rewrite the inequality in (a) as

$$\frac{\boldsymbol{y}'\boldsymbol{A}\boldsymbol{y}}{(\boldsymbol{y}'\boldsymbol{x})^2} \geq \frac{1}{\boldsymbol{x}'\boldsymbol{A}^{-1}\boldsymbol{x}} = \psi(\boldsymbol{A}).$$

Since this holds for all $\boldsymbol{y}$, (b) follows. Equality holds if and only if $\boldsymbol{y}$ is a multiple of $\boldsymbol{A}^{-1}\boldsymbol{x}$.
(c) The expression under (b) is a so-called *quasilinear* representation. It expresses the *nonlinear* function $\phi(\boldsymbol{x}) := (\boldsymbol{x}'\boldsymbol{A}^{-1}\boldsymbol{x})^{-1}$ as an envelope of *linear* functions of $\boldsymbol{A}$. We will have a number of occasions to demonstrate the usefulness of this technique. Here we have

$$\psi(\boldsymbol{A}+\boldsymbol{B}) = \min_{\boldsymbol{y}} \frac{\boldsymbol{y}'(\boldsymbol{A}+\boldsymbol{B})\boldsymbol{y}}{(\boldsymbol{y}'\boldsymbol{x})^2} \geq \min_{\boldsymbol{y}} \frac{\boldsymbol{y}'\boldsymbol{A}\boldsymbol{y}}{(\boldsymbol{y}'\boldsymbol{x})^2} + \min_{\boldsymbol{y}} \frac{\boldsymbol{y}'\boldsymbol{B}\boldsymbol{y}}{(\boldsymbol{y}'\boldsymbol{x})^2} = \psi(\boldsymbol{A}) + \psi(\boldsymbol{B}),$$

and hence,

$$\frac{1}{\psi(\boldsymbol{A}+\boldsymbol{B})} \leq \frac{1}{\psi(\boldsymbol{A})+\psi(\boldsymbol{B})} = \frac{(\psi(\boldsymbol{A}))^{-1}(\psi(\boldsymbol{B}))^{-1}}{(\psi(\boldsymbol{A}))^{-1}+(\psi(\boldsymbol{B}))^{-1}}.$$

Exercise 12.4 (Cauchy's inequality)
(a) Show that

$$\left(\sum_{i=1}^{n} x_i\right)^2 \leq n\sum_{i=1}^{n} x_i^2$$

with equality if and only if $x_1 = x_2 = \cdots = x_n$ (*Cauchy*).
(b) If all eigenvalues of $\boldsymbol{A}$ are real, show that $|(1/n)\operatorname{tr}\boldsymbol{A}| \leq \left((1/n)\operatorname{tr}\boldsymbol{A}^2\right)^{1/2}$, with equality if and only if the eigenvalues of the $n \times n$ matrix $\boldsymbol{A}$ are all equal.
(c) If $\boldsymbol{A}$ is symmetric and $\boldsymbol{A} \neq \mathbf{O}$, show that

$$\operatorname{rk}(\boldsymbol{A}) \geq \frac{(\operatorname{tr}\boldsymbol{A})^2}{\operatorname{tr}\boldsymbol{A}^2}.$$

Solution
(a) Let $\boldsymbol{\imath}$ denote the vector of ones. Then $\sum_i x_i = \boldsymbol{\imath}'\boldsymbol{x}$ and $\sum_i x_i^2 = \boldsymbol{x}'\boldsymbol{x}$. We wish to prove that $(\boldsymbol{\imath}'\boldsymbol{x})^2 \leq n\boldsymbol{x}'\boldsymbol{x}$, which we rewrite as $\boldsymbol{x}'\boldsymbol{\imath}\boldsymbol{\imath}'\boldsymbol{x} \leq n\boldsymbol{x}'\boldsymbol{x}$, or as $\boldsymbol{x}'\boldsymbol{A}\boldsymbol{x} \geq 0$, where $\boldsymbol{A} := \boldsymbol{I}_n - (1/n)\boldsymbol{\imath}\boldsymbol{\imath}'$. The result now follows from the fact that $\boldsymbol{A}$ is symmetric idempotent, hence positive semidefinite. Equality occurs if and only if $\boldsymbol{A}\boldsymbol{x} = \mathbf{0}$, that is, if and only $x_i = \boldsymbol{\imath}'\boldsymbol{x}/n$ for all i.
(b) Let $\{\lambda_i\}$ denote the eigenvalues of $\boldsymbol{A}$. Then, $\operatorname{tr}\boldsymbol{A} = \sum_i \lambda_i$ and $\operatorname{tr}\boldsymbol{A}^2 = \sum_i \lambda_i^2$. Application of Cauchy's inequality (a) gives the result.
(c) Let $r := \operatorname{rk}(\boldsymbol{A})$, and let $\mu_1, \dots, \mu_r$ denote the nonzero eigenvalues of $\boldsymbol{A}$. Then, by Cauchy's inequality, $(\sum_{i=1}^r \mu_i)^2 \leq r\sum_{i=1}^r \mu_i^2$, and hence

$$r \geq \frac{(\sum_{i=1}^r \mu_i)^2}{\sum_{i=1}^r \mu_i^2} = \frac{(\operatorname{tr}\boldsymbol{A})^2}{\operatorname{tr}\boldsymbol{A}^2}.$$

Equality occurs if and only if $\boldsymbol{A}$ is proportional to a symmetric idempotent matrix.

Exercise 12.5 (Cauchy-Schwarz, trace version) Let $\boldsymbol{A}$ and $\boldsymbol{B}$ be two matrices of the same order. Show that:
(a) $(\operatorname{tr} \boldsymbol{A}'\boldsymbol{B})^2 \leq (\operatorname{tr} \boldsymbol{A}'\boldsymbol{A})(\operatorname{tr} \boldsymbol{B}'\boldsymbol{B})$ with equality if and only if one of the matrices $\boldsymbol{A}$ and $\boldsymbol{B}$ is a multiple of the other;
(b) $\operatorname{tr}(\boldsymbol{A}'\boldsymbol{B})^2 \leq \operatorname{tr}(\boldsymbol{A}'\boldsymbol{A}\boldsymbol{B}'\boldsymbol{B})$ with equality if and only if $\boldsymbol{A}\boldsymbol{B}'$ is symmetric;
(c) $\operatorname{tr}(\boldsymbol{A}'\boldsymbol{B})^2 \leq \operatorname{tr}(\boldsymbol{A}\boldsymbol{A}'\boldsymbol{B}\boldsymbol{B}')$ with equality if and only if $\boldsymbol{A}'\boldsymbol{B}$ is symmetric.

Solution
(a) Let $\boldsymbol{a} := \operatorname{vec} \boldsymbol{A}$ and $\boldsymbol{b} := \operatorname{vec} \boldsymbol{B}$ and apply Cauchy-Schwarz.
(b) Let $\tilde{\boldsymbol{A}} := \boldsymbol{A}\boldsymbol{B}'$ and $\tilde{\boldsymbol{B}} := \boldsymbol{B}\boldsymbol{A}'$ and apply (a) to the matrices $\tilde{\boldsymbol{A}}$ and $\tilde{\boldsymbol{B}}$. This gives

$$(\operatorname{tr} \boldsymbol{B}\boldsymbol{A}'\boldsymbol{B}\boldsymbol{A}')^2 \leq (\operatorname{tr} \boldsymbol{B}\boldsymbol{A}'\boldsymbol{A}\boldsymbol{B}')(\operatorname{tr} \boldsymbol{A}\boldsymbol{B}'\boldsymbol{B}\boldsymbol{A}'),$$

implying (b).
(c) This follows from (b) and the fact that $\operatorname{tr}(\boldsymbol{A}'\boldsymbol{B})^2 = \operatorname{tr}(\boldsymbol{A}\boldsymbol{B}')^2$:

$$\begin{aligned}\operatorname{tr}(\boldsymbol{A}'\boldsymbol{B})^2 &= \operatorname{tr}(\boldsymbol{A}'\boldsymbol{B}\boldsymbol{A}'\boldsymbol{B}) = \operatorname{tr}(\boldsymbol{B}'\boldsymbol{A}\boldsymbol{B}'\boldsymbol{A}) \\ &= \operatorname{tr}(\boldsymbol{A}\boldsymbol{B}')^2 \leq \operatorname{tr}(\boldsymbol{A}\boldsymbol{A}'\boldsymbol{B}\boldsymbol{B}').\end{aligned}$$

Exercise 12.6 (Schur's inequality) Let $\boldsymbol{A}$ be a square real matrix. Prove Schur's inequality, $\operatorname{tr} \boldsymbol{A}^2 \leq \operatorname{tr} \boldsymbol{A}'\boldsymbol{A}$ with equality if and only if $\boldsymbol{A}$ is symmetric.

Solution
We use (again) the fact that $\operatorname{tr} \boldsymbol{B}'\boldsymbol{B} \geq 0$ with equality if and only if $\boldsymbol{B} = \mathbf{O}$. Let $\boldsymbol{B} := \boldsymbol{A} - \boldsymbol{A}'$. This is a skew-symmetric matrix, because $\boldsymbol{B}' = -\boldsymbol{B}$. Then,

$$\begin{aligned}\operatorname{tr} \boldsymbol{B}'\boldsymbol{B} &= \operatorname{tr}(\boldsymbol{A} - \boldsymbol{A}')'(\boldsymbol{A} - \boldsymbol{A}') = \operatorname{tr} \boldsymbol{A}'\boldsymbol{A} - \operatorname{tr} \boldsymbol{A}'\boldsymbol{A}' - \operatorname{tr} \boldsymbol{A}\boldsymbol{A} + \operatorname{tr} \boldsymbol{A}\boldsymbol{A}' \\ &= 2 \operatorname{tr} \boldsymbol{A}'\boldsymbol{A} - 2 \operatorname{tr} \boldsymbol{A}^2 \geq 0,\end{aligned}$$

with equality if and only if $\boldsymbol{A} - \boldsymbol{A}' = \mathbf{O}$. (An alternative proof, using the commutation matrix, was provided in Exercise 11.14(b).)

12.2 Positive (semi)definite matrix inequalities

Exercise 12.7 (The fundamental determinantal inequality)
(a) Let $\boldsymbol{A}$ and $\boldsymbol{B}$ be positive semidefinite matrices. Show that $|\boldsymbol{A} + \boldsymbol{B}| \geq |\boldsymbol{A}| + |\boldsymbol{B}|$.
(b) When does equality occur?

Solution
If both $\boldsymbol{A}$ and $\boldsymbol{B}$ are singular, then the result is trivially true. Suppose that one (or both) of the two matrices is nonsingular, say $\boldsymbol{A}$, and let $\boldsymbol{C} := \boldsymbol{A}^{-1/2}\boldsymbol{B}\boldsymbol{A}^{-1/2}$. Then,

$$\begin{aligned}|\boldsymbol{A} + \boldsymbol{B}| - |\boldsymbol{A}| - |\boldsymbol{B}| &= |\boldsymbol{A}^{1/2}(\boldsymbol{I} + \boldsymbol{C})\boldsymbol{A}^{1/2}| - |\boldsymbol{A}| - |\boldsymbol{A}^{1/2}\boldsymbol{C}\boldsymbol{A}^{1/2}| \\ &= |\boldsymbol{A}| \left(|\boldsymbol{I} + \boldsymbol{C}| - 1 - |\boldsymbol{C}|\right).\end{aligned}$$

It thus suffices to show, for any positive semidefinite matrix C, that $|I+C|-1-|C|\geq 0$. Let $\lambda_1,\dots,\lambda_n$ be the eigenvalues of C. Then we must show that, for $\lambda_i\geq 0$,

$$\prod_{i=1}^{n}(1+\lambda_i)-1-\prod_{i=1}^{n}\lambda_i\geq 0.$$

This can be proved by expanding the product $\prod_i(1+\lambda_i)$. Alternatively, it can be proved by induction, as follows. For $n=1$ we have equality. For $n=2$, we have

$$(1+\lambda_1)(1+\lambda_2)-1-\lambda_1\lambda_2=\lambda_1+\lambda_2\geq 0.$$

Now suppose the result is true for $n-1$. Then,

$$\begin{aligned}\prod_{i=1}^{n}(1+\lambda_i)-1-\prod_{i=1}^{n}\lambda_i&=(1+\lambda_n)\prod_{i=1}^{n-1}(1+\lambda_i)-1-\lambda_n\prod_{i=1}^{n-1}\lambda_i\\&\geq(1+\lambda_n)(1+\prod_{i=1}^{n-1}\lambda_i)-1-\lambda_n\prod_{i=1}^{n-1}\lambda_i=\lambda_n+\prod_{i=1}^{n-1}\lambda_i\geq 0.\end{aligned}$$

(b) Equality occurs if and only if either $n=1$ or $|A+B|=0$ or $A=\mathbf{O}$ or $B=\mathbf{O}$. If $n=1$, equality is obvious. If $n\geq 2$, we distinguish three cases:
(i) $|A|=|B|=0$. Equality then occurs if and only if $|A+B|=0$.
(ii) $|A|>0$ and $|B|\geq 0$. There is equality if and only if $\prod_{i=1}^{n}(1+\lambda_i)=1+\prod_{i=1}^{n}\lambda_i$, where the $\lambda_i\geq 0$ are defined under (a). We wish to show that this equality holds true if and only if all λ_i are zero. If all λ_i are zero, then (trivially) equality holds. If at least one of the λ_i is positive, then

$$\prod_{i=1}^{n}(1+\lambda_i)\geq 1+\sum_{i=1}^{n}\lambda_i+\prod_{i=1}^{n}\lambda_i>1+\prod_{i=1}^{n}\lambda_i,$$

and equality does not hold. We conclude that equality holds true if and only if all λ_i are zero, that is, if and only $B=\mathbf{O}$.
(iii) $|A|\geq 0$ and $|B|>0$. By a similar argument we find that equality occurs if and only if $A=\mathbf{O}$.

Exercise 12.8 (Determinantal inequality, special case)
(a) Let A and B be positive semidefinite matrices and let $A\geq B$. Show that $|A|\geq|B|$.
(b) Show that equality occurs if and only if A and B are nonsingular and $A=B$, or (trivially) if A and B are both singular.

Solution
(a) Let $C:=A-B$, and apply Exercise 12.7. Then, $|A|=|B+C|\geq|B|$.
(b) Equality occurs if and only if $|A-B|=0$ and, in addition, one of the following four conditions holds: $n=1$ or $|A|=0$ or $A=B$ or $B=\mathbf{O}$. Hence, equality occurs if and only if $A=B$ or $|A|=|A-B|=0$. In fact, by Exercise 8.41, $|A|=0$ implies that both $|B|$ and $|A-B|$ vanish.

Exercise 12.9 (Condition for $A = I$) Let $O \leq A \leq I$. (This means that both A and $I - A$ are positive semidefinite.) Show that $A = I$ if and only if $|A| = 1$.

Solution

We apply Exercise 12.8. Since $I > O$, $A \geq O$, and $I \geq A$, we have $|I| \geq |A|$ with equality if and only if $A = I$.

***Exercise 12.10 (Lines in the plane)** Let A be a set of $n \geq 3$ elements, and let $A_1, \dots, A_m$ be proper subsets of A, such that every pair of elements of A is contained in precisely one set A_j.

(a) Give two examples for $n = 4$, and represent these examples graphically.

(b) Show that $m \geq n$.

(c) Prove that it is not possible to arrange n points in the plane in such a way that every line through two points also passes through a third, unless they all lie on the same line (*Sylvester*).

Solution

(a) We can have: $A_1 = \{1,2\}$, $A_2 = \{2,3\}$, $A_3 = \{3,4\}$, $A_4 = \{4,1\}$, $A_5 = \{1,3\}$, $A_6 = \{2,4\}$. Another possibility is: $A_1 = \{1,2,3\}$, $A_2 = \{3,4\}$, $A_3 = \{4,1\}$, $A_4 = \{2,4\}$. This is illustrated in Figure 12.1, where subsets are represented by alignments.

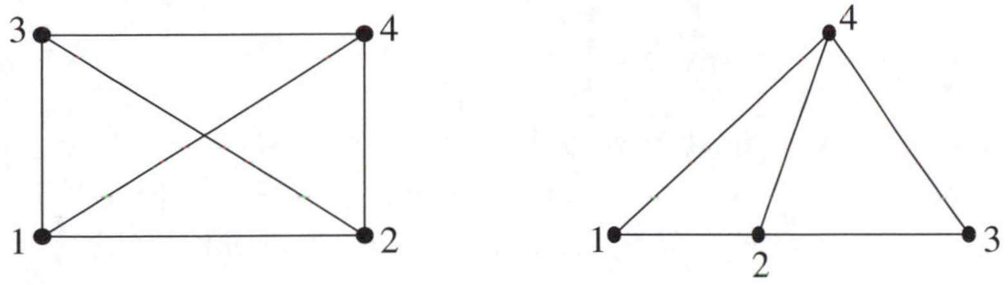

Figure 12.1 — Two examples for $n = 4$.

(b) For $x_i \in A$, let r_i denote the number of sets A_j containing x_i. Define the $n \times m$ matrix $B := (b_{ij})$ with

$$b_{ij} := \begin{cases} 1 & \text{if } x_i \in A_j, \\ 0 & \text{if } x_i \notin A_j. \end{cases}$$

for $i = 1, \dots, n$, $j = 1, \dots, m$. Now consider the $n \times n$ matrix BB'. For $k \neq i$ we have $\sum_j b_{ij} b_{kj} = 1$, because every pair of elements of A is contained in precisely one set A_j. For $k = i$ we have $\sum_j b_{ij}^2 = r_i$ by the definition of r_i. Hence,

$$BB' = \begin{pmatrix} r_1 & 1 & \dots & 1 \\ 1 & r_2 & \dots & 1 \\ \vdots & \vdots & & \vdots \\ 1 & 1 & \dots & r_n \end{pmatrix} = R - I_n + \imath\imath',$$

where $\boldsymbol{R} := \text{diag}(r_1, r_2, \dots, r_n)$ and $\boldsymbol{\imath}$ denotes the $n \times 1$ vector of ones. (Compare the matrix $\boldsymbol{BB}'$ with the equicorrelation matrix of Exercise 8.74.) Now, since $2 \le r_i < m$, the matrix $\boldsymbol{R} - \boldsymbol{I}_n$ is positive definite. Also, the matrix $\boldsymbol{\imath\imath}'$ is positive semidefinite. Hence, by Exercise 8.8(b), $\boldsymbol{BB}'$ is positive definite. This implies that $\text{rk}(\boldsymbol{B}) = \text{rk}(\boldsymbol{BB}') = n$, and hence that $n \le m$.
(c) Sylvester's statement is just another way of formulating result (b).

Exercise 12.11 (Arithmetic-geometric mean inequality)
(a) Show that $(\prod_i \lambda_i)^{1/n} \le (1/n)\sum_i \lambda_i$ for any set of nonnegative numbers $\lambda_1, \dots, \lambda_n$, with equality if and only if all λ_i are the same (*Euclid*).
(b) Use (a) to show that $|\boldsymbol{A}|^{1/n} \le (1/n) \operatorname{tr} \boldsymbol{A}$ for any positive semidefinite $n \times n$ matrix $\boldsymbol{A}$.
(c) Show that equality in (b) occurs if and only if $\boldsymbol{A} = \alpha \boldsymbol{I}_n$ for some $\alpha \ge 0$.

Solution
(a) There are many proofs of this fundamental inequality. We establish the result via calculus. If one of the λ_i is zero, then the result is trivially true. Thus assume that all λ_i are positive. Define the function

$$\varphi(\lambda_1, \dots, \lambda_n) := \frac{1}{n}\sum_{i=1}^{n} \lambda_i - \left(\prod_{i=1}^{n} \lambda_i\right)^{1/n}.$$

Differentiating φ gives

$$\frac{\partial \varphi}{\partial \lambda_j} = \frac{1}{n} - \frac{1}{n\lambda_j}\left(\prod_{i=1}^{n} \lambda_i\right)^{1/n} \qquad (j = 1, \dots, n).$$

Setting the partial derivatives equal to zero, we obtain $\lambda_j = (\prod_i \lambda_i)^{1/n}$ for all j, and hence $\lambda_1 = \lambda_2 = \cdots = \lambda_n$. At such points, $\varphi(\lambda_1, \dots, \lambda_n) = 0$. Since $(\prod_i \lambda_i)^{1/n}$ is concave, $\varphi(\lambda_1, \dots, \lambda_n)$ is convex. Hence, φ has a global minimum at every point where $\lambda_1 = \lambda_2 = \cdots = \lambda_n$.
(b) Consider $\lambda_1, \dots, \lambda_n$ as eigenvalues of $\boldsymbol{A}$, and the result follows from (a) and the fact that $|\boldsymbol{A}| = \prod_i \lambda_i$ and $\operatorname{tr} \boldsymbol{A} = \sum_i \lambda_i$.
(c) Equality occurs if and only if $\lambda_1 = \lambda_2 = \cdots = \lambda_n$. If $\boldsymbol{A} = \alpha \boldsymbol{I}_n$, then all eigenvalues of $\boldsymbol{A}$ are clearly equal. Conversely, if all eigenvalues are equal, then $\boldsymbol{S}'\boldsymbol{AS} = \alpha \boldsymbol{I}$ for some orthogonal matrix $\boldsymbol{S}$, implying that $\boldsymbol{A} = \alpha \boldsymbol{SS}' = \alpha \boldsymbol{I}_n$. (We provide a different solution to this fundamental inequality in Exercise 13.67.)

Exercise 12.12 (Quasilinear representation of $|\boldsymbol{A}|^{1/n}$) Let $\boldsymbol{A}$ be a positive semidefinite $n \times n$ matrix.
(a) Show that $(1/n) \operatorname{tr} \boldsymbol{AX} \ge |\boldsymbol{A}|^{1/n}$ for every $n \times n$ matrix $\boldsymbol{X} > \mathbf{O}$ satisfying $|\boldsymbol{X}| = 1$.
(b) Show that equality occurs if and only if $\boldsymbol{X} = |\boldsymbol{A}|^{1/n}\boldsymbol{A}^{-1}$ or $\boldsymbol{A} = \mathbf{O}$.

Solution
(a) If $\boldsymbol{A} = \mathbf{O}$, the result is trivial. Assume $\boldsymbol{A} \ne \mathbf{O}$, and define $\boldsymbol{B} := \boldsymbol{X}^{1/2}\boldsymbol{AX}^{1/2}$. Then $\boldsymbol{B} \ge \mathbf{O}$, and hence, by Exercise 12.11, $|\boldsymbol{B}|^{1/n} \le (1/n) \operatorname{tr} \boldsymbol{B}$, that is, $|\boldsymbol{X}^{1/2}\boldsymbol{AX}^{1/2}|^{1/n} \le (1/n) \operatorname{tr} \boldsymbol{X}^{1/2}\boldsymbol{AX}^{1/2}$. Since $|\boldsymbol{X}| = 1$, this becomes $|\boldsymbol{A}|^{1/n} \le (1/n) \operatorname{tr} \boldsymbol{AX}$.

(b) Equality occurs if and only if $\boldsymbol{B} = \alpha \boldsymbol{I}_n$ for some $\alpha \geq 0$, that is, if and only if $\boldsymbol{X}^{1/2}\boldsymbol{A}\boldsymbol{X}^{1/2} = \alpha \boldsymbol{I}_n$. If $\alpha = 0$, then $\boldsymbol{A} = \mathbf{O}$. If $\alpha \neq 0$, then $\boldsymbol{A} = \alpha \boldsymbol{X}^{-1}$, so that $\boldsymbol{X}$ is a multiple of $\boldsymbol{A}^{-1}$. The requirement $|\boldsymbol{X}| = 1$ then gives $\boldsymbol{X} = |\boldsymbol{A}|^{1/n}\boldsymbol{A}^{-1}$. (A solution along different lines is provided in Exercise 13.68.)

Exercise 12.13 (Minkowski's inequality)
(a) Use the quasilinear representation of Exercise 12.12 to show that

$$|\boldsymbol{A}+\boldsymbol{B}|^{1/n} \geq |\boldsymbol{A}|^{1/n} + |\boldsymbol{B}|^{1/n}$$

for every two positive semidefinite $n \times n$ matrices $\boldsymbol{A} \neq \mathbf{O}$ and $\boldsymbol{B} \neq \mathbf{O}$.
(b) When does equality occur?

Solution
(a) If $|\boldsymbol{A}| = 0$, $|\boldsymbol{B}| > 0$, it follows immediately that $|\boldsymbol{A}+\boldsymbol{B}| > |\boldsymbol{B}|$. Similarly, if $|\boldsymbol{A}| > 0$, $|\boldsymbol{B}| = 0$, it follows that $|\boldsymbol{A}+\boldsymbol{B}| > |\boldsymbol{A}|$. And, if $|\boldsymbol{A}| = |\boldsymbol{B}| = 0$, we have $|\boldsymbol{A}+\boldsymbol{B}| \geq 0$. Hence, if $\boldsymbol{A}$ or $\boldsymbol{B}$ is singular, the inequality holds. Assume next that both $\boldsymbol{A}$ and $\boldsymbol{B}$ are positive definite. Using the quasilinear representation of Exercise 12.12 gives

$$\begin{aligned}|\boldsymbol{A}+\boldsymbol{B}|^{1/n} &= \min_{\boldsymbol{X}}(1/n)\operatorname{tr}(\boldsymbol{A}+\boldsymbol{B})\boldsymbol{X} \\ &\geq \min_{\boldsymbol{X}}(1/n)\operatorname{tr}\boldsymbol{A}\boldsymbol{X} + \min_{\boldsymbol{X}}(1/n)\operatorname{tr}\boldsymbol{B}\boldsymbol{X} \\ &= |\boldsymbol{A}|^{1/n} + |\boldsymbol{B}|^{1/n},\end{aligned}$$

where the minimum is taken over all positive definite $\boldsymbol{X}$ satisfying $|\boldsymbol{X}| = 1$.
(b) If $\boldsymbol{A}$ and $\boldsymbol{B}$ are both singular, equality occurs if and only if $|\boldsymbol{A}+\boldsymbol{B}| = 0$. If only one of the two matrices $\boldsymbol{A}$ and $\boldsymbol{B}$ is singular, then equality can only occur when $n = 1$, since we have assumed that $\boldsymbol{A} \neq \mathbf{O}$ and $\boldsymbol{B} \neq \mathbf{O}$; see Exercise 12.12. If both $\boldsymbol{A}$ and $\boldsymbol{B}$ are nonsingular, then equality occurs only if the same $\boldsymbol{X}$ minimizes $(1/n)\operatorname{tr}\boldsymbol{A}\boldsymbol{X}$, $(1/n)\operatorname{tr}\boldsymbol{B}\boldsymbol{X}$ and $(1/n)\operatorname{tr}(\boldsymbol{A}+\boldsymbol{B})\boldsymbol{X}$, which implies that $\boldsymbol{A}^{-1}$, $\boldsymbol{B}^{-1}$ and $(\boldsymbol{A}+\boldsymbol{B})^{-1}$ must be proportional, and hence that $\boldsymbol{A}$ and $\boldsymbol{B}$ must be proportional.

***Exercise 12.14 (Trace inequality, 1)** Let $\boldsymbol{A}$ and $\boldsymbol{B}$ be positive semidefinite $n \times n$ matrices.
(a) Show that $0 \leq \operatorname{tr}\boldsymbol{A}\boldsymbol{B} \leq (\operatorname{tr}\boldsymbol{A})(\operatorname{tr}\boldsymbol{B})$.
(b) Show that $\sqrt{\operatorname{tr}\boldsymbol{A}\boldsymbol{B}} \leq (\operatorname{tr}\boldsymbol{A} + \operatorname{tr}\boldsymbol{B})/2$.
(c) When does equality in (b) occur?

Solution
Let $\boldsymbol{S}$ be an orthogonal matrix such that $\boldsymbol{S}'\boldsymbol{A}\boldsymbol{S} = \boldsymbol{\Lambda}$ (diagonal), and let $\boldsymbol{C} := \boldsymbol{S}'\boldsymbol{B}\boldsymbol{S}$. Note that $\boldsymbol{\Lambda}$ is diagonal with nonnegative diagonal elements, and that $\boldsymbol{C}$ is positive semidefinite. Then,

$$\operatorname{tr}\boldsymbol{A} = \sum_{i=1}^{n}\lambda_i, \quad \operatorname{tr}\boldsymbol{B} = \operatorname{tr}\boldsymbol{C} = \sum_{i=1}^{n}c_{ii}, \quad \operatorname{tr}\boldsymbol{A}\boldsymbol{B} = \operatorname{tr}\boldsymbol{\Lambda}\boldsymbol{C} = \sum_{i=1}^{n}\lambda_i c_{ii}.$$

(a) It is clear that $\operatorname{tr} \boldsymbol{AB} = \sum_i \lambda_i c_{ii} \geq 0$. Also,

$$(\operatorname{tr} \boldsymbol{A})(\operatorname{tr} \boldsymbol{B}) - \operatorname{tr} \boldsymbol{AB} = (\sum_{i=1}^{n} \lambda_i)(\sum_{i=1}^{n} c_{ii}) - \sum_{i=1}^{n} \lambda_i c_{ii} = \sum_{i \neq j} \lambda_i c_{jj} \geq 0.$$

(b) Here we have

$$(\operatorname{tr} \boldsymbol{A} + \operatorname{tr} \boldsymbol{B})^2 - 4 \operatorname{tr} \boldsymbol{AB} = (\operatorname{tr} \boldsymbol{A} - \operatorname{tr} \boldsymbol{B})^2 + 4((\operatorname{tr} \boldsymbol{A})(\operatorname{tr} \boldsymbol{B}) - \operatorname{tr} \boldsymbol{AB}) \geq 0.$$

(c) This occurs (trivially) if $\boldsymbol{A} = \mathbf{O}$ and $\operatorname{tr} \boldsymbol{B} = 0$, or if $\boldsymbol{B} = \mathbf{O}$ and $\operatorname{tr} \boldsymbol{A} = 0$, but also if $\boldsymbol{A} = \boldsymbol{B} = \boldsymbol{a}\boldsymbol{a}'$ for some vector $\boldsymbol{a} \neq \mathbf{0}$. To prove this, let $\boldsymbol{A} \neq \mathbf{O}$ and $\boldsymbol{B} \neq \mathbf{O}$. Then equality occurs if and only if

$$\left(\sum_{i=1}^{n} \lambda_i - \sum_{i=1}^{n} c_{ii}\right)^2 + 4\left(\left(\sum_{i=1}^{n} \lambda_i\right)\left(\sum_{i=1}^{n} c_{ii}\right) - \sum_{i=1}^{n} \lambda_i c_{ii}\right) = 0,$$

that is, if and only if $\sum_i \lambda_i = \sum_i c_{ii}$ and $\lambda_i c_{jj} = 0$ for all $i \neq j$. Consider the latter condition. Since $\operatorname{rk}(\boldsymbol{A}) \geq 1$, at least one of the λ's, say λ_i, is nonzero. This implies that $c_{jj} = 0$ for all $j \neq i$, so that $\operatorname{rk}(\boldsymbol{C}) \leq 1$. Since $\boldsymbol{C} \neq \mathbf{O}$, this gives $\operatorname{rk}(\boldsymbol{C}) = 1$. Similarly we obtain $\operatorname{rk}(\boldsymbol{\Lambda}) = 1$. Hence, $\boldsymbol{A} = \boldsymbol{a}\boldsymbol{a}'$ and $\boldsymbol{B} = \boldsymbol{b}\boldsymbol{b}'$ for some $\boldsymbol{a} \neq \mathbf{0}$, $\boldsymbol{b} \neq \mathbf{0}$. Equality in (b) then implies that $(\boldsymbol{a}'\boldsymbol{b})^2 = (\boldsymbol{a}'\boldsymbol{a})(\boldsymbol{b}'\boldsymbol{b})$ and $\boldsymbol{a}'\boldsymbol{a} = \boldsymbol{b}'\boldsymbol{b}$, and hence that $\boldsymbol{a}\boldsymbol{a}' = \boldsymbol{b}\boldsymbol{b}'$.

Exercise 12.15 (Cauchy-Schwarz, determinantal version) Let $\boldsymbol{A}$ and $\boldsymbol{B}$ be two matrices of the same order. Show that $|\boldsymbol{A}'\boldsymbol{B}|^2 \leq |\boldsymbol{A}'\boldsymbol{A}||\boldsymbol{B}'\boldsymbol{B}|$ with equality if and only if $\boldsymbol{A}'\boldsymbol{A}$ or $\boldsymbol{B}'\boldsymbol{B}$ is singular, or if $\boldsymbol{B} = \boldsymbol{A}\boldsymbol{Q}$ for some nonsingular matrix $\boldsymbol{Q}$.

Solution

If $|\boldsymbol{A}'\boldsymbol{B}| = 0$, the result is trivial. Assume that $|\boldsymbol{A}'\boldsymbol{B}| \neq 0$. Then both $\boldsymbol{A}$ and $\boldsymbol{B}$ have full column rank, so that $\boldsymbol{A}'\boldsymbol{A}$ and $\boldsymbol{B}'\boldsymbol{B}$ are nonsingular. Now define

$$\boldsymbol{C} := \boldsymbol{B}'\boldsymbol{A}(\boldsymbol{A}'\boldsymbol{A})^{-1}\boldsymbol{A}'\boldsymbol{B} \quad \text{and} \quad \boldsymbol{D} := \boldsymbol{B}'(\boldsymbol{I} - \boldsymbol{A}(\boldsymbol{A}'\boldsymbol{A})^{-1}\boldsymbol{A}')\boldsymbol{B},$$

and notice that $\boldsymbol{C}$ is positive definite and $\boldsymbol{D}$ positive semidefinite (because $\boldsymbol{I} - \boldsymbol{A}(\boldsymbol{A}'\boldsymbol{A})^{-1}\boldsymbol{A}'$ is idempotent). Since, by Exercise 12.7, $|\boldsymbol{C}+\boldsymbol{D}| \geq |\boldsymbol{C}|$ with equality if and only if $\boldsymbol{D} = \mathbf{O}$, we obtain

$$|\boldsymbol{B}'\boldsymbol{B}| \geq |\boldsymbol{B}'\boldsymbol{A}(\boldsymbol{A}'\boldsymbol{A})^{-1}\boldsymbol{A}'\boldsymbol{B}| = |\boldsymbol{A}'\boldsymbol{B}|^2|\boldsymbol{A}'\boldsymbol{A}|^{-1}$$

with equality if and only if $\boldsymbol{B}'(\boldsymbol{I} - \boldsymbol{A}(\boldsymbol{A}'\boldsymbol{A})^{-1}\boldsymbol{A}')\boldsymbol{B} = \mathbf{O}$, that is, if and only if $(\boldsymbol{I} - \boldsymbol{A}(\boldsymbol{A}'\boldsymbol{A})^{-1}\boldsymbol{A}')\boldsymbol{B} = \mathbf{O}$.

Exercise 12.16 (Inequality for the inverse) Let $\boldsymbol{A}$ and $\boldsymbol{B}$ be positive definite. Show that $\boldsymbol{A} > \boldsymbol{B}$ if and only if $\boldsymbol{B}^{-1} > \boldsymbol{A}^{-1}$.

Solution

Let $\boldsymbol{A}$ and $\boldsymbol{B}$ be of order $n \times n$. We use the simultaneous reduction to diagonal form, provided by Exercise 8.37. Thus, there exist a nonsingular matrix $\boldsymbol{T}$ and a positive definite diagonal matrix $\boldsymbol{\Lambda} = \text{diag}(\lambda_1, \dots, \lambda_n)$ such that $\boldsymbol{A} = \boldsymbol{T}\boldsymbol{T}'$ and $\boldsymbol{B} = \boldsymbol{T}\boldsymbol{\Lambda}\boldsymbol{T}'$. Then,

$$\boldsymbol{A} - \boldsymbol{B} = \boldsymbol{T}(\boldsymbol{I}_n - \boldsymbol{\Lambda})\boldsymbol{T}', \quad \boldsymbol{B}^{-1} - \boldsymbol{A}^{-1} = \boldsymbol{T}'^{-1}(\boldsymbol{\Lambda}^{-1} - \boldsymbol{I}_n)\boldsymbol{T}^{-1}.$$

If $\boldsymbol{A} - \boldsymbol{B}$ is positive definite, then $\boldsymbol{I}_n - \boldsymbol{\Lambda}$ is positive definite as well and hence $0 < \lambda_i < 1$ $(i = 1, \dots, n)$. This implies that $\boldsymbol{\Lambda}^{-1} - \boldsymbol{I}_n$ is positive definite and hence that $\boldsymbol{B}^{-1} - \boldsymbol{A}^{-1}$ is positive definite.

***Exercise 12.17 (Kantorovich's inequality)**
(a) Show that $\lambda^2 - (a+b)\lambda + ab \leq 0$ for all $\lambda \in [a, b]$.
(b) Let $\boldsymbol{A}$ be a positive definite $n \times n$ matrix with eigenvalues $\lambda_1 \geq \lambda_2 \geq \dots \geq \lambda_n > 0$. Use (a) to show that the matrix

$$(\lambda_1 + \lambda_n)\boldsymbol{I}_n - \boldsymbol{A} - (\lambda_1\lambda_n)\boldsymbol{A}^{-1}$$

is positive semidefinite of rank $\leq n - 2$.
(c) Use Schur's inequality (Exercise 12.6) and (b) to show that

$$1 \leq (\boldsymbol{x}'\boldsymbol{A}\boldsymbol{x})(\boldsymbol{x}'\boldsymbol{A}^{-1}\boldsymbol{x}) \leq \frac{(\lambda_1 + \lambda_n)^2}{4\lambda_1\lambda_n}$$

for every positive definite $n \times n$ matrix $\boldsymbol{A}$ and every $n \times 1$ vector $\boldsymbol{x}$ satisfying $\boldsymbol{x}'\boldsymbol{x} = 1$ (*Kantorovich*).

Solution
(a) This follows from the fact that the function $\varphi(\lambda) := \lambda^2 - (a+b)\lambda + ab$ satisfies $\varphi(a) = \varphi(b) = 0$ and has a minimum at $\lambda = (a+b)/2$. (Compare Kato's lemma in Exercise 8.18.)
(b) Since $\lambda_i \in [\lambda_n, \lambda_1]$ for all i, we obtain from (a), $\lambda_i^2 - (\lambda_1 + \lambda_n)\lambda_i + \lambda_1\lambda_n \leq 0$ and hence, dividing by λ_i,

$$(\lambda_1 + \lambda_n) - \lambda_i - (\lambda_1\lambda_n)\lambda_i^{-1} \geq 0 \quad (i = 1, \dots, n)$$

with equality if and only if $\lambda_i = \lambda_1$ or $\lambda_i = \lambda_n$. Let $\boldsymbol{\Lambda} := \text{diag}(\lambda_1, \dots, \lambda_n)$, and write $\boldsymbol{A} = \boldsymbol{S}\boldsymbol{\Lambda}\boldsymbol{S}'$ where $\boldsymbol{S}$ is orthogonal. Then,

$$(\lambda_1 + \lambda_n)\boldsymbol{I}_n - \boldsymbol{A} - (\lambda_1\lambda_n)\boldsymbol{A}^{-1} = \boldsymbol{S}\left((\lambda_1 + \lambda_n)\boldsymbol{I}_n - \boldsymbol{\Lambda} - (\lambda_1\lambda_n)\boldsymbol{\Lambda}^{-1}\right)\boldsymbol{S}' \geq \mathbf{O}.$$

Since (at least) two of the eigenvalues of the matrix $(\lambda_1 + \lambda_n)\boldsymbol{I}_n - \boldsymbol{A} - (\lambda_1\lambda_n)\boldsymbol{A}^{-1}$ are zero, its rank is $\leq n - 2$.
(c) We first prove the inequality $1 \leq (\boldsymbol{x}'\boldsymbol{A}\boldsymbol{x})(\boldsymbol{x}'\boldsymbol{A}^{-1}\boldsymbol{x})$. Let $\boldsymbol{B} := \boldsymbol{A}^{1/2}\boldsymbol{x}\boldsymbol{x}'\boldsymbol{A}^{-1/2}$. Then,

$$\text{tr}\,\boldsymbol{B}^2 = \text{tr}\left(\boldsymbol{A}^{1/2}\boldsymbol{x}\boldsymbol{x}'\boldsymbol{A}^{-1/2}\boldsymbol{A}^{1/2}\boldsymbol{x}\boldsymbol{x}'\boldsymbol{A}^{-1/2}\right) = (\boldsymbol{x}'\boldsymbol{x})^2 = 1$$

and

$$\text{tr}\,\boldsymbol{B}'\boldsymbol{B} = \text{tr}\left(\boldsymbol{A}^{-1/2}\boldsymbol{x}\boldsymbol{x}'\boldsymbol{A}^{1/2}\boldsymbol{A}^{1/2}\boldsymbol{x}\boldsymbol{x}'\boldsymbol{A}^{-1/2}\right) = (\boldsymbol{x}'\boldsymbol{A}\boldsymbol{x})(\boldsymbol{x}'\boldsymbol{A}^{-1}\boldsymbol{x}).$$

Since $\text{tr}\,\boldsymbol{B}^2 \leq \text{tr}\,\boldsymbol{B}'\boldsymbol{B}$ (Schur's inequality), we obtain the first inequality. (Notice that equality occurs if and only if $\boldsymbol{B}$ is symmetric, that is, if and only if $\boldsymbol{x}$ is an eigenvector of $\boldsymbol{A}$.)

The second equality is proved using (b). Since $(\lambda_1+\lambda_n)\boldsymbol{I}_n-\boldsymbol{A}-(\lambda_1\lambda_n)\boldsymbol{A}^{-1}$ is positive semidefinite, we have

$$(\lambda_1+\lambda_n)-\boldsymbol{x}'\boldsymbol{A}\boldsymbol{x}-(\lambda_1\lambda_n)\boldsymbol{x}'\boldsymbol{A}^{-1}\boldsymbol{x}\geq 0$$

for every $\boldsymbol{x}$ satisfying $\boldsymbol{x}'\boldsymbol{x}=1$. Multiplying by $\boldsymbol{x}'\boldsymbol{A}\boldsymbol{x}$ yields

$$\begin{aligned}(\lambda_1\lambda_n)(\boldsymbol{x}'\boldsymbol{A}\boldsymbol{x})(\boldsymbol{x}'\boldsymbol{A}^{-1}\boldsymbol{x}) &\leq (\lambda_1+\lambda_n)\boldsymbol{x}'\boldsymbol{A}\boldsymbol{x}-(\boldsymbol{x}'\boldsymbol{A}\boldsymbol{x})^2\\ &= -\left(\boldsymbol{x}'\boldsymbol{A}\boldsymbol{x}-\frac{\lambda_1+\lambda_n}{2}\right)^2+\left(\frac{\lambda_1+\lambda_n}{2}\right)^2\leq\frac{(\lambda_1+\lambda_n)^2}{4},\end{aligned}$$

and the second inequality follows as well. (Equality occurs here if and only if $\boldsymbol{A}=\alpha\boldsymbol{I}_n$ for some $\alpha>0$.)

Exercise 12.18 (Inequality when $\boldsymbol{A}'\boldsymbol{B}=\boldsymbol{I}$) For any two matrices $\boldsymbol{A}$ and $\boldsymbol{B}$ satisfying $\boldsymbol{A}'\boldsymbol{B}=\boldsymbol{I}$, show that

$$\boldsymbol{A}'\boldsymbol{A}\geq(\boldsymbol{B}'\boldsymbol{B})^{-1}\quad\text{and}\quad\boldsymbol{B}'\boldsymbol{B}\geq(\boldsymbol{A}'\boldsymbol{A})^{-1}.$$

Solution

The trick is to consider the idempotent symmetric matrix $\boldsymbol{M}:=\boldsymbol{I}-\boldsymbol{B}(\boldsymbol{B}'\boldsymbol{B})^{-1}\boldsymbol{B}'$. This matrix is positive semidefinite, and hence

$$\mathbf{O}\leq\boldsymbol{A}'\boldsymbol{M}\boldsymbol{A}=\boldsymbol{A}'\boldsymbol{A}-\boldsymbol{A}'\boldsymbol{B}(\boldsymbol{B}'\boldsymbol{B})^{-1}\boldsymbol{B}'\boldsymbol{A}=\boldsymbol{A}'\boldsymbol{A}-(\boldsymbol{B}'\boldsymbol{B})^{-1},$$

since $\boldsymbol{A}'\boldsymbol{B}=\boldsymbol{B}'\boldsymbol{A}=\boldsymbol{I}$. The second result is proved analogously.

*__Exercise 12.19 (Unequal powers)__ Let $\boldsymbol{A}$ and $\boldsymbol{B}$ be positive semidefinite matrices and let $\boldsymbol{A}\geq\boldsymbol{B}$.
(a) Show that $\boldsymbol{A}^{1/2}\geq\boldsymbol{B}^{1/2}$.
(b) Show that it is not true, in general, that $\boldsymbol{A}^2\geq\boldsymbol{B}^2$.
(c) However, if $\boldsymbol{A}$ and $\boldsymbol{B}$ commute (that is, $\boldsymbol{A}\boldsymbol{B}=\boldsymbol{B}\boldsymbol{A}$), then show that $\boldsymbol{A}^k\geq\boldsymbol{B}^k$ for $k=2,3,\dots$.

Solution

(a) Let $\boldsymbol{C}:=\boldsymbol{A}^{1/2}-\boldsymbol{B}^{1/2}$. We will show that all eigenvalues of $\boldsymbol{C}$ are nonnegative. We have

$$\begin{aligned}\mathbf{O}\leq\boldsymbol{A}-\boldsymbol{B}&=\boldsymbol{A}-(\boldsymbol{A}^{1/2}-\boldsymbol{C})^2=\boldsymbol{A}-(\boldsymbol{A}-\boldsymbol{A}^{1/2}\boldsymbol{C}-\boldsymbol{C}\boldsymbol{A}^{1/2}+\boldsymbol{C}^2)\\ &=\boldsymbol{A}^{1/2}\boldsymbol{C}+\boldsymbol{C}\boldsymbol{A}^{1/2}-\boldsymbol{C}^2\leq\boldsymbol{A}^{1/2}\boldsymbol{C}+\boldsymbol{C}\boldsymbol{A}^{1/2},\end{aligned}$$

because $\boldsymbol{C}$ is symmetric and hence $\boldsymbol{C}^2=\boldsymbol{C}'\boldsymbol{C}\geq\mathbf{O}$. Now, let λ be an eigenvalue of $\boldsymbol{C}$, such that $\boldsymbol{C}\boldsymbol{x}=\lambda\boldsymbol{x}$. Then,

$$0\leq\boldsymbol{x}'(\boldsymbol{A}^{1/2}\boldsymbol{C}+\boldsymbol{C}\boldsymbol{A}^{1/2})\boldsymbol{x}=2\boldsymbol{x}'\boldsymbol{A}^{1/2}\boldsymbol{C}\boldsymbol{x}=2\lambda(\boldsymbol{x}'\boldsymbol{A}^{1/2}\boldsymbol{x}).$$

If $|\boldsymbol{A}| > 0$, then $\boldsymbol{A}$ and $\boldsymbol{A}^{1/2}$ are positive definite, and hence $\boldsymbol{x}'\boldsymbol{A}^{1/2}\boldsymbol{x} > 0$. In that case, $\lambda \geq 0$, which is what we wish to demonstrate.

If $|\boldsymbol{A}| = 0$, then a continuity argument applies. Since $\boldsymbol{A} + \epsilon\boldsymbol{I} > \mathbf{O}$ for all $\epsilon > 0$, the previous argument shows that $(\boldsymbol{A} + \epsilon\boldsymbol{I})^{1/2} \geq \boldsymbol{B}^{1/2}$ for all $\epsilon > 0$. Let $\boldsymbol{S}$ be an orthogonal matrix such that $\boldsymbol{S}'\boldsymbol{A}\boldsymbol{S} = \boldsymbol{\Lambda}$ (diagonal). Then, $(\boldsymbol{A} + \epsilon\boldsymbol{I})^{1/2} = \boldsymbol{S}(\boldsymbol{\Lambda} + \epsilon\boldsymbol{I})^{1/2}\boldsymbol{S}'$. Since $\boldsymbol{\Lambda} + \epsilon\boldsymbol{I} \to \boldsymbol{\Lambda}$ as $\epsilon \to 0$, it follows that $(\boldsymbol{A} + \epsilon\boldsymbol{I})^{1/2} \to \boldsymbol{A}^{1/2}$. Hence, $\boldsymbol{A}^{1/2} \geq \boldsymbol{B}^{1/2}$.

(b) We take

$$\boldsymbol{A} = \begin{pmatrix} 2 & 1 \\ 1 & 1 \end{pmatrix} \quad \text{and} \quad \boldsymbol{B} = \begin{pmatrix} 1 & 0 \\ 0 & 0 \end{pmatrix}.$$

Then $\boldsymbol{A} \geq \boldsymbol{B} \geq \mathbf{O}$, but $|\boldsymbol{A}^2 - \boldsymbol{B}^2| = -1$.

(c) If $\boldsymbol{A}$ and $\boldsymbol{B}$ commute, then there is a *single* orthogonal matrix $\boldsymbol{S}$ that diagonalizes both $\boldsymbol{A}$ and $\boldsymbol{B}$ (Exercise 7.51):

$$\boldsymbol{S}'\boldsymbol{A}\boldsymbol{S} = \operatorname{diag}(\lambda_1, \dots, \lambda_n), \quad \boldsymbol{S}'\boldsymbol{B}\boldsymbol{S} = \operatorname{diag}(\mu_1, \dots, \mu_n).$$

Since $\boldsymbol{A} \geq \boldsymbol{B}$, it follows that $\lambda_i \geq \mu_i$ for all i. Hence, $\lambda_i^k \geq \mu_i^k \geq 0$, and

$$\begin{aligned} \boldsymbol{S}'(\boldsymbol{A}^k - \boldsymbol{B}^k)\boldsymbol{S} &= \boldsymbol{S}'\boldsymbol{A}^k\boldsymbol{S} - \boldsymbol{S}'\boldsymbol{B}^k\boldsymbol{S} = (\boldsymbol{S}'\boldsymbol{A}\boldsymbol{S})^k - (\boldsymbol{S}'\boldsymbol{B}\boldsymbol{S})^k \\ &= \operatorname{diag}(\lambda_1^k - \mu_1^k, \dots, \lambda_n^k - \mu_n^k) \geq \mathbf{O}. \end{aligned}$$

Exercise 12.20 (Bound for $\log|\boldsymbol{A}|$) Let $\boldsymbol{A}$ be a positive definite $n \times n$ matrix. Show that

$$\log|\boldsymbol{A}| \leq \operatorname{tr} \boldsymbol{A} - n,$$

with equality if and only if $\boldsymbol{A} = \boldsymbol{I}_n$.

Solution

Consider the function $\phi(\lambda) := \lambda - 1 - \log\lambda$ for $\lambda > 0$. Differentiating, we obtain $\phi'(\lambda) = 1 - 1/\lambda$ and $\phi''(\lambda) = 1/\lambda^2 > 0$. Hence, a minimum occurs at $\lambda = 1$, and hence $\log\lambda \leq \lambda - 1$ for every $\lambda > 0$, with equality if and only if $\lambda = 1$. Now, let $\lambda_1, \dots, \lambda_n$ be the eigenvalues of $\boldsymbol{A}$. Then,

$$\log\lambda_i \leq \lambda_i - 1 \quad (i = 1, \dots, n),$$

which gives

$$\begin{aligned} \log|\boldsymbol{A}| &= \log\prod_{i=1}^n \lambda_i = \sum_{i=1}^n \log\lambda_i \leq \sum_{i=1}^n (\lambda_i - 1) \\ &= \sum_{i=1}^n \lambda_i - n = \operatorname{tr} \boldsymbol{A} - n. \end{aligned}$$

Equality occurs if and only if all λ_i are equal to 1, that is, when $\boldsymbol{A} = \boldsymbol{I}_n$.

Alternatively, we can write

$$\exp(\operatorname{tr} \boldsymbol{A} - n) = \operatorname{etr}(\boldsymbol{A} - \boldsymbol{I}_n) = |\exp(\boldsymbol{A} - \boldsymbol{I}_n)| \geq |\boldsymbol{A}|,$$

since $\exp(\lambda_i - 1) \geq \lambda_i$ for $\lambda_i > 0$ (with equality if and only if $\lambda_i = 1$ for all i), using the fact that the exponential function is convex.

Exercise 12.21 (Concavity of $\log|\boldsymbol{A}|$)
(a) For every $\lambda > 0$ and $0 < \alpha < 1$, show that $\lambda^\alpha \leq \alpha\lambda + 1 - \alpha$, with equality if and only if $\lambda = 1$.
(b) For any $\boldsymbol{A} \geq \mathbf{O}$ and $\boldsymbol{B} \geq \mathbf{O}$ of the same order, show that

$$|\boldsymbol{A}|^\alpha |\boldsymbol{B}|^{1-\alpha} \leq |\alpha \boldsymbol{A} + (1-\alpha)\boldsymbol{B}|$$

for every $0 < \alpha < 1$.
(c) When does equality occur?

Solution
(a) Define $\phi(\lambda) := \alpha\lambda + 1 - \alpha - \lambda^\alpha$. Then, $\phi'(\lambda) = \alpha(1 - \lambda^{-(1-\alpha)})$ and $\phi''(\lambda) = \alpha(1-\alpha)\lambda^{-(2-\alpha)} > 0$. Hence, a minimum occurs at $\lambda = 1$, implying that $\phi(\lambda) \geq \phi(1) = 0$. (Alternatively we may take the arithmetic mean of λ and 1, then the geometric mean, and use the arithmetic-geometric mean inequality of Exercise 12.11(a).)
(b) If $|\boldsymbol{A}| = 0$ or $|\boldsymbol{B}| = 0$ the result is trivial. Assume that $|\boldsymbol{A}| > 0$ and $|\boldsymbol{B}| > 0$. Let $\boldsymbol{C} := \boldsymbol{B}^{-1/2}\boldsymbol{A}\boldsymbol{B}^{-1/2}$ with eigenvalues $\lambda_1, \dots, \lambda_n$. Then $\boldsymbol{C} > \mathbf{O}$ and hence $\lambda_i > 0$ for all i. Thus, using (a),

$$\lambda_i^\alpha \leq \alpha\lambda_i + (1-\alpha) \quad (i = 1, \dots, n).$$

Multiplying both sides over all i now yields

$$|\boldsymbol{C}|^\alpha = \prod_{i=1}^n \lambda_i^\alpha \leq \prod_{i=1}^n (\alpha\lambda_i + (1-\alpha)) = |\alpha\boldsymbol{C} + (1-\alpha)\boldsymbol{I}_n|.$$

Hence,

$$\begin{aligned} |\boldsymbol{A}|^\alpha |\boldsymbol{B}|^{1-\alpha} &= |\boldsymbol{B}||\boldsymbol{C}|^\alpha \leq |\boldsymbol{B}||\alpha\boldsymbol{C} + (1-\alpha)\boldsymbol{I}_n| \\ &= |\alpha\boldsymbol{B}^{1/2}\boldsymbol{C}\boldsymbol{B}^{1/2} + (1-\alpha)\boldsymbol{B}| = |\alpha\boldsymbol{A} + (1-\alpha)\boldsymbol{B}|. \end{aligned}$$

(c) We distinguish between two cases. First, let $|\alpha\boldsymbol{A} + (1-\alpha)\boldsymbol{B}| = 0$. Then either $|\boldsymbol{A}| = 0$ or $|\boldsymbol{B}| = 0$ (or both), and equality occurs. Next, let $|\alpha\boldsymbol{A} + (1-\alpha)\boldsymbol{B}| > 0$. For equality we must have $|\boldsymbol{A}| > 0$ and $|\boldsymbol{B}| > 0$. Equality then holds if $\lambda_i^\alpha = \alpha\lambda_i + 1 - \alpha$ for *every* i, that is, if and only if $\lambda_i = 1$ $(i = 1, \dots, n)$. This in turn is the case if and only if $\boldsymbol{C} = \boldsymbol{I}_n$, that is, if and only if $\boldsymbol{A} = \boldsymbol{B}$. Hence, equality holds if and only if $|\alpha\boldsymbol{A} + (1-\alpha)\boldsymbol{B}| = 0$ or $\boldsymbol{A} = \boldsymbol{B}$. (A solution using matrix calculus is provided in Exercise 13.66.)

Exercise 12.22 (Implication of concavity)
(a) Let $\alpha_i > 0$, $\sum_i \alpha_i = 1$ and $\boldsymbol{A}_i > \mathbf{O}$ for $i = 1, \dots, k$. Show that

$$|\boldsymbol{A}_1|^{\alpha_1}|\boldsymbol{A}_2|^{\alpha_2} \dots |\boldsymbol{A}_k|^{\alpha_k} \leq |\alpha_1\boldsymbol{A}_1 + \alpha_2\boldsymbol{A}_2 + \dots + \alpha_k\boldsymbol{A}_k|.$$

(b) When does equality occur?

Solution

(a) We have already proved the result for $k = 2$ (Exercise 12.21). Now proceed by induction on k. Let $k \geq 3$. We write

$$\alpha_1 \boldsymbol{A}_1 + \cdots + \alpha_k \boldsymbol{A}_k = (1 - \alpha_k)\boldsymbol{B} + \alpha_k \boldsymbol{A}_k$$

with

$$\boldsymbol{B} := \beta_1 \boldsymbol{A}_1 + \cdots + \beta_{k-1} \boldsymbol{A}_{k-1} \quad \text{and} \quad \beta_j := \frac{\alpha_j}{1 - \alpha_k} \quad (j = 1, \ldots, k-1).$$

Since $\boldsymbol{B}$ is positive definite, it follows that

$$|\alpha_1 \boldsymbol{A}_1 + \cdots + \alpha_k \boldsymbol{A}_k| = |(1 - \alpha_k)\boldsymbol{B} + \alpha_k \boldsymbol{A}_k| \geq |\boldsymbol{B}|^{1-\alpha_k} |\boldsymbol{A}_k|^{\alpha_k}.$$

We note that the weights β_j in $\boldsymbol{B}$ sum to one. Applying the induction hypothesis, we have

$$|\boldsymbol{B}| \geq |\boldsymbol{A}_1|^{\beta_1} \ldots |\boldsymbol{A}_{k-1}|^{\beta_{k-1}},$$

and hence

$$\begin{aligned} |\alpha_1 \boldsymbol{A}_1 + \cdots + \alpha_k \boldsymbol{A}_k| &\geq |\boldsymbol{A}_1|^{\beta_1(1-\alpha_k)} \ldots |\boldsymbol{A}_{k-1}|^{\beta_{k-1}(1-\alpha_k)} |\boldsymbol{A}_k|^{\alpha_k} \\ &= |\boldsymbol{A}_1|^{\alpha_1} \ldots |\boldsymbol{A}_k|^{\alpha_k}. \end{aligned}$$

(b) Equality occurs if and only if $\boldsymbol{A}_1 = \cdots = \boldsymbol{A}_k$.

Exercise 12.23 (Positive definiteness of bordered matrix) Let $\boldsymbol{A}$ be a positive definite $n \times n$ matrix, and let $\boldsymbol{B}$ be the $(n+1) \times (n+1)$ bordered matrix

$$\boldsymbol{B} := \begin{pmatrix} \boldsymbol{A} & \boldsymbol{b} \\ \boldsymbol{b}' & \alpha \end{pmatrix}.$$

Show that:

(a) $|\boldsymbol{B}| \leq \alpha |\boldsymbol{A}|$ with equality if and only if $\boldsymbol{b} = \boldsymbol{0}$;

(b) $\boldsymbol{B}$ is positive definite if and only if $|\boldsymbol{B}| > 0$.

Solution

(a) We already know from Exercise 5.30(a) that $|\boldsymbol{B}| = |\boldsymbol{A}|(\alpha - \boldsymbol{b}'\boldsymbol{A}^{-1}\boldsymbol{b})$. This implies (a).

(b) To prove (b), we need elements of the proof of this determinantal equality. Thus, define

$$\boldsymbol{P} := \begin{pmatrix} \boldsymbol{I}_n & -\boldsymbol{A}^{-1}\boldsymbol{b} \\ \boldsymbol{0}' & 1 \end{pmatrix}, \quad \text{implying} \quad \boldsymbol{P}'\boldsymbol{B}\boldsymbol{P} = \begin{pmatrix} \boldsymbol{A} & \boldsymbol{0} \\ \boldsymbol{0}' & \alpha - \boldsymbol{b}'\boldsymbol{A}^{-1}\boldsymbol{b} \end{pmatrix}.$$

Then, $|\boldsymbol{B}| = |\boldsymbol{P}'\boldsymbol{B}\boldsymbol{P}| = |\boldsymbol{A}|(\alpha - \boldsymbol{b}'\boldsymbol{A}^{-1}\boldsymbol{b})$. Now notice that $|\boldsymbol{B}| > 0$ if and only if $\alpha - \boldsymbol{b}'\boldsymbol{A}^{-1}\boldsymbol{b} > 0$, which is the case if and only if $\boldsymbol{P}'\boldsymbol{B}\boldsymbol{P}$ is positive definite. This in turn is true if and only if $\boldsymbol{B}$ is positive definite. (Compare the proof of Exercise 8.31.)

Exercise 12.24 (Positive semidefiniteness of bordered matrix) Let $\boldsymbol{A}$ be a positive semidefinite $n \times n$ matrix, and let $\boldsymbol{B}$ be the $(n+1) \times (n+1)$ bordered matrix

$$\boldsymbol{B} := \begin{pmatrix} \boldsymbol{A} & \boldsymbol{b} \\ \boldsymbol{b}' & \alpha \end{pmatrix}.$$

(a) Show that $\boldsymbol{B}$ is positive semidefinite if and only if $\alpha \geq 0$ and $\alpha\boldsymbol{A} - \boldsymbol{b}\boldsymbol{b}'$ is positive semidefinite.
(b) Obtain the result of Exercise 12.23 as a special case.

Solution
(a) Consider the quadratic form $\boldsymbol{x}'\boldsymbol{B}\boldsymbol{x}$ and partition $\boldsymbol{x} = (\boldsymbol{x}_1', x_2)'$ where x_2 is a scalar. Then,

$$\phi(x_2) := \boldsymbol{x}'\boldsymbol{B}\boldsymbol{x} = \boldsymbol{x}_1'\boldsymbol{A}\boldsymbol{x}_1 + 2x_2\boldsymbol{b}'\boldsymbol{x}_1 + \alpha x_2^2.$$

If $\alpha > 0$ we minimize ϕ with respect x_2 and find

$$\boldsymbol{x}'\boldsymbol{B}\boldsymbol{x} \geq \boldsymbol{x}_1'\boldsymbol{A}\boldsymbol{x}_1 - \frac{(\boldsymbol{b}'\boldsymbol{x}_1)^2}{\alpha} = \frac{1}{\alpha}\boldsymbol{x}_1'\left(\alpha\boldsymbol{A} - \boldsymbol{b}\boldsymbol{b}'\right)\boldsymbol{x}_1.$$

Hence, if $\alpha > 0$, then $\boldsymbol{B} \geq \mathbf{O}$ if and only if $\alpha\boldsymbol{A} - \boldsymbol{b}\boldsymbol{b}' \geq \mathbf{O}$. If $\alpha < 0$, then $\boldsymbol{B}$ cannot be positive semidefinite, because a positive semidefinite matrix must have nonnegative diagonal elements. If $\alpha = 0$, then $\boldsymbol{B} \geq \mathbf{O}$ if and only if $\boldsymbol{b} = \mathbf{0}$.
(b) If $\boldsymbol{A} > \mathbf{O}$, then $\boldsymbol{B} > \mathbf{O}$ if and only if $\alpha > 0$ and $\alpha\boldsymbol{A} - \boldsymbol{b}\boldsymbol{b}' > \mathbf{O}$. We write

$$\alpha\boldsymbol{A} - \boldsymbol{b}\boldsymbol{b}' = \boldsymbol{A}^{1/2}\left(\alpha\boldsymbol{I}_n - \boldsymbol{A}^{-1/2}\boldsymbol{b}\boldsymbol{b}'\boldsymbol{A}^{-1/2}\right)\boldsymbol{A}^{1/2},$$

which is positive definite if and only if all eigenvalues of $\alpha\boldsymbol{I}_n - \boldsymbol{A}^{-1/2}\boldsymbol{b}\boldsymbol{b}'\boldsymbol{A}^{-1/2}$ are positive. The eigenvalues are α ($n-1$ times) and $\alpha - \boldsymbol{b}'\boldsymbol{A}^{-1}\boldsymbol{b}$ (once). Hence, $\boldsymbol{B} > \mathbf{O}$ if and only if $\alpha - \boldsymbol{b}'\boldsymbol{A}^{-1}\boldsymbol{b} > 0$. Since $|\boldsymbol{A}| > 0$ and $|\boldsymbol{B}| = |\boldsymbol{A}|(\alpha - \boldsymbol{b}'\boldsymbol{A}^{-1}\boldsymbol{b}) > 0$, the result follows.

Exercise 12.25 (Bordered matrix, special case) Consider the matrix

$$\boldsymbol{B} := \begin{pmatrix} \boldsymbol{A} & \boldsymbol{b} \\ \boldsymbol{b}' & \boldsymbol{b}'\boldsymbol{A}^{-1}\boldsymbol{b} \end{pmatrix},$$

where $\boldsymbol{A}$ is positive definite.
(a) Show that $\boldsymbol{B}$ is positive semidefinite and singular.
(b) Find the eigenvector associated with the zero eigenvalue.

Solution
In the proof of Exercise 12.23, let $\alpha := \boldsymbol{b}'\boldsymbol{A}^{-1}\boldsymbol{b}$. Then,

$$\boldsymbol{P}'\boldsymbol{B}\boldsymbol{P} = \begin{pmatrix} \boldsymbol{A} & \mathbf{0} \\ \mathbf{0}' & 0 \end{pmatrix},$$

implying that $\boldsymbol{B}$ is positive semidefinite and singular.
(b) Let $(\boldsymbol{x}' : \xi)'$ be the required eigenvector (unique up to a scalar). Then we need to solve

$$\boldsymbol{A}\boldsymbol{x} + \xi\boldsymbol{b} = \mathbf{0}, \quad \boldsymbol{b}'\boldsymbol{x} + \xi(\boldsymbol{b}'\boldsymbol{A}^{-1}\boldsymbol{b}) = 0.$$

This gives $\boldsymbol{x} = -\boldsymbol{A}^{-1}\boldsymbol{b}$ and $\xi = 1$. Notice that this is the last column of $\boldsymbol{P}$.

Exercise 12.26 (Hadamard's inequality)
(a) Let $\boldsymbol{A} := (a_{ij})$ be a positive definite $n \times n$ matrix. Show that $|\boldsymbol{A}| \leq \prod_{i=1}^n a_{ii}$ with equality if and only if $\boldsymbol{A}$ is diagonal.
(b) Use (a) to show that

$$|\boldsymbol{A}|^2 \leq \prod_{i=1}^n \left(\sum_{j=1}^n a_{ij}^2 \right).$$

for any $n \times n$ matrix $\boldsymbol{A}$ (*Hadamard*).
(c) When does Hadamard's inequality become an equality?

Solution
(a) Let $\boldsymbol{A}_{(k)}$ denote the k-th leading principal submatrix of $\boldsymbol{A}$, that is, the $k \times k$ matrix, containing only the elements a_{ij} for $i, j = 1, \ldots, k$. Note that $\boldsymbol{A}_{(1)} = a_{11}$ and $\boldsymbol{A}_{(n)} = \boldsymbol{A}$. Now, using Exercise 12.23(a), we obtain

$$\begin{aligned} |\boldsymbol{A}_{(n)}| &\leq a_{nn}|\boldsymbol{A}_{(n-1)}| \leq a_{nn}a_{n-1,n-1}|\boldsymbol{A}_{(n-2)}| \leq \cdots \\ &\leq a_{nn}a_{n-1,n-1} \cdots a_{22}|\boldsymbol{A}_{(1)}| = a_{nn}a_{n-1,n-1} \cdots a_{22}a_{11}. \end{aligned}$$

Equality at the first step of this sequence of inequalities occurs if and only if all nondiagonal elements in the n-th row and the n-th column vanish. Equality at the first and second steps occurs if and only if, in addition, all nondiagonal elements in the $(n-1)$-th row and the $(n-1)$-th column vanish. Continuing in this way, we see that equality occurs if and only if all nondiagonal elements vanish.
(b) If $|\boldsymbol{A}| = 0$, the inequality is trivial. If $|\boldsymbol{A}| \neq 0$, then $\boldsymbol{AA}'$ is positive definite. Then, using (a),

$$|\boldsymbol{A}|^2 = |\boldsymbol{AA}'| \leq \prod_{i=1}^n (\boldsymbol{AA}')_{ii} = \prod_{i=1}^n \left(\sum_{j=1}^n a_{ij}^2 \right).$$

(c) If $|\boldsymbol{A}| = 0$, then equality occurs if and only if $\sum_{j=1}^n a_{ij}^2 = 0$ for some i, that is, if and only if $\boldsymbol{A}$ contains a row of zeros. If $|\boldsymbol{A}| \neq 0$, equality occurs if and only if $\boldsymbol{AA}'$ is diagonal.

Exercise 12.27 (When is a symmetric matrix diagonal?)
(a) We know from Exercise 12.26(a) that, if $\boldsymbol{A}$ is a positive definite $n \times n$ matrix, then, $|\boldsymbol{A}| = \prod_{i=1}^n a_{ii}$ if and only if $\boldsymbol{A}$ is diagonal. If $\boldsymbol{A}$ is merely symmetric, show that this result is still true for $n = 2$, but not in general for $n \geq 3$.
(b) Now show that a symmetric matrix is diagonal if and only if its eigenvalues and its diagonal elements coincide.

Solution

(a) If $n = 2$, then $|\boldsymbol{A}| = a_{11}a_{22} - a_{12}^2$, and this is equal to $a_{11}a_{22}$ if and only $a_{12} = 0$. If $n = 3$, then the matrix

$$\boldsymbol{A} = \begin{pmatrix} 2 & 3 & 3 \\ 3 & 2 & 3 \\ 3 & 3 & 2 \end{pmatrix}$$

has eigenvalues are -1, -1, and 8. Hence, $|\boldsymbol{A}| = 8$. The product of its diagonal elements is also 8. But $\boldsymbol{A}$ is not diagonal. (An important practical lesson can be learned from this example. If a matrix result holds for $n = 2$, then it does not necessarily hold generally. However, if it holds for $n = 3$, then there is a good chance that it holds generally. This is not a theorem, but is true nonetheless.)

(b) Let $\boldsymbol{A} := (a_{ij})$ be a symmetric $n \times n$ matrix. The "only if" part is trivial. To prove the "if" part, we assume that $\lambda_i(\boldsymbol{A}) = a_{ii}$ $(i = 1, \dots, n)$, and consider the matrix $\boldsymbol{B} = \boldsymbol{A} + \alpha\boldsymbol{I}$, where $\alpha > 0$ is such that $\boldsymbol{B}$ is positive definite. Then,

$$\lambda_i(\boldsymbol{B}) = \lambda_i(\boldsymbol{A}) + \alpha = a_{ii} + \alpha = b_{ii} \quad (i = 1, \dots, n),$$

and hence

$$|\boldsymbol{B}| = \prod_{i=1}^{n} \lambda_i(\boldsymbol{B}) = \prod_{i=1}^{n} b_{ii}.$$

It then follows from Exercise 12.26(a) that $\boldsymbol{B}$ is diagonal, and hence that $\boldsymbol{A}$ is diagonal.

Exercise 12.28 (Trace inequality, 2)

(a) If $\boldsymbol{A}$ is positive definite, show that $\boldsymbol{A} + \boldsymbol{A}^{-1} - 2\boldsymbol{I}$ is positive semidefinite.

(b) When is the matrix positive definite?

(c) Let $\boldsymbol{A} > \mathbf{O}$ and $\boldsymbol{B} > \mathbf{O}$, both of order n. Use (a) to show that

$$\operatorname{tr}\left((\boldsymbol{A}^{-1} - \boldsymbol{B}^{-1})(\boldsymbol{A} - \boldsymbol{B})\right) \leq 0.$$

Solution

For a scalar $\lambda > 0$, we have $\lambda + \lambda^{-1} - 2 = (\lambda - 1)^2/\lambda \geq 0$ with equality if and only if $\lambda = 1$. Let $\boldsymbol{S}$ be an orthogonal matrix such that $\boldsymbol{S}'\boldsymbol{A}\boldsymbol{S} = \boldsymbol{\Lambda}$ (diagonal). Then, $\boldsymbol{A} + \boldsymbol{A}^{-1} - 2\boldsymbol{I} = \boldsymbol{S}\left(\boldsymbol{\Lambda} + \boldsymbol{\Lambda}^{-1} - 2\boldsymbol{I}\right)\boldsymbol{S}'$ is positive semidefinite if and only if $\boldsymbol{\Lambda} + \boldsymbol{\Lambda}^{-1} - 2\boldsymbol{I}$ is positive semidefinite. The latter matrix is diagonal with nonnegative diagonal elements. This proves (a).

(b) The matrix is positive definite if and only if it is nonsingular, that is, if and only if *none* of the eigenvalues of $\boldsymbol{A}$ are equal to one.

(c) We write

$$\begin{aligned} \operatorname{tr}\left((\boldsymbol{A}^{-1} - \boldsymbol{B}^{-1})(\boldsymbol{A} - \boldsymbol{B})\right) &= \operatorname{tr}\left(\boldsymbol{I} - \boldsymbol{A}^{-1}\boldsymbol{B} - \boldsymbol{B}^{-1}\boldsymbol{A} + \boldsymbol{I}\right) \\ &= -\operatorname{tr}\left(\boldsymbol{C} + \boldsymbol{C}^{-1} - 2\boldsymbol{I}\right) \leq 0, \end{aligned}$$

where $\boldsymbol{C} = \boldsymbol{A}^{-1/2}\boldsymbol{B}\boldsymbol{A}^{-1/2}$.

Exercise 12.29 (OLS and GLS) Let V be a positive definite $n \times n$ matrix, and let X be an $n \times k$ matrix with $\operatorname{rk}(X) = k$. Show that

$$(X'X)^{-1}X'VX(X'X)^{-1} \geq (X'V^{-1}X)^{-1},$$

(a) using Exercise 12.18;
(b) by considering the matrix $M := V^{-1/2}X(X'V^{-1}X)^{-1}X'V^{-1/2}$.
(c) Can you explain the title "OLS and GLS" of this exercise? (Conditions for equality are provided in Exercise 8.69.)

Solution
(a) Let $A := V^{1/2}X(X'X)^{-1}$ and $B := V^{-1/2}X$. Then $A'B = I$ and hence Exercise 12.18 yields

$$(X'X)^{-1}X'VX(X'X)^{-1} = A'A \geq (B'B)^{-1} = (X'V^{-1}X)^{-1}.$$

(b) The matrix M is symmetric idempotent, and hence $I - M$ is also symmetric idempotent. Thus,

$$O \leq V^{1/2}(I - M)V^{1/2} = V - X(X'V^{-1}X)^{-1}X'.$$

Now premultiply by $(X'X)^{-1}X'$ and postmultiply by $X(X'X)^{-1}$.
(c) In the linear regression model $y = X\beta + u$ with $u \sim \mathrm{N}(0, V)$, the best linear unbiased estimator of β is given by $\tilde{\beta} := (X'V^{-1}X)^{-1}X'V^{-1}y$ with variance $(X'V^{-1}X)^{-1}$. This is the generalized least-squares (GLS) estimator. The ordinary least-squares (OLS) estimator $\hat{\beta} := (X'X)^{-1}X'y$ is also linear and unbiased, but not *best*, that is, $\operatorname{var}(\tilde{\beta}) \leq \operatorname{var}(\hat{\beta})$. Hence,

$$(X'V^{-1}X)^{-1} \leq (X'X)^{-1}X' \operatorname{var}(y)X(X'X)^{-1} = (X'X)^{-1}X'VX(X'X)^{-1}.$$

Exercise 12.30 (Bound for $\log|A|$, revisited) Show that

$$\frac{|A + B|}{|A|} \leq \exp(\operatorname{tr}(A^{-1}B)),$$

where A and $A + B$ are positive definite, with equality if and only if $B = O$.

Solution
Assume that A and B are of order n. It follows from Exercise 12.20 that

$$\log|I_n + B| \leq \operatorname{tr}(I_n + B) - n = \operatorname{tr} B,$$

when $I_n + B > O$, with equality if and only if $B = O$. Hence,

$$|I_n + B| = \exp(\log|I_n + B|) \leq \exp(\operatorname{tr} B).$$

This shows that the result holds for $A = I_n$. To prove the general result, let $C := A^{-1/2}BA^{-1/2}$. Then,

$$\frac{|A + B|}{|A|} = |A^{-1/2}(A + B)A^{-1/2}| = |I_n + C| \leq \exp(\operatorname{tr} C) = \exp(\operatorname{tr}(A^{-1}B)),$$

with equality if and only if $C = O$, that is, if and only if $B = O$.

Exercise 12.31 (Olkin's inequality)
(a) Let $\boldsymbol{A}$ be positive definite and $\boldsymbol{B}$ symmetric such that $|\boldsymbol{A}+\boldsymbol{B}| \neq 0$. Show that

$$(\boldsymbol{A}+\boldsymbol{B})^{-1}\boldsymbol{B}(\boldsymbol{A}+\boldsymbol{B})^{-1} \leq \boldsymbol{A}^{-1} - (\boldsymbol{A}+\boldsymbol{B})^{-1}.$$

(b) Show that the inequality is strict if and only if $\boldsymbol{B}$ is nonsingular.

Solution
(a) The trick is to try and rephrase this problem so that we are left with an inequality in one matrix rather than two. This is achieved by defining $\boldsymbol{C} := \boldsymbol{A}^{-1/2}\boldsymbol{B}\boldsymbol{A}^{-1/2}$. This is a symmetric matrix and well-defined, since $\boldsymbol{A}$ is positive definite. Also, the matrix $\boldsymbol{I}+\boldsymbol{C} = \boldsymbol{A}^{-1/2}(\boldsymbol{A}+\boldsymbol{B})\boldsymbol{A}^{-1/2}$ is nonsingular, since $\boldsymbol{A}+\boldsymbol{B}$ is nonsingular. Now,

$$\begin{aligned}
&\boldsymbol{A}^{-1} - (\boldsymbol{A}+\boldsymbol{B})^{-1} - (\boldsymbol{A}+\boldsymbol{B})^{-1}\boldsymbol{B}(\boldsymbol{A}+\boldsymbol{B})^{-1} \\
&\quad = \boldsymbol{A}^{-1} - \boldsymbol{A}^{-1/2}(\boldsymbol{I}+\boldsymbol{C})^{-1}\boldsymbol{A}^{-1/2} - \boldsymbol{A}^{-1/2}(\boldsymbol{I}+\boldsymbol{C})^{-1}\boldsymbol{C}(\boldsymbol{I}+\boldsymbol{C})^{-1}\boldsymbol{A}^{-1/2} \\
&\quad = \boldsymbol{A}^{-1/2}(\boldsymbol{I}+\boldsymbol{C})^{-1}\left((\boldsymbol{I}+\boldsymbol{C})^2 - (\boldsymbol{I}+\boldsymbol{C}) - \boldsymbol{C}\right)(\boldsymbol{I}+\boldsymbol{C})^{-1}\boldsymbol{A}^{-1/2} \\
&\quad = \boldsymbol{A}^{-1/2}(\boldsymbol{I}+\boldsymbol{C})^{-1}\boldsymbol{C}^2(\boldsymbol{I}+\boldsymbol{C})^{-1}\boldsymbol{A}^{-1/2} \geq \mathbf{O},
\end{aligned}$$

because $\boldsymbol{C}^2$ is positive semidefinite.
(b) The inequality is strict if and only if $\boldsymbol{C}$ is nonsingular, that is, if and only if $\boldsymbol{B}$ is nonsingular.

Exercise 12.32 (Positive definiteness of Hadamard product) Let $\boldsymbol{A}$ and $\boldsymbol{B}$ be square $n \times n$ matrices. The *Hadamard product* $\boldsymbol{A} \odot \boldsymbol{B}$ is defined as the $n \times n$ matrix whose ij-th element is $a_{ij}b_{ij}$. This is the element-by-element matrix product.
(a) Let $\boldsymbol{\lambda} := (\lambda_1, \dots, \lambda_n)'$ and $\boldsymbol{\Lambda} := \operatorname{diag}(\lambda_1, \dots, \lambda_n)$. Show that

$$\boldsymbol{\lambda}'(\boldsymbol{A} \odot \boldsymbol{B})\boldsymbol{\lambda} = \operatorname{tr} \boldsymbol{A}\boldsymbol{\Lambda}\boldsymbol{B}'\boldsymbol{\Lambda}.$$

(b) If $\boldsymbol{A} > \mathbf{O}$ and $\boldsymbol{B} > \mathbf{O}$, show that $\boldsymbol{A} \odot \boldsymbol{B} > \mathbf{O}$.

Solution
(a) We write

$$\begin{aligned}
\operatorname{tr} \boldsymbol{A}\boldsymbol{\Lambda}\boldsymbol{B}'\boldsymbol{\Lambda} &= \sum_i (\boldsymbol{A}\boldsymbol{\Lambda}\boldsymbol{B}'\boldsymbol{\Lambda})_{ii} = \sum_i \boldsymbol{e}_i'\boldsymbol{A}\boldsymbol{\Lambda}\boldsymbol{B}'\boldsymbol{\Lambda}\boldsymbol{e}_i = \sum_i \lambda_i \boldsymbol{e}_i'\boldsymbol{A}\boldsymbol{\Lambda}\boldsymbol{B}'\boldsymbol{e}_i \\
&= \sum_{ij} \lambda_i\lambda_j a_{ij}b_{ij} = \boldsymbol{\lambda}'(\boldsymbol{A} \odot \boldsymbol{B})\boldsymbol{\lambda}.
\end{aligned}$$

(b) Let $\boldsymbol{x} := (x_1, \dots, x_n)'$ be an arbitrary $n \times 1$ vector, and let $\boldsymbol{X} := \operatorname{diag}(x_1, \dots, x_n)$. Then, using (a),

$$\boldsymbol{x}'(\boldsymbol{A} \odot \boldsymbol{B})\boldsymbol{x} = \operatorname{tr} \boldsymbol{A}\boldsymbol{X}\boldsymbol{B}\boldsymbol{X} = \operatorname{tr}(\boldsymbol{A}^{1/2}\boldsymbol{X}\boldsymbol{B}^{1/2})(\boldsymbol{B}^{1/2}\boldsymbol{X}\boldsymbol{A}^{1/2}) = \operatorname{tr} \boldsymbol{C}\boldsymbol{C}' \geq 0,$$

where $\boldsymbol{C} = \boldsymbol{A}^{1/2}\boldsymbol{X}\boldsymbol{B}^{1/2}$. Equality implies that $\boldsymbol{C} = \mathbf{O}$, and hence that $\boldsymbol{X} = \mathbf{O}$, that is, $\boldsymbol{x} = \mathbf{0}$. We conclude that $\boldsymbol{x}'(\boldsymbol{A} \odot \boldsymbol{B})\boldsymbol{x} > 0$ for every $\boldsymbol{x} \neq \mathbf{0}$, and hence that $\boldsymbol{A} \odot \boldsymbol{B}$ is positive definite.

12.3 Inequalities derived from the Schur complement

Exercise 12.33 (Schur complement: basic inequality) Let A be a positive definite $n \times n$ matrix and let B be an $n \times m$ matrix. Show that, for any symmetric $m \times m$ matrix X,

$$Z := \begin{pmatrix} A & B \\ B' & X \end{pmatrix} \geq O \iff X \geq B'A^{-1}B,$$

and that, if one inequality is strict, the other is strict as well.

Solution
We write the equality

$$\begin{pmatrix} I & O \\ -B'A^{-1} & I \end{pmatrix} \begin{pmatrix} A & B \\ B' & X \end{pmatrix} \begin{pmatrix} I & -A^{-1}B \\ O & I \end{pmatrix} = \begin{pmatrix} A & O \\ O & X - B'A^{-1}B \end{pmatrix},$$

or, for short, $P'ZP = \Delta$. Since $|P| \neq 0$, $Z \geq O$ if and only if $\Delta \geq O$ (Exercise 8.28). Further, since $A > O$, $\Delta \geq O$ if and only if $X - B'A^{-1}B \geq O$ (Exercise 8.44). To prove the strict inequality, the same argument applies, all inequalities now being strict.

Exercise 12.34 (Fischer's inequality, again) As in Exercise 8.46, consider

$$Z := \begin{pmatrix} A & B \\ B' & D \end{pmatrix} > O.$$

(a) Show that $|Z| \leq |A||D|$ with equality if and only if $B = O$.
(b) If B is a square matrix, show that $|B|^2 < |A||D|$.

Solution
(a) Since $Z > O$, it follows that $A > O$ and $D > O$ (Exercise 8.30), and $D - B'A^{-1}B > O$ (Exercise 12.33). Hence, using the decomposition of Exercise 12.33,

$$|Z| = |A||D - B'A^{-1}B| \leq |A||D|,$$

since

$$|D| = |(D - B'A^{-1}B) + B'A^{-1}B| \geq |D - B'A^{-1}B|,$$

using Exercise 12.7. Equality occurs if and only if the last inequality is an equality, that is, if and only if $B'A^{-1}B = O$. This, in turn, happens if and only if $B = O$.
(b) Since $D - B'A^{-1}B > O$, we have, using Exercise 12.7,

$$\begin{aligned} |D| &= |(D - B'A^{-1}B) + B'A^{-1}B| \geq |D - B'A^{-1}B| + |B'A^{-1}B| \\ &> |B'A^{-1}B| = |B|^2|A|^{-1}. \end{aligned}$$

Multiplying both sides by $|A|$ gives $|A||D| > |B|^2$.

Exercise 12.35 (A positive semidefinite matrix) Show that

$$\begin{pmatrix} \boldsymbol{I} & \boldsymbol{A} \\ \boldsymbol{A}' & \boldsymbol{A}'\boldsymbol{A} \end{pmatrix} \geq \mathrm{O}$$

for any matrix $\boldsymbol{A}$.

Solution

The easiest solution is to notice that

$$\begin{pmatrix} \boldsymbol{I} & \boldsymbol{A} \\ \boldsymbol{A}' & \boldsymbol{A}'\boldsymbol{A} \end{pmatrix} = (\boldsymbol{I} : \boldsymbol{A})'(\boldsymbol{I} : \boldsymbol{A}) \geq \mathrm{O}.$$

Alternatively, we may invoke Exercise 12.33. The partitioned matrix is positive semidefinite if and only if $\boldsymbol{A}'\boldsymbol{A} \geq \boldsymbol{A}'\boldsymbol{I}^{-1}\boldsymbol{A}$, and this is obviously the case.

Exercise 12.36 (OLS and GLS, continued) Let $\boldsymbol{V}$ be a positive definite $n \times n$ matrix, and let $\boldsymbol{X}$ be an $n \times k$ matrix with $\operatorname{rk}(\boldsymbol{X}) = k$.
(a) Show that $\boldsymbol{X}(\boldsymbol{X}'\boldsymbol{V}^{-1}\boldsymbol{X})^{-1}\boldsymbol{X}' \leq \boldsymbol{V}$.
(b) Conclude that $(\boldsymbol{X}'\boldsymbol{V}^{-1}\boldsymbol{X})^{-1} \leq \boldsymbol{X}'\boldsymbol{V}\boldsymbol{X}$ for any $\boldsymbol{X}$ satisfying $\boldsymbol{X}'\boldsymbol{X} = \boldsymbol{I}_k$.

Solution

(a) It follows from Exercise 12.33 that

$$\begin{pmatrix} \boldsymbol{V} & \boldsymbol{X} \\ \boldsymbol{X}' & \boldsymbol{X}'\boldsymbol{V}^{-1}\boldsymbol{X} \end{pmatrix} \geq \mathrm{O}.$$

An immediate consequence is that

$$\begin{pmatrix} \boldsymbol{X}'\boldsymbol{V}^{-1}\boldsymbol{X} & \boldsymbol{X}' \\ \boldsymbol{X} & \boldsymbol{V} \end{pmatrix} \geq \mathrm{O}.$$

Now take the Schur complement in this matrix. This shows that

$$\boldsymbol{V} \geq \boldsymbol{X}(\boldsymbol{X}'\boldsymbol{V}^{-1}\boldsymbol{X})^{-1}\boldsymbol{X}'.$$

(b) This follows from (a) by premultiplying both sides by $\boldsymbol{X}'$ and postmultiplying by $\boldsymbol{X}$. (Notice that (a) implies, but is not implied by, the inequality in Exercise 12.29. Also compare (b) with Kantorovich's inequality in Exercise 12.17.)

Exercise 12.37 (Another positive semidefinite matrix) Let $\boldsymbol{A}$ and $\boldsymbol{B}$ be matrices of order $m \times n$.
(a) Show that

$$\begin{pmatrix} \boldsymbol{I}_m + \boldsymbol{A}\boldsymbol{A}' & \boldsymbol{A}+\boldsymbol{B} \\ (\boldsymbol{A}+\boldsymbol{B})' & \boldsymbol{I}_n + \boldsymbol{B}'\boldsymbol{B} \end{pmatrix} \geq \mathrm{O}.$$

(b) Use the Schur complement to show that

$$\boldsymbol{I}_n + \boldsymbol{B}'\boldsymbol{B} \geq (\boldsymbol{A}+\boldsymbol{B})'(\boldsymbol{I}_m + \boldsymbol{A}\boldsymbol{A}')^{-1}(\boldsymbol{A}+\boldsymbol{B}).$$

(c) If $\boldsymbol{A}$ and $\boldsymbol{B}$ are square matrices, show that

$$|\boldsymbol{A}+\boldsymbol{B}|^2 \leq |\boldsymbol{I}_n + \boldsymbol{B}'\boldsymbol{B}||\boldsymbol{I}_m + \boldsymbol{A}\boldsymbol{A}'|.$$

Solution

(a) This follows from the relationship

$$\begin{pmatrix} \boldsymbol{I}_m & \boldsymbol{A} \\ \boldsymbol{B}' & \boldsymbol{I}_n \end{pmatrix} \begin{pmatrix} \boldsymbol{I}_m & \boldsymbol{B} \\ \boldsymbol{A}' & \boldsymbol{I}_n \end{pmatrix} = \begin{pmatrix} \boldsymbol{I}_m + \boldsymbol{A}\boldsymbol{A}' & \boldsymbol{A}+\boldsymbol{B} \\ (\boldsymbol{A}+\boldsymbol{B})' & \boldsymbol{I}_n + \boldsymbol{B}'\boldsymbol{B} \end{pmatrix}.$$

(b) This follows directly from Exercise 12.33.

(c) This follows from (b).

Exercise 12.38 (An inequality equivalence) Let $\boldsymbol{A} > \mathbf{O}$ and $\boldsymbol{B} > \mathbf{O}$. Show that

$$\begin{pmatrix} \boldsymbol{A}+\boldsymbol{B} & \boldsymbol{A} \\ \boldsymbol{A} & \boldsymbol{A}+\boldsymbol{X} \end{pmatrix} \geq \mathbf{O} \iff \boldsymbol{X} \geq -(\boldsymbol{A}^{-1}+\boldsymbol{B}^{-1})^{-1}.$$

Solution

By Exercise 12.33 the partitioned matrix is positive semidefinite if and only if $\boldsymbol{A}+\boldsymbol{X} \geq \boldsymbol{A}(\boldsymbol{A}+\boldsymbol{B})^{-1}\boldsymbol{A}$. To prove the result we must therefore demonstrate that

$$\boldsymbol{A}(\boldsymbol{A}+\boldsymbol{B})^{-1}\boldsymbol{A} - \boldsymbol{A} = -(\boldsymbol{A}^{-1}+\boldsymbol{B}^{-1})^{-1},$$

or, equivalently, that

$$(\boldsymbol{A}^{-1}+\boldsymbol{B}^{-1})(\boldsymbol{A} - \boldsymbol{A}(\boldsymbol{A}+\boldsymbol{B})^{-1}\boldsymbol{A}) = \boldsymbol{I}.$$

Multiplying out the left-hand side shows that we need to prove that

$$(\boldsymbol{A}+\boldsymbol{B})^{-1}\boldsymbol{A} - \boldsymbol{B}^{-1}\boldsymbol{A} + \boldsymbol{B}^{-1}\boldsymbol{A}(\boldsymbol{A}+\boldsymbol{B})^{-1}\boldsymbol{A} = \mathbf{O}.$$

(Almost always, when you need to prove $\boldsymbol{A} = \boldsymbol{B}$, try proving $\boldsymbol{A} - \boldsymbol{B} = \mathbf{O}$ instead!) Now postmultiply both sides of the equation by $\boldsymbol{A}^{-1}(\boldsymbol{A}+\boldsymbol{B})$, and the result follows.

12.4 Inequalities concerning eigenvalues

Exercise 12.39 (Bounds of Rayleigh quotient, continued) Let $\boldsymbol{A}$ be a symmetric $n \times n$ matrix with eigenvalues $\lambda_1 \geq \lambda_2 \geq \cdots \geq \lambda_n$.

(a) Show that the Rayleigh quotient $\boldsymbol{x}'\boldsymbol{A}\boldsymbol{x}/\boldsymbol{x}'\boldsymbol{x}$ is bounded by

$$\lambda_n \leq \frac{\boldsymbol{x}'\boldsymbol{A}\boldsymbol{x}}{\boldsymbol{x}'\boldsymbol{x}} \leq \lambda_1.$$

(b) Can the bounds of $\boldsymbol{x}'\boldsymbol{A}\boldsymbol{x}/\boldsymbol{x}'\boldsymbol{x}$ be achieved?

(c) (Quasilinear representation) Show that we may express λ_1 and λ_n as

$$\lambda_1 = \max_{\boldsymbol{x}} \frac{\boldsymbol{x}'\boldsymbol{A}\boldsymbol{x}}{\boldsymbol{x}'\boldsymbol{x}} \quad \text{and} \quad \lambda_n = \min_{\boldsymbol{x}} \frac{\boldsymbol{x}'\boldsymbol{A}\boldsymbol{x}}{\boldsymbol{x}'\boldsymbol{x}}.$$

What potential use is this quasilinear representation?

Solution

(a) Let $\boldsymbol{S}$ be an orthogonal $n \times n$ matrix such that $\boldsymbol{S}'\boldsymbol{A}\boldsymbol{S} = \boldsymbol{\Lambda} = \operatorname{diag}(\lambda_1, \lambda_2, \dots, \lambda_n)$, and let $\boldsymbol{y} = \boldsymbol{S}'\boldsymbol{x}$. Since $\lambda_1 \boldsymbol{y}'\boldsymbol{y} \geq \boldsymbol{y}'\boldsymbol{\Lambda}\boldsymbol{y} \geq \lambda_n \boldsymbol{y}'\boldsymbol{y}$, we obtain $\lambda_1 \boldsymbol{x}'\boldsymbol{x} \geq \boldsymbol{x}'\boldsymbol{A}\boldsymbol{x} \geq \lambda_n \boldsymbol{x}'\boldsymbol{x}$, because $\boldsymbol{x}'\boldsymbol{A}\boldsymbol{x} = \boldsymbol{y}'\boldsymbol{\Lambda}\boldsymbol{y}$ and $\boldsymbol{x}'\boldsymbol{x} = \boldsymbol{y}'\boldsymbol{y}$.

(b) Yes, by choosing $\boldsymbol{x}$ to be an eigenvector associated with λ_1 or λ_n.

(c) This follows from (a) and (b). Thus, as in Exercise 12.3, we may represent λ_1 and λ_n (two nonlinear functions of $\boldsymbol{A}$) as an envelope of linear functions of $\boldsymbol{A}$. An immediate application follows in the next exercise.

Exercise 12.40 (Applications of the quasilinear representation) Let $\boldsymbol{A}$ and $\boldsymbol{B}$ be symmetric $n \times n$ matrices.

(a) Use the quasilinear representations in Exercise 12.39 to show that

$$\lambda_1(\boldsymbol{A}+\boldsymbol{B}) \leq \lambda_1(\boldsymbol{A}) + \lambda_1(\boldsymbol{B}) \quad \text{and} \quad \lambda_n(\boldsymbol{A}+\boldsymbol{B}) \geq \lambda_n(\boldsymbol{A}) + \lambda_n(\boldsymbol{B}).$$

(b) If, in addition, $\boldsymbol{B}$ is positive semidefinite, show that

$$\lambda_1(\boldsymbol{A}+\boldsymbol{B}) \geq \lambda_1(\boldsymbol{A}) \quad \text{and} \quad \lambda_n(\boldsymbol{A}+\boldsymbol{B}) \geq \lambda_n(\boldsymbol{A}).$$

Solution

(a) We have

$$\begin{aligned} \lambda_1(\boldsymbol{A}+\boldsymbol{B}) &= \max_{\boldsymbol{x}} \left(\frac{\boldsymbol{x}'\boldsymbol{A}\boldsymbol{x}}{\boldsymbol{x}'\boldsymbol{x}} + \frac{\boldsymbol{x}'\boldsymbol{B}\boldsymbol{x}}{\boldsymbol{x}'\boldsymbol{x}} \right) \\ &\leq \max_{\boldsymbol{x}} \frac{\boldsymbol{x}'\boldsymbol{A}\boldsymbol{x}}{\boldsymbol{x}'\boldsymbol{x}} + \max_{\boldsymbol{x}} \frac{\boldsymbol{x}'\boldsymbol{B}\boldsymbol{x}}{\boldsymbol{x}'\boldsymbol{x}} = \lambda_1(\boldsymbol{A}) + \lambda_1(\boldsymbol{B}). \end{aligned}$$

The proof that $\lambda_n(\boldsymbol{A}+\boldsymbol{B}) \geq \lambda_n(\boldsymbol{A}) + \lambda_n(\boldsymbol{B})$ proceeds similarly.

(b) To prove the result for λ_1, we write

$$\begin{aligned} \lambda_1(\boldsymbol{A}+\boldsymbol{B}) &= \max_{\boldsymbol{x}} \left(\frac{\boldsymbol{x}'\boldsymbol{A}\boldsymbol{x}}{\boldsymbol{x}'\boldsymbol{x}} + \frac{\boldsymbol{x}'\boldsymbol{B}\boldsymbol{x}}{\boldsymbol{x}'\boldsymbol{x}} \right) \\ &\geq \max_{\boldsymbol{x}} \frac{\boldsymbol{x}'\boldsymbol{A}\boldsymbol{x}}{\boldsymbol{x}'\boldsymbol{x}} + \min_{\boldsymbol{x}} \frac{\boldsymbol{x}'\boldsymbol{B}\boldsymbol{x}}{\boldsymbol{x}'\boldsymbol{x}} = \lambda_1(\boldsymbol{A}) + \lambda_n(\boldsymbol{B}). \end{aligned}$$

Since $\lambda_n(\boldsymbol{B}) \geq 0$, we see that $\lambda_1(\boldsymbol{A}+\boldsymbol{B}) \geq \lambda_1(\boldsymbol{A})$ if $\boldsymbol{B}$ is positive semidefinite. The result for λ_n follows directly from (a), because $\lambda_n(\boldsymbol{B}) \geq 0$.

Exercise 12.41 (Convexity of λ_1, concavity of λ_n) For any two symmetric matrices $\boldsymbol{A}$ and $\boldsymbol{B}$ of order $n \times n$ and $0 \leq \alpha \leq 1$, show that

$$\begin{aligned} \lambda_1(\alpha\boldsymbol{A} + (1-\alpha)\boldsymbol{B}) &\leq \alpha\lambda_1(\boldsymbol{A}) + (1-\alpha)\lambda_1(\boldsymbol{B}), \\ \lambda_n(\alpha\boldsymbol{A} + (1-\alpha)\boldsymbol{B}) &\geq \alpha\lambda_n(\boldsymbol{A}) + (1-\alpha)\lambda_n(\boldsymbol{B}). \end{aligned}$$

Hence, λ_1 is convex and λ_n is concave on the space of symmetric matrices.

Solution

Using the quasilinear representation (Exercise 12.39), we obtain

$$\begin{aligned}\lambda_1(\alpha\boldsymbol{A}+(1-\alpha)\boldsymbol{B}) &= \max_{\boldsymbol{x}} \frac{\boldsymbol{x}'(\alpha\boldsymbol{A}+(1-\alpha)\boldsymbol{B})\boldsymbol{x}}{\boldsymbol{x}'\boldsymbol{x}} \\ &\le \alpha \max_{\boldsymbol{x}} \frac{\boldsymbol{x}'\boldsymbol{A}\boldsymbol{x}}{\boldsymbol{x}'\boldsymbol{x}} + (1-\alpha)\max_{\boldsymbol{x}} \frac{\boldsymbol{x}'\boldsymbol{B}\boldsymbol{x}}{\boldsymbol{x}'\boldsymbol{x}} \\ &= \alpha\lambda_1(\boldsymbol{A}) + (1-\alpha)\lambda_1(\boldsymbol{B}).\end{aligned}$$

The analogue for λ_n is proved similarly.

Exercise 12.42 (Variational description of eigenvalues) Let $\boldsymbol{A}$ be a symmetric $n \times n$ matrix with eigenvalues $\lambda_1 \ge \lambda_2 \ge \cdots \ge \lambda_n$. Let $\boldsymbol{S} := (\boldsymbol{s}_1, \boldsymbol{s}_2, \dots, \boldsymbol{s}_n)$ be an orthogonal $n \times n$ matrix that diagonalizes $\boldsymbol{A}$, so that $\boldsymbol{S}'\boldsymbol{A}\boldsymbol{S} = \operatorname{diag}(\lambda_1, \lambda_2, \dots, \lambda_n)$. Show that

$$\lambda_k = \max_{\boldsymbol{R}_{k-1}'\boldsymbol{x}=\boldsymbol{0}} \frac{\boldsymbol{x}'\boldsymbol{A}\boldsymbol{x}}{\boldsymbol{x}'\boldsymbol{x}} = \min_{\boldsymbol{T}_{k+1}'\boldsymbol{x}=\boldsymbol{0}} \frac{\boldsymbol{x}'\boldsymbol{A}\boldsymbol{x}}{\boldsymbol{x}'\boldsymbol{x}} \quad (k = 1, \dots, n),$$

where

$$\boldsymbol{R}_k := (\boldsymbol{s}_1, \boldsymbol{s}_2, \dots, \boldsymbol{s}_k) \quad \text{and} \quad \boldsymbol{T}_k := (\boldsymbol{s}_k, \boldsymbol{s}_{k+1}, \dots, \boldsymbol{s}_n),$$

and we agree to interpret $\boldsymbol{R}_0$ and $\boldsymbol{T}_{n+1}$ as "empty" in the sense that the restrictions $\boldsymbol{R}_0'\boldsymbol{x} = \boldsymbol{0}$ and $\boldsymbol{T}_{n+1}'\boldsymbol{x} = \boldsymbol{0}$ do not impose a restriction on $\boldsymbol{x}$.

Solution

We only prove the first representation of λ_k. Let $\boldsymbol{y} := \boldsymbol{S}'\boldsymbol{x}$. Partition $\boldsymbol{S}$ and $\boldsymbol{y}$ as

$$\boldsymbol{S} = (\boldsymbol{R}_{k-1} : \boldsymbol{T}_k) \quad \text{and} \quad \boldsymbol{y} = \begin{pmatrix} \boldsymbol{y}_1 \\ \boldsymbol{y}_2 \end{pmatrix}.$$

Then, we may express $\boldsymbol{x}$ as $\boldsymbol{x} = \boldsymbol{S}\boldsymbol{y} = \boldsymbol{R}_{k-1}\boldsymbol{y}_1 + \boldsymbol{T}_k\boldsymbol{y}_2$. Hence, using $\boldsymbol{R}_{k-1}'\boldsymbol{T}_k = \boldsymbol{O}$,

$$\boldsymbol{R}_{k-1}'\boldsymbol{x} = \boldsymbol{0} \iff \boldsymbol{y}_1 = \boldsymbol{0} \iff \boldsymbol{x} = \boldsymbol{T}_k\boldsymbol{y}_2.$$

It follows that

$$\max_{\boldsymbol{R}_{k-1}'\boldsymbol{x}=\boldsymbol{0}} \frac{\boldsymbol{x}'\boldsymbol{A}\boldsymbol{x}}{\boldsymbol{x}'\boldsymbol{x}} = \max_{\boldsymbol{x}=\boldsymbol{T}_k\boldsymbol{y}_2} \frac{\boldsymbol{x}'\boldsymbol{A}\boldsymbol{x}}{\boldsymbol{x}'\boldsymbol{x}} = \max_{\boldsymbol{y}_2} \frac{\boldsymbol{y}_2'(\boldsymbol{T}_k'\boldsymbol{A}\boldsymbol{T}_k)\boldsymbol{y}_2}{\boldsymbol{y}_2'\boldsymbol{y}_2} = \lambda_k,$$

since $\boldsymbol{T}_k'\boldsymbol{A}\boldsymbol{T}_k = \operatorname{diag}(\lambda_k, \lambda_{k+1}, \dots, \lambda_n)$.

Exercise 12.43 (Variational description, generalized) Let $\boldsymbol{A}$ be a symmetric $n \times n$ matrix with eigenvalues $\lambda_1 \ge \lambda_2 \ge \cdots \ge \lambda_n$. Show that, for every $n \times (k-1)$ matrix $\boldsymbol{B}$ and $n \times (n-k)$ matrix $\boldsymbol{C}$,

$$\min_{\boldsymbol{C}'\boldsymbol{x}=\boldsymbol{0}} \frac{\boldsymbol{x}'\boldsymbol{A}\boldsymbol{x}}{\boldsymbol{x}'\boldsymbol{x}} \le \lambda_k \le \max_{\boldsymbol{B}'\boldsymbol{x}=\boldsymbol{0}} \frac{\boldsymbol{x}'\boldsymbol{A}\boldsymbol{x}}{\boldsymbol{x}'\boldsymbol{x}}.$$

Solution

Let $\boldsymbol{B}$ be an arbitrary $n \times (k-1)$ matrix, and denote (normalized) eigenvectors associated with the eigenvalues $\lambda_1, \dots, \lambda_n$ of $\boldsymbol{A}$ by $\boldsymbol{s}_1, \boldsymbol{s}_2, \dots, \boldsymbol{s}_n$. Let $\boldsymbol{R} := (\boldsymbol{s}_1, \boldsymbol{s}_2, \dots, \boldsymbol{s}_k)$, so that

$$\boldsymbol{R}'\boldsymbol{A}\boldsymbol{R} = \operatorname{diag}(\lambda_1, \lambda_2, \dots, \lambda_k), \quad \boldsymbol{R}'\boldsymbol{R} = \boldsymbol{I}_k.$$

Now consider the $(k-1) \times k$ matrix $\boldsymbol{B}'\boldsymbol{R}$. Since the rank of $\boldsymbol{B}'\boldsymbol{R}$ cannot exceed $k-1$, its k columns are linearly dependent. Thus $\boldsymbol{B}'\boldsymbol{R}\boldsymbol{p} = \boldsymbol{0}$ for some $k \times 1$ vector $\boldsymbol{p} \neq \boldsymbol{0}$. Then, choosing $\boldsymbol{x} = \boldsymbol{R}\boldsymbol{p}$, we obtain

$$\max_{\boldsymbol{B}'\boldsymbol{x}=\boldsymbol{0}} \frac{\boldsymbol{x}'\boldsymbol{A}\boldsymbol{x}}{\boldsymbol{x}'\boldsymbol{x}} \geq \frac{\boldsymbol{p}'(\boldsymbol{R}'\boldsymbol{A}\boldsymbol{R})\boldsymbol{p}}{\boldsymbol{p}'\boldsymbol{p}} \geq \lambda_k.$$

The proof of the second inequality is similar.

Exercise 12.44 (Fischer's min-max theorem) Let $\boldsymbol{A}$ be a symmetric $n \times n$ matrix with eigenvalues $\lambda_1 \geq \lambda_2 \geq \dots \geq \lambda_n$. Obtain a quasilinear representation of the eigenvalues, that is, show that λ_k can be expressed as

$$\lambda_k = \min_{\boldsymbol{B}'\boldsymbol{B}=\boldsymbol{I}_{k-1}} \max_{\boldsymbol{B}'\boldsymbol{x}=\boldsymbol{0}} \frac{\boldsymbol{x}'\boldsymbol{A}\boldsymbol{x}}{\boldsymbol{x}'\boldsymbol{x}},$$

and equivalently as

$$\lambda_k = \max_{\boldsymbol{C}'\boldsymbol{C}=\boldsymbol{I}_{n-k}} \min_{\boldsymbol{C}'\boldsymbol{x}=\boldsymbol{0}} \frac{\boldsymbol{x}'\boldsymbol{A}\boldsymbol{x}}{\boldsymbol{x}'\boldsymbol{x}},$$

where, as the notation indicates, $\boldsymbol{B}$ is an $n \times (k-1)$ matrix and $\boldsymbol{C}$ is an $n \times (n-k)$ matrix.

Solution

The solution is now simple, because we have the preliminary Exercises 12.42 and 12.43 at our disposal. Let $\boldsymbol{\Lambda}_{k-1} := \operatorname{diag}(\lambda_1, \lambda_2, \dots, \lambda_{k-1})$, and let $\boldsymbol{R}_{k-1}$ be a semi-orthogonal $n \times (k-1)$ matrix satisfying

$$\boldsymbol{A}\boldsymbol{R}_{k-1} = \boldsymbol{R}_{k-1}\boldsymbol{\Lambda}_{k-1}, \quad \boldsymbol{R}_{k-1}'\boldsymbol{R}_{k-1} = \boldsymbol{I}_{k-1}.$$

Now define

$$\phi(\boldsymbol{B}) := \max_{\boldsymbol{B}'\boldsymbol{x}=\boldsymbol{0}} \frac{\boldsymbol{x}'\boldsymbol{A}\boldsymbol{x}}{\boldsymbol{x}'\boldsymbol{x}}.$$

Then we obtain, using Exercise 12.42, $\lambda_k = \phi(\boldsymbol{R}_{k-1}) \geq \min_{\boldsymbol{B}'\boldsymbol{B}=\boldsymbol{I}_{k-1}} \phi(\boldsymbol{B})$, because $\boldsymbol{R}_{k-1}$ obviously satisfies the constraint $\boldsymbol{R}_{k-1}'\boldsymbol{R}_{k-1} = \boldsymbol{I}_{k-1}$. Also, Exercise 12.43 shows that $\lambda_k \leq \phi(\boldsymbol{B})$ for every $\boldsymbol{B}$, and hence in particular for every semi-orthogonal $\boldsymbol{B}$. We have thus demonstrated that λ_k is both larger and smaller than $\min_{\boldsymbol{B}'\boldsymbol{B}=\boldsymbol{I}_{k-1}} \phi(\boldsymbol{B})$; hence equality follows. The second result is proved in a similar fashion.

Exercise 12.45 (Monotonicity of eigenvalue function) Generalize Exercise 12.40(b) by showing that, for any symmetric matrix $\boldsymbol{A}$ and positive semidefinite matrix $\boldsymbol{B}$,

$$\lambda_k(\boldsymbol{A}+\boldsymbol{B}) \geq \lambda_k(\boldsymbol{A}) \quad (k = 1, 2, \dots, n).$$

If $\boldsymbol{B}$ is positive definite, show that the inequality is strict.

Solution

For any $n \times (n-k)$ matrix $\boldsymbol{C}$ we have

$$\begin{aligned}\min_{\boldsymbol{C}'\boldsymbol{x}=\boldsymbol{0}} \frac{\boldsymbol{x}'(\boldsymbol{A}+\boldsymbol{B})\boldsymbol{x}}{\boldsymbol{x}'\boldsymbol{x}} &= \min_{\boldsymbol{C}'\boldsymbol{x}=\boldsymbol{0}} \left(\frac{\boldsymbol{x}'\boldsymbol{A}\boldsymbol{x}}{\boldsymbol{x}'\boldsymbol{x}} + \frac{\boldsymbol{x}'\boldsymbol{B}\boldsymbol{x}}{\boldsymbol{x}'\boldsymbol{x}}\right) \\ &\geq \min_{\boldsymbol{C}'\boldsymbol{x}=\boldsymbol{0}} \frac{\boldsymbol{x}'\boldsymbol{A}\boldsymbol{x}}{\boldsymbol{x}'\boldsymbol{x}} + \min_{\boldsymbol{C}'\boldsymbol{x}=\boldsymbol{0}} \frac{\boldsymbol{x}'\boldsymbol{B}\boldsymbol{x}}{\boldsymbol{x}'\boldsymbol{x}} \\ &\geq \min_{\boldsymbol{C}'\boldsymbol{x}=\boldsymbol{0}} \frac{\boldsymbol{x}'\boldsymbol{A}\boldsymbol{x}}{\boldsymbol{x}'\boldsymbol{x}} + \lambda_n(\boldsymbol{B}),\end{aligned}$$

because $\min_{\boldsymbol{C}'\boldsymbol{x}=\boldsymbol{0}}(\boldsymbol{x}'\boldsymbol{B}\boldsymbol{x}/\boldsymbol{x}'\boldsymbol{x}) \geq \min_{\boldsymbol{x}}(\boldsymbol{x}'\boldsymbol{B}\boldsymbol{x}/\boldsymbol{x}'\boldsymbol{x}) = \lambda_n(\boldsymbol{B})$. Hence, by Fischer's min-max theorem,

$$\begin{aligned}\lambda_k(\boldsymbol{A}+\boldsymbol{B}) &= \max_{\boldsymbol{C}'\boldsymbol{C}=\boldsymbol{I}_{n-k}} \min_{\boldsymbol{C}'\boldsymbol{x}=\boldsymbol{0}} \frac{\boldsymbol{x}'(\boldsymbol{A}+\boldsymbol{B})\boldsymbol{x}}{\boldsymbol{x}'\boldsymbol{x}} \\ &\geq \max_{\boldsymbol{C}'\boldsymbol{C}=\boldsymbol{I}_{n-k}} \min_{\boldsymbol{C}'\boldsymbol{x}=\boldsymbol{0}} \frac{\boldsymbol{x}'\boldsymbol{A}\boldsymbol{x}}{\boldsymbol{x}'\boldsymbol{x}} + \lambda_n(\boldsymbol{B}) = \lambda_k(\boldsymbol{A}) + \lambda_n(\boldsymbol{B}) \geq \lambda_k(\boldsymbol{A}),\end{aligned}$$

since $\boldsymbol{B}$ is positive semidefinite. If $\boldsymbol{B}$ is positive definite, then $\lambda_n(\boldsymbol{B}) > 0$ and the last inequality is strict.

***Exercise 12.46 (Poincaré's separation theorem)** Let $\boldsymbol{A}$ be a symmetric $n \times n$ matrix with eigenvalues $\lambda_1 \geq \lambda_2 \geq \cdots \geq \lambda_n$, and let $\boldsymbol{G}$ be a semi-orthogonal $n \times r$ matrix $(1 \leq r \leq n)$, so that $\boldsymbol{G}'\boldsymbol{G} = \boldsymbol{I}_r$. Show that the eigenvalues $\mu_1 \geq \mu_2 \geq \cdots \geq \mu_r$ of $\boldsymbol{G}'\boldsymbol{A}\boldsymbol{G}$ satisfy

$$\lambda_{n-r+k} \leq \mu_k \leq \lambda_k \quad (k = 1, 2, \ldots, r).$$

Solution

We do not need the full force of Fischer's theorem. The two preliminary results in Exercises 12.42 and 12.43 suffice. Let $1 \leq k \leq r$ and let $\boldsymbol{R}$ be a semi-orthogonal $n \times (k-1)$ matrix whose columns are eigenvectors of $\boldsymbol{A}$ associated with $\lambda_1, \lambda_2, \ldots, \lambda_{k-1}$. (Again, we agree to interpret $\boldsymbol{R}$ as "empty" when $k = 1$, in the sense that the restriction $\boldsymbol{R}'\boldsymbol{x} = \boldsymbol{0}$ does not impose a restriction on $\boldsymbol{x}$.) Then,

$$\lambda_k = \max_{\boldsymbol{R}'\boldsymbol{x}=\boldsymbol{0}} \frac{\boldsymbol{x}'\boldsymbol{A}\boldsymbol{x}}{\boldsymbol{x}'\boldsymbol{x}} \geq \max_{\substack{\boldsymbol{R}'\boldsymbol{x}=\boldsymbol{0} \\ \boldsymbol{x}=\boldsymbol{G}\boldsymbol{y}}} \frac{\boldsymbol{x}'\boldsymbol{A}\boldsymbol{x}}{\boldsymbol{x}'\boldsymbol{x}} = \max_{\boldsymbol{R}'\boldsymbol{G}\boldsymbol{y}=\boldsymbol{0}} \frac{\boldsymbol{y}'\boldsymbol{G}'\boldsymbol{A}\boldsymbol{G}\boldsymbol{y}}{\boldsymbol{y}'\boldsymbol{y}} \geq \mu_k,$$

where the first equality follows from Exercise 12.42, and the last inequality from Exercise 12.43.

Next, let $n - r + 1 \leq k \leq n$, and let $\boldsymbol{T}$ be a semi-orthogonal $n \times (n-k)$ matrix whose columns are eigenvectors of $\boldsymbol{A}$ associated with $\lambda_{k+1}, \ldots, \lambda_n$. (Of course, $\boldsymbol{T}$ will be interpreted as "empty" when $k = n$, in the sense that the restriction $\boldsymbol{T}'\boldsymbol{x} = \boldsymbol{0}$ does not impose a restriction on $\boldsymbol{x}$.) Then we obtain in the same way

$$\lambda_k = \min_{\boldsymbol{T}'\boldsymbol{x}=\boldsymbol{0}} \frac{\boldsymbol{x}'\boldsymbol{A}\boldsymbol{x}}{\boldsymbol{x}'\boldsymbol{x}} \leq \min_{\substack{\boldsymbol{T}'\boldsymbol{x}=\boldsymbol{0} \\ \boldsymbol{x}=\boldsymbol{G}\boldsymbol{y}}} \frac{\boldsymbol{x}'\boldsymbol{A}\boldsymbol{x}}{\boldsymbol{x}'\boldsymbol{x}} = \min_{\boldsymbol{T}'\boldsymbol{G}\boldsymbol{y}=\boldsymbol{0}} \frac{\boldsymbol{y}'\boldsymbol{G}'\boldsymbol{A}\boldsymbol{G}\boldsymbol{y}}{\boldsymbol{y}'\boldsymbol{y}} \leq \mu_{r-n+k}.$$

The last inequality is tricky. We know from Exercise 12.43 that $\boldsymbol{y}'\boldsymbol{G}'\boldsymbol{A}\boldsymbol{G}\boldsymbol{y}/\boldsymbol{y}'\boldsymbol{y} \leq \mu_k$ for every vector $\boldsymbol{y}$ satisfying $\boldsymbol{C}'\boldsymbol{y} = \mathbf{0}$, where $\boldsymbol{C}$ is an $r \times (r-k)$ matrix. The matrix $\boldsymbol{G}'\boldsymbol{T}$ has $(n-k)$ columns, not $(r-k)$; hence there are $(n-r)$ additional restrictions on $\boldsymbol{y}$ and the upper bound changes from μ_k to μ_{r-n+k}. We now rewrite the inequality $\lambda_k \leq \mu_{r-n+k}$ as $\lambda_{n-r+k} \leq \mu_k$, and this completes the second half of the proof.

Exercise 12.47 (Poincaré applied, 1) Let $\boldsymbol{A}$ be a symmetric $n \times n$ matrix with eigenvalues $\lambda_1 \geq \lambda_2 \geq \cdots \geq \lambda_n$, and let $\boldsymbol{M}$ be an idempotent symmetric $n \times n$ matrix of rank r $(1 \leq r \leq n)$. Denote the eigenvalues of the $n \times n$ matrix $\boldsymbol{MAM}$, apart from $n-r$ zeros, by $\mu_1 \geq \mu_2 \geq \cdots \geq \mu_r$. Use Poincaré's separation theorem to show that

$$\lambda_{n-r+k} \leq \mu_k \leq \lambda_k \quad (k = 1, 2, \ldots, r).$$

Solution
This is an immediate consequence (in fact a reformulation) of Poincaré's theorem. Write $\boldsymbol{M} = \boldsymbol{G}\boldsymbol{G}'$ with $\boldsymbol{G}'\boldsymbol{G} = \boldsymbol{I}_r$ (see Exercise 8.66), and note that $\boldsymbol{G}\boldsymbol{G}'\boldsymbol{A}\boldsymbol{G}\boldsymbol{G}'$ and $\boldsymbol{G}'\boldsymbol{A}\boldsymbol{G}$ have the same eigenvalues, apart from $n-r$ zeros (Exercise 7.25(b)).

Exercise 12.48 (Poincaré applied, 2) Let $\boldsymbol{A}$ be a symmetric $n \times n$ matrix with eigenvalues $\lambda_1(\boldsymbol{A}) \geq \lambda_2(\boldsymbol{A}) \geq \cdots \geq \lambda_n(\boldsymbol{A})$, and let $\boldsymbol{A}_{(r)}$ be an $r \times r$ principal submatrix of $\boldsymbol{A}$ (not necessarily a leading principal submatrix) with eigenvalues $\lambda_1(\boldsymbol{A}_{(r)}) \geq \lambda_2(\boldsymbol{A}_{(r)}) \geq \cdots \geq \lambda_r(\boldsymbol{A}_{(r)})$.
(a) Use Poincaré's separation theorem to show that

$$\lambda_{n-r+k}(\boldsymbol{A}) \leq \lambda_k(\boldsymbol{A}_{(r)}) \leq \lambda_k(\boldsymbol{A}) \quad (k = 1, 2, \ldots, r).$$

(b) In particular, show that

$$\begin{aligned}\lambda_n(\boldsymbol{A}_{(n)}) &\leq \lambda_{n-1}(\boldsymbol{A}_{(n-1)}) \leq \lambda_{n-1}(\boldsymbol{A}_{(n)}) \leq \lambda_{n-2}(\boldsymbol{A}_{(n-1)}) \\ &\leq \cdots \leq \lambda_1(\boldsymbol{A}_{(n-1)}) \leq \lambda_1(\boldsymbol{A}_{(n)}).\end{aligned}$$

Solution
(a) Let $\boldsymbol{G}$ be the $n \times r$ matrix $\boldsymbol{G} := (\boldsymbol{I}_r : \mathbf{O})'$ or a row permutation thereof. Then $\boldsymbol{G}'\boldsymbol{G} = \boldsymbol{I}_r$ and $\boldsymbol{G}'\boldsymbol{A}\boldsymbol{G}$ is an $r \times r$ principal submatrix of $\boldsymbol{A}$. The result then follows from Poincaré's theorem.
(b) Letting $r = n-1$ in (a), we see that $\lambda_{k+1}(\boldsymbol{A}_{(n)}) \leq \lambda_k(\boldsymbol{A}_{(n-1)}) \leq \lambda_k(\boldsymbol{A}_{(n)})$ for $1 \leq k \leq n-1$.

Exercise 12.49 (Bounds for $\operatorname{tr} \boldsymbol{A}_{(r)}$**)** Let $\boldsymbol{A}$ be a symmetric $n \times n$ matrix with eigenvalues $\lambda_1 \geq \lambda_2 \geq \cdots \geq \lambda_n$.
(a) Show that

$$\max_{\boldsymbol{X}'\boldsymbol{X}=\boldsymbol{I}_r} \operatorname{tr} \boldsymbol{X}'\boldsymbol{A}\boldsymbol{X} = \sum_{k=1}^{r} \lambda_k \quad \text{and} \quad \min_{\boldsymbol{X}'\boldsymbol{X}=\boldsymbol{I}_r} \operatorname{tr} \boldsymbol{X}'\boldsymbol{A}\boldsymbol{X} = \sum_{k=1}^{r} \lambda_{n-r+k}.$$

(b) In particular, defining for $r = 1, 2, \dots, n$,

$$A_{(r)} := \begin{pmatrix} a_{11} & \dots & a_{1r} \\ \vdots & & \vdots \\ a_{r1} & \dots & a_{rr} \end{pmatrix},$$

show that

$$\sum_{k=1}^{r} \lambda_{n-r+k} \leq \operatorname{tr} A_{(r)} \leq \sum_{k=1}^{r} \lambda_k.$$

Solution

(a) Denote the r eigenvalues of $X'AX$ by $\mu_1 \geq \mu_2 \geq \dots \geq \mu_r$. Then, Poincaré's theorem gives

$$\sum_{k=1}^{r} \lambda_{n-r+k} \leq \sum_{k=1}^{r} \mu_k \leq \sum_{k=1}^{r} \lambda_k.$$

Noting that $\sum_{k=1}^{r} \mu_k = \operatorname{tr} X'AX$, and that the bounds can be attained by suitable choices of X, (a) follows.

(b) Take $X := (I_r : \mathrm{O})'$ in (a).

Exercise 12.50 (Bounds for $|A_{(r)}|$) Let A be a positive definite $n \times n$ matrix with eigenvalues $\lambda_1 \geq \lambda_2 \geq \dots \geq \lambda_n$.

(a) Show that

$$\max_{X'X=I_r} |X'AX| = \prod_{k=1}^{r} \lambda_k \quad \text{and} \quad \min_{X'X=I_r} |X'AX| = \prod_{k=1}^{r} \lambda_{n-r+k}.$$

(b) In particular, letting $A_{(r)}$ be as defined in Exercise 12.49, show that

$$\prod_{k=1}^{r} \lambda_{n-r+k} \leq |A_{(r)}| \leq \prod_{k=1}^{r} \lambda_k.$$

Solution

(a) Let $\mu_1 \geq \mu_2 \geq \dots \geq \mu_r$ be the eigenvalues of $X'AX$. Poincaré's theorem implies

$$\prod_{k=1}^{r} \lambda_{n-r+k} \leq \prod_{k=1}^{r} \mu_k \leq \prod_{k=1}^{r} \lambda_k.$$

Then, since $\prod_{k=1}^{r} \mu_k = |X'AX|$, and the bounds can be attained by suitable choices of X, the result follows.

(b) Take $X := (I_r : \mathrm{O})'$ in (a).

Exercise 12.51 (A consequence of Hadamard's inequality) Let $A = (a_{ij})$ be a positive definite $n \times n$ matrix with eigenvalues $\lambda_1 \geq \lambda_2 \geq \dots \geq \lambda_n$. Show that

$$\prod_{k=1}^{r} \lambda_{n-r+k} \leq \prod_{k=1}^{r} a_{kk} \quad (r = 1, \dots, n).$$

Solution

Let $A_{(r)}$ be as defined in Exercise 12.49. We know from Exercise 12.26(a) that $|A_{(r)}| \leq \prod_{k=1}^{r} a_{kk}$. We also know from Exercise 12.50 that $\prod_{k=1}^{r} \lambda_{n-r+k} \leq |A_{(r)}|$. The result follows from these two inequalities.

Notes

The classic treatise on inequalities is Hardy, Littlewood, and Pólya's (1952) monumental monograph. Useful references are also Beckenbach and Bellman (1961), Magnus and Neudecker (1999, Chapter 11), and Zhan (2002). The idea of expressing a nonlinear function as an envelope of linear functions (quasilinearization) is due to Minkowski. Exercise 12.10 was first discussed by Sylvester in 1893; the presented proof comes from Aigner and Ziegler (1999, p. 46).

13

Matrix calculus

Let us first establish the notation. This is important, because bad notation is a serious obstacle to elegant mathematics and coherent exposition, and it can be misleading. If $\boldsymbol{f}$ is an $m \times 1$ vector function of an $n \times 1$ vector $\boldsymbol{x}$, then the *derivative* (or *Jacobian matrix*) of $\boldsymbol{f}$ is the $m \times n$ matrix

$$\mathrm{D}\boldsymbol{f}(\boldsymbol{x}) := \frac{\partial \boldsymbol{f}(\boldsymbol{x})}{\partial \boldsymbol{x}'}, \tag{13.1}$$

the elements of which are the partial derivatives $\partial f_i(\boldsymbol{x})/\partial x_j$, $i = 1, \dots, m$, $j = 1, \dots, n$. There is no controversy about this definition. It implies, inter alia, that when $\boldsymbol{y} = \boldsymbol{A}\boldsymbol{x}$, then $\partial \boldsymbol{y}/\partial \boldsymbol{x}' = \boldsymbol{A}$ (when $\boldsymbol{A}$ is a matrix of constants). It also implies that for a scalar function $\varphi(\boldsymbol{x})$, the derivative $\partial \varphi(\boldsymbol{x})/\partial \boldsymbol{x}'$ is a *row* vector, not a column vector.

Now consider an $m \times p$ *matrix* function $\boldsymbol{F}$ of an $n \times q$ *matrix* of variables $\boldsymbol{X}$. Clearly, the derivative is a matrix containing all $mpnq$ partial derivatives. Also, (13.1) should be a special case of the more general definition. The most obvious and elegant definition is

$$\mathrm{D}\boldsymbol{F}(\boldsymbol{X}) := \frac{\partial \operatorname{vec} \boldsymbol{F}(\boldsymbol{X})}{\partial (\operatorname{vec} \boldsymbol{X})'}, \tag{13.2}$$

which is an $mp \times nq$ matrix. As a result, if $\boldsymbol{F}$ is a function of a scalar x ($n = q = 1$), then $\mathrm{D}\boldsymbol{F}(x) = \partial \operatorname{vec} \boldsymbol{F}(x)/\partial x$, an $mp \times 1$ column vector. If φ is a scalar function of a matrix $\boldsymbol{X}$ ($m = p = 1$), then $\mathrm{D}\varphi(\boldsymbol{X}) = \partial \varphi(\boldsymbol{X})/\partial(\operatorname{vec} \boldsymbol{X})'$, a $1 \times nq$ row vector. The choice of ordering in (13.2) is not arbitrary. For example, the derivative of the scalar function $\varphi(\boldsymbol{X}) = \operatorname{tr}(\boldsymbol{X})$ is not $\mathrm{D}\varphi(\boldsymbol{X}) = \boldsymbol{I}_n$, but $\mathrm{D}\varphi(\boldsymbol{X}) = (\operatorname{vec} \boldsymbol{I}_n)'$.

For practical rather than theoretical reasons, the treatment of matrix calculus is based on *differentials* rather than derivatives. An important advantage is the following. Let $\boldsymbol{f}(\boldsymbol{x})$ be an $m \times 1$ vector function of an $n \times 1$ vector $\boldsymbol{x}$. Then the derivative $\mathrm{D}\boldsymbol{f}(\boldsymbol{x})$ is an $m \times n$ matrix, but the differential $\mathrm{d}\boldsymbol{f}(\boldsymbol{x})$ remains an $m \times 1$ vector. The advantage is even larger for matrices: $\mathrm{d}\boldsymbol{F}(\boldsymbol{X})$ has the same dimension as $\boldsymbol{F}$, irrespective of the dimension of $\boldsymbol{X}$.

Unless specified otherwise, φ denotes a scalar function, $\boldsymbol{f}$ a vector function, and $\boldsymbol{F}$ a matrix function. Also, x denotes a scalar argument, $\boldsymbol{x}$ a vector argument, and $\boldsymbol{X}$ a matrix argument. For example, we write

$$\varphi(x) = x^2, \quad \varphi(\boldsymbol{x}) = \boldsymbol{a}'\boldsymbol{x}, \quad \varphi(\boldsymbol{X}) = \operatorname{tr} \boldsymbol{X}'\boldsymbol{X},$$
$$\boldsymbol{f}(x) = (x, x^2)', \quad \boldsymbol{f}(\boldsymbol{x}) = \boldsymbol{A}\boldsymbol{x}, \quad \boldsymbol{f}(\boldsymbol{X}) = \boldsymbol{X}\boldsymbol{a},$$
$$\boldsymbol{F}(x) = x^2\boldsymbol{I}_m, \quad \boldsymbol{F}(\boldsymbol{x}) = \boldsymbol{x}\boldsymbol{x}', \quad \boldsymbol{F}(\boldsymbol{X}) = \boldsymbol{X}'.$$

There is a possibility of confusion between the $'$ sign for derivative and transpose. Thus, the vector $\boldsymbol{f}(\boldsymbol{x})'$ will denote the transpose of $\boldsymbol{f}(\boldsymbol{x})$, while $\boldsymbol{f}'(\boldsymbol{x})$ will denote its derivative, and the same for scalar and matrix functions. However, we try and avoid the use of the $'$ sign for derivatives of vector or matrix functions.

Note carefully that all functions and variables in this chapter are real; that is, we only consider real-valued functions φ, $\boldsymbol{f}$, and $\boldsymbol{F}$ defined on a subset of $\mathbb{R}$, $\mathbb{R}^n$, or $\mathbb{R}^{n\times q}$. Special care needs to be taken when differentiating complex functions or real functions of complex variables, and we will not deal with these problems in this chapter.

In the one-dimensional case, the equation

$$\lim_{u\to 0} \frac{\varphi(x+u) - \varphi(x)}{u} = \varphi'(x)$$

defines the derivative of φ at x. Rewriting the equation gives

$$\varphi(x+u) = \varphi(x) + \varphi'(x)u + r_x(u),$$

where the remainder term $r_x(u)$ satisfies $r_x(u)/u \to 0$ as $u \to 0$. We now define the (first) differential of φ at x (with increment u) as $\mathrm{d}\varphi(x; u) = \varphi'(x)u$. For example, for $\varphi(x) = x^2$, we obtain $\mathrm{d}\varphi(x; u) = 2xu$. In practice we write $\mathrm{d}x$ instead of u, so that $\mathrm{d}\varphi(x) = \varphi'(x)\,\mathrm{d}x$ and, in the case $\varphi(x) = x^2$, $\mathrm{d}\varphi(x) = 2x\,\mathrm{d}x$. The double use of the symbol "d" requires careful justification, which is not provided in this chapter.

In the vector case we have

$$\boldsymbol{f}(\boldsymbol{x}+\boldsymbol{u}) = \boldsymbol{f}(\boldsymbol{x}) + (\mathrm{D}\boldsymbol{f}(\boldsymbol{x}))\boldsymbol{u} + \boldsymbol{r}_{\boldsymbol{x}}(\boldsymbol{u})$$

and the (first) differential is defined as $\mathrm{d}\boldsymbol{f}(\boldsymbol{x}; \boldsymbol{u}) = (\mathrm{D}\boldsymbol{f}(\boldsymbol{x}))\boldsymbol{u}$. The matrix case is obtained from the vector case by writing $\boldsymbol{f} := \operatorname{vec} \boldsymbol{F}$ and $\boldsymbol{x} := \operatorname{vec} \boldsymbol{X}$.

We need three crucial results: two identification results and one invariance result. The first identification result shows that the first derivative can be obtained (identified) from the first differential. We have

$$\mathrm{d}\boldsymbol{f}(\boldsymbol{x}) = \boldsymbol{A}(\boldsymbol{x})\,\mathrm{d}\boldsymbol{x} \iff \mathrm{D}\boldsymbol{f}(\boldsymbol{x}) = \boldsymbol{A}(\boldsymbol{x}),$$

where $\boldsymbol{A}(\boldsymbol{x})$, as the notation indicates, will in general depend on $\boldsymbol{x}$. More generally,

$$\mathrm{d}\operatorname{vec} \boldsymbol{F}(\boldsymbol{X}) = \boldsymbol{A}(\boldsymbol{X})\,\mathrm{d}\operatorname{vec} \boldsymbol{X} \iff \mathrm{D}\boldsymbol{F}(\boldsymbol{X}) = \boldsymbol{A}(\boldsymbol{X}). \tag{13.3}$$

For example, when $\varphi(\boldsymbol{x}) = \boldsymbol{x}'\boldsymbol{A}\boldsymbol{x}$ ($\boldsymbol{A} = \boldsymbol{A}'$), then $\mathrm{d}\varphi = 2\boldsymbol{x}'\boldsymbol{A}\,\mathrm{d}\boldsymbol{x}$. Hence, $\mathrm{D}\varphi(\boldsymbol{x}) = 2\boldsymbol{x}'\boldsymbol{A}$.

The second identification result shows that the second derivative can be obtained (identified) from the second differential. We have

$$\mathrm{d}^2\varphi(\boldsymbol{x}) = (\mathrm{d}\boldsymbol{x})'\boldsymbol{B}(\boldsymbol{x})\,\mathrm{d}\boldsymbol{x} \iff \mathrm{H}\varphi(\boldsymbol{x}) = \frac{1}{2}(\boldsymbol{B}(\boldsymbol{x}) + \boldsymbol{B}(\boldsymbol{x})'), \tag{13.4}$$

where $\mathrm{H}\varphi(\boldsymbol{x})$ denotes the *Hessian matrix* with typical element $\partial^2\varphi/\partial x_i \partial x_j$. Notice that we present (13.4) only for scalar functions. It is possible to extend the result to vector functions and matrix functions, but this is seldom required. For example, when $\varphi(\boldsymbol{x}) = \boldsymbol{x}'\boldsymbol{A}\boldsymbol{x}$ $(\boldsymbol{A} = \boldsymbol{A}')$, then $\mathrm{d}\varphi = 2\boldsymbol{x}'\boldsymbol{A}\,\mathrm{d}\boldsymbol{x}$ and

$$\mathrm{d}^2\varphi = 2\,\mathrm{d}\big(\boldsymbol{x}'\boldsymbol{A}\,\mathrm{d}\boldsymbol{x}\big) = 2(\mathrm{d}\boldsymbol{x})'\boldsymbol{A}\,\mathrm{d}\boldsymbol{x} + 2\boldsymbol{x}'\boldsymbol{A}\,\mathrm{d}^2\boldsymbol{x} = 2(\mathrm{d}\boldsymbol{x})'\boldsymbol{A}\,\mathrm{d}\boldsymbol{x},$$

because $\mathrm{d}^2\boldsymbol{x} = \boldsymbol{0}$, since $\boldsymbol{x}$ (trivially) is a linear function of $\boldsymbol{x}$. Hence, $\mathrm{H}\varphi(\boldsymbol{x}) = 2\boldsymbol{A}$. In this case the matrix $\boldsymbol{B} = 2\boldsymbol{A}$ is symmetric but this need not be the case in general. The Hessian matrix, however, *must* be symmetric, so we have to make it symmetric, as in (13.4).

The invariance result is essentially the chain rule. The chain rule tells us that the derivative of a composite function $h(x) = g(f(x))$ is given by

$$\mathrm{D}h(x) = \mathrm{D}g(f(x))\,\mathrm{D}f(x).$$

The equivalent result for differentials is called *Cauchy's rule of invariance*, and states that

$$\mathrm{d}h(x; u) = \mathrm{d}g(f(x); \mathrm{d}f(x; u)).$$

This looks more complicated than it is. For example, when $\varphi(x) = \sin x^2$, we can take $g(y) = \sin y$ and $f(x) = x^2$, so that $\mathrm{D}\varphi(x) = (\cos x^2)(2x)$. The differential is

$$\mathrm{d}\varphi = (\cos x^2)\,\mathrm{d}x^2 = (\cos x^2)(2x\,\mathrm{d}x).$$

Cauchy's rule thus allows sequential determination of the differential.

Special care needs to be taken when dealing with the second differential and the Hessian matrix of composite functions. Cauchy's invariance result is not applicable here. For example, if $\varphi(y) = \sin y$, then $\mathrm{d}\varphi = (\cos y)\,\mathrm{d}y$ and

$$\mathrm{d}^2\varphi = \mathrm{d}((\cos y)\,\mathrm{d}y) = (\mathrm{d}\cos y)\,\mathrm{d}y + (\cos y)\,\mathrm{d}^2y = -(\sin y)(\mathrm{d}y)^2,$$

because $\mathrm{d}^2y = 0$. However, if we are now told that $y = x^2$, then it is still true, by Cauchy's invariance rule, that $\mathrm{d}\varphi = (\cos y)\,\mathrm{d}x^2 = 2x(\cos x^2)\,\mathrm{d}x$, but for the second differential we have $\mathrm{d}^2\varphi \neq -(\sin y)(\mathrm{d}x^2)^2 = -4x^2(\sin x^2)(\mathrm{d}x)^2$. The reason is that d^2y is no longer zero. There exists a chain rule for Hessian matrices, but in practice the simplest and safest procedure is to go back to the first differential. Then,

$$\begin{aligned}\mathrm{d}^2\varphi &= \mathrm{d}((\cos y)\,\mathrm{d}y) = -(\sin y)(\mathrm{d}y)^2 + (\cos y)\,\mathrm{d}^2y \\ &= -(\sin x^2)(\mathrm{d}x^2)^2 + (\cos x^2)\,\mathrm{d}^2x^2 = -4(\sin x^2)(x\,\mathrm{d}x)^2 + 2(\cos x^2)(\mathrm{d}x)^2 \\ &= \left(-4x^2\sin x^2 + 2\cos x^2\right)(\mathrm{d}x)^2.\end{aligned}$$

This works in precisely the same way for vector and matrix functions.

A major use of matrix calculus is in problems of optimization. Suppose we wish to minimize a scalar function $\varphi(\boldsymbol{X})$. We compute

$$\mathrm{d}\varphi = \sum_{ij} \frac{\partial \varphi}{\partial x_{ij}} \mathrm{d}x_{ij} = \operatorname{tr} \boldsymbol{A}' \mathrm{d}\boldsymbol{X},$$

where $\boldsymbol{A}$ will in general depend on $\boldsymbol{X}$, unless the function is linear. The first-order condition is thus $\boldsymbol{A}(\boldsymbol{X}) = \mathbf{O}$. In order to verify that the solution is a (local or global) minimum, various conditions are available. We only mention that if $\mathrm{d}^2\varphi \geq 0$, then φ is convex, and hence φ has a global minimum at the point where $\mathrm{d}\varphi = 0$; and, if $\mathrm{d}^2\varphi > 0$ for all $\mathrm{d}\boldsymbol{X} \neq \mathbf{O}$, then φ is *strictly* convex, so that φ has a strict global minimum at $\mathrm{d}\varphi = 0$.

More difficult is constrained optimization. This usually takes the form of minimizing $\varphi(\boldsymbol{X})$ subject to a matrix constraint $\boldsymbol{G}(\boldsymbol{X}) = \mathbf{O}$. We then define the Lagrangian function

$$\psi(\boldsymbol{X}) = \varphi(\boldsymbol{X}) - \operatorname{tr} \boldsymbol{L}'\boldsymbol{G}(\boldsymbol{X}),$$

where $\boldsymbol{L}$ is a matrix of Lagrange multipliers. (If $\boldsymbol{G}(\boldsymbol{X})$ happens to be symmetric, we may take $\boldsymbol{L}$ symmetric too.) If ψ is (strictly) convex, then φ has a (strict) global minimum at the point where $\mathrm{d}\psi = 0$ under the constraint $\boldsymbol{G}(\boldsymbol{X}) = \mathbf{O}$. The simplest case where this occurs is when φ is (strictly) convex and all constraints are linear.

In the first seven sections of this chapter we practice the use of the first differential and the first derivative. First we practice with the use of differentials (Section 13.1), then we discuss simple scalar, vector, and matrix functions (Sections 13.2–13.4), and then some more interesting functions: the inverse (Section 13.5), the exponential and logarithmic function (Section 13.6), and the determinant (Section 13.7).

The next two sections contain two important applications of matrix calculus. First, the evaluation of Jacobians. If $\boldsymbol{Y}$ is a one-to-one function of $\boldsymbol{X}$, then $\boldsymbol{J} := \partial \operatorname{vec} \boldsymbol{Y} / \partial (\operatorname{vec} \boldsymbol{X})'$ is the Jacobian matrix of the transformation and the absolute value of $\det(\boldsymbol{J})$ is the *Jacobian*. In Section 13.8 we show how matrix calculus can be used to obtain Jacobians, also (and in particular) when the matrix argument is symmetric. A second application is sensitivity analysis. Here we typically ask how an estimator or predictor changes with respect to small changes in some of its components, for example, how the OLS estimator $\hat{\boldsymbol{\beta}} := (\boldsymbol{X}'\boldsymbol{X})^{-1}\boldsymbol{X}'\boldsymbol{y}$ changes with ("is sensitive to") small perturbations in $\boldsymbol{X}$. In Section 13.9 several examples demonstrate this approach.

Up to this point we did not need the second differential and the Hessian matrix. These are developed in Section 13.10.

Two further applications of matrix calculus are presented in the final three sections. Our third application is (constrained) optimization, which we demonstrate with least-squares problems, best linear (and quadratic) unbiased estimation (Section 13.11), and some simple maximum likelihood cases (Section 13.12). Finally, we consider inequalities. Every inequality can be considered as an optimization problem, because showing that $\varphi(\boldsymbol{x}) \geq 0$ for all $\boldsymbol{x}$ in S is equivalent to showing that the minimum of $\varphi(\boldsymbol{x})$ over all $\boldsymbol{x}$ in S is equal to zero. Thus, matrix calculus can often be fruitfully applied in proving inequalities (and even equalities, see Exercise 13.69).

13.1 Basic properties of differentials

Exercise 13.1 (Sum rules of differential) Let α be a constant, $\boldsymbol{A}$ a matrix of constants, and let $\boldsymbol{F}$ and $\boldsymbol{G}$ be two matrix functions of the same order. Show that:
(a) $\mathrm{d}\boldsymbol{A} = \mathbf{O}$;
(b) $\mathrm{d}(\alpha \boldsymbol{F}) = \alpha \, \mathrm{d}\boldsymbol{F}$;
(c) $\mathrm{d}(\boldsymbol{F} + \boldsymbol{G}) = \mathrm{d}\boldsymbol{F} + \mathrm{d}\boldsymbol{G}$;
(d) $\mathrm{d}(\boldsymbol{F} - \boldsymbol{G}) = \mathrm{d}\boldsymbol{F} - \mathrm{d}\boldsymbol{G}$;
(e) $\mathrm{d}\,\mathrm{tr}\,\boldsymbol{F} = \mathrm{tr}(\mathrm{d}\boldsymbol{F})$ ($\boldsymbol{F}$ square).

Solution
(a) Let $\varphi(x) := \alpha$ be a constant scalar function. Then its derivative $\varphi'(x)$ is zero, and hence $\mathrm{d}\varphi = \varphi'(x)\,\mathrm{d}x = 0$. The same holds for the matrix function, because the differential of a matrix is a matrix of differentials.
(b) This follows from the scalar result that $\mathrm{d}(\alpha\varphi(x)) = \alpha\,\mathrm{d}\varphi(x)$.
(c) Let us formally prove the case of a scalar function of a vector. Let $\varphi(\boldsymbol{x}) := f(\boldsymbol{x}) + g(\boldsymbol{x})$. Then,

$$\begin{aligned}
\mathrm{d}\varphi(\boldsymbol{x};\boldsymbol{u}) &= \sum_j u_j \mathrm{D}_j \varphi(\boldsymbol{x}) = \sum_j u_j \left(\mathrm{D}_j f(\boldsymbol{x}) + \mathrm{D}_j g(\boldsymbol{x})\right) \\
&= \sum_j u_j \mathrm{D}_j f(\boldsymbol{x}) + \sum_j u_j \mathrm{D}_j g(\boldsymbol{x}) = \mathrm{d}f(\boldsymbol{x};\boldsymbol{u}) + \mathrm{d}g(\boldsymbol{x};\boldsymbol{u}).
\end{aligned}$$

The matrix case then follows immediately.
(d)–(e) These are proved similarly. Since the derivative of a sum is the sum of the derivatives (linearity), the same holds for differentials.

Exercise 13.2 (Permutations of linear operators) For any matrix function $\boldsymbol{F}$, show that:
(a) $\mathrm{d}(\boldsymbol{F}') = (\mathrm{d}\boldsymbol{F})'$;
(b) $\mathrm{d}(\mathrm{vec}\,\boldsymbol{F}) = \mathrm{vec}(\mathrm{d}\boldsymbol{F})$.

Solution
Both results follow from the fact that the differential of a vector (matrix) is the vector (matrix) of differentials.

Exercise 13.3 (Product rules of differential) For any two conformable matrix functions $\boldsymbol{F}$ and $\boldsymbol{G}$, show that:
(a) $\mathrm{d}(\boldsymbol{F}\boldsymbol{G}) = (\mathrm{d}\boldsymbol{F})\boldsymbol{G} + \boldsymbol{F}(\mathrm{d}\boldsymbol{G})$;
(b) $\mathrm{d}(\boldsymbol{F} \otimes \boldsymbol{G}) = (\mathrm{d}\boldsymbol{F}) \otimes \boldsymbol{G} + \boldsymbol{F} \otimes (\mathrm{d}\boldsymbol{G})$.

Solution
(a) We have

$$\begin{aligned}(\mathrm{d}(\boldsymbol{F}\boldsymbol{G}))_{ij} &= \mathrm{d}(\boldsymbol{F}\boldsymbol{G})_{ij} = \mathrm{d}\sum_k f_{ik}g_{kj} = \sum_k \mathrm{d}(f_{ik}g_{kj})\\ &= \sum_k ((\mathrm{d}f_{ik})g_{kj} + f_{ik}\,\mathrm{d}g_{kj}) = \sum_k (\mathrm{d}f_{ik})g_{kj} + \sum_k f_{ik}\,\mathrm{d}g_{kj}\\ &= ((\mathrm{d}\boldsymbol{F})\boldsymbol{G})_{ij} + (\boldsymbol{F}\,\mathrm{d}\boldsymbol{G})_{ij}.\end{aligned}$$

(b) For a typical element of $\boldsymbol{F}\otimes\boldsymbol{G}$, say $f_{ij}g_{st}$, we have

$$\mathrm{d}(f_{ij}g_{st}) = (\mathrm{d}f_{ij})g_{st} + f_{ij}\,\mathrm{d}g_{st},$$

and the result follows.

13.2 Scalar functions

Exercise 13.4 (Linear, quadratic, and bilinear forms, vectors) Let $\boldsymbol{a}$ be a vector of constants and $\boldsymbol{A}$ a matrix of constants. Obtain the differential $\mathrm{d}\varphi$ and the derivative $\mathrm{D}\varphi$ of the following scalar functions:
(a) $\varphi(\boldsymbol{x}) := \boldsymbol{a}'\boldsymbol{x}$;
(b) $\varphi(\boldsymbol{x}) := \boldsymbol{x}'\boldsymbol{A}\boldsymbol{x}$;
(c) $\varphi(\boldsymbol{x}_1,\boldsymbol{x}_2) := \boldsymbol{x}_1'\boldsymbol{A}\boldsymbol{x}_2$, a *bilinear form* in $\boldsymbol{x}_1$ and $\boldsymbol{x}_2$.

Solution
(a) From $\mathrm{d}\varphi = \boldsymbol{a}'\,\mathrm{d}\boldsymbol{x}$, it follows that $\mathrm{D}\varphi = \boldsymbol{a}'$.
(b) We have $\mathrm{d}\varphi = (\mathrm{d}\boldsymbol{x})'\boldsymbol{A}\boldsymbol{x} + \boldsymbol{x}'\boldsymbol{A}\,\mathrm{d}\boldsymbol{x} = \boldsymbol{x}'(\boldsymbol{A}+\boldsymbol{A}')\,\mathrm{d}\boldsymbol{x}$, and hence $\mathrm{D}\varphi = \boldsymbol{x}'(\boldsymbol{A}+\boldsymbol{A}')$. In quadratic forms there is no loss in generality if we take the matrix to be symmetric. If $\boldsymbol{A}$ is symmetric, the derivative reduces to $\mathrm{D}\varphi = 2\boldsymbol{x}'\boldsymbol{A}$, which agrees with the scalar case $\varphi(x) := ax^2$ with derivative $\mathrm{D}\varphi = 2ax$. (In general, it is a good idea to check vector and matrix derivatives with the scalar case.) The reason why we present also the derivative for the general, nonsymmetric case is that it is sometimes unpractical to first rewrite the quadratic form in its symmetric version.
(c) Let $\boldsymbol{x} := (\boldsymbol{x}_1', \boldsymbol{x}_2')'$. Then,

$$\begin{aligned}\mathrm{d}\varphi &= (\mathrm{d}\boldsymbol{x}_1)'\boldsymbol{A}\boldsymbol{x}_2 + \boldsymbol{x}_1'\boldsymbol{A}\,\mathrm{d}\boldsymbol{x}_2 = \boldsymbol{x}_2'\boldsymbol{A}'\,\mathrm{d}\boldsymbol{x}_1 + \boldsymbol{x}_1'\boldsymbol{A}\,\mathrm{d}\boldsymbol{x}_2\\ &= (\boldsymbol{x}_1', \boldsymbol{x}_2')\begin{pmatrix}\mathbf{O} & \boldsymbol{A}\\ \boldsymbol{A}' & \mathbf{O}\end{pmatrix}\begin{pmatrix}\mathrm{d}\boldsymbol{x}_1\\ \mathrm{d}\boldsymbol{x}_2\end{pmatrix} = \boldsymbol{x}'\boldsymbol{C}\,\mathrm{d}\boldsymbol{x}, \quad \text{where } \boldsymbol{C} := \begin{pmatrix}\mathbf{O} & \boldsymbol{A}\\ \boldsymbol{A}' & \mathbf{O}\end{pmatrix},\end{aligned}$$

implying that

$$\mathrm{D}\varphi = \partial\varphi/\partial\boldsymbol{x}' = \boldsymbol{x}'\boldsymbol{C} = (\boldsymbol{x}_2'\boldsymbol{A}' : \boldsymbol{x}_1'\boldsymbol{A}).$$

Exercise 13.5 (On the unit sphere) If $\boldsymbol{x}'\boldsymbol{x} = 1$ on an open subset S in $\mathbb{R}^n$, show that $\boldsymbol{x}'\,\mathrm{d}\boldsymbol{x} = 0$ on S.

Solution
If $\boldsymbol{x}'\boldsymbol{x} = 1$ at $\boldsymbol{x}$ *and* in a neighborhood of $\boldsymbol{x}$, then

$$0 = \mathrm{d}(\boldsymbol{x}'\boldsymbol{x}) = (\mathrm{d}\boldsymbol{x})'\boldsymbol{x} + \boldsymbol{x}'\,\mathrm{d}\boldsymbol{x} = 2\boldsymbol{x}'\,\mathrm{d}\boldsymbol{x},$$

and the result follows.

Exercise 13.6 (Bilinear and quadratic forms, matrices) Let $\boldsymbol{a}$ and $\boldsymbol{b}$ be two vectors of constants. Find the differential and derivative of the following scalar functions:
(a) $\varphi(\boldsymbol{X}) = \boldsymbol{a}'\boldsymbol{X}\boldsymbol{b}$, a bilinear form in $\boldsymbol{a}$ and $\boldsymbol{b}$;
(b) $\varphi(\boldsymbol{X}) = \boldsymbol{a}'\boldsymbol{X}\boldsymbol{X}'\boldsymbol{a}$;
(c) $\varphi(\boldsymbol{X}) = \boldsymbol{a}'\boldsymbol{X}'\boldsymbol{X}\boldsymbol{a}$.

Solution
(a) The differential is simply $\mathrm{d}\varphi = \boldsymbol{a}'(\mathrm{d}\boldsymbol{X})\boldsymbol{b}$. To obtain the derivative we have to write $\mathrm{d}\varphi = (\operatorname{vec}\boldsymbol{A})'\,\mathrm{d}\operatorname{vec}\boldsymbol{X}$ for some matrix $\boldsymbol{A}$. Hence, we rewrite $\mathrm{d}\varphi$ as

$$\mathrm{d}\varphi = \boldsymbol{a}'(\mathrm{d}\boldsymbol{X})\boldsymbol{b} = (\boldsymbol{b}' \otimes \boldsymbol{a}')\,\mathrm{d}\operatorname{vec}\boldsymbol{X}$$

with derivative

$$\mathrm{D}\varphi(\boldsymbol{X}) = \frac{\partial\varphi}{\partial(\operatorname{vec}\boldsymbol{X})'} = (\boldsymbol{b} \otimes \boldsymbol{a})'.$$

(b) We have

$$\begin{aligned}\mathrm{d}\varphi &= \boldsymbol{a}'(\mathrm{d}\boldsymbol{X})\boldsymbol{X}'\boldsymbol{a} + \boldsymbol{a}'\boldsymbol{X}(\mathrm{d}\boldsymbol{X})'\boldsymbol{a} = 2\boldsymbol{a}'(\mathrm{d}\boldsymbol{X})\boldsymbol{X}'\boldsymbol{a}\\ &= 2(\boldsymbol{a}'\boldsymbol{X} \otimes \boldsymbol{a}')\,\mathrm{d}\operatorname{vec}\boldsymbol{X},\end{aligned}$$

so that

$$\mathrm{D}\varphi(\boldsymbol{X}) = \frac{\partial\varphi(\boldsymbol{X})}{\partial(\operatorname{vec}\boldsymbol{X})'} = 2(\boldsymbol{X}'\boldsymbol{a} \otimes \boldsymbol{a})'.$$

(c) Similarly,

$$\mathrm{d}\varphi = \boldsymbol{a}'(\mathrm{d}\boldsymbol{X})'\boldsymbol{X}\boldsymbol{a} + \boldsymbol{a}'\boldsymbol{X}'(\mathrm{d}\boldsymbol{X})\boldsymbol{a} = 2\boldsymbol{a}'\boldsymbol{X}'(\mathrm{d}\boldsymbol{X})\boldsymbol{a} = 2(\boldsymbol{a}' \otimes \boldsymbol{a}'\boldsymbol{X}')\,\mathrm{d}\operatorname{vec}\boldsymbol{X},$$

yielding $\mathrm{D}\varphi(\boldsymbol{X}) = 2(\boldsymbol{a} \otimes \boldsymbol{X}\boldsymbol{a})'$.

Exercise 13.7 (Differential and trace) For a scalar function φ with differential $\mathrm{d}\varphi = \operatorname{tr}(\boldsymbol{A}'\,\mathrm{d}\boldsymbol{X})$, show that $\mathrm{D}\varphi(\boldsymbol{X}) = (\operatorname{vec}\boldsymbol{A})'$.

Solution
This is a very useful property, and simple to prove:

$$\mathrm{d}\varphi = \operatorname{tr}\boldsymbol{A}'\,\mathrm{d}\boldsymbol{X} = (\operatorname{vec}\boldsymbol{A})'\,\mathrm{d}\operatorname{vec}\boldsymbol{X} \iff \mathrm{D}\varphi(\boldsymbol{X}) = (\operatorname{vec}\boldsymbol{A})'.$$

Exercise 13.8 (Trace of powers, 1) Use Exercise 13.7 to obtain the differential and derivative of:
(a) $\varphi(\boldsymbol{X}) := \operatorname{tr}\boldsymbol{X}$;

(b) $\varphi(\boldsymbol{X}) := \operatorname{tr} \boldsymbol{X}^2$;
(c) $\varphi(\boldsymbol{X}) := \operatorname{tr} \boldsymbol{X}^p$.

Solution
(a) First,

$$\mathrm{d}\varphi = \mathrm{d}(\operatorname{tr} \boldsymbol{X}) = \operatorname{tr}(\mathrm{d}\boldsymbol{X}) = \operatorname{tr}(\boldsymbol{I}\,\mathrm{d}\boldsymbol{X}) \implies \mathrm{D}\varphi = (\operatorname{vec} \boldsymbol{I})'.$$

(b) Next,

$$\mathrm{d}\varphi = \mathrm{d}\operatorname{tr} \boldsymbol{X}^2 = \operatorname{tr}(\mathrm{d}\boldsymbol{X})\boldsymbol{X} + \operatorname{tr} \boldsymbol{X}\,\mathrm{d}\boldsymbol{X} = 2\operatorname{tr} \boldsymbol{X}\,\mathrm{d}\boldsymbol{X} \implies \mathrm{D}\varphi = 2(\operatorname{vec} \boldsymbol{X}')'.$$

(Notice the transpose of $\boldsymbol{X}$. This corresponds to the rule in Exercise 13.7 and also to the fact that $\partial \operatorname{tr} \boldsymbol{X}^2/\partial x_{ij} = 2x_{ji}$.)
(c) Finally,

$$\begin{aligned}\mathrm{d}\varphi &= \operatorname{tr} \boldsymbol{X}^p = \operatorname{tr}(\mathrm{d}\boldsymbol{X})\boldsymbol{X}^{p-1} + \operatorname{tr} \boldsymbol{X}(\mathrm{d}\boldsymbol{X})\boldsymbol{X}^{p-2} + \cdots + \operatorname{tr} \boldsymbol{X}^{p-1}(\mathrm{d}\boldsymbol{X}) \\ &= p\operatorname{tr} \boldsymbol{X}^{p-1}\,\mathrm{d}\boldsymbol{X},\end{aligned}$$

implying that

$$\mathrm{D}\varphi = p(\operatorname{vec}(\boldsymbol{X}')^{p-1})'.$$

Exercise 13.9 (Trace of powers, 2) Find the differential and derivative of:
(a) $\varphi(\boldsymbol{X}) := \operatorname{tr} \boldsymbol{X}'\boldsymbol{X}$;
(b) $\varphi(\boldsymbol{X}) := \operatorname{tr}(\boldsymbol{X}'\boldsymbol{X})^p$;
(c) $\varphi(\boldsymbol{X}) := \operatorname{tr}(\boldsymbol{X}\boldsymbol{X}')^p$.
(d) What is the difference between the derivatives in (c) and (b)?

Solution
(a) From

$$\mathrm{d}\varphi = \operatorname{tr}(\mathrm{d}\boldsymbol{X})'\boldsymbol{X} + \operatorname{tr} \boldsymbol{X}'\,\mathrm{d}\boldsymbol{X} = 2\operatorname{tr} \boldsymbol{X}'\,\mathrm{d}\boldsymbol{X}$$

it follows that $\mathrm{D}\varphi(\boldsymbol{X}) = 2(\operatorname{vec} \boldsymbol{X})'$.
(b) More generally,

$$\begin{aligned}\mathrm{d}\varphi &= \operatorname{tr}(\mathrm{d}(\boldsymbol{X}'\boldsymbol{X}))(\boldsymbol{X}'\boldsymbol{X})^{p-1} + \cdots + \operatorname{tr}(\boldsymbol{X}'\boldsymbol{X})^{p-1}\,\mathrm{d}(\boldsymbol{X}'\boldsymbol{X}) \\ &= p\operatorname{tr}(\boldsymbol{X}'\boldsymbol{X})^{p-1}\,\mathrm{d}(\boldsymbol{X}'\boldsymbol{X}) = p\operatorname{tr}(\boldsymbol{X}'\boldsymbol{X})^{p-1}(\mathrm{d}\boldsymbol{X})'\boldsymbol{X} + p\operatorname{tr}(\boldsymbol{X}'\boldsymbol{X})^{p-1}\boldsymbol{X}'\,\mathrm{d}\boldsymbol{X} \\ &= 2p\operatorname{tr}(\boldsymbol{X}'\boldsymbol{X})^{p-1}\boldsymbol{X}'\,\mathrm{d}\boldsymbol{X},\end{aligned}$$

with derivative

$$\mathrm{D}\varphi(\boldsymbol{X}) = 2p(\operatorname{vec} \boldsymbol{X}(\boldsymbol{X}'\boldsymbol{X})^{p-1})'.$$

(c) Similarly,

$$\mathrm{d}\varphi = p\operatorname{tr}(\boldsymbol{X}\boldsymbol{X}')^{p-1}(\mathrm{d}\boldsymbol{X}\boldsymbol{X}') = 2p\operatorname{tr} \boldsymbol{X}'(\boldsymbol{X}\boldsymbol{X}')^{p-1}\,\mathrm{d}\boldsymbol{X}$$

implies

$$\mathrm{D}\varphi(\boldsymbol{X}) = 2p(\operatorname{vec}(\boldsymbol{X}\boldsymbol{X}')^{p-1}\boldsymbol{X})'.$$

(d) There is no difference between the two derivatives, because

$$\operatorname{tr}(\boldsymbol{X}'\boldsymbol{X})^p = \operatorname{tr}(\boldsymbol{X}'\boldsymbol{X})\cdots(\boldsymbol{X}'\boldsymbol{X}) = \operatorname{tr}\boldsymbol{X}'(\boldsymbol{X}\boldsymbol{X}')\cdots(\boldsymbol{X}\boldsymbol{X}')\boldsymbol{X} = \operatorname{tr}(\boldsymbol{X}\boldsymbol{X}')^p$$

and

$$\boldsymbol{X}(\boldsymbol{X}'\boldsymbol{X})^{p-1} = \boldsymbol{X}(\boldsymbol{X}'\boldsymbol{X})\cdots(\boldsymbol{X}'\boldsymbol{X}) = (\boldsymbol{X}\boldsymbol{X}')\cdots(\boldsymbol{X}\boldsymbol{X}')\boldsymbol{X} = (\boldsymbol{X}\boldsymbol{X}')^{p-1}\boldsymbol{X}.$$

Exercise 13.10 (Linear and quadratic matrix forms) Let $\boldsymbol{A}$ and $\boldsymbol{B}$ be two matrices of constants. Find the differential and derivative of:
(a) $\varphi(\boldsymbol{X}) := \operatorname{tr}\boldsymbol{A}\boldsymbol{X}$;
(b) $\varphi(\boldsymbol{X}) := \operatorname{tr}\boldsymbol{X}\boldsymbol{A}\boldsymbol{X}'\boldsymbol{B}$;
(c) $\varphi(\boldsymbol{X}) := \operatorname{tr}\boldsymbol{X}\boldsymbol{A}\boldsymbol{X}\boldsymbol{B}$.

Solution
(a) From $\mathrm{d}\varphi = \operatorname{tr}\boldsymbol{A}\,\mathrm{d}\boldsymbol{X}$, we find $\mathrm{D}\varphi(\boldsymbol{X}) = (\operatorname{vec}\boldsymbol{A}')'$, in accordance with Exercise 13.7.
(b) From

$$\begin{aligned}\mathrm{d}\varphi &= \operatorname{tr}(\mathrm{d}\boldsymbol{X})\boldsymbol{A}\boldsymbol{X}'\boldsymbol{B} + \operatorname{tr}\boldsymbol{X}\boldsymbol{A}(\mathrm{d}\boldsymbol{X})'\boldsymbol{B} = \operatorname{tr}\boldsymbol{A}\boldsymbol{X}'\boldsymbol{B}\,\mathrm{d}\boldsymbol{X} + \operatorname{tr}\boldsymbol{A}'\boldsymbol{X}'\boldsymbol{B}'(\mathrm{d}\boldsymbol{X})\\ &= \operatorname{tr}(\boldsymbol{A}\boldsymbol{X}'\boldsymbol{B} + \boldsymbol{A}'\boldsymbol{X}'\boldsymbol{B}')\,\mathrm{d}\boldsymbol{X},\end{aligned}$$

we obtain

$$\mathrm{D}\varphi(\boldsymbol{X}) = (\operatorname{vec}(\boldsymbol{B}'\boldsymbol{X}\boldsymbol{A}' + \boldsymbol{B}\boldsymbol{X}\boldsymbol{A}))'.$$

(c) And,

$$\mathrm{d}\varphi = \operatorname{tr}(\mathrm{d}\boldsymbol{X})\boldsymbol{A}\boldsymbol{X}\boldsymbol{B} + \operatorname{tr}\boldsymbol{X}\boldsymbol{A}(\mathrm{d}\boldsymbol{X})\boldsymbol{B} = \operatorname{tr}(\boldsymbol{A}\boldsymbol{X}\boldsymbol{B} + \boldsymbol{B}\boldsymbol{X}\boldsymbol{A})\,\mathrm{d}\boldsymbol{X}$$

yields

$$\mathrm{D}\varphi(\boldsymbol{X}) = \left(\operatorname{vec}(\boldsymbol{A}\boldsymbol{X}\boldsymbol{B} + \boldsymbol{B}\boldsymbol{X}\boldsymbol{A})'\right)'.$$

Exercise 13.11 (Sum of squares) Let $\varphi(\boldsymbol{X})$ be defined as the sum of the squares of all elements in $\boldsymbol{X}$. Obtain $\mathrm{d}\varphi$ and $\mathrm{D}\varphi$.

Solution
The trick here is to work with the *matrix* $\boldsymbol{X}$ rather than with the individual *elements* of $\boldsymbol{X}$. Thus we write

$$\varphi(\boldsymbol{X}) = \sum_i \sum_j x_{ij}^2 = \operatorname{tr}\boldsymbol{X}'\boldsymbol{X}$$

and hence $\mathrm{d}\varphi = 2\operatorname{tr}\boldsymbol{X}'\,\mathrm{d}\boldsymbol{X}$, and $\mathrm{D}\varphi(\boldsymbol{X}) = 2(\operatorname{vec}\boldsymbol{X})'$.

Exercise 13.12 (A selector function) Let $\varphi(\boldsymbol{X})$ be defined as the ij-th element of $\boldsymbol{X}^2$. Obtain $\mathrm{d}\varphi$ and $\mathrm{D}\varphi$.

Solution
As in Exercise 13.11, we want to work with the matrix $\boldsymbol{X}$, rather than with its elements. Let $\boldsymbol{e}_i$ denote the i-th unit vector, having 1 in its i-th position and zeros elsewhere. Then, $\varphi(\boldsymbol{X}) = \boldsymbol{e}_i'\boldsymbol{X}^2\boldsymbol{e}_j$ and

$$\mathrm{d}\varphi = \boldsymbol{e}_i'(\mathrm{d}\boldsymbol{X})\boldsymbol{X}\boldsymbol{e}_j + \boldsymbol{e}_i'\boldsymbol{X}(\mathrm{d}\boldsymbol{X})\boldsymbol{e}_j = \operatorname{tr}(\boldsymbol{X}\boldsymbol{e}_j\boldsymbol{e}_i' + \boldsymbol{e}_j\boldsymbol{e}_i'\boldsymbol{X})\,\mathrm{d}\boldsymbol{X},$$

so that the derivative takes the form

$$\mathrm{D}\varphi(\boldsymbol{X}) = (\operatorname{vec}(\boldsymbol{e}_i(\boldsymbol{X}\boldsymbol{e}_j)' + (\boldsymbol{X}'\boldsymbol{e}_i)\boldsymbol{e}_j'))' = (\operatorname{vec}(\boldsymbol{e}_i\boldsymbol{x}_{\bullet j}' + \boldsymbol{x}_{i\bullet}\boldsymbol{e}_j'))'.$$

13.3 Vector functions

Exercise 13.13 (Vector functions of a vector, 1) Obtain the differential and derivative of the vector functions:
(a) $\boldsymbol{f}(\boldsymbol{x}) := \boldsymbol{A}\boldsymbol{x}$ ($\boldsymbol{A}$ constant);
(b) $\boldsymbol{f}(\boldsymbol{x}) := \boldsymbol{A}\boldsymbol{g}(\boldsymbol{x})$ ($\boldsymbol{A}$ constant).
(c) What happens in (a) if the elements of $\boldsymbol{A}$ also depend on $\boldsymbol{x}$?

Solution
(a) Since $\mathrm{d}\boldsymbol{f} = \boldsymbol{A}\,\mathrm{d}\boldsymbol{x}$, we have $\mathrm{D}\boldsymbol{f}(\boldsymbol{x}) = \boldsymbol{A}$.
(b) Now we have

$$\mathrm{d}\boldsymbol{f} = \boldsymbol{A}\,\mathrm{d}\boldsymbol{g}(\boldsymbol{x}) = \boldsymbol{A}(\mathrm{D}\boldsymbol{g}(\boldsymbol{x}))\,\mathrm{d}\boldsymbol{x},$$

so that

$$\mathrm{D}\boldsymbol{f}(\boldsymbol{x}) = \boldsymbol{A}\mathrm{D}\boldsymbol{g}(\boldsymbol{x}).$$

(c) If $\boldsymbol{f}(\boldsymbol{x}) = \boldsymbol{A}(\boldsymbol{x})\boldsymbol{x}$, then

$$\begin{aligned}\mathrm{d}\boldsymbol{f} &= (\mathrm{d}\boldsymbol{A})\boldsymbol{x} + \boldsymbol{A}\,\mathrm{d}\boldsymbol{x} = (\boldsymbol{x}' \otimes \boldsymbol{I})\,\mathrm{d}\operatorname{vec}\boldsymbol{A} + \boldsymbol{A}\,\mathrm{d}\boldsymbol{x}\\ &= \left((\boldsymbol{x}' \otimes \boldsymbol{I})\frac{\partial \operatorname{vec}\boldsymbol{A}}{\partial \boldsymbol{x}'} + \boldsymbol{A}\right)\mathrm{d}\boldsymbol{x},\end{aligned}$$

implying that

$$\mathrm{D}\boldsymbol{f}(\boldsymbol{x}) = \frac{\partial \boldsymbol{f}(\boldsymbol{x})}{\partial \boldsymbol{x}'} = (\boldsymbol{x}' \otimes \boldsymbol{I})\frac{\partial \operatorname{vec}\boldsymbol{A}}{\partial \boldsymbol{x}'} + \boldsymbol{A}.$$

Exercise 13.14 (Vector functions of a vector, 2)
(a) Let $\boldsymbol{f}(\boldsymbol{x}) := (\boldsymbol{x}'\boldsymbol{x})\boldsymbol{a}$, where $\boldsymbol{a}$ is a vector of constants. Find the differential and derivative.
(b) What happens if $\boldsymbol{a}$ also depends on $\boldsymbol{x}$?

Solution
(a) From $\mathrm{d}\boldsymbol{f} = (2\boldsymbol{x}'\,\mathrm{d}\boldsymbol{x})\boldsymbol{a} = 2\boldsymbol{a}\boldsymbol{x}'\,\mathrm{d}\boldsymbol{x}$, we obtain $\mathrm{D}\boldsymbol{f}(\boldsymbol{x}) = 2\boldsymbol{a}\boldsymbol{x}'$.
(b) If $\boldsymbol{a} = \boldsymbol{a}(\boldsymbol{x})$, then

$$\begin{aligned}\mathrm{d}\boldsymbol{f} &= (\mathrm{d}\boldsymbol{x}'\boldsymbol{x})\boldsymbol{a} + (\boldsymbol{x}'\boldsymbol{x})\,\mathrm{d}\boldsymbol{a} = (2\boldsymbol{x}'\,\mathrm{d}\boldsymbol{x})\boldsymbol{a} + \boldsymbol{x}'\boldsymbol{x}(\mathrm{D}\boldsymbol{a}(\boldsymbol{x}))\,\mathrm{d}\boldsymbol{x}\\ &= (2\boldsymbol{a}\boldsymbol{x}' + \boldsymbol{x}'\boldsymbol{x}\mathrm{D}\boldsymbol{a}(\boldsymbol{x}))\,\mathrm{d}\boldsymbol{x}\end{aligned}$$

so that

$$\mathrm{D}\boldsymbol{f}(\boldsymbol{x}) = 2\boldsymbol{a}\boldsymbol{x}' + \boldsymbol{x}'\boldsymbol{x}\mathrm{D}\boldsymbol{a}(\boldsymbol{x}).$$

Exercise 13.15 (Vector functions of a matrix) Let $\boldsymbol{a}$ be a vector of constants. Find the differential and derivative of the vector functions:
(a) $\boldsymbol{f}(\boldsymbol{X}) := \boldsymbol{X}\boldsymbol{a}$;
(b) $\boldsymbol{f}(\boldsymbol{X}) := \boldsymbol{X}'\boldsymbol{a}$.

Solution
(a) We have

$$\mathrm{d}\boldsymbol{f} = (\mathrm{d}\boldsymbol{X})\boldsymbol{a} = (\boldsymbol{a}' \otimes \boldsymbol{I})\,\mathrm{d}\mathrm{vec}\,\boldsymbol{X},$$

and hence

$$\mathrm{D}\boldsymbol{f}(\boldsymbol{x}) = \frac{\partial \boldsymbol{f}(\boldsymbol{x})}{\partial(\mathrm{vec}\,\boldsymbol{X})'} = \boldsymbol{a}' \otimes \boldsymbol{I}.$$

(b) Similarly,

$$\begin{aligned}\mathrm{d}\boldsymbol{f} &= (\mathrm{d}\boldsymbol{X})'\boldsymbol{a} = \mathrm{vec}\left((\mathrm{d}\boldsymbol{X})'\boldsymbol{a}\right)\\ &= \mathrm{vec}\left(\boldsymbol{a}'\,\mathrm{d}\boldsymbol{X}\right) = (\boldsymbol{I} \otimes \boldsymbol{a}')\,\mathrm{d}\mathrm{vec}\,\boldsymbol{X},\end{aligned}$$

so that

$$\mathrm{D}\boldsymbol{f}(\boldsymbol{X}) = \boldsymbol{I} \otimes \boldsymbol{a}'.$$

13.4 Matrix functions

Exercise 13.16 (Matrix function of a vector) Obtain the differential and derivative of $\boldsymbol{F}(\boldsymbol{x}) := \boldsymbol{x}\boldsymbol{x}'$.

Solution
Since $\mathrm{d}\boldsymbol{F} = (\mathrm{d}\boldsymbol{x})\boldsymbol{x}' + \boldsymbol{x}(\mathrm{d}\boldsymbol{x})'$, we find

$$\mathrm{d}\mathrm{vec}\,\boldsymbol{F} = (\boldsymbol{x} \otimes \boldsymbol{I})\,\mathrm{d}\mathrm{vec}\,\boldsymbol{x} + (\boldsymbol{I} \otimes \boldsymbol{x})\,\mathrm{d}\mathrm{vec}\,\boldsymbol{x}' = (\boldsymbol{x} \otimes \boldsymbol{I} + \boldsymbol{I} \otimes \boldsymbol{x})\,\mathrm{d}\boldsymbol{x},$$

so that

$$\mathrm{D}\boldsymbol{F} = \frac{\partial\,\mathrm{vec}\,\boldsymbol{F}(\boldsymbol{x})}{\partial \boldsymbol{x}'} = \boldsymbol{x} \otimes \boldsymbol{I} + \boldsymbol{I} \otimes \boldsymbol{x}.$$

Exercise 13.17 (Linear matrix function of a matrix) What is the differential of the matrix function $\boldsymbol{F}(\boldsymbol{X}) := \boldsymbol{A}\boldsymbol{X}\boldsymbol{B}$, where $\boldsymbol{A}$ and $\boldsymbol{B}$ are two matrices of constants? What is the derivative?

Solution
From $\mathrm{d}\boldsymbol{F} = \boldsymbol{A}(\mathrm{d}\boldsymbol{X})\boldsymbol{B}$ we find, after vectorizing,

$$\mathrm{d}\operatorname{vec}\boldsymbol{F} = (\boldsymbol{B}' \otimes \boldsymbol{A})\,\mathrm{d}\operatorname{vec}\boldsymbol{X},$$

and hence

$$\mathrm{D}\boldsymbol{F}(\boldsymbol{X}) = \frac{\partial \operatorname{vec}\boldsymbol{F}(\boldsymbol{X})}{\partial(\operatorname{vec}\boldsymbol{X})'} = \boldsymbol{B}' \otimes \boldsymbol{A}.$$

Exercise 13.18 (Powers) Find the differential and derivative of the powers:
(a) $\boldsymbol{F}(\boldsymbol{X}) := \boldsymbol{X}$;
(b) $\boldsymbol{F}(\boldsymbol{X}) := \boldsymbol{X}^2$;
(c) $\boldsymbol{F}(\boldsymbol{X}) := \boldsymbol{X}^p$.

Solution
(a) Let $\boldsymbol{X}$ be an $m \times n$ matrix. Since $\mathrm{d}\boldsymbol{F} = \mathrm{d}\boldsymbol{X}$, we find $\mathrm{d}\operatorname{vec}\boldsymbol{F} = \mathrm{d}\operatorname{vec}\boldsymbol{X}$ and hence

$$\mathrm{D}\boldsymbol{F}(\boldsymbol{X}) = \frac{\partial \operatorname{vec}\boldsymbol{F}}{\partial(\operatorname{vec}\boldsymbol{X})'} = \boldsymbol{I}_{mn},$$

as of course we should.
(b) Let $\boldsymbol{X}$ be a square matrix of order n. Then,

$$\mathrm{d}\boldsymbol{F} = (\mathrm{d}\boldsymbol{X})\boldsymbol{X} + \boldsymbol{X}\,\mathrm{d}\boldsymbol{X},$$

and hence

$$\mathrm{d}\operatorname{vec}\boldsymbol{F} = (\boldsymbol{X}' \otimes \boldsymbol{I}_n + \boldsymbol{I}_n \otimes \boldsymbol{X})\,\mathrm{d}\operatorname{vec}\boldsymbol{X},$$

so that

$$\mathrm{D}\boldsymbol{F}(\boldsymbol{X}) = \frac{\partial \operatorname{vec}\boldsymbol{F}}{\partial(\operatorname{vec}\boldsymbol{X})'} = \boldsymbol{X}' \otimes \boldsymbol{I}_n + \boldsymbol{I}_n \otimes \boldsymbol{X}.$$

(c) Generalizing (b) gives

$$\mathrm{d}\boldsymbol{F} = (\mathrm{d}\boldsymbol{X})\boldsymbol{X}^{p-1} + \cdots + \boldsymbol{X}^{p-1}(\mathrm{d}\boldsymbol{X}) = \sum_{j=1}^{p} \boldsymbol{X}^{j-1}(\mathrm{d}\boldsymbol{X})\boldsymbol{X}^{p-j}.$$

Taking vecs,

$$\mathrm{d}\operatorname{vec}\boldsymbol{F} = \left(\sum_{j=1}^{p}(\boldsymbol{X}')^{p-j} \otimes \boldsymbol{X}^{j-1}\right)\mathrm{d}\operatorname{vec}\boldsymbol{X},$$

which leads to

$$\mathrm{D}\boldsymbol{F}(\boldsymbol{X}) = \sum_{j=1}^{p} (\boldsymbol{X}')^{p-j} \otimes \boldsymbol{X}^{j-1}.$$

Notice that $\mathrm{d}\boldsymbol{F}$ is equal to $\boldsymbol{C}\{\boldsymbol{X}^{p-1}, \mathrm{d}\boldsymbol{X}\}$ in the notation of Exercise 9.9, which is the term linear in $\mathrm{d}\boldsymbol{X}$ in the expansion of $(\boldsymbol{X} + \mathrm{d}\boldsymbol{X})^p - \boldsymbol{X}^p$.

Exercise 13.19 (Involving the transpose) If $\boldsymbol{X}$ is an $m \times n$ matrix, obtain the differential and derivative of:
(a) $\boldsymbol{F}(\boldsymbol{X}) := \boldsymbol{X}'$;
(b) $\boldsymbol{F}(\boldsymbol{X}) := \boldsymbol{X}'\boldsymbol{X}$;
(c) $\boldsymbol{F}(\boldsymbol{X}) := \boldsymbol{X}\boldsymbol{X}'$.

Solution
(a) Since $\mathrm{d}\boldsymbol{F} = (\mathrm{d}\boldsymbol{X})'$, we have

$$\mathrm{d}\operatorname{vec}\boldsymbol{F} = \mathrm{d}\operatorname{vec}\boldsymbol{X}' = \boldsymbol{K}_{mn}\,\mathrm{d}\operatorname{vec}\boldsymbol{X}$$

and hence $\mathrm{D}\boldsymbol{F}(\boldsymbol{X}) = \boldsymbol{K}_{mn}$, the commutation matrix.
(b) The differential is $\mathrm{d}\boldsymbol{F} = (\mathrm{d}\boldsymbol{X})'\boldsymbol{X} + \boldsymbol{X}'(\mathrm{d}\boldsymbol{X})$, so that

$$\begin{aligned}\mathrm{d}\operatorname{vec}\boldsymbol{F} &= (\boldsymbol{X}' \otimes \boldsymbol{I}_n)\,\mathrm{d}\operatorname{vec}\boldsymbol{X}' + (\boldsymbol{I}_n \otimes \boldsymbol{X}')\,\mathrm{d}\operatorname{vec}\boldsymbol{X}\\ &= (\boldsymbol{X}' \otimes \boldsymbol{I}_n)\boldsymbol{K}_{mn}\,\mathrm{d}\operatorname{vec}\boldsymbol{X} + (\boldsymbol{I}_n \otimes \boldsymbol{X}')\,\mathrm{d}\operatorname{vec}\boldsymbol{X}\\ &= (\boldsymbol{I}_{n^2} + \boldsymbol{K}_n)(\boldsymbol{I}_n \otimes \boldsymbol{X}')\,\mathrm{d}\operatorname{vec}\boldsymbol{X}\end{aligned}$$

and

$$\mathrm{D}\boldsymbol{F}(\boldsymbol{X}) = (\boldsymbol{I}_{n^2} + \boldsymbol{K}_n)(\boldsymbol{I}_n \otimes \boldsymbol{X}').$$

(c) Similarly, $\mathrm{d}\boldsymbol{F} = (\mathrm{d}\boldsymbol{X})\boldsymbol{X}' + \boldsymbol{X}(\mathrm{d}\boldsymbol{X})'$, so that

$$\begin{aligned}\mathrm{d}\operatorname{vec}\boldsymbol{F} &= (\boldsymbol{X} \otimes \boldsymbol{I}_m)\,\mathrm{d}\operatorname{vec}\boldsymbol{X} + (\boldsymbol{I}_m \otimes \boldsymbol{X})\,\mathrm{d}\operatorname{vec}\boldsymbol{X}'\\ &= (\boldsymbol{X} \otimes \boldsymbol{I}_m)\,\mathrm{d}\operatorname{vec}\boldsymbol{X} + (\boldsymbol{I}_m \otimes \boldsymbol{X})\boldsymbol{K}_{mn}\,\mathrm{d}\operatorname{vec}\boldsymbol{X}\\ &= (\boldsymbol{I}_{m^2} + \boldsymbol{K}_m)(\boldsymbol{X} \otimes \boldsymbol{I}_m)\,\mathrm{d}\operatorname{vec}\boldsymbol{X}\end{aligned}$$

and

$$\mathrm{D}\boldsymbol{F}(\boldsymbol{X}) = (\boldsymbol{I}_{m^2} + \boldsymbol{K}_m)(\boldsymbol{X} \otimes \boldsymbol{I}_m).$$

Exercise 13.20 (Matrix quadratic forms) Let $\boldsymbol{A}$ be a matrix of constants. Find the differential and derivative of:
(a) $\boldsymbol{F}(\boldsymbol{X}) := \boldsymbol{X}\boldsymbol{A}\boldsymbol{X}'$ $\quad(\boldsymbol{A} = \boldsymbol{A}')$;
(b) $\boldsymbol{F}(\boldsymbol{X}) := \boldsymbol{X}'\boldsymbol{A}\boldsymbol{X}$ $\quad(\boldsymbol{A} = \boldsymbol{A}')$;
(c) $\boldsymbol{F}(\boldsymbol{X}) := \boldsymbol{X}\boldsymbol{A}\boldsymbol{X}$;
(d) $\boldsymbol{F}(\boldsymbol{X}) := \boldsymbol{X}'\boldsymbol{A}\boldsymbol{X}'$.

Solution
Let $\boldsymbol{X}$ be an $m \times n$ matrix.
(a) From $\mathrm{d}\boldsymbol{F} = (\mathrm{d}\boldsymbol{X})\boldsymbol{A}\boldsymbol{X}' + \boldsymbol{X}\boldsymbol{A}(\mathrm{d}\boldsymbol{X})'$, we find

$$\begin{aligned}\mathrm{d}\operatorname{vec}\boldsymbol{F} &= (\boldsymbol{X}\boldsymbol{A} \otimes \boldsymbol{I}_m + (\boldsymbol{I}_m \otimes \boldsymbol{X}\boldsymbol{A})\boldsymbol{K}_{mn})\,\mathrm{d}\operatorname{vec}\boldsymbol{X}\\ &= (\boldsymbol{I}_{m^2} + \boldsymbol{K}_m)(\boldsymbol{X}\boldsymbol{A} \otimes \boldsymbol{I}_m)\,\mathrm{d}\operatorname{vec}\boldsymbol{X}\end{aligned}$$

and

$$\mathrm{D}\boldsymbol{F}(\boldsymbol{X}) = (\boldsymbol{I}_{m^2} + \boldsymbol{K}_m)(\boldsymbol{X}\boldsymbol{A} \otimes \boldsymbol{I}_m).$$

(b) Similarly, $\mathrm{d}\operatorname{vec}\boldsymbol{F} = (\boldsymbol{I}_{n^2} + \boldsymbol{K}_n)(\boldsymbol{I}_n \otimes \boldsymbol{X}'\boldsymbol{A})\,\mathrm{d}\operatorname{vec}\boldsymbol{X}$, so that

$$\mathrm{D}\boldsymbol{F}(\boldsymbol{X}) = (\boldsymbol{I}_{n^2} + \boldsymbol{K}_n)(\boldsymbol{I}_n \otimes \boldsymbol{X}'\boldsymbol{A}).$$

(c) From $\mathrm{d}\boldsymbol{F} = (\mathrm{d}\boldsymbol{X})\boldsymbol{A}\boldsymbol{X} + \boldsymbol{X}\boldsymbol{A}(\mathrm{d}\boldsymbol{X})$, we obtain

$$\mathrm{d}\operatorname{vec}\boldsymbol{F} = (\boldsymbol{X}'\boldsymbol{A}' \otimes \boldsymbol{I}_m + \boldsymbol{I}_n \otimes \boldsymbol{X}\boldsymbol{A})\,\mathrm{d}\operatorname{vec}\boldsymbol{X},$$

and hence

$$\mathrm{D}\boldsymbol{F}(\boldsymbol{X}) = \boldsymbol{X}'\boldsymbol{A}' \otimes \boldsymbol{I}_m + \boldsymbol{I}_n \otimes \boldsymbol{X}\boldsymbol{A}.$$

(d) Finally, $\mathrm{d}\boldsymbol{F} = (\mathrm{d}\boldsymbol{X})'\boldsymbol{A}\boldsymbol{X}' + \boldsymbol{X}'\boldsymbol{A}(\mathrm{d}\boldsymbol{X})'$ gives

$$\begin{aligned}\mathrm{d}\operatorname{vec}\boldsymbol{F} &= (\boldsymbol{X}\boldsymbol{A}' \otimes \boldsymbol{I}_n + \boldsymbol{I}_m \otimes \boldsymbol{X}'\boldsymbol{A})\,\mathrm{d}\operatorname{vec}\boldsymbol{X}'\\ &= (\boldsymbol{X}\boldsymbol{A}' \otimes \boldsymbol{I}_n + \boldsymbol{I}_m \otimes \boldsymbol{X}'\boldsymbol{A})\boldsymbol{K}_{mn}\,\mathrm{d}\operatorname{vec}\boldsymbol{X},\end{aligned}$$

so that

$$\mathrm{D}\boldsymbol{F}(\boldsymbol{X}) = (\boldsymbol{X}\boldsymbol{A}' \otimes \boldsymbol{I}_n + \boldsymbol{I}_m \otimes \boldsymbol{X}'\boldsymbol{A})\boldsymbol{K}_{mn}.$$

13.5 The inverse

Exercise 13.21 (Differential of the inverse)
(a) Show that the differential of $\boldsymbol{F}(\boldsymbol{X}) := \boldsymbol{X}^{-1}$ is given by

$$\mathrm{d}\boldsymbol{X}^{-1} = -\boldsymbol{X}^{-1}(\mathrm{d}\boldsymbol{X})\boldsymbol{X}^{-1}.$$

(b) When is $\mathrm{d}\boldsymbol{X}^{-1}$ nonsingular?

Solution
(a) This is a "once seen, never forgotten" solution. Since $\boldsymbol{X}^{-1}\boldsymbol{X} = \boldsymbol{I}$, we have

$$\mathrm{d}(\boldsymbol{X}^{-1}\boldsymbol{X}) = (\mathrm{d}\boldsymbol{X}^{-1})\boldsymbol{X} + \boldsymbol{X}^{-1}\,\mathrm{d}\boldsymbol{X} = \mathbf{O}.$$

Postmultiplying by $\boldsymbol{X}^{-1}$ then gives the result immediately. (This important result occurs so often that it will be used without reference. Notice how the scalar result $\varphi(x) := 1/x$ with $\varphi'(x) = -1/x^2$ generalizes to the matrix case.)
(b) When $|\mathrm{d}\boldsymbol{X}| \neq 0$.

Exercise 13.22 (Scalar functions involving the inverse) Let $\boldsymbol{a}$ be a vector of constants and $\boldsymbol{A}$ a matrix of constants. Let $\boldsymbol{X}$ be a nonsingular $n \times n$ matrix. Find the differential

and the derivative of the following scalar functions:
(a) $\varphi(\boldsymbol{X}) := \operatorname{tr} \boldsymbol{A}\boldsymbol{X}^{-1}$;
(b) $\varphi(\boldsymbol{X}) := \boldsymbol{a}'\boldsymbol{X}^{-1}\boldsymbol{a}$.

Solution
(a) Since

$$\mathrm{d}\varphi = \operatorname{tr} \boldsymbol{A}(\mathrm{d}\boldsymbol{X}^{-1}) = -\operatorname{tr} \boldsymbol{A}\boldsymbol{X}^{-1}(\mathrm{d}\boldsymbol{X})\boldsymbol{X}^{-1} = -\operatorname{tr} \boldsymbol{X}^{-1}\boldsymbol{A}\boldsymbol{X}^{-1}\,\mathrm{d}\boldsymbol{X},$$

we find

$$\mathrm{D}\varphi = -(\operatorname{vec}(\boldsymbol{X}^{-1}\boldsymbol{A}\boldsymbol{X}^{-1})')'.$$

(b) Here we have

$$\begin{aligned}\mathrm{d}\varphi &= \boldsymbol{a}'(\mathrm{d}\boldsymbol{X}^{-1})\boldsymbol{a} = -\boldsymbol{a}'\boldsymbol{X}^{-1}(\mathrm{d}\boldsymbol{X})\boldsymbol{X}^{-1}\boldsymbol{a}\\ &= -(\boldsymbol{a}'\boldsymbol{X}'^{-1} \otimes \boldsymbol{a}'\boldsymbol{X}^{-1})\,\mathrm{d}\operatorname{vec}\boldsymbol{X} = -(\boldsymbol{X}^{-1}\boldsymbol{a} \otimes \boldsymbol{X}'^{-1}\boldsymbol{a})'\,\mathrm{d}\operatorname{vec}\boldsymbol{X},\end{aligned}$$

and hence

$$\mathrm{D}\varphi = -(\boldsymbol{X}^{-1}\boldsymbol{a} \otimes \boldsymbol{X}'^{-1}\boldsymbol{a})'.$$

Exercise 13.23 (Relationship between $\mathrm{d}\boldsymbol{X}^{-1}$ and $\mathrm{d}\boldsymbol{X}$, trace) Show that $\operatorname{tr} \boldsymbol{X}^{-1}\,\mathrm{d}\boldsymbol{X} = -\operatorname{tr} \boldsymbol{X}\,\mathrm{d}\boldsymbol{X}^{-1}$.

Solution
Since $\mathrm{d}\boldsymbol{X}^{-1} = -\boldsymbol{X}^{-1}(\mathrm{d}\boldsymbol{X})\boldsymbol{X}^{-1}$, it follows that

$$\operatorname{tr} \boldsymbol{X}\,\mathrm{d}\boldsymbol{X}^{-1} = -\operatorname{tr} \boldsymbol{X}\boldsymbol{X}^{-1}(\mathrm{d}\boldsymbol{X})\boldsymbol{X}^{-1} = -\operatorname{tr} \boldsymbol{X}^{-1}\,\mathrm{d}\boldsymbol{X}.$$

Exercise 13.24 (Differential of an idempotent matrix) Let $\boldsymbol{X} := (\boldsymbol{x}_1, \dots, \boldsymbol{x}_k)$ be an $n \times k$ matrix of rank k, and define $\boldsymbol{M} := \boldsymbol{I}_n - \boldsymbol{X}(\boldsymbol{X}'\boldsymbol{X})^{-1}\boldsymbol{X}'$.
(a) Obtain the differential and derivative of $\boldsymbol{M}$.
(b) Obtain the differential and derivative of $\boldsymbol{M}$ with respect to $\boldsymbol{x}_j$.

Solution
(a) We have

$$\begin{aligned}\mathrm{d}\boldsymbol{M} &= -\left((\mathrm{d}\boldsymbol{X})(\boldsymbol{X}'\boldsymbol{X})^{-1}\boldsymbol{X}' + \boldsymbol{X}(\mathrm{d}(\boldsymbol{X}'\boldsymbol{X})^{-1})\boldsymbol{X}' + \boldsymbol{X}(\boldsymbol{X}'\boldsymbol{X})^{-1}(\mathrm{d}\boldsymbol{X})'\right)\\ &= -(\mathrm{d}\boldsymbol{X})(\boldsymbol{X}'\boldsymbol{X})^{-1}\boldsymbol{X}' + \boldsymbol{X}(\boldsymbol{X}'\boldsymbol{X})^{-1}(\mathrm{d}(\boldsymbol{X}'\boldsymbol{X}))(\boldsymbol{X}'\boldsymbol{X})^{-1}\boldsymbol{X}'\\ &\quad - \boldsymbol{X}(\boldsymbol{X}'\boldsymbol{X})^{-1}(\mathrm{d}\boldsymbol{X})'\\ &= -(\mathrm{d}\boldsymbol{X})(\boldsymbol{X}'\boldsymbol{X})^{-1}\boldsymbol{X}' + \boldsymbol{X}(\boldsymbol{X}'\boldsymbol{X})^{-1}(\mathrm{d}\boldsymbol{X})'\boldsymbol{X}(\boldsymbol{X}'\boldsymbol{X})^{-1}\boldsymbol{X}'\\ &\quad + \boldsymbol{X}(\boldsymbol{X}'\boldsymbol{X})^{-1}\boldsymbol{X}'(\mathrm{d}\boldsymbol{X})(\boldsymbol{X}'\boldsymbol{X})^{-1}\boldsymbol{X}' - \boldsymbol{X}(\boldsymbol{X}'\boldsymbol{X})^{-1}(\mathrm{d}\boldsymbol{X})'\\ &= -\boldsymbol{M}(\mathrm{d}\boldsymbol{X})(\boldsymbol{X}'\boldsymbol{X})^{-1}\boldsymbol{X}' - \boldsymbol{X}(\boldsymbol{X}'\boldsymbol{X})^{-1}(\mathrm{d}\boldsymbol{X})'\boldsymbol{M}.\end{aligned}$$

Hence,

$$\begin{aligned}\mathrm{d}\operatorname{vec} \boldsymbol{M} &= -(\boldsymbol{X}(\boldsymbol{X}'\boldsymbol{X})^{-1} \otimes \boldsymbol{M})\,\mathrm{d}\operatorname{vec} \boldsymbol{X} - (\boldsymbol{M} \otimes \boldsymbol{X}(\boldsymbol{X}'\boldsymbol{X})^{-1})\,\mathrm{d}\operatorname{vec} \boldsymbol{X}' \\ &= -\left(\boldsymbol{X}(\boldsymbol{X}'\boldsymbol{X})^{-1} \otimes \boldsymbol{M} + (\boldsymbol{M} \otimes \boldsymbol{X}(\boldsymbol{X}'\boldsymbol{X})^{-1})\boldsymbol{K}_{nk}\right)\mathrm{d}\operatorname{vec} \boldsymbol{X} \\ &= -(\boldsymbol{I}_{n^2} + \boldsymbol{K}_n)(\boldsymbol{X}(\boldsymbol{X}'\boldsymbol{X})^{-1} \otimes \boldsymbol{M})\,\mathrm{d}\operatorname{vec} \boldsymbol{X},\end{aligned}$$

so that the derivative is given by

$$\frac{\partial \operatorname{vec} \boldsymbol{M}}{\partial (\operatorname{vec} \boldsymbol{X})'} = -(\boldsymbol{I}_{n^2} + \boldsymbol{K}_n)(\boldsymbol{X}(\boldsymbol{X}'\boldsymbol{X})^{-1} \otimes \boldsymbol{M}).$$

(b) The crucial step here is to realize that we can write $\mathrm{d}\boldsymbol{X} = (\mathrm{d}\boldsymbol{x}_j)\boldsymbol{e}_j'$, when only $\boldsymbol{x}_j$ varies. (Recall that $\boldsymbol{e}_j$ is the vector with 1 in the j-th position and zeros elsewhere.) Thus,

$$\mathrm{d}\boldsymbol{M} = -\boldsymbol{M}(\mathrm{d}\boldsymbol{x}_j)\boldsymbol{e}_j'(\boldsymbol{X}'\boldsymbol{X})^{-1}\boldsymbol{X}' - \boldsymbol{X}(\boldsymbol{X}'\boldsymbol{X})^{-1}\boldsymbol{e}_j(\mathrm{d}\boldsymbol{x}_j)'\boldsymbol{M}$$

and

$$\begin{aligned}\mathrm{d}\operatorname{vec} \boldsymbol{M} &= -(\boldsymbol{I}_{n^2} + \boldsymbol{K}_n)(\boldsymbol{X}(\boldsymbol{X}'\boldsymbol{X})^{-1} \otimes \boldsymbol{M})(\boldsymbol{e}_j \otimes \mathrm{d}\boldsymbol{x}_j) \\ &= -(\boldsymbol{I}_{n^2} + \boldsymbol{K}_n)(\boldsymbol{X}(\boldsymbol{X}'\boldsymbol{X})^{-1}\boldsymbol{e}_j \otimes \boldsymbol{M})\,\mathrm{d}\boldsymbol{x}_j.\end{aligned}$$

The derivative is therefore

$$\frac{\partial \operatorname{vec} \boldsymbol{M}}{\partial \boldsymbol{x}_j'} = -(\boldsymbol{I}_{n^2} + \boldsymbol{K}_n)(\boldsymbol{X}(\boldsymbol{X}'\boldsymbol{X})^{-1}\boldsymbol{e}_j \otimes \boldsymbol{M}).$$

Exercise 13.25 (Matrix functions involving a (symmetric) inverse) Let $\boldsymbol{A}$ and $\boldsymbol{B}$ be two matrices of constants. Find the differential and derivative of the following nonlinear matrix functions:
(a) $\boldsymbol{F}(\boldsymbol{X}) := \boldsymbol{A}\boldsymbol{X}^{-1}\boldsymbol{B}$;
(b) $\boldsymbol{F}(\boldsymbol{X}) := \boldsymbol{A}\boldsymbol{X}^{-1}\boldsymbol{A}'$ when $\boldsymbol{X}$ is known to be symmetric.

Solution
(a) The differential is given by $\mathrm{d}\boldsymbol{F} = \boldsymbol{A}(\mathrm{d}\boldsymbol{X}^{-1})\boldsymbol{B} = -\boldsymbol{A}\boldsymbol{X}^{-1}(\mathrm{d}\boldsymbol{X})\boldsymbol{X}^{-1}\boldsymbol{B}$. Hence,

$$\mathrm{d}\operatorname{vec} \boldsymbol{F} = -(\boldsymbol{B}'\boldsymbol{X}'^{-1} \otimes \boldsymbol{A}\boldsymbol{X}^{-1})\,\mathrm{d}\operatorname{vec} \boldsymbol{X}$$

and

$$\mathrm{D}\boldsymbol{F}(\boldsymbol{X}) = -(\boldsymbol{B}'\boldsymbol{X}'^{-1} \otimes \boldsymbol{A}\boldsymbol{X}^{-1})\,\mathrm{d}\operatorname{vec} \boldsymbol{X}.$$

(b) From $\mathrm{d}\boldsymbol{F} = \boldsymbol{A}(\mathrm{d}\boldsymbol{X}^{-1})\boldsymbol{A}' = -\boldsymbol{A}\boldsymbol{X}^{-1}(\mathrm{d}\boldsymbol{X})\boldsymbol{X}^{-1}\boldsymbol{A}'$, we obtain

$$\mathrm{d}\operatorname{vec} \boldsymbol{F} = -(\boldsymbol{A}\boldsymbol{X}^{-1} \otimes \boldsymbol{A}\boldsymbol{X}^{-1})\,\mathrm{d}\operatorname{vec} \boldsymbol{X} = -(\boldsymbol{A}\boldsymbol{X}^{-1} \otimes \boldsymbol{A}\boldsymbol{X}^{-1})\boldsymbol{D}_n\,\mathrm{d}\operatorname{vech}(\boldsymbol{X}),$$

where $\boldsymbol{D}_n$ denotes the duplication matrix. This then yields

$$\mathrm{D}\boldsymbol{F}(\boldsymbol{X}) := \frac{\partial \operatorname{vec} \boldsymbol{F}(\boldsymbol{X})}{\partial (\operatorname{vech}(\boldsymbol{X}))'} = -(\boldsymbol{A}\boldsymbol{X}^{-1} \otimes \boldsymbol{A}\boldsymbol{X}^{-1})\boldsymbol{D}_n.$$

This is the first exercise where we obtain the derivative with respect to a symmetric matrix $\boldsymbol{X}$. Since $\boldsymbol{X}$ is symmetric, say of order n, its n^2 elements cannot move independently. The symmetry imposes $n(n-1)/2$ restrictions. The "free" elements are precisely the $n(n+1)/2$ elements in $\operatorname{vech}(\boldsymbol{X})$, and the derivative is therefore defined by considering $\boldsymbol{F}$ as a function of $\operatorname{vech}(\boldsymbol{X})$ and not as a function of $\operatorname{vec}\boldsymbol{X}$.

Exercise 13.26 (Sum of all elements)
(a) Let $\varphi(\boldsymbol{X})$ be the sum of the n^2 elements of $\boldsymbol{X}^{-1}$. Obtain $\mathrm{d}\varphi$ and $\mathrm{D}\varphi$.
(b) How do the results change when $\boldsymbol{X}$ is known to be symmetric?

Solution
(a) Let $\boldsymbol{\imath}$ denote the vector of ones. Then $\varphi(\boldsymbol{X}) = \boldsymbol{\imath}'\boldsymbol{X}^{-1}\boldsymbol{\imath}$, and $\mathrm{d}\varphi = \boldsymbol{\imath}'(\mathrm{d}\boldsymbol{X}^{-1})\boldsymbol{\imath} = -\boldsymbol{\imath}'\boldsymbol{X}^{-1}(\mathrm{d}\boldsymbol{X})\boldsymbol{X}^{-1}\boldsymbol{\imath}$. Hence,

$$\mathrm{d}\varphi = -(\boldsymbol{X}^{-1}\boldsymbol{\imath} \otimes \boldsymbol{X}'^{-1}\boldsymbol{\imath})' \,\mathrm{dvec}\,\boldsymbol{X}, \quad \mathrm{D}\varphi(\boldsymbol{X}) = -\left(\boldsymbol{X}^{-1}\boldsymbol{\imath} \otimes \boldsymbol{X}'^{-1}\boldsymbol{\imath}\right)'.$$

(b) If $\boldsymbol{X}$ is symmetric, then $\operatorname{vec}\boldsymbol{X} = \boldsymbol{D}_n \operatorname{vech}(\boldsymbol{X})$, and

$$\mathrm{d}\varphi = -\left(\boldsymbol{X}^{-1}\boldsymbol{\imath} \otimes \boldsymbol{X}'^{-1}\boldsymbol{\imath}\right)' \boldsymbol{D}_n \,\mathrm{dvech}(\boldsymbol{X}), \quad \mathrm{D}\varphi(\boldsymbol{X}) = -\left(\boldsymbol{X}^{-1}\boldsymbol{\imath} \otimes \boldsymbol{X}'^{-1}\boldsymbol{\imath}\right)' \boldsymbol{D}_n.$$

Exercise 13.27 (Selector from the inverse) Let $\boldsymbol{X}$ be an $m \times n$ matrix of rank n, and let $\boldsymbol{F}(\boldsymbol{X})$ be the $n \times (n-1)$ matrix function defined as $(\boldsymbol{X}'\boldsymbol{X})^{-1}$ with the last column deleted. Obtain $\mathrm{d}\boldsymbol{F}$ and $\mathrm{D}\boldsymbol{F}$.

Solution
Let $\boldsymbol{S}$ be the $n \times (n-1)$ selection matrix defined as $\boldsymbol{S} := (\boldsymbol{I}_{n-1} : \boldsymbol{0})'$, so that $\boldsymbol{F}(\boldsymbol{X})$ can be expressed as $\boldsymbol{F}(\boldsymbol{X}) = (\boldsymbol{X}'\boldsymbol{X})^{-1}\boldsymbol{S}$. Then,

$$\begin{aligned}\mathrm{d}\boldsymbol{F} &= -(\boldsymbol{X}'\boldsymbol{X})^{-1}(\mathrm{d}(\boldsymbol{X}'\boldsymbol{X}))(\boldsymbol{X}'\boldsymbol{X})^{-1}\boldsymbol{S} \\ &= -(\boldsymbol{X}'\boldsymbol{X})^{-1}(\mathrm{d}\boldsymbol{X})'\boldsymbol{X}\boldsymbol{F} - (\boldsymbol{X}'\boldsymbol{X})^{-1}\boldsymbol{X}'(\mathrm{d}\boldsymbol{X})\boldsymbol{F}.\end{aligned}$$

Taking vecs we obtain

$$\begin{aligned}\mathrm{dvec}\,\boldsymbol{F} &= -(\boldsymbol{F}'\boldsymbol{X}' \otimes (\boldsymbol{X}'\boldsymbol{X})^{-1})\,\mathrm{dvec}\,\boldsymbol{X}' - (\boldsymbol{F}' \otimes (\boldsymbol{X}'\boldsymbol{X})^{-1}\boldsymbol{X}')\,\mathrm{dvec}\,\boldsymbol{X} \\ &= -((\boldsymbol{F}'\boldsymbol{X}' \otimes (\boldsymbol{X}'\boldsymbol{X})^{-1})\boldsymbol{K}_{mn} + \boldsymbol{F}' \otimes (\boldsymbol{X}'\boldsymbol{X})^{-1}\boldsymbol{X}')\,\mathrm{dvec}\,\boldsymbol{X} \\ &= -(\boldsymbol{F}' \otimes (\boldsymbol{X}'\boldsymbol{X})^{-1})(\boldsymbol{I}_{n^2} + \boldsymbol{K}_n)(\boldsymbol{I}_n \otimes \boldsymbol{X}')\,\mathrm{dvec}\,\boldsymbol{X},\end{aligned}$$

and hence

$$\mathrm{D}\boldsymbol{F} = -(\boldsymbol{F}' \otimes (\boldsymbol{X}'\boldsymbol{X})^{-1})(\boldsymbol{I}_{n^2} + \boldsymbol{K}_n)(\boldsymbol{I}_n \otimes \boldsymbol{X}').$$

13.6 Exponential and logarithm

Exercise 13.28 (The exponential, special case) By analogy to the power series $e^x = \sum_{k=0}^{\infty} x^k/k!$, which converges for all x, we have written the exponential of a square matrix $\boldsymbol{X}$ as

$$\exp(\boldsymbol{X}) := \sum_{k=0}^{\infty} \frac{1}{k!}\boldsymbol{X}^k,$$

and shown that it is well-defined for every $\boldsymbol{X}$, real or complex; see Exercise 9.19(b).

Now show that, for any square matrix $\boldsymbol{A}$ of constants and for every x,

$$\mathrm{d}e^{x\boldsymbol{A}} = \boldsymbol{A}e^{x\boldsymbol{A}}\,\mathrm{d}x.$$

Solution
We have

$$\begin{aligned}\mathrm{d}e^{x\boldsymbol{A}} &= \sum_{k=0}^{\infty}\frac{1}{k!}(\mathrm{d}x^k)\boldsymbol{A}^k = \sum_{k=0}^{\infty}\frac{1}{k!}kx^{k-1}\boldsymbol{A}^k\,\mathrm{d}x \\ &= \sum_{k=1}^{\infty}\frac{1}{(k-1)!}x^{k-1}\boldsymbol{A}^k\,\mathrm{d}x = \boldsymbol{A}\sum_{k=0}^{\infty}\frac{1}{k!}(x\boldsymbol{A})^k\,\mathrm{d}x = \boldsymbol{A}e^{x\boldsymbol{A}}\,\mathrm{d}x.\end{aligned}$$

Exercise 13.29 (The exponential, general case) More generally, show that

$$\mathrm{d}(e^{\boldsymbol{X}}) = \sum_{k=0}^{\infty}\frac{1}{(k+1)!}\sum_{j=0}^{k}\boldsymbol{X}^j(\mathrm{d}\boldsymbol{X})\boldsymbol{X}^{k-j} \quad\text{and}\quad \operatorname{tr}\mathrm{d}(e^{\boldsymbol{X}}) = \operatorname{tr}(e^{\boldsymbol{X}}\,\mathrm{d}\boldsymbol{X}).$$

Solution
Using the definition of $e^{\boldsymbol{X}}$,

$$\begin{aligned}\mathrm{d}(e^{\boldsymbol{X}}) &= \sum_{k=0}^{\infty}\frac{1}{k!}\,\mathrm{d}\boldsymbol{X}^k = \sum_{k=1}^{\infty}\frac{1}{k!}\sum_{j=0}^{k-1}\boldsymbol{X}^j(\mathrm{d}\boldsymbol{X})\boldsymbol{X}^{k-j-1} \\ &= \sum_{k=0}^{\infty}\frac{1}{(k+1)!}\sum_{j=0}^{k}\boldsymbol{X}^j(\mathrm{d}\boldsymbol{X})\boldsymbol{X}^{k-j},\end{aligned}$$

and hence

$$\begin{aligned}\operatorname{tr}\mathrm{d}(e^{\boldsymbol{X}}) &= \sum_{k=0}^{\infty}\frac{1}{(k+1)!}(k+1)\operatorname{tr}(\boldsymbol{X}^k\,\mathrm{d}\boldsymbol{X}) \\ &= \operatorname{tr}\left(\sum_{k=0}^{\infty}\frac{1}{k!}\boldsymbol{X}^k\,\mathrm{d}\boldsymbol{X}\right) = \operatorname{tr}(e^{\boldsymbol{X}}\,\mathrm{d}\boldsymbol{X}).\end{aligned}$$

Exercise 13.30 (The logarithm, special case) Similarly, by analogy to the power series $\log(1-x) = -\sum_{k=1}^{\infty} x^k/k$, we have

$$\log(\boldsymbol{I}_n - \boldsymbol{X}) = -\sum_{k=1}^{\infty}\frac{1}{k}\boldsymbol{X}^k,$$

which converges absolutely for every $n \times n$ matrix X satisfying $\varrho(X) < 1$, where $\varrho(\cdot)$ denotes the spectral radius; see Exercises 9.8(b) and 9.19(c). Show that, for any square matrix A of constants and every x satisfying $|x|\varrho(A) < 1$,

$$\mathrm{d}\log(I_n - xA) = -A(I_n - xA)^{-1}\,\mathrm{d}x.$$

Solution
This follows from

$$\begin{aligned}\mathrm{d}\log(I_n - xA) &= -\sum_{k=1}^{\infty}\frac{1}{k}(\mathrm{d}x^k)A^k = -\sum_{k=1}^{\infty}\frac{1}{k}kx^{k-1}A^k\,\mathrm{d}x\\ &= -A\sum_{k=1}^{\infty}(xA)^{k-1}\,\mathrm{d}x = -A\sum_{k=0}^{\infty}(xA)^k\,\mathrm{d}x = -A(I_n - xA)^{-1}\,\mathrm{d}x.\end{aligned}$$

Exercise 13.31 (The logarithm, general case) More generally, if $\varrho(X) < 1$, show that

$$\mathrm{d}\log(I_n - X) = -\sum_{k=0}^{\infty}\frac{1}{k+1}\sum_{j=0}^{k}X^j(\mathrm{d}X)X^{k-j}$$

and

$$\mathrm{tr}(\mathrm{d}\log(I_n - X)) = -\,\mathrm{tr}((I_n - X)^{-1}\,\mathrm{d}X).$$

Solution
(a) In general,

$$\begin{aligned}\mathrm{d}\log(I_n - X) &= -\sum_{k=1}^{\infty}\frac{1}{k}\,\mathrm{d}X^k = -\sum_{k=1}^{\infty}\frac{1}{k}\sum_{j=0}^{k-1}X^j(\mathrm{d}X)X^{k-j-1}\\ &= -\sum_{k=0}^{\infty}\frac{1}{k+1}\sum_{j=0}^{k}X^j(\mathrm{d}X)X^{k-j},\end{aligned}$$

and, taking the trace,

$$\begin{aligned}\mathrm{tr}(\mathrm{d}\log(I_n - X)) &= -\sum_{k=0}^{\infty}\frac{1}{k+1}(k+1)\,\mathrm{tr}\,X^k\,\mathrm{d}X\\ &= -\,\mathrm{tr}\left(\sum_{k=0}^{\infty}X^k\,\mathrm{d}X\right) = -\,\mathrm{tr}(I_n - X)^{-1}\,\mathrm{d}X.\end{aligned}$$

13.7 The determinant

***Exercise 13.32 (Differential of the determinant)** At points where X is nonsingular, show that the scalar function $\varphi(X) := |X|$ has differential

$$\mathrm{d}|X| = |X|\,\mathrm{tr}\,X^{-1}\,\mathrm{d}X,$$

and obtain the derivative.

Solution

We have emphasized several times that, when evaluating differentials, one should always try to work with matrices rather than with elements of matrices. This, however, is not always possible. Here is an example where, regrettably, we have to rely on the elements of $\boldsymbol{X}$.

Recall that the minor of x_{ij} is the determinant of the $(n-1)\times(n-1)$ submatrix of $\boldsymbol{X}$ obtained by deleting the i-th row and the j-th column, and the cofactor c_{ij} of x_{ij} is $(-1)^{i+j}$ times the minor. The cofactors can be put into an $n\times n$ matrix $\boldsymbol{C} := (c_{ij})$. We have proved in Exercise 4.37(c) that $\boldsymbol{C}'\boldsymbol{X} = |\boldsymbol{X}|\boldsymbol{I}_n$. In particular,

$$|\boldsymbol{X}| = \sum_{i=1}^{n} c_{ij}x_{ij} \quad (j = 1, \dots, n).$$

The crucial step is to realize that, for given j, $c_{1j}, \dots, c_{nj}$ do not depend on x_{ij}. This gives

$$\frac{\partial|\boldsymbol{X}|}{\partial x_{ij}} = \frac{\partial}{\partial x_{ij}}(c_{1j}x_{1j} + c_{2j}x_{2j} + \dots + c_{nj}x_{nj}) = c_{ij},$$

and hence

$$\mathrm{d}|\boldsymbol{X}| = \sum_{i=1}^{n}\sum_{j=1}^{n} c_{ij}\,\mathrm{d}x_{ij} = \operatorname{tr}\boldsymbol{C}'\,\mathrm{d}\boldsymbol{X} = |\boldsymbol{X}|\operatorname{tr}\boldsymbol{X}^{-1}\,\mathrm{d}\boldsymbol{X},$$

because $\boldsymbol{C}' = |\boldsymbol{X}|\boldsymbol{X}^{-1}$. The derivative follows immediately. It is

$$\frac{\partial|\boldsymbol{X}|}{\partial(\operatorname{vec}\boldsymbol{X})'} = |\boldsymbol{X}|(\operatorname{vec}\boldsymbol{X}'^{-1})'.$$

Exercise 13.33 (The vanishing d$|\boldsymbol{X}|$) Show that $\mathrm{d}|\boldsymbol{X}| = 0$ at points where the $n\times n$ matrix $\boldsymbol{X}$ has rank $\leq n-2$.

Solution

Suppose that $\operatorname{rk}(\boldsymbol{X}) = r \leq n-2$. Let us think (for a moment) of the matrix $\boldsymbol{X}$ as a matrix of constants, except for the element x_{ij}. Suppose we perturb x_{ij} by an amount ϵ. The rank of the perturbed matrix $\tilde{\boldsymbol{X}}$ can only be $r+1$, r, or $r-1$, and hence $\operatorname{rk}(\tilde{\boldsymbol{X}}) \leq n-1$, so that $|\tilde{\boldsymbol{X}}| = 0$. This shows that

$$\frac{\partial|\boldsymbol{X}|}{\partial x_{ij}} = 0.$$

Since this holds for all i and all j, it follows that the differential vanishes. (The determinant $|\boldsymbol{X}|$ is "locally constant" in this case, namely zero.)

Exercise 13.34 (Determinant of a matrix function, 1) Let $\boldsymbol{A}$ and $\boldsymbol{B}$ be two matrices of constants. Find the differential and derivative of:
(a) $\varphi(\boldsymbol{X}) := |\boldsymbol{A}\boldsymbol{X}\boldsymbol{B}|$ (if $\boldsymbol{A}\boldsymbol{X}\boldsymbol{B}$ is nonsingular);
(b) $\varphi(\boldsymbol{X}) := |\boldsymbol{A}\boldsymbol{X}^{-1}\boldsymbol{B}|$ (if $\boldsymbol{X}$ and $\boldsymbol{A}\boldsymbol{X}^{-1}\boldsymbol{B}$ are nonsingular).

Solution
(a) The differential is

$$\begin{aligned}\mathrm{d}|\boldsymbol{AXB}| &= |\boldsymbol{AXB}|\operatorname{tr}(\boldsymbol{AXB})^{-1}\mathrm{d}(\boldsymbol{AXB})\\ &= |\boldsymbol{AXB}|\operatorname{tr}(\boldsymbol{AXB})^{-1}\boldsymbol{A}(\mathrm{d}\boldsymbol{X})\boldsymbol{B}\\ &= |\boldsymbol{AXB}|\operatorname{tr}\boldsymbol{B}(\boldsymbol{AXB})^{-1}\boldsymbol{A}\,\mathrm{d}\boldsymbol{X}.\end{aligned}$$

Hence,

$$\frac{\partial|\boldsymbol{AXB}|}{\partial(\operatorname{vec}\boldsymbol{X})'} = |\boldsymbol{AXB}|(\operatorname{vec}(\boldsymbol{A}'(\boldsymbol{AXB})'^{-1}\boldsymbol{B}'))'.$$

(b) Similarly,

$$\begin{aligned}\mathrm{d}|\boldsymbol{AX}^{-1}\boldsymbol{B}| &= |\boldsymbol{AX}^{-1}\boldsymbol{B}|\operatorname{tr}(\boldsymbol{AX}^{-1}\boldsymbol{B})^{-1}\boldsymbol{A}(\mathrm{d}\boldsymbol{X}^{-1})\boldsymbol{B}\\ &= -|\boldsymbol{AX}^{-1}\boldsymbol{B}|\operatorname{tr}(\boldsymbol{AX}^{-1}\boldsymbol{B})^{-1}\boldsymbol{AX}^{-1}(\mathrm{d}\boldsymbol{X})\boldsymbol{X}^{-1}\boldsymbol{B}\\ &= -|\boldsymbol{AX}^{-1}\boldsymbol{B}|\operatorname{tr}\boldsymbol{X}^{-1}\boldsymbol{B}(\boldsymbol{AX}^{-1}\boldsymbol{B})^{-1}\boldsymbol{AX}^{-1}\,\mathrm{d}\boldsymbol{X},\end{aligned}$$

so that

$$\frac{\partial|\boldsymbol{AX}^{-1}\boldsymbol{B}|}{\partial(\operatorname{vec}\boldsymbol{X})'} = -|\boldsymbol{AX}^{-1}\boldsymbol{B}|(\operatorname{vec}(\boldsymbol{X}^{-1}\boldsymbol{B}(\boldsymbol{AX}^{-1}\boldsymbol{B})^{-1}\boldsymbol{AX}^{-1})')'.$$

Exercise 13.35 (Determinant of a matrix function, 2) Find the differential and derivative of:
(a) $\varphi(\boldsymbol{X}) := |\boldsymbol{XX}'|$ $\quad(\boldsymbol{XX}'$ nonsingular);
(b) $\varphi(\boldsymbol{X}) := |\boldsymbol{X}'\boldsymbol{X}|$ $\quad(\boldsymbol{X}'\boldsymbol{X}$ nonsingular);
(c) $\varphi(\boldsymbol{X}) := |\boldsymbol{X}^2|$ $\quad(\boldsymbol{X}$ nonsingular);
(d) $\varphi(\boldsymbol{X}) := |\boldsymbol{X}^p|$ $\quad(\boldsymbol{X}$ nonsingular).

Solution
(a) The differential is

$$\begin{aligned}\mathrm{d}|\boldsymbol{XX}'| &= |\boldsymbol{XX}'|\operatorname{tr}(\boldsymbol{XX}')^{-1}\mathrm{d}(\boldsymbol{XX}')\\ &= |\boldsymbol{XX}'|\operatorname{tr}(\boldsymbol{XX}')^{-1}((\mathrm{d}\boldsymbol{X})\boldsymbol{X}' + \boldsymbol{X}(\mathrm{d}\boldsymbol{X})')\\ &= |\boldsymbol{XX}'|(\operatorname{tr}(\boldsymbol{XX}')^{-1}(\mathrm{d}\boldsymbol{X})\boldsymbol{X}' + \operatorname{tr}(\boldsymbol{XX}')^{-1}\boldsymbol{X}(\mathrm{d}\boldsymbol{X})')\\ &= |\boldsymbol{XX}'|(\operatorname{tr}(\boldsymbol{XX}')^{-1}(\mathrm{d}\boldsymbol{X})\boldsymbol{X}' + \operatorname{tr}(\mathrm{d}\boldsymbol{X})\boldsymbol{X}'(\boldsymbol{XX}')^{-1})\\ &= 2|\boldsymbol{XX}'|\operatorname{tr}\boldsymbol{X}'(\boldsymbol{XX}')^{-1}\,\mathrm{d}\boldsymbol{X}.\end{aligned}$$

Hence,

$$\frac{\partial|\boldsymbol{XX}'|}{\partial(\operatorname{vec}\boldsymbol{X})'} = 2|\boldsymbol{XX}'|(\operatorname{vec}(\boldsymbol{XX}')^{-1}\boldsymbol{X})'.$$

(b) Similarly,

$$\begin{aligned}\mathrm{d}|\boldsymbol{X}'\boldsymbol{X}| &= |\boldsymbol{X}'\boldsymbol{X}|\,\mathrm{tr}(\boldsymbol{X}'\boldsymbol{X})^{-1}\,\mathrm{d}(\boldsymbol{X}'\boldsymbol{X})\\ &= 2|\boldsymbol{X}'\boldsymbol{X}|\,\mathrm{tr}(\boldsymbol{X}'\boldsymbol{X})^{-1}\boldsymbol{X}'\,\mathrm{d}\boldsymbol{X},\end{aligned}$$

implying

$$\frac{\partial|\boldsymbol{X}'\boldsymbol{X}|}{\partial(\mathrm{vec}\,\boldsymbol{X})'} = 2|\boldsymbol{X}'\boldsymbol{X}|(\mathrm{vec}\,\boldsymbol{X}(\boldsymbol{X}'\boldsymbol{X})^{-1})'.$$

(c) Further,

$$\mathrm{d}|\boldsymbol{X}^2| = \mathrm{d}|\boldsymbol{X}|^2 = 2|\boldsymbol{X}|\,\mathrm{d}|\boldsymbol{X}| = 2|\boldsymbol{X}|^2\,\mathrm{tr}\,\boldsymbol{X}^{-1}\,\mathrm{d}\boldsymbol{X},$$

giving

$$\frac{\partial|\boldsymbol{X}^2|}{\partial(\mathrm{vec}\,\boldsymbol{X})'} = 2|\boldsymbol{X}|^2(\mathrm{vec}\,\boldsymbol{X}'^{-1})'.$$

(d) And, similarly,

$$\mathrm{d}|\boldsymbol{X}^p| = \mathrm{d}|\boldsymbol{X}|^p = p|\boldsymbol{X}|^{p-1}\,\mathrm{d}|\boldsymbol{X}| = p|\boldsymbol{X}|^p\,\mathrm{tr}\,\boldsymbol{X}^{-1}\,\mathrm{d}\boldsymbol{X},$$

with

$$\frac{\partial|\boldsymbol{X}^p|}{\partial(\mathrm{vec}\,\boldsymbol{X})'} = p|\boldsymbol{X}|^p(\mathrm{vec}\,\boldsymbol{X}'^{-1})'.$$

Exercise 13.36 (Differential of $\log|\boldsymbol{X}|$)
(a) For $|\boldsymbol{X}| > 0$, show that

$$\mathrm{d}\log|\boldsymbol{X}| = \mathrm{tr}\,\boldsymbol{X}^{-1}\,\mathrm{d}\boldsymbol{X}$$

and obtain the derivative.
(b) Find the differential and derivative of $\varphi(\boldsymbol{X}) := \log|\boldsymbol{X}'\boldsymbol{A}\boldsymbol{X}|$ for $|\boldsymbol{X}'\boldsymbol{A}\boldsymbol{X}| > 0$.

Solution
(a) We have

$$\mathrm{d}\log|\boldsymbol{X}| = \frac{1}{|\boldsymbol{X}|}\,\mathrm{d}|\boldsymbol{X}| = \frac{1}{|\boldsymbol{X}|}|\boldsymbol{X}|\,\mathrm{tr}\,\boldsymbol{X}^{-1}\,\mathrm{d}\boldsymbol{X} = \mathrm{tr}\,\boldsymbol{X}^{-1}\,\mathrm{d}\boldsymbol{X},$$

with derivative

$$\frac{\partial\log|\boldsymbol{X}|}{\partial(\mathrm{vec}\,\boldsymbol{X})'} = (\mathrm{vec}\,\boldsymbol{X}'^{-1})'.$$

(b) Using (a), we then find

$$\begin{aligned}\mathrm{d}\log|\boldsymbol{X}'\boldsymbol{A}\boldsymbol{X}| &= \mathrm{tr}(\boldsymbol{X}'\boldsymbol{A}\boldsymbol{X})^{-1}\,\mathrm{d}(\boldsymbol{X}'\boldsymbol{A}\boldsymbol{X})\\ &= \mathrm{tr}(\boldsymbol{X}'\boldsymbol{A}\boldsymbol{X})^{-1}(\mathrm{d}\boldsymbol{X})'\boldsymbol{A}\boldsymbol{X} + \mathrm{tr}(\boldsymbol{X}'\boldsymbol{A}\boldsymbol{X})^{-1}\boldsymbol{X}'\boldsymbol{A}\,\mathrm{d}\boldsymbol{X}\\ &= \mathrm{tr}((\boldsymbol{X}'\boldsymbol{A}'\boldsymbol{X})^{-1}\boldsymbol{X}'\boldsymbol{A}' + (\boldsymbol{X}'\boldsymbol{A}\boldsymbol{X})^{-1}\boldsymbol{X}'\boldsymbol{A})\,\mathrm{d}\boldsymbol{X},\end{aligned}$$

with derivative

$$\frac{\partial \log |\boldsymbol{X}'\boldsymbol{A}\boldsymbol{X}|}{\partial(\operatorname{vec}\boldsymbol{X})'} = (\operatorname{vec}((\boldsymbol{X}'\boldsymbol{A}'\boldsymbol{X})^{-1}\boldsymbol{X}'\boldsymbol{A}' + (\boldsymbol{X}'\boldsymbol{A}\boldsymbol{X})^{-1}\boldsymbol{X}'\boldsymbol{A})')'.$$

13.8 Jacobians

Exercise 13.37 (Jacobians and linear transformations) Let $\boldsymbol{A}$ and $\boldsymbol{B}$ be two matrices of constants.
(a) Find the Jacobian of the transformation $\boldsymbol{Y} := \boldsymbol{A}\boldsymbol{X}\boldsymbol{B}$, where $\boldsymbol{A}$ and $\boldsymbol{B}$ are square $n \times n$ matrices.
(b) Now suppose $\boldsymbol{X}$ is symmetric. Find the Jacobian of the transformation $\boldsymbol{Y} := \boldsymbol{A}\boldsymbol{X}\boldsymbol{A}'$ ($|\boldsymbol{A}| \neq 0$).

Solution
(a) We take the differential and obtain $\mathrm{d}\boldsymbol{Y} = \boldsymbol{A}(\mathrm{d}\boldsymbol{X})\boldsymbol{B}$, so that

$$\mathrm{d}\operatorname{vec}\boldsymbol{Y} = (\boldsymbol{B}' \otimes \boldsymbol{A})\,\mathrm{d}\operatorname{vec}\boldsymbol{X}.$$

The Jacobian matrix (the derivative) $\boldsymbol{J}(\boldsymbol{Y},\boldsymbol{X})$ of the transformation from $\boldsymbol{X}$ to $\boldsymbol{Y}$ is therefore $\boldsymbol{B}' \otimes \boldsymbol{A}$, and its determinant is $\det(\boldsymbol{J}) = |\boldsymbol{A}|^n|\boldsymbol{B}|^n$. The absolute value $|\det(\boldsymbol{J})|$ is the Jacobian of the transformation.
(b) Now, $\mathrm{d}\boldsymbol{Y} = \boldsymbol{A}(\mathrm{d}\boldsymbol{X})\boldsymbol{A}'$, so that $\mathrm{d}\operatorname{vec}\boldsymbol{Y} = (\boldsymbol{A} \otimes \boldsymbol{A})\,\mathrm{d}\operatorname{vec}\boldsymbol{X}$. Both $\boldsymbol{X}$ and $\boldsymbol{Y}$ are symmetric, say of order n. Hence, $\operatorname{vec}\boldsymbol{X} = \boldsymbol{D}_n \operatorname{vech}(\boldsymbol{X})$ and, using Exercise 11.27(a), $\operatorname{vech}(\boldsymbol{Y}) = \boldsymbol{D}_n^+ \operatorname{vec}\boldsymbol{Y}$. This gives

$$\mathrm{d}\operatorname{vech}(\boldsymbol{Y}) = \boldsymbol{D}_n^+\,\mathrm{d}\operatorname{vec}\boldsymbol{Y} = \boldsymbol{D}_n^+(\boldsymbol{A} \otimes \boldsymbol{A})\,\mathrm{d}\operatorname{vec}\boldsymbol{X} = \boldsymbol{D}_n^+(\boldsymbol{A} \otimes \boldsymbol{A})\boldsymbol{D}_n\,\mathrm{d}\operatorname{vech}(\boldsymbol{X}).$$

The Jacobian matrix of the transformation between the $\frac{1}{2}n(n+1)$ variables y_{ij} and the $\frac{1}{2}n(n+1)$ variables x_{ij} is then given by $\boldsymbol{J} = \boldsymbol{D}_n^+(\boldsymbol{A} \otimes \boldsymbol{A})\boldsymbol{D}_n$, and the determinant is $\det(\boldsymbol{J}) = |\boldsymbol{D}_n^+(\boldsymbol{A} \otimes \boldsymbol{A})\boldsymbol{D}_n| = |\boldsymbol{A}|^{n+1}$, using Exercise 11.33(c). The absolute value $|\det(\boldsymbol{J})|$ is the Jacobian of the transformation.

Exercise 13.38 (Jacobian of inverse transformation, 1)
(a) Obtain the Jacobian of the transformation $\boldsymbol{Y} := \boldsymbol{X}^{-1}$.
(b) How is the result affected when $\boldsymbol{X}$ is known to be symmetric?

Solution
(a) From $\mathrm{d}\boldsymbol{Y} = \mathrm{d}\boldsymbol{X}^{-1} = -\boldsymbol{X}^{-1}(\mathrm{d}\boldsymbol{X})\boldsymbol{X}^{-1}$, we find

$$\mathrm{d}\operatorname{vec}\boldsymbol{Y} = -(\boldsymbol{X}'^{-1} \otimes \boldsymbol{X}^{-1})\,\mathrm{d}\operatorname{vec}\boldsymbol{X}$$

and, using Exercise 10.12(b), the determinant is

$$\det(\boldsymbol{J}) = |-(\boldsymbol{X}'^{-1} \otimes \boldsymbol{X}^{-1})| = (-1)^n|\boldsymbol{X}|^{-2n},$$

where n denotes the order of $\boldsymbol{X}$. The Jacobian is $|\det(\boldsymbol{J})| = |\boldsymbol{X}|^{-2n}$.
(b) If $\boldsymbol{X}$ is symmetric, then so is $\boldsymbol{Y}$. As in Exercise 13.37, we write

$$\mathrm{d}\operatorname{vec}(\boldsymbol{Y}) = \boldsymbol{D}_n^+\,\mathrm{d}\operatorname{vec}\boldsymbol{Y} = -\boldsymbol{D}_n^+(\boldsymbol{X}^{-1} \otimes \boldsymbol{X}^{-1})\boldsymbol{D}_n\,\mathrm{d}\operatorname{vech}(\boldsymbol{X})$$

with determinant

$$\det(\boldsymbol{J}) = |-\boldsymbol{D}_n^+(\boldsymbol{X}^{-1} \otimes \boldsymbol{X}^{-1})\boldsymbol{D}_n| = (-1)^{\frac{1}{2}n(n+1)}|\boldsymbol{X}^{-1}|^{n+1}.$$

Hence, the Jacobian is $|\det(\boldsymbol{J})| = |\det(\boldsymbol{X})|^{-(n+1)}$.

Exercise 13.39 (Jacobian of inverse transformation, 2) Find the Jacobian of the transformation $\boldsymbol{Y} := |\boldsymbol{X}|\boldsymbol{X}^{-1}$.

Solution

We first find the differential,

$$\mathrm{d}\boldsymbol{Y} = (\mathrm{d}|\boldsymbol{X}|)\boldsymbol{X}^{-1} + |\boldsymbol{X}|\,\mathrm{d}\boldsymbol{X}^{-1} = |\boldsymbol{X}|(\operatorname{tr}\boldsymbol{X}^{-1}\,\mathrm{d}\boldsymbol{X})\boldsymbol{X}^{-1} - |\boldsymbol{X}|\boldsymbol{X}^{-1}(\mathrm{d}\boldsymbol{X})\boldsymbol{X}^{-1}.$$

Taking vecs,

$$\begin{aligned}\mathrm{d}\operatorname{vec}\boldsymbol{Y} &= |\boldsymbol{X}|((\operatorname{vec}\boldsymbol{X}^{-1})(\operatorname{vec}\boldsymbol{X}'^{-1})' - \boldsymbol{X}'^{-1} \otimes \boldsymbol{X}^{-1})\,\mathrm{d}\operatorname{vec}\boldsymbol{X} \\ &= -|\boldsymbol{X}|(\boldsymbol{I}_n \otimes \boldsymbol{X}^{-1})(\boldsymbol{I}_{n^2} - (\operatorname{vec}\boldsymbol{I}_n)(\operatorname{vec}\boldsymbol{I}_n)')(\boldsymbol{X}'^{-1} \otimes \boldsymbol{I}_n)\,\mathrm{d}\operatorname{vec}\boldsymbol{X}.\end{aligned}$$

Since $|\boldsymbol{I}_{n^2} - (\operatorname{vec}\boldsymbol{I}_n)(\operatorname{vec}\boldsymbol{I}_n)'| = -(n-1)$ (Exercise 7.36), we find

$$\boldsymbol{J} = \frac{\partial \operatorname{vec}\boldsymbol{Y}}{\partial(\operatorname{vec}\boldsymbol{X})'} = (-1)^{n^2}|\boldsymbol{X}|^{n^2}|\boldsymbol{X}|^{-n}(-(n-1))|\boldsymbol{X}|^{-n} = (-1)^{n^2+1}(n-1)|\boldsymbol{X}|^{n(n-2)}$$

so that the Jacobian equals $|\boldsymbol{J}| = (n-1)|\det(\boldsymbol{X})|^{n(n-2)}$.

Exercise 13.40 (Jacobians and linear structures) Consider the relation between s variables y_{ij} and s variables x_{ij} given by $\boldsymbol{Y} := \boldsymbol{F}(\boldsymbol{X})$, where $\boldsymbol{X} \in \mathrm{L}(\boldsymbol{\Delta}_1)$ and

$$\boldsymbol{Y} \in \mathrm{L}(\boldsymbol{\Delta}_2) \quad \text{for every } \boldsymbol{X} \in \mathrm{L}(\boldsymbol{\Delta}_1).$$

Assume that the dimensions of $\mathrm{L}(\boldsymbol{\Delta}_1)$ and $\mathrm{L}(\boldsymbol{\Delta}_2)$ are both equal to s. Show that the Jacobian matrix of the transformation from $\boldsymbol{X}$ to $\boldsymbol{Y}$ is given by

$$\boldsymbol{\Delta}_2^+ \frac{\partial \operatorname{vec}\boldsymbol{Y}}{\partial(\operatorname{vec}\boldsymbol{X})'}\boldsymbol{\Delta}_1,$$

so that the Jacobian is given by the absolute value of its determinant.

Solution

Using the notation of Section 11.4, we write $\boldsymbol{\Delta}_1\boldsymbol{\psi}_1(\boldsymbol{X}) = \operatorname{vec}\boldsymbol{X}$ and $\boldsymbol{\Delta}_2\boldsymbol{\psi}_2(\boldsymbol{Y}) = \operatorname{vec}\boldsymbol{Y}$. Then, $\boldsymbol{\psi}_2(\boldsymbol{Y}) = \boldsymbol{\Delta}_2^+\operatorname{vec}\boldsymbol{Y}$, and, upon taking the differential,

$$\begin{aligned}\mathrm{d}\boldsymbol{\psi}_2(\boldsymbol{Y}) = \boldsymbol{\Delta}_2^+\,\mathrm{d}\operatorname{vec}\boldsymbol{Y} &= \boldsymbol{\Delta}_2^+\frac{\partial \operatorname{vec}\boldsymbol{Y}}{\partial(\operatorname{vec}\boldsymbol{X})'}\,\mathrm{d}\operatorname{vec}\boldsymbol{X} \\ &= \boldsymbol{\Delta}_2^+\frac{\partial \operatorname{vec}\boldsymbol{Y}}{\partial(\operatorname{vec}\boldsymbol{X})'}\boldsymbol{\Delta}_1\,\mathrm{d}\boldsymbol{\psi}_1(\boldsymbol{X}).\end{aligned}$$

Hence,

$$J = \frac{\partial \psi_2(\boldsymbol{Y})}{\partial (\psi_1(\boldsymbol{X}))'} = \boldsymbol{\Delta}_2^+ \frac{\partial \operatorname{vec} \boldsymbol{Y}}{\partial (\operatorname{vec} \boldsymbol{X})'} \boldsymbol{\Delta}_1,$$

and the Jacobian is given by $|\det(\boldsymbol{J})|$.

13.9 Sensitivity analysis in regression models

Exercise 13.41 (Sensitivity of OLS) Consider the linear regression model $\boldsymbol{y} = \boldsymbol{X}\boldsymbol{\beta} + \boldsymbol{\varepsilon}$, where $\boldsymbol{X} := (\boldsymbol{x}_1, \dots, \boldsymbol{x}_k)$ is an $n \times k$ matrix of regressors, $\boldsymbol{y}$ is an $n \times 1$ vector of random observations, and $\boldsymbol{\beta}$ is a $k \times 1$ vector of unknown coefficients.
(a) Obtain the differential and derivative of $\hat{\boldsymbol{\beta}} := (\boldsymbol{X}'\boldsymbol{X})^{-1}\boldsymbol{X}'\boldsymbol{y}$ with respect to $\boldsymbol{X}$. The estimator is called the (ordinary) least-squares (OLS) estimator, and the derivative with respect to $\boldsymbol{X}$ is called the *sensitivity* of $\hat{\boldsymbol{\beta}}$ with respect to $\boldsymbol{X}$.
(b) Obtain also the sensitivity of $\hat{\boldsymbol{\beta}}$ with respect to $\boldsymbol{x}_j$.

Solution
(a) Taking the differential of $\hat{\boldsymbol{\beta}}$ gives

$$\begin{aligned}
\mathrm{d}\hat{\boldsymbol{\beta}} &= (\mathrm{d}(\boldsymbol{X}'\boldsymbol{X})^{-1})\boldsymbol{X}'\boldsymbol{y} + (\boldsymbol{X}'\boldsymbol{X})^{-1}(\mathrm{d}\boldsymbol{X})'\boldsymbol{y} \\
&= -(\boldsymbol{X}'\boldsymbol{X})^{-1}(\mathrm{d}\boldsymbol{X}'\boldsymbol{X})(\boldsymbol{X}'\boldsymbol{X})^{-1}\boldsymbol{X}'\boldsymbol{y} + (\boldsymbol{X}'\boldsymbol{X})^{-1}(\mathrm{d}\boldsymbol{X})'\boldsymbol{y} \\
&= -(\boldsymbol{X}'\boldsymbol{X})^{-1}(\mathrm{d}\boldsymbol{X})'\boldsymbol{X}\hat{\boldsymbol{\beta}} - (\boldsymbol{X}'\boldsymbol{X})^{-1}\boldsymbol{X}'(\mathrm{d}\boldsymbol{X})\hat{\boldsymbol{\beta}} + (\boldsymbol{X}'\boldsymbol{X})^{-1}(\mathrm{d}\boldsymbol{X})'\boldsymbol{y} \\
&= (\boldsymbol{X}'\boldsymbol{X})^{-1}(\mathrm{d}\boldsymbol{X})'\hat{\boldsymbol{\varepsilon}} - (\boldsymbol{X}'\boldsymbol{X})^{-1}\boldsymbol{X}'(\mathrm{d}\boldsymbol{X})\hat{\boldsymbol{\beta}},
\end{aligned}$$

where $\hat{\boldsymbol{\varepsilon}} := \boldsymbol{y} - \boldsymbol{X}\hat{\boldsymbol{\beta}}$ denotes the vector of residuals. Hence, using the commutation matrix,

$$\begin{aligned}
\mathrm{d}\hat{\boldsymbol{\beta}} = \mathrm{d}\operatorname{vec}\hat{\boldsymbol{\beta}} &= (\hat{\boldsymbol{\varepsilon}}' \otimes (\boldsymbol{X}'\boldsymbol{X})^{-1})\,\mathrm{d}\operatorname{vec}\boldsymbol{X}' - (\hat{\boldsymbol{\beta}}' \otimes (\boldsymbol{X}'\boldsymbol{X})^{-1}\boldsymbol{X}')\,\mathrm{d}\operatorname{vec}\boldsymbol{X} \\
&= ((\hat{\boldsymbol{\varepsilon}}' \otimes (\boldsymbol{X}'\boldsymbol{X})^{-1})\boldsymbol{K}_{nk} - \hat{\boldsymbol{\beta}}' \otimes (\boldsymbol{X}'\boldsymbol{X})^{-1}\boldsymbol{X}')\,\mathrm{d}\operatorname{vec}\boldsymbol{X} \\
&= ((\boldsymbol{X}'\boldsymbol{X})^{-1} \otimes \hat{\boldsymbol{\varepsilon}}' - \hat{\boldsymbol{\beta}}' \otimes (\boldsymbol{X}'\boldsymbol{X})^{-1}\boldsymbol{X}')\,\mathrm{d}\operatorname{vec}\boldsymbol{X},
\end{aligned}$$

so that

$$\frac{\partial \hat{\boldsymbol{\beta}}}{\partial (\operatorname{vec}\boldsymbol{X})'} = (\boldsymbol{X}'\boldsymbol{X})^{-1} \otimes \hat{\boldsymbol{\varepsilon}}' - \hat{\boldsymbol{\beta}}' \otimes (\boldsymbol{X}'\boldsymbol{X})^{-1}\boldsymbol{X}'.$$

(b) If only $\boldsymbol{x}_j$ is perturbed, we can write $\mathrm{d}\boldsymbol{X} = (\mathrm{d}\boldsymbol{x}_j)\boldsymbol{e}_j'$, and hence

$$\begin{aligned}
\mathrm{d}\hat{\boldsymbol{\beta}} &= ((\boldsymbol{X}'\boldsymbol{X})^{-1} \otimes \hat{\boldsymbol{\varepsilon}}' - \hat{\boldsymbol{\beta}}' \otimes (\boldsymbol{X}'\boldsymbol{X})^{-1}\boldsymbol{X}')(\boldsymbol{e}_j \otimes \mathrm{d}\boldsymbol{x}_j) \\
&= ((\boldsymbol{X}'\boldsymbol{X})^{-1}\boldsymbol{e}_j \otimes \hat{\boldsymbol{\varepsilon}}' - \hat{\beta}_j \otimes (\boldsymbol{X}'\boldsymbol{X})^{-1}\boldsymbol{X}')\,\mathrm{d}\boldsymbol{x}_j \\
&= -(\boldsymbol{X}'\boldsymbol{X})^{-1}(\hat{\beta}_j\boldsymbol{X}' - \boldsymbol{e}_j\hat{\boldsymbol{\varepsilon}}')\,\mathrm{d}\boldsymbol{x}_j,
\end{aligned}$$

so that the derivative simplifies to

$$\frac{\partial \hat{\beta}}{\partial x_j'} = -(X'X)^{-1}(\hat{\beta}_j X' - e_j \hat{\varepsilon}').$$

Exercise 13.42 (Sensitivity of residuals)
(a) Now obtain the sensitivity of the residual vector $\hat{\varepsilon}$ with respect to X.
(b) Also obtain the sensitivity of $\hat{\varepsilon}$ with respect to x_j.

Solution
We have

$$\hat{\varepsilon} = y - X\hat{\beta} = y - X(X'X)^{-1}X'y = (I_n - X(X'X)^{-1}X')y = My,$$

where $M = I_n - X(X'X)^{-1}X'$. We know from Exercise 13.24 that

$$\mathrm{d}M = -M(\mathrm{d}X)(X'X)^{-1}X' - X(X'X)^{-1}(\mathrm{d}X)'M.$$

Hence,

$$\begin{aligned}\mathrm{d}\hat{\varepsilon} &= (\mathrm{d}M)y = -M(\mathrm{d}X)\hat{\beta} - X(X'X)^{-1}(\mathrm{d}X)'\hat{\varepsilon} \\ &= -(\hat{\beta}' \otimes M)\,\mathrm{d}\,\mathrm{vec}\, X - \mathrm{vec}\left(\hat{\varepsilon}'(\mathrm{d}X)(X'X)^{-1}X'\right) \\ &= \left(-\hat{\beta}' \otimes M - X(X'X)^{-1} \otimes \hat{\varepsilon}'\right)\mathrm{d}\,\mathrm{vec}\, X,\end{aligned}$$

so that

$$\frac{\partial \hat{\varepsilon}}{\partial (\mathrm{vec}\, X)'} = -\hat{\beta}' \otimes M - X(X'X)^{-1} \otimes \hat{\varepsilon}'.$$

(b) If $\mathrm{d}X = (\mathrm{d}x_j)e_j'$, then

$$\begin{aligned}\mathrm{d}\hat{\varepsilon} &= -(\hat{\beta}' \otimes M + X(X'X)^{-1} \otimes \hat{\varepsilon}')(e_j \otimes \mathrm{d}x_j) \\ &= -(\hat{\beta}_j M + X(X'X)^{-1}e_j\hat{\varepsilon}')\,\mathrm{d}x_j\end{aligned}$$

and

$$\frac{\partial \hat{\varepsilon}}{\partial x_j'} = -(\hat{\beta}_j M + X(X'X)^{-1}e_j\hat{\varepsilon}').$$

Exercise 13.43 (Sensitivity of GLS) Next consider the model $y = X\beta + u$ with $\mathrm{E}(u) = 0$ and $\mathrm{var}(u) = \Omega$, where Ω is positive definite and depends on a single parameter α. The GLS (generalized least-squares) estimator of β is

$$\hat{\beta} := (X'\Omega^{-1}X)^{-1}X'\Omega^{-1}y.$$

Obtain the sensitivity of $\hat{\beta}$ with respect to α.

Solution
Taking the differential yields

$$\begin{aligned}
\mathrm{d}\hat{\beta} &= \left(\mathrm{d}(X'\Omega^{-1}X)^{-1}\right) X'\Omega^{-1}y + (X'\Omega^{-1}X)^{-1}X'(\mathrm{d}\Omega^{-1})y \\
&= -(X'\Omega^{-1}X)^{-1}X'(\mathrm{d}\Omega^{-1})X(X'\Omega^{-1}X)^{-1}X'\Omega^{-1}y \\
&\quad - (X'\Omega^{-1}X)^{-1}X'\Omega^{-1}(\mathrm{d}\Omega)\Omega^{-1}y \\
&= (X'\Omega^{-1}X)^{-1}X'\Omega^{-1}(\mathrm{d}\Omega)\Omega^{-1}X\hat{\beta} - (X'\Omega^{-1}X)^{-1}X'\Omega^{-1}(\mathrm{d}\Omega)\Omega^{-1}y \\
&= -(X'\Omega^{-1}X)^{-1}X'\Omega^{-1}(\mathrm{d}\Omega)\Omega^{-1}\hat{u},
\end{aligned}$$

where $\hat{u} := y - X\hat{\beta}$. Hence,

$$\begin{aligned}
\mathrm{d}\hat{\beta} &= -(\hat{u}'\Omega^{-1} \otimes (X'\Omega^{-1}X)^{-1}X'\Omega^{-1})\,\mathrm{d}\operatorname{vec}\Omega \\
&= -(\hat{u}'\Omega^{-1} \otimes (X'\Omega^{-1}X)^{-1}X'\Omega^{-1})\frac{\partial \operatorname{vec}\Omega}{\partial \alpha}\,\mathrm{d}\alpha,
\end{aligned}$$

and

$$\frac{\partial\hat{\beta}}{\partial\alpha} = -(\hat{u}'\Omega^{-1} \otimes (X'\Omega^{-1}X)^{-1}X'\Omega^{-1})\frac{\partial \operatorname{vec}\Omega}{\partial \alpha}.$$

***Exercise 13.44 (Bayesian sensitivity)** Let $y = X\beta + u$, where $u \sim \mathrm{N}(0, \Omega)$ and Ω is positive definite. Suppose there is prior information on β, say $\beta \sim \mathrm{N}(\underline{\beta}, \underline{H}^{-1})$, where $\underline{H}$ is positive definite. Then the posterior distribution of β is $\beta \sim \mathrm{N}(\overline{\beta}, \overline{H}^{-1})$, where

$$\overline{\beta} := \overline{H}^{-1}(\underline{H}\,\underline{\beta} + X'\Omega^{-1}y), \qquad \overline{H} := \underline{H} + X'\Omega^{-1}X.$$

Determine the sensitivity of the posterior expectation $\overline{\beta}$ with respect to the prior moments $\underline{\beta}$ and $\underline{H}^{-1}$.

Solution
We have

$$\begin{aligned}
\mathrm{d}\overline{\beta} &= (\mathrm{d}\overline{H}^{-1})(\underline{H}\,\underline{\beta} + X'\Omega^{-1}y) + \overline{H}^{-1}\,\mathrm{d}(\underline{H}\,\underline{\beta}) \\
&= -\overline{H}^{-1}(\mathrm{d}\overline{H})\overline{H}^{-1}(\underline{H}\,\underline{\beta} + X'\Omega^{-1}y) + \overline{H}^{-1}(\mathrm{d}\underline{H})\underline{\beta} + \overline{H}^{-1}\underline{H}\,\mathrm{d}\underline{\beta} \\
&= -\overline{H}^{-1}(\mathrm{d}\underline{H})\overline{\beta} + \overline{H}^{-1}(\mathrm{d}\underline{H})\underline{\beta} + \overline{H}^{-1}\underline{H}\,\mathrm{d}\underline{\beta} \\
&= \overline{H}^{-1}(\mathrm{d}\underline{H})(\underline{\beta} - \overline{\beta}) + \overline{H}^{-1}\underline{H}\,\mathrm{d}\underline{\beta} \\
&= -\overline{H}^{-1}\underline{H}(\mathrm{d}\underline{H}^{-1})\underline{H}(\underline{\beta} - \overline{\beta}) + \overline{H}^{-1}\underline{H}\,\mathrm{d}\underline{\beta} \\
&= ((\overline{\beta} - \underline{\beta})'\underline{H} \otimes \overline{H}^{-1}\underline{H})\,\mathrm{d}\operatorname{vec}\underline{H}^{-1} + \overline{H}^{-1}\underline{H}\,\mathrm{d}\underline{\beta} \\
&= ((\overline{\beta} - \underline{\beta})'\underline{H} \otimes \overline{H}^{-1}\underline{H})D_k\,\mathrm{dvech}(\underline{H}^{-1}) + \overline{H}^{-1}\underline{H}\,\mathrm{d}\underline{\beta},
\end{aligned}$$

where D_k denotes the duplication matrix. Hence,

$$\frac{\partial \overline{\beta}}{\partial (\operatorname{vech}(\underline{H}^{-1}))'} = ((\overline{\beta} - \underline{\beta})'\underline{H} \otimes \overline{H}^{-1}\underline{H})D_k$$

and

$$\frac{\partial \overline{\beta}}{\partial \underline{\beta}'} = \overline{H}^{-1}\underline{H} = (I + \underline{H}^{-1}X'\Omega^{-1}X)^{-1}.$$

13.10 The Hessian matrix

Exercise 13.45 (Hessian of linear form) Let a be a vector of constants, and A and B two matrices of constants. Find the second differential and the Hessian matrix of the linear functions:
(a) $\varphi(X) := a'x$;
(b) $\varphi(X) := \operatorname{tr} AXB$.

Solution
(a) We have $\mathrm{d}\varphi = a'\,\mathrm{d}x$ and hence $\mathrm{d}^2\varphi = 0$. As a result, the Hessian matrix is the $n \times n$ null matrix (if x is an $n \times 1$ vector).
(b) Similarly, $\mathrm{d}\varphi = \operatorname{tr} A(\mathrm{d}X)B$ and $\mathrm{d}^2\varphi = 0$. The Hessian is the $mn \times mn$ null matrix (if X is an $m \times n$ matrix).

Exercise 13.46 (Hessian of quadratic form, 1) Find the second differential and the Hessian matrix of $\varphi(x) := x'Ax$, where A is a matrix of constants, not necessarily symmetric.

Solution
Now we have

$$\mathrm{d}\varphi = (\mathrm{d}x)'Ax + x'A\,\mathrm{d}x = x'(A + A')\,\mathrm{d}x$$

and

$$\mathrm{d}^2\varphi = (\mathrm{d}x)'(A + A')\,\mathrm{d}x.$$

Since the matrix $A + A'$ is already symmetric, the Hessian is $\mathrm{H}\varphi(x) = A + A'$.

Exercise 13.47 (Identification of the Hessian, 1) Let A and B be two matrices of constants. Let X be an $m \times n$ matrix. Find the Hessian matrix of:
(a) $\varphi(X) := \operatorname{tr} X'X$;
(b) $\varphi(X) := \operatorname{tr} AX'BX$.
(c) (Identification) Show that

$$\mathrm{d}^2\varphi(X) = \operatorname{tr} A(\mathrm{d}X)'B(\mathrm{d}X) \iff \mathrm{H}\varphi(X) = \frac{1}{2}(A' \otimes B + A \otimes B'),$$

where A and B may depend on X.

Solution
(a) From $\mathrm{d}\varphi = \operatorname{tr}(\mathrm{d}\boldsymbol{X})'\boldsymbol{X} + \operatorname{tr}\boldsymbol{X}'\,\mathrm{d}\boldsymbol{X} = 2\operatorname{tr}\boldsymbol{X}'\,\mathrm{d}\boldsymbol{X}$, we obtain

$$\mathrm{d}^2\varphi = 2\operatorname{tr}(\mathrm{d}\boldsymbol{X})'(\mathrm{d}\boldsymbol{X}) = 2(\mathrm{d}\operatorname{vec}\boldsymbol{X})'(\mathrm{d}\operatorname{vec}\boldsymbol{X}),$$

implying that

$$\mathrm{H}\varphi(\boldsymbol{X}) = \frac{\partial^2\varphi(\boldsymbol{X})}{\partial(\operatorname{vec}\boldsymbol{X})\partial(\operatorname{vec}\boldsymbol{X})'} = 2\boldsymbol{I}_{mn}.$$

(b) Similarly, $\mathrm{d}\varphi = \operatorname{tr}\boldsymbol{A}(\mathrm{d}\boldsymbol{X})'\boldsymbol{B}\boldsymbol{X} + \operatorname{tr}\boldsymbol{A}\boldsymbol{X}'\boldsymbol{B}(\mathrm{d}\boldsymbol{X})$ and $\mathrm{d}^2\varphi = 2\operatorname{tr}\boldsymbol{A}(\mathrm{d}\boldsymbol{X})'\boldsymbol{B}(\mathrm{d}\boldsymbol{X})$. Now, since $\operatorname{tr}\boldsymbol{ABCD} = (\operatorname{vec}\boldsymbol{B}')'(\boldsymbol{A}'\otimes\boldsymbol{C})\operatorname{vec}\boldsymbol{D}$ (Exercise 10.20(b)), we obtain

$$\mathrm{d}^2\varphi = 2(\mathrm{d}\operatorname{vec}\boldsymbol{X})'(\boldsymbol{A}'\otimes\boldsymbol{B})(\mathrm{d}\operatorname{vec}\boldsymbol{X}).$$

Since the Hessian matrix *must* be symmetric, we find

$$\mathrm{H}\varphi(\boldsymbol{X}) = \boldsymbol{A}'\otimes\boldsymbol{B} + \boldsymbol{A}\otimes\boldsymbol{B}'.$$

Notice that $\boldsymbol{A}$ and $\boldsymbol{B}$ must be square matrices, of orders $n\times n$ and $m\times m$, respectively.
(c) More generally,

$$\mathrm{d}^2\varphi = \operatorname{tr}\boldsymbol{A}(\mathrm{d}\boldsymbol{X})'\boldsymbol{B}(\mathrm{d}\boldsymbol{X}) = (\mathrm{d}\operatorname{vec}\boldsymbol{X})'(\boldsymbol{A}'\otimes\boldsymbol{B})\,\mathrm{d}\operatorname{vec}\boldsymbol{X}$$

implies, and is implied by,

$$\mathrm{H}\varphi(\boldsymbol{X}) = \frac{1}{2}(\boldsymbol{A}'\otimes\boldsymbol{B} + \boldsymbol{A}\otimes\boldsymbol{B}').$$

This result is useful in many applications.

Exercise 13.48 (Identification of the Hessian, 2) Let $\boldsymbol{A}$ and $\boldsymbol{B}$ be two matrices of constants. Find the Hessian matrix of:
(a) $\varphi(\boldsymbol{X}) := \operatorname{tr}\boldsymbol{X}^2$ ($\boldsymbol{X}$ of order $n\times n$);
(b) $\varphi(\boldsymbol{X}) := \operatorname{tr}\boldsymbol{AXBX}$ ($\boldsymbol{X}$ of order $m\times n$).
(c) (Identification) Show that

$$\mathrm{d}^2\varphi(\boldsymbol{X}) = \operatorname{tr}\boldsymbol{A}(\mathrm{d}\boldsymbol{X})\boldsymbol{B}(\mathrm{d}\boldsymbol{X}) \iff \mathrm{H}\varphi(\boldsymbol{X}) = \frac{1}{2}\boldsymbol{K}_{nm}(\boldsymbol{A}'\otimes\boldsymbol{B} + \boldsymbol{B}'\otimes\boldsymbol{A}),$$

where $\boldsymbol{A}$ and $\boldsymbol{B}$ may depend on the $m\times n$ matrix $\boldsymbol{X}$.

Solution
(a) From $\mathrm{d}\varphi = \operatorname{tr}(\mathrm{d}\boldsymbol{X})\boldsymbol{X} + \operatorname{tr}\boldsymbol{X}(\mathrm{d}\boldsymbol{X}) = 2\operatorname{tr}\boldsymbol{X}\,\mathrm{d}\boldsymbol{X}$, we find

$$\mathrm{d}^2\varphi = 2\operatorname{tr}(\mathrm{d}\boldsymbol{X})(\mathrm{d}\boldsymbol{X}) = 2(\mathrm{d}\operatorname{vec}\boldsymbol{X}')'(\mathrm{d}\operatorname{vec}\boldsymbol{X}) = 2(\mathrm{d}\operatorname{vec}\boldsymbol{X})'\boldsymbol{K}_n\,\mathrm{d}\operatorname{vec}\boldsymbol{X}.$$

Since $\boldsymbol{K}_n$ is symmetric, $\mathrm{H}\varphi(\boldsymbol{X}) = 2\boldsymbol{K}_n$.
(b) Now we have

$$\begin{aligned}\mathrm{d}^2\varphi(\boldsymbol{X}) &= 2\operatorname{tr}\boldsymbol{A}(\mathrm{d}\boldsymbol{X})\boldsymbol{B}(\mathrm{d}\boldsymbol{X}) = 2(\mathrm{d}\operatorname{vec}\boldsymbol{X}')'(\boldsymbol{A}'\otimes\boldsymbol{B})\,\mathrm{d}\operatorname{vec}\boldsymbol{X}\\ &= 2(\mathrm{d}\operatorname{vec}\boldsymbol{X})'\boldsymbol{K}_{nm}(\boldsymbol{A}'\otimes\boldsymbol{B})\,\mathrm{d}\operatorname{vec}\boldsymbol{X}\end{aligned}$$

with Hessian matrix (symmetric!)

$$\mathrm{H}\varphi(\boldsymbol{X}) = \boldsymbol{K}_{nm}(\boldsymbol{A}' \otimes \boldsymbol{B}) + (\boldsymbol{A} \otimes \boldsymbol{B}')\boldsymbol{K}_{mn} = \boldsymbol{K}_{nm}(\boldsymbol{A}' \otimes \boldsymbol{B} + \boldsymbol{B}' \otimes \boldsymbol{A}).$$

(c) In general,

$$\mathrm{d}^2\varphi(\boldsymbol{X}) = \operatorname{tr} \boldsymbol{A}(\mathrm{d}\boldsymbol{X})\boldsymbol{B}(\mathrm{d}\boldsymbol{X}) = (\mathrm{dvec}\,\boldsymbol{X})'\boldsymbol{K}_{nm}(\boldsymbol{A}' \otimes \boldsymbol{B})\,\mathrm{dvec}\,\boldsymbol{X}$$

implies, and is implied by,

$$\mathrm{H}\varphi(\boldsymbol{X}) = \frac{1}{2}(\boldsymbol{K}_{nm}(\boldsymbol{A}' \otimes \boldsymbol{B}) + (\boldsymbol{A} \otimes \boldsymbol{B}')\boldsymbol{K}_{mn}) = \frac{1}{2}\boldsymbol{K}_{nm}(\boldsymbol{A}' \otimes \boldsymbol{B} + \boldsymbol{B}' \otimes \boldsymbol{A}).$$

Exercise 13.49 (Hessian of $\boldsymbol{a}'\boldsymbol{X}\boldsymbol{X}'\boldsymbol{a}$) Find the Hessian matrix of $\varphi(\boldsymbol{X}) := \boldsymbol{a}'\boldsymbol{X}\boldsymbol{X}'\boldsymbol{a}$, where $\boldsymbol{a}$ is a vector of constants.

Solution

The first differential is

$$\mathrm{d}\varphi = \boldsymbol{a}'(\mathrm{d}\boldsymbol{X})\boldsymbol{X}'\boldsymbol{a} + \boldsymbol{a}'\boldsymbol{X}(\mathrm{d}\boldsymbol{X})'\boldsymbol{a} = 2\boldsymbol{a}'(\mathrm{d}\boldsymbol{X})\boldsymbol{X}'\boldsymbol{a},$$

and the second differential

$$\mathrm{d}^2\varphi = 2\boldsymbol{a}'(\mathrm{d}\boldsymbol{X})(\mathrm{d}\boldsymbol{X})'\boldsymbol{a} = 2\operatorname{tr}(\mathrm{d}\boldsymbol{X})'\boldsymbol{a}\boldsymbol{a}'(\mathrm{d}\boldsymbol{X}).$$

This is of the form $\mathrm{d}^2\varphi = \operatorname{tr} \boldsymbol{A}(\mathrm{d}\boldsymbol{X})'\boldsymbol{B}(\mathrm{d}\boldsymbol{X})$, where $\boldsymbol{A} := 2\boldsymbol{I}$ and $\boldsymbol{B} := \boldsymbol{a}\boldsymbol{a}'$, and the Hessian thus follows from Exercise 13.47; it is $\mathrm{H}\varphi(\boldsymbol{X}) = 2(\boldsymbol{I} \otimes \boldsymbol{a}\boldsymbol{a}')$.

Exercise 13.50 (Hessian of $\operatorname{tr} \boldsymbol{X}^{-1}$) Find the Hessian matrix of $\varphi(\boldsymbol{X}) := \operatorname{tr} \boldsymbol{X}^{-1}$, where $\boldsymbol{X}$ is a nonsingular matrix of order $n \times n$.

Solution

We take differentials twice and obtain from $\mathrm{d}\boldsymbol{X}^{-1} = -\boldsymbol{X}^{-1}(\mathrm{d}\boldsymbol{X})\boldsymbol{X}^{-1}$,

$$\begin{aligned}\mathrm{d}^2\boldsymbol{X}^{-1} &= -(\mathrm{d}\boldsymbol{X}^{-1})(\mathrm{d}\boldsymbol{X})\boldsymbol{X}^{-1} - \boldsymbol{X}^{-1}(\mathrm{d}\boldsymbol{X})\,\mathrm{d}\boldsymbol{X}^{-1} \\ &= \boldsymbol{X}^{-1}(\mathrm{d}\boldsymbol{X})\boldsymbol{X}^{-1}(\mathrm{d}\boldsymbol{X})\boldsymbol{X}^{-1} + \boldsymbol{X}^{-1}(\mathrm{d}\boldsymbol{X})\boldsymbol{X}^{-1}(\mathrm{d}\boldsymbol{X})\boldsymbol{X}^{-1}.\end{aligned}$$

Hence,

$$\mathrm{d}^2\mathrm{tr}\,\boldsymbol{X}^{-1} = \mathrm{tr}\,\mathrm{d}^2\boldsymbol{X}^{-1} = 2\operatorname{tr}\boldsymbol{X}^{-2}(\mathrm{d}\boldsymbol{X})\boldsymbol{X}^{-1}(\mathrm{d}\boldsymbol{X})$$

and the Hessian follows from Exercise 13.48 as

$$\mathrm{H}\varphi(\boldsymbol{X}) = \boldsymbol{K}_n(\boldsymbol{X}'^{-2} \otimes \boldsymbol{X}^{-1} + \boldsymbol{X}'^{-1} \otimes \boldsymbol{X}^{-2}).$$

Exercise 13.51 (Hessian of $|\boldsymbol{X}|$) Obtain the Hessian matrix of $\varphi(\boldsymbol{X}) := |\boldsymbol{X}|$.

Solution
From $\mathrm{d}|\boldsymbol{X}| = |\boldsymbol{X}| \operatorname{tr} \boldsymbol{X}^{-1} \mathrm{d}\boldsymbol{X}$, we obtain

$$\begin{aligned}
\mathrm{d}^2|\boldsymbol{X}| &= (\mathrm{d}|\boldsymbol{X}|) \operatorname{tr} \boldsymbol{X}^{-1} \mathrm{d}\boldsymbol{X} + |\boldsymbol{X}| \operatorname{tr}(\mathrm{d}\boldsymbol{X}^{-1}) \mathrm{d}\boldsymbol{X} \\
&= |\boldsymbol{X}|(\operatorname{tr} \boldsymbol{X}^{-1} \mathrm{d}\boldsymbol{X})^2 - |\boldsymbol{X}| \operatorname{tr} \boldsymbol{X}^{-1}(\mathrm{d}\boldsymbol{X})\boldsymbol{X}^{-1} \mathrm{d}\boldsymbol{X} \\
&= |\boldsymbol{X}|(\mathrm{d}\operatorname{vec} \boldsymbol{X})'(\operatorname{vec} \boldsymbol{X}'^{-1})(\operatorname{vec} \boldsymbol{X}'^{-1})' \mathrm{d}\operatorname{vec} \boldsymbol{X} \\
&\quad - |\boldsymbol{X}|(\mathrm{d}\operatorname{vec} \boldsymbol{X}')'(\boldsymbol{X}'^{-1} \otimes \boldsymbol{X}^{-1}) \mathrm{d}\operatorname{vec} \boldsymbol{X} \\
&= -|\boldsymbol{X}|(\mathrm{d}\operatorname{vec} \boldsymbol{X})' \left(\boldsymbol{K}_n(\boldsymbol{X}'^{-1} \otimes \boldsymbol{X}^{-1}) - (\operatorname{vec} \boldsymbol{X}'^{-1})(\operatorname{vec} \boldsymbol{X}'^{-1})'\right) \mathrm{d}\operatorname{vec} \boldsymbol{X},
\end{aligned}$$

and, since $\boldsymbol{K}_n(\boldsymbol{X}'^{-1} \otimes \boldsymbol{X}^{-1})$ is symmetric, we find

$$\mathrm{H}\varphi(\boldsymbol{X}) = -|\boldsymbol{X}| \left(\boldsymbol{K}_n(\boldsymbol{X}'^{-1} \otimes \boldsymbol{X}^{-1}) - (\operatorname{vec} \boldsymbol{X}'^{-1})(\operatorname{vec} \boldsymbol{X}'^{-1})'\right).$$

Exercise 13.52 (Hessian of $\log|\boldsymbol{X}|$) Let $\boldsymbol{X}$ be an $n \times n$ matrix with $|\boldsymbol{X}| > 0$. Find the Hessian of $\varphi(\boldsymbol{X}) := \log|\boldsymbol{X}|$.

Solution
Since $\mathrm{d}\varphi = \operatorname{tr} \boldsymbol{X}^{-1} \mathrm{d}\boldsymbol{X}$, we find

$$\mathrm{d}^2\varphi = -\operatorname{tr} \boldsymbol{X}^{-1}(\mathrm{d}\boldsymbol{X})\boldsymbol{X}^{-1} \mathrm{d}\boldsymbol{X},$$

and the Hessian follows from Exercise 13.48 as

$$\mathrm{H}\varphi(\boldsymbol{X}) = -\boldsymbol{K}_n(\boldsymbol{X}'^{-1} \otimes \boldsymbol{X}^{-1}).$$

Exercise 13.53 (Hessian of quadratic form, 2) Let $\boldsymbol{f}(\boldsymbol{x})$ be an $m \times 1$ vector function of a $n \times 1$ vector $\boldsymbol{x}$, and let $\boldsymbol{A}$ be a symmetric $m \times m$ matrix of constants. Obtain the Hessian matrix of $\varphi(\boldsymbol{x}) := \boldsymbol{f}(\boldsymbol{x})'\boldsymbol{A}\boldsymbol{f}(\boldsymbol{x})$.

Solution
We have

$$\mathrm{d}\varphi = (\mathrm{d}\boldsymbol{f})'\boldsymbol{A}\boldsymbol{f} + \boldsymbol{f}'\boldsymbol{A}(\mathrm{d}\boldsymbol{f}) = 2\boldsymbol{f}'\boldsymbol{A}\,\mathrm{d}\boldsymbol{f}$$

and

$$\mathrm{d}^2\varphi = 2(\mathrm{d}\boldsymbol{f})'\boldsymbol{A}\,\mathrm{d}\boldsymbol{f} + 2\boldsymbol{f}'\boldsymbol{A}\,\mathrm{d}^2\boldsymbol{f}.$$

One of the good things about matrix calculus using differentials is that you can do it sequentially, like here. So, we first evaluate $\mathrm{d}\boldsymbol{f}$ and $\mathrm{d}^2\boldsymbol{f}$:

$$\mathrm{d}\boldsymbol{f} = \boldsymbol{C}(\mathrm{d}\boldsymbol{x}), \quad \boldsymbol{C} := \frac{\partial \boldsymbol{f}(\boldsymbol{x})}{\partial \boldsymbol{x}'}.$$

Note that $\boldsymbol{C}$ is an $m \times n$ matrix. The tricky part is $\mathrm{d}^2\boldsymbol{f}$. We define

$$\boldsymbol{B}_i := \mathrm{H}f_i(\boldsymbol{x}) = \frac{\partial^2 f_i(\boldsymbol{x})}{\partial \boldsymbol{x} \partial \boldsymbol{x}'} \quad (i = 1, \dots, m).$$

Notice that $\boldsymbol{B}_i$ must be symmetric, because it is the Hessian matrix of $f_i(\boldsymbol{x})$. Then, $\mathrm{d}^2\boldsymbol{f}$ is an $m \times 1$ vector whose i-th component equals $(\mathrm{d}\boldsymbol{x})'\boldsymbol{B}_i(\mathrm{d}\boldsymbol{x})$.

Now, let $\boldsymbol{g}(\boldsymbol{x}) := \boldsymbol{A}\boldsymbol{f}(\boldsymbol{x})$. Then,

$$\begin{aligned}
\mathrm{d}^2\varphi &= 2(\mathrm{d}\boldsymbol{f})'\boldsymbol{A}\,\mathrm{d}\boldsymbol{f} + 2\boldsymbol{f}'\boldsymbol{A}\,\mathrm{d}^2\boldsymbol{f} \\
&= 2(\mathrm{d}\boldsymbol{x})'\boldsymbol{C}'\boldsymbol{A}\boldsymbol{C}(\mathrm{d}\boldsymbol{x}) + 2\boldsymbol{g}(\boldsymbol{x})' \begin{pmatrix} (\mathrm{d}\boldsymbol{x})'\boldsymbol{B}_1(\mathrm{d}\boldsymbol{x}) \\ \vdots \\ (\mathrm{d}\boldsymbol{x})'\boldsymbol{B}_m(\mathrm{d}\boldsymbol{x}) \end{pmatrix} \\
&= 2(\mathrm{d}\boldsymbol{x})'\boldsymbol{C}'\boldsymbol{A}\boldsymbol{C}(\mathrm{d}\boldsymbol{x}) + 2(\mathrm{d}\boldsymbol{x})' \left(\sum_i g_i(\boldsymbol{x})\boldsymbol{B}_i(\boldsymbol{x}) \right) (\mathrm{d}\boldsymbol{x}) \\
&= 2(\mathrm{d}\boldsymbol{x})' \left(\boldsymbol{C}'\boldsymbol{A}\boldsymbol{C} + \sum_i g_i(\boldsymbol{x})\boldsymbol{B}_i(\boldsymbol{x}) \right) (\mathrm{d}\boldsymbol{x})
\end{aligned}$$

This gives the Hessian matrix

$$\mathrm{H}\varphi(\boldsymbol{x}) = 2 \left(\boldsymbol{C}'\boldsymbol{A}\boldsymbol{C} + \sum_i g_i(\boldsymbol{x})\boldsymbol{B}_i(\boldsymbol{x}) \right).$$

Notice that in matrix calculus, we always try as much as possible to work with whole matrices and not with elements, but sometimes one has to go back to the elements. Here there is no alternative.

13.11 Least squares and best linear unbiased estimation

Exercise 13.54 (Least squares) Given an $n \times k$ matrix $\boldsymbol{X}$ of rank k and an $n \times 1$ vector $\boldsymbol{y}$, find the unique $k \times 1$ vector $\boldsymbol{\beta}$ that minimizes $(\boldsymbol{y} - \boldsymbol{X}\boldsymbol{\beta})'(\boldsymbol{y} - \boldsymbol{X}\boldsymbol{\beta})$.

Solution
Let $\varphi(\boldsymbol{\beta}) := (\boldsymbol{y} - \boldsymbol{X}\boldsymbol{\beta})'(\boldsymbol{y} - \boldsymbol{X}\boldsymbol{\beta})$. Then,

$$\mathrm{d}\varphi = 2(\boldsymbol{y} - \boldsymbol{X}\boldsymbol{\beta})'\,\mathrm{d}(\boldsymbol{y} - \boldsymbol{X}\boldsymbol{\beta}) = -2(\boldsymbol{y} - \boldsymbol{X}\boldsymbol{\beta})'\boldsymbol{X}\,\mathrm{d}\boldsymbol{\beta},$$

so that $\mathrm{d}\varphi = 0$ implies that $\boldsymbol{X}'(\boldsymbol{y} - \boldsymbol{X}\boldsymbol{\beta}) = \boldsymbol{0}$, that is, $\boldsymbol{X}'\boldsymbol{X}\boldsymbol{\beta} = \boldsymbol{X}'\boldsymbol{y}$. Since $\mathrm{rk}(\boldsymbol{X}) = k$, this equation has a unique solution, $\hat{\boldsymbol{\beta}} = (\boldsymbol{X}'\boldsymbol{X})^{-1}\boldsymbol{X}'\boldsymbol{y}$.

To prove that this solution is a minimum, it suffices to note that $\varphi(\boldsymbol{\beta})$ is convex. Equivalently, we can compute $\mathrm{d}^2\varphi = 2(\mathrm{d}\boldsymbol{\beta})'\boldsymbol{X}'\boldsymbol{X}\,\mathrm{d}\boldsymbol{\beta}$, and notice that the Hessian matrix $\mathrm{H}\varphi = 2\boldsymbol{X}'\boldsymbol{X}$ is positive definite. This implies that φ is strictly convex.

Exercise 13.55 (Generalized least-squares) Under the same conditions, find the vector β that minimizes $(y - X\beta)'\Omega^{-1}(y - X\beta)$, where Ω is a positive definite $n \times n$ matrix.

Solution

Let $\tilde{y} := \Omega^{-1/2}y$ and $\tilde{X} := \Omega^{-1/2}X$. Then, minimizing $(y - X\beta)'\Omega^{-1}(y - X\beta)$ is equivalent to minimizing $(\tilde{y} - \tilde{X}\beta)'(\tilde{y} - \tilde{X}\beta)$. The solution is given in Exercise 13.54:

$$\hat{\beta} = (\tilde{X}'\tilde{X})^{-1}\tilde{X}'\tilde{y} = (X'\Omega^{-1}X)^{-1}X'\Omega^{-1}y.$$

Exercise 13.56 (Constrained least-squares) Next, under the same conditions, minimize $(y - X\beta)'\Omega^{-1}(y - X\beta)$ under the constraint $R'\beta = c$, where R is a $k \times r$ matrix of rank r.

Solution

Define the Lagrangian function

$$\psi(\beta) := \frac{1}{2}(y - X\beta)'\Omega^{-1}(y - X\beta) - l'(R'\beta - c),$$

where l is an $r \times 1$ vector of Lagrange multipliers. Taking the differential of ψ gives

$$\begin{aligned} \mathrm{d}\psi &= (y - X\beta)'\Omega^{-1}\,\mathrm{d}(y - X\beta) - l'R'\,\mathrm{d}\beta \\ &= -((y - X\beta)'\Omega^{-1}X + l'R')\,\mathrm{d}\beta. \end{aligned}$$

The first-order conditions are therefore

$$X'\Omega^{-1}X\beta - Rl = X'\Omega^{-1}y, \quad R'\beta = c.$$

We can write these two equations as

$$\begin{pmatrix} X'\Omega^{-1}X & R \\ R' & O \end{pmatrix}\begin{pmatrix} \beta \\ -l \end{pmatrix} = \begin{pmatrix} X'\Omega^{-1}y \\ c \end{pmatrix},$$

and solve by inverting the partitioned matrix; see Exercise 8.50. Let us try and solve the first-order conditions without inverting a partitioned matrix. We are interested in solving for β, but in constrained problems of this type we (almost) always have to solve first for l and then for β. We could premultiply the first condition by R' (since $R'R$ is nonsingular). This would solve l in terms of β,

$$l = (R'R)^{-1}R'X'\Omega^{-1}X\beta - (R'R)^{-1}R'X'\Omega^{-1}y,$$

but, since we do not know $R'X'\Omega^{-1}X\beta$, we do not obtain a full solution for l in this way. We must use the fact that, although β is not known, $R'\beta$ is known. This is achieved by premultiplying the first condition by $R'(X'\Omega^{-1}X)^{-1}$, giving

$$R'\beta - R'(X'\Omega^{-1}X)^{-1}Rl = R'(X'\Omega^{-1}X)^{-1}X'\Omega^{-1}y.$$

The matrix $R'(X'\Omega^{-1}X)^{-1}R$ is nonsingular. (For any positive definite matrix A, we have $\operatorname{rk}(B'AB) = \operatorname{rk}(B)$, see Exercise 8.26(a).) Denote the unconstrained solution by

$\hat{\beta} = (X'\Omega^{-1}X)^{-1}X'\Omega^{-1}y$. Then, since $R'\beta = c$, we find the solution for l as

$$\tilde{l} = (R'(X'\Omega^{-1}X)^{-1}R)^{-1}(c - R'\hat{\beta})$$

and hence the constrained solution for β as

$$\begin{aligned}\tilde{\beta} &= (X\Omega^{-1}X)^{-1}R\tilde{l} + \hat{\beta} \\ &= \hat{\beta} + (X'\Omega^{-1}X)^{-1}R(R'(X'\Omega^{-1}X)^{-1}R)^{-1}(c - R'\hat{\beta}).\end{aligned}$$

Since ψ is strictly convex, the solution $\tilde{\beta}$ provides a strict constrained global minimum.

Exercise 13.57 (Gauss-Markov theorem) Let X be a given $n \times k$ matrix of rank k. Find the $k \times n$ matrix G that minimizes $\operatorname{tr} GG'$ subject to the constraint $GX = I_k$.

Solution

We consider the Lagrangian function

$$\psi(G) := \frac{1}{2}\operatorname{tr} GG' - \operatorname{tr} L'(GX - I_k),$$

where L is a $k \times k$ matrix of Lagrange multipliers. Taking the differential of ψ with respect to G yields

$$\begin{aligned}\mathrm{d}\psi &= \frac{1}{2}\operatorname{tr}(\mathrm{d}G)G' + \frac{1}{2}\operatorname{tr} G(\mathrm{d}G)' - \operatorname{tr} L'(\mathrm{d}G)X \\ &= \operatorname{tr} G'\,\mathrm{d}G - \operatorname{tr} XL'\,\mathrm{d}G = \operatorname{tr}(G' - XL')\,\mathrm{d}G.\end{aligned}$$

The first-order conditions are

$$G' = XL', \quad GX = I_k.$$

To solve the two conditions for G and L, we (again) solve first for L. From $I_k = GX = LX'X$, we find

$$\hat{L} = (X'X)^{-1}, \quad \hat{G} = \hat{L}X' = (X'X)^{-1}X'.$$

Since ψ is strictly convex, $\frac{1}{2}\operatorname{tr} GG'$ has a strict global minimum at $\hat{G} = (X'X)^{-1}X'$ under the constraint $GX = I_k$. (Notice that $\hat{G} = X^+$. In fact we could have *defined* the MP-inverse through its least-squares property.)

Exercise 13.58 (Aitken's theorem) Let X be a given $n \times k$ matrix of rank k, let Ω be a positive definite $n \times n$ matrix, and let W be a given $m \times k$ matrix. Find the $m \times n$ matrix G that minimizes $\operatorname{tr} G\Omega G'$ subject to the constraint $GX = W$.

Solution

We define the Lagrangian function

$$\psi(G) := \frac{1}{2}\operatorname{tr} G\Omega G' - \operatorname{tr} L'(GX - W)$$

where $\boldsymbol{L}$ is an $m \times k$ matrix of Lagrange multipliers. Taking the differential of ψ with respect to $\boldsymbol{G}$ yields

$$\begin{aligned}\mathrm{d}\psi &= \frac{1}{2}\operatorname{tr}(\mathrm{d}\boldsymbol{G})\boldsymbol{\Omega}\boldsymbol{G}' + \frac{1}{2}\operatorname{tr}\boldsymbol{G}\boldsymbol{\Omega}(\mathrm{d}\boldsymbol{G})' - \operatorname{tr}\boldsymbol{L}'(\mathrm{d}\boldsymbol{G})\boldsymbol{X} \\ &= \operatorname{tr}\boldsymbol{\Omega}\boldsymbol{G}'\,\mathrm{d}\boldsymbol{G} - \operatorname{tr}\boldsymbol{X}\boldsymbol{L}'\,\mathrm{d}\boldsymbol{G} = \operatorname{tr}(\boldsymbol{\Omega}\boldsymbol{G}' - \boldsymbol{X}\boldsymbol{L}')\,\mathrm{d}\boldsymbol{G}.\end{aligned}$$

Hence, the first-order conditions are

$$\boldsymbol{\Omega}\boldsymbol{G}' = \boldsymbol{X}\boldsymbol{L}', \quad \boldsymbol{G}\boldsymbol{X} = \boldsymbol{W}.$$

We now write

$$\boldsymbol{W} = \boldsymbol{G}\boldsymbol{X} = (\boldsymbol{L}\boldsymbol{X}'\boldsymbol{\Omega}^{-1})\boldsymbol{X} = \boldsymbol{L}(\boldsymbol{X}'\boldsymbol{\Omega}^{-1}\boldsymbol{X}).$$

Solving $\boldsymbol{L}$ gives $\hat{\boldsymbol{L}} = \boldsymbol{W}(\boldsymbol{X}'\boldsymbol{\Omega}^{-1}\boldsymbol{X})^{-1}$ and hence

$$\hat{\boldsymbol{G}} = \hat{\boldsymbol{L}}\boldsymbol{X}'\boldsymbol{\Omega}^{-1} = \boldsymbol{W}(\boldsymbol{X}'\boldsymbol{\Omega}^{-1}\boldsymbol{X})^{-1}\boldsymbol{X}'\boldsymbol{\Omega}^{-1}.$$

Since ψ is strictly convex, $\hat{\boldsymbol{G}}$ provides the constrained minimum.

***Exercise 13.59 (Multicollinearity)** Let $\boldsymbol{X}$ be a given $n \times k$ matrix, and let $\boldsymbol{\Omega}$ be a positive definite $n \times n$ matrix. Without the assumption that $\operatorname{rk}(\boldsymbol{X}) = k$, minimize $\operatorname{tr}\boldsymbol{G}\boldsymbol{\Omega}\boldsymbol{G}'$ under the constraint $\boldsymbol{G}\boldsymbol{X} = \boldsymbol{X}$.

Solution

We define the Lagrangian function

$$\psi(\boldsymbol{G}) := \frac{1}{2}\operatorname{tr}\boldsymbol{G}\boldsymbol{\Omega}\boldsymbol{G}' - \operatorname{tr}\boldsymbol{L}'(\boldsymbol{G}\boldsymbol{X} - \boldsymbol{X}),$$

where $\boldsymbol{L}$ is an $n \times k$ matrix of Lagrange multipliers. Taking the differential gives

$$\begin{aligned}\mathrm{d}\psi &= \frac{1}{2}\operatorname{tr}(\mathrm{d}\boldsymbol{G})\boldsymbol{\Omega}\boldsymbol{G}' + \frac{1}{2}\operatorname{tr}\boldsymbol{G}\boldsymbol{\Omega}(\mathrm{d}\boldsymbol{G})' - \operatorname{tr}\boldsymbol{L}'(\mathrm{d}\boldsymbol{G})\boldsymbol{X} \\ &= \operatorname{tr}(\boldsymbol{\Omega}\boldsymbol{G}' - \boldsymbol{X}\boldsymbol{L}')\,\mathrm{d}\boldsymbol{G},\end{aligned}$$

from which we obtain the first-order conditions as

$$\boldsymbol{\Omega}\boldsymbol{G}' = \boldsymbol{X}\boldsymbol{L}', \quad \boldsymbol{G}\boldsymbol{X} = \boldsymbol{X}.$$

Since $\boldsymbol{G} = \boldsymbol{L}\boldsymbol{X}'\boldsymbol{\Omega}^{-1}$, we can write

$$\boldsymbol{X} = \boldsymbol{G}\boldsymbol{X} = \boldsymbol{L}\boldsymbol{X}'\boldsymbol{\Omega}^{-1}\boldsymbol{X}.$$

Since $\boldsymbol{X}'\boldsymbol{\Omega}^{-1}\boldsymbol{X}$ can be singular, it is not immediately obvious that this equation has any solution for $\boldsymbol{L}$. So, let us show that it does. By Exercise 10.49(a), a necessary and sufficient condition for the equation $\boldsymbol{L}\boldsymbol{B} = \boldsymbol{C}$ to have a solution is that $\boldsymbol{C}\boldsymbol{B}^+\boldsymbol{B} = \boldsymbol{C}$. In the above case, we need to demonstrate that

$$\boldsymbol{X}(\boldsymbol{X}'\boldsymbol{\Omega}^{-1}\boldsymbol{X})^+\boldsymbol{X}'\boldsymbol{\Omega}^{-1}\boldsymbol{X} = \boldsymbol{X},$$

or, letting $\tilde{\boldsymbol{X}} := \boldsymbol{\Omega}^{-1/2}\boldsymbol{X}$, that

$$\tilde{\boldsymbol{X}}(\tilde{\boldsymbol{X}}'\tilde{\boldsymbol{X}})^+\tilde{\boldsymbol{X}}'\tilde{\boldsymbol{X}} = \tilde{\boldsymbol{X}}.$$

But this is a well-known result (Exercise 10.30(a)). Hence, the equation $\boldsymbol{L}\boldsymbol{X}'\boldsymbol{\Omega}^{-1}\boldsymbol{X} = \boldsymbol{X}$ does have a solution. This solution, however, is not unique, unless $\boldsymbol{X}$ has full column rank. The general solution is given by

$$\hat{\boldsymbol{L}} = \boldsymbol{X}(\boldsymbol{X}'\boldsymbol{\Omega}^{-1}\boldsymbol{X})^+ + \boldsymbol{Q}(\boldsymbol{I}_k - (\boldsymbol{X}'\boldsymbol{\Omega}^{-1}\boldsymbol{X})(\boldsymbol{X}'\boldsymbol{\Omega}^{-1}\boldsymbol{X})^+),$$

where $\boldsymbol{Q}$ is an arbitrary $n \times k$ matrix. Even though $\hat{\boldsymbol{L}}$ is not unique, the matrix $\hat{\boldsymbol{L}}\boldsymbol{X}'$ *is* unique, namely $\hat{\boldsymbol{L}}\boldsymbol{X}' = \boldsymbol{X}(\boldsymbol{X}'\boldsymbol{\Omega}^{-1}\boldsymbol{X})^+\boldsymbol{X}'$, and hence

$$\hat{G} = \hat{\boldsymbol{L}}\boldsymbol{X}'\boldsymbol{\Omega}^{-1} = \boldsymbol{X}(\boldsymbol{X}'\boldsymbol{\Omega}^{-1}\boldsymbol{X})^+\boldsymbol{X}'\boldsymbol{\Omega}^{-1}.$$

Again, we see that ψ is convex, so that the first-order conditions define a minimum.

***Exercise 13.60 (Quadratic estimation of σ^2)** Let $\boldsymbol{X}$ be an $n \times k$ matrix of rank $r \leq k$, and let $\boldsymbol{V}$ be a positive semidefinite matrix of order n. Solve the constrained problem

$$\begin{aligned} &\text{minimize} \quad \frac{1}{n}\operatorname{tr}\boldsymbol{V}^2 \\ &\text{subject to} \quad \boldsymbol{V}\boldsymbol{X} = \mathbf{O}, \quad \operatorname{tr}\boldsymbol{V} = 1. \end{aligned}$$

(This problem relates to the best positive, quadratic, and unbiased estimation of σ^2 in the linear model $\boldsymbol{y} = \boldsymbol{X}\boldsymbol{\beta} + \boldsymbol{\varepsilon}$ with $\boldsymbol{\varepsilon} \sim \mathrm{N}(\mathbf{0}, \sigma^2\boldsymbol{I}_n)$.)

Solution

Since we require that $\boldsymbol{V}$ be positive semidefinite, we write $\boldsymbol{V} = \boldsymbol{T}'\boldsymbol{T}$, where $\boldsymbol{T}$ is a square matrix of order n. The constrained problem then becomes:

$$\begin{aligned} &\text{minimize} \quad \frac{1}{n}\operatorname{tr}(\boldsymbol{T}'\boldsymbol{T})^2 \\ &\text{subject to} \quad \boldsymbol{T}\boldsymbol{X} = \mathbf{O}, \quad \operatorname{tr}\boldsymbol{T}'\boldsymbol{T} = 1. \end{aligned}$$

Form the Lagrangian function

$$\psi(\boldsymbol{T}) := \frac{1}{4}\operatorname{tr}(\boldsymbol{T}'\boldsymbol{T})^2 - \frac{1}{2}\lambda(\operatorname{tr}\boldsymbol{T}'\boldsymbol{T} - 1) - \operatorname{tr}\boldsymbol{L}'\boldsymbol{T}\boldsymbol{X},$$

where λ is a Lagrange multiplier and $\boldsymbol{L}$ is a matrix of Lagrange multipliers. Taking the differential of ψ gives

$$\begin{aligned} \mathrm{d}\psi &= \frac{1}{2}\operatorname{tr}\boldsymbol{T}\boldsymbol{T}'\boldsymbol{T}(\mathrm{d}\boldsymbol{T})' + \frac{1}{2}\operatorname{tr}\boldsymbol{T}'\boldsymbol{T}\boldsymbol{T}'(\mathrm{d}\boldsymbol{T}) \\ &\quad - \frac{1}{2}\lambda\left(\operatorname{tr}(\mathrm{d}\boldsymbol{T})'\boldsymbol{T} + \operatorname{tr}\boldsymbol{T}'\,\mathrm{d}\boldsymbol{T}\right) - \operatorname{tr}\boldsymbol{L}'(\mathrm{d}\boldsymbol{T})\boldsymbol{X} \\ &= \operatorname{tr}\boldsymbol{T}'\boldsymbol{T}\boldsymbol{T}'\,\mathrm{d}\boldsymbol{T} - \lambda\operatorname{tr}\boldsymbol{T}'\,\mathrm{d}\boldsymbol{T} - \operatorname{tr}\boldsymbol{X}\boldsymbol{L}'\,\mathrm{d}\boldsymbol{T}, \end{aligned}$$

from which we obtain the first-order conditions

$$T'TT' = \lambda T' + XL', \quad \operatorname{tr} T'T = 1, \quad TX = \mathrm{O}.$$

Premultiplying the first condition byX' and using $TX = \mathrm{O}$, we obtain $X'XL' = \mathrm{O}$, so that $XL' = \mathrm{O}$, and hence

$$T'TT' = \lambda T'.$$

This implies that $(T'T)^2 = \lambda T'T$ and hence that $\lambda > 0$. Now, define $B := (1/\lambda)T'T$. Then we can rewrite the conditions as

$$B^2 = B, \quad \operatorname{tr} B = 1/\lambda, \quad BX = \mathrm{O}.$$

The matrix B is thus an idempotent symmetric matrix. Now, since $\operatorname{tr}(T'T)^2 = \lambda$, it appears that we must choose λ as small as possible; that is, we must choose the rank of B as large as possible. The only constraint on the rank of B is $BX = \mathrm{O}$, which implies that $\operatorname{rk}(B) \leq n - r$, where r is the rank of X. Since we wish to maximize $\operatorname{rk}(B)$ we take

$$1/\lambda = \operatorname{rk}(B) = n - r.$$

Then, using Exercise 10.42(b), we find $\hat{B} = I_n - XX^+$, and hence

$$\hat{V} = \hat{T}'\hat{T} = \lambda\hat{B} = \frac{1}{n-r}(I_n - XX^+).$$

13.12 Maximum likelihood estimation

***Exercise 13.61 (Symmetry ignored)** Let the random $m \times 1$ vectors $y_1, y_2, \ldots, y_n$ be independently and identically distributed such that

$$y_i \sim \mathrm{N}_m(\mu, \Omega) \quad (i = 1, \ldots, n),$$

where Ω is positive definite, and let $n \geq m + 1$. The maximum likelihood estimators of μ and Ω are

$$\hat{\mu} = \frac{1}{n}\sum_{i=1}^{n} y_i = \bar{y} \quad \text{and} \quad \hat{\Omega} = \frac{1}{n}\sum_{i=1}^{n}(y_i - \bar{y})(y_i - \bar{y})'.$$

Prove this well-known result, ignoring the fact that Ω is symmetric.

Solution

The log-likelihood function is

$$\ell(\mu, \Omega) = -\frac{1}{2}mn\log(2\pi) - \frac{1}{2}n\log|\Omega| - \frac{1}{2}\operatorname{tr}\Omega^{-1}Z,$$

where

$$Z = \sum_{i=1}^{n}(y_i - \mu)(y_i - \mu)'.$$

The first differential of ℓ is

$$\begin{aligned}
\mathrm{d}\ell &= -\frac{1}{2} n \,\mathrm{d}\log|\boldsymbol{\Omega}| - \frac{1}{2}\operatorname{tr}(\mathrm{d}\boldsymbol{\Omega}^{-1})\boldsymbol{Z} - \frac{1}{2}\operatorname{tr}\boldsymbol{\Omega}^{-1}\,\mathrm{d}\boldsymbol{Z} \\
&= -\frac{1}{2} n \operatorname{tr}\boldsymbol{\Omega}^{-1}\,\mathrm{d}\boldsymbol{\Omega} + \frac{1}{2}\operatorname{tr}\boldsymbol{\Omega}^{-1}(\mathrm{d}\boldsymbol{\Omega})\boldsymbol{\Omega}^{-1}\boldsymbol{Z} \\
&\quad + \frac{1}{2}\operatorname{tr}\boldsymbol{\Omega}^{-1}\left(\sum_i (\boldsymbol{y}_i - \boldsymbol{\mu})(\mathrm{d}\boldsymbol{\mu})' + (\mathrm{d}\boldsymbol{\mu})\sum_i (\boldsymbol{y}_i - \boldsymbol{\mu})'\right) \\
&= \frac{1}{2}\operatorname{tr}(\mathrm{d}\boldsymbol{\Omega})\boldsymbol{\Omega}^{-1}(\boldsymbol{Z} - n\boldsymbol{\Omega})\boldsymbol{\Omega}^{-1} + (\mathrm{d}\boldsymbol{\mu})'\boldsymbol{\Omega}^{-1}\sum_i (\boldsymbol{y}_i - \boldsymbol{\mu}) \\
&= \frac{1}{2}\operatorname{tr}(\mathrm{d}\boldsymbol{\Omega})\boldsymbol{\Omega}^{-1}(\boldsymbol{Z} - n\boldsymbol{\Omega})\boldsymbol{\Omega}^{-1} + n(\mathrm{d}\boldsymbol{\mu})'\boldsymbol{\Omega}^{-1}(\bar{\boldsymbol{y}} - \boldsymbol{\mu}).
\end{aligned}$$

Ignoring the symmetry constraint on $\boldsymbol{\Omega}$ gives the first-order conditions,

$$\boldsymbol{\Omega}^{-1}(\boldsymbol{Z} - n\boldsymbol{\Omega})\boldsymbol{\Omega}^{-1} = \mathbf{O}, \quad \boldsymbol{\Omega}^{-1}(\bar{\boldsymbol{y}} - \boldsymbol{\mu}) = \mathbf{0},$$

from which the maximum likelihood estimators follow. To prove that we have in fact found the maximum of ℓ, we take the differential again:

$$\begin{aligned}
\mathrm{d}^2\ell &= \frac{1}{2}\operatorname{tr}(\mathrm{d}\boldsymbol{\Omega})(\mathrm{d}\boldsymbol{\Omega}^{-1})(\boldsymbol{Z} - n\boldsymbol{\Omega})\boldsymbol{\Omega}^{-1} + \frac{1}{2}\operatorname{tr}(\mathrm{d}\boldsymbol{\Omega})\boldsymbol{\Omega}^{-1}(\boldsymbol{Z} - n\boldsymbol{\Omega})\,\mathrm{d}\boldsymbol{\Omega}^{-1} \\
&\quad + \frac{1}{2}\operatorname{tr}(\mathrm{d}\boldsymbol{\Omega})\boldsymbol{\Omega}^{-1}(\mathrm{d}\boldsymbol{Z} - n\,\mathrm{d}\boldsymbol{\Omega})\boldsymbol{\Omega}^{-1} + n(\mathrm{d}\boldsymbol{\mu})'(\mathrm{d}\boldsymbol{\Omega}^{-1})(\bar{\boldsymbol{y}} - \boldsymbol{\mu}) \\
&\quad - n(\mathrm{d}\boldsymbol{\mu})'\boldsymbol{\Omega}^{-1}\,\mathrm{d}\boldsymbol{\mu}.
\end{aligned}$$

At the point $(\hat{\boldsymbol{\mu}}, \hat{\boldsymbol{\Omega}})$ we have $\hat{\boldsymbol{\mu}} = \bar{\boldsymbol{y}}$, $\hat{\boldsymbol{Z}} - n\hat{\boldsymbol{\Omega}} = \mathbf{O}$, and

$$\mathrm{d}\hat{\boldsymbol{Z}} = -\sum_i \left((\mathrm{d}\boldsymbol{\mu})(\boldsymbol{y}_i - \hat{\boldsymbol{\mu}})' + (\boldsymbol{y}_i - \hat{\boldsymbol{\mu}})(\mathrm{d}\boldsymbol{\mu})'\right) = \mathbf{O},$$

since $\sum_i \boldsymbol{y}_i = n\hat{\boldsymbol{\mu}}$. Hence,

$$\mathrm{d}^2\ell(\hat{\boldsymbol{\mu}}, \hat{\boldsymbol{\Omega}}) = -\frac{n}{2}\operatorname{tr}(\mathrm{d}\boldsymbol{\Omega})\hat{\boldsymbol{\Omega}}^{-1}(\mathrm{d}\boldsymbol{\Omega})\hat{\boldsymbol{\Omega}}^{-1} - n(\mathrm{d}\boldsymbol{\mu})'\hat{\boldsymbol{\Omega}}^{-1}\,\mathrm{d}\boldsymbol{\mu} < 0$$

unless $\mathrm{d}\boldsymbol{\mu} = \mathbf{0}$ and $\mathrm{d}\boldsymbol{\Omega} = \mathbf{O}$. It follows that ℓ has a strict local maximum at $(\hat{\boldsymbol{\mu}}, \hat{\boldsymbol{\Omega}})$.

Exercise 13.62 (Symmetry: implicit treatment) Exercise 13.61 shows that, even if we do not impose symmetry (or positive definiteness) on $\boldsymbol{\Omega}$, the solution $\hat{\boldsymbol{\Omega}}$ is symmetric and positive semidefinite (in fact, positive definite with probability 1). Hence, there is no need to impose symmetry at this stage. (But to derive the information matrix, we do need a proper treatment of symmetry, see Exercise 13.65.) Prove the results of Exercise 13.61 again, but now taking symmetry *implicitly* into account, that is, by taking the differential with respect to $\operatorname{vech}(\boldsymbol{\Omega})$.

Solution

Using the expression for $\mathrm{d}\ell$ obtained in Exercise 13.61, we have

$$\begin{aligned}\mathrm{d}\ell &= \frac{1}{2}\operatorname{tr}(\mathrm{d}\boldsymbol{\Omega})\boldsymbol{\Omega}^{-1}(\boldsymbol{Z}-n\boldsymbol{\Omega})\boldsymbol{\Omega}^{-1} + n(\mathrm{d}\boldsymbol{\mu})'\boldsymbol{\Omega}^{-1}(\bar{\boldsymbol{y}}-\boldsymbol{\mu}) \\ &= \frac{1}{2}(\operatorname{vec}\mathrm{d}\boldsymbol{\Omega})'(\boldsymbol{\Omega}^{-1}\otimes\boldsymbol{\Omega}^{-1})\operatorname{vec}(\boldsymbol{Z}-n\boldsymbol{\Omega}) + n(\mathrm{d}\boldsymbol{\mu})'\boldsymbol{\Omega}^{-1}(\bar{\boldsymbol{y}}-\boldsymbol{\mu}) \\ &= \frac{1}{2}(\mathrm{d}\operatorname{vech}(\boldsymbol{\Omega}))'\boldsymbol{D}_m'(\boldsymbol{\Omega}^{-1}\otimes\boldsymbol{\Omega}^{-1})\operatorname{vec}(\boldsymbol{Z}-n\boldsymbol{\Omega}) + n(\mathrm{d}\boldsymbol{\mu})'\boldsymbol{\Omega}^{-1}(\bar{\boldsymbol{y}}-\boldsymbol{\mu}),\end{aligned}$$

where $\boldsymbol{D}_m$ is the duplication matrix. The first-order conditions are

$$\boldsymbol{\Omega}^{-1}(\bar{\boldsymbol{y}}-\boldsymbol{\mu}) = \boldsymbol{0}, \quad \boldsymbol{D}_m'(\boldsymbol{\Omega}^{-1}\otimes\boldsymbol{\Omega}^{-1})\operatorname{vec}(\boldsymbol{Z}-n\boldsymbol{\Omega}) = \boldsymbol{0}.$$

The first condition implies that $\hat{\boldsymbol{\mu}} = \bar{\boldsymbol{y}}$; the second condition can be written as

$$\boldsymbol{D}_m'(\boldsymbol{\Omega}^{-1}\otimes\boldsymbol{\Omega}^{-1})\boldsymbol{D}_m\operatorname{vech}(\boldsymbol{Z}-n\boldsymbol{\Omega}) = \boldsymbol{0},$$

because $\boldsymbol{Z}-n\boldsymbol{\Omega}$ is symmetric. Now, $\boldsymbol{D}_m'(\boldsymbol{\Omega}^{-1}\otimes\boldsymbol{\Omega}^{-1})\boldsymbol{D}_m$ is nonsingular (Exercise 11.34(a)), and so is $\boldsymbol{D}_m'(\hat{\boldsymbol{\Omega}}^{-1}\otimes\hat{\boldsymbol{\Omega}}^{-1})\boldsymbol{D}_m$ with probability 1 when $n \geq m+1$. Hence, $\operatorname{vech}(\hat{\boldsymbol{Z}}-n\hat{\boldsymbol{\Omega}}) = \boldsymbol{0}$. Using again the symmetry of $\hat{\boldsymbol{Z}}$ and $\hat{\boldsymbol{\Omega}}$, we obtain

$$\hat{\boldsymbol{\Omega}} = \frac{1}{n}\hat{\boldsymbol{Z}} = \frac{1}{n}\sum_{i=1}^{n}(\boldsymbol{y}_i-\bar{\boldsymbol{y}})(\boldsymbol{y}_i-\bar{\boldsymbol{y}})'.$$

Exercise 13.63 (Symmetry: explicit treatment) Now prove the same result again using an *explicit* treatment of symmetry, that is, by including the restriction $\boldsymbol{\Omega} = \boldsymbol{\Omega}'$.

Solution

Our starting point now is the Lagrangian function

$$\psi(\boldsymbol{\mu},\boldsymbol{\Omega}) := -\frac{1}{2}mn\log(2\pi) - \frac{1}{2}n\log|\boldsymbol{\Omega}| - \frac{1}{2}\operatorname{tr}\boldsymbol{\Omega}^{-1}\boldsymbol{Z} - \operatorname{tr}\boldsymbol{L}'(\boldsymbol{\Omega}-\boldsymbol{\Omega}'),$$

where $\boldsymbol{L}$ is an $m\times m$ matrix of Lagrange multipliers. Taking the differential yields

$$\mathrm{d}\psi = \frac{1}{2}\operatorname{tr}(\mathrm{d}\boldsymbol{\Omega})\boldsymbol{\Omega}^{-1}(\boldsymbol{Z}-n\boldsymbol{\Omega})\boldsymbol{\Omega}^{-1} + \operatorname{tr}(\boldsymbol{L}-\boldsymbol{L}')\,\mathrm{d}\boldsymbol{\Omega} + n(\mathrm{d}\boldsymbol{\mu})'\boldsymbol{\Omega}^{-1}(\bar{\boldsymbol{y}}-\boldsymbol{\mu}),$$

so that the first-order conditions are

$$\frac{1}{2}\boldsymbol{\Omega}^{-1}(\boldsymbol{Z}-n\boldsymbol{\Omega})\boldsymbol{\Omega}^{-1} + \boldsymbol{L}-\boldsymbol{L}' = \mathbf{O}, \quad \boldsymbol{\Omega}^{-1}(\bar{\boldsymbol{y}}-\boldsymbol{\mu}) = \boldsymbol{0}, \quad \boldsymbol{\Omega} = \boldsymbol{\Omega}'.$$

These three equations imply that $\hat{\boldsymbol{\mu}} = \bar{\boldsymbol{y}}$, and, since $\boldsymbol{\Omega}$ and $\boldsymbol{Z}$ are symmetric, that $\boldsymbol{L}-\boldsymbol{L}'$ is symmetric, that is, that $\boldsymbol{L} = \mathbf{O}$. Hence, $\boldsymbol{\Omega}^{-1}(\boldsymbol{Z}-n\boldsymbol{\Omega})\boldsymbol{\Omega}^{-1} = \mathbf{O}$, giving the required results.

Exercise 13.64 (Treatment of positive definiteness) Finally we may impose both symmetry *and* positive definiteness on $\boldsymbol{\Omega}$ by writing $\boldsymbol{\Omega} = \boldsymbol{T}'\boldsymbol{T}$, $\boldsymbol{T}$ square. Show that this approach leads to the same results again.

Solution
We have

$$
\begin{aligned}
\mathrm{d}\ell &= \frac{1}{2}\operatorname{tr}(\mathrm{d}\boldsymbol{\Omega})\boldsymbol{\Omega}^{-1}(\boldsymbol{Z}-n\boldsymbol{\Omega})\boldsymbol{\Omega}^{-1} + n(\mathrm{d}\boldsymbol{\mu})'\boldsymbol{\Omega}^{-1}(\bar{\boldsymbol{y}}-\boldsymbol{\mu}) \\
&= \frac{1}{2}\operatorname{tr}(\mathrm{d}\boldsymbol{T}'\boldsymbol{T})\boldsymbol{\Omega}^{-1}(\boldsymbol{Z}-n\boldsymbol{\Omega})\boldsymbol{\Omega}^{-1} + n(\mathrm{d}\boldsymbol{\mu})'\boldsymbol{\Omega}^{-1}(\bar{\boldsymbol{y}}-\boldsymbol{\mu}) \\
&= \frac{1}{2}\operatorname{tr}\left((\mathrm{d}\boldsymbol{T})'\boldsymbol{T}+\boldsymbol{T}'\,\mathrm{d}\boldsymbol{T})\boldsymbol{\Omega}^{-1}(\boldsymbol{Z}-n\boldsymbol{\Omega})\boldsymbol{\Omega}^{-1}\right) \\
&\quad + n(\mathrm{d}\boldsymbol{\mu})'\boldsymbol{\Omega}^{-1}(\bar{\boldsymbol{y}}-\boldsymbol{\mu}) \\
&= \operatorname{tr}\left(\boldsymbol{\Omega}^{-1}(\boldsymbol{Z}-n\boldsymbol{\Omega})\boldsymbol{\Omega}^{-1}\boldsymbol{T}'\,\mathrm{d}\boldsymbol{T}\right) + n(\mathrm{d}\boldsymbol{\mu})'\boldsymbol{\Omega}^{-1}(\bar{\boldsymbol{y}}-\boldsymbol{\mu}).
\end{aligned}
$$

The first-order conditions are

$$\boldsymbol{\Omega}^{-1}(\boldsymbol{Z}-n\boldsymbol{\Omega})\boldsymbol{\Omega}^{-1}\boldsymbol{T}' = \mathbf{O}, \quad \boldsymbol{\Omega}^{-1}(\bar{\boldsymbol{y}}-\boldsymbol{\mu}) = \mathbf{0},$$

from which it follows that $\hat{\boldsymbol{\mu}} = \bar{\boldsymbol{y}}$ and $\hat{\boldsymbol{\Omega}} = \hat{\boldsymbol{T}}'\hat{\boldsymbol{T}} = (1/n)\hat{\boldsymbol{Z}}$.

***Exercise 13.65 (Information matrix)** Consider again the log-likelihood function $\ell(\boldsymbol{\theta})$, where $\boldsymbol{\theta} := (\boldsymbol{\mu}', (\operatorname{vech}(\boldsymbol{\Omega}))')'$. Then

$$\mathcal{H}(\boldsymbol{\theta}) := \frac{\partial^2 \ell(\boldsymbol{\theta})}{\partial\boldsymbol{\theta}\partial\boldsymbol{\theta}'} \quad \text{and} \quad \boldsymbol{\mathcal{I}} := -\operatorname{E}(\mathcal{H}(\boldsymbol{\theta}))$$

denote the *Hessian matrix* of the log-likelihood function and the *information matrix*, respectively.
(a) Obtain the information matrix $\boldsymbol{\mathcal{I}}$ of $\boldsymbol{\mu}$ and $\operatorname{vech}(\boldsymbol{\Omega})$, taking the symmetry of $\boldsymbol{\Omega}$ implicitly into account, using the duplication matrix. In particular, show that

$$\boldsymbol{\mathcal{I}} = n\begin{pmatrix} \boldsymbol{\Omega}^{-1} & \mathbf{O} \\ \mathbf{O} & \frac{1}{2}\boldsymbol{D}_m'(\boldsymbol{\Omega}^{-1}\otimes\boldsymbol{\Omega}^{-1})\boldsymbol{D}_m \end{pmatrix}.$$

(b) From (a), obtain

$$n\boldsymbol{\mathcal{I}}^{-1} = \begin{pmatrix} \boldsymbol{\Omega} & \mathbf{O} \\ \mathbf{O} & 2\boldsymbol{D}_m^{+}(\boldsymbol{\Omega}\otimes\boldsymbol{\Omega})\boldsymbol{D}_m^{+\prime} \end{pmatrix}.$$

Solution
(a) Since $\boldsymbol{\Omega}$ is a linear function of $\operatorname{vech}(\boldsymbol{\Omega})$, we have $\mathrm{d}^2\boldsymbol{\Omega} = \mathbf{O}$ and hence the second differential of $\ell(\boldsymbol{\mu}, \operatorname{vech}(\boldsymbol{\Omega}))$ is given by

$$
\begin{aligned}
\mathrm{d}^2\ell(\boldsymbol{\mu}, \operatorname{vech}(\boldsymbol{\Omega})) &= \frac{1}{2}\operatorname{tr}(\mathrm{d}\boldsymbol{\Omega})(\mathrm{d}\boldsymbol{\Omega}^{-1})(\boldsymbol{Z}-n\boldsymbol{\Omega})\boldsymbol{\Omega}^{-1} \\
&\quad + \frac{1}{2}\operatorname{tr}(\mathrm{d}\boldsymbol{\Omega})\boldsymbol{\Omega}^{-1}(\boldsymbol{Z}-n\boldsymbol{\Omega})\,\mathrm{d}\boldsymbol{\Omega}^{-1} + \frac{1}{2}\operatorname{tr}(\mathrm{d}\boldsymbol{\Omega})\boldsymbol{\Omega}^{-1}(\mathrm{d}\boldsymbol{Z}-n\,\mathrm{d}\boldsymbol{\Omega})\boldsymbol{\Omega}^{-1} \\
&\quad + n(\mathrm{d}\boldsymbol{\mu})'(\mathrm{d}\boldsymbol{\Omega}^{-1})(\bar{\boldsymbol{y}}-\boldsymbol{\mu}) - n(\mathrm{d}\boldsymbol{\mu})'\boldsymbol{\Omega}^{-1}\,\mathrm{d}\boldsymbol{\mu}.
\end{aligned}
$$

Notice that we do not at this stage evaluate $\mathrm{d}^2\ell$ completely in terms of $\mathrm{d}\boldsymbol{\mu}$ and $\mathrm{d}\operatorname{vech}(\boldsymbol{\Omega})$; this is unnecessary because, upon taking expectations, we find immediately

$$-\operatorname{E}\left(\mathrm{d}^2\ell(\boldsymbol{\mu}, \operatorname{vech}(\boldsymbol{\Omega}))\right) = \frac{n}{2}\operatorname{tr}(\mathrm{d}\boldsymbol{\Omega})\boldsymbol{\Omega}^{-1}(\mathrm{d}\boldsymbol{\Omega})\boldsymbol{\Omega}^{-1} + n(\mathrm{d}\boldsymbol{\mu})'\boldsymbol{\Omega}^{-1}\,\mathrm{d}\boldsymbol{\mu},$$

from the following three facts. First, since $\boldsymbol{y}_i \sim \mathrm{N}_m(\boldsymbol{\mu}, \boldsymbol{\Omega})$ $(i = 1, \dots, n)$, we obtain $\operatorname{E}(\bar{\boldsymbol{y}}) = \boldsymbol{\mu}$. Second,

$$\operatorname{E}(\boldsymbol{Z}) = \operatorname{E}\left(\sum_{i=1}^{n}(\boldsymbol{y}_i - \boldsymbol{\mu})(\boldsymbol{y}_i - \boldsymbol{\mu})'\right) = n\boldsymbol{\Omega}.$$

And, third,

$$\operatorname{E}(\mathrm{d}\boldsymbol{Z}) = -\sum_{i=1}^{n}\operatorname{E}\left((\mathrm{d}\boldsymbol{\mu})(\boldsymbol{y}_i - \boldsymbol{\mu})' + (\boldsymbol{y}_i - \boldsymbol{\mu})(\mathrm{d}\boldsymbol{\mu})'\right) = \mathbf{O}.$$

We now use the duplication matrix and obtain

$$\begin{aligned}-\operatorname{E}\left(\mathrm{d}^2\ell(\boldsymbol{\mu}, \operatorname{vech}(\boldsymbol{\Omega}))\right) &= \frac{n}{2}(\operatorname{vec}\mathrm{d}\boldsymbol{\Omega})'(\boldsymbol{\Omega}^{-1} \otimes \boldsymbol{\Omega}^{-1})\operatorname{vec}\mathrm{d}\boldsymbol{\Omega} + n(\mathrm{d}\boldsymbol{\mu})'\boldsymbol{\Omega}^{-1}\,\mathrm{d}\boldsymbol{\mu} \\ &= \frac{n}{2}(\mathrm{d}\operatorname{vech}(\boldsymbol{\Omega}))'\boldsymbol{D}_m'(\boldsymbol{\Omega}^{-1} \otimes \boldsymbol{\Omega}^{-1})\boldsymbol{D}_m\,\mathrm{d}\operatorname{vech}(\boldsymbol{\Omega}) + n(\mathrm{d}\boldsymbol{\mu})'\boldsymbol{\Omega}^{-1}\,\mathrm{d}\boldsymbol{\mu}.\end{aligned}$$

Hence, the information matrix for $\boldsymbol{\mu}$ and $\operatorname{vech}(\boldsymbol{\Omega})$ is

$$\boldsymbol{\mathcal{I}} = n\begin{pmatrix}\boldsymbol{\Omega}^{-1} & \mathbf{O} \\ \mathbf{O} & \frac{1}{2}\boldsymbol{D}_m'(\boldsymbol{\Omega}^{-1} \otimes \boldsymbol{\Omega}^{-1})\boldsymbol{D}_m\end{pmatrix}.$$

(b) Its inverse is obtained from Exercise 11.34(b). We have

$$n\boldsymbol{\mathcal{I}}^{-1} = \begin{pmatrix}\boldsymbol{\Omega} & \mathbf{O} \\ \mathbf{O} & 2\boldsymbol{D}_m^+(\boldsymbol{\Omega} \otimes \boldsymbol{\Omega})\boldsymbol{D}_m^{+\prime}\end{pmatrix}.$$

13.13 Inequalities and equalities

Exercise 13.66 (Concavity?) Let $\boldsymbol{X}$ be a positive definite $n \times n$ matrix. Show that:
(a) $\log|\boldsymbol{X}|$ is concave;
(b) $|\boldsymbol{X}|$ is neither convex nor concave;
(c) $|\boldsymbol{X}|^{1/n}$ is concave for $n \geq 2$.

Solution
(a) Since $\mathrm{d}\log|\boldsymbol{X}| = \operatorname{tr}\boldsymbol{X}^{-1}\,\mathrm{d}\boldsymbol{X}$, we see that

$$\mathrm{d}^2\log|\boldsymbol{X}| = -\operatorname{tr}\boldsymbol{X}^{-1}(\mathrm{d}\boldsymbol{X})\boldsymbol{X}^{-1}\,\mathrm{d}\boldsymbol{X} = -(\mathrm{d}\operatorname{vec}\boldsymbol{X})'(\boldsymbol{X}^{-1} \otimes \boldsymbol{X}^{-1})\,\mathrm{d}\operatorname{vec}\boldsymbol{X} < 0$$

for all $\mathrm{d}\boldsymbol{X} \neq 0$. Hence, $\log|\boldsymbol{X}|$ is concave.
(b) If $|\boldsymbol{X}|$ were convex or concave on the set of positive definite matrices, then the function

$$\varphi(\boldsymbol{A}, \boldsymbol{B}) := \alpha|\boldsymbol{A}| + (1-\alpha)|\boldsymbol{B}| - |\alpha\boldsymbol{A} + (1-\alpha)\boldsymbol{B}|$$

would be nonnegative (convex) or nonpositive (concave) for every $\boldsymbol{A}$ and $\boldsymbol{B}$, and every $\alpha \in (0,1)$. To show that $|\boldsymbol{X}|$ is neither convex nor concave, let $\alpha = 1/2$, $\beta > 0$, and

$$\boldsymbol{A} = \begin{pmatrix} 1 & 0 \\ 0 & 1 \end{pmatrix} \quad \text{and} \quad \boldsymbol{B} = \begin{pmatrix} \beta & 0 \\ 0 & 5 \end{pmatrix}.$$

Then,

$$\alpha|\boldsymbol{A}| + (1-\alpha)|\boldsymbol{B}| - |\alpha\boldsymbol{A} + (1-\alpha)\boldsymbol{B}| = \beta - 1,$$

which is positive for $\beta > 1$ and negative for $0 < \beta < 1$.
(c) From

$$\mathrm{d}|\boldsymbol{X}|^{1/n} = \frac{1}{n}|\boldsymbol{X}|^{(1/n)-1}|\boldsymbol{X}| \operatorname{tr} \boldsymbol{X}^{-1}\,\mathrm{d}\boldsymbol{X} = \frac{1}{n}|\boldsymbol{X}|^{1/n} \operatorname{tr} \boldsymbol{X}^{-1}\,\mathrm{d}\boldsymbol{X},$$

we obtain

$$\begin{aligned}
\mathrm{d}^2|\boldsymbol{X}|^{1/n} &= \frac{1}{n}(\mathrm{d}|\boldsymbol{X}|^{1/n}) \operatorname{tr} \boldsymbol{X}^{-1}\,\mathrm{d}\boldsymbol{X} + \frac{1}{n}|\boldsymbol{X}|^{1/n} \operatorname{tr}(\mathrm{d}\boldsymbol{X}^{-1})\,\mathrm{d}\boldsymbol{X} \\
&= \frac{1}{n^2}|\boldsymbol{X}|^{1/n}(\operatorname{tr} \boldsymbol{X}^{-1}\,\mathrm{d}\boldsymbol{X})^2 - \frac{1}{n}|\boldsymbol{X}|^{1/n} \operatorname{tr}(\boldsymbol{X}^{-1}\,\mathrm{d}\boldsymbol{X})^2 \\
&= -\frac{1}{n}|\boldsymbol{X}|^{1/n}\left(\operatorname{tr}(\boldsymbol{X}^{-1}\,\mathrm{d}\boldsymbol{X})^2 - \frac{1}{n}(\operatorname{tr} \boldsymbol{X}^{-1}\,\mathrm{d}\boldsymbol{X})^2\right) \\
&= -\frac{1}{n}|\boldsymbol{X}|^{1/n}(\mathrm{d}\operatorname{vec} \boldsymbol{X})'\left(\boldsymbol{X}^{-1} \otimes \boldsymbol{X}^{-1} - \frac{1}{n}(\operatorname{vec} \boldsymbol{X}^{-1})(\operatorname{vec} \boldsymbol{X}^{-1})'\right)\mathrm{d}\operatorname{vec} \boldsymbol{X} \leq 0
\end{aligned}$$

for all $\mathrm{d}\boldsymbol{X} \neq \mathbf{O}$; see Exercise 10.21.

Exercise 13.67 (Arithmetic-geometric mean inequality, revisited)
(a) Show that $|\boldsymbol{X}|^{1/n} \leq (1/n) \operatorname{tr} \boldsymbol{X}$ for every $n \times n$ positive semidefinite matrix $\boldsymbol{X}$. (Compare Exercise 12.11.)
(b) When does equality occur?

Solution
(a) Assume first that $|\boldsymbol{X}| \neq 0$, so that $\boldsymbol{X}$ is positive definite. Write $\boldsymbol{X} = \boldsymbol{T}'\boldsymbol{T}$, where $\boldsymbol{T}$ is a square $n \times n$ matrix. This forces the solution matrix $\boldsymbol{X}$ to be positive definite. Now define

$$\varphi(\boldsymbol{T}) := \frac{1}{n} \operatorname{tr} \boldsymbol{T}'\boldsymbol{T} - |\boldsymbol{T}|^{2/n}.$$

We wish to minimize φ, and show that the minimum is zero. Taking the differential of φ gives

$$\begin{aligned}
\mathrm{d}\varphi &= \frac{2}{n} \operatorname{tr} \boldsymbol{T}'\,\mathrm{d}\boldsymbol{T} - \frac{2}{n}|\boldsymbol{T}|^{\frac{2}{n}-1}\,\mathrm{d}|\boldsymbol{T}|, \\
&= \frac{2}{n} \operatorname{tr} \boldsymbol{T}'\,\mathrm{d}\boldsymbol{T} - \frac{2}{n}|\boldsymbol{T}|^{(2/n)-1}|\boldsymbol{T}| \operatorname{tr} \boldsymbol{T}^{-1}\,\mathrm{d}\boldsymbol{T} \\
&= \frac{2}{n} \operatorname{tr}(\boldsymbol{T}' - |\boldsymbol{T}|^{2/n}\boldsymbol{T}^{-1})\,\mathrm{d}\boldsymbol{T},
\end{aligned}$$

so that the first-order condition is $T' = |T|^{2/n} T^{-1}$. This implies $T'T = |T|^{2/n} I_n$, that is, $\tilde{X} = \alpha I_n$ for some $\alpha > 0$. The value of φ is then

$$\tilde{\varphi} = \varphi(\tilde{T}) = \frac{1}{n} \operatorname{tr} \tilde{X} - |\tilde{X}|^{1/n} = \alpha - \alpha = 0.$$

If $|X| = 0$, then $\operatorname{tr} X \geq 0$ for every positive semidefinite X with equality if and only if $X = O$ (Exercise 8.8(a)).

From Exercise 13.66, we know that $|X|^{1/n}$ is concave. Hence, the function $(1/n) \operatorname{tr} X - |X|^{1/n}$ is convex, and thus has a minimum at points where the derivative vanishes.
(b) Equality occurs if and only if $X = \alpha I_n$ for some $\alpha \geq 0$.

*__Exercise 13.68 (Lower bound of $(1/n) \operatorname{tr} AX$)__ Let A be a positive semidefinite $n \times n$ matrix.
(a) Show that $(1/n) \operatorname{tr} AX \geq |A|^{1/n}$ for every positive definite $n \times n$ matrix X satisfying $|X| = 1$.
(b) When does equality occur? (Compare the solution to the same problem in Exercise 12.12.)

Solution
(a) This can be proved as an extension of Exercise 13.67 by letting $B := X^{1/2} A X^{1/2}$, thus producing the inequality $(1/n) \operatorname{tr} AX \geq |A|^{1/n} |X|^{1/n}$ with equality if and only if $A = O$ or $X = \alpha A^{-1}$ for some $\alpha > 0$.

A direct proof will be instructive. We view the inequality as the solution of the following constrained minimization problem in X:

$$\text{minimize} \quad \frac{1}{n} \operatorname{tr} AX$$
$$\text{subject to} \quad \log |X| = 0, \quad X \text{ positive definite},$$

where A is a given positive semidefinite $n \times n$ matrix. If $A = O$, then both sides of the inequality are zero, so that the inequality is trivially satisfied. Hence, we assume $A \neq O$.

To take the positive definiteness of X explicitly into account we write $X = T'T$, where T is a square matrix of order n. The minimization problem then becomes

$$\text{minimize} \quad \frac{1}{n} \operatorname{tr} TAT'$$
$$\text{subject to} \quad \log |T|^2 = 0.$$

As usual, we define the Lagrangian function

$$\psi(T) := \frac{1}{n} \operatorname{tr} TAT' - \lambda \log |T|^2$$

and take differentials. This yields

$$\begin{aligned} \mathrm{d}\psi(T) &= \frac{2}{n} \operatorname{tr}(\mathrm{d}T) AT' - 2\lambda \operatorname{tr} T^{-1} \mathrm{d}T \\ &= 2 \operatorname{tr}((1/n) AT' - \lambda T^{-1}) \, \mathrm{d}T. \end{aligned}$$

The first-order conditions are

$$\frac{1}{n}\boldsymbol{A}\boldsymbol{T}' = \lambda \boldsymbol{T}^{-1}, \quad |\boldsymbol{T}|^2 = 1.$$

We postmultiply both sides of the first condition by $n\boldsymbol{T}'^{-1}$. This gives

$$\boldsymbol{A} = n\lambda(\boldsymbol{T}'\boldsymbol{T})^{-1},$$

which shows that $\lambda > 0$ and that $\boldsymbol{A}$ is nonsingular. (If $\lambda = 0$, then $\boldsymbol{A}$ is the null matrix, which we have excluded.) Taking determinants on both sides of this equation, we obtain $|\boldsymbol{A}| = (n\lambda)^n|\boldsymbol{T}|^{-2} = (n\lambda)^n$, because $|\boldsymbol{T}|^2 = 1$. Hence,

$$\boldsymbol{T}'\boldsymbol{T} = (n\lambda)\boldsymbol{A}^{-1} = |\boldsymbol{A}|^{1/n}\boldsymbol{A}^{-1}.$$

Since $\operatorname{tr}\boldsymbol{T}\boldsymbol{A}\boldsymbol{T}'$ is convex, $\log|\boldsymbol{T}|^2 = \log|\boldsymbol{T}'\boldsymbol{T}|$ is concave (Exercise 13.66), and $\lambda > 0$, it follows that $\psi(\boldsymbol{T})$ is convex. Hence, $(1/n)\operatorname{tr}\boldsymbol{T}\boldsymbol{A}\boldsymbol{T}'$ has a global minimum under the constraint at every point where $\boldsymbol{T}'\boldsymbol{T} = |\boldsymbol{A}|^{1/n}\boldsymbol{A}^{-1}$. The constrained minimum is

$$\frac{1}{n}\operatorname{tr}\boldsymbol{T}\boldsymbol{A}\boldsymbol{T}' = \frac{1}{n}\operatorname{tr}|\boldsymbol{A}|^{1/n}\boldsymbol{A}^{-1}\boldsymbol{A} = |\boldsymbol{A}|^{1/n}.$$

(b) Equality occurs when $\boldsymbol{A} = \mathbf{O}$ or $\boldsymbol{X} = |\boldsymbol{A}|^{1/n}\boldsymbol{A}^{-1}$.

Exercise 13.69 (An equality obtained from calculus) The previous exercises show that matrix calculus can be used — at least in principle — to prove inequalities. We now show that it can also be of use in proving equalities. The idea is simple. If we want to prove the equality $\boldsymbol{F}(\boldsymbol{X}) = \mathbf{O}$ for all $\boldsymbol{X}$, then it suffices to show that $\mathrm{d}\boldsymbol{F} = \mathbf{O}$ and that $\boldsymbol{F}(\boldsymbol{X}) = \mathbf{O}$ for *one* suitably chosen $\boldsymbol{X}$. Here is an example.

Let $\boldsymbol{X}$ be an $n \times k$ matrix with $\operatorname{rk}(\boldsymbol{X}) = k$, $\boldsymbol{A}$ an $n \times (n-k)$ matrix with rank $\operatorname{rk}(\boldsymbol{A}) = n - k$, and $\boldsymbol{\Omega}$ a positive definite $n \times n$ matrix. If $\boldsymbol{A}'\boldsymbol{X} = \mathbf{O}$, then show that

$$|\boldsymbol{A}'\boldsymbol{\Omega}\boldsymbol{A}||\boldsymbol{X}'\boldsymbol{X}| = |\boldsymbol{A}'\boldsymbol{A}||\boldsymbol{X}'\boldsymbol{\Omega}^{-1}\boldsymbol{X}||\boldsymbol{\Omega}|.$$

Solution

Consider the function

$$\varphi(\boldsymbol{\Omega}) := \frac{|\boldsymbol{X}'\boldsymbol{\Omega}^{-1}\boldsymbol{X}||\boldsymbol{\Omega}|}{|\boldsymbol{A}'\boldsymbol{\Omega}\boldsymbol{A}|}.$$

Then,

$$\log\varphi(\boldsymbol{\Omega}) = \log|\boldsymbol{X}'\boldsymbol{\Omega}^{-1}\boldsymbol{X}| + \log|\boldsymbol{\Omega}| - \log|\boldsymbol{A}'\boldsymbol{\Omega}\boldsymbol{A}|.$$

Taking the differential with respect to $\boldsymbol{\Omega}$ gives

$$\mathrm{d}\log\varphi = \operatorname{tr}\left(\boldsymbol{\Omega}^{-1} - \boldsymbol{\Omega}^{-1}\boldsymbol{X}(\boldsymbol{X}'\boldsymbol{\Omega}^{-1}\boldsymbol{X})^{-1}\boldsymbol{X}'\boldsymbol{\Omega}^{-1} - \boldsymbol{A}(\boldsymbol{A}'\boldsymbol{\Omega}\boldsymbol{A})^{-1}\boldsymbol{A}'\right)\mathrm{d}\boldsymbol{\Omega}.$$

Now suppose that we can demonstrate that $\boldsymbol{A}'\boldsymbol{X} = \mathbf{O}$ implies that

$$\boldsymbol{F}(\boldsymbol{\Omega}) := \boldsymbol{\Omega}^{-1} - \boldsymbol{\Omega}^{-1}\boldsymbol{X}(\boldsymbol{X}'\boldsymbol{\Omega}^{-1}\boldsymbol{X})^{-1}\boldsymbol{X}'\boldsymbol{\Omega}^{-1} - \boldsymbol{A}(\boldsymbol{A}'\boldsymbol{\Omega}\boldsymbol{A})^{-1}\boldsymbol{A}' = \mathbf{O}.$$

Then $\mathrm{d}\log\varphi = 0$ and hence φ does not depend on $\boldsymbol{\Omega}$. This in turn implies that $\varphi(\boldsymbol{\Omega}) = \varphi(\boldsymbol{I})$ for all $\boldsymbol{\Omega}$, and the result follows.

Thus, let us show that $\boldsymbol{F}(\boldsymbol{\Omega}) = \mathbf{O}$ whenever $\boldsymbol{A}'\boldsymbol{X} = \mathbf{O}$. Let $\tilde{\boldsymbol{A}} := \boldsymbol{\Omega}^{1/2}\boldsymbol{A}$ and $\tilde{\boldsymbol{X}} := \boldsymbol{\Omega}^{-1/2}\boldsymbol{X}$. It suffices to show that

$$\tilde{\boldsymbol{X}}(\tilde{\boldsymbol{X}}'\tilde{\boldsymbol{X}})^{-1}\tilde{\boldsymbol{X}}' + \tilde{\boldsymbol{A}}(\tilde{\boldsymbol{A}}'\tilde{\boldsymbol{A}})^{-1}\tilde{\boldsymbol{A}}' = \boldsymbol{I}_n$$

whenever $\tilde{\boldsymbol{A}}'\tilde{\boldsymbol{X}} = \mathbf{O}$. But this follows from Exercise 8.67, using the fact that $\operatorname{rk}(\tilde{\boldsymbol{A}}) + \operatorname{rk}(\tilde{\boldsymbol{X}}) = \operatorname{rk}(\boldsymbol{A}) + \operatorname{rk}(\boldsymbol{X}) = n$.

Notes

A thorough exposition of the theory of matrix differential calculus is provided in Magnus and Neudecker (1999). The present chapter emphasizes the practical aspects of the theory.

Some of the results on maximum likelihood estimation (Section 13.12) will return in the *Econometric Exercises* volume by Abadir, Heijmans, and Magnus (2006, Chapters 11 and 12), where we demonstrate the use of some statistical shortcuts, like sufficiency.

Jacobians can also be derived using differential forms, a tool regularly employed in differential geometry. For example, see Rudin (1976, Chapter 10) or Muirhead (1982, Chapter 2) for an introduction, or Lang (1995) for a more advanced treatment. Muirhead (1982) also provides applications to statistics.

Appendix A: Some mathematical tools

This appendix collects mathematical tools that are needed in the main text. In addition, it gives a brief description of some essential background topics. It is assumed that the reader knows elementary calculus. The topics are grouped in four sections. First, we consider some useful methods of indirect proofs. Second, we introduce elementary results for complex numbers and polynomials. The third topic concerns series expansions. Finally, some further calculus is presented.

A.1 Some methods of indirect proof

Perhaps the most fundamental of all mathematical tools is the construction of a proof. When a direct proof is hard to obtain, there are indirect methods that can often help. In this section, we will denote a statement by p (such as "I like this book"), and another by q (such as "matrix algebra is interesting"). The negation of p will be denoted by $\neg p$. The statement "p and q" is denoted by $p \wedge q$, and the statement "p or q (or both)" is denoted by $p \vee q$. The statements $\neg(p \vee q)$ and $\neg p \wedge \neg q$ are equivalent: the negation transforms p, q into $\neg p, \neg q$ and $\vee$ into $\wedge$. This is the equivalent of *De Morgan's law* for sets, where p and q would be sets, $\neg p$ the complement of p, $p \vee q$ the union of the sets, and $p \wedge q$ their intersection. Clearly, $\neg(\neg p)$ is the same as p, and the operation $\vee$ is commutative (hence $\wedge$ is too) so that $p \vee q$ is equivalent to $q \vee p$.

We will explore equivalent ways of formulating that p implies q, denoted by $p \implies q$, meaning that if statement p holds then q will hold too: p is therefore *sufficient* for q ("if p then q"). The truth of $p \implies q$ is equivalent to the truth of $\neg p \vee q$: the claim $p \implies q$ is violated if and only if we have $p \wedge \neg q$.

The first alternative formulation of $p \implies q$ is $\neg q \implies \neg p$, meaning that if statement q does not hold then p will not hold either: q is therefore *necessary* for p ("p only if q"). A proof that starts by presuming $\neg q$ and then shows that it leads to $\neg p$, is called a *proof by contrapositive*.

The second way of establishing that $p \implies q$ is through a *proof by contradiction*. It proceeds by showing that if one were to assume $\neg q$ and p simultaneously, a contradiction would occur; for example, $s \wedge \neg s$ where s is some statement. Therefore, $\neg q \wedge p$ is false, and its negation $q \vee \neg p$ holds, which is precisely the required $p \implies q$. Notice the difference with the previous method of proof, where no contradictory statements ever arose.

The third method of indirect proof is of a different nature, and can sometimes lead to errors if not treated carefully. The previous two methods are examples of *proofs by deduction*. A *proof by induction* is one that takes the following structure. Suppose that $n \in \mathbb{N}$, and that we wish to prove a statement s_n (such as $p \implies q$) for all $n \in \mathbb{N}$. If s_1 is true and if we can show that $s_n \implies s_{n+1}$, then s_n holds for all $n \in \mathbb{N}$. Caution should be exercised in defining what n stands for, so that s_1 is not a trivial or empty statement.

Finally, we have used the terms "p is equivalent to q" and "p if and only if q". These can be abbreviated by $p \iff q$, which happens when $q \implies p$ and $p \implies q$ simultaneously: p is necessary *and* sufficient for q.

A.2 Primer on complex numbers and polynomials

A number u is said to be *complex* if it can be expressed in the *rectangular (Cartesian) form*

$$u = a + ib,$$

where i is the imaginary unit satisfying $\mathrm{i}^2 = -1$, $\mathrm{Re}(u) := a \in \mathbb{R}$ is the *real part* of u, and $\mathrm{Im}(u) := b \in \mathbb{R}$ is the *imaginary part* of u. An alternative expression for this complex number $u \in \mathbb{C}$ is the *polar form*

$$u = |u| \left(\cos(\theta) + \mathrm{i}\sin(\theta)\right),$$

where the *modulus* (or *absolute value*) of u, denoted by $|u|$, is defined as the nonnegative square root of $a^2 + b^2$, and $\arg(u) := \theta = \tan^{-1}(b/a)$ is the *argument* of u.

Euler's formula, $\exp(\mathrm{i}\theta) = \cos(\theta) + \mathrm{i}\sin(\theta)$, allows us to rewrite the polar form as

$$u = |u|\, \mathrm{e}^{\mathrm{i}\theta},$$

where e^x is understood to refer to be the *exponential function* $\exp(x) := \sum_{j=0}^{\infty} x^j/j!$, and

$$j! := \prod_{k=1}^{j} k = 1 \times 2 \times \cdots \times j$$

is the *factorial function*. Empty products like $\prod_{k=1}^{0} k$ are equal to 1 by convention; hence $0! = 1$. A similar formulation applies to matrices, and is known as the *polar decomposition*.

Any complex number $u = a + \mathrm{i}b = |u|\, \mathrm{e}^{\mathrm{i}\theta}$ can be represented graphically on the *complex plane*, depicted in Figure A.1. The Cartesian coordinates of a point representing u are (a, b), with the horizontal and vertical axes measuring the real and imaginary parts of u, respectively. A complex number can therefore be thought of as a two-dimensional vector of real numbers. The polar coordinates representing u are $(|u|, \theta)$, respectively the length and the angle of a ray joining the point u to the origin. Positive values of θ are conventionally measured anticlockwise from the positive horizontal axis, and negative values clockwise.

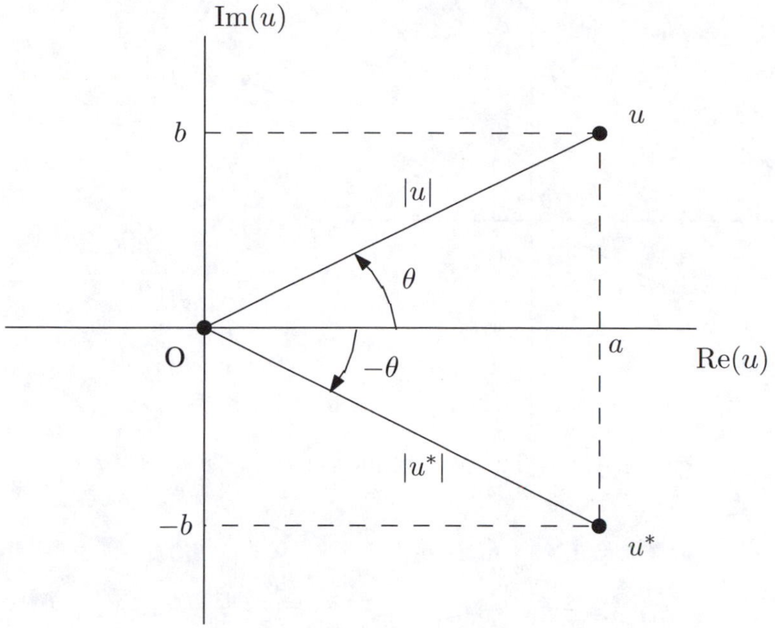

Figure A.1 — Rectangular and polar coordinates of a complex number and its conjugate.

We also see that $\tan(\theta) = b/a$. The *complex conjugate* of the number u is $u^* = a - \mathrm{i}b = |u|\,\mathrm{e}^{-\mathrm{i}\theta}$, the reflection of point u across the horizontal axis. The product of the conjugate pair,

$$u \cdot u^* = |u|\,\mathrm{e}^{\mathrm{i}\theta}\,|u|\,\mathrm{e}^{-\mathrm{i}\theta} = |u|^2 = a^2 + b^2,$$

is always nonnegative.

Euler's formula clarifies and provides a simple proof of *de Moivre's theorem*, which states that

$$u^\nu = \left(|u|\,(\cos(\theta) + \mathrm{i}\sin(\theta))\right)^\nu = |u|^\nu\,(\cos(\nu\theta) + \mathrm{i}\sin(\nu\theta))$$

for any complex ν. A direct consequence of this theorem and Euler's formula is that the equation $x^2 = u$ (where $u = |u|\,\mathrm{e}^{\mathrm{i}\theta}$ is a complex number and x is a *complex variable*) has the two solutions

$$x_1 = \sqrt{|u|}\mathrm{e}^{\mathrm{i}\theta/2} \quad \text{and} \quad x_2 = -\sqrt{|u|}\mathrm{e}^{\mathrm{i}\theta/2} = \sqrt{|u|}\mathrm{e}^{\mathrm{i}(\pi+\theta/2)},$$

using the fact that $\mathrm{e}^{\mathrm{i}\pi} = -1$. These are shown in Figure A.2. The square-root function is *multiple-valued.* In fact, there are infinitely-many solutions of the form $x_{j+1} = \sqrt{|u|}\mathrm{e}^{\mathrm{i}(\pi j+\theta/2)}$, $j = 0, 1, \ldots$, but they have the same rectangular coordinates as either x_1 or x_2. Therefore, we restrict our attention to the solutions having $0 \le \arg(x) < 2\pi$. The solution x_1 is called the *principal value* of this multiple-valued function. Note that when $\theta = 0$, we have $u = u^* = |u|$ and $x = \pm\sqrt{|u|}$, with the positive square root x_1 as the principal value. Similarly, when $\theta = \pi$, we have $u = u^* = -|u|$ and $x = \pm\mathrm{i}\sqrt{|u|}$. If, in addition, $|u| = 1$, the principal valueof $\sqrt{-1}$ is i.

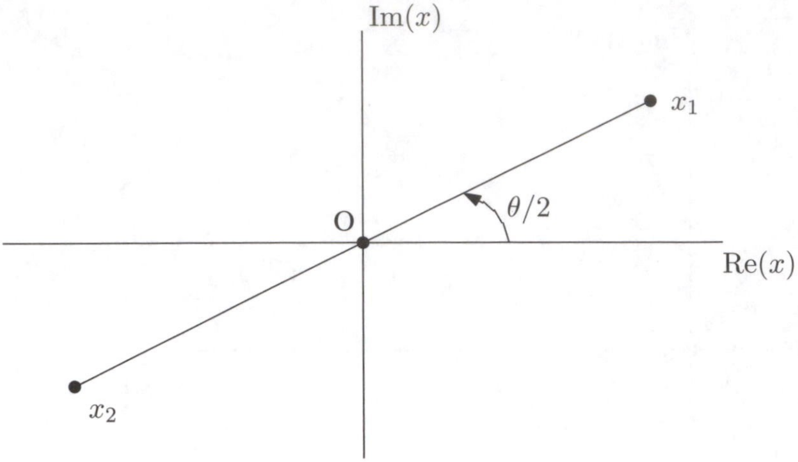

Figure A.2 — The two solutions to $x^2 = u$.

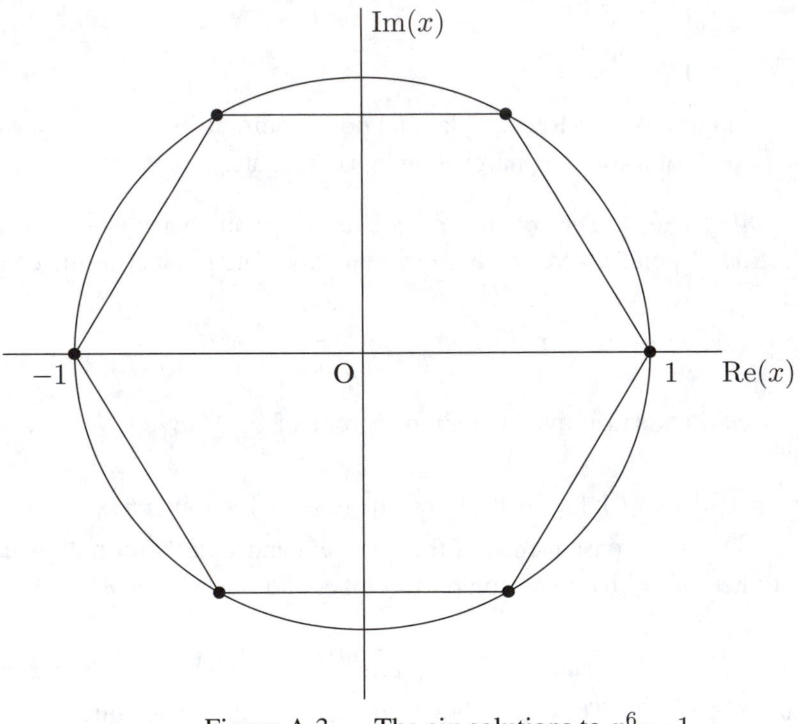

Figure A.3 — The six solutions to $x^6 = 1$.

Similarly, the n *roots of unity*, which solve the equation $x^n = 1$, are given by $x_{j+1} = e^{2ij\pi/n}$, where $n \in \mathbb{N}$ and $j = 0, 1, ..., n-1$. For $n = 6$, these roots are depicted by the points on the unit circle of Figure A.3. These points are the vertices of the symmetric hexagon in the figure. The displayed circle of radius one, which is centered around the origin, is called *the unit circle*. More generally, a circle of unit radius centered around some point (not necessarily the origin) is called *a unit circle*.

The two equations in x that we have just considered are examples of a polynomial equation. A function of the form

$$P_n(x) := \sum_{j=0}^{n} p_j x^j = p_0 + p_1 x + \cdots + p_n x^n$$

is called a *polynomial of degree* (or *order*) n in the variable x, when $p_n \neq 0$ and the p_j are all finite constants. When $p_n = 1$, we have a *monic* polynomial, an example of this being the characteristic polynomial of a matrix. Polynomials of degrees n_1 and n_2 can be multiplied with one another, yielding a polynomial of degree $n_1 + n_2$. For example,

$$(1+x)\left(1-x^2\right) = 1 + x - x^2 - x^3.$$

If a polynomial does not vanish identically (that is, if $P_n(x) \neq 0$ for at least one x), then it can divide another polynomial, such as

$$\frac{2 + x - x^2 - x^3}{1 - x^2} = \frac{1}{1 - x^2} + \frac{1 + x - x^2 - x^3}{1 - x^2} = \frac{1}{1 - x^2} + 1 + x.$$

The fraction $1/(1-x^2)$ is called the *remainder of the division*. The *fundamental theorem of algebra* states that $P_n(x) := \sum_{j=0}^{n} p_j x^j$ can always be factored as a product of linear polynomials,

$$P_n(x) = p_n \prod_{i=1}^{n} (x - \lambda_i) = p_n (x - \lambda_1) \ldots (x - \lambda_n),$$

where the $\lambda_i \in \mathbb{C}$ are the constants that solve the equation $P_n(x) = 0$, and are known as the *roots* of this equation. Notice two features. First, there are no remainders from the division of $P_n(x)$ by any of its factors. Second, the equation has exactly n roots, when the λ_i are allowed to be complex; see the example of $x^n - 1 = 0$ in the previous paragraph. *Repeated* (or *multiple*) *roots* occur when two or more of the roots λ_i are equal; these are included in the count of the n roots. If λ_i is not repeated, then it is a *simple root*. For example,

$$1 + x - x^2 - x^3 = -(x - 1)(x + 1)^2$$

has the repeated root -1 (twice), and the simple root 1. Finally, let $f(x)$ be a continuous but otherwise unspecified function. The only functional solution to $f(x) + f(y) = f(x + y)$, called *Hamel's equation*, is $f(x) = px$ where p is a constant.

A.3 Series expansions

Polynomials were defined in the previous section. Not all functions are, however, expressible as polynomials of a finite order n. If, by allowing $n \to \infty$, we are able to express a function $f(x)$ as

$$f(x) = \sum_{j=0}^{\infty} a_j (x - b)^j,$$

then we obtain what is known as a *power series* representation of $f(x)$ about the point $x = b$. More generally, an *infinite series* representation of $f(x)$ is a sum of the type

$$f(x) = \sum_{j=0}^{\infty} g_j(x),$$

where $g_j(x)$ is a sequence of functions for $j = 0, 1, \ldots,$ and $S_n(x) := \sum_{j=0}^{n-1} g_j(x)$ is known as the *partial sum* of the first n terms of the series.

Before we consider $n \to \infty$, we briefly discuss sequences and limits. Then, we consider infinite series and their properties: types of convergence, special series, expansions of functions, and multiple series.

A.3.1 Sequences and limits

The *maximum* of a set of real numbers $\{x_1, \ldots, x_n\}$ is denoted by $\max_i \{x_i\}$ and is the largest element in this set. If the sequence is infinitely long, the maximum may not exist. For example, the set of values of x_i in the interval $[0, 1)$ have a smallest element, the *minimum* $\min_i \{x_i\} = 0$, but no maximum. The *supremum* $\sup_i \{x_i\}$ is the smallest upper bound on $\{x_1, \ldots, x_n\}$, and may not be a member of this set. In the previous example, the supremum is $\sup_i \{x_i\} = 1$ while the *infimum* is $\inf_i \{x_i\} = 0 = \min_i \{x_i\}$. Note that $\sup_i \{x_i\} = -\inf_i \{-x_i\}$, but that it is not necessarily the case that $\max_i \{x_i\} = -\min_i \{-x_i\}$. Also,

$$\sup_i \{a + bx_i\} = \begin{cases} a + b \inf_i \{x_i\} & (b \le 0), \\ a + b \sup_i \{x_i\} & (b \ge 0), \end{cases}$$

for $a, b \in \mathbb{R}$.

We briefly consider sets. A collection $\mathcal{A}$ of sets is said to *cover* a set B when $B \subset \cup_{A \in \mathcal{A}} A$. When this collection contains only a finite number of sets, we denote it by $\mathcal{A}_\varphi$. Let B be a set made up of some real numbers, and suppose that each collection $\mathcal{A}$ of open sets covering B has a finite subcollection $\mathcal{A}_\varphi$ able to cover B. Then B is said to be *compact*.

A sequence of real numbers is *bounded* if $\inf_i \{x_i\} > -\infty$ and $\sup_i \{x_i\} < \infty$. These finite bounds are members of the sequence if and only if it is compact. This is a variant of the *Heine-Borel* theorem. An implication is the *Bolzano-Weierstrass* theorem, which states that every bounded sequence in $\mathbb{R}$ contains a convergent subsequence.

A possibly surprising result is that there always exists a rational number q between any two real numbers x and y. The rationals are therefore said to be *dense* in the reals. This implies that one can represent any real number as the limit of a sequence of rationals.

Let $\{x_i\}_{i=1}^{\infty}$ be an infinite sequence of numbers. If for every $\epsilon > 0$ there exists a constant $n_\epsilon > 0$ such that

$$|x_n - x_m| < \epsilon \quad \text{for all } m, n > n_\epsilon,$$

then $\{x_i\}_{i=1}^{\infty}$ is called a *Cauchy sequence*. If $x_i \in \mathbb{R}$, then a sequence $\{x_i\}_{i=1}^{\infty}$ converges if and only if it is a Cauchy sequence, and the condition for convergence is known as *Cauchy's criterion*. The set $\mathbb{R}$ is then said to be *complete*. If $x_i \in \mathbb{Q}$, the equivalence breaks down: a Cauchy sequence of rationals may not be converging to a rational number, as seen in the previous paragraph. The set $\mathbb{Q}$ is *incomplete*.

A.3.2 Convergence of series

We can now analyze the convergence of series of complex numbers. It suffices to consider series of real numbers, since $\sum_{j=0}^{\infty}(a_j + \mathrm{i}b_j)$ converges if and only if both real series $\sum_{j=0}^{\infty} a_j$ and $\sum_{j=0}^{\infty} b_j$ converge.

An infinite series *converges* if the limit of its partial sums exists and is finite, that is, if $\lim_{n\to\infty} S_n(x) = S_\infty(x)$ where $|S_\infty(x)| < \infty$. Otherwise, the series is *nonconvergent*. If convergence occurs only for some values of x, then this set of values is called the *convergence region* of the series. A series $\sum_{j=0}^{\infty} g_j(x)$ is *absolutely convergent* if $\sum_{j=0}^{\infty} |g_j(x)|$ converges. If $\sum_{j=0}^{\infty} g_j(x)$ converges but $\sum_{j=0}^{\infty} |g_j(x)|$ does not, then the series is *conditionally convergent*. For example, the *logarithmic series*

$$\log(1+x) = x\sum_{j=0}^{\infty}\frac{(-x)^j}{j+1}$$

converges to $\log 2$ for $x = 1$, but not absolutely so:

$$\lim_{x\to1^-}\sum_{j=0}^{\infty}\frac{|-1|^j}{j+1}\left|x^{j+1}\right| = \lim_{x\to1^-} x\sum_{j=0}^{\infty}\frac{x^j}{j+1} = \lim_{x\to1^-} -\log(1-x) = \infty.$$

This example illustrates some key properties. A necessary (but not always sufficient) condition for the convergence of $\sum_{j=0}^{\infty} g_j(x)$ is that $\lim_{j\to\infty} g_j(x) = 0$. It is also a sufficient condition for the convergence of *alternating series* defined by

$$\sum_{j=0}^{\infty}(-1)^j g_j(x),$$

where $g_j(x) \geq 0$. When $g_j(x) \geq g_{j+1}(x) \geq 0$ and $\lim_{j\to\infty} g_j(x) = 0$, the convergence of alternating series can be seen from calculating the partial sums of $(-1)^j g_j(x)$. In general, a sufficient condition for the absolute convergence of $\sum_{j=0}^{\infty} g_j(x)$ is that there is a $\delta > 0$ such that $j^{1+\delta} g_j(x)$ has a finite limit as $j \to \infty$, meaning that the terms $g_j(x)$ decline at least as fast as $1/j^{1+\delta}$.

If the power series $f(x) := \sum_{j=0}^{\infty} a_j(x-b)^j$ converges for all $|x-b| < r$ (that is, within a circle of radius r centered around the point $x = b$ in the complex plane), and r is the largest value for which this convergence holds, then r is called the *radius of convergence*. Power series have the pleasant property that they converge *absolutely* within (but not on) their radius of convergence. The same convergence also holds for their term-by-term or *termwise* derivative, and $\sum_{j=1}^{\infty} j a_j(x-b)^{j-1}$ is the derivative of the function represented by the original series. The same is true for their termwise integrals.

An infinite series may be nonconvergent but nonetheless *summable*, meaning that it represents a finite function. Such series are often encountered in econometrics and statistics, for example in the form of Edgeworth expansions of distribution functions or, more generally, asymptotic expansions to be considered in Section A.3.4 below. One method for working out the sum of a nonconvergent series is as follows. If the average of the partial sums,

$$S_{n,1} := \frac{1}{n}\sum_{i=1}^{n} S_i, \quad n = 1, 2, \ldots,$$

converges to $S_{\infty,1}$ then the original series $S_\infty := \sum_{j=0}^{\infty} g_j(x)$ is *Cesàro-summable-1* (C-1) to $S_{\infty,1}$. (The reason for using C-1, rather than just C, is that the process can be repeated by defining $S_{n,m} := \frac{1}{n}\sum_{i=1}^{n} S_{i,m-1}$ for $m = 2, 3, \ldots$ if $\lim_{n\to\infty} S_{n,m-1}$ does not exist.) A simple example is

$$\tfrac{1}{2} = \tfrac{1}{1+1} = 1 - 1 + 1 - 1 + \ldots,$$

where

$$S_n = \begin{cases} 1 \ (n \text{ odd}) \\ 0 \ (n \text{ even}) \end{cases} \implies S_{n,1} = \begin{cases} \frac{n+1}{2n} & (n \text{ odd}) \\ \frac{1}{2} & (n \text{ even}), \end{cases}$$

hence converging to 1/2 as expected. To be applicable, Cesàro-summability requires a *consistency condition*, namely that the method of summation leads to the same result as $\lim_{n\to\infty} \sum_{j=0}^{n} g_j(x)$ when this series is convergent. In our example, this condition is satisfied because the *geometric progression* $\sum_{j=0}^{\infty}(-x)^j$ converges to $(1+x)^{-1}$ when $|x| < 1$.

Knowing that a series is summable can lead to a relaxation of the sufficient condition for convergence seen earlier. *Hardy's convergence theorem* states that a sufficient condition for the convergence of a C-1 summable series $\sum_{j=0}^{\infty} g_j(x)$ is that $\lim_{j\to\infty} j g_j(x) = c$ (a finite constant), that is, the terms need only decline as fast as $1/j$. Notice that the convergence may not be absolute, as the example of log 2 has illustrated.

A.3.3 Special series

We next discuss some prominent functions whose series expansions are commonly encountered. The stated radii of convergence for these power series follow from the previous section. All the series considered here can be regarded as a generalization of the exponential series introduced in Section A.2, $e^x = \sum_{j=0}^{\infty} x^j/j!$, which converges absolutely for all $|x| < \infty$. In this appendix, we adopt the alternative approach of defining new series by taking the exponential as the first building block then adding in some gamma-type function of the index j. Before we tackle these other series, we define the *gamma* (or *generalized factorial*) *function*

$$\Gamma(\nu) := \int_0^\infty t^{\nu-1} e^{-t}\, dt, \quad \nu \in \mathbb{R}_+.$$

Integrating by parts leads to the recursion $\Gamma(\nu) = (\nu-1)\Gamma(\nu-1)$, with $\Gamma(1) = 1$. This recursion is used to extend the definition to any real ν except $0, -1, \ldots$. When the argument of the function is a natural number, this is just the factorial function seen earlier,

$$\Gamma(n) = (n-1)(n-2)\dots 1 = (n-1)!$$

with $0! = 1$. The *binomial coefficients* can be written as

$$\binom{\nu}{j} := \frac{(\nu)(\nu-1)\dots(\nu-j+1)}{j!} = \frac{\Gamma(\nu+1)}{\Gamma(\nu-j+1)j!},$$

for $j = 0, 1, \dots$ and $\nu \in \mathbb{R}$. When ν takes the values $-1, -2, \dots$, that is, when $-\nu \in \mathbb{N}$, the ratio of gamma functions is understood to denote the limit obtained by using the recursion $\Gamma(\nu+1) = \nu\Gamma(\nu)$ repeatedly j times. The binomial coefficient is sometimes also written as the *combination symbol* C_j^ν, which is related to the *permutation symbol* P_j^ν by

$$\binom{\nu}{j} \equiv \mathrm{C}_j^\nu \equiv \frac{\mathrm{P}_j^\nu}{j!}.$$

We now introduce various generalizations of the exponential series.

First, for $\nu \in \mathbb{R}$, the *binomial series*

$$(1+x)^\nu = \sum_{j=0}^{\infty} \binom{\nu}{j} x^j = \sum_{j=0}^{\infty} \frac{\Gamma(\nu+1)}{\Gamma(\nu-j+1)} \cdot \frac{x^j}{j!}$$

converges absolutely for $|x| < 1$. It also converges absolutely when $|x| = 1$ and $\nu \in \mathbb{R}_+$. The series is summable for all $x \in \mathbb{C} \setminus \{-1\}$ when $\nu \in \mathbb{R}_-$ (an illustration is in the previous section), and for all $x \in \mathbb{C}$ when $\nu \in \mathbb{R}_+$. Note that in the excluded case of $x = -1$ when $\nu \in \mathbb{R}_-$, the signs of the terms in the binomial series do *not* alternate as $j \to \infty$.

The second generalization is the logarithmic series introduced in Section A.3.2,

$$\log(1+x) = x \sum_{j=0}^{\infty} \frac{(-x)^j}{j+1} = x \sum_{j=0}^{\infty} \frac{j!j!}{(j+1)!} \cdot \frac{(-x)^j}{j!},$$

which converges absolutely for $|x| < 1$. It also converges conditionally for $x = 1$, but not for $x = -1$. The *logarithmic function* is defined more generally by $\log(\mathrm{e}^x) := x$, such that it is the inverse of the exponential function, and is multiple-valued. This is because $x = x\mathrm{e}^{2\mathrm{i}\pi j}$ for $j = 0, 1, \dots$, implying that

$$\log(x) = \log\left(|x|\mathrm{e}^{\mathrm{i}(\theta+2\pi j)}\right) = \log|x| + \mathrm{i}(\theta + 2\pi j),$$

which is the rectangular (Cartesian) form of the complex function. We restrict our attention to the principal value of the function, which is conventionally taken to be $\log|x| + \mathrm{i}\theta$.

Now define the *hyperbolic functions*

$$\cosh(x) := \frac{\mathrm{e}^x + \mathrm{e}^{-x}}{2}, \ \sinh(x) := \frac{\mathrm{e}^x - \mathrm{e}^{-x}}{2}, \ \tanh(x) := \frac{\sinh(x)}{\cosh(x)} = 1 - \frac{2\mathrm{e}^{-2x}}{1+\mathrm{e}^{-2x}},$$

and the corresponding *trigonometric functions*

$$\cos(x) := \cosh(\mathrm{i}x), \quad \sin(x) := \frac{\sinh(\mathrm{i}x)}{\mathrm{i}}, \quad \tan(x) := \frac{\sin(x)}{\cos(x)}.$$

Important properties follow from these definitions. First, it is easy to see that $\mathrm{d}\sinh(x)/\,\mathrm{d}x = \cosh(x)$. Also, simple addition yields

$$\cos(x) + \mathrm{i}\sin(x) = \mathrm{e}^{\mathrm{i}x},$$

which is Euler's formula, stated earlier in Section A.2. From the definition in terms of e^x, we also see that the cosine is an *even function* (that is, it satisfies $f(-x) = f(x)$ for all x) whereas the sine is an *odd function* (that is, it satisfies $f(-x) = -f(x)$ for all x). These functions also have series expansions that are inherited from e^x. For example,

$$\begin{aligned}\cosh(x) &= \sum_{j=0}^{\infty} \frac{\left(x^j + (-x)^j\right)/2}{j!} \\ &= \sum_{k=0}^{\infty} \frac{\left(x^{2k} + (-x)^{2k}\right)/2}{(2k)!} + \sum_{k=0}^{\infty} \frac{\left(x^{2k+1} + (-x)^{2k+1}\right)/2}{(2k+1)!} \\ &= \sum_{k=0}^{\infty} \frac{x^{2k}}{(2k)!}\end{aligned}$$

by splitting the series into two: one where the power of x is even ($2k$) and another where it is odd ($2k+1$). Similarly,

$$\sinh(x) = \sum_{j=0}^{\infty} \frac{\left(x^j - (-x)^j\right)/2}{j!} = \sum_{k=0}^{\infty} \frac{x^{2k+1}}{(2k+1)!},$$

where both the $\sinh(x)$ series and the $\cosh(x)$ series converge absolutely for all $|x| < \infty$. Merging and/or splitting series is allowed for series that are absolutely convergent, but not for series that are conditionally convergent.

Finally, *inverse hyperbolic functions* can be defined in terms of the inverse of the exponential, namely the logarithmic function. We have

$$\cosh^{-1}(x) := \log(x + \sqrt{x^2 - 1}), \quad \sinh^{-1}(x) := \log(x + \sqrt{x^2 + 1}),$$

and

$$\tanh^{-1}(x) := \frac{1}{2}\log\left(\frac{1+x}{1-x}\right) = \frac{1}{2}\log\left(1 + \frac{2x}{1-x}\right).$$

One may check this by verifying that $\cosh(\log(x + \sqrt{x^2 - 1})) = x$, using the definition of hyperbolic functions. Because of the logarithmic series, the convergence of the expansions of these inverse hyperbolic functions will depend on the magnitude of x. For example, the equality after the definition of $\tanh^{-1}(x)$ suggests two different expansions, the first one being

$$\tanh^{-1}(x) = \frac{\log(1+x) - \log(1-x)}{2} = \sum_{k=0}^{\infty} \frac{x^{2k+1}}{2k+1},$$

which converges absolutely for $|x| < 1$. Similar relations apply to inverse trigonometric functions.

A.3.4 Expansions of functions

An important question has been hinted at in the previous section: does each function have a single series representation? We saw that in general the answer is no, the exponential (and hence hyperbolic) being a rare exception. Not only can one expand functions in different power series $f(x) = \sum_{j=0}^{\infty} a_j (x - b)^j$ centered around a variety of values of b (see Taylor series later), but there are also *asymptotic expansions* that are valid for, say, real $x \to \infty$ (different expansions usually apply for $x \to -\infty$, and some more if we allow x to be complex). These take the form $f(x) = \sum_{j=0}^{\infty} g_j(x)$ where, for $k \in \mathbb{N}$, the ratio $g_{j+k}(x)/g_j(x)$ is decreasing in x as $x \to \infty$. For example,

$$(1+x)^{\nu} = x^{\nu} \sum_{j=0}^{\infty} \binom{\nu}{j} \frac{1}{x^j}$$

is the asymptotic expansion of the left-hand side function. Before we can tackle the specifics of the different expansions of functions, we need to introduce some tools.

We say that a function $f(x)$ is *of order smaller than* x^{α}, written as $f(x) = o(x^{\alpha})$, if $\lim_{x\to\infty} f(x)/x^{\alpha} = 0$, where α is a constant. This definition gives a strict upper bound; a weaker upper bound is given by the following definition. We say that a function $f(x)$ is *at most of order* x^{α}, written as $f(x) = O(x^{\alpha})$, if $f(x)/x^{\alpha}$ is bounded as $x \to \infty$; that is, if for all $x > b$ (a constant) there exists a finite constant c such that

$$\left| \frac{f(x)}{x^{\alpha}} \right| \le c.$$

It should be borne in mind that orders of magnitude are inequality (not equivalence) relations. For example, if $f(x) = o(x^{\alpha})$, then it is also $o\left(x^{\alpha+\delta}\right)$ for any $\delta > 0$. The following relations hold:

- $f(x) = o(x^{\alpha})$ implies (but is not implied by) $f(x) = O(x^{\alpha})$;
- if $f(x) = O(x^{\alpha})$ and $g(x) = O\left(x^{\beta}\right)$, then $f(x)g(x) = O\left(x^{\alpha+\beta}\right)$ and $f(x) + g(x) = O(x^{\max\{\alpha,\beta\}})$, and similarly when O is replaced by o throughout;
- if $f(x) = o(x^{\alpha})$ and $g(x) = O\left(x^{\beta}\right)$, then $f(x)g(x) = o\left(x^{\alpha+\beta}\right)$;
- if $f(x) = o(x^{\alpha})$ and $g(x) = O(x^{\alpha})$, then $f(x) + g(x) = O(x^{\alpha})$.

These relations can be illustrated with simple functions like $f(x) = 3x^2 + x$.

Sometimes, the expression $f(x) = O(x^{\alpha})$ is not sufficiently precise for the required purpose, since it is an inequality relation. The mathematical (not statistical) symbol $\sim$ denotes the *asymptotic equivalence* of the two sides of $f(x) \sim g(x)$, that is, $f(x)/g(x) \to 1$ as $x \to \infty$. The first term of a series expansion, arranged by orders of magnitude, is called its *leading term*. In the previous example, we have $f(x) = 3x^2 + x \sim 3x^2$, so that $3x^2$ is the leading term as $x \to \infty$. This could have been written as $f(x) = O(x^2)$ without reference to the constant 3, which is less informative, though often adequate. As an example of a useful asymptotic expansion, we have *Stirling's series*,

$$\Gamma(x) = \sqrt{2\pi} \mathrm{e}^{-x+(x-1/2)\log(x)} \left(1 + \frac{1}{12x} + \frac{1}{288x^2} + O\left(\frac{1}{x^3}\right)\right)$$

for $x \to \infty$, implying

$$\frac{\Gamma(x+a)}{\Gamma(x+b)} = x^{a-b}\left(1+\frac{(a-b)(a+b-1)}{2x}+O\left(\frac{1}{x^2}\right)\right) \sim x^{a-b}.$$

These formulae facilitate the derivation of the convergence radii stated in the previous section.

All these concepts can be generalized to expansions around any point other than ∞. For example, the leading term of $f(x) = 3x^2 + x$ as $x \to 0$ becomes the latter term, since $f(x)/x \to 1$ as $x \to 0$, and therefore $f(x) = O(x)$ as $x \to 0$.

If a function $f(x)$ is differentiable an infinite number of times in an open neighborhood of a point b, then it has the *Taylor series* representation

$$f(x) = \sum_{j=0}^{\infty} f^{(j)}(b)\frac{(x-b)^j}{j!},$$

where $f^{(j)}(b)$ is the j-th derivative of $f(x)$ evaluated at $x = b$. *Maclaurin's expansion* is the special case obtained by choosing the point $x = 0$. Taylor's series implies that we can write

$$f(x) = \sum_{j=0}^{n-1} f^{(j)}(b)\frac{(x-b)^j}{j!} + O\left((x-b)^n\right).$$

Taylor's theorem states that for a real-valued function to have this latter representation, it need only be differentiable n times in the closed interval between x and b, and the $O\left((x-b)^n\right)$ remainder term is of the form $f^{(n)}(c)(x-c)^n/n!$ for some point c in between x and b. The expansion is said to be up to order $n-1$, and the remainder follows from the *mean-value theorem*: a real-valued function $f(x)$, continuous over $[a, b]$ and differentiable over (a, b), will have at least one point $c \in (a, b)$ such that $f'(c) = \left(f(b) - f(a)\right)/(b-a)$, meaning that $f'(c)$ equals the slope of the chord joining $f(b)$ to $f(a)$.

One important implication is a method of calculating $\lim_{x\to b} g(x)/h(x)$ when $g(b) = h(b) = 0$, known as *l'Hôpital's rule*. It states that if $g(x)$ and $h(x)$ are differentiable in an open neighborhood of $x = b$, then

$$\lim_{x\to b}\frac{g(x)}{h(x)} = \lim_{x\to b}\frac{g'(x)}{h'(x)}.$$

If $g'(b) = h'(b) = 0$, then the process can be repeated with further derivatives. It is assumed that the first nonzero derivative $g^{(j)}(b) \neq 0$ corresponds to $h^{(j)}(b) \neq 0$. The rule also applies if we had $\lim_{x\to b} |g(x)| = \lim_{x\to b} |h(x)| = \infty$, by working with the reciprocal of these functions (since $\lim_{x\to b} 1/g(x) = \lim_{x\to b} 1/h(x) = 0$). This also shows that it is not necessary for $g(x)$ and $h(x)$ to be differentiable at the point $x = b$, so long as they are differentiable around it.

A.3.5 Multiple series, products, and their relation

Suppose we have a sum over more than one index, called a *multiple series*. If this sum is absolutely convergent, then any two sums in this series may be exchanged. This is a manifestation of a more general result due to Fubini (for integrals) and Tonelli (for measures). Convergent multiple series are a recursive generalization of double series, so that the latter provide a convenient standard form. Rearrange the summand terms of the absolutely convergent $\sum_{j=0}^{\infty}\sum_{k=0}^{\infty} g_{j,k}(x)$ into the array

$$\begin{matrix} g_{0,0}(x) & g_{0,1}(x) & \dots \\ g_{1,0}(x) & g_{1,1}(x) & \dots \\ \vdots & \vdots & \end{matrix}$$

These infinite double sums may be transformed into the infinite sum of a finite series. The former representation consists of summing over the successive rows of the array, whereas the latter calculates the sum diagonally. For example, using a south-west to north-east diagonal, we have

$$\sum_{j=0}^{\infty}\sum_{k=0}^{\infty} g_{j,k}(x) = \sum_{j=0}^{\infty}\sum_{k=0}^{j} g_{j-k,k}(x),$$

which is one way of rewriting the double sum.

Infinite products are related to infinite series. The infinite product $\prod_{j=0}^{\infty}(1 + g_j(x))$ converges absolutely if and only if $\sum_{j=0}^{\infty} g_j(x)$ converges absolutely. However, further care is needed in handling multiple products. For example, $\sum_i \sum_j f_i g_j = \sum_i f_i \sum_j g_j$, but

$$\prod_{i=1}^{m}\prod_{j=1}^{n}(f_i g_j) = \left(\prod_{i=1}^{m} f_i^n\right)\prod_{j=1}^{n} g_j \neq \left(\prod_{i=1}^{m} f_i\right)\prod_{j=1}^{n} g_j$$

for $n \neq 1$. In the case of products, parentheses are needed to avoid ambiguity.

A.4 Further calculus

This section contains some further results on calculus: linear difference equations, convexity, and constrained optimization.

A.4.1 Linear difference equations

Let $\{x_1, \dots, x_n\}$ be a sequence of variables. Suppose they are related by the *linear difference equation*

$$x_i = c + a_1 x_{i-1} + \dots + a_p x_{i-p} \quad (i = p+1, \dots, n),$$

where $p < n$ and p is the *order* of this equation. We assume that the coefficients a and c do not depend on x. The values $\{x_1, \dots, x_p\}$ are called the *initial values* (or *boundary conditions*), because they initialize the sequence and allow the recursive calculation of x_{p+1}, followed by x_{p+2}, and so on. Given the initial values, one can solve explicitly for the complete sequence. We now show this by means of matrix algebra.

Define

$$\boldsymbol{y}_i := \begin{pmatrix} x_{i-p+1} \\ \vdots \\ x_i \end{pmatrix}, \quad \boldsymbol{A} := \begin{pmatrix} 0 & 1 & 0 & \dots & 0 & 0 \\ 0 & 0 & 1 & \dots & 0 & 0 \\ 0 & 0 & 0 & \dots & 0 & 0 \\ \vdots & \vdots & \vdots & & \vdots & \vdots \\ 0 & 0 & 0 & \dots & 0 & 1 \\ a_p & a_{p-1} & a_{p-2} & \dots & a_2 & a_1 \end{pmatrix}, \quad \boldsymbol{c} := \begin{pmatrix} 0 \\ \vdots \\ 0 \\ c \end{pmatrix},$$

so that the p-th order difference equation can be written as $\boldsymbol{y}_i = \boldsymbol{c} + \boldsymbol{A}\boldsymbol{y}_{i-1}$, which is a first-order difference equation in the vector $\boldsymbol{y}_i$. Repeated substitution gives the solution

$$\boldsymbol{y}_i = \boldsymbol{c} + \boldsymbol{A}(\boldsymbol{c} + \boldsymbol{A}\boldsymbol{y}_{i-2}) = \dots = \left(\sum_{j=0}^{i-p-1} \boldsymbol{A}^j \right) \boldsymbol{c} + \boldsymbol{A}^{i-p}\boldsymbol{y}_p$$

in terms of the vector of initial values $\boldsymbol{y}_p$. The square matrix $\boldsymbol{A}$ is known as the *companion matrix* for the *characteristic equation*

$$\lambda^p - a_1\lambda^{p-1} - \dots - a_p = 0,$$

whose coefficients arise from the left-hand side of the reformulated difference equation

$$x_i - a_1 x_{i-1} - \dots - a_p x_{i-p} = c.$$

The eigenvalues of $\boldsymbol{A}$ and the roots of the characteristic equation coincide, and they can be used to decompose powers of $\boldsymbol{A}$ explicitly, for example by a Jordan decomposition.

A.4.2 Convexity

A *linear combination* of the elements of $\{x_1, \dots, x_n\}$ is written as $\sum_{i=1}^n a_i x_i$, where the a_i are constants. If $\sum_{i=1}^n a_i = 1$, we call this linear combination a *weighted average*. If, furthermore, $a_i \geq 0$ for all i, hence $a_i \in [0, 1]$, we have a *convex combination*. Similar definitions apply to integrals like $\int_b^c a(t)x(t)\,\mathrm{d}t$.

A real-valued function $f(x)$ defined on an interval is said to be *convex* if

$$f(ax_1 + (1-a)x_2) \leq af(x_1) + (1-a)f(x_2)$$

for every $a \in (0, 1)$ and every pair of distinct points x_1 and x_2 in that interval. The function is *strictly convex* if the inequality holds strictly. If $f(x)$ is twice differentiable on an open interval I, then $f(x)$ is convex if and only if $f''(x) \geq 0$ for every $x \in I$. A function $f(x)$ is (strictly) *concave* if and only if $-f(x)$ is (strictly) convex.

A.4.3 Constrained optimization

Suppose that a real-valued function $f(x)$ is being minimized over a compact space S. Then we write $\operatorname{argmin}_{x \in S} f(x) = \hat{x}$ (or occasionally $\tilde{x}$) for the points at which the minimum of the function occurs, and $\min_{x \in S} f(x) = f(\hat{x})$ for the *global* minimum of the function.

This global minimum is *strict* if there is only one such point $\hat{x}$. If the space is not compact, then one should use inf instead of min.

We now consider the problem of optimizing a function subject to restrictions, both differentiable. Let f be a real-valued function defined on a set S in $\mathbb{R}^n$. We consider the minimization of $f(\boldsymbol{x})$ subject to m constraints, say $g_1(\boldsymbol{x}) = 0, \dots, g_m(\boldsymbol{x}) = 0$, and we write:

$$\begin{aligned} &\text{minimize} \quad f(\boldsymbol{x}) \\ &\text{subject to} \quad \boldsymbol{g}(\boldsymbol{x}) = \boldsymbol{0}, \end{aligned}$$

where $\boldsymbol{g} := (g_1, g_2, \dots, g_m)'$ and $\boldsymbol{x} := (x_1, x_2, \dots, x_n)'$. This is known as a *constrained minimization problem*, and the most convenient way of solving it is, in general, to use the *Lagrange multiplier theory*. Let Γ denote the subset of S on which $\boldsymbol{g}$ vanishes, that is, $\Gamma = \{\boldsymbol{x} : \boldsymbol{x} \in S,\, \boldsymbol{g}(\boldsymbol{x}) = \boldsymbol{0}\}$, and let $\boldsymbol{c}$ be a point of Γ. We say that:

- f has a local minimum at $\boldsymbol{c}$ under the constraint $\boldsymbol{g}(\boldsymbol{x}) = \boldsymbol{0}$, if there exists a neighborhood $B(\boldsymbol{c})$ of the point $\boldsymbol{c}$ such that $f(\boldsymbol{x}) \geq f(\boldsymbol{c})$ for all $\boldsymbol{x} \in \Gamma \cap B(\boldsymbol{c})$;
- f has a strict local minimum at $\boldsymbol{c}$ under the constraint $\boldsymbol{g}(\boldsymbol{x}) = \boldsymbol{0}$, if we can choose $B(\boldsymbol{c})$ such that $f(\boldsymbol{x}) > f(\boldsymbol{c})$ for all $\boldsymbol{x} \in \Gamma \cap B(\boldsymbol{c})$, $\boldsymbol{x} \neq \boldsymbol{c}$;
- f has a global minimum at $\boldsymbol{c}$ under the constraint $\boldsymbol{g}(\boldsymbol{x}) = \boldsymbol{0}$, if $f(\boldsymbol{x}) \geq f(\boldsymbol{c})$ for all $\boldsymbol{x} \in \Gamma$;
- f has a strict global minimum at $\boldsymbol{c}$ under the constraint $\boldsymbol{g}(\boldsymbol{x}) = \boldsymbol{0}$, if $f(\boldsymbol{x}) > f(\boldsymbol{c})$ for all $\boldsymbol{x} \in \Gamma$, $\boldsymbol{x} \neq \boldsymbol{c}$.

Lagrange's theorem gives a necessary condition for a constrained minimum to occur at a given point, and establishes the validity of the following formal method ("Lagrange's multiplier method") for obtaining *necessary* conditions for an extremum subject to equality constraints. We first define the *Lagrangian function* ψ by

$$\psi(\boldsymbol{x}) := f(\boldsymbol{x}) - \boldsymbol{l}'\boldsymbol{g}(\boldsymbol{x}),$$

where $\boldsymbol{l}$ is an $m \times 1$ vector of constants $\lambda_1, \dots, \lambda_m$, called the *Lagrange multipliers*; one multiplier is introduced for each constraint. Next we differentiate ψ with respect to $\boldsymbol{x}$ and set the result equal to zero. Together with the m constraints we thus obtain the following system of $n + m$ equations (the *first-order conditions*):

$$\begin{aligned} \mathrm{d}\psi(\boldsymbol{x}) &= 0 \quad \text{for every } \mathrm{d}\boldsymbol{x} \\ \boldsymbol{g}(\boldsymbol{x}) &= \boldsymbol{0}. \end{aligned}$$

We then try to solve this system of $n + m$ equations in $n + m$ unknowns, and we write the solutions as $\hat{\lambda}_1, \dots, \hat{\lambda}_m$ and $\hat{x}_1, \dots, \hat{x}_n$. The points $\hat{\boldsymbol{x}} = (\hat{x}_1, \dots, \hat{x}_n)'$ obtained in this way are called *critical points*, and among them are any points of S at which constrained minima or maxima occur.

As a simple example, consider the case where $n = 2$ and $m = 1$:

$$\begin{aligned} &\text{minimize} \quad f(x, y) \\ &\text{subject to} \quad g(x, y) = 0. \end{aligned}$$

We form the Lagrangian function

$$\psi(x, y) := f(x, y) - \lambda g(x, y),$$

and differentiate ψ with respect to x and y. This gives

$$\begin{aligned} \mathrm{d}\psi &= \left(\frac{\partial f}{\partial x}\,\mathrm{d}x + \frac{\partial f}{\partial y}\,\mathrm{d}y\right) - \lambda\left(\frac{\partial g}{\partial x}\,\mathrm{d}x + \frac{\partial g}{\partial y}\,\mathrm{d}y\right) \\ &= \left(\frac{\partial f}{\partial x} - \lambda\frac{\partial g}{\partial x}\right)\mathrm{d}x + \left(\frac{\partial f}{\partial y} - \lambda\frac{\partial g}{\partial y}\right)\mathrm{d}y, \end{aligned}$$

leading to the first-order conditions

$$\frac{\partial f}{\partial x} = \lambda\frac{\partial g}{\partial x}, \quad \frac{\partial f}{\partial y} = \lambda\frac{\partial g}{\partial y}, \quad g(x, y) = 0,$$

which can be conveniently rewritten as

$$\frac{\partial f/\partial x}{\partial g/\partial x} = \frac{\partial f/\partial y}{\partial g/\partial y} = \hat{\lambda}, \quad g(\hat{x}, \hat{y}) = 0.$$

The Lagrange multiplier $\hat{\lambda}$ measures the rate at which the optimal value of the objective function f changes with respect to a small change in the value of the constraint g.

Of course, the question remains whether a given critical point actually yields a minimum, maximum, or neither. To investigate whether a given critical point actually yields a minimum, maximum, or neither, it is often practical to proceed on an *ad hoc* basis. If this fails, the following criterion provides sufficient conditions to ensure the existence of a constrained minimum or maximum at a critical point.

Bordered determinantal criterion: Let $\mathbf{c}$ be an interior point of S, such that f and $\boldsymbol{g}$ are twice differentiable at $\mathbf{c}$, and the $m \times n$ Jacobian matrix $\mathrm{D}\boldsymbol{g}(\boldsymbol{c})$ has full row rank m. Assume that the first-order conditions,

$$\begin{aligned} \mathrm{d}\psi(\boldsymbol{c}) &= 0 \quad \text{for every } \mathrm{d}\boldsymbol{x} \\ \boldsymbol{g}(\boldsymbol{c}) &= \mathbf{0}, \end{aligned}$$

hold, and let $\boldsymbol{\Delta}_r$ be the symmetric $(m + r) \times (m + r)$ matrix

$$\boldsymbol{\Delta}_r := \begin{pmatrix} \mathbf{O} & \boldsymbol{B}_r \\ \boldsymbol{B}_r' & \boldsymbol{A}_{rr} \end{pmatrix} \quad (r = 1, \dots, n),$$

where $\boldsymbol{A}_{rr}$ is the $r \times r$ matrix in the north-west corner of

$$\boldsymbol{A} := \mathrm{H}f(\boldsymbol{c}) - \sum_{i=1}^{m} \lambda_i \mathrm{H}g_i(\boldsymbol{c}),$$

the matrices $\mathrm{H}f(\boldsymbol{c})$ and $\mathrm{H}g_i(\boldsymbol{c})$ denote Hessian matrices (second derivatives), and $\boldsymbol{B}_r$ is the $m \times r$ matrix whose columns are the first r columns of $\boldsymbol{B} := \mathrm{D}\boldsymbol{g}(\boldsymbol{c})$. Assume that $|\boldsymbol{B}_m| \neq 0$. (This can always be achieved by renumbering the variables, if necessary.) If

$$(-1)^m |\boldsymbol{\Delta}_r| > 0 \quad (r = m+1, \dots, n),$$

then f has a strict local minimum at $\boldsymbol{c}$ under the constraint $\boldsymbol{g}(\boldsymbol{x}) = \mathbf{0}$; if

$$(-1)^r |\boldsymbol{\Delta}_r| > 0 \quad (r = m+1, \dots, n),$$

then f has a strict local maximum at $\boldsymbol{c}$ under the constraint $\boldsymbol{g}(\boldsymbol{x}) = \mathbf{0}$.

Lagrange's theorem gives *necessary* conditions for a local (and hence also for a global) constrained extremum to occur at a given point. The bordered determinantal criterion gives *sufficient* conditions for a local constrained extremum. To find sufficient conditions for a global constrained extremum, it is often convenient to impose appropriate convexity (concavity) conditions.

Criterion under convexity: If the first-order conditions are satisfied, that is,

$$\mathrm{d}\psi(\boldsymbol{c}) = 0 \quad \text{for every } \mathrm{d}\boldsymbol{x}$$
$$\boldsymbol{g}(\boldsymbol{c}) = \mathbf{0},$$

and ψ is (strictly) convex on S, then $\boldsymbol{f}$ has a (strict) global minimum at $\boldsymbol{c}$ under the constraint $\boldsymbol{g}(\boldsymbol{x}) = \mathbf{0}$. (Of course, if ψ is (strictly) concave on S, then f has a (strict) global maximum at $\boldsymbol{c}$ under the constraint.)

To prove that the Lagrangian function ψ is (strictly) convex or (strictly) concave, several criteria exist. In particular, if the constraints $g_1(\boldsymbol{x}), \dots, g_m(\boldsymbol{x})$ are all linear, and $f(\boldsymbol{x})$ is (strictly) convex, then $\psi(\boldsymbol{x})$ is (strictly) convex. More generally, if the functions $\hat{\lambda}_1 g_1(\boldsymbol{x}), \dots, \hat{\lambda}_m g_m(\boldsymbol{x})$ are all concave (that is, for $i = 1, 2, \dots, m$, either $g_i(\boldsymbol{x})$ is concave and $\hat{\lambda}_i \geq 0$, or $g_i(\boldsymbol{x})$ is convex and $\hat{\lambda}_i \leq 0$), and if $f(\boldsymbol{x})$ is convex, then $\psi(\boldsymbol{x})$ is convex; furthermore, if at least one of these $m+1$ conditions is *strict*, then $\psi(\boldsymbol{x})$ is strictly convex.

Finally, we consider the case where there is a matrix (rather than a vector) of constraints. Let $f(\boldsymbol{X})$ be the function to be minimized subject to $\boldsymbol{G}(\boldsymbol{X}) = \mathbf{O}$, where $\boldsymbol{X}$ is an $n \times q$ matrix and $\boldsymbol{G}$ is an $m \times p$ matrix function. To solve the problem

$$\text{minimize} \quad f(\boldsymbol{X})$$
$$\text{subject to} \quad \boldsymbol{G}(\boldsymbol{X}) = \mathbf{O},$$

we introduce mp multipliers λ_{ij} (one for each constraint $g_{ij}(\boldsymbol{X}) = 0$, and define the $m \times p$ matrix of Lagrange multipliers $\boldsymbol{L} := (\lambda_{ij})$. The Lagrangian function then takes the convenient form $\psi(\boldsymbol{X}) := f(\boldsymbol{X}) - \operatorname{tr} \boldsymbol{L}'\boldsymbol{G}(\boldsymbol{X})$.

Notes

In Section A.1, we have not introduced truth tables, which can be used to establish the validity of the rules of indirect proof. Further material on this section can be found in Binmore (1980).

Analysis (typically complex analysis) is a branch of mathematics that has evolved out of calculus. Most of the material covered in Sections A.2–A.3 can be found in more depth in Whittaker and Watson (1996). Section A.3.1 requires some extra results, which are in Binmore (1981). All the series considered as generalizations of e^x in Section A.3.3 are a special case of the generalized hypergeometric series; see Whittaker and Watson (1996) or Abadir (1999) for a brief introduction.

In Section A.3.4, we have not dwelled on differentiability in the case of complex-valued functions. A complex function that is differentiable is called *analytic*. It will satisfy the *Cauchy-Riemann equations*, which ensure that differentiating $f(x)$ with respect to $\text{Re}(x)$, then with respect to $\text{Im}(x)$, will yield the same result as when the derivatives are performed in the reverse order. As a result of these equations, a complex function that is differentiable once will be differentiable an infinite number of times. This is why we have defined Taylor's infinite series for complex functions, but switched to real functions when we considered a function that is differentiable only up to order n.

A function defined by a series, which is convergent and analytic in some domain, may have its definition extended to some further domain by a process called analytic continuation. This can provide an alternative proof to the result we stated in Section A.3.3, about the binomial series being summable for all $x \in \mathbb{C}\backslash\{-1\}$.

For Section A.4, details on difference equations can be found in Spiegel (1971), and convexity and optimization in Magnus and Neudecker (1999).

Appendix B: Notation

In Abadir and Magnus (2002) we proposed a standard for notation in econometrics. The consistent use of the proposed notation in our volumes shows that it is in fact practical. The only adaptation we have made is to use $\boldsymbol{A}_{(k)}$ rather than $\boldsymbol{A}_k$ for a $k \times k$ leading principal submatrix of the matrix $\boldsymbol{A}$. The notational conventions described below only apply to the material actually covered in this volume. Further notation will be introduced, as needed, as the series develops. Authors of articles and books who wish to adopt our notation may consult the *Econometric Exercises* website,

http://us.cambridge.org/economics/ee/econometricexercises.htm

where we explain in detail how to implement all notational conventions in a LaTeX or Scientific Workplace environment.

B.1 Vectors and matrices

Vectors are lowercase and matrices are uppercase symbols. Moreover, both vectors and matrices are written in bold-italic. Thus, $\boldsymbol{a}$, $\boldsymbol{b}$,..., $\boldsymbol{z}$ denote (column) vectors and $\boldsymbol{A}$, $\boldsymbol{B}$,..., $\boldsymbol{Z}$ denote matrices. Vectors can also be denoted by Greek lowercase letters: $\boldsymbol{\alpha}$,..., $\boldsymbol{\omega}$, and matrices by Greek uppercase letters, such as $\boldsymbol{\Gamma}$, $\boldsymbol{\Theta}$, or $\boldsymbol{\Omega}$. We write

$$\boldsymbol{a} = \begin{pmatrix} a_1 \\ a_2 \\ \vdots \\ a_n \end{pmatrix} \quad \text{and} \quad \boldsymbol{A} = \begin{pmatrix} a_{11} & a_{12} & \dots & a_{1n} \\ a_{21} & a_{22} & \dots & a_{2n} \\ \vdots & \vdots & & \vdots \\ a_{m1} & a_{m2} & \dots & a_{mn} \end{pmatrix}$$

for an $n \times 1$ vector $\boldsymbol{a}$ and an $m \times n$ matrix $\boldsymbol{A}$. When we have a choice, we define a matrix in such a way that the number of rows (m) exceeds or equals the number of columns (n).

We write $\boldsymbol{A} = (a_{ij})$ or $\boldsymbol{A} = (\boldsymbol{A})_{ij}$ to denote a typical element of the matrix $\boldsymbol{A}$. The n columns of $\boldsymbol{A}$ are denoted by $\boldsymbol{a}_{\bullet 1}$, $\boldsymbol{a}_{\bullet 2}$, …, $\boldsymbol{a}_{\bullet n}$, and the m rows by $\boldsymbol{a}'_{1\bullet}$, $\boldsymbol{a}'_{2\bullet}$, …, $\boldsymbol{a}'_{m\bullet}$, where transpose is denoted by a prime. Hence,

$$\boldsymbol{A} = (\boldsymbol{a}_{\bullet 1}, \boldsymbol{a}_{\bullet 2}, \dots, \boldsymbol{a}_{\bullet n}) \quad \text{and} \quad \boldsymbol{A}' = (\boldsymbol{a}_{1\bullet}, \boldsymbol{a}_{2\bullet}, \dots, \boldsymbol{a}_{m\bullet}) .$$

However, we write $\boldsymbol{A} = (\boldsymbol{a}_1, \boldsymbol{a}_2, \dots, \boldsymbol{a}_n)$, and occasionally $\boldsymbol{A}' = (\boldsymbol{a}_1, \boldsymbol{a}_2, \dots, \boldsymbol{a}_m)$, when there is no possibility of confusion. A vector $\boldsymbol{a}$ denotes a column and $\boldsymbol{a}'$ denotes a row.

Special vectors and matrices. Some special vectors are:

$\mathbf{0}$, $\mathbf{0}_n$	null vector $(0, 0, \dots, 0)'$ of order $n \times 1$
$\boldsymbol{\imath}$, $\boldsymbol{\imath}_n$	sum vector $(1, 1, \dots, 1)'$ or order $n \times 1$
$\boldsymbol{e}_i$	unit vector, i-th column of identity matrix $\boldsymbol{I}$.

Special matrices are:

$\mathbf{O}$, $\mathbf{O}_{mn}$, $\mathbf{O}_{m,n}$	null matrix of order $m \times n$
$\boldsymbol{I}$, $\boldsymbol{I}_n$	identity matrix of order $n \times n$
$\boldsymbol{K}_{mn}$	commutation matrix
$\boldsymbol{K}_n$	$\boldsymbol{K}_{nn}$
$\boldsymbol{N}_n$	symmetrizer matrix $\frac{1}{2}(\boldsymbol{I}_{n^2} + \boldsymbol{K}_n)$
$\boldsymbol{D}_n$	duplication matrix
$\boldsymbol{J}_k(\lambda)$	Jordan block of order $k \times k$.

Note that the null vector $\mathbf{0}$ is smaller than the null matrix $\mathbf{O}$.

Ordering of eigenvalues. If an $n \times n$ matrix $\boldsymbol{A}$ is symmetric, then its eigenvalues are real and can be ordered. We shall order the eigenvalues as

$$\lambda_1 \geq \lambda_2 \geq \dots \geq \lambda_n,$$

since there are many cases where it is desirable that λ_1 denotes the largest eigenvalue. If $\boldsymbol{A}$ is not symmetric, its eigenvalues are in general complex. The moduli $|\lambda_1|, \dots, |\lambda_n|$ are, however, real. The largest of these is called the *spectral radius* of $\boldsymbol{A}$, denoted $\varrho(\boldsymbol{A})$.

Operations on matrix $\boldsymbol{A}$ and vector $\boldsymbol{a}$. Let $\boldsymbol{A}$ be a real $m \times n$ matrix of rank r. Then, $\boldsymbol{A}$ can be viewed as a collection of n columns in $\mathbb{R}^m$, but also as a collection of m rows in $\mathbb{R}^n$. Thus, associated with $\boldsymbol{A}$ are two vector spaces, the collection of columns and the collection of rows. In each of the two spaces there are two subspaces of special importance. The *column space* of $\boldsymbol{A}$, denoted col $\boldsymbol{A}$ or col$(\boldsymbol{A})$, consists of all linear combinations of the columns,

$$\operatorname{col} \boldsymbol{A} = \{\boldsymbol{x} \in \mathbb{R}^m : \boldsymbol{x} = \boldsymbol{A}\boldsymbol{y} \text{ for some } \boldsymbol{y} \in \mathbb{R}^n\}.$$

The dimension of col $\boldsymbol{A}$ is $\dim(\operatorname{col} \boldsymbol{A}) = r$. The *kernel* (or *null space*) of $\boldsymbol{A}$, denoted ker $\boldsymbol{A}$ or ker$(\boldsymbol{A})$, is the set $\ker \boldsymbol{A} = \{\boldsymbol{y} \in \mathbb{R}^n : \boldsymbol{A}\boldsymbol{y} = \mathbf{0}\}$ with dimension $\dim(\ker \boldsymbol{A}) = n - r$. The column space and kernel of $\boldsymbol{A}'$ are defined in the same way. The two kernels are more commonly known as *orthogonal complements*: $\operatorname{col}^\perp(\boldsymbol{A}) = \ker \boldsymbol{A}'$ and $\operatorname{col}^\perp(\boldsymbol{A}') = \ker \boldsymbol{A}$.

Two vectors $\boldsymbol{x}$ and $\boldsymbol{a}$ for which $\boldsymbol{x}'\boldsymbol{a} = 0$ are *orthogonal*, and we write $\boldsymbol{x} \perp \boldsymbol{a}$. If $\boldsymbol{x}$ is orthogonal to all columns of $\boldsymbol{A}$, we write $\boldsymbol{x} \perp \boldsymbol{A}$. Thus, $\operatorname{col}^{\perp}(\boldsymbol{A}) = \{\boldsymbol{x} : \boldsymbol{x} \perp \boldsymbol{A}\}$ with dimension $\dim(\operatorname{col}^{\perp} \boldsymbol{A}) = m - r$. A basis of $\operatorname{col}^{\perp}(\boldsymbol{A})$ is denoted $\boldsymbol{A}_{\perp}$. Hence, $\boldsymbol{A}_{\perp}$ denotes any $m \times (m - r)$ matrix with full column rank, satisfying $\boldsymbol{A}'\boldsymbol{A}_{\perp} = \mathbf{O}$. The following standard operations are used:

$\boldsymbol{A}'$	transpose
$\boldsymbol{A}^{-1}$	inverse
$\boldsymbol{A}^{+}$	Moore-Penrose inverse
$\boldsymbol{A}^{-}$	generalized inverse (satisfying only $\boldsymbol{A}\boldsymbol{A}^{-}\boldsymbol{A} = \boldsymbol{A}$)
$\operatorname{dg} \boldsymbol{A}$, $\operatorname{dg}(\boldsymbol{A})$	diagonal matrix containing the diagonal elements of $\boldsymbol{A}$
$\operatorname{diag}(a_1, \ldots, a_n)$	diagonal matrix with $a_1, \ldots, a_n$ on the diagonal
$\operatorname{diag}(\boldsymbol{A}_1, \ldots, \boldsymbol{A}_n)$	block-diagonal matrix with $\boldsymbol{A}_1, \ldots, \boldsymbol{A}_n$ on the diagonal
$\boldsymbol{A}^2$	$\boldsymbol{A}\boldsymbol{A}$
$\boldsymbol{A}^p$	p-th power
$\boldsymbol{A}^{1/2}$	(unique) positive semidefinite square root of $\boldsymbol{A} \geq \mathbf{O}$
$\boldsymbol{A}^{\#}$	adjoint (matrix)
$\boldsymbol{A}^{*}$	conjugate transpose
$\boldsymbol{A}_{ij}$	submatrix
$\boldsymbol{A}_{(k)}$	leading principal submatrix of order $k \times k$
$(\boldsymbol{A}, \boldsymbol{B})$, $(\boldsymbol{A} : \boldsymbol{B})$	partitioned matrix
$\operatorname{vec} \boldsymbol{A}$, $\operatorname{vec}(\boldsymbol{A})$	vec-operator
$\operatorname{vech} \boldsymbol{A}$, $\operatorname{vech}(\boldsymbol{A})$	half-vec containing a_{ij} $(i \geq j)$
$\operatorname{rk}(\boldsymbol{A})$	rank
λ_i, $\lambda_i(\boldsymbol{A})$	i-th eigenvalue (of $\boldsymbol{A}$)
$\operatorname{tr} \boldsymbol{A}$, $\operatorname{tr}(\boldsymbol{A})$	trace
$\operatorname{etr} \boldsymbol{A}$, $\operatorname{etr}(\boldsymbol{A})$	$\exp(\operatorname{tr} \boldsymbol{A})$
$\|\boldsymbol{A}\|$, $\det \boldsymbol{A}$, $\det(\boldsymbol{A})$	determinant
$\|\boldsymbol{A}\|$	norm of matrix $(\sqrt{(\operatorname{tr} \boldsymbol{A}^{*}\boldsymbol{A})})$
$\|\boldsymbol{a}\|$	norm of vector $(\sqrt{(\boldsymbol{a}^{*}\boldsymbol{a})})$
$\boldsymbol{a}_{\circ}$	normalization of $\boldsymbol{a}$ (such that $\|\boldsymbol{a}_{\circ}\| = 1$)
$\bar{x}$	average of components of $\boldsymbol{x}$
$\boldsymbol{a} \geq \boldsymbol{b}$, $\boldsymbol{b} \leq \boldsymbol{a}$	$a_i \geq b_i$ for all i
$\boldsymbol{a} > \boldsymbol{b}$, $\boldsymbol{b} < \boldsymbol{a}$	$a_i > b_i$ for all i
$\boldsymbol{A} \geq \boldsymbol{B}$, $\boldsymbol{B} \leq \boldsymbol{A}$	$\boldsymbol{A} - \boldsymbol{B}$ positive semidefinite
$\boldsymbol{A} > \boldsymbol{B}$, $\boldsymbol{B} < \boldsymbol{A}$	$\boldsymbol{A} - \boldsymbol{B}$ positive definite
$\boldsymbol{A} \otimes \boldsymbol{B}$	Kronecker product
$\boldsymbol{A} \odot \boldsymbol{B}$	Hadamard product.

A few words of explanation on some of the symbols is required. First, the square root of a positive semidefinite matrix $\boldsymbol{A} = \boldsymbol{S}\boldsymbol{\Lambda}\boldsymbol{S}'$ ($\boldsymbol{S}$ orthogonal, $\boldsymbol{\Lambda}$ diagonal) is defined here as the unique matrix $\boldsymbol{A}^{1/2} = \boldsymbol{S}\boldsymbol{\Lambda}^{1/2}\boldsymbol{S}'$. Next, the conjugate transpose of a complex-valued matrix $\boldsymbol{A} := \boldsymbol{A}_1 + \mathrm{i}\boldsymbol{A}_2$ ($\boldsymbol{A}_1$ and $\boldsymbol{A}_2$ real) is thus given by $\boldsymbol{A}^{*} = \boldsymbol{A}_1' - \mathrm{i}\boldsymbol{A}_2'$. Then, ambiguity can arise between the symbol $|\cdot|$ for determinant and the same symbol for absolute value, for example in the calculation of Jacobians or in the multivariate transformation theorem. This ambiguity can be avoided by writing $|\det \boldsymbol{A}|$ for the absolute value of a determinant. Finally, possible confusion could arise between the notation $\boldsymbol{a} > \boldsymbol{0}$ and $\boldsymbol{A} > \mathbf{O}$. The first means that each element of $\boldsymbol{a}$ is positive, while the second does *not* mean that each element of $\boldsymbol{A}$ is positive, but rather than $\boldsymbol{A}$ is positive definite.

Occasional notation. As we have seen above, we denote a leading principal submatrix of $\boldsymbol{A}$ by $\boldsymbol{A}_{(k)}$, and a general submatrix by $\boldsymbol{A}_{ij}$, so that we can write

$$\boldsymbol{A} := \begin{pmatrix} \boldsymbol{A}_{11} & \boldsymbol{A}_{12} \\ \boldsymbol{A}_{21} & \boldsymbol{A}_{22} \end{pmatrix}.$$

If $\boldsymbol{A}_{11}$ is square and nonsingular, we denote the Schur complement of $\boldsymbol{A}_{11}$ by $\boldsymbol{A}_{22|1} := \boldsymbol{A}_{22} - \boldsymbol{A}_{21}\boldsymbol{A}_{11}^{-1}\boldsymbol{A}_{12}$. This notation, however, does not suffice. Occasionally, we shall use $\boldsymbol{A}_{(ij)}$, $\boldsymbol{A}^{(j)}$, or similar expressions to denote special matrix functions of $\boldsymbol{A}$, defined as needed in the special context. Thus, $\boldsymbol{A}_{(ij)}$ might denote the $(n-1)\times(n-1)$ matrix obtained from the $n \times n$ matrix $\boldsymbol{A}$ by deleting row i and column j, and $\boldsymbol{A}^{(j)}$ might mean the matrix obtained from $\boldsymbol{A}$ when the j-th column is replaced by some vector $\boldsymbol{b}$.

Parentheses and brackets. We try to minimize on the use of parentheses and brackets, unless this leads to ambiguities. Thus, we write $\operatorname{tr} \boldsymbol{AB}$ instead of $\operatorname{tr}(\boldsymbol{AB})$, and $\mathrm{d}\boldsymbol{XY}$ instead of $\mathrm{d}(\boldsymbol{XY})$. In particular, $\operatorname{tr} \boldsymbol{AB}$ (a scalar) does not equal $(\operatorname{tr} \boldsymbol{A})\boldsymbol{B}$ (a matrix), and $\mathrm{d}\boldsymbol{XY}$ does not equal $(\mathrm{d}\boldsymbol{X})\boldsymbol{Y}$. For expectation and variance we shall, however, always write $\mathrm{E}(x)$ and $\operatorname{var}(x)$.

B.2 Mathematical symbols, functions, and operators

Definitions and implications. We denote definitions, implications, convergence, and transformations by

$\equiv$	identity, equivalence
$a := b$	defines a in terms of b
$\Longrightarrow$	implies
$\Longleftrightarrow$	if and only if
$\to, \quad \longrightarrow$	converges to
$x \to c^+, \quad x \downarrow c$	x converges to c from above
$x \to c^-, \quad x \uparrow c$	x converges to c from below
$x \mapsto y$	transformation from x to y.

We write $f(x) \approx g(x)$ if the two functions are approximately equal in some sense depending on the context. If $f(x)$ is proportional to $g(x)$ we write $f(x) \propto g(x)$. We say that "$f(x)$ is at most of order $g(x)$" and write $f(x) = O(g(x))$, if $|f(x)/g(x)|$ is bounded above in some neighborhood of $x = c$ (possibly $c = \pm\infty$), and we say that "$f(x)$ is of order less than $g(x)$" and write $f(x) = o(g(x))$, if $f(x)/g(x) \to 0$ when $x \to c$. Finally, we write $f(x) \sim g(x)$ if $f(x)/g(x) \to 1$ when $x \to c$. The two functions are then said to be *asymptotically equal*. Notice that when $f(x)$ and $g(x)$ are asymptotically equal, then $f(x) \approx g(x)$ and also $f(x) = O(g(x))$, but not vice versa.

Sets. The usual sets are denoted as follows:

$\mathbb{N}$	natural numbers $1, 2, \ldots$
$\mathbb{Z}$	integers $\ldots, -2, -1, 0, 1, 2, \ldots$
$\mathbb{Q}$	rational numbers
$\mathbb{R}$	real numbers
$\mathbb{C}$	complex numbers.

Superscripts denote the dimension and subscripts the relevant subset. For example, $\mathbb{R}^2 = \mathbb{R} \times \mathbb{R}$ denotes the real plane, $\mathbb{R}^n$ the set of real $n \times 1$ vectors, and $\mathbb{R}^{m \times n}$ the set of real $m \times n$ matrices. The set $\mathbb{R}^n_+$ denotes the positive orthant of $\mathbb{R}^n$, while $\mathbb{Z}_+$ denotes the set of positive integers (hence, $\mathbb{Z}_+ = \mathbb{N}$) and $\mathbb{Z}_{0,+}$ denotes the nonnegative integers. The set $\mathbb{C}^{n \times n}$ denotes the complex $n \times n$ matrices.

Set differences are denoted by a backslash. For example, $\mathbb{N} = \mathbb{Z}_{0,+} \backslash \{0\}$. Real-line intervals defined by x in $a \le x < b$ are denoted by $[a, b)$. Occasionally it might be unclear whether (a, b) indicates a real-line interval or a point in $\mathbb{R}^2$. In that case the interval $a < x < b$ can alternatively be written as $]a, b[$.

Sequences are special ordered sets. They are delimited, as usual, by braces (curly brackets). It is often convenient to write $\{\boldsymbol{Z}_j\}_m^n$ (or simply $\{\boldsymbol{Z}_j\}$) for the sequence of matrices $\boldsymbol{Z}_m, \boldsymbol{Z}_{m+1}, \ldots, \boldsymbol{Z}_n$.

The space l_2 consists of real (or complex) sequences $(x_1, x_2, \ldots)$ satisfying $\sum_{i=1}^{\infty} |x_i|^2 < \infty$, while the space L_2 contains all real (or complex) variables x satisfying $\int |x(t)|^2 \,\mathrm{d}t < \infty$.

Other set-related symbols are:

$\in$	belongs to
$\notin$	does not belong to
$\{x : x \in S, x \text{ satisfies } \mathcal{P}\}$	set of all elements of S with property $\mathcal{P}$
$\subseteq$	is a subset of
$\subset$	is a proper subset of
$\cup$	union
$\cap$	intersection
$\emptyset$	empty set
A^c	complement of A
$B \backslash A$	$B \cap A^c$.

Functions. We denote functions by:

$f: S \to T$	function defined on S with values in T
$f, g, \varphi, \psi, \vartheta$	scalar-valued function
$\boldsymbol{f}, \boldsymbol{g}$	vector-valued function
$\boldsymbol{F}, \boldsymbol{G}$	matrix-valued function
$\boldsymbol{g} \circ \boldsymbol{f}, \boldsymbol{G} \circ \boldsymbol{F}$	composite function
$g * f$	convolution $(g * f)(x) = \int_{-\infty}^{\infty} g(y) f(x - y) \, \mathrm{d}y$.

Two special functions are the gamma (generalized factorial) function, $\Gamma(x)$, satisfying $\Gamma(x + 1) = x\Gamma(x)$, and the beta function $B(x, y) := \Gamma(x)\Gamma(y)/\Gamma(x + y)$.

Derivatives and differentials. The treatment of lowercase single-letter constants is somewhat controversial. For example, the base of natural logarithms e and the imaginary unit i are often written as e and i. The same applies to operators (such as the derivative operator d — often written as d). We recommend the use of i, e, and d, in order to avoid potential confusion with variables (such as the index i in $i = 1, \ldots, n$ or the distance $d(\cdot, \cdot)$). Thus, for differentials and derivatives, we write:

d	differential
d^n	n-th order differential
$\mathrm{D}_j \varphi(\boldsymbol{x})$	partial derivative, $\partial \varphi(\boldsymbol{x}) / \partial x_j$
$\mathrm{D}_j f_i(\boldsymbol{x})$	partial derivative, $\partial f_i(\boldsymbol{x}) / \partial x_j$
$\mathrm{D}^2_{kj} \varphi(\boldsymbol{x})$	second-order partial derivative, $\partial \mathrm{D}_j \varphi(\boldsymbol{x}) / \partial x_k$
$\mathrm{D}^2_{kj} f_i(\boldsymbol{x})$	second-order partial derivative, $\partial \mathrm{D}_j f_i(\boldsymbol{x}) / \partial x_k$
$\varphi^{(n)}(x)$	n-th order derivative of $\varphi(x)$
$\mathrm{D}\varphi(\boldsymbol{x}), \partial \varphi(\boldsymbol{x}) / \partial \boldsymbol{x}'$	derivative of $\varphi(\boldsymbol{x})$
$\mathrm{D}\boldsymbol{f}(\boldsymbol{x}), \partial \boldsymbol{f}(\boldsymbol{x}) / \partial \boldsymbol{x}'$	derivative (Jacobian matrix) of $\boldsymbol{f}(\boldsymbol{x})$
$\mathrm{D}\boldsymbol{F}(\boldsymbol{X})$	derivative (Jacobian matrix) of $\boldsymbol{F}(\boldsymbol{X})$
$\partial \operatorname{vec} \boldsymbol{F}(\boldsymbol{X}) / \partial (\operatorname{vec} \boldsymbol{X})'$	derivative of $\boldsymbol{F}(\boldsymbol{X})$, alternative notation
$\nabla \varphi, \nabla \boldsymbol{f}, \nabla \boldsymbol{F}$	gradient (transpose of derivative)
$\mathrm{H}\varphi(\boldsymbol{x}), \partial^2 \varphi(\boldsymbol{x}) / \partial \boldsymbol{x} \partial \boldsymbol{x}'$	second derivative (Hessian matrix) of $\varphi(\boldsymbol{x})$
$[f(x)]_a^b, \ f(x)\|_a^b$	$f(b) - f(a)$.

Instead of $\varphi^{(1)}(x)$ and $\varphi^{(2)}(x)$, we may write the more common $\varphi'(x)$ and $\varphi''(x)$, but otherwise we prefer to reserve the prime for matrix transposes rather than derivatives. To emphasize the difference between transpose and derivative, we write $\boldsymbol{f}'(\boldsymbol{x})$ for the derivative of $\boldsymbol{f}$ and $\boldsymbol{f}(\boldsymbol{x})'$ for the transpose.

Other mathematical symbols. Various other symbols in common use are:

i	imaginary unit
e, exp	exponential
log	natural logarithm

$\log_a$	logarithm to the base a
!	factorial
$\binom{\nu}{j}$	binomial coefficient
δ_{ij}	Kronecker delta: equals 1 if $i = j$, 0 otherwise
$\text{sgn}(x)$	sign of x
$\lfloor x \rfloor$, $\text{int}(x)$	integer part of x, that is, largest integer $\leq x$
$1_{\mathcal{K}}$	indicator function (1, not I): equals 1 if condition $\mathcal{K}$ is satisfied, 0 otherwise
$\|x\|$	absolute value (modulus) of scalar $x \in \mathbb{C}$
x^*	complex conjugate of scalar $x \in \mathbb{C}$
$\text{Re}(x)$	real part of x
$\text{Im}(x)$	imaginary part of x
$\arg(x)$	argument of x.

Statistical symbols. We do not use many statistical symbols in this volume. The ones we use are:

$\sim$	is distributed as
$\Pr$	probability
$\text{E}(\cdot)$	expectation
$\text{var}(\cdot)$	variance
$\ell(\boldsymbol{\theta})$	log-likelihood function
$\boldsymbol{\mathcal{H}}(\boldsymbol{\theta})$	Hessian matrix
$\boldsymbol{\mathcal{I}}(\boldsymbol{\theta})$	(Fisher) Information matrix
$\text{N}(\boldsymbol{\mu}, \boldsymbol{\Omega})$, $\text{N}_m(\boldsymbol{\mu}, \boldsymbol{\Omega})$	m-dimensional normal distribution
$\text{W}_m(n, \boldsymbol{V}, \boldsymbol{M}'\boldsymbol{M})$	Wishart distribution
$\text{W}_m(n, \boldsymbol{V})$	central Wishart distribution ($\boldsymbol{M} = \mathbf{O}$).

Bibliography

Abadir, K. M. (1999). An introduction to hypergeometric functions for economists, *Econometric Reviews*, 18, 287–330.

Abadir, K. M., R. D. H. Heijmans, and J. R. Magnus (2006). *Statistics*, Econometric Exercises Series, Volume 2, Cambridge University Press, New York.

Abadir, K. M. and J. R. Magnus (2002). Notation in econometrics: a proposal for a standard, *Econometrics Journal*, 5, 76–90.

Aigner, M. and G. M. Ziegler (1999). *Proofs from the Book*, 2nd corrected printing, Springer-Verlag, Berlin

Ayres, F. Jr (1962). *Matrices*, Schaum's Outline Series, McGraw-Hill, New York.

Beaton, A. E. (1964). *The Use of Special Matrix Operators in Statistical Calculus*, Ed.D. thesis, Harvard University. Reprinted as *Educational Testing Service Research Bulletin*, 64–51, Princeton.

Beckenbach, E. F. and R. Bellman (1961). *Inequalities*, Springer-Verlag, Berlin.

Bellman, R. (1970). *Introduction to Matrix Analysis*, 2nd edition, McGraw-Hill, New York.

Binmore, K. G. (1980). *Logic, Sets and Numbers*, Cambridge University Press, Cambridge.

Binmore, K. G. (1981). *Topological Ideas*, Cambridge University Press, Cambridge.

Bretscher, O. (1997). *Linear Algebra with Applications*, Prentice-Hall, Upper Saddle River, New Jersey.

Bronson, R. (1989). *Theory and Problems of Matrix Operations*, Schaum's Outline Series, McGraw-Hill, New York.

Browne, M. W. (1974). Generalized least squares estimators in the analysis of covariance structures, *South African Statistical Journal*, 8, 1–24. Reprinted in: *Latent Variables in Socioeconomic Models* (eds D. J. Aigner and A. S. Goldberger), North-Holland, Amsterdam, 205–226.

Dempster, A. P. (1969). *Elements of Continuous Multivariate Analysis*, Addison-Wesley, Reading.

Driscoll, M. F. and W. R. Gundberg (1986). A history of the development of Craig's theorem, *The American Statistician*, 40, 65–70.

Gantmacher, F. R. (1959). *The Theory of Matrices*, 2 volumes, Chelsea, New York.

Graybill, F. A. and G. Marsaglia (1957). Idempotent matrices and quadratic forms in the general linear hypothesis, *Annals of Mathematical Statistics*, 28, 678–686.

Hadley, G. (1961). *Linear Algebra*, Addison-Wesley, Reading, Mass.

Halmos, P. R. (1974). *Finite-Dimensional Vector Spaces*, Springer-Verlag, New York.

Hardy, G. H., J. E. Littlewood and G. Pólya (1952). *Inequalities*, 2nd edition, Cambridge University Press, Cambridge.

Harville, D. A. (2001). *Matrix Algebra: Exercises and Solutions*, Springer-Verlag, New York.

Hedayat, A. and W. D. Wallis (1978). Hadamard matrices and their applications, *Annals of Statistics*, 6, 1184–1238.

Horn, R. A. and C. R. Johnson (1985). *Matrix Analysis*, Cambridge University Press, New York.

Horn, R. A. and C. R. Johnson (1991). *Topics in Matrix Analysis*, Cambridge University Press, Cambridge.

Kay, D. C. (1988). *Tensor Calculus*, Schaum's Outline Series, McGraw-Hill, New York.

Koopmans, T. C., H. Rubin and R. B. Leipnik (1950). Measuring the equation systems of dynamic economics, in: *Statistical Inference in Dynamic Economic Models* (ed. T. C. Koopmans), Cowles Foundation for Research in Economics, Monograph 10, John Wiley, New York, Chapter 2.

Kostrikin, A. I. and Yu. I. Manin (1981). *Linear Algebra and Geometry*, Gordon and Breach Science Publishers, New York.

Kreyszig, E. (1978). *Introductory Functional Analysis with Applications*, John Wiley, New York.

Lang, S. (1995). *Differential and Riemannian Manifolds*, 3rd edition, Springer-Verlag, Berlin.

Lipschutz, S. (1989). *3000 Solved Problems in Linear Algebra*, Schaum's Solved Problems Series, McGraw-Hill, New York.

Lipschutz, S. and M. Lipson (2001). *Theory and Problems of Linear Algebra*, 3rd edition, Schaum's Outline Series, McGraw-Hill, New York.

Liu, S. and W. Polasek (1995). An equivalence relation for two symmetric idempotent matrices, *Econometric Theory*, 11, 638. Solution (by H. Neudecker) in: *Econometric Theory*, 12, 590.

MacDuffee, C. C. (1946). *The Theory of Matrices*, Chelsea, New York.

Magnus, J. R. (1988). *Linear Structures*, Charles Griffin & Company, London and Oxford University Press, New York.

Magnus, J. R. (1990). On the fundamental bordered matrix of linear estimation, in: *Advanced Lectures In Quantitative Economics* (ed. F. van der Ploeg), Academic Press, London, 583–604.

Magnus, J. R. and H. Neudecker (1979). The commutation matrix: some properties and applications, *The Annals of Statistics*, 7, 381–394.

Magnus, J. R. and H. Neudecker (1980). The elimination matrix: some lemmas and applications, *SIAM Journal on Algebraic and Discrete Methods*, 1, 422–449.

Magnus, J. R. and H. Neudecker (1999). *Matrix Differential Calculus with Applications in Statistics and Econometrics*, revised edition, Wiley, Chichester/New York.

McCullagh, P. (1987). *Tensor Methods in Statistics*, Chapman and Hall, London.

Mirsky, L. (1955). *An Introduction to Linear Algebra*, Oxford University Press, London.

Moore, E. H. (1920). On the reciprocal of the general algebraic matrix (Abstract), *Bulletin of the American Mathematical Society*, 26, 394–395.

Moore, E. H. (1935). *General Analysis*, Memoirs of the American Philosophical Society, Volume I, American Philosophical Society, Philadelphia.

Muirhead, R. J. (1982). *Aspects of Multivariate Statistical Theory*, Wiley, New York.

Ortega, J. M. (1987). *Matrix Theory: A Second Course*, Plenum Press, New York.

Penrose, R. (1955). A generalized inverse for matrices, *Proceedings of the Cambridge Philosophical Society*, 51, 406–413.

Penrose, R. (1956). On best approximate solutions of linear matrix equations, *Proceedings of the Cambridge Philosophical Society*, 52, 17–19.

Pollock, D. S. G. (1979). *The Algebra of Econometrics*, Wiley, New York.

Prasolov, V. V. (1994). *Problems and Theorems in Linear Algebra*, Translations of Mathematical Monographs, Vol. 134, American Mathematical Society, Providence, Rhode Island

Proskuryakov, I. V. (1978). *Problems in Linear Algebra*, Mir Publishers, Moscow.

Rao, C. R. and S. K. Mitra (1971). *Generalized Inverse of Matrices and Its Applications*, Wiley, New York.

Roth, W. E. (1934). On direct product matrices, *Bulletin of the American Mathematical Society*, 40, 461–468.

Rudin, W. (1976). *Principles of Mathematical Analysis*, 3rd edition, McGraw-Hill, New York.

Shilov, G. E. (1974). *Elementary Functional Analysis*, MIT Press, Cambridge, Mass.

Spiegel, M. R. (1971). *Calculus of Finite Differences and Difference Equations*, Schaum's Outline Series, McGraw-Hill, New York.

Whittaker, E. T. and G. N. Watson (1996). *A Course of Modern Analysis*, 4th edition, Cambridge University Press, Cambridge.

Zhan, X. (2002). *Matrix Inequalities*, Springer-Verlag, Berlin.

Zhang, F. (1996). *Linear Algebra: Challenging Problems for Students*, The Johns Hopkins University Press, Baltimore.

Zhang, F. (1999). *Matrix Theory: Basic Results and Techniques*, Springer-Verlag, New York.

Index